TABLE OF CONTENTS

The California Firearm, Knife, and Weapon Law Compendium

-

GUNS
KNIVES
OTHER WEAPONS

-

USE
SAFETY
OWNERSHIP
LAW

-

FULL TEXT OF ALL THE GUN, KNIFE, AND WEAPONS LAWS IN THE CALIFORNIA CODE

-

First Edition - 2010

Authored by: Robert Todd Bergin, Esq.
www.cagunlaw.com

Pointed In!™ Press
Las Vegas, NV
www.pointedin.com

Proudly written and published in the United States of America
by Robert Todd Bergin, Esq.
www.cagunlaw.com
Published by Pointed In!™ Press
www.pointedin.com
ISBN 978-0-615-35406-4 $19.95
First Publication: Winter 2010

DISCLAIMER - WARNING - READ FIRST!

Nothing contained in this book is to be considered as the rendering of legal advice. This book, and all information herein, is intended solely for educational purposes.

The author has extensively researched the information contained in this book. However, neither the author, the publisher, nor any distributors and/or retailers assume any liability or responsibility for the use of the information contained in this book or on the website. Furthermore, neither the author, the publisher, nor any distributors and/or retailers assume any liability or responsibility for errors, omissions, inaccuracies, misinterpretations, etc., that might be found in this book

<u>THIS BOOK IS NOT LEGAL ADVICE</u>. This book contains interpretations and opinions of the author only, and not legal advice. The reader must realize that the law is always changing, and therefore, it is virtually impossible for any single book to be complete at any given time. The author emphasizes the importance of seeking legal counsel for any questions you may have about a specific situation. Regretfully, the author is unavailable to answer individual questions regarding California law or to provide legal advice of any kind. Finally, any and all warranties, either expressed or implied, are specifically disclaimed.

ABOUT THE AUTHOR

Todd Bergin is an attorney in Orange County, California. He earned his law degree from Whittier Law School, in Costa Mesa, California. Prior to law school, Mr. Bergin first attended Marshall University in Huntington, West Virginia, but ultimately finished his undergraduate work at the University of Kentucky, in Lexington, Kentucky.

Prior to attending college, Mr. Bergin went to a small private high school in West Virginia. While Mr. Bergin primarily grew up in Huntington, West Virginia, he had also lived in Chicago, Illinois, Atlanta, Georgia, Montgomery, Alabama, Lexington, Kentucky, and Charleston, South Carolina. Mr. Bergin has also spent a great deal of time in the Washington, D.C., area, including Scientist's Cliffs in Calvert County, Maryland.

For the past eleven years, Mr. Bergin has called Orange County, California, home. For how much longer, we shall see, if the law does not begin to change for the better for the State and the people of California.

Mr. Bergin was raised by a conservative yet anti-gun mother. He was the one kid on the street who was not allowed to have toy guns as a child and was forced to improvise with wooden sticks shaped like guns. While remaining indifferent to firearm-related issues most of his life, Mr. Bergin began to get interested in firearms.

Prior to buying his first handgun, a GLOCK 23, Mr. Bergin sought out training to become proficient with firearms. He has since become very proficient with firearms, and prefers a 1911 over any other handgun, but is most fond of his Benelli M4 shotgun.

Mr. Bergin's training and interest did not stop there. He has since become a very active participant in the gun culture, having been extensively trained in the use of handguns, shotguns, and rifles, and continues to train to this day on a very regular basis. Mr. Bergin's handgun training has focused primarily on the use of the handgun from concealment, and he holds concealed permits in many states, and yes, including California.

Mr. Bergin is also a life member at a nationally recognized firearm training institute in southern Nevada, and since joining, has averaged roughly one class per month. Mr. Bergin is also a member of many organizations dedicated to protecting the Second Amendment, including a Life Member of the National Rifle Association, Life Member of the California Pistol and Rifle Association, Life Membership of the Jews for the Preservation of Firearms Ownership, Life Member of the Second Amendment Foundation, Life Member of the California Rifle and Pistol Association, and a member of the Gun Owners of California and Gun Owners of Nevada. Mr. Bergin also is a donor to the Calguns Foundation.

The California Firearm, Knife, and Weapon Law Compendium is Mr. Bergin's first work as an author.

Mr. Bergin invites you to visit his website at www.cagunlaw.com for updates and ordering information. You may also contact Mr. Bergin at gunlawsnow@gmail.com. However, Mr. Bergin is unavailable to answer individual questions or provide legal advice of any kind about California law.

ACKNOWLEDGMENTS

This book is the result of many factors, and a variety of people deserve my sincerest appreciation in completing this project.

First, I appreciate my wife Jessica's patience and her belief in me to see this project to the end. Thank you for standing by me all these years.

Second, thank you to my mother, Teri, has been instrumental to all of my successes in life.

Also, a thank you to other supporting family, including my children, Madison and Parker, as well as my brother and sister, Tyler and Taite.

Further, I would like to thank Greg Block, a Southern California local firearm instructor, all-around legal guru, and friend. Greg was instrumental in providing his thoughts and feedback regarding the information contained in this book. Greg took the time out of his day to review my book with a critical eye, and to provide feedback, answer questions, and provide direction to me as I worked through the daunting task of writing this book. Thank you for all of your time and consideration.

Last but certainly not least, my sincerest appreciation to Linda Giles. Linda has been a close, personal friend of our family for over thirty years. Without her assistance, I may have never made it past sentence diagrams in the seventh grade. She was the first person to review this book with a critical eye, and I am quite confident that never in her wildest dreams did she ever, ever think she would read so much about California firearms law, or any firearms law in general for that matter. Thank you for always being there for me and my family, and for being a good friend.

PURPOSE OF THIS BOOK

This book was written for anyone who will be handling, using, and/or owning some type of firearm, such as a rifle, shotgun, or handgun, or some type of knife or other weapon. Basically, this book is for everyone, even for those who do not plan to handle any of the above, as none of us have the privilege of looking into the future and knowing whether or not we would ever be in a situation where there exists a firearm or other type of deadly weapon. As such, it is all of our responsibility to be knowledgeable of the law, as well as have an understanding of basic safety issues, should we find ourselves in such a situation.

While the overall theme of this book is the lawful use and ownership of firearms, this book will also briefly touch upon the lawful ownership of other dangerous or deadly weapons, as well as knives. Where the text of this book does not address certain dangerous or deadly weapons or explosives, the law regarding these items as provided by the California State Legislature can be found in the appendix of this book. However, most everything that is relevant to most readers is included in the text of this book.

There are many reasons to read a book that discusses the law as it relates to firearms, knives, and other items and weapons that are considered dangerous and/or deadly weapons, and explosives. However, there is no need to speculate and discuss all the reasons one may be reading this book, but in all probability, the reason one would read a book such as this is because they desire to conduct their behavior as a person respectful of the laws. Basically, they want to keep their butt out of trouble. One keeps free of trouble by knowing and understanding the laws that relate to their activities.

Many readers of this book may be new to the self-defense and/or "gun culture,"[1] and may currently be considering firearm ownership, knife ownership, or both, and they want to possess more information about the law as it pertains to the weapons they may be considering. Some readers may already be part of the culture, and may already own many of the firearms and/or weapons discussed in this book, and attach importance to being knowledgeable of the current law. Either way, you have selected the appropriate book in obtaining current information on the law of firearms and weapons as it exists in California.

---

[1]The first time I heard the term "gun culture" was in a book by John Ross entitled *Unintended Consequences*. This may be one of the finest books I have ever read, and I highly recommend it to anyone who thinks they may be part of the "gun culture."

However, if you currently find yourself in legal trouble regarding improper ownership, use, storage, transport, or some other issue, with any of the weapons this book addresses, please accept my best wishes and appreciation in choosing this text to assist you. But please, as soon as possible, seek and obtain competent legal counsel. Do not depend on this book to assist you in your legal troubles. Sure, it can guide you regarding some basic considerations, but a talented attorney, well-versed in firearms, knife, or weapon law and with a strong criminal defense background will better assist you in your troubles. As explained at the beginning of the book, **THIS BOOK IS NOT LEGAL ADVICE**. Period.

Either way, you have chosen this book because you are interested in a decent understanding of the firearm laws, knife laws, and "other" weapon laws in the State of California. You desire some sort of explanation of the laws in terms that are clear, concise, and in plain English. You wish to avoid trouble with the law yet enjoy to the fullest what rights you have left in regards to both firearms and knives. Further, you wish to have a single text that provides you with all of the above.

It is my desire that this book assists you with your goal of obtaining a better understanding of the law as it pertains to firearms, knives, and other weapons.

While this book is quite comprehensive, keep in mind that neither this book, and likely no other book, contains each and every federal, state, and local law and ordinances as they relate to knives and firearms. There are so many laws at all levels that creating one single book to cover it all and remain current would be an exercise in futility. Furthermore, the law changes often, and it is a difficult task for the author of a publication such as this to keep the book 100% current.

However, every effort has been made to keep this book current and accurate. Also, **this book will always be a "work in progress."** Laws change often, and in particular, firearms laws change often. Updated versions of this book will make every effort to keep up with the most recent changes. Furthermore, this book includes interpretations of the law. Every effort was made to discover each and every nuance, each and every source of information to accurately interpret each law addressed in this book. A worry when writing a book such as this is that something was missed. Despite checking each and every statute for cases that may impact the interpretation, and double-checking, and even triple-checking *everything*, is it possible something may not have been discovered, leading to a mistake being made? Certainly. Readers are encouraged to forward any discoveries they may have that impact the laws as presented in this book to the author for consideration.

In any event, this book covers most of the laws that the average person needs to know in order to lawfully handle, use, or own a knife or firearm, such as what requirements exist for one who desires to purchasing a firearm or a knife, or to carry or use the same. Additionally, a large portion of this book covers the concealed carry laws of California with some basic, practical considerations for all those who are considering whether or not to carry a concealed weapon.

Aside from brief mention in various parts of this book, this text does not extensively cover laws as they pertain to law enforcement or military individuals, or hunters and the laws regulating hunting. This book was primarily written for, and assumes that the reader is, an average firearm, knife, and/or weapon owner who have not lost his ability to own and/or handle firearms under the law, and for those who are subject to exceptions in the law by virtue of serving our country, the state, any particular locality, or by operation of law.

However, there is an abundance of material in this book that is included that goes much further into the law than traditional firearm books. Instead of leaving out information that some may find valuable, this book was designed to be overly inclusive so that the readers may choose for themselves what is important and what may be ignored.

Included in the text of this book are over 2300 footnotes. This was a dilemma for the author, as using footnotes, especially as extensively as found in this book, can interfere with the flow of the text. However, a driving factor that led to this book being written was that most books of this nature lack any emphasis on the source for the assertions that are made, or an endnote is given and the endnote has five or six code sections and the reader has to try to figure it all out. Therefore, the author elected to leave the footnotes intact, no matter how trivial or repetitive. The reader will find a footnote attached to almost each and every assertion.

Please understand, that as tempting as it was to provide scathing commentary about the California Legislature and the direction that this state is moving politically, this book is not intended to put forth a political agenda. There are simply too many bad laws, potential laws that are bad, and too many arguments to address, and quite often, these events move much too quickly for commentary in a book. Instead, there are numerous online chat forums and blogs dealing with such issues. At some point, the author of this book may have something along those lines at his website, www.cagunlaw.com, but for now, the author is not involved in any political criticisms or commentary, aside from perhaps a slight indulgence here or there.

Instead, this book mainly discusses the laws regarding firearms, knives, and other weapons in a practical, informational sense. If it appears knife issues were slighted, they weren't. There simply are not many knife laws, and the knife laws rarely change. Knives, at least in California, are just not heavily regulated.

Additionally, and in all probability, people are more interested in firearm law than they are in laws regarding knives and other weapons. And while that consideration may be true, it seems logical to include a discussion regarding knives and other weapons in any book that addresses firearms, as most of the people that are into firearms tend to also be interested in knives and other weapons, at least to some degree. Certainly, if there are issues regarding weapons other than firearms, those readers will enjoy the convenience of owning a book that covers the current laws and common issues of all weapons.

In any event, the author hopes that the reader finds in this book a more comprehensive book regarding firearm, knife, and weapon law than has ever existed. It is the author's desire that this book serves to answer all of the reader's questions and concerns regarding the weapons laws addressed in this book.

WARNING - READ THIS NOW!

This book regards and includes only California law and some, but not all, federal laws, as well as commentary for each. This book does not make a point to include extensive discussions of federal law or local laws and ordinances. While there may be some reference to federal law and local ordinances, please be aware that these are selected references, and the author of this book by no means intended the book to be all-inclusive.

This book does not concern the laws of states other than California. While there may be a reference to laws of another state, such reference would be only to compare or contrast a law in California. Otherwise, this book strictly concerns California law and mainly focuses on what may be found in the Penal Code. If you need information regarding the laws of another state or need more information on Federal Law, this book is not a resource to satisfy those needs.

This book is not designed to provide specific legal advice. Instead, it is designed to provide the reader with a general overview of the law regarding firearms, knives, and other weapons. If you need legal advice, please do not rely on this book to provide the legal advice for your situation. Seek out adequate legal counsel to address your needs, as they likely go beyond the text and commentary as provided in this book.

As a prudent gun enthusiast, you are responsible to observe and obey all applicable federal, state, and local laws and regulations pertaining to the handling, use, and ownership of firearms.

A great deal of time and consideration has gone into this text to provide the reader with both the relevant laws pertaining to firearms, knife, and other weapons handling, use, and ownership under federal, state, and local laws, along with commentary designed to translate the laws from legalese to regular, everyday terms that most readers will find they can understand. But keep in mind, such efforts were strictly to provide this book as an educational text, and not as legal advice.

Despite the care and attention dedicated to this text, please realize that neither the author, the publisher, nor any distributor or retailer, provides any guarantees or warranties of any kind, either expressed or implied. The commentary of the relevant law is simply that - commentary. Such commentary should not be considered to be legal advice or a restatement of the law.

Please also understand that all the federal laws and state laws relevant to the use, handling, and the ownership of firearms, knives, and other weapons, are voluminous, and it would be a daunting task to provide each and every law, word for word, along with commentary. Therefore, it is important for you, the reader, to understand that this text is simply a summary of such laws, that no representations are made by either the author, publisher, any distributor or retailer, that this book includes all laws and regulations. The author, publisher, distributors and retailers expressly disclaim any and all potential liability that could ever exist from the reader's reliance upon information as provided in this text.

Furthermore, new bills are introduced every year to further restrict firearm use, ownership, and transfer. Many politicians and government figures have been quite frank regarding their interest to eliminate our rights under the Second Amendment. It is your responsibility as a citizen to pay attention to pending legislation and to observe and obey it if signed into law. It is also your responsibility, to yourself, your children, and future gun enthusiasts not yet born, to consider the right to bear arms when casting a ballot at the voting booth.

Additionally, laws addressed in this book, and in particular, the firearm laws, are subject to change at any moment, and by the time you read this book, changes have likely occurred. This book is also a "work in progress," and while every effort was made in researching each and every statute and applicable case to provide an interpretation of the law, the potential that something was overlooked always exists. Readers that question a particular interpretation of the law are encouraged to consult an attorney to answer their questions, compare the interpretation to other books on the subject, and, to contact the author of this book to discuss.

Also included in this book is a fairly thorough discussion on basic firearm safety consideration and firearm competency. However, it is important to understand that despite the detailed discussion regarding firearms safety and the basic use of a firearm, this text is not a training manual, nor is this book an adequate substitute for such. This book is likely not complete as firearm safety is concerned. Basic firearm safety considerations, are included in this text because the unfortunate reality is that for many individuals, safety is often overlooked. Will this book get through to such individuals? Perhaps not. But such considerations are here for them should they care to read it.

The author strongly suggests anyone who intends to purchase, own, use, or handle a firearm to seek out training from a professional in his or her local area prior to doing so. There is no reason at all that a firearm should ever be in the hands of someone who does not know even the most basic firearm safety considerations, such as to always treat the firearm as if it were loaded, knowing to keep the finger off the trigger, pointing the firearm in a safe direction, even if unloaded, and knowing how to safely check to see if a firearm is loaded and, if necessary, safely unload a firearm.

Finally, the author and publisher, or any reseller, retailer, or distributor assume no liability for any damages or negligence that may occur through the reader's use of firearms, knives, or other weapons, or any information included in this text. Regarding firearms, they should generally be handled only at a designated firing range under carefully controlled conditions. Readers of this text fully accept the responsibility for any and all accidents, damages and injuries that might occur from the handling and use of firearms or knives.

Thank you for your interest in this book. A great deal of time has gone into researching the material, sorting through and analyzing the law, and preparing it in a format that the reader can enjoy and understand. Hopefully it will answer all of your questions.

Part One

Organization of the Government

CHAPTER ONE

Federal and State Government in the United States

The United States of America is a federal district republic that consists of a federal district (Washington, D.C.), and fifty states. Our nation was established, or rather, was "constituted," by a document called the United States Constitution, which is the supreme law of the land. Each of the fifty states has its own individual constitution as well.

At the federal level, there are three branches of government: the Legislative branch, the Executive branch, and the Judicial branch. The State of California also has the same three branches of government that operate at the state level.

The Legislative branch consists of Congress at the federal level, and the state legislature at the state level, as well as all agencies which were created and serve Congress and the state legislature. At the federal level, the Executive branch consists of the President of the United States, and, at the state level, the Governor. Finally, the Judicial branch consists of the Supreme Court and all federal courts at the federal level, and the State Supreme Courts and the lower courts at the state level.

The Legislative branch passes laws which, at the federal level, are presented to the President, and at the state level, the state legislature presents laws to the Governor. Those laws are either signed by the President and the Governor, or they are vetoed (rejected), and either do not become laws, or are enacted by meeting the voting requirements to override the veto. Various agencies created by Congress or the state legislature then administer the laws.

More often than not, these laws, which are usually in the form of statues, are incomplete. It would be impossible to write laws that cover every contingency; that is, for every type of situation that could arise from a given subject matter. Here we find the duties of the Judiciary, which considers the questions about whether laws were broken by interpreting the law and applying it to a set of facts of a given situation. Quite often, courts that make up the Judiciary also determine if the law is a violation of either the federal or state constitution. Decisions of the courts then become the law, often known as "case law" or "common law", and these decisions sort of "fill in the blanks" where the statute may have been incomplete, vague, or somehow inadequate to address a given set of facts.

The federal judiciary is broken up into districts, and each district interprets the law for the states that make up its district. California is in the ninth district, which also includes Alaska, Hawaii, Arizona, Nevada, Washington, Oregon, Idaho, and Montana. Decisions rendered in one district apply only to the states that fall within that district, which can often lead to extremely different laws across the states. The only federal court that creates law that applies to the entire United States as a whole is the Supreme Court.

The United States Constitution

The United States Constitution is the supreme law of the land. It was created on September 17, 1787, and ratified June 21, 1788, and its purpose was to provide the structure and to organize the government of the United States and to define the relationship of the federal government to the individual states and the citizens (and even non-citizens) of the United States. Further, the Constitution was created to outline the powers and duties of each branch of the federal government as discussed above. The Constitution can be amended and has been numerous times. The first ten amendments are known as The Bill of Rights.

The Bill of Rights

The Bill of Rights was introduced by James Madison and was ratified December 15, 1791. The ten amendments were designed to protect the citizens from persecutions of their freedoms and culture and to affirm their rights by virtue of being an American citizen. The protections and/or rights include the right to free speech under the First Amendment; protections from unreasonable search and seizure under the Fourth Amendment; the right to due process; the right against self-incrimination; and other protections under the Fifth Amendment; various rights and protections that apply to criminal prosecutions, as provided under the Sixth Amendment; and of course, the right to keep and bear arms, as provided under the Second Amendment.

Of course, there are other protections and rights provided by the amendments in The Bill of Rights that are not mentioned, and they are also very important, and one should become familiar with those basic protections and rights. The Bill of Rights is included in the Appendices to this book.

The Second Amendment

While the Second Amendment appears very simple, it could be argued that no other Amendment has created so many different interpretations and so much heated debate over its meaning. The Amendment is as follows:

> *"A well regulated Militia, being necessary to the security of a free State, the right of the people to keep and bear Arms, shall not be infringed."*

The terms "well regulated," "Militia," and "bear arms," have, over the last several years, been subject to extensive debate because issues that involve availability of firearms, self-defense, concealed carry, and the like, have become very hot button issues.

One of the most recent cases was *District of Columbia v. Heller.*[2] After hearing the merits of this case, the Supreme Court ruled that "the Second Amendment protects the individual right to possess a firearm unconnected with service in a militia, and to use that arm for traditionally lawful purposes, such as self-defense within the home." Basically, the Supreme Court declared as unconstitutional the District of Columbia's long time ban against fully assembled handguns to be lawfully kept in the home of its citizens.

As it stands, *Heller* did not answer many questions concerning firearm laws in this nation, and since Heller, the courts at all levels have seen an increase in lawsuits pertaining to firearm issues.

The Second Amendment is undoubtedly the most hotly contested amendment included in the Bill of Rights. Politicians, mainly from the left, routinely distort the intentions of the Second Amendment for political gain, and, along with typical scare tactics, continue to push their agenda to limit or completely restrict firearms. There are currently many unconstitutional laws on the books regarding firearms that we must all live by, and it can take decades to reverse the damage caused by these bad laws.

How will these recent cases impact the firearm laws in the State of California and elsewhere? Well, in the immediate future, very little. Changing laws takes time. Fortunately, many lawsuits have been filed in California, and across this nation, in the wake of *Heller.* Only time will tell, however, if the rights that have eroded away will ever be returned to us.

---

[2] *District of Columbia v. Heller,* 128 S Ct. 2783 (2008).

Legislative Law

Statutes are laws that have been codified. In California, state statutes can be found in the California Code. The California Legislature maintains a website where the code can be found in its entirety. The California Code is massive. In print, the code comprises a large series of books that is ever-growing.

Each statute is called a "section," and is often represented by a symbol, "§"; There is generally no rhyme or reason as to whether the word "section" is used instead of the symbol §. In fact, throughout the California code, you see both, and in this book, you will see both used.

For your reference, the California Penal Code regarding firearm, knife, and weapon law is included in its entirety in the appendices.

Executive Law

Agencies of the United States or the State of California have the power to pass laws if first authorized by Congress or the state legislature. The regulations passed must fall within the scope of their powers, and must be constitutional.

The series of regulations as enacted by the various federal agencies can be found in the Code of Federal Regulations. In California, agency regulations are codified and included in the California Code, with a handful of regulations found elsewhere. As stated above, the state legislature keeps updated code online for our convenience.

One must also be aware of executive orders, both by the President of the United States and by the Governor of California. Presidential executive orders can be found online, as well as the executive orders enacted by the Governor.

Judicial Law

Judicial law, or court rulings, is often called "case law" or "common law." Case law has the same force and effect as the laws mentioned above, and generally interprets statues, administrative law and regulations, and applies such law to specific facts that arise from disputes and conflicts. Case law is the most volatile area of law, as it can change daily and vary from district to district, state to state, more than the other law. While statutes and regulations tend to be easier to find, read, and understand, case law tends to be harder to find, harder to read, and more difficult to understand. Case law is generally tailored very narrowly to address specific issues that pertain to a specific case, and therefore quite often appear incomplete, and many times leave open more questions than answers.

If you have questions in regards to case law, or any other law, it is best to consult an attorney for a translation of the meaning of the decision.

Federal Law v. State Law

Federal laws are the laws of the United States and apply everywhere within the United States. Laws of the State of California apply only to those individuals who are within the borders of California. However, both sets of laws apply and both sets of laws must be observed.

Keep in mind, that this book is about California law. While this book at times touches briefly on various key federal laws, please remember that by no means is this book comprehensive regarding federal law, and in fact, it may even be grossly inadequate if you are looking for a study of federal law as it pertains to firearms, knives, and other weapons. However, very common federal law considerations that were selected for this book are included where applicable.

By reading this book, one will learn that, for the most part, California law is specific in that it applies to almost everything you do regard firearms, knives, and other weapons, if such laws even exist. On the other hand, federal law tends to address broader issues, such as prohibited weapons, imported weapons, defining people who are prohibited from owning guns, and the like. You will look to California law to determine issues such as buying and transporting firearms, concealed carry, self-defense issues, and even more prohibited places.

CHAPTER TWO

California Law

The California Constitution

The original constitution for the State of California was created in November 1849. Statehood followed in 1850. However, the current constitution for the State of California was ratified on May 7, 1879. The California constitution is one of the longest constitutions in the world, which is one of two reasons why the text of the California constitution is not included in the appendices of this book.

Interestingly enough, but not surprisingly, the California constitution is one of the few state constitutions that offers no guarantee to the individual right to bear arms.[3] This is the second reason the text of the California constitution is not included in this book. Most states explicitly state such a right in their Constitution. Five other states do not have constitutional protections for the right to bear arms, which include Iowa, Maryland, Minnesota, New Jersey, and New York.

California Firearms and Deadly Weapons Law

"*To disarm the people is the most effectual way to enslave them.*"
- George Mason

Unfortunately, California is home to the nation's most oppressive firearm and weapon laws. There is an abundance of law that centers around telling you what you cannot own, what you cannot do, and limiting your rights in various ways. Many of these laws are extremely confusing. If you are not paying attention to what you are doing, you can accidentally break a law without even realizing they have violated the law. And the fact of the matter is that in almost all situations, ignorance of the law is no defense to breaking the law.

If you have read any of the firearm and weapon laws for the State of California in an effort to comply with the law, and you wound up confused, exhausted, and with questions unanswered, you are not alone. While California firearm laws are mainly written by attorneys, many of these laws are difficult for

---

[3]See *Kasler v. Lockyer*, 2 P.3d 581 (Cal. 2000), which holds that no "right to bear arms" exists under the California Constitution.

even the most talented attorneys to try to understand and translate. It is completely understandable for anyone to have difficulty in understanding California firearms and weapon laws as written by the state legislature.

Despite the confusion, the prudent firearm, knife, or weapon owner will do his best to be aware of the laws, have an understanding of the laws to the best of his abilities, and will respect the laws by observing and obeying such laws. It is important to obey the laws, even if you ultimately disagree with a particular law, and even if the law appears to be unconstitutional.

In California, most dangerous weapon laws can be found in The California Code. The California Code contains all of the statutes enacted by the state legislature. Within the California Code are codes such as the Vehicle Code, Civil Code, Education Code, Penal Code, and many, many more codes. The bulk of dangerous weapons laws, including firearms law, can be found in Part 4, Title 2 of the Penal Code, which is known as the "Dangerous Weapons Control Law."[4] Title 2 consists of six chapters dealing with firearms, machine guns, the Roberti-Roos Assault Weapons Control Act of 1989, the .50 Caliber BMG Regulation Act of 2004, destructive devices, ammunition, booby traps, body armor certification, tear gas weapons, firearm devices, and miscellaneous items such as BB guns, blowguns, picketing, stun guns, and Handgun Safety Certificates, commonly known as "HSC."

Also, there are laws regarding firearms and other weapons sprinkled throughout other areas of the California Code, and such laws may be found in the Business and Professions Code, the Civil Code, the Code of Civil Procedure, the Education Code, the Elections Code, the Family Code, the Financial Code, the Fish and Game Code, the Government Code, the Health and Safety Code, the Insurance Code, the Military and Veterans Code, the Penal Code, the Public Contracts Code, the Public Resources Code, the Vehicle Code, the Water Code, and the Welfare and Institutions Code.

For reference, the back of this book contains selected laws related to the use, possession, purchase, ownership, and transfer laws regarding firearms, knives, and other weapons as found throughout the California Code.

---

[4]Penal Code § 12000 et seq.

State Preemption

In California, firearm laws are primarily made at the state level by the California Legislature. This concept that an entire set of laws are intended to be made at only one level, such as firearms laws in California being made at the state legislature level, is called "preemption." Preemption of any law usually exists in order to create uniform laws that everyone must abide by, so there is less confusion of the laws which makes it easier for citizens to have an understanding of the law.

Currently, 46 states have enacted preemption laws so as to prevent more restrictive local ordinances regarding firearms. The four states that do not have preemption laws include Hawaii, Illinois, Nebraska, and Massachusetts, although Massachusetts allows only local ordinances that are first approved by the state legislature. Further, Connecticut, Massachusetts, New Jersey, and New York have preemption based upon judicial rulings but no preemption based upon statute.

Without preemption, counties, towns, municipalities, etc., could make their own gun laws that either intentionally or inadvertently conflicted or restricted the laws that were made at the state legislative level. This would be a nightmare and completely unacceptable for citizens attempting to conduct their lives in accordance with the law, as they would have too many laws to follow, many laws that conflict with it being unclear which laws were controlling, etc.

Despite the fact that California firearm laws are considered by the legislature to be preempted, the California Constitution provides that "[a] county or city may make and enforce within its limits all local, police, sanitary, and other ordinances and regulations not in conflict with general laws."[5] Therefore, a local government's power is as broad as the state legislature's power, and a city or county may act to protect the welfare of its residents, including the regulation of firearms.[6]

Therefore, only ordinances enacted that conflict with state law are prohibited.[7] Still, in this state, there are renegade lawmakers that still attempt to create laws despite preemption. A number of years ago In San Francisco,

---

[5] California Constitution, Article XI § 7.

[6] *Candid Enterprises v. Grossmont Union High School District*, 705 P.2d 876, 882 (Cal. 1985); *Galvan v. Superior Court of San Francisco*, 452 P.2d 930 (Cal. 1969).

[7] *Sherwin Williams Co v. City of Los Angeles*, 844 P.2d 534 (Cal. 1993).

Proposition H was proposed and passed by the San Francisco Board of Supervisors. This measure basically banned the manufacture, distribution, sale, and transfer of firearms and ammunition within the City of San Francisco.

Ultimately this law was challenged, and the California Supreme Court wisely ruled that Proposition H violated California law, stating that local officials do not have the authority to ban firearms from law-abiding residents. Despite the ruling, there are lawmakers at all levels in California willing to attempt to restrict or ban firearms despite California's preemption.

Please note that knives and other weapons are not subject to preemption. This means that these items can be regulated at the local level, and quite often, regulations regarding knives in particular can catch owners off-guard and land them in legal hot water. Be sure to check local laws and regulations regarding such items.

Part Two

Persons Prohibited from Ownership, Possession, and Use of Firearms

CHAPTER THREE

Buying, Possessing, and Owning Firearms in California

Who May Buy, Own, Use, or Possess Firearms and Ammunition in California

Those Who are Legal Age

In California, anyone who is legal age may buy, own, use, or possess a firearm. In much of the country, "legal age" means 18 years of age. However, in California, in order to buy a firearm, "legal age" is 18 years of age for a rifle or shotgun, and 21 years of age for a handgun.[8] There are no restrictions as to how many firearms a person is allowed to own. In general, firearms in California need not be registered. However, California does require registration of handguns, assault weapons, machineguns, and .50 BMG rifles. There are no permits involved with buying, owning, or possessing firearms in California.

If you are visiting California but you are a citizen of another state, you will not be permitted to buy a firearm anywhere in California. The exception to this prohibition is if you are buying directly from a licensed firearm dealer or through a licensed firearm dealer from a private party. This dealer must holds a federal firearm license ("FFL") and who will ship your purchase to a licensed gun dealer with an FFL in your state of residence. Such buyers will go through the purchase requirements in their state of residence as well as take possession of their firearm in their own state of residence.

Minors and Juveniles

In California, a minor is someone who is under the age of 18.[9] Federal law uses the term "juvenile," which has the same meaning as the definition of the word "minor" under California law.[10] There are three types of law that apply to minors and firearms, including California law, federal law, and local or municipal law. Only California law and some federal law are discussed in this book. There are just too

---

[8]Penal Code § 12072 (b).

[9]Family Code § 6500.

[10]18 U.S.C. § 922 (x)(5).

many counties and cities to keep up with. If you have a concern about a particular municipality and the laws governing that municipality, the laws are likely online, as just about every municipality has a web site. Google is your friend when looking for such laws and ordinances.

In order to avoid confusion for everyone involved, this book will use the appropriate term when discussing either federal or state law. In other words, when this book addresses state law, the term used will be "minor," and when addressing federal law, the term used will be "juvenile."

Federal Law as it Pertains to Juveniles

It shall be unlawful for any person who is a juvenile to knowingly possess a handgun or ammunition that is suitable for use only in a handgun.[11] However, there are exceptions.[12] First, a juvenile may be in temporary possession of or may use a handgun and/or handgun ammunition in the course of employment, such as in the course of ranching or farming related to the activities at the residence of the juvenile, as long as the juvenile first has the permission of the land owner or lessee.[13] The same exists for the juvenile who is temporarily engaged in target practice, hunting, or a course of instruction in the safe and lawful use of a handgun.[14]

Further, a juvenile may temporarily possess and/or use a handgun and/or handgun ammunition if prior written consent of the juvenile's parent or guardian is given, provided that the parent or guardian themselves is not prohibited by federal, state, or local law from possessing a firearm.[15] The written consent must remain on the juvenile's person at all times when the handgun is in the possession of the juvenile.[16]

A juvenile may also possess a handgun and/or handgun ammunition if they

[11] 18 U.S.C. § 922 (x)(2)(A) and (B).

[12] 18 U.S.C. § 922 (x)(3).

[13] 18 U.S.C. § 922 (x)(3)(A)(i).

[14] 18 U.S.C. § 922 (x)(3)(A)(i).

[15] 18 U.S.C. § 922 (x)(3)(A)(ii).

[16] 18 U.S.C. § 922 (x)(3)(A)(iii).

are a member of the Armed Forces of the United States or the National Guard and who possess or is armed with a handgun in the line of duty.[17] Juveniles may also possess a handgun and/or handgun ammunition if used in self-defense of the juvenile or other persons against an intruder into the residence of the juvenile or a residence where the juvenile is an invited guest.[18]

Finally, a juvenile is subject to the exceptions if they take a handgun or handgun ammunition subject to a transfer by inheritance of title; however, they may not take possession legally until they are of legal age.[19]

In any of the scenarios above, where a juvenile is in temporary custody of a handgun and/or handgun ammunition, he must transport the handgun unloaded and in a locked container when traveling to and from the activity, and must also observe all state and local gun laws.[20]

A juvenile who violates federal law regarding possession of a handgun and/or handgun ammunition may be fined and imprisoned not more than one year, or both.[21] The good news for the juvenile is that if the offense he is charged with is possession of either a handgun or handgun ammunition, or both, and that juvenile has not been convicted in any court of an offense or adjudicated as a juvenile delinquent, the punishment will be probation.[22] A violation of probation may result in incarceration.[23]

California Law as it Pertains to Minors - Possession and Use of Handguns

The general rule is that a minor shall not possess a pistol, revolver, or

---

[17] 18 U.S.C. § 922 (x)(3)((B).

[18] 18 U.S.C. § 922 (x)(3)(D).

[19] 18 U.S.C. § 922 (x)(3)(C).

[20] 18 U.S.C. § 922 (x)(3)(A)(ii)(I).

[21] 18 U.S.C. § 924 (a)(6)(A)(i).

[22] 18 U.S.C. §§ 924 (a)(6)(A)(I), 924 (a)(6)(A)(ii)(I) and (II).

[23] 18 U.S.C. § 924 (a)(6)(A)(i).

other firearm capable of being concealed upon the person.[24] A minor may also not possess live ammunition.[25] Even under strict California law as it pertains to minors, exceptions exist for both possession of firearms and possession of live ammunition.[26]

Intra-Familial Handgun Transfer - California law allows a parent to permanently transfer ownership in a handgun to their child who is aged 18 or older. The parent must file a Report of Operation of Law or Intra-Familial Handgun Transaction with the DOJ and submit the required fees.

Accompanied by a Parent - If the minor is accompanied by a parent or legal guardian, and the minor is actively engaged in, or is in direct transit to or from a lawful, recreational sport, including, but not limited to, competitive shooting, or agricultural, ranching, or hunting activity, or a motion picture, television, or video production, or entertainment or theatrical event, the nature of which involves the use of a firearm, the minor may possess and use the handgun.[27]

Written Permission - Additionally, if the minor is taking part in any of the above described activities, but instead is with a responsible adult, and the minor has the prior written consent of a parent or legal guardian, the minor may possess and use a handgun.[28] A "responsible adult" means a person at least 21 years of age who is not prohibited by state or federal law from possessing, receiving, owning, or purchasing a firearm.[29]

Minors 16 Years of Age or Older - Another exception exists for the minor who is at least 16 years of age, has the prior written consent of a parent or legal guardian, and taking part in activities described above, the minor need not be

---

[24]Penal Code § 12101 (a)(1).

[25]Penal Code § 12101 (b)(1).

[26]Penal Code § 12101 (a)(2).

[27]Penal Code § 12101 (a)(2)(A).

[28]Penal Code § 12101 (a)(2)(B).

[29]Penal Code § 12101 (e).

accompanied by a parent, legal guardian, or responsible adult.[30]

Possession on Private Land - Finally, for the minor engaged in the above described activities, and with parental consent or consent from a legal guardian, the minor may possess and use a handgun on lands owned or lawfully possessed by a parent or legal guardian.[31]

Live Ammunition - There are also exceptions for a minor's possession of live ammunition.[32] For live ammunition exceptions, the minor must be subject to one of the following exceptions: that he must have written consent from a parent or legal guardian[33] that he must be accompanied by a parent or legal guardian,[34] or the minor is actively engaged in, or is going to or from a lawful activity as described above.[35] California laws regarding minors and live ammunition is discussed in greater detail below.

Violation of Prohibition - A minor who violates any of the above may be punished by imprisonment in the state prison or county jail if he has previously been found guilty of violating the state laws discussed above as they pertain to minors, been previously found guilty of either the long list of violent crimes listed in Penal Code § 12021.1, a violation regarding the making, possessing, selling, or importing prohibited weapons pursuant to Penal Code § 12020, or of machinegun or silencer possession violations.[36] Further, custodial parents or the legal guardians of a convicted minor may be required to participate in classes on parenting education.[37]

---

[30]Penal Code § 12101 (a)(2)(C).

[31]Penal Code § 12101 (a)(2)(D).

[32]Penal Code § 12101 (b)(2).

[33]Penal Code § 12101 (b)(2)(A).

[34]Penal Code § 12101 (b)(2)(B).

[35]Penal Code § 12101 (b)(2)(C).

[36]Penal Code § 12101 (c).

[37]Penal Code § 12101 (d); Regarding parenting education classes, see Welfare and Institutions Code §§ 601 et seq., and 16507.7.

California Law as it Pertains to Minors - Loans and Transfers of Handguns

No person, corporation, or firm shall sell, loan, or transfer a firearm to a minor.[38] Violation of this law shall be punished by imprisonment in a county jail not exceeding one year or in the state prison, or by a fine not to exceed $1,000, or by both.[39] Exceptions exist regarding a loan of a handgun to a minor, as long as all of the following four conditions exist.[40]

Written Consent - The minor must have written consent of his parent or legal guardian that is presented at the time of, or prior to the time of, the loan, or is accompanied by the parent or legal guardian at the time the loan is made.[41]

Legitimate Purpose - The minor is being loaned the handgun for the purpose of engaging in lawful recreational sports, including, but not limited to, competitive shooting, or agricultural ranching, or hunting activity, or a motion picture, television, or video production, or entertainment or theatrical event, the nature of which involves the use of a firearm.[42]

Duration of Loan - The duration of the loan does not exceed the amount of time that is reasonably necessary to engage in the activity, the purpose of which was the reason to make the loan.[43]

Maximum Loan Term - The loan my not exceed 10 days.[44]

Another exception exists, however, known as the Intra-Familial Handgun Transfer. California law allows a parent to permanently transfer ownership in a

---

[38]Penal Code § 12072 (a)(3).

[39]Penal Code § 12072 (g)(3)(B).

[40]Penal Code § 12078 (p)(2).

[41]Penal Code § 12078 (p)(2)(A).

[42]Penal Code § 12078 (p)(2)(B).

[43]Penal Code § 12078 (p)(2)(C).

[44]Penal Code § 12078 (p)(2)(D).

handgun to their child who is aged 18 or older. The parent must file a Report of Operation of Law or Intra-Familial Handgun Transaction with the DOJ and submit the required fees.

Finally, it is not the intent of the Legislature, in enacting the laws discussed above regarding firearms, either to expand or narrow the current statutory or judicial authority as to the rights of minors to be loaned or possess a firearm for the purpose of self-defense or defense of others.[45]

California Law as it Pertains to Minors - Rifles and Shotguns

No person, corporation, or firm shall sell, loan, or transfer a firearm to a minor.[46] As usual, exceptions exist to this law in regard to rifles and shotguns.[47]

Express Permission - An exception exists for the loan of a firearm that is not a handgun with the express permission of the parent or legal guardian of the minor, if the loan does not exceed 30 days in duration and is for a lawful purpose.[48]

Distinguish the exception here as opposed to the handgun exception, in that with handguns, the permission must be *written*. The loan may be for as long as 30 days, instead of merely 10 days or as long as the specified activity lasts, whichever comes first.

Legitimate Purpose - The loan may be for *any* lawful purpose, instead of just for the specified purposes.

Transfer of Ownership - Other exceptions to this law include transfers or loans of firearms that are not handguns to a minor by a parent or legal guardian[49] and transfers or loans of the same to the minor by a grandparent if the transfer is done with the express (not written) permission of the parent or legal guardian of

---

[45]Penal Code § 12101 (f).

[46]Penal Code § 12072 (a)(3).

[47]Penal Code § 12072 (g)(1).

[48]Penal Code § 12078 (p)(1).

[49]Penal Code § 12078 (p)(4).

the minor.[50]

California Law as it Pertains to Minors - Assault Weapons and .50 BMG Rifles

No person who is under the age of 18 years may register or possess an assault weapon or .50 BMG rifle.[51]

California Law as it Pertains to Minors - Live Ammunition of Any Kind

A minor shall not possess live ammunition.[52] Exceptions exist for the application of this law, and **only one** of the following need exist.[53]

Written Consent - An exception exists for the minor who has written consent of a parent or legal guardian to possess live ammunition.[54]

Accompanied by Parent or Guardian - An exception exists for the minor who is accompanied by a parent or legal guardian.[55]

Legitimate Purpose - An exception exists for the minor who is actively engaged in, or is going to or from a lawful, recreational sport, including but not limited to, competitive shooting, or agricultural, ranching, or hunting activity, the nature of which involves the use of a firearm.[56]

Violation of Prohibition - As discussed above, the first conviction is a

---

[50]Penal Code § 12078 (p)(5).

[51]Penal Code § 12078 (d).

[52]Penal Code § 12101 (b)(1).

[53]Penal Code § 12101 (b)(2).

[54]Penal Code § 12101 (b)(2)(A).

[55]Penal Code § 12101 (b)(2)(B).

[56]Penal Code § 12101 (b)(2)(C).

misdemeanor.[57] However, if the minor had been previously convicted of either a violent felony,[58] a violation regarding the making, possessing, selling, or importing prohibited weapons,[59] a machinegun or silencer possession violation, or a previous violation of the law regarding minors possessing handguns or ammunition,[60] the punishment could be imprisonment in the state prison or in a county jail.[61] Also, custodial parents or the legal guardians of the minor may be required to participate in classes on parenting education.[62]

Selling Ammunition to Minors

No person, corporation, or dealer may sell any ammunition or reloaded ammunition to a person under 18 years of age.[63] Further, no person, corporation, or dealer may sell any ammunition or reloaded ammunition designed and intended for use in a handgun to a person under 21 years of age.[64] Where ammunition or reloaded ammunition may be used in both a rifle and a handgun, it may be sold to a person who is at least 18 years of age, but less than 21 years of age, if the vendor reasonably believes that the ammunition is being acquired for the use in a rifle and not a handgun.[65]

Sellers of ammunition may protect themselves when selling ammunition to a potential buyer by demanding proof of identification. Proof that the seller

---

[57]Penal Code § 12101 (c)(2).

[58]See Penal Code § 12021.1 regarding violent felonies applicable to this prohibition.

[59]See Penal Code § 12020 regarding prohibited weapons.

[60]See Penal Code § 12101 regarding minors violating handgun and ammunition laws.

[61]Penal Code § 12021 (c).

[62]Penal Code § 12101 (d); Regarding parenting education classes, see Welfare and Institutions Code §§ 601 et seq., and 16507.7.

[63]Penal Code § 12316 (a)(1) and (a)(1)(A)..

[64]Penal Code § 12316 (a)(1)(B).

[65]Penal Code § 12316 (a)(1)(B).

demanded proof of age, and was shown an identification card, and therefore acted in reasonable reliance upon that identification card, provides the seller the facts necessary to defend any criminal prosecution to the laws against selling ammunition to minors.[66] A violation of the prohibitions on selling ammunition to minors shall be punished by imprisonment in a county jail for a term not to exceed six months, or by a fine not to exceed $1,000, or by both.[67] The term "ammunition" does not include blanks.[68]

Supplies, Delivers, or Gives Ammunition to Minor

Any person, corporation, or dealer who supplies, delivers, or gives any ammunition to a minor who he or she knows, or using reasonable care should know, is prohibited from possessing that ammunition at the time is guilty of a misdemeanor, and subject to jail time and a financial penalty.[69]

For the purposes of the laws discussed above as they pertain to minors, "ammunition" includes, but is not limited to, any bullet, cartridge, magazine, clip, speed loader, autoloader, or a projectile capable of being fired from a firearm with a deadly consequence.[70] Also, "ammunition" does not include "blanks."[71]

Those Prohibited by California Law From Buying, Owning, Using, or Possessing Firearms in California

Those with Prior Felony Convictions

Any person who has been convicted of a felony under the laws of the United States, the State of California, or any other state, government, or country, and who owns, purchases, receives, or has in his or her possession or under his or

[66]Penal Code § 12316 (a)(2).

[67]Penal Code § 12316 (a)(3).

[68]Penal Code § 12316 (a)(2).

[69]Penal Code § 12316 (a)(1)(C).

[70]Penal Code § 12316 (b)(2).

[71]Penal Code § 12316 (b)(2).

her custody or control any firearm is guilty of a felony.[72] For purposes of this prohibition, California defines a "firearm" as not just a complete, working firearm, but also the frame of a firearm or the receiver of a firearm.[73]

However, if the conviction was in a federal court for a federal crime, California's prohibition regarding felons and firearms applies only if the conviction of a like offense under California law can only result in imposition of felony punishment,[74] or the defendant was sentenced to a federal correctional facility for more than 30 days, or received a fine of more than one thousand dollars ($1,000), or received both punishments.[75]

Individuals in this category may also not possess ammunition.

Those Convicted of Certain Violent Firearm Offenses

California law also specifically prohibits those convicted of specified offenses from firearm ownership, regardless if the conviction was a misdemeanor conviction or a felony conviction.[76] For purposes of this prohibition, California defines a "firearm" as not just a complete, working firearm, but also the frame of a firearm or the receiver of a firearm.[77]

These specific offenses include the following:

- an assault upon the person of another with a deadly weapon or instrument other than a firearm or by any means of force likely to produce great bodily injury[78]
- an assault upon the person of another with a firearm

[72]Penal Code § 12021(a)(1).

[73]Penal Code § 12001 (k).

[74]Penal Code § 12021 (f)(1).

[75]Penal Code § 12021 (f)(2).

[76]Penal Code § 12021 (a)(1).

[77]Penal Code § 12001 (k).

[78]Penal Code §§ 12001.6 (a); 245 (a)(1); 12021.1 (b)(27).

(assault with a deadly weapon)[79]

- an assault with a firearm, semiautomatic firearm, assault weapon, machinegun, or .50 BMG rifle upon the person of a peace officer or firefighter, and who knows or reasonably should know that the victim is a peace officer or firefighter engaged in the performance of his or her duties, while such officer or firefighter is actually engaged in the performance of their duties (assault with a firearm)[80]
- the discharge of a firearm at an inhabited dwelling house, occupied building, vehicle, aircraft, or inhabited housecar or camper[81]
- for any person who, except in self-defense, in the presence of any other person, draws or exhibits any firearm, whether loaded or unloaded, in a rude, angry, or threatening manner, or who in any manner, unlawfully uses a firearm in any fight or quarrel (brandishing)[82]
- any person who, in the immediate presence of a peace officer, draws or exhibits any firearm, whether loaded or not, in a rude, angry, or threatening manner, and who knows or should know that the officer is engaged in his duties, who is convicted of such, is thereafter prohibited from owning, possessing, or using a firearm, and having such in his custody or control (brandishing in the presence of a police officer)[83]

It should be noted that where any person brandishes a firearm, that is, a person who, except in self-defense, in the presence of any other person, draws or exhibits any firearm, whether loaded or unloaded, in a rude, angry, or threatening manner, or who in any manner, unlawfully uses a firearm in any fight or quarrel, is guilty of a misdemeanor if it is their first offense for brandishing. However, any

---

[79]Penal Code §§ 12001.6 (a); 245 (a)(2); 12021.1 (b)(27).

[80]Penal Code §§ 12001.6 (a); 245 (d)(1), (2), and (3); 12021.1 (b)(27).

[81]Penal Code §§12001.6 (b); 246; 12021.1 (b)(27).

[82]Penal Code §§12001.6 (c); 417 (a)(2).

[83]Penal Code §§ 12001.6 (d); 417 (c); 12021.1(b)(27).

convictions thereafter for brandishing will result in a felony charge.[84]

Individuals in this category may also not possess ammunition.

Those Convicted of Certain Other Offenses

Any person who has been previously convicted of any of the offenses listed below and who owns, has in his possession, or has under his control any firearm is also guilty of a felony.[85] For purposes of this prohibition, California defines a "firearm" as not just a complete, working firearm, but also the frame of a firearm or the receiver of a firearm.[86]

The offenses that form the basis for the prohibition include the following:

- Murder or involuntary manslaughter
- Mayhem
- Rape
- Sodomy by force, violence, duress, menace, or threat of great bodily harm
- Oral copulation by force, violence, duress, menace, or threat of great bodily harm
- Lewd acts on a child under the age of 14 years
- Any felony punishable by death or imprisonment in the state prison for life
- Any other felony in which the defendant inflicts great bodily injury on any person, other than an accomplice, that has been charged and proven, or any felony in which the defendant uses a firearm which use has been charged and proven
- Attempted murder
- Assault with intent to commit rape or robbery
- Assault with a deadly weapon or instrument on a peace officer
- Assault by a life prisoner on a non-inmate
- Arson
- Exploding a destructive device or any explosive with intent to injure

---

[84] Penal Code § 12021.1 (b)(29).

[85] Penal Code § 12021.1 (a) and (b).

[86] Penal Code § 12001 (k).

- Exploding a destructive device or any explosive causing great bodily injury
- Exploding a destructive device or any explosive with the intent to murder
- Robbery
- Kidnapping
- Taking of a hostage by an inmate of a state prison
- Attempt to commit a felony punishable by death or imprisonment in the state prison for life
- Any felony in which the defendant personally used a dangerous or deadly weapon
- Escape from a state prison by use of force or violence
- Assault with a deadly weapon or force likely to produce great bodily injury
- Any felony violation while participating in criminal street gang crimes
- Any attempt to commit a crime listed above, other than an assault
- Any offense enumerated in Penal Code § 12001.6 (a), (b), or (d), as listed and discussed above
- Carjacking
- Any offense enumerated in Penal Code 12001.6 (c), if the person has two or more convictions for violating 417 (a)(2)

Individuals in this category may also not possess ammunition.

Possession of Ammunition by Prohibited Persons

No person who is prohibited from owning or possessing a firearm because of a conviction of an offense in the previous three categories shall own, possess, or have under his or her custody or control, any ammunition or reloaded ammunition.[87] A violation is a misdemeanor punishable by imprisonment in a county jail not to exceed one year or in the state prison, by a fine not to exceed $1,000, or by both.[88]

However, a violation of this law regarding the prohibition for ammunition possession is justifiable if all of the following conditions are met:

---

[87]Penal Code § 12316 (b)(1).

[88]Penal Code § 12316 (b)(3).

- the person found or took the ammunition or reloaded ammunition from a person who was committing a crime against him[89]
- he kept it for long enough as necessary to deliver or transport it to a law enforcement agency for them to dispose of[90]
- the person's prohibition is solely because of a previous violation of Penal Code 12021[91] and is not the result of other prohibitions

At trial, the trier of fact shall determine whether the defendant is subject to the exemption,[92] and the defendant has the burden of proof by a preponderance of the evidence that he or she is subject to the exemption.[93]

Minors Convicted of Felony or Certain Violent Firearm Offenses

Minors with felony convictions or convictions for the violent firearms offenses as those listed in Penal Code § 12001.6 (as discussed above) that were prosecuted as an adult in an adult court of law, may not own, have in their possession, or have under their custody or control any firearm.[94]

Those Who are Addicted to the Use of Any Narcotic Drug

Any person who is addicted to the use of any narcotic drug and who owns, purchases, receives, or has in his or her possession or under his or her custody or control any firearm is guilty of a felony.[95] "Narcotic drugs" include drugs such as cocaine, crack, heroin, morphine, and the like. It is important to note that marijuana

---

89 Penal Code § 12316 (d)(1)(A).

90 Penal Code § 12316 (d)(1)(B).

91 Penal Code § 12316 (d)(1)(C); see Penal Code § 12021.

92 Penal Code § 12316 (d)(2); see also Penal Code § 12316 (d).

93 Penal Code § 12316 (d)(3).

94 Penal Code § 12021 (b).

95 Penal Code § 12021 (a)(1).

is not defined as a narcotic in regards to this law.[96] However, federal law prohibits users of marijuana from possessing, owning, purchasing, receiving, or having within their custody or control any firearms.[97]

Regardless of whether you are a drug addict or not, the law has strict punishments for those individuals found in the unlawful possession of narcotics while armed with a loaded firearm. Specifically, every person who is "armed with" a loaded, operable firearm, while also unlawfully possessing a substance containing cocaine or with a cocaine base, a substance containing methamphetamine, a substance with PCP, whether liquid or not, or a hand-rolled cigarette with PCP, is guilty of a felony that is punishable by imprisonment in the state prison for two, three, or four years.[98] "Armed with" is defined as "being available for immediate offensive and defensive use."[99]

A problem exists with the word "addicted." What does that mean, exactly? Courts have defined the term to mean that the person need not be in an actual state of withdrawal, but that the individual is "emotionally dependent" on the drug in the sense that he experiences a compulsive need to continue its use, has a tolerance to its effects such that he may require larger and more potent doses.[100]

Those Convicted of Other Various Misdemeanors - 10 Year Prohibition

The Penal Code also provides that individuals convicted of certain misdemeanors will lose their right to own, purchase, receive, or have in their possession or under their custody or control, any firearm for a period of ten years, along with the potential of paying up to $1,000 in penalties.[101] The offenses include:

- Making reasonable threats of injury to person or property of any officer or employee of any public or private institution, or any other public officer or employee, to do or refrain from doing an

---

[96] Health and Safety Code § 11019.

[97] 18 U.S.C. § 922 (g)(3) and 21 U.S.C. § 802.

[98] Health and Safety Code § 11370.1 (a).

[99] Health and Safety Code § 11370.1 (a).

[100] *People v. Washington*, (1965) 237 Cal.App.2d 59, 68.

[101] Penal Code § 12021 (c)(1).

act in performance of their duties[102]

- Making threats to kill or seriously injure specifically named public employees (the list is extensive, please see the code section)[103]
- Witness and victim intimidation, with or without a deadly weapon[104]
- Making threats of violence against witnesses, victims, or informants, or threats to destroy their property[105]
- Disarming or attempting to disarm a police officer while that officer is engaged in the performance of his lawful duties[106]
- Unlawfully bringing a firearm or other weapon into any state or local public building[107]
- Unlawfully bringing or possessing a loaded firearm into specifically named public buildings (the list is extensive, please see the code sections)[108]
- Knowingly transferring possession and control of firearms to criminal street gang members[109]
- Assaulting another individual, i.e., attempt, coupled with the present ability, to commit a violent injury on the person of another[110]
- Committing a battery against another individual, i.e., any willful or unlawful use of force of violence upon the person of another[111]

---

[102]Penal Code § 71.

[103]Penal Code § 76.

[104]Penal Code §§ 136.1, 136.5.

[105]Penal Code § 140.

[106]Penal Code § 148 (d).

[107]Penal Code § 171b.

[108]Penal Code §§ 171c and 171d.

[109]Penal Code § 186.28.

[110]Penal Code §§ 240 and 241.

[111]Penal Code §§ 242 and 243.

- Committing a sexual battery upon the person of another.[112]
- Assaulting another individual with a stun gun or "less lethal weapon" (see Glossary or Penal Code § 12601)[113]
- Assault with a deadly weapon or instrument other than a firearm or by means of force likely to produce great bodily injury upon another, including school employees[114]
- Unlawful discharge of a firearm in a grossly negligent manner that could result in death or injury to another person[115]
- Willfully and maliciously discharging a firearm at an unoccupied aircraft, motor vehicle, uninhabited building or dwelling house.[116] This does not include shooting at abandoned vehicles, unoccupied vehicles, uninhabited buildings, or a dwelling house with the permission of the owner[117]
- Wilfully inflicting corporal injury upon one's spouse, former spouse, cohabitant, former cohabitant, or the mother or father of their child, resulting in a traumatic condition[118]
- Intentionally and knowingly violating a protective order to prevent domestic violence[119]
- Drawing or exhibiting any deadly weapon in a rude, angry, or threatening manner, or who unlawfully uses a deadly weapon in a fight or quarrel[120]
- The crime of drawing or exhibiting any firearm or deadly weapon

---

[112]Penal Code § 243.4.

[113]Penal Code § 244.5.

[114]Penal Code §§ 245 and 245.5.

[115]Penal Code § 246.3.

[116]Penal Code § 247.

[117]Penal Code § 247.

[118]Penal Code § 273.5.

[119]Penal Code § 273.6.

[120]Penal Code § 417.

and actually inflicting serious bodily injury[121]

- Making threats designed to terrorize others, whether such threats can actually be committed or not[122]
- Violating the Gun Free School Zone Act of 1995 (discussed in depth later in this book), but basically bringing or possessing a firearm on the grounds of any public or private school, community college, university, or simply bringing or possessing the firearm in any area considered a school zone[123]
- Committing the act of stalking (the willful, malicious, and repeated following or harassment of that person with the intent to cause that person to be fearful for their safety[124]
- Carrying a loaded firearm with the intent to commit a felony[125]
- Carrying a loaded firearm with the intent to assault another[126]
- Allowing another person to discharge a firearm from a vehicle while you are driving the vehicle,[127] or willfully and maliciously discharging a firearm from a motor vehicle[128]
- Committing criminal possession of a firearm while carrying a firearm in a public place or on any public street while masked so as to hide their identity[129]
- A licensed dealer transferring a firearm to a person not of legal age to possess such[130]
- Selling to a minor a pistol, revolver, or other firearm capable of

---

[121]Penal Code § 417.6.

[122]Penal Code § 422.

[123]Penal Code § 626.9.

[124]Penal Code § 646.9.

[125]Penal Code § 12023.

[126]Penal Code § 12024.

[127]Penal Code § 12034 (b).

[128]Penal Code § 12034 (d)

[129]Penal Code § 12040.

[130]Penal Code § 12072 (b).

being concealed upon the person[131]

- Possessing or knowingly transporting a machinegun[132]
- Knowingly possessing handgun ammunition designed primarily to penetrate metal or armor[133]
- Picketing or attending other informational activities in a public place relating to a concerted refusal to work while carrying a firearm concealed, on the person, within a vehicle under his or her control, carries some other type of deadly weapon, and/or wears the uniform of a peace officer, whether or not the person is a peace officer[134]
- Possession of a firearm by a person declared mentally ill[135]
- Transferring a firearm to a person declared mentally ill[136]
- Bringing a firearm into a Youth Authority or county juvenile facility[137]

Those Who are on Probation

Any person who, as an express condition of probation, is prohibited or restricted from owning, possessing, controlling, receiving, or purchasing a firearm and who owns, purchases, receives, or has in his or her possession or under his or her custody or control, any firearm is guilty of a public offense, with punishment being up to a year in jail or in the state prison, and up to $1000 fine, or both.[138] The court must notify the person subject to the prohibition of such prohibition.[139]

---

[131]Penal Code § 12100 (repealed).

[132]Penal Code § 12220.

[133]Penal Code § 12320.

[134]Penal Code § 12590.

[135]Welfare & Institutions Code §§ 8100 and 8103.

[136]Welfare & Institutions Code § 8101.

[137]Welfare and Institutions Code §§ 871.5 and 1001.5

[138]Penal Code § 12021 (d)(1).

[139]Penal Code § 12021 (d)(1).

Those Who are Subject to a Protective Order, Temporary Restraining Order, or Injunction

Courts have at their disposal a variety of orders to address different situations.[140] Quite often, orders are designed to require certain individuals to stay away from other individuals, to stay away from certain property or residences, to refrain from committing certain acts, or to prohibit threatening situations and acts of violence. Such orders may be temporary or permanent.

It is very common for protective orders to include prohibitions on the ownership, purchase, or receipt of a firearm, or even having a firearm under the custody or control of those subject to the protective order. The order should explicitly state any terms of the order, including any prohibitions on firearms. If the person subject to a protective order that includes firearm prohibitions already owns firearms, he will be ordered to surrender them to the police or sell them to a licenced firearms dealer.

Protective orders can be issued pursuant to a variety of code sections and for a variety of reasons.[141] To violate knowingly a protective order is considered a misdemeanor (some violations are felonies), with punishment and penalty including imprisonment in a county jail or state prison not to exceed one year, and by a fine not to exceed $1,000.[142]

A violation of a protective order may be justified for a variety of reasons, such as the person subject to the order found the firearm, or took away a firearm from a person who was committing a crime against them, who then lawfully transported the firearm to a local law enforcement agency.[143]

A recently signed bill authorizes the issuance of a search warrant to seize a firearm possessed by a person subject to a protective order that prohibits firearms

---

[140]See Code of Civil Procedure §§ 527.6 and 527.8; Family Code § 6218; Penal Code §§ 136.2 and 646.91; Welfare and Institutions Code § 15657.03.

[141]See Code of Civil Procedure §§ 527.6 and 527.8; Family Code § 6218; Penal Code §§ 136.2 and 646.91; Welfare and Institutions Code § 15657.03.

[142]Penal Code § 12021 (g)(1).

[143]Penal Code § 12021 (h).

possession or if he is arrested in connection with a domestic violence incident.[144]

Those Adjudicated as a Ward of the Court

Any person who has committed certain enumerated violations and is subsequently adjudged a ward of the juvenile court shall not own, or have in his custody or control, any firearm until the age of 30 years.[145] The enumerated violations include serious felonies, sexual offenses, drug offenses, and the like.[146]

Those Admitted to Mental Facility

A person shall not have in his possession or under his custody or control, or purchase or receive, or attempt to purchase or receive, any firearm whatsoever or any other deadly weapon, if he has been admitted to a facility and is receiving inpatient treatment and, in the opinion of the attending health professional who is primarily responsible for the patient's treatment of a mental disorder, is a danger to self or others, as specified by law,[147] even in situations where the patient has voluntarily consented to that treatment.[148] A person is not subject to this prohibition once he is discharged from the facility.[149]

The California Legislature provided a few key definitions to assist in our understanding of the laws discussed above.

"Discharge" does not include a simply a leave of absence from the facility.[150] The patient must actually be discharged by the hospital following the end of treatment. "A deadly weapon" means any weapon, the possession or concealed

---

[144]Assembly Bill ("AB") No. 532.

[145]Penal Code § 12021 (e).

[146]See Welfare and Institutions Code § 707 (b); Penal Code §§ 1203.073, 12021 (c)(1), 12025 (a), 12031 (a), and 12034 (a).

[147]See Welfare and Institutions Code §§ 5150, 5250, and 5300.

[148]Welfare and Institutions Code § 8100 (a).

[149]Welfare and Institutions Code § 8100 (a).

[150]Welfare and Institutions Code § 8100 (c).

carry of which is prohibited by the Penal Code.[151] A person who is a "danger to self" is a person who has made a serious threat of, or attempted, suicide with the use of a firearm or other deadly weapon.[152]

Violations of these prohibitions are misdemeanors.[153]

Mental hospitals, health facilities, or other institutions, or treating health professionals or psychotherapists who provide reports are civilly immune for making any report required or authorized.[154]

A recently signed bill authorizes courts to issue search warrants to seize firearms where, upon a finding of sufficient probable cause, the weapon is owned by or in the possession of a person detained for a mental health examination.[155]

Those Who Inform a Psychotherapist of Threats to Others

A person shall not have in their possession or under their custody or control, or purchase or receive, or attempt to purchase or receive, any firearms whatsoever or any other deadly weapon for a period of six months whenever he communicates to a licensed psychotherapist a serious threat of physical violence against a reasonably foreseeable victim or victims.[156] The six-month prohibition begins when the psychotherapist reports to the local law enforcement agency the identity of the person making the threat.[157]

This prohibition does not apply unless the psychotherapist actually informs

---

[151] See Penal Code § 12020.

[152] Welfare and Institutions Code § 8100 (f).

[153] Welfare and Institutions Code § 8100 (g).

[154] Welfare and Institutions Code § 8108.

[155] Assembly Bill ("AB") 532.

[156] Welfare and Institutions Code § 8100 (b)(1).

[157] Welfare and Institutions Code § 8100 (b)(1).

local law enforcement of the threat.[158] However, a licensed psychotherapist is required to immediately report to a local law enforcement agency the identity of any person who made such threats.[159] Then, the Department of Justice will notify by certified mail, return receipt requested, a person who has become subject to this prohibition as a result of threats made.[160]

The notification sent by the Department of Justice will state the conditions of the prohibition, and will include the start date and end date of the prohibition.[161] The notification will also inform the individual that he may petition the court for an order permitting the person to own, possess, control, receive, or purchase a firearm.[162] Should he choose to petition the superior court, he must prove, by a preponderance of the evidence, that he (the "petitioner") is likely to use firearms or other deadly weapons in a safe and lawful manner.[163] The petition must be filed in the county of residence.[164]

Mental hospitals, health facilities, or other institutions, or treating health professionals or psychotherapists who provide reports are civilly immune for making any report required or authorized.[165]

Those Affected by Mental Disorder or Illness and Mentally Disordered Sex Offenders

No person who has been adjudicated by a court of any state to be a danger to others as a result of a mental disorder or mental illness, or who has been adjudicated to be a mentally disordered sex offender, shall purchase or receive, or

---

[158] Welfare and Institutions Code § 8100 (b)(1).

[159] Welfare and Institutions Code § 8105 (c).

[160] Welfare and Institutions Code § 8100 (b)(2).

[161] Welfare and Institutions Code § 8100 (b)(2)(A).

[162] Welfare and Institutions Code § 8100 (b)(2)(B).

[163] Welfare and Institutions Code §§ 8100 (b)(1) and (b)(3).

[164] Welfare and Institutions Code § 8100 (b)(3).

[165] Welfare and Institutions Code § 8108.

attempt to purchase or receive, or have in his possession, custody, or control any firearm or any other deadly weapon.[166] Such people may regain the right to a firearm if there has been issued to the person a certificate by the court of adjudication upon release from treatment or at a later date stating that the person may possess a firearm or any other deadly weapon without endangering others, if the person has not, subsequent to the issuance of the certificate, again been adjudicated by a court to be a danger to others as a result of a mental disorder or illness.[167]

In the above scenario, the court will immediately notify the Department of Justice when an individual is prohibited from firearms and other deadly weapons.[168] Furthermore, the court will notify the Department of Justice if a certificate has been issued that removes the prohibition.[169]

Mental hospitals, health facilities, or other institutions, or treating health professionals or psychotherapists who provide reports are civilly immune for making any report required or authorized.[170]

Those Found Not Guilty by Reason of Insanity

No person who has been found not guilty by reason of insanity of a wide variety of violent and/or very serious felonies shall purchase or receive, or attempt to purchase and receive, or have in his possession or under his custody or control any firearm or any other deadly weapon.[171] The court will immediately notify the Department of Justice of the court order finding a person to be subject to this prohibition.[172] This individual may at some point possess a firearm or other deadly

---

[166]Welfare and Institutions Code § 8103 (a)(1).

[167]Welfare and Institutions Code § 8103 (a)(1).

[168]Welfare and Institutions Code § 8103 (a)(2).

[169]Welfare and Institutions Code § 8103 (a)(2).

[170]Welfare and Institutions Code § 8108.

[171]Welfare and Institutions Code § 8103 (b)(1). For the extensive list of felonies applicable to this prohibition, see Welfare and Institutions Code § 8103 (b)(1),

[172]Welfare and Institutions Code §§ 8103 (b)(2) and (c)(2).

weapon if the court of commitment has found the person to have recovered sanity under the law.[173] The court will notify the Department of Justice of any restored rights by way of restored sanity.[174]

It is important to note, however, that if the crime for which one was found not guilty by reason of insanity is an enumerated offense as found in Welfare and Institutions Code § 8103 (b)(1), he will be unable to have his rights restored, even if the court finds he has recovered their sanity.[175]

Those Found Mentally Incompetent to Stand Trial

No person found by a court to be mentally incompetent to stand trial shall purchase or receive, or attempt to purchase and receive, or shall have in his or her possession, custody, or control any firearm or any other deadly weapon.[176] The court will immediately notify the Department of Justice of any such finding.[177] Rights may be restored if there is a finding that the person has recovered his competence, and such a finding must be sent by the court to the Department of Justice.[178]

Those Placed Under Conservatorship by a Court

No person who has been placed under conservatorship by a court after a determination that the person is gravely disabled as a result of a mental disorder or impairment by chronic alcoholism shall purchase or receive, or attempt to purchase or receive, or shall have in his possession, custody, or control any firearm or any other deadly weapon while under the conservatorship if, at the time the conservatorship was ordered or at a later date, the court which imposed the conservatorship found that possession of a firearm or any other deadly weapon by

---

[173]Welfare and Institutions Code § 8103 (c)(1).

[174]Welfare and Institutions Code § 8103 (c)(2).

[175]Welfare and Institutions Code § 8103 (c)(1).

[176]Welfare and Institutions Code § 8103 (d)(1).

[177]Welfare and Institutions Code § 8103 (d)(2).

[178]Welfare and Institutions Code § 8103 (d)(1) and (d)(2).

the person would present a danger to the safety of the person or to others.[179] Upon imposing the conservatorship, the court will notify the person of this prohibition,[180] and will also notify the Department of Justice of the same.[181] Such notice will include dates if imposition and the date the conservatorship is to end.[182] If the conservatorship ends prior to the initial termination date, the court shall immediately notify the Department of Justice that possession of a firearm or any other deadly weapon by the person would no longer present a danger to the safety of the person or to others.[183]

All information provided to the Department of Justice regarding the conservatorship and its prohibitions is to be kept confidential, separate, and apart from all other records maintained from the Department of Justice, to be used only to determine firearms and other deadly weapon eligibility, and all such information is to be destroyed upon receipt by the Department of Justice of notice of termination of the conservatorship.[184]

Those Arrested, Confined, and Treated as Danger to Themselves or Others, and Those Certified for Intensive Treatment

No person who has been taken into custody because he is a danger to himself or to others as a result of a mental disorder, or is otherwise gravely disabled, who is later evaluated and admitted because that person is indeed a danger to himself or to others or is otherwise certified for intensive treatment, shall own, possess, control, receive, or purchase, or attempt to own, possess, control, receive, or purchase any firearm for a period of five years after the person is released from the facility.[185]

---

[179]Welfare and Institutions Code § 8103 (e)(1).

[180]Welfare and Institutions Code § 8103 (e)(1).

[181]Welfare and Institutions Code § 8103 (e)(1).

[182]Welfare and Institutions Code § 8103 (e)(2).

[183]Welfare and Institutions Code § 8103 (e)(2).

[184]Welfare and Institutions Code § 8103 (e)(3).

[185]Welfare and Institutions Code §§ 8103 (f)(1) and 8103 (g)(1).

The facility that accepts the person as a patient is to inform immediately the Department of Justice of the identity of the patient and the legal grounds upon which the person was admitted to the facility.[186] This report is to be kept confidential, and aside for court purposes, it is to be used to determine only the eligibility of the person to own, possess, control, receive, or purchase a firearm.[187]

However, the person subject to this prohibition has a right to petition the superior court in the appropriate county for a hearing and request for an order to restore his rights to firearms and other deadly weapons. Only if that court determines that the prosecution has failed to meet its burden of proof will the petitioner's rights will be restored.[188] Prior to or upon discharge, the facility is to inform the person that he is prohibited from firearms for a period of five years and must also inform the person that he has the right to request a hearing from the court for an order removing the prohibition.[189] The facility is to provide the patient with a form prescribed by the Department of Justice that allows the patient to request such hearing.[190] If the patient requests, the facility is required to submit the form on behalf of the patient.[191]

Mental hospitals, health facilities, or other institutions, or treating health professionals or psychotherapists who provide reports are civilly immune for making any report required or authorized.[192]

<u>Confiscation of Weapons of Detained or Apprehended Person for Mental Evaluation</u>

When a person has been detained or apprehended for examination of his mental examination or who is a person described in Welfare and Institutions Code

---

[186]Welfare and Institutions Code §§ 8103 (f)(2) and 8103 (g)(2).

[187]Welfare and Institutions Code §§ 8103 (f)(2) and 8103 (g)(2).

[188]Welfare and Institutions Code §§ 8103 (f)(1), (f)(5), (f)(6), 8103 (g)(4).

[189]Welfare and Institutions Code §§ 8103 (f)(3), 8103 (g)(3).

[190]Welfare and Institutions Code §§ 8103 (f)(3) and 8103 (g)(3).

[191]Welfare and Institutions Code §§ 8103 (f)(3) and 8103 (g)(3).

[192]Welfare and Institutions Code § 8108.

§§ 8100 or 8103 (as discussed above), and is found to own, have in his possession or control, any firearm or any other deadly weapon, such will be confiscated by any law enforcement agency or peace officer, who shall retain custody of the weapon.[193] The law enforcement agency or peace officer responsible for confiscation will notify the person of confiscation and of the procedure for the return of the weapon, as will the professional person in charge of the mental health care facility, or his designee at the mental health care facility.[194]

Upon that person's release, the law enforcement agency that has possession of a seized firearm or other deadly weapon has 30 days to initiate a petition in the superior court for a hearing to determine whether the return of the firearm or other deadly weapon would be likely to result in endangering the person or others.[195] The law enforcement agency must give notice of such hearing to the person whose weapon was confiscated.[196] If law enforcement fails to initiate the hearing, it shall make the weapon available for return.[197] If that person fails to attend the hearing, a default judgment will be entered in favor of the law enforcement agency petition, and the person will be deemed to have forfeited the confiscated weapon.[198]

Felony Driving Conviction

As discussed above, if one is convicted of a felony, he is forever prohibited from purchasing, possessing, owning, controlling, and handling firearms. This is true for those convicted of a felony traffic offense, such as felony drunk driving. This is a very common way the average citizen forever loses his right to legally handle firearms.

---

[193] Welfare and Institutions Code § 8102 (a).

[194] Welfare and Institutions Code § 8102 (b).

[195] Welfare and Institutions Code § 8102 (c).

[196] Welfare and Institutions Code § 8102 (c).

[197] Welfare and Institutions Code § 8102 (d).

[198] Welfare and Institutions Code § 8102 (e).

Who May Not Buy, Own, Use, or Possess Firearms in California, (or Any Other State) Under to Federal Law

Pursuant to federal law, it is unlawful for any of the following individuals to possess any firearm or ammunition:[199]

- one who has been convicted in any court of a crime by imprisonment for a term exceeding one year (a felony), even if time served was actually less[200]
- one who is a fugitive from justice[201]
- one who is an unlawful user of or addicted to any controlled substance as defined in the Controlled Substances Act (includes marijuana)[202]
- one who has been adjudicated as a mental defective or who has been committed to a mental institution[203]
- one who is illegally or unlawfully in the United States or who has been admitted to the United States under a nonimmigrant visa, unless that nonimmigrant was admitted to the United States for lawful hunting or sporting purposes or is in possession of a hunting license or permit lawfully issued in the United States, is an official representative of a foreign government who is accredited to the United States Government or the Government's mission to an international organization having its headquarters in the United States, is *en route* to or from another country to which that alien is accredited, an official of a foreign government or a distinguished foreign visitor who has been so designated by the Department of State, or a foreign law enforcement officer of a friendly foreign government entering the United States on official law enforcement business[204]

---

199 18 U.S.C. § 922 (g).

200 18 U.S.C. § 922 (g)(1).

201 18 U.S.C. § 922 (g)(2).

202 18 U.S.C. § 922 (g)(3) and 21 U.S.C. § 802.

203 18 U.S.C. § 922 (g)(4).

204 18 U.S.C. § 922 (g)(5), 8 U.S.C. § 1101 (a)(26), 18 U.S.C. § 922 (y)(2)(A) and (B).

- one who has been discharged from the Armed Forces under dishonorable conditions[205]
- one who, having been a citizen of the United States, has renounced his citizenship[206]
- one who is subject to a court order that was issued after a hearing of which such person received actual notice and which such person had an opportunity to participate, or was restrained from harassing, stalking, or threatening an intimate partner or person, or engaging in other conduct that would place an intimate partner in reasonable fear of bodily injury to the partner or child and includes a finding that such person represents a credible threat to the physical safety of such intimate partner or child or, by its terms, explicitly prohibits the use, attempted use, or threatened use of physical force against such intimate partner or child that would reasonably be expected to cause bodily injury[207]
- one who has been convicted in any court of a misdemeanor crime of domestic violence[208]
- employees of any of the persons above who are subject to federal firearms prohibitions if having a firearm is required for their employment[209]

Any of the above federal offenses may subject the offender to a fine and up to ten years in a federal prison.[210]

Also under federal law, one who is under indictment for a crime punishable by imprisonment for a term exceeding one year may not ship or transport any firearm or ammunition or receive any firearm or ammunition which has been

---

[205] 18 U.S.C. § 922 (g)(6).

[206] 18 U.S.C. § 922 (g)(7).

[207] 18 U.S.C. § 922 (g)(8)(A), (B), and (C).

[208] 18 U.S.C. § 922 (g)(9).

[209] 18 U.S.C. § 922 (h).

[210] 18 U.S.C. § 924 (a)(2).

shipped or transported.[211] Note that this prohibition does not prevent the person under indictment from maintaining possession of firearms or ammunition he has in their custody and control at the time of indictment.

Restoration of Rights

Included with several of the prohibited categories above were the means that one can remove the prohibition imposed upon him. However, several still need to be addressed. For one who happens to be in a prohibited category and desires the restoration of their rights in regards to firearms, it cannot be stressed enough that they seek competent legal counsel in working through the problem.

Restoration of Rights for Convicted Felons Who Used Deadly Weapon in Commission of Crime

There are firearm prohibitions imposed on those convicted of most felonies and many misdemeanors. For those who were convicted of a felony, and a firearm or other deadly weapon was used in the commission of the crime, it is very unlikely they will ever have your rights restored. The California Supreme Court has stated that in creating the Dangerous Weapons Control Act, the intent of the Legislature is clear in that the Legislature wanted to limit as far as possible the use of instruments commonly associated with criminal activity and, specifically, to minimize the danger to public safety arising from the free access to firearms that can be used for crimes of violence.[212] The law presumes the danger is greater when the person possessing the concealable firearm has previously been convicted of a felony.

If you are a felon and you used a dangerous weapon in the commission of a federal crime, the only way to restore your rights to a firearm would be to seek a Presidential pardon for your crime. The State of California must recognize a Presidential pardon, as subordinate governments may not hinder the supreme power of the President.[213]

---

[211] 18 U.S.C. § 922 (n).

[212] *People v. Ratcliff* (1990) 223 Cal.App.3d 1401, 1409; see also *People v. Bell* (1989) 49 Cal.3d 502, 544 [262 Cal.Rptr. 1, 778 P.2d 129].

[213] *Bradford v. Cardoza* (1987) 195 Cal.App3d 361, 365; *Bjerkan v. United States* (7th Cir. 1975) 529 F.2d 125, 127.

Restoration of Rights for Convicted Felons Who Did Not Use Deadly Weapon in Commission of Crime in Violation of State Law

Those who are convicted felons who did not use a deadly weapon in the commission of the crime may seek to have their rights to firearms and other deadly weapons restored. The procedure for restoration of rights and application for pardon is included in the Penal Code.[214] It would be best to seek competent legal counsel to assist anyone seeking the restoration of any rights. Also, it is important that the person, when discharged, must live an honest and upright life, conduct himself with sobriety and industry, exhibit a good moral character, and conform to and obey the laws of the land, as that is expected of those seeking restoration.[215]

Restoration of Rights for Individuals with a Misdemeanor Conviction Listed in Penal Code § 12021 (c)(1)

As discussed above, the general rule is that those with a misdemeanor conviction for crimes listed in Penal Code § 12021 (c)(1) are prohibited from owning firearms and other deadly weapons for ten years. The individual may petition the court for relief from this prohibition, but may only petition the court once for such relief.[216] After the hearing, the court may reduce or eliminate the prohibition, impose conditions on reduction or elimination of the prohibition, or otherwise grant relief from the prohibition as the court deems appropriate.[217]

The burden will be on the petitioner (the one convicted of the misdemeanor), and the court must find by a preponderance of the evidence that the petitioner is likely to use a firearm in a safe and lawful manner.[218] Also, the court will inquire as to whether the petitioner is within a prohibited class as discussed above, such as one with prior felony convictions, convictions of other dangerous crimes, subject to prohibitions due to probation conditions, subject to an injunction, restraining order, or other protective order with firearms and deadly weapons

---

[214]See Penal Code § 4852.01 through § 4852.21.

[215]Penal Code § 4852.05.

[216]Penal Code § 12021 (c)(3).

[217]Penal Code § 12021 (c)(3).

[210]Penal Code § 12021 (c)(3)(A).

prohibitions, or prohibited because of mental disorders as discussed above.[219]

The court, in making its decision, will consider the interest of justice, any relevant evidence, and the totality of the circumstances.[220] The legislature has given the courts broad discretion in fashioning appropriate relief when such is warranted.[221] However, courts are not required to grant relief to any particular petitioner.[222]

It is important to mention that law enforcement officials who enforce prohibitions against an individual who has been granted relief from the prohibition are immune from any liability from false arrest arising from the enforcement of the prohibition unless that person has in his possession at the time of arrest a certified copy of the court order that granted the person relief from the prohibition.[223]

One other instance exists that might provide relief from the ten-year prohibition. If one is employed as a peace officer and whose employment and livelihood is dependent on the ability to legally possess a firearm, and whose prohibition is because of a conviction of either domestic spousal violence, a violation of a protective order to prevent the same, or a stalking crime, he may petition the court for relief.[224] The procedures, hearing, and potential relief are the same as outlined above.[225]

Restoration of Rights for Peace Officers

Originally under California law and as it currently exists under the Penal

[219]Penal Code § 12021 (c)(3)(B).

[220]Penal Code § 12021 (c)(3)(C)(ii).

[221]Penal Code § 12021 (c)(3)(C)(ii).

[222]Penal Code § 12021 (c)(3)(C)(ii).

[223]Penal Code § 12021 (c)(4).

[224]Penal Code § 12021 (c)(2).

[225]Penal Code § 12021 (c)

Code, any person employed as a peace officer as specified by law[226] whose employment or livelihood is dependent on the ability to possess legally a firearm, and who becomes subject to the prohibition because of a misdemeanor conviction for spousal abuse or domestic violence,[227] the intentional or knowingly violation of a protective order,[228] or a stalking crime,[229] may petition the court only once for relief from this prohibition.[230] If possible, the matter is to be heard in front of the same judge who sentenced the petitioner.[231] The court also has broad discretion on how to handle the original prohibition, whether to eliminate it, reduce it, or modify it.[232]

However, under Federal Law, which trumps California law, those peace officers convicted of a misdemeanor of domestic violence may not regain their rights.[233]

Restoration of Rights for Those Prohibited Under Federal Law

A person who is prohibited from possessing, shipping, transporting, or receiving firearms or ammunition may make application to the Attorney General for relief from the disabilities imposed by Federal laws with respect to those acts regarding firearms.[234]

The Attorney General may grant such relief if it is established to his satisfaction that the circumstances regarding the disability, and the applicant's record

---

[226]See Penal Code §§ 830.1, 830.2, 830.31, 830.32, 830.33, and 830.5 regarding peace officers relevant to this point.

[227]See Penal Code § 273.5, now rendered unconstitutional.

[228]See Penal Code § 273.6.

[229]See Penal Code § 646.9.

[230]Penal Code § 12021 (c)(2).

[231]Penal Code § 12021 (c)(2).

[232]Penal Code § 12021 (c)(2); see also Penal Code § 12021 (c)(2)(C)(ii).

[233]See *United States v. Hayes* 555 U.S. __ (2009).

[234]18 U.S.C. § 925 (c).

and reputation, are such that the applicant will not likely act in a manner dangerous to public safety and that the granting of the relief would not be contrary to the public interest.[235]

Any person whose application for relief from disabilities is denied by the Attorney General may file a petition with the United States District Court for the district in which he resides for a judicial review of such denial.[236] The court may in its discretion admit additional evidence where failure to do so would result in a miscarriage of justice.[237]

A licensed importer, licensed manufacturer, licensed dealer, or licensed collector conducting lawful operations who applies for relief from the disabilities incurred by law, shall not be barred by such disability from further operations under his license pending final action on an application for relief filed pursuant to this section.[238]

When the Attorney General grants relief to any person, he shall promptly publish a notice regarding the relief given in the Federal Register notice of such action, together with the reasons stated therefor.[239]

---

[235] 18 U.S.C. § 925 (c).

[236] 18 U.S.C. § 925 (c).

[237] 18 U.S.C. § 925 (c).

[238] 18 U.S.C. § 925 (c).

[239] 18 U.S.C. § 925 (c).

Part Three

Firearms, Ammunition, and Firearms Related Devices That Are Prohibited or Controlled in California

CHAPTER FOUR

Firearms That Are Prohibited or Controlled in California

"*This may be considered as the true palladium of liberty....The right of self defense is the first law of nature: in most governments it has been the study of rulers to confine this right within the narrowest limits possible. Wherever standing armies are kept up, and the right of the people to keep and bear arms is, under any color or pretext whatsoever, prohibited, liberty, if not already annihilated, is on the brink of destruction.*" - St. George Tucker

As would be expected, there are quite a few types of firearms in California that are prohibited or controlled to such a degree that for all intents and purposes, they are prohibited. Certain types of ammunition are also prohibited or controlled in California, as are many other deadly and non-deadly weapons. This chapter discusses in detail the prohibitions on and control of firearms, ammunition, and firearms related items in California. Chapter Nine discusses prohibitions and controls of other deadly and non-deadly weapons.

Some prohibitions, if violated, are felonies, such as the prohibition on assault rifles, .50 BMG rifles, and machineguns. Other prohibitions, if violated, may result only in misdemeanor convictions.

A word of warning: any person within the State of California dealing with any firearms or weapons of any kind must be fully aware of these prohibitions, as ignorance of the law is no defense to breaking it. Any person stands a chance of conviction the item they possess within the state has features that make it illegal.[240] Because many of the violations regarding certain weapons are felonies, a conviction for violating the prohibition will result in a permanent loss of freedom regarding the ownership of firearms.

Another word of warning: for the purposes of many of the firearm prohibitions addressed below, a violation of that section as to each firearm, weapon, or device is considered a distinct and separate offense.[241] Please be aware that many

---

[240]See *People v. Lanham* (1991) 230 Cal.App.3d 1396, 1405; *People v. Valencia* (1989) 214 Cal.App.3d 1410, 1416; *In re Jorge M.* (1998) 66 Cal.App.4th 809, 820; *People v. Rubalcava* (2000) 23 Cal.4th 322.

[241]Penal Code § 12001 (l).

localities pass their own laws and ordinances regarding firearms, and one must be aware of such prohibitions. Be sure to contact local authorities or a competent attorney for details or to get answers to any questions you may have.

One final note, it is important to realize that advertising the sale of any prohibited items is punishable. Specifically, for any person to advertise any prohibited firearms in any newspaper, magazine, circular, form letter, or open publication that is published, distributed, or circulated in this state, or on any billboard, card, label, or other advertising medium, or by means of any other advertising device, is unlawful in California.[242]

As with most laws discussed in this book, here are limited exceptions to the prohibitions. Where an exception exists, the exception will be discussed in detail.

Short-Barreled Shotguns and Short Barreled Rifles

Any person in this state who manufactures, imports into the state, keeps for sale, offers or exposes for sale, or who gives, lends, or possesses any short-barreled shotgun or short-barreled rifle is punishable by imprisonment in a county jail not to exceed one year or in the state prison.[243]

A "short-barreled shotgun" means any of the following:[244]

- a firearm which is designed or redesigned to fire a fixed shotgun shell and having a barrel or barrels of less than 18 inches in length
- a firearm which has an overall length of less than 26 inches and which is designed or redesigned to fire a fixed shotgun shell
- any weapon made from a shotgun, whether by alteration, modification, or otherwise, if that weapon, as modified, has an overall length of less than 26 inches or a barrel or barrels of less than 18 inches in length
- any device which may be readily restored to fire a fixed shotgun shell which, when so restored, is a device as

---

[242]Penal Code § 12020.5.

[243]Penal Code § 12020 (a) and (a)(1); see also Penal Code § 12001.5.

[244]Penal Code § 12020 (c)(1)(A) through (E).

described in the above three bullet points

- any part, or combination of parts, designed and intended to convert a device into a device as described in the first three bullet points, or any combination of parts from which such a device can be readily assembled if those parts are in the possession or under the control of the same person

Beware! Simply having what would otherwise be a short-barreled shotgun in your possession, only disassembled, constitutes the offense. It is common myth that having all the parts of a banned weapon, just not assembled, allows the person to keep the weapon and remain in compliance with the law. That is incorrect, and the person who takes such a path is in violation and is risking everything.

A "short-barreled rifle" means any of the following:[245]

- a rifle having a barrel length of less than 16 inches in length
- a rifle with an overall length of less than 26 inches
- any weapon made from a rifle, whether by alteration, modification, or otherwise, if that weapon, as modified, has an overall length of less than 26 inches or a barrel or barrels of less than 18 inches in length
- any device which may be readily restored to fire a fixed cartridge which, when so restored, is a device as described above
- any part, or combination of parts, designed and intended to convert a device into a device as described above, or any combination of parts from which such a device can be readily assembled if those parts are in the possession or under the control of the same person

Such as with the short-barreled shotgun, one may not legally possess a short-barreled rifle simply by keeping it disassembled.

Federal law makes it unlawful for any person, other than one who is properly licensed, to transport in interstate commerce any short-barreled rifles or

---

[245]Penal Code § 12020 (c)(2)(A) through (E).

short-barreled shotguns.[246] Both federal law and California law have the same measurements for determining short-barreled rifles and short-barreled shotguns.[247] Whoever knowingly violates this prohibition shall be fined, imprisoned not more than five years, or both.[248]

Of course, exceptions under California law exist to the prohibitions on short-barreled rifles and short-barreled shotguns.[249]

The prohibitions above do not apply in the following circumstances:[250]

- the sale to, purchase by, or possession of either short-barreled rifles or short-barreled shotguns by specified law enforcement agencies for specific authorized duties
- when authorized by the Department of Justice ("DOJ") by way of obtaining a permit[251]

Permits may be granted by the DOJ upon a showing of "good cause" and determination that granting the permit will not endanger the public safety.[252] Permits are good for only one year, and therefore must be renewed annually.[253] "Good cause," for the purpose of permitting short-barreled rifles and shotguns, is limited to permits for the manufacture, possession, or use with blank cartridges, solely for props in entertainment productions, or the manufacture, exposing for sale, keeping for sale, sale of, importation or lending of short-barreled rifles and shotguns to authorized law enforcement agencies by authorized dealers or manufacturers.[254]

---

[246] 18 U.S.C. § 922 (a)(4).

[247] 25 U.S.C. § 5845 (a).

[248] 18 U.S.C. § 924 (a)(1) and (a)(1)(D).

[249] Penal Code § 12020 (b).

[250] Penal Code § 12020 (b), (b)(1) and (b)(2).

[251] See Penal Code § 12095.

[252] Penal Code § 12095 (a).

[253] Penal Code § 12095 (a).

[254] Penal Code § 12095 (b).

Applications for permits must be in writing, complete with all the information as requested by the DOJ, and submitted with the appropriate fee.[255] The permit must be kept by the permit holder or at the place where the weapons are kept, and open to inspection by any peace officer or other DOJ designated person.[256] A unique identifying number shall be placed or stamped on each weapon, either by the permit holder or by the DOJ.[257] Annual inspections will be conducted for security and safe storage purposes, as well as to reconcile the inventory of permitted weapons, unless there are fewer than five weapons on the permit, in which case, the inspection may occur as little as once every five years unless the DOJ decides otherwise.[258]

Permits may be revoked at any time when it appears that the need for the permit has ceased, or that the permit holder has not exercised great care in retaining custody of any weapons possessed under the permit.[259]

Machineguns[260]

A machinegun is any weapon which shoots, is designed to shoot, or can readily be restored to shoot, automatically, more than one shot, without manual reloading, by a single pull of the trigger.[261] This includes the frame or receiver of any such weapon, any part designed and intended solely and exclusively, or combination of parts designed and intended, for use in converting a weapon into a machine gun, and any combination of parts from which a machinegun can be assembled if such parts are in possession or under the control of a person.[262]

---

[255] Penal Code § 12096.

[256] Penal Code § 12097 (a).

[257] Penal Code § 12097 (b).

[258] Penal Code § 12099 (a) and (b).

[259] Penal Code § 12098.

[260] Please do not be annoyed at the use of the word "machinegun" instead of the words "machine gun," as such spelling is used almost exclusively throughout the Penal Code by the California Legislature.

[261] Penal Code § 12200.

[262] Penal Code § 12200.

Note that one may not have all the components to assemble a machinegun and keep the various parts disassembled in his possession to avoid a violation of the prohibition.[263] Also note that federal law prohibits the possession or transfer of machineguns, with very serious punishment and penalties, including a potential ten year term in a federal prison.[264]

Assault Weapons

The California Legislature identifies assault weapons several ways. The first is a designated list of specific weapons it has declared to be assault weapons. This is oftentimes referred to as aa "list based" definition.

The second is a features list, often referred to as a "features-based" definition. Basically, if a weapon has a certain feature or a combination of certain features, it is considered by the state to be an assault weapon.[265]

Any person who, within this state, manufactures or causes to be manufactured, distributes, transports, imports into the state, keeps for sale, offers or exposes for sale, or who gives or lends an assault weapon is guilty of a felony, with a conviction leading to punishment in the state prison for 4, 6, or 8 years.[266] Any transfer to a minor will result in a sentence enhancement of one year, meaning prison terms of 5, 7, or 9 years.[267]

Note that having an assault weapon, but only disassembled, is still a prohibited firearm in the eyes of the law.[268]

Because these weapons are so popular, so heavily regulated, and cause so much confusion, a lengthier, more detailed discussion can be found in Chapter Seven.

---

[263]*People v. Hale* (1974) 43 Cal.App.3d 353, 356.

[264]18 U.S.C. § 922 (o), and § 924 (a)(2).

[265]See Penal Code §§ 12276 and 12276.1.

[266]Penal Code § 12280 (a).

[267]Penal Code § 12280 (b)

[268]*People v. Hale* (1974) 43 Cal.App.3d 353, 356.

.50 BMG Rifle

A .50 BMG rifle is a center fire rifle that can fire a .50 BMG cartridge and is not already declared an assault weapon or machinegun by the state.[269] Any person who, within this state, manufactures or causes to be manufactured, distributes, transports, imports into the state, keeps for sale, offers or exposes for sale, or who gives or lends a .50 BMG rifle is guilty of a felony, with a conviction leading to punishment in the state prison for 4, 6, or 8 years.[270] Any transfer to a minor will result in a sentence enhancement of one year, meaning prison terms of 5, 7, or 9 years.[271]

Unsafe Handguns

As of January 1, 2001, any person in the state who manufactures, causes to be manufactured, imports into the state for sale, keeps for sale, offers or exposes for sale, gives, or lends, any unsafe handgun shall be punished in the county jail not exceeding one year.[272] An important note is that violations of this law are cumulative with respect to each handgun, meaning, each unsafe handgun is a separate misdemeanor.[273]

An unsafe handgun means any pistol, revolver, or other firearm capable of being concealed upon the person, for which <u>any</u> of the following is true:[274]

- For a **revolver**:[275]
    - It does not have a safety device, that, either automatically (in the case of a double-action firing mechanism), or by manual operation (in the case of a

---

[269] Penal Code § 12278 (a); see also Penal Code §§ 12276, 12276.1, 12276.5, and 12200.

[270] Penal Code § 12280 (a).

[271] Penal Code § 12280 (b)

[272] Penal Code § 12125 (a).

[273] Penal Code § 12125 (c).

[274] Penal Code § 12126.

[275] Penal Code § 12126 (a).

single-action firing mechanism), causes the hammer to retract to a point where the firing pin does not rest upon the primer of the cartridge

- It does not meet the firing requirements or drop safety requirements as required (discussed below)

- For a **pistol**:[276]
  - It does not have a positive manually operated safety device
  - It does not meet the firing requirements or drop safety requirements as required (discussed below)
  - It must have a chamber load indicator if it is a center-fire semi-automatic pistol
  - It must have a magazine disconnect mechanism if it is a center-fire semi-automatic pistol
  - It need only have a magazine disconnect mechanism, if it is a rimfire semi-automatic pistol, and only if it has a detachable magazine
  - **Microstamping:** Was supposed to take effect on January 1, 2010 but **is not currently law**. The law was supposed to be that all semi-automatic pistols that are not on the pre-approved roster of semi-automatic pistols must be designed and equipped with a microscopic array of characters that identify the make, model, and serial number of the pistol. These numbers must be etched or stamped in two places on the interior surface or internal working parts of the pistol, and that are transferred by imprinting on each cartridge case when the firearm is fired.[277] The law also states that for all intents and purposes the microstamping technology must be "patent free,"[278] and because all current microstamping is protected by patents, the law is not in effect.

A "semi-automatic pistol" means a pistol that operates by using the energy

[276]Penal Code § 12126 (b).

[277]Penal Code § 12126 (b)(7).

[278]Penal Code § 12126 (b)(7).

of the explosive in a fixed cartridge to extract a fired cartridge and then chamber a fresh cartridge with each single pull of the trigger.[279]

A "chamber load indicator" is a device that plainly indicates that a cartridge is in the firing chamber. To satisfy the definition, it must be readily visible, has text or graphics incorporated into the firearm next to the indicator itself, and must indicate to a reasonably foreseeable adult user of the pistol whether the cartridge is actually in the firing chamber. Further, the text or graphics must be such that the user will understand what he is are looking at without having to refer to a user's manual or other resource to interpret it.[280]

A "magazine disconnect mechanism" is a mechanism that prevents a semi-automatic pistol that has a detachable magazine from operating to strike the primer of ammunition in the firing chamber when a detachable magazine is not inserted in the pistol.[281] Translation: a magazine disconnect mechanism makes the firearm, if there is no magazine in the firearm, it will be unable fire.

These days, if a center-fire semi-automatic handgun does not have both a magazine disconnect mechanism and a chamber load indicator, it will not be permitted to be tested as discussed below, and will automatically be deemed an "unsafe handgun," and not permitted legally in California.[282] The same applies for a rimfire semi-automatic handgun that does not have a magazine disconnect mechanism but does have a detachable magazine.[283]

Firing Requirements for Handguns[284]

The California legislature has, for several years, required a firing requirement for handguns that must be passed in order for a firearm to be

---

[279]Penal Code § 12126 (c).

[280]Penal Code § 12126 (c).

[281]Penal Code § 12126 (d).

[282]Penal Code § 12130 (d)(1) and (2).

[283]Penal Code § 12130 (d)(3).

[284]Penal Code § 12127; The authority that supports the entire discussion regarding this requirement may be found in this code section.

considered a "safe handgun," and therefore not prohibited in California.

This is a test in which the manufacturer provides three handguns of the make and model for which certification is sought to an independent testing laboratory. This laboratory must be certified by the Attorney General.[285] The handguns that are provided must not be refined or modified in any way, and must be representative of the handguns that would be offered for retail sale if certification is granted. The same applies for the magazines used in the firearms.

The laboratory testers will fire 600 rounds from each gun. They will stop after every 50 rounds to allow the weapon to cool, and they will stop as needed to reload. The handgun passes the test of each if the three test handguns are able to fire the first 20 rounds without a malfunction (unless the malfunction is caused by the ammunition itself) and the handgun is able to fire the full 600 rounds with no more than six malfunctions (unless the malfunction is caused by the ammunition itself). If the handgun, after 600 rounds fired, exhibits any cracks or breakage of an operating part such that the user has an increased risk of injury, the handgun will fail.

Drop Safety Requirement for Handguns[286]

The drop safety requirement for handguns is conducted only after the firing requirement is completed. If the handgun passes the firing requirements, the same laboratory will subject the same three handguns to a drop test. The drop test begins with the insertion of a primed case to be inserted into the chamber. The firearm will be dropped from just over a meter onto a solid concrete slab from a fixture, rather than by hand. Any safety will be disengaged. Six drops will be performed to hit various sides of the handgun. The handgun will pass the test provided that none of the guns on any of the drops fires the primer.

Roster of Approved Firearms

As of 2001, the Department of Justice began compiling, publishing, and thereafter maintaining a roster listing all of the pistols, revolvers, and other firearms that are capable of being concealed upon the person that have been tested by a

---

[285]Penal Code § 12127; for certification by the Attorney General, see Penal Code § 12130.

[286]Penal Code § 12128; The authority that supports the entire discussion regarding this requirement may be found in this code section.

certified testing laboratory, have been determined not to be unsafe handguns, and may be sold in this state.[287] The roster lists the manufacturer, model number, and model name.

If a purchaser of a handgun attempts to purchase a handgun that is not listed on the roster, and at some point during the purchasing process, the handgun is added to the roster, the purchaser will be able to finish the purchase.[288] If the purchaser of a handgun attempts to purchase a handgun that is on the roster, but is removed from the roster during the purchasing process, the purchaser will not be able to take possession of the handgun.[289] A firearm may be removed from the roster if someone along the chain of custody of the firearm fails to pay the fees as imposed by the Department.[290] In conclusion, it is possible that a firearm that is safe pursuant to standards set by the Department may be excluded if fees are not paid by the manufacturer, the dealer, or anyone who is listed in the code as being subject to the fees. Suits are pending to challenge the "unsafe handgun" laws as unconstitutional, as firearms may be deemed "unsafe" simply by failing to pay the fee, when the fee has nothing to do with whether a handgun is safe or not.

The Department may retest up to 5% of the handgun models annually, subject to the same tests as described above.[291] If the handgun is removed from the list due to failing a test, it may only be tested one more time for reinstatement.[292] If it fails again, it is forever banned.

It is possible that a firearm that is similar to a firearm that is already listed be deemed a safe handgun.[293] However, it may only differ in the following ways: finish, material used to make the grips, the shape or texture of the grips (as long as it does not affect dimensions or functioning of any part of the gun), or other purely

---

[287] Penal Code § 12131.

[288] Penal Code § 12131 (b)(3)

[289] Penal Code § 12131 (b)(3).

[290] Penal Code § 12131 (a), (b)(1) and (2).

[291] Penal Code § 12131 (c), (d), and (e).

[292] Penal Code § 12131 (f) and (g).

[293] Penal Code § 12131.5.

cosmetic features.[294] The manufacturer, not the purchaser, must apply to the Department to have a firearm added to the roster as a similar firearm to one that is already on the roster.[295]

Cases Where Unsafe Handgun Laws are Inapplicable

There are situations where the "unsafe handgun" laws are inapplicable, and include the following:[296]

- private party transfers
- a bequest from an immediate family member residing out of state; handgun must still be registered with the DOJ
- the firearm is a curio or relic[297]
- transfers of the firearm to and from gunsmith for repair
- transfers to and from pawnbroker
- use of such in Olympic sporting events
- use of such as props in entertainment industry
- manufacturing of or importing prototypes for the sole purpose of testing to determine if it is an "unsafe handgun" or not[298]
- sale or purchase of an unsafe handgun by the DOJ, any police department, sheriffs' official, any marshals' office, the Youth and Adult Correctional Agency, the California Highway Patrol, any district attorney's office, or any military, state or federal, for the use in the discharge of their duties[299]
- sale to or purchase by sworn members of any of the above law enforcement agencies[300]

---

[294]Penal Code § 12131.5 (a).

[295]Penal Code § 12131.5 (b).

[296]Penal Code § 12132.

[297]See also Penal Code § 12125 (b)(3).

[298]Penal Code § 12125 (b)(1).

[299]Penal Code § 12125 (b)(4).

[300]Penal Code § 12125 (b)(4).

Cane Gun

A cane gun is any firearm mounted or enclosed in a stick, staff, rod, crutch, or similar device, designed to be, or capable of being used as, an aid in walking, if the firearm may be fired while mounted or enclosed therein.[301]

Wallet Gun

A wallet gun is any firearm mounted or enclosed in a case, resembling a wallet, designed to be capable of being carried in a pocket or a purse, if the firearm may be fired while mounted or enclosed in the case.[302]

Undetectable Firearm

An undetectable firearm means any weapon which, after the removal of grips, stocks, and magazines, is not detectable by walk-through metal detectors, does not generate an image that accurately depicts the shape of the component by X-ray machines that are commonly found at airports, and are oftentimes fabricated by compounds such as barium sulfate.[303]

Any Firearm Which is Not Immediately Recognizable as a Firearm

This is simply any firearm that by some sort of camouflage or trick is not recognizable.

Zip Gun

A zip gun is a weapon or device that was not imported as a firearm by an importer licensed under federal law,[304] was not originally designed to be a firearm by a manufacturer licensed under the same federal law, no tax was paid on the

---

[301]Penal Code § 12020 (c)(5).

[302]Penal Code § 12020 (c)(4).

[303]Penal Code § 12020 (c)(22).

[304]See 18 U.S.C. § 921 et seq.

weapon or device, no exemption from the tax was granted,[305] and it is made or altered to expel a projectile by the force of an explosion or some other form of combustion.[306]

Imitation Firearms

Imitation firearms are not per se prohibited, but there are governmental controls on the transferability and modification of imitation firearms. First, an "imitation firearm" means any BB device, toy gun, replica of a firearm, or other device that is so substantially similar in coloration and overall appearance to an existing firearm as to lead a reasonable person to perceive that the device is a firearm.[307]

Furnishing an imitation firearm to a minor is a misdemeanor, which includes a loan or a transfer that does not involve a sale.[308] To change, alter, remove, or obliterate any coloration or markings on an imitation firearm to make it look more like a real firearm is a misdemeanor.[309] An exception to the prohibitions on changing, altering, removing, or obliterating markings on a firearm exist only for entertainment productions.[310]

No person may openly display or expose an imitation firearm in a public place.[311] Violation is an infraction punishable by a fine of $100 for the first offense, and $300 for the second offense.[312] A third and any subsequent offense is a misdemeanor.[313]

---

[305] See Section 4181 and Subchapters F and G of 26 U.S.C. § 32.

[306] Penal Code § 12020 (c)(10) and (c)(10)(A) through (D).

[307] Penal Code § 12550 (c).

[308] Penal Code § 12552 (a) and (b).

[309] Penal Code § 12553 (a).

[310] Penal Code § 12553 (a)(2).

[311] Penal Code § 12556 (a).

[312] Penal Code § 12556 (b).

[313] Penal Code § 12556 (c).

A "public place" is defined as an area open to the public and includes streets, sidewalks, bridges, alleys, plazas, parks, driveways, front yards, parking lots, automobiles (whether moving or not), and buildings open to the general public, including those that serve food and drink, or provide entertainment, and the doorways and entrances to buildings or dwellings, and shall include public schools and a public or private college or university.[314]

Exceptions apply to the government controls when the imitation firearm is:[315]

- packaged or concealed so that it is not subject to public viewing[316]
- displayed or exposed in the course of commerce, including commercial film or video productions, or for service, repair, or restoration of the imitation firearm[317]
- used in a theatrical production, a motion picture, video, television, or stage production[318]
- used in conjunction with a certified or regulated public or private shooting range[319]
- used in conjunction with lawful hunting, or lawful pest control activities[320]
- used or possessed at certified or regulated public or private shooting ranges[321]
- used at fairs, exhibitions, expositions, or other similar activities for which a permit has been obtained from a local or state government[322]

---

[314]Penal Code § 12556 (e).

[315]Penal Code § 12556 (d).

[316]Penal Code § 12556 (d)(1).

[317]Penal Code § 12556 (d)(2).

[318]Penal Code § 12556 (d)(3).

[319]Penal Code § 12556 (d)(4).

[320]Penal Code § 12556 (d)(5).

[321]Penal Code § 12556 (d)(6).

[322]Penal Code § 12556 (d)(7).

- used in military, civil defense, or civil activities, including flag ceremonies, color guards, parades, award presentations, historical re-enactments, and memorials[323]
- used for public display authorized by public or private schools or displays that are part of museum collections[324]
- used in parades, ceremonies, or other similar activities for which a permit has been obtained from a state or local government[325]
- displayed on a wall plaque or in a presentation case[326]
- used in areas where the discharge of a firearm is lawful[327]
- where the entire exterior surface is white, bright red, bright orange, or some other bright color, or a combination of bright colors, or where the entire device is made of transparent or translucent materials, to allow unmistakable observation of the device's complete contents.[328] Note, however, that federal law allows a mere "orange tip," but California does not, as the entire surface must be colored, transparent, or translucent.[329]

Finally, brandishing an imitation firearm, that is, drawing or exhibiting, in a threatening manner, except in self-defense, in such a way that a reasonable person would have an apprehension of fear or bodily harm, is guilty of a misdemeanor and punishable in the county jail for no less than 30 days.[330]

---

[323] Penal Code § 12556 (d)(8).

[324] Penal Code § 12556 (d)(9).

[325] Penal Code § 12556 (d)(10).

[326] Penal Code § 12556 (d)(11).

[327] Penal Code § 12556 (d)(12).

[328] Penal Code § 12556 (d)(13).

[329] Penal Code § 12556 (d)(13).

[330] Penal Code § 417.4.

Unconventional Pistols

Unconventional pistols are prohibited in California.[331] An unconventional pistol is a firearm that does not have a rifled bore and has a barrel or barrels of less than 18 inches in length or has an overall length of less than 26 inches.[332]

Brightly Colored Firearms

Any person who, for commercial purposes, purchases, sells, manufactures, ships, transports, distributes, or receives a firearm, where the coloration of the exterior surface of the firearm is bright orange or bright green, either singly, in combination, or as the predominant color in combination with other colors in any pattern, is liable for a civil fine in an action brought by the city attorney or the county district attorney of not more than $10,000.[333]

Firearms Greater than .60 Caliber

Any firearm of a caliber greater than 0.60 caliber which fires fixed ammunition, or any ammunition therefor, other than a shotgun (smooth or rifled bore) conforming to a definition of a "destructive device,"[334] shotgun ammunition (single projection or shot), antique rifle, or an antique cannon.[335] This is considered to be a "destructive device."[336]

"Antique cannon" means any cannon manufactured before January 1, 1899, which has been rendered incapable of firing or for which ammunition is no longer manufactured in the United States and is not readily available in the ordinary channels of commercial trade.[337] "Antique rifle" means a firearm conforming to the

---

[331]Penal Code § 12020 (a)(1).

[332]Penal Code § 12020 (c)(12).

[333]Penal Code § 12020.3.

[334]See 27 C.F.R. § 479.11 (b).

[335]Penal Code § 12301 (a)(3).

[336]Penal Code § 12301 (a).

[337]Penal Code § 12301 (a)(3).

definition of "antique firearm."[338]

Complete Prohibited Firearms Kept Disassembled

The parts of any prohibited firearm that have been disassembled, but all the parts are readily available to be reassembled, are considered by the law to be a firearm.[339] To take a prohibited weapon apart in an attempt to circumvent the law may seem clever at first, but it is indeed illegal, and it is highly advised that one does not commit such act. It simply is not worth it.

---

[338]Penal Code § 12301 (a)(3); see also 27 C.F.R. § 479.11 for definition of "antique firearm".

[339]*People v. Hale*, (1974) 43 Cal.App. 3d 353, 356.

CHAPTER FIVE

Prohibited Ammunition in California

The California Legislature has set out prohibitions and controls on various types of ammunition. Please read this section carefully and observe all laws.

It should be noted that it is unlawful in California for any person to advertise any of the ammunition discussed below in any newspaper, magazine, circular, form letter, or open publication that is published, distributed, or circulated in this state, or on any billboard, card, label, or other advertising medium, or by means of any other advertising device.[340]

Metal or Armor-Penetrating Bullets

Any person, firm, or corporation who, within this state *knowingly possesses* any handgun ammunition designed primarily to penetrate metal or armor is guilty of a public offense and upon conviction thereof shall be punished in the state prison, or in the county jail for a term not to exceed one year, or by a fine not to exceed $5,000, or by both.[341]

However, any person, firm, or corporation who, within this state, manufactures, imports, sells, offers to sell, or knowingly transports any handgun ammunition designed primarily to penetrate metal or armor is guilty of a felony and upon conviction thereof shall be punished by imprisonment in the state prison, or by a fine not to exceed $5,000, or by both.[342]

Notice that this law pertains to handgun ammunition only. "Handgun ammunition," for the purposes of these prohibitions, means ammunition principally for use in pistols, revolvers, and other firearms capable of being concealed upon the person, and notwithstanding that the ammunition may also be used in some rifles.[343]

---

[340]Penal Code § 12020.5.

[341]Penal Code § 12320.

[342]Penal Code § 12321.

[343]Penal Code § 12323 (a).

Furthermore, this prohibition regards ammunition, except for shotgun shells or ammunition that is primarily designed for use in rifles, that is designed primarily to penetrate a body vest or body shield.[344] It is important to understand that this prohibition pertains to ammunition primarily used in handguns. If the ammunition is primarily used in rifles, it is not subject to the ban.

Typical characteristics of metal or armor-penetrating ammunition are generally ammunition that has a projectile or projectile core constructed entirely from one or a combination of tungsten alloys, steel, iron, brass, beryllium copper, or depleted uranium, or ammunition that is primarily designed, by virtue of its shape, cross-sectional density, or any coating applied thereto, to breach or penetrate a body vest or body shield when fired from a handgun.[345]

Exceptions exist for the United States Armed Forces and National Guard, as well as any law enforcement that has a valid permit for destructive devices and explosives.[346] Another exception will be made for one who finds this sort of ammunition, if they are not in the class of people prohibited from possessing firearms, and so long as they are transporting the ammunition to a law enforcement agency for disposition according to law.[347] Those involved in the manufacture of ammunition under contracts approved by agencies of the state or federal government are also not subject to the prohibition on metal or armor-penetrating ammunition.[348]

If one is in possession of metal or armor-piercing ammunition that has had the propellant removed or primer that has been permanently deactivated, he will not be in violation of this law.[349]

---

[344]Penal Code § 12323 (b).

[345]Penal Code § 12323 (b)(1) and (2).

[346]Penal Code § 12322 (a); see also Penal Code § 12305 regarding permits.

[347]Penal Code § 12322 (b); see also Penal Code §§ 12021, 12021.1, 12316 (b)(1), and Welfare and Institutions Code §§ 8100 and 8103 regarding those prohibited from possession of firearms.

[348]Penal Code § 12325.

[349]Penal Code § 12324.

Finally, any person who, while armed with a firearm in the commission or attempted commission of any felony, has in his or her immediate possession ammunition for the firearm designed primarily to penetrate metal or armor, shall upon conviction, receive a sentence enhancement by an additional term of 3, 4, or 10 years.[350] The court will impose the 4-year term, absent aggravating or mitigating circumstances, and shall state the reasons for its enhancement choice on the record at the time of sentencing.[351]

Ammunition Greater than .60 Caliber

Any person, firm, or corporation who, within this state, sells, offers for sale, or knowingly transports any destructive device, other than fixed ammunition of a caliber greater than .60 caliber, is guilty of a public offense and upon conviction shall be guilty of a misdemeanor and punished accordingly.[352] A second or subsequent conviction has the same punishment with higher fines.[353] No person convicted of a violation regarding this ammunition will be granted probation, and sentences shall not be suspended by the court.[354]

Ammunition that is a caliber greater than .60 is considered a "destructive device" under the Penal Code.

Explosive Bullets

Explosive bullets are any bullets that contain or carry an explosive agent.[355] The manufacture, importation, sale, offer to sell, gift, loan, or possession of the same is prohibited in California.[356] Note that for the purposes of this prohibition, a bullet containing or carrying an explosive agent is not a destructive device as defined in

---

[350]Penal Code § 12022.2.

[351]Penal Code § 12022.2.

[352]Penal Code § 12304.

[353]Penal Code § 12304.

[354]Penal Code § 12311.

[355]Penal Code § 12020 (a)(1).

[356]Penal Code § 12020 (a)(1).

other parts of the Penal Code.[357]

Flechette Darts

A flechette dart is a dart capable of being fired from a firearm that measures approximately one inch in length, with tail fins that take up approximately five-sixteenths of an inch of the body.[358] The manufacture, importation, sale, offer to sell, gift, loan, or possession of flechette darts is prohibited in California.[359]

Tracer Ammunition

Tracer ammunition is considered by the state of California to be a "destructive device." The definition of "destructive device" includes any projectile containing any explosive or incendiary material or any other chemical substance, including, but not limited to, that which is commonly known as tracer or incendiary ammunition.[360] However, tracer ammunition made for shotguns is neither considered a "destructive device," nor is it banned in California.[361]

Those who possess tracer ammunition within this state are guilty of a public offense and upon conviction shall be imprisoned in the county jail for up to a year, or in the state prison, or by a fine up to $10,000, or both.[362] Those who offer tracer ammunition for sale, sell tracer ammunition, or transport it, have committed a felony and are subject to a term in the state prison for 2, 3, or 4 years.[363] No person convicted of a violation regarding this ammunition will be granted probation, and sentences shall not be suspended by the court.[364]

---

357 Penal Code § 12020 (a)(4); see also Penal Code § 12301.

358 Penal Code § 12020 (c)(6).

359 Penal Code § 12020 (a)(1).

360 Penal Code § 12301 (a)(1).

361 Penal Code §§ 12020 (b)(6) and 12301 (a)(1).

362 Penal Code § 12303.

363 Penal Code § 12303.6.

364 Penal Code § 12311.

CHAPTER SIX

Firearms Related Items and Devices Prohibited in California

The California Legislature has set out prohibitions and controls on various types of ammunition. Please read this section carefully and observe all laws.

Before discussing prohibited firearms related items and devices, it is important to note that it is unlawful for any person to advertise any of these items in any newspaper, magazine, circular, form letter, or open publication that is published, distributed, or circulated in this state, or on any billboard, card, label, or other advertising medium, or by means of any other advertising device.[365]

High-Capacity Magazines

Outside of California, most magazines that accompany a firearm at the time of purchase have a capacity greater than 10 bullets. Such magazines, outside of California, are called "standard capacity magazines." However, that is outside of California.

In California, the definition of a "large-capacity magazine" or "high capacity magazine" is any ammunition feeding device with the capacity to accept more than 10 rounds.[366]

California law prohibits any large-capacity magazines from being manufactured, imported into the state, offered or kept for sale, given, lent, or possessed, and this prohibition applies from January 1, 2000, to the present day.[367] For some, one important factor is whether the magazines that were here prior to January 1, 2001, because if they were, they are considered "grandfathered in," so there is no ban on possession for these devices that were already here.

There are a few exceptions to the ban on the possession, manufacture,

---

[365]Penal Code § 12020.5.

[366]Penal Code § 12020 (c)(25).

[367]Penal Code § 12020 (a)(2).

sale, import, or transfer of large-capacity magazines:[368]

- to or by authorized law enforcement agencies
- to or by authorized law enforcement officers
- to or by licensed gun dealers
- lawful loans (person is not prohibited from possession, and possession will occur where it is not prohibited and remain there for the duration of the loan)
- giving or lending such to gunsmith or licensed gun dealer for maintenance, repair, or modification; return of the same to the rightful owner
- authorized manufacture of such for sale outside of state
- props for entertainment purposes
- large-capacity magazines that have been permanently altered to hold only 10 rounds[369]
- .22 caliber tube ammunition feeding devices[370]
- authorized armored vehicle companies and employees
- import of high-capacity magazine that was previously in the state lawfully and the owner is simply returning to the state with the same device
- those with special permits issued by the Department
- a tubular device that is contained in a lever-action[371]

<u>Permits Issued for Large Capacity Magazines in California</u>

Upon a showing of good cause, the DOJ may issue permits for the possession, transportation, or sale between a licensed person[372] and an out-of-state client, of large capacity magazines.[373]

---

[368]Penal Code § 12020 (b)(19) through (32).

[369]Penal Code § 12020 (c)(25)(A).

[370]Penal Code § 12020 (c)(25)(B).

[371]Penal Code § 12020 (c)(25)(C).

[372]See Penal Code § 12071 regarding licensed person.

[373]Penal Code § 12079 (a); see also Penal Code § 12020 (c)(25) for definition of "large capacity magazine".

Federal Law and High Capacity Magazines

The famous and unpopular Federal Assault Weapons Ban, passed by Congress and signed by then President Bill Clinton on September 13, 1994, both defined and banned "large capacity ammunition feeding devices," which applied to magazines or other ammunition feeding devices. The ban set the limit of rounds at 10 rounds. This entire ban has expired. So under federal law, "large capacity magazines" or "high capacity magazines" (the author likes calling them "standard capacity magazines") are still legal under federal law, but may be regulated under state law.

Sniperscopes

Any person who knowingly buys, sells, receives, disposes of, conceals, or has in his possession a sniperscope shall be guilty of a misdemeanor, punishable by a fine not to exceed $1000 or by imprisonment in the county jail for not more than one year, or by both.[374] A "sniperscope" is defined as any attachment, device, or similar contrivance designed for or adaptable to use on a firearm which, through the use of a projected infrared light source and electronic telescope, enables the operator thereof visually to determine and locate the presence of objects during the nighttime.[375]

This prohibition on sniperscopes does not apply to the authorized use or possession of such by a member of the armed forces of the United States, or by police officers, peace officers, or law enforcement officers with proper authorization.[376] Also, a sniperscope used solely for scientific research or educational purposes is not prohibited.[377]

Camouflaging Firearm Containers

Camouflaging firearm containers are prohibited in California[378] and are

[374]Penal Code § 468.

[375]Penal Code § 468.

[376]Penal Code § 468.

[377]Penal Code § 468.

[378]Penal Code § 12020 (a)(1).

defined as a container which meets the three following characteristics:[379] designed and intended to enclose a firearm, is designed and intended to allow the firing of the enclosed firearm by external controls while the firearm is in the container, and is not readily recognizable as a firearm. This is not to include any camouflaging covering used while engaged in lawful hunting or while going to or returning from a lawful hunting expedition.[380]

Multiburst Trigger Activators

Multiburst trigger activators are prohibited in California.[381] A multiburst trigger activator is defined as a device designed or redesigned to be attached to a semi-automatic firearm which allows the firearm to discharge two or more shots in a burst by activating the device.[382] It can also mean a manual or power-driven trigger activating device constructed and designed so that when attached to a semi-automatic firearm, it increases the rate of fire of that firearm.[383]

Body Vests

Body vests are not prohibited as many of the other items in this list, but it is important to realize that there are significant penalties for wearing a body vest while carrying out a crime.

Any person who wears a body vest in the commission or attempted commission of a violent offense[384] shall, upon conviction of that crime, in addition and consecutive to the punishment prescribed for the crime, be punished by an additional term of one, two, or five years.[385] The court shall order the two-year

---

[379] Penal Code § 12020 (c)(9).

[380] Penal Code § 12020 (c)(9)(C).

[381] Penal Code § 12020 (a)(1).

[382] Penal Code § 12020 (c)(23) and (c)(23)(A).

[383] Penal Code § 12020 (c)(23) and (c)(23)(B).

[384] See Penal Code § 12021.1 for violent offenses applicable to this prohibition.

[385] Penal Code § 12022.2.

sentence enhancement unless there are circumstances in aggravation or mitigation, which the court will consider best serve the interests of justice, and the court shall state the reasons for the enhancement choice on the record at the time of sentencing.[386]

For the purposes of this prohibition, "body vest" means any bullet-resistant material intended to provide ballistic and trauma protection for the wearer.[387]

Body Armor

Under the Penal Code as it is currently written (and deemed unconstitutional), absent an exception, any person who has been convicted of a violent felony[388] under the laws of the United States, the State of California, or any other state, government, or country, who purchases, owns, or possesses body armor[389], except as authorized, is guilty of a felony, punishable by imprisonment in a state prison for 16 months, or two or three years.[390]

Note, however, that Penal Code § 12370 has been deemed unconstitutional due to vagueness, because the law does not provide fair notice of which protective body vests constitute the body armor made illegal by the statute.[391] Therefore, the law as stated immediately above is void.

Masks

A person commits criminal possession of a firearm when he or she carries a firearm in a public place or on any public street while masked so as to hide his or

---

386 Penal Code § 12022.2.

387 Penal Code § 12022.2.

388 See Penal Code § 667.5.

389 See 11 C.C.R. § 942 for definition of "body armor".

390 Penal Code § 12370 (a).

391 See *People v. Saleem*, Filed December 17, 2009 in the Court of Appeal of the State of California, Second Appellate District, Division Three, Case Number B204646.

her identity.[392] However, this prohibition on wearing masks while armed in public places or public streets does not apply to the following:[393]

- a peace officer who is in the performance of his or her duties[394]
- full-time paid peace officers of other states and the federal government when carrying out official duties in this state[395]
- any person summoned by any of the officers in the above two exceptions to assist in making arrests on preserving the peace while he or she is actually engaged in assisting that officer[396]
- the possession of an unloaded firearm or a firearm loaded with blank ammunition by an authorized participant in an entertainment production when the use of the firearm is lawful and is part of that production[397]
- the possession of a firearm by a licensed hunter while actually engaged in lawful hunting, or while going directly to or returning directly from the hunting expedition[398]

Silencers

Silencers are strictly prohibited in California, and any person, firm, or corporation who, within this state, possesses a silencer is guilty of a felony and is subject to imprisonment in the state prison and a fine up to $10,000.[399]

The term "silencer" is defined to mean any device or attachment of any kind designed, used, or intended for use in silencing, diminishing, or muffling the report of a firearm, and may include any combination of parts, designed or

---

[392]Penal Code § 12040 (a).

[393]Penal Code § 12040 (c).

[394]Penal Code § 12040 (c)(1).

[395]Penal Code § 12040 (c)(2).

[396]Penal Code § 12040 (c)(3).

[397]Penal Code § 12040 (c)(4).

[398]Penal Code § 12040 (c)(5).

[399]Penal Code § 12520.

redesigned, and intended for use in assembling a silencer or fabricating a silencer and any part intended only for the use in such assembly or fabrication.[400]

There are exceptions to the prohibition on the possession of silencers in California.[401] Certain authorized California law enforcement, state or federal military or naval forces, when discharging their official duties are permitted to possess silencers.[402] Authorized dealers and manufacturers who are manufacturing, transporting, or selling silencers to the authorized possessors described above may also possess silencers.[403]

Exceptions to the Prohibitions on the Firearms and Ammunition Listed Above

Under both state and federal law exist limited exceptions to the prohibitions on the firearms and ammunition that are discussed above.[404]

Antique Firearm and Ammunition Exception

The prohibitions discussed above do not apply to any antique firearm or antique ammunition. An "antique firearm," for the purposes of these prohibitions, means any firearm not designed or redesigned for using rimfire or conventional center-fire ignition with fixed ammunition and manufactured in or before 1898 (including any matchlock, flintlock, percussion cap, or similar type of ignition system or replica thereof, whether actually manufactured before or after the year 1898), and also any firearm using fixed ammunition manufactured in or before 1898, for which ammunition is no longer manufactured in the United States and is not readily available in the ordinary channels of commercial trade.[405]

It is important to note that if your firearm was made after 1898, but the

---

[400] Penal Code § 12500.

[401] Penal Code § 12501.

[402] Penal Code § 12501.

[403] Penal Code § 12501 (c).

[404] See Penal Code § 12020 (b).

[405] Penal Code § 12020 (b)(5).

exact model was being made prior to 1898, it falls within the exception.[406] However, this does not include replicas of firearms manufactured today that were also manufactured prior to 1898.

"Curio or Relic"

A similar exception exists for firearms and ammunition that are "curio or relic" as defined in 27 C.F.R. 478.11, and only applies to persons who are permitted to possess such items pursuant to 18 U.S.C. 44.[407] Please note, that those who take title by way of bequest or intestate succession but are prohibited from owning, possessing, or handling firearms, may indeed maintain title for up to one year, but may not at any time take possession of the firearms, even though they are considered curio or relic.[408] At some point during the year, the person prohibited from taking possession must transfer title to the firearms by way of sale, gift, or other disposition.[409]

Other Exceptions

Other exceptions include:

- firearms that are possessed by federal, state, and local historical societies, museums, and institutional collections, which are open to the public provided that these instruments or devices are properly housed, secured from unauthorized handling, and, if the instrument or device is a firearm, unloaded[410]
- instruments or devices, other than short-barreled rifles or short-barreled shotguns, used in entertainment productions by authorized employees[411]
- instruments or devices, other than short-barreled rifles or short-barreled shotguns, that are sold by, manufactured by, exposed or

[406]Penal Code § 12020 (b)(5).

[407]Penal Code § 12020 (b)(7).

[408]Penal Code § 12020 (b)(7).

[409]Penal Code § 12020 (b)(7).

[410]Penal Code § 12020 (b)(9).

[411]Penal Code § 12020 (b)(10).

kept for sale by, possessed by, imported by, or lent by persons who are in the business of selling instruments or devices to either the historical societies, or entertainment production entitles as discussed above[412]

- the sale to, possession of, or purchase of any weapon, device, or ammunition, other than a short-barreled shotgun or short-barreled rifle, by any federal, state, county, city and county, or city agency that is charged with law enforcement, or the possession of the same by peace officers when on duty and the use of such is authorized and is within the course and scope of their duties[413]
- weapons, devices, and ammunition, other than short-barreled rifles and short-barreled shotguns, that are sold by, manufactured by, exposed or kept for sale by, possessed by, imported by, or lent by, persons who are in the business of selling weapons, devices, and ammunition that are otherwise prohibited in California to law enforcement agencies as discussed above, when engaging in transactions with those entities[414]
- possession of any of the above except for firearms by any person who is not prohibited from possessing firearms if the possession is not any longer than necessary to transport the item to law enforcement for disposal, and the transport is conducted according to law[415]
- possession of any prohibited firearm as listed above so long that it is found and possessed by a person who is not prohibited from possessing firearms, the possession was not for any longer than necessary to turn it over to law enforcement for disposal, that they are transporting the firearm according to law, and they give prior notice to the law enforcement entity that they are bringing the firearm in for disposal[416]
- possession of any weapon, device, or ammunition, by a forensic laboratory or any authorized agent or employee thereof in the

[412]Penal Code § 12020 (b)(11).

[413]Penal Code § 12020 (b)(12).

[414]Penal Code § 12020 (b)(13).

[415]Penal Code § 12020 (b)(16).

[416]Penal Code § 12020 (b)(17).

course and scope of his or her authorized activities[417]

- any other weapon as defined in 26 U.S.C. § 5845 and which is in the possession of a person permitted to possess the weapons pursuant to the federal Gun Control Act of 1968 (Public Law 90-618)[418]

Various Specified Prohibited Weapons and Items as Nuisances

Except as provided otherwise,[419] short-barreled rifles, short-barreled shotguns, wallet gun, cane gun, undetectable firearm, firearm that is not immediately recognizable as a firearm, camouflaging firearm container, multiburst trigger activator, zip gun, or unconventional pistol, as defined in the Penal Code,[420] are nuisances, and the Attorney General, district attorney, or city attorney, may bring an action to enjoin the manufacture of, importation of, keeping for sale of, offering or exposing for sale, giving, lending, or possession of, any of the foregoing items.[421]

These weapons shall be subject to confiscation and summary destruction whenever found in the state, and shall be destroyed in the manner as other weapons,[422] except that upon the certification of a judge or of the district attorney that the ends of justice will be subserved thereby, the weapon shall be preserved until the necessity for its use ceases.[423]

---

[417]Penal Code § 12020 (b)(18).

[418]Penal Code § 12020 (b)(8).

[419]See Penal Code § 12020 for exceptions to this law.

[420]See Penal Code § 12020 for definitions of the weapons listed.

[421]Penal Code § 12029.

[422]See Penal Code § 12028 regarding destruction of weapons that are deemed a nuisance.

[423]Penal Code § 12029.

CHAPTER SEVEN

"Assault Weapons" and .50 BMG Rifles

"The Constitution shall never be construed to prevent the people of the United States who are peaceable citizens from keeping their own arms." - Samuel Adams

As previously discussed, the rather unpopular Federal Assault Weapons Ban, passed by Congress and signed by then President Bill Clinton on September 13, 1994. This law both defined and banned "assault weapons," which applied to various firearms, either by name or by characteristics of the firearm. The good news for some is that this ban expired in its entirety in 2004. The bad news is, very little changed for Californians when the ban expired.

The California Legislature, in their infinite wisdom, found and declared that the proliferation and use of assault weapons, .50 BMG rifles, and .50 BMG ammunition (".50 BMG") poses a threat to the health, safety, and security of all citizens of California.[424] The original restrictions put forth by the Legislature were based upon a finding that each assault weapon has such a high rate of fire and capacity for firepower that its function as a legitimate sports or recreational firearm is substantially outweighed by the danger that it can be used to kill and injure human beings.[425]

As for the .50 BMG, the California Legislature found and declared that such a firearm was a clear and present terrorist threat to the health, safety, and security of all residents of and visitors to California, because of the high capacity for long distance and highly destructive firepower.[426] Critical to their line of reasoning is what they viewed as an unacceptable risk to the death and serious injury of human beings, destruction or serious damage of vital public and private buildings, civilian, police and military vehicles, power generation and transmission facilities, petrochemical production and storage, and the transportation infrastructure.[427]

---

[424] Penal Code § 12275.5 (a) and (b).

[425] Penal Code § 12275.5 (a).

[426] Penal Code § 12275.5 (b).

[427] Penal Code § 12275.5 (b).

Therefore, the intent of the legislature was to place restrictions on the use of assault weapons and .50 BMG such that they are practically outlawed. The legislature also established a registration and permit procedure for the lawful sale and possession of assault weapons and .50 BMG rifles.[428] While it may be of minimal importance because many of us do not agree, but the legislature did not intend to place restrictions on the use of those weapons which are primarily designed and intended for hunting, target practice, or other legitimate sports or recreational activities.[429]

The bottom line is that the legislature has created laws that basically state that once a firearm is deemed an "assault weapon," its lawful owner will be unable to buy, sell, or give it away. Further, it is difficult, or rather virtually impossible, for the lawful owner to pass it onto his children when he dies. The same applies to .50 BMG rifles.

To ensure the public is aware of the strict prohibitions on assault weapons and .50 BMG rifles, the state legislature conducts a public education and notification program regarding assault weapons and .50 BMG rifles and the registration of such weapons, including information bulletins sent to law enforcement agencies, and the use of public service announcements in a variety of media approaches, such as posters and pamphlets, and the like.[430]

Be aware that some localities attempt to create bans of their own and likely are much less aggressive in notifying the public than the DOJ. San Francisco in particular seems to enjoy pushing the limits of the law with their own prohibitions. Such laws may indeed conflict with state law and ultimately be considered unconstitutional. However, one must be aware of such local laws (beyond the scope of this book), and abide by them, as violating such laws, even if ultimately deemed unconstitutional, can still buy a citizen a great deal of trouble.

In any event, being aware of the intent of those in the state legislature who, through their actions, claim to know what is best for the law-abiding citizen, and by having a generalized idea of the limitations put upon the lawful assault weapon owner and his or her ability to transfer the weapon, we can move forward to

---

[428]Penal Code § 12275.5.

[429]Penal Code § 12275.5.

[430]Penal Code § 12289 (a).

discuss the various bans in place and the weapons that are banned and controlled in California.

Assault Weapons

California assault weapon law is very broad, difficult to understand, and with many parts of the law open to varying interpretations, which is a problem for the firearms owner who wants to remain in compliance with the law while at the same time exercising his Second Amendment rights. Assault weapons are the most highly regulated category of firearms under California law, aside for perhaps pistols.

Anyone who lives in California, who intends to travel to or through California, before handling a firearm that may be considered an assault weapon under California law, ought to have a good understanding of the law, as well as know whether or not the firearm he is handling is prohibited. Penalties and punishments regarding violations of assault weapons laws can be severe, and it is easy for the person who is not exercising caution to wind up in trouble with the law.

A common offense associated with assault weapons is a violation of the California prohibitions on large capacity magazines as discussed above. Typical assault weapons generally are sold with magazines greater than 10 rounds. One must be mindful about this prohibition because the penalties can be severe.

To make situations more difficult for the firearm enthusiast, there are three categories of assault weapon under California law. The first category includes firearms listed in the Roberti-Roos assault weapons list,[431] which was created when, in 1989, the California Legislature passed the Roberti-Roos Assault Weapons Control Act. The second category of assault weapons includes AK and AR-15 series of firearms, often referred to as the "Kasler list."[432] Finally, the third category of assault weapons is defined by specific generic characteristics.[433]

The constitutionality of the Assault Weapons Control Act of 1989 has already been challenged, and in 2000 the California Supreme Court upheld the

---

[431]Penal Code § 12276 (a), (b), and (c).

[432]Penal Code § 12276 (e) and (f).

[433]Penal Code § 12276.1; Senate Bill ("SB") 23.

Act.[434] The United States Supreme Court ultimately refused to hear the case upon appeal.

When considering the constitutionality of the Act, the California Supreme Court declared the identification of weapons by a "series" in trying to determine if they were indeed assault weapons (or not), a very difficult task for the average person. In deciding another case in 2001, the California Supreme Court created specific requirements to identify the assault weapons that were part of the "series."[435] This decision required that firearms that were banned in California that were part of the "series" had to be listed by make and model in the California Code. The list created, as discussed above, is commonly referred to as the "Kasler list." A side note: the court was silent as to assault weapons that were defined by features.

Over the years, there were various windows of time where those with "assault weapons" of any kind could be registered and kept legally in the state. Any window of time to register any of these firearms has now closed, and the Department does not allow any registration of assault weapons absent special circumstances or exceptions, which are few and far between.

At this point in time, the Attorney General lacks authority to petition a superior court to determine that a potential assault weapon should be banned, as the authority to do so expired on January 1, 2007.[436] At this time, the assault weapon list may only be modified (a firearm removed or added to the list) by the state legislature.[437] It is now almost 10 years from the last additions to the list, and it is unlikely that any more firearms will be added to the list, as the generic characteristics method appears to be the preferred method of identifying assault weapons.

So, to review, there are generally three categories of assault weapons: those identified in the Roberti-Roos Assault Weapons Control Act of 1989 ("list-

---

[434]See *Kasler v. Lockyer* 23 Cal.4th 472, 97 Cal.Rptr.2d 334.

[435]See *Harrott v. County of Kings* (2001) 25 Cal.4th 1138, 25 P.3d 649, 108 Cal.Rptr.2d 445.

[436]Penal Code § 12276.5.

[437]Penal Code § 12276.5.

based ban"), the "Kasler list" (also part of the "list-based ban"), that being the AK and AR-15 series of weapons added in 2000, and the generic characteristics definitions ("generic characteristics ban") under SB 23, effective January 1, 2000.

Category 1 - Roberti-Roos Assault Weapons Control Act of 1989[438]

At the time the Roberti-Roos Assault Weapons Control Act was enacted, the legislature defined assault weapons as the types, series, and models listed because they believed at the time that this was the most effective way to identify and restrict a specific class of semiautomatic weapons.[439]

Firearms that are designated as an "assault weapon" under this act are as follows:[440]

- All of the following specified **rifles**:
  - All AK series including, but not limited to, the models identified as follows:
    - Made in China AK, AKM, AKS, AK47, AK47S, 56, 56S, 84S, and 86S
    - Norinco 56, 56S, 84S, and 86S
    - Poly Technologies AKS and AK47
    - MAADI AK47 and ARM
  - UZI and Galil
  - Beretta AR-70
  - CETME Sporter
  - Colt AR-15 series
  - Daewoo K-1, K-2, Max 1, Max 2, AR 100, and AR 110C
  - Fabrique Nationale FAL, LAR, FNC, 308 Match, and Sporter. (8) MAS 223
  - HK-91, HK-93, HK-94, and HK-PSG-1
  - The following MAC types:
    - RPB Industries Inc. sM10 and sM11
    - SWD Incorporated M11
  - SKS with detachable magazine
  - SIG AMT, PE-57, SG 550, and SG 551

---

[438]Penal Code § 12276 (a), (b), and (c).

[439]Penal Code § 12276 (f).

[440]Penal Code § 12276 (a) through (c).

- Springfield Armory BM59 and SAR-48
- Sterling MK-6
- Steyer AUG
- Valmet M62S, M71S, and M78S
- Armalite AR-180
- Bushmaster Assault Rifle
- Calico M-900
- J&R ENG M-68
- Weaver Arms Nighthawk

- All of the following specified **pistols**:
  - UZI
  - Encom MP-9 and MP-45
  - The following MAC types:
    - RPB Industries Inc. sM10 and sM11
    - SWD Incorporated M-11
    - Advance Armament Inc. M-11
    - Military Armament Corp. Ingram —11
  - Intratec TEC-9
  - Sites Spectre
  - Sterling MK-7
  - Calico M-950
  - Bushmaster Pistol
- All of the following specified **shotguns**:
  - Franchi SPAS 12 and LAW 12
  - Striker 12
  - The Streetsweeper type S/S Inc. SS/12

Weapons found in this list are considered Category I assault weapons, and were controlled as of December 31, 1991.[441] "Controlled" means that they could not be legally purchased, kept for sale, offered for sale, exposed for sale, given, lent, manufactured, distributed, or imported. At this point in time, the only thing a California resident to do with firearms that are found in Category I that were not registered on or before March 31, 1992, that still physically exist within the state, are to properly surrender to law enforcement.[442]

---

[441]See California Attorney General Assault Weapons Identification Guide, 3rd Edition, November 2001.

[442]See Penal Code § 12288.

Category 2 - Kasler List[443]

In addition to the list above in Category 1, any firearm that was declared by the court[444] to be an assault weapon or that was already specified as an assault weapon in the list promulgated pursuant to court order was to be deemed an assault weapon.[445] Further, the term "series" includes all other models that are only variations, with minor differences, of those models listed above, regardless of manufacturer.[446]

The Supreme Court upheld the constitutionality of the Roberti-Roos Assault Weapons Control Act of 1989 in the Kasler decision, which in turn took effect on August 16, 2000. Effective on that day, firearm models that are variations of the AK or AR-15, with only minor differences from those two models, are indeed considered assault weapons and banned in California. To be grand-fathered in, and therefore possessed legally in California, they must have been registered as assault weapons on or before January 23, 2001. At this point, the only legal option for Category 2 assault weapons that were not registered by January 23, 2001, is to surrender the weapon to law enforcement according to law.[447]

The following list represents the *Kasler v. Lockyear* Assault Weapon List.[448] Please note that the following list does not also include the list under the Roberti-Roos Assault Weapons Control Act of 1989.

AK Series Weapons

- American Arms
  - AK-Y 39
  - AK-F 39
  - AK-C 47

---

[443]Penal Code § 12276 (e).

[444]See Penal Code § 12276.5.

[445]Penal Code § 12276 (d).

[446]Penal Code § 12276 (e).

[447]See California Attorney General Assault Weapons Identification Guide, 3rd Edition, November 2001; also see Penal Code § 12288.

[448]As provided by the California Department of Justice.

- AK-F 47
- Arsenal
  - SLR (all)
  - SLG (all)
- B-West
  - AK-47 (all)
- Hesse Arms
  - Model 47 (all)
  - Wieger STG 940 Rifle
- Inter Ordnance - Monroe, NC
  - RPK
  - M-97
  - AK-47 (all)
- Kalashnikov USA
  - Hunter Rifle / Saiga
- MAADI CO
  - MISR (all)
  - MISTER (all)
- MARS
  - Pistol
- Mitchell Arms, Inc.
  - M-90
  - AK-47 (all)
  - AK-47 Cal .308 (all)
  - M-76
  - RPK
- Norinco
  - 86 (all)
  - 81 S (all)
  - RPK Rifle
  - NHM 90, 90-2, 91 Sport
  - AK-47 (all)
  - MAK 90
  - Hunter Rifle
- Ohio Ordnance Works (o.o.w.)
  - ROMAK 991
  - AK-74
- Valmet
  - Hunter Rifle
  - 76 S

- WUM
    - WUM (all)

AR-15 Series Weapons

- American Spirit
    - USA Model
- Armalite
    - AR 10 (all)
    - M15 (all)
    - Golden Eagle
- Bushmaster
    - XM15 (all)
- Colt
    - Law Enforcement (6920)
    - Match Target (all)
    - Sporter (all)
- Dalphon
    - B.F.D.
- DPMS
    - Panther (all)
- Eagle Arms
    - M15 (all)
    - EA-15 A2 H-Bar
    - EA-15 E1
- Frankford Arsenal
    - AR-15 (all)
- Hesse Arms
    - HAR 15 A2
- Knights
    - SR-15 (all)
    - SR-25 (all)
    - RAS (all)
- Les Baer
    - Ultimate AR (all)
- Olympic Arms
    - AR-15
    - Car-97
    - PCR (all)
- Ordnance, Inc.
    - AR-15

- Palmetto
  - SGA (all)
- Professional Ordnance, Inc.
  - Carbon 15 Rifle
  - Carbon 15 Pistol
- PWA
  - All models
- Rock River Arms
  - Standard A-2
  - Car A2
  - Standard A-4 Flattop
  - Car A4 Flattop
  - NM A2 - DCM Legal
  - LE Tactical Carbine
- Wilson Combat
  - AR-15

Category 3 - Prohibited Assault Weapons Identified by Generic Characteristics[449]

As discussed above, in 1999 the California Legislature passed Senate Bill 23 (SB 23), which took effect on January 1, 2000.[450] This bill worked to expand the existing assault weapon ban as defined under the Roberti-Roos Assault Weapons Control Act of 1989, by creating a list of generic characteristics that, if included on the weapon, would define it as an assault weapon under California law, and therefore subject to the ban.

Category 3 assault weapons were controlled as of January 1, 2000, and must have been registered as assault weapons on or before December 31, 2000 to be legally possessed in California. There was a one year window after that, open until December 31, 2001, where a person arrested for possession of an unregistered Category 3 assault weapon between December 31, 2000, and December 31, 2001, could have it registered and reduce the charge to an infraction pursuant to the Penal Code at the time. As of January 1, 2002, the only legal option for Category 3 assault weapons that are not registered is to surrender them to law

---

[449] Penal Code § 12276.1.

[450] Penal Code § 12276.1 (e).

enforcement according to law.[451]

Penal Code § 12276 includes the list of generic characteristics. It states that an "assault weapon" shall also mean any of the following:[452]

Rifles:

- a semiautomatic, centerfire rifle that has the capacity to accept a detachable magazine and any one of the following:
  - a pistol-grip that protrudes conspicuously beneath the action of the weapon
  - a thumbhole stock
  - a folding or telescoping stock
  - a grenade launcher or flare launcher
  - a flash suppressor
  - a forward pistol grip
- a semiautomatic, centerfire rifle that has a fixed magazine with the capacity to accept more than 10 rounds
- a semiautomatic centerfire rifle that has an overall length of less than 30 inches

Pistols:

- a semiautomatic pistol that has the capacity to accept a detachable magazine and any one of the following:
  - a threaded barrel, capable of accepting a flash suppressor, forward handgrip, or silencer
  - a second handgrip
  - a shroud that is attached to, or partially or completely encircles, the barrel that allows the bearer to fire the weapon without burning his or her hand, except a slide that encloses the barrel
  - the capacity to accept a detachable magazine at some location outside of the pistol grip
- a semiautomatic pistol with a fixed magazine that has the capacity to accept more than 10 rounds

---

[451] See Penal Code § 12288.

[452] Penal Code § 12276.1 (a)(1) through (8).

Shotguns:

- a semiautomatic shotgun that has <u>both</u> of the following:
  - a folding or telescoping stock
  - a pistol-grip that protrudes conspicuously beneath the action of the weapon, thumbhole stock, or vertical handgrip
- a semiautomatic shotgun that has the ability to accept a detachable magazine
- any shotgun with a revolving cylinder

Assault Weapon Exceptions

Exceptions[453] to the above apply in two situations, those being antique firearms[454] and specified pistols intended to be used only for Olympic target shooting purposes.[455]

Assault Weapon Definitions

For the purposes of the generic characteristics ban discussed above, the following terms apply:

- "magazine" shall mean any ammunition feeding device[456]
- "capacity to accept more than 10 rounds" shall mean capable of accommodating more than 10 rounds, but shall not be construed to include a feeding device that has been permanently altered so that it cannot accommodate more than 10 rounds
- "antique firearm" means any firearm manufactured prior to January 1, 1899[457]
- "detachable magazine" means any ammunition feeding device that can be removed readily from the firearm with neither disassembly of the firearm action nor use of a tool being required. A bullet or

---

[453]Penal Code § 12276.1 (c).

[454]Penal Code § 12276.1 (c)(1).

[455]Penal Code § 12276.1 (c)(2); see also Penal Code § 12276.1 (b) and Penal Code § 12276.1 (c)(3).

[456]Penal Code § 12276.1 (d)(1).

[457]Penal Code § 12276.1 (d)(3).

- ammunition cartridge is considered a tool. Ammunition feeding device includes any belted or linked ammunition, but does not include clips, en bloc clips, or stripper clips that load cartridges into the magazine[458]
- "flash suppressor" means any device designed, intended, or that functions to perceptibly reduce or redirect muzzle flash from the shooter's field of vision[459]
- "forward pistol-grip" means a grip that allows for a pistol-style grasp forward of the trigger[460]
- "pistol-grip that protrudes conspicuously beneath the action of the weapon" means a grip that allows for a pistol-style grasp in which the web of the trigger hand (between the thumb and index finger) can be placed below the top of the exposed portion of the trigger while firing[461]
- "thumbhole stock" means a stock with a hole that allows the thumb of the trigger hand to penetrate into or through the stock while firing[462]

Before discussing any of the items included in this section, please be aware that it is illegal in California for any person to advertise any of these firearms in any newspaper, magazine, circular, form letter, or open publication that is published, distributed, or circulated in this state, or on any billboard, card, label, or other advertising medium, or by means of any other advertising device.[463]

California Legal Assault Rifles

The California Supreme Court basically ruled in 2001[464] that a

---

[458] 11 C.C.R. § 5469 (2009).

[459] 11 C.C.R. § 5469 (2009).

[460] 11 C.C.R. § 5469 (2009).

[461] 11 C.C.R. § 5469 (2009).

[462] 11 C.C.R. § 5469 (2009).

[463] Penal Code § 12020.5.

[464] See *Harrott v. County of Kings* 54 Cal.Rptr.2d 145 Cal.App. 5 Dist., 1996.

semiautomatic firearm is not a "series" assault weapon under the Penal Code[465] unless the firearm was first included in the list promulgated by the California Attorney General according to law.[466] However, the authority for the California Attorney General to add weapons to the list expired on January 1, 2007.

Therefore, under California law, one may possess what is commonly known as an assault weapon that is "California legal." A "California legal rifle" is simply an AR-15 or AK-47 rifle that has a lower receiver that is not included on either the Roberti-Roos List or the Kasler List, oftentimes known as an "off-list lower receiver" and also equipped with either a "bullet button" magazine release or a "Prince 50" magazine release.

The bullet button magazine release or Prince 50 is key because it prevents the magazine from being detachable without a tool. The bullet button device allows the tip of a bullet to work as the tool to release the magazine, and the Prince 50 allows an Allen wrench to release the magazine. Fortunately, under the law, a single bullet is considered a "tool." Keep in mind that the magazines may still only hold ten rounds.

.50 BMG Rifles

A ".50 BMG rifle," as defined by the legislature, is a center-fire rifle that can fire a .50 BMG cartridge and is not already defined as either a machinegun or an assault weapon pursuant to the other three categories of assault weapons.[467] A ".50 BMG cartridge," as defined by the legislature, is a cartridge that is designed and intended to be fired from a center-fire rifle and that meets all of the following criteria:[468]

- it has an overall length of 5.54 inches from the base to the tip of the bullet
- the bullet diameter for the cartridge is from .510 to, and including, .511 inch
- the case base diameter for the cartridge is from .800 inch to, and

[465] See Penal Code § 12276 (e).

[466] See Penal Code § 12276.5 (h).

[467] Penal Code § 12278 (a).

[468] Penal Code § 12278 (b).

including, .804 inch

- the cartridge case length is 3.91 inches

The legislature does not consider, in its definition of a .50 BMG rifle, any antique firearm (a firearm manufactured prior to January 1, 1899),[469] nor any curio or relic as defined under federal law.[470]

Violations of the Ban on Assault Weapons and .50 BMG Rifles

For the purposes of the violations of the ban on assault weapons and .50 BMG rifle, the term "person" means any individual, partnership, corporation, limited liability company, association, or any other group or entity, regardless of how it was created.[471]

Basically, any person who, within this state, manufacturers, causes to be manufactured, distributes, transports, or imports into the state, keeps for sale, offers or exposes for sale, or who gives or lends any assault weapon or any .50 BMG rifle, absent an exception or permitting, is guilty of a felony, with punishment being anywhere from four to eight years.[472] A one year sentence enhancement applies for anyone who transfers, lends, sells, or gives an assault weapon or .50 BMG rifle to a minor, meaning the sentence will range from five years to nine years.[473] Violations of these laws can result in a severe punishment.

Generally, each assault weapon and/or .50 BMG rifle is a distinct and separate offense.[474] Also, note that the above does not address mere "possession" of an assault weapon or .50 BMG rifle (please note that the use of the word "mere" is not to minimize the importance of the law or compliance with the law).

If the case is a first violation and the amount of weapons is only two, the

---

[469]Penal Code § 12278 (d).

[470]Penal Code § 12278 (c); for federal law definitions of "curio and relic," see Section 178.11 of Title 27 of the Code of Federal Regulations (27 C.F.R. § 178.11).

[471]Penal Code § 12277.

[472]Penal Code § 12280 (a)(1).

[473]Penal Code § 12280 (a)(2).

[474]Penal Code § 12280 (a)(3).

two rifles will not each be considered a distinct and separate offense, and the punishment and/or penalties will be much less severe.[475]

California Legal .50 BMG Rifles

While technically, .50 BMG rifles are banned for all intents and purposes, there are clever entrepreneurs in the marketplace that are selling rifles that fire ammunition that is just slightly smaller than as defined by law that ban .50 BMG rifles.

Possession Offenses for Assault Weapons and .50 BMG Rifle

As for a possession offense regarding an assault weapon, any person who, within the State of California, possesses any assault weapon, absent any exceptions or permitting, shall be punished by imprisonment in a county jail for a period not exceeding one year, or by imprisonment in the state prison.[476] This punishment is typical of a misdemeanor or a low level felony.

However, and this is a big "however," if this is the person's first violation of the possession ban, the offense will simply be deemed an infraction, and the penalty will be a fine not to exceed $500 if the person was found in possession of no more than two unregistered assault weapons[477] and the person meets all of the following requirements:[478]

- the person proves that he or she is lawfully in possession of the assault weapon prior to the date it was defined as an assault weapon[479]
- the person has not previously been convicted of a violation of the law regarding banned assault weapons
- the person was found to be in possession of the assault weapon within one year following the end of the one-year registration

---

[475]Penal Code § 12280 (a)(3).

[476]Penal Code § 12280 (b).

[477]See Penal Code § 12285 regarding registration of assault weapons and .50 BMG.

[478]Penal Code § 12280 (b) and (b)(1) through (b)(4).

[479]See Penal Code §§ 12276, 12276.1, or 12276.5.

period[480]

- the person relinquished the firearm to authorities[481] for it to be destroyed[482]

If one is found with an assault weapon while committing another crime, there will be a sentence enhancement of one year on top of the prescribed punishments and other sentence enhancements will apply.[483]

For those persons who, within this state, possess any .50 BMG rifle, absent an exception or a valid, current permit, shall be punished by a fine of $1,000, imprisonment in a county jail for a period not to exceed one year, or by both.[484] However, a first violation of this provision is punishable as an infraction, and the person will be fined no more than $500 if the person was found in possession of no more than two firearms that are not registered[485] and if the person meets the following conditions:[486]

- the person proves that he or she lawfully possessed the .50 BMG rifle prior to January 1, 2005
- the person has not previously been convicted of violating the ban on possession of .50 BMG rifle
- the person was found to be in possession of the .50 BMG rifle within one year following the end of the .50 BMG rifle registration period[487]

Firearms seized pursuant to the ban from a person who is guilty of only an infraction as discussed above will have his rifle returned to him, unless the court

---

[480] See Penal Code § 12285 (a).

[481] See Penal Code § 12288.

[482] See Penal Code § 12028.

[483] Penal Code § 12280 (d).

[484] Penal Code § 12280 (c).

[485] See Penal Code § 12285 regarding registration of assault weapons and .50 BMG.

[486] Penal Code § 12280 (c) and (c)(1) through (3).

[487] See Penal Code § 12285 (a).

finds that, in the interest of public safety (and after notice and a hearing), that the .50 BMG rifle should be destroyed.[488] Of course, .50 BMG rifles found on the person who does not meet the above will indeed be destroyed.[489] If one is found with a .50 BMG rifle while committing another crime, there will be a sentence enhancement of one year on top of the prescribed punishments and other sentence enhancements will apply.[490]

Exceptions, Exemptions, and Permits for Assault Weapons and .50 BMG Rifle

Exemptions for Law Enforcement

The ban on assault weapons and .50 BMG rifle shall not apply to the sale to, purchase by, importation of, or possession of assault weapons or .50 BMG rifle by the Department of Justice, police departments, sheriffs' offices, marshals' offices, the Department of Corrections and Rehabilitation, the Department of the California Highway Patrol, district attorney's offices, Department of Fish and Game, Department of Parks and Recreation, or the military or naval forces of this state or of the United States, or any federal law enforcement agency for the use and discharge of their official duties.[491]

Also, law enforcement, specifically, sworn peace officer members of those agencies specified above may possess and/or use assault weapons and .50 BMG rifles whether on or off duty.[492] These sworn peace officer members may accept delivery, accept transfer, or purchase an assault weapon or .50 BMG rifle, if they have the required authorization, meaning, verifiable written certification from the head of the agency identifying the possessor-officer.[493] The weapon must be properly registered

---

[488] Penal Code § 12280 (c)(4); also see Penal Code § 12028 regarding destroying banned weapons.

[489] Penal Code § 12280 (c)(4).

[490] Penal Code § 12280 (d).

[491] Penal Code § 12280 (e).

[492] Penal Code § 12280 (f)(1).

[493] Penal Code § 12280 (f)(2).

under the law.[494]

Exemptions for Citizens

The penalties and punishment for possession of an assault weapon would not apply to the possession of an assault weapon during the 90-day period immediately following the date a particular weapon was specified as an assault weapon,[495] or during the one-year period after the date it was defined as an assault weapon,[496] if all of the following apply:[497]

- the person is eligible to register the particular assault weapon
- the person lawfully possessed the particular assault weapon prior to the date it was specified as an assault weapon, or prior to the date it was defined as an assault weapon
- the person is otherwise in compliance with the Penal Code in regard to assault weapons

Those Who Are Permit Holders

The prohibitions regarding the manufacture of assault weapons and .50 BMG rifles shall not apply to persons who are issued permits[498] if the manufacture of the prohibited weapons is to sell[499] to exempt law enforcement entities discussed above,[500] permits issued for other reasons,[501] entities outside of the state who have a federal firearms dealer's license solely for the purpose of distribution to federal

---

[494]Penal Code § 12280 (f)(2).

[495]See Penal Code § 12276.5.

[496]See Penal Code § 12276.1.

[497]Penal Code 12280 (g), and (g)(1) through (3).

[498]See Penal Code § 12287.

[499]Penal Code § 12280 (h).

[500]Penal Code § 12280 (h) and (h)(1).

[501]Penal Code § 12280 (h) and (h)(2); see also Penal Code §§ 12286 and 12287.

military and federal law enforcement agencies,[502] federal military and law enforcement agencies,[503] law enforcement and military agencies of other states,[504] and foreign governments and agencies approved by the United States State Department.[505]

Exemptions that Exist by Operation of Law

The prohibitions against a person within the State of California from manufacturing, causing to be manufactured, distributing, transporting, or importing, keeping for sale, offering or exposing for sale, or giving or lending of an assault weapon or .50 BMG rifle, do not apply if that person is the executor or administrator of an estate that includes such a weapon if that weapon is legally registered[506] or was possessed and disposed of as authorized by the probate court, or is as otherwise permitted under the Roberti-Roos Assault Weapons Control Act of 1989.[507]

The prohibitions against possession and the conditions that allow it under normal circumstances are not applicable, again, where the person is the executor or administrator of an estate that includes an assault weapon or a .50 BMG rifle that is properly registered,[508] or was properly possessed and disposed of as set forth by the probate court.[509]

---

[502]Penal Code § 12280 (h) and (h)(3).

[503]Penal Code 12280 (h) and (h)(4).

[504]Penal Code § 12280 (h)(5).

[505]Penal Code § 12280 (h) and (h)(6).

[506]See Penal Code § 12285.

[507]Penal Code § 12280 (i).

[508]See Penal Code § 12285.

[509]Penal Code § 12280 (j).

Exceptions for Loans of an Assault Weapon or .50 BMG Rifle

The prohibition against lending an assault weapon does not apply when:[510]

- the person who is loaning the firearm lawfully possesses the assault weapon or .50 BMG rifle and it is properly registered, if all of the following apply:[511]
    - the person to whom the assault weapon or .50 BMG rifle is lent is 18 years of age or over and is not otherwise prohibited by state or federal law from possessing, receiving, owning, or purchasing a firearm
    - the person to whom the assault weapon or .50 BMG rifle is lent remains in the presence of the registered possessor of the weapon
    - the assault weapon or .50 BMG rifle is possessed at any of the following locations:
        - while on a target range that holds a regulatory or business license for the purpose of practicing shooting at that target range
        - while on the premises of a target range of a public or private club or organization organized for the purpose of practicing shooting at targets
        - while attending any exhibition, display, or educational project that is about firearms and is sponsored by, conducted under the auspices of, or approved by a law enforcement agency or nationally or state-recognized entity that fosters proficiency in, or promotes education about firearms
- the return of an assault weapon or .50 BMG rifle to the registered possessor, or the lawful possessor, which is lent the same[512]

It follows that the possession of an assault weapon or .50 BMG rifle by a

[510]Penal Code § 12280 (k).

[511]Penal Code § 12280 (k)(1).

[512]Penal Code § 12280 (k)(2).

person is not prohibited under the Assault Weapons Act if the person is lent a firearm as discussed above.[513]

Exceptions for Non-Residents

None of the previous prohibitions concerning assault weapons and .50 BMG rifles[514] as discussed above apply to the possession and importation of such weapons into the state if all of the following conditions are met:[515]

- the person is attending or going directly to or coming directly from an organized competitive match or league competition that involves the use of an assault weapon or .50 BMG rifle
- the competition or match is conducted on the premises of one of the following:
    - while on a target range that holds a regulatory or business license for the purpose of practicing shooting at that target range
    - while on the premises of a target range of a public or private club or organization organized for the purpose of practicing shooting at targets
- the match or competition is sponsored by, conducted under the auspices of, or approved by a law enforcement agency or nationally or state-recognized entity that fosters proficiency in, or promotes education about firearms
- the assault weapon or .50 BMG rifle is lawfully transported in accordance with law[516]
- the person is 18 years of age and over and is not in a class of persons prohibited from possessing firearms because of a violent offense[517] or a serious mental issue.[518]

---

[513]Penal Code § 12280 (l).

[514]See Penal Code § 12280 (a), (b), and (c).

[515]Penal Code § 12280 (m).

[516]See Penal Code §§ 12026.1 and 12026.2.

[517]See Penal Code §§ 12021 and 12021.1.

[518]See Welfare and Institutions Code §§ 8100 and 8103.

Other Exceptions

The exceptions to the prohibitions on only the **possession** of an assault weapon or .50 BMG rifle are numerous and include:[519]

- any person who lawfully acquired his assault weapon before June 1, 1989, or his .50 BMG rifle before January 1, 2005, and who is permitted to use it outside of normal lawful uses,[520]
- a person who is permitted to manufacture and/or sell assault weapons or .50 BMG rifles[521]
- any person that falls under the previous two exceptions who is acting in accordance with his permit[522]
- a person who is the registered owner of an assault weapon or .50 BMG rifle when he is possessing it in accordance with law, as follows:[523]
  - the person is possessing it at his residence, place of business, or other property owned by that person, or on property owned by another with the owner's express permission[524]
  - while on the premises of a target range or a public or private club or organization organized for the purpose of practicing shooting at targets[525]
  - while on a target range that holds a regulatory or business license for the purposes of practicing shooting at that target range[526]
  - while on the premises of a shooting club which is

---

519 Penal Code § 12280 (n).

520 Penal Code §§ 12280 (n)(1), 12286, and 12287; see also 12285 (c).

521 Penal Code §§ 12280 (n)(1); 12286 and 12287; see also 12285 (c).

522 Penal Code § 12280 (n)(2); see also Penal Code §§ 12285, 12286, and 12287.

523 Penal Code § 12280 (p); see also Penal Code § 12285 (c).

524 Penal Code § 12285 (c)(1).

525 Penal Code § 12285 (c)(2).

526 Penal Code § 12285 (c)(3).

licensed pursuant to the Fish and Game Code[527]

- while attending any exhibition, display, or educational project which is about firearms and which is sponsored by, conducted under the auspices of, or approved by a law enforcement agency or a nationally recognized entity that fosters proficiency in, or promotes education about, firearms[528]
- while on publicly owned land if the possession and use of the assault weapon or .50 BMG rifle is specifically permitted by the managing agency of the land[529]
- while transporting the assault weapon or .50 BMG rifle between any of the places mentioned above, or to any licensed gun dealer[530] for lawful servicing and repair,[531] so long as the assault weapon is properly transported as defined by the law[532]

The exceptions to all of the prohibitions for an assault weapon or .50 BMG rifle, **including** possession, manufacture, cause to be manufactured, distribution, transportation, importation, keep for sale, offer or exposes for sale, or who gives or lends such, apply in the following situations:[533]

- a person who is acting in accordance with laws regarding

---

[527]Penal Code § 12285 (c)(4)

[528]Penal Code § 12285 (c)(5).

[529]Penal Code § 12285 (c)(6). Please note that you may or may not be allowed to bring the weapon on land held by the Bureau of Land Management, and one should consult the Bureau prior to bringing the weapon onto the land. Further, whether or not one can take weapons into National Parks has been at issue over the last few years, as it used to be prohibited, then it was allowed, and now, it may or may not be allowed, depending on the prevailing political winds. Check with the National Park Service prior to bringing weapons onto National Park Land.

[530]See Penal Code § 12290 regarding "licensed gun dealer".

[531]See Penal Code § 12290 (h).

[532]Penal Code § 12285 (c)(7); see also Penal Code § 12026.1 regarding lawful transport of the weapon.

[533]Penal Code § 12280 (o).

registration of such weapons[534]

- a person who is acting in accordance with both the laws regarding registration of assault weapons and .50 BMG rifles,[535] but also with the laws regarding his permit[536]

The prohibitions against the **import** of an assault weapon or .50 BMG rifle do not apply to one who is in lawful possession of a properly registered weapon in California who is returning home.[537]

The prohibitions on the sale of assault weapons or .50 BMG rifles are inapplicable to persons who are issued permits[538] to any of the following:[539]

- exempt law enforcement entities[540]
- entities and persons who have been issued permits[541]
- federal military and law enforcement agencies
- law enforcement and military agencies of other states
- foreign governments and agencies approved by the United States State Department
- officers who are authorized to possess assault weapons and .50 BMG rifles[542]

Unlawful Possession of Assault Weapon or .50 BMG Rifle as a Nuisance

If a person does not have lawful possession of an assault weapon or .50

---

[534]See Penal Code § 12285.

[535]See Penal Code § 12285.

[536]See Penal Code §§ 12286, 12287, and 12290.

[537]Penal Code § 12280 (q); see also Penal Code § 12285 (c).

[538]See Penal Code § 12287.

[539]Penal Code § 12280 (t).

[540]See Penal Code § 12280 (e).

[541]See Penal Code §§ 12286 and 12287.

[542]See Penal Code § 12280 (f).

BMG rifle within the State of California, it may be deemed a public nuisance.[543] Instead of a criminal prosecution, a prosecuting attorney may choose to bring a civil action or reach a civil compromise in any superior court to enjoin the possession of the weapon that is the public nuisance.[544]

If this is the case, and the prosecuting attorney makes a motion in the superior court, he may ask for the imposition of a civil fine not to exceed $300 for the first weapon deemed a public nuisance and up to $100 for each additional weapon deemed a public nuisance.[545] Any weapon deemed a public nuisance shall be destroyed in a manner so that it may no longer be used, unless the court finds that preservation of the weapon is in the interest of justice.[546]

It is important to note that automatically, upon the conviction of any misdemeanor or felony involving the illegal possession or use of an assault weapon, the weapon shall be deemed a public nuisance and disposed of.[547]

Registration of Assault Weapons and .50 BMG Rifles

Only people who possessed their assault weapon or .50 BMG rifle(s) at the time they were banned under California law, and who properly registered the weapon within the grace period as prescribed by the law, can legally own an assault weapon[548] or a .50 BMG rifle.[549] The registration was extensive, as it required a description of the firearm to identify it uniquely, including all identification marks, the full name, address, date of birth, and thumbprint of the owner, and any other information the Department deemed appropriate.[550]

---

[543]Penal Code § 12282 (a).

[544]Penal Code § 12282 (a).

[545]Penal Code § 12282 (b).

[546]Penal Code § 12282 (c).

[547]Penal Code § 12282 (d); see also Penal Code § 12028 (d) regarding disposal of a weapon deemed a nuisance.

[548]Penal Code § 12285 (a)(1).

[549]Penal Code § 12285 (a)(2).

[550]Penal Code § 12285 (a).

Registration of an assault weapon or .50 BMG rifle was simple. A form could be obtained from many firearms dealers, a local law enforcement office, such as a police department, or directly from the Department of Justice. The card had to be completed and was to include a thumbprint professionally taken at a local law enforcement agency, with a payment of $20.

Any failure to register an assault weapon or .50 BMG rifle ultimately meant that any such weapon possessed in California would be a felony with the offense being possession of an unregistered assault weapon or .50 BMG rifle. You have two choices if you find yourself in this situation. One may either properly relinquish the firearm to local authorities or apply for a special permit from the Department. One other option exists, and in rare circumstances, you may be able to alter or modify permanently the firearm in an attempt to remove it from being characterized as an assault weapon.

If your registration is or was approved, it is wise to keep permanently a copy of the registration letter with the firearm. This way, if you are stopped for any reason, at any place, you have proof of registration.

Other Assault Weapons and .50 BMG Rifle Issues

Date of Designation of Weapon as Assault Weapon

The date a firearm is an assault weapon for purposes of the ban is the earliest of the following:[551]

- the effective date of an amendment to the Category Two assault weapons (named/list-based ban) that adds the designation of the specified firearm[552]
- the effective date of the addition to the Category One assault weapons (named/list-based ban) promulgated according to law[553]
- the operative date of amendment to the Category Three assault weapons (generic characteristics ban)[554]

---

[551]Penal Code § 12280 (u).

[552]Penal Code § 12280 (u)(1); see also Penal Code § 12276.

[553]Penal Code § 12280 (u)(2); see also Penal Code § 12276.5.

[554]Penal Code § 12280 (u)(3); see also Penal Code § 12276.1.

Joint Registration of Assault Weapons and .50 BMG Rifles

The Department of Justice's registration procedures provide the option of joint registration for assault weapons and .50 BMG rifles that are owned by family members residing in the same household.[555] This allows multiple persons within a family of legally possessing and using the registered weapon.

Re-Registration of Assault Weapons and .50 BMG Rifles

Any person who registered a firearm as an assault weapon pursuant to the provisions of law in effect prior to January 1, 2000, where the assault weapon is thereafter defined as an assault weapon pursuant to the "generic characteristics" ban[556] shall be deemed to have registered the weapon, and does not need to re-register the weapon.[557]

Further, any person who legally registered a firearm as an assault weapon pursuant to the law in effect prior to January 1, 2005, where the assault weapon is thereafter defined as a .50 BMG rifle,[558] shall be deemed to have registered the weapon and need not re-register the weapon.[559]

Assault Weapon and .50 BMG Rifle Transfers Between Persons

No assault weapon that is lawfully registered[560] and possessed may be sold or transferred to anyone within this state other than to a licensed gun dealer.[561] No .50 BMG rifle properly possessed may be sold or transferred to anyone within this

---

555 Penal Code § 12285 (e).

556 See Penal Code § 12276.1 regarding "generic characteristics" ban.

557 Penal Code § 12285 (g)(1).

558 See Penal Code § 12278 regarding definition of .50 BMG rifle.

559 Penal Code § 12285 (g)(2).

560 Penal Code § 12285.

561 Penal Code § 12285 (b)(1); see also Penal Code § 12290 (c) and Penal Code § 12288 regarding "licensed gun dealers".

state other than to a licensed gun dealer.[562]

Assault Weapon and .50 BMG Rifle Transfers Between Gun Dealers - Any licensed gun dealer[563] who lawfully possesses an assault weapon or .50 BMG rifle,[564] in addition to other authorized uses,[565] may transport the firearm between dealers or out of state if that person is permitted to under federal law,[566] display it at any gun show licensed by a state or local governmental entity, sell it to a resident outside the state, or sell it to a person who has been issued a permit,[567] but any transporting must be done as required by the laws regarding lawful travel with a firearm.[568]

Transfer of Assault Weapon or .50 BMG Rifle to Minor

No person who is under the age of 18 years may register or possess an assault weapon or .50 BMG rifle.[569]

Transfer to Person with Mental Issues

No person who is prohibited by state or federal law from possessing, receiving, owning, or purchasing a firearm may register or possess an assault weapon or .50 BMG rifle.[570]

---

[562]Penal Code § 12285 (b)(3); see also Penal Code § 12290 (c) and § 12288 regarding "licensed gun dealers".

[563]See Penal Code §§ 12290 (c), 12071, and 12287.

[564]See Penal Code § 12285.

[565]See Penal Code § 12285.

[566]See National Firearms Act.

[567]See Penal Code § 12286.

[568]Penal Code § 12290 (a); see also Penal Code § 12026.1.

[569]Penal Code § 12285 (d).

[570]Penal Code § 12285 (d).

Acquired Through Bequest or Intestate Succession

Any person who obtains title by bequest or intestate succession to a properly registered assault weapon or an assault weapon that was possessed through a peace officer exemption, shall, within 90 days, render the weapon permanently inoperable, sell the weapon to a licensed gun dealer, obtain a permit from the Department,[571] or remove the weapon from the state.[572] The same options apply for a person who obtains title to a .50 BMG rifle that was properly registered or was possessed through a peace officer exemption, except that the person acquiring the .50 BMG rifle has 180 days from receipt of the weapon to act,[573] whereas the person acquiring the assault weapon has only 90 days.

Situations Where a Lawfully Possessed Firearm is Declared an Assault Weapon

If a firearm you currently (and lawfully) possess is subsequently declared to be an assault weapon,[574] you shall, within 90 days, render the weapon permanently inoperable, sell the weapon to a licensed gun dealer, obtain a permit from the Department,[575] or remove the weapon from the state.[576]

Important exception: A person who lawfully possessed a firearm that was subsequently declared to be an assault weapon pursuant to the "list-based ban"[577] may alternatively register the firearm within 90 days (the typical grace period that the Department has given in the past) of the declaration issued.[578]

---

[571]See Penal Code § 12230 et seq.

[572]Penal Code § 12285 (b)(1).

[573]Penal Code § 12285 (b)(3).

[574]See Penal Code §§ 12276.1 and 12276.5.

[575]See Penal Code § 12230 et seq.

[576]Penal Code § 12285 (b)(1).

[577]See Penal Code §§ 12276 and 12276.1.

[578]Penal Code § 12285 (b)(1); see also Penal Code § 12276.5.

Moving Into the State with Assault Weapon or .50 BMG Rifle

A person moving into California, who is otherwise in lawful possession of an assault weapon or .50 BMG rifle, shall do one of the following:[579]

- Prior to bringing the assault weapon into this state, that person shall first obtain a permit from the Department of Justice[580]
- The person shall cause the assault weapon to be delivered to a licensed gun dealer.[581] If the person then obtains a permit from the Department, the dealer shall redeliver the assault weapon to the person.[582] However, if the licensed gun dealer is prohibited from delivering the assault weapon because the permit is denied, or for any other reason, the dealer shall properly possess or properly dispose of the assault weapon according to law.[583]
- leave it out of state

Using and Traveling with Properly Registered Assault Weapons and .50 BMG Rifles

Yes, this is somewhat of a rehash of the discussion above about permitted acts by a person in lawful possession of an assault weapon or .50 BMG rifle, But, for good measure, we address it once again just to be clear. Call it a "belt and suspenders" approach, if you will, but this topic is very important because the way the law is written, it is very easy for one in lawful possession of an assault weapon or .50 BMG rifle to wander outside the permissible bounds as set by the legislature.

As it stands, any person who has registered an assault weapon or registered .50 BMG rifle according to law may possess it only under any of the

---

579 Penal Code §§ 12285 (b)(2) and 12285 (b)(4).

580 Penal Code §§ 12285 (b)(2)(A) and 12285 (b)(4)(A); for registration process, see Penal Code § 12230 et seq.

581 See Penal Code § 12285 (b)(2)(B) and (b)(4)(B); see also Penal Code § 12290 and 18 U.S.C. § 44 regarding "licensed gun dealers"

582 Penal Code § 12285 (b)(2)(B) and (b)(4)(B).

583 Penal Code § 12285 (b)(1)(B) and (b)(4)(B).

following conditions unless a permit allowing for additional uses is first obtained:[584]

- at that person's residence, place of business, or other property owned by that person, or on property owned by another and with that owner's express permission[585]
- while on the premises of a target range of a public or private club or organization organized for the purpose of practice shooting at targets[586]
- while on a target range that holds a regulatory or business license for the purpose of practicing shooting at the target range[587]
- while on the premises of a shooting club which is licensed pursuant to the Fish and Game Code[588]
- While attending any exhibition, display, or educational project which is about firearms and which is sponsored by, conducted under the auspices of, or approved by a law enforcement agency or a nationally or state-recognized entity that fosters proficiency in, or promotes education about, firearms[589]
- while on publicly owned land if the possession and use of the assault weapon or .50 BMG rifle is specifically permitted by the managing agency of the land.[590]
- while **transporting** the assault weapon or .50 BMG rifle between

---

[584]Penal Code § 12285 (c); see also Penal Code § 12286 regarding special permits.

[585]Penal Code § 12285 (c)(1).

[586]Penal Code § 12285 (c)(2).

[587]Penal Code § 12285 (c)(3).

[588]Penal Code § 12285 (c)(4).

[589]Penal Code § 12285 (c)(5).

[590]Penal Code § 12285 (c)(6). Please note that you may or may not be allowed to bring the weapon on land held by the Bureau of Land Management, and one should consult the Bureau prior to bringing the weapon onto the land. Further, whether or not one can take weapons into National Parks has been at issue, as it used to be prohibited, then it was allowed, and now, it may or may not be allowed, depending on the prevailing political winds. Check with the National Park Service prior to bringing weapons onto National Park Land.

any of the places mentioned above, or to any licensed gun dealer[591] for lawful servicing and repair,[592] so long as the assault weapon is properly transported as defined by the law[593]

Transporting a Legally Possessed Assault Weapon or .50 BMG Rifle

As stated above, a person with legal possession of an assault weapon or .50 BMG rifle may transport the same between any of the permitted places (also discussed above), or to any licensed gun dealer for service and repair.

For a person who is over the age of 18 years of age (those under 18 years of age may not possess an assault weapon or .50 BMG rifle) and who resides or is temporarily within the state, and who is a citizen of the United States,[594] to transport an assault weapon or .50 BMG rifle lawfully within his vehicle, it must be locked in the vehicle's trunk or in a locked container in the vehicle other than the utility or glove compartment,[595] the firearm must be carried by the person directly to or from any motor vehicle for any lawful purpose, and, while carrying the firearm, the firearm is contained within a locked container.[596]

A "locked container" means a secure container which is fully enclosed and locked by a padlock, key lock, combination lock, or similar locking device.[597] Because it needs only to be a "secure container," the container may be metal, plastic, nylon, etc. As long as it may be locked by one of the prescribed lock types, it would be considered a secure container.

---

591 See Penal Code § 12290 regarding "licensed gun dealer".

592 See Penal Code § 12290 (h).

593 Penal Code § 12285 (c)(7); see also Penal Code § 12026.1 regarding lawful transport of the weapon.

594 Penal Code § 12026.1 (a).

595 Penal Code § 12026.1 (a)(1)

596 Penal Code § 12026.1 (a)(2).

597 Penal Code § 12026.1 (c).

Transfer of Assault Weapon or .50 BMG Rifle to a Firearms Dealer for Sale or Repair

A person may transfer an assault weapon or .50 BMG rifle to any licensed firearms dealer, so long as it is properly registered or a special permit exists for the person to have the weapon, for service or repair.[598] If the gunsmith is not also a "licensed firearms dealer" as defined by law, he may not accept the firearm for repair from the unlicensed person. Instead, the firearm will need to be transferred to a licensed firearms dealer, and that dealer will transfer the firearm to the gunsmith for you.[599] The gunsmith who accepts the transfer must be a gunsmith who is in the dealer's employ, or a gunsmith with whom the dealer has contracted with for gun-smithing services,[600] and must be properly licensed by the federal government and hold a business license.[601]

For these laws, a "licensed gun dealer" is a person who is properly licensed[602] and who has a permit to sell assault weapons or .50 BMG rifles.[603]

Relinquishing Assault Weapon or .50 BMG Rifle to Law Enforcement

Any individual may arrange in advance to relinquish an assault weapon or a .50 BMG rifle to a police or sheriff's department.[604] The firearm that is relinquished should be transported to authorities in accordance with law.[605]

---

[598]Penal Code § 12285 (c)(7); see also Penal Code § 12026.1 regarding lawful transport of the weapon.

[599]Penal Code § 12290 (b)(1) and (2).

[600]Penal Code § 12290 (b)(2)(A) and (B).

[601]Penal Code § 12290 (b)(2)(B)(i) and (ii).

[602]See Penal Code § 12071 regarding licensing of gun dealers.

[603]See Penal Code § 12287 regarding permits to sell assault weapons and .50 BMG rifles.

[604]Penal Code § 12288.

[605]Penal Code § 12288; see also Penal Code § 12026.1 for details on transporting firearms in accordance with law.

Modifications of Assault Weapons

Prior to bringing the would-be "assault weapon" into the State of California, you permanently remove one of the defined generic characteristics[606] from the firearm so that it brings the firearm outside the definition of an "assault weapon," and it is not also included as a named assault weapon on the list of assault weapons in California,[607] the firearm will no longer be prohibited in California and may be lawfully possessed, used, transferred, and the like, because the firearm will no longer fall within the definitions of "assault weapon," as set forth by the state legislature.

However, if you modify a firearm that is not already an assault weapon, and modify it such that it would now fall under the ban because generic characteristics[608] were somehow added, the firearm will likely then fall within the ban and be an unlawful, unregistered assault weapon. At this time, there is no codified law regarding this issue, and the only case law has been dismissed and remanded for review[609], so this is merely a prediction of what would happen if you modified a previously lawful firearm and created a firearm that would ordinarily be banned under the generic characteristics ban.

Permits Issued for Assault Weapons and .50 BMG Rifles

Any person who has a lawfully registered assault weapon or .50 BMG rifle in the State of California, who wishes to use the firearm in a fashion that is different than specified as permitted uses,[610] shall first obtain a permit from the Department of Justice in the same manner as prescribed by law.[611] No permit will be issued to

---

[606]See Penal Code § 12276.1 regarding generic characteristics of assault weapons.

[607]See Penal Code § 12276 regarding list of named assault weapons.

[608]See Penal Code § 12276.1 regarding generic characteristics of assault weapons.

[609]*People v. Dingman* (1996) 47 Cal.App.4th 1068.

[610]See Penal Code § 12285 (c) regarding specific permitted uses of lawfully possessed assault weapons and .50 BMG rifles.

[611]See Penal Code § 12230 regarding authority of DOJ to issue permit.

an applicant who is not at least 18 years of age.[612]

The Department of Justice issues permits only for good cause.[613] Permits may only be for the manufacture for or sale of assault weapons or .50 BMG rifles to any of the following:[614]

- authorized law enforcement agencies[615]
- entities and person who have been issued permits[616]
- entities outside of the State of California who have, in effect, a federal firearm's dealer's license (FFL) solely for the purpose of distribution to an authorized entity[617]
- federal law enforcement and military agencies[618]
- law enforcement and military agencies of other states[619]
- foreign governments and agencies approved by the United States State Department[620]

Permits are generally not issued for those of us who are decent, law-abiding citizens, who would just like to own such weapons, despite having spotless records and are good, upstanding citizens of this country. It is just too much to trust us, the decent, law-abiding citizen.

---

[612]Penal Code § 12230.

[613]Penal Code § 12287 (a).

[614]Penal Code § 12287 (a).

[615]Penal Code § 12287 (a)(1); see also Penal Code § 12280 (f) regarding authorized law enforcement agencies.

[616]Penal Code § 12287 (a)(2); see also Penal Code §§ 12286 and 12287 regarding entitles with permits.

[617]Penal Code § 12287 (a)(3); see also Penal Code § 12287 (a)(4) and (6) for authorized entities.

[618]Penal Code § 12287 (a)(4).

[619]Penal Code § 12287 (a)(5).

[620]Penal Code § 12287 (a)(6).

Permit Process

The authority to issue permits, as well as revoke permits, is completely the discretion of the DOJ.[621] Applications for permits must be filed in writing with complete information as required by the DOJ.[622] The permits will be uniform throughout the state, as will the application forms, which are provided by the DOJ.[623] A fee is required, both for the initial application, and for any renewals, which are required yearly, as the permit is only valid for one year.[624] The fee may vary from year to year, but is designed to cover only the expenses involved with processing the application and issuing the permit.[625]

Revocation of Permit

A revocation of a permit may occur by the DOJ at any time when it appears the need for the firearms has ceased or that the holder of the permit has used the firearms for purposes other than as allowed in the permit, or, that the holder of the permit has not exercised great care in retaining custody of any of the weapons possessed under the permit.[626]

Annual Inspection of Permit Holder's Facilities and Inventory

The DOJ shall, for every person, firm, or corporation to whom a permit is issued, annually conduct an inspection for security and safe storage purposes, and to reconcile inventory.[627] However, should the permit allow less than five assault weapons or .50 BMG rifles, the DOJ may conduct irregular inspections, perhaps

[621]Penal Code § 12287 (b); see also Penal Code § 12230 and 12233.

[622]Penal Code § 12231.

[623]Penal Code § 12231.

[624]Penal Code § 12231.

[625]Penal Code § 12231.

[626]Penal Code § 12233.

[627]Penal Code § 12289.5 (a).

even as little as once every five years, at their discretion.[628]

Broadcasting Registration or Permit on Police Radio

No peace officer or dispatcher shall broadcast over a police radio that an individual has registered or has obtained a permit to possess, an assault weapon or .50 BMG rifle, unless there exists a reason to believe in good faith that one of the following conditions exist:[629]

- the individual with the permit has or may be engaged in criminal conduct[630]
- the police are responding to a call in which the person allegedly committing a criminal violation may gain access to the assault weapon or .50 BMG rifle[631]
- the victim, witness, or person who reported to police may be using the assault weapon or .50 BMG rifle to hold the person allegedly committing the crime, or may be using the weapon in self-defense or defense of others[632]

A peace officer is not prohibited from broadcasting over a police radio that an individual has not registered, or not obtained a permit to possess an assault weapon.[633] Also, this prohibition does not also prohibit transmission of ownership status over law enforcement computers or any other form of communication that is legally accessible only to peace officers or other authorized personnel.[634]

---

[628]Penal Code § 12289.5 (b).

[629]Penal Code § 12288.5 (a).

[630]Penal Code § 12288.5 (a)(1).

[631]Penal Code § 12288.5 (a)(2).

[632]Penal Code § 12288.5 (a)(3).

[633]Penal Code § 12285 (b).

[634]Penal Code § 12285 (c).

CHAPTER EIGHT

Machineguns

Machineguns

Machineguns are both prohibited and heavily regulated in California, under both state and federal law. For all intents and purposes, they are completely banned in California, absent very limited circumstances.

Machinegun Violations

Possession of Machineguns

Any person, firm, or corporation who, within the Sate of California, possesses or knowingly transports a machinegun, absent authorization, is guilty of a public offense and subject to imprisonment in the state prison, a fine of $10,000, or by both.[635]

Conversion of Firearm into Machinegun and Sale of Machinegun

Any person, firm, or corporation who, within the State of California, intentionally converts a firearm into a machinegun, or who sells, offers for sale, or knowingly manufactures a machinegun, absent authorization, is punishable in the state prison for four, six, or eight years.[636]

Unlawful Possession of Machinegun As Public Nuisance

It shall be a public nuisance to possess any machinegun in violation of law.[637] The Attorney General, or any local city or county prosecutor may bring an action to enjoin the possession of a machinegun. Upon determination of the court, any machinegun found in violation of the chapter will be surrendered to the DOJ for

---

[635]Penal Code § 12220 (a).

[636]Penal Code § 12220 (b).

[637]Penal Code § 12251.

disposal according to law.[638]

Permits for Machineguns

The California Legislature has given the authority to issue permits for the possession, manufacture, and transportation of machineguns only upon a satisfactory showing that good cause exists for the issuance of a permit to the applicant.[639] No applicant under the age of 18 years will be granted a permit.[640]

Application for Machinegun Permit

Permits must be kept by every person, firm, or corporation, either on their person or at the place where the firearms are kept.[641] The permit shall be open to inspection by any peace officer or other person designated by the DOJ.[642] Also, the DOJ will conduct annual inspections for security and safe storage purposes, and to reconcile the inventory of weapons on the permit,[643] unless the permit allows for less than five weapons, and then the inspection may only occur once (or more) every five years, as determined by the DOJ and at their discretion.[644]

Annual Inspections of Machinegun Permit Holders Facility

The DOJ shall, for every person, firm, or corporation to whom a permit is issued, annually conduct an inspection for security and safe storage purposes and to reconcile inventory.[645] However, should the permit allow less than five assault weapons or .50 BMG rifles, the DOJ may conduct irregular inspections, perhaps

---

[638]Penal Code § 12251.

[639]Penal Code § 12230.

[640]Penal Code § 12230.

[641]Penal Code § 12232.

[642]Penal Code § 12232.

[643]Penal Code § 12234 (a).

[644]Penal Code § 12234 (b).

[645]Penal Code § 12234 (a).

even as little as once every five years, at their discretion.[646]

Revocation of Machinegun Permit

Revocations of permits may occur by the DOJ at any time when it appears the need for the firearms has ceased or that the holder of the permit has used the firearms for purposes other than as allowed in the permit, or, that the holder of the permit has not exercised great care in retaining custody of any of the weapons possessed under the permit.[647]

Licenses to Sell Machineguns

The DOJ may grant one-year licenses to sell machineguns, subject to all of the following conditions:[648]

- the business shall be carried on only in the place designated in the license[649]
- the license or certified copy thereof must be displayed on the premises where it may easily be read[650]
- no machinegun shall be delivered to any person not authorized to receive the machinegun[651]
- complete records of sale with information required by the DOJ must be kept and available for inspection at any time[652]

All applications for licenses will be made in writing, on forms prescribed by the DOJ, with the appropriate fee.[653]

---

[646]Penal Code § 12234 (b).

[647]Penal Code § 12233.

[648]Penal Code § 12250 (a).

[649]Penal Code § 12250 (a)(1).

[650]Penal Code § 12250 (a)(2).

[651]Penal Code § 12250 (a)(3).

[652]Penal Code § 12250 (a)(4).

[653]Penal Code § 12250 (b).

Exemptions to Machinegun Prohibitions

No machinegun prohibitions as discussed above, or the need to obtain permitting or licensing, shall apply to any of the following:[654]

- the sale to, purchase by, or possession of machine guns by the police departments, sheriffs' offices, marshals' offices, district attorneys' offices, the CHP, the DOJ, the Department of Corrections for use by their Special Emergency Response Teams and Law Enforcement Liaison/Investigations Unit, or the military of the United States, if purchased for the use in the discharge of their official duties, provided the sale is carried out according to law by a permitted person who is properly licensed[655]
- the possession and use by the police departments, sheriffs' offices, marshals' offices, district attorneys' offices, the CHP, the DOJ, the Department of Corrections for use by their Special Emergency Response Teams and Law Enforcement Liaison/Investigations Unit authorities if within the scope of their duties[656]

---

[654]Penal Code § 12201.

[655]Penal Code § 12201 (a); see also Penal Code §§ 12230 and 12250.

[656]Penal Code § 12201 (b).

Part Four

Prohibited and/or Controlled Weapons and Devices in California

CHAPTER NINE

Other Weapons, Items, and Devices That are Prohibited and/or Controlled in California

Under California law, there are many weapons, items, and other devices that are practically outlawed or controlled. For these items, some exceptions exist. Please read this section carefully. At the end of this section is a list of places where most of these weapons are prohibited or restricted and controlled.

Also note that, as with other prohibited weapons and weapons-related items, it is illegal for any person to advertise any of the following weapons, items, and devices in any newspaper, magazine, circular, form letter, or open publication that is published, distributed, or circulated in this state, or on any billboard, card, label, or other advertising medium, or by means of any other advertising device.[657]

Switchblade Knives

Every person who possesses in the passenger's or driver's area of any motor vehicle in any public place open to the public, carries upon his or her person, and every person who sells, offers for sale, exposes for sale, loans, transfers, or gives to any other person a switchblade knife having a blade of two or more inches in length is guilty of a misdemeanor.[658]

A "switchblade knife" is a knife having the appearance of a pocketknife and includes a spring-blade knife, snap-blade knife, gravity knife or any other similar type knife, the blade or blades of which are two or more inches in length and which can be released automatically by a flick of a button, pressure on the handle, flip of the wrist, or other mechanical device, or is released by the weight of the blade or by any type of mechanism whatsoever, but does not include a knife that opens with one hand utilizing thumb pressure applied solely to the blade of the knife or a thumb stud attached to the blade, provided that the knife has a detent or other mechanism that provides resistance that must be overcome in opening the blade, or that biases

---

[657]Penal Code § 12020.5.

[658]Penal Code § 653k.

the blade back toward its closed position.[659]

Note that this prohibition basically prohibits "butterfly" or "balisong" style knives that have a blade in excess of 2" long. However, it does not prohibit knives that open with one hand utilizing thumb pressure that must be applied solely to the blade of the knife, nor does it prohibit knives with a thumb stud attached to the blade, so long as the knife has a detent or some other mechanism that provides a measure of resistance. Also, knives that are generally opened with the flick of the wrist after the blade has been opened are illegal, as a knife is only a gravity knife if it can easily be opened with the flick of the wrist from a closed position.[660]

Undetectable Knives

It is a misdemeanor to manufacture, knowingly import into the state for commercial sale, knowingly export out of this state for commercial sale of any kind, to keep for commercial sale, offer or expose for sale, any undetectable knife.[661] An "undetectable knife" means any knife or other instrument with or without a handguard that is capable of ready use as a stabbing weapon that may inflict great bodily injury or death that is commercially manufactured to be used as a weapon and is not detectable by a metal detector or magnetometer, either handheld or otherwise, that is set at standard calibration.[662]

Exceptions include manufacture or importation of undetectable knives for sale to a law enforcement or military entity with a valid purchase order issued by the agency or department,[663] and federal, state, and local historical societies, museums, and the like, which are open to the public, so long as such weapons are housed and secured from unauthorized handling.[664]

Because of what the legislature found to be a widespread problem

---

[659]Penal Code § 653k.

[660]See *In Re Roderick S.* 125 Cal.App.3rd 48.

[661]Penal Code § 12001.1 (a).

[662]Penal Code § 12001.1 (a).

[663]Penal Code § 12001.1 (c).

[664]Penal Code § 12001.1 (d).

concerning knives that were undetectable, the legislature enacted a law that required all knives or other instruments with or without a handguard that are capable of ready use as a stabbing weapon that may inflict great bodily injury or death that are commercially manufactured in this state to be manufactured to include materials that will ensure that they are detectable by a metal detector or magnetometer, either handheld or otherwise, that is set at standard calibration.[665]

Ballistic Knives

Possession, manufacture, import, sale of, gift of, or lending any ballistic knives is prohibited in California.[666] A "ballistic knife" is defined as a device that propels a knifelike blade as a projectile by means of a coil spring, elastic material, or compressed gas, but does not include any device which propels an arrow or a bolt by means of any common bow, compound bow, crossbow, or underwater speargun.[667]

Nunchaku

California law prohibits the possession, manufacture, import, offer to sell, lend, or give a nunchaku, which is defined as an instrument consisting of two or more sticks, clubs, bars, or rods to be used as handles, connected by a rope, cord, wire, or chain, in the design of a weapon used in connection with the practice of a system of self-defense such as karate.[668] However, possession of a nunchaku on the premises of a school which holds a regulatory or business license and teaches the art of self-defense, or the manufacture of a nunchaku to be sold to such entity, is permitted in California.[669]

Metal Knuckles

To manufacture, import, offer to sell, lend, give, or possess metal knuckles is prohibited in California. Metal knuckles are defined as any device or instrument

---

[665]Penal Code § 12001.1 (b).

[666]Penal Code § 12020 (a)(2).

[667]Penal Code § 12020 (c)(8).

[668]Penal Code § 12020 (a)(1) and (c)(3).

[669]Penal Code § 12020 (b)(3) and (b)(4).

made wholly or partially of metal which is worn for purposes of offense or defense in or on the hand and which either protects the wearer's hand while striking a blow or increases the force of impact from the blow or injury to the individual receiving the blow.[670] The metal contained in the device may help support the hand or fist, provide a shield to protect it, or consist of projections or studs which would contact the individual receiving a blow.[671]

Composite Knuckles

Any person in this state who possesses, commercially manufactures, causes to be commercially manufactured, or who knowingly imports into the state for commercial sale, keeps for commercial sale, or offers or exposes for commercial sale, any composite knuckles or hard wooden knuckles is guilty of a misdemeanor.[672] "Composite knuckles" or "hard wooden knuckles" means any device made wholly or partially of composite materials, other than a medically prescribed prosthetic, that is not a metal knuckle[673] that is worn for purposes of offense or defense in or on the hand, and that either protects the wearer's hand while striking a blow or increases the force of impact from the blow or injury to the person receiving the blow.[674]

"Hard wooden knuckles" means any device or instrument made wholly or partially of wood or paper products that is not a metal knuckle[675] that is worn for purposes of offense or defense in or on the hand, and that either protects the wearer's hand while striking a blow, or increases the force of impact from the blow or injury to the individual receiving the blow.[676]

The composite materials, wood, or paper products contained in the device may help support the hand or fist, provide a shield to protect it, or consist of

---

[670] Penal Code § 12020 (a)(1) and (c)(7).

[671] Penal Code § 12020 (c)(7).

[672] Penal Code § 12020.1.

[673] As defined by Penal Code § 12020 (c)(7).

[674] Penal Code § 12020.1.

[675] As defined by Penal Code § 12020 (c)(7).

[676] Penal Code § 12020.1.

projections or studs that would contact the individual receiving a blow.[677]

Distinguish this from metal knuckles above. The manufacture, import, offer to sell, lend, give, or possession for any reason of any metal knuckles is prohibited in California. However, to possess, manufacture, or import "hard knuckles," whether plastic or wood, is not prohibited in California as long as such acts are not for a commercial purpose. If they are made, imported, loaned, given, or otherwise possessed for a non-commercial purpose, "hard knuckles" are not prohibited in California.

Belt Buckle Knives

California law prohibits the manufacture, import, gift of, sale of, loan of, or possession of belt buckle knives. A belt buckle knife is defined as a knife which is made an integral part of a belt buckle and consists of a blade with a length of at least 2.5 inches.[678]

Leaded Canes

California prohibits the manufacture of, gift of, import of, sale of, loan of, or possession of leaded canes. A leaded cane is defined as a staff, crutch, stick, rod, pole, or similar device, unnaturally weighted with lead.[679]

Shurikens

The possession, manufacture, sale, offer to sell, gift of, loan of, or import of a shuriken in California is prohibited.[680] A "shuriken" is defined as any instrument, without handles, consisting of a metal plate having three or more radiating points with one or more sharp edges and designed in the shape of a polygon, trefoil, cross, star, diamond, or other geometric shape for use as a weapon for throwing.[681]

---

[677]Penal Code § 12020.1.

[678]Penal Code § 12020 (a)(1) and (c)(13).

[679]Penal Code § 12020 (a)(1) and (c)(17).

[680]Penal Code § 12020 (a)(1).

[681]Penal Code § 12020 (c)(11).

Lipstick Case Knife

California law prohibits the possession, manufacture, sale of, gift or loan of, or import of lipstick case knives. A lipstick case knife is defined as a knife enclosed within and made an integral part of a lipstick case.[682]

Cane Sword

California law prohibits the possession, manufacture, sale of, gift or loan of, or import of cane swords.[683] A "cane sword" is a cane, swagger stick, stick, staff, rod, pole, umbrella, or similar device, having concealed within it a blade that may be used as a sword or stiletto.[684]

Shobi-Zue

California law prohibits the possession, manufacture, sale of, gift or loan of, or import of a shobi-zue.[685] A "shobi-zue" is a staff, crutch, stick, rod, or pole concealing a knife or blade within it which may be exposed by a flip of the wrist or by a mechanical action.[686]

Air-Gauged Knives

California law prohibits the possession of, import of, sale of, gift or loan of, or manufacture of air-gauged knives.[687] An "air-gauged knife" is defined as a device that appears to be an air gauge but has concealed within it a pointed, metallic shaft that is designed to be a stabbing instrument which is exposed by mechanical action or gravity, and which locks into place when extended.[688]

---

[682]Penal Code § 12020 (a)(1) and (c)(14).

[683]Penal Code § 12020 (a)(1).

[684]Penal Code § 12020 (c)(15).

[685]Penal Code § 12020 (a)(1).

[686]Penal Code § 12020 (c)(16).

[687]Penal Code § 12020 (a)(1).

[688]Penal Code § 12020 (c)(18).

Blowguns

Any person who knowingly manufactures, sells, offers for sale, possesses, or uses a blowgun or blowgun ammunition in California is guilty of a misdemeanor.[689] A "blowgun" is defined as a hollow tube designed and intended to be used as a tube through which a dart is propelled by the force of the breath of the user.[690] "Blowgun ammunition" is defined as a dart that is designed and intended for use in a blowgun.[691]

Exceptions apply for the possession and use of blowguns and blowgun ammunition by zookeepers, animal control officers, personnel of the Department of Fish and Game, properly authorized humane officers,[692] or veterinarians in the course and scope of their business in order to administer medicine to animals.[693]

Writing Pen Knives

California law prohibits the possession, import of, sale, gift, loan, or manufacture of writing pen knives, which are defined as a device that appears to be a writing pen but has concealed within it a pointed, metallic shaft that is designed to be a stabbing instrument which is exposed by mechanical action or gravity, which when activated locks into place when extended, or, the pointed, metallic shaft is exposed by the removal of the cap or cover on the device.[694]

Explosive Substances

Any person who carries concealed upon his or her person any explosive substance, other than fixed ammunition, is punishable by imprisonment in a county

---

[689] Penal Code § 12582.

[690] Penal Code § 12580.

[691] Penal Code § 12581.

[692] See Corporations Code § 14502 regarding authorized humane officers.

[693] Penal Code § 12583.

[694] Penal Code § 12020 (a)(1) and (c)(19).

jail not exceeding one year or in the state prison.[695]

Dirk or Dagger

Any person who carries concealed upon his or her person any dirk or dagger is punishable by imprisonment in a county jail not exceeding one year or in the state prison.[696] A "dagger" is a generic term that basically covers a dirk, stiletto, or poniard.[697] A dirk is arguably the same thing, as it is defined as a straight knife or other instrument with or without a hand-guard that is capable or ready for use as a stabbing weapon that may inflict great bodily injury or death only if the blade of the knife is exposed and into the locked position.[698]

A knife, such as a non-locking folding knife or a basic pocket knife, is not considered a "dirk" or a "dagger," for the purposes of the laws prohibiting concealed carry, unless somehow the blade of the knife is exposed and locked into position.[699] Additionally, a knife carried in a sheath or some other case that attaches to the waist is not a concealed weapon, nor are small "pocketknives" that are obviously designed to be carried in the pocket in a closed state, and which cannot be used until there have been several intervening manipulations.[700]

Because there is such a large variety of knives, the test for a dirk or a dagger is whether it is "capable of ready use," and any knife that requires some sort of action to bring it into a position where it could be effectively used is not a dirk or dagger, and is therefore not prohibited.

---

[695]Penal Code § 12020 (a)(3).

[696]Penal Code § 12020 (a)(4).

[697]*People v. McClure* 160 Cal.Rptr. 83, 98 Cal.App.3d Supp. 31.

[698]*People v. McClure* 160 Cal.Rptr. 83, 98 Cal.App.3d Supp. 31.

[699]*In Re George W.* (App.2 Dist. 1998) 80 Cal.Rptr.2d 868, 68 Cal.App.4th 1208.

[700]*In Re. Luke W.*, (App. 1 Dist. 2001) 105 Cal.Rptr.2d 905, 88 Cal.App.4th 650.

Blackjacks and Weapons Similar to Blackjacks

Any person who manufactures, imports into the state, keeps for sale, offers or exposes for sale, gives, lends, or possesses a blackjack, slungshot, billy, sandclub, sap, or sandbag, is punishable by imprisonment in the county jail not exceeding one year or in the state prison.[701] A nunchaku is considered a blackjack.[702]

Metal Military Practice Handgrenades or Metal Replica Handgrenade

California law has a prohibition on the manufacture, importation, sale, offer for sale, expose for sale, gift, loan, or possession of any metal military practice handgrenades or metal replica handgrenades.[703] However, there are no prohibitions on any plastic toy handgrenade, any metal military practice handgrenade, or any metal replica handgrenade that is a relic, curio, memorabilia, or display item, that is filled with a permanent inert substance that is otherwise permanently altered in a manner that prevents modification for use as a grenade.[704]

The first offense for a violation of the law regarding handgrenades shall be punishable only as an infraction as long as the offender is not an active participant in a criminal street gang.[705]

Less Lethal Weapons

Persons living or traveling in California are not necessarily prohibited from possessing "less lethal weapons," but must be aware of the laws regarding them.

Under California law, an authorized peace officer or an authorized custodial

---

[701] Penal Code § 12020 (a)(1).

[702] 56 Op.Atty.Gen. 506, 9-30-73.

[703] Penal Code § 12020 (a)(1).

[704] Penal Code § 12020 (b)(15).

[705] Penal Code § 12020 (b)(4); see also Street Terrorism and Enforcement and Prevention Act (Chapter 11 (commencing with Penal Code § 186.20) of Title 7 of Part 1).

officer[706] may purchase, possess, or transport any less lethal weapon or less lethal ammunition, and may do so only under the terms and conditions as are specified by his or her employing agency.[707]

A "less lethal weapon" is defined as any device that is designed to, or that has been converted to, expel or propel less lethal ammunition by any action, mechanism, or process for the purpose of incapacitating, immobilizing, or stunning a human being through the infliction of any less than lethal impairment of physical condition, function, or senses, including physical pain or discomfort.[708] The weapon need not leave any lasting or permanent incapacitation, discomfort, pain, or other injury or disability in order to be qualified as falling under the definition of "less lethal weapon."[709]

The definition of "less lethal weapon" includes the frame or receiver of any weapon defined as a "less lethal weapon," but does not include any of the following unless the part or weapon has been converted as a defined "less lethal weapon":[710]

- a pistol, revolver, or firearm[711]
- a machinegun[712]
- rifle or shotgun using fixed ammunition consisting of standard primer and powder not capable of being concealed upon the person[713]
- pistols, rifles, and shotguns that are firearms having a barrel less than 0.18 inches in diameter and that are designed to expel a

---

[706]See Penal Code § 830 et seq. regarding applicable custodial officers.

[707]Penal Code § 12600.

[708]Penal Code § 12601 (a).

[709]Penal Code § 12601 (a).

[710]Penal Code § 12601 (b).

[711]Penal Code § 12601 (b)(1); see also Penal Code § 12001 regarding definition of a "pistol, revolver, or firearm".

[712]Penal Code § 12601 (b)(2); see also Penal Code § 12200 regarding definition of "machinegun".

[713]Penal Code § 12601 (b)(3).

projectile by any mechanical means or by compressed air or gas[714]

- when used as designed or intended by the manufacturer, any weapon commonly regarded as a toy gun, and that as such is incapable of inflicting any impairment of physical condition, function, or senses[715]
- a destructive device[716]
- a tear gas weapon[717]
- a bow or crossbow designed to shoot arrows[718]
- a device commonly known as a slingshot[719]
- a device designed for the firing of stud cartridges, explosive rivets, or similar industrial ammunition[720]
- a device designed for signaling, illumination, or safety[721]
- an assault weapon[722]

"Less lethal ammunition" means any ammunition that is designed to be used in any less lethal weapon or any other kind of weapon and when used is designed to immobilize, incapacitate, or stun a human being through the infliction of any less than lethal impairment of physical condition, function, or senses, including physical pain or discomfort.[723]

---

[714]Penal Code § 12601 (b)(4).

[715]Penal Code § 12601 (b)(5).

[716]Penal Code § 12601 (b)(6); see also Penal Code § 12301 regarding definition of "destructive device".

[717]Penal Code § 12601 (b)(7); see also Penal Code § 12402 regarding definition of "tear gas".

[718]Penal Code § 12601 (b)(8).

[719]Penal Code § 12601 (b)(9).

[720]Penal Code § 12601 (b)(10).

[721]Penal Code § 12601 (b)(11).

[722]Penal Code § 12601 (b)(12); see also Penal Code §§ 12276 and 12276.1 for definition of "assault weapon".

[723]Penal Code § 12601 (c).

Any person who sells a less lethal weapon to a person under the age of 18 years of age is guilty of a misdemeanor, punishable by imprisonment in the county jail for up to six months or by a fine of not more than $1000, or by both.[724] Any other violation of the laws regarding less lethal weapons is a misdemeanor.[725]

Stun Guns

Any person may purchase, possess, or use a stun gun, aside from the following prohibited persons:[726]

- no person convicted of a felony or any crime involving an assault under the laws of the United States, of the State of California, or any other state, government, or country shall purchase, possess, or use stun guns[727]
- no person convicted of misuse of a stun gun[728] shall purchase, possess, or use stun guns[729]
- no person who is addicted to any narcotic drug shall purchase, possess, or use a stun gun[730]
- Minors: no person shall sell or furnish any stun gun to a minor unless that minor is at least 16 years of age and has the written consent of his or her parent or legal guardian.[731]

Manufacturers of stun guns must include with each stun gun the name of the manufacturer stamped on the gun,[732] as well as a serial number as applied by the

---

[724]Penal Code § 12655.

[725]Penal Code § 12653.

[726]Penal Code § 12651.

[727]Penal Code § 12651 (a).

[728]See Penal Code § 244.5 regarding misuse of a stun gun.

[729]Penal Code § 12651 (a).

[730]Penal Code § 12651 (b).

[731]Penal Code § 12651 (c) and (d).

[732]Penal Code § 12652 (a).

manufacturer.[733] Also, every stun gun sold in California must include an instruction booklet, and each stun gun sold without a booklet is a separate offense with a fine of $50.[734]

Violation of the laws regarding stun guns is a public offense punishable by a $50 fine for the first offense, with subsequent violations being considered a misdemeanor.[735] And, unless otherwise specified, any violation of the laws regarding stun guns is a misdemeanor.[736]

BB Device

Every person who sells to a minor any BB device is guilty of a misdemeanor.[737] Also, every person who furnishes (loans or a transfer without a sale[738]) any BB device to any minor, without the express or implied permission of the parent or legal guardian of the minor, is guilty of a misdemeanor.[739]

While BB devices are not prohibited in California, there are certain prohibitions on their transferability and modification. First, the definition of "imitation firearm" includes a BB device that is so substantially similar in coloration and overall appearance to an existing firearm as to lead a reasonable person to perceive that the device is a firearm.[740]

To change, alter, remove, or obliterate any coloration or markings on any BB device to make it look more like a real firearm is a misdemeanor.[741] An

---

[733]Penal Code § 12652 (b).

[734]Penal Code § 12654.

[735]Penal Code § 12651 (c).

[736]Penal Code § 12653.

[737]Penal Code § 12551.

[738]Penal Code § 12552 (b).

[739]Penal Code § 12552 (a).

[740]Penal Code § 12550 (c).

[741]Penal Code § 12553 (a).

exception to the prohibitions on changing, altering, removing, or obliterating markings on a BB devices exist for entertainment productions.[742]

Open display of BB devices is subject to prohibitions.[743] No person may openly display or expose an imitation firearm in a public place.[744] Violation is an infraction punishable by a fine of $100 for the first offense and $300 for the second offense.[745] A third and any subsequent offense is a misdemeanor.[746]

A "public place" is defined as an area open to the public and includes streets, sidewalks, bridges, alleys, plazas, parks, driveways, front yards, parking lots, automobiles (whether moving or not), and buildings open to the general public, including those that serve food and drink, or provide entertainment, and the doorways and entrances to buildings or dwellings, and shall include public schools and a public or private college or university.[747]

Exceptions apply when the BB device is:[748]

- packaged or concealed so that it is not subject to public viewing[749]
- displayed or exposed in the course of commerce, including commercial film or video productions, or for service, repair, or restoration of the imitation firearm[750]
- used in a theatrical production, a motion picture, video, television,

---

742 Penal Code § 12553 (a)(2).

743 Penal Code § 12556.

744 Penal Code § 12556 (a).

745 Penal Code § 12556 (b).

746 Penal Code § 12556 (c).

747 Penal Code § 12556 (e).

748 Penal Code § 12556 (d).

749 Penal Code § 12556 (d)(1).

750 Penal Code § 12556 (d)(2).

or stage production[751]

- used in conjunction with a certified or regulated public or private shooting range[752]
- used in conjunction with lawful hunting, or lawful pest control activities[753]
- used or possessed at certified or regulated public or private shooting ranges[754]
- used at fairs, exhibitions, expositions, or other similar activities for which a permit has been obtained from a local or state government[755]
- used in military, civil defense, or civil activities, including flag ceremonies, color guards, parades, award presentations, historical re-enactments, and memorials[756]
- used for public display authorized by public or private schools or displays that are part of museum collections[757]
- used in parades, ceremonies, or other similar activities for which a permit has been obtained from a state or local government[758]
- displayed on a wall plaque or in a presentation case[759]
- used in areas where the discharge of a firearm is lawful[760]
- where the entire exterior surface is white, bright red, bright orange, or some other bright color, or a combination of bright colors, or where the entire device is made of transparent or

---

[751]Penal Code § 12556 (d)(3).

[752]Penal Code § 12556 (d)(4).

[753]Penal Code § 12556 (d)(5).

[754]Penal Code § 12556 (d)(6).

[755]Penal Code § 12556 (d)(7).

[756]Penal Code § 12556 (d)(8).

[757]Penal Code § 12556 (d)(9).

[758]Penal Code § 12556 (d)(10).

[759]Penal Code § 12556 (d)(11).

[760]Penal Code § 12556 (d)(12).

translucent materials, to allow unmistakable observation of the device's complete contents.[761] Note, however, that federal law allows a mere "orange tip," but California does not, as the entire surface must be colored, transparent, or translucent.[762]

Finally, brandishing a BB device, that is, drawing or exhibiting, in a threatening manner, except in self-defense, in such a way that a reasonable person would have an apprehension of fear or bodily harm, is guilty of a misdemeanor and punishable in the county jail for no less than 30 days.[763]

Tear Gas

Notwithstanding any other law, any person may purchase, possess, or use tear gas and tear gas weapons for the projection or release of tear gas, if the tear gas and tear gas weapons are used solely for self-defense purposes.[764] However, no person shall purchase, possess, or use any tear gas weapon that expels a projectile, or that expels the tear gas by any method other than an aerosol spray, or that contains more than 2.5 ounces net weight of aerosol spray.[765]

Typical "tear gas" products available to the public include bottles of mace, pepper spray, and other typical irritants that are manufactured and offered for sale to the public for self-defense purposes. Such items are typically found in local firearms retail establishments.

"Tear gas" is defined as all liquid, gaseous, or solid substances intended to produce temporary physical discomfort or permanent injury through being vaporized or otherwise dispersed in the air.[766] This does not include any substance

---

[761]Penal Code § 12556 (d)(13).

[762]Penal Code § 12556 (d)(13).

[763]Penal Code § 417.4.

[764]Penal Code § 12403.7.

[765]Penal Code § 12403.7 (e)(1).

[766]Penal Code § 12401.

registered as an economic poison,[767] provided that such substance is not intended to be used to produce discomfort or injury to human beings.[768]

A "tear gas weapon" includes any shell, cartridge, or bomb capable of being discharged or exploded, when the discharge or explosion will cause or permit the release or emission of tear gasses.[769] "Tear gas weapon" also includes any revolvers, pistols, fountain pen guns, billies, or other form of device, portable or fixed, intended for the projection or release of tear gas, except those regularly manufactured and sold for use with firearm ammunition.[770]

The following persons may not purchase, possess, or use tear gas or tear gas weapons:[771]

- a person who has been convicted of a felony[772]
- a person who has been convicted of a crime of assault[773]
- a person who is addicted to any narcotic drug[774]

Minors and Tear Gas

Prohibitions regarding tear gas and tear gas weapons with minors include:

- no person shall sell or furnish any tear gas or tear gas weapon to a minor[775]
- no person who is a minor shall purchase, possess, or use tear gas

---

[767]See Agricultural Code § 12751 et seq., regarding "economic poisons."

[768]Penal Code § 12401.

[769]Penal Code § 12402 (a).

[770]Penal Code § 12402 (b).

[771]Penal Code § 12403.7 (a) and (b).

[772]Penal Code § 12403.7 (a).

[773]Penal Code 12403.7 (a).

[774]Penal Code § 12403.7 (b).

[775]Penal Code § 12403.7 (c).

or tear gas weapons[776]

Exceptions exist. A minor who has attained the age of 16 years may purchase or possess tear gas or a tear gas weapon if he or she is accompanied by a parent or guardian, or who has the written consent of the same,[777] and a retailer may sell tear gas or a tear gas weapon to the same so long as he is presented with a statement of consent signed by the parent or guardian.[778]

Any civil liability of a minor arising out of his or her misuse of tear gas or a tear gas weapon (that is, using it for anything other than self-defense), is imposed upon the person, parent, or guardian who signed the statement of consent, and that person shall be jointly and severally liable with the minor for any damages proximately resulting from the negligent or wrongful act or omission of the minor in the misuse of the tear gas.[779]

Other Considerations Regarding Tear Gas

Other issues regarding tear gas and tear gas weapons include the requirement that all tear gas containers and tear gas weapons include a label that states: "WARNING: The use of this substance or device for any other purpose other than self-defense is a crime under the law."[780] The label shall also include a date on which the useful life of the tear gas weapon expires.[781] Every tear gas weapon sold, transported, or possessed shall bear the name of the manufacturer and a serial number applied by that manufacturer.[782]

Every tear gas container or weapon shall also be accompanied at the time

[776]Penal Code § 12403.7 (d).

[777]Penal Code § 12403.8 (a).

[778]Penal Code § 12403.8 (b).

[779]Penal Code § 12403.8 (c).

[780]Penal Code § 12403.7 (e)(2).

[781]Penal Code § 12403.7 (e)(3).

[782]Penal Code § 12421.

of purchase by printed instructions for use,[783] an insert including directions for use, first aid information, safety and storage information, and an explanation of the legal ramifications of improper use of the product.[784]

Tear Gas Offenses

Any person who uses tear gas or tear gas weapons except in self-defense is guilty of a public offense and is punishable by imprisonment in a state prison for 16 months, two or three years (felony conviction), or in a county jail not to exceed one year or by a fine not to exceed $1000 (misdemeanor conviction), or by both.[785] If the victim is a peace officer,[786] who is engaged in his or her official duties and the person committing the offense knows or reasonably should know that the victim is a police officer, the offense is a felony and is punishable by imprisonment in a state prison for 16 months or two or three years, or by a fine of $1000, or by both.[787]

Any person, firm, or corporation who, within California, knowingly sells or offers for sale, possesses, or transports any tear gas or tear gas weapon, except as permitted by law, is guilty of a public offense that may result in imprisonment in a county jail for no more than one year or by a fine not to exceed $2000, or by both.[788]

Any person who changes, alters, removes, or obliterates the name of the manufacturer, serial number, or any other mark of identification on any tear gas weapon, is guilty of a public offense and, upon conviction, shall be punished by imprisonment in the state prison or by a fine of not more than $2000, or by both.[789] Further, possession of the same is considered to be presumptive evidence that the possessor is the person who actually changed, altered, removed, or obliterated the

[783]Penal Code § 12403.7 (e)(4).

[784]Penal Code § 12403.7 (e)(4) and (f).

[785]Penal Code § 12403.7 (g).

[786]See Penal Code § 830 et seq., regarding definition of "peace officer."

[787]Penal Code § 12403.7 (g).

[788]Penal Code § 12420.

[789]Penal Code § 12422.

manufacturer's name or serial number.[790]

Exemptions to Tear Gas Limitations

As addressed above, the only tear gas weapon available to the average citizen is such that only discharges an aerosol spray, and is available only in a form that contains more than 2.5 ounces net weight of aerosol spray.[791] However, a wide variety of exemptions exist to this limitation for the following:

- peace officers[792] may purchase, possess, transport, or use any tear gas or tear gas weapon if they have satisfactorily completed a course of instruction on the use of tear gas[793]
- military, naval forces of this state, of the United States, or any federal law enforcement may purchase, possess, or transport any tear gas or tear gas weapon for the official use in the discharge of their duties[794]
- properly licensed[795] private investigators or private patrol operators,[796] or uniformed patrolmen employees of a private patrol operator, may purchase, possess, or transport any tear gas weapon, if it is used solely for defensive purposes in the course of the activity for which their license was issued and if the person has satisfactorily completed an approved course of instruction in the use of tear gas.[797]
- custodial officers of any county may lawfully carry tear gas weapons only while on duty, but may carry tear gas weapons

---

[790]Penal Code § 12422.

[791]Penal Code § 12403.7 (e)(2).

[792]See Penal Code § 830 et seq., regarding definition of "peace officer".

[793]Penal Code § 12403.

[794]Penal Code § 12403.1.

[795]See Business and Professions Code § 7500 et seq., regarding licensing of patrol operators and private investigators.

[796]Penal Code § 12403.5.

[797]Penal Code § 12403.5.

while off duty in accordance with all other laws.[798]

Permits for Tear Gas and Tear Gas Weapons

Good Cause Required - The Department of Justice may issue a permit for the possession and transportation of tear gas or tear gas weapons that are not intended or certified for personal self-defense purposes, but will require proof of good cause exists for the issuance of the permit.[799]

Protective Systems Allowed - Permits may be issued to allow the applicant to install, maintain, and operate a protective system involving the use of tear gas or tear gas weapons in any place which is accurately and completely described in the application for the permit.[800]

Applications - Applications will be in writing with details to be provided as required by the Department of Justice,[801] and may be made for multiple offices or branches in a single application.[802]

Display of Permit - Every person, firm, or corporation to whom a permit has been issued shall either carry the permit on their person, or keep it in a place as described on the permit, and be open to inspection by any peace officer or other person as designated by the authority issuing the permit.[803]

Revocation of Permit - Permits may be revoked or suspended by the issuing authority at any time when it appears that the need supporting the issuance of the permit has ceased, or the holder of the permit engaged in an unlawful business or occupation, or has wrongfully made use of the tear gas or tear gas weapon or the

---

[798]Penal Code § 12403.9; see also Penal Code § 12403.

[799]Penal Code § 12423.

[800]Penal Code § 12423.

[801]Penal Code § 12424.

[802]Penal Code § 12424.5.

[803]Penal Code § 12425.

permit issued.[804]

Boobytraps

Except as provided elsewhere and according to law,[805] any person who assembles, maintains, places, or causes to be placed a boobytrap device[806] is guilty of a felony punishable by imprisonment in the state prison for two, three, or five years.[807] A "boobytrap" means any concealed or camouflaged device designed to cause great bodily injury when triggered by an action of any unsuspecting person coming across the device, and may include, but is not limited to, guns, ammunition, or explosive devices attached to trip wires or other triggering mechanisms, sharpened stakes, and lines or wire with hooks attached.[808]

Possession of any boobytrap device with the intent to use the device as a boobytrap is punishable in a state prison, or in a county jail, not exceeding one year, or by a fine of $5000, or both.[809]

Destructive Devices and Explosives

Any person, firm, or corporation who, within the State of California, possesses any destructive device, other than fixed ammunition of a caliber greater than 0.60 caliber, is guilty of a public offense and upon conviction shall be punished by imprisonment in the county jail for up to one year, or in state prison, or by a fine not to exceed $10,000, or by both.[810]

---

[804] Penal Code § 12426.

[805] See Penal Code § 12301 regarding exceptions.

[806] See Penal Code § 12355 (c) for definition of "boobytrap device".

[807] Penal Code § 12355 (a).

[808] Penal Code § 12355 (c).

[809] Penal Code § 12355 (b).

[810] Penal Code § 12303.

The term "destructive device" includes any of the following weapons:[811]

- any projectile containing any explosive or incendiary material or any other chemical substance, including, but not limited to, that which is commonly known as tracer or incendiary ammunition, except tracer ammunition manufactured for use in shotguns[812]
- any bomb, grenade, explosive missile, or similar device or any launching device therefor[813]
- Any weapon of a caliber greater than 0.60 caliber which fires fixed ammunition, or any ammunition therefor, other than a shotgun (smooth or rifled bore) conforming to a definition of a "destructive device,"[814] shotgun ammunition (single projection or shot), antique rifle, or an antique cannon.[815] "Antique cannon" means any cannon manufactured before January 1, 1899, which has been rendered incapable of firing or for which ammunition is no longer manufactured in the United States and is not readily available in the ordinary channels of commercial trade.[816] "Antique rifle" means a firearm conforming to the definition of "antique firearm."[817]
- any rocket, rocket-propelled projectile, or similar device of a diameter greater than 0.60 inch, or any launching device therefor, and any rocket, rocket-propelled projectile, or similar device containing any explosive or incendiary material or any other chemical substance, other than the propellant for that device, except those devices designed primarily for emergency or distress signaling purposes[818]

---

[811]Penal Code § 12301 (a).

[812]Penal Code § 12301 (a)(1).

[813]Penal Code § 12301 (a)(1).

[814]See 27 C.F.R. § 479.11 (b).

[815]Penal Code § 12301 (a)(3).

[816]Penal Code § 12301 (a)(3).

[817]Penal Code § 12301 (a)(3); see also 27 C.F.R. § 479.11 for definition of "antique firearm".

[818]Penal Code § 12301 (a)(4).

- any breakable container which contains a flammable liquid with a flashpoint of 150 degrees Fahrenheit or less and has a wick or similar device capable of being ignited, except for a device which is commercially manufactured primarily for the purpose of illumination.[819] An example of this would be a Molotov cocktail
- any sealed device containing dry ice (CO_2) or other chemically reactive substances assembled for the purpose of causing an explosion by chemical reaction[820]

Unlawful Activities with Destructive Devices and Explosives

Possession in Public

Every person who recklessly or maliciously has in his or her possession any destructive device or any explosive on a public street or highway, in or near any theater, hall, school, college, church, hotel, other public building, or private habitation, in, on, or near any aircraft, railway passenger train, car, cable road or cable car, vessel engaged in carrying passengers for hire, or other public place ordinarily passed by human beings, is guilty of a felony, and shall be punishable by imprisonment in the state prison for two, four, or six years.[821] Exceptions apply, see below.

Wrongful Possession

Every person who possesses, explodes, ignites, or attempts to explode or ignite any destructive device or any explosive with intent to injure, intimidate, or terrify any person, or with intent to wrongfully injure or destroy any property, is guilty of a felony, and shall be punished by imprisonment in the state prison for a period of three, five, or seven years.[822]

---

[819] Penal Code § 12301 (a)(5).

[820] Penal Code § 12301 (b)(6).

[821] Penal Code § 12303.2.

[822] Penal Code § 12303.3.

Sale, Transfer, and Transport Offenses

Any person, firm, or corporation who, within the State of California, sells, offers for sale, or knowingly transports any destructive device, other than fixed ammunition of a caliber greater than 0.60 caliber, is guilty of a felony and is punishable by imprisonment in the state prison for two, three, or four years.[823] Exceptions apply, see below.

Common Carrier Offenses

Every person who willfully does any of the following is guilty of a felony and is punishable by imprisonment in the state prison for two, four, or six years:[824]

- carries a destructive device or explosive onto any vehicle that transports passengers for hire[825]
- places or carries any explosive or destructive device while on board of any vehicle that transports passengers for hire[826]
- places any explosive or destructive device in any baggage which is later checked with any common carrier[827]

Other Serious Felony Offenses

Other offenses that are all felonies include:

- attempt to explode or ignite destructive device or explosive with intent to murder[828]
- exploding or igniting destructive device causing bodily injury[829]
- exploding or igniting destructive device or explosive device

---

[823]Penal Code § 12303.6.

[824]Penal Code § 12303.1.

[825]Penal Code § 12303.1 (a).

[826]Penal Code § 12303.1 (b).

[827]Penal Code § 12303.1 (c).

[828]Penal Code § 12308.

[829]Penal Code § 12309.

causing death, mayhem, or great bodily injury[830]

- possession (absent a permit) of materials with intent to make destructive device or explosive[831]

Any person who is convicted of any of the offenses as described above will not be granted probation, and the execution of the sentence imposed by the court will not be suspended.[832]

Destructive Device as Nuisance

The possession of any destructive device shall be deemed to be a public nuisance and a government attorney may bring an action in superior court to enjoin the possession of the device.[833] Upon a finding by the court of a violation, the destructive device shall be surrendered to authorities for disposal.[834]

Exemptions for Destructive Devices and Explosives

There is no prohibition on the sale to, purchase by, possession, transportation, storage, or use of destructive devices by:[835]

- any peace officer,[836] peace officer in the DOJ, while on duty and acting within the course and scope of his or her employment[837]
- any member of the military or National Guard, while on duty and acting within the course and scope of his or her employment[838]
- firefighters, fire department, and fire protection agencies, while on

[830]Penal Code § 12310.

[831]Penal Code § 12312.

[832]Penal Code § 12311.

[833]Penal Code § 12307.

[834]Penal Code § 12307.

[835]Penal Code § 12302.

[836]See Penal Code §§ 830.1 or 830.2 for authorized peace officers.

[837]Penal Code § 12302 (a).

[838]Penal Code § 12302 (b).

the duty and acting within the course and scope of their employment in the course of fire suppression[839]

Permits for Destructive Devices and Explosives

Permits are available for dealers, manufacturers, importers, and exporters of destructive devices, as well as entertainment studios using destructive devices in the conduct of its business.[840] Permits are issued by the Department of Justice.[841] All applications must be in writing and include complete information as requested by the Department.[842] The Department issues the forms to apply for the permit, and also issues the permit, both of which shall be uniform throughout the State of California.[843] There is a fee when applying and renewing, and every permit must be renewed annually.[844]

Permits will not be issued to prohibited persons, such as:[845]

- a person who has been convicted of a felony[846]
- a person who is addicted to the use of any narcotic drug[847]
- is prohibited from state or federal law from possessing, receiving, owning, or purchasing a firearm[848]

Inspections by a person appointed by the Department of Justice to conduct

---

[839]Penal Code § 12302 (b).

[840]Penal Code § 12305 (a).

[841]Penal Code § 12305 (b).

[842]Penal Code § 12305 (c).

[843]Penal Code § 12305 (d).

[844]Penal Code § 12305 (e).

[845]Penal Code § 12305 (b).

[846]Penal Code § 12305 (b)(1).

[847]Penal Code § 12305 (b)(2).

[848]Penal Code § 12305 (b)(3).

inspections will occur yearly;[849] unless the permit is for less than five devices, these inspections may then occur irregularly, even as little as once every five years.[850] The purpose of the inspection is to inspect the security and safe storage of the devices as well as to reconcile the inventory of devices.[851]

Various Specified Prohibited Weapons as Nuisances

Except as provided otherwise,[852] blackjacks, slungshots, billies, nunchakus, sandclubs, sandbags, shurikens, metal knuckles, any ballistic knife, belt buckle knife, leaded cane, lipstick case knife, cane sword, shobi-zue, air gauge knife, writing pen knife, metal practice handgrenade or metal replica handgrenade, sap, or sandbag, as defined in the Penal Code,[853] are considered under the law to be nuisances, and the Attorney General, district attorney, or city attorney, may bring an action to enjoin the manufacture of, importation of, keeping for sale of, offering or exposing for sale, giving, lending, or possession of, any of the foregoing items.[854]

These weapons shall be subject to confiscation and summary destruction whenever found in the state and shall be destroyed in the manner as other weapons,[855] except that upon the certification of a judge or of the district attorney that the ends of justice will be subserved thereby, the weapon shall be preserved until the necessity for its use ceases.[856]

---

[849]Penal Code § 12305 (f).

[850]Penal Code § 12305 (g).

[851]Penal Code § 12305 (f) and (g).

[852]See Penal Code § 12020 for exceptions to this law.

[853]See Penal Code § 12020 for definitions of the weapons listed.

[854]Penal Code § 12029.

[855]See Penal Code § 12028 regarding destruction of weapons designated as a nuisance.

[856]Penal Code § 12029.

Places With Prohibitions

State Buildings

Any person who brings or possesses any deadly weapon,[857] knife with a blade length in excess of four inches, the blade of which is fixed or capable of being fixed in an unguarded position by the use of one or two hands, any unauthorized tear gas weapon, any taser or stun gun,[858] any instrument that propels a metal projectile, such as a BB or pellet, through the force of air pressure, CO2 pressure, or spring action, or any spot marker or paint gun, and firearm within any state or local public building or at any meeting required to be opened to the public[859] is guilty of a public offense punishable by imprisonment in a county jail for not more than one year, or in the state prison.[860]

This prohibition does not apply to the following:[861]

- authorized peace officers,[862] a full-time paid peace officer of another state or federal government on official business, or any person summoned to assist any of the above[863]
- any person who possesses weapons in, or transports weapons into, a court of law for use as evidence,[864] so long as he is not a party to an action pending in a court of law, unless he is a peace

---

[857]See Penal Code §§ 653k and 12020 for extensive list, most of which are discussed in this chapter.

[858]See Penal Code § 244.5.

[859]See Chapter 9 (commencing with § 54950) of Part 1 of Division 2 of Title 5 of, or Article 9 (commencing with § 11120) of Chapter 1 of Part 1 of Division 3 of Title 2 of, the Government Code.

[860]Penal Code § 171b (a) and (a)(1).

[861]Penal Code § 171b (b).

[862]See Penal Code § 830 et seq.

[863]Penal Code § 171b (b)(2)(A).

[864]Penal Code § 171b (b)(1).

officer as described above[865]

- a person with permission to possess that weapon granted in writing by a duly authorized official who is in charge of the security of the state or local government building[866]
- a person who lawfully resides in, lawfully owns, or is in lawful possession of, that building with respect to those portions of the building that are not owned or leased by the state or local government[867]
- private investigators or alarm company agents who have been hired by the owner or manager of the building[868]
- a person who, for the purpose of sale or trade, brings any weapon that may otherwise be lawfully possessed, into a gun show,[869] or who brings a weapon for the purposes of an authorized public exhibition at a gun show[870]

A "state or local public building" means a building that meets all of the following criteria:[871]

- it is a building or part of a building owned or leased by the state or local government, if state or local public employees are regularly present for the purposes of performing their official duties, and includes, but is not limited to, a building that contains a courtroom[872]
- it is not also a building or facility, or a part thereof, of any of the following:[873]

---

[865]Penal Code § 171b (b)(2)(B).

[866]Penal Code § 171b (b)(4).

[867]Penal Code § 171b (b)(5).

[868]Penal Code § 171b (b)(6).

[869]Penal Code § 171b (b)(7)(A); see also Penal Code §§ 12071.1 and 12071.4.

[870]Penal Code § 171b (b)(7)(B); see also Penal Code §§ 12071.1 and 12071.4.

[871]Penal Code § 171b (c).

[872]Penal Code § 171b (c)(1).

[873]Penal Code § 171b (c)(2).

- state capitol, legislative offices, Governor's office, offices or residence of a constitutional officer, Governor's mansion, other residence of the Governor, residence of the immediate family of any of the above[874]
- public or private schools, public or private colleges or universities, playgrounds, and youth centers[875]
- it is a building not regularly used, and not intended to be used, by state or local employees as a place of residence[876]

<u>Airports and Airplanes, and Passenger Vessel Terminals</u>

One must be concerned with both federal law and state law when considering airports, airplanes, and passenger vessel terminals.

Under California law, it is unlawful for any person knowingly to possess, within any sterile area of an airport or passenger vessel terminal, any knife with a blade length in excess of four inches, the blade of which is fixed, or is capable of being fixed, in an unguarded position by the use of one or two hands, any box cutter or straight razor, any military practice hand grenade, any metal replica hand grenade, any plastic replica hand grenade, any imitation firearm,[877] any unauthorized tear gas weapon, any taser or stun gun,[878] any instrument that expels a metallic projectile, such as a BB or pellet, through the force of air pressure, CO2 pressure, or spring action, or any spot marker gun or paint gun, or any ammunition.[879]

---

[874]Penal Code § 171b (c)(2); see also Penal Code §§ 171c, 171d.

[875]Penal Code § 171b (c)(2); see also Penal Code §§ 626.9, 626.95, and 626.10.

[876]Penal Code § 171b (c)(3).

[877]See Penal Code § 417.4.

[878]See Penal Code § 244.5.

[879]Penal Code § 171.5 (b), (b)(1), (b)(8), and (b)(12); see also Penal Code § 12316 for definition of ammunition.

Persons who are exempt include:[880]

- authorized peace officers,[881] a full-time paid peace officer of another state or federal government on official business, or any person summoned to assist any of the above[882]
- a member of the military forces of this state or the federal government engaged in the performance of his duties[883]
- a person who has authorization to possess a prohibited weapon,[884] granted in writing by an airport security coordinator[885] who is responsible for the security of the airport
- a person, including employees of a licensed contract guard service, authorized to possess a weapon granted in writing by a person discharging the duties of Facility Security Officer or Company Security Officer pursuant to an approved United States Coast Guard facility security plan, and who is responsible for the security of the passenger vessel terminal[886]

Under California law, violation of this prohibition is a misdemeanor, punishable by time in jail not exceeding six months, or by a fine of no more than $1000, or both.[887] Under federal law, the punishment can be up to five years in prison and a $25,000 penalty.

For the purposes of the prohibitions of firearms and other weapons at airports, airplanes, and passenger vessel terminals, the following definitions apply:[888]

---

[880] Penal Code § 171.5 (d).

[881] See Penal Code § 830 et seq.

[882] Penal Code § 171.5 (d)(1).

[883] Penal Code § 171.5 (d)(1).

[884] See Penal Code § 171.5 (c) for list of prohibited weapons.

[885] See 49 C.F.R. § 1542.3 for those designated as responsible for security at the airport.

[886] Penal Code § 171.5 (d)(3).

[887] Penal Code § 171.5 (e).

[888] Penal Code § 171.5 (a).

- "airport" means an airport, with a secure area, that regularly serves an air carrier holding a certificate issued by the United States Secretary of Transportation[889]
- "passenger vessel terminal" means only that portion of a harbor or port facility[890] with a secured area that regularly serves scheduled commuter or passenger operations[891]
- "sterile area" means a portion of an airport defined in the airport security program to which access generally is controlled through the screening of persons and property,[892] or a portion of any passenger vessel terminal to which, pursuant to law,[893] access is generally controlled in a manner consistent with the passenger vessel terminal.[894]

Federal Buildings and Courthouses

Federal Buildings - Absent an exemption, any person who knowingly possesses or causes to be present a firearm or other dangerous weapon in a Federal facility (other than a Federal court facility), or attempts to do so, shall be fined or imprisoned not more than one year, or both.[895] If the possession or causation of a firearm to be present in a Federal facility or attempt to do such is coupled with the intent that the firearm or other dangerous weapon be used in the commission of a crime, the punishment is imprisonment for not more than 5 years and a fine, or both.[896]

The exemption of the first prohibition discussed above includes the

---

[889]Penal Code § 171.5 (a)(1).

[890]See 33 C.F.R. § 105.105 (a)(2) regarding harbor or port facilities.

[891]Penal Code § 171.5 (a)(2).

[892]See 49 C.F.R. § 1540.5.

[893]See 33 C.F.R. §§ 105.255 (a)(1), 105.255 (c)(1), and 105.260 (a).

[894]Penal Code § 171.5 (a)(3).

[895]18 U.S.C. § 930 (a).

[896]18 U.S.C. § 930 (b).

following persons:[897]

- the lawful performance of official duties by an officer, agent, or employee of the United States, a State, or a political subdivision thereof, who is authorized by law to engage in or supervise the prevention, detection, investigation, or prosecution of any violation of law[898]
- the possession of a firearm or other dangerous weapon by a Federal official or a member of the military if such possession is authorized by law[899]
- the lawful carrying of firearms or other dangerous weapons in a Federal facility incident to hunting or other lawful purposes[900]

Federal Courthouses - Absent an exemption, whoever knowingly possesses or causes to be present a firearm or other dangerous weapon in a Federal court facility, or attempts to do so, shall be fined and imprisoned not more than two years, or both.[901] Exemptions include:[902]

- the lawful performance of official duties by an officer, agent, or employee of the United States, a State, or a political subdivision thereof, who is authorized by law to engage in or supervise the prevention, detection, investigation, or prosecution of any violation of law[903]
- the possession of a firearm or other dangerous weapon by a Federal official or a member of the military if such possession is authorized by law

A "federal facility." for the purposes of these prohibitions, means a building or part thereof owned or leased by the Federal Government, where Federal

---

897 18 U.S.C. § 930 (d).

898 18 U.S.C. § 930 (d)(1).

899 18 U.S.C. § 930 (d)(2).

900 18 U.S.C. § 930 (d)(3).

901 18 U.S.C. § 930 (e)(1).

902 18 U.S.C. § 930 (e)(2).

903 18 U.S.C. § 930 (d)(1).

employees are regularly present for the purpose of performing their official duties.[904]

A "dangerous weapon" means a weapon, device, instrument, material, or substance, animate or inanimate, that is used for, or is readily capable of, causing death or serious bodily injury, except that such term does not include a pocket knife with a blade of less than 2 ½ inches in length.[905]

The term "federal court facility" means the courtroom, judges' chambers, witness rooms, jury deliberation rooms, attorney conference rooms, prisoner holding cells, offices of the court clerks, the United States attorney, and the United States marshal, probation and parole offices, and adjoining corridors of any court of the United States.[906]

Notice concerning the prohibitions in Federal facility and courthouses shall be posted conspicuously at each public entrance to each facility or courthouse, and no person shall be convicted of an offense with respect to a federal facility if such notice is not posted at such facility, unless the person had actual notice prior to the offense.[907]

---

904 18 U.S.C. § 930 (g)(1).

905 18 U.S.C. § 930 (g)(2).

906 18 U.S.C. § 930 (g)(2).

907 18 U.S.C. § 930 (h).

Part Five

Firearms, Knife, and Weapons Offenses in California

CHAPTER TEN

Common Weapons Offenses

There are quite a few firearms related offenses associated with owning and possessing firearms. Be sure to read the chapters on the "concealed firearm law" and the "loaded firearm law," as they discuss various offenses that are not included in this chapter. Additionally, other firearms and weapons offenses are scattered throughout this entire book but are not repeated in this chapter.

Prohibited Transfers of Firearms

In California, no person, corporation, or firm, or dealer shall knowingly supply, deliver, sell, or give possession or control of a firearm to any person who is prohibited by law from handling firearms in any fashion.[908] A transfer may not occur if the transferor even has cause to believe the person is within any of the prohibited classes.[909]

For the purposes of this prohibition, a "firearm" includes a complete firearm, and also includes either the frame or the receiver of a firearm.[910]

The law prohibits any transfers to prohibited persons, which include individuals who have been convicted of a violent felony,[911] have been determined to have a mental disorder such that they fall under the prohibitions,[912] or who are a minor.[913] The law also prohibits otherwise lawful transfers, but where the transferor knows or has reason to know that the transferee is not the actual purchaser or transferee, and only intends to turn around and complete an unlawful

---

[908]Penal Code § 12072 (a)(1), (2), (3), and (4); see also Penal Code §§ 12021 and 12021.1, and Welfare and Institutions Code §§ 8100 and 8103.

[909]Penal Code § 12072 (a)(2); see also Penal Code §§ 12021 and 12021.1, and Welfare and Institutions Code §§ 8100 and 8103.

[910]See Penal Code § 12001 (c) and (k).

[911]Penal Code § 12072 (a)(1); see also Penal Code §§ 12021 and 12021.1.

[912]See Welfare and Institutions Code §§ 8100 and 8103.

[913]Penal Code § 12072.

transfer to a prohibited person in an attempt to skirt the law.[914]

Finally, it is a violation of law for any person, corporation, or dealer to acquire a firearm for the purpose of selling, transferring, or loaning the firearm, if he or she intends to avoid requirements regarding private party transfers or any exemptions thereto,[915] to transfer unlawfully the firearm (handgun) to a minor,[916] to avoid the mandatory ten-day waiting period as prescribed by law,[917] to avoid dealer/licensee requirements to report to the DOJ of an acquisition of a firearm (handgun),[918] or to avoid dealing properly with a firearm if the transferee fails take possession of the firearm within 30 days after a background check.[919]

Alteration of Identification Marks on Firearms

Any person who changes, alters, removes, or obliterates the name of the maker, model, manufacturer's number, or other mark of identification, including any distinguishing number or mark assigned by the DOJ on any pistol, revolver, or to any other firearm, shall be punished by imprisonment in a state prison.[920] However, making such changes to identification marks is not punishable if one has first secured written permission from the department to make such a change.[921]

Placing Marks on Firearm

Despite the prohibition against alteration of marks on a firearm, any person may place or stamp on any pistol, revolver, or other firearm any number or

---

[914]Penal Code § 12073 (a)(4).

[915]Penal Code §§ 12072 (a)(5), 12072 (a)(5)(B)(i) and (ii); see also Penal Code § 12072 (d).

[916]Penal Code § 12072 (a)(5)(A); see also Penal Code § 12072 (b).

[917]Penal Code § 12072 (a)(5)(A); see also Penal Code § 12072 (c).

[918]Penal Code § 12072 (a)(6); see also Penal Code § 12071 (b)(18).

[919]Penal Code § 12072 (a)(7); see also Penal Code § 12071 (b)(19).

[920]Penal Code § 12090.

[921]Penal Code § 12090.

identifying indicium, provided the new marking leaves the original markings intact.[922] Also, original numbers and markings that may have been accidentally damaged may be restored with DOJ authorization.[923]

DOJ Assignment of Identification Marks on a Firearm

On a side note, the DOJ may, upon request, assign a distinguishing number or mark of identification to any firearm when it is without such, or to a firearm that has had its markings destroyed or obliterated.[924]

Knowingly Purchasing Firearm with Altered Markings

Any person with knowledge of any change, alteration, removal, or obliteration of marks, who buys, receives, disposes of, sells, offers for sale, or has in his or her possession any pistol, revolver, or other firearm which has had the name of the makers, model, or the manufacturer's number or other mark of identification, including any distinguishing number or mark assigned by the DOJ changed, altered, removed, or obliterated, is guilty of a misdemeanor.[925] Note that this prohibition does not include shotguns and rifles.

Ownership in a firearm that is a pistol, revolver, or other firearm capable of being concealed upon the person may not be transferred if it is missing any of the following: the name of the manufacturer, the manufacturer's make or model, manufacturer's serial number, or the identification number or mark assigned to the firearm by the DOJ pursuant to law.[926] Note that this prohibition does not include shotguns and rifles.

Exceptions

The prohibitions on knowingly purchasing a firearm with altered markings

---

[922]Penal Code § 12093.

[923]Penal Code § 12093.

[924]Penal Code § 12092.

[925]Penal Code § 12094 (a).

[926]Penal Code § 12072 (a)(8)(A) and (B); see also Penal Code § 12092 regarding the DOJ assignment of identification numbers.

does not apply in the following situations:[927]

- the acquisition or possession by any member of the US military while on duty and acting within the course and scope of employment[928]
- the acquisition or possession by any peace officer[929] while on duty and acting within the course and scope of employment[930]
- the acquisition or possession by any employee of a forensic laboratory, while on duty and acting in the course and scope of employment[931]
- the possession and disposition by a person who meets <u>all</u> of the following:[932]
    - he is not prohibited by state or federal law from possessing, receiving, owning, or purchasing a firearm[933]
    - the person possessed the firearm no longer than necessary to deliver it to the proper authorities so they could properly dispose of it[934]
    - if the person is transporting the firearm, the person is transporting it in order to deliver it to the proper authorities for disposition[935]
    - if the person is transporting the firearm, he has first given notice to the law enforcement agency that he intends to deliver it to that he is bringing a firearm in for

---

927 Penal Code § 12094 (a).

928 Penal Code § 12094 (a)(1).

929 See Penal Code § 830 et seq.

930 Penal Code § 12094 (a)(2).

931 Penal Code § 12094 (a)(3).

932 Penal Code § 12094 (a)(4).

933 Penal Code § 12094 (b)(4)(A).

934 Penal Code § 12094 (b)(4)(B).

935 Penal Code § 12094 (b)(4)(C).

disposition[936]

- the firearm is properly transported in a locked container[937]

Gross Negligent Discharge of Firearm or BB Device

Except as otherwise may be authorized by law, any person who willfully discharges a firearm or a BB device in a grossly negligent manner which could result in injury or death to a person is guilty of a public offense and subject to punishment by imprisonment in a county jail not exceeding one year, or by imprisonment in the state prison.[938]

Brandishing a Weapon

Every person who, except in self-defense, in the presence of any other person, draws or exhibits any deadly weapon whatsoever, other than a firearm, in a rude, angry, or threatening manner, or who in any manner, unlawfully uses a deadly weapon other than a firearm in any fight or quarrel is guilty of a misdemeanor, punishable by imprisonment in a county jail for not less than 30 days.[939]

Brandishing a Firearm

Every person who, except in self-defense, in the presence of any other person, draws or exhibits any firearm, whether loaded or unloaded, in a rude, angry, or threatening manner, or who in any manner, unlawfully uses a firearm in any fight or quarrel is punishable as follows:[940]

- if the firearm is a pistol, revolver, or other firearm capable of being concealed upon the person, by imprisonment in a county jail for not less than three months and not more than one year, by a

---

[936]Penal Code § 12094 (b)(4)(D).

[937]Penal Code § 12094 (b)(4)(E); see also Penal Code § 12026.2 regarding transporting a firearm in a locked container according to law.

[938]Penal Code § 246.3 (a) and (b).

[939]Penal Code § 417 (a)(1).

[940]Penal Code § 417 (a)(2).

fine not to exceed $1000, or by both[941]

- for any other firearms, the crime is a misdemeanor, punishable by imprisonment in a county jail for not less than three months[942]

Every person who, except in self-defense, in the presence of any other person, draws or exhibits any loaded firearm in a rude, angry, or threatening manner, or who, in any manner, unlawfully uses any loaded firearm in any fight or quarrel upon the grounds of any day care center,[943] or any facility where programs, including day care programs or recreational programs are being conducted for persons under the age of 18 years, including programs conducted by non-profit organizations, during the hours they are open for use, is guilty of a misdemeanor or of a felony depending on the circumstances.[944]

To brandish a firearm in the immediate presence of a peace officer is also punished as a misdemeanor.[945] Finally, for the gang-bangers, to brandish in the presence of someone in the process of cleaning up graffiti or vandalism is guilty of a misdemeanor.[946]

Brandishing an Imitation Firearm

Every person who, except in self-defense, draws or exhibits an imitation firearm[947] in a threatening manner against another in such a way to cause a reasonable person apprehension or fear of bodily harm is guilty of a misdemeanor punishable by imprisonment in a county jail for a term of not less than 30 days.[948]

---

[941]Penal Code § 417 (a)(2)(A).

[942]Penal Code § 417 (a)(2)(B).

[943]As defined in Health and Safety Code § 1596.76.

[944]Penal Code § 417 (b).

[945]Penal Code § 417 (c).

[946]Penal Code § 417 (d).

[947]As defined in Penal Code § 12550.

[948]Penal Code § 417.4.

Discharge of Firearm Along Public Roads and Highways

Every person who shoots any firearm from or upon a public road or highway is guilty of a misdemeanor.[949]

Weapons on School Grounds

Any person, unless authorized by law, who brings or possesses any dirk, dagger, ice pick, knife having a blade longer than 2 ½ inches, folding knife with a blade that locks into place, a razor with an unguarded blade, a taser, or a stun gun,[950] any instrument that expels a metallic projectile such as a BB or a pellet, through the force of air pressure, CO2 pressure, or spring action, or any spot marker gun, upon the grounds of, or within, any public or private school providing instruction in kindergarten or any grades 1 through 12, inclusive, is guilty of a public offense, punishable by imprisonment in a county jail not exceeding one year, or by imprisonment in the state prison.[951]

With the same stipulations as above, unless authorized by law, except upon the grounds of any private university, the University of California, the California State University, or the California Community Colleges is also guilty of a public offense, punishable by imprisonment in a county jail not exceeding one year, or by imprisonment in the state prison.[952]

Interstate Travel with Firearms

It is very possible that the firearm laws in another state are much more restrictive than the firearm laws in your state.[953] So, taking a family trip with firearms in the car could lead to problems.

Protections exist, however, for the traveler in what is known as the

---

[949] Penal Code § 374c.

[950] As defined by Penal Code § 244.5 (a).

[951] Penal Code § 626.10 (a).

[952] Penal Code § 626.10 (b).

[953] Of course, California has the most restrictive firearms laws in the nation, as we all know.

Firearms Owners' Protection Act ("FOPA").[954] This act revised many of the statutes in the famous 1968 Gun Control Act.[955]

Included in the FOPA is the "Safe Passage Provision"[956] which applies to any person not prohibited under federal law from possessing firearms. Persons who travel from one place to another for any lawful activity cannot be arrested for a firearm offense in a state that has strict gun control laws if the traveler is just passing through, with only short stops for food and gas, and the firearms and ammunition are not immediately accessible, unloaded, and, in the case of a vehicle without a compartment separate from the driver's compartment, in a locked container.[957]

At this time, it is unclear if this provision applies to transportation of firearms through the District of Columbia. Also, the provision is silent regarding the definition of "unloaded," so the best bet is to have the firearm completely unloaded and even go so far as store the ammunition completely separate and apart from the firearm to best avoid any potential trouble with law enforcement.

---

[954] See 18 U.S.C. § 921 et seq.

[955] See 18 U.S.C. § 44.

[956] See 18 U.S.C. § 926A.

[957] 18 U.S.C. § 926A.

CHAPTER ELEVEN

The Concealed Firearm Law

One of the most common offenses concerning firearms is that they are carried or transported improperly. Please be aware that the concealed firearm law[958] does not depend on whether the firearm is loaded or unloaded, and therefore applies to all firearms. The concealed firearm law is inapplicable in many situations, and also many exemptions exist to the concealed firearm law, and all are discussed in detail later in this chapter. Please be familiar with both the concealed firearm law and the loaded firearm law before traveling about with firearms.

Because the definition of a firearm under the "concealed firearm law" includes "any pistol, revolver, or other firearm capable of being concealed upon the person," it is important to understand that this means all handguns, any firearms or devices with a barrel length of under 16 inches in length, or are designed to be interchanged with a barrel less than 16 inches in length.[959] Also included in the concealed firearm law are any rocket, rocket propelled projectile launcher, or similar device containing any explosive or incendiary material whether or not the device is designed for emergency or distress signaling purposes.[960] Finally, nothing shall prevent a device to be subject to the concealed firearm law that is found to be a short-barreled rifle or short-barreled shotgun.[961]

Violation of Concealed Firearm Law

A person is guilty of carrying a concealed firearm when he or she does any of the following with any pistol, revolver, or other firearm capable of being concealed upon the person without a proper permit:[962]

- carries concealed within any vehicle which is under his or her

---

[958]See Penal Code § 12025 regarding the concealed firearm law.

[959]Penal Code § 12021 (a)(1).

[960]Penal Code § 12021 (d).

[961]Penal Code § 12021 (f); see also Penal Code § 12020 regarding definition of short-barreled rifle and short-barreled shotgun.

[962]Penal Code § 12025 (a).

control or direction[963]

- carries concealed upon his or her person[964]
- causes to be carried concealed within any vehicle in which he or she is an occupant[965]

A person who carries a firearm openly in a belt holster is not carrying a firearm as "concealed" within the meaning of the concealed firearm law.[966]

However, if a person who carries a firearm in a personal carry bag, such as a purse, backpack, briefcase, belly-pack, or the like, that person is carrying a gun on their person under the law as it is written. The law does not distinguish between carrying a firearm in a purse or carrying a firearm stuffed in the waistband of a pair of pants or holstered in a concealed holster. Under the concealed firearm law, all of these examples are considered "carry."[967]

Further, if any part of a firearm is concealed, the firearm will likely be considered concealed under the law, as only partial concealment of a firearm is required.[968] Additionally, a firearm disassembled into two or more parts still constitutes an operable weapon within the meaning of the Dangerous Weapon Control Law.[969] It follows that if any part of a disassembled firearm is concealed, the person is in violation of the concealed firearm law.

Punishment for Violating Concealed Firearm Law

Carrying a concealed firearm in violation of the concealed firearm law[970] is

---

963 Penal Code § 12025 (a)(1).

964 Penal Code § 12025 (a)(2).

965 Penal Code § 12025 (a)(3).

966 Penal Code § 12025 (f); see also Penal Code § 12025 regarding the concealed firearm law and offenses.

967 See *People v. Smith*, (1946) 72 Cal.App.2d Supp. 875, 879.

968 See *People v. Koehn*, 25 Cal.App.3d 799, 802 [102 Cal.Rptr. 102].

969 See *People v. Ekberg*, 94 Cal.App.2d 613, 616-617 [211 P.2d 316].

970 See Penal Code 12025 regarding the concealed firearm law.

very serious, and in many circumstances, it is punishable as a felony, with serious prison time.[971] However, in many circumstances, violation of the concealed firearm law may be punishable as a misdemeanor, with up to $1000 in fines, and/or imprisonment in the state prison or county jail for up to one year.[972]

Concealed Firearm Law and Private Property

The concealed firearm law[973] shall not apply or affect any citizen of the United States or legal resident over the age of 18 years who resides or is temporarily within this state, and who is not prohibited from possessing firearms,[974] who carries, either openly or concealed, anywhere within the citizen's or legal resident's place of residence, place of business, or on private property owned or lawfully possessed by the citizen or legal resident, any pistol, revolver, or other firearm capable of being concealed upon the person.[975] Also, no permit is required to carry concealed in these specified places.[976] However, a business vehicle is not a "place of business," for those of you who use a vehicle as your workplace.[977]

Please be mindful that one who desires to carry concealed legally under the concealed firearm law[978] must be mindful of the loaded firearm law[979] as discussed in Chapter Twelve, as the concealed firearm law is a separate offense from the

---

[971]See Penal Code § 12025 (b)(1) through (4) regarding felony offenses and details regarding same.

[972]See Penal Code § 12025 (b)(5) through (7), (d), and (e) regarding misdemeanor offenses and details regarding same.

[973]See Penal Code § 12025.

[974]See Penal Code §§ 12021 and 12021.1, and Welfare and Institutions Code §§ 8100 and 8103 regarding prohibited persons.

[975]Penal Code § 12026 (a).

[976]Penal Code § 12026 (b).

[977]See *People v. Wooten* (App. 5 Dist. 1985) 214 Cal.Rptr. 36, 168 Cal.App.3d 168.

[978]See Penal Code § 12025.

[979]See Penal Code § 12031 regarding the loaded firearm law.

loaded firearm law.[980]

Justification of Violation of Concealed Firearms Law

A violation of the concealed firearm law[981] is justifiable when a person who possesses a firearm reasonably believes that he or she is in grave danger because of circumstances forming the basis of a current restraining order issued by a court against another person or persons who have been found to pose a threat to his or her life or safety.[982] This justification does not exist in circumstances involving a mutual restraining order[983] absent a factual finding of a specific threat to the person's life or safety.[984]

Upon a trial for violation of the concealed firearm law,[985] and upon the defense of justification for violation, a jury shall determine whether the defendant was acting out of a reasonable belief that he or she was in grave danger.[986]

Properly Transporting Pistols, Revolvers, and Other Firearms Capable of Being Concealed Upon the Person

The concealed firearm law[987] shall not be construed to prohibit any citizen of the United States over the age of 18 years who resides or is temporarily within this state, and who is not prohibited from possession, receipt of, owning, or purchasing a firearm, from transporting or carrying any pistol, revolver, or other firearm capable of being concealed upon the person, provided that the following

---

[980]Penal Code § 12026 (c); see also Penal Code § 12031 regarding loaded firearm laws.

[981]See Penal Code § 12025 regarding the concealed firearm law.

[982]Penal Code § 12025.5 (a).

[983]See Family Code § 6200 et seq., regarding mutual restraining orders applicable here.

[984]Penal Code § 12025.5 (a).

[985]See Penal Code § 12025 regarding the concealed firearm law.

[986]Penal Code § 12025.5 (a).

[987]See Penal Code § 12025 regarding the concealed firearms law.

applies to the firearm:[988]

- the firearm is within a motor vehicle and it is locked in the vehicle's trunk or in a locked container in the vehicle other than the utility, center console, or glove compartment,[989] and to be sure, any compartment within the driver-passenger area
- the firearm is carried by the person directly to or from any motor vehicle for any lawful purpose and, while carrying the firearm, the firearm is contained in the locked container[990]

A "locked container" as defined by the Penal Code and as applied to the concealed firearm law[991] means a secure container that is fully enclosed and locked by a padlock, key lock, combination lock, or similar locking device.[992]

Exemptions and Exceptions to the Concealed Firearm Law

Many exemptions and exceptions exist for the concealed firearm law. Please review all exemptions and exceptions very carefully and before transporting a firearm on your person to make sure that the exemption or exception actually applies in your situation, as many of the exemptions and exceptions have several conditions and/or rely on other laws for it to apply. It is always wise to consult a well-versed attorney before choosing a course of direction to take, as you may find you misunderstood the exception or exception.

Also, if none of the exemptions or exceptions discussed below apply, the firearm, while being transported to or from a place, must be unloaded, kept in a locked container,[993] and the course of travel shall include only those deviations between authorized locations as are reasonably necessary under the

---

[988]Penal Code § 12026.1 (a).

[989]Penal Code § 12026.1 (a)(1).

[990]Penal Code § 12026.1 (a)(2).

[991]See Penal Code § 12025 regarding the concealed firearm law.

[992]Penal Code § 12026.1 (c).

[993]See Penal Code § 12026.2 (d) regarding definition of "locked container".

circumstances.[994]

A "locked container," for the purposes of these exemptions, means a secure container which is fully enclosed and locked by a padlock, keylock, combination lock, or similar device, but does not include the utility or glove compartment in a motor vehicle, even if the utility or glove compartment locks.[995] That is a very important consideration, as many people fall into the trap of thinking the utility or glove compartment is an acceptable place to transport lawfully a firearm.

The concealed firearm law does not apply to, or affect, any of the following:[996]

- the possession of a firearm in authorized entertainment production or while going to or from that production[997]
- the possession of a firearm in a locked container by a member of a club or organization that is organized for the purpose of collecting or lawfully displaying firearms, while that member is at a meeting of the club or organization, or going to or from[998]
- the transport of a firearm by a participant going to or from a recognized safety or hunter safety class, or a recognized sporting event involving that firearm[999]
- the transportation of a firearm by a person who is a United States citizen who is over 18 years of age going to and from his residence, place of business, or other private property[1000]
- the transportation of a firearm by any United States citizen who is over 18 years of age when going directly to, or directly from, a fixed place of business or private residential property for the

[994]Penal Code § 12026.2 (b).

[995]Penal Code § 12026.2 (d).

[996]Penal Code § 12026.2 (a).

[997]Penal Code § 12026.2 (a)(1).

[998]Penal Code § 12026.2 (a)(2).

[999]Penal Code § 12026.2 (a)(3).

[1000]Penal Code § 12026.2 (a)(4).

purpose of lawful repair or the lawful transfer, sale, or loan of that firearm[1001]

- the transportation of a firearm by any United States citizen who is over 18 years of age when going directly from the place where that person lawfully received the firearm to his personal residence, place of business, or to private property owned or lawfully possessed by that person[1002]
- the transportation of a firearm by a person when going directly to, or coming directly from, a gun show, swap meet, or similar event to which the public is invited, for the purpose of displaying that firearm in a lawful manner[1003]
- the transportation of a firearm by an authorized agent or employee of a supplier of firearms when going directly to, or coming directly from, an authorized entertainment production[1004]
- the transportation of a firearm by a person when going directly to for from a target range which holds a regulatory or business license for the purpose of shooting at targets with that firearm at that target range[1005]
- the transportation of a firearm by a person when going directly to or from a place designated by a person authorized to issue concealed carry licenses,[1006] when done at the request of the issuing agency so that agency can determine whether or not a license should be issued to that person carrying the firearm[1007]
- the transportation of a firearm by a person when going directly to or from a lawful camping activity for the purpose of having the firearm available for lawful personal protection while at the lawful

---

[1001] Penal Code § 12026.2 (a)(5).

[1002] Penal Code § 12026.2 (a)(6).

[1003] Penal Code § 12026.2 (a)(7).

[1004] Penal Code § 12026.2 (a)(8).

[1005] Penal Code § 12026.2 (a)(9).

[1006] See Penal Code § 12050 regarding concealed carry licenses.

[1007] Penal Code § 12026.2 (a)(10).

campsite.[1008] Note: this shall not be construed to override the statutory authority granted to the Department of Parks and Recreation or any other state or local governmental agencies to promulgate rules and regulations governing the administration of parks and campgrounds[1009] (this means you must be aware of other rules and regulations established that may conflict with this exception, as those rules and regulations will be what you must abide by)

- the transportation of a firearm by a person in order to participate in an infrequent transfer of a firearm,[1010] or, who is taking title of the firearm that is not a handgun by operation of law[1011]
- the transportation of a firearm that is not a handgun by a person in order to have it sent lawfully from within the State of California to lawful receipt outside the State of California ("dealer to dealer transfer)[1012]
- the transportation of a firearm by a person when going directly to or from a gun show or event[1013] for the purpose of lawfully transferring, selling, or loaning that firearm when neither the transferor (firearm owner) or transferee (firearm purchaser) is a licensed dealer of firearms[1014]
- the transportation of a firearm by a person in order to consummate a sale, loan, delivery, or transfer of a firearm to authorized representatives of government entities where the

[1008] Penal Code § 12026.2 (a)(11).

[1009] Penal Code § 12026.2 (a)(11).

[1010] See Penal Code § 12078 (c) regarding infrequent transfer of a firearm.

[1011] Penal Code § 12026.2 (a)(12); see also § 12078 (l) regarding taking a firearm by operation of law.

[1012] Penal Code § 12026.2 (a)(13); see also Penal Code § 12078 (l), and Penal Code § 12078 (f) regarding lawful transfers under federal law.

[1013] See 27 C.F.R. § 478.11 regarding the definition of a gun show or event.

[1014] Penal Code § 12026.2 (a)(14); see also Penal Code § 12072 (d) regarding proper transfers under the exemption.

acquisition of the firearm from a private individual is authorized[1015]

- the transportation of a firearm by a person who finds the firearm and who wishes to dispose of the firearm in accordance with law by turning that firearm over to law enforcement[1016]
- the transportation of a firearm by a personal handgun importer[1017]
- the transportation of a firearm by a person who finds a firearm and is transporting it to a law enforcement agency for disposition according to law, provided he gives prior notice to the agency that he is bringing the weapon in for disposal[1018]
- the transportation of a firearm by a collector[1019] whose licensed premises are within the State of California, who acquires a pistol, revolver, or other firearm capable of being concealed upon the person that is a curio or relic[1020]outside of California, who takes actual possession of the firearm outside of this state according to law,[1021] and transports the firearm into this state, who, within 5 days of transport into the state, reports the acquisition to the department as prescribed[1022]
- the transportation of a firearm by a person for the purpose of obtaining an identification number or mark assigned for that firearm according to law[1023]

[1015]Penal Code § 12026.2 (a)(15); see also Penal Code § 12078 (a)(6).

[1016]Penal Code § 12026.2 (a)(16); see also Civil Code § 2080 et seq., regarding lost or abandoned property.

[1017]Penal Code § 12026.2 (a)(17); see also Penal Code § 12072 (f)(2) regarding personal handgun importers.

[1018]Penal Code § 12026.2 (a)(18).

[1019]See 18 U.S.C. § 921 et seq., regarding definition of "collector" as applicable here.

[1020]See 27 C.F.R. § 478.11 regarding definition of "curio or relic".

[1021]See 18 U.S.C. § 923 (j) regarding taking lawful possession outside of the state.

[1022]Penal Code § 12026.2 (a)(19).

[1023]Penal Code § 12026.2 (a)(20); see also Penal Code § 12092 regarding lawfully obtaining an identification number or mark for a firearm.

Be very careful with the above exceptions. While doing the above does not violate the *concealed* firearm law, such activity may very well violate the *loaded* firearm law. For instance, the exceptions above where you may transport a firearm to and from various places may not violate the concealed firearm law, but if the firearm is loaded, may violate the loaded firearm law.

Finally, the California Legislature did not intend for these exemptions to prohibit or limit the otherwise lawful carrying or transportation of any handgun, which includes pistols, revolvers, or other firearms capable of being concealed upon the person.[1024]

Persons Who Are Exempt from Concealed Firearm Law

The concealed firearm law[1025] does not apply to, or affect, any of the following:[1026]

- various peace officers[1027]
- the possession or transportation of unloaded pistols, revolvers, or other firearms capable of being concealed upon the person as merchandise by a person who is properly licensed to be engaged in the business of manufacturing, importing, wholesaling, repairing, or dealing in firearms, or his authorized agent while engaged in the lawful course of business[1028]
- members of the military or National Guard when on duty, or those organizations which are authorized by law to purchase or receive those weapons from the United States or this state[1029]
- duly authorized military or civil organizations when parading and

---

[1024]Penal Code § 12026.2 (c).

[1025]See Penal Code § 12025 regarding concealed firearm law.

[1026]Penal Code 12027.

[1027]Penal Code § 12027 (a)(1), (a)(2), and (a)(3); see the actual code sections for extensive list of exempted peace officers and considerations regarding same.

[1028]Penal Code § 12027 (b).

[1029]Penal Code § 12027 (c).

going to and from the parade[1030]

- guards or messengers of common carriers, banks, and other financial institutions while actually employed in and about the shipment, transportation, or delivery of any money, treasure, bullion, bonds, or other items of value within the state[1031]
- members of any club or organization organized for shooting at targets upon established target ranges, when participating in such activities, or going to and from[1032]
- licensed hunters or fisherman when engaged in such activities, or going to and from[1033]
- transportation of unloaded firearms by a person operating a common carrier or an authorized agent or employee thereof when transported in conformance with applicable federal law[1034]
- specific retired federal agents upon approval by the sheriff of the county in which they reside[1035]
- a person with a valid concealed weapons permit ("CCW")[1036]

[1030]Penal Code § 12027 (d).

[1031]Penal Code § 12027 (e).

[1032]Penal Code § 12027 (f).

[1033]Penal Code § 12027 (g).

[1034]Penal Code § 12027 (h).

[1035]Penal Code § 12027 (i); see the actual code section for extensive list of exempted federal agents and considerations regarding same.

[1036]Penal Code § 12027 (j); see also Penal Code § 12050 et seq., regarding those with valid CCWs.

CHAPTER TWELVE

The Loaded Firearm Law

The loaded firearm law[1037] is a prohibition on carrying a loaded firearm around in public places. Of course, to violate this law, the firearm must be loaded. One should be aware that if he has a concealed firearm that is loaded and does not fall into an exemption, he may be charged with two offenses, as both the concealed firearm law and the loaded firearm laws were violated. Therefore, the individual transporting a firearm must be keenly aware of both laws, and abide accordingly.

Firearms that apply to the loaded firearm law are basically handguns, which includes pistols, revolvers, and any firearms capable of being concealed upon the person, as well as rifles and shotguns whether or not they are modified to be concealable. This means that all firearms, basically, including any rocket, rocket propelled projectile launchers, or any similar devices containing any explosive or incendiary materials, whether or not the device is designed for emergency or distress signaling purposes, fall under the loaded firearm law.[1038]

Violations of the Loaded Firearm Law

A person is guilty of carrying a loaded firearm when he or she carries a loaded firearm on his or her person or in a vehicle while in any public place or on any public street in an incorporated city or in any public place or on any public street in a prohibited area of unincorporated territory.[1039]

The key here is that the loaded firearm is carried in a public place. If the loaded firearm is carried on private property owned or lawfully possessed by the person in possession of the firearm, there is no violation of the loaded firearm law. Keep in mind that despite the fact that inside your vehicle might seem like your private property, if the vehicle is taken onto a public street, the vehicle does not shield the person form the loaded firearm law.

[1037]Penal Code § 12031, for all intents and purposes, within this book will be called the "loaded firearm law".

[1038]See Penal Code § 12001 (a)(1), (d), and Penal Code § 12020 (c) for definitions.

[1039]Penal Code § 12031 (a)(1).

Very common loaded firearm law violations include:

- carrying a loaded firearm in your vehicle
- carrying a loaded firearm on your person
- carrying a loaded firearm concealed, such as in your purse, backpack, belly-pack, or suitcase
- carrying a loaded firearm in your trunk
- carrying a loaded firearm in your glove box
- carrying a loaded firearm in a locked container in your trunk or vehicle in any other place

Keep in mind that it makes no difference under the law as to you had knowledge the firearm was loaded or not and you stand a good chance of arrest for violation of this law.

What Constitutes "Loaded" for the Purposes of the Loaded Firearm Law?

A firearm shall be deemed to be loaded for the purposes of the loaded firearm law when there is an unexpended cartridge or shell, consisting of a case that holds a charge of powder and a bullet or shot, in, or attached in any manner to, the firearm, including, but not limited to, in the firing chamber, magazine, or clip thereof attached to the firearm.[1040] A muzzle-loader firearm shall be deemed to be loaded when it is capped or primed and has a powder charge and a ball or shot in the barrel or cylinder.[1041]

The law is silent as to whether a loaded magazine, if detached from the firearm but contained in the same container as the firearm, would be considered "loaded" for the purposes of the loaded firearm law. An argument could be made that ammunition was attached to the firearm by virtue of being kept in the same locked container, so the prudent traveler would probably not put himself or herself in such a situation.

California courts have also addressed the question of what the meaning of "loaded" was for the purposes of the loaded firearm law. The courts concluded that if the firearm had ammunition where it was ready for firing, it was loaded, such as ammunition loaded in a magazine. This can be distinguished from ammunition that

---

[1040]Penal Code § 12031 (g).

[1041]Penal Code § 12031 (g).

is stored in some sort of storage space, such as inside a rifle or shotgun stock, which is not considered "loaded" for the purposes of the law.[1042]

Common Motor Vehicle Loaded Firearm Law Violations

Carrying Firearm to and From Car

One violates the loaded firearm law if they carry the firearm to or from a motor vehicle, even if for a lawful purpose, if the firearm is not contained within a locked container.[1043]

Allowing Loaded Firearm in Vehicle

It is a misdemeanor for a driver of any motor vehicle or the owner of any motor vehicle, whether or not the owner of the vehicle is occupying the vehicle, knowingly to permit any other person to carry into or bring into the vehicle a firearm in violation of the loaded firearm law,[1044] or to possess a loaded rifle or shotgun in any vehicle or conveyance or its attachments which are standing on or along or is being driven on or along any public highway or other way that is open to the public.[1045]

Discharge of Firearm from Vehicle, Driver or Owner Violation

Any driver or owner of any vehicle, whether or not the owner of the vehicle is occupying the vehicle, who knowingly permits any other person to discharge a firearm from the vehicle is punishable by imprisonment in the county jail for not more than one year, or in state prison for 16 months or two or three years.[1046]

[1042] *People v. Clark*, (1996) 45 Cal.App.4th 1147, 1154.

[1043] Penal Code § 12026.1 (a)(2).

[1044] See Penal Code § 12031 regarding loaded firearm law.

[1045] Penal Code § 12034 (a); see also Fish and Game Code § 2006.

[1046] Penal Code § 12034 (b).

Discharge of Firearm from Vehicle, Person Shooting Firearm Violator

Any person who willfully and maliciously discharges a firearm from a motor vehicle at another person other than an occupant of a motor vehicle is guilty of a felony with a punishment of three, five, or seven years in the state prison.[1047]

Except as provided otherwise,[1048] any person who willfully discharges a firearm from a motor vehicle is guilty of a public offense punishable by imprisonment in the county jail for not more than one year or in the state prison.[1049] This section would apply in situations such as where one was caught firing upon road signs while being driven along a roadway, and would likely not be the only offense the person would be charged with if caught participating in such an act.

Justifiable Violation of Loaded Firearm Law

Self-Defense or Defense of Others Justification

A violation for the loaded firearm law may be justified under circumstances where it would otherwise be lawful, by a person who reasonably believes that the person or property of himself or herself or of another is in immediate, grave danger, and that the carrying of the weapon is necessary for the preservation of that person or property.[1050] The word "immediate," as used above, means the brief interval before and after the local law enforcement agency, when reasonably possible, has been notified of the danger and before the arrival of its assistance.[1051]

So, in a situation where there is an immediate danger, you are required to call the police and during the time from when the danger started, until the time the police arrive, you may be justified in violating the loaded firearm law.

However, one must be mindful about what the law considers acceptable force when protecting personal property, such as a car, or a bike parked on the

---

[1047]Penal Code § 12034 (c).

[1048]See Fish and Game Code § 3002.

[1049]Penal Code § 12034 (d).

[1050]Penal Code § 12031 (j)(1).

[1051]Penal Code § 12031 (j)(1).

front porch, and what the law considers acceptable force when protecting real property, such as a trespass onto private land, or an intrusion into someone's private residence. Please carefully read Chapter 28 of this book for more information on this matter.

Restraining Order Violation Justification

A violation of the loaded firearms law is justifiable when a person who possesses a firearm reasonably believes that he or she is in grave danger because of circumstances forming the basis of a current restraining order issued by a court against another person or persons who have been found to pose a threat to his or her life or safety.[1052] However, this justification does not apply when the circumstances involve a mutual restraining order,[1053] absent a factual finding of a specific threat to the person's life or safety.[1054]

The California Legislature did not intend to limit, restrict, or narrow the application of current statutory or judicial authority to apply this or other justifications to defendants charged with violating the loaded firearm law or of committing similar offenses.[1055]

Upon a trial for violating the loaded firearm law, and upon the defense of justification based upon a potential restraining order violation, the trier of fact shall determine whether the defendant was acting out of a reasonable belief that he or she was in grave danger.[1056]

Punishment and Penalties for Violating the Loaded Firearm Law

Carrying a loaded firearm in violation of the loaded firearm law[1057] is

---

[1052]Penal Code § 12031 (j)(2).

[1053]See Family Code § 6200 et seq., regarding mutual restraining orders referred to here.

[1054]Penal Code § 12031 (j)(2).

[1055]Penal Code § 12031 (j)(2).

[1056]Penal Code § 12031 (j)(2).

[1057]Penal Code § 12031.

punishable as either a felony or a misdemeanor.[1058] Of course, an exception applies within the private residence of one who lawfully possesses a firearm, unless a child under the age of 18 is present.

If the person has previously been convicted of a felony, the firearm was stolen and the person in possession knew or had reasonable cause to believe it was stolen, the person was an active participant in criminal gang activity, or is within the class of people prohibited from possessing firearms, the violation is a felony.[1059] Other violations may be considered misdemeanors.[1060] The California Legislature does not intend for the loaded firearm law to preclude prosecution under other more serious violations of the code,[1061] or any other law with a greater penalty than as provided under the loaded firearms law.[1062] It is the prosecutor's discretion as to how to prosecute firearms violations, and under what code sections.

Warrantless Arrest for Violation of Loaded Firearm Law Allowed

A peace officer may make an arrest without a warrant when the person violated the loaded firearm law, even if not in the officer's presence,[1063] and whenever the officer has reasonable cause to believe that the person to be arrested has violated the loaded firearm law, whether or not it was actually violated.[1064]

Further, in order to determine whether a firearm is loaded for the purpose of enforcing the loaded firearm law, peace officers are authorized to examine any firearm carried by anyone on his or her person or in a vehicle while in any public place or on any public street in an incorporated city or prohibited area of an unincorporated territory, and refusal to allow a peace officer to inspect a firearm

---

[1058] Penal Code § 12031 (a)(2).

[1059] Penal Code § 12031 (a)(2)(A) through (D).

[1060] Penal Code § 12031 (a)(2)(E) through (G).

[1061] See Penal Code §§ 12021 and 12021.1, and Welfare and Institutions Code §§ 8100 and 8103 regarding more serious violations.

[1062] Penal Code § 12031 (a)(4).

[1063] Penal Code § 12031 (a)(5)(A)(i).

[1064] Penal Code § 12031 (a)(5)(A)(ii).

constitutes probable cause for arrest for violation of the loaded firearm law.[1065] For the purposes of this law, "prohibited area" means any place where it is unlawful to discharge a weapon.[1066]

Exemptions to Loaded Firearm Law

Private Place of Business Exemption

Nothing in the loaded firearm law shall prevent any person engaged in any lawful business, including a nonprofit organization, or any officer, employee, or agent authorized by that person for lawful purposes connected with that business, from having a loaded firearm within the person's place of business, or any person in lawful possession of private property from having a loaded firearm on that property.[1067]

Private Residence Exemption

Nothing in the loaded firearms law shall prevent any person from having a loaded weapon, if it is otherwise lawful, at his or her place of residence, including any temporary residence or campsite, as long as there is not a child under the age of 18 present.[1068]

Making a Lawful Citizen's Arrest Exemption

Nothing in the loaded firearm law shall preclude the carrying of a loaded firearm by any person while engaged in the act of making or attempting to make a lawful arrest.[1069]

[1065]Penal Code § 12031 (e).

[1066]Penal Code § 12031 (f).

[1067]Penal Code § 12031 (h).

[1068]Penal Code § 12031 (l).

[1069]Penal Code § 12031 (k).

Other Exemptions

The loaded firearm law does not apply to any of the following:[1070]

- specified peace officers under certain conditions[1071]
- members of the military forces while engaged in the performance of their duties[1072]
- persons who are using target ranges for the purpose of practice shooting with a firearm or who are members of shooting clubs while hunting on the premises of those clubs[1073]
- those carrying pistols, revolvers, and other firearms capable of being concealed upon the person by persons who have their concealed weapons permit (CCWs)[1074]
- armored vehicle guards[1075] if hired prior to January 1, 1977, or, if hired on or after that date, have received a firearms qualification card from the Department of Consumer Affairs, and only when acting within the course and scope of their employment[1076]
- specific retired federal agents upon approval of the sheriff of the county in which they reside[1077]
- those who have completed a regular course in firearms training approved by the Commission on Peace Officer Standards and Training[1078]

[1070]Penal Code § 12031 (b).

[1071]Penal Code § 12031 (b)(1) through (3); see the actual code sections for extensive list of exempted peace officers and considerations regarding same.

[1072]Penal Code § 12031 (b)(4).

[1073]Penal Code § 12031 (b)(5).

[1074]Penal Code § 12031 (b)(6).

[1075]See Business and Professions Code § 7521 regarding definition of "armored vehicle guards".

[1076]Penal Code § 12031 (b)(7).

[1077]Penal Code § 12031 (b)(8); see the actual code sections for extensive list of exempted federal agents and considerations regarding same.

[1078]Penal Code § 12031 (c); see actual code section for extensive list of exempted individuals under this section, and considerations regarding same.

- those who have been issued a certificate[1079] by the Department of Consumer Affairs who are acting within the course and scope of their employment, including:[1080]
    - guards or messengers of common carriers, banks, and other financial institutions[1081]
    - guards of contract carriers operating armored vehicles[1082]
    - licensed private investigators and private patrol operators[1083]
    - uniformed security guards or night watch persons employed by any public agency[1084]
    - other uniformed security guards and alarm agents (please note that cities and counties may enact their own ordinances with requirements on alarm agents)[1085]
    - uniformed employees of private patrol operators and private investigators[1086]

Exemption for Emergency or Distress Signaling Purposes

Nothing in the loaded firearm law shall prevent any person from storing above any vessel or aircraft any loaded or unloaded rocket, rocket-propelled

---

[1079]See Penal Code § 12033 for certificates issued to security guards, armored vehicle guards, private investigators, etc.; see § 12031 (d) for full list.

[1080]Penal Code § 12031 (d); see also Penal Code § 12033 for certificates issued by the Department of Consumer Affairs.

[1081]Penal Code § 12031 (d)(1).

[1082]Penal Code § 12031 (d)(2); applies to those with authority from California Highway Patrol or Public Utilities Commission.

[1083]Penal Code § 12031 (d)(3); see also Business and Professions Code § 7512 et seq., for private investigators and private patrol operators, and Business and Professions Code § 7590 et seq., for alarm company operators.

[1084]Penal Code § 12031 (d)(4).

[1085]Penal Code § 12031 (d)(5).

[1086]Penal Code § 12031 (d)(6); see also Business and Professions Code § 7513 et seq., regarding licenses for these persons.

projectile launcher, or similar device designed primarily for emergency or distress signaling purposes, or from possessing such a device while in a permitted hunting area or traveling to and from such a hunting area while carrying a valid California permit or license to hunt.[1087]

[1087]Penal Code § 12031.1.

CHAPTER THIRTEEN

Other Offenses

Criminal Storage of a Firearm

The following definitions are applicable to the offense of criminal storage of a firearm.[1088]

- "locking device" means a device that is designed to prevent the firearm from functioning and when applied to the firearm, renders the firearm inoperable[1089]
- "loaded firearm" means a firearm that has an unexpended cartridge or shell, consisting of a case that holds a charge of powder and a bullet or shot, in, or attached in any manner to, the firearm, including, but not limited to, in the firing chamber, magazine, or clip thereof attached to the firearm, but in the case of a muzzle loader, the firearm is deemed loaded when it is capped or primed and has a powder charge and a ball or shot in the barrel or cylinder[1090]
- "child" means a person under the age of 18[1091]
- "great bodily injury" means a significant or substantial physical injury[1092]
- "locked container" means a secure container which is fully enclosed and locked by a padlock, keylock, combination lock, or similar locking device, but does not include the utility or glove compartment of a motor vehicle[1093]
- "off-premises means premises other than the premises where the

---

1088Penal Code §§ 12035 (a) and 12036 (a).

1089Penal Code §§ 12035 (a)(1) and 12306 (a)(1).

1090Penal Code § 12035 (a)(2); see also Penal Code § 12031 (g).

1091Penal Code §§ 12035 (a)(3) and 12036 (a)(2).

1092Penal Code § 12035 (a)(4); see also Penal Code § 12022.7 (f).

1093Penal Code §§ 12035 (a)(5) and 12036 (a)(4); see also Penal Code § 12026.2 (d).

firearm was stored[1094]

Criminal storage of a firearm is a very common offense that oftentimes ends with tragic circumstances. Basically, these are situations where a firearm is not properly stored and a child obtains possession of a firearm and ultimately hurts himself or another person. There are two degrees of "criminal storage of a firearm," a first degree criminal storage of a firearm and a second degree criminal storage of a firearm.

"Criminal Storage of a Firearm in the First Degree"

Criminal storage of a firearm in the first degree occurs when a person keeps any loaded firearm within any premises that is under his or her custody or control and he or she knows or reasonably should know that a child is likely to gain access to the firearm without the permission of the child's parent or legal guardian and the child gains access to the firearm and thereby causes death or great bodily injury to himself, herself, or any other person.[1095]

"Criminal Storage of a Firearm in the Second Degree"

Criminal storage of a firearm in the second degree is the same as with the first degree, only that the damage the child does to himself, herself, or another person is less than great bodily injury, or the child simply carries the firearm either to a public place and/or commits the offense of "brandishing."[1096]

Situations Where Criminal Storage of a Firearm is Inapplicable

Criminal storage of a firearm shall not apply when any of the following occurs:[1097]

- the child obtains the firearm as the result of an illegal entry to any

---

[1094] Penal Code § 12036 (a)(3).

[1095] Penal Code § 12035 (b)(1).

[1096] Penal Code § 12035 (b)(2); see also Penal Code § 417 regarding brandishing violations.

[1097] Penal Code § 12035 (c).

premises by the person[1098]

- the firearm is kept in a locked container or in a location that a reasonable person would believe to be secure[1099]
- the firearm is carried on the person or within such a close proximity thereto that the individual can readily retrieve and use the firearm as if carried on the person[1100]
- the firearm is locked with a locking device that has rendered the firearm inoperable[1101]
- the person is a peace officer or a member of the armed forces or National Guard and the child obtains the firearm during, or incidental to, the performance of the person's duties[1102]
- the child obtains, or obtains and discharges, the firearm in a lawful act of self-defense or defense of another person or persons[1103]
- the person who keeps a loaded firearm on any premise that is under his or her custody or control has no reasonable expectation, based upon objective facts and circumstances, that a child is likely to be present on the premises[1104]

Punishment and Penalties for Criminal Storage of a Firearm[1105]

Criminal storage of a firearm in the first degree may be either a felony or a misdemeanor, with punishment being as slight as imprisonment in a county jail for not more than one year and/or a fine of up to $1000, a misdemeanor, to imprisonment in the state prison for 16 months, or two or three years, by a fine not

---

[1098] Penal Code § 12035 (c)(1).

[1099] Penal Code § 12035 (c)(2).

[1100] Penal Code § 12035 (c)(3).

[1101] Penal Code § 12035 (c)(4).

[1102] Penal Code § 12035 (c)(5).

[1103] Penal Code § 12035 (c)(6).

[1104] Penal Code § 12035 (c)(7).

[1105] Penal Code § 12035 (d).

exceeding $10,000, or by both, a felony.[1106]

Criminal storage of a firearm in the second degree is a misdemeanor, and is punishable by a jail term of not exceeding one year, and/or a fine of up to $1000.[1107]

Adult Commits Offense Where Child Carries Firearms Off Premises

Child Carrying a Handgun Off-Premises

A person who keeps a pistol, revolver, or other firearm capable of being concealed upon the person, loaded or unloaded, within any premises that are under his or her custody or control, and he or she knows or reasonably should know that a child is likely to gain access to that firearm without the permission of the child's parent or legal guardian, and the child obtains access to that firearm and thereafter carries that firearm off-premises, shall be guilty of a misdemeanor (up to a year in jail and/or up to $1000 fine).[1108]

Child Carrying Any Firearm Off-Premises and Onto School Grounds

A person who keeps any firearm within any premises that are under his or her custody or control and he or she knows or reasonably should know that a child is likely to gain access to the firearm without the permission of the child's parent or legal guardian and the child obtains access to the firearm and thereafter carries that firearm off-premises to any public or private preschool, elementary school, middle school, high school, or to any school-sponsored event, activity, or performance, whether occurring on school grounds or elsewhere, shall be punished by imprisonment in the county jail not exceeding one year, and/or a fine not exceeding $5000.[1109]

Any pistol, revolver, or other firearm capable of being concealed upon the

---

[1106]Penal Code § 12035 (d)(1).

[1107]Penal Code § 12035 (d)(2).

[1108]Penal Code § 12036 (b).

[1109]Penal Code § 12036 (c).

person that is involved in any of the two offenses above shall be deemed "used in the commission of any misdemeanor as provided in this code or any felony," and will be confiscated by the authorities as a nuisance and disposed of according to law.[1110]

Exceptions

Offenses when a child carries a firearm off-premises shall not apply when any of the following occurs:[1111]

- the child obtains the firearm as the result of an illegal entry to any premises by the person[1112]
- the firearm is kept in a locked container or in a location that a reasonable person would believe to be secure[1113]
- the firearm is carried on the person or within such a close proximity thereto that the individual can readily retrieve and use the firearm as if carried on the person[1114]
- the firearm is locked with a locking device that has rendered the firearm inoperable[1115]
- the person is a peace officer or a member of the armed forces or National Guard and the child obtains the firearm during, or incidental to, the performance of the person's duties[1116]
- the child obtains, or obtains and discharges, the firearm in a lawful act of self-defense or defense of another person or persons[1117]
- the person who keeps a loaded firearm on any premise that is under his or her custody or control has no reasonable

[1110]Penal Code § 12036 (d); see also Penal Code § 12028 (b) regarding "pistol, revolver, or other firearm capable of being concealed upon the person" as nuisance.

[1111]Penal Code § 12035 (c).

[1112]Penal Code § 12036 (e)(1).

[1113]Penal Code § 12036 (e)(2).

[1114]Penal Code § 12036 (e)(4).

[1115]Penal Code § 12036 (e)(3).

[1116]Penal Code § 12036 (e)(5).

[1117]Penal Code § 12036 (e)(6).

expectation, based upon objective facts and circumstances, that a child is likely to be present on the premises[1118]

Penalties to Child for Carrying Firearm or Weapon Onto School Grounds

A pupil shall be immediately suspended from school and may be recommended for expulsion for possessing, selling, or otherwise furnishing a firearm, knife, explosive, or other dangerous object, absent written permission from the proper authorities.[1119] This includes an imitation firearm that is so substantially similar in physical properties to an existing firearm as to lead a reasonable person to conclude that the replica is a firearm.[1120] Expulsion is guaranteed for the pupil found in possession of a firearm at any of the prohibited places.[1121]

These prohibitions include having any of these items on school grounds,[1122] while going to or coming from school,[1123] during the lunch period whether or not on campus,[1124] or during, or while going to or coming from, any school-sponsored activity.[1125]

Other Considerations

Incident Reports Regarding Gunshot Wounds to Minors

Each law enforcement agency investigating an incident shall report to the State Department of Health Services any information obtained that reasonably

---

[1118]Penal Code § 12036 (e)(7).

[1119]Education Code §§ 48900 and 48900 (a)(2)(b); see also Penal Code § 48915 (a), (a)(2), and (c)(2) for knives, (c), (c)(1), and (5) for firearms.

[1120]Education Code § 48900 (m).

[1121]Education Code § 48915.7.

[1122]Education Code § 48900 (s)(1).

[1123]Education Code § 48900 (s)(2).

[1124]Education Code § 48900 (s)(3).

[1125]Education Code § 48900 (s)(4).

supports the conclusion that[1126] a child 18 years of age or younger suffered an unintentional or self-inflicted gunshot wound inflicted by a firearm that was sold or transferred in this state, or manufactured in this state,[1127] and that as a result of that incident the child died, suffered serious injury, or was treated by a medical professional.[1128]

Legislative Intent Regarding Prosecutions for Offense of Criminal Storage of a Firearm

If the person who allegedly committed the offense of criminal storage of a firearm, and the person is the parent or guardian of a child who is injured or who dies as the result of an accidental shooting, the district attorney shall consider, among other factors, the impact of the injury or death on the person alleged to have violated the law when deciding whether to prosecute an alleged violation.[1129]

It is the Legislature's intent that a parent or guardian of a child who is injured or who dies as the result of an accidental shooting shall be prosecuted only in those instances in which the parent or guardian behaved in a grossly negligent manner or where similarly egregious circumstances exist.[1130]

Despite that, it is not the Legislature's intent to otherwise restrict, in any manner, the factors that a district attorney may consider when deciding whether or not to prosecute alleged violations regarding the criminal storage of a firearm.[1131]

Other Prosecution Considerations

No Arrest for Seven Days Following Shooting - If the person who allegedly committed the offense of criminal storage of a firearm is the parent of a child who is injured or who dies as the result of an accidental shooting, no arrest of the person

---

[1126]Penal Code § 12088.5.

[1127]Penal Code § 12088.5 (a).

[1128]Penal Code § 12088.5 (b).

[1129]Penal Code §§ 12035 (e) and 12036 (f)

[1130]Penal Code §§ 12035 (e) and 12036 (f).

[1131]Penal Code §§ 12035 (e) and 12036 (f).

for the alleged violation shall occur until at least seven days after the date upon which the accidental shooting occurred.[1132] In addition, a law enforcement officer shall consider the health status of a child who suffers great bodily injury as the result of an accidental shooting prior to arresting a person for a violation of this law, if the person to be arrested is indeed the child's parent or guardian.[1133]

The intent behind the considerations above is to encourage law enforcement officials to delay the arrest of a parent or guardian of a seriously injured child while the child remains on life-support equipment or is in similarly critical medial condition.[1134]

Violator Had Attended Firearm Safety Training Course - The fact that the person who allegedly committed the offense of criminal storage of a firearm had attended a firearm safety training course prior to the purchase of the firearm that is obtained by the child shall be considered a mitigating factor by a district attorney when he or she is deciding whether to prosecute the alleged violation.[1135] Also, in any action or trial commenced for criminal storage of a firearm, the fact that the person who allegedly violated the law attended a firearm safety training course prior to the purchase of the firearm shall be admissible.[1136]

Licensed Dealer Warnings to Adult Regarding Child Access to Firearms to Notify and Educate Firearms Owners

All licensees and dealers of firearms[1137] shall post conspicuously within the licensed premises the following three warnings in block letters not less than one inch in height:[1138]

[1132]Penal Code §§ 12035 (f) and 12036 (g).

[1133]Penal Code §§ 12035 (f) and 12036 (g).

[1134]Penal Code §§ 12035 (f) and 12036 (g).

[1135]Penal Code §§ 12035 (g)(1) and 12036 (h)(1).

[1136]Penal Code §§ 12035 (g)(2) and 12036 (h)(1).

[1137]See Penal Code 12071.

[1138]Penal Code §§ 12035 (h) and 12036 (i); see also Penal Code § 12071 (b)(7) regarding the same, and for the exact language to be used.

The first warning is as follows:[1139]

"IF YOU KEEP A LOADED FIREARM WITHIN ANY PREMISES UNDER YOUR CUSTODY OR CONTROL, AND A PERSON UNDER 18 YEARS OF AGE OBTAINS IT AND USES IT, RESULTING IN INJURY OR DEATH, OR CARRIES IT TO A PUBLIC PLACE, YOU MAY BE GUILTY OF A MISDEMEANOR OR A FELONY UNLESS YOU STORED THE FIREARM IN A LOCKED CONTAINER OR LOCKED THE FIREARM WITH A LOCKING DEVICE, TO KEEP IT FROM TEMPORARILY FUNCTIONING."

The second warning is as follows:[1140]

"IF YOU KEEP A PISTOL, REVOLVER, OR OTHER FIREARM CAPABLE OF BEING CONCEALED UPON THE PERSON, WITHIN ANY PREMISES UNDER YOUR CUSTODY OR CONTROL, AND A PERSON UNDER 18 YEARS OF AGE GAINS ACCESS TO THE FIREARM, AND CARRIES IT OFF-PREMISES, YOU MAY BE GUILTY OF A MISDEMEANOR, UNLESS YOU STORED THE FIREARM IN A LOCKED CONTAINER, OR LOCKED THE FIREARM WITH A LOCKING DEVICE, TO KEEP IT FROM TEMPORARILY FUNCTIONING."

Finally, the third warning required to be posted at a licensee's or dealer's business:[1141]

"IF YOU KEEP ANY FIREARM WITHIN ANY PREMISES UNDER YOUR CUSTODY OR CONTROL, AND A PERSON UNDER 18 YEARS OF AGE GAINS ACCESS TO THE FIREARM, AND CARRIES IT OFF-PREMISES TO A SCHOOL OR SCHOOL-SPONSORED EVENT, YOU MAY BE GUILTY OF A MISDEMEANOR, INCLUDING A FINE OF UP TO FIVE THOUSAND DOLLARS ($5,000), UNLESS YOU STORED THE FIREARM IN A LOCKED CONTAINER, OR LOCKED THE FIREARM WITH A LOCKING DEVICE."

[1139] Penal Code § 12071 (b)(7)(A).

[1140] Penal Code § 12071 (b)(7)(B).

[1141] Penal Code § 12071 (b)(7)(C).

Failure to post the signs is a misdemeanor and the licensee is subject to lose his license.

Suspension or Delay of Minor's Driver's License for Firearms Offenses

For each conviction of a minor who commits a public offense involving a pistol, revolver, or other firearm capable of being concealed upon the person, the court may suspend the minor's driving privilege for five years.[1142] If the convicted minor is too young to have a license, the five years may be delayed until the minor becomes legally eligible to drive, at which time the five years begins to toll.[1143] Each subsequent offense may mean the addition of one more year of delay for the license.[1144]

The minor may reduce the delay up to 50% in acquiring a license by participating in approved community service.[1145] One hour's worth of community service will remove one day of the delay.[1146]

If the minor already has a driver's license, the license will be surrendered to the court, and the court, within 10 days, will notify the DOJ.[1147] However, the court, in considering a suspension or delay in the minor's driver's license privileges, will consider if a personal or family hardship exists that requires the person to have a driver's license for his or her own, or a member of his or her family, employment or medically related purposes.[1148]

[1142] Penal Code § 13202.4 (a)(1).

[1143] Penal Code § 13202.4 (a)(1).

[1144] Penal Code § 13202.4 (a)(1).

[1145] Penal Code § 13202.4 (a)(2)(A).

[1146] Penal Code § 13202.4 (a)(2)(B).

[1147] Penal Code § 13202.4 (b).

[1148] Penal Code § 13202.4 (c).

Part Six

Licenses to Carry a Firearm in California

CHAPTER FOURTEEN

Carry Licenses in California

-

Concealed Carry and Open Carry

As is generally known, especially for gun owners in California, is that California is a "may issue" state in regards to licenses to carry a firearm, whether openly or concealed. This means that you may or may not get a license, the licensing authority of the county you live in may or may not approve your application, etc. Some counties issue concealed carry licenses ("CCWs"), some counties issue both CCWs and open carry licenses, and some counties do not issue either.

The licensing authority, in more cases than not, is the sheriff of the county. However, the chief or other head of a municipal police department of any city may enter into an agreement as to who will process all applications for licenses, renewals of licenses, and amendments to carry licenses.[1149] In some counties, both the sheriff and the local police department may be responsible for issuing carry licenses. Check with local authorities for more information. The sheriff (or other licensing authority) has extremely broad discretion concerning the issuance of concealed weapon licenses.[1150]

There are several specific fundamental requirements to getting a carry license in California. These specific requirements are not all you will need to successfully acquire a carry license, but if you do not have any of these three, you likely will not be approved for a carry license.

First, you must live in a county where you even stand a chance to get a carry license. For instance, if you live in San Francisco County, you will not be granted a carry license, period. However, if you live in Humboldt County, the odds are high that you will be granted a carry license.

Second, you must be of good moral character. You will have to provide character references and submit to a fairly significant background check. If you have

---

[1149]Penal Code § 12050 (g).

[1150]*Gifford v. City of Los Angeles* 106 Cal.Rptr.2d 164, 88 Cal.App.4th 801.

a criminal record, questionable references, or other shady information in your background, you stand a good chance for denial of a carry license. Carry licenses are never issued if the DOJ determines that the person is prohibited from state or federal law from possessing, receiving, owning, or purchasing a firearm.[1151]

Third, and most importantly, "good cause" must exist for the issuance of the carry license. Good cause is the licensing authorities tool for denial of carry license, because good cause could mean anything to anyone. However, the "good cause" required by any licensing authority must be uniform within the county as to what is required by the applicant. However, "good cause" does not have to be uniform from county to county across the state. This is a real problem for the citizens of California, and it is currently being challenged in the courts.

Oftentimes, it can serve your interests in getting a carry license to research ahead of time what "good cause" the licensing authority in your county will need to see before approving your application and ultimately issuing you a carry license. Simply call the local sheriff to inquire. Also, a great deal of information may be found online about this issue.

Please note that the law, anywhere it discusses licenses to carry, is fairly specific in that it covers a "pistol, revolver, or other firearm capable of being concealed upon the person." This does not mean that a concealed carry or open carry license would not include a rifle or shotgun. In certain circumstances, sheriffs will list a rifle or a shotgun on a license. This is primarily done in rural counties for farmers or ranchers who want to keep their firearms loaded when moving from one properly to another when traveling on public roads.

While on the public road, the long gun must be concealed. It need not be concealed on private lands, so a "gun rack" in the back window of a pickup truck may be utilized while on private land, but may not be utilized on public roads. Also, the long gun must be unloaded when left in the vehicle.

Concealed Carry License Laws

The sheriff of a county, upon proof that the person applying is of good moral character, that good cause exists for the issuance, and that the person

---

[1151] Penal Code § 12050 (d).

applying is either a resident within the county where he is applying,[1152] or spends a substantial period of time in the applicant's principal place of employment or business in the county where he is applying,[1153] and has completed a course of training as prescribed by law, may issue to that person a license to carry a handgun, which is basically a pistol, revolver, or other firearm capable of being concealed upon the person in one of two formats to be discussed below.[1154]

In some instances, the authority to issue the license may be the chief or other head of a municipal police department of any city or city and county.[1155] This is why, in this book, the sheriff, chief of police, or other authorized authority is referred to as "licensing authority." Otherwise, the requirements are the same as above for the licensing authority to issue a carry license.[1156]

Two Formats of Licenses - Open Carry and Concealed Carry

As stated above, the licensing authority may issue either an open carry or a concealed carry license, depending on what the applicant desires.

Concealed Carry Licenses

The licensing authority may issue a license to carry a handgun concealed, which includes pistols, revolvers, or other firearms capable of being concealed upon the person.[1157] A California license will allow you to carry in other specific states.

Open Carry Licenses

The licensing authority may issue a license to carry openly in limited

---

1152 Penal Code § 12050 (a)(1)(D)(I).

1153 Penal Code § (a)(1)(D)(ii).

1154 Penal Code § 12050 (a)(1)(A).

1155 Penal Code § 12050 (a)(1)(B); see Penal Code § 12050 (a)(2)(A)(ii) regarding other limitations on licenses granted not on residency, but on employment in or business in county that the applicant does not reside in.

1156 Penal Code § 12050 (a)(1)(B).

1157 Penal Code § 12050 (a)(1)(A)(I).

circumstances. Only where the population of the county in which the city is located is less than 200,000 persons according to the most recent federal decennial census,[1158] a license to carry loaded and exposed in that county a handgun, including pistols, revolvers, or other firearms capable of being concealed on the person may be issued.[1159] Therefore, an open carry license issued in Inyo County will not allow the license holder to carry openly in San Francisco County.

Recently, a bill was signed into law to clarify a problem with the previous laws that called into question exactly where an open carry license allowed the license holder to open carry, with the law stating that the license holder may carry openly only as allowed by the license and only in the county where the license was issued.[1160] This is evident now in the Penal Code.[1161]

Note: there is nothing in the Penal Code that makes it illegal to carry openly an unloaded firearm anywhere in California. Additionally, there is nothing in the Penal Code that prohibits carrying a loaded magazine separate from the handgun.

In the last few years, the online community has been buzzing with stories detailing the episodes where citizens have chosen to carry an unloaded handgun openly. However, do so at your own peril. Also, should you choose to tempt fate, be sure to be aware of all restricted or prohibited areas.

Licenses for Certain Law Enforcement - The licensing authority, upon proof of good moral character, and that good cause exists for the issuance, and that the person applying is a person who has been deputized or appointed as a peace officer[1162] by that sheriff, chief of police, etc., may issue to that person a license to

---

[1158]There are usually two census reports that *could* be considered, federal, or the California census as taken by the California Department of Finance. For the purpose of this law, however, the federal report is used. This is true, despite claims from the Department of Finance that the US Census is consistently under-reported.

[1159]Penal Code §§ 12050 (a)(1)(A)(ii) and 12050 (a)(1)(B)(ii).

[1160]Assembly Bill ("AB") No. 1363.

[1161]See the 2010 Penal Code § 12050 (a)(1)(A)(ii) and (a)(1)(B)(ii).

[1162]See Penal Code § 830.6 (a) and (b) for peace officers to whom this law applies.

carry and waive the fees.[1163] The fact that the person is a peace officer is not supposed to have an impact on the process and requirements for the issuance of a carry license.[1164]

Publication of Licensing Requirements

Each licensing authority shall publish and make available a written policy summarizing the requirements in obtaining a carry license, whether the license is an open carry license or a concealed carry license.[1165]

Training for New Applicants

For new license applicants, the course of training may be:[1166]

- any course acceptable to the licensing authority
- shall not exceed 16 hours, subject to exception
- shall include instruction on firearm safety
- shall include instruction on the law regarding the permissible use of a firearm

Despite the above law that the course not exceed 16 hours, the local licensing authority may require further education and training, such as requiring a community college course certified by the Commission on Peace Officer Standards and Training and up to a maximum of 24 hours of education and training, but only if required uniformly of all license applicants without exception.[1167]

Training for Renewal Applicants

For renewal applicants, the course of training may be:[1168]

- any course acceptable to the licensing authority

[1163]Penal Code § 12050 (a)(1)(C).

[1164]Penal Code § 12050 (a)(1)(C).

[1165]Penal Code § 12050.2.

[1166]Penal Code § 12050 (a)(1)(E)(i)

[1167]Penal Code § 12050 (a)(1)(E)(i).

[1168]Penal Code § 12050 (a)(1)(E)(ii).

- shall be no less than four hours
- shall include instruction on firearm safety
- shall include instruction on the law regarding permissible use of a firearm

Term of License

Two-Year Licenses - Generally, a carry license is valid for a period of only two years.[1169]

Three-Year Licenses - The following individuals who are granted a license will receive one valid license for three years:[1170]

- a judge of a California court of record (this is the only instance where a resident of another state could get a California CCW, because a judge of a California court of record could live and be a resident across the state line in Nevada or Oregon)
- a full-time court commissioner of a California court of record
- a judge of a federal court
- a magistrate of a federal court

Four-Year Licenses - Finally, a license not to exceed four years may be issued to a custodial officer who is an employee of the sheriff, except that the license shall be invalid upon the conclusion of the person's employment if the four-year period has not otherwise expired or any other condition imposed pursuant to the licensing law does not limit the validity of the license for a shorter period of time.[1171]

Restrictions on Licenses

Any license may include any reasonable restrictions or conditions which the issuing authority deems warranted, including restrictions on the time, place, manner,

---

[1169]Penal Code § 12050 (a)(2)(A)(i).

[1170]Penal Code § 12050 (a)(2)(C).

[1171]Penal Code § 12050 (a)(2)(D); see also Penal Code § 831.5 regarding custodial officers employed by the sheriff.

and circumstances under which the person may carry a firearm.[1172] Any restrictions imposed will be indicated on any license issued.[1173]

Standard Application for Carry License, and Amendments Thereto

The application form for a carry license is a standard form, whether the application is to amend a license, apply for a license, and shall be uniform throughout the state, as prescribed by the Attorney General.[1174] All applications will include a section summarizing the statutory provisions of state law that result in the automatic denial of a license.[1175]

The forms shall contain a provision whereby the applicant attests to the truth of the statements contained in the application.[1176] Generally, applicants shall not be required to complete any additional application or form for a license, or to provide any information other than that which is necessary to complete the standard application form, or to clarify or interpret information provided by the applicant on the standard application form.[1177]

For instance, if the applicant is applying for a license in Orange County, he will likely be asked for a business license and a bank statement to support information provided regarding his "good cause" for getting a license. If the applicant is unable to supply this information, the applicant will likely be denied a license.

Information Required for a Carry License

Information required by the applicant when completing the standard application form for either a license, a renewal of a license, or to amend the license,

---

[1172]Penal Code § 12050 (b).

[1173]Penal Code § 12050 (c).

[1174]Penal Code § 12051 (a)(1) and (a)(3)(A).

[1175]Penal Code § 12051 (a)(3)(A).

[1176]Penal Code § 12051 (a)(3)(B).

[1177]Penal Code § 12051 (a)(3)(C).

will include, but is not limited to, the following:[1178]

- full name
- occupation
- residence address
- business address
- age / date of birth
- height
- weight
- color of eyes and hair
- reason for desiring a license to carry the weapon

All applicants shall be filed in writing, and signed by the applicant.[1179]

Lying on the Application

Generally, any person who files an application knowing that the statements on the contained therein are false is guilty of a misdemeanor.[1180] However, any person who knowingly makes a false statement on the application regarding any of the following shall be guilty of a felony:[1181]

- the denial or revocation of a carry license[1182]
- the denial of an amendment to a carry license[1183]
- a criminal conviction[1184]
- a finding of not guilty by reason of insanity[1185]
- the use of a controlled substance[1186]

[1178] Penal Code § 12051 (a)(1).

[1179] Penal Code § 12051 (a)(1).

[1180] Penal Code § 12051 (b).

[1181] Penal Code § 12051 (c).

[1182] Penal Code § 12051 (c)(1).

[1183] Penal Code § 12051 (c)(1).

[1184] Penal Code § 12051 (c)(2).

[1185] Penal Code § 12051 (c)(3).

[1186] Penal Code § 12051 (c)(4).

- a dishonorable discharge from the military[1187]
- a commitment to a mental institution[1188]
- a renunciation of United States citizenship[1189]

Fingerprints Required with Application

The fingerprints of each applicant shall be taken and two copies on forms prescribed by the DOJ shall be forwarded to the department.[1190]

Upon receipt of the fingerprints and the fee,[1191] the department shall promptly furnish the forwarding licensing authority a report of all data and information pertaining to any applicant of which there is a record in its office, including information as to whether the person is prohibited by state or federal law from possessing, receiving, owning, or purchasing a firearm.[1192] No license shall be issued by any licensing authority until after receipt of the report from the department.[1193] New fingerprints are not required for renewals and amendments.[1194]

Information Contained on an Issued License

The license issued to the licensee may be laminated.[1195] Any license issued upon the application shall set forth all of the following information:[1196]

[1187]Penal Code § 12051 (c)(5).

[1188]Penal Code § 12051 (c)(6).

[1189]Penal Code § 12051 (c)(7).

[1190]Penal Code § 12052 (a).

[1191]See Penal Code § 12054 regarding fees.

[1192]Penal Code § 12052 (a).

[1193]Penal code § 12052 (a).

[1194]Penal Code § 12052 (b) and (c).

[1195]Penal Code § 12051 (a)(1).

[1196]Penal Code § 12051 (a)(1).

- full name
- occupation
- residence address
- business address
- age / date of birth
- height
- weight
- color of eyes and hair
- reason for desiring a license to carry the weapon

Notice of Approval or Denial of License

The licensing authority shall give written notice to the applicant indicating if the license is approved or denied within 90 days of the initial application for a new license or a license renewal, or 30 days after receipt of the applicant's criminal background check from the DOJ, whichever is later.[1197]

Applications to Amend License

Applications for amendments to licenses shall be filed in writing and signed by the applicant, and shall state what type of amendment is sought, and the reason for desiring the amendment.[1198] There are several reasons a licensee may want or may be required to amend their license, including:[1199]

- add or delete authority to carry a particular firearm[1200]
- authorize the licensee to carry a particular firearm[1201]
- authorize the licensee to carry the firearm openly[1202]
- change any restrictions or conditions on the license, including

---

[1197]Penal Code § 12052.5.

[1198]Penal Code § 12051 (a)(2); see also § 12050 (f)(1).

[1199]Penal Code § 12050 (f)(1).

[1200]Penal Code § 12050 (f)(1)(A).

[1201]Penal Code § 12050 (f)(1)(B).

[1202]Penal Code § 12050 (f)(1)(C); see also Penal Code §§ 12050 (a)(1)(A)(ii) and (a)(1)(B)(ii) regarding requirements for an open carry permit.

time, place, manner, circumstances, or conditions[1203]

- change of address,[1204] as licensees are required to notify the issuing authority in writing within 10 days of any change in the licensee's place of residence[1205]

Anytime a licensing authority amends the license, a new license shall be issued to the licensee reflecting the amendments.[1206] Another important item for the licensee to understand is that amending the license does not extend the original expiration date of the license, and the license shall be subject to renewal at the same time as if the license had not been amended.[1207] Similarly, an application to amend a license does not constitute an application for renewal of the license.[1208]

Fees for Application and Amendment of Carry License

Except as discussed below, and as pursuant to the Penal Code,[1209] no requirement, charge, assessment, fee, or condition that requires the payment of any additional funds by the applicant may be imposed by any licensing authority as a condition of the application for a license.[1210] That being said, the only fees the applicant should encounter in the process of obtaining a carry license are discussed below.

New License Fees - Each applicant for a new license or for the renewal of a license shall pay, at the time of filing his or her application, a fee determined by the DOJ not to exceed the application processing costs of the DOJ for the direct costs

---

1203 Penal Code § 12050 (f)(1)(D).

1204 Penal Code § 12050 (f)(2).

1205 Penal Code § 12050 (f)(4)(A).

1206 Penal Code § 12050 (f)(3).

1207 Penal Code § 12050 (f)(5).

1208 Penal Code § 12050 (f)(6).

1209 See Penal Code § 12054.

1210 Penal Code § 12054 (d).

of furnishing the report.[1211] The licensing authority may charge an additional fee in the amount equal to the actual costs for processing the application for a new license, excluding fingerprint and training costs, but in no case to exceed $100.[1212]

Up to the first 20% of the additional local fee may be collected upon the filing of the initial application, with the balance of the fee to be collected only upon issuance of the license.[1213] DOJ fees will increase from year to year based upon th annual cost-of-living adjustments approved by the legislature.[1214] Local fees may be increased at a rate not to exceed any increase in the California Consumer Price Index as compiled and reported by the California Department of Industrial Relations.[1215]

Renewal License Fees - The local licensing authority may charge an additional fee, not to exceed $25, for processing the application for a license renewal.[1216]

Amended License Fees - The local licensing authority may charge a fee, not to exceed $10, to process a request to amend a license[1217] except that the fee may be increased at a rate not to exceed any increase in the California Consumer Price Index.[1218]

Psychological Testing Fees - The Penal Code is quite silent as to a psychological testing requirement for a carry permit, but it does address fees for such, if any issuing authority demands psychological testing prior to issuing a license.

[1211] Penal Code § 12054 (a).

[1212] Penal Code § 12054 (a).

[1213] Penal Code § 12054 (a).

[1214] Penal Code § 12054 (a).

[1215] Penal Code § 12054 (a).

[1216] Penal Code § 12054 (a).

[1217] See Penal Code § 12050 (f).

[1218] Penal Code § 12054 (b).

If psychological testing on the initial application is required by the licensing authority, the license applicant shall be referred to a licensed psychologist used by the licensing authority for the psychological testing of its own employees.[1219] The applicant may be charged for the actual cost of the testing in an amount not to exceed $150.[1220]

Any additional psychological testing of the applicant seeking license renewal shall be required only if there is some compelling evidence to indicate that a test is necessary, and that cost shall not exceed $150 to the applicant.[1221]

Revocation and Early Expiration of Carry License

Licensee Joins Class of Prohibited Persons - The license shall be revoked by the local licensing authority if at any time either the local licensing authority is notified by the DOJ that a licensee is prohibited by state or federal law from owning or purchasing firearms, or the local licensing authority determines that on its own.[1222] If the DOJ discovers this at any time, the local licensing authority will be immediately notified of the determination.[1223] If the local licensing authority revokes the license, the DOJ shall be notified of the revocation.[1224]

Move from County of Issuance - A concealed license may not be revoked simply because a licensee who is licensed to carry a handgun changes his or her place of residence to another county, so long as the licensee has not breached any conditions or restrictions set forth in the license and has not joined the class of prohibited persons.[1225] However, any two-year civilian concealed license issued shall expire 90 days after the licensee moves from the county of issuance if the licensee's

---

[1219]Penal Code § 12054 (c).

[1220]Penal Code § 12054 (c).

[1221]Penal Code § 12054 (c).

[1222]Penal Code § 12050 (e)(1).

[1223]Penal Code § 12050 (e)(2).

[1224]Penal Code § 12050 (e)(3); see also Penal Code § 12053 regarding authority to require local issuing agency to notify the DOJ.

[1225]Penal Code § 12050 (f)(4)(B).

place of residence, rather than their employment or place of business, was the means to satisfy the resident requirement for the license.[1226] An individual who bears a license for open carry will find that if he changes his residency to another county, his license is revoked immediately.[1227]

Records Maintained by the Licensing Authority

Records will be kept by the licensing authority, and the licensing authority shall forward a copy of the same to the DOJ.[1228] The records that shall be maintained in both the office of the licensing authority and the DOJ include:[1229]

- the denial of a license[1230]
- the denial of an amendment to a license[1231]
- the issuance of a license[1232]
- the amendment of a license[1233]
- the revocation of a license[1234]

Also, keep in mind that the sheriff has a legal right to make public the names of the person to whom he has issued concealed weapons permits because the names of such persons are information contained in public records which are not confidential.[1235]

[1226] Penal Code § 12050 (f)(4)(B).

[1227] Penal Code § 12050 (f)(4)(C).

[1228] Penal Code § 12053 (b).

[1229] Penal Code § 12053 (a) and (b).

[1230] Penal Code § 12053 (a)(1) and (b)(1).

[1231] Penal Code § 12053 (a)(2) and (b)(2).

[1232] Penal Code § 12053 (a)(3) and (b)(3).

[1233] Penal Code § 12053 (a)(4) and (b)(4).

[1234] Penal Code § 12053 (a)(5) and (b)(5).

[1235] 62 Op.Atty.Gen. 402, 8-7-79.

Special Considerations for Licenses Acquired for Business Reasons in County Where Applicant Does Not Reside

Licenses granted to applicants who do not live in the county of issuance, and instead acquired their license because their employment or business was in the county where they applied for the license, have some very unique characteristics that drastically limit the license as opposed to the licenses as discussed above.

License Term - The license issued on the basis of employment or business is located in another county, and the issuing authority is the county where the business is, and not where the applicant resides, is valid only for any period of time not to exceed 90 days from the date of the license.[1236]

Where License is Valid - The license is valid only in the county in which the license was originally issued.[1237] This means that unlike the other licenses which allow the licensee to carry throughout the entire state, this license only allows the licensee to carry only in the county where he was issued the license.

Notice to Authorities - With this license, the licensee shall give a copy of the license to the licensing authority in the county where he or she resides.[1238] To be sure that this notice is given, the licensing authority that is actually issuing the license shall clearly notify the licensee of this obligation.[1239]

Renewal of License - Any application to renew or extend the validity of, or reissue, the license may be granted only upon the concurrence of the licensing authority that originally issued the license and the licensing authority of the county in which the licensee resides.[1240]

"Principal Place of Employment or Business" - In order to be issued a license for this reason, an applicant's principal place of employment or business means that the applicant is physically present in the jurisdiction during a substantial

---

[1236]Penal Code § 12050 (a)(2)(A)(ii).

[1237]Penal Code § 12050 (a)(2)(A)(ii).

[1238]Penal Code § 12050 (a)(2)(A)(ii).

[1239]Penal Code § 12050 (a)(2)(A)(ii).

[1240]Penal Code § 12050 (a)(2)(A)(ii).

part of his or her working hours for purposes of that employment or business.[1241]

Concealed Carry for Retired Peace Officers

In many cases, retired peace officers may be able to carry concealed once retired.

Certificates with Approval to Carry Concealed and Loaded - Any peace officer who retired after January 1, 1981, who was previously employed by specific agencies,[1242] shall have an endorsement on the identification certificate stating that the issuing agency approves the officer's carrying of a concealed and loaded firearm.[1243] Any peace officer[1244] who retired prior to January 1, 1981, is authorized to carry a concealed and loaded firearm if the agency issued the officer an identification certificate and the certificate has not been stamped "No CCW privilege."[1245] Peace officers who are not listed in the cited Penal Code sections above, who were authorized to, and did, carry firearms during the course and scope of their employment as peace officers, shall have an endorsement on the identification certificate stating that the issuing agency approves the officer's carrying of a concealed and loaded firearm.[1246]

Denial of Privilege to Carry Concealed and Loaded - An identification certificate authorizing the officer to carry a concealed and loaded firearm or an endorsement on the certificate may be permanently revoked or denied by the issuing agency only upon a showing of good cause, which shall be determined at a hearing.[1247]

[1241] Penal Code § 12050 (a)(3).

[1242] See Penal Code §§ 830.1, 830.2, or 830.5 (c).

[1243] Penal Code § 12027.1(a)(1)(A)(i).

[1244] See Penal Code §§ 830.1, 830.2, or 830.5 (c).

[1245] Penal code § 12027 (a)(1)(A)(ii); see also Penal Code § 12027 (a)(2) regarding the stamped certificate.

[1246] Penal Code § 12027.1 (a)(1)(A)(iii).

[1247] Penal Code § 12027.1 (a)(1)(B) and (b)(1); see also Penal Code § 12027 (d).

Further, an identification certificate authorizing the officer to carry a concealed or loaded firearm or an endorsement on the certificate may be immediately and temporarily revoked by the issuing agency when the conduct of the retired peace officer compromises safety.[1248] Notice shall be effective upon personal service or upon receipt of the notice that was sent by first-class mail, postage prepaid, return receipt requested, to the retiree's last known place of residence.[1249] The retiree shall have 15 days to respond to the notification and request a hearing to determine if the temporary revocation shall become permanent.[1250] A retiree who fails to respond to the notice shall forfeit his or her right to a hearing and the authority of the officer to carry a firearm shall be permanently revoked.[1251] The retired peace officer shall immediately return the identification certificate to the issuing agency.[1252] If a hearing is requested, good cause for permanent revocation shall be determined at the hearing.[1253] The hearing shall be held no later than 120 days after the request by the retired officer for a hearing is received.[1254] The retiree may elect to waive his or her right to a hearing and instead immediately return the identification to the issuing agency.[1255]

A retired peace officer may have his or her privilege to carry a concealed and loaded firearm revoked or denied by violating any departmental rule, or state or federal law that, if violated by an officer on active duty, would result in that officer's arrest, suspension, or removal from the agency.[1256]

Good Cause - An identification certificate authorizing the officer to carry a concealed and loaded firearm or an endorsement may be permanently revoked or

---

[1248] Penal Code § 12027.1 (a)(1)(C).

[1249] Penal Code § 12027.1 (a)(1)(C).

[1250] Penal Code § 12027.1 (a)(1)(C).

[1251] Penal Code § 12027.1 (a)(1)(C).

[1252] Penal Code § 12027.1 (a)(1)(C).

[1253] Penal Code § 12027.1 (a)(1)(C).

[1254] Penal Code § 12027.1 (a)(1)(C).

[1255] Penal Code § 12027.1 (a)(1)(C).

[1256] Penal Code § 12027.1 (a)(2).

denied by the issuing agency only upon a showing of good cause, which shall ultimately be determined at a hearing.[1257]

Notice of Hearing - Notice of the hearing shall be served personally on the retiree or sent by first-class mail, postage prepaid, return receipt requested to the retiree's last known place of residence.[1258] Upon the date the agency receives the signed registered receipt or upon the date the notice is served personally on the retiree, the retiree shall then have 15 days in which to respond to the notification.[1259] A retired peace officer who fails to respond to the notice of the hearing shall forfeit his or her right to respond.[1260]

Denial Prior to Hearing - An identification certificate authorizing the officer to carry a concealed or loaded firearm or an endorsement may be denied prior to a hearing.[1261] If a hearing is not conducted prior to the denial of an endorsement, the retired officer, within 15 days of the denial, shall have the right to request a hearing, and if he fails to do so, shall forfeit his or her right to a hearing on the matter.[1262]

Hearing - Any hearing for revocation of the endorsement shall be held before a three-member hearing board.[1263] One member of the board shall be selected by the issuing agency, and one member shall be selected by the retired peace officer or his or her employee organization.[1264] The third member shall be selected jointly by the issuing agency and the retired peace officer or his or her employee organization.[1265] Any decision by the board shall be binding on the agency

---

[1257]Penal Code § 12027.1 (b)(1).

[1258]Penal Code § 12027.1 (b)(2).

[1259]Penal Code § 120271. (b)(2).

[1260]Penal Code § 12027.1 (b)(2).

[1261]Penal Code § 12027.1 (b)(3).

[1262]Penal Code § 12027.1 (b)(3).

[1263]Penal Code § 12027.1 (d).

[1264]Penal Code § 12027.1 (d).

[1265]Penal Code § 12027.1 (d).

and the retired peace officer.[1266] No peace officer who is retired after January 1, 1989, because of a psychological disability shall be issued an endorsement to carry a concealed and loaded firearm.[1267]

Surrender of Identification Certificate - A retired peace officer, when notified of the revocation of his or her privilege to carry a concealed and loaded firearm, after the hearing, or upon forfeiting his or her right to a hearing, shall immediately surrender to the issuing agency his or her identification certificate.[1268] The issuing authority shall then issue a new identification certificate without the endorsement.[1269] However, if the officer retired prior to January 1, 1981, and was at the time of his or her retirement a specified peace officer,[1270] the issuing agency shall stamp on the identification certificate "No CCW privilege."[1271]

Resources for Those Who Carry Concealed - There are many resources on the internet for those who carry concealed, and one must be very wary of information they gather from the internet because oftentimes it can be wrong. It is simply not worth it to gather incorrect information and risk arrest. There exists one exceptional site dedicated to concealed carry in California, and it may be found at www.calccw.com. This site is very active with dedicated CCW holders who closely follow the law and discuss the latest developments.

Reciprocity - States that Recognize a California CCW Permit

A valid, current California concealed carry permit will allow you to carry in the following states: Alaska, Arizona, Idaho, Indiana, Kentucky, Michigan, Missouri, Montana, Oklahoma, South Dakota, Tennessee, Texas, and Utah. However, California law does not apply in these states, you must follow the law of the state you are in. Also, open carry licenses in California are not valid for open carry in another state. California does not recognize the CCW from any other state.

1266 Penal Code § 12027.1 (d).

1267 Penal Code § 12027.1 (e).

1268 Penal Code § 12027.1 (c).

1269 Penal Code § 12027.1 (c).

1270 See Penal Code §§ 830.1, 830.2, and 830.5 (c).

1271 Penal Code § 12027.1 (c).

Part Seven

Prohibited Places to Transport or Possess Firearms in California

CHAPTER FIFTEEN

Places Where *Firearms* Are Prohibited in California

In California, both under federal and state law, there are places where firearms are prohibited. This chapter will address these places. One must be careful not to carry firearms into these places, as both the reaction by law enforcement and the penalties for the violation can be quite severe. Additionally, it is common for those found carrying a firearm into these prohibited places, are also found in violation of the concealed firearm law and/or the loaded firearm law as well.

Public and Private Schools - Kindergarten through 12th Grade

School Zone Possession Prohibition

A "school zone" has been created under both federal law[1272] and California law[1273] to define an area around schools and colleges where firearms are prohibited. In 1995, the California Legislature enacted the California Gun-Free School Zone Act.[1274] It states that any person who possesses a firearm in a place that the person knows, or reasonably should know, is a school zone is guilty of a felony.[1275] Punishment for violation of state law is harsh, and includes imprisonment in the state prison for two, three, or five years.[1276] Violation of the federal law regarding school zones is generally a felony offense punishable by up to five years in prison and up to a $5000 fine, or both, but if prosecuted as a misdemeanor, than up to $5000 penalty only.[1277]

It is important to note that the "school zone," applies only to public and

---

[1272] 18 U.S.C. § 921 (a)(25).

[1273] Penal Code § 626.9.

[1274] Penal Code § 626.9.

[1275] See Penal Code § 626.9 (e)(1) for definition of "school zone".

[1276] Penal Code § 626.9 (b); see also Penal Code § 626.9 (e)(1) regarding punishment in the state prison.

[1277] 18 U.S.C. § 924 (a)(4).

private schools with students in kindergarten through 12th grade.

Exceptions Applicable to the Prohibitions for BOTH Schools K-12 and Colleges and Universities

Keep in mind that exceptions or exemptions that exist under California law may not apply to federal law, and which law is tougher is the law that the traveler must be primarily concerned with. If one brings a firearm into a school zone and they are not otherwise violating California law, they may still be violating federal law. Or vice versa.

California law provides exceptions to the California Gun-Free School Zone Act of 1995.[1278]

Residence, Place of Business, or Private Property

A firearm may be possessed in a "school zone" as long as it is possessed within a place of residence, place of business, or on private property so long as none of these places is also part of the school grounds, and possession of the firearm is otherwise lawful.[1279] This means that if an individual is on private property, in a private residence, or in a place of business, and possesses the firearm in violation of any other law, the protection is lost, and the person will also be guilty of violating the School Zone Act. This is a serious matter for the violator. Also realize that public sidewalks do not fall under this exception.[1280] The person that falls under this exception will not be in violation of federal law.[1281]

Unloaded, Locked in Container, Locked in Trunk

An unloaded pistol, revolver, or other firearm capable of being concealed on the person may be possessed in a "school zone" as long as it is being legally transported in a locked container.[1282] Remember, a "locked container" is a secure

---

[1278] Penal Code § 626.9 (c).

[1279] Penal Code § 626.9 (c)(1).

[1280] *People v. Tapia* (1995) 129 Cal.App. 4th 1153.

[1281] See 18 U.S.C. § 922 (q).

[1282] Penal Code § 626.9 (c)(2).

container which is fully enclosed and locked with a padlock or similar style lock.[1283] The person that falls under this exception will not be in violation of federal law.[1284]

It is important to note that also allowed is the lawful transportation of <u>any</u> other firearm, so long as the firearms are being transported in accordance with state law, meaning they are in a locked container or a locked gun rack.[1285] The person that falls under this exception will not be in violation of federal law.

<u>Permission</u>

One does not violate the School Zone Act if he first has the written permission of the school district superintendent, his or her designee, or equivalent school authority.[1286] The person that falls under this exception will not be in violation of federal law.[1287]

<u>Reasonable Belief of Grave Danger - Restraining Order Situations</u>

A person may lawfully possess a firearm within a "school zone" so long as that person has a reasonable belief that he or she is in grave danger because of the circumstances forming the basis of a current restraining order issued by a court against another person or persons who have been found to pose a threat to his or her life or safety.[1288] This is not applicable in the case of mutual restraining orders absent a factual finding of a specific threat to the person's life or safety.[1289] Upon trial of a violation of the School Zone Act, the trier of fact shall determine whether the defendant was acting out of a reasonable belief that he or she was in grave

---

1283 See Penal Code § 12026.1 (c) regarding definition of "locked container".

1284 See 18 U.S.C. § 922 (q).

1285 Penal Code § 626.9 (c)(2).

1286 Penal Code § 626.9 (b); see also Penal Code § 12316 (c).

1287 See 18 U.S.C. § 922 (q).

1288 Penal Code § 626.9 (c)(3).

1289 Penal Code § 626.9 (c)(3); see also Family Code § 6200 et seq.

danger.[1290] This exception is inapplicable under federal law. Therefore, the individual who commits this offense will not be prosecuted for a violation under state law, but they may be prosecuted for a violation under federal law.

Those with an Exemption

When a person falls under certain exemptions from the prohibition of carrying a concealed firearm, he is not violating the School Zone Act when he otherwise lawfully carries his firearm.[1291] The individuals to whom this exemption applies to include the following individuals:

Peace Officers - An exemption exists for the duly appointed peace officer,[1292] full-time paid peace officers of another state or federal government who are carrying out their official duties while in California, or any person summoned by these officers to assist in making arrests or preserving the peace while he or she is actually engaged in assisting the officer.[1293]

Additionally, honorably retired peace officers may be authorized to carry a concealed or loaded firearm according to law.[1294] The person who falls under these peace officer exceptions will not be in violation of federal law.[1295]

Persons with a Carry Permit - An exemption exists from all school and college prohibitions for those who hold a valid, current California carry license, either open or concealed.[1296] The person who falls under the carry license

---

[1290] Penal Code § 626.9 (c)(3).

[1291] Penal Code § 626.9 (c)(4); see also Penal Code § 12027 (b), (d), (e), and (h).

[1292] See Penal Code § 830 et seq., regarding duly appointed peace officers.

[1293] Penal Code § 626.9 (l).

[1294] See Penal Code § 12027 (a) and (l), and Penal Code § 12031 (b)(1) and (b)(8).

[1295] See 18 U.S.C. § 922 (q).

[1296] Penal Code § 626.9 (l); see also Penal Code § 12050 et seq., regarding carry licenses in California.

exception will not be in violation of federal law.[1297] Yes, you read that correctly.

Persons in the Firearms Business - those properly licensed in the business of manufacturing, importing, wholesaling, repairing, or dealing in firearms, or their authorized representative or agent while engaged in the lawful course of the business, so long as the firearms are unloaded.[1298] The person who falls under this exception will not be in violation of federal law.[1299]

Persons in the Military - those who are duly authorized military or civil organizations, while parading, or the members thereof when going to and from the places of meeting of their respective organizations, or are otherwise engaged in the performance of their duties.[1300] The person who falls under this exception will not be in violation of federal law.[1301]

Armored Guards and Messengers - those who are guards or messengers of common carriers, banks, and other financial institutions while actually employed in and about the shipment, transportation, or delivery of anything of substantial value.[1302] The person who falls under this exception will not be in violation of federal law.[1303]

Security Guards - The prohibitions above do not apply to the security guard with authorization to carry a loaded firearm according to law,[1304] as an exemption exists if they are properly licensed.[1305] The person who falls under this

---

[1297]See 18 U.S.C. § 922 (q).

[1298]Penal Code § 626.9 (c)(4); see also Penal Code § 12027 (b).

[1299]See 18 U.S.C. § 922 (q).

[1300]Penal Code § 626.9 (c)(4) and (l); see also Penal Code § 12027 (d).

[1301]See 18 U.S.C. 922 (q).

[1302]Penal Code § 626.9 (c)(4) and (l); see also Penal Code § 12027 (e), and Business and Professions Code § 7521.

[1303]See 18 U.S.C. § 922 (q).

[1304]See Penal Code § 12031.

[1305]Penal Code § 626.9 (m).

exception will not be in violation of federal law.[1306]

Common Carriers - Those persons operating a licensed common carrier or an authorized agent or employee thereof when transported in conformance with applicable federal law.[1307] The firearms must be unloaded and transported according to law.[1308] The person who falls under this exception will not be in violation of federal law.[1309]

Violations of the Prohibition on Firearm Possession in School Gun Zone

Punishment for Possession on the Grounds of the School

Any person who violates the prohibition on firearm possession in a school gun zone[1310] by possessing a firearm in, or on the grounds of, a public or private school providing instruction in kindergarten or grades 1 to 12, inclusive, shall be punished by imprisonment in the state prison for two, three, or five years.[1311]

Punishment for Possession Within 1000 Feet of the School

Any person who violates the prohibition on firearms possession in a school gun zone[1312] by possessing a firearm within a distance of 1000 feet from the grounds of a public or private school providing instruction in kindergarten or grades 1 to 12, inclusive, shall be punished as follows:[1313]

- by imprisonment in the state prison for two, three, or five years,

---

[1306] See 18 U.S.C. § 922 (q).

[1307] Penal Code § 626.9 (c)(4); see also Penal Code § 12027 (h).

[1308] See Penal Code § 12027 (h).

[1309] See 18 U.S.C. § 922 (q).

[1310] See Penal Code § 626.9 (b).

[1311] Penal Code § 626.9 (f)(1).

[1312] See Penal Code § 626.9 (b).

[1313] Penal Code § 626.9 (f)(2).

if any of the following circumstances apply:[1314]

- if the person has been previously convicted of a felony, or any crime made punishable by Chapter 1 (commencing with § 12000) of Title 2 Part 4 of the Penal Code[1315]
- if the person is a prohibited person from possessing firearms under specific laws[1316]
- if the firearm is any pistol, revolver, or other firearm capable of being concealed upon the person and the offense is punished as a felony for violation of the concealed firearm law[1317]

- by imprisonment in a county jail for not more than one year or by imprisonment in the state prison for two, three, or five years, in all cases other than those specified immediately above[1318]

California Law - School Gun Zone Discharge of Firearm Prohibition

It shall be unlawful for any person, with reckless disregard for the safety of another, to discharge, or attempt to discharge, a firearm in a school zone.[1319] However, this prohibition does not apply to the discharge of a firearm to the extent that the act occurs within a place of residence, place of business, or private property, so long as the possession of the firearm is otherwise lawful.[1320]

[1314]Penal Code § 626.9 (f)(2)(A).

[1315]Penal Code § 626.9 (f)(2)(A)(I).

[1316]Penal Code § 626.9 (f)(2)(A)(ii); see also Penal Code §§ 12021 and 12021.1, and Welfare and Institutions Code §§ 8100 and 8103 regarding specific violations applicable to this law.

[1317]Penal Code § 626.9 (f)(2)(A)(iii); see also Penal Code § 12025 regarding concealed firearm law.

[1318]Penal Code § 626.9 (f)(2)(B); see also Penal Code § 626.9 (f)(1)(A) for exceptions referred to here.

[1319]Penal Code § 626.9 (d); see also Penal Code § 626.9 (b) and (e).

[1320]Penal Code § 626.9 (d); see also Penal Code § 626.9 (c)(1).

Violation of California School Gun Zone Discharge of Firearm Prohibition

Any person who violates this prohibition and discharges a firearm with the reckless disregard for the safety of another within a school zone shall be punished by imprisonment in the state prison for three, five, or seven years.[1321]

For the purposes of determining the penalty to be imposed for violation of these "school zone" prohibitions, the court may consider a written report from the DOJ containing information from its records showing prior convictions, and such communication is prima facie evidence of the convictions, if the defendant admits them, regardless of whether or not the complaint commencing the proceedings has alleged prior convictions.[1322]

In closing, it should be noted that none of the above prohibitions applies to an existing shooting range at a public or private school.[1323]

Public and Private Colleges and Universities

Loaded Firearm on Campus

Any person who brings or possesses a loaded firearm upon the grounds of a campus of, or buildings owned or operated for student housing, teaching, research, or administration by, a public or private university or college, that are contiguous or are clearly marked university property, shall be punished by imprisonment in the state prison for two, three, or four years.[1324]

Any Unloaded Firearm on Campus

Any person who brings or possesses any unloaded firearm upon the grounds of a campus of, or buildings owned or operated for student housing, teaching, research, or administration by, a public or private university or college, that are contiguous or are clearly marked university property, shall be punished by

---

[1321]Penal Code § 626.9 (f)(3); see also Penal Code § 626.9 (d).

[1322]Penal Code § 626.9 (b).

[1323]Penal Code § 626.9 (n).

[1324]Penal Code § 626.9 (h).

imprisonment in the state prison for one, two, or three years.[1325]

An exception to these prohibitions includes written permission of the university or college president, his or her designee, or equivalent university or college authority.[1326] Other exceptions that are discussed above in this chapter that apply to K-12 schools also apply to colleges and universities.[1327] For good measure, that list includes:

- residences, businesses, and private property
- unloaded firearms properly stored when transported
- those with carry permits, concealed or open carry
- those with written permission from relevant school officials
- certain peace officers
- certain security guards and retired peace officers
- properly licensed armored vehicle guards
- military personnel

For the purposes of determining the penalty to be imposed for violation of these prohibitions, the court may consider a written report from the DOJ containing information from its records showing prior convictions, and such communication is prima facie evidence of the convictions, if the defendant admits them, regardless of whether or not the complaint commencing the proceedings has alleged prior convictions.[1328]

Universities and colleges shall post prominent notices at primary entrances on noncontiguous property stating that firearms are prohibited on that property.[1329] However, notice need not be posted regarding the proscribed conduct.[1330]

It should be noted that none of the above prohibitions applies to an

---

[1325] Penal Code § 626.9 (i).

[1326] Penal Code § 626.9 (h).

[1327] See Penal Code § 626.9 (h).

[1328] Penal Code § 626.9 (b).

[1329] Penal Code § 626.9 (h).

[1330] Penal Code § 626.9 (k).

existing shooting range at a public or private college or university.[1331]

Definitions Applicable to the Prohibitions for Schools, Colleges, and Universities Under California Law

A "school zone" means an area in, or on the grounds of, a public or private school providing instruction in kindergarten or grades 1 to 12, inclusive, or within a distance of 1000 feet from the grounds of the public or private school.[1332]

1000 feet is quite a distance, and is likely much further than most people realize. If one is looking at a person who is standing 1000 feet away, the person off in the distance will be reduced to the size of a speck; that is, they will be almost impossible to see. 1000 feet is equal to 3 and 1/3 football fields. Keep this in mind when traveling near potential school zones, as 1000 feet is indeed the law, and a person traveling into the school zone in violation of the Act may be punished, even if 1000 feet is a very unreasonable distance and difficult to ascertain when traveling about town.

"Firearm" means any device, designed to be used as a weapon, from which is expelled through a barrel, a projectile by the force of any explosion or other form of combustion.[1333]

"Locked container" means a secure container which is fully enclosed and locked by a padlock, key lock, combination lock, or similar locking device.[1334]

For the purposes of the law in regards to schools and colleges, a firearm shall be deemed "loaded" when there is an unexpended cartridge or shell, consisting of a case that holds a charge of powder and a bullet or shot, in, or attached in any manner to, the firearm, including, but not limited to, in the firing chamber, magazine, or clip thereof attached to the firearm.[1335] For a muzzle loader, it shall be deemed loaded when it is capped or primed and has a powder charge and ball or shot in the

---

[1331] Penal Code § 626.9 (n).

[1332] Penal Code § 626.9 (e)(1).

[1333] Penal Code § 626.9 (e)(2); see also Penal Code § 12001 (b).

[1334] Penal Code § 626.9 (e)(3); see also Penal Code § 12026.1 (c).

[1335] Penal Code § 626.9 (j).

barrel or cylinder.[1336]

"University" means the University of California, and includes any affiliated institution thereof and any campus or facility owned, operated, or controlled by the Regents of the University of California.[1337]

"State university" means any California state university, and includes any campus or facility owned, operated, or controlled by the Trustees of the California State University.[1338]

"Community College" means any public community college established pursuant to the Education Code.[1339]

"School" means any public or private elementary school, junior high school, four-year high school, senior high school, adult school or any branch thereof, opportunity school, continuation high school, regional occupational center, evening high school, or technical school or any public right-of-way situated immediately adjacent to school property or any other place if a teacher and one or more pupils are required to be at that place in connection with assigned school activities.[1340]

A "safe school zone," not to be confused with the gun-free school zone, is an area that encompasses any of the following places during regular school hours or within 60 minutes before or after the school day or 60 minutes before or after a school-sponsored activity at the schoolsite:[1341]

- within 100 feet of a bus stop, whether or not a public transit bus stop, that has been publicly designated by the school district as a schoolbus stop - this definition applies only if the school district

---

[1336]Penal Code § 626.9 (j).

[1337]Penal Code § 626 (a)(1).

[1338]Penal Code § 626 (a)(2).

[1339]Penal Code § 626 (a)(3).

[1340]Penal Code § 626 (a)(4).

[1341]Penal Code § 626 (c)(2).

has chosen to mark the bus stop as a school bus stop[1342]

- within 1500 feet of a school, as designated by the school district[1343]

Loaded Firearm on Playground

If, while on a playground, any person who, except in self-defense, brandishes a firearm, whether unloaded or not, or violates the concealed firearm law or loaded firearm law, shall be punished by imprisonment in the state prison for one, two, or three years, or in a county jail for not more than one year.[1344]

A "playground" means any park or recreational area specifically designed to be used by children that has play equipment installed, including public grounds designed for athletic activities such as baseball, football, soccer, or basketball, or any similar facility located on public or private school grounds, or on city or county parks.[1345]

State and local authorities are encouraged to cause signs to be posted around playgrounds giving warning of prohibition of the possession of firearms upon the grounds or within playgrounds.[1346]

Keep in mind, the individuals who fall within an exception or are exempted from either the concealed firearm law or loaded firearm law, may carry as prescribed by law.

Loaded Firearm at Youth Centers

If, while at any youth center, public or private, during hours in which the facility is open for business, classes, or school-related programs, or at any time when minors are using the facility, any person who, except in self-defense, brandishes a

---

[1342]Penal Code § 626 (c)(2)(A).

[1343]Penal Code § 626 (c)(2)(B).

[1344]Penal Code § 626.95 (a); see also Penal Code §§ 417 (a)(2), (b), 12025 or 12031.

[1345]Penal Code § 626.95 (c)(1).

[1346]Penal Code § 626.95 (b).

firearm, whether unloaded or not, or violates the concealed firearm law or loaded firearm law, shall be punished by imprisonment in the state prison for one, two, or three years, or in a county jail for not more than one year.[1347]

"Youth center" means any public or private facility that is used to host recreational or social activities for minors while minors are present.[1348]

State and local authorities are encouraged to cause signs to be posted around playgrounds giving warning of prohibition of the possession of firearms upon the grounds or within playgrounds.[1349]

Keep in mind, if you fall within an exception or are exempted from either the concealed firearm law or loaded firearm law, you may carry as prescribed by law.

Loaded Firearm at Gun Shows

No person at a gun show or event, other than security personnel or sworn peace officers, shall possess at the same time both a firearm and ammunition that is designed to be fired in the firearm.[1350] Of course, vendors having those items at the show for sale or exhibition are exempt from this prohibition.[1351] Those with carry permits, open or CCW, are not exempted from this prohibition.

Federal Buildings and Courthouses

Federal Buildings

Absent an exemption, any person who knowingly possesses or causes to be present a firearm or other dangerous weapon in a Federal facility (other than a Federal court facility), or attempts to do so, shall be fined or imprisoned not more

---

[1347]Penal Code § 626.95 (a); see also Penal Code §§ 417 (a)(2), (b), 12025 or 12031.

[1348]Penal Code § 626.95 (c)(2).

[1349]Penal Code § 626.95 (b).

[1350]Penal Code § 12071.4 (g).

[1351]Penal Code § 12071.4 (g).

than 1 year, or both.[1352] If the possession or causation of a firearm in a Federal facility or attempt to do such is coupled with the intent that the firearm or other dangerous weapon be used in the commission of a crime, the punishment is imprisonment for not more than 5 years and a fine, or both.[1353]

The exemption of the first prohibition discussed above include the following persons:[1354]

- the lawful performance of official duties by an officer, agent, or employee of the United States, a State, or a political subdivision thereof, who is authorized by law to engage in or supervise the prevention, detection, investigation, or prosecution of any violation of law[1355]
- the possession of a firearm or other dangerous weapon by a Federal official or a member of the military if such possession is authorized by law[1356]
- the lawful carrying of firearms or other dangerous weapons in a Federal facility incident to hunting or other lawful purposes[1357]

Notice: there is no exemption for those with a carry license, either open carry or CCW.

Federal Courthouse

Absent an exemption, whoever knowingly possesses or causes to be present a firearm or other dangerous weapon in a Federal court facility, or attempts to do so, shall be fined and imprisoned not more than 2 years, or both.[1358]

1352 18 U.S.C. § 930 (a).

1353 18 U.S.C. § 930 (b).

1354 18 U.S.C. § 930 (d).

1355 18 U.S.C. § 930 (d)(1).

1356 18 U.S.C. § 930 (d)(2).

1357 18 U.S.C. § 930 (d)(3).

1358 18 U.S.C. § 930 (e)(1).

Exemptions include:[1359]

- the lawful performance of official duties by an officer, agent, or employee of the United States, a State, or a political subdivision thereof, who is authorized by law to engage in or supervise the prevention, detection, investigation, or prosecution of any violation of law[1360]
- the possession of a firearm or other dangerous weapon by a Federal official or a member of the military if such possession is authorized by law

Notice: there is no exemption for those with a carry license, either open carry or CCW.

A "federal facility," for the purposes of these prohibitions, means a building or part thereof owned or leased by the Federal Government, where Federal employees are regularly present for the purpose of performing their official duties.[1361]

A "dangerous weapon" means a weapon, device, instrument, material, or substance, animate or inanimate, that is used for, or is readily capable of, causing death or serious bodily injury, except that such term does not include a pocket knife with a blade of less than 2 ½ inches in length.[1362]

The term "federal court facility" means the courtroom, judges' chambers, witness rooms, jury deliberation rooms, attorney conference rooms, prisoner holding cells, offices of the court clerks, the United States attorney, and the United States marshal, probation and parole offices, and adjoining corridors of any court of the United States.[1363]

Notice concerning the prohibitions in Federal facility and courthouses shall

---

[1359] 18 U.S.C. § 930 (e)(2).

[1360] 18 U.S.C. § 930 (d)(1).

[1361] 18 U.S.C. § 930 (g)(1).

[1362] 18 U.S.C. § 930 (g)(2).

[1363] 18 U.S.C. § 930 (g)(2).

be posted conspicuously at each public entrance to each facility or courthouse, and no person shall be convicted of an offense with respect to a federal facility if such notice is not posted at such facility, unless the person had actual notice prior to the offense.[1364]

National Parks

The issue regarding firearms in national parks has been in the spotlight over the last few years, and as of February 22, 2010, one may lawfully carry a firearm in national parks and national wildlife refuges just as they would lawfully carry anywhere else in the state. Basically, state law governs.

State Government Buildings

Any person who brings or possesses any firearm within any state or local public building or at any meeting required to be opened to the public[1365] is guilty of a public offense punishable by imprisonment in a county jail for not more than one year, or in the state prison.[1366]

This prohibition does not apply to the following:[1367]

- authorized peace officers,[1368] retired peace officers with a concealed carry permit,[1369] a full-time paid peace officer of another state or federal government on official business, or any person summoned to assist any of the above[1370]
- any person who possesses weapons in, or transports weapons

[1364] 18 U.S.C. § 930 (h).

[1365] See Chapter 9 (commencing with § 54950) of Part 1 of Division 2 of Title 5 of, or Article 9 (commencing with § 11120) of Chapter 1 of Part 1 of Division 3 of Title 2 of, the Government Code.

[1366] Penal Code § 171b (a) and (a)(1).

[1367] Penal Code § 171b (b).

[1368] See Penal Code § 830 et seq.

[1369] See Penal Code § 12027 (a).

[1370] Penal Code § 171b (b)(2)(A).

into, a court of law for use as evidence,[1371] so long as they are not a party to an action pending in a court of law, unless they are a peace officer as described above[1372]

- a person who holds a valid carry license[1373]
- a person with permission to possess that weapon granted in writing by a duly authorized official who is in charge of the security of the state or local government building[1374]
- a person who lawfully resides in, lawfully owns, or is in lawful possession of, that building with respect to those portions of the building that are not owned or leased by the state or local government[1375]
- private investigators or alarm company agents who have been hired by the owner or manager of the building[1376]
- a person who, for the purpose of sale or trade, brings any weapon that may otherwise be lawfully possessed, into a gun show,[1377] or who brings a weapon for the purposes of an authorized public exhibition at a gun show[1378]

A "state or local public building" means a building that meets all of the following criteria:[1379]

- it is a building or part of a building owned or leased by the state or local government, if state or local public employees are

---

[1371]Penal Code § 171b (b)(1).

[1372]Penal Code § 171b (b)(2)(B).

[1373]Penal Code § 171b (b)(3).

[1374]Penal Code § 171b (b)(4).

[1375]Penal Code § 171b (b)(5).

[1376]Penal Code § 171b (b)(6).

[1377]Penal Code § 171b (b)(7)(A); see also Penal Code §§ 12071.1 and 12071.4.

[1378]Penal Code § 171b (b)(7)(B); see also Penal Code §§ 12071.1 and 12071.4.

[1379]Penal Code § 171b (c).

regularly present for the purposes of performing their official duties, and includes, but is not limited to, a building that contains a courtroom[1380]

- it is not also a building or facility, or a part thereof, of any of the following:[1381]
    - state capitol, legislative offices, Governor's office, offices or residence of a constitutional officer, Governor's mansion, other residence of the Governor, residence of the immediate family of any of the above[1382]
    - public or private schools, public or private colleges or universities, playgrounds, and youth centers[1383]
    - it is a building not regularly used, and not intended to be used, by state or local employees as a place of residence[1384]

State Courthouses

Notice that state courthouses are not included specifically in the prohibitions listed above. In California, as a general rule, one with a CCW may carry in a state courthouse. However, most courthouses have a security checkpoint at each public entrance with metal detectors, and most will not allow weapons into the building unless the individual is active law enforcement while on duty. The only courthouses that still allow CCWs to carry while in the building are likely found in rural areas where there are fewer people and firearms are more accepted as a part of life than they are in the urban centers.

Two options exist for state courthouses. First, one can simply lock up his firearm and avoid any hassles altogether. Second, one can call ahead to the courthouse and inquire as to whether CCW holders may utilize the Sheriff's secure storage. Apparently, there are courthouses that do this, including several Los

---

1380 Penal Code § 171b (c)(1).

1381 Penal Code § 171b (c)(2).

1382 Penal Code § 171b (c)(2); see also Penal Code §§ 171c, 171d.

1383 Penal Code § 171b (c)(2); see also Penal Code §§ 626.9, 626.95, and 626.10.

1384 Penal Code § 171b (c)(3).

Angeles courthouses.

For the permit holder who selects the second option, be sure to be discreet about the firearm. It might be best to speak to a security officer prior to passing through the metal detector to inform him about the weapon and its being carried lawfully, and that a call was placed prior to arrival so courthouse authorities would expect the permit holder's arrival at the courthouse, and that the weapon will be placed in the Sheriff's secure storage.

Other State Government Buildings and Related Places

For the purposes of this section on government buildings, which are discussed under two Penal Code Sections,[1385] a firearm shall be deemed loaded whenever both the firearm and the unexpended ammunition capable of being discharged from such firearm are in the immediate possession of the same person.[1386]

In order to determine whether the firearm is loaded or not in enforcing these provisions,[1387] peace officers are authorized to examine any firearm carried by anyone on his person or in a vehicle while in any place or on the grounds of any place in or on which the possession of a loaded firearm is prohibited by the law.[1388] Refusal to allow a peace officer to inspect a firearm in this situation constitutes probable cause for arrest for violation of the law.[1389]

Government Buildings: any person who brings a loaded firearm into, or possesses a loaded firearm within, the State Capitol, any legislative office, any office of the Governor or other constitutional officer, or any hearing room in which any committee of the Senate or Assembly is conducting a hearing, or upon the grounds of the State Capitol,[1390] shall be punished by imprisonment in the county jail for a

---

[1385]Penal Code § 171c and 171d.

[1386]Penal Code § 171e.

[1387]Penal Code § 171c and 171d.

[1388]Penal Code § 171e; see also Penal Code §§ 171c and 171d.

[1389]Penal Code § 171e; see also Penal Code §§ 171c and 171d.

[1390]See Penal Code § 171c for coordinates.

period of not more than one year, a fine of not more than $1000, or both, or by imprisonment in the state prison.[1391]

Persons exempt include:[1392]

- authorized peace officers,[1393] a full-time paid peace officer of another state or federal government on official business, or any person summoned to assist any of the above[1394]
- a member of the military forces of this state or the federal government engaged in the performance of his duties[1395]
- a person who holds a valid carry license[1396]

Residences of Government Officials: any person shall be punished by imprisonment in a county jail for not more than one year, by a fine of not more than $1000, or by both, or by imprisonment in the state prison, if he or she does any of the following:[1397]

- brings a loaded firearm into, or possesses a loaded firearm within, the Governor's Mansion, or any other residence of the Governor, the residence of any other constitutional officer, or the residence of any Member of the Legislature[1398]
- brings a loaded firearm upon, or possesses a loaded firearm upon, the grounds of the Governor's Mansion, or any other residence of the Governor, the residence of the Governor, the residence of any constitutional officer, or the residence of any Member of the Legislature[1399]

[1391] Penal Code § 171c.

[1392] Penal Code § 171c.

[1393] See Penal Code § 830 et seq.

[1394] Penal Code § 171c.

[1395] Penal Code § 171c.

[1396] Penal Code § 171c.

[1397] Penal Code § 171d.

[1398] Penal Code § 171d (a).

[1399] Penal Code § 171d (b).

Persons exempt include:[1400]

- authorized peace officers,[1401] a full-time paid peace officer of another state or federal government on official business, or any person summoned to assist any of the above[1402]
- a member of the military forces of this state or the federal government engaged in the performance of his duties[1403]
- a person who holds a valid carry license[1404]
- the Governor/constitutional officer/Member of the Legislature, or any member of his or her immediate family with the Governor/constitutional officer/Member of the Legislature's permission

Polling Places

Any person in possession of a firearm or any uniformed peace officer, private guard, or security personnel, or any person who is wearing a uniform of a peace officer, private guard, or security personnel, who is stationed in the immediate vicinity of, or posted at, a polling place without written authorization of the appropriate city or county elections official is punishable by a fine not exceeding $10,000, by imprisonment in the state prison for 16 months, two or three years, or in a county jail not exceeding one year, or by both the fine and imprisonment.[1405]

Exempted persons include:[1406]

- armed uniformed guard or security personnel who are at the polling place to cast their vote[1407]

[1400]Penal Code § 171d.

[1401]See Penal Code § 830 et seq.

[1402]Penal Code § 171d.

[1403]Penal Code § 171d.

[1404]Penal Code § 171d.

[1405]Elections Code § 18544 (a).

[1406]Elections Code § 18544 (b).

[1407]Elections Code § 18544 (b)(1).

- a peace officer who is conducting official business in the course and scope of his employment or who is there to cast a vote[1408]
- a private guard or security personnel hired or arranged for by a city or county elections official[1409]
- a private guard or security personnel hired or arranged for by the owner or manager of the facility or property in which the polling place is located so long as that person is hired regularly and not just on days when elections are held[1410]

Notice: those with carry permits do not have an exemption for polling places.

Airports and Airplanes, and Passenger Vessel Terminals

One must be concerned with both federal law and state law when considering airports, airplanes, and passenger vessel terminals.

Under California law, it is unlawful for any person knowingly to possess, within any sterile area of an airport or passenger vessel terminal, any firearm, any frame, receiver, barrel, or magazine of a firearm, and any ammunition.[1411]

Persons who are exempt include:[1412]

- authorized peace officers,[1413] a full-time paid peace officer of another state or federal government on official business, or any person summoned to assist any of the above[1414]
- a member of the military forces of this state or the federal

---

[1408]Elections Code § 18544 (b)(2).

[1409]Elections Code § 18544 (b)(3).

[1410]Elections Code § 18544 (b)(4).

[1411]Penal Code § 171.5 (b), (b)(1), (b)(8), and (b)(12); see also Penal Code § 12316 for definition of ammunition.

[1412]Penal Code § 171.5 (d).

[1413]See Penal Code § 830 et seq.

[1414]Penal Code § 171.5 (d)(1).

government engaged in the performance of his duties[1415]

- a person who has authorization to possess a prohibited weapon,[1416] granted in writing by an airport security coordinator[1417] who is responsible for the security of the airport
- a person, including employees of a licensed contract guard service, authorized to possess a weapon granted in writing by a person discharging the duties of Facility Security Officer or Company Security Officer pursuant to an approved United States Coast Guard facility security plan, and who is responsible for the security of the passenger vessel terminal[1418]

Under California law, violation of this prohibition is a misdemeanor, punishable by time in jail not exceeding six months, or by a fine of no more than $1000, or both.[1419] Under federal law, the punishment can be as serious as five years in prison and a $25,000 penalty, a felony.[1420]

However, nothing in the state law prohibition is intended to affect existing state or federal law regarding the transportation of firearms in airplanes in checked in luggage, or the possession of the prohibited weapons[1421] in areas that are not "sterile areas."[1422]

For the purposes of the prohibitions of firearms at airports, airplanes, and passenger vessel terminals, the following definitions apply:[1423]

1415 Penal Code § 171.5 (d)(1).

1416 See Penal Code § 171.5 (c) for list of prohibited weapons.

1417 See 49 C.F.R. § 1542.3 for those designated as responsible for security at the airport.

1418 Penal Code § 171.5 (d)(3).

1419 Penal Code § 171.5 (e).

1420 See 49 U.S.C. App. 1472 (l).

1421 See Penal Code § 171.5 (c) for a list of prohibited weapons.

1422 Penal Code § 171.5 (g).

1423 Penal Code § 171.5 (a).

- "airport" means an airport, with a secure area, that regularly serves an air carrier holding a certificate issued by the United States Secretary of Transportation[1424]
- "passenger vessel terminal" means only that portion of a harbor or port facility[1425] with a secured area that regularly serves scheduled commuter or passenger operations[1426]
- "sterile area" means a portion of an airport defined in the airport security program to which access generally is controlled through the screening of persons and property,[1427] or a portion of any passenger vessel terminal to which, pursuant to law,[1428] access is generally controlled in a manner consistent with the passenger vessel terminal.[1429]

Important Consideration for Those With Carry Permits Regarding Airports and Passenger Vessel Terminals

An important item to notice about the above laws, exceptions, and exemptions regarding airports and passenger vessel terminals is that those with carry permits, whether open or concealed, are not exempt. In addition, the "sterile area" as defined, could be interpreted and likely would be interpreted as meaning even the "loop" that one drives around when picking up people at the airport. Quite often, cars are subject to a stop and search. Therefore, simply driving into the airport to pick someone up is technically entering a sterile area. Please use caution when visiting an airport and lock up your firearms and transport them as someone who does not have a carry permit would be required under the law.

Amtrak Trains

While there may be some legal authority creating a prohibition on firearms

---

[1424]Penal Code § 171.5 (a)(1).

[1425]See 33 C.F.R. § 105.105 (a)(2) regarding harbor or port facilities.

[1426]Penal Code § 171.5 (a)(2).

[1427]See 49 C.F.R. § 1540.5.

[1428]See 33 C.F.R. §§ 105.255 (a)(1), 105.255 (c)(1), and 105.260 (a).

[1429]Penal Code § 171.5 (a)(3).

and other deadly weapons on Amtrak trains, none was discovered while researching this book. However, research did discover correspondence from Amtrak officials that demonstrated their desire that only "qualified active law enforcement officers employed by a local, state, federal, or railroad law enforcement agency on official business be permitted to carry aboard Amtrak trains." Further, the officials stated that each situation requires prior approval by Amtrak Police.

County Parks and Fairs

Many counties have restrictions and prohibitions regarding firearms and dangerous weapons in county parks or county fairs. Prior to taking any of these items into a county park or fair, it is best to check with local authorities for the latest information. Research for information on this topic revealed that CCW permit holders are not welcome at the Orange County Fair with their weapon.

State Parks

There is not an abundance of authority regarding any prohibitions in California State Parks. However, one can contact the California State Parks - Public Safety Division at (916) 651-0403 and inquire.

At the time of writing this book, it appears that weapons, firearms, and traps are prohibited in California State Parks,[1430] except that there exists limited exemptions for firearms possessed by the following:

- California peace officers who are otherwise permitted to carry firearms
- honorably retired California peace officers with CCW privileges
- California citizens with CCW privileges

This policy may change, so anyone visiting a California State Park should call to inquire before assuming the above policy is still in effect.

Locally Defined Prohibited Areas

Many counties, cities, and other municipalities have local restrictions and prohibitions regarding firearms and dangerous weapons. Prior to taking any of these items into a place that might be considered sensitive to local authorities, it is best

---

[1430]See 14 C.C.R. § 4313.

to check with those authorities for the latest information.

Traps exist for the careless traveler who possesses firearms, and the carry permit holder, whether open or concealed. Not only are there places discussed above with prohibitions, but also consider National Parks, National Forests, land maintained by the Bureau of Land Management (BLM Land), National Monuments, National Historic Trails, National Recreation Areas, National Historic Sites, National Memorials, etc. The list goes on and on. Be sure to inquire with the appropriate authorities before making any assumptions.

Private Businesses That Prohibit Weapons

There is no California law that prohibits carry permit holders from carrying into a private establishment. In fact, even if there is a posting at the door that expressly forbids the weapon, to ignore the sign and enter while carrying is not a violation of law.

However, a person who ignores such a warning may be asked to leave, and any refusal for any reason may lead to an arrest for trespassing.[1431]

[1431]See Penal Code § 602 (o) regarding trespassing after refusing to leave.

Part Eight

Transfer of Firearms in California

CHAPTER SIXTEEN

Transfer of Firearms in California

License Required to Transfer Firearms in California

The main issue regarding the transfer of firearms in California is that the law is designed to prevent non-licensed individuals from conducting a firearms business. In order to prevent this, the California Legislature basically created laws that allow a person without a license to transfer firearms, or transfer a firearm or firearms under other specific exceptions, but only if those transfers are infrequent.

Thus, a very common problem for firearms owners who are not licensed dealers is what to do with the firearm if they no longer wish to keep it, or may no longer possess it for whatever reason. There are several ways to transfer or dispose of a firearm in California when the firearm is no longer wanted.

A "transfer" may be one of several acts. The owner may transfer it through a sale. Or, the owner may want to transfer ownership by way of a gift to another person. In California, as in most states, even a loan of a firearm would be considered a transfer of that firearm.

A "transferor" is the person making the sale, loan, or gift. The "transferee" is the buyer, person being loaned the firearm, or the person to whom the gift is being given.

The general rule In California is no person shall sell, lease, or transfer firearms unless he or she has been issued a license,[1432] and any such person violating this prohibition is guilty of a misdemeanor.

Many of the exceptions still require the person transferring the firearm to go through a licensed firearms dealer and conform to requirements on most deliveries, sales, transfers, or loans of firearms. However, several exceptions allow the transferor to avoid transferring a firearm through a firearms dealer and also allow the transferor to bypass typical regulations, such as the 10 day waiting period and background. This is all discussed in detail below.

[1432]A license pursuant to Penal Code § 12071.

Finally, as discussed elsewhere in this book, there are prohibitions on the transfer of certain types of firearms. This too is discussed at length in this chapter.

Exceptions Allowing Individuals Not Licensed to Transfer Firearms

Exceptions exist that allow individuals not licensed to transfer firearms. Some are free from the requirement that the transfer must be conducted through a licensed firearms dealer. Exceptions apply to the following situations.[1433]

Operation of Law / Court Judgment

The law allows for the sale, lease, or transfer of any firearm by any person acting pursuant to operation of law, a court order, or pursuant to the Enforcement of Judgments Law,[1434] or by a person who liquidates a personal firearm collection to satisfy a court judgment.[1435]

"Operation of law" includes, but is not limited to, the following:[1436]

- the executor or administrator of an estate, if the estate includes firearms[1437]
- a secured creditor or an agent or employee thereof when the firearms are possessed as collateral for, or as the result of, a default under a security agreement under the Commercial Code[1438]
- a levying officer[1439]
- a receiver performing his or her functions as a receiver, if the

---

[1433]Penal Code § 12070 (b).

[1434]See Code of Civil Procedure § 680.010 et seq. (Title 9 Part 2).

[1435]Penal Code § 12070 (b)(1).

[1436]Penal Code § 12070 (c)(2).

[1437]Penal Code § 12070 (c)(2)(A).

[1438]Penal Code § 12070 (c)(2)(B).

[1439]See Code of Civil Procedure §§ 481.140, 511.060, and 680.260 regarding levying officers.

receivership estate includes firearms[1440]

- a trustee in bankruptcy performing his or her duties, if the bankruptcy estate includes firearms[1441]
- an assignee for the benefit of creditors performing his or her functions as an assignee, if the assignment includes firearms[1442]
- a transmutation of property between spouses according to law[1443]
- firearms received by the family of a peace officer or deputy sheriff from a local agency pursuant to law[1444]
- the transfer of a firearm by a law enforcement agency to the person who found the firearm where the delivery is to the person as the finder of the firearm pursuant to law[1445]

Surrender or Sale to Law Enforcement

The surrender or sale of a firearm to a law enforcement agency or other agency in a government buy-back program[1446] will not violate the prohibition of a transfer by an unlicensed individual.[1447] In most cases, the requirement to transfer through a licensed dealer, the ten day waiting period, and the HSC requirement will not apply.[1448]

[1440]Penal Code § 12070 (c)(2)(D).

[1441]Penal Code § 12070 (c)(2)(E).

[1442]Penal Code § 12070 (c)(2)(F).

[1443]Penal Code § 12070 (c)(2)(G); see also Family Code § 850.

[1444]Penal Code § 12070 (c)(2)(H); see also Government Code § 50081.

[1445]Penal Code § 12070 (c)(2)(I); see also Article 1 (commencing with § 2080) of Chapter 4 of Division 3 of the Civil Code.

[1446]See Penal Code § 12078 (a)(3).

[1447]Penal Code § 12070 (b)(2); see also Penal Code §§ 12078 (a)(3), 186.22a (e), and 12028.

[1448]Penal Code § 12078 (a)(6).

Intestate Succession

The sale, lease, or transfer of a firearm by a person who obtains title to the firearm by intestate succession or by bequest or as a surviving spouse is permitted,[1449] provided the person disposes of the firearm within 60 days of receipt of the firearm.[1450]

Infrequent Sale / Transfer

As stated above, the general rule In California is that no person shall sell, lease, or transfer firearms unless he or she has been issued a license,[1451] and any such person violating this prohibition is guilty of a misdemeanor.[1452] However, this prohibition does not include the infrequent sale, lease, or transfer of firearms.[1453]

The infrequent sale of a firearm that is a pistol, revolver, or other firearm capable of being concealed upon the person is any transfer, so long as the transferee does not transfer more than six firearm transactions per calendar year (between January 1 and December 31).[1454] A "transaction" is a single sale, lease, or transfer of any number of pistols, revolvers, or other firearms capable of being concealed upon the person.[1455] For any firearms that are not pistols, revolvers, or other firearms capable of being concealed upon the person, infrequent means "occasional and without regularity."[1456]

So, regarding handguns, one may actually transfer more than six firearms in a year, so long as there are no more than six transactions, and all other laws

---

[1449] See Chapter 1 (commencing with § 13500) of Part 2 of Division 8 of the Probate Code.

[1450] Penal Code § 12070 (b)(3).

[1451] A license pursuant to Penal Code § 12071.

[1452] Penal Code § 12070 (a).

[1453] Penal Code § 12070 (b)(4).

[1454] Penal Code § 12070 (c)(1)(A).

[1455] Penal Code § 12070 (c)(1)(A).

[1456] Penal Code § 12070 (c)(1)(B).

regarding the transfer or firearms are respected.

Obviously, the rule regarding firearms that are not handguns and the like is vague and open to interpretation, as the transactions must be occasional and without regularity. If the transactions of long guns would be legal if the firearms in question were pistols, revolvers, etc., then it is likely a safe bet that the transactions in question were lawful. However, it may be best to consult a competent attorney for advice, as exceptions to the infrequent transfer laws may apply to the situation.[1457]

Gun Show Traders

The sale, lease, or transfer of used firearms other than handguns, which includes pistols, revolvers, or other firearms capable of being concealed upon the person, at gun shows or events[1458] by a person other than a licensee or dealer are permitted, provided the person has a valid federal firearms license (FFL) and a current certificate of eligibility issued by the DOJ,[1459] and provided all the sales, leases, or transfers comply with specific provisions of law.[1460] This means that neither party to the transaction holds a California issued dealer's license,[1461] and the parties to the transaction complete the sale, loan, or transfer through a licensed firearms dealer.[1462]

The person who utilizes this exception may not participate in such deals at more than 12 gun shows or events in any calender year and shall not sell, lease, or transfer more than 15 used firearms other than pistols, revolvers, or other firearms capable of being concealed upon the person at any single gun show or event.[1463] Also, in no event shall the person sell more than 75 used firearms other

---

[1457]Penal Code § 12070 (c)(1)(B).

[1458]Pursuant to Penal Code § 12071.

[1459]Pursuant to Penal Code § 12071.

[1460]See Penal Code § 12072 (d).

[1461]See Penal Code § 12071.

[1462]Penal Code § 12070 (b)(5); see also Penal Code § 12082.

[1463]Penal Code § 12070 (b)(5).

than pistols, revolvers, or other firearms capable of being concealed upon the person in any calendar year.[1464]

The person that fits into this exception is known as a "Gun Show Trader."[1465] A "used firearm," in regards to gun show traders, means a firearm that has been previously sold at retail and is more than three years old.[1466]

<u>Importers and Manufacturers of Firearms</u>

Deliveries, sales, or transfers of firearms between or to importers and manufacturers of firearms licensed to engage in business under federal law[1467] are not prohibited.[1468] Also, the sale, delivery, or transfer of firearms by manufacturers or importers properly licensed under federal law[1469] are not prohibited.[1470]

<u>Transfers Involving Law Enforcement</u>

Deliveries and transfers of firearms, or surrender thereof, to law enforcement agencies, or between law enforcement agencies, or otherwise according to law when a party is a law enforcement agency, are not subject to the prohibitions under the law.[1471] Transfers of firearms to paid, full-time police officers who are properly identified are not required to be held for the ten-day waiting

---

[1464]Penal Code § 12070 (b)(5).

[1465]Penal Code § 12070 (b)(5).

[1466]Penal Code § 12070 (b)(5).

[1467]See Chapter 44 (commencing with § 921) of Title 18 of the United States Code and the regulations issued pursuant thereto.

[1468]Penal Code § 12070 (b)(6).

[1469]See Chapter 44 (commencing with § 921) of Title 18 of the United States Code and the regulations issued pursuant thereto as it pertains to dealers or wholesalers.

[1470]Penal Code § 12070 (b)(7).

[1471]Penal Code § 12070 (b)(8); see also Penal Code §§ 12028, 12028.5, and 12030.

period, and do not require the presentation of a Handgun Safety Certificate.[1472] Some other officers are also exempt from either the ten-day wait or the HSC requirement, see the Penal Code for details.[1473]

Loans of Firearms for Target Shooting

The loan of a firearm for the purposes of shooting at targets; if the loan occurs on the premises of a target facility which holds a business or regulatory license or on the premises of any club or organization organized for the purposes of practicing shooting at targets upon established ranges, whether public or private, if the firearm is at all times kept within the premises of the target range or on the premises of the club or organization.[1474]

Further, the infrequent loan of firearms between persons who are personally known to each other for any lawful purpose, so long as the loan does not exceed 30 days in duration, is allowed.[1475]

However, if the loan is for a lawful purpose, the person or firearms facility loaning the firearm is in the presence of the person being loaned the firearm at all times, the loan does not exceed 3 days in duration, the person receiving the firearm is not in a prohibited class, is 18 years of age or older, and the person loaning the firearm is 18 years of age or older, the requirement to transfer through a licensed dealer, as well as the HSC requirement, do not apply.[1476]

Manufacturers, Importers, and Wholesalers Under Federal Law

Sales, deliveries, or transfers of firearms by manufacturers, importers, or

---

[1472]Penal Code § 12078 (a)(1) through (5); see also Penal Code § 12801 regarding the Handgun Safety Certificate requirement.

[1473]Penal Code § 12078 (a)(2) through (6).

[1474]Penal Code § 12070 (b)(9); see also Penal Code § 12078 (h).

[1475]Penal Code § 12078 (d)(1).

[1476]Penal Code § 12078 (d)(2) and (h).

wholesalers properly licensed under federal law[1477] to persons who reside outside this state who are also licensed under federal law[1478] are not prohibited if the sale, delivery, or transfer is in accordance with federal law,[1479] or transfers going the other direction, if in accordance with federal law.[1480]

Transfers Between Those in the Firearms Business

Sales, deliveries, or transfers of firearms by wholesalers to dealers are not prohibited.[1481] Also, the delivery, sale, or transfer of an unloaded firearm by one wholesaler to another wholesaler if that firearm is intended as merchandise in the receiving wholesaler's business is not prohibited.[1482]

Sales by Out of State Transferors to Licensed Dealers

Sales, deliveries, or transfers of firearms by persons who reside outside this state to persons licensed in California[1483] are not prohibited if the sale, delivery, or transfer is in accordance with federal law.[1484] This includes transfers, sales, or deliveries going out of state as well.[1485]

1477 See Chapter 44 (commencing with § 921) of Title 18 of the United States Code and the regulations issued pursuant thereto.

1478 See Chapter 44 (commencing with § 921) of Title 18 of the United States Code and the regulations issued pursuant thereto.

1479 Penal Code § 12070 (b)(10); see also Chapter 44 (commencing with § 921) of Title 18 of the United States Code and the regulations issued pursuant thereto.

1480 Penal Code § 12070 (b)(11); see also Chapter 44 (commencing with § 921) of Title 18 of the United States Code and the regulations issued pursuant thereto.

1481 Penal Code § 12070 (b)(12).

1482 Penal Code § 12070 (b)(15).

1483 See Penal Code § 12071.

1484 Penal Code § 12070 (b)(13); see also Chapter 44 (commencing with § 921) of Title 18 of the United States Code and the regulations issued pursuant thereto.

1485 Penal Code § 12070 (b)(14); see also See Chapter 44 (commencing with § 921) of Title 18 of the United States Code and the regulations issued pursuant thereto.

Entertainment Prop Loans

The prohibitions on transfers, sales, and loans does not apply to loans of an unloaded firearm or the loan of a firearm loaded with blank cartridges for use solely as a prop for a motion picture, television, or video production or entertainment or theatrical event.[1486] Quite often, loans for entertainment purposes need not be conducted through a dealer and may not be subject to the ten-day waiting period or the HSC requirement, so long as the loans are infrequent.[1487]

Curio and Relic

The prohibitions do not include the delivery of an unloaded firearm that is a curio or relic[1488] by a person licensed as a collector under federal law[1489] who holds a current certificate of eligibility issued pursuant to California law.[1490]

Generally, firearms that are considered antique or curio/relic firearms are freely transferable; that is, they need not be transferred through a licensed dealer and are not subject to the ten-day waiting period, so long as they are not handguns and at least 50 years old.[1491] Be careful, as replicas of curio/relic firearms are required to be transferred through a dealer with the applicable ten-day waiting period.[1492] Transfers must be infrequent.[1493]

[1486]Penal Code § 12070 (b)(16).

[1487]Penal Code § 12078 (s).

[1488]As defined in 27 C.F.R. § 478.11.

[1489]See Chapter 44 (commencing with § 921) of Title 18 of the United States Code and the regulations issued pursuant thereto.

[1490]Penal Code § 12070 (b)(17); see also Penal Code § 12071 regarding certificate of eligibility.

[1491]Penal Code § 12078 (t)(1).

[1492]Penal Code § 12078 (t)(2).

[1493]Penal Code § 12078 (t)(2).

Private Party Transfers Through a Firearms Dealer

A person shall complete any sale, loan,[1494] or transfer of a firearm through a person licensed[1495] in order to complete the transfer according to law when neither party is licensed.[1496] This is commonly known as a "private party transfer."

All formalities that exist and are required by law for purchases of firearms by those not licensed from licensed dealers must be recognized and followed in a private party transfer. All the same paperwork will be processed, and even the dealer will hold the firearm for the mandatory 10 day waiting period, at which time it may be delivered barring any other reasons why it may not be delivered.[1497]

Keep in mind, that a dealer who does not sell, transfer, or keep an inventory of handguns is not required by law to process private party transfers of handguns.[1498]

Finally, a violation of any of the laws regarding private party transfers[1499] is a misdemeanor.[1500]

Fees for Transfer of Firearm by Private Parties

Either the transferor or transferee may be required by the dealer to pay a fee not to exceed $10 per firearm, and no other fees may be demanded unless

---

[1494] This does not include loans where they are otherwise allowed by law, as discussed throughout this book.

[1495] See Penal Code § 12071 regarding persons licensed to transfer firearms.

[1496] Penal Code § 12082 (a); see also Penal Code § 12072 (d) regarding transfers, sales, or loans between two persons who are unlicensed.

[1497] Penal Code § 12082 (a); see also Penal Code § 12072 (d) regarding waiting period.

[1498] Penal Code § 12082 (c).

[1499] Pursuant to Penal Code § 12082.

[1500] Penal Code § 12082 (d).

pursuant to law[1501] and forwarded to the DOJ.[1502] If a dealer elects to, he may charge a smaller fee or no fee at all.[1503]

Inability to Legally Deliver Firearm

If the dealer is unable to deliver legally the firearm to the purchaser or transferee or the person being loaned the firearm, the dealer shall, without waiting for the conclusion of the waiting period,[1504] return the firearm to the transferor, unless doing so would violate the law against the transfer of a firearm to a prohibited person.[1505]

In the case where the dealer cannot give the firearm to the intended transferee, and is prohibited from returning it to the original transferor, the dealer must deliver the firearm to the sheriff or other local authorities who shall then dispose of the firearm according to law.[1506]

Regulations for Private Party Transfer Established by Attorney General

The Attorney General adopts regulations to do all of the following:[1507]

- allow the seller or transferor to complete a sale, loan, or transfer through a dealer, and allow such person and the dealer to comply with requirements in the law regarding transfers[1508] and to

---

[1501] See Penal Code §§ 12076, 12076.5, 12088.9, and 12805 regarding allowable additional fees to be forwarded to DOJ.

[1502] Penal Code § 12082 (a).

[1503] Penal Code § 12082 (a).

[1504] See Penal Code §§ 12071 and 12072.

[1505] Penal Code § 12082 (a); see also Penal Code § 12072 (a) regarding transfer of firearm to prohibited person.

[1506] Penal Code § 12082 (a); see also Penal Code §§ 12028 and 12032 regarding disposal of firearm by law enforcement according to law.

[1507] Penal Code § 12082 (b).

[1508] See Penal Code §§ 12071, 12072, 12076, and 12077 regarding transfers.

preserve the confidentiality of those records[1509]

- where a personal handgun importer is selling or transferring a pistol, revolver, or other firearm capable of being concealed upon the person to comply with the law regarding private party transfers,[1510] where the firearm cannot be delivered to the transferee and must be returned to the personal handgun importer, the DOJ will have sufficient information about that personal handgun importer so that a record of his or her ownership can be maintained in the registry as provided by law[1511]
- ensure that the register or record of electronic transfer shall state the name and address of the transferor of the firearm and whether or not the person is a personal handgun importer, in addition to any other information required by law[1512]

Other Instances Where Firearms Transfer May Occur Without a Licensed Firearms Dealer

Transfers Between Immediate Family Members

Transfers between immediate family members are permitted without going through a licensed firearms dealer.[1513] "Immediate family members" include parent and child, and grandparent and grandchild.[1514] The transfers must be infrequent.[1515] If the firearm is a handgun, the person taking possession must, within 30 days of receipt of the firearm, properly register the handgun by notifying the DOJ with all required information, and the person must have an HSC, as well as be 18 years of

1509Penal Code § 12082 (b)(1).

1510See Penal Code § 12072 (f)(2)(A)(ii).

1511Penal Code 12082 (b)(2); see also Penal Code § 11106 (c).

1512Penal Code § 12082 (b)(3); see also Penal Code § 12077 regarding additional information required.

1513See Penal Code § 12078 (c).

1514Penal Code § 12078 (3)(A) and (B).

1515Penal Code § 12078 (c)(1) and (2).

age or older.[1516]

California law also allows an immediate family member who resides out-of-state to bequest a non-approved handgun to a family member who resides in California, provided the magazine capacity does not exceed ten rounds and is accompanied by a letter stating the intent of the family member who resides out-of-state. The DOJ still requires the handgun be registered pursuant to law.

Transfers Between Spouses

A person may transfer a firearm to his or her spouse by changing the nature of the property from community property to separate property, or separate property to community property, or even one spouse's separate property to the other spouse's separate property, as allowed by law through what is called "transmutation."[1517] In order for the transmutation to be upheld if challenged, the transferring spouse must sign in writing consenting to the transfer and change in status of their property.

After the death of one spouse, the firearms will pass to the surviving spouse, and need not be transferred through a firearms dealer.[1518]

In either of these situations, however, the spouse must report the transfer and provide all required information to the DOJ within 30 days of taking possession of the firearm and must pay the applicable fees, if any.[1519] The HSC is required if the firearm is a handgun, as well as registration with the DOJ.[1520]

Transfers to Historical Societies and Museums

The state or federal government, and even private citizens, may transfer

---

[1516]Penal Code § 12078 (c)(2)(A) through (C).

[1517]Penal Code § 12078 (l) and (u)(2)(G); see also Family Code §§ 850 and 852 regarding transmutation.

[1518]Penal Code § 12078 (c) and (u)(2)(H); see also Probate Code § 13500 et seq.

[1519]Penal Code § 12078.

[1520]Penal Code § 12078.

firearms to historical societies and museums without going through a licensed firearms dealer, and need not comply with the law regarding the background check and ten day waiting period, subject to certain conditions.[1521]

Sales Out of State to Those Properly Licensed

A person may transfer a firearm to a person outside California who is licensed under federal law (FFL), so long as the transfer is in accordance with federal law.[1522]

Firearms Turned in for Service or Repair

Firearms transferred for service or repair or not required to be transferred through a licensed dealer, and also are not subject to the ten-day waiting period or the HSC requirement.[1523]

Importers and Manufacturers

Transactions regarding firearms between importers and manufacturers are not required to be conducted through a licensed firearms dealer and are not subject to the ten-day waiting period or the HSC requirement.[1524]

Loans Between Hunters

The requirement that transfers be conducted through a licensed dealer does not apply to loans of a firearm that is not a handgun to a licensed hunter for use by that person for a period of time not to exceed the duration of the hunting season for which that firearm is to be used.[1525]

[1521] Penal Code § 12078 (a)(7) and (8); see same for list of conditions on transfer.

[1522] Penal Code § 12078 (f); see also Chapter 44 (commencing with Section 921) of Title 18 of the United States Code regarding persons licensed under federal law and requirements under federal law on firearms transfers.

[1523] Penal Code § 12078 (e).

[1524] Penal Code § 12078 (b).

[1525] Penal Code § 12078 (q).

Part Nine

Buying Firearms, Firearms Safety Devices, and Firearms Safes in California

CHAPTER SEVENTEEN

Buying Firearms in California

In California, between the years 1982 and 2004, the average firearm denial rate for transactions processed was 1%.[1526] Despite that, the prospective buyer needs to read this chapter carefully and comply with all laws and regulations when buying firearms in California.

Handguns

In California, no handgun may be delivered unless the purchaser, transferee, or person being loaned the firearm presents documentation indicating that he or she is a California resident.[1527] Dealers will keep a copy of this documentation, which may be proven by providing either a utility bill from the last three months, a residential lease, a property deed, or military permanent duty station orders indicating assignment within the state.[1528]

Other statutory requirements for buying a handgun include the requirements that the potential handgun buyer first obtain a "Handgun Safety Certificate" often referred to as an "HSC," as well as successfully completing the "Safe Handling Demonstration."

The HSC is absolutely required to purchase a handgun in any transaction. There is no way around it, as the law states that no person shall purchase or receive any handgun, aside from an antique firearm, without a valid HSC.[1529]

One selling, loaning, or transferring a handgun ought to be certain the person he is transferring the handgun to has an HSC. The law states that no person shall sell, deliver, loan, or transfer any handgun, aside from an antique firearm, to any

---

[1526] Department of Justice Statistics.

[1527] Penal Code § 12071 (b)(8)(C).

[1528] Penal Code § 12071 (b)(8)(C).

[1529] Penal Code § 12801 (b)(1); see also 18 U.S.C. § 921 regarding antique firearms.

person who does not have a valid HSC.[1530] Note that this law even applies to loans of handguns.

The Safe Handling demonstration is also required when buying any handgun. No firearms dealer may deliver a handgun unless the recipient performs a safe handling demonstration with that handgun.[1531] The details of this requirement are outlined in the section following the HSC requirements below.

A violation of any of the above laws is a misdemeanor.[1532]

Handgun Safety Certificate, or "HSC"

It is the intent of the Legislature to require that persons who obtain handguns have a basic familiarity with those firearms, including, but not limited to, the safe handling and storage of those firearms.[1533] It is important to note, however, that it is not the intent of the Legislature to require an HSC for the mere possession of a firearm.[1534]

Since January 1, 2003, the law has been that no handgun shall be delivered unless the purchaser, transferee, or person being loaned a handgun presents an HSC.[1535] It is important to note that no HSC will be issued to any person who is under the age of 18.[1536]

An instruction manual, written in both English and Spanish, is provided by the legislature to the firearms dealers, who in turn will make it available to the

---

[1530]Penal Code § 12801 (b)(2); see also 18 U.S.C. § 921 regarding antique firearms.

[1531]Penal Code § 12071 (b)(8)(D).

[1532]Penal Code § 12801 (c).

[1533]Penal Code § 12800.

[1534]Penal Code § 12800.

[1535]Penal Code § 12072(c)(5)(B).

[1536]Penal Code § 12803 (b).

general public.[1537] The test will also be provided by the legislature, and be in both English and Spanish.[1538] Should a person taking a test be illiterate, the examination will be administered orally.[1539] Further, if the person taking the test is unable to read English or Spanish, the test may be applied orally by a translator.[1540]

Topics covered by the test will cover, at a minimum:[1541]

- the laws applicable to carrying and handling firearms, particularly handguns
- the responsibilities of ownership of firearms, particularly handguns
- current law as it relates to the private sale and transfer of firearms
- current laws as it relates to the permissible use of lethal force;
- what constitutes safe firearm storage
- issues associated with bringing a handgun into the home
- prevention strategies to address issues associated with bringing a firearm into the home

An applicant for an HSC shall successfully pass the multiple-choice test with a passing grade of at least 75%, and any person receiving a passing grade on the test shall immediately be issued an HSC by the instructor.[1542] An applicant who fails to pass the test on the first attempt will be given additional instructional materials by the instructor, such as a videotape or a booklet.[1543] The person must wait at least 24 hours before attempting the test a second time, and the second test will be a different version of the test and must be administered by the same instructor absent permission by the department upon a showing of good cause.[1544]

[1537]Penal Code § 12804 (a).

[1538]Penal Code § 12804 (c)(1).

[1539]Penal Code § 12804 (c)(1).

[1540]Penal Code § 12804 (c)(2).

[1541]Penal Code § 12804 (c)(1)(A) through (G).

[1542]Penal Code § 12805 (a).

[1543]Penal Code § 12805 (b).

[1544]Penal Code § 12805 (b).

HSC Exam Fees

Fees for the exam may include a charge of $25 by the certified instructor.[1545] $10 of this fee goes to the instructor, and $15 goes to the DOJ.[1546] Renewals of the HSC, which expires after five years from the date it is issued, come at a cost of $25 as well.[1547] If you lose your HSC, it may be replaced by the issuing instructor at a cost of $15.[1548]

Personal information that will appear on the HSC include a unique HSC identification number, the holder's full name, date of birth, drivers license or state identification number, the holder's signature, the signature of the issuing instructor, and the date of issuance.[1549]

There are many individuals that, when properly identified, are exempted from the HSC requirements.[1550] Individuals that are exempt from the HSC requirement are also exempt from the Safe Handling Demonstration.[1551]

Exemptions to the HSC

Individuals that are exempt from the HSC requirements are as follows:[1552]

- any active or honorably retired peace officers
- any active or honorably retired federal peace officers
- any reserve peace officer
- any person who has successfully completed course of training for

---

[1545]Penal Code § 12805 (c).

[1546]Penal Code § 12805 (c) and (e).

[1547]Penal Code §§ 12805 (d); 12806 (b).

[1548]Penal Code § 12808.

[1549]Penal Code § 12806 (a)(1) through (7).

[1550]Penal Code § 12807 (a).

[1551]Penal Code § 12071 (b)(8)(J).

[1552]Penal Code § 12807 (a)(1) through (12).

peace officers[1553]

- a firearms dealer licensed in the state who is acting in the course and scope of his or her activities as a person licensed to deal in firearms
- a federally licensed collector who is acquiring or being loaned a handgun that is a curio or relic under federal law[1554]
- a person to whom a handgun is being returned, where the person receiving the firearm is the owner of the firearm
- a family member of a fallen peace officer or deputy sheriff from a local agency who receives a firearm as part of the personal effects carried in the line of duty by the officer (such firearm will likely be made inoperable)[1555]
- any individual who has a valid concealed weapons permit
- an active, or honorably retired member of the United States Armed Forces, National Guard, Air National Guard, or any reserve component of the United States
- any person who is authorized to carry loaded firearms as a patrol special police officer, animal control officers and zookeepers, harbor police officers, guards or messengers of common carriers, banks, etc., private investigators, private patrol operators, uniformed security guards, night watch persons, and uniformed alarm agents[1556]
- persons who are holders of a special weapons permit issued by the DOJ, such as those permitted to deal with short barreled shotguns, short barreled rifles, and machineguns[1557]

There are also exceptions for taking title or possession of a handgun by operation of law in a representative capacity.[1558] However, if the person wishes to transfer title ownership of the handguns to himself in a personal capacity, he will

---

[1553]See Penal Code § 832.

[1554]See 27 C.F.R. § 478.11.

[1555]See Government Code § 50081.

[1556]See Penal Code § 12031 (c) and (d).

[1557]See Penal Code §§ 12095, 12230, 12250, and 12305.

[1558]Penal Code § 12807 (b).

need an HSC first.[1559] These individuals include:[1560]

- the executor or administrator of an estate
- a secured creditor or an agent or employee thereof when the firearms are possessed as collateral for, or as a result of, or an agent or employee thereof when the firearms are possessed as collateral for, or as a result of, a default under a security agreement under the Commercial Code
- a levying officer[1561]
- a receiver performing his or her functions as a receiver
- a trustee in bankruptcy performing his or her duties
- an assignee for the benefit of creditors performing his or her functions as an assignee

Prohibited Acts Regarding the HSC

There are some prohibited acts regarding HSCs. Any person who alters, counterfeits, or falsifies an HSC, or who uses or attempts to use any altered, counterfeited, or falsified HSC to purchase a handgun is guilty of a misdemeanor.[1562] Also, no person may commit an act of collusion.[1563] An act of collusion is a violation that shall be punished by imprisonment in a county jail not exceeding one year or in the state prison, or by a fine not to exceed $1,000, or both.[1564] Collusion may be any of the following:[1565]

- answering a test applicant's questions during an objective test relating to firearms safety
- knowingly grading the examination falsely
- providing an advance copy of the test to the applicant
- taking or allowing another person to take the basic firearms safety

---

[1559] Penal Code § 12807 (b).

[1560] Penal Code § 12807 (b)(1) through (6).

[1561] See Code of Civil Procedure §§ 481.140, 511.060, or 680.260.

[1562] Penal Code § 12802 (b).

[1563] Penal Code §§ 12802 (a); 12072 (e).

[1564] Penal Code §§ 12072 (g)(3) and 12072 (g)(3)(A).

[1565] Penal Code § 12072 (e)(1) through (9).

course for one who is the applicant for a basic firearms safety certificate or handgun safety certificate

- allowing another to take the objective test for the applicant, purchaser, or transferee
- using or allowing another to use one's identification, proof of residency, or thumbprint
- allowing others to give unauthorized assistance during an examination
- reference to unauthorized materials during the examination and cheating by the applicant
- providing originals or photocopies of the objective test, or any version thereof, to any person other than as authorized by the department

Safe Handling Demonstration

As stated above, no firearms dealer may deliver a handgun unless the recipient performs a safe handling demonstration with that handgun.[1566] The purchaser shall perform the safe handling demonstration for a department-certified instructor.[1567]

The demonstration shall commence with the handgun unloaded and locked with the firearm safety device with which it is required to be delivered, if applicable.[1568] While maintaining muzzle awareness, that is, the firearm is pointed in a safe direction, preferably down at the ground, and while maintaining trigger discipline, which is the trigger finger remaining outside of the trigger guard and along the side of the handgun frame at all times, the handgun recipient shall correctly and safely perform the following:[1569]

- If the handgun is a semiautomatic pistol:
  - remove the magazine
  - lock the slide back; if the model of firearm does not

[1566]Penal Code § 12071 (b)(8)(D).

[1567]Penal Code § 12071 (b)(8)(G).

[1568]Penal Code § 12071 (b)(8)(D).

[1569]Penal Code § 12071 (b)(8)(D), (b)(8)(D)(i)(I) through (XII), (b)(8)(D)(ii)(VIII), and (b)(8)(D)(iii)(I) through (VII).

allow the slide to be locked back, pull the slide back, visually and physically check the chamber to ensure that it is clear

- visually and physically inspect the chamber to ensure that the handgun is unloaded
- remove the firearm safety device, if applicable. If the firearm safety device prevents any of the previous steps, remove the device during the appropriate step
- load one bright orange, red, or other readily identifiable dummy round into the magazine. An empty cartridge casing with an empty primer pocket may be used instead
- insert the magazine into the magazine well of the firearm
- manipulate the slide release or pull back and release the slide
- remove the magazine
- visually inspect the chamber to reveal that a round can be chambered with the magazine removed
- lock the slide back to eject the dummy round. If the slide does not lock, check to ensure that the chamber is unloaded.
- apply the safety, if applicable
- apply the firearms safety device, if applicable

- If the handgun is a double-action revolver:
    - open the cylinder
    - visually and physically inspect each chamber to ensure that the revolver is unloaded
    - remove the firearm safety device, if applicable. If the firearm safety device prevents any of the previous steps, remove the device during the appropriate step
    - while maintaining muzzle awareness and trigger discipline, load a dummy round into a chamber of the cylinder and rotate the cylinder so that the round is in the next-to-fire position
    - close the cylinder
    - open the cylinder and eject the round
    - visually and physically inspect each chamber to ensure that the revolver is unloaded
    - apply the firearm safety device, if applicable
- If the handgun is a single-action revolver
    - open the loading gate

- visually and physically inspect each chamber to ensure the firearm is unloaded
- remove the firearm safety device, if applicable. If the firearm safety device prevents any of the previous steps, remove the device during the appropriate step
- load a dummy round into the cylinder. Close the loading gate and rotate the cylinder so that the round is in the next-to-fire position
- open the loading gate and unload the revolver
- visually and physically inspect each chamber to ensure that the revolver is unloaded
- apply the firearm safety device, if applicable

Also during this process, the purchaser of the handgun shall receive instruction regarding how to render that handgun safe in the event of a jam.[1570]

Please note that no demonstration will be required if the dealer is returning the handgun to the owner of that handgun.[1571] The firearms dealer shall sign, date, and keep on file as proof of compliance an affidavit stating that the requirements of the safe handling demonstration have been met.[1572] The purchaser must also sign the affidavit.[1573]

Department-Certified Instructor

To administer the safe handling demonstration, as well as administer the HSC test and issue an HSC to one who passed the test, one must be a department-certified instructor and meet the requirements as set forth by the Department of Justice.[1574]

[1570]Penal Code § 12071 (b)(7)(J).

[1571]Penal Code § 12071 (b)(8)(H).

[1572]Penal Code § 12071 (b)(7)(F).

[1573]Penal Code § 12071 (b)(7)(F).

[1574]Penal Code § 12071 (b)(7)(I); see also Penal Code § 12804.

Firearm Safety Devices

All firearms, including handguns, that are sold or transferred in this state by a licensed firearms dealer, including private party transfers through a dealer, and all firearms manufactured in this state, shall include or be accompanied by a firearms safety device that is listed on the Department of Justice's roster of approved firearms safety devices, and that is identified as appropriate for that firearm by reference to either the manufacturer and model of the firearm, or to the physical characteristics of the firearm that match those listed on the roster for use with the device.[1575] Exceptions to this rule do exist, particularly if you own a gun safe that is certified by the Department of Justice.[1576] Please see Chapter Eighteen for more on firearms safety devices and safes and the exceptions.

One Handgun Every 30 Days

No person shall make an application to purchase more than one pistol, revolver, or other firearm capable of being concealed upon the person ("handgun") within any 30-day period.[1577]

Exceptions exist for the following:[1578]

- any law enforcement agency
- any agency duly authorized to perform law enforcement duties
- any state or local correctional facility
- any private security company licensed to do business in California
- any person who is properly identified as a full time paid peace officer,[1579] and who is authorized to, and does carry a firearm during the course and scope of his or her employment as a peace officer
- any motion picture, television, or video production company or entertainment or theatrical company whose production by its nature involves the use of a firearm

---

1575 Penal Code § 12088.1 (a).

1576 Penal Code § 12088.1 (d) and (e).

1577 Penal Code § 12072 (a)(9).

1578 Penal Code § 12072 (a)(9)(B)(i) through (xii).

1579 See Penal Code § 830 et seq.

- any person who may receive it through an infrequent transfer by gift, bequest, intestate succession, or other means by one individual to another if both individuals are members of the same immediate family (parent and child or grandparent and grandchild), so long as the person taking possession files a report with the DOJ that includes information concerning himself or herself, how title was obtained and from whom, and a description of the firearm in question, the person has the required HSC, and the person is at least 18 years of age or older[1580]
- any loan transaction conducted through a licensed firearms dealer
- any person who is a licensed collector pursuant to 18 U.S.C. § 921 et seq., and who has a current certificate of eligibility issued to him or her by the DOJ[1581]
- the exchange of a handgun where the dealer purchased that firearm from the person seeking the exchange within the 30-day period immediately preceding the date of exchange or replacement
- the replacement of a handgun where the original purchase was lost or stolen, and the person reported that firearm lost or stolen prior to the completion of the new application to purchase
- the return of any handgun to the person or its owner

Violations of 30-Day Law

A first violation of the one handgun per 30-day law, such as an attempt to purchase two handguns within 30 days, is considered an infraction and punishable by a fine of $50.[1582] A second violation is also an infraction, but punishable by a fine of $100.[1583] A third and any subsequent violation is a misdemeanor.[1584] Each and every attempt to purchase in violation of this law is considered a separate

---

[1580]See Penal Code § 12078 (c)(2) and (3).

[1581]See Penal Code § 12071.

[1582]Penal Code § 12072 (g)(5)(A).

[1583]Penal Code § 12072 (g)(5)(B).

[1584]Penal Code § 12072 (g)(5)(C).

offense.[1585]

Dealers may not deliver the handgun to a person in violation of this law, and will be notified of such by the DOJ if an individual is determined to have applied to purchase more than one handgun in 30 days.[1586]

Shotguns and Rifles

An HSC is not required for the purchase of a shotgun or rifle. Also, shotguns and rifles are not subject to any requirement that a buyer may only buy one every thirty days.

Other Requirements When Purchasing a Firearms

Waiting Period

No firearm shall be delivered within 10 days of the application to purchase.[1587] The way the 10 days is calculated is by taking the time that the application is complete, and counting out ten 24-hour periods. At that point, the purchaser may take possession of his purchase. If the DOJ sends the application back due to a deficiency in the application, an incomplete fee is not paid, etc., the 10 day waiting period restarts once the corrections are made or fee is paid.[1588] During the ten-day waiting period, the DOJ will conduct the background checks.

Identification for Proof of Identify, Age, and Residency

As discussed above, to purchase a handgun, you must be at least 21 years of age, and you must be 18 years of age to purchase a rifle or shotgun.[1589] No dealer shall deliver a firearm to a person unless that person presents clear evidence of his

---

[1585] Penal Code § 12072 (g)(5)(D).

[1586] Penal Code § 12072 (c)(6).

[1587] Penal Code § 12071 (b)(3) and (b)(3)(A).

[1588] Penal Code § 12071 (b)(3)(A).

[1589] Penal Code § 12072 (b).

or her identity and age.[1590] "Clear evidence of his or her identity and age" may be either a valid California driver's license or a valid California identification card as issued by the Department of Motor Vehicles.[1591]

Background Checks

The department shall examine its records, as well as those records that it is authorized to request from the State Department of Mental Health, in order to determine if the purchaser is prohibited by state or federal law from possessing, receiving, owning, or purchasing a firearm.[1592] The DOJ will also participate in the National Instant Criminal Background Check System ("NICS"), and if a person is determined to be prohibited from acquiring a firearm under federal law, the DOJ will notify local authorities of the potential sale and will notify the dealer that the sale may not go through.[1593]

Background Check Fees

The DOJ collects a few, as will most dealers by adding an administrative charge. If you buy or receive more than one shotgun or rifle on the same date in a single transaction, the DOJ will charge only one fee.

Background Check Forms

The Department of Justice shall prescribe the form of the register and the record of electronic transfer.[1594]

For handguns, the register or record of electronic transfer shall include:[1595]

- the date and time of sale
- make of handgun

[1590]Penal Code § 12072 (c) and (c)(3).

[1591]Penal Code § 12071 (c)(1), (c)(1)(A) and (B).

[1592]Penal Code § 12076 (d)(1).

[1593]Penal Code § 12076 (d)(2) and (3).

[1594]Penal Code § 12077 (a); see also Penal Code § 12074.

[1595]Penal Code § 12077 (b)(1).

- peace officer exemption status,[1596] if applicable, along with the agency name
- dealer waiting period exemption,[1597] if applicable
- dangerous weapons permit holder waiting period exemption,[1598] if applicable
- curio and relic waiting period exemption[1599], if applicable
- California Firearms Dealer number[1600]
- the purchaser's HSC number
- manufacturer's name if stamped on the handgun
- model name or number, if stamped on the handgun
- serial number, or other numbers if stamped on the handgun
- any identification or mark assigned to the handgun whenever a firearm is without a manufacturer's number, whether it was made that way or the number was later destroyed or obliterated[1601]
- caliber
- type of handgun
- whether the handgun is new or used
- barrel length
- color of the handgun
- full name of the purchaser
- purchaser's complete date of birth
- purchaser's local address (if current address is temporary, complete permanent address is required)
- identification of the purchaser
- purchaser's place of birth (state or country)
- purchaser's complete telephone number
- purchaser's occupation
- purchaser's sex
- purchaser's physical description

[1596] See Penal Code § 12078 (a).

[1597] See Penal Code § 12078 (n).

[1598] See Penal Code § 12078 (r).

[1599] See Penal Code § 12078 (t).

[1600] See Penal Code § 12071.

[1601] See Penal Code § 12092.

- all legal names and aliases ever used by the purchaser
- signature of purchaser
- signature of salesperson as a witness of the signature of purchaser
- salesperson's certificate of eligibility number
- name and address of the dealer or firm selling the handgun as displayed on the dealer's license
- the establishment number, if assigned
- the dealer's complete business telephone number
- any information as required for loans of handguns[1602]
- any information required to determine if the purchaser has already applied to purchase a firearm in the previous 30 days
- a statement of penalties for any person signing a fictitious name or address for knowingly furnishing any incorrect information or for knowingly omitting any information required to be provided for the register

The purchaser of a handgun shall also provide his or her right thumbprint on the register in a manner as prescribed by the department.[1603] The firearms dealer shall record on the register the date that the handgun is to be delivered.[1604]

For the purchase of a handgun, the register and the record of electronic transfer will also include a series of "yes/no" questions that operate to disqualify a person automatically from legally purchasing a firearm, as they are deemed a prohibited person.[1605] Such questions include (but may include more in the future) whether the person has:[1606]

- a felony conviction
- committed other violent offenses[1607]
- whether the person has had mental issues as discussed above under prohibited persons

---

[1602]See Penal Code § 12082.

[1603]Penal Code § 12077 (b)(2).

[1604]Penal Code § 12077 (b)(3).

[1605]Penal Code § 12077 (b)(1).

[1606]Penal Code § 12077 (b)(1).

[1607]See Penal Code § 12021.1.

- whether the person has been adjudicated as not guilty by reason of insanity
- whether the person has been placed under conservatorship by a court

For the purchase of a rifle or shotgun, all of the same is required as for handguns, with a few exceptions.[1608] For rifles and shotguns, the register or record for electronic transfer will not require the following:

- make of the firearm
- an HSC number
- manufacturer's name if stamped on the firearm
- model name or number, if stamped on the firearm
- serial number
- an identification mark or number as provided by the DOJ
- caliber
- type of firearm
- if the firearm is new or used
- barrel length
- color of firearm

Also, shotguns and rifles allow for one extra exemption from the ten-day waiting period, that being an auction or event waiting period exemption for infrequent sales or transfers at auctions or similar events conducted by nonprofit mutual or public benefit corporations or donations for these auctions or similar events.[1609]

Of course, the differences between the requirements for handguns and the requirements for shotguns and rifles regards the fact that handguns in California are permanently registered with the Department of Justice, while rifles and shotguns are not.

Common Situations Prohibiting the Purchase of Firearms

In addition to prohibitions discussed earlier in this book, two more prohibitions exist that are very common.

[1608] Penal Code § 12077 (c)(1), (2), and (3).

[1609] See Penal Code § 12078 (g)(1), (2), and (3).

Felony Driving Record

As discussed above, if one is convicted of a felony, he is forever prohibited from purchasing, possessing, owning, controlling, and handling firearms. This is true for those convicted of a felony traffic offense, such as felony drunk driving. This is a very common way the average citizen loses his right to handle firearms legally.

Invalid Driver's License

In California, to purchase a firearm, you must possess a valid driver's license (or identification card) issued by the California Department of Motor Vehicles ("DMV"). Also, if a license is suspended for any reason, a prospective purchaser of a firearm will be unable to purchase a firearm.

Ammunition Purchasing Requirements[1610]

Up until February 1, 2011, there are no requirements or processes required of retail dealers when selling handgun ammunition. However, that changes on February 1, 2011. At that point, all vendors of handgun ammunition will be required to:

- maintain records containing certain identifying information about the purchaser and the ammunition being sold, and
- store handgun ammunition so that it is inaccessible to purchasers without the assistance of the vendor

The law will also require that handgun ammunition sales be completed in face-to-face transactions (no mail order), prohibits person subject to gang injunctions from purchasing handgun ammunition, and prohibiting handgun ammunition sales to any person the seller knows or has cause to believe is prohibited from possessing handgun ammunition. Also, a person prohibited from possessing handgun ammunition will not be able to be employed in a capacity where they will be expected to handle handgun ammunition.

The information required from the buyer of handgun ammunition includes the right thumbprint of the purchaser or transferee, the date of the sale or other transaction, the purchaser's or transferee's driver's license or other identification number and the state in which it was issued, the brand, type, and amount of

---

[1610]This authority for this entire section is found in Assembly Bill ("AB") 962, and may also be found codified in Penal Code § 12060 and § 12061.

ammunition sold or otherwise transferred, the purchaser's or transferee's signature, the name of the salesperson who processed the sale, the purchaser's or transferee's full residential address and telephone number, and the purchaser's or transferee's date of birth.

Further, the records of each transaction shall be maintained on the premises of the vendor for a period of not less than five years from the date of the recorded transfer and subject to inspection by law enforcement upon demand.

Any violation of the above or failure to comply is a misdemeanor.

CHAPTER EIGHTEEN

Firearms Safety Devices and Gun Safes

An extensive area in the Penal Code known as the "Aroner-Scott-Hayden Firearms Safety Act of 1999,"[1611] concerns firearms safety devices. The Act creates standards and requirements on safety devices, including requirements of purchase or prior ownership when buying a firearm.

In enacting this Act, the State Legislature found that, in the years 1987 to 1996, nearly 2,200 children in the United States under the age of 15 died in unintentional shootings, and that in 1996 alone, 138 had been shot and killed unintentionally (averaging 11 children every month, one child every three days).[1612] Upon review, the legislature also discovered the United States leads the industrialized world in the rates of children and youth lost to unintentional, firearms-related deaths, so much so that the rate in the United States was nine times higher than in 25 other industrialized countries combined.[1613] Further, the legislature discovered that nearly eight times the number of unintentional deaths of children under 15 are shot but do not actually result in death, because of successes in U.S. hospital emergency rooms.[1614]

The legislature also depended on other studies in considering this Act. A study of unintentional firearm deaths among children in California found that unintentional gunshot wounds most often involve handguns.[1615] Another study relied on by the legislature was in the December 1995 issue of the *Archives of Pediatric and Adolescent Medicine*, which found that children as young as three years old are strong enough to fire most commercially available handguns.[1616]

[1611] Penal Code § 12087; see also Penal Code §§ 12087 through 12088.9.

[1612] Penal Code § 12087.5.

[1613] Penal Code § 12087.5 (b).

[1614] Penal Code § 12087 (c).

[1615] Penal Code § 12087.5 (d).

[1616] Penal Code § 12087.5 (e).

The Government Accounting Office ("GAO"), in a March 1991 study estimated that 31% of accidental deaths caused by firearms might have been prevented by the addition of two safety devices: a child-resistant safety device that automatically engages, and a device that indicates whether the gun is loaded.[1617] Further studies by the GAO revealed that for all unintentional firearms-related fatalities of children 6 years of age that occurred between 1988 and 1989, 8% could have been prevented had the firearm been equipped with a child-resistant safety device.[1618]

The legislature declared that firearms were the only products manufactured in the United States that were not subject to minimum safety standards.[1619] The legislature also relied upon a 1997 public opinion poll that 74% of Americans support safety regulation of the firearms agency.[1620] Finally, the legislature pointed out that, at the time, some of the available trigger locks and other similar devices were inadequate to prevent the accidental discharge of firearms to which they were attached, or to prevent young children from gaining access to the firearm.[1621]

Please keep in mind that it is not the intent of this book to dispute the above findings and declarations of the California Legislature. Much of the above could easily be argued. The point of this book is to report, discuss, and analyze the law as it exists.

Also note: compliance with the requirements as set forth in the Firearms Safety Act shall not relieve any person from liability to any other person as may be imposed pursuant to common law, statutory law, or local ordinance.[1622]

Definitions Applicable to the Firearms Safety Act of 1999

A "firearms safety device" means a device other than a gun safe that locks

---

[1617] Penal Code § 12087.5 (f).

[1618] Penal Code § 12087.5 (f).

[1619] Penal Code § 12087.5 (g).

[1620] Penal Code § 12087.5 (h).

[1621] Penal Code § 12087.5 (i).

[1622] Penal Code § 12088.7.

and is designed to prevent children and unauthorized users from firing a firearm.[1623] Such device may be installed on a firearm, be incorporated into the design of the firearm, or prevent access to the firearm.[1624]

A "gun safe" means a locking container that fully contains and secures one or more firearms, and that meets the standards for gun safes as provided by law.[1625]

A "long gun safe" means a locking container designed to fully contain and secure a rifle[1626] or a shotgun[1627] that has a locking system consisting of either a mechanical combination lock or an electronic combination lock that has at least 1000 possible unique combinations consisting of a minimum of three numbers, letters, or symbols per combination, and that is listed on the roster maintained by the DOJ.[1628]

Requirement to Include Firearms Safety Devices with All Firearms Purchases

The California Legislature requires that all firearms sold or transferred in this state by a licensed firearms dealer, including private party transfers that pass through the dealer, as well as with all firearms manufactured in the State of California, will include or be accompanied by a firearms safety device that is listed on the department's roster of approved firearms safety devices and that is identified as appropriate for that firearm by reference to either the manufacturer and the model of the firearm, or to the physical characteristics of the firearm that match those listed on the roster for use with the device.[1629]

[1623] Penal Code § 12087.6 (a).

[1624] Penal Code § 12087.6 (a).

[1625] Penal Code § 12087.6 (b); see also Penal Code § 12088.2 regarding standards for gun safes.

[1626] See Penal Code § 12020 (c)(20) regarding meaning of "rifle".

[1627] See Penal Code § 12020 (c)(21) regarding meaning of "shotgun".

[1628] Penal Code § 12087.6 (c); see also Penal Code § 12088 regarding roster maintained by the DOJ.

[1629] Penal Code § 12088.1 (a).

Federal law states that it shall be unlawful for any licensed importer, licensed manufacturer, or licensed dealer to sell, deliver, or transfer any handgun to any person other than any person licensed under federal law, unless the transferee is provided with a secure gun storage or safety device[1630] for that handgun.[1631]

Under federal law, a "secure gun storage or safety device" means either:[1632]

- a device that, when installed on a firearm is designed to prevent the firearm from being operated without first deactivating the device
- a device incorporated into the design of the firearm that is designed to prevent the operation of the firearm by anyone not having access to the device
- a safe, gun safe, gun case, lock box, or other device that is designed to be or can be used to store a firearm and that is designed to be unlocked only by means of a key, a combination, or other similar means

Exemption from California Requirement to Include Firearms Safety Device in Sale of Rifle or Shotgun

The sale or transfer of a firearm that is not a handgun shall be exempt from the requirement to include a firearms safety device if both of the following apply:[1633]

- the purchaser or transferee owns a gun safe that meets the standards pursuant to the Firearms Safety Act[1634]
- the purchaser or transferee presents an original receipt for the purchase of a gun safe, or other proof of purchase or ownership of the gun safe to the firearms dealer[1635]

[1630]As defined in 18 U.S.C. § 921 (a)(34).

[1631]18 U.S.C. § 922 (z)(1).

[1632]18 U.S.C. § 922 (z)(34)(A) through (C).

[1633]Penal Code § 12088.1 (d).

[1634]Penal Code § 12088.1 (d)(1); see also Penal Code § 12088.2 regarding safety standards for firearms safety devices and gun safes.

[1635]Penal Code § 12088.1 (d)(2).

Gun safes shall not be required to be tested, and therefore may meet the standards without appearing on the DOJ roster.[1636] For those buying shotguns or rifles (not handguns) who provide proof by providing an original receipt or other proof of purchase or ownership, such proof shall be copied by the dealer and maintained with the dealer records to demonstrate compliance with the Act.[1637]

All of the following may apply (instead of the above) to exempt the sale or transfer of a shotgun or rifle from the requirement that the sale include an approved firearms safety device:[1638]

- the purchase of the approved safety device as proven by the buyer or transferee by presenting the proof of purchase must show a purchase that is no more than 30 days prior to the day the purchaser or transferee takes possession of the firearm[1639]
- the purchaser or transferee presents the approved safety device to the firearms dealer when picking up the firearm[1640]
- the purchaser or transferee presents the original receipt that shows the date of purchase, the name and model number of the safety device[1641]
- the firearms dealer verifies that all of the above (the three points directly above) have been satisfied[1642]
- the firearms dealer maintains a copy of the receipt as part of the record for sale[1643]

[1636]Penal Code § 12088.1 (d)(1).

[1637]Penal Code § 12088.1 (d)(2).

[1638]Penal Code § 12088.1 (e).

[1639]Penal Code § 12088.1 (e)(1).

[1640]Penal Code § 12088.1 (e)(2).

[1641]Penal Code § 12088.1 (e)(3).

[1642]Penal Code § 12088.1 (e)(4).

[1643]Penal Code § 12088.1 (e)(5).

Violation of Requirement to Sell or Transfer Firearm With Firearms Safety Device

Under California law, any violation of this requirement is punishable by a fine of $1000 for the first violation, the ineligibility of the dealer to sell firearms for thirty days plus a $1000 fine for the second violation, and upon the third violation, permanent ineligibility to sell firearms within the State of California.[1644]

Inapplicability of Firearms Safety Act of 1999

This Act does not apply to the commerce of any firearm defined as an "antique firearm."[1645] Also, this Act does not apply to the commerce of any firearm intended to be used by a salaried, full-time peace officer[1646] for the purposes of law enforcement.[1647] However, nothing in the Act shall preclude local governments, local agencies, or state law enforcement agencies from requiring their peace officers to store their firearms in gun safes and/or attach firearms safety devices to those firearms.[1648]

Approved Firearms Safety Devices

Certification of Laboratories to Test Firearms Safety Devices

The DOJ shall certify laboratories to verify compliance with standards for firearms safety devices pursuant to the Firearms Safety Act.[1649] The DOJ may charge the laboratories that seek certification a fee to be certified to perform testing at the request of the DOJ.[1650]

[1644]Penal Code § 12088.6.

[1645]Penal Code § 12088.8 (a); see also 18 U.S.C. § 921 (a) regarding definition of "antique firearm".

[1646]See Penal Code § 830 et seq., regarding definitions of "salaried, full-time peace officers".

[1647]Penal Code § 12088.8 (b).

[1648]Penal Code § 12088.8 (b).

[1649]Penal Code § 12088 (a).

[1650]Penal Code § 12088 (b).

Testing of Firearms Safety Devices

The certified laboratory will, at the expense of the manufacturer of the safety device, or the dealer interested in selling the safety device, test the device and submit a copy of the final test directly to the DOJ along with a sample device.[1651] The DOJ will then report to the manufacturer and/or dealer of the results, and the status as to whether the device can be sold in California.[1652]

Roster of Approved Firearms Safety Devices

Beginning on July 1, 2001, the DOJ began to compile, publish, and maintain a roster listing all of the firearm safety devices that have been tested by certified testing laboratories, and have been determined to meet the department's standards for firearm safety devices that may be sold in California.[1653] For each firearms safety device, the roster will include the manufacturer's name, model number, and model name of the device.[1654]

Retesting of Firearms Safety Devices

From time to time, the DOJ may randomly retest samples obtained from sources other than directly from the manufacturer of the firearms safety device to ensure compliance with the requirements under the Firearms Safety Act.[1655] Such retesting will be done with brand new, unused firearms safety devices only, and will be taken from samples that are still in the manufacturer's original, unopened package.[1656]

Violation to Sell Firearms Safety Device Not on Roster

No person shall keep for commercial sale, offer, or expose for commercial

---

[1651]Penal Code § 12088 (c).

[1652]Penal Code § 12088 (c).

[1653]Penal Code § 12088 (d).

[1654]Penal Code § 12088 (e).

[1655]Penal Code § 12088 (f).

[1656]Penal Code § 12088 (g).

sale, or commercially sell any firearms safety device that is not listed on the roster,[1657] or that does not comply with the standards for firearms safety devices.[1658] Firearms safety devices that may be distributed as part of an organized safety program may also not be distributed if not on the roster or the device simply does not meet the standards as provided by law.[1659]

Violations may be prosecuted by the Attorney General, a district or city attorney,[1660] and may be punishable by a civil fine of up to $500 for a first violation.[1661] A second violation that occurs within five years of the date of the first violation is a civil fine of up to $1000, and if committed by a licensed firearms dealer, the dealer shall be ineligible to sell firearms in the State of California for 30 days.[1662] A third and subsequent violation that occurs within five years of two or more previous offenses is punishable by a fine of $5000, and, if the violation is committed by a licensed firearms dealer, that dealer shall be permanently ineligible to sell firearms in the state.[1663]

Warning Label Requirement

All firearms sold by a dealer or through a dealer as a private party transfer will also include certain warning labels.[1664] To be more precise, the packaging of any firearm and any descriptive materials that accompany any firearm sold or transferred in this state, or delivered for sale in this state, by any licensed manufacturer, or

---

[1657]See Penal Code § 12088 (d) regarding the DOJ roster.

[1658]Penal Code § 12088.15 (a); see also Penal Code § 12088.2 regarding standards for firearms safety devices.

[1659]Penal Code § 12088.15 (b); see also Penal Code § 12088 (d) regarding the DOJ roster, and Penal Code § 12088.2 regarding safety standards for firearms safety devices.

[1660]Penal Code § 12088.15 (f).

[1661]Penal Code § 12088.15 (e).

[1662]Penal Code § 12088.15 (e).

[1663]Penal Code § 12088.15 (e).

[1664]Penal. Code § 12088.1 (b); see also Penal Code § 12088.3 regarding warning labels.

licensed dealer, shall bear a label containing the following warning statement:[1665]

> "WARNING: Children are attracted to and can operate firearms that can cause severe injuries or death. Prevent child access by always keeping guns locked away and unloaded when not in use. If you keep a loaded firearm where a child obtains and improperly uses it, you may be fined or sent to prison."

A "yellow triangle" containing an exclamation mark shall appear immediately before the word "WARNING" on the label.[1666]

Firearms may be sold or transferred without any accompanying packaging, and in such a case, the warning label or notice shall be affixed to the firearm itself by a prescribed method.[1667]

The warning statement that is required shall be displayed in its entirety on the principal display panel of the firearms package, and on any descriptive materials that accompany the firearm.[1668] The warning will be displayed in both English and Spanish and will be in conspicuous and legible type in contrast by typography, layout, or color with other printed matter on that package or descriptive materials in a prescribed manner under federal law.[1669]

Violation of Requirement to Sell or Transfer Firearm With Proper Warning Labels

Any violation of the warning label requirement is punishable by a fine of $1000 for the first violation, the ineligibility of the dealer to sell firearms for thirty days plus a $1000 fine for the second violation, and upon the third violation,

---

[1665] Penal Code § 12088.3 (a) and (c).

[1666] Penal Code § 12088.3 (a).

[1667] Penal Code § 12088.3 (b).

[1668] Penal Code § 12088.3 (a) and (c)

[1669] Penal Code § 12088.3 (2); see also 16 C.F.R. § 1500.121 et seq., regarding federal regulations addressing warnings accompanying the sale of firearms.

permanent ineligibility to sell firearms within the State of California.[1670]

Long-Gun Safes

All long-gun safes commercially sold or transferred in this state, or manufactured in this state for sale in this state, that do not meet the standards for gun safes,[1671] shall be accompanied by the following warning:[1672]

> "WARNING: This gun safe does not meet the safety standards for gun safes specified in California Penal Code Section 12088.2. It does not satisfy the requirements of Penal Code 12099.1, which mandates that all firearms sold in California must be accompanied by a firearms safety device or proof of ownership, as required by law, of a gun safe that meets the Section 12088.2 minimum safety standards developed by the California Attorney General."

This warning shall be conspicuously displayed in its entirety, in both English and Spanish,[1673] on the principal display panel of the gun safe's package, on any descriptive materials that accompany the gun safe, and on a label affixed to the front of the gun safe.[1674] The warning shall be in conspicuous and legible type in contrast to typography, layout, or color with other printed matter on the package or descriptive materials in a manner consistent with federal law.[1675]

Long-Gun Safes Must Comply with Safety Standards

No long-gun safe may be manufactured in this state for sale in this state that does not comply with the standards for gun safes adopted pursuant to the Penal

---

[1670]Penal Code § 12088.6.

[1671]Penal Code § 12088.1 (c)(1); see also Penal Code § 12088.2.

[1672]Penal Code § 12088.1 (c)(1).

[1673]Penal Code § 12088.1 (c)(3).

[1674]Penal Code § 12088.1 (c)(2).

[1675]Penal Code § 12088.1 (c)(3); see also 16 C.F.R. § 1500.121 regarding federal regulations of warnings on packaging.

Code[1676] unless the long-gun safe is labeled by the manufacturer consistent with requirements under the Firearms Safety Act.[1677]

Violations of Law Pertaining to Long-Gun Safes

Any person who keeps for commercial sale, offers, or exposes for commercial sale, or who commercially sells a long-gun safe that does not comply with the standards[1678] for gun safes is in violation of the law,[1679] and is punishable as described below,[1680] unless the long gun safe is labeled as prescribed by law.[1681]

Also, any person who keeps for commercial sale, offers, or exposes for commercial sale, or who commercially sells a long-gun safe that does not comply with the standards[1682] for gun safes, and who removes or causes to be removed from the long-gun safe, the label required[1683] is punishable as described below.[1684]

Violations may be prosecuted by the Attorney General, a district or city attorney,[1685] and may be punishable by a civil fine of up to $500 for a first

---

[1676]See Penal Code § 12088.2.

[1677]Penal Code § 12088.15 (c); see also Penal Code § 12088.1 regarding labels to be included by the manufacturer.

[1678]See Penal Code § 12088.2 regarding standards for gun safes.

[1679]Specifically, in violation of Penal Code § 12088.15.

[1680]See Penal Code § 12088.15 regarding punishment for violation.

[1681]Penal Code § 12088.15 (d)(1); see also Penal Code § 12088.1 regarding properly labeled long-gun safes.

[1682]See Penal Code § 12088.2 regarding standards for gun safes.

[1683]See Penal Code § 12088.1 regarding appropriate labeling required by the Penal Code.

[1684]Penal Code § 12088.15 (c)(2); see also Penal Code § 12088.15 regarding punishment for violation.

[1685]Penal Code § 12088.15 (f).

violation.[1686] A second violation that occurs within five years of the date of the first violation is a civil fine of up to $1000, and if committed by a licensed firearms dealer, the dealer shall be ineligible to sell firearms in the State of California for 30 days.[1687] A third and subsequent violation that occurs within five years of two or more previous offenses is punishable by a fine of $5000, and, if the violation is committed by a licensed firearms dealer, that dealer shall be permanently ineligible to sell firearms in the state.[1688]

Safety Standards for Firearms Safety Devices and Gun Safes

The Attorney General develops regulations to implement minimum safety standards for firearms safety devices and gun safes to reduce significantly the risk of firearms-related injuries to children 17 years of age and younger, and the final standard shall do all of the following:[1689]

- address the risk of injury from unintentional gunshot wounds[1690]
- address the risk of injury from self-inflicted gunshot wounds by unauthorized users[1691]
- include provisions to ensure that all firearms safety devices and gun safes are reusable and of adequate quality and construction to prevent children and unauthorized users from firing the firearm and to ensure that these devices cannot be readily removed from the firearm, or that the firearm cannot be readily removed from the gun safe except by an authorized user utilizing the key, combination, or other method of access intended by the manufacturer of the device[1692]

[1686] Penal Code § 12088.15 (e).

[1687] Penal Code § 12088.15 (e).

[1688] Penal Code § 12088.15 (e).

[1689] Penal Code § 12088.2 (a).

[1690] Penal Code § 12088.2 (a)(1).

[1691] Penal Code § 12088.2 (a)(2).

[1692] Penal Code § 12088.2 (a)(3).

Nonconforming Firearms Safety Devices and Gun Safes

If the Attorney General determines that a gun safe or firearms safety device subject to the provisions of the Firearms Safety Act sold after January 1, 2002, does not conform with the standards as discussed above,[1693] the Attorney General may order the recall and replacement of the gun safe or firearms safety device, or order that the same be brought into conformity with those requirements.[1694] If the device cannot be separated from the firearm without damaging the firearm, the Attorney General may order the recall and replacement of the firearm.[1695] If the firearms safety device can be separated and reattached to the firearm without damage to the firearm, the licensed manufacturer or dealer shall immediately provide a conforming replacement.[1696]

[1693]See Penal Code §§ 12088.1 (a) and 12088.2.

[1694]Penal Code § 12088.4.

[1695]Penal Code § 12088.4.

[1696]Penal Code § 12088.4.

Part Ten

California Licensed Dealers, Manufacturers, and Gun Shows

CHAPTER NINETEEN

Persons Licensed to Sell Firearms in California

Licensed Dealers - Requirements and Prohibitions

In California, before any person can become engaged in the business of dealing in firearms, that person must be a properly licensed "dealer" under California law.[1697] Even a properly licensed dealer in California must adhere to a voluminous amount of federal laws, as well as local laws and regulations, both of which are beyond the scope of this book. Instead, this book will provide a breakdown of California law regarding dealers as found in the Penal Code.[1698]

Licensed Dealer Defined

A "licensee" is a person who is licensed to sell firearms pursuant to law,[1699] and a "dealer means a person who has all of the following:[1700]

- a valid federal firearms license[1701]
- any regulatory or business license, or licenses, required by local government[1702]
- a valid seller's permit issued by the State Board of Equalization[1703]
- a certificate of eligibility issued by the DOJ[1704]

[1697]See Penal Code § 12071.

[1698]Penal Code sections addressing licensed dealers consist of Penal Code §§ 12071 through 12084.

[1699]Penal Code § 12071 (a)(1).

[1700]Penal Code § 12071 (a)(1).

[1701]Penal Code § 12071 (a)(1)(A).

[1702]Penal Code § 12071 (a)(1)(B).

[1703]Penal Code § 12071 (a)(1)(C).

[1704]Penal Code § 12071 (a)(1)(D); see also Penal Code § 12071 (a)(4) regarding certificate of eligibility.

- a license issued in the format as prescribed by law[1705]
- is among those recorded in the centralized list[1706]

Centralized List of Licensees

There are two centralized lists applicable to this chapter on licensed firearms dealers in California. The first centralized list regards all persons licensed to sell firearms pursuant to California law.[1707] The second centralized list regards exempted federal firearms licensees.[1708] This section addresses the list regarding persons licensed to sell firearms pursuant to California law. A section further in this chapter addresses the centralized list of exempted federal firearms licensees.

The DOJ shall maintain a centralized list of all persons licensed pursuant to law,[1709] and the DOJ may remove from this list any person who knowingly or with gross negligence violates any of the requirements imposed on him or her as a licensee,[1710] or whose license has expired or been revoked.[1711] Upon removal of a dealer from the list, notification shall be provided to local law enforcement and licensing authorities in the jurisdiction where the dealer's business is located.[1712]

Information compiled from the list shall be made available, upon request, for the following purposes only:[1713]

[1705]Penal Code § 12071 (a)(1)(E); see also Penal Code § 12071 (a)(6) regarding the prescribed format of a license.

[1706]Penal Code § 12071 (a)(1)(F); see also Penal Code § 12071 (e) regarded centralized list.

[1707]See Penal Code § 12071.

[1708]See Penal Code § 12083.

[1709]See Penal Code § 12071 (a)(1)(A) through (E).

[1710]Penal Code § 12071 (e)(1).

[1711]Penal Code § 12071 (e)(2).

[1712]Penal Code § 12071 (e)(1).

[1713]Penal Code § 12071 (e)(3).

- for law enforcement purposes[1714]
- when the information is requested by a person licensed under federal law[1715] to deal in firearms for determining the validity of the license for firearms shipments[1716]
- when information is requested by a person promoting, sponsoring, operating, or otherwise organizing a show or event as defined by law,[1717] or its successor, who possesses a valid certificate of eligibility issued according to law,[1718] if that information is requested by the person to determine the eligibility of a prospective participant in a gun show or event to conduct transactions as a firearms dealer[1719]

Information provided as outlined above shall be limited in scope to information necessary to corroborate an individual's current license status as being one of the following:[1720]

- a person licensed under the law[1721]
- a person licensed under federal law[1722] and who is not subject to the requirements that he or she be licensed according to California law[1723]

[1714]Penal Code § 12071 (e)(3)(A).

[1715]See Chapter 44 (commencing with Section 921) of Title 18 U.S.C.

[1716]Penal Code § 12071 (e)(3)(B).

[1717]See 27 C.F.R. § 478.100.

[1718]See Penal Code § 12071.1.

[1719]Penal Code § 12071 (e)(3)(C); see also Penal Code § 12071 (b)(1)(B).

[1720]Penal Code § 12071 (e)(4).

[1721]Penal Code § 12071 (e)(4)(A); see also Penal Code § 12071 (a)(1)(A) through (E).

[1722]See Chapter 44 (commencing with § 921) of Title 18 of the U.S.C.

[1723]Penal Code § 12071 (e)(4)(B); see also Penal Code § 12071 (a)(1)(A) through (E).

Authority to Accept Applications for a License

The duly constituted local licensing authority shall accept applications for, and may grant licenses permitting, licensees to sell firearms at retail within the locality.[1724] Fees may be collected by the local licensing authorities to recover their full costs of processing applications for licenses.[1725]

Must be Licensed by Federal Government

No license shall be granted to any applicant who fails to provide a copy of his or her federal firearms license (FFL), valid seller's permit issued by the State Board of Equalization, and the certificate of eligibility.[1726]

Denial of License

The duly constituted local licensing authority shall inform applicants who are denied licenses of the reasons for the denial in writing.[1727]

Certificate of Eligibility

A person may request a certificate of eligibility from the DOJ, which will examine its records and records available to it in the National Instant Criminal Background Check System in order to determine if the applicant is prohibited from state or federal law from possessing, receiving, owning, or purchasing a firearm and issue a certificate to the applicant if the DOJ's records indicate that the applicant is not a person who is prohibited from state or federal law from possessing firearms.[1728] Applications can be found at licensed dealers or on the DOJ website.[1729]

[1724]Penal Code § 12071 (a)(2).

[1725]Penal Code § 12071 (a)(7).

[1726]Penal Code § 12071 (a)(3); see also Penal Code § 12071 (a)(4) regarding certificate of eligibility.

[1727]Penal Code § 12071 (a)(2).

[1728]Penal Code § 12071 (a)(4); see also Penal Code § 12077.5.

[1729]Penal Code § 12071 (e).

Fees for the certificate of eligibility program will be collected from applicants to recover the full costs of administering the program.[1730] The fee was established at $20 but is permitted to be increased as permitted by law.[1731]

The application must be notarized.[1732] Only upon receiving the complete,[1733] notarized application and applicable fee, the DOJ will examine its records to determine if the applicant is prohibited from state or federal law from possessing, receiving, owning, or purchasing a firearm.[1734]

The applicant will be notified by mail of the DOJ's determination as either eligible or ineligible as of the date the check was completed.[1735] The DOJ is immune from liability arising out of the performance of the firearms eligibility check, or the reliance upon the same.[1736]

No person or agency may require or request another person to obtain a firearms eligibility check or notification of a firearms eligibility check, since to do such is a misdemeanor.[1737] The application will state the prohibition on other persons or agencies to require or request such clearly on its face.[1738]

Duration of License, Form of License, and Display of License

A license granted by the duly constituted local licensing authority shall be valid for not more than one year from the date of issuance and shall be in one of the

[1730]Penal Code § 12071 (a)(5); see also Penal Code § 12077.5 (b).

[1731]Penal Code § 12077.5 (b).

[1732]Penal Code § 12077.5 (c).

[1733]See Penal Code § 12077.5 (d).

[1734]Penal Code § 12077.5 (c)(1).

[1735]Penal Code § 12077.5 (c)(2).

[1736]Penal Code § 12077.5 (f).

[1737]Penal Code § 12077.5 (g).

[1738]Penal Code § 12077.5 (h).

following forms:[1739]

- in the form prescribed by the Attorney General[1740]
- a regulatory or business license that states on its face "Valid for Retail Sales of Firearms" and is endorsed by the signature of the issuing authority[1741]
- a letter from the duly constituted licensing authority having primary jurisdiction for the applicant's intended business location stating that the jurisdiction does not require any form of regulatory or business license or does not otherwise restrict or regulate the sale of firearms[1742]

A license or copy thereof, certified by the issuing authority, shall be displayed on the premises where it can be easily seen.[1743]

Requirements and Prohibitions on Licensed Dealers

A license is subject to forfeiture for a breach of any of the following prohibitions and requirements.[1744]

Notification to DOJ of License Issuance or Renewal

The licensee shall, upon the issuance or renewal of a license, submit a copy of the same to the DOJ.[1745]

Notification to DOJ of Firearm (Handgun) Acquisition

On the date of receipt, the licensee shall report to the DOJ, in a format

---

[1739]Penal Code § 12071 (a)(6).

[1740]Penal Code § 12071 (a)(6)(A).

[1741]Penal Code § 12071 (a)(6)(B).

[1742]Penal Code § 12071 (a)(6)(C).

[1743]Penal Code § 12071 (b)(2).

[1744]Penal Code § 12071 (b).

[1745]Penal Code § 12071 (b)(16).

prescribed by the DOJ, the acquisition by the licensee of the ownership of the pistol, revolver, or other firearm capable of being concealed upon the person.[1746] However, this need not be done if it is a dealer-to-dealer transfer, or the dealer is transferring a firearm to himself, pursuant to applicable laws.[1747]

The dealer need not notify the DOJ of such acquisitions involving an acquisition from a wholesaler,[1748] the dealer is also licensed as a secondhand dealer pursuant to law,[1749] the dealer acquired the firearm from a person who is licensed as a manufacturer or importer to engage in those activities,[1750] or the dealer acquired the firearm from a person who resides outside this state yet holds a federal firearms license.[1751]

Notification to DOJ Regarding Non-Delivery of Firearm

The licensee shall forward, in a format as prescribed by the DOJ, information as required by the DOJ on any firearm that is not delivered within the prescribed time period, which is currently 30 days from the date the licensee contacts the NICS regarding a potential firearms sale.[1752]

Firearms Transaction Record Available to Law Enforcement

The licensee shall maintain and make available for inspection during business hours to any peace officer, authorized local law enforcement employee, or DOJ

[1746]Penal Code § 12071 (b)(18).

[1747]Penal Code § 12071 (b)(18)(B)(i); see also Penal Code § 12078 (n) regarding applicable transfers.

[1748]Penal Code § 12071 (b)(18)(B)(ii).

[1749]Penal Code § 12071 (b)(18)(B)(iii); see also Business and Professions Code § 21625 et seq., regarding secondhand dealer licensees.

[1750]Penal Code § 12071 (b)(18)(B)(iv); see also 18 U.S.C. § 921 et seq., regarding federally licensed manufacturers and importers.

[1751]Penal Code § 12071 (b)(18)(B)(v); see also Chapter 44 (commencing with § 921) of Title 18 of the United States Code regarding federally licensed firearms dealers.

[1752]Penal Code § 12071 (b)(19); see also 27 C.F.R. § 478.102 (c).

employee designated by the Attorney General, upon the presentation of proper I.D., a firearms transaction record.[1753] A "firearms transaction record" is a record containing the same information as required by law.[1754]

Business Conducted on Licensed Dealer's Premises

Except as provided by law,[1755] the business shall be conducted only in the buildings designated in the license.[1756]

Secure Storage of Firearms

Except as provided by law,[1757] all firearms that are in the inventory of the licensee shall be kept within the licensed location.[1758] Also, unless provided otherwise by law,[1759] any time when the licensee is not open for business, all inventory firearms shall be stored in the licensed location, and secured by one of the following methods for each individual firearm:[1760]

- store the firearm in a secure facility that is a part of, or that constitutes, the licensee's business premises
- secure the firearm with a hardened steel rod or cable of at least 1/8 inch thick in diameter through the trigger guard of the firearm, with the steel rod or cable being secured with a hardened steel lock with a shackle, which is protected or shielded from the use of a boltcutter and the rod or cable being anchored in a manner that prevents the removal of the firearm from the

---

[1753] Penal Code § 12071 (b)(17).

[1754] Penal Code § 12071 (c)(4)(A); see also 27 C.F.R. §§ 478.124 (a), 478.124a, and 478.125 (e).

[1755] See Penal Code § 12071 (b)(1)(B) and (C) for exceptions.

[1756] Penal Code § 12071 (b)(1)(A).

[1757] See Penal Code § 12071 (b)(1)(B) and (C).

[1758] Penal Code § 12071 (b)(13).

[1759] See Penal Code § 12071 (b)(1)(B) and (C).

[1760] Penal Code § 12071 (b)(14).

premises[1761]

- store the firearm in a locked fireproof safe or vault in the licensee's business premises[1762]

Local licensing authorities in an unincorporated area of a county or within a city may impose security requirements that are more strict or are at a higher standard than those specified above.[1763]

Upon written request from a licensee, the licensing authority may grant an exemption from compliance with the requirements listed above regarding storage and security of firearms if the licensee is unable to comply with those requirements because of local ordinances, covenants, lease conditions, or similar circumstances that are not under the control of the licensee.[1764]

The above standards shall not apply to a licensee organized as a nonprofit public benefit or mutual benefit corporation organized under the Corporations Code[1765] so long as both of the following conditions are satisfied:[1766]

- the corporation obtained the dealer's license solely and exclusively to assist that corporation or local chapters of that corporation in conducting auctions or similar events at which the firearms are auctioned to fund the activities of that corporation or the local chapters of the corporation[1767]
- the firearms are not pistols, revolvers, or other firearms capable of being concealed upon the person[1768]

[1761]Penal Code § 12071 (b)(14)(B).

[1762]Penal Code § 12071 (b)(14)(C).

[1763]Penal Code § 12071 (b)(15).

[1764]See Penal Code § 12071 (d).

[1765]See Part 2 (commencing with § 5110) or Part 3 (commencing with § 7110) of Division 2 of the Corporations Code.

[1766]Penal Code § 12071 (h).

[1767]Penal Code § 12071 (h)(1).

[1768]Penal Code § 12071 (h)(2).

Business Conducted at Gun Shows and Events

A person properly licensed[1769] may take possession of firearms and commence preparation of registers for the sale, delivery, or transfer of firearms at gun shows or events,[1770] or its successor, if the gun show or event is not conducted from any motorized or towed vehicle,[1771] and the person conducting business under this law shall be entitled to conduct business as authorized at any gun show or event in the state without regard to the jurisdiction within this state, provided he complies with all applicable laws, including, but not limited to, the waiting period[1772] and all applicable local laws, regulations, and fees, if any, and the person shall display his license,[1773] or a facsimile thereof, at any gun show or event.[1774]

Transfers at Charity Benefits and Events

A person properly licensed[1775] may engage in the sale and transfer of firearms other than pistols, revolvers, or other firearms capable of being concealed upon the person, at specified events (charity benefits and the like),[1776] subject to the prohibitions and restrictions contained in the law addressing such events,[1777] and such person may accept delivery of firearms other than pistols, revolvers, and other firearms capable of being concealed upon the person, outside the building designated in the license, provided the firearms are being donated for the purpose of a sale or

---

[1769]Pursuant to § 12071 (a).

[1770]See 27 C.F.R. § 478.100 for definition of gun shows or events.

[1771]Penal Code § 12071 (b)(1)(B).

[1772]See Penal Code § 12071 (b)(3)(A) regarding waiting period.

[1773]As prescribed under Penal Code § 12071 (a).

[1774]Penal Code § 12071 (b)(1)(B).

[1775]Pursuant to § 12071 (a).

[1776]See Penal Code § 12078 (g) for specified events.

[1777]See Penal Code § 12078 (g).

transfer at an auction or similar event as specified by law.[1778]

Places Where Transfers May Lawfully Occur

The firearm may be delivered to the purchaser, transferee, or person being loaned the firearm at one of the following places:[1779]

- the building specified in the license[1780]
- at a gun show or event,[1781] or charity type benefit[1782]
- the place of residence of, the fixed place of business of, or on private property owned or lawfully possessed by, the purchaser, transferee, or person being loaned the firearm[1783]

Waiting Period and Other Requirements Prior to Transfer

No firearm shall be delivered:[1784]

- within 10 days of the application to purchase, or, after notice by the DOJ,[1785] within 10 days of the submission to the department of any correction to the application, or within 10 days of the submission to the department of any fee required by the DOJ,[1786] whichever is later[1787]

[1778]Penal Code § 12071 (b)(1)(C); see also Penal Code § 12078 (g) for specified events.

[1779]Penal Code § 12071 (b)(1)(D).

[1780]Penal Code § 12071 (b)(1)(D)(i).

[1781]See Penal Code § 12071 (b)(1)(B).

[1782]Penal Code § 12071 (b)(1)(D)(ii); see Penal Code § 12071 (b)(1)(C).

[1783]Penal Code § 12071 (b)(1)(D)(iii).

[1784]Penal Code § 12071 (b)(3).

[1785]See Penal Code § 12076 (d).

[1786]See Penal Code § 12076 (e).

[1787]Penal Code § 12071 (b)(3)(A).

- unless unloaded and securely wrapped or unloaded and in a locked container[1788]
- unless the purchaser, transferee or person being loaned the firearm presents clear evidence of his or her identity and age to the dealer[1789]

Denial of Ability to Transfer Firearm

When the dealer is notified by the DOJ that the person is prohibited by state or federal law from possessing, owning, purchasing, or receiving a firearm, the dealer shall make available to the person of a prohibited class a prohibited notice and transfer form, provided by the DOJ, stating that the person is prohibited from owning and possessing a firearm, and that person may obtain from the DOJ the reason for the prohibition.[1790]

Reporting Requirements for Loss or Theft of Firearm

Within 48 hours of discovery by the licensee, the licensee shall report to the appropriate local law enforcement agency the loss or theft of any firearm that is merchandise of the licensee, any firearm that the licensee takes possession of pursuant to law,[1791] or any firearm kept at the licensee's place of business.[1792]

Prohibited Advertising and Required Postings

No pistol, revolver, or other firearm or imitation thereof capable of being concealed upon the person, or placard advertising the sale or transfer thereof, shall be displayed in any part of the premises where it can readily be seen from the outside.[1793] In addition, there are six postings that must be posted conspicuously within the licensed premises that are firearms warnings, and these postings must be

---

[1788] Penal Code § 12071 (b)(3)(B).

[1789] Penal Code § 12071 (b)(3)(C).

[1790] Penal Code § 12071 (b)(3)(D).

[1791] See Penal Code § 12082.

[1792] Penal Code § 12071 (b)(13).

[1793] Penal Code § 12071 (b)(4).

in block letters of not less than one inch in height.[1794]

Licensees must also post conspicuously within the licensed premises a detailed list of each of the following regarding fees, which may not be misstated:[1795]

- all charges required by governmental agencies for processing firearm transfers are required by Sections 12076, 12082, and 12086[1796]
- all fees that the licensee charges pursuant to Sections 12082 and 12086[1797]

Timely Process of Transactions

The licensee shall agree to and shall act properly and promptly in processing firearms transactions pursuant to law.[1798]

Certificates of Eligibility for Employees

Firearms dealers may require any agent who handles, sells, or delivers firearms to obtain and provide to the dealer a certificate of eligibility from the DOJ pursuant to law,[1799] and such agent or employee shall provide on the application, the name and California firearms dealer number of the firearms dealer with whom he or she is employed.[1800]

The DOJ shall notify the firearms dealer in the event that the agent or employee who has a certificate of eligibility if he or she becomes prohibited from

---

[1794]Penal Code § 12071 (b)(7); see also Penal Code § 12071 (b)(7)(A) through (F) for exact wording of the required postings.

[1795]Penal Code § 12071 (b)(11); see also Penal Code § 12071 (b)(12).

[1796]Penal Code § 12071 (b)(11)(A).

[1797]Penal Code § 12071 (b)(11)(B).

[1798]Penal Code § 12071 (b)(5); see also Penal Code § 12082.

[1799]See Penal Code § 12071 (a)(4).

[1800]Penal Code § 12071 (b)(20)(A).

possessing firearms.[1801]

If the local jurisdiction requires a background check on the agents and employees of the firearms dealer, the agent or employee shall obtain such, prior to handing firearms during the employ of the dealer.[1802] Local jurisdictions may also conduct an additional background check[1803] or may prohibit employment based on a criminal history that does not appear as part of obtaining a certificate of eligibility, provided however, that the local jurisdiction may not charge a fee for the additional criminal history check.[1804] Finally, local jurisdictions may enact ordinances imposing additional conditions on licensees with regards to agents.[1805]

Licensee Monitoring of Employees

The licensee shall prohibit any agent who the licensee knows, or reasonably should know, is within a class of persons prohibited from possessing firearms[1806] from coming into contact with any firearm that is not secured and from accessing any key, combination, code, or other means to open any of the locking devices as required by law.[1807]

Other Requirements

The licensee shall comply with the following:[1808]

- requirements regarding register and record of sale to be kept by

---

[1801]Penal Code § 12071 (b)(20)(B).

[1802]Penal Code § 12071 (b)(20)(C); see also Penal Code § 12071 (b)(20)(A).

[1803]Pursuant to Penal Code § 11105.

[1804]Penal Code § 12071 (b)(20)(D).

[1805]Penal Code § 12071 (b)(20)(F).

[1806]Pursuant to Penal Code §§ 12021 and 12021.1, or Welfare and Institutions Code §§ 8100 or 8103.

[1807]Penal Code § 12071 (b)(20)(E); see also Penal Code § 12071 (b)(20)(G)(ii) regarding secure firearms.

[1808]Penal Code § 12071 (b)(6).

firearms dealer[1809]

- requirements on format and procedure dealing with firearms purchaser information, as well as applicable fees[1810]
- requirements regarding the record of electronic transfers[1811]
- prohibitions regarding the sale of ammunition to a minor or a person prohibited from possessing a firearm[1812]
- other requirements regarding deliveries of firearms[1813]
- comply with all requirements regarding safe handling demonstration and handgun safety certificates[1814]
- requirements to offer to provide purchasers or transferees of a firearm, or one being loaned a firearm, with a copy of a pamphlet,[1815] at a price to be added to the sales price of the firearm[1816]
- no participating in any acts of collusion[1817]

Definitions Relevant to Requirements on Licensees and Agents

The following definitions are relevant to the requirements discussed above regarding licensees and agents.[1818]

[1809]Penal Code § 12071 (b)(6); see also Penal Code § 12073.

[1810]Penal Code § 12071 (b)(6); see also Penal Code § 12076.

[1811]Penal Code § 12071 (b)(6); see also Penal Code § 12077.

[1812]Penal Code § 12071 (b)(6); see also Penal Code § 12316.

[1813]Penal Code § 12071 (b)(6); see also Penal Code § 12072 (a), (b), and (f)(1).

[1814]Penal Code § 12071 (b)(8).

[1815]As described in Penal Code § 12080.

[1816]Penal Code § 12071 (b)(9).

[1817]Penal Code § 12071 (b)(10).

[1818]Penal Code § 12071 (b)(20)(G).

An "agent" is an employee of the licensee.[1819]

"Secured" means a firearm that is made inoperable in one or more of the following ways:[1820]

- the firearm is inoperable because it is secured by a firearms safety device listed on the DOJ's roster of approved firearms safety devices pursuant to law[1821]
- the firearm is stored in a locked gun safe or long-gun safe which meets the standards for department-approved gun safes set forth in the Penal Code[1822]
- the firearm is stored in a distinct locked room or area in the building that is used to store the firearms that can only be unlocked by key, a combination, or other means[1823]
- the firearm is secured with a hardened steel rod or cable that is at least 1/8 inch in diameter through the trigger guard of the firearm, with the steel rod or cable being secured with a hardened steel lock that has a shackle, the lock and shackle being protected or shielded from the use of a boltcutter and the rod or cable being anchored in a manner that prevents the removal of the firearm from the premises[1824]

"Clear evidence of his or her identity and age" means either a valid California driver's license[1825] or a valid California identification card issued by the DMV.[1826]

[1819]Penal Code § 12071 (b)(20)(G)(i).

[1820]Penal Code § 12071 (b)(20)(G)(ii).

[1821]Penal Code § 12071 (b)(20)(G)(I); see also Penal Code § 12088 (d).

[1822]Penal Code § 12071 (b)(20)(G)(II); see also Penal Code § 12088.2.

[1823]Penal Code § 12071 (b)(20)(G)(III).

[1824]Penal Code § 12071 (b)(20)(G)(IV).

[1825]Penal Code § 12071 (c)(1)(A).

[1826]Penal Code § 12071 (c)(1)(B).

"Secure facility," as it pertains to the laws covered in this chapter, means a building that meets all of the following requirements:[1827]

- all perimeter doors shall meet one of the following:[1828]
  - a windowless steel security door equipped with a dead bolt and a doorknob lock[1829]
  - a windowed metal door that is equipped with both a dead bolt and a doorknob lock, and, if the window has an opening of five inches or more measured in any direction, the window shall be covered with steel bars of at least ½ inch diameter or metal grating of at least 9 gauge affixed to the exterior or interior of the door[1830]
  - a metal grate that is padlocked and affixed to the licensee's premises independent of the door and doorframe[1831]
- all windows are covered with steel bars[1832]
- heating, ventilating, air-conditioning, and service openings are secured with steel bars, metal grating, or an alarm system[1833]
- any metal screens have spaces no larger than three inches wide measured in any direction[1834]
- all steel bars shall be no further than six inches apart[1835]

"Licensed premises," "licensed place of business," "licensee's place of

---

[1827]Penal Code § 12071 (c)(2).

[1828]Penal Code § 12071 (c)(2)(A).

[1829]Penal Code § 12071 (c)(2)(A)(i).

[1830]Penal Code § 12071 (c)(2)(A)(ii).

[1831]Penal Code § 12071 (c)(2)(A)(iii).

[1832]Penal Code § 12071 (c)(2)(B).

[1833]Penal Code § 12071 (c)(2)(C).

[1834]Penal Code § 12071 (c)(2)(D).

[1835]Penal Code § 12071 (c)(2)(E).

business," etc., means the building designated in the license.[1836]

Department of Justice Inspections of Licensees

The DOJ may inspect dealers to ensure compliance with all of the requirements and prohibitions as discussed above.[1837] An annual fee may be assessed by the DOJ, not to exceed $115, to cover the reasonable cost of maintaining the centralized list,[1838] including the cost of inspections.[1839] The applicant is responsible for providing evidence to the DOJ that the jurisdiction In which the business is located has the inspection program.[1840]

The DOJ shall maintain and make available upon request information concerning the number of inspections conducted and the amount of fees collected, a listing of exempted jurisdictions, the number of dealers removed from the centralized list, and the number of dealers found to have violated the prohibitions and/or regulations listed above with knowledge or gross negligence.[1841]

Register or Record of Sales Required to Be Kept by Firearms Dealer

As required by the DOJ, every dealer shall keep a register or record of electronic transfer in which shall be entered the information as required by law.[1842] A violation is a misdemeanor.[1843]

The register is in a uniform format, and is printed by a State Printer, who, upon issuing the non-transferable register to the dealer, shall forward to the DOJ

[1836]Penal Code § 12071 (c)(3).

[1837]Penal Code § 12071 (f).

[1838]See Penal Code § 12071 (e), regarding centralized list.

[1839]Penal Code § 12071 (f).

[1840]Penal Code § 12071 (f).

[1841]Penal Code § 12071 (g); see also Penal Code § 12071 (e) and (f).

[1842]Penal Code § 12073 (a); see also Penal Code § 12077 regarding required information.

[1843]Penal Code § 12073 (c).

the name of the business and the address of the business of the dealer, along with the series and sheet numbers of the register.[1844] Should the dealer move his business to a different location, he shall notify the DOJ of the move in writing within 48 hours.[1845]

However, in the following circumstances, the dealer need not keep a register or record of electronic transfer, as customarily required by law:[1846]

- the delivery, sale, or transfer of an unloaded firearm that is not a handgun by a dealer to another dealer upon proof of compliance with law regarding obtaining an electronic verification number[1847]
- the delivery, sale, or transfer of an unloaded firearm by a dealer to another dealer if that firearm is intended as merchandise in the receiving dealer's business and upon proof of compliance with the requirements regarding an electronic verification number[1848]
- the delivery, sale, or transfer of an unloaded firearm by a dealer to a person licensed as an importer or manufacturer under federal law[1849]
- the delivery, sale, or transfer of an unloaded firearm by a dealer who sells, transfers, or delivers the firearm to a person who resides outside this state who is licensed pursuant to federal law[1850]
- the delivery, sale, or transfer of an unloaded firearm by a dealer to a wholesaler if that firearm is being returned to the wholesaler and is intended as merchandise in the wholesaler's business[1851]

[1844]Penal Code § 12075.

[1845]Penal Code § 12075.

[1846]Penal Code § 12073 (b).

[1847]Penal Code § 12073 (b)(1); see also Penal Code § 12072 (f)(1).

[1848]Penal Code § 12073 (b)(2); see also Penal Code § 12072 (f)(1).

[1849]Penal Code § 12073 (b)(3); see also Chapter 44 (commencing with § 921) of Title 18 of the United States Code.

[1850]Penal Code § 12073 (b)(4); see also Chapter 44 (commencing with § 921) of Title 18 of the United States Code.

[1851]Penal Code § 12073 (b)(5).

- the delivery, sale, or transfer of an unloaded firearm that is not a handgun by a dealer to himself or herself[1852]
- the loan of an unloaded firearm by a dealer who has a licensed target facility if the loan is made at that facility for the purposes of target shooting, and as long as the firearm does not leave the facility[1853]
- the delivery of an unloaded firearm by a dealer to a gunsmith for service or repair[1854]
- the return of an unloaded firearm to the owner of that firearm by a dealer, if the owner initially delivered the firearm to the dealer for service and repair[1855]
- the loan of an unloaded firearm by a dealer to a person who possesses a valid entertainment firearms permit,[1856] so long as the use is solely as a prop in an entertainment production[1857]
- the loan of an unloaded firearm by a dealer to a consultant-evaluator, if the loan does not exceed 45 days from the date of delivery of the firearm by the dealer to the consultant-evaluator[1858]

DOJ Centralized List of Exempted Federal Firearms Licensees

Centralized List Defined, and Application to Be Placed on the List

As of January 1, 2008, the DOJ was required to keep a centralized list of persons who identify themselves as being licensed under federal law[1859] as a dealer,

---

[1852]Penal Code § 12073 (b)(6).

[1853]Penal Code § 12073 (b)(7).

[1854]Penal Code § 12073 (b)(8).

[1855]Penal Code § 12073 (b)(9).

[1856]See Penal Code § 12081 regarding entertainment firearms permit.

[1857]Penal Code § 12073 (b)(10).

[1858]Penal Code § 12073 (b)(11).

[1859]See Chapter 44 (commencing with § 921) of Title 18 of the United States Code.

pawnbroker, importer, or manufacturer of firearms whose licensed premises are within the State of California and who declare to the DOJ an exemption from the firearms licensing requirements in the Penal Code.[1860] The list is known as the "centralized list of exempted federal firearms licensees," and, to qualify for placement on the centralized list, an applicant shall do all of the following:[1861]

- possess a valid federal firearms license[1862] as a dealer, pawnbroker, importer, or manufacturer of firearms
- maintain eligibility under California law to possess firearms by possessing a current, valid certificate of eligibility[1863]
- maintain with the DOJ a signed declaration enumerating the applicant's statutory exemptions from California licensing requirements[1864]

Any person who furnishes a fictitious name, knowingly furnishes any incorrect information, or knowingly omits any information for the declaration as required above is guilty of a misdemeanor.[1865]

Fees for Applying to Be Included on the List

There is an annual fee of $115 to cover the costs of maintaining the centralized list of exempted federal firearms licensees, conducting inspections in accordance with law, and for the cost of maintaining the firearm shipment verification number system as defined by law.[1866] Fees may be increased at a rate

---

[1860]Penal Code § 12083 (a); see also Penal Code § 12070 regarding state licensing requirements.

[1861]Penal Code § 12083 (a).

[1862]Pursuant to Chapter 44 (commencing with § 921) of Title 18 of the United States Code.

[1863]Penal Code § 12083 (a)(2); see also Penal Code § 12071 regarding certificate of eligibility.

[1864]Penal Code § 12083 (a)(4); see also Penal Code § 12070 regarding licensing requirements by the State of California.

[1865]Penal Code § 12083 (a)(3).

[1866]Penal Code § 12083 (b); see also Penal Code § 12072 (f) regarding firearm shipment verification number system.

not to exceed the increase in the California Consumer Price Index.[1867]

Transfers of Firearms Involving Exempted Licensees

Any person licensed under federal law[1868] as a dealer, pawnbroker, importer, or manufacturer of firearms whose licensed premises are within this state shall not import or receive firearms from any source unless listed on the centralized list of firearms dealers,[1869] or the centralized list of exempted federal firearms licensees,[1870] or the centralized list of firearms manufacturers.[1871] Violation is a misdemeanor.[1872]

Record Keeping by Exempted Federal Firearms Licensees

All persons on the centralized list of exempted federal firearms licensees shall record and keep on file for three years the verification number that shall accompany firearms received from other federal licensees.[1873] A violation of this requirement is cause for immediate removal from the centralized list.[1874]

Information Compiled from List of Exempted Federal Firearms Licensees

Information compiled from the list shall be made available for the following purposes:[1875]

- requests from local, state, and federal law enforcing agencies and

---

[1867]Penal Code § 12083 (b).

[1868]See Chapter 44 (commencing with § 921) of Title 18 of the United States Code.

[1869]Pursuant to Penal Code § 12071.

[1870]Pursuant to Penal Code § 12083 (a).

[1871]Penal Code § 12083 (c)(1); see also Penal Code § 12086 (f).

[1872]Penal Code § 12083 (c)(2).

[1873]Penal Code § 12083 (d)(1); see also Penal Code § 12072 (f).

[1874]Penal Code § 12083 (d)(2).

[1875]Penal Code § 12083 (e).

- the duly constituted local authorities[1876]
- when the information is requested by a person licensed under federal law[1877] for determining the validity of the license for firearms shipments[1878]

DOJ Inspection of Premises

The DOJ may conduct onsite inspections at the business premises of a person on the centralized list to determine compliance with firearms laws.[1879] The DOJ will work with the ATF to ensure that licensees are not subject to duplicative inspections.[1880] During the inspections, the following firearms records shall be made available for review:[1881]

- federal records[1882] and the bound book containing information as required by law[1883]
- issued verification numbers[1884]
- any other records requested by the DOJ to determine compliance with law[1885]

1876 Penal Code § 12083 (e)(1).

1877 See Chapter 44 (commencing with § 921) of Title 18 of the United States Code.

1878 Penal Code § 12083 (e)(2).

1879 Penal Code § 12083 (f); see also Article 4 (commencing with Section 12070) of Chapter 1 of Title 2 of Part 4 of the Penal Code.

1880 Penal Code § 12083 (f).

1881 Penal Code § 12083 (f).

1882 See 27 C.F.R. § 417.125 (a).

1883 Penal Code § 12083 (f)(1); see also 27 C.F.R. §§ 478.124a and 478.125 (e) regarding information required to be kept in bound book.

1884 Penal Code § 12083 (f)(2); see also Penal Code § 12072 (f) regarding verification numbers.

1885 Penal Code § 12083 (f)(3); see also Penal Code § 12083.

Removal from Centralized List of Exempted Federal Firearms Licensees

The DOJ may remove from the centralized list any person who violates any of the above requirements and prohibitions set onto those licensees whose application was approved and were put onto the list.[1886]

The California Firearms Licensee Check (CFLC) Program

The DOJ is required to establish and maintain a centralized list of persons who are federally licensed as dealers, pawnbrokers, importers, or manufacturers of firearms with licensed premises within the State of California who are also exempt from the firearms dealer licensing requirements.[1887] The list is known as the Centralized List of Exempted Federal Firearms Licensees ("CLEFFL").[1888] This law does not affect California firearms dealers who were currently listed on either the centralized list of firearms dealers or the centralized list of firearms manufacturers.[1889]

The intent of the program is to ensure that the intended recipient of a firearms purchase or transfer currently meets all California requirements for lawfully dealing in firearms.

Beginning on July 1, 2008, all federal firearms license holders ("FFLs") (other than Type 03 and 06) were prohibited from delivering, selling, or transferring a firearm (excluding curio & relic long guns) to FFLs in California unless, prior to delivery, the person intending to deliver, sell, or transfer the firearm first obtains a

---

[1886]Penal Code § 12083 (g).

[1887]Penal Code § 12083; see also Penal Code § 12070 and California Department of Justice - Division of Law Enforcement - Information Bulletin Number 2008-BOF-01 entitled "Centralized List of Exempted Firearms Licensees and the California Firearms Licensee Check Program".

[1888]California Department of Justice - Division of Law Enforcement - Information Bulletin Number 2008-BOF-01 entitled "Centralized List of Exempted Firearms Licensees and the California Firearms Licensee Check Program".

[1889]California Department of Justice - Division of Law Enforcement - Information Bulletin Number 2008-BOF-01 entitled "Centralized List of Exempted Firearms Licensees and the California Firearms Licensee Check Program".

verification number from the DOJ.[1890] This includes firearm dealers and manufacturers who are active on the DOJ centralized list, who transfer firearms to another FFL within the State of California.[1891] This also includes transfers that occur at gun shows.[1892]

To implement this new requirement, the DOJ has developed the California Firearms Licensee Check (CFLC) program which allows FFLs to obtain firearms shipment verification numbers via the internet prior to shipping firearms to any FFL in California.[1893] Should the FFL not have an internet connection, the FFL may obtain a verification number by calling the DOJ at (916) 263-8100 or by a fax request at (916) 263-0790.[1894]

As of January 1, 2008, it is unlawful for an FFL (type 01, 02, 07, 08, 09, 10, or 11) to receive firearms in accordance with their status as an FFL unless they are on one of the Centralized Lists, those being either the Exempted Federal Firearms Licensees, Firearms Dealers, or Firearm Manufacturers.[1895]

[1890]Penal Code § 12072 (f)(1); California Department of Justice - Division of Law Enforcement - Information Bulletin Number 2008-BOF-01 entitled "Centralized List of Exempted Firearms Licensees and the California Firearms Licensee Check Program".

[1891]California Department of Justice - Division of Law Enforcement - Information Bulletin Number 2008-BOF-01 entitled "Centralized List of Exempted Firearms Licensees and the California Firearms Licensee Check Program".

[1892]California Department of Justice - Division of Law Enforcement - Information Bulletin 2008-BOF-05 entitled "California Firearms Licensee Check (CFLC) Program".

[1893]California Department of Justice - Division of Law Enforcement - Information Bulletin Number 2008-BOF-01 entitled "Centralized List of Exempted Firearms Licensees and the California Firearms Licensee Check Program".

[1894]California Department of Justice - Division of Law Enforcement - Information Bulletin Number 2008-BOF-01 entitled "Centralized List of Exempted Firearms Licensees and the California Firearms Licensee Check Program".

[1895]California Department of Justice - Division of Law Enforcement - Information Bulletin Number 2008-BOF-01 entitled "Centralized List of Exempted Firearms Licensees and the California Firearms Licensee Check Program"; see also Penal Code § 12083(c)(1).

Placement on the Centralized List of Exempted Federal Firearms Licensees

To be placed on the list, an applicant must possess a valid federal firearms license as a dealer, pawnbroker, importer, or manufacturer of firearms, possess a valid Certificate of Eligibility issued by the DOJ, and complete and submit the Application and the § 12070 Penal Code Exemption Declaration for Centralized List of Exempted Federal Firearms Licensees.[1896] Fees include an initial application fee of $73 for the Certificate of Eligibility, with an annual renewal fee of $22, and an annual fee of $115 for the Application and Declaration.[1897]

Practical Information Regarding the CFLC Program

First, there are no costs or fees associated with the CFLC program, with either enrolling into the program or acquiring the verification number.[1898] Also, the program applies only to transactions between FFLs, meaning, if one of the parties is not an FFL, the program does not apply.[1899]

To receive a firearm, the person must be listed on either the Centralized List of Firearms Dealers,[1900] or the Centralized List of Exempted Federal Firearms Licensees.[1901] The verification number, which is a unique number, is a five-digit number.[1902] Once approved, the DOJ will provide a Firearms Shipment Approval

---

[1896] California Department of Justice - Division of Law Enforcement - Information Bulletin Number 2008-BOF-01 entitled "Centralized List of Exempted Firearms Licensees and the California Firearms Licensee Check Program".

[1897] California Department of Justice - Division of Law Enforcement - Information Bulletin Number 2008-BOF-01 entitled "Centralized List of Exempted Firearms Licensees and the California Firearms Licensee Check Program".

[1898] California Firearms Licensee Check (CFLC) Program - Frequently Asked Questions.

[1899] California Firearms Licensee Check (CFLC) Program - Frequently Asked Questions.

[1900] See Penal Code § 12071.

[1901] See Penal Code § 12083 (c)(1).

[1902] Penal Code § 12072 (f)(1)(C).

Letter to the shipper that must be included with the firearm.[1903] If the party being shipped the firearm is not a licensed dealer, but is an FFL on the DOJ's Centralized List of exempt FFLs, that party must retain each Firearms Shipment Approval Letter for three years.[1904]

When a person wants to ship or transfer a firearm to another California FFL, he must first obtain the Firearms Shipment Letter, and before that person can obtain such a letter, he must be enrolled in the CFLC program.[1905] Even FFLs located out of state must enroll in the CFLC program.[1906]

Once enrolled, the FFL can access the CFLC database 24 hours per day, seven days per week.[1907]

Each and every shipment or transfer of firearms must be accompanied with a new Firearms Shipment Approval Letter, but any number of firearms may be included in the shipment and still only one letter is required.[1908]

Should an approved order change, such as additional firearms are going to be shipped, the order will be canceled, etc., the FFL must obtain a Firearms Shipment Modification/Cancellation Form, and complete and submit it to the DOJ.[1909]

[1903]Penal Code § 12072 (f)(1)(A).

[1904]Penal Code § 12083 (d)(1).

[1905]California Firearms Licensee Check (CFLC) Program - Frequently Asked Questions.

[1906]California Firearms Licensee Check (CFLC) Program - Frequently Asked Questions.

[1907]California Firearms Licensee Check (CFLC) Program - Frequently Asked Questions.

[1908]California Firearms Licensee Check (CFLC) Program - Frequently Asked Questions.

[1909]California Firearms Licensee Check (CFLC) Program - Frequently Asked Questions.

CHAPTER TWENTY

Dealer's Record of Sale

In California, the Department of Justice is the entity that determines the method by which a dealer shall submit firearm purchaser information.[1910] As of January 1, 2003, unless permitted by the DOJ, electronic transfer is the exclusive means by which purchaser information is transmitted to the DOJ, and telephonic transfers shall not be permitted for information regarding the sales of firearms.[1911]

In completing the record of electronic transfer, the purchaser shall be required to present clear evidence of his or her identity and age[1912] to the dealer, and the dealer shall require that person to sign his current legal name to the record of electronic transfer.[1913] Further, the salesperson shall affix his or her signature to the record of electronic transfer as a witness to the signature and identification of the purchaser.[1914]

Any person furnishing a fictitious name or address or who otherwise knowingly furnishes any incorrect information or knowingly omits any information required to be provided for the electronic transfer is guilty of a misdemeanor.[1915] However, if the person is prohibited from obtaining a firearm[1916] and who knowingly furnishes a fictitious name or address, or knowingly furnishes any incorrect information or knowingly omits any information required by the register shall be guilty of a misdemeanor or felony with the punishment ranging from as little as under a year in the county jail or state prison, and as much as a state prison term

---

[1910]Penal Code § 12076 (a)(1).

[1911]Penal Code § 12076 (a)(3).

[1912]As defined in Penal Code § 12071.

[1913]Penal Code § 12076 (c)(1).

[1914]Penal Code § 12076 (c)(1).

[1915]Penal Code § 12076 (c)(1).

[1916]Pursuant to Penal Code §§ 12021 or 12021.1, or Welfare and Institutions Code §§ 8100 or 8103.

of 18 months.[1917]

The record of applicant information shall be transmitted to the DOJ in Sacramento by electronic transfer on the same date of the application to purchase.[1918]

The original of each record of electronic transfer is to be retained by the dealer in consecutive order.[1919] Each original operates as the permanent record of the transaction and shall be retained for not less than three years from the date of the last transaction and is to be made available for the inspection of any peace officer, DOJ employee designated by the Attorney General, or agent of the ATF, upon the presentation of proper identification.[1920] However, no information shall be compiled therefrom regarding the purchasers or other transferees of firearms that are not pistols, revolvers, or other firearms capable of being concealed upon the person.[1921]

Should the purchaser request a copy of the record of electronic transfer, the dealer is to fulfill the request.[1922]

In the event the transaction is a private party transfer,[1923] a copy shall be provided to the seller or purchaser by the dealer, upon request.[1924] The dealer shall redact all of the purchaser's personal information[1925] from the seller's copy, and the

---

[1917]Penal Code § 12076 (c)(1).

[1918]Penal Code § 12076 (c)(2).

[1919]Penal Code § 12076 (c)(3).

[1920]Penal Code § 12076 (c)(3).

[1921]Penal Code § 12076 (c)(3).

[1922]Penal Code § 12076 (c)(4).

[1923]Pursuant to Penal Code § 12082.

[1924]Penal Code § 12076 (c)(5).

[1925]As required pursuant to Penal Code § 12077 (b)(1) and (c)(1).

seller's personal information from the purchaser's copy.[1926]

Fees for the electronic transfer may include a fee not to exceed $14 by the dealer, and any additional fees as required by the DOJ to reimburse the DOJ for carrying out the entire process.[1927]

Only one fee shall be charged for a single transaction on the same date for the sale of any number of firearms that are not pistols, revolvers, or other firearms capable of being concealed upon the person or for the taking of possession of those firearms.[1928] A reduced fee will be charged for firearms that are pistols, revolvers, or other firearms that are capable of being concealed.[1929]

Finally, only one fee shall be charged for a single transaction on the same date for taking title or possession of any number of firearms if they are being taken by operation of law,[1930] or by an infrequent transfer of a firearm by gift, bequest, intestate succession, or other means by those who are immediate family members.[1931]

[1926]Penal Code § 12076 (c)(5).

[1927]Penal Code § 12076 (e) and (f).

[1928]Penal Code § 12076 (i)(1).

[1929]Penal Code § 12076 (i)(2).

[1930]See Penal Code §§ 12078 (i).

[1931]Penal Code § 12076 (j); see also Penal Code § 12078 (c) and 12071 (b)(18).

CHAPTER TWENTY-ONE

Licenses to Manufacture of Firearms in California

As of January 1, 1999, no person, firm, or corporation licensed to manufacture firearms under federal law[1932] may manufacture firearms within this state unless licensed according to law.[1933] However, this does not apply to a person licensed to manufacture firearms under federal law[1934] within California to a manufacturer who manufactures fewer than 100 firearms in a calendar year within this state.[1935]

The Penal Code contains regulations for the licensing of persons who desire to manufacture firearms in the State of California.[1936] A detailed discussion is needed to address those regulations as they exist in the code.

To manufacture firearms in California, a person must be a licensee. A "licensee," for the purposes of getting a license to manufacture firearms, means a person, firm, or corporation that meets the requirements in two separate Penal Code sections.[1937] Basically, those two Penal Code sections require that the person must have a "license"[1938] as well as inclusion among those recorded in a "centralized list" of licensed manufacturers[1939] in order to be a licensee to manufacture firearms.

[1932]See 18 U.S.C. § 921 et seq., regarding federal firearms licensees.

[1933]Penal Code § 12085 (a); see Penal Code § 12086 regarding California licensing.

[1934]See 18 U.S.C. § 921 et seq., regarding federal firearms licensees.

[1935]Penal Code § 12085 (b).

[1936]See Penal Code § 12086.

[1937]Penal Code § 12086 (a)(1); see also Penal Code § 12086 (b)(2) and (f).

[1938]See Penal Code 12086 (a)(1)(a) and (b)(2).

[1939]Penal Code § 12086 (a)(1); see also Penal Code § 12086 (f) regarding the centralized list and those recorded in the centralized list.

Centralized List of Licensees

The DOJ shall maintain a centralized list of all persons licensed to manufacture firearms in California, which shall be provided annually to each police department and county sheriff within the state.[1940]

License to Manufacture

The DOJ shall accept applications for, and shall grant licenses permitting, the manufacture of firearms within this state.[1941] No license shall be granted by the department unless and until the applicant presents proof that he or she has all of the following:[1942]

- a valid license to manufacture firearms issued by the federal government (an FFL)[1943]
- any regulatory or business license, or licenses, required by the local government[1944]
- a valid seller's permit or resale certificate issued by the State Board of Equalization, if applicable[1945]
- a certificate of eligibility issued by the DOJ as required by law[1946]

Fees for License to Manufacture - Fees collected are used to administer the licensing system, as well as prosecuting violations of the laws regarding the manufacture of firearms, so, as with other permits and licensing, these fees are not tied strictly to processing applications.[1947] Costs to recoup in the fees include the

---

[1940] Penal Code § 12086 (f)(1).

[1941] Penal Code § 12086 (b)(1).

[1942] Penal Code § 12086 (b)(2).

[1943] Penal Code § 12086 (b)(2)(A); see also 18 U.S.C. § 921 et seq., regarding federal firearms licensing.

[1944] Penal Code § 12086 (b)(2)(B).

[1945] Penal Code § 12086 (b)(2)(C).

[1946] Penal Code § 12086 (b)(2)(D); see also Penal Code § 12071 (a)(4) regarding certificate of eligibility.

[1947] Penal Code § 12086 (b)(3).

cost to inspect and maintain a centralized list of licensed firearm manufacturers.[1948]

Fees for licensed manufacturers who produce fewer than 500 firearms in a calendar year in this state shall not exceed $250 per year, or the actual costs of inspections and maintaining a centralized list as discussed above, whichever is less.[1949]

Duration of License - A license granted by the DOJ shall be valid for no more than one year from the date of issuance and shall be in the form prescribed by the Attorney General.[1950]

Denial of License to Manufacture - The department shall inform applicants who are denied licenses of the reasons for the denial in writing.[1951]

Prohibitions on and Requirements of Licensees

The following requirements and prohibitions are imposed on all licensees.[1952]

Where Business is to Be Conducted - The business shall be conducted only in the buildings designated in the license.[1953]

Display of License - The license, or a copy thereof, certified by the DOJ, shall be displayed on the premises where it can easily be seen.[1954]

Reporting Stolen Firearms

When a licensee discovers that a firearm has been stolen or is missing from

---

[1948] Penal Code § 12086 (b)(3).

[1949] Penal Code § 12086 (b)(3).

[1950] Penal Code § 12086 (b)(3).

[1951] Penal Code § 12086 (b)(1).

[1952] Penal Code § 12086 (c).

[1953] Penal Code § 12086 (c)(1).

[1954] Penal Code § 12086 (c)(2).

the licensee's premises, the licensee shall report the loss or theft within 48 hours of the discovery to all of the following.[1955]

- the DOJ, in a manner prescribed by the DOJ[1956]
- the federal Bureau of Alcohol, Tobacco, and Firearms[1957]
- the local police department[1958]
- if there is no local police department, the county sheriff of the county where the license is valid[1959]

Employees Have Certificates of Eligibility

The licensee shall require each employee obtain a certificate of eligibility,[1960] which shall be renewed annually, prior to being allowed to come into contact with any firearm.[1961]

No Prohibited Persons Handing Firearms

The licensee shall prohibit any employee who the licensee knows, or reasonably should know, is prohibited from state or federal law from possessing, receiving, owning, or purchasing a firearm from coming into contact with any firearm.[1962]

Identification Marks on Manufactured Firearms

Each firearm manufactured in this state shall be identified with a unique serial number stamped onto the firearm utilizing the method of compression

---

[1955] Penal Code § 12086 (c)(3).

[1956] Penal Code § 12086 (c)(3)(A).

[1957] Penal Code § 12086 (c)(3)(B).

[1958] Penal Code § 12086 (c)(3)(C).

[1959] Penal Code § 12086 (c)(3)(D).

[1960] See Penal Code § 12071 (a)(4) regarding certificates of eligibility.

[1961] Penal Code § 12086 (c)(4)(A).

[1962] Penal Code § 12086 (c)(4)(B).

stamping.[1963] The licensee shall stamp the serial number onto the firearm within one business day of the time the receiver or frame is manufactured,[1964] and the licensee shall not use the same serial number for more than one firearm.[1965]

Finally, licensed manufacturers who produce fewer than 500 firearms in a calendar year within this state may serialize long guns only by utilizing a method of compression stamping or by engraving the serial number onto the firearm.[1966]

Record Keeping of Firearms Manufactured

The licensee shall record the type, model, caliber, or gauge, and serial number of each firearm manufactured or acquired, and the date of the manufacture or acquisition, within one business day of the manufacture or acquisition.[1967] Such records shall be maintained permanently within the building designated in the license,[1968] and backup copies of the records, whether electronic or hard copy, shall be made at least once per month.[1969] These backup records shall be maintained in a separate facility from the original records.[1970]

For at least 10 years, the licensee shall maintain records of all firearms that are lost or stolen, as prescribed by the DOJ.[1971]

Building in License Made Available for Inspection

The licensee shall allow the DOJ to inspect the building designated in the

---

[1963]Penal Code § 12086 (c)(5)(A).

[1964]Penal Code § 12086 (c)(5)(C).

[1965]Penal Code § 12086 (c)(5)(D).

[1966]Penal Code § 12086 (c)(5)(B).

[1967]Penal Code § 12086 (c)(6)(A).

[1968]Penal Code § 12086 (c)(6)(B).

[1969]Penal Code § 12086 (c)(6)(C).

[1970]Penal Code § 12086 (c)(6)(C).

[1971]Penal Code § 12086 (c)(10).

license to ensure compliance with the requirements put on licensees.[1972] The licensee shall also allow any peace officer, authorized law enforcement employee, or DOJ employee designated by the Attorney General, upon the presentation of proper identification, to inspect facilities and records during business hours to ensure compliance with the requirements set forth onto licensees.[1973]

Maintain a Secure Facility

The licensee shall store in a secure facility all firearms manufactured and all barrels for firearms manufactured.[1974] A "secure facility," as used in this area of the law as it applies to licensees to manufacture firearms, means that the facility satisfies all of the following:[1975]

- the facility is equipped with a burglar alarm with central monitoring[1976]
- all perimeter entries to areas in which firearms are stored other than doors, including windows and skylights, are secured with steel window guards or an audible, silent, or sonic alarm to detect entry[1977]
- all perimeter doorways are designed in one of the following ways:[1978]
  - a windowless security door equipped with both a deadbolt lock and doorknob lock[1979]
  - a windowed metal door equipped with both a deadbolt and a doorknob lock, as long as the window, if greater than 5 inches in either direction, is covered with steel

---

1972 Penal Code § 12086 (c)(7)(A).

1973 Penal Code § 12086 (c)(7)(B).

1974 Penal Code § 12086 (c)(8).

1975 Penal Code § 12086 (d).

1976 Penal Code § 12086 (d)(1).

1977 Penal Code § 12086 (d)(2).

1978 Penal Code § 12086 (d)(3).

1979 Penal Code § 12086 (d)(3)(A).

bars of at least one-half inch diameter or metal grating of at least nine gauge affixed to the exterior or interior of the door[1980]

- a metal grate that is padlocked and affixed to the licensee's premises independent of the door and doorframe[1981]
- hinges and hasps attached to doors by welding, riveting, or bolting with nuts on the inside of the door[1982]
- hinges and hasps installed so that they cannot be removed when the doors are closed and locked[1983]

- heating, ventilating, air-conditioning, and service openings are secured with steel bars, metal grating, or an alarm system[1984]
- steel bars used to satisfy the requirements are not capable of being entered by any person[1985]
- perimeter walls of rooms in which firearms are stored are constructed of concrete of at least 10-gauge expended steel wire mesh utilized with typical wood frame and drywall construction, and if there is no vault to store firearms, the facility shall use an exterior security-type door along with a high security, single-key deadbolt, or other door that is more secure, with firearms stored in a separate room away from any general living area or work area[1986]
- perimeter doorways, including the loading dock area, are locked at all times when not attended by paid employees or contracted employees, including security guards[1987]

[1980]Penal Code § 12086 (d)(3)(B).

[1981]Penal Code § 12086 (d)(3)(C).

[1982]Penal Code § 12086 (d)(3)(D).

[1983]Penal Code § 12086 (d)(3)(E).

[1984]Penal Code § 12086 (d)(4).

[1985]Penal Code § 12086 (d)(5).

[1986]Penal Code § 12086 (d)(7).

[1987]Penal Code § 12086 (d)(8).

- except when a firearm is being tested, any ammunition on the premises is removed from all manufactured guns and stored in a separate and locked room, cabinet, or box away from the storage area for the firearms, unless the ammunition is stored with a firearm within a locked safe[1988]

One exception to all of the above items that establish a "secure facility" is for manufacturers of less than 500 firearms per year. They may instead design a security plan that is approved by the DOJ or the federal Bureau of Alcohol, Tobacco, and Firearms.[1989]

If a plan is approved by the ATF, the plan must be filed with the DOJ and the local police department or sheriff if there is no local police department.[1990] If the plan is approved by the DOJ, the licensee must file the plan with the local police department or sheriff if there is no local police department.[1991]

Notification of Local Law Enforcement of License

The licensee shall notify the chief of police or other head of the municipal police department where the building designated in the license is located that the licensee is manufacturing firearms within that city or county at that location contained in the license.[1992] In the absence of any local police department, the licensee shall notify the county sheriff of the same.[1993]

Revocation of License

Any licensee who violates the provisions above may have his license

---

[1988] Penal Code § 12086 (d)(9).

[1989] Penal Code § 12086 (e).

[1990] Penal Code § 12086 (e)(1).

[1991] Penal Code § 12086 (e)(2).

[1992] Penal Code § 12086 (c)(9)(A).

[1993] Penal Code § 12086 (c)(9)(B).

revoked,[1994] and in the case of those licensees who knowingly or with gross negligence violate the above three times will become permanently ineligible to obtain a license to manufacture in California.[1995]

Upon revocation, notification shall be provided to local law enforcement authorities in the jurisdiction where the licensee's business is located, as well as to the ATF.[1996]

Licensed Manufacturer Discontinuing Operations

If a person, firm, or corporation required to be licensed under California law to manufacture firearms, and ultimately ceases operations, then the following records shall be forwarded to the ATF within three days of the closure of the business:[1997]

- records regarding the type, model, caliber, or gauge, and serial number of each firearm manufactured or acquired, and the date of acquisition[1998]
- records of all firearms lost or stolen[1999]

[1994]Penal Code § 12086 (f)(2).

[1995]Penal Code § 12086 (f)(3).

[1996]Penal Code § 12086 (g)(1).

[1997]Penal Code § 12085 (c).

[1998]Penal Code § 12085 (c); see also Penal Code § 12086 (c)(6)(A) regarding records kept by the licensee, and Penal Code § 12086 requiring such records to be kept.

[1999]Penal Code § 12085 (c); see also Penal Code § 12086 (c)(10) regarding records kept by the licensee, and Penal Code § 12086 requiring such records to be kept.

CHAPTER TWENTY-TWO

Gun Shows

Not surprisingly, gun shows in California are heavily regulated. The area of the law dealing with gun shows is often overlooked most books addressing the firearms laws of any particular state. For good measure, this book address the California Legislature's regulation of gun shows as contained in the Penal Code.[2000]

A "licensed gun show producer" (or "producer," as used in this chapter in this book), means a person who has been issued a certificate of eligibility by the DOJ pursuant to state law.[2001] A gun show may not be produced if the persons wishing to produce it do not have a certificate of eligibility first.[2002]

Gun Show Requirements for Producers of Gun Shows

Certificate of Eligibility Regulated by Department of Justice

The DOJ shall adopt regulations to administer the certificate of eligibility program and shall recover the full costs of administering the program by fees assessed on applicants who apply for certificates.[2003] It is also the intent of the California Legislature that the certificate of eligibility program for gun shows[2004] be incorporated into the certificate of eligibility program under Penal Code § 12071 to the maximum extent practicable.[2005]

Requirements for Certificate of Eligibility

No person shall produce, promote, sponsor, operate, or otherwise

---

[2000] See Penal Code §§ 12071, 12071.1, and 12071.4.

[2001] Penal Code § 12071.1 (c); see also Penal Code § 12071.1 (a), for laws pertaining to issuing a certificate of eligibility.

[2002] See Penal Code § 12071, 12071.1, and 12071.4.

[2003] Penal Code § 12071.1 (d).

[2004] See Penal Code § 12071.1.

[2005] Penal Code § 12071.1 (q).

organize a gun show or event[2006] unless that person possesses a valid certificate of eligibility from the DOJ.[2007] Unless the DOJ's records indicate that the applicant is a person prohibited from possessing firearms, a certificate of eligibility shall be issued by the DOJ to an applicant provided the applicant does all of the following:[2008]

- certifies that he or she is familiar with the provisions in the Penal Code,[2009] which includes the Gun Show Enforcement and Security Act of 2000
- ensures that liability insurance is in effect for the duration of the event or show in an amount of not less than one million dollars ($1,000,000)[2010]
- provides an annual list of the gun shows or events that the applicant plans to promote, produce, sponsor, operate, or otherwise organize during the year for which the certificate of eligibility is issued, including the date, time, and location of the gun shows or events,[2011] and if there exist any changes or additional gun shows will be promoted, sponsored, operated, or otherwise organized, the producer will notify the DOJ within 30 days of the change[2012]

Fee for Certificate of Eligibility - A licensed gun show producer shall be assessed an annual fee of $85 by the DOJ.[2013]

Requirements for Producing Gun Show After Certificate Issued - The producer of a gun show or event shall be responsible for informing prospective gun

---

[2006]See Penal Code § 12071 (b)(1)(B) for specified gun shows or events.

[2007]Penal Code § 12071.1 (a).

[2008]Penal Code § 12071.1 (a).

[2009]See Penal Code §§ 12071.1 and 12071.4.

[2010]Penal Code § 12071.1 (a)(2).

[2011]Penal Code § 12071.1 (a)(3).

[2012]Penal Code § 12071.1 (b).

[2013]Penal Code § 12071.1 (d).

show vendors of the requirements discussed below concerning vendor information[2014] and the annual event and security plan,[2015] as well as the Gun Show Enforcement and Security Act of 2000.[2016]

Vendor Information - Prior to the commencement of a gun show or event, the producer shall, upon written request, within 48 hours, or a later time specified by the requesting law enforcement agency, make available to the requesting law enforcement agency with jurisdiction over the facility, shall supply a complete and accurate list of all persons, entities, and organizations that have leased or rented, or are known to the producer to intend to lease or rent, any table, display space, or area at the gun show or event for the purpose of selling, leasing, or transferring firearms.[2017]

Also, upon a written request, for every day the gun show or event operates, and within 24 hours, or a later time as specified by the requesting law enforcement agency, the same information must be supplied.[2018]

In addition to the above information that must be turned over to requesting law enforcement agencies, the producer must also provide, if requested, the following information relative to a vendor who offers for sale firearms manufactured after December 31, 1898:[2019]

- his or her complete name
- his or her complete driver's license or identification number

The information must also be submitted to the DOJ. The producer shall, within seven calendar days of the commencement or event, but not later than noon on Friday for a show or event held on a weekend, submit a list of all prospective vendors and designated firearms transfer agents who are licensed firearms dealers

---

[2014]See Penal Code § 12071.1 (f) and (g).

[2015]See Penal Code § 12071.1 (h) and (i).

[2016]Penal Code § 12071.1 (j); see also Penal Code § 12071.4 regarding Gun Show Enforcement and Security Act of 2000.

[2017]Penal Code § 12071.1 (f).

[2018]Penal Code § 12071.1 (f).

[2019]Penal Code § 12071.1 (g).

to the DOJ for the purpose of determining whether these prospective vendors and designated firearms transfer agents possess valid licenses and are thus eligible to participate as licensed dealers at the gun show or event.[2020]

The DOJ shall examine its records and if it determines that a dealer's license is not valid, it shall notify the show or event producer of that fact prior to the commencement of the gun show or event.[2021]

Annual Event and Security Plan - No gun show or event shall commence unless all of the requirements as discussed below, regarding an annual event and security plan, are met.[2022] The producer and facility manager shall prepare an annual event and security plan and schedule that shall include, at a minimum, the following:[2023]

- the type of shows or events including, but not limited to, antique or general firearms[2024]
- the estimated number of vendors offering firearms for sale or display[2025]
- the estimated number of attendees[2026]
- the number of entrances and exits at the gun show or event site[2027]
- the location, dates, and times of the shows or events[2028]
- the contact person and telephone number for both the producer

---

[2020] Penal Code § 12071.1 (k).

[2021] Penal Code § 12071.1 (k).

[2022] Penal Code § 12071.1 (i).

[2023] Penal Code § 12071.1 (h).

[2024] Penal Code § 12071.1 (h)(1).

[2025] Penal Code § 12071.1 (h)(2).

[2026] Penal Code § 12071.1 (h)(3).

[2027] Penal Code § 12071.1 (h)(4).

[2028] Penal Code § 12071.1 (h)(5).

and the facility[2029]

- the number of sworn peace officers employed by the producer or the facilities manager who will be present at the show or event[2030]
- the number of nonsworn security personnel employed by the producer or the facility's manager who will be present at the show or event[2031]

The annual event and security plan shall be submitted by either the producer or the facility's manager to the DOJ and the law enforcement agency with jurisdiction over the facility.[2032] Not later than 15 days prior to the commencement of the gun show or event, the producer shall submit to the DOJ, the law enforcement agency with jurisdiction over the facility site, and the facility's manager, a revised event and security plan if significant changes have been made since the annual plan was submitted, including a revised list of vendors that the producer knows, or reasonably should know, will be renting tables, space, or otherwise participating in the gun show or event.[2033]

The event and security plan shall be approved by the facility's manager prior to the event or show after consultation with the law enforcement agency with jurisdiction over the facility.[2034]

Other Requirements in Producing a Gun Show - There are several other requirements that must be fulfilled before a gun show or event may commence, including:[2035]

- producers shall have written contracts with all gun show vendors

---

2029 Penal Code § 12071.1 (h)(6).

2030 Penal Code § 12071.1 (h)(7).

2031 Penal Code § 12071.1 (h)(8).

2032 Penal Code § 12071.1 (i).

2033 Penal Code § 12071.1 (i).

2034 Penal Code § 12071.1 (i).

2035 Penal Code § 12071.1 (m), (o), and (p).

selling firearms at the show or event[2036]

- producers shall post, in a readily visible location at each entrance to the parking lot at the show, signage that states: "The transfer of firearms on the parking lot of this facility is a crime."[2037]
- producers shall require that signs be posted in a readily visible location at each public entrance to the show containing, but not limited to, the following notices:[2038]
    - "This gun show follows all federal, state, and local firearms and weapons laws without exception."[2039]
    - "All firearms carried onto the premises by members of the public shall be checked, cleared of any ammunition, secured in a manner that prevents them from being operated, and an identification tag or sticker will be attached to the firearm prior to the person being allowed admittance to the show."[2040]
    - "No member of the public under the age of 18 years shall be admitted to the show unless accompanied by a parent, grandparent, or legal guardian."[2041]
    - "All firearms transfers between private parties at the show shall be conducted through a licensed dealer in accordance with the applicable state and federal laws."[2042]
    - "Persons possessing firearms on this facility must have in their immediate possession government-issued photo identification, and display it upon request to any security officer or any peace officer, as defined in Section

---

[2036]Penal Code § 12071.1 (m).

[2037]Penal Code § 12071.1 (p).

[2038]Penal Code § 12071.1 (o).

[2039]Penal Code § 12071.1 (o)(1).

[2040]Penal Code § 12071.1 (o)(2).

[2041]Penal Code § 12071.1 (o)(3).

[2042]Penal Code § 12071.1 (o)(4).

830."[2043]

Gun Show Producers Who Fail to Comply with Requirements

A willful failure by a gun show producer to comply with any of the requirements in the laws regarding gun shows,[2044] except for the posting of required signs, shall be guilty of a misdemeanor punishable by a fine not to exceed $2000, and shall render the producer ineligible for a gun show producer license for one year from the date of conviction.[2045]

The willful failure of a gun show producer to post signs as required by the laws regarding gun shows[2046] shall be guilty of a misdemeanor punishable by a fine not to exceed $1000 for the first offense and not to exceed $2000 for the second and subsequent offenses, and again, shall render the producer ineligible for a gun show producer license for one year from the date of conviction.[2047]

Multiple violations charged pursuant to law[2048] that arise from more than one gun show or event shall be grounds for suspension of a producer's certificate of eligibility pending adjudication of the violations.[2049]

If a producer fails to inform prospective gun show vendors of the requirements under the gun show laws as they are required to,[2050] or fails to inform them of applicable provisions of the Gun Show Enforcement and Security Act of

---

[2043] Penal Code § 12071.1 (o)(5); see also Penal Code § 830 for relevant peace officers with authority to demand identification at the gun show.

[2044] See Penal Code §§ 12071, 12071.1, and 12071.4.

[2045] Penal Code § 12071.1 (e)(1).

[2046] See Penal Code §§ 12071, 12071.1, and 12071.4.

[2047] Penal Code § 12071.1 (e)(2).

[2048] See Penal Code § 12071.1 (e)(1) and (2) regarding violations.

[2049] Penal Code § 12071.1 (e)(3).

[2050] See Penal Code 12071.1 (j).

2000 as required,[2051] or fails to provide vendor information to the DOJ, the gun show or event will not commence until those requirements are met.[2052]

Gun Show Requirements for Vendors at Gun Shows

All gun show vendors shall certify in writing to the producer that they:[2053]

- will not display, possess, or offer for sale any firearms, knives, or weapons for which possession or sale is prohibited[2054]
- acknowledge that they are responsible for knowing and complying with all applicable federal, state, and local laws dealing with the possession and transfer of firearms[2055]
- will not engage in activities that incite or encourage hate crimes[2056]
- will process all transfers of firearms through licensed firearms dealers as required by law[2057]
- will verify that all firearms in their possession at the show or event will be unloaded, and that the firearms will be secured in a manner than prevents them from being operated except for brief periods when the mechanical condition of a firearm is being demonstrated to a prospective buyer[2058]
- will not display or possess black powder, or offer it for sale[2059]
- have complied with requirements that the vendor provide to the producer all information relative to the vendor, the vendor's employees, and other persons, compensated or not, who will be

---

[2051] See Penal Code § 12071.1 (k).

[2052] Penal Code § 12071.1 (m).

[2053] Penal Code § 12071.4 (b).

[2054] Penal Code § 12071.4 (b)(1).

[2055] Penal Code § 12071.4 (b)(2).

[2056] Penal Code § 12071.4 (b)(3).

[2057] Penal Code § 12071.4 (b)(4).

[2058] Penal Code § 12071.4 (b)(5).

[2059] Penal Code § 12071.4 (b)(6).

working or otherwise providing services to the public at the vendor's display space if firearms manufactured after December 31, 1898, will be offered for sale there, including the following information:[2060]

- his or her complete name
- his or her driver's license or state issued identification card number
- his or her date of birth

The information in the last point above shall be kept by the producer at the show's or event's onsite headquarters for the duration of the show or event, and at the producer's regular place of business for two weeks after the conclusion of the show or event, and shall make the information available upon request to any sworn peace officer for the purposes of the officer's official law enforcement duties.[2061]

Vendors must also wear name tags that indicate their first and last name.[2062]

Licensed Firearms Dealer Who Are Gun Show Vendors Who Fail to Comply with Requirements - If a licensed firearms dealer fails to cooperate with the producer or fails to comply with the applicable requirements[2063] regarding gun shows or the Gun Show Enforcement and Security Act of 2000,[2064] that person shall not be allowed to participate in that gun show or event.[2065]

Gun Show Requirements for Attendees at Gun Shows

Yes, there are requirements for people who wish to attend a gun show.

No Loaded Firearms at Gun Show - No person at a gun show or event, other than security personnel or sworn peace officers, shall possess at the same

---

[2060] Penal Code § 12071.4 (b)(6); see also Penal Code § 12071.4 (e).

[2061] Penal Code § 12071.4 (e)(3).

[2062] Penal Code § 12071.4 (f).

[2063] See Penal Code § 12071.1.

[2064] See Penal Code § 12071.4.

[2065] Penal Code § 12071.1 (l).

time both a firearm and ammunition that is designed to be fired in the firearm.[2066] Of course, vendors having those items at the show for sale or exhibition are exempt from this prohibition.[2067] Those with carry permits, open or CCW, are not exempted from this prohibition.

Must be 18 Years of Age to Attend Without Adult - No member of the public who is under the age of 18 years of age shall be admitted to, or be permitted to remain at, a gun show or event unless accompanied by a parent or legal guardian, and such person under the age of 18 shall be accompanied by his or her parent, grandparent, or legal guardian, while at the show or event.[2068]

Must Check, Clear, and Render Inoperable Any Firearms Brought to Event - All firearms carried onto the premises of a gun show or event by members of the public shall be checked, cleared, cleared of any ammunition, and secured in a manner that prevents them from being operated, prior to that person being allowed admittance to the show.[2069]

Must Mark Any Firearms Brought to Event - Persons, other than show or event security personnel, sworn peace officers, or vendors, who bring firearms into the gun show or onto event premises must apply an identification tag or sticker to their firearm and shall sign in ink the tag or sticker that is attached to the firearm prior to being allowed admittance to the show or event.[2070]

The identification tag or sticker applied to the firearm shall state that all firearms transfers between private parties at the show or event shall be conducted through a licensed dealer in accordance with applicable state and federal laws.[2071] The person possessing the firearm shall complete and include his printed name, signature, and identification number from the gun owner's government-issued photo

---

[2066] Penal Code § 12071.4 (g).

[2067] Penal Code § 12071.4 (g).

[2068] Penal Code § 12071.4 (h).

[2069] Penal Code § 12071.4 (j).

[2070] Penal Code § 12071.4 (i) and (j).

[2071] Penal Code § 12071.4 (j).

identification prior to attaching the tag to the firearm.[2072]

Identification Readily Available for Those Possessing Firearms - All persons possessing firearms at the gun show or event shall have in his or her immediate possession government-issued photo identification and shall produce it and display it upon request to any security officer or peace officer.[2073]

Attendee Violation of Laws - Unless otherwise provided by law, a first violation by an attendee of any of the above is an infraction; any second or subsequent violation is a misdemeanor, unless on the first violation the attendee knows he or she to be in violation, which makes the first violation a misdemeanor instead of an infraction.[2074]

[2072] Penal Code § 12071.4 (j).

[2073] Penal Code § 12071.4 (k).

[2074] Penal Code § 12071.4 (l).

Part Eleven

Encounters with Law Enforcement, and Privately Owned Firearms and Other Weapons in the Custody of Law Enforcement

CHAPTER TWENTY-THREE

Encounters with Law Enforcement While Armed or While Transporting Firearms or Other Weapons

One should always minimize the amount of exposure he has to problems with law enforcement while carrying or transporting firearms. Most interactions with law enforcement for the average citizen deals with traffic stops, where the person has committed some offense and has been pulled over.

Knowing this, one should be careful to drive safely at all times with perhaps additional focus while armed and/or while transporting firearms. One should make sure they obey all traffic laws and also make sure the car is operating properly before starting the journey, such as checking the headlights to ensure they are working properly, as well as the turn signals. Such malfunctions prompt many traffic stops.

Assault weapons, handguns, and .50 BMG rifle must be unloaded and locked as prescribed by law. Shotguns and rifles in general need not be locked up but must be unloaded. However, if they are not locked up and in plain view, one can expect scrutiny from any law enforcement officer who notices the weapon during the traffic stop.

Finally, it is important to understand that during a traffic stop, the officer may not know the Penal Code line by line. They are likely not well-versed in the concealed carry laws, laws regarding assault weapons, that is, what you may or may not legally possess, and the like. Because they likely do not have a firm understanding of all of these laws, it is easy for someone who knows the laws to get frustrated with the officer rather quickly. Avoid allowing that frustration to create a truly adversarial situation. If any person in an encounter with law enforcement leaves the scene in handcuffs, there is a 100% guarantee it will not be the officer. Be cooperative and understanding.

Traffic Stops by Law Enforcement

The prudent traveler will always travel with his firearms being stored and/or transported according to law. This will eliminate most problems with law enforcement.

For those who are CCW holders and armed at the time of an encounter with a law enforcement officer, a requirement exists to notify the officer of at the time of the stop as to your status as a CCW and that you are armed. A great way of notifying the officer of your status, during a traffic stop, is to have your driver's license ready, along with the CCW license, and your hands on the steering wheel. There is no need to say anything; simply hand both licenses to the officer. He will choose how to proceed. Likely, he will inquire as to where the firearm is. Tell him. Also, ask permission before retrieving your registration and proof of insurance. Most officers know that getting a CCW license in California is a major feat, and the odds are that you are an individual that they need not be concerned with. However, that does not mean that you lower protocol. If anything, the fact that the officer now knows you are armed is argument enough to raise protocol, meaning, elevate the courtesy and respect you are giving to the officer. In the end, doing such will help more than hurt your situation.

Whether or not you are a CCW holder, you need not incriminate yourself, as you have a right to refuse any questioning. However, if you refuse to answer questions, there is a high probability of a major confrontation with the law enforcement officer. If you choose to answer the officer's questions, be sure to answer any questions you choose to answer truthfully. To lie is only going to make matters worse. If you believe you will be arrested, or you know you cannot truthfully answer a question without being arrested, simply say nothing or state that you will not answer any questions without first having an opportunity to consult your attorney.

It is important to realize that a CCW holder need not reveal their CCW status to a law enforcement officer if, at the time of the encounter, they are unarmed. Further, if you are a CCW holder, and your firearm is locked away according to law, such that if you did not have a CCW, you would be lawfully traveling with the weapon, you need not reveal either your CCW status or that a weapon exists in your car.

Law Enforcement Search of Your Vehicle

It is fairly common that at some point during a traffic stop, the law enforcement officer will ask to search your vehicle. The general rule of thumb is to refuse the search. You need not give consent. If they choose to search your vehicle anyway, do not get in the way. Allow them to do their job, and be respectful, so as to lower the odds of escalating the confrontation to an arrest.

CHAPTER TWENTY-FOUR

Privately Owned Firearms (and other Deadly Weapons) in the Custody of Law Enforcement and Other Agencies

Domestic Violence Situations

Authority to Confiscate Firearm or Other Deadly Weapon

Any officer with authorization[2075] who is at the scene of a domestic violence incident involving threat to human life or a physical assault shall take temporary custody of any firearm or other deadly weapon in plain sight or discovered pursuant to a consensual or other lawful search as necessary for the protection of the peace officer or other persons present.[2076]

Receipt for Confiscated Firearm or Deadly Weapon

Upon taking custody of the firearm or other deadly weapon, the officer shall give the owner or person who possessed the firearm a receipt, which shall describe the firearm or other deadly weapon and list any identification or serial number on the firearm.[2077] The receipt shall indicate where the firearm or other deadly weapon may be recovered, the time limit for recovery,[2078] and the date after which the owner or possessor can recover the firearm or other deadly weapon.[2079] No firearm or other deadly weapon shall be held less than 48 hours in domestic violence situations.[2080]

[2075]See Penal Code §§ 830.1, 830.2, 830.6, 830.31, 830.32, 830.5, and any other officer listed in Penal Code § 12028.5 (b), regarding officers with authorization.

[2076]Penal Code § 12028.5 (b).

[2077]Penal Code § 12028.5 (b); see also Penal Code § 12028.7 (a) for detailed information regarding the receipt.

[2078]See Penal Code § 12028.5 regarding time limit for recovery.

[2079]Penal Code § 12028.5 (b); see also Penal Code § 12028.7 (b).

[2080]Penal Code § 12028.5 (b).

Any campus peace officer[2081] who takes custody of a firearm or other deadly weapon during a domestic violence situation shall deliver the item within 24 hours to the city police department or sheriff's office in the jurisdiction where the college or school is located.[2082]

Return of Confiscated Weapon

Unless provided otherwise by law,[2083] if a firearm or other deadly weapon is not retained for use as evidence related to criminal charges brought as a result of the domestic violence incident, or it is not retained because it was illegally possessed, the firearm or deadly weapon shall be made available to the owner or person who was in lawful possession 48 hours after the seizure or as soon thereafter as possible, but no later than 5 business days afer the owner or person who was in lawful possession demonstrates compliance with the law as it pertains to applying to receive a confiscated firearm.[2084]

However, if it is discovered that the firearm or other deadly weapon that was confiscated during a domestic disturbance call was indeed stolen, it shall be restored to the lawful owner, as soon as its use for evidence has been served, upon his or her identification of the firearm or other deadly weapon and proof of ownership, and after the law enforcement has complied with the law relating to the return of a firearm or other deadly weapon in its possession.[2085]

Confiscated Firearm As Nuisance

Any firearm or other deadly weapon that was taken into custody and held

---

[2081] See Penal Code § 830.2 (a) and (b).

[2082] Penal Code § 12028.5 (c).

[2083] See Penal Code § 12028.5 (f).

[2084] Penal Code § 12028.5 (b); see also Penal Code § 12021.3 regarding application to recover firearm in the custody and control of law enforcement or a court.

[2085] Penal Code § 12028.5 (d); see also Penal Code § 12021.3 regarding process and application for recovery of a firearm in the custody and control of law enforcement or a court by the rightful, lawful owner.

by specified peace officers[2086] for longer than 12 months and not recovered by the owner or person who has lawful possession at the time it was taken into custody shall be considered a nuisance and sold or destroyed as provided by law.[2087] However, firearms or other deadly weapons not recovered in 12 months due to an extended hearing process[2088] are not subject to destruction until the court issues its decision, and then only if the court does not order the return of the firearm or other deadly weapon to the owner.[2089]

Petition to Refuse Return to Owner

In those cases in which a law enforcement agency has reasonable cause to believe that return of the firearm or other deadly weapon would be likely to result in endangering the victim or the person reporting the assault or threat, the agency shall advise the owner of the firearm or other deadly weapon, and within 60 days of the date of seizure, initiate a petition in superior court to determine if the firearm or other deadly weapon should be returned.[2090] The law enforcement agency may make an ex parte application stating good cause for an order extending the time to file a petition,[2091] and, including any extension of time granted pursuant to an ex parte request, a petition must be filed within 90 days of the date of seizure of the firearm or other deadly weapon.[2092]

Notice of Hearing When Refusing Return of Firearm

The law enforcement agency shall inform the owner or person who had lawful possession of the firearm or other deadly weapon, at that person's last known address by registered mail, return receipt requested, that he or she has 30 days

---

[2086]See Penal Code § 830.2 (a), (f), 830.31 (d), 830.5, and 12028.5 (e) regarding specified peace officers.

[2087]Penal Code § 12028.5 (e); see also Penal Code § 12028 (c) regarding firearm as nuisance, and disposal thereof.

[2088]See Penal Code § 12028.5 (j).

[2089]Penal Code § 12028.5 (e).

[2090]Penal Code § 12028.5 (f).

[2091]Penal Code § 12028.5 (f).

[2092]Penal Code § 12028.5 (f).

from the date of receipt of the notice to respond to the court clerk to confirm his or her desire for a hearing, and that the failure to respond shall result in a default order forfeiting the confiscated firearm or other deadly weapon.[2093] The person's last known address will be used as it will be presumed to be the address provided to the law enforcement officer by that person at the time of the domestic violence incident.[2094] In the event that person does not live at that address, the law enforcement agency shall make a diligent, good faith effort to learn the whereabouts of the person and to comply with these notification requirements.[2095]

Hearing - If the person requests a hearing, the court clerk shall set a hearing no later than 30 days from receipt of that request, and shall notify the person, the law enforcement agency involved, and the district attorney of the date, time, and place of hearing.[2096] Unless it is shown by a preponderance of the evidence that the return of the firearm or other deadly weapon would result in endangering the victim or the person reporting the assault or threat, the court shall order the return of the firearm or other deadly weapon and shall award reasonable attorney's fees to the prevailing party.[2097]

Default and Disposal of Weapon - If the person does not request a hearing or does not otherwise respond within 30 days of the receipt of the notice, the law enforcement agency may file a petition for an order of default and may dispose of the firearm or other deadly weapon according to law.[2098]

Appeal - If, at the hearing, the court does not order the return of the firearm or other deadly weapon to the owner or person who had lawful possession, that person may petition the court for a second hearing within 12 months from the

---

[2093] Penal Code § 12028.5 (g).

[2094] Penal Code § 12028.5 (g).

[2095] Penal Code § 12028.5 (g).

[2096] Penal Code § 12028.5 (h).

[2097] Penal Code § 12028.5 (h); see also (b).

[2098] Penal Code § 12028.5 (i); see also Penal Code § 12028 regarding disposal of firearm or other deadly weapon.

date of the initial hearing.[2099] If there is a petition for a second hearing, unless it is shown by clear and convincing evidence that the return of the firearm or other deadly weapon would result in endangering the victim or the person reporting the assault or threat, the court shall order the return of the firearm or other deadly weapon and shall award reasonable attorney's fees to the prevailing party.[2100] If the owner or person who had lawful possession does not petition the court for appeal, the firearm or other deadly weapon will be disposed of according to law.[2101]

Attorney's Fees After Action - A civil action or proceeding for the return of a firearm or ammunition, or other deadly weapon that was seized by authorities and not returned according to law, the court shall award reasonable attorney's fees to the prevailing party.[2102]

It is important to note that the Legislature does not intend the law enforcement agency, or the individual law enforcement officer, to be liable for any act in good faith in confiscating or maintaining custody of the firearm or other deadly weapon.[2103]

Important Definitions Regarding Confiscation of Firearms in Domestic Violence Situations

A couple of definitions are important to the laws regarding firearms and other deadly weapons and their confiscation during domestic violence situations.[2104]

"Domestic violence" means abuse perpetrated against any of the following persons:[2105]

[2099] Penal Code § 12028.5 (j).

[2100] Penal Code § 12028.5 (j); see also (b).

[2101] Penal Code § 12028.5 (j); see also Penal Code § 12028 regarding disposal of firearm or other deadly weapon.

[2102] Penal Code § 12028.5 (b); see also (h).

[2103] Penal Code § 12028.5 (k).

[2104] See Penal Code § 12028.5 (a) for complete list of definitions.

[2105] Penal Code § 12028.5 (a)(2).

- a spouse or former spouse[2106]
- a cohabitant or former cohabitant[2107]
- a person with whom the respondent is having or has had a dating or engagement relationship[2108]
- a person with whom the respondent has had a child, where the presumption applies that the male parent is the father of the child of the female parent[2109]
- a child of a party or child who is subject of an action under the Uniform Parentage Act,[2110] where the presumption applies that the male parent is the father of the child to be protected[2111]
- any other person related by consanguinity or affinity within the second degree[2112]

"Deadly weapon" means any weapon, the possession or concealed carrying of which is prohibited by law.[2113]

Firearms Retained as Exhibits in Criminal Actions

Notwithstanding any provision of law or of any local ordinance to the contrary, when any firearm is in the possession of any officer of the State of California, or of any local or county agency, or University of California or California State University campus peace officer agency, and the firearm is an exhibit in any criminal action or proceeding which is no longer needed or is unclaimed or abandoned property, which has been in the possession of the officer for at least 180

[2106]Penal Code § 12028.5 (a)(2)(A).

[2107]Penal Code § 12028.5 (a)(2)(B).

[2108]Penal Code § 12028.5 (a)(2)(C).

[2109]Penal Code § 12028.5 (a)(2)(D); see also Uniform Parentage Act (Part 3 (commencing with § 7600) of Division 12 of the Family Code).

[2110]See Part 3 (commencing with § 7600) of Division 12 of the Family Code.

[2111]Penal Code § 12028.5 (a)(2)(E).

[2112]Penal Code § 12028.5 (a)(2)(F).

[2113]Penal Code § 12028.5 (a)(3); see also Penal Code § 12020 regarding weapons that are prohibited from possession or concealed carry thereof.

days, the firearm shall be destroyed, or sold, as provided for by law.[2114]

However, any firearm in the possession of the Department of Fish and Game or which was used in the violation of any provision of the Fish and Game Code shall not be required to be disposed of as discussed above.[2115]

Firearms Retained Following Traffic Accidents

It is very common for firearms to wind up in the hands of law enforcement because of a traffic accident. If there are injured parties who are removed from the scene, it is the job of the law enforcement officers to take and inventory the contents of the vehicle. If there are firearms in the vehicle, they will take and inventory the firearms as well. Individuals who have guns in the custody of law enforcement agencies following a traffic accident will have to go through the regular channels to request the return of their firearms.

Disposition of Seized or Abandoned Firearms

Seized or abandoned firearms may be destroyed, sold at auction to FFLs, or given to the military.[2116]

Declaration and Disposal of Firearm or Other Weapon as Nuisance

The unlawful carrying upon the person of any explosive substance, other than fixed ammunition, dirk, or dagger, as provided by law,[2117] the unlawful carrying of a concealed handgun in violation of law,[2118] and the unlawful possession or carrying of any switchblade knife with a blade exceeding two inches,[2119] is a

---

[2114] Penal Code § 12032; see also Penal Code § 12028 regarding disposal of a firearm according to law.

[2115] Penal Code § 12032.

[2116] See Penal Code §§ 12028, 12028.5, and 12030.

[2117] See Penal Code § 12020 regarding weapons addressed by this law.

[2118] See Penal Code § 12025 regarding concealed firearms law.

[2119] See Penal Code § 653k regarding switchblade knife prohibitions.

nuisance.[2120]

Also, firearms of any nature owned or possessed in violation of the following laws, are considered a nuisance:[2121]

- offenses which involve the violent use of a firearm[2122]
- firearms in the custody of any person who has two or more convictions for brandishing a firearm[2123]
- firearms carried in violation of the concealed firearms law[2124]
- handguns possessed by a minor in violation of law[2125]
- firearms involved in violation of law by those prohibited persons with mental conditions[2126]
- firearms possessed by other prohibited persons[2127]
- firearms used in the commission or attempted commission of any misdemeanor or felony in the Penal Code, even if committed by a juvenile where the crime would have been a misdemeanor or felony if he or she were an adult[2128]

However, the firearm is not a nuisance if the firearm owner disposes of his or her firearm according to law.[2129] A firearm is also not a nuisance that is in the

---

[2120] Penal Code § 12028 (a).

[2121] Penal Code § 12028 (b)(1).

[2122] Penal Code § 12028 (b)(1); see also Penal Code § 12021 (a)(1); see also Penal Code § 12001.6.

[2123] Penal Code § 12028 (b)(1); see also Penal Code 12021 (a)(2); see also Penal Code § 417 (a)(2).

[2124] Penal Code § 12028 (b)(1); see also Penal Code § 12021.1.

[2125] Penal Code § 12028 (b)(1); see also Penal Code § 12101.

[2126] Penal Code § 12028 (b)(1); see also Chapter 3 of Division 5 of the Welfare and Institutions Code (commencing with § 8100).

[2127] Penal Code § 12028 (b)(1); see also Penal Code § 12021 (c)(1).

[2128] Penal Code § 12028 (b)(1).

[2129] Penal Code § 12028 (b)(2); see also Penal Code § 12021 (d)(2) regarding lawfully disposing of the firearm that would otherwise be deemed a nuisance.

possession of the Department of Fish and Game after being confiscated because it was used in violation of the Fish and Game Code.[2130]

Any weapon deemed a nuisance[2131] shall be surrendered to the local authorities[2132] for disposal according to law, including destruction.[2133] No weapon that has been stolen will be destroyed unless reasonable notice is given to its lawful owner, if his identity and address can reasonably be ascertained.[2134]

Other Means of Disposal of Firearms and Other Weapons

Any law enforcement agency which has custody of any firearms, or any parts of any firearms, which are subject to destruction as required by law[2135] may, in lieu of destroying the weapons, retain and use any of them as may be useful in carrying out the official duties of the agency, or upon approval of the court, may release them to any other law enforcement agency for use in carrying out the official duties of that agency, or may turn over to the criminalistics laboratory of the DOJ or the criminalistics laboratory of a police department, sheriff's office, or district attorney's office, any weapons which may be useful in carrying out the official duties of their respective agencies.[2136]

However, any such firearm, or part of a firearm, when it is no longer needed by the agency, shall be destroyed, unless they were previously donated to the California National Guard military museum and resource center, in which case,

---

[2130]Penal Code § 12028 (e).

[2131]For weapons deemed a nuisance under Penal Code § 12028 (a) and (b).

[2132]See Penal Code 12028 (c) for list of appropriate local authorities.

[2133]See Penal Code § 12028 (c) for disposal of the nuisance, and Penal Code § 12028 (d) for destruction of the nuisance.

[2134]Penal Code § 12028 (f).

[2135]According to "law", meaning, Chapter 1 - Firearms, of the California Penal Code.

[2136]Penal Code § 12030 (b).

they must be disposed of according to the Military and Veterans Code.[2137]

Weapons Sent to Training Academy in Lieu of Destruction

Any law enforcement agency which has custody of any firearms, or any parts of any firearms, which are subject to destruction as required by law[2138] may, in lieu of destroying the firearms, obtain an order from the superior court directing the release of the firearms to the sheriff.[2139] The sheriff shall enter those weapons into the Automated Firearms System (AFS), via the California Law Enforcement Telecommunications System (CLETS), with a complete description of each weapon, including the make, type, category, caliber, and serial number of the firearms, and the name of the academy receiving the weapon into the AFS miscellaneous field.[2140]

The sheriff shall then release the weapons to the basic training academy certified by the Commission on Peace Officer Standards and Training, so that the firearms may be used for instructional purposes in the certified courses.[2141] However, "destructive devices"[2142] are not considered "firearms" or "weapons" for the purposes of this law.[2143]

All firearms released to an academy shall be under the care, custody, and control of the particular academy.[2144] Any firearm, or any part of any firearm, which is not destroyed, and is donated and used in this fashion, shall be returned to the law enforcement agency which had original custody of the firearm when it is no longer needed by the basic training academy, or when the basic training academy is

---

[2137]Penal Code § 12030 (c); see also Military and Veterans Code § 179 regarding disposal of firearms and other weapons.

[2138]According to "law", meaning, Chapter 1 - Firearms, of the California Penal Code.

[2139]Penal Code § 12030 (d).

[2140]Penal Code § 12030 (d).

[2141]Penal Code § 12030 (d).

[2142]See Penal Code § 12301.

[2143]Penal Code § 12030 (d).

[2144]Penal Code § 12030 (d).

no longer certified by the commission.[2145]

Upon return, the law enforcement agency shall, on the date of the return, enter into the Automated Firearms System (AFS), via the California Law Enforcement Telecommunications System (CLETS), a complete description of each weapon, including the make, type, category, caliber, and serial number of the firearm, and the name of the entity returning the firearm.[2146]

Finally, any law enforcement agency that retains custody of any firearm pursuant to this section or that destroys a firearm pursuant to law[2147] shall notify the DOJ of the retention or destruction, included with a complete description of the firearm, the name of the manufacturer or brand name, model, caliber, and serial number.[2148]

[2145]Penal Code § 12030 (d).

[2146]Penal Code § 12030 (d).

[2147]See Penal Code § 12028 regarding disposal of firearm according to law.

[2148]Penal Code § 12030 (e).

CHAPTER TWENTY-FIVE

Applying to DOJ for Return of Seized or Stolen Firearm

At some point, firearms may end up being in the custody and control of law enforcement, and for a variety of reasons. Quite commonly, firearms are stolen from their rightful owner and ultimately make their way into the hands of law enforcement. However, firearms, as discussed above, may be taken from the rightful owner by law enforcement in situations such as confiscation during a domestic violence incident, being turned over in compliance with a protective order, restraining order, or other type of injunction, or they were used in a crime of some sort, such as armed robbery, to something as seemingly innocent as unlawfully carrying the firearm in violation of the concealed firearm law or the loaded firearm law.

Keep All Firearms Records

It is commonly known that many law enforcement agencies at all levels make it very difficult for the rightful owner to have a seized or stolen firearm returned to him without hassle, despite the process being fairly straight-forward. Many local authorities will require a proof of ownership of the firearm, with the original purchase receipt acting as sufficient proof of ownership. Therefore, it is best that all sales receipts and other records are kept in a safe place along with other important documents.

Applying for Return of Firearm

Basically, any person who claims title to any firearm that is in the custody or control of a court or law enforcement agency and who wishes to have the firearm returned to him or her shall make application for a determination by the DOJ as to whether he or she is eligible to possess a firearm.[2149] Before the DOJ will do an eligibility check, the application must be complete and include any applicable fees as discussed below.[2150] The application shall include the following:[2151]

- the applicant's name, address, date and place of birth, gender,

[2149] Penal Code § 12021.3 (a)(1).

[2150] Penal. Code § 12021.3 (d).

[2151] Penal Code § 12021.3 (a)(1).

telephone number, and complete address[2152]

- whether the applicant is a United States citizen; if not, the applicant shall also provide his country of citizenship and his alien registration or I-94 number[2153]
- if the firearm is a handgun, the firearm's make, model, caliber, barrel length, handgun type, country of origin, and serial number[2154]
- for residents of California, the applicant's valid California driver's license number or valid California identification card number[2155]
- for nonresidents of California, a copy of the applicant's military identification with orders indicating that the individual is stationed in California, a copy of his valid driver's license or identification card; all copies shall be notarized[2156]
- the name of the court or law enforcement holding the firearm[2157]
- the signature of the applicant and the date of the signature[2158]

Lying on Application for Return for Firearm

Any person furnishing a fictitious name or address or knowingly furnishing any incorrect information or knowingly omitting any information required to be provided for the application, including any notarized information, is guilty of a misdemeanor.[2159]

[2152]Penal Code § 12021.3 (a)(1)(A).

[2153]Penal Code § 12021.3 (a)(1)(B).

[2154]Penal Code § 12021.3 (a)(1)(C).

[2155]Penal Code § 12021.3 (a)(1)(D).

[2156]Penal Code § 12021.3 (a)(1)(D).

[2157]Penal Code § 12021.3 (a)(1)(E).

[2158]Penal Code § 12021.3 (a)(1)(F).

[2159]Penal Code § 12021.3 (a)(1)(G) and (a)(3).

Sale of Firearm in Possession of Law Enforcement

A person who owns a firearm that is in the custody of a court or law enforcement agency and who does not wish to obtain possession of the firearm, and the firearm is an otherwise legal firearm, and the person otherwise has a right to title of the firearm, shall be entitled to sell or transfer title of the firearm to a licensed dealer.[2160]

Requirements on Law Enforcement to Return Firearm

No law enforcement agency or court that has taken custody of any firearm may return the firearm to any individual unless the following requirements are satisfied:[2161]

- that individual presents to the agency or court notification of a determination[2162] by the DOJ that the person is eligible to possess firearms[2163]
- if the agency or court has direct access to the Automated Firearms System, the agency or court has verified that the firearm is not listed as stolen,[2164] and that the firearm has been recorded in the Automated Firearms System in the name of the individual that seeks its return[2165]
- if the firearm has been reported lost or stolen,[2166] a law enforcement agency shall notify the owner or person entitled to possession according to law,[2167] who in turn shall provide proof

---

[2160]Penal Code § 12021.3 (a)(2); see also Penal Code § 12071 regarding licensed dealers.

[2161]Penal Code § 12021.3 (b).

[2162]See Penal Code § 12021.3 (e).

[2163]Penal. Code § 12021.3 (b)(1).

[2164]See Penal Code § 11108.

[2165]Penal. Code § 12021.3 (b)(2).

[2166]See Penal Code § 11108.

[2167]See Penal Code § 11108.5.

of eligibility to possess a firearm[2168]

Fees

The local law enforcement agency may charge the rightful owner or person entitled to possession of the firearm the fees as allowed by law.[2169] However, individuals who are applying for a background check to retrieve a firearm that comes into the custody or control of the court or law enforcement agency shall be exempt from the fees provided that the court or agency determines that the firearm was reported stolen to a law enforcement agency prior to the date the firearm came into the custody and control of the court or law enforcement agency or within 5 business days of the firearm being stolen from its owner.[2170] The court or law enforcement agency shall notify the DOJ of this exemption whenever it occurs.[2171]

The DOJ shall establish a fee of $20 per request for return of a firearm, plus a $3 charge for each additional handgun being processed as part of the request to return a firearm.[2172] Fees may increase annually by using the California Consumer Price Index and shall be rounded to the nearest dollar.[2173]

Local agencies may impose charges equal to the administrative costs related to the seizure, impounding, storage, or release of firearms, and shall not exceed the actual costs incurred for the expenses directly related to the same.[2174] These administrative fees may be waived by the local agency upon verifiable proof that the firearm was reported stolen at the time the firearm came into the custody or control of the law enforcement agency.[2175] The following apply to any administrative

---

[2168]Penal. Code § 12021.3 (b)(3); see also Penal Code § 12021.3 (e).

[2169]Penal. Code § 12021.3 (b)(3); see also Penal Code § 12021.3 (j) regarding allowable fees.

[2170]Penal. Code § 12021.3 (b)(3).

[2171]Penal. Code § 12021.3 (b)(3).

[2172]Penal Code § 12021.3 (c).

[2173]Penal. Code § 12021.3 (c).

[2174]Penal Code § 12021.3 (j)(1).

[2175]Penal Code § 12021.3 (j)(1).

costs charged by the local agency:[2176]

- the charges shall only be imposed on the person claiming title to the firearms[2177]
- any charges shall be collected by the local agency only from the person claiming title to the firearm[2178]
- the charges shall be in addition to any other charges authorized or imposed pursuant to law[2179]
- no charge may be imposed for any hearing or appeal relating to the removal, impound, storage, or release of a firearm unless that hearing or appeal was requested in writing by the legal owner of the firearm, and the charge may be imposed only upon the person requesting that hearing or appeal[2180]

No costs for any hearing or appeal related to the release of a firearm shall be charged to the legal owner who redeems the firearm unless the legal owner voluntarily requests the post storage hearing or appeal.[2181] No local agency shall require a legal owner to request a post-storage hearing as a requirement for release of the firearm to the legal owner.[2182]

Notification of Eligibility to Receive Firearm

If the DOJ determines that the applicant is eligible to possess the firearm, the DOJ shall provide the applicant with written notification that includes the following:[2183]

2176 Penal Code § 12021.3 (j)(2).

2177 Penal Code § 12021.3 (j)(2)(A).

2178 Penal Code § 12021.3 (j)(2)(B).

2179 Penal Code § 12021.3 (j)(2)(C); see also Penal Code § 12021.3 regarding other charges pursuant to law.

2180 Penal Code § 12021.3 (j)(2)(D).

2181 Penal Code § 12021.3 (j)(3).

2182 Penal Code § 12021.3 (j)(3).

2183 Penal Code § 12021.3 (e)(1).

- the identity of the applicant[2184]
- a statement that the applicant is eligible to possess a firearm[2185]
- if the firearm is a handgun, a description of the handgun by make, model, and serial number[2186]

Time to Process Application

The DOJ shall have 30 days from the date of receipt to complete the background check unless delayed by circumstances beyond the control of the DOJ.[2187] If the firearm is a handgun, the DOJ shall enter a record of the handgun into the Automated Firearms System.[2188]

Denial of Application

If the DOJ denies the application, and the firearm is otherwise a legal firearm, the DOJ shall notify the applicant of the denial and provide a form for the applicant to use to sell or transfer the firearm to a licensed dealer.[2189] The applicant may contact the DOJ and inquire as to the reasons that formed the basis for the denial.[2190]

If a law enforcement agency determines that the applicant is the legal owner of any firearm deposited with the law enforcement agency and is prohibited from possessing any firearm and the firearm is an otherwise legal firearm, the applicant shall be entitled to sell or transfer the firearm to a licensed dealer.[2191]

[2184] Penal Code § 12021.3 (e)(1)(A).

[2185] Penal Code § 12021.3 (e)(1)(B).

[2186] Penal Code § 12021.3 (e)(1)(C).

[2187] Penal Code § 12021.3 (e)(3).

[2188] Penal Code § 12021.3 (e)(2).

[2189] Penal Code § 12021.3 (f); see also Penal Code § 12071 regarding licensed dealers.

[2190] Penal Code § 12021.3 (f).

[2191] Penal Code § 12021.3 (i)(1); see also Penal Code § 12071 regarding licensed dealers.

Time Courts and Law Enforcement May Hold Firearm

Notwithstanding any other provisions of law, no law enforcement agency or court shall be required to retain a firearm for more than 180 days after the owner of the firearm has been notified by the court or agency that the firearm has been made available for return.[2192] An unclaimed firearm may be disposed of after the 180-day period has expired.[2193]

Information Retained by the Department

Notwithstanding any other provision of law,[2194] the DOJ may retain personal information about an applicant in connection with a claim for a firearm that is not a handgun to allow for law enforcement confirmation of compliance with the law[2195] and may include personal identifying information regarding the individual applying for the clearance, but may not include information that identifies any particular firearm that is not a handgun.[2196]

No Licensed Dealer Transfer Required

None of the requirements[2197] regarding private party transfers or transfers between persons who are not licensed dealers shall apply to deliveries, transfers, or returns of firearms made by a court or a law enforcement agency when carrying out the return of a confiscated, lost, or stolen firearm to its lawful owner.[2198]

[2192] Penal Code § 12021.3 (g).

[2193] Penal Code § 12021.3 (g).

[2194] See Penal Code § 11106.

[2195] Specifically, in compliance with Penal Code § 12021.3.

[2196] Penal Code § 12021.3 (h).

[2197] See Penal Code §§ 12070 (a) and 12070 (d) regarding licensed dealers involved in transfer.

[2198] Penal Code § 12021.3 (i)(3) and (4).

Part Twelve

Self-Defense and Defense of Others in California

CHAPTER TWENTY-SIX

Self-Defense in California

Obviously, someone who may lawfully possess, handle, use, own, or be in control of a firearm may use such to defend himself in California. They may also use other weapons that they possess legally.

Interestingly enough, even prohibited persons who are not allowed to own, possess, handle, or use a firearm under either state or federal law have exceptions (in both state and federal law) created by the courts to allow them to use a firearm in self-defense or defense of others. The California Supreme Court outlined several circumstances where otherwise prohibited people may use a firearm.[2199] Those circumstances include:

- the prohibited person did not have a preconceived design or plan to obtain the firearm[2200]
- the firearm was made available to them by virtue of someone else's actions[2201]
- they possessed the firearm only long enough as necessary to use the firearm in defense to repel the attack[2202]
- the use of the firearm by the prohibited person is of last resort; that is, there is no other option[2203]
- the prohibited person cannot have substantially contributed to the situation[2204]
- the prohibited person cannot create a greater danger by obtaining and using a firearm than the danger he is supposed to be trying to

---

[2199]See *People v. King* (1978) 22 Cal.3d 12, 24; *People v. Pepper* (1996) 41 Cal.App.4th 1029, 1035.

[2200]See *People v. King* (1978) 22 Cal.3d 12.

[2201]See *People v. King* (1978) 22 Cal.3d 12.

[2202]See *People v. King* (1978) 22 Cal.3d 12.

[2203]See *People v. King* (1978) 22 Cal.3d 12.

[2204]See *People v. Pepper* (1996) 41 Cal.App.4th 1029.

avoid[2205]

Federal law uses the same circumstances to create the rule, but adds that those prohibited under federal law from possessing a firearm must not be reckless in placing themselves in situations where it might be possible to need to use a firearm in self-defense.[2206]

Defense of Self

Lawful resistance to the commission of a public offense may be made[2207] by the party about to be injured[2208] or by other parties.[2209] Resistence sufficient to prevent the offense may be made by the party about to be injured[2210] to prevent an offense against his person, or his family, or some member thereof.[2211]

In California, there is no clear cut rule regarding self-defense, and instead, the rules of self-defense were created primarily by a mix of statutes and what is known as "case law," that is, law that was created by virtue of court decisions involving various cases over the years. Simply put, self-defense is the subject of statutory and case law.[2212]

Generally, in order for a person to defend himself using deadly force, that person must have an actual belief (that is, genuine and honest), and that belief is reasonable, he is indeed in imminent danger of death or great bodily injury as the result of an unlawful attack, and that the person's act of self-defense is necessary to prevent the injury, and that a reasonable person under the same circumstances

---

[2205] See *People v. Pepper* (1996) 41 Cal.App.4th 1029.

[2206] See *U.S. v. Sahakian* (9th Cir. 1992) 965 F.2d 740; U.S. v. Lemon (9th Cir. 1987) 824 F.2d 763.

[2207] Penal Code § 692.

[2208] Penal Code § 692 1.

[2209] Penal Code § 692 2.

[2210] Penal Code § 693.

[2211] Penal Code § 693 1.

[2212] *People v. Aris* (1989) 215 Cal.App.3d 1178, 1185.

would have the same perception and would have acted similarly.[2213]

There are several keywords in the statement above, which must be examined carefully. The keywords include the following:

- honest and reasonable belief
- they are in imminent danger
- death or great bodily injury
- an unlawful attack
- self-defense is necessary (must be reasonable)
- reasonable person would have acted the same way

Honest and Reasonable Belief

Honest Belief - To use deadly force in California as a means of self-defense, a person must have an "honest" belief that he is

1) in imminent danger, and
2) at risk of death or great bodily injury, from
3) an unlawful attack, and
4) self-defense is necessary to prevent death or great bodily injury to himself

If the facts do not lead an average person, or a jury, to conclude that a person who used deadly self-defense could honestly believe all four of the above points, that person could be in both civilly and criminally liable.

Reasonable Belief - The situation must create a sense that all four of the other elements listed above are true and must cause a "reasonable person" to conclude likewise. A "reasonable person" would be the average, prudent citizen. What would that person do if in that situation? This is known as the "reasonable person standard." Generally, the reasonable person is likely to be the "average jury member," because again, that will be who is determining whether or not it was reasonable for one to use deadly self-defense.

Honest and Reasonable Belief Considerations

If the jury ultimately determined that the person had an honest belief of any of the above criteria (imminent danger, risk of death or great bodily injury, an

---

[2213] See *People v. Aris* (1989) 215 Cal.App.3d 1178, 1186.

unlawful attack, self-defense was necessary), however, it was unreasonable to have that any one of those beliefs, that person cannot be convicted of homicide. Instead, that person will be convicted of voluntary manslaughter, if his acts caused death, or he will be convicted of assault and/or battery if the person survived the defensive acts.[2214]

Fortunately, prior threats are to be considered when determining the reasonableness of the self-defense used.[2215] If the person that was killed or injured had made threats against the defendant prior to his actions, the jury is to consider such threats when considering the reasonableness of the defensive actions taken.

Also, when considering reasonableness, jury members must consider how the situation appeared to the person who defended himself, and not how they themselves would have seen it.[2216]

Imminent Danger

To justify the use of deadly force as self-defense, the danger to one's life or physical well-being must be imminent. "Imminent" means "likely to occur at any moment" or "impending." Mere fear that the danger will be become imminent at a later time is not imminent.[2217]

One Very Important Consideration

One must be aware that the Penal Code does not allow one person, in self-defense, defense of others, or defense of property, to shoot to kill or shoot to wound. The purpose of the self-defense laws is to allow a person in danger to shoot to stop the threat that put that person in fear for their life, or the life of another. Once the threat stops, the shooting must end. Otherwise, one risks becoming the aggressor and thereby facing criminal charges.

[2214]See *People v. Flannel* (1979) 25 Cal.3d 668, 674-680, [160 Cal.Rptr.84, 603 P.2d 1]

[2215]See *People v. Pena* (1984) 141 Cal.App. 3d 462.

[2216]See *People v. Dawson* (1948) 88 Cal.App.2d 85, 96, *People v. Torres* (1949) 94 Cal.App.2d 146, 151; CALJIC 5.51.

[2217]*People v. Aris* (1989) 215 Cal.App.3d 1178, 1188, 1192, overruled on other grounds.

Defense of Others

Regarding the defense of others, such as your immediate family, the general rule is that one may use as much force to defend other people as it would take to defend oneself under the same threat.[2218]

Reasonable Force

The force allowed by a person forced to use self-defense to protect himself must be no more than what is reasonably necessary[2219] to cause the attacker to repel the attack. Force that goes beyond what is reasonable to repel the attack is excessive force, and the person forced to defend himself who chooses to use excessive force has exposure to criminal and civil liability.

Transition from Self-Defense to Attack

It is unlawful for someone forced to defend himself, when he realizes the attacker has been repelled, to continue the fight, such that the person defending himself becomes an attacker. Also, the person who was forced to defend himself cannot serve up some of his own justice by further attacking the original attacker as a means to punish him or her.

Pursuit of Attacker That Has Been Repelled

Only when the fleeing attacker continues represents a real and reasonable threat of death or serious injury to the victim or other potential victims if he or she is chased down to continue the altercation.

Castle Doctrine

In many states, there is a rule called the "castle doctrine," that designates one's home, and in some states, one's car or any other place legally occupied, as a place where one may enjoy existing free of illegal trespassing, harm, or violent attack. Where the castle doctrine applies, the use of any force that results in the death of the attacker may be defended as justifiable.

[2218] See Civil Code § 50; see also Penal Code §§ 197, 692, 693, 694.

[2219] Civil Code § 50; see also Penal Code §§ 197, 692, 693.

Fortunately, this is one part of the law where the California Legislature has it (somewhat) right. In California, there is no duty to retreat from the home, as any person using force intended or likely to cause death or great bodily injury within his or her residence shall be presumed to have held a reasonable fear of imminent peril of death or great bodily injury to self, family, or a member of the household when that force is used against another person, not a member of the family or household, who unlawfully and forcibly enters the residence and the person using the force knew or had reason to believe that an unlawful and forcible entry had occurred.[2220]

Important elements to consider from the above rule include:

1) the person unlawfully or forcibly enters or entered the residence
2) the person is not a member of the family or household
3) the person using self-defense knows or has reason to believe force was used to enter the home

All three elements must be present. If so, such circumstances create a rebuttable presumption that the homicide was justifiable.[2221] That it is "rebuttable" means that a prosecutor may try to prove that one of the elements was not present, and therefore, the homicide was not justifiable. Of course, the defendant will be given an opportunity to bolster his or her case that the presumption should apply, by providing more facts to bolster that position.

Another situation that has led to problems for many defendants is that the entry into the residence must be "unlawful." Using deadly self-defense against police trying to make an arrest or in attempting to prevent a person who has a right to be in the residence spells trouble for any defendant.

Duty to Retreat / Stand Your Ground Under the Castle Doctrine

Another rule is that a defendant is not required to retreat . . . he or she is entitled to stand his or her ground and defend himself or herself, and, if reasonably necessary, to pursue the assailant until the danger has passed; this is so even if safety could have been achieved by retreating.[2222]

It should be noted, however, that it has been held by California courts that

---

[2220]Penal Code § 198.5.

[2221]See Penal Code § 197.

[2222]CALCRIM 506.

burglaries that do not reasonably create fear of great bodily harm are not sufficient cause for the extraction of human life.[2223]

Stand Your Ground

In California, there is no "stand your ground" statute as there is in a few other states, but case law suggests that if a person is attacked there is no duty for that person to retreat, regardless of where that person is. Such a victim may stand his ground to defend himself and use such force is as reasonable considering the circumstances.[2224]

Preventing Crime

More often than not, the first responders to any crime are ordinary, average citizens, and not law enforcement. Some first responders have carry permits, concealed or open. However, this section is for all potential first responders - that is, this section is for everyone.

Several crimes outlined by the courts are such that ordinary, average citizens, with or without carry permits, may get involved and attempt to prevent a crime. Such crimes that allow deadly force by average citizen first responders include:

- felonies where there is a serious danger of death or great bodily harm to self or others
- situations where one attempts to suppress a riot or keep the peace
- situations where a person has already committed a felony involving danger of death or great bodily harm

A few bits of wisdom may be offered concerning the above situations. First, it would be very unwise to attempt to suppress a riot or keep the peace. Just stay out of it. Go somewhere else. Seriously.

Regarding situations where there is serious danger of death or great bodily harm to self or others is a common scenario discussed by those who are into self-

---

[2223] *People v. Ceballos* 12 Cal.3d 470 (1974).

[2224] *People v. Clark* (1982) 130 Cal.App.3d 371, 380, overruled on other grounds.

defense training. While it would be great to save others, one should seriously consider whether or not to get involved. Late responders, such as police officers, likely will not know that a person who chooses to defend himself or others, or to attempt to stop a crime, is not part of the crime. If that good Samaritan has a firearm out, shooting or not, or has some other weapon or is in the mode of attack, the responding law enforcement may fire upon that person. Seriously consider whether it is worth getting involved. Sometimes it is best to let the professionals handle situations like this, and instead, hunker down, be prepared to engage the criminal if he comes towards you or your family, and ride out the situation.

Your family will appreciate having you alive instead of in a body bag.

Not only that, but if for those who choose to get involved, there are no immunities that are extended to police officers for mistakes. Therefore, if a good Samaritan makes a mistake in his perception as to who is the bad guy or who is the good guy, or accidentally shoots innocent people, he may incur both criminal and civil liability.

In most cases, one with a firearm is responsible for every bullet that travels downrange, past the intended recipient. However, in self-defense situations, if the person who is defending himself is doing so lawfully, he will not incur criminal liability if a missed shot accidentally hits an innocent person.[2225]

Justifiable Homicide

According to statute, homicide is justifiable when committed by any person in the following cases:[2226]

- when resisting any attempt to murder any person, or to commit a felony, or to do some great bodily injury upon any person; or[2227]
- when committed in defense of habitation, property, or person, against one who manifestly intends or endeavors, by violence or surprise, to commit a felony, or against one who manifestly intends and endeavors, in a violent, riotous or tumultuous manner, to enter the habitation of another for the purpose of

---

[2225] *People v. Matthews*, (1979) 91 Cal.App.3d 1018, 1024.

[2226] Penal Code § 197.

[2227] Penal Code § 197 1.

offering violence to any person therein; or,[2228]

- when committed in the lawful defense of such person, or of a wife or husband, parent, child, master, mistress, or servant of such person, when there is reasonable ground to apprehend a design to commit a felony or to do some great bodily injury, and imminent danger of such design being accomplished; but such person, or the person in whose behalf the defense was made, if he was the assailant or engaged in mutual combat, must really and in good faith have endeavored to decline any further struggle before the homicide was committed; or[2229]
- when necessarily committed in attempting, by lawful ways and means, to apprehend any person for any felony committed, or in lawfully suppressing any riot, or in lawfully keeping or preserving the peace[2230]

Of course, the discussion proceeding this section involves case law that interprets and adds to this statutory definition on justifiable homicide by providing the certain elements that must exist before deadly self-defense is warranted. One must take into account all the information above when considering potential self-defense strategies in a given situation.

Excusable Homicide

Homicide may also be excusable in situations that are not really self-defense, but for reference, the statutory excusable homicide law is included here.

Homicide is excusable in the following cases:[2231]

- when committed by accident and misfortune, or in doing any other lawful act by lawful means, with usual and ordinary caution, and without any unlawful intent[2232]
- When committed by accident or misfortune, in the heat of

[2228]Penal Code § 197 2.

[2229]Penal Code § 197 3.

[2230]Penal Code § 197 4.

[2231]Penal Code § 195.

[2232]Penal Code § 195 1.

passion, upon any sudden and sufficient provocation, or upon a sudden combat, when no undue advantage is taken, nor any dangerous weapons is used, and when the killing is not done in a cruel or unusual manner[2233]

[2233]Penal Code § 195 2.

CHAPTER TWENTY-SEVEN

Defense of Property in California

In order to understand the law regarding defense of property, one must first understand the difference between what is considered under the law to be "real property" and what is "personal property."

The most basic definition of "real property" is "land and all things attached to it." This would include your house, a shed in the back yard, a flagpole sticking out of the ground in front of your home, and the like.

The most basic definition of "personal property" is "anything that is not real property is personal property and personal property is anything that is not nailed into, dug into, or built onto the land." This would include a dining room table in your home, a leather chair in the living room, your silverware, firearms kept in a safe in your home, and the like.

Protecting Property with Deadly Force

Personal Property - One may not use deadly force, or even force that is likely to cause great bodily injury, in protecting his personal property. The use of a firearm or a knife, or some other deadly weapon, in protecting personal property is generally not allowed, as the use of such would be considered deadly force.

Real Property - One may use deadly force to protect real property in situations where there is a danger of death or great bodily injury to the individuals present on the real property.

Also, the rightful owner or possessor of the land, such as a lessee, may use force to eject a trespasser if it appears that the trespasser will either damage the property or injure those rightfully on the property, so long as the trespasser is first asked to leave the property and given a reasonable time to vacate the property.[2234] The amount of force that may be used is only which is reasonably necessary to eject the trespasser.[2235]

[2234] *People v. Miller* (1946) 72 Cal..App.2d 602, 606.

[2235] *People v. Miller* (1946) 72 Cal..App.2d 602.

Boobytraps on Real Property - As previously discussed, except as provided elsewhere and according to law,[2236] any person who assembles, maintains, places, or causes to be placed a boobytrap device[2237] is guilty of a felony punishable by imprisonment in the state prison for two, three, or five years.[2238] A "boobytrap" means any concealed or camouflaged device designed to cause great bodily injury when triggered by an action of any unsuspecting person coming across the device, and may include, but is not limited to, guns, ammunition, or explosive devices attached to trip wires or other triggering mechanisms, sharpened stakes, and lines or wire with hooks attached.[2239]

Possession of any boobytrap device with the intent to use the device as a boobytrap is punishable in a state prison, or in a county jail, not exceeding one year, or by a fine of $5000, or both.[2240]

The problem with boobytraps is that they imperil the lives of children, firemen, and policemen acting within the scope of their employment, along with others.[2241] Boobytraps are silent instrumentalities of death, dealing death to the innocent and the criminal intruder without the slightest warning and are considered brutally savage and inhuman.[2242]

Therefore, the lawful citizen should refrain from setting boobytraps to protect real or personal property.

[2236] See Penal Code § 12301 regarding exceptions.

[2237] See Penal Code § 12355 (c) for definition of "boobytrap device".

[2238] Penal Code § 12355 (a).

[2239] Penal Code § 12355 (c).

[2240] Penal Code § 12355 (b).

[2241] *People v. Ceballos* (1974) 12 Cal.3d 470, 477.

[2242] See *People v. Ceballos* (1974) 12 Cal.3d 470, 477.

Part Thirteen

Everything Else Regarding California Firearms and Weapon Law

CHAPTER TWENTY-EIGHT

Miscellaneous California Firearms Laws and Considerations

DOJ Pamphlet Summarizing Firearms Laws

The DOJ prepares a pamphlet which summarizes California firearms laws as they pertain to persons other than law enforcement officers or members of the armed services.[2243] Included in the pamphlet are the following matters:[2244]

- lawful possession[2245]
- licensing procedures[2246]
- transportation and use of firearms[2247]
- acquisition of hunting licenses[2248]
- the safe handling and use of firearms[2249]
- various methods of safe storage and child-proofing of firearms[2250]
- the availability of firearms safety programs and devices[2251]
- the responsibilities of firearms ownership[2252]
- the operation of various types of firearms[2253]

[2243]Penal Code § 12080 (a).

[2244]Penal Code § 12080 (b).

[2245]Penal Code § 12080 (b)(1).

[2246]Penal Code § 12080 (b)(2).

[2247]Penal Code § 12080 (b)(3).

[2248]Penal Code § 12080 (b)(4).

[2249]Penal Code § 12080 (b)(5).

[2250]Penal Code § 12080 (b)(6).

[2251]Penal Code § 12080 (b)(7).

[2252]Penal Code § 12080 (b)(8).

[2253]Penal Code § 12080 (b)(9).

- the lawful use of deadly force[2254]

These pamphlets are offered at actual cost to firearms dealers[2255] who shall have copies of the most current version available for sale to retail purchasers or transferees of firearms.[2256] This pamphlet is intended to provide a general summary of laws applicable to firearms and is not designed to provide individual guidance for specific areas.[2257]

Individuals having specific questions about issues addressed in the pamphlet shall be directed to contact their local law enforcement agency or private counsel.[2258] This applies to readers of this book as well.

The DOJ or any other public entity shall be immune from any liability arising from the drafting, publication, or dissemination of the pamphlet or any reliance upon it.[2259]

Attorney General Report Regarding Use of Firearms in Crime

The Attorney General shall provide the Legislature on or before April 15 of each year, commencing in 1998, a written report on the specific types of firearms used in the commission of crimes based upon information obtained from state and local crime laboratories and shall include all of the following information regarding crimes in which firearms were used:[2260]

- a description of the relative occurrence of firearms most frequently used in the commission of violent crimes, distinguishing whether the firearms used were handguns, rifles, shotguns, assault

---

[2254]Penal Code § 12080 (b)(10).

[2255]See Penal Code § 12071 regarding licensed dealers applicable to this law.

[2256]Penal Code § 12080 (c).

[2257]Penal Code § 12080 (c).

[2258]Penal Code § 12080 (c).

[2259]Penal Code § 12080 (d).

[2260]Penal Code § 12039.

weapons, or other related types of weapons[2261]

- a description of specific types of firearms that are used in homicides or street gang and drug trafficking crimes[2262]
- the frequency with which stolen firearms were used in the commission of the crimes[2263]
- the frequency with which fully automatic firearms were used in the commission of crimes[2264]
- any trends of importance such as those involving specialized ammunition or firearm modifications, such as conversion to a fully automatic weapon, removal of a serial number, shortening of barrel, or use of a suppressor[2265]

Prohibited Armed Persons File

The Attorney General maintains an online database that is known as the Prohibited Armed Persons File.[2266] The purpose of this file is to cross-reference persons who have ownership or possession of a firearm on or after January 1, 1991, as indicated by a record in the Consolidated Firearms Information System, and who, subsequent to the date of that ownership or possession of a firearm, fall within a class of persons who are prohibited from owning or possessing a firearm.[2267]

The information contained in the Prohibited Armed Persons File shall only be available to those entities specified in, and pursuant to, California Penal Code § 11105, through the California Law Enforcement Telecommunication System (CLETS), for the purpose of determining if persons are armed and prohibited from

---

[2261] Penal Code § 12039 (a).

[2262] Penal Code § 12039 (b).

[2263] Penal Code § 12039 (c).

[2264] Penal Code § 12039 (d).

[2265] Penal Code § 12039 (e).

[2266] Penal Code § 12010 (a).

[2267] Penal Code § 12010 (a).

possessing firearms.[2268]

Upon entry into the Automated Criminal History System of a disposition for a conviction of any felony, a conviction for any firearms-prohibiting charge[2269] or other charge,[2270] a firearm prohibition due to a mental condition,[2271] or any firearms possession prohibition identified by the federal National Instant Check System (NICS), the DOJ shall determine if the subject has an entry in the Consolidated Firearms Information System indicating possession or ownership of a firearm on or after January 1, 1991, or an assault weapon registration, or a .50 BMG rifle registration.[2272]

Upon an entry into any department automated information system that is used for the identification process, persons who are prohibited by state or federal law from acquiring, owning, or possessing firearms, the department shall determine if those subjects have an entry in the Consolidated Firearms Information System indicating ownership or possession of a firearm on or after January 1, 1991, or an assault weapon registration, or a .50 BMG rifle registration.[2273]

If the DOJ determines that, after considering the above, the subject has an entry in the Consolidated Firearms Information System indicating possession or ownership of a firearm on or after January 1, 1991, or an assault weapon registration, or a .50 BMG rifle registration, the following information will be entered into the Prohibited Armed Person File:[2274]

- the subject's name[2275]

[2268]Penal Code § 12010 (b).

[2269]See Penal Code § 12021.

[2270]See Penal Code § 12021.1.

[2271]See Welfare and Institutions Code §§ 8100 and 8103.

[2272]Penal Code § 12011 (a).

[2273]Penal Code § 12011 (b).

[2274]Penal Code § 12011 (c).

[2275]Penal Code § 12011 (c)(1).

- the subject's date of birth[2276]
- the subject's physical description[2277]
- any other identifying information regarding the subject that is deemed necessary by the Attorney General[2278]
- a description of all firearms owned or possessed by the subject, as reflected by the Consolidated Firearms Information System[2279]

Entertainment Firearms Permits

The DOJ provides those in the entertainment industry a permit so their productions involving firearms can be done so legally.[2280]

Who May Apply for Permit - Any person who is at least 21 years of age may apply for an entertainment firearms permit from the DOJ that authorizes the permit holder to possess firearms loaned to him or her for use solely as a prop in a motion picture, television, video, theatrical, or other entertainment production or event.[2281] Upon receipt of the initial or renewal application, the DOJ will examine its records, records the DOJ is authorized to request and review from the State Department of Mental Health,[2282] and records of the National Instant Criminal Background Check System (NCIS),[2283] in order to determine if the applicant is prohibited from possessing or receiving firearms.[2284]

The DOJ shall issue an entertainment firearms permit only if the records

---

[2276]Penal Code § 12011 (c)(2).

[2277]Penal Code § 12011 (c)(3).

[2278]Penal Code § 12011 (c)(4).

[2279]Penal Code § 12011 (c)(5).

[2280]See Penal Code § 12081 regarding entertainment permits.

[2281]Penal Code § 12081 (a).

[2282]See Welfare and Institutions Code § 8104 regarding authorization of the DOJ to request and review records from the State Department of Mental Health.

[2283]See 18 U.S.C. 922 regarding records in the NICS.

[2284]Penal Code § 12081 (a).

indicate that the applicant is not prohibited from possessing or receiving firearms pursuant to any federal, state, or local law.[2285]

Duration of License - An entertainment firearms permit issued by the DOJ shall be valid for one year from the date of issuance.[2286] If at any time during that year the permit holder becomes prohibited from possessing or receiving firearms pursuant to any federal, state, or local law, his or her entertainment firearms permit shall no longer be valid.[2287]

Information Required on Entertainment Firearms Permits - Requests for entertainment firearms permits shall be made on application forms prescribed by the DOJ that require applicant information, including, but not limited to, the following:[2288]

- complete name[2289]
- residential and mailing address[2290]
- telephone number[2291]
- date of birth[2292]
- place of birth[2293]
- country of citizenship and, if other than the United States, alien number or admission number[2294]
- valid driver's license number or valid identification card number

---

[2285] Penal Code § 12081 (a).

[2286] Penal Code § 12081 (f).

[2287] Penal Code § 12081 (f).

[2288] Penal Code § 12081 (b)(1).

[2289] Penal Code § 12081 (b)(1)(A).

[2290] Penal Code § 12081 (b)(1)(B).

[2291] Penal Code § 12081 (b)(1)(C).

[2292] Penal Code § 12081 (b)(1)(D).

[2293] Penal Code § 12081 (b)(1)(E).

[2294] Penal Code § 12081 (b)(1)(F).

issued by the California DMV[2295]
- Social Security Number[2296]
- signature[2297]

An initial application for an entertainment firearms permit shall require the submission of fingerprint images and related information in a manner as prescribed by the DOJ, for the purpose of obtaining information as to the existence and nature of a record of state or federal level convictions and state or federal level arrests for which the DOJ establishes that the individual was released on bail or on his or her own recognizance pending trial as needed to determine whether the applicant may be issued the permit.[2298] Requests for federal level criminal offender record information received by the Department of Justice pursuant to this section shall be forwarded by the DOJ to the FBI.[2299]

The DOJ shall also review the criminal offender record information[2300] for entertainment firearms permit applicants,[2301] and subsequent arrests[2302] to determine the continuing validity of the permit for all entertainment firearms permit holders.[2303]

Lying on Entertainment Permit Application - Any person who furnishes a fictitious name or address, knowingly furnishes any incorrect information, or knowingly omits any information required to be provided on the application is guilty

---

2295 Penal Code § 12081 (b)(1)(G).

2296 Penal Code § 12081 (b)(1)(H).

2297 Penal Code § 12081 (b)(1)(I).

2298 Penal Code § 12081 (b)(3).

2299 Penal Code § 12081 (b)(3).

2300 See Penal Code § 11105 regarding criminal record information.

2301 Penal Code § 12081 (b)(4).

2302 See Penal Code § 11105.2 regarding records of subsequent arrests.

2303 Penal Code § 12081 (b)(5).

of a misdemeanor.[2304]

Fees Involved with the Entertainment Firearms Permit - All applications must be submitted with the appropriate fee,[2305] as the DOJ shall recover the full costs of administering the program by assessing the following application fees:[2306]

- for the initial application: $104[2307]
- for each annual renewal application: $29[2308]

The DOJ will annually review and shall adjust the fees if necessary to fund fully, but not to exceed the actual costs of, the permit program, including enforcement of the program.[2309]

Finally, those who hold an entertainment firearms permit are the only permit holders in California who are exempt from the background check provisions under the Brady Act.

Airline Travel with Firearms[2310]

When traveling by air, a firearms owner must declare and check any firearms he wants to be stored and returned after the flight. Ammunition need not be declared.

All firearms must be unloaded and kept in a hard-sided container. The container must be locked. A locked container is defined as one that completely secures the firearms from access by anyone other than the owner. Cases that can be pulled open with very little effort are not considered locked containers.

[2304] Penal Code § 12081 (b)(6).

[2305] Penal Code § 12081 (b)(2).

[2306] Penal Code § 12081 (c).

[2307] Penal Code § 12081 (c)(1).

[2308] Penal Code § 12081 (c)(2).

[2309] Penal Code § 12081 (e).

[2310] This entire section is as provided by the Transportation Security Administration.

Any key or combination must be provided to the security officer if he choose to inspect the container. The owner should remain present during the screening to take the key back. If the owner is not present at the time the officer chooses to inspect the container, the container will not be placed on the plane.

Ammunition must be securely packed in fiber (such as cardboard), wood, or metal boxes or other packaging that is specifically designed to carry small amounts of ammunition. Magazines or clips are not allowed to be used for packing ammunition unless they completely and securely enclose the ammunition, such as containers that securely cover the exposed portions of the magazine or by securely placing the magazine in a pouch, holder, holster, or lanyard.

Ammunition may be stored in the same hard-sided case as the firearm, so long as it is also packed as described above.

Black powder or percussion caps are not allowed on the plane whatsoever.

Violations of these provisions are dealt with through severe punishment and penalties of up to $10,000 per violation.

Airlines have their own additional requirements on the carriage of firearms and the amount of ammunition that one may transport in checked baggage. It is important to contact the carrier prior to traveling to inquire about their individual policies.

Part Fourteen

Firearms Safety Considerations

CHAPTER TWENTY-NINE

Firearms and Weapons Safety

Whether you are pro-gun or anti-gun, one point every citizen can likely agree on is that gun safety is of paramount concern. In 2005, 3,424 people died in California from firearm-related injuries, and 4,533 people were hospitalized for non-fatal gunshot wounds in California.[2311]

No firearms related book would be complete without a few words on firearms safety and the safe handling of firearms.

Basic Firearms Safety Considerations

1. Treat each and every firearm as if it were loaded. When you first handle any firearm, be sure to inspect it to determine if it is loaded or unloaded. If you do not know how to check a particular gun as to whether it is loaded or not, you should leave it alone and seek assistance from someone who is more knowledgeable about that gun. To insure your safety and the safety of those around you, it is always best to assume that a gun is loaded, even if you think it is unloaded, and even if you have already checked it. By doing this, you will create a habit of handling a gun safely. It will be second-nature to handle a gun as if it were loaded. It is important to always respect the firearm, and to understand the dangers presented by someone who improperly handles a firearm.

2. Never point the muzzle of the firearm towards any object that you are unwilling to destroy. Always keep the muzzle of the gun pointed in a safe direction. The best place to point a firearm is a direction where an accidental discharge (commonly called a negligent discharge, or "ND"), of the firearm will not cause injury or damage to yourself or others. Never quit paying attention to where you or others are pointing a firearm. It is never amusing, and is instead very dangerous, and in very poor taste, to point a firearm at yourself, another person, or an animal that you do not intend to shoot. Again, it is important to always respect the firearm, and to understand the dangers presented by someone who improperly handles a firearm.

[2311] California Department of Health Services, Epidemiology and Prevention for Injury Control Branch (EPIC), Firearm Injuries in California (2008).

3. Keep your finger off the trigger at all times while handling a firearm up until the point in time that you are pointed in at your target and ready to fire. Keep your trigger finger outside the trigger guard that surrounds the trigger until you are ready to fire. The best place for the finger is along the frame of the weapon, with the tip of the finger resting gently on top of the reference point, which is usually a slide stop, a screw, or some other physical feature along the side of the frame, which is actually simply holding the finger down the side of the frame or receiver. That way, if you were to drop the gun for any reason, or suddenly grip the firearm for any reason, you do not inadvertently apply pressure to the trigger.

If you choose to handle a firearm in the fashion described above, it will actually become uncomfortable to hold a firearm with your finger on the trigger. You will create a level of consciousness of where your finger is that you will not have to give much thought. For some, this is very similar to wearing a seat belt when in an automobile. Some people are so aware of the safety risks of not wearing a seat belt that they cannot even sit in a car comfortably without the seat belt on, even if the car is not moving and is not going to move. If they are in a car, the seat belt will be on. They will do this without even giving it any thought.

The proper handling of a firearm is the same. If you handle a firearm properly, after some time of doing so, you will ultimately develop a level of consciousness that allows you to respect a firearm without having to give it any thought; it will be natural.

4. Be aware of your target and everything around and behind it. A prudent shooter will check the areas around, behind, and in front of a target to ensure that the area is safe before shooting.

When you fire a gun, rarely does the bullet stop at the target. Instead, the bullet travels downrange somewhere before coming to a rest. If there is someone or something downrange that you do not want to shoot at, you should not be shooting at that target. If you are ever in doubt of what is downrange, it is prudent to not shoot the firearm at all. Most importantly, before shooting any firearm, get a good sense of where all the people are around you. Check behind you, in front of you, and to your sides. Check this area regularly so as to raise the safety level for yourself and others around you.

5. Penetration and Zone of Danger Information. In general, a residential home is built with walls that are constructed with two layers of 5/8 inch sheet rock. It is safe to assume that just about any type of bullet, no matter how small and powerless or how big and powerful, will penetrate the sheet rock and continue to travel out the other side. Consider this when handling a firearm at your home and you are either unsure of what is on the other side of the structure, or you know what is on the other side and know it is something you would prefer not to point a gun at or shoot at.

Further, the range of typical rifle bullets can be as short as 4500 feet to as high as 17,000 feet. This is nearly a mile to over three miles! Pistol rounds do not travel as far, generally with a range of about 4500 feet to as high as 7500 feet. The range of a shotgun is much shorter, with ranges from about 700 feet to 2,500 feet. So, in considering what is behind your target, a safe rule of thumb is to assume that at a minimum, the typical downrange zone of danger if you fire a gun is one mile.

Additional Firearms Safety Considerations

Consider your attitude on any day that you might be handling a firearm. If you have had a bad day, are angry, troubled, or even if you simply did not get a good night's rest the night before, perhaps you should not be handling a firearm as your judgment and ability to focus on safety may be impaired.

Transport guns and ammunition in a safe, secure, and legal fashion. Store guns and ammunition safely, securely, and legally. Just because you are off doing other things and are not currently dealing with your firearm, safety considerations still exist. The responsible firearms owner will spend good time considering just how to store his firearms and ammunition. Ideally, firearms and ammunition are never stored together.

Consider using a firearms safety device on your firearms that will prevent the weapon from being fired until unlocked. Common devices are trigger locks and cable locks. All firearms and ammunition should be stored in some sort of locked container, or, better yet, in a gun safe. The more you lock up your firearm, the less chance there is that the firearm will be involved in some sort of unfortunate situation.

Shoot only where it is safe and legal.

Learn how your firearm functions and how to operate properly the firearm. It is amazing how many people do not know how their firearm functions. For instance, it is shocking how many people do not know what a "trigger reset" is. A gun owner who has no clue what a trigger reset is does not fully understand how his firearm works. If you do not know what the trigger reset is, what other things do you not know? As a firearms owner, it is your responsibility to know.

As a gun owner, you have a great responsibility to yourself and others to become thoroughly familiar with your firearm and how to handle it in a safe fashion. You should be able to identify the various parts of your firearm, and how to maintain them in safe, working condition. You should know how to load the firearm, unload the firearm, and clear the inevitable malfunction from your gun. Various firearms operate differently, so you should become inherently familiar with each and every firearm you own.

When shooting with friends, never assume their firearm functions the same as firearms you are already familiar with. There are many resources to answer any questions you may have regarding a particular firearm. If you bought the firearm, included with it should have been an owner's manual and field strip guide. A field strip guide provides detail regarding taking the gun apart for routine cleaning and maintenance, as well as problem solving. Furthermore, such information is on the manufacturer's website, or contact either the manufacturer directly or locate a local gunsmith. A responsible firearms enthusiast who plans on handling firearms in any regards will insist on taking a class prior to handling the particular firearm. Find a local gun club or organization that either has classes for novices or can recommend local classes for novices. People who are part of the gun culture are usually very friendly and eager to help newcomers participate in the sport.

Learn how to confirm that the firearm is safe to shoot and confirm each and every time you pick up your firearm.

Learn how to check to be sure the barrel is clear of obstructions.

Never handline firearms while under the influence of drugs or alcohol. Any chemical impairments coupled with the handling and./or use of a firearm greatly increases the odds of a bad situation. Drugs, even some over-the-counter drugs and prescription drugs, as well as alcohol, can dramatically impair your judgment as well as mental functions and physical coordination.

Further, no celebration exists that justifies shooting a firearm in happiness and celebration. It is common in other countries to fire a gun into the air in celebration of New Year's Eve or other national holidays. Any responsible firearms owner will refuse to participate and even strongly discourage such activity.

Whatever goes up, must come down. And a bullet fired into the air will ultimately return to earth and could seriously injure or kill someone.

At all times while handling firearms, you and others around you should wear ear and eye protection, and should dress appropriately for a day of shooting.

The loud noise, often called the report, can cause permanent hearing damage. Further, the debris, including the shell casing of a bullet, unfired powder, and hot gas, all of which are emitted each time most types of firearms are fired, can result in injuries to your eyes.

If you are shooting with others, consider wearing fitted clothing. Open-collared shirts and blouses will allow a discharged shell casing to travel down into the garment, and ultimately trapping that shell, often referred to as "hot brass," to be pinned up against your body where it will burn your skin. Hot brass cools very quickly, but some people tend to dance around in an attempt to create space between the skin and the hot brass. This can be very dangerous to everyone involved, as such excitement could cause someone involved to be distracted at the same moment as pulling the trigger. Wear appropriate clothing when you plan to shoot a firearm in the presence of others who are also shooting firearms.

Safety Considerations and Children

These considerations are important even if you do not keep a firearm in the house. Many people do, and accidents tend to happen in someone else's house.

Always lock up firearms and/or render them inoperable with a firearms safety device of your choosing. Do so even if you do not have children, but make sure to do so if you have children. Small children are able to work firearms.

Test yourself. Pick up an unloaded firearm with your opposite hand; that is, if you are left-handed, pick it up right-handed, and vice versa. Unless you have been trained otherwise, your trigger finger will automatically rest on the trigger. A child will pick up a firearm in the same fashion, no matter which hand he uses. This is a very scary thought.

Talk to your children about firearms at an age they can begin to appreciate what you are telling them. A four year old will understand basic considerations about "staying away" from things, such as ovens and irons. Therefore, he can learn to stay away from firearms.

Some considerations for you to discuss with children so they know who to handle a situation where they happen upon a firearm includes:

1. Stopping everything.
2. Do not touch the gun.
3. Leave the area immediately.
4. Tell a parent about the gun right away.

If you intend to teach your children how to handle firearms safely, do so with toy firearms, such as made by popular brands as "Nerf," that make little rubber and foam projectiles. Teach your child with toys such as this about safe handling of firearms, how and where to point them, and when not to point them, etc.

The bottom line is, educate your child. Do not scare them. Educate them. Help them appreciate and respect the dangers but not fear the tool.

Final Safety Considerations

Are some of these considerations repetitive of the above comments? Most likely. But when dealing with safety considerations, one cannot over-emphasize enough.

Whenever you pick up or are handed a gun, make sure it is unloaded. If you are being handed a gun, ask that it be unloaded and the action open before being handled to you.

Do not ever leave firearms unattended, unloaded or not, unless locked up safely in a secure container.

Never load a gun until you are ready to use it, and unload it when you are finished using it.

Use only ammunition intended for your gun. Usually the caliber is marked on the barrel, and it must match the markings on the ammo box and ammo cartridge.

Wear adequate eye protection when shooting.

Wear adequate hearing protection when shooting.

Wear adequate clothing when shooting.

Never shoot while drinking or taking drugs, even prescription medications if they have adverse effects on your perception or judgment.

CHAPTER THIRTY

Firearms Competency

All Firearms Owners and Their Families Should Seek Training

As the heading above states, everyone who handles or is around firearms should seek training and at least obtain minimal skills in safely handling firearms. As a person handling firearms, one should ask himself if he is truly competent in the handling of firearms? A simple self-assessment is a great idea when considering competence.

Many industries, including the military, consider the "four levels of competence," which is a very common training evaluation model first published in 1959. This model includes the four levels of confidence, including:

- **Unconscious Incompetence**: The person is unaware that he cannot perform a task.
- **Conscious Incompetence**: The person is aware of the task, but cannot do it.
- **Conscious Competence**: The person is able to think through something step by step and can perform the task.
- **Unconscious Competence**: The person can do the task without thinking about the intermediate steps.

Complete an assessment of yourself, considering each and every firearm or weapon you own. Consider: what level of training are you with the various firearms that you own?

A prudent firearms owner will receive enough training to bring himself into a consciously competent or unconsciously competent firearms user, for both his safety and the safety of those around him.

But do not just stop there. Do what you can to educate those around you, including your children, once they are old enough to learn and appreciate the rewards, but also the dangers, of handling firearms.

The bottom line is: **seek adequate training. Today.**

Part Fifteen

Appendices

Appendix One

Glossary

.50 BMG rifle:	a center-fire rifle that can fire a .50 BMG cartridge and is not already defined as an assault weapon or a machinegun. This definition does not include any "antique firearm" or any firearm defined under federal law as a curio/relic
.50 BMG cartridge:	a cartridge that is designed and intended to be fired from a center-fire rifle and that has an overall length of 5.54 inches from the base to the tip of the bullet, the bullet diameter for the cartridge is from .510 to, and including, .511 inch, the case base diameter for the cartridge is from .800 inch to and including .804 inch, and the cartridge case length is 3.91 inches
AG:	Attorney General
Air gauge knife:	a device that appears to be an air gauge but has concealed within it a pointed, metallic shaft that is designed to be a stabbing instrument which is exposed by mechanical action or gravity, and which locks into place when extended
Ammunition:	projectiles, such as bullets and shot, together with their fuses and primers, that can be fired from guns or otherwise propelled
Antique cannon:	any cannon manufactured prior to January 1, 1899, which has been rendered incapable of firing or for which ammunition is no longer made in the United States and is otherwise not readily available in the ordinary channels of commercial trade
Antique firearm:	generally, any firearm manufactured prior to January 1, 1899

Automatic firearm: an automatic firearm continues to self-load and fire as long as the trigger is held back and a supply of ammunition is present. In an automatic firearm, one pull on the trigger may result in multiple shots being fired

Ballistic knife: a device that propels a knifelike blade as a projectile by means of a coil spring, elastic material, or compressed gas. Ballistic knife does not include any device which propels an arrow or a bolt by means of a common bow, compound bow, crossbow, or underwater speargun

Ballistic identification system: includes, but not limited to, any automated image analysis system that is capable of storing firearm ballistic markings and tracing those markings to the firearm that produced them

BATFE: Bureau of Alcohol, Tobacco, and Firearms Enforcement

BB device: any instrument that expels a projectile, such as a BB or a pellet, not exceeding 6mm caliber, through the force of air pressure, gas pressure, or spring action, or any spot marker gun

Belt buckle knife: a knife that is made an integral part of a belt buckle and consists of a blade with a length of at least 2.5 inches

Blowgun: a hollow tube designed and intended to be used as a tube through which a dart is propelled by the force of the breath of the user

Blowgun ammunition: a dart designed and intended for use in a blowgun

Caliber: the caliber of a firearm is the approximate diameter of the bore measured before rifling (or the diameter of a circle formed by the tops of the rifling lands)

Camouflaging firearm container:	a container that meets all of the following criteria: it is designed and intended to enclose a firearm; it is designed and intended to allow the firing of the enclosed firearm by external controls while the firearm is in the container; it is not readily recognizable as containing a firearm. Does not include any camouflaging covering used while engaged in lawful hunting or while going to or returning from a lawful hunting expedition
Cane gun:	any firearm mounted or enclosed in a stick, staff, rod, crutch, or similar device, designed to be, or capable of being used as, an aid in walking, if the firearm may be fired while mounted or enclosed therein
Cane sword:	a cane, swagger stick, stick, staff, rod, pole, umbrella, or similar device, having concealed within it a blade that may be used as a sword or a stiletto
CCW:	Carry Concealed Weapon
CDL:	California Driver's License
Chamber load indicator:	a device that plainly indicates that a cartridge is in the firing chamber. Device satisfies this condition if it is readily visible, has incorporated or adjacent explanatory text or graphics, or both, and is designed and intended to indicate to a reasonably foreseeable adult user of the pistol without having to reference a user's manual or other resource
Child:	a person under 18 years of age
COE:	Certificate of Eligibility
DOJ:	Department of Justice; oftentimes in the Penal Code (and in this book), the DOJ is referred to as "the department"

DROS:	Dealer Record of Sale
FFL:	Federal Firearms License (or Licensee)
Firearm:	any device designed to be used as a weapon from which is expelled through a barrel a projectile by the force of any explosion or other form of combustion
Firearms safety device:	a device other than a gun safe that locks and is designed to prevent children and unauthorized users from firing a firearm. Device may be installed on firearm, incorporated into design of the firearm, or prevent access to firearm
Flash suppressor:	any device designed, intended, or that functions to perceptibly reduce or redirect muzzle flash from the shooter's field of vision
Flechette dart:	a dart, capable of being fired from a firearm, that measures approximately one inch in length, with tail fins that take up approximately 5/16 of an inch of the body
Forearm:	the forward position of a two-part stock which is usually under the barrel
Gunsmith:	a person who is a licensed dealer who is engaged primarily in the business of repairing firearms, or making or fitting special barrels, stocks, or trigger mechanisms to firearms, or the agent or employee of that person
Handgun:	In California, generally a handgun is any pistol, revolver, or firearm capable of being concealed upon the person; further, a handgun is any device designed to be used as a weapon, from which is expelled a projectile by the force of any explosion, or other form of combustion, and that has a barrel less than 16 inches in length. These terms also include any device that has a barrel 16 inches or more in length which is designed to be interchanged with a barrel less than 16 inches in length

Hard knuckles: any device or instrument made wholly or partially of plastic or of wood, composite, or paper materials that is not a metal knuckle that is worn for the purpose of offense or defense in or on the hand, that either protects the wearer's hand while striking a blow or increases the force of impact from the blow or injury to the individual receiving the blow. The plastic, wood, composite, or paper products contained in the device may help support the hand or fist, provide a shield to protect it, or consist of projections or studs that would contact the individual receiving the blow

HSC: otherwise known as a "handgun safety certificate," is issued by the DOJ and is required to be obtained prior to lawfully purchasing a firearm in California

Imitation firearm: means any BB device, toy gun, replica of a firearm, or other device that is so substantially similar in coloration and overall appearance to an existing firearm as to lead a reasonable person to perceive that the device is a firearm

Infrequent transfer: for pistols, revolvers, and other concealable firearms: less than 6 transactions per calendar year. For firearms other than pistols, revolvers, and other concealable firearms, occasional and without regularity

Large capacity magazine: any ammunition feeding device with the capacity to accept more than 10 rounds, but not including a feeding device that has been permanently altered so it cannot accommodate more than 10 rounds, a .22 caliber tube ammunition feeding device, or a tubular magazine that is contained in a lever action firearm

Leaded cane: a staff, crutch, stick, rod, pole, or similar device, unnaturally weighted with lead

Less lethal ammunition: any ammo that (1) is designed to be used in any less lethal weapon or any other kind of weapon (including, but not limited to, firearms, pistols, revolvers, shotguns, rifles, and spring, compressed air, and compressed gas weapons) and (2) when used in the less lethal weapon or other weapon designed to immobilize or incapacitate or stun a human being through the infliction of any less than lethal impairment of physical condition, function, or senses, including physical pain or discomfort

Less lethal weapon: any device that is designed to, or that has been converted to expel or propel less lethal ammunition by any action, mechanism, or process for the purpose of incapacitating, immobilizing, or stunning a human being through the infliction of any less than lethal impairment of physical condition, function, or senses, including physical pain or discomfort. It is not necessary that a weapon leave any lasting or permanent incapacitation, discomfort, pain, or other injury or disability in order to qualify as a less lethal weapon

Lipstick case knife: a knife enclosed within and made an integral part of a lipstick case

Loaded firearm: generally, a firearm shall be deemed to be "loaded" when both the firearm and the unexpended ammunition capable of being discharged from the firearm are in the immediate possession of the same person. It may also mean a firearm that has an unexpended cartridge or shell, consisting of a case that holds a charge of powder and a bullet or shot, in, or attached in any manner to, the firearm, including, but not limited to, in the firing chamber, magazine, or clip thereof attached to the firearm; except that a muzzle-loader firearm shall be deemed loaded when it is capped or primed and has a powder charge and ball or shot in the barrel or cylinder.

Locked container: a secure container which is fully enclosed and locked by a padlock, key lock, combination lock, or similar locking device

Locking device: a device that is designed to prevent the firearm from functioning and when applied to the firearm, renders the firearm inoperable

Magazine: any ammunition feeding device

Magazine disconnect: a mechanism that prevents a semiautomatic pistol that has a detachable magazine from operating to strike the primer of ammo in the firing chamber when a detachable magazine is not inserted in the semiautomatic pistol

Magazine, fixed: a magazine which remains affixed to the firearm during loading. Frequently a fixed magazine is charged (loaded) from a clip (en block or stripper) of cartridges inserted through the open breech into the magazine

Magazine, detachable: an ammunition feeding device that can be removed readily from the firearm with neither disassembly of the firearm action nor use of a tool being required. A bullet or ammunition cartridge is considered a tool. Ammunition feeding device includes any belted or linked ammunition, but does not include clips, en bloc clips, or stripper clips that load cartridges into the magazine

Malfunction: a failure to feed, fire, or eject a round properly, or failure of the pistol to accept or eject the magazine, or failure of pistol slide to remain open after the magazine has been expended

Metal knuckles: any device or instrument made wholly or partially of metal which is worn for purposes of offense or defense in or on the hand and which either protects the wearer's hand while striking a blow or increases the force of impact from the blow or injury to the individual receiving the blow. The metal contained in the device may help support the hand or fist, provide a shield to protect it, or consist of projections or studs which would contact the individual receiving the blow

Minor: a person under 18 years of age

Multiburst trigger activator:	either a device designed or redesigned to be attached to a semiautomatic firearm which allows the firearm to discharge two or more shots in a burst by activating the device, or a manual or power-driven trigger activating device constructed and designed so that when attached to a semiautomatic firearm it increases the rate of fire of that firearm
Nunchaku:	an instrument consisting of two or more sticks, clubs, bars or rods to be used as handles, connected by a rope, cord, wire, or chain, in the design of a weapon and used in connection with the practice of a system of self-defense such as karate
PC:	Penal Code
Pistol grip, conspicuously protruding:	a grip that allows for a pistol style grasp in which the web of the trigger hand (between the thumb and index finger) can be placed below the top of the exposed portion of the trigger while firing
Pistol grip, forward:	a grip that allows for a pistol style grasp forward of the trigger
Public place:	an area open to the public and includes streets, sidewalks, bridges, alleys, plazas, parks, driveways, front yards, parking lots, automobiles, whether moving or not, and buildings open to the general public, including those that serve food or drink, or provide entertainment, and the doorways and entrances to buildings or dwellings, and shall include public schools and a public or private college or university
Receiver:	the basic unit of a firearm which houses the firing and breech mechanism and to which the barrel and stock are assembled. The receiver may consist of two sections. In some autoloading pistols and other firearms, the terms receiver and frame are used interchangeably

Receiver, lower:	in a receiver composed of two parts, the lower receiver usually contains the trigger and firing mechanism
Receiver, upper:	in a receiver composed of two parts, the upper receiver usually contains the barrel and breech mechanism
Rifle:	a weapon designed or redesigned, made or remade, and intended to be fired from the shoulder and designed or redesigned and made or remade to use the energy of the explosive in a fixed cartridge to fire only a single projectile through a rifled bore for each single pull of the trigger
Semiautomatic firearm:	a firearm which is self-loading but not self-firing. A single pull on the trigger results in a single shot being fired
Semiautomatic pistol:	a pistol where the operating mode of which uses the energy of the explosive in a fixed cartridge to extract a fired cartridge and chamber a fresh cartridge with each single pull of the trigger
Shobi-zue:	a staff, crutch, stick, rod, or pole concealing a knife or blade within it which may be exposed by a flip of the wrist or by a mechanical action
Short-barreled rifle:	a rifle having a barrel or barrels of less than 16 inches in length
Short-barreled shotgun:	a firearm which is designed or redesigned to fire a fixed shotgun shell and having a barrel or barrels of less than 18 inches in length
Shotgun:	a weapon designed or redesigned, made or remade, and intended to be fired from the shoulder and designed or redesigned and made or remade to use the energy of the explosive in a fixed shotgun shell to fire through a smooth bore either a number of projectiles (ball shot) or a single projectile for each pull of the trigger

Shuriken: any instrument, without handles, consisting of a metal plate having three or more radiating points with one or more sharp edges and designed in the shape of a polygon, trefoil, cross, star, diamond, or other geometric shape for the use as a weapon for throwing

Silencer: any device or attachment of any kind designed, used, or intended for use in silencing, diminishing, or muffling the report of a firearm. The term "silencer" also includes any combination of parts, designed or redesigned, and intended for use in assembling a silencer or fabricating a silencer and any part intended only for use in such assembly or fabrication

State of domicile: the state where a person has his or her true, fixed, and permanent home and principal residence and to which he or she has manifested the intention of returning whenever he or she is absent

Stock: the part of a rifle, carbine, or shotgun to which the barrel assembly is attached and which provides a means for holding the weapon to the shoulder

Stun gun: any item, except a less lethal weapon as defined in 12601, used or intended to be used as either an offensive or defensive weapon that is capable of temporarily immobilizing a person by the infliction of an electrical charge

Stock, collapsing: a stock which is shortened by allowing one section to telescope into another

Stock, folding: a stock which is hinged to the receiver to allow the stock to be folded next to the receiver to reduce the overall length of the firearm

Stock, thumbhole: a stock with a hole that allows the thumb of the trigger hand to penetrate into or through the stock when firing

Tear gas: all liquid, gaseous, or solid substances intended to produce temporary physical discomfort or permanent injury by being vaporized or otherwise dispersed in the air, but does not apply to, and shall not include, any substance registered as an economic poison per the Agricultural Code provided that such substance is not intended to be used to produce discomfort or injury to human beings

Unconventional pistol: a firearm that does not have a rifled bore and has a barrel or barrels of less than 18 inches in length or has an overall length of less than 26 inches

Undetectable firearm: any weapon which meets one of the following requirements: when, after removal of grips, stocks, and magazines, it is not as detectable as the Security Exemplar, by walk-through metal detectors calibrated and operated to detect the Security Exemplar; or, when any major component of which, when subjected to inspection by the types of Xray machines commonly used at airports, does not generate an image that accurately depicts the shape of the component. Barium sulfate or other compounds may be used in the fabrication of the component

Undetectable knife: any knife or other instrument with or without a handguard that is capable of ready use as a stabbing weapon that may inflict great bodily injury or death that is commercially manufactured to be used as a weapon AND is not detectable by a metal detector or magnetometer

Wallet gun: any firearm mounted or enclosed in a case, resembling a wallet, designed to be or capable of being carried in a pocket or purse, if the firearm may be fired while mounted or enclosed in the case

Writing pen knife: a device that appears to be a writing pen but has concealed within it a pointed, metallic shaft that is designed to be a stabbing instrument which is exposed by mechanical action or gravity which locks into place when extended or the pointed, metallic shaft is exposed by the removal of the cap or cover on the device

Zip gun: any weapon or device which meets all of the following criteria: it was not imported as a firearm by an FFL; it was not originally designed to be a firearm by an FFL; no tax was paid on the weapon or device nor was an exemption from paying the tax granted; it is made or altered to expel a projectile by the force of an explosion or other form of combustion

Appendix Two

California Code

-

Firearms, Knives, and Other Weapons Laws

Business and Professions Code

Business and Professions Code § 7500.

This chapter of the Business and Professions Code constitutes the chapter on repossessors. It may be cited as the "Collateral Recovery Act."

Business and Professions Code § 7500.1.

The following terms as used in this chapter have the meaning expressed in this Section.

(a) "Advertisement" means any written or printed communication, including a directory listing, except a free telephone directory listing that does not allow space for a license number.

(b) "Assignment" means a written authorization by the legal owner, lienholder, lessor or lessee, or the agent of any of them, to skip trace, locate, or repossess or to collect money payment in lieu of repossession of, any collateral, including, but not limited to, collateral registered under the Vehicle Code that is subject to a security agreement that contains a repossession clause. "Assignment" also means a written authorization by an employer to recover any collateral entrusted to an employee or former employee if the possessor is wrongfully in possession of the collateral. A photocopy, facsimile copy, or electronic copy of an assignment shall have the same force and effect as an original written assignment.

(c) "Bureau" means the Bureau of Security and Investigative Services.

(d) "Chief" means the Chief of the Bureau of Security and Investigative Services.

(e) "Collateral" means any vehicle, boat, recreational vehicle, motor home, appliance, or other property that is subject to a security agreement.

(f) "Combustibles" means any substance or article that is capable of undergoing combustion or catching fire, or that is flammable, if retained.

(g) "Dangerous drugs" means any controlled substances as defined in Chapter 2 (commencing with Section 11053) of Division 10 of the Health and Safety Code.

(h) "Deadly weapon" means and includes any instrument or weapon of the kind commonly known as a blackjack, slungshot, billy, sandclub, sandbag, metal knuckles, dirk, dagger, pistol, or revolver, or any other firearm, any knife having a blade longer than five inches, any razor with an unguarded blade, and any metal pipe or bar used or intended to be used as a club.

(i) "Debtor" means any person obligated under a security agreement.

(j) "Department" means the Department of Consumer Affairs.

(k) "Director" means the Director of Consumer Affairs.

(l) "Health hazard" means any personal effects which if retained would produce an unsanitary or unhealthful condition.

(m) "Legal owner" means a person holding a security interest in any collateral that is subject to a security agreement, a lien against any collateral, or an interest in any collateral that is subject to a lease agreement.

(n) "Licensee" means an individual, partnership, limited liability company, or corporation licensed under this chapter as a repossession agency.

(o) "Multiple licensee" means a repossession agency holding more than one repossession license under this chapter, with one fictitious trade style and ownership, conducting repossession business from additional licensed locations other than the location shown on the original license.

(p) "Person" includes any individual, partnership, limited liability company, or corporation.

(q) "Personal effects" means any property that is not the property of the legal owner.

(r) "Private building" means and includes any dwelling, outbuilding, or other enclosed structure.

(s) "Qualified certificate holder" or "qualified manager" is a person who possesses a valid qualification certificate in accordance with the provisions of Article 5 (commencing with Section 7504) and is in active control or management of, and who is a director of, the licensee's place of business.

(t) "Registrant" means a person registered under this chapter.

(u) "Secured area" means and includes any fenced and locked area.

(v) "Security agreement" means an obligation, pledge, mortgage, chattel mortgage, lease agreement, deposit, or lien, given by a debtor as security for payment or performance of his or her debt, by furnishing the creditor with a recourse to be used in case of failure in the principal obligation. "Security agreement" also includes a bailment where an employer-employee relationship exists or existed between the bailor and the bailee.

(w) "Services" means any duty or labor to be rendered by one person for another.

(x) "Violent act" means any act that results in bodily harm or injury to any party involved.

(y) The amendments made to this section during the 2005-06 Regular Session shall not be deemed to exempt any person from the provisions of this chapter.

Business and Professions Code § 7507.9.

Personal effects shall be removed from the collateral, including any personal effect that is mounted but detachable from the collateral by a release mechanism. A complete and accurate inventory of the personal effects shall be made, and the personal effects shall be labeled and stored by the licensee for a minimum of 60 days in a secure manner, except those personal effects removed by or in the presence of the debtor or the party in possession of the collateral at the time of the repossession. If the licensee or the licensee's agent cannot determine whether the property attached to the collateral is a personal effect or a part of the collateral, then that fact shall be noted on the inventory and the licensee or agent shall not be obligated to remove the item from the collateral, unless the item can be removed without the use of tools, in which case it shall be removed and inventoried. The licensee or the licensee's agent shall notify the debtor that if the debtor takes the position that an item is a personal effect, then the debtor shall contact the legal owner to resolve the issue.

(a) The date and time the inventory is made shall be indicated. The permanent records of the licensee shall indicate the name of the employee or registrant who performed the inventory.

(b) The following items of personal effects are items determined to present a danger or health hazard when recovered by the licensee and shall be disposed of in the following manner:

(1) Deadly weapons and dangerous drugs shall be turned over to any law enforcement agency for retention. These items shall be entered on the inventory and a notation shall be made as to the date and the time and the place the deadly weapon or dangerous drug was turned over to the law enforcement agency, and a receipt from the law enforcement agency shall be maintained in the records of the repossession agency.

(2) Combustibles shall be inventoried and noted as "disposed of, dangerous combustible," and the item shall be disposed of in a reasonable and safe manner.

(3) Food and other health hazard items shall be inventoried and noted as "disposed of, health hazard," and disposed of in a reasonable and safe manner.

(c) Personal effects may be disposed of after being held for at least 60 days. The inventory, and adequate information as to how, when, and to whom the personal effects were disposed of, shall be filed in the permanent records of the licensee.

(d) The inventory shall include the name, address, business hours, and telephone number of the repossession agency to contact for recovering the personal effects and an itemization of all personal effects removal and storage charges that will be made by the repossession agency. The inventory shall also include the following statement: "Please be advised that the property listed on this inventory will be disposed of by the repossession agency after being held for 60 days from the date of this notice IF UNCLAIMED."

(e) The inventory shall be provided to a debtor not later than 48 hours after the recovery of the collateral, except that if:

(1) The 48-hour period encompasses a Saturday, Sunday, or postal holiday, the inventory shall be provided no later than 72 hours after the recovery of the collateral.

(2) The 48-hour period encompasses a Saturday or Sunday and a postal holiday, the inventory shall be provided no later than 96 hours after the recovery of the collateral.

(3) Inventory resulting from repossession of a yacht, motor home, or travel trailer is such that it shall take at least four hours to inventory, then the inventory shall be provided no later than 96 hours after the recovery of the collateral. When the 96-hour period encompasses a Saturday, Sunday, or postal holiday, the inventory shall be provided no later than 120 hours after the recovery of the collateral.

(f) Environmental, Olympic, special interest, or other license plates issued pursuant to Article 8 (commencing with Section 5000), Article 8.4 (commencing with Section 5060) or Article 8.5 (commencing with Section 5100) of Chapter 1 of Division 3 of the Vehicle Code that remain the personal effects of the debtor shall be removed from the collateral and inventoried pursuant to this section. If the plates are not claimed by the debtor within 60 days, they shall be effectively destroyed and the licensee shall, within 30 days thereafter, notify the Department of Motor Vehicles of their effective destruction on a form promulgated by the chief that has been approved as to form by the Director of the Department of Motor Vehicles.

(g) The notice may be given by regular mail addressed to the last known address of the debtor or by personal service at the option of the repossession agency.

(h) The debtor may waive the preparation and presentation of an inventory if the debtor redeems the personal effects or other personal property not covered by a security interest within the time period for the notices required by this section and signs a statement that he or she has received all the property.

(i) If personal effects or other personal property not covered by a security agreement are to be released to someone other than the debtor, the repossession agency may request written authorization to do so from either the debtor or the legal owner.

(j) The inventory shall be a confidential document. A licensee shall only disclose the contents of the inventory under the following circumstances:

(1) In response to the order of a court having jurisdiction to issue the order.

(2) In compliance with a lawful subpoena issued by a court of competent jurisdiction.

(3) When the debtor has consented in writing to the release and the written consent is signed and dated by the debtor subsequent to the repossession and states the entity or entities to whom the contents of the inventory may be disclosed.

Business and Professions Code § 7510.1.

In addition to any other remedies authorized by this chapter, the director may suspend or revoke a repossession agency license, a qualification certificate, or registration issued under this chapter if the director determines that the licensee or the licensee's manager, if an individual, or if the licensee is a person other than an individual, that any of its officers, partners, registrants, employees, or its manager, has:

(a) Made any false statement or given any false information in connection with an application for a license, qualification certificate, or registration, or a renewal or reinstatement thereof.

(b) Violated any provisions of this chapter.

(c) Violated any rule of the director adopted pursuant to authority contained in this chapter.

(d) Been convicted of a felony or any crime substantially related to the repossession agency business including illegally using, carrying, or possessing a deadly weapon.

(e) Committed or permitted any registrant or employee to commit any act while the license was expired which would be cause for the suspension or revocation of a license, or grounds for the denial of an application for a license.

(f) Unlawfully committed assault, battery, or kidnapping, or used force or violence on any person.

(g) Knowingly violated, or advised, encouraged, or assisted the violation of any court order or injunction in the course of business as a licensee. (h) Been convicted of a violation of Section 148 of the Penal Code, resisting or obstructing a public officer.

(i) Committed any act which is a ground for denial of an application for license under this chapter.

(j) Committed any act prohibited by Chapter 1.5 (commencing with Section 630) of Title 15 of Part 1 of the Penal Code.

(k) Committed any act in the course of the licensee's business constituting dishonesty or fraud, including, but not limited to:

(1) Knowingly making a false statement relating to evidence or information obtained in the course of employment or while under contract, or knowingly publishing a slander or a libel in the course of business.

(2) Using illegal means in the collection or attempted collection of a debt or obligation.

(l) Represented that the licensee has an office and conducts business at a specific address when that is not the case.

Business and Professions Code § 7512.

This chapter may be cited as the Private Investigator Act.

Business and Professions Code § 7512.1.

As used in this chapter, "director" means the Director of Consumer Affairs, unless the context indicates otherwise.

Business and Professions Code § 7512.2.

The director shall administer and enforce the provisions of this chapter.

Business and Professions Code § 7512.3.

As used in this chapter, "person" includes any individual, firm, company, association, organization, partnership, and corporation.

Business and Professions Code § 7512.4.

As used in this chapter, "bureau" means the Bureau of Security and Investigative Services.

Business and Professions Code § 7512.5.

As used in this chapter, "chief" means the Chief of the Bureau of Security and Investigative Services.

Business and Professions Code § 7512.6.

As used in this chapter, "licensee" means a person licensed under this chapter.

Business and Professions Code § 7512.7.

As used in this chapter, "manager" means the individual under whose direction, control, charge, or management the business of a licensee is operated.

Business and Professions Code § 7512.10.

As used in this chapter, "employer" means a person who employs an individual for wages or salary, lists the individual on the employer's payroll records, and withholds all legally required deductions and contributions.

Business and Professions Code § 7512.11.

As used in this chapter, "employee" means an individual who works for an employer, is listed on the employer's payroll records, and is under the employer's direction and control.

Business and Professions Code § 7512.12.

As used in this chapter, "employer-employee" relationship means a relationship in which an individual works for another, the individual's name appears on the payroll records of the employer, and the employee is under the direction and control of the employer.

Business and Professions Code § 7512.13.

As used in this chapter, "firearm permit" includes "firearms permit," "firearms qualification card," "firearms qualification," and "firearms qualification permit."

Business and Professions Code § 7521.5.

(a) A private investigator may provide services to protect a person, but not property, which is incidental to an investigation for which the private investigator has been previously hired to perform.

(b) If the private investigator provides those services, he or she shall comply with the requirements of Article 4 (commencing with Section 7540), as those provisions relate to the carrying of firearms and the receipt of a valid firearms qualification card from the bureau.

(c) If the private investigator provides those services, he or she shall comply with the requirements of Sections 7583.39, 7583.40, and 7583.41, as those provisions relate to the maintenance of an insurance policy.

(d) If the private investigator provides those services, he or she shall be subject to the jurisdiction of the disciplinary review committee, pursuant to Section 7581.2, only with respect to violation of the law or regulations relating to firearms.

(e) If a person acts for, or on behalf of a private investigator in providing those services, that person shall be an employee of the private investigator, as defined by Section 7512.11, and there shall be an employer-employee relationship, as defined in Section 7512.12, and that person shall comply with the requirements of this section with the exception of the maintenance of an insurance policy.

Business and Professions Code § 7522.

This chapter does not apply to:

(a) A person employed exclusively and regularly by any employer who does not provide contract security services for other entities or persons, in connection with the affairs of such employer only and where there exists an employer-employee relationship if that person at no time carries or uses any deadly weapon in the performance of his or her duties. For purposes of this subdivision, "deadly weapon" is defined to include any instrument or weapon of the kind commonly known as a blackjack, slungshot, billy, sandclub, sandbag, metal knuckles, any dirk, dagger, pistol, revolver, or any other firearm, any knife having a blade longer than five inches, any razor with an unguarded blade and any metal pipe or bar used or intended to be used as a club.

(b) An officer or employee of the United States of America, or of this state or a political subdivision thereof, while the officer or employee is engaged in the performance of his or her official duties, including uniformed peace officers employed part time by a public agency pursuant to a written agreement between a chief of police or sheriff and the public agency, provided the part-time employment does not exceed 50 hours in any calendar month.

(c) A person engaged exclusively in the business of obtaining and furnishing information as to the financial rating of persons.

(d) A charitable philanthropic society or association duly incorporated under the laws of this state which is organized and maintained for the public good and not for private profit.

(e) An attorney at law in performing his or her duties as an attorney at law.

(f) Admitted insurers and agents and insurance brokers licensed by the state, performing duties in connection with insurance transacted by them.

(g) Any bank subject to the jurisdiction of the Commissioner of Financial Institutions of the State of California under Division 1 (commencing with Section 99) of the Financial Code or the Comptroller of Currency of the United States.

(h) A person engaged solely in the business of securing information about persons or property from public records.

(i) A peace officer of this state or a political subdivision thereof while the peace officer is employed by a private employer to engage in off-duty employment in accordance with Section 1126 of the Government Code. However, nothing herein shall exempt a peace officer who either contracts for his or her services or the services of others as a private investigator or contracts for his or her services as or is employed as an armed private investigator. For purposes of this subdivision, "armed private investigator" means an individual who carries or uses a firearm in the course and scope of that contract or employment.

(j) A licensed insurance adjuster in performing his or her duties within the scope of his or her license as an insurance adjuster.

(k) Any savings association subject to the jurisdiction of the Commissioner of Financial Institutions or the Office of Thrift Supervision.

(l) Any secured creditor engaged in the repossession of the creditor's collateral and any lessor engaged in the repossession of leased property in which it claims an interest.

(m) The act of serving process by an individual who is registered as a process server pursuant to Section 22350.

(n)(1) A person or business engaged in conducting objective observations of consumer purchases of products or services in the public environments of a business establishment by the use of a preestablished questionnaire, provided that person or business entity does not engage in any other activity that requires licensure pursuant to this chapter. The questionnaire may include objective comments.

(2) If a preestablished questionnaire is used as a basis, but not the sole basis, for disciplining or discharging an employee, or for conducting an interview with the employee that might result in the employee being terminated, the employer shall provide the employee with a copy of that questionnaire using the same procedures that an employer is required to follow under Section 2930 of the Labor Code for providing an employee with a copy of a shopping investigator's report. This subdivision does not exempt from this chapter a person or business described in paragraph (1) if a preestablished questionnaire of that person or business is used as the sole basis for evaluating an employee's work performance.

(o) Any joint labor-management committee established pursuant to the federal Labor Management Cooperation Act of 1978 (Section 175a of Title 29 of the United States Code), or its employees, where either the committee or employee is performing a function authorized by the Labor Management Cooperation Act of 1978, which includes, but is not limited, to monitoring public works projects to ensure that employers are complying with federal and state public works laws.

Business and Professions Code § 7542.

Every licensee and qualified manager who in the course of his or her employment or business carries a deadly weapon shall complete a course of training in the exercise of the powers to arrest as specified in Section 7583.7 and a course of training in the carrying and use of firearms as specified in Article 4 (commencing with Section 7583) of Chapter 11.5. No licensee or qualified manager shall carry or use a firearm unless he or she has met the requirements of Sections 7583.23, 7583.28, and 7583.29 and has in his or her possession a valid firearms qualification card as provided in Section 7583.30. A licensee or qualified manager who possesses a valid firearms qualification card shall comply with and be subject to the provisions of Sections 7583.31, 7583.32, and 7583.37.

Business and Professions Code § 7561.1.

The director may deny, suspend, or revoke a license issued under this chapter if he or she determines that the licensee or his or her manager, if an individual, or if the licensee is a person other than an individual, that any of its officers, directors, partners, or its manager, has:

(a) Made any false statement or given any false information in connection with an application for a license or a renewal or reinstatement of a license.

(b) Violated any provisions of this chapter.

(c) Violated any rule of the director adopted pursuant to the authority contained in this chapter.

(d) Been convicted of any act or crime constituting grounds for denial of licensure under Section 480, including illegally using, carrying, or possessing a deadly weapon.

(e) Impersonated, or permitted or aided and abetted an employee to impersonate a law enforcement officer or employee of the United States of America, or of any state or political subdivision thereof.

(f) Committed or permitted any employee to commit any act, while the license was expired which would be cause for the suspension or revocation of a license, or grounds for the denial of an application for a license.

(g) Willfully failed or refused to render to a client services or a report as agreed between the parties and for which compensation has been paid or tendered in accordance with the agreement of the parties.

(h) Committed assault, battery, or kidnapping, or using force or violence on any person, without proper justification.

(i) Knowingly violated, or advised, encouraged, or assisted the violation of any court order or injunction in the course of business as a licensee.

(j) Acted as a runner or capper for any attorney.

(k) Been convicted of a violation of Section 148 of the Penal Code.

(l) Committed any act which is a ground for denial of an application for a license under this chapter.

(m) Committed any act prohibited by Chapter 1.5 (commencing with Section 630) of Title 15 of Part 1 of the Penal Code.

(n) Purchased, possessed, or transported any tear gas weapon except as authorized by law. A violation of this subdivision may be punished by the suspension of a license for a period to be determined by the director.

(o) Been convicted of a violation of Section 95.3 of the Penal Code.

Business and Professions Code § 7566.

The director may assess administrative fines against any licensee, registrant, or firearms qualification cardholder for failure to notify the bureau within 30 days of any change of residence or business address. The principal place of business may be at a home or at a business address, but it shall be the place at which the licensee maintains a permanent office.

(a) The fine shall be twenty-five dollars ($25) for each violation by a licensee.

(b) The fine shall be fifteen dollars ($15) for each violation by a registrant or a firearms qualification cardholder.

Business and Professions Code § 7580.

This chapter may be cited as the Private Security Services Act.

Business and Professions Code § 7580.1.

As used in this chapter, "director" means the Director of Consumer Affairs, unless the context indicates otherwise.

Business and Professions Code § 7580.2.

The director shall administer and enforce the provisions of this chapter.

Business and Professions Code § 7580.3.

As used in this chapter, "person" includes any individual, firm, company, association, organization, partnership, and corporation.

Business and Professions Code § 7580.4.

As used in this chapter, "bureau" means the Bureau of Security and Investigative Services.

Business and Professions Code § 7580.5.

As used in this chapter, "chief" means the Chief of the Bureau of Security and Investigative Services.

Business and Professions Code § 7580.6.

As used in this chapter, "licensee" means a person licensed under this chapter and includes, but is not limited to, private patrol operator and armored contract carrier.

Business and Professions Code § 7580.7.

As used in this chapter, "manager" means the individual under whose direction, control, charge, or management the business of a licensee is operated.

Business and Professions Code § 7580.8.

As used in this chapter, "employer" means a person who employs an individual for wages or salary, lists the individual on the employer's payroll records, and withholds all legally required deductions and contributions.

Business and Professions Code § 7580.9.

As used in this chapter, "employee" means an individual who works for an employer, is listed on the employer's payroll records, and is under the employer's direction and control.

Business and Professions Code § 7580.10.

As used in this chapter, "employer-employee" relationship means a relationship in which an individual works for another, the individual's name appears on the payroll records of the employer, and the employee is under the direction and control of the employer.

Business and Professions Code § 7580.11.

As used in this chapter, "firearm permit" includes "firearms permit," "firearms qualification card," "firearms qualification," and "firearms qualification permit."

Business and Professions Code § 7581.

The director may adopt and enforce reasonable rules, as follows:

(a) Classifying licensees according to the type of business regulated by this chapter in which they are engaged, including, but not limited to, persons employed by any lawful business as security guards or patrolpersons, and armored contract carriers and limiting the field and scope of the operations of a licensee to those in which he or she is classified and qualified to engage.

(b) Fixing the qualifications of licensees and managers, in addition to those prescribed in this chapter, necessary to promote and protect the public welfare.

(c) Carrying out generally the provisions of this chapter, including regulation of the conduct of licensees.

(d) Establishing the qualifications that any person employed by a private patrol operator or any lawful business as a security guard or patrolperson, or employed by an armored contract carrier, must meet as a condition of becoming eligible to carry firearms pursuant to subdivision (d) of Section 12031 of the Penal Code.

(e) Requiring each uniformed employee of a private patrol operator and each armored vehicle guard, as defined in this chapter, and any other person employed and compensated by a private patrol operator or any lawful business as a security guard or patrolperson and who in the course of this employment carries a deadly weapon to be registered with the bureau upon application on a form prescribed by the director accompanied by the registration fee and by two classifiable sets of fingerprints of the applicant or its equivalent as determined by the director and approved by the Department of Justice, establishing the term of the registration for a period of not less than two nor more than four years, and providing for the renewal thereof upon proper application and payment of the renewal fee. The director may, after opportunity for a hearing, refuse this registration to any person who lacks good moral character, and may impose reasonable additional requirements as are necessary to meet local needs that are not inconsistent with the provisions of this chapter.

(f) Establishing procedures whereby the local authorities of any city, county, or city and county may file charges with, or any person in this state, may file a complaint with the director alleging that any licensed private patrol operator, registered security guard, or patrolperson, or anyone who is an applicant for registration or licensure with the bureau, fails to meet standards for registration or licensure, or violates any provision of this chapter, and providing further for the investigation of the charges and a response to the charging or complaining party in the manner described in subdivision (b) of Section 129.

(g) Requiring private patrol operators and any lawful business to maintain detailed records identifying all firearms in their possession or under their control, and the employees or persons authorized to carry or have access to those firearms.

Business and Professions Code § 7581.1.

The Governor shall appoint two private security disciplinary review committees, and may remove any member of a disciplinary review committee for misconduct, incompetency, or neglect of duty. One committee shall meet in the southern portion of the state and the other committee shall meet in the northern portion of the state. Each disciplinary review committee shall consist of five members. Of the five members, one member shall be actively engaged in the business of a licensed private patrol operator, one member shall be actively engaged in the business of a firearm training facility, one member shall be actively engaged in the business of a registered security guard, and two members shall be public members. None of the public members shall be licensees or registrants or engaged in any business or profession in which any part of the fees, compensation, or revenue thereof, is derived from any licensee. Each committee shall meet every 60 days or more or less frequently as may be required. The members shall be paid per diem pursuant to Section 103 and shall be reimbursed for actual travel expenses. The members shall be appointed for a term of four years.

Business and Professions Code § 7581.2.

Each disciplinary review committee shall perform the following functions as they pertain to private patrol operators, security guards, firearm qualification cardholders, firearm training facilities, firearm training instructors, baton training facilities, and baton training instructors, as licensed, certified, or registered by the bureau under this chapter, and proprietary security officers, as registered by the bureau under Chapter 11.4 (commencing with Section 7574):

(a) Affirm, rescind, or modify all appealed decisions which concern administrative fines assessed by the director.

(b) Affirm, rescind, or modify all appealed decisions which concern denials, revocations, or suspensions of a license, certificate, or registration except denials, revocations, or suspensions ordered by the director in accordance with Chapter 5 (commencing with Section 11500) of Division 3 of Title 2 of the Government Code.

Business and Professions Code § 7581.3.

A private patrol operator, qualified manager of a private patrol operator, security guard, firearm qualification cardholder, firearm training facility, firearm training instructor, baton training facility, or baton training instructor may request a review by a disciplinary review committee to contest the assessment of an administrative fine or to appeal a denial, revocation, or suspension of a license, certificate, or registration unless the denial, revocation, or suspension is ordered by the director in accordance with Chapter 5 (commencing with Section 11500) of Part 1 of Division 3 of Title 2 of the Government Code. A request for a review shall be by written notice to the bureau within 30 days of the issuance of the citation and assessment, denial, revocation, or suspension. Following a review by a disciplinary review committee, the appellant shall be notified within 30 days, in writing, by regular mail, of the committee's decision. If the appellant disagrees with the decision made by a disciplinary review committee, he or she may request a hearing in accordance with Chapter 5 (commencing with Section 11500) of Part 1 of Division 3 of Title 2 of the Government Code. A request for a hearing following a decision by a disciplinary review committee shall be by written notice to the bureau within 30 days following notice of the committee's decision. If the appellant does not request a hearing within 30 days, the review committee's decision shall become final.

Business and Professions Code § 7582.

No person shall engage in a business regulated by this chapter; act or assume to act as, or represent himself or herself to be, a licensee unless he or she is licensed under this chapter; and no person shall falsely represent that he or she is employed by a licensee.

Business and Professions Code § 7582.05.

(a) Notwithstanding any other provision of law, any person engaging in a business as a private patrol operator who violates Section 7582 is guilty of an infraction subject to the procedures described in Sections 19.6 and 19.7 of the Penal Code under either of the following circumstances:

(1) A complaint or a written notice to appear in court pursuant to Chapter 5c (commencing with Section 853.5) of Title 3 of Part 2 of the Penal Code is filed in court charging the offense as an infraction unless the defendant, at the time he or she is arraigned, after being advised of his or her rights, elects to have the case proceed as a misdemeanor.

(2) The court, with the consent of the defendant and the prosecution, determines that the offense is an infraction in which event the case shall proceed as if the defendant has been arraigned on an infraction complaint.

(b) This section does not apply to a violation of Section 7582 if the defendant has had his or her license previously revoked or suspended.

(c) Notwithstanding any other provision of law, a violation of Section 7582, which is an infraction, is punishable by a fine of one thousand dollars ($1,000). No portion of the fine may be suspended by the court unless as a condition of that suspension the defendant is required to submit proof of a current valid license for the profession of private patrol operator which was the basis for his or her conviction.

Business and Professions Code § 7582.1.

(a) A private patrol operator, or operator of a private patrol service, within the meaning of this chapter is a person, other than an armored contract carrier, who, for any consideration whatsoever: Agrees to furnish, or furnishes, a watchman, guard, patrolperson, or other person to protect persons or property or to prevent the theft, unlawful taking, loss, embezzlement, misappropriation, or concealment of any goods, wares, merchandise, money, bonds, stocks, notes, documents, papers, or property of any kind; or performs the service of a watchman, guard, patrolperson, or other person, for any of these purposes.

(b) A person licensed as a private patrol operator only may not make any investigation or investigations except those that are incidental to the theft, loss, embezzlement, misappropriation, or concealment of any property, or any other thing enumerated in this section, which he or she has been hired or engaged to protect, guard, or watch.

(c) An armored contract carrier within the meaning of this chapter is a contract carrier operating armored vehicles pursuant to California Highway Patrol and Public Utilities Commission authority.

(d) An armored vehicle guard within the meaning of this chapter is any person employed by an armored contract carrier who in the course of that employment carries a deadly weapon.

(e) A security guard or security officer, within the meaning of this chapter, is an employee of a private patrol operator, or an employee of a lawful business or public agency who is not exempted pursuant to Section 7582.2, who performs the functions as described in subdivision (a) on or about the premises owned or controlled by the customer of the private patrol operator or by the guard's employer or in the company of persons being protected.

(f) A street patrolperson, within the meaning of this chapter, is a security guard or security officer employed by a private patrol operator who performs the functions described in subdivision (a) by street patrol service utilizing foot patrol, motor patrol, or other means of transportation in public areas, streets or public thoroughfares in order to serve multiple customers. "Street patrolperson" does not include management or supervisory employees of the private patrol operator moving from one customer location to another to inspect personnel or security guard or security officers.

Business and Professions Code § 7582.2.

This chapter does not apply to the following:

(a) A person who does not meet the requirements to be a proprietary private security officer, as defined in Section 7574.1, and is employed exclusively and regularly by any employer who does not provide contract security services for other entities or persons, in connection with the affairs of the employer only and where there exists an employer-employee relationship if that person at no time carries or uses any deadly weapon in the performance of his or her duties. For purposes of this subdivision, "deadly weapon" is defined to include any instrument or weapon of the kind commonly known as a blackjack, slungshot, billy, sandclub, sandbag, metal knuckles, any dirk, dagger, pistol, revolver, or any other firearm, any knife having a blade longer than five inches, any razor with an unguarded blade and any metal pipe or bar used or intended to be used as a club.

(b) An officer or employee of the United States of America, or of this state or a political subdivision thereof, while the officer or employee is engaged in the performance of his or her official duties, including uniformed peace officers employed part time by a public agency pursuant to a written agreement between a chief of police or sheriff and the public agency, provided the part-time employment does not exceed 50 hours in any calendar month.

(c) A person engaged exclusively in the business of obtaining and furnishing information as to the financial rating of persons.

(d) A charitable philanthropic society or association duly incorporated under the laws of this state that is organized and maintained for the public good and not for private profit.

(e) Patrol special police officers appointed by the police commission of any city, county, or city and county under the express terms of its charter who also under the express terms of the charter

(1) are subject to suspension or dismissal after a hearing on charges duly filed with the commission after a fair and impartial trial,

(2) must be not less than 18 years of age nor more than 40 years of age,

(3) must possess physical qualifications prescribed by the commission, and

(4) are designated by the police commission as the owners of a certain beat or territory as may be fixed from time to time by the police commission.

(f) An attorney at law in performing his or her duties as an attorney at law.

(g) A collection agency or an employee thereof while acting within the scope of his or her employment, while making an investigation incidental to the business of the agency, including an investigation of the location of a debtor or his or her property where the contract with an assignor creditor is for the collection of claims owed or due or asserted to be owed or due or the equivalent thereof.

(h) Admitted insurers and agents and insurance brokers licensed by the state, performing duties in connection with insurance transacted by them.

(i) Any bank subject to the jurisdiction of the Commissioner of Financial Institutions of the State of California under Division 1 (commencing with Section 99) of the Financial Code or the Comptroller of Currency of the United States.

(j) A person engaged solely in the business of securing information about persons or property from public records.

(k) A peace officer of this state or a political subdivision thereof while the peace officer is employed by a private employer to engage in off-duty employment in accordance with Section 1126 of the Government Code. However, nothing herein shall exempt such peace officer who either contracts for his or her services or the services of others as a private patrol operator or contracts for his or her services as or is employed as an armed private security officer. For purposes of this subdivision, "armed security officer" means an individual who carries or uses a firearm in the course and scope of that contract or employment.

(l) A retired peace officer of the state or political subdivision thereof when the retired peace officer is employed by a private employer in employment approved by the chief law enforcement officer of the jurisdiction where the employment takes place, provided that the retired officer is in a uniform of a public law enforcement agency, has registered with the bureau on a form approved by the director, and has met any training requirements or their equivalent as established for security personnel under Section 7583.5. This officer may not carry a loaded or concealed firearm unless he or she is exempted under the provisions of subdivision (a) of Section 12027 of the Penal Code or paragraph (1) of subdivision (b) of Section 12031 of the Penal Code or has met the requirements set forth in Section 12033 of the Penal Code. However, nothing herein shall exempt the retired peace officer who contracts for his or her services or the services of others as a private patrol operator.

(m) A licensed insurance adjuster in performing his or her duties within the scope of his or her license as an insurance adjuster.

(n) Any savings association subject to the jurisdiction of the Commissioner of Financial Institutions or the Office of Thrift Supervision.

(o) Any secured creditor engaged in the repossession of the creditor's collateral and any lessor engaged in the repossession of leased property in which it claims an interest.

(p) A peace officer in his or her official police uniform acting in accordance with subdivisions (c) and (d) of Section 70 of the Penal Code.

(q) An unarmed, uniformed security person employed exclusively and regularly by a motion picture studio facility employer who does not provide contract security services for other entities or persons in connection with the affairs of that employer only and where there exists an employer-employee relationship if that person at no time carries or uses any deadly weapon, as defined in subdivision (a), in the performance of his or her duties, which may include, but are not limited to, the following business purposes:

(1) The screening and monitoring access of employees of the same employer.

(2) The screening and monitoring access of prearranged and preauthorized invited guests.

(3) The screening and monitoring of vendors and suppliers.

(4) Patrolling the private property facilities for the safety and welfare of all who have been legitimately authorized to have access to the facility.

(r) The changes made to this section by the act adding this subdivision during the 2005-06 Regular Session of the Legislature shall apply as follows:

(1) On and after July 1, 2006, to a person hired as a security officer on and after January 1, 2006.

(2) On and after January 1, 2007, to a person hired as a security officer before January 1, 2006.

Business and Professions Code § 7582.3.

(a) Unless specifically exempted by Section 7582.2, no person shall engage in the business of private patrol operator, as defined in Section 7582.1, unless that person has applied for and received a license to engage in that business pursuant to this chapter.

(b) Any person who violates any provision of this chapter or who conspires with another person to violate any provision of this chapter relating to private patrol operator licensure, or who knowingly engages a nonexempt unlicensed person is guilty of a misdemeanor punishable by a fine of five thousand dollars ($5,000) or by imprisonment in the county jail not to exceed one year, or by both that fine and imprisonment.

(c) A proceeding to impose the fine specified in subdivision (b) may be brought in any court of competent jurisdiction in the name of the people of the State of California by the Attorney General or by any district attorney or city attorney, or with the consent of the district attorney, the city prosecutor in any city or city and county having a full-time city prosecutor for the jurisdiction in which the violation occurred. If the action is brought by the district attorney, the penalty collected shall be paid to the treasurer of the county in which the judgment is entered. If the action is brought by a city attorney or city prosecutor, one-half of the penalty collected shall be paid to the treasurer of the city in which the judgment was entered and one-half to the treasurer of the county in which the judgment was entered. If the action is brought by the Attorney General, all of the penalty collected shall be deposited in the Private Security Services Fund.

(d) Any person who:

(1) acts as or represents himself or herself to be a private patrol operator under this chapter when that person is not a licensee under this chapter;

(2) falsely represents that he or she is employed by a licensee under this chapter when that person is not employed by a licensee under this chapter;

(3) carries a badge, identification card, or business card, indicating that he or she is a licensee under this chapter when that

person is not a licensee under this chapter;

(4) uses a letterhead or other written or electronically generated materials indicating that he or she is a licensee under this chapter when that person is not a licensee under this chapter; or

(5) advertises that he or she is a licensee under this chapter when that person is not a licensee, is guilty of a misdemeanor that is punishable by a fine of ten thousand dollars ($10,000) or by imprisonment in a county jail for not more than one year, or by both that fine and imprisonment.

(e) A proceeding to impose the fine specified in subdivision (d) may be brought in any court of competent jurisdiction in the name of the people of the State of California by the Attorney General or by any district attorney or city attorney, or with the consent of the district attorney, the city prosecutor in any city or city and county having a full-time city prosecutor for the jurisdiction in which the violation occurred. If the action is brought by the district attorney, the penalty collected shall be paid to the treasurer of the county in which the judgment is entered. If the action is brought by a city attorney or city prosecutor, one-half of the penalty collected shall be paid to the treasurer of the city in which the judgment was entered and one-half to the treasurer of the county in which the judgment was entered. If the action is brought by the Attorney General, all of the penalty collected shall be deposited in the Private Security Services Fund.

(f) Any person who is convicted of a violation of the provisions of this section shall not be issued a license under this chapter, within one year following that conviction.

(g) Any person who is convicted of a violation of subdivision (a), (b), or (d) shall not be issued a license for a period of one year following a first conviction and shall not be issued a license for a period of five years following a second or subsequent conviction of subdivision (a), (b), or (d), or any combination of subdivision (a), (b), or (d).

(h) The chief shall gather evidence of violations of this chapter and of any rule or regulation established pursuant to this chapter by persons engaged in the business of private patrol operator who fail to obtain licenses and shall gather evidence of violations and furnish that evidence to prosecuting officers of any county or city for the purpose of prosecuting all violations occurring within their jurisdiction.

(i) The prosecuting officer of any county or city shall prosecute all violations of this chapter occurring within his or her jurisdiction.

Business and Professions Code § 7582.4.

(a) The superior court in and for the county in which any person has engaged or is about to engage in any act which constitutes a violation of Section 7582.3 may, upon a petition filed by the bureau with the approval of the director, issue an injunction or other appropriate order restraining this conduct and may impose a civil fine not exceeding ten thousand dollars ($10,000). The proceedings under this section shall be governed by Chapter 3 (commencing with Section 525) of Title 7 of Part 2 of the Code of Civil Procedure, except that there shall be no requirement to allege facts necessary to show or tending to show lack of adequate remedy at law or irreparable injury.

(b) The superior court for the county in which any person has engaged in any act which constitutes a violation of Section 7582.3 may, upon a petition filed by the bureau with the approval of the director, order this person to make restitution to persons injured as a result of the violation.

(c) The court may order a person subject to an injunction or restraining order, provided for in subdivision (a), or subject to an order requiring restitution pursuant to subdivision (b), to reimburse the bureau for expenses incurred by the bureau in its investigation related to its petition.

(d) A proceeding to impose the fine specified in subdivision (a) or to enjoin the unlicensed operation may be brought in any court of competent jurisdiction in the name of the people of the State of California by the Attorney General, or by any district attorney or city attorney, or, with the consent of the district attorney, the city prosecutor in any city or city and county having a full-time city prosecutor, for the jurisdiction in which the violation occurred. If the action is brought by the district attorney, the penalty collected shall be paid to the treasurer of the county in which the judgment is entered. If the action is brought by a city attorney or city prosecutor, one-half of the penalty collected shall be paid to the treasurer of the city in which the judgment was entered and one-half to the treasurer of the county in which the judgment was entered. If the action is brought by the Attorney General, all of the penalty collected shall be deposited in the Private Security Services Fund.

(e) The remedy provided for by this section shall be in addition to any other remedy provided for in this chapter.

Business and Professions Code § 7582.5.

(a) The provisions of this chapter shall not prevent the local authorities of any city, county, or city and county, by ordinance and within the exercise of the police power of the city, county, or city and county from imposing local regulations upon any street patrol service or street patrol special officers requiring registration with an agency to be designated by the city, county, or city and county, including in the registration full information as to the identification and employment and subject to the right of the city, county, or city and county to allocate certain portions of the territory in the city, county, or city and county within which the activities of any street patrol service or person shall be confined. Any city, county, or city and county may refuse registration to any person of bad moral character and may impose reasonable additional requirements as are necessary to meet local needs and are not inconsistent with the provisions of this chapter.

(b) The provisions of this chapter shall not prevent the local authorities of any city, county, or city and county, by ordinance and within the exercise of the police power of the city, county, or city and county from imposing local regulations upon any employees of a private patrol operator who are unable to furnish evidence of current registration pursuant to subdivision (f) of Section 7581.

(c) The provisions of this chapter shall not prevent the local authorities of any city, county, or city and county, by ordinance and within the exercise of the police power of the city, county, or city and county from requiring private patrol operators and their employees to register their name and file a copy of their state identification card with the city, county, or city and county. No fee may be charged and no application may be required by the city, county, or city and county for this registration.

(d) The provisions of this chapter shall not prevent the local authorities in any city, county, or city and county, by ordinance and within the exercise of the police power of the city, county, or city and county from imposing reasonable additional requirements necessary to regulate and control protection dogs according to their local needs and not inconsistent with the provisions of this chapter.

Business and Professions Code § 7582.6.

An application for a license under this chapter shall be on a form prescribed by the director and accompanied by the application fee provided by this chapter.

Business and Professions Code § 7582.7.

An application shall be verified and shall include:

(a) The full name and business address of the applicant.

(b) The name under which the applicant intends to do business.

(c) A statement as to the general nature of the business in which the applicant intends to engage.

(d) A statement as to the type of license for which the applicant is applying.

(e) A verified statement of his or her experience qualifications.

(f)(1) If the applicant is an individual, a qualified manager, partner of a partnership, or officer of a corporation designated in subdivision (i), one personal identification form provided by the bureau upon which shall appear a photograph taken within one year immediately preceding the date of the filing of the application together with two legible sets of fingerprints, one set of which shall be forwarded to the Federal Bureau of Investigation for purposes of a background check, on a form approved by the Department of Justice, and a personal description of each person, respectively. The identification form shall include residence addresses and employment history for the previous five years and be signed under penalty of perjury.

(2) The bureau may impose a fee not to exceed three dollars ($3) for processing classifiable fingerprint cards submitted by applicants, excluding those submitted into an electronic fingerprint system using electronic fingerprint technology.

(g) In addition, if the applicant for a license is an individual, the application shall list all other names known as or used during the past 10 years and shall state that the applicant is to be personally and actively in charge of the business for which the license is sought, or if any other qualified manager is to be actively in charge of the business, the application shall be subscribed, verified, and signed by the applicant, under penalty of perjury, and if any other person is to be actively in charge of the business, the application shall also be subscribed, verified, and signed by that person under penalty of perjury.

(h) If the applicants for license are copartners, the application shall state the true names and addresses of all partners and the name of the partner to be actively in charge of the business for which the license is sought; and list all other names known as or used during the past 10 years, or if a qualified manager other than a partner is to be actively in charge of the business, then the application shall be subscribed, verified, and signed by all of the partners under penalty of perjury, and if any other person is to be actively in charge of the business, the application shall also be subscribed, verified, and signed by that person, under penalty of perjury, under penalty of perjury by all of the partners and qualified manager, or by all of the partners or the qualified manager.

(i) If the applicant for license is a corporation, the application shall state the true names, and complete residence addresses of the chief executive officer, secretary, chief financial officer, and any other corporate officer who will be active in the business to be licensed. The application shall also state the name and address of the designated person to be actively in charge of the business for which the license is sought. The application shall be subscribed, verified, and signed by a duly authorized officer of the applicant and by the qualified manager thereof, under penalty of perjury.

(j) Any other information, evidence, statements, or documents as may be required by the director.

Business and Professions Code § 7582.8.

Before an application for a license or registration is granted, the applicant for a license or his or her manager or the applicant for a security guard registration shall meet all of the following:

(a) Be at least 18 years of age.

(b) Not have committed acts or crimes constituting grounds for denial of a license under Section 480.

(c) Comply with the requirements specified in this chapter for the particular license or registration for which an application is made.

(d) Comply with other qualifications as the director may fix by rule.

(e) In lieu of meeting any other training-related requirements of this section, an applicant may apply for licensure or registration if he or she has completed comparable military training as documented by submission of Verification of Military Experience and Training (V-MET) records.

Business and Professions Code § 7582.9.

The director may require an applicant or his or her manager, to demonstrate his or her qualifications by a written or oral examination, or a combination of both.

Business and Professions Code § 7582.10.

Payment of the application fee prescribed by this chapter entitles an applicant or his or her manager to one examination without further charge. If the person fails to pass the examination, he or she shall not be eligible for any subsequent examination except upon payment of the reexamination fee prescribed by this chapter for each subsequent examination.

Business and Professions Code § 7582.11.

The chief shall issue a license, the form and content of which shall be determined by the chief in accordance with Section 164. In addition, the chief shall issue a "Certificate of Licensure" to any licensee, upon request and upon the payment of a fee of fifty dollars ($50).

Business and Professions Code § 7582.12.

(a) The license shall at all times be posted in a conspicuous place in the principal place of business of the licensee.

(b) The director may assess a fine of two hundred fifty dollars ($250) per violation of subdivision (a).

Business and Professions Code § 7582.13.

Upon the issuance of a license, a pocket card of the size, design, and content determined by the director shall be issued to each licensee, if an individual, or if the licensee is a person other than an individual, to its manager and to each of its officers and partners. The pocket card is evidence that the licensee is licensed pursuant to this chapter. The card shall contain the signature of the licensee, signature of the chief, and a photograph of the licensee, or bearer of the card, if the licensee is other than an individual. The card shall clearly state that the person is licensed as a private patrol operator or is the manager or officer of the licensee. The applicant may request to be issued an enhanced pocket card that shall be composed of a durable material and may incorporate technologically advanced security features. The bureau may charge a fee sufficient to reimburse the department's costs for furnishing the enhanced pocket card. The fee charged may not exceed the actual costs for system development, maintenance, and processing necessary to provide this service, and may not exceed six dollars ($6). If the applicant does not request an enhanced card, the department shall issue a standard card at no cost. When a person to whom a card is issued terminates his or her position, office, or association with the licensee, the card shall be surrendered to the licensee and within five days thereafter shall be mailed or delivered by the licensee to the bureau for cancellation. Every person, while engaged in any activity for which registration is required, shall display their valid pocket card as provided by regulation.

Business and Professions Code § 7582.14.

A license issued under this chapter is not assignable.

Business and Professions Code § 7582.15.

A licensee shall at all times be legally responsible for the good conduct in the business of each of his or her employees or agents, including his or her manager.

Business and Professions Code § 7582.16.

Each licensee shall maintain a record containing information relative to his or her employees as may be prescribed by the director.

Business and Professions Code § 7582.17.

No licensee shall conduct a business under a fictitious or other business name unless and until he or she has obtained the written authorization of the bureau to do so. The bureau shall not authorize the use of a fictitious or other business name which is so similar to that of a public officer or agency or of that used by another licensee that the public may be confused or misled thereby. The authorization shall require, as a condition precedent to the use of any fictitious name, that the licensee comply with Chapter 5 (commencing with Section 17900) of Part 3 of Division 7. A licensee desiring to conduct his or her business under more than one fictitious business name shall obtain the authorization of the bureau in the manner prescribed in this section for the use of each name. The licensee shall pay a fee of twenty-five dollars ($25) for each authorization to use an additional fictitious business name and for each change in the use of a fictitious business name. If the original license is issued in a nonfictitious name and authorization is requested to have the license reissued in a fictitious business name the licensee shall pay a fee of twenty-five dollars ($25) for the authorization.

Business and Professions Code § 7582.18.

Each licensee shall file with the bureau the complete address of his or her principal place of business including the name and number of the street, or, if the street where the business is located is not numbered, the number of the post office box. The director may require the filing of other information for the purpose of identifying the principal place of business.

Business and Professions Code § 7582.19

(a) A licensee shall notify the bureau within 30 days of any change in its corporate officers or of any addition of a new partner.

(b) Applications, on forms prescribed by the director, shall be submitted by all new officers and partners. The director may suspend or revoke a license issued under this chapter if the director determines that the new officer or partner of a licensee has committed any of the acts constituting grounds to deny an application for a license or to take disciplinary action against a licensee pursuant to Section 7582.24 or 7582.25 respectively.

Business and Professions Code § 7582.20.

(a) Every advertisement by a licensee soliciting or advertising business shall contain his or her name, address, and license number as they appear in the records of the bureau. For the purpose of this section, "advertisement" includes any business card, stationery, brochure, flyer, circular, newsletter, fax form, printed or published paid advertisement in any media form, or telephone book listing. Every advertisement by a licensee soliciting or advertising the licensee's business shall contain his or her business name, business address or business telephone number, and license number, as they appear in the records of the bureau.

(b) The director may assess a fine of two hundred fifty dollars ($250) per violation of subdivision (a).

Business and Professions Code § 7582.21.

(a) A licensee shall not advertise or conduct business from any location other than that shown on the records of the bureau as his or her principal place of business unless he or she has received a branch office certificate for the location after compliance with the provisions of this chapter and any additional requirements necessary for the protection of the public as the director may by regulation prescribe. A licensee shall notify the bureau in writing within 10 days after closing or changing the location of a branch office.

(b) The director may assess a fine of five hundred dollars ($500) for the first violation of subdivision (a) and one thousand dollars ($1,000) for each violation thereafter.

Business and Professions Code § 7582.22.

(a) The business of each licensee shall be operated under the active direction, control, charge, or management, in this state, of the licensee, if he or she is qualified, or the person who is qualified to act as the licensee's manager, if the licensee is not qualified. Any licensee conducting business in this state whose primary office is located outside of this state shall do both of the following:

(1) Maintain an office in this state operated under the active direction, control, charge, or management of a qualified manager.

(2) Maintain at the office in this state all records required under this chapter and under rules adopted by the bureau.

(b) No person shall act as a qualified manager of a licensee until he or she has complied with each of the following:

(1) Demonstrated his or her qualifications by a written or oral examination, or a combination of both, if required by the director.

(2) Made a satisfactory showing to the director that he or she has the qualifications prescribed in Section 7582.8 and that none of the facts stated in Section 7582.24 or 7582.25 exist as to him or her.

Business and Professions Code § 7582.23.

(a) In case of the death of a person licensed as an individual, a member of the immediate family of the deceased licensee shall be entitled to continue the business under the same license for 120 days following the death of the licensee, provided that written application for permission is made to the bureau within 30 days following the death of the licensee. At the end of the 120-day period, the license shall be automatically canceled. If no request is received within the 30-day period, the license shall be automatically canceled at the end of that period.

(b) If the manager, who has qualified as provided in Section 7582.22, ceases for any reason whatsoever to be connected with the licensee to whom the license is issued, the licensee shall notify the bureau in writing 30 days from this cessation. If the notice of cessation is filed timely, the license shall remain in force for a period of 90 days after cessation or for an additional period, not to exceed one year, as approved by the director, pending the qualification of another manager as provided in this chapter. After the 90-day period or additional period, as approved by the director, the license shall be automatically suspended, unless the bureau receives written notification that the license is under the active charge of a qualified manager. If the licensee fails to notify the bureau within the 30-day period, his or her license shall be automatically suspended and may be reinstated only upon the filing of an application for reinstatement, payment of the reinstatement fee, and the qualification of a manager as provided in this chapter.

(c) In the case of the death or disassociation of a partner of an entity licensed as a partnership, the licensee shall notify the bureau, in writing, within 30 days from the death or disassociation of the individual. If notice is given, the license shall remain in force for 90 days following the death or disassociation. At the end of this period the license shall be automatically canceled. If the licensee fails to notify the bureau within the 30-day period, the license shall be automatically canceled.

(d) A license extended under this section is subject to all other provisions of this chapter.

Business and Professions Code § 7582.24.

After a hearing the director may deny a license unless the applicant makes a showing satisfactory to the director that the applicant, if an individual, has not, or if the applicant is a person other than an individual, that its manager and each of its officers have not:

(a) Committed any act, which, if committed by a licensee, would be a ground for the suspension or revocation of a license under this chapter.

(b) Committed any act constituting dishonesty or fraud.

(c) Committed any act or crime constituting grounds for denial of licensure under Section 480, including illegally using, carrying, or possessing a deadly weapon.

(d) Been refused a license under this chapter or had a license revoked.

(e) Been an officer, partner, or manager of any person who has been refused a license under this chapter or whose license has been revoked.

(f) While unlicensed committed, or aided and abetted the commission of, any act for which a license is required by this chapter.

(g) Knowingly made any false statement in his or her application.

Business and Professions Code § 7582.25.

The director may refuse to issue any license provided for in this chapter to any person:

(a) Who has had any license revoked, or whose license is under suspension, or has failed to renew his or her license while it was under suspension.

(b) If any member of any partnership, or any officer or director of any corporation, or any officer or person acting in a managerial capacity of any firm or association has had any license issued to him or her revoked, or whose license is under suspension, or who has failed to renew his or her license while it was under suspension.

(c) If any member of the partnership, or any officer or director of the corporation, or any officer or person acting in a managerial capacity of the firm or association, was either a member of any partnership, or an officer or director of any corporation, or an officer or person acting in a managerial capacity of any firm or association, whose license has been revoked, or whose license is under suspension, or who failed to renew a license while it was under suspension, and while acting as such member, officer, director, or person acting in a managerial capacity participated in any of the prohibited acts for which any such license was revoked or suspended.

Business and Professions Code § 7582.26.

(a) Any licensee or officer, director, partner, or manager of a licensee may divulge to any law enforcement officer or district attorney, or his or her representative, any information he or she may acquire as to any criminal offense, but he or she shall not divulge to any other person, except as he or she may be required by law so to do, any information acquired by him or her except at the direction of the employer or client for whom the information was obtained.

(b) No licensee or officer, director, partner, manager, or employee of a licensee shall knowingly make any false report to his or her employer or client for whom information was being obtained.

(c) No written report shall be submitted to a client except by the licensee, qualifying manager, or a person authorized by one or either of them, and the person submitting the report shall exercise diligence in ascertaining whether or not the facts and information in the report are true and correct.

(d) No licensee, or officer, director, partner, manager, or employee of a licensee, shall use a title, or wear a uniform, or use an insignia, or use an identification card, or make any statement with the intent to give an impression that he or she is connected in any way with the federal government, a state government, or any political subdivision of a state government.

(e) No licensee, or officer, director, partner, manager, or employee of a licensee, shall enter any private building or portion thereof, except premises commonly accessible to the public, without the consent of the owner or of the person in legal possession thereof.

(f) No private patrol licensee or officer, director, partner, manager, or employee of a private patrol licensee shall use or wear a badge, except while engaged in guard or patrol work and while wearing a distinctive uniform. A private patrol licensee or officer, director, partner, manager, or employee of a private patrol licensee wearing a distinctive uniform shall wear a patch on each shoulder of his or her uniform that reads "private security" and that includes the name of the private patrol company by which the person is employed or for which the person is a representative and a badge or cloth patch on the upper left breast of the uniform. All patches and badges worn on a distinctive uniform shall be of a standard design approved by the director and shall be clearly visible. The director may assess a fine of two hundred fifty dollars ($250) per violation of this subdivision.

(g) No licensee shall permit an employee or agent in his or her own name to advertise, engage clients, furnish reports or present bills to clients, or in any manner whatever conduct business for which a license is required under this chapter. All business of the licensee shall be conducted in the name of and under the control of the licensee.

(h) No licensee shall use a fictitious name in connection with the official activities of the licensee's business.

(i) No private patrol operator licensee or officer, director, partner, or manager of a private patrol operator licensee, or person required to be registered as a security guard pursuant to this chapter shall use or wear a baton or exposed firearm as authorized by this chapter unless he or she is wearing a uniform which complies with the requirements of Section 7582.27.

Business and Professions Code § 7582.27.

(a) Any person referred to in subdivision (i) of Section 7582.26 who uses or wears a baton or exposed firearm as authorized pursuant to this chapter shall wear a patch on each arm that reads "private security" and that includes the name of the company by which the person is employed or for which the person is a representative. The patch shall be clearly visible at all times. The patches of a private patrol operator licensee, or his or her employees or representatives shall be of a standard design approved by the director.

(b) The director may assess a fine of two hundred fifty dollars ($250) per violation of subdivision (a).

Business and Professions Code § 7582.28.

(a) Any badge or cap insignia worn by a person who is a licensee, officer, director, partner, manager, or employee of a licensee shall be of a design approved by the director, and shall bear on its face a distinctive word indicating the name of the licensee and an employee number by which the person may be identified by the licensee. The provisions of this section shall not be construed to authorize persons to wear badges who are prohibited by Section 7582.26 from wearing badges.

(b) The director may assess a fine of two hundred fifty dollars ($250) per violation of subdivision (a).

Business and Professions Code § 7583.

For purposes of this article, "licensee" means a licensed private patrol operator.

Business and Professions Code § 7583.2.

No person licensed as a private patrol operator shall do any of the following:

(a) Fail to properly maintain an accurate and current record of all firearms or other deadly weapons that are in the possession of the licensee or of any employee while on duty. Within seven days after a licensee or his or her employees discover that a deadly weapon that has been recorded as being in his or her possession has been misplaced, lost, or stolen, or is in any other way missing, the licensee or his or her manager shall mail or deliver to any local law enforcement agency that has jurisdiction, a written report concerning the incident. The report shall describe fully the circumstances surrounding the incident, any injuries or damages incurred, the identity of all participants, and whether a police investigation was conducted.

(b) Fail to properly maintain an accurate and current record of the name, address, commencing date of employment, and position of each employee, and the date of termination of employment when an employee is terminated.

(c) Fail to properly maintain an accurate and current record of proof of completion by each employee of the licensee of the course of training in the exercise of the power to arrest as required by Section 7583.5, the security officer skills training required by subdivision (b) of Section 7583.6, and the annual practice and review required by subdivision (f) of Section 7583.6.

(d) Fail to certify an employee's completion of the course of training in the exercise of the power to arrest prior to placing the employee at a duty station.

(e) Fail to certify proof of current and valid registration for each employee who is subject to registration.

(f) Permit any employee to carry a firearm or other deadly weapon without first ascertaining that the employee is proficient in the use of each weapon to be carried. With respect to firearms, evidence of proficiency shall include a certificate from a firearm training facility approved by the director certifying that the employee is proficient in the use of that specified caliber of firearm and a current and valid firearm qualification permit issued by the department. With respect to other deadly weapons, evidence of proficiency shall include a certificate from a training facility approved by the director certifying that the employee is proficient in the use of that particular deadly weapon.

(g) Fail to deliver to the director a written report describing fully the circumstances surrounding the discharge of any firearm, or physical altercation with a member of the public while on duty, by a licensee or any officer, partner, or employee of a licensee while acting within the course and scope of his or her employment within seven days after the incident. For the purposes of this subdivision, a report shall be required only for physical altercations that result in any of the following:

(1) the arrest of a security guard,

(2) the filing of a police report by a member of the public,

(3) injury on the part of a member of the public that requires medical attention, or

(4) the discharge, suspension, or reprimand of a security guard by his or her employer. The report shall include, but not be limited to, a description of any injuries or damages incurred, the identity of all participants, and whether a police investigation was conducted. Any report may be investigated by the director to determine if any disciplinary action is necessary.

(h) Fail to notify the bureau in writing and within 30 days that a manager previously qualified pursuant to this chapter is no longer connected with the licensee.

(i) Fail to administer to each registered employee of the licensee, the review or practice training required by subdivision (f) of Section 7583.6.

Business and Professions Code § 7583.3.

No person required to be registered as a security guard pursuant to this chapter shall do any of the following:

(a) Fail to carry on his or her person, while on duty, a valid and current security guard registration card.

(b) Fail to carry on his or her person a valid and current firearms permit when carrying a firearm on duty.

(c) Carry or use a firearm unless he or she possesses a valid and current firearms permit issued pursuant to this chapter.

(d) Fail to report to his or her employer within 24 hours of the incident the circumstances surrounding any incident involving the discharge of any firearm in which he or she is involved while acting within the course and scope of his or her employment.

Business and Professions Code § 7583.4.

Any person registered as a security guard or patrolperson shall deliver to the director a written report describing fully the circumstances surrounding any incident involving the discharge of any firearm in which he or she was involved while acting within the course and scope of his or her employment, within seven days after the incident. The report shall be made on a form prescribed by the director which shall include, but not be limited to, the following:

(a) The name, address, and date of birth of the guard or patrolperson.

(b) The registration number of the guard or patrolperson.

(c) The firearm permit number and baton permit number of the guard or patrolperson, if applicable.

(d) The name of the employer of the person.

(e) The description of any injuries and damages that occurred.

(f) The identity of all participants in the incident.

(g) Whether a police investigation was conducted relating to the incident.

(h) The date and location of the incident. Any report may be investigated by the director to determine if any disciplinary action is necessary. A copy of the report delivered to the director pursuant to this section shall also be delivered within seven days of the incident to the local police or sheriff's department which has jurisdiction over the geographic area where the incident occurred.

Business and Professions Code § 7583.5.

(a) Every licensee and any person employed and compensated by a licensee, other lawful business or public agency as a security guard or patrolperson, and who in the course of that employment or business carries a firearm, shall complete a course of training in the exercise of the powers to arrest and a course of training in the carrying and use of firearms. This subdivision shall not apply to armored vehicle guards hired prior to January 1, 1977. Armored vehicle guards hired on or after January 1, 1977, shall complete a course of training in the carrying and use of firearms, but shall not be required to complete a course of training in the exercise of the powers to arrest. The course of training in the carrying and use of firearms shall not be required of any employee who is not required or permitted by a licensee to carry or use firearms. The course in the carrying and use of firearms and the course of training in the exercise of the powers to arrest shall meet the standards which shall be prescribed by the Department of Consumer Affairs. The department shall encourage restraint and caution in the use of firearms.

(b) No uniformed employee of a licensee shall carry or use any firearm unless the employee has in his or her possession a valid firearm qualification card.

Business and Professions Code § 7583.8.

No employee of a licensee who performs the function of a security guard or security patrolperson shall be issued a registration card until there is proper certification by the instructor that the exercise of the power to arrest course has been taught and the employee's certification that the instruction was received has been delivered to the department. Except as provided in subdivision (f) of Section 7583.9, no security guard registration shall be issued until a criminal history background check has been completed pursuant to subdivision (e) of Section 7583.9 and a determination has been made by the bureau.

Business and Professions Code § 7583.9.

(a) Upon accepting employment by a private patrol operator, any employee who performs the function of a security guard or security patrolperson who is not currently registered with the bureau, shall complete an application for registration on a form as prescribed by the director, and obtain two classifiable fingerprint cards for submission to the Department of Justice. The applicant shall submit the application, the registration fee, and his or her fingerprints to the bureau. The bureau shall forward the classifiable fingerprint cards to the Department of Justice. The Department of Justice shall forward one classifiable fingerprint card to the Federal Bureau of Investigation for purposes of a background check.

(b) If a private patrol operator pays the application fee on behalf of the applicant, nothing in this section shall preclude the private patrol operator from withholding the amount of the fee from the applicant's compensation.

(c) The licensee shall maintain supplies of applications and fingerprint cards that shall be provided by the bureau upon request.

(d) In lieu of classifiable fingerprint cards provided for in this section, the bureau may authorize applicants to submit their fingerprints into an electronic fingerprinting system administered by the Department of Justice. Applicants who submit their fingerprints by electronic means shall have their fingerprints entered into the system through a terminal operated by a law enforcement agency or other facility authorized by the Department of Justice to conduct electronic fingerprinting. The enforcement agency responsible for operating the terminal may charge a fee sufficient to reimburse it for the costs incurred in providing this service.

(e) Upon receipt of an applicant's electronic or hard card fingerprints as provided in this section, the Department of Justice shall disseminate the following information to the bureau:

(1) Every conviction rendered against the applicant.

(2) Every arrest for an offense for which the applicant is presently awaiting trial, whether the applicant is incarcerated or has been released on bail or on his or her own recognizance pending trial.

(f)(1) The requirement in subdivision (a) to submit a fingerprint card does not apply to any of the following:

(A) A currently employed, full-time peace officer holding peace officer status under Chapter 4.5 (commencing with Section 830) of Title 3 of Part 2 of the Penal Code.

(B) A level I or level II reserve officer under paragraphs (1) and (2) of subdivision (a) of Section 832.6 of the Penal Code.

(2) An individual listed in subparagraph (A) or (B) of paragraph (1) may immediately perform the functions of a security guard or security patrolperson provided that he or she has submitted an application, the applicable fees, and his or her fingerprints, if required to submit fingerprints pursuant to subdivision (a), to the bureau for a security guard registration.

(3) This subdivision does not apply to a peace officer required to obtain a firearm qualification card pursuant to Section 7583.12.

(g) Peace officers exempt from the submission of classifiable fingerprints pursuant to subdivision (f) shall submit verification of their active duty peace officer status to the bureau with their application for registration. A photocopy of the front and back of their peace officer identification badge shall be adequate verification.

(h) Peace officers exempt from the submission of classifiable fingerprints pursuant to subdivision (f) shall report a change in their active duty peace officer status to the bureau within 72 hours of the change in active duty peace officer status.

(i)(1) Peace officers exempt from obtaining a firearm qualification card pursuant to subdivision (c) of Section 7583.12 shall submit to the bureau with their application for registration a letter of approval from his or her primary employer authorizing him or her to carry a firearm while working as a security guard or security officer.

(2) For purposes of this section, "primary employer" means a public safety agency currently employing a peace officer subject to this section.

(j) In addition to the amount authorized pursuant to Section 7570.1, the bureau may impose an additional fee not to exceed three dollars ($3) for processing classifiable fingerprint cards submitted by applicants excluding those submitted into an electronic fingerprint system using electronic fingerprint technology.

(k) An employee shall, on the first day of employment, display to the client his or her registration card if it is feasible and practical to comply with this disclosure requirement. The employee shall thereafter display to the client his or her registration card upon the request of the client.

Business and Professions Code § 7583.12.

(a) No employee of a licensee shall carry or use a firearm unless the employee has in his or her possession both of the following:

(1) A valid guard registration card issued pursuant to this chapter.

(2) A valid firearm qualification card issued pursuant to this chapter.

(b) Paragraph (2) of subdivision (a) shall not apply to a duly appointed peace officer, as defined in Chapter 4.5 (commencing with Section 830) of Title 3 of Part 2 of the Penal Code, who meets all of the following:

(1) He or she has successfully completed a course of study in the use of firearms.

(2) He or she is authorized to carry a concealed firearm in the course and scope of his or her employment pursuant to subdivision (a) of Section 12027 of the Penal Code.

(3) He or she has proof that he or she has applied to the bureau for a firearms qualification card.

(c) (1) This section shall not apply to a duly appointed peace officer, as defined in Chapter 4.5 (commencing with Section 830) of Title 3 of Part 2 of the Penal Code, who has written approval from his or her primary employer, as defined in paragraph (2) of subdivision (i) of Section 7583.9, to carry a firearm while working as a security guard or security officer.

(2) A peace officer exempt under this subdivision shall carry on his or her person a letter of approval from his or her primary employer authorizing him or her to carry a firearm while working as a security guard or security officer.

Business and Professions Code § 7583.13.

(a) The bureau, upon receipt of a criminal offense record or record of a subsequent arrest from the Department of Justice, shall make an immediate determination of fitness of

(1) applicants for registration under this article, or

(2) applicants for firearm qualification cards, when information contained in the records of the Department of Justice makes this determination possible. Applications of those determined to be unfit shall be immediately denied.

(b) The bureau shall keep a current and accurate record of the individuals who have applied for and been denied registration under this article or a firearms qualification card. A list consisting of individual names and other pertinent identifying information may be made of those individuals who have been denied registration. The list may be updated bimonthly and made available to interested licensees and law enforcement agencies.

Business and Professions Code § 7583.15.

If the director determines that continued employment of an applicant, firearms qualification cardholder, or registrant, in his or her current capacity, may present an undue hazard to the public safety, the licensee, upon proper notification from the director, shall suspend the applicant, firearms qualification cardholder, or registrant from employment in that capacity. A registrant, firearms qualification card holder, or applicant may request a review by the Private Security Disciplinary Review Committee as set forth in Section 7581.3 to appeal the suspension.

Business and Professions Code § 7583.18.

A qualified manager who complies with Section 7582.22 is not required to register under this article..

Business and Professions Code § 7583.20.

(a) A registration issued under this chapter expires two years following the date of issuance or on the assigned renewal date. Every security guard issued a registration under this chapter that expires on or after January 1, 1997, and who is also issued or renews a firearms qualification card on or after January 1, 1997, shall be placed on a cyclical renewal so that the registration expires on the expiration date of the firearms qualification card. Notwithstanding any other provision of law, the bureau is authorized to extend or shorten the first term of registration following January 1, 1997, and to prorate the required registration fee in order to implement this cyclical renewal. At least 60 days prior to the expiration, a registrant seeking to renew a security guard registration shall forward to the bureau a completed registration renewal application and the renewal fee. The renewal application shall be on a form prescribed by the director, dated and signed by the applicant, certifying under penalty of perjury that the information in the application is true and correct.

(b) The licensee shall provide to any employee information regarding procedures for renewal or registration.

(c) In the event a registrant fails to request a renewal of his or her registration as provided for in this chapter, the registration shall expire as indicated on the registration. If the registration is renewed within 60 days after its expiration, the registrant, as a condition precedent to renewal, shall pay the renewal fee and the delinquency fee.

(d) The delinquency fee is 50 percent of the renewal fee in effect on the date of expiration, but not less than twenty-five dollars ($25).

(e) If the renewed registration card has not been delivered to the registrant prior to the expiration of the prior registration, the registrant may present evidence of renewal to substantiate continued registration for a period not to exceed 90 days after the date of expiration.

(f) A registration may not be renewed or reinstated unless a registrant meets both of the following requirements:

(1) All fines assessed pursuant to Section 7587.7 and not resolved in accordance with the provisions of that section have been paid.

(2) On and after July 1, 2005, the registrant certifies, on a form prescribed by the bureau, that he or she has completed the 32 hours of the training required by subdivision (b) of Section 7583.6.

Business and Professions Code § 7583.22.

(a) A licensee, qualified manager of a licensee, or security guard who, in the course of his or her employment, may be required to carry a firearm shall, prior to carrying a firearm, do both of the following:

(1) Complete a course of training in the carrying and use of firearms.

(2) Receive a firearms qualification card or be otherwise qualified to carry a firearm as provided in Section 7583.12.

(b) A licensee shall not permit an employee to carry or use a loaded or unloaded firearm, whether or not it is serviceable or operative, unless the employee possesses a valid and current firearms qualification card issued by the bureau or is so otherwise qualified to carry a firearm as provided in Section 7583.12.

(c) A pocket card issued by the bureau pursuant to Section 7582.13 may also serve as a firearms qualification card if so indicated on the face of the card.

(d) Paragraph (1) of subdivision (a) shall not apply to a peace officer as defined in Chapter 4.5 (commencing with Section 830) of Title 3 of Part 2 of the Penal Code, who has successfully completed a course of study in the use of firearms.

(e) This section shall become operative on January 1, 1998.

Business and Professions Code § 7583.23.

The bureau shall issue a firearms permit when all of the following conditions are satisfied:

(a) The applicant is a licensee, a qualified manager of a licensee, or a registered uniformed security guard.

(b) A certified firearms training instructor has certified that the applicant has successfully completed a written examination prepared by the bureau and training course in the carrying and use of firearms approved by the bureau.

(c) The applicant has filed with the bureau a classifiable fingerprint card, a completed application for a firearms permit on a form prescribed by the director, dated and signed by the applicant, certifying under penalty of perjury that the information in the application is true and correct.

(d) The bureau has determined, after investigation, that the carrying and use of a firearm by the applicant, in the course of his or her duties, presents no apparent threat to the public safety, or that the carrying and use of a firearm by the applicant is not in violation of the Penal Code.

(e) The applicant has produced evidence to the firearm training facility that he or she is a citizen of the United States or has permanent legal alien status in the United States. Evidence of citizenship or permanent legal alien status shall be that deemed sufficient by the bureau to ensure compliance with federal laws prohibiting possession of firearms by persons unlawfully in the United States and may include, but not be limited to, Department of Justice, Immigration and Naturalization Service Form I-151 or I-551, Alien Registration Receipt Card, naturalization documents, or birth certificates evidencing lawful residence or status in the United States.

(f) The application is accompanied by the application fees prescribed in this chapter.

Business and Professions Code § 7583.24.

(a) The bureau shall not issue a firearm permit if the applicant is prohibited from possessing, receiving, owning, or purchasing a firearm pursuant to state or federal law.

(b) Before issuing an initial firearm permit the bureau shall provide the Department of Justice with the name, address, social security number, and fingerprints of the applicant.

(c) The Department of Justice shall inform the bureau, within 60 days from receipt of the information specified in subdivision (b), of the applicant's eligibility to possess, receive, purchase, or own a firearm pursuant to state and federal law.

(d) An applicant who has been denied a firearm permit based upon subdivision (a) may reapply for the permit after the prohibition expires. The bureau shall treat this application as an initial application and shall follow the required screening process as specified in this section.

Business and Professions Code § 7583.25.

(a) The bureau shall not renew a firearm permit if the applicant is prohibited from possessing, receiving, purchasing, or owning a firearm pursuant to state or federal law.

(b) Before renewing a firearm permit, the bureau shall provide the Department of Justice with the information necessary to identify the renewal applicant. No firearm permit shall be renewed if the expiration date of the permit is between October 1, 1993, and October 1, 1994, unless the application for renewal is also accompanied by a classifiable fingerprint card and the fingerprint processing fees for that card.

(c) The Department of Justice shall inform the bureau, within 30 days of receipt of the information specified in subdivision (b), of the renewal applicant's eligibility to possess, receive, purchase, or own a firearm pursuant to state and federal law.

(d) An applicant who is denied a firearm permit renewal based upon subdivision (a) may reapply for the permit after the prohibition expires. The bureau shall treat this as an initial application and shall follow the screening process specified in Section 7583.24.

Business and Professions Code § 7583.26.

(a) The Department of Justice may charge the bureau a fee sufficient to reimburse the department's costs for furnishing firearm eligibility information upon submission of the application for issuance or renewal of a firearm permit. The fee charged shall not exceed the actual costs for system development, maintenance, and processing necessary to provide this service.

(b) The bureau shall collect the fee described in subdivision (a) for all initial and renewal applications for firearm permits. 7583.27. A firearm permit shall be automatically revoked if at any time the Department of Justice notifies the bureau that the holder of the firearm permit is prohibited from possessing, receiving, or purchasing a firearm pursuant to state or federal law. Following the automatic revocation, an administrative hearing shall be provided upon written request to the bureau in accordance with Chapter 5 (commencing with Section 11500) of Part 1 of Division 3 of Title 2 of the Government Code.

Business and Professions Code § 7583.27.

A firearm permit shall be automatically revoked if at any time the Department of Justice notifies the bureau that the holder of the firearm permit is prohibited from possessing, receiving, or purchasing a firearm pursuant to state or federal law. Following the automatic revocation, an administrative hearing shall be provided upon written request to the bureau in accordance with Chapter 5 (commencing with Section 11500) of Part 1 of Division 3 of Title 2 of the Government Code.

Business and Professions Code § 7583.28.

If an applicant fails to complete his or her application within one year after it has been filed, the application shall be considered to be abandoned. An application submitted subsequent to the abandonment of the former application shall be treated as a new application.

Business and Professions Code § 7583.29.

If a firearms permit is denied, the denial of the permit shall be in writing and shall describe the basis for the denial. The denial shall inform the applicant that if he or she desires a review by a disciplinary review committee to contest the denial, the review shall be requested of the director within 30 days following notice of the issuance of the denial. However, no review or hearing shall be granted to an individual who is otherwise prohibited by law from carrying a firearm.

Business and Professions Code § 7583.30.

The firearms qualification card, if issued, shall be mailed to the applicant at the address which appears on the application. In the event of the loss or destruction of the card, the cardholder may apply to the bureau for a certified replacement of the card, stating the circumstances surrounding the loss, and pay a ten dollar ($10) certification fee, whereupon the bureau shall issue a certified replacement of the card.

Business and Professions Code § 7583.31.

A firearms qualification card does not authorize the holder thereof to carry a pistol, revolver, or other firearm capable of being concealed upon the person in a concealed manner pursuant to Section 12050 of the Penal Code.

Business and Professions Code § 7583.32.

(a) A firearms qualification card expires two years from the date of issuance, if not renewed. A person who wishes to renew a firearms qualification card shall file an application for renewal at least 60 days prior to the card's expiration. A person whose card has expired shall not carry a firearm until he or she has been issued a renewal card by the bureau.

(b) The bureau shall not renew a firearms qualification card unless all of the following conditions are satisfied:

(1) The cardholder has filed with the bureau a completed application for renewal of a firearms qualification card, on a form

prescribed by the director, dated and signed by the applicant under penalty of perjury certifying that the information on the application is true and correct.

(2) The applicant has requalified on the range and has successfully passed a written examination based on course content as specified in the firearms training manual approved by the department and taught at a training facility approved by the bureau.

(3) The application is accompanied by a firearms requalification fee as prescribed in this chapter.

(4) The applicant has produced evidence to the firearm training facility, either upon receiving his or her original qualification card or upon filing for renewal of that card, that he or she is a citizen of the United States or has permanent legal alien status in the United States. Evidence of citizenship or permanent legal alien status is that deemed sufficient by the bureau to ensure compliance with federal laws prohibiting possession of firearms by persons unlawfully in the United States and may include, but not be limited to, Department of Justice, Immigration and Naturalization Service Form I-151 or I-551, Alien Registration Receipt Card, naturalization documents, or birth certificates evidencing lawful residence or status in the United States.

(c) An expired firearms qualification card may not be renewed. A person with an expired registration is required to apply for a new firearms qualification in the manner required of persons not previously registered. A person whose card has expired shall not carry a firearm until he or she has been issued a new firearms qualification card by the bureau.

Business and Professions Code § 7583.33.

(a) Any licensee, qualified manager, or a registered uniformed security guard who wishes to carry a baton in the performance of his or her duties, shall qualify to carry the weapon pursuant to Article 5 (commencing with Section 7585).

(b) Subdivision (a) does not apply to a peace officer as defined in Chapter 4.5 (commencing with Section 830) of Title 3 of Part 2 of the Penal Code who has successfully completed a course of study in the use of batons.

Business and Professions Code § 7583.34.

A licensee shall not permit any employee to carry a baton prior to ascertaining that the employee is proficient in the use of the weapon. Evidence of proficiency shall include a certificate from a baton training facility approved by the bureau which certifies that the employee is proficient in the use of the baton.

Business and Professions Code § 7583.35.

Every licensee, qualified manager, or a registered uniformed security guard, who in the course of his or her employment carries tear gas or any other nonlethal chemical agent, shall complete the required course pursuant to Section 12403.5 of the Penal Code.

Business and Professions Code § 7583.36.

A licensee shall not permit any employee to carry tear gas or any other nonlethal chemical agent prior to ascertaining that the employee is proficient in the use of tear gas or other nonlethal chemical agent. Evidence of proficiency shall include a certificate from a training facility approved by the Department of Consumer Affairs, Bureau of Security and Investigative Services that the person is proficient in the use of tear gas or any other nonlethal chemical agent.

Business and Professions Code § 7583.37.

The director may assess fines as enumerated in Article 7 (commencing with Section 7587). Assessment of administrative fines shall be independent of any other action by the bureau or any local, state, or federal governmental agency that may result from a violation of this article. In addition to other prohibited acts under this chapter, no licensee, qualified manager, or registered security guard shall, during the course and scope of licensed activity, do any of the following:

(a) Carry any inoperable, replica, or other simulated firearm.

(b) Use a firearm in violation of the law, or in knowing violation of the standards for the carrying and usage of firearms as taught in the course of training in the carrying and use of firearms. Unlawful or prohibited uses of firearms shall include, but not be limited to, the following:

(1) Illegally using, carrying, or possessing a dangerous weapon.

(2) Brandishing a weapon.

(3) Drawing a weapon without proper cause.

(4) Provoking a shooting incident without cause.

(5) Carrying or using a firearm while on duty while under the influence of alcohol or dangerous drugs.

(6) Carrying or using a firearm of a caliber for which a firearms permit has not been issued by the bureau.

(c) Carry or use a baton in the performance of his or her duties, unless he or she has in his or her possession a valid baton certificate issued pursuant to Section 7585.14.

(d) Carry or use tear gas or any other nonlethal chemical agent in the performance of his or her duties unless he or she has in his or her possession proof of completion of a course in the carrying and use of tear gas or any other nonlethal chemical agent.

(e) Carry a concealed pistol, revolver, or other firearm capable of being concealed upon the person unless one of the following circumstances applies:

(1) The person has been issued a permit to carry a pistol, revolver, or other firearm capable of being concealed upon the person in a concealed manner by a local law enforcement agency pursuant to Section 12050 of the Penal Code.

(2) The person is employed as a guard or messenger of a common carrier, bank, or other financial institution and he or she carries the weapon while actually employed in and about the shipment, transportation, or delivery of any money, treasure, bullion, bonds, or other thing of value within this state, as specified in subdivision (e) of Section 12027 of the Penal Code.

(3) The person is an honorably retired peace officer authorized to carry a concealed firearm pursuant to subdivision (a) or (i) of Section 12027 of the Penal Code.

(4) The person is a duly appointed peace officer, as defined in Chapter 4.5 (commencing with Section 830) of Title 3 of Part 2 of the Penal Code, who is authorized to carry a concealed firearm in the course and scope of his or her employment pursuant to

subdivision (a) of Section 12027 of the Penal Code.

Business and Professions Code § 7583.39.

No private patrol operator who employs a security guard who carries a firearm as part of his or her duties shall engage in any of the practices for which he or she is required to be licensed by this chapter, unless he or she maintains an insurance policy as defined in Section 7583.40.

Business and Professions Code § 7585.

The course of training in the carrying and usage of firearms, the satisfactory completion of which shall be required of applicants who wish to obtain a firearms qualification card, shall be in the format prescribed by the Department of Consumer Affairs as delineated in the bureau's "Firearms Training Manual." The course of training contained in the manual shall include, but not be limited to, the following:

(a) Moral and legal aspects of firearms usage.

(b) Firearms nomenclature and maintenance.

(c) Weapon handling and shooting fundamentals.

(d) Emergency procedures.

(e) Prequalification range training, including the firing of practice rounds.

(f) Qualification course of fire.

(g) Examination which has been provided by the bureau of the subject matter taught.

Business and Professions Code § 7585.1.

For purposes of this article, "firearms course" means the firearms training course as outlined in Section 7585.

Business and Professions Code § 7585.2.

The firearms requalification course shall consist of the successful completion of a firearms requalification course approved by the bureau.

Business and Professions Code § 7585.3.

(a) Any institution, firm, or individual wishing the approval of the bureau to offer the firearms course shall complete an application for certification as a firearms training facility. The application shall be in a form prescribed by the chief and shall include, but not be limited to, the following information:

(1) The name, business address, and telephone number of the institution, firm, or individual.

(2) A detailed description of the places, days, and times the course will be offered.

(3) An estimate of the minimum and maximum class size.

(4) The location and description of the range facilities.

(5) The name or names of the firearms training instructors who will teach the course who have been certified by the bureau, and their certificate numbers, if available.

(b) The application shall be accompanied by the fee prescribed in this chapter.

Business and Professions Code § 7585.4.

Upon approval by the bureau of a firearms training facility, the chief shall issue to the facility a "Firearms Training Facility Certificate." The certificate is valid only when the firearms training facility has in its employ a firearms training instructor who has been certified by the bureau. The certificate shall be posted in a conspicuous place at the facility.

Business and Professions Code § 7585.5.

(a) Any individual who desires certification by the bureau to instruct a firearms course shall complete an application for a firearms training instructor certificate. An application shall be made on a form provided by the bureau.

(b) An applicant for a firearms training instructor certificate shall meet the following minimum qualifications:

(1) Possess an associate of arts degree in the administration of justice or one year of teaching or training experience in firearms or the equivalent thereof.

(2) Possess a police or security firearms instructor training certificate issued by the National Rifle Association or a firearms instructor training certificate issued by a federal, state, or local agency.

(c) The application shall be accompanied by the fee prescribed in this chapter.

(d) Upon approval by the bureau of an applicant for certification as a firearms training instructor, the chief shall issue to the applicant a "Firearms Training Instructor Certificate." The certificate shall be posted at the training site.

Business and Professions Code § 7585.6.

(a) All firearms course material provided to the certificate holder in the "Firearms Training Manual" issued by the bureau shall be covered in each class session. Any course textbook or manual developed to be used by a firearm training facility as a course in the carrying and usage of firearms shall include the aspects of employee restraint and defensive missions of security guards in addition to following the format delineated in the bureau's "Firearms Training Manual" and shall be examined and approved by the bureau prior to use. Once the bureau has approved the textbooks or manuals, all firearm training facilities shall be required to instruct in accordance with one of the textbooks or manuals. In no event shall the class instruction total less than eight hours for the initial firearms qualification. The range instruction for the initial firearms qualification shall not exceed eight hours and shall cover the following subjects:

(1) Range safety and procedure.

(2) Demonstration and dry firing.

(3) Practice rounds.

(4) Qualification firing.

(b) If a person fails to successfully complete the range instruction, that person may, at the discretion of the firearms training facility, continue range instruction for an additional eight hours. However, the person shall, in order to receive a firearms qualification card, be required to successfully pass the range instruction within 30 days of the passage of the classroom instruction. (c) Prior to range instruction a person shall participate in the classroom instruction and pass a bureau-developed examination of the subject matter with a minimum score of 85 percent. If a person fails to pass the written examination, he or she shall once more participate in the entire classroom instruction prior to retaking the examination. In no event shall a firearm instructor review the examination question by question with a person, allow a person to review the examination questions and answers, or in any manner assist a person with the examination.

Business and Professions Code § 7585.7.

(a) Each firearms training facility shall be required to retain for two years the following information regarding each student:

(1) The student's name.

(2) The date of course completion.

(3) Any information regarding the passage or failure of the firearms training course.

(4) The instructor's name.

(5) The make and caliber of the qualifying weapon.

(6) The range scores.

(7) The written examination scores.

(b) Records shall be made available for examination by the bureau on demand.

(c) Each firearm training facility shall have a written procedure for the security of the written examination which shall be made available for inspection by the bureau on demand.

Business and Professions Code § 7585.8.

(a) Each firearm training facility shall, prior to allowing any person to participate in the course of training in the carrying and usage of firearms, verify and certify on the firearms qualification application that they have seen documentation verifying that the person to whom they are providing firearms training is a citizen of the United States or possesses permanent legal alien status in the United States in accordance with Sections 7583.23 and 7596.7.

(b) During calendar year 1985, each firearm training facility shall, prior to allowing any person to participate in the requalification course in the carrying and usage of firearms, verify and certify on the firearm requalification application that they have seen documentation verifying that the person to whom they are providing firearms training is a citizen of the United States or possesses permanent legal alien status in the United States in accordance with Sections 7583.32 and 7596.3.

Business and Professions Code § 7585.9.

(a) The course of training in the carrying and usage of the baton, the satisfactory completion of which shall be required of applicants who wish to obtain a baton permit, shall be in the format prescribed by the Department of Consumer Affairs as delineated in the bureau's "Baton Training Manual." The course of training contained in the manual shall include, but not be limited to, the following subjects:

(1) Moral and legal aspects of baton usage.

(2) Use of force.

(3) Baton familiarization and uses.

(4) First aid for baton injuries.

(5) Fundamentals of baton handling.

(A) Stances and grips.

(B) Target areas.

(C) Defensive techniques.

(D) Control techniques.

(E) Arrest and control techniques.

(6) Examination of the subject matter as taught in the classroom and as provided by the bureau.

(b) The baton training outline distributed by the Department of Justice shall be recognized as an approved outline for the baton training course until January 1, 1984, or until the bureau distributes the "Baton Training Manual."

Business and Professions Code § 7585.10.

For purposes of this article "a baton course" means the baton training course as outlined in Section 7585.9.

Business and Professions Code § 7585.11.

(a) Any institution, firm, or individual wishing approval of the bureau to offer the baton course shall complete an application for certification as a baton training facility. The application shall be in a form prescribed by the chief and shall include, but not be limited to, all of the following information:

(1) The name, business address, and telephone number of the institution, firm or individual.

(2) A detailed description of the places, days, and times the course will be offered.

(3) An estimate of the minimum and maximum class size.

(4) Location and description of the facilities.

(5) The name or names of the baton instructors who will teach the course who have been certified by the bureau, and their certificate numbers if available.

(b) The application shall be accompanied by the fee prescribed in this chapter.

(c) No approval shall be given, and no certification shall be issued, to a baton training facility until a baton training instructor who has been certified by the bureau has been approved to teach the course.

(d) Upon approval by the bureau of a baton training facility, the chief shall issue to the facility a "Baton Training Facility Certificate." The certificate is valid only when the baton training facility has in its employ a baton training instructor who has been certified by the bureau. The certificate shall be posted in a conspicuous place at the facility.

Business and Professions Code § 7585.12.

Any individual who desires certification by the bureau to instruct the baton course shall complete an application for a baton training instructor certificate. An application shall be made on a form provided by the bureau. An applicant for a baton training instructor certificate shall meet the following minimum qualifications:

(a) Possess an associate of arts degree in the administration of justice or the equivalent thereof.

(b) Possess a baton instructor certificate issued by a federal, state, or local agency or one year of verifiable baton teaching or training experience or the equivalent thereof to be determined by the chief.

(c) The application shall be accompanied by the fee prescribed in this chapter.

(d) Upon approval by the bureau of an applicant for certification as a baton training instructor, the chief shall issue to the applicant a "Baton Training Instructor Certificate." The certificate shall be posted at the baton training site.

Business and Professions Code § 7585.13.

All baton course material provided to the certificate holder in the "Baton Training Manual" issued by the bureau shall be covered in each class session. In no event shall the class instruction for the course required for baton certification total less than eight hours.

Business and Professions Code § 7585.14.

(a) A baton training facility shall issue a bureau-developed baton permit to any person who successfully completes a baton training course as described in Section 7585.9 and possesses a valid security guard registration card issued pursuant to Article 4 (commencing with Section 7583) or who has made application for that registration card. The permit is valid only when the holder possesses a valid guard registration card.

(b) The bureau shall issue baton permits to a baton training facility, in good standing, upon request and upon payment of the fees as set forth in this chapter.

(c) Each baton training facility shall submit to the bureau, on forms as prescribed by the director, no later than five working days following the issuance of a permit for each person, the name, address, bureau registration or license number, date of birth, and baton permit number of each person issued a permit.

Business and Professions Code § 7585.15.

(a) Each baton training facility shall be required to retain for two years the following information regarding each student:

(1) The student's name.

(2) The date of course completion.

(3) Any information regarding the passage or failure of the baton training course.

(4) The instructor's name.

(5) Written examination scores.

(b) Records shall be made available for examination by the bureau on demand.

(c) Each baton training facility shall have a written procedure for the security of the examinations and the baton certificates which shall be made available for inspection by the bureau on demand.

Business and Professions Code § 7585.16.

In the event of the loss, theft, or destruction of a baton permit, a permit holder may request the bureau to issue a replacement permit. The request shall be in writing, shall state the circumstances surrounding the loss, theft, or destruction of the permit and the name of the instructor, training facility, and date of instruction relating to the issuance of the original baton permit. The request shall be accompanied by a five dollar ($5) replacement fee. The bureau may issue a replacement baton permit upon verification of successful baton training.

Business and Professions Code § 7585.17.

Each firearms training facility or baton training facility shall notify the bureau within five working days whenever any training instructor certified by the bureau is employed or ceases to be employed with the training facility.

Business and Professions Code § 7585.18.

Each firearms training facility, firearms training instructor, baton training facility, or baton training instructor shall report to the bureau the name of any person who, while taking the course, demonstrated that the carrying and usage of a firearm or the carrying and usage of a baton by that person would present an undue hazard to the safety of the public. The report shall contain the name and address of the student, the name of the student's employer, if available, and the reasons or specific incident which caused the certificate holder to make the report. All substantiating documents, including, but not limited to, an affidavit from the instructor regarding the incident, or reasons, shall be included in the report.

Business and Professions Code § 7585.19.

(a) The chief may refuse to issue or may cancel a previously issued firearms training facility certificate, firearms training instructor certificate, baton training facility certificate, or baton training instructor certificate, or may assess fines pursuant to Section

7587.7, on the grounds that one or more instructors have done any of the following:

(1) Failed to maintain the records required by Section 7585.7 or 7585.15.

(2) Failed to submit the records to the bureau as required by Section 7585.14.

(3) Given inaccurate instructions regarding the laws of California and the regulations of the bureau, including, but not limited to, the necessity of an individual to possess a valid firearms qualification card issued by the bureau prior to carrying any firearm; or the necessity of an individual to possess a valid baton permit issued by the bureau prior to carrying any baton.

(4) Used improper caution while instructing students, so as to endanger the safety of students.

(5) Failed to instruct completely in accordance with the bureau's "Firearms Training Manual" as required by Section 7585.6.

(6) Failed to instruct completely in accordance with the bureau's "Baton Training Manual" as required by Section 7585.9.

(7) Allowed a noncertified instructor to teach any portion of the firearms course, including range qualification. This does not include range coaches employed to assist the instructor.

(8) Allowed a noncertified instructor to teach any portion of the baton course.

(9) Falsified any application for registration, firearms qualification card, firearms requalification permit, or baton certificate.

(10) Failed to inform the bureau of any range or classroom incident as required by Section 7585.18. (11) Failed to notify the bureau of any change of employment pursuant to Section 7585.17.

(12) Made any false statement of fact required to be revealed in the application for certification as a firearms training facility or as a firearms training instructor.

(b) Fines shall not be assessed on firearms training facilities which are a part of the California community college system.

Business and Professions Code § 7585.20.

(a) A firearms training facility certificate, a firearms training instructor certificate, a baton training facility certificate, or a baton training instructor certificate which expires on or after January 1, 1985, shall be placed on a cyclical renewal and shall expire two years following the date of issuance or assigned renewal date. In order to implement the cyclical renewal, the population of licensees mentioned in this section shall be divided into 24 equal groups, the licenses of each group to expire on the last day of each successive month. Notwithstanding any other provision of law, the bureau shall have authority to extend or shorten the first term of licensure following January 1, 1985, and to prorate the required license fee in order to implement this cyclical renewal. To renew an unexpired certificate, the certificate holder shall apply for renewal on a form prescribed by the director and pay the renewal fee prescribed by this chapter.

(b) If renewal is granted, evidence of renewal of the certificate that the director may prescribe shall be issued to the certificate holder.

(c) In the event the certificate holder fails to renew his or her training facility certificate, the certificate shall be automatically canceled, but may be reinstated within three years of the date of cancellation upon application for reinstatement and upon the payment of the reinstatement fee provided by this chapter. In the event the certificate holder fails to renew his or her training instructor certificate, the certificate shall be automatically canceled, but may be reinstated within 30 days of the date of cancellation upon application for reinstatement and upon the payment of the reinstatement fee provided by this chapter. Reinstatement of a canceled certificate shall not prohibit the bringing of disciplinary proceedings for any act committed in violation of this chapter during the period the certificate is canceled.

(d) A firearms training facility, a firearms training instructor, a baton training facility, or a baton training instructor whose certificate has not been renewed may obtain a new license only upon compliance with all of the provisions of this article relating to the issuance of an original certificate.

(e) A firearms training facility, firearms training instructor, baton training facility, or a baton training instructor certificate shall not be renewed until any and all fines assessed pursuant to Section 7587.7 and not resolved in accordance with the provisions of that section have been paid.

Business and Professions Code § 7586.

A private patrol operator license, branch office certificate, and pocket card issued under this chapter expires two years following the date of issuance or on the assigned renewal date. Every private patrol operator issued a license under this chapter that expires on or after January 1, 1997, and who is also issued or renews a firearms qualification card on or after January 1, 1997, shall be placed on a cyclical renewal so that the license expires on the expiration date of the firearms qualification card. Notwithstanding any other provision of law, the bureau is authorized to extend or shorten the first term of licensure following January 1, 1997, and to prorate the required license fee in order to implement this cyclical renewal.

Business and Professions Code § 7586.1.

(a) To renew an unexpired license or certificate, the licensee shall, on or before the date on which it would otherwise expire, apply for renewal on a form prescribed by the director, and pay the renewal fee prescribed by this chapter. On renewal, such evidence of renewal of the license or certificate as the director may prescribe, and renewal pocket cards for the persons mentioned in Section 7582.13, shall be issued to the licensee.

(b) A license or certificate shall not be renewed until any and all fines assessed pursuant to Section 7587.7 and not resolved in accordance with the provisions of that section have been paid.

Business and Professions Code § 7586.2.

Except as otherwise provided in this article, an expired license or branch office certificate may be renewed at any time within three years after its expiration on filing of application for renewal on a form prescribed by the director, and payment of the renewal fee in effect on the last preceding regular renewal date. If the license or certificate is renewed more than 30 days after its expiration, the licensee, as a condition precedent to renewal, shall also pay the delinquency fee prescribed in this chapter. Renewal under this section shall be effective on the date on which the application is filed, on the date on which the renewal fee is paid, or on the date on which the delinquency fee, if any, is paid, whichever last occurs. If so renewed, the license or certificate shall continue in effect through the date provided in Section 7586 which next occurs after the effective date of the renewal, when it shall expire if it is not again renewed. Renewal of a license or certificate shall not prohibit the bringing of disciplinary proceedings for an act committed before the effective date of the renewal.

Business and Professions Code § 7586.3.

A suspended license or branch office certificate is subject to expiration and shall be renewed as provided in this article, but renewal of the license does not entitle the licensee, while the license remains suspended and until it is reinstated, to engage in the licensed activity, or in any other activity, or in any other activity or conduct in violation of the order or judgment by which the license was suspended, and renewal of the branch office certificate does not entitle the licensee, while the certificate remains suspended, and until it is reinstated, to engage in the licensed activity at the location for which the certificate was issued, or to engage in any other activity or conduct in violation of the order or judgment by which the certificate was suspended.

Business and Professions Code § 7586.4.

A revoked license or branch office certificate is subject to expiration as provided in this article, but it may not be renewed. If it is reinstated after its expiration, the licensee, as a condition precedent to its reinstatement, shall pay a reinstatement fee in an amount equal to the renewal fee in effect on the last regular renewal date before the date on which it is reinstated, plus the delinquency fee, if any, accrued at the time of its revocation.

Business and Professions Code § 7586.5.

A license or branch office certificate which is not renewed within three years after its expiration may not be renewed, restored, reinstated, or reissued thereafter. The holder of the license or certificate may obtain a new license or certificate only on compliance with all of the provisions of this chapter relating to the issuance of an original license or certificate.

Business and Professions Code § 7587.

Except as otherwise required to comply with the provisions of Section 7581.3 or Article 6 (commencing with Section 7586), the proceedings under this article shall be conducted in accordance with Chapter 5 (commencing with Section 11500) of Part 1 of Division 3 of Title 2 of the Government Code, and the director shall have all the powers granted therein.

Business and Professions Code § 7587.1.

Notwithstanding Section 477, a firearm qualification card and a baton permit shall be considered a license subject to the terms of this section. Notwithstanding the assessment or payment of fines for any violations of this chapter, the director may deny, suspend, or revoke a license issued under this chapter if he or she determines that the licensee or his or her manager, if an individual, or if the licensee is a person other than an individual, that any of its officers, directors, partners, or its manager, has:

(a) Made any false statement or given any false information in connection with an application for a license or a renewal or reinstatement of a license.

(b) Violated any provisions of this chapter.

(c) Violated any rule of the director adopted pursuant to the authority contained in this chapter.

(d) Committed any act or crime constituting grounds for denial of licensure under Section 480, including illegally using, carrying, or possessing a deadly weapon.

(e) Impersonated, or permitted or aided and abetted an employee to impersonate a law enforcement officer or employee of the United States of America, or of any state or political subdivision thereof.

(f) Committed or permitted any employee to commit any act, while the license was expired which would be cause for the suspension or revocation of a license, or grounds for the denial of an application for a license.

(g) Willfully failed or refused to render to a client services or a report as agreed between the parties and for which compensation has been paid or tendered in accordance with the agreement of the parties.

(h) Committed assault, battery, or kidnapping, or used force or violence on any person, without proper justification.

(i) Knowingly violated, or advised, encouraged, or assisted the violation of any court order or injunction in the course of business as a licensee.

(j) Acted as a runner or capper for any attorney.

(k) Been convicted of a violation of Section 148 of the Penal Code.

(l) Committed any act which is a ground for denial of an application for a license under this chapter.

(m) Committed any act prohibited by Chapter 1.5 (commencing with Section 630) of Title 15 of Part 1 of the Penal Code.

(n) Purchased, possessed, or transported any tear gas weapon except as authorized by law. A violation of this subdivision may be punished by the suspension of a license for a period to be determined by the director.

(o) Been convicted of a violation of Section 95.3 of the Penal Code.

Business and Professions Code § 7587.15.

Notwithstanding any other provision of law, the director may assess a fine of up to five thousand dollars ($5,000) per violation against any licensee for a failure to comply with subdivision (e) of Section 7583.2 or Section 7583.11. In addition, the director may deny, suspend, or revoke a license issued under this chapter for a failure to comply with Section 7583.11. 7587.2. Any person who knowingly makes a false statement in his or her application for a license or registration as a security guard is guilty of a misdemeanor. 7587.3. The director may suspend or revoke a license issued under this chapter if he or she determines that the licensee or his or her manager, if an individual, or if the licensee is a person other than an individual, that any of its officers, directors, partners, or its manager, has:

(a) Used any letterhead, advertisement, or other printed matter, or in any manner whatever represented that he or she is an instrumentality of the federal government, a state, or any political subdivision thereof.

(b) Used a name different from that under which he or she is currently licensed in any advertisement, solicitation, or contract for business.

Business and Professions Code § 7587.4.

The director may suspend or revoke a license issued under this chapter if he or she determines that the licensee or his or her manager, if an individual, or if the licensee is a person other than an individual, that any of its officers, directors, partners, or its manager, has committed any act in the course of the licensee's business constituting dishonesty or fraud. "Dishonesty or fraud" as used in this section, includes, in addition to other acts not specifically enumerated herein:

(a) Knowingly making a false statement relating to evidence or information obtained in the course of employment, or knowingly publishing a slander or a libel in the course of business.

(b) Using illegal means in the collection or attempted collection of a debt or obligation.

(c) Manufacture of evidence.

(d) Acceptance of employment adverse to a client or former client relating to a matter with respect to which the licensee has obtained confidential formation by reason of or in the course of his or her employment by the client or former client.

Business and Professions Code § 7587.5.

The record of conviction, or a certified copy thereof, shall be conclusive evidence of the conviction as that term is used in this article, Section 7582.24, or Section 480. A plea or verdict of guilty or a conviction following a plea of nolo contendere is deemed to be a conviction within the meaning of this article, Section 7582.24, or Section 480. The director may order the license suspended or revoked, or may decline to issue a license, when the time for appeal has elapsed, or the judgment of conviction has been affirmed on appeal or when an order granting probation is made suspending the imposition of sentence, irrespective of a subsequent order under the provisions of Section 1203.4 of the Penal Code allowing the person to withdraw his or her plea of guilty and to enter a plea of not guilty, or setting aside the verdict of guilty, or dismissing the accusation, information, or indictment.

Business and Professions Code § 7587.6.

The director, in lieu of suspending or revoking a license issued under this chapter for violations of Sections 7587.1, 7587.3, and 7587.4, may impose a civil penalty not to exceed five hundred dollars ($500) upon a licensee, if the director determines that this action better serves the purposes of this chapter.

Business and Professions Code § 7587.7.

If, upon investigation, the director determines a licensee, including a corporation, or registrant is in violation of Section 7583.2, 7583.3, 7583.37, 7585.19, 7587.2, or 7587.14, the director may issue a citation to the licensee or registrant. The citation shall be in writing and shall describe with particularity the nature of the violation, including specific reference to the provision of law determined to have been violated. If the director deems it appropriate, the citation may contain an order of abatement fixing a reasonable time for abatement of the violation and may contain an assessment of an administrative fine. The amount of the fine shall in no event exceed two thousand five hundred dollars ($2,500) or as otherwise provided in this chapter, whichever is less. A citation or fine assessment shall inform the licensee or registrant that if he or she contests the finding of a violation, they may request a review by a disciplinary review committee in accordance with Section 7581.3. If a review is not requested pursuant to this section, payment of any fine shall not constitute an admission of the violation charged. If a review is not allowed under this chapter, a licensee or registrant may request a hearing in accordance with the provisions of Chapter 5 (commencing with Section 11500) of Part 1 of Division 3 of Title 2 of the Government Code if he or she wishes to contest the findings of a violation, and if a hearing is not requested, payment of any fines shall not constitute an admission of the violation charged. If the licensee or registrant neither requests a review, nor pays the assessed fine within 30 days of the assessment, the license or registration of the person shall not be renewed pursuant to the provisions of this chapter until the assessed fine is paid. Administrative fines collected pursuant to this article shall be deposited in the Private Security Services Fund, which fund is hereby created to carry out the purposes of this chapter.

Business and Professions Code § 7587.8.

The director may assess fines for the following acts pursuant to Article 4 (commencing with Section 7583) only as follows:

(a) Violation of subdivisions (a), (b), and (c) of Section 7583.2; one hundred dollars ($100) per violation.

(b) Violation of subdivisions (h) and (i) of Section 7583.2; one hundred dollars ($100) for the first violation and two hundred fifty dollars ($250) per violation for each violation thereafter.

(c) Violation of subdivision (d) of Section 7583.2; one hundred dollars ($100) per violation.

(d) Violation of subdivision (g) of Section 7583.2; five hundred dollars ($500) for the first violation and one thousand five hundred dollars ($1,500) per violation for each violation thereafter.

(e) Violation of subdivision (f) of Section 7583.2; two thousand five hundred dollars ($2,500) per violation, notwithstanding any other provision of law.

Business and Professions Code § 7587.9.

The director may assess fines for the following acts pursuant to Article 4 (commencing with Section 7583) only as follows:

(a) Violation of subdivisions (a) and (b) of Section 7583.3; twenty-five dollars ($25) for the first violation and fifty dollars ($50) per violation for each violation thereafter.

(b) Violation of subdivision (c) of Section 7583.3; two hundred fifty dollars ($250) for the first violation and five hundred dollars ($500) per violation for each violation thereafter.

(c) Violation of Section 7583.4; two hundred fifty dollars ($250) for the first violation and five hundred dollars ($500) per violation for each violation thereafter.

Business and Professions Code § 7587.10.

The director may assess fines for the following acts pursuant to Article 4 (commencing with Section 7583) only as follows:

(a) Violation of subdivisions (c) and (d) of Section 7583.37; one hundred dollars ($100) for the first violation and two hundred dollars ($200) for each violation thereafter.

(b) Violation of subdivision (a) of Section 7583.37; one hundred dollars ($100) for the first violation and five hundred dollars ($500) for each violation thereafter.

(c) Violation of subdivision (e) of Section 7583.37; one thousand dollars ($1000).

(d) Violation of subdivision (b) of Section 7583.37; one thousand dollars ($1000) for the first violation and suspension of a firearm qualification card for six months for each violation thereafter.

Business and Professions Code § 7587.12.

The director may assess fines for the following acts only as follows:

(a) Violations of paragraph (1), (2), (11), or (12) of subdivision (a) of Section 7585.19; one hundred dollars ($100) for the first violation and five hundred dollars ($500) for subsequent violations.

(b) Violations of paragraph (3), (7), (8), or (10) of subdivision (a) of Section 7585.19; five hundred dollars ($500) for each violation.

(c) Violations of paragraph (6) of subdivision (a) of Section 7585.19; two hundred fifty dollars ($250) for each hour shortened.

(d) Violations of paragraph (4) of subdivision (a) of Section 7585.19; five hundred dollars ($500) for each violation.

(e) Violations of paragraph (5) of subdivision (a) of Section 7585.19; five hundred dollars ($500) for every hour the course has been shortened.

(f) Violations of paragraph (9) of subdivision (a) of Section 7585.19; one thousand dollars ($1,000) for each violation.

Business and Professions Code § 7587.13.

Any person who knowingly falsifies the fingerprints or photographs submitted pursuant to any provision of this chapter is guilty of a felony. Any person who violates any of the other provisions of this chapter is guilty of a misdemeanor punishable by a fine not to exceed one thousand dollars ($1,000) or by imprisonment in the county jail not to exceed one year, or by both such fine and imprisonment.

Business and Professions Code § 7587.14.

The director may assess administrative fines against any licensee, registrant, or firearms qualification cardholder for failure to notify the bureau within 30 days of any change of residence or business address. The principal place of business may be at a home or at a business address, but it shall be the place at which the licensee maintains a permanent office.

(a) The fine shall be twenty-five dollars ($25) for the first violation and fifty dollars ($50) per violation for each violation thereafter by a licensee.

(b) The fine shall be fifty dollars ($50) for each violation by a registrant or a firearms qualification cardholder.

Business and Professions Code § 7588.

The fees prescribed by this chapter are as follows:

(a) The application and examination fee for an original license for a private patrol operator may not exceed five hundred dollars ($500).

(b) The application fee for an original branch office certificate for a private patrol operator may not exceed two hundred fifty dollars ($250).

(c) The fee for an original license for a private patrol operator may not exceed seven hundred dollars ($700).

(d) The renewal fee is as follows:

(1) For a license as a private patrol operator, the fee may not exceed seven hundred dollars ($700).

(2) For a combination license as a private investigator under Chapter 11.3 (commencing with Section 7512) and private patrol operator, AC or DC prefix, the fee may not exceed six hundred dollars ($600).

(3) For a branch office certificate for a combination private investigator under Chapter 11.3 (commencing with Section 7512) and private patrol operator, the fee may not exceed forty dollars ($40), and for a private patrol operator, the fee may not exceed seventy-five dollars ($75).

(e) The delinquency fee is 50 percent of the renewal fee in effect on the date of expiration.

(f) A reinstatement fee is equal to the amount of the renewal fee plus the regular delinquency fee.

(g) The fee for reexamination of an applicant or his or her manager shall be the actual cost to the bureau for developing, purchasing, grading, and administering each examination.

(h) Registration fees pursuant to this chapter are as follows:

(1) A registration fee for a security guard shall not exceed fifty dollars ($50).

(2) A security guard registration renewal fee shall not exceed thirty-five dollars ($35).

(i) Fees to carry out other provisions of this chapter are as follows:

(1) A firearms qualification fee may not exceed eighty dollars ($80).

(2) A firearms requalification fee may not exceed sixty dollars ($60).

(3) An initial baton certification fee may not exceed fifty dollars ($50).

(4) An application fee and renewal fee for certification as a firearms training facility or a baton training facility may not exceed five hundred dollars ($500).

(5) An application fee and renewal fee for certification as a firearms training instructor or a baton training instructor may not exceed two hundred fifty dollars ($250).

Business and Professions Code § 7588.2.

(a) A peace officer of this state or a political subdivision thereof who engages in off-duty employment solely and exclusively as a security guard or security officer, and who is required to be registered as a security guard or security officer pursuant to this chapter, shall only be subject to the fees required by subdivision (h) of Section 7588.

(b) A peace officer shall also be subject to the fees required by paragraphs (1) and (2) of subdivision (i) of Section 7588 if the peace officer carries or uses a firearm as part of the off-duty employment and has not received approval of his or her primary employer, as defined in paragraph (2) of subdivision (i) of Section 7583.9, to carry a firearm while working as a security guard or security officer, and has not submitted verification of that approval to the bureau pursuant to subdivision (i) of Section 7583.9.

Business and Professions Code § 7590.

This chapter constitutes the chapter on alarm company operators and alarm agents. It may be cited as the Alarm Company Act.

Business and Professions Code § 7590.1.

The following terms as used in this chapter have the meaning expressed in this article:

(a) "Person" means any individual, firm, company, association, organization, partnership, limited liability company, or corporation.

(b) "Department" means the Department of Consumer Affairs.

(c) "Director" means the Director of Consumer Affairs.

(d) "Bureau" means the Bureau of Security and Investigative Services.

(e) "Chief" means the Chief of the Bureau of Security and Investigative Services.

(f) "Employer" means a person who employs an individual for wages or salary, lists the individual on the employer's payroll records, and withholds all legally required deductions and contributions.

(g) "Employee" means an individual who works for an employer, is listed on the employer's payroll records, and is under the employer's direction and control.

(h) "Employer-employee relationship" means an individual who works for another and where the individual's name appears on the payroll records of the employer.

(i) "Licensee" means a business entity, whether an individual, partnership, or corporation licensed under this chapter.

(j) "Qualified manager" means an individual who is in active control, management, and direction of the licensee's business, and who is in possession of a current and valid qualified manager's certificate pursuant to this chapter.

(k) "Registrant" means any person registered or who has applied for registration under this chapter.

(l) "Branch office" means any location, other than the principal place of business of the licensee, which is licensed as set forth in Article 11 (commencing with Section 7599.20).

(m) "Branch office manager" means an individual designated by the qualified manager to manage the licensee's branch office and who has met the requirements as set forth in Article 11 (commencing with Section 7599.20).

(n) "Alarm system" means an assembly of equipment and devices arranged to signal the presence of a hazard requiring urgent attention and to which police are expected to respond.

(o) "Alarm agent" means a person employed by an alarm company operator whose duties include selling on premises, altering, installing, maintaining, moving, repairing, replacing, servicing, responding, or monitoring an alarm system, or a person who manages or supervises a person employed by an alarm company to perform any of the duties described in this subdivision or any person in training for any of the duties described in this subdivision.

(p) "Deadly weapon" means and includes any instrument or weapon of the kind commonly known as a blackjack, slungshot, billy, sandclub, sandbag, metal knuckles; any dirk, dagger, pistol, revolver, or any other firearm; any knife having a blade longer than five inches; any razor with an unguarded blade; or any metal pipe or bar used or intended to be used as a club.

(q) "Firearms permit" means a permit issued by the bureau, pursuant to Article 6 (commencing with Section 7596), to a licensee, a qualified manager, or an alarm agent, to carry an exposed firearm while on duty.

(r)(1) "Advertisement" means:

(A) Any written or printed communication for the purpose of soliciting, describing, or promoting the licensed business of the licensee, including a brochure, letter, pamphlet, newspaper, periodical, publication, or other writing.

(B) A directory listing caused or permitted by the licensee which indicates his or her licensed activity.

(C) A radio, television, or similar airwave transmission which solicits or promotes the licensed business of the licensee.

(2) "Advertisement" does not include any of the following:

(A) Any printing or writing used on buildings, vehicles, uniforms, badges, or other property where the purpose of the printing or writing is identification.

(B) Any printing or writing on communications, memoranda, or any other writings used in the ordinary course of business where the sole purpose of the writing is other than the solicitation or promotion of business.

(C) Any printing or writing on novelty objects used in the promotion of the licensee's business where the printing of the information required by this chapter would be impractical due to the available area or surface.

(s) "Residential sales agreement" means and includes an agreement between an alarm company operator and an owner or tenant for the purchase of an alarm system to be utilized in the personal residence of the owner or tenant.

(t) "Firearm permit" means and includes "firearms permit," "firearms qualification card," "firearms qualification," and "firearms qualification permit."

Business and Professions Code § 7590.2.

An "alarm company operator" means any person who, for any consideration whatsoever, engages in business or accepts employment to install, maintain, alter, sell on premises, monitor, or service alarm systems or who responds to alarm systems except for any alarm agent. "Alarm company operator," includes any entity that is retained by a licensed alarm company operator , a customer, or any other person or entity, to monitor one or more alarm systems, whether or not the entity performs any other duties within the definition of an alarm company operator. The provisions of this chapter, to the extent that they can be made applicable, shall be applicable to the duties and functions performed in monitoring alarm systems. A person licensed as an alarm company operator may not conduct any investigation or investigations except those that are incidental to personal injury, or the theft, loss, embezzlement, misappropriation, or concealment of any property, or any other thing enumerated in this section, which he or she has been hired or engaged to protect.

Business and Professions Code § 7590.3.

This chapter does not apply to:

(a) A person employed exclusively and regularly by any employer who does not provide contract alarm services for other entities or persons, in connection with the affairs of that employer only and where there exists an employer-employee relationship. A person so employed shall at no time carry or use any deadly weapon in the performance of his or her duties.

(b) An officer or employee of the United States of America, or of this state or a political subdivision thereof, while the officer or employee is engaged in the performance of his or her official duties, including uniformed peace officers employed part time by a public agency pursuant to a written agreement between a chief of police or sheriff and the public agency.

(c) Patrol special police officers appointed by the police commission of any city, county, or city and county under the express terms of its charter.

(d) A licensed private patrol operator or any employee of a licensed private patrol operator who is employed as a security guard, security officer, or street patrol person as defined in Section 7582.1 and who is employed to respond to alarm systems.

Business and Professions Code § 7590.5.

Notwithstanding any other requirements for licensure as an alarm company operator or for registration as an alarm agent pursuant to this chapter, an applicant for an alarm company operator license or an alarm agent registration shall be at least 18 years of age. This section shall apply only to applications for licensure or registration or applications for renewal of that licensure or registration submitted to the bureau on or after January 1, 1991.

Business and Professions Code § 7591.

There is in the Department of Consumer Affairs a Bureau of Security and Investigative Services. The bureau is under the supervision and control of the director. The director shall administer and enforce the provisions of this chapter.

Business and Professions Code § 7591.1.

The Governor shall appoint a chief of the bureau at a salary to be fixed in accordance with Section 12080.3 of the Government Code. The chief shall serve under the direction and supervision of the director.

Business and Professions Code § 7591.2.

Every power and duty granted to or imposed upon the director under this chapter may be delegated to the chief, except that the director may not delegate authority to adopt or otherwise act upon any proposed decision of a hearing officer after a hearing under the provisions of Chapter 5 (commencing with Section 11500) of Part 1 of Division 3 of Title 2 of the Government Code. The chief may delegate any power or duty granted to or imposed upon him or her under this chapter to the deputy chief, to the assistant chief, or to any inspection, investigation, or auditing personnel of the bureau.

Business and Professions Code § 7591.3.

The director, in accordance with the State Civil Service Act, and Section 159.5, may appoint and fix the compensation of such clerical, inspection, investigation, and auditing personnel, as well as an assistant chief, as may be necessary to carry out the provisions of this chapter. Except as otherwise provided in Section 159.5, all personnel shall perform their respective duties under the supervision and direction of the chief.

Business and Professions Code § 7591.4.

The chief shall gather evidence of violations of this chapter and of any rule or regulation established under this chapter by unlicensed persons who engage in a business for which a license is required under this chapter and shall furnish the same to prosecuting officers of any county or city or city and county for the purpose of prosecuting those violations.

Business and Professions Code § 7591.5.

It shall be the duty of the chief to initiate and conduct investigations into the business operations of alarm company operators on his or her own motion, if the alarm company operator is not operating in accordance with the provisions of this chapter, or there has been a written complaint to the bureau about the actions and conduct of the alarm company operator or his or her employees or agents.

Business and Professions Code § 7591.6.

The director, taking into consideration the recommendations of the advisory board, may establish and enforce such rules and regulations as may be reasonable and necessary for the examination and licensing of applicants, for the conduct of licensees, and for the general enforcement of the various provisions of this chapter in the protection of the public.

Business and Professions Code § 7591.7.

The chief or his or her designee may inspect, examine, or investigate the relevant records, books, accounts, and files created and maintained by the alarm company operator. The chief shall have access to those relevant business records, not including client information relating to the operational integrity of the alarm system, necessary to the examination for the purpose of performing a random audit to determine compliance with the provisions of this chapter.

Business and Professions Code § 7591.8.

The director may automatically suspend a license, registration, or firearm qualification card if it is determined that the continued possession of such a license, registration, or card by the licensee, registrant, or card holder presents an undue hazard to public safety which may result in substantial injury to another. A licensee, registrant, or firearm qualification card holder may request a review by the Alarm Company Operator Disciplinary Review Committee as set forth in Section 7591.19 to appeal the suspension.

Business and Professions Code § 7591.9.

If, upon investigation, the chief determines that an alarm company operator, a qualified manager, or an alarm agent is in violation of Sections 7597.1, 7597.2, 7597.3, 7597.5, 7597.6, 7598.51, 7598.53, 7599.32, 7599.33, 7599.34, 7599.36, 7599.37, 7599.38, 7599.39, 7599.40, 7599.41, 7599.42, 7599.43, 7599.44, 7599.45, 7599.46, 7599.47, 7599.48, 7599.49, 7599.50, 7599.51, 7599.52, 7599.53, 7599.54, 7599.55, 7599.58, and 7599.59, the director may issue a citation to, and fine, the alarm company operator, qualified manager, or alarm agent. The citation and fine assessment shall be in writing and shall describe with particularity the nature of the violation, including specific reference to the provision of law determined to have been violated. The citation shall contain an order of abatement fixing a reasonable time for abatement of the violation and may contain assessment of an administrative fine. The amount of the fine for any single investigation or audit of an alarm company operator, a qualified manager, or an alarm agent shall not exceed two thousand five hundred dollars ($2,500). A citation and fine assessment shall inform the alarm company operator, qualified manager, or alarm agent that if he or she desires a review by the Alarm Company Operator Disciplinary Review Committee, the review shall be requested by written notice to the chief within 30 days of the issuance of the citation and assessment, as appropriate. If a review is not requested pursuant to this section, payment of any fine shall not constitute an admission of the violation charged. A review shall be held pursuant to the provisions of Section 7591.19. If the alarm company operator, qualified manager, or alarm agent fails to request a review or fails to pay the assessed fine within 30 days of the assessment, the license, certificate, or registration shall not be renewed pursuant to the provisions of this chapter until the assessed fine is paid. Administrative fines collected pursuant to this section shall be deposited in the Private Investigator Fund.

Business and Professions Code § 7591.10.

(a) The director may deny a license, certificate, or registration regulated by this chapter on the grounds that the applicant has done any of the following:

(1) Knowingly made a false statement of fact required to be revealed in the application for a license.

(2) Been convicted of a crime. A conviction within the meaning of this section means a plea or verdict of guilty or a conviction following a plea of nolo contendere. Any action which the bureau is permitted to take following the establishment of a conviction may be taken when the time for appeal has elapsed, or the judgment of conviction has been affirmed on appeal, or when an order granting probation is made suspending the imposition of sentence, irrespective of a subsequent order under the provisions of Section 1203.4 of the Penal Code.

(3) Done any act involving dishonesty, fraud, or deceit with the intent to substantially benefit himself, herself, or another, or to substantially injure another.

(4) Done any act which if done by a licensee would be grounds for suspension or revocation of a license.

(5) Done any act without a license for which a license is required under this chapter.

(6) Been refused a license under this chapter or had a license revoked.

(7) Been an officer, partner, or manager of any person who has been refused a license under this chapter or whose license has been suspended or revoked. The bureau may deny a license, certificate, or registration pursuant to this section only if the crime or act is substantially related to the qualifications, functions, or duties of the license, certificate, or registration for which application has been made. The denial of a license, certificate, or registration shall be in writing and shall describe the basis for the denial. The denial shall inform the applicant that if he or she desires a review by the disciplinary review committee the review shall be requested within 30 days of the issuance of the denial. A review shall be held pursuant to the provisions of Section 7591.19.

(b) Notwithstanding any other provision of this chapter, no person shall be denied a license, certificate, or registration solely on the basis that he or she has been convicted of a felony, if he or she has obtained a certificate of rehabilitation pursuant to Chapter 3.5 (commencing with Section 4852.01) of Title 6 of Part 3 of the Penal Code, or solely on the basis that he or she has been convicted of a misdemeanor, if he or she has met all applicable requirements of the criteria of rehabilitation as provided in Section 7591.12.

Business and Professions Code § 7591.11.

The bureau shall deny a firearms permit, pursuant to Section 12021 of the Penal Code, to any licensee, qualified manager, or alarm agent who has been convicted of a felony, unless the felony conviction has been reduced pursuant to Section 17 of the Penal Code or the person has been pardoned by the Governor. The licensee, qualified manager, or alarm agent shall not have a right to a review or a hearing if the denial is made pursuant to this section.

Business and Professions Code § 7591.12.

(a) When considering the denial, suspension, or revocation of a license, certificate, or registration, for which application has been made under this chapter, the chief, in evaluating the rehabilitation of the applicant and his or her present eligibility for a license, certificate, or registration shall consider all the following criteria:

(1) The nature and severity of the act or crime under consideration as grounds for denial.

(2) Total criminal record.

(3) Evidence of any act committed subsequent to the act or crime under consideration as grounds for a denial, suspension, or revocation which also could be considered as grounds for denial under Section 7591.10.

(4) The time that has elapsed since commission of the act or crime referred to in paragraph (1) or (2).

(5) The extent to which the applicant has complied with any terms of parole, probation, restitution, or any other sanctions

lawfully imposed against the applicant.

(6) Evidence, if any, of rehabilitation submitted by the applicant.

(b) When considering a petition for reinstatement of a license, certificate, or registration, the chief shall evaluate evidence of rehabilitation, considering those criteria of rehabilitation listed in subdivision (a).

Business and Professions Code § 7591.17.

The Governor shall appoint an Alarm Company Operator Disciplinary Review Committee. The disciplinary review committee shall consist of three members who are actively engaged in business as licensed alarm company operators and two public members. The committee shall meet every 60 days, or more or less frequently as may be required. The members shall be paid per diem pursuant to Section 103 and shall be reimbursed for actual travel expenses. The members shall serve at the pleasure of the Governor.

Business and Professions Code § 7591.18.

The Alarm Company Operator Disciplinary Review Committee shall perform the following functions:

(a) Affirm, rescind, or modify all appealed decisions concerning administrative fines assessed by the bureau against alarm company operators or their employees.

(b) Affirm, rescind, or modify all appealed decisions concerning denial, revocation, or suspension of licenses, and certificates, registrations, or permits issued by the bureau, except denials or suspensions ordered by the director in accordance with Chapter 5 (commencing with Section 11500) of Division 3 of Title 2 of the Government Code.

Business and Professions Code § 7591.19.

(a)(1) An alarm company operator, qualified manager, or alarm agent may request a review by the Alarm Company Operator Disciplinary Review Committee to contest the assessment of an administrative fine or to appeal a denial, revocation, or suspension unless the denial or suspension is ordered by the director in accordance with Chapter 5 (commencing with Section 11500) of Part 1 of Division 3 of Title 2 of the Government Code or in accordance with Section 7591.8 of this code.

(2) A request for a review shall be by written notice to the bureau within 30 days of the issuance of the citation and assessment, denial, or suspension.

(3) Following a review by the disciplinary review committee, the appellant shall be notified within 30 days, in writing, by regular mail, of the committee's decision.

(4) If the appellant disagrees with the decision made by the Alarm Company Operator Disciplinary Review Committee, he or she may request a hearing as outlined in subdivision (b). A request for a hearing following a decision by the disciplinary review committee shall be by written notice to the bureau within 30 days of the committee's decision.

(5) If the appellant does not request a hearing within 30 days, the review committee's decision shall become final.

(b)(1) An alarm company operator, qualified manager, or alarm agent may request a hearing in accordance with Chapter 5 (commencing with Section 11500) of Part 1 of Division 3 of Title 2 of the Government Code if he or she contests an assessment of an administrative fine, or to appeal a denial, suspension, or revocation. A hearing may also be requested if the appellant disagrees with the decision made by the Alarm Company Operator Disciplinary Review Committee.

(2) A request for a hearing shall be by written notice to the bureau within 30 days of the issuance of the decision by the review committee. A hearing pursuant to this subdivision shall be available only after a reviewby the disciplinary review committee.

Business and Professions Code § 7591.20.

The disciplinary review committee shall be provided all evidence used by the bureau in reaching its decision prior to hearing an appeal.

Business and Professions Code § 7593.

An application for an alarm company operator license shall be made in writing to, and filed with, the chief in the form that may be required by the director and shall be accompanied by the original license fee prescribed by this chapter. The chief may require the submission of any other relevant information, evidence, statements, or documents. Every application for an alarm company operator license shall state, among other things that may be required, the name of the applicant with the name under which the applicant will do business, and the location by street and number, and city of the office of the business for which the license is sought. All information obtained on the application shall be confidential pursuant to the Information Practices Act of 1977 (Chapter 1 (commencing with Section 1798) of Title 1.8 of Part 4 of Division 3 of the Civil Code) and shall not be released to the public except for the registrant's full name, the employer's name and address, and the registration number. Nothing in this section shall preclude the release of information to the public regarding the status of an operator's license, or the release of information to law enforcement agencies or other governmental agencies for other authorized purposes. No license shall be issued in any fictitious name which may be confused with or which is similar to any federal, state, county, or municipal governmental function or agency or to any law enforcement agency, or in any name which may tend to describe any business function or enterprise not actually engaged in by the applicant.

Business and Professions Code § 7593.1.

(a) Each individual applicant and each qualified manager, partner of a partnership, and designated officers of a corporation shall submit with the application, one personal identification form provided by the chief upon which shall appear a photograph taken within one year immediately preceding the date of the filing of the application together with two legible sets of fingerprints, one set of which shall be forwarded to the Federal Bureau of Investigation for purposes of a background check, and personal description of each such person, respectively. The identification form shall include residence addresses and employment history for the previous five years.

(b) The bureau may impose a fee not to exceed three dollars ($3) for processing classifiable fingerprint cards submitted by applicants excluding those submitted into an electronic fingerprint system using electronic fingerprint technology.

Business and Professions Code § 7593.2.

If the applicant for license is an individual, the application shall state the full name of the individual, the full residence address of the applicant, and that the applicant is to be personally and actively in charge of the business for which the license is sought; or if any other qualified manager is to be actively in charge of the business, the application shall so state and set forth the name of that person. The application shall be subscribed, verified, and signed by the applicant, under penalty of perjury.

Business and Professions Code § 7593.3.

If the applicants for license are copartners, the application shall state the true names and addresses of all the general partners and the name of the partner to be actively in charge of the business for which the license is sought; or if a qualified manager other than a partner is to be actively in charge of the business then the application shall state the name and address of that person. The application shall be subscribed, verified, and signed under penalty of perjury by all of the general partners.

Business and Professions Code § 7593.4.

If the applicant for license is a corporation, the application shall state the true names and complete residence addresses of the chief executive officer, secretary, chief financial officer, and any other corporate officer who will be active in the business to be licensed. A copy of the articles of incorporation issued by the Secretary of State shall be supplied to the bureau upon request. The application shall also state the name and address of the designated person to be actively in charge of the business for which the license is sought. The application shall be subscribed, verified, and signed by a duly authorized officer of the applicant under penalty of perjury.

Business and Professions Code § 7593.6.

The director may refuse to issue a license to any applicant pending final disposition of any investigation of criminal activity or of any disciplinary action previously filed against the person or applicant or against any qualified manager, partner, or officer of the applicant. A new alarm company operator license, qualified manager certificate, or alarm agent registration shall be subject to payment of any and all fines assessed pursuant to this section and not resolved in accordance with the provisions of this section and payment of all applicable fees.

Business and Professions Code § 7593.11.

An alarm company operator license issued under this chapter expires two years following the date of issuance or on the assigned renewal date. Every alarm company operator issued a license under this chapter that expires on or after January 1, 1997, and who is also issued or renews a firearms qualification card on or after January 1, 1997, shall be placed on a cyclical renewal so that the license expires on the expiration date of the firearms qualification card. Notwithstanding any other provision of law, the bureau is authorized to extend or shorten the first term of licensure following January 1, 1997, and to prorate the required license fee in order to implement this cyclical renewal. To renew an unexpired license or certificate, the licensee shall apply for renewal on a form prescribed by the director, pay all fines assessed pursuant to Section 7591.9 and not resolved in accordance with the provisions of that section, and pay the renewal fee. On renewal, evidence of renewal of the license or certificate that the director may prescribe shall be issued to the licensee. The bureau shall send to each licensee a notice of renewal at least 45 calendar days prior to the expiration of each license.

Business and Professions Code § 7596.

Every person licensed, registered, or designated under this chapter, who in the course of his or her employment carries a firearm, shall complete a course of training in the carrying and use of firearms and shall receive a firearms qualification card prior to the carrying of such a firearm and shall complete a course in the exercise of the powers to arrest. A registration card issued by the bureau pursuant to Section 7598.14 may also serve as a firearms qualification card if so indicated on the face of the card.

Business and Professions Code § 7596.3.

The director shall issue a firearms permit when all of the following conditions exist:

(a) The applicant is a licensee, a qualified manager of a licensee, a designated branch office manager of a licensee, or a registered alarm agent.

(b) The applicant has filed with the bureau a classifiable fingerprint card, a completed application for a firearms permit on a form prescribed by the director, dated and signed by the applicant, certifying under penalty of perjury that the information in the application is true and correct.

(c) A certified firearms training instructor certifies that the applicant has successfully completed the bureau-approved training course in the carrying and use of firearms.

(d) The applicant has provided the bureau with evidence that the applicant has completed a course in the exercise of the powers to arrest.

(e) The bureau has determined, after investigation, that the carrying and use of a firearm by the applicant, in the course of his or her duties, presents no apparent threat to the public safety, or the carrying and use of a firearm by the applicant is not in violation of the Penal Code.

(f) The applicant has produced evidence to the firearm training facility that he or she is a citizen of the United States or has permanent legal alien status in the United States. Evidence of citizenship or permanent legal alien status shall be that deemed sufficient by the bureau to ensure compliance with federal laws prohibiting possession of firearms by persons unlawfully in the United States and may include, but not be limited to, Department of Justice, Immigration and Naturalization Service Form I-151 or I-551, Alien Registration Receipt Card, naturalization documents, or birth certificates evidencing lawful residence or status in the United States.

(g) The application is accompanied by the fee prescribed in this chapter.

Business and Professions Code § 7596.4.

If a firearms permit is denied, the denial of the permit shall be in writing and shall describe the basis for the denial. The denial shall inform the applicant that if he or she desires a review by the Alarm Company Operator Disciplinary Review Committee or a hearing to contest the denial, the review or hearing shall be requested within 30 days of the issuance of the denial. A review or hearing shall be held pursuant to Section

Business and Professions Code § 7591.19.

However, no review or hearing shall be granted to an individual who is otherwise prohibited by law from carrying a firearm.

Business and Professions Code § 7596.5.

The firearms qualification card shall be mailed to the applicant at the address which appears on the application. In the event of the loss or destruction of the card, the cardholder may apply to the bureau for a certified replacement of the card, stating the circumstances surrounding the loss, and pay a ten dollar ($10) certification fee, whereupon, the bureau shall issue a certified replacement of the card.

Business and Professions Code § 7596.6.

A firearms qualification card does not authorize the holder thereof to carry a pistol, revolver, or other firearm capable of being concealed upon the person in a concealed manner pursuant to Section 12050 of the Penal Code.

Business and Professions Code § 7596.7.

A firearms qualification card expires two years from the date of issuance, if not renewed. A person who wishes to renew a firearms qualification card shall file an application for renewal at least 60 days prior to the card's expiration. A person whose card has expired shall not carry a firearm until he or she has been issued a renewal card by the bureau. The director shall not renew a firearms qualification card unless all of the following conditions exist:

(a) The cardholder has filed with the bureau a completed application for renewal of a firearms qualification card, on a form prescribed by the director, dated and signed by the applicant under penalty of perjury certifying that the information on the application is true and correct.

(b) The application is accompanied by a firearms requalification fee as prescribed in this chapter.

(c) The applicant has requalified on the range and has successfully passed a written examination based on course content as specified in the firearms training manual approved by the department and taught at a training facility approved by the bureau.

(d) During calendar year 1985, the applicant has produced evidence to the firearm training facility, either upon receiving his or her original qualification card or upon filing for renewal of that card, that he or she is a citizen of the United States or has permanent legal alien status in the United States. Such evidence of citizenship or permanent legal alien status is that deemed sufficient by the bureau to ensure compliance with federal laws prohibiting possession of firearms by persons unlawfully in the United States and may include, but not be limited to, Department of Justice, Immigration and Naturalization Service Form I-151 or I-551, Alien Registration Receipt Card, naturalization documents, or birth certificates evidencing lawful residence or status in the United States.

(e) An expired firearms qualification card may not be renewed. A person with an expired firearms qualification card is required to apply for a new card in the manner required of persons not previously registered. A person whose card has expired shall not carry a firearm until he or she has been issued a new firearms qualification card by the bureau.

Business and Professions Code § 7596.8.

(a) Effective October 1, 1993, the bureau shall not issue a firearm permit if the applicant is prohibited from possessing, receiving, owning, or purchasing a firearm pursuant to state or federal law.

(b) Before issuing an initial firearm permit the bureau shall provide the Department of Justice with the name, address, social security number, and fingerprints of the applicant.

(c) The Department of Justice shall inform the bureau, within 60 days from receipt of the information specified in subdivision (b), of the applicant's eligibility to possess, receive, purchase, or own a firearm pursuant to state and federal law.

(d) An applicant who has been denied a firearm permit based upon subdivision (a) may reapply for the permit after the prohibition expires. The bureau shall treat this application as an initial application and shall follow the required screening process as specified in this section.

Business and Professions Code § 7596.81.

(a) Effective October 1, 1993, the bureau shall not renew a firearm permit if the applicant is prohibited from possessing, receiving, purchasing, or owning a firearm pursuant to state or federal law.

(b) Before renewing a firearm permit, the bureau shall provide the Department of Justice with the information necessary to identify the renewal applicant. No firearm permit shall be renewed if the expiration date of the permit is between October 1, 1993, and October 1, 1994, unless the application for renewal is also accompanied by a classifiable fingerprint card and the fingerprint processing fees for that card.

(c) The Department of Justice shall inform the bureau, within 30 days of receipt of the information specified in subdivision (b), of the renewal applicant's eligibility under state and federal law to possess, receive, purchase, or own a firearm.

(d) An applicant who is denied a firearm permit renewal based upon subdivision (a) may reapply for the permit after the prohibition expires. The bureau shall treat this as an initial application and shall follow the screening process specified in Section 7596.8.

Business and Professions Code § 7596.82.

(a) The Department of Justice may charge the bureau a fee sufficient to reimburse the department's costs for furnishing firearm eligibility information upon submission of the application for issuance or renewal of a firearm permit. The fee charged shall not exceed the actual costs for system development, maintenance, and processing necessary to provide this service.

(b) The bureau shall collect the fee described in subdivision (a) for all initial and renewal applications for firearm permits.

Business and Professions Code § 7596.83.

A firearm permit shall be automatically revoked if at any time the Department of Justice notifies the bureau that the holder of the firearm permit is prohibited from possessing, receiving, or purchasing a firearm pursuant to state or federal law. Following the automatic revocation, an administrative hearing shall be provided upon written request to the bureau in accordance with Chapter 5 (commencing with Section 11500) of Part 1 of Division 3 of Title 2 of the Government Code.

Business and Professions Code § 7596.12.

Every person licensed, registered, or designated under this chapter, who in the course of his or her employment carries tear gas, or any other nonlethal chemical agent, shall complete the course required pursuant to Section 12403.5 of the Penal Code.

Business and Professions Code § 7596.13.

A licensee shall not permit any employee to carry tear gas, or any other nonlethal chemical agent, prior to ascertaining that the employee is proficient in the use of tear gas or other nonlethal chemical agent. Evidence of proficiency shall include a certificate from a POST-approved or Department of Justice-approved training facility that the person is proficient in the use of tear gas or other nonlethal chemical agent.

Business and Professions Code § 7597.

The director may assess fines as enumerated in this article pursuant to Section 7591.9. Assessment of administrative fines shall be independent of any other action by the bureau or any local, state, or federal governmental agency which may result from a violation of this article.

Business and Professions Code § 7597.1.

(a) No licensee, qualified manager, branch office manager, or alarm agent shall carry, use, or possess a loaded or unloaded firearm in the course and scope of his or her employment, whether or not it is serviceable or operative, unless he or she has in his or her possession a valid and current firearms qualification card issued to him or her by the bureau. The card shall be shown to any peace officer or bureau representative upon demand.

(b) Subdivision (a) shall not apply to a duly appointed peace officer, as defined in Chapter 4.5 (commencing with Section 830) of Title 3 of Part 2 of the Penal Code, who meets all of the following:

(1) He or she has successfully completed a course of study in the use of firearms.

(2) He or she is authorized to carry a concealed firearm in the course and scope of his or her employment pursuant to subdivision (a) of Section 12027 of the Penal Code.

(3) He or she has proof that he or she has applied to the bureau for a firearms qualification card. (c) A fine of twenty-five dollars ($25) may be assessed for the first violation of this section and a fine of one hundred dollars ($100) for each subsequent violation.

Business and Professions Code § 7597.2.

No licensee, qualified manager, branch office manager, or alarm agent shall carry any inoperable, replica, or other simulated firearm. A violation of this section shall result in a fine of twenty-five dollars ($25) for the first violation and a fine of one hundred dollars ($100) for each subsequent violation.

Business and Professions Code § 7597.3.

No licensee, qualified manager, branch office manager, or alarm agent shall use a firearm which is in violation of law, or in knowing violation of the standards for carrying and usage of firearms, as taught in the course of training in the carrying and use of firearms, including, but not limited to:

(a) Illegally using, carrying, or possessing a dangerous weapon.

(b) Brandishing a weapon.

(c) Drawing a weapon without proper cause.

(d) Provoking a shooting incident without cause.

(e) Carrying or using a firearm while on duty under the influence of alcohol or dangerous drugs.

(f) Carrying or using a firearm of a caliber for which a bureau firearms permit has not been issued. A fine of one hundred dollars ($100) may be assessed for the first violation of this section and a fine of five hundred dollars ($500) for each subsequent violation.

Business and Professions Code § 7597.5.

No licensee, qualified manager, branch office manager, or alarm agent shall carry or use tear gas or any other nonlethal chemical agent in the performance of his or her duties, unless he or she has in his or her possession proof of completion of a course in the carrying and use of tear gas or other nonlethal chemical agent. A fine of twenty-five dollars ($25) may be assessed for the first violation of this section and a fine of one hundred dollars ($100) for each subsequent violation.

Business and Professions Code § 7597.6.

(a) No licensee, qualified manager, branch office manager, or alarm agent shall carry a pistol, revolver, or other firearm capable of being concealed upon the person in a concealed manner unless one of the following circumstances apply:

(1) The person has been issued a permit to carry that firearm in a concealed manner by a local law enforcement agency pursuant to Section 12050 of the Penal Code.

(2) The person is an honorably retired peace officer authorized to carry a concealed firearm pursuant to subdivision (a) or (i) of Section 12027 of the Penal Code.

(3) The person is a duly appointed peace officer, as defined in Chapter 4.5 (commencing with Section 830) of Title 3 of Part 2 of the Penal Code, who is authorized to carry a concealed firearm in the course and scope of his or her employment pursuant to

subdivision (a) of Section 12027 of the Penal Code.

(b) A fine of five hundred dollars ($500) may be assessed for each violation of subdivision (a).

Business and Professions Code § 7598.1.

Every person entering the employ of a licensee, performing the function of an alarm agent who responds to alarm systems shall complete a course in the exercise of the powers to arrest, prior to being assigned to a duty location responding to an alarm system. Evidence of completion shall consist of certification by the licensee or instructor that the exercise of the powers to arrest course has been taught, the date the course was taught, and certification by the employee that the instruction was received. Evidence of completion of the powers to arrest shall be maintained in the licensee's employee records and made available to the bureau upon request. A qualified manager is not required to register under this article.

Business and Professions Code § 7598.2.

The course of training in the exercise of the power to arrest may be administered, tested, and certified by any licensee. The department may approve any person or school to teach the course in the exercise of the power to arrest. The course of training shall be approximately two hours in length and cover the following topics:

(a) Responsibilities and ethics in citizen arrest.

(b) Relationship with the public police in arrest.

(c) Limitations on security guard power to arrest.

(d) Restrictions on searches and seizures.

(e) Criminal and civil liabilities.

(1) Personal liability.

(2) Employer liability.

The department shall make available a guide book as a standard for teaching the course in the exercise of the power to arrest. The department shall encourage additional training and may provide a training guide recommending additional courses.

Business and Professions Code § 7598.3.

No employee of a licensee performing the function of an alarm agent who responds to alarm systems shall be issued a firearms qualification card until proper certification by the instructor that the exercise of the power to arrest course has been taught and the employee's certification that the instruction was received has been delivered to the department.

Business and Professions Code § 7598.4.

(a) Within three working days after commencing employment, any employee performing the function of alarm agent, who is not currently registered with the bureau, shall submit to the bureau a completed application for registration, two classifiable fingerprint cards, one set of which shall be forwarded to the Federal Bureau of Investigation for purposes of a background check, and the appropriate registration fee. All information obtained on the application shall be confidential pursuant to the Information Practices Act of 1977 (Chapter 1 (commencing with Section 1798) of Title 1.8 of Part 4 of Division 3 of the Civil Code) and shall not be released to the public except for the registrant's full name, the employer's name and address, and the registration number. Nothing in this section shall preclude the release of information to the public regarding the status of a registrant, or the release of information to law enforcement agencies or other governmental agencies for other authorized purposes.

(b) No application is required to be submitted if the employee terminated employment within the three working days. "Within three working days" means 72 hours from the time an employee is first compensated for alarm agent services by a licensee.

(c) The bureau may impose a fee not to exceed three dollars ($3) for processing classifiable fingerprint cards submitted by applicants, excluding those submitted into an electronic fingerprint system using electronic fingerprint technology.

Business and Professions Code § 7598.5.

The application for registration under this article shall be on a form prescribed by the director and shall be accompanied by the fee as prescribed in this chapter.

Business and Professions Code § 7598.6.

The application shall be verified and shall include the following:

(a) The full name, residence address, telephone number, and date of birth of the employee.

(b) The name, address, telephone number, and license number of the employer and the date the employment commenced.

(c) A statement as to whether the employee has been convicted of a misdemeanor, excluding minor traffic violations.

(d) A statement as to whether the employee has been convicted of a felony.

Business and Professions Code § 7598.7.

(a) Except as provided in subdivision (b), an employee of a licensee may be assigned to work with a temporary application for registration until the bureau issues a registration card or denies the application for registration. A temporary application for registration shall be a copy of the initial application. Any alarm agent employee assigned to work must carry either a temporary application for registration or a valid registration. A temporary application for registration shall in no event be valid for more than 120 days. However, the director may extend the expiration date beyond the 120 days if there is an abnormal delay in processing applications for registration. For purposes of this section, the 120-day period shall commence on the date the applicant signs and submits the application.

(b) Notwithstanding subdivision (a), an employee who has been convicted of a crime prior to applying for registration shall not be issued a temporary application for registration and shall not be assigned to work as an alarm agent until the bureau issues a permanent registration card. This subdivision shall apply only if the applicant for registration has disclosed the conviction to the bureau on his or her application form, or if the fact of the conviction has come to the attention of the bureau through official court or other governmental documents.

Business and Professions Code § 7598.8.

No employee of a licensee shall carry or use a firearm unless the employee has in his or her possession a valid alarm agent registration card and a valid firearm qualification card issued pursuant to this chapter.

Business and Professions Code § 7598.9.

The bureau, upon receipt of a criminal offense record or record of a subsequent arrest from the California Department of Justice, shall make an immediate determination of fitness for registration of applicants for registration or firearms qualification permit, when information contained in the records of the Department of Justice makes such a determination possible. Applications for registration of those determined to be unfit shall be immediately denied. The bureau shall keep a current and accurate record of the individuals who have applied for and been denied registration or firearms qualification permits. A listing consisting of individual names and other pertinent identifying information may be made of those individuals who have been denied. The listing may be updated bimonthly and made available to interested licensees and law enforcement agencies.

Business and Professions Code § 7598.11.

If the chief determines that an applicant's criminal history contains arrest information for which there appears no disposition, the chief shall issue a notice to the applicant allowing the applicant 45 days for the applicant to provide documentation concerning the disposition of the arrest or arrests. The notice shall be sent to the applicant and shall provide sufficient information to assist the applicant in complying with the chief's request. If the applicant fails to respond within 45 days, the applicant's employment shall be automatically suspended until the bureau obtains the necessary documentation to approve or deny the application.

Business and Professions Code § 7598.12.

If the director determines that continued employment of an applicant or registrant, in his or her current capacity, may present an undue hazard to public safety, the licensee, upon proper notification from the director, shall suspend the applicant or registrant from employment in that capacity. A registrant or applicant may request a review by the Alarm Company Disciplinary Review Committee as set forth in Section 7591.19 to appeal the suspension.

Business and Professions Code § 7598.14.

Upon approval of an application for registration, the chief shall cause to be issued to the applicant, at his or her last known address, a registration card in a form approved by the director. A photo identification card shall be issued upon written request of the applicant, submission of two recent photographs of the applicant, and payment of the fee. The applicant may request to be issued an enhanced pocket card that shall be composed of a durable material and may incorporate technologically advanced security features. The bureau may charge a fee sufficient to reimburse the department's costs for furnishing the enhanced license. The fee charged may not exceed the actual costs for system development, maintenance, and processing necessary to provide this service, and may not exceed six dollars ($6). If the applicant does not request an enhanced card, the department shall issue a standard card at no cost to the applicant. In the event of the loss or destruction of the card, the cardholder may apply to the bureau for a certified replacement of the card, stating the circumstances surrounding the loss, and pay a ten dollar ($10) certification fee, whereupon the bureau shall issue a certified replacement of the card. Every person, while engaged in any activity for which registration is required, shall display their valid pocket card as provided by regulation.

Business and Professions Code § 7598.16.

A licensee shall at all times be responsible for ascertaining that his or her employees subject to registration are currently registered or have made proper application for registration as provided in this article. The licensee may not have in his or her employment a person whose registration has expired, or been revoked, denied, suspended, or canceled.

Business and Professions Code § 7598.17.

A registration issued under this chapter expires two years following the date of issuance or on the assigned renewal date. Every alarm agent issued a registration under this chapter that expires on or after January 1, 1997, and who is also issued or renews a firearms qualification card on or after January 1, 1997, shall be placed on a cyclical renewal so that the registration expires on the expiration date of the firearms qualification card. Notwithstanding any other provision of law, the bureau is authorized to extend or shorten the first term of registration following January 1, 1997, and to prorate the required registration fee in order to implement this cyclical renewal. At least 60 days prior to the expiration of a registration, a registrant who desires to renew his or her registration shall forward to the bureau a copy of his or her current registration card, along with the renewal fee as set forth in this chapter, to the bureau for renewal of his or her registration. The licensee shall provide to any employee information regarding procedures for renewal of registration. An expired registration may be renewed provided the registrant files a renewal application on a form prescribed by the director and the renewal and delinquency fees prescribed by this chapter are returned to the bureau within 60 days of the expiration date of the registration. A firearms permit is not valid while the registration is expired. A registration not renewed within 60 days following its expiration may not be renewed thereafter. The holder of the expired registration may obtain a new registration only on compliance with all of the provisions of this chapter relating to the issuance of an original registration. The delinquency fee is 50 percent of the renewal fee in effect on the date of expiration, but not less than twenty-five dollars ($25). The holder of an expired registration shall not engage in the activity for which a registration is required until the bureau issues a renewal registration. If the renewed registration card has not been delivered to the registrant, prior to the date of expiration of the prior registration, the registrant may present evidence of renewal to substantiate continued registration, for a period not to exceed 90 days after the date of expiration. A registration may not be renewed or reinstated until all fines assessed pursuant to Section 7591.9 and not resolved in accordance with the provisions of that section have been paid. A new registration shall be issued subject to payment of all fines assessed pursuant to Section 7591.9 and not resolved in accordance with the provisions of Section

7591.9 and payment of all applicable fees.

Business and Professions Code § 7598.50.

The director may assess fines as enumerated in this article pursuant to Section 7591.9. Assessment of administrative fines shall be independent of any other action by the bureau, or any local, state, or federal governmental agency, which may result from a violation of this article.

Business and Professions Code § 7598.51.

An alarm agent shall carry on his or her person, while on duty, either a valid and current registration card or a temporary application for registration. A fine of ten dollars ($10) may be assessed for the first violation of this section and a fine of twenty-five dollars ($25) for each subsequent violation.

Business and Professions Code § 7598.53.

An alarm agent who responds to an alarm system shall wear a prominently displayed patch or other designation which clearly identifies the name of the licensee. An alarm agent who carries a deadly weapon while responding to an alarm system shall wear a recognizable uniform with a prominently displayed patch or other designation which clearly identifies the name of the licensee. The uniform must be distinguishable from the uniforms worn by local regular law enforcement officers. A violation of this section may result in a fine of twenty-five dollars ($25) for each violation.

Business and Professions Code § 7599.30.

The director may assess fines for any violation as enumerated in this article, pursuant to Section 7591.9. Assessment of administrative fines shall be independent of any other action by the bureau or any local, state, or federal governmental agency which may result from a violation of this article.

Business and Professions Code § 7599.31.

For purposes of this article, "licensee" means an alarm company operator. A licensee shall at all times be responsible for those actions of his or her employees, including his or her qualified manager, performed in violation of this chapter, when acting within the course and scope of his or her employment.

Business and Professions Code § 7599.32.

(a) A licensee shall notify the bureau within 30 days of any change of its officers required to be named pursuant to Section 7593.4 and of any addition of a new partner.

(b) Applications, on forms prescribed by the director, shall be submitted by all new officers and partners. The director may suspend or revoke a license issued under this chapter if the director determines that the new officer or partner has committed any act which constitutes grounds for the denial of a license pursuant to Section 7591.10.

(c) A Notice of Warning may be issued for the first violation of this section and a fine of twenty-five dollars ($25) for each subsequent violation.

Business and Professions Code § 7599.40.

No licensee shall allow any employee to carry a firearm or other deadly weapon without first ascertaining that the employee is proficient in the use of each weapon to be carried. A current and valid firearm qualification card which indicates the specific caliber of the firearm which may be carried shall be deemed evidence of proficiency. A firearm qualification permit is not valid unless the employee holds a valid, current registration card. With respect to other deadly weapons, evidence of proficiency shall include a certificate from a training facility, certifying that the employee is proficient in the use of that particular deadly weapon. A violation of this section may result in a fine of two hundred fifty dollars ($250) for each violation.

Business and Professions Code § 7599.41.

A licensee shall maintain an accurate and current record of all firearms or other deadly weapons that are in the possession of the licensee, or of any employee of the licensee, while on duty. The record shall contain the make, model, and serial number, or a description of any other deadly weapon, and the name of the person who has title of ownership. A violation of this section may result in a fine of twenty-five dollars ($25) for each violation.

Business and Professions Code § 7599.42.

Within seven days after any violent incident, involving a dangerous weapon, which has been caused by or occurred upon a licensee or any officer, partner, qualified manager, or employee of a licensee, while acting within the course and scope of his or her employment, that results in bodily injury to any person or death of any person involved in that incident or of any discharge of a weapon, excluding any discharge which occurs on the range, the licensee or his or her manager shall mail or deliver to the chief a detailed report of the incident. The report shall describe fully the circumstances surrounding the incident, any injuries or damages incurred, the identity of all participants, and whether a police investigation was conducted. A violation of this section may result in a fine of twenty-five dollars ($25) for the first violation and one hundred dollars ($100) for each subsequent violation.

Business and Professions Code § 7599.59.

The director may assess administrative fines against any licensee, qualified certificate holder, firearms qualification card holder, or registrant for failure to notify the bureau within 30 days of any change of residence or business address. (a) The fine shall be twenty-five dollars ($25) for each violation by a licensee or qualified certificate holder. (b) The fine shall be fifteen dollars ($15) for each violation by a firearms qualification card holder or registrant.

Business and Professions Code § 7599.70.

Effective July 1, 1998, the bureau shall establish and assess fees and penalties for licensure and registration as follows:

(a) A company license application fee may not exceed thirty-five dollars ($35).

(b) An original license fee for an alarm company operator license may not exceed two hundred eighty dollars ($280). A renewal fee for an alarm company operator license may not exceed three hundred thirty-five dollars ($335).

(c) A qualified manager application and examination fee may not exceed one hundred five dollars ($105).

(d) A renewal fee for a qualified manager may not exceed one hundred twenty dollars ($120).

(e) An original license fee and renewal fee for a branch office certificate may not exceed thirty-five dollars ($35).

(f) Notwithstanding Section 163.5, the reinstatement fee as required by Sections 7593.12 and 7598.17 is the amount equal to the renewal fee plus a penalty of 50 percent thereof.

(g) A fee for reexamination of an applicant for a qualified manager may not exceed two hundred forty dollars ($240).

(h) An initial registration fee for an alarm agent may not exceed seventeen dollars ($17).

(i) A registration renewal fee for an alarm agent may not exceed seven dollars ($7).

(j) A firearms qualification fee may not exceed eighty dollars ($80) and a firearms requalification fee may not exceed sixty dollars ($60).

(k) The fingerprint processing fee is that amount charged the bureau by the Department of Justice.

(l) The processing fee required pursuant to Sections 7593.7 and 7598.14 is the amount equal to the expenses incurred to provide a photo identification card.

(m) The fee for a "Certificate of Licensure" may not exceed fifty dollars ($50).

(n) The delinquency fee is 50 percent of the renewal fee in effect on the date of expiration, but not less than twenty-five dollars ($25).

Business and Professions Code § 17533.9.

It shall be unlawful for any person, firm, corporation, or association, in any newspaper, magazine, circular, form letter, or open publication, published, distributed, or circulated in this state, including over the Internet, or on any billboard, card, label, or other advertising medium, or by means of any other advertising device, to advertise the sale of tear gas, tear gas devices, and tear gas weapons, as defined in Sections 12401 and 12402 of the Penal Code, unless there is conspicuously displayed or stated in connection with the name and description of that tear gas, or those tear gas weapons or devices, a direct and unequivocal statement that will clearly indicate that possession or transportation of tear gas and tear gas weapons or devices is prohibited by law unless specifically exempted or permitted pursuant to the authority contained in Chapter 4 (commencing with Section 12401) of Title 2 of Part 4 of the Penal Code.

Business and Professions Code § 17534.5.

Unless otherwise expressly provided, the remedies or penalties provided by this chapter are cumulative to each other and to the remedies or penalties available under all other laws of this state.

Business and Professions Code § 17535.

Any person, corporation, firm, partnership, joint stock company, or any other association or organization which violates or proposes to violate this chapter may be enjoined by any court of competent jurisdiction. The court may make such orders or judgments, including the appointment of a receiver, as may be necessary to prevent the use or employment by any person, corporation, firm, partnership, joint stock company, or any other association or organization of any practices which violate this chapter, or which may be necessary to restore to any person in interest any money or property, real or personal, which may have been acquired by means of any practice in this chapter declared to be unlawful. Actions for injunction under this section may be prosecuted by the Attorney General or any district attorney, county counsel, city attorney, or city prosecutor in this state in the name of the people of the State of California upon their own complaint or upon the complaint of any board, officer, person, corporation or association or by any person who has suffered injury in fact and has lost money or property as a result of a violation of this chapter. Any person may pursue representative claims or relief on behalf of others only if the claimant meets the standing requirements of this section and complies with Section 382 of the Code of Civil Procedure, but these limitations do not apply to claims brought under this chapter by the Attorney General, or any district attorney, county counsel, city attorney, or city prosecutor in this state.

Business and Professions Code § 17535.5.

(a) Any person who intentionally violates any injunction issued pursuant to Section 17535 shall be liable for a civil penalty not to exceed six thousand dollars ($6,000) for each violation. Where the conduct constituting a violation is of a continuing nature, each day of such conduct is a separate and distinct violation. In determining the amount of the civil penalty, the court shall consider all relevant circumstances, including, but not limited to, the extent of harm caused by the conduct constituting a violation, the nature and persistence of such conduct, the length of time over which the conduct occurred, the assets, liabilities and net worth of the person, whether corporate or individual, and any corrective action taken by the defendant.

(b) The civil penalty prescribed by this section shall be assessed and recovered in a civil action brought in any county in which the violation occurs or where the injunction was issued in the name of the people of the State of California by the Attorney General or by any district attorney, county counsel, or city attorney in any court of competent jurisdiction within his jurisdiction without regard to the county from which the original injunction was issued. An action brought pursuant to this section to recover such civil penalties shall take special precedence over all civil matters on the calendar of the court except those matters to which equal precedence on the calendar is granted by law.

(c) If such an action is brought by the Attorney General, one-half of the penalty collected pursuant to this section shall be paid to the treasurer of the county in which the judgment was entered, and one-half to the State Treasurer. If brought by a district attorney or county counsel, the entire amount of the penalty collected shall be paid to the treasurer of the county in which the judgment is entered. If brought by a city attorney or city prosecutor, one-half of the penalty shall be paid to the treasurer of the county in which the judgment was entered and one-half to the city.

(d) If the action is brought at the request of a board within the Department of Consumer Affairs or a local consumer affairs agency, the court shall determine the reasonable expenses incurred by the board or local agency in the investigation and prosecution of the action. Before any penalty collected is paid out pursuant to subdivision (c), the amount of such reasonable expenses incurred by the board shall be paid to the State Treasurer for deposit in the special fund of the board described in Section 205. If the board has no such special fund, the moneys shall be paid to the State Treasurer. The amount of such reasonable expenses incurred by a local consumer affairs agency shall be paid to the general fund of the municipality or county which funds the local agency.

Business and Professions Code § 17536.

(a) Any person who violates any provision of this chapter shall be liable for a civil penalty not to exceed two thousand five hundred dollars ($2,500) for each violation, which shall be assessed and recovered in a civil action brought in the name of the people of the State of California by the Attorney General or by any district attorney, county counsel, or city attorney in any court of competent jurisdiction.

(b) The court shall impose a civil penalty for each violation of this chapter. In assessing the amount of the civil penalty, the court shall consider any one or more of the relevant circumstances presented by any of the parties to the case, including, but not limited to, the following: the nature and seriousness of the misconduct, the number of violations, the persistence of the misconduct, the length of time over which the misconduct occurred, the willfulness of the defendant's misconduct, and the defendant's assets, liabilities, and net worth.

(c) If the action is brought by the Attorney General, one-half of the penalty collected shall be paid to the treasurer of the county in which the judgment was entered, and one-half to the State Treasurer. If brought by a district attorney or county counsel, the entire amount of penalty collected shall be paid to the treasurer of the county in which the judgment was entered. If brought by a city attorney or city prosecutor, one-half of the penalty shall be paid to the treasurer of the county and one-half to the city. The aforementioned funds shall be for the exclusive use by the Attorney General, district attorney, county counsel, and city attorney for the enforcement of consumer protection laws.

(d) If the action is brought at the request of a board within the Department of Consumer Affairs or a local consumer affairs agency, the court shall determine the reasonable expenses incurred by the board or local agency in the investigation and prosecution of the action. Before any penalty collected is paid out pursuant to subdivision (c), the amount of such reasonable expenses incurred by the board shall be paid to the State Treasurer for deposit in the special fund of the board described in Section 205. If the board has no such special fund the moneys shall be paid to the State Treasurer. The amount of such reasonable expenses incurred by a local consumer affairs agency shall be paid to the general fund of the municipality which funds the local agency.

(e) As applied to the penalties for acts in violation of Section 17530, the remedies provided by this section and Section 17534 are mutually exclusive.

Business and Professions Code § 17536.5.

If a violation of this chapter is alleged or the application or construction of this chapter is in issue in any proceeding in the Supreme Court of California, a state court of appeal, or the appellate division of a superior court, each person filing any brief or petition with the court in that proceeding shall serve, within three days of filing with the court, a copy of that brief or petition on the Attorney General, directed to the attention of the Consumer Law Section at a service address designated on the Attorney General's official Web site for service of papers under this section or, if no service address is designated, at the Attorney General's office in San Francisco, California, and on the district attorney of the county in which the lower court action or proceeding was originally filed. Upon the Attorney General's or district attorney's request, each person who has filed any other document, including all or a portion of the appellate record, with the court in addition to a brief or petition shall provide a copy of that document without charge to the Attorney General or the district attorney within five days of the request. The time for service may be extended by the Chief Justice or presiding justice or judge for good cause shown. No judgment or relief, temporary or permanent, shall be granted or opinion issued until proof of service of the petition or brief on the Attorney General and district attorney is filed with the court.

Business and Professions Code § 21625.

It is the intent of the Legislature in enacting this article to curtail the dissemination of stolen property and to facilitate the recovery of stolen property by means of a uniform, statewide, state-administered program of regulation of persons whose principal business is the buying, selling, trading, auctioning, or taking in pawn of tangible personal property and to aid the State Board of Equalization to detect possible sales tax evasion. Further, it is the intent of the Legislature in enacting this article to require the uniform statewide reporting of tangible personal property acquired by persons whose principal business is the buying, selling, trading, auctioning, or taking in pawn of tangible personal property, unless the property or the transaction is specifically exempt herein, for the purpose of correlating these reports with other reports of city, county, and city and county law enforcement agencies and further utilizing the services of the Department of Justice to aid in tracing and recovering stolen property. Further, it is the intent of the Legislature that this article shall not be superseded or supplanted by the provisions of any ordinance or charter of any city, county, or city and county.

Business and Professions Code § 21626.

(a) A "secondhand dealer," as used in this article, means and includes any person, copartnership, firm, or corporation whose business includes buying, selling, trading, taking in pawn, accepting for sale on consignment, accepting for auctioning, or auctioning secondhand tangible personal property. A "secondhand dealer" does not include a "coin dealer" or participants at gun shows or events, as defined in Section 478.100 of Title 27 of the Code of Federal Regulations, or its successor, who are not required to be licensed pursuant to Section 12071 of the Penal Code, who are acting in compliance with the requirements of Section 12070 and subdivision (d) of Section 12072 of the Penal Code, and who are not a "Gun Show Trader," as described in paragraph (5) of subdivision (b) of Section 12070 of the Penal Code.

(b) As used in this section, a "coin dealer" means any person, firm, partnership, or corporation whose principal business is the buying, selling, and trading of coins, monetized bullion, or commercial grade ingots of gold, or silver, or other precious metals.

Business and Professions Code § 21628.

Every secondhand dealer or coin dealer described in Section 21626 shall report daily, or on the first working day after receipt or purchase of the property, on forms either approved or provided at actual cost by the Department of Justice, all tangible personal property which he or she has purchased, taken in trade, taken in pawn, accepted for sale on consignment, or accepted for auctioning, to the chief of police or to the sheriff, in accordance with the provisions of Sections 21630 and 21633 and subdivision (j) of this section. The report shall be legible, prepared in English, completed where applicable, and include, but not be limited to, the following information:

(a) The name and current address of the intended seller or pledger of the property.

(b) The identification of the intended seller or pledger. The identification of the seller or pledger of the property shall be verified by the person taking the information. The verification shall be valid if the person taking the information reasonably relies on any one of the following documents, provided that the document is currently valid or has been issued within five years and contains a photograph or description, or both, of the person named on it, is signed by the person, and bears a serial or other identifying number:

(1) A passport of the United States.

(2) A driver's license issued by any state, or Canada.

(3) An identification card issued by any state.

(4) An identification card issued by the United States.

(5) A passport from any other country in addition to another item of identification bearing an address.

(c) A complete and reasonably accurate description of serialized property, including, but not limited to, the following: serial number and other identifying marks or symbols, owner-applied numbers, manufacturer's named brand, and model name or number. Watches need not be disassembled when special skill or special tools are required to obtain the required information, unless specifically requested to do so by a peace officer. A special tool does not include a penknife, caseknife, or similar instrument and disassembling a watch with a penknife, caseknife, or similar instrument does not constitute a special skill. In all instances where the required information may be obtained by removal of a watchband, then the watchband shall be removed. The cost associated with opening the watch shall be borne by the pawnbroker, secondhand dealer, or customer.

(d) A complete and reasonably accurate description of nonserialized property, including, but not limited to, the following: size, color, material, manufacturer's pattern name (when known), owner-applied numbers and personalized inscriptions and other identifying marks or symbols. Watches need not be disassembled when special skill or special tools are required to obtain the required information, unless specifically requested to do so by a peace officer. A special tool does not include a penknife, caseknife, or similar instrument and disassembling a watch with a penknife, caseknife, or similar instrument does not constitute a special skill. In all instances where the required information may be obtained by removal of a watchband, then the watchband shall be removed. The cost associated with opening the watch shall be borne by the pawnbroker, secondhand dealer, or customer.

(e) A certification by the intended seller or pledger that he or she is the owner of the property or has the authority of the owner to sell or pledge the property.

(f) A certification by the intended seller or pledger that to his or her knowledge and belief the information is true and complete.

(g) A legible fingerprint taken from the intended seller or pledger, as prescribed by the Department of Justice. This requirement does not apply to a coin dealer, unless required pursuant to local regulation.

(h) When a secondhand dealer complies with all of the provisions of this section, he or she shall be deemed to have received from the seller or pledger adequate evidence of authority to sell or pledge the property for all purposes included in this article, and Division 8 (commencing with Section 21000) of the Financial Code. In enacting this subdivision, it is the intent of the Legislature that its provisions shall not adversely affect the implementation of, or prosecution under, any provision of the Penal Code.

(i) Any person who conducts business as a secondhand dealer at any gun show or event, as defined in Section 478.100 of Title 27 of the Code of Federal Regulations, or its successor, outside the jurisdiction that issued the secondhand dealer license in accordance with subdivision (d) of Section 21641, may be required to submit a duplicate of the transaction report prepared pursuant to this section to the local law enforcement agency where the gun show or event is conducted.

(j)(1) The Department of Justice shall, in consultation with appropriate local law enforcement agencies, develop clear and comprehensive descriptive categories denoting tangible personal property subject to the reporting requirements of this section. These categories shall be incorporated by secondhand dealers and coin dealers described in Section 21626 for purposes of the reporting requirements set forth herein. Any required report shall be transmitted by electronic means. The Department of Justice and local law enforcement agencies, in consultation with representatives from the secondhand dealer and coin dealer businesses, shall develop a standard format to be used statewide to transmit this report electronically.

(2) Twelve months after the format and the categories described in paragraph (1) have been developed, each secondhand dealer and coin dealer shall electronically report using this format the information required by this section under these reporting categories. Until that time, each secondhand dealer and coin dealer may either continue to report this information using existing forms and procedures or may begin electronically reporting this information under the reporting categories and using the format described in paragraph (1) as soon as each has been developed.

(3) A coin dealer who engages in less than 10 transactions each week in which he or she has purchased, taken in trade, taken in pawn, accepted for sale or consignment, or accepted for auctioning tangible personal property, shall report the information required by this section under the reporting categories described in paragraph (1) on a form developed by the Attorney General that the coin dealer shall transmit each day by facsimile transmission or by mail to the chief of police or sheriff. A transaction shall consist of not more than one item. Nothing in this section shall prohibit up to 10 transactions with the same customer per week, provided that the cumulative total per week for all customers does not exceed 10 transactions. Until that form is developed, these coin dealers shall continue to report information required by this section using existing forms and procedures. If these transactions increase to 10 per week, the coin dealer shall electronically report using the format described in paragraph (1) the information required by this section beginning six months after his or her transactions exceed 10 per week or 12 months after the format described in paragraph (1) has been developed, whichever occurs

later.

(4) For purposes of this subdivision, "item" shall mean any single physical article. However, with respect to a commonly accepted grouping of articles that are purchased as a set, including, but not limited to, a pair of earrings or place settings of china, silverware, or other tableware, "item" shall mean that commonly accepted grouping.

(5) Nothing in this subdivision shall be construed as excepting a secondhand dealer from the fingerprinting requirement of subdivision (g).

Business and Professions Code § 21628.1.

Notwithstanding Section 21628, except for firearms, submission of transaction reports are not required to be submitted to the local law enforcement agency if the report of an acquisition of the same property from the same customer has been submitted within the preceding 12 months, except when submission of the reports is specifically requested in writing by the local licensing authority.

Business and Professions Code § 21641.

(a) The chief of police, the sheriff or, where appropriate, the police commission, shall accept an application for and grant a license permitting the licensee to engage in the business of secondhand dealer, as defined in Section 21626, to an applicant who has not been convicted of an attempt to receive stolen property or any other offense involving stolen property. Prior to the granting of a license, the licensing authority shall submit the application to the Department of Justice. If the Department of Justice does not comment on the application within 30 days thereafter, the licensing authority may grant the applicant a license. All forms for application and licensure, and license renewal, shall be prescribed and provided by the Department of Justice. A fee may be charged to the applicant as specified by the Department of Justice and the local licensing authority for processing the initial license application.

(b) For the purposes of this section, "convicted" means a plea or verdict of guilty or a conviction following a plea of nolo contendere.

(c) Notwithstanding subdivisions (a) and (b), no person shall be denied a secondhand dealer's license solely on the grounds that he or she violated any provision contained in Article 4 (commencing with Section 21625) or Article 5 (commencing with Section 21650) of this chapter, or any provision contained in Chapter 2 (commencing with Section 21200) of Division 8 of the Financial Code, unless the violation demonstrates a pattern of conduct.

(d) Any person licensed as a firearms dealer pursuant to Section 12071 of the Penal Code, who is conducting business at gun shows or events pursuant to subparagraph (B) of paragraph (1) of subdivision (b) of Section 12071 of the Penal Code, and who has a valid secondhand dealer license granted by the appropriate local authorities in the jurisdiction where the firearms dealer license has been granted, shall be authorized to conduct business as a secondhand dealer at any gun show or event, as defined in Section 478.100 of Title 27 of the Code of Federal Regulations, or its successor, without regard to the jurisdiction within this state that issued the secondhand dealer license pursuant to subdivision (a) of this section. No additional fees or separate secondhand dealer license shall be required by any agency having jurisdiction over the locality where the gun show or event is conducted. However, the person shall otherwise be subject to, and comply with, the requirements of this article when he or she acts as a secondhand dealer at the gun show or event to the same extent as if he or she were licensed as a secondhand dealer in the jurisdiction in which the gun show or event is being conducted.

Business and Professions Code § 21642.

(a) A license granted pursuant to Section 21641 shall be renewable the second year from the date of issue, and every other year thereafter, upon the filing of a renewal application and the payment of a license renewal fee specified by the licensing authority. The Department of Justice may also charge a fee of not more than twelve dollars ($12) but not to exceed the actual processing costs of the department. After the department establishes a fee sufficient to reimburse the department for processing costs, the fee charged shall increase at a rate not to exceed the legislatively approved annual cost-of-living adjustments for the department's budget. The licensing authority shall collect the fee and transmit the fee and a copy of the renewed license to the Department of Justice.

(b) The license shall be subject to forfeiture by the licensing authority and the licensee's activities as a secondhand dealer shall be subject to being enjoined pursuant to Section 21646 for breach of any of the following conditions:

(1) The business shall be carried on only at the location designated on the license. The license shall designate all locations where property belonging to the business is stored. Property of the business may be stored at locations not designated on the license only with the written consent of the local licensing authority.

(2) The license or a copy thereof, certified by the licensing authority, shall be displayed on the premises in plain view of the public.

(3) The licensee shall not engage in any act which the licensee knows to be in violation of this article.

(4) The licensee shall not be convicted of an attempt to receive stolen property or any other offense involving stolen property. For the purposes of this paragraph, "convicted" means a plea or verdict of guilty or a conviction following a plea of nolo contendere. Any action which the chief of police, the sheriff or, where appropriate, the police commission, is permitted to take following the establishment of a conviction may be taken when the time for appeal has elapsed, or the judgment of conviction has been affirmed on appeal, or when an order granting probation is made suspending the imposition of sentence, irrespective of a subsequent order under the provisions of Section 1203.4 of the Penal Code.

(c) Notwithstanding subdivisions (a) and (b), no person shall have his or her renewal application for a secondhand dealer's license denied, nor shall his or her secondhand dealer's license be forfeited solely on the grounds that he or she violated any provision contained in Article 4 (commencing with Section 21625) or Article 5 (commencing with Section 21650) of this chapter, or any provision contained in Chapter 2 (commencing with Section 21200) of Division 8 of the Financial Code, unless the violation demonstrates a pattern of conduct.

Business and Professions Code § 21643.

No transactions that require reporting under Section 21628 shall be engaged in with a minor.

Business and Professions Code § 21645.

A violation of any provision of this article under circumstances where a person knows or should have known that a violation was being committed is a misdemeanor punishable as follows: (a) For the first offense, a fine of up to one thousand five hundred dollars ($1,500) or imprisonment in the county jail up to two months, or both. (b) For the second offense, a fine of up to five thousand dollars ($5,000) or imprisonment in the county jail up to four months, or both. (c) For the third, and any subsequent offense, a fine of up to twenty-five thousand dollars ($25,000) or imprisonment in the county jail up to six months, or both.

Business and Professions Code § 21646.

The district attorney or the Attorney General, in the name of the people of the State of California, may bring an action to enjoin the violation or the threatened violation of any provision of this article or of any regulation made pertaining to the provisions of this article. Any proceeding brought hereunder shall be governed in all respects by the provisions of Chapter 3 (commencing with Section 525) of Title 7 of Part 2 of the Code of Civil Procedure.

Business and Professions Code § 23425.

For the purposes of this article "club" means:

(a) Any chapter, aerie, parlor, lodge, or other local unit of an American national fraternal organization which has as the owner, lessee, or occupant thereof operated an establishment for fraternal purposes. An American national fraternal organization as used in this subdivision shall actively operate in not less than 20 states of the Union and have not less than 175 local units in those 20 states, and shall have been in active continuous existence for not less than 20 years.

(b) Any hall or building association of a local unit mentioned in subdivision (a), all of the capital stock of which is owned by the local unit or the members thereof, and which operates the clubroom facilities of the local unit.

Business and Professions Code § 23428.2.

For the purposes of this article "club" also means any rod and gun club which is a nonprofit organization belonging to a recognized national association of rod or gun clubs, and which has more than 100 bona fide regular members, each of whom is required to pay regular membership dues of not less than five dollars ($5) each year, and which owns, maintains, or operates a clubhouse and has continuously operated a clubhouse for not less than three years.

Business and Professions Code § 23430.

The department may issue one club license to any club as defined in this article.

Civil Code

Civil Code § 50.

Section Fifty. Any necessary force may be used to protect from wrongful injury the person or property of oneself, or of a wife, husband, child, parent, or other relative, or member of one's family, or of a ward, servant, master, or guest.

Civil Code § 846.

An owner of any estate or any other interest in real property, whether possessory or nonpossessory, owes no duty of care to keep the premises safe for entry or use by others for any recreational purpose or to give any warning of hazardous conditions, uses of, structures, or activities on such premises to persons entering for such purpose, except as provided in this section. A "recreational purpose," as used in this section, includes such activities as fishing, hunting, camping, water sports, hiking, spelunking, sport parachuting, riding, including animal riding, snowmobiling, and all other types of vehicular riding, rock collecting, sightseeing, picnicking, nature study, nature contacting, recreational gardening, gleaning, hang gliding, winter sports, and viewing or enjoying historical, archaeological, scenic, natural, or scientific sites. An owner of any estate or any other interest in real property, whether possessory or nonpossessory, who gives permission to another for entry or use for the above purpose upon the premises does not thereby

(a) extend any assurance that the premises are safe for such purpose, or

(b) constitute the person to whom permission has been granted the legal status of an invitee or licensee to whom a duty of care is owed, or

(c) assume responsibility for or incur liability for any injury to person or property caused by any act of such person to whom permission has been granted except as provided in this section. This section does not limit the liability which otherwise exists (a) for willful or malicious failure to guard or warn against a dangerous condition, use, structure or activity; or (b) for injury suffered in any case where permission to enter for the above purpose was granted for a consideration other than the consideration, if any, paid to said landowner by the state, or where consideration has been received from others for the same purpose; or (c) to any persons who are expressly invited rather than merely permitted to come upon the premises by the landowner.

Nothing in this section creates a duty of care or ground of liability for injury to person or property.

Civil Code § 847.

(a) An owner, including, but not limited to, a public entity, as defined in Section 811.2 of the Government Code, of any estate or any other interest in real property, whether possessory or nonpossessory, shall not be liable to any person for any injury or death that occurs upon that property during the course of or after the commission of any of the felonies set forth in subdivision (b) by the injured or deceased person.

(b) The felonies to which the provisions of this section apply are the following:

(1) Murder or voluntary manslaughter;

(2) mayhem;

(3) rape;

(4) sodomy by force, violence, duress, menace, or threat of great bodily harm;

(5) oral copulation by force, violence, duress, menace, or threat of great bodily harm;

(6) lewd acts on a child under the age of 14 years;

(7) any felony punishable by death or imprisonment in the state prison for life;

(8) any other felony in which the defendant inflicts great bodily injury on any person, other than an accomplice, or any felony in which the defendant uses a firearm;

(9) attempted murder;

(10) assault with intent to commit rape or robbery;

(11) assault with a deadly weapon or instrument on a peace officer;

(12) assault by a life prisoner on a noninmate;

(13) assault with a deadly weapon by an inmate;

(14) arson;

(15) exploding a destructive device or any explosive with intent to injure;

(16) exploding a destructive device or any explosive causing great bodily injury;

(17) exploding a destructive device or any explosive with intent to murder;

(18) burglary;

(19) robbery;

(20) kidnapping;

(21) taking of a hostage by an inmate of a state prison;

(22) any felony in which the defendant personally used a dangerous or deadly weapon;

(23) selling, furnishing, administering, or providing heroin, cocaine, or phencyclidine (PCP) to a minor;

(24) grand theft as defined in Sections 487 and 487a of the Penal Code; and

(25) any attempt to commit a crime listed in this subdivision other than an assault.

(c) The limitation on liability conferred by this section arises at the moment the injured or deceased person commences the felony or attempted felony and extends to the moment the injured or deceased person is no longer upon the property.

(d) The limitation on liability conferred by this section applies only when the injured or deceased person's conduct in furtherance of the commission of a felony specified in subdivision (b) proximately or legally causes the injury or death.

(e) The limitation on liability conferred by this section arises only upon the charge of a felony listed in subdivision (b) and the subsequent conviction of that felony or a lesser included felony or misdemeanor arising from a charge of a felony listed in subdivision (b). During the pendency of any such criminal action, a civil action alleging this liability shall be abated and the statute of limitations on the civil cause of action shall be tolled.

(f) This section does not limit the liability of an owner or an owner's agent which otherwise exists for willful, wanton, or criminal conduct, or for willful or malicious failure to guard or warn against a dangerous condition, use, structure, or activity.

(g) The limitation on liability provided by this section shall be in addition to any other available defense.

Civil Code § 1708.

Every person is bound, without contract, to abstain from injuring the person or property of another, or infringing upon any of his or her rights.

Civil Code § 1708.5.

(a) A person commits a sexual battery who does any of the following:

(1) Acts with the intent to cause a harmful or offensive contact with an intimate part of another, and a sexually offensive contact with that person directly or indirectly results.

(2) Acts with the intent to cause a harmful or offensive contact with another by use of his or her intimate part, and a sexually offensive contact with that person directly or indirectly results.

(3) Acts to cause an imminent apprehension of the conduct described in paragraph (1) or (2), and a sexually offensive contact with that person directly or indirectly results.

(b) A person who commits a sexual battery upon another is liable to that person for damages, including, but not limited to, general damages, special damages, and punitive damages.

(c) The court in an action pursuant to this section may award equitable relief, including, but not limited to, an injunction, costs, and any other relief the court deems proper.

(d) For the purposes of this section "intimate part" means the sexual organ, anus, groin, or buttocks of any person, or the breast of a female.

(e) The rights and remedies provided in this section are in addition to any other rights and remedies provided by law.

(f) For purposes of this section "offensive contact" means contact that offends a reasonable sense of personal dignity.

Civil Code § 1708.6.

(a) A person is liable for the tort of domestic violence if the plaintiff proves both of the following elements:

(1) The infliction of injury upon the plaintiff resulting from abuse, as defined in subdivision (a) of Section 13700 of the Penal Code.

(2) The abuse was committed by the defendant, a person having a relationship with the plaintiff as defined in subdivision (b) of Section 13700 of the Penal Code.

(b) A person who commits an act of domestic violence upon another is liable to that person for damages, including, but not limited to, general damages, special damages, and punitive damages pursuant to Section 3294.

(c) The court, in an action pursuant to this section, may grant to a prevailing plaintiff equitable relief, an injunction, costs, and any other relief that the court deems proper, including reasonable attorney's fees.

(d) The rights and remedies provided in this section are in addition to any other rights and remedies provided by law.

(e) The time for commencement of an action under this section is governed by Section 340.15 of the Code of Civil Procedure.

Civil Code § 1708.7.

(a) A person is liable for the tort of stalking when the plaintiff proves all of the following elements of the tort:

(1) The defendant engaged in a pattern of conduct the intent of which was to follow, alarm, or harass the plaintiff. In order to establish this element, the plaintiff shall be required to support his or her allegations with independent corroborating evidence.

(2) As a result of that pattern of conduct, the plaintiff reasonably feared for his or her safety, or the safety of an immediate family member. For purposes of this paragraph, "immediate family" means a spouse, parent, child, any person related by consanguinity or affinity within the second degree, or any person who regularly resides, or, within the six months preceding any portion of the pattern of conduct, regularly resided, in the plaintiff's household.

(3) One of the following:

(A) The defendant, as a part of the pattern of conduct specified in paragraph (1), made a credible threat with the intent to place the plaintiff in reasonable fear for his or her safety, or the safety of an immediate family member and, on at least one occasion, the plaintiff clearly and definitively demanded that the defendant cease and abate his or her pattern of conduct and the defendant persisted in his or her pattern of conduct.

(B) The defendant violated a restraining order, including, but not limited to, any order issued pursuant to Section 527.6 of the Code of Civil Procedure, prohibiting any act described in subdivision (a).

(b) For the purposes of this section:

(1) "Pattern of conduct" means conduct composed of a series of acts over a period of time, however short, evidencing a continuity of purpose. Constitutionally protected activity is not included within the meaning of "pattern of conduct."

(2) "Credible threat" means a verbal or written threat, including that communicated by means of an electronic communication device, or a threat implied by a pattern of conduct or a combination of verbal, written, or electronically communicated statements and conduct, made with the intent and apparent ability to carry out the threat so as to cause the person who is the target of the threat to reasonably fear for his or her safety or the safety of his or her immediate family.

(3) "Electronic communication device" includes, but is not limited to, telephones, cellular telephones, computers, video recorders, fax machines, or pagers. "Electronic communication" has the same meaning as the term defined in Subsection 12 of Section 2510 of Title 18 of the United States Code.

(4) "Harass" means a knowing and willful course of conduct directed at a specific person which seriously alarms, annoys, torments, or terrorizes the person, and which serves no legitimate purpose. The course of conduct must be such as would cause a

reasonable person to suffer substantial emotional distress, and must actually cause substantial emotional distress to the person. (c) A person who commits the tort of stalking upon another is liable to that person for damages, including, but not limited to, general damages, special damages, and punitive damages pursuant to Section 3294.

(d) In an action pursuant to this section, the court may grant equitable relief, including, but not limited to, an injunction.

(e) The rights and remedies provided in this section are cumulative and in addition to any other rights and remedies provided by law.

(f) This section shall not be construed to impair any constitutionally protected activity, including, but not limited to, speech, protest, and assembly.

Civil Code § 1709.

One who willfully deceives another with intent to induce him to alter his position to his injury or risk, is liable for any damage which he thereby suffers.

Civil Code § 1710.

A deceit, within the meaning of the last section, is either:

1. The suggestion, as a fact, of that which is not true, by one who does not believe it to be true;

2. The assertion, as a fact, of that which is not true, by one who has no reasonable ground for believing it to be true;

3. The suppression of a fact, by one who is bound to disclose it, or who gives information of other facts which are likely to mislead for want of communication of that fact; or,

4. A promise, made without any intention of performing it.

Civil Code § 1710.1.

Any person who, with intent to defraud, sells or disposes of a radio, piano, phonograph, sewing machine, washing machine, typewriter, adding machine, comptometer, bicycle, firearm, safe, vacuum cleaner, dictaphone, watch, watch movement, watchcase, or any other mechanical or electrical device, appliance, contrivance, material, piece of apparatus or equipment, from which the manufacturer's nameplate, serial number or any other distinguishing number or identification mark has been removed, defaced, covered, altered or destroyed, is civilly liable to the manufacturer in the sum of five hundred dollars ($500) per transaction and civilly liable to the purchaser for treble the actual damages sustained by the purchaser. This section does not apply to those cases or instances where any of the changes or alterations enumerated in this section have been customarily made or done as an established practice in the ordinary and regular conduct of business by the original manufacturer or his duly appointed direct representative or under specific authorization from the original manufacturer.

Civil Code § 1714.

(a) Everyone is responsible, not only for the result of his or her willful acts, but also for an injury occasioned to another by his or her want of ordinary care or skill in the management of his or her property or person, except so far as the latter has, willfully or by want of ordinary care, brought the injury upon himself or herself. The design, distribution, or marketing of firearms and ammunition is not exempt from the duty to use ordinary care and skill that is required by this section. The extent of liability in these cases is defined by the Title on Compensatory Relief.

(b) It is the intent of the Legislature to abrogate the holdings in cases such as Vesely v. Sager (1971) 5 Cal.3d 153, Bernhard v. Harrah's Club (1976) 16 Cal.3d 313, and Coulter v. Superior Court (1978) 21 Cal.3d 144 and to reinstate the prior judicial interpretation of this section as it relates to proximate cause for injuries incurred as a result of furnishing alcoholic beverages to an intoxicated person, namely that the furnishing of alcoholic beverages is not the proximate cause of injuries resulting from intoxication, but rather the consumption of alcoholic beverages is the proximate cause of injuries inflicted upon another by an intoxicated person.

(c) No social host who furnishes alcoholic beverages to any person may be held legally accountable for damages suffered by that person, or for injury to the person or property of, or death of, any third person, resulting from the consumption of those beverages.

Civil Code § 1714.01.

(a) Domestic partners shall be entitled to recover damages for negligent infliction of emotional distress to the same extent that spouses are entitled to do so under California law.

(b) For the purpose of this section, "domestic partners" has the meaning provided in Section 297 of the Family Code.

Civil Code § 1714.1.

(a) Any act of willful misconduct of a minor that results in injury or death to another person or in any injury to the property of another shall be imputed to the parent or guardian having custody and control of the minor for all purposes of civil damages, and the parent or guardian having custody and control shall be jointly and severally liable with the minor for any damages resulting from the willful misconduct. Subject to the provisions of subdivision (c), the joint and several liability of the parent or guardian having custody and control of a minor under this subdivision shall not exceed twenty-five thousand dollars ($25,000) for each tort of the minor, and in the case of injury to a person, imputed liability shall be further limited to medical, dental and hospital expenses incurred by the injured person, not to exceed twenty-five thousand dollars ($25,000). The liability imposed by this section is in addition to any liability now imposed by law.

(b) Any act of willful misconduct of a minor that results in the defacement of property of another with paint or a similar substance shall be imputed to the parent or guardian having custody and control of the minor for all purposes of civil damages, including court costs, and attorney's fees, to the prevailing party, and the parent or guardian having custody and control shall be jointly and severally liable with the minor for any damages resulting from the willful misconduct, not to exceed twenty-five thousand dollars ($25,000), except as provided in subdivision (c), for each tort of the minor.

(c) The amounts listed in subdivisions (a) and (b) shall be adjusted every two years by the Judicial Council to reflect any increases in the cost of living in California, as indicated by the annual average of the California Consumer Price Index. The Judicial Council shall round this adjusted amount up or down to the nearest hundred dollars. On or before July 1 of each odd-numbered year, the Judicial Council shall compute and publish the amounts listed in subdivisions (a) and (b), as adjusted according to this subdivision.

(d) The maximum liability imposed by this section is the maximum liability authorized under this section at the time that the act of willful misconduct by a minor was committed.

(e) Nothing in this section shall impose liability on an insurer for a loss caused by the willful act of the insured for purposes of Section 533 of the Insurance Code. An insurer shall not be liable for the conduct imputed to a parent or guardian by this section for any amount in excess of ten thousand dollars ($10,000).

Civil Code § 1714.3.

Civil liability for any injury to the person or property of another proximately caused by the discharge of a firearm by a minor under the age of 18 years shall be imputed to a parent or guardian having custody and control of the minor for all purposes of civil damages, and such parent or guardian shall be jointly and severally liable with such minor for any damages resulting from such act, if such parent or guardian either permitted the minor to have the firearm or left the firearm in a place accessible to the minor. The liability imposed by this section is in addition to any liability otherwise imposed by law. However, no person, or group of persons collectively, shall incur liability under this section in any amount exceeding thirty thousand dollars ($30,000) for injury to or death of one person as a result of any one occurrence or, subject to the limit as to one person, exceeding sixty thousand dollars ($60,000) for injury to or death of all persons as a result of any one such occurrence.

Civil Code § 1714.45.

(a) In a product liability action, a manufacturer or seller shall not be liable if both of the following apply:

(1) The product is inherently unsafe and the product is known to be unsafe by the ordinary consumer who consumes the product with the ordinary knowledge common to the community.

(2) The product is a common consumer product intended for personal consumption, such as sugar, castor oil, alcohol, and butter, as identified in comment i to Section 402A of the Restatement (Second) of Torts.

(b) This section does not exempt the manufacture or sale of tobacco products by tobacco manufacturers and their successors in interest from product liability actions, but does exempt the sale or distribution of tobacco products by any other person, including, but not limited to, retailers or distributors.

(c) For purposes of this section, the term "product liability action" means any action for injury or death caused by a product, except that the term does not include an action based on a manufacturing defect or breach of an express warranty.

(d) This section is intended to be declarative of and does not alter or amend existing California law, including Cronin v. J.B.E. Olson Corp. (1972), 8 Cal. 3d 121, and shall apply to all product liability actions pending on, or commenced after, January 1, 1988.

(e) This section does not apply to, and never applied to, an action brought by a public entity to recover the value of benefits provided to individuals injured by a tobacco-related illness caused by the tortious conduct of a tobacco company or its successor in interest, including, but not limited to, an action brought pursuant to Section 14124.71 of the Welfare and Institutions Code. In the action brought by a public entity, the fact that the injured individual's claim against the defendant may be barred by a prior version of this section shall not be a defense. This subdivision does not constitute a change in, but is declaratory of, existing law relating to tobacco products.

(f) It is the intention of the Legislature in enacting the amendments to subdivisions (a) and (b) of this section adopted at the 1997-98 Regular Session to declare that there exists no statutory bar to tobacco-related personal injury, wrongful death, or other tort claims against tobacco manufacturers and their successors in interest by California smokers or others who have suffered or incurred injuries, damages, or costs arising from the promotion, marketing, sale, or consumption of tobacco products. It is also the intention of the Legislature to clarify that those claims that were or are brought shall be determined on their merits, without the imposition of any claim of statutory bar or categorical defense. (g) This section shall not be construed to grant immunity to a tobacco industry research organization.

Civil Code § 3479.

Anything which is injurious to health, including, but not limited to, the illegal sale of controlled substances, or is indecent or offensive to the senses, or an obstruction to the free use of property, so as to interfere with the comfortable enjoyment of life or property, or unlawfully obstructs the free passage or use, in the customary manner, of any navigable lake, or river, bay, stream, canal, or basin, or any public park, square, street, or highway, is a nuisance.

Civil Code § 3480.

Section Thirty-four Hundred and Eighty. A public nuisance is one which affects at the same time an entire community or neighborhood, or any considerable number of persons, although the extent of the annoyance or damage inflicted upon individuals may be unequal.

Civil Code § 3481.

Every nuisance not included in the definition of the last section is private.

Civil Code § 3482.

Nothing which is done or maintained under the express authority of a statute can be deemed a nuisance.

Civil Code § 3482.1.

(a) As used in this section:

(1) "Person" means an individual, proprietorship, partnership, corporation, club, or other legal entity.

(2) "Sport shooting range" or "range" means an area designed and operated for the use of rifles, shotguns, pistols, silhouettes,

skeet, trap, black powder, or any other similar sport or law enforcement training purpose.

(3) "Indoor shooting range" means a totally enclosed facility designed to offer a totally controlled shooting environment that includes impenetrable walls, floor and ceiling, adequate ventilation and lighting systems, and acoustical treatment for sound attenuation suitable for the range's approved use.

(4) "Nighttime" means between the hours of 10 p.m. and 7 a.m.

(b)(1) Except as provided in subdivision (f), a person who operates or uses a sport shooting range in this state shall not be subject to civil liability or criminal prosecution in any matter relating to noise or noise pollution resulting from the operation or use of the range if the range is in compliance with any noise control laws or ordinances that applied to the range and its operation at the time construction or operation of the range was approved by a local public entity having jurisdiction in the matter, or if there were no such laws or ordinances that applied to the range and its operation at that time.

(2) Except as provided in subdivision (f), a person who operates or uses a sport shooting range or law enforcement training range is not subject to an action for nuisance, and a court shall not enjoin the use or operation of a range, on the basis of noise or noise pollution if the range is in compliance with any noise control laws or ordinances that applied to the range and its operation at the time construction or operation of the range was approved by a local public entity having jurisdiction in the matter, or if there were no such laws or ordinances that applied to the range and its operation at that time.

(3) Rules or regulations adopted by any state department or agency for limiting levels of noise in terms of decibel level which may occur in the outdoor atmosphere shall not apply to a sport shooting range exempted from liability under this section.

(c) A person who acquires title to or who owns real property adversely affected by the use of property with a permanently located and improved sport shooting range may not maintain a nuisance action with respect to noise or noise pollution against the person who owns the range to restrain, enjoin, or impede the use of the range where there has been no substantial change in the nature or use of the range. This section does not prohibit actions for negligence or recklessness in the operation of the range or by a person using the range.

(d) A sport shooting range that is in operation and not in violation of existing law at the time of the enactment of an ordinance described in subdivision (b) shall be permitted to continue in operation even if the operation of the sport shooting range at a later date does not conform to a new ordinance or an amendment to an existing ordinance if there has been no substantial change in the nature or use of the range. Nothing in this section shall be construed to limit the authority of a local agency to enforce any term of a conditional use permit.

(e) Except as otherwise provided in this section, this section does not prohibit a local public entity having jurisdiction in the matter from regulating the location and construction of a sport shooting range after the effective date of this section.

(f) This section does not prohibit a local public entity having jurisdiction in the matter from requiring that noise levels at the nearest residential property line to a range not exceed the level of normal city street noise which shall not be more than 60 decibels for nighttime shooting. The subdivision does not abrogate any existing local standards for nighttime shooting. The operator of a sport shooting range shall not unreasonably refuse to use trees, shrubs, or barriers, when appropriate, to mitigate the noise generated by nighttime shooting. For the purpose of this section, a reasonable effort to mitigate is an action that can be accomplished in a manner and at a cost that does not impose an unreasonable financial burden upon the operator of the range.

(g) This section does not apply to indoor shooting ranges.

(h) This section does not apply to a range in existence prior to January 1, 1998, that is operated for law enforcement training purposes by a county of the sixth class if the range is located without the boundaries of that county and within the boundaries of another county. This subdivision shall become operative on July 1, 1999.

Civil Code § 3483.

Every successive owner of property who neglects to abate a continuing nuisance upon, or in the use of, such property, created by a former owner, is liable therefor in the same manner as the one who first created it.

Civil Code § 3484.

The abatement of a nuisance does not prejudice the right of any person to recover damages for its past existence.

Civil Code § 3485.

(a) To abate the nuisance caused by illegal conduct involving an unlawful weapons or ammunition purpose on real property, the city prosecutor or city attorney may file, in the name of the people, an action for unlawful detainer against any person who is in violation of the nuisance or illegal purpose provisions of subdivision 4 of Section 1161 of the Code of Civil Procedure, with respect to that unlawful weapons or ammunition purpose. In filing this action, which shall be based upon an arrest report or other report by a law enforcement agency, reporting an offense committed on the property and documented by the observations of a police officer, the city prosecutor or city attorney shall use the procedures set forth in Chapter 4 (commencing with Section 1159) of Title 3 of Part 3 of the Code of Civil Procedure, except that in cases filed under this section, the following also shall apply:

(1)(A) Prior to filing an action pursuant to this section, the city prosecutor or city attorney shall give 30 calendar days' written notice to the owner, requiring the owner to file an action for the removal of the person who is in violation of the nuisance or illegal purpose provisions of subdivision 4 of Section 1161 of the Code of Civil Procedure with respect to an unlawful weapons or ammunition purpose.

(B) This notice shall include sufficient documentation establishing a violation of the nuisance or illegal purpose provisions of subdivision 4 of Section 1161 of the Code of Civil Procedure and shall be served upon the owner and the tenant in accordance with subdivision (e).

(C) The notice to the tenant shall also include on the bottom of its front page, in at least 14-point bold type, the following: "Notice to Tenant: This notice is not a notice of eviction. However, you should know that an eviction action may soon be filed in court against you for an unlawful weapons or ammunition activity, as described above. You should call (insert name and telephone number of the city attorney or prosecutor pursuing the action) or a legal assistance provider to stop the eviction action if any of the following is applicable:

(i) You are not the person named in this notice.

(ii) The person named in the notice does not live with you.

(iii) The person named in the notice has permanently moved.

(iv) You do not know the person named in the notice.

(v) You have any other legal defense or legal reason to stop the eviction action. A list of legal assistance providers is attached to this notice. Some provide free legal help if you are eligible."

(D) The owner shall, within 30 calendar days of the mailing of the written notice, either provide the city prosecutor or city attorney with all relevant information pertaining to the unlawful detainer case, or provide a written explanation setting forth any safety-related reasons for noncompliance, and an assignment to the city prosecutor or city attorney of the right to bring an unlawful detainer action against the tenant.

(E) The assignment shall be on a form provided by the city prosecutor or city attorney and may contain a provision for costs of investigation, discovery, and reasonable attorney's fees, in an amount not to exceed six hundred dollars ($600).

(F) If the city prosecutor or city attorney accepts the assignment of the right of the owner to bring the unlawful detainer action, the owner shall retain all other rights and duties, including the handling of the tenant's personal property, following issuance of the writ of possession and its delivery to and execution by the appropriate agency.

(2) Upon the failure of the owner to file an action pursuant to this section, or to respond to the city prosecutor or city attorney as provided in paragraph (1), or having filed an action, if the owner fails to prosecute it diligently and in good faith, the city prosecutor or city attorney may file and prosecute the action, and join the owner as a defendant in the action. This action shall have precedence over any similar proceeding thereafter brought by the owner, or to one previously brought by the owner and not prosecuted diligently and in good faith. Service of the summons and complaint upon the defendant owner shall be in accordance with Sections 415.10, 415.20, 415.30, 415.40, and 415.50 of the Code of Civil Procedure.

(3) If a jury or court finds the defendant tenant guilty of unlawful detainer in a case filed pursuant to paragraph (2), the city prosecutor or city attorney may be awarded costs, including the costs of investigation and discovery and reasonable attorney's fees. These costs shall be assessed against the defendant owner, to whom notice was directed pursuant to paragraph (1), and once an abstract of judgment is recorded, it shall constitute a lien on the subject real property.

(4) This article shall not prevent a local governing body from adopting and enforcing laws, consistent with this article, relating to weapons or ammunition abatement. If local laws duplicate or supplement this article, this article shall be construed as providing alternative remedies and not preempting the field.

(5) This article shall not prevent a tenant from receiving relief against a forfeiture of a lease pursuant to Section 1179 of the Code of Civil Procedure. (b) In any proceeding brought under this section, the court may, upon a showing of good cause, issue a partial eviction ordering the removal of any person, including, but not limited to, members of the tenant's household if the court finds that the person has engaged in the activities described in subdivision (a). Persons removed pursuant to this section may be permanently barred from returning to or reentering any portion of the entire premises. The court may further order as an express condition of the tenancy that the remaining tenants shall not give permission to or invite any person who has been removed pursuant to this subdivision to return to or reenter any portion of the entire premises.

(c) For purposes of this section, "unlawful weapons or ammunition purpose" means the illegal use, manufacture, causing to be manufactured, importation, possession, possession for sale, sale, furnishing, or giving away of any of the following:

(1) A firearm, as defined in subdivision (b) of Section 12001 of the Penal Code.

(2) Any ammunition, as defined in paragraph (2) of subdivision (b) of Section 12316 or subdivisions (a) and (b) of Section 12323 of the Penal Code.

(3) Any assault weapon, as defined in Section 12276, 12276.1, or 12276.5 of the Penal Code.

(4) Any .50 BMG rifle, as defined in Section 12278 of the Penal Code.

(5) Any tear gas weapon, as defined in Section 12402 of the Penal Code.

(d) Notwithstanding subdivision (b) of Section 68097.2 of the Government Code, a public entity may waive all or part of the costs incurred in furnishing the testimony of a peace officer in an unlawful detainer action brought pursuant to this section.

(e) The notice and documentation described in paragraph (1) of subdivision (a) shall be given in writing and may be given either by personal delivery or by deposit in the United States mail in a sealed envelope, postage prepaid, addressed to the owner at the address known to the public entity giving the notice, or as shown on the last equalized assessment roll, if not known. Separate notice of not less than 30 calendar days and documentation shall be provided to the tenant in accordance with this subdivision. Service by mail shall be deemed to be completed at the time of deposit in the United States mail. Proof of giving the notice may be made by a declaration signed under penalty of perjury by any employee of the public entity which shows service in conformity with this section.

(f) This section shall apply only to the following courts:

(1) In the County of Los Angeles, any court having jurisdiction over unlawful detainer cases involving real property situated in the City of Los Angeles or the City of Long Beach.

(2) In the County of San Diego, any court having jurisdiction over unlawful detainer cases involving real property situated in the City of San Diego.

(3) In the County of Alameda, any court with jurisdiction over unlawful detainer cases involving real property situated in the City of Oakland.

(4) In the County of Sacramento, any court with jurisdiction over unlawful detainer cases involving real property situated in the City of Sacramento.

(g)(1) The city attorney and city prosecutor of each participating jurisdiction shall provide to the Judicial Council the following information:

(A) The number of notices provided pursuant to paragraph (1) of subdivision (a).

(B) The number of cases filed by an owner, upon notice.

(C) The number of assignments executed by owners to the city attorney or city prosecutor.

(D) The number of three-day, 30-day, or 60-day notices issued by the city attorney or city prosecutor.

(E) The number of cases filed by the city attorney or city prosecutor.

(F) The number of times that an owner is joined as a defendant pursuant to this section.

(G) As to each case filed by an owner, the city attorney, or the city prosecutor, the following information:

(i) The number of judgments ordering an eviction or partial eviction, and specifying whether each was a default judgment, stipulated judgment, or judgment following trial.

(ii) The number of cases, listed by separate categories, in which the case was withdrawn or in which the tenant prevailed.

(iii) The number of other dispositions, and specifying the disposition.

(iv) The number of defendants represented by counsel.

(v) Whether the case was a trial by the court or a trial by a jury.

(vi) Whether an appeal was taken, and, if so, the result of the appeal.

(vii) The number of cases in which partial eviction was requested, and the number of cases in which the court ordered a partial eviction.

(H) As to each case in which a notice was issued, but no case was filed, the following information:

(i) The number of instances in which a tenant voluntarily vacated.

(ii) The number of instances in which a tenant vacated a unit prior to the providing of the notice.

(iii) The number of cases in which the notice provided pursuant to subdivision (a) was erroneously sent to the tenant. This shall include a list of the reasons, if known, for the erroneously sent notice, such as reliance on information on the suspected violator's name or address that was incorrect, a clerical error, or any other reason.

(iv) The number of other resolutions, and specifying the type of resolution.

(2)(A) Information compiled pursuant to this section shall be reported annually to the Judicial Council on or before January 30 of each year.

(B) The Judicial Council shall thereafter submit a brief report to the Senate and Assembly Committees on Judiciary on or before April 15, 2009, summarizing the information collected pursuant to this section and evaluating the merits of the pilot programs established by this section. The report for this section may be combined with the Judicial Council report submitted for the pilot program established by Section 11571.1 of the Health and Safety Code.

(h) This section shall remain in effect only until January 1, 2010, and as of that date is repealed, unless a later enacted statute, that is enacted before January 1, 2010, deletes or extends that date.

Code of Civil Procedure

Code of Civil Procedure § 525.

An injunction is a writ or order requiring a person to refrain from a particular act. It may be granted by the court in which the action is brought, or by a judge thereof; and when granted by a judge, it may be enforced as an order of the court.

Code of Civil Procedure § 527.6.

(a) A person who has suffered harassment as defined in subdivision (b) may seek a temporary restraining order and an injunction prohibiting harassment as provided in this section.

(b) For the purposes of this section, "harassment" is unlawful violence, a credible threat of violence, or a knowing and willful course of conduct directed at a specific person that seriously alarms, annoys, or harasses the person, and that serves no legitimate purpose. The course of conduct must be such as would cause a reasonable person to suffer substantial emotional distress, and must actually cause substantial emotional distress to the plaintiff. As used in this subdivision:

(1) "Unlawful violence" is any assault or battery, or stalking as prohibited in Section 646.9 of the Penal Code, but shall not include lawful acts of self-defense or defense of others.

(2) "Credible threat of violence" is a knowing and willful statement or course of conduct that would place a reasonable person in fear for his or her safety, or the safety of his or her immediate family, and that serves no legitimate purpose.

(3) "Course of conduct" is a pattern of conduct composed of a series of acts over a period of time, however short, evidencing a continuity of purpose, including following or stalking an individual, making harassing telephone calls to an individual, or sending harassing correspondence to an individual by any means, including, but not limited to, the use of public or private mails, interoffice mail, fax, or computer e-mail. Constitutionally protected activity is not included within the meaning of "course of conduct."

(c) Upon filing a petition for an injunction under this section, the plaintiff may obtain a temporary restraining order in accordance with Section 527, except to the extent this section provides a rule that is inconsistent. A temporary restraining order may be issued with or without notice upon an affidavit that, to the satisfaction of the court, shows reasonable proof of harassment of the plaintiff by the defendant, and that great or irreparable harm would result to the plaintiff. In the discretion of the court, and on a showing of good cause, a temporary restraining order or injunction, issued under this section may include other named family or household members who reside with the plaintiff. A temporary restraining order issued under this section shall remain in effect, at the court's discretion, for a period not to exceed 15 days, or, if the court extends the time for hearing under subdivision (d), not to exceed 22 days, unless otherwise modified or terminated by the court.

(d) Within 15 days, or, if good cause appears to the court, 22 days from the date the temporary restraining order is issued, a hearing shall be held on the petition for the injunction. The defendant may file a response that explains, excuses, justifies, or denies the alleged harassment or may file a cross-complaint under this section. At the hearing, the judge shall receive any testimony that is relevant, and may make an independent inquiry. If the judge finds by clear and convincing evidence that unlawful harassment exists, an injunction shall issue prohibiting the harassment. An injunction issued pursuant to this section shall have a duration of not more than three years. At any time within the three months before the expiration of the injunction, the plaintiff may apply for a renewal of the injunction by filing a new petition for an injunction under this section.

(e) This section does not preclude either party from representation by private counsel or from appearing on the party's own behalf.

(f) In a proceeding under this section if there are allegations or threats of domestic violence, a support person may accompany a party in court and, if the party is not represented by an attorney, may sit with the party at the table that is generally reserved for the party and the party's attorney. The support person is present to provide moral and emotional support for a person who alleges he or she is a victim of domestic violence. The support person is not present as a legal adviser and may not provide legal advice. The support person may assist the person who alleges he or she is a victim of domestic violence in feeling more confident that he or she will not be injured or threatened by the other party during the proceedings if the person who alleges he or she is a victim of domestic violence and the other party are required to be present in close proximity. This subdivision does not preclude the court from exercising its discretion to remove the support person from the courtroom if the court believes the support person is prompting, swaying, or influencing the party assisted by the support person.

(g) Upon the filing of a petition for an injunction under this section, the defendant shall be personally served with a copy of the petition, temporary restraining order, if any, and notice of hearing of the petition. Service shall be made at least five days before the hearing. The court may for good cause, on motion of the plaintiff or on its own motion, shorten the time for service on the defendant.

(h) The court shall order the plaintiff or the attorney for the plaintiff to deliver a copy of each temporary restraining order or injunction, or modification or termination thereof, granted under this section, by the close of the business day on which the order was granted, to the law enforcement agencies within the court's discretion as are requested by the plaintiff. Each appropriate law enforcement agency shall make available information as to the existence and current status of these orders to law enforcement officers responding to the scene of reported harassment. An order issued under this section shall, on request of the plaintiff, be served on the defendant, whether or not the defendant has been taken into custody, by any law enforcement officer who is present at the scene of reported harassment involving the parties to the proceeding. The plaintiff shall provide the officer with an endorsed copy of the order and a proof of service that the officer shall complete and send to the issuing court. Upon receiving information at the scene of an incident of harassment that a protective order has been issued under this section, or that a person who has been taken into custody is the subject of an order, if the protected person cannot produce a certified copy of the order, a law enforcement officer shall immediately attempt to verify the existence of the order. If the law enforcement officer determines that a protective order has been issued, but not served, the officer shall immediately notify the defendant of the terms of the order and shall at that time also enforce the order. Verbal notice of the terms of the order shall constitute service of the order and is sufficient notice for the purposes of this section and for the purposes of Section 273.6 and subdivision (g) of Section 12021 of the Penal Code.

(i) The prevailing party in any action brought under this section may be awarded court costs and attorney's fees, if any.

(j) Any willful disobedience of any temporary restraining order or injunction granted under this section is punishable pursuant to Section 273.6 of the Penal Code.

(k)(1) A person subject to a protective order issued under this section shall not own, possess, purchase, receive, or attempt to purchase or receive a firearm while the protective order is in effect.

(2) The court shall order a person subject to a protective order issued under this section to relinquish any firearms he or she owns or possesses pursuant to Section 527.9.

(3) Every person who owns, possesses, purchases or receives, or attempts to purchase or receive a firearm while the protective order is in effect is punishable pursuant to subdivision (g) of Section 12021 of the Penal Code.

(l) This section does not apply to any action or proceeding covered by Title 1.6C (commencing with Section 1788) of the Civil Code or by Division 10 (commencing with Section 6200) of the Family Code. This section does not preclude a plaintiff from using other existing civil remedies.

(m) The Judicial Council shall promulgate forms and instructions therefor, and rules for service of process, scheduling of hearings, and any other matters required by this section. The petition and response forms shall be simple and concise, and their use by parties in actions brought pursuant to this section shall be mandatory.

(n) A temporary restraining order or injunction relating to harassment or domestic violence issued by a court pursuant to this section shall be issued on forms adopted by the Judicial Council of California and that have been approved by the Department of Justice pursuant to subdivision (i) of Section 6380 of the Family Code. However, the fact that an order issued by a court pursuant to this section was not issued on forms adopted by the Judicial Council and approved by the Department of Justice shall not, in and of itself, make the order unenforceable.

(o) Information on any temporary restraining order or injunction relating to harassment or domestic violence issued by a court pursuant to this section shall be transmitted to the Department of Justice in accordance with subdivision (b) of Section 6380 of the Family Code.

(p) There is no filing fee for a petition that alleges that a person has inflicted or threatened violence against the petitioner, or stalked the petitioner, or acted or spoken in any other manner that has placed the petitioner in reasonable fear of violence, and that seeks a protective or restraining order or injunction restraining stalking or future violence or threats of violence, in any action brought pursuant to this section. No fee shall be paid for a subpoena filed in connection with a petition alleging these acts. No fee shall be paid for filing a response to a petition alleging these acts.

(q)(1) Subject to paragraph (4) of subdivision (b) of Section 6103.2 of the Government Code, there shall be no fee for the service of process of a protective order, restraining order, or injunction to be issued, if any of the following conditions apply:

(A) The protective order, restraining order, or injunction issued pursuant to this section is based upon stalking, as prohibited by Section 646.9 of the Penal Code.

(B) The protective order, restraining order, or injunction issued pursuant to this section is based upon a credible threat of violence.

(C) The protective order, restraining order, or injunction is issued pursuant to Section 6222 of the Family Code.

(2) The Judicial Council shall prepare and develop application forms for applicants who wish to avail themselves of the services described in this subdivision.

Code of Civil Procedure § 527.7.

(a) It shall be unlawful for any group, association, organization, society, or other assemblage of two or more persons to meet and to advocate, and to take substantial action in furtherance of, the commission of an unlawful act of violence or force directed to and likely to produce the imminent and unlawful infliction of serious bodily injury or death of another person within this state.

(b) Whenever it reasonably appears that any group, association, society, or other assemblage of two or more persons has met and taken substantial action in furtherance of the commission of an act of violence made unlawful by subdivision (a) and will engage in those acts in the future, any aggrieved individual may bring a civil action in the superior court to enjoin the advocacy of the commission of any act of violence made unlawful by subdivision (a) at any future meeting or meetings. Upon a proper showing by clear and convincing evidence, a permanent or preliminary injunction, restraining order, or writ of mandate shall be granted.

(c) Whenever it appears that an action brought under this section was groundless and brought in bad faith for the purpose of harassment, the trial court or any appellate court may award to the defendant attorney's fees and court costs incurred for the purpose of defending the action.

Code of Civil Procedure § 527.8.

(a) Any employer, whose employee has suffered unlawful violence or a credible threat of violence from any individual, that can reasonably be construed to be carried out or to have been carried out at the workplace, may seek a temporary restraining order and an injunction on behalf of the employee and, at the discretion of the court, any number of other employees at the workplace, and, if appropriate, other employees at other workplaces of the employer.

(b) For the purposes of this section:

(1) "Unlawful violence" is any assault or battery, or stalking as prohibited in Section 646.9 of the Penal Code, but shall not include lawful acts of self-defense or defense of others.

(2) "Credible threat of violence" is a knowing and willful statement or course of conduct that would place a reasonable person in fear for his or her safety, or the safety of his or her immediate family, and that serves no legitimate purpose.

(3) "Course of conduct" is a pattern of conduct composed of a series of acts over a period of time, however short, evidencing a continuity of purpose, including following or stalking an employee to or from the place of work; entering the workplace; following an employee during hours of employment; making telephone calls to an employee; or sending correspondence to an employee by any means, including, but not limited to, the use of the public or private mails, interoffice mail, fax, or computer e-mail.

(c) This section does not permit a court to issue a temporary restraining order or injunction prohibiting speech or other activities that are constitutionally protected, or otherwise protected by Section 527.3 or any other provision of law.

(d) For purposes of this section, the terms "employer" and "employee" mean persons defined in Section 350 of the Labor

Code. "Employer" also includes a federal agency, the state, a state agency, a city, county, or district, and a private, public, or quasi-public corporation, or any public agency thereof or therein. "Employee" also includes the members of boards of directors of private, public, and quasi-public corporations and elected and appointed public officers. For purposes of this section only, "employee" also includes a volunteer or independent contractor who performs services for the employer at the employer's worksite.

(e) Upon filing a petition for an injunction under this section, the plaintiff may obtain a temporary restraining order in accordance with subdivision (a) of Section 527, if the plaintiff also files an affidavit that, to the satisfaction of the court, shows reasonable proof that an employee has suffered unlawful violence or a credible threat of violence by the defendant, and that great or irreparable harm would result to an employee. In the discretion of the court, and on a showing of good cause, a temporary restraining order or injunction issued under this section may include other named family or household members who reside with the employee, or other persons employed at his or her workplace or workplaces. A temporary restraining order granted under this section shall remain in effect, at the court's discretion, for a period not to exceed 15 days, unless otherwise modified or terminated by the court.

(f) Within 15 days of the filing of the petition, a hearing shall be held on the petition for the injunction. The defendant may file a response that explains, excuses, justifies, or denies the alleged unlawful violence or credible threats of violence or may file a cross-complaint under this section. At the hearing, the judge shall receive any testimony that is relevant and may make an independent inquiry. Moreover, if the defendant is a current employee of the entity requesting the injunction, the judge shall receive evidence concerning the employer's decision to retain, terminate, or otherwise discipline the defendant. If the judge finds by clear and convincing evidence that the defendant engaged in unlawful violence or made a credible threat of violence, an injunction shall issue prohibiting further unlawful violence or threats of violence. An injunction issued pursuant to this section shall have a duration of not more than three years. At any time within the three months before the expiration of the injunction, the plaintiff may apply for a renewal of the injunction by filing a new petition for an injunction under this section.

(g) This section does not preclude either party from representation by private counsel or from appearing on his or her own behalf.

(h) Upon filing of a petition for an injunction under this section, the defendant shall be personally served with a copy of the petition, temporary restraining order, if any, and notice of hearing of the petition. Service shall be made at least five days before the hearing. The court may, for good cause, on motion of the plaintiff or on its own motion, shorten the time for service on the defendant.

(i)(1) The court shall order the plaintiff or the attorney for the plaintiff to deliver a copy of each temporary restraining order or injunction, or modification or termination thereof, granted under this section, by the close of the business day on which the order was granted, to the law enforcement agencies within the court's discretion as are requested by the plaintiff. Each appropriate law enforcement agency shall make available information as to the existence and current status of these orders to law enforcement officers responding to the scene of reported unlawful violence or a credible threat of violence.

(2) At the request of the plaintiff, an order issued under this section shall be served on the defendant, regardless of whether the defendant has been taken into custody, by any law enforcement officer who is present at the scene of reported unlawful violence or a credible threat of violence involving the parties to the proceedings. The plaintiff shall provide the officer with an endorsed copy of the order and proof of service that the officer shall complete and send to the issuing court.

(3) Upon receiving information at the scene of an incident of unlawful violence or a credible threat of violence that a protective order has been issued under this section, or that a person who has been taken into custody is the subject of an order, if the plaintiff or the protected person cannot produce an endorsed copy of the order, a law enforcement officer shall immediately attempt to verify the existence of the order.

(4) If the law enforcement officer determines that a protective order has been issued, but not served, the officer shall immediately notify the defendant of the terms of the order and obtain the defendant's address. The law enforcement officer shall at that time also enforce the order, but may not arrest or take the defendant into custody for acts in violation of the order that were committed prior to the verbal notice of the terms and conditions of the order. The law enforcement officer's verbal notice of the terms of the order shall constitute service of the order and constitutes sufficient notice for the purposes of this section and for the purposes of Section 273.6 and subdivision (g) of Section 12021 of the Penal Code. The plaintiff shall mail an endorsed copy of the order to the defendant's mailing address provided to the law enforcement officer within one business day of the reported incident of unlawful violence or a credible threat of violence at which a verbal notice of the terms of the order was provided by a law enforcement officer.

(j)(1) A person subject to a protective order issued under this section shall not own, possess, purchase, receive, or attempt to purchase or receive a firearm while the protective order is in effect.

(2) The court shall order a person subject to a protective order issued under this section to relinquish any firearms he or she owns or possesses pursuant to Section 527.9.

(3) Every person who owns, possesses, purchases or receives, or attempts to purchase or receive a firearm while the protective order is in effect is punishable pursuant to subdivision (g) of Section 12021 of the Penal Code.

(k) Any intentional disobedience of any temporary restraining order or injunction granted under this section is punishable pursuant to Section 273.6 of the Penal Code.

(l) Nothing in this section may be construed as expanding, diminishing, altering, or modifying the duty, if any, of an employer to provide a safe workplace for employees and other persons.

(m) The Judicial Council shall develop forms, instructions, and rules for scheduling of hearings and other procedures established pursuant to this section. The forms for the petition and response shall be simple and concise, and their use by parties in actions brought pursuant to this section shall be mandatory.

(n) A temporary restraining order or injunction relating to harassment or domestic violence issued by a court pursuant to this section shall be issued on forms adopted by the Judicial Council of California and that have been approved by the Department of Justice pursuant to subdivision (i) of Section 6380 of the Family Code. However, the fact that an order issued by a court pursuant to this section was not issued on forms adopted by the Judicial Council and approved by the Department of Justice shall not, in and of itself, make the order unenforceable.

(o) Information on any temporary restraining order or injunction relating to harassment or domestic violence issued by a court pursuant to this section shall be transmitted to the Department of Justice in accordance with subdivision (b) of Section 6380 of the

Family Code.

(p) There is no filing fee for a petition that alleges that a person has inflicted or threatened violence against an employee of the petitioner, or stalked the employee, or acted or spoken in any other manner that has placed the employee in reasonable fear of violence, and that seeks a protective or restraining order or injunction restraining stalking or future violence or threats of violence, in any action brought pursuant to this section. No fee shall be paid for a subpoena filed in connection with a petition alleging these acts. No fee shall be paid for filing a response to a petition alleging these acts.

(q)(1) Subject to paragraph (4) of subdivision (b) of Section 6103.2 of the Government Code, there shall be no fee for the service of process of a temporary restraining order or injunction to be issued pursuant to this section if either of the following conditions apply:

(A) The temporary restraining order or injunction issued pursuant to this section is based upon stalking, as prohibited by Section 646.9 of the Penal Code.

(B) The temporary restraining order or injunction issued pursuant to this section is based upon a credible threat of violence.

(2) The Judicial Council shall prepare and develop application forms for applicants who wish to avail themselves of the services described in this subdivision.

Code of Civil Procedure § 527.9.

(a) A person subject to a temporary restraining order or injunction issued pursuant to Section 527.6 or 527.8 of the Code of Civil Procedure, or subject to a restraining order issued pursuant to Section 136.2 of the Penal Code, or Section 15657.03 of the Welfare and Institutions Code, shall relinquish the firearm pursuant to this section.

(b) Upon the issuance of a protective order pursuant to subdivision (a), the court shall order the person to relinquish any firearm in that person's immediate possession or control, or subject to that person's immediate possession or control, within 24 hours of being served with the order, either by surrendering the firearm to the control of local law enforcement officials, or by selling the firearm to a licensed gun dealer, as specified in Section 12071 of the Penal Code. A person ordered to relinquish any firearm pursuant to this subdivision shall file with the court a receipt showing the firearm was surrendered to the local law enforcement agency or sold to a licensed gun dealer within 48 hours after receiving the order. In the event that it is necessary to continue the date of any hearing due to a request for a relinquishment order pursuant to this section, the court shall ensure that all applicable protective orders described in Section 6218 of the Family Code remain in effect or bifurcate the issues and grant the permanent restraining order pending the date of the hearing.

(c) A local law enforcement agency may charge the person subject to the order or injunction a fee for the storage of any firearm relinquished pursuant to this section. The fee shall not exceed the actual cost incurred by the local law enforcement agency for the storage of the firearm. For purposes of this subdivision, "actual cost" means expenses directly related to taking possession of a firearm, storing the firearm, and surrendering possession of the firearm to a licensed dealer as defined in Section 12071 of the Penal Code or to the person relinquishing the firearm.

(d) The restraining order requiring a person to relinquish a firearm pursuant to subdivision (b) shall state on its face that the respondent is prohibited from owning, possessing, purchasing, or receiving a firearm while the protective order is in effect and that the firearm shall be relinquished to the local law enforcement agency for that jurisdiction or sold to a licensed gun dealer, and that proof of surrender or sale shall be filed with the court within a specified period of receipt of the order. The order shall also state on its face the expiration date for relinquishment. Nothing in this section shall limit a respondent's right under existing law to petition the court at a later date for modification of the order.

(e) The restraining order requiring a person to relinquish a firearm pursuant to subdivision (b) shall prohibit the person from possessing or controlling any firearm for the duration of the order. At the expiration of the order, the local law enforcement agency shall return possession of any surrendered firearm to the respondent, within five days after the expiration of the relinquishment order, unless the local law enforcement agency determines that

(1) the firearm has been stolen,

(2) the respondent is prohibited from possessing a firearm because the respondent is in any prohibited class for the possession of firearms, as defined in Sections 12021 and 12021.1 of the Penal Code and Sections 8100 and 8103 of the Welfare and Institutions Code, or

(3) another successive restraining order is used against the respondent under this section. If the local law enforcement agency determines that the respondent is the legal owner of any firearm deposited with the local law enforcement agency and is prohibited from possessing any firearm, the respondent shall be entitled to sell or transfer the firearm to a licensed dealer as defined in Section 12071 of the Penal Code. If the firearm has been stolen, the firearm shall be restored to the lawful owner upon his or her identification of the firearm and proof of ownership.

(f) The court may, as part of the relinquishment order, grant an exemption from the relinquishment requirements of this section for a particular firearm if the respondent can show that a particular firearm is necessary as a condition of continued employment and that the current employer is unable to reassign the respondent to another position where a firearm is unnecessary. If an exemption is granted pursuant to this subdivision, the order shall provide that the firearm shall be in the physical possession of the respondent only during scheduled work hours and during travel to and from his or her place of employment. In any case involving a peace officer who as a condition of employment and whose personal safety depends on the ability to carry a firearm, a court may allow the peace officer to continue to carry a firearm, either on duty or off duty, if the court finds by a preponderance of the evidence that the officer does not pose a threat of harm. Prior to making this finding, the court shall require a mandatory psychological evaluation of the peace officer and may require the peace officer to enter into counseling or other remedial treatment program to deal with any propensity for domestic violence.

(g) During the period of the relinquishment order, a respondent is entitled to make one sale of all firearms that are in the possession of a local law enforcement agency pursuant to this section. A licensed gun dealer, who presents a local law enforcement agency with a bill of sale indicating that all firearms owned by the respondent that are in the possession of the local law enforcement agency have been sold by the respondent to the licensed gun dealer, shall be given possession of those firearms, at the location where a respondent's firearms are stored, within five days of presenting the local law enforcement agency with a bill of sale.

Commercial Code

Commercial Code § 14500.

This title extends to all corporations heretofore formed and existing for the prevention of cruelty to children or animals, but do not extend or apply to any association, society, or corporation that uses or specifies a name or style of the same, or substantially the same, as that of any previously existing society or corporation in this state organized for a like purpose.

Commercial Code § 14501.

Every society, incorporated and organized for the prevention of cruelty to animals, or for the prevention of cruelty to children, may, in each city, or city and county, or county, where the society exists, while actively engaged in enforcing the provisions of laws of this state, now or hereafter enacted, for the prevention of cruelty to animals, or children, or arresting, or prosecuting offenders thereunder or preventing cruelty to animals or children, be paid as compensation therefor, from the city or county, or city and county general fund, by the board of supervisors or other governing body thereof, a sum not exceeding five hundred dollars ($500) per calendar month, in the same manner as other claims against said city or county, or city and county, are paid.

Commercial Code § 14502.

(a)(1)(A)(i) On and after July 1, 1996, no entity, other than a humane society or society for the prevention of cruelty to animals, shall be eligible to apply for an appointment of any individual as a level 1 or level 2 humane officer, the duty of which shall be the enforcement of the laws for the prevention of cruelty to animals.

(ii) On and after July 1, 1996, only a person who meets the requirements of this section may be appointed as, or perform the duties of, a humane officer.

(iii) Any person appointed as a humane officer prior to July 1, 1996, may continue to serve as a humane officer until the expiration of the term of appointment only if the appointing agency maintains records pursuant to subparagraph (C) documenting that both the appointing agency and the humane officer meet the requirements of this section.

(B) Each humane society or society for the prevention of cruelty to animals that makes application to the court for the appointment of an individual to act as a level 1 or level 2 humane officer for the humane society or society for the prevention of cruelty to animals shall provide with the application documentation that demonstrates that the person has satisfactorily completed the training requirements set forth in subdivision (i).

(C) Each humane society or society for the prevention of cruelty to animals for which an individual is acting as a level 1 or level 2 humane officer shall maintain complete and accurate records documenting that the individual has successfully completed all requirements established in this section and shall make those records available, upon request, to the superior court, the Attorney General, or any entity duly authorized to review that information, including the State Humane Association of California. The records shall include the full name and address of each level 1 or level 2 humane officer.

(2) Any corporation incorporated for the purpose of the prevention of cruelty to animals that possesses insurance of at least one million dollars ($1,000,000) for liability for bodily injury or property damage may, six months after the date of its incorporation and by resolution of its board of directors or trustees duly entered on its minutes, appoint any number of persons, who shall be citizens of the State of California, as humane officers, provided that the individuals to be appointed have met the training guidelines set forth in subdivision (i).

(3) Each appointment of a humane officer shall be by separate resolution. The resolution shall state the full name and address of the appointing agency, the full name of the person so appointed, and the fact that he or she is a citizen of the State of California, and shall also designate the number of the badge to be allotted to the officer.

(b) The humane society or society for the prevention of cruelty to animals shall recommend any appointee to the judge of the superior court in and for the county or city and county in which the humane society is incorporated, and shall deliver to the judge a copy of the resolution appointing the person, duly certified to be correct by the president and secretary of the corporation and attested by its seal, together with the fingerprints of the appointee taken on standard 8X8-inch cards, proof of the society's proper incorporation in compliance with Part 9 (commencing with Section 10400) of Division 2, a copy of the society's liability for bodily injury or property damage insurance policy in the amount of at least one million dollars ($1,000,000), and documentation establishing that the appointee has satisfactorily completed the training requirements set forth in this section.

(c) The judge shall send a copy of the resolution, together with the fingerprints of the appointee, to the Department of Justice, which shall thereupon submit to the judge, in writing, a report of the record in its possession, if any, of the appointee. If the Department of Justice has no record of the appointee, it shall so report to the judge in writing.

(d) Upon receipt of the report the judge shall review the matter of the appointee's qualifications and fitness to act as a humane officer and, if he or she reaffirms the appointment, shall so state on a court order confirming the appointment. The appointee shall thereupon file a certified copy of the reviewed court order in the office of the county clerk of the county or city and county and shall, at the same time, take and subscribe the oath of office prescribed for constables or other peace officers.

(e) The county clerk shall thereupon immediately enter in a book to be kept in his or her office and designated "Record of Humane Officers" the name of the officer, the name of the agency appointing him or her, the number of his or her badge, the name of the judge appointing him or her, and the date of the filing. At the time of the filing the county clerk shall collect from the officer a fee of five dollars ($5), which shall be in full for all services to be performed by the county clerk under this section.

(f) All appointments of humane officers shall automatically expire if the society disbands or legally dissolves. In addition, all appointments of humane officers shall automatically expire within three years from the date on which the certified copy of the court order was filed with the county clerk. Officers whose appointments are about to expire may only be reappointed after satisfactorily completing the continuing education and training set forth in this section.

(g)(1) The corporation appointing an officer may revoke an appointment at any time by filing in the office of the county clerk in which the appointment of the officer is recorded a copy of the revocation in writing under the letterhead of the corporation and duly certified by its executive officer. Upon the filing the county clerk shall enter the fact of the revocation and the date of the filing thereof opposite the name of the officer in the record of humane officers.

(2) Notwithstanding paragraph (1), a revocation hearing may be initiated by petition from any duly authorized sheriff or local police agency or the State Humane Association of California. The petition shall show cause why an appointment should be revoked and shall be made to the superior court in the jurisdiction of the appointment.

(h) The corporation or local humane society appointing the humane officer shall pay the training expenses of the humane officer attending the training required pursuant to this section.

(i)(1)(A) A level 1 humane officer is not a peace officer, but may exercise the powers of a peace officer at all places within the state in order to prevent the perpetration of any act of cruelty upon any animal and to that end may summon to his or her aid any bystander. A level 1 humane officer may use reasonable force necessary to prevent the perpetration of any act of cruelty upon any animal.

(B) A level 1 humane officer may make arrests for the violation of any penal law of this state relating to or affecting animals in the same manner as any peace officer and may also serve search warrants.

(C) A level 1 humane officer is authorized to carry firearms while exercising the duties of a humane officer, upon satisfactory completion of the training specified in subparagraph (D) and the basic training for a level 1 reserve officer by the Commission on Peace Officer Standards and Training pursuant to Section 13510.1 of the Penal Code.

(D) A level 1 humane officer shall, prior to appointment, provide evidence satisfactory to the appointing agency that he or she has successfully completed courses of training in the following subjects:

(i) At least 20 hours of a course of training in animal care sponsored or provided by an accredited postsecondary institution or any other provider approved by the California Veterinary Medical Association, the focus of which shall be the identification of disease, injury, and neglect in domestic animals and livestock.

(ii) At least 40 hours of a course of training in the state humane laws relating to the powers and duties of a humane officer, sponsored or provided by an accredited postsecondary institution, law enforcement agency, or the State Humane Association of California.

(E) A person may not be appointed as a level 1 humane officer until he or she has satisfied the requirements in Sections 1029, 1030, and 1031 of the Government Code. A humane society or society for the prevention of cruelty to animals shall complete a background investigation, using standards defined by the Commission on Peace Officer Standards and Training as guidelines for all level 1 humane officer appointments.

(F) In order to be eligible for reappointment, a level 1 humane officer shall complete ongoing weapons training and range qualifications at least every six months pursuant to subdivision (s) of Section 830.3 of the Penal Code and shall, every three years, complete 40 hours of continuing education and training relating to the powers and duties of a humane officer, which education and training shall be provided by an accredited postsecondary institution, law enforcement agency, or the State Humane Association of California.

(G)(i) Notwithstanding any other provision of this section, a level 1 humane officer may carry firearms only if authorized by, and only under the terms and conditions specified by, his or her appointing agency.

(ii) Notwithstanding any other provision of this section, a level 1 humane officer shall not be authorized to carry firearms unless and until his or her appointing agency has adopted a policy on the use of deadly force by its officers and the officer has been instructed in that policy.

(2)(A) A level 2 humane officer is not a peace officer, but may exercise the powers of a peace officer at all places within the state in order to prevent the perpetration of any act of cruelty upon any animal and to that end may summon to his or her aid any bystander. A level 2 humane officer may use reasonable force necessary to prevent the perpetration of any act of cruelty upon any animal.

(B) A level 2 humane officer may make arrests for the violation of any penal law of this state relating to or affecting animals in the same manner as any peace officer and may serve search warrants during the course and within the scope of employment, upon the successful completion of a course relating to the exercise of the police powers specified in Section 832 of the Penal Code, except the power to carry and use firearms.

(C) A level 2 humane officer is not authorized to carry firearms. (D) A level 2 humane officer shall, prior to appointment, provide evidence satisfactory to the appointing agency that he or she has successfully completed courses of training in the following subjects:

(i) At least 20 hours of a course of training in animal care sponsored or provided by an accredited postsecondary institution or any other provider approved by the California Veterinary Medical Association, the focus of which is the identification of disease, injury, and neglect in domestic animals and livestock.

(ii) At least 40 hours of a course of training in the state humane laws relating to the powers and duties of a humane officer, sponsored or provided by an accredited postsecondary institution, law enforcement agency, or the State Humane Association of California.

(E) In order to be eligible for reappointment, a level 2 humane officer shall, every three years, complete 40 hours of continuing education and training relating to the powers and duties of a humane officer, which education and training shall be provided by an accredited postsecondary institution, law enforcement agency, or the State Humane Association of California.

(j) Every humane officer shall, when making an arrest, exhibit and expose a suitable badge to be adopted by the corporation under this title of which he or she is a member which shall bear its name and a number. Uniforms worn by humane officers shall prominently display the name of the appointing agency. Humane officer uniforms shall not display the words "state" or "California," unless part of the appointing agency's incorporated name.

(k) Any person resisting a humane officer in the performance of his or her duty as provided in this section, is guilty of a misdemeanor. Any person who has not been appointed and qualified as a humane officer as provided in this section, or whose appointment has been revoked as provided in this section, or whose appointment, having expired, has not been renewed as provided in this section, who shall represent himself or herself to be or shall attempt to act as an officer shall be guilty of a misdemeanor.

(l) No humane officer shall serve a search warrant without providing prior notice to local law enforcement agencies operating within that jurisdiction.

(m) Any humane society, society for the prevention of cruelty to animals, or person, who knowingly provides a court with false or forged documentation for the appointment of a humane officer, is guilty of a misdemeanor and shall be punished by a fine of up to ten thousand dollars ($10,000).

(n) A humane society or a society for the prevention of cruelty to animals shall notify the sheriff of the county in which the society is incorporated, prior to appointing a humane officer, of the society' s intent to enforce laws for the prevention of cruelty to animals. Humane societies or societies for the prevention of cruelty to animals incorporated and enforcing animal cruelty laws prior to January 1, 1996, that intend to continue to enforce those laws, shall notify the sheriff of the county in which the society is incorporated by March 1, 1996.

(o) Except as otherwise provided by this section, a humane officer shall serve only in the county in which he or she is appointed. A humane officer may serve temporarily in a county other than that in which he or she is appointed if the humane officer gives notice requesting consent to the sheriff of the county in which he or she intends to serve, and acquires consent from the sheriff of the county in which he or she intends to serve, or from a person authorized by the sheriff to give that consent. A sheriff shall promptly respond to any request by a humane officer to serve in his or her jurisdiction and any request shall not be unreasonably denied.

Commercial Code § 14503.

The governing body of a local agency, by ordinance, may authorize employees of public pounds, societies for the prevention of cruelty to animals, and humane societies, who have qualified as humane officers pursuant to Section 14502, and which societies or pounds have contracted with such local agency to provide animal care or protection services, to issue notices to appear in court pursuant to Chapter 5c (commencing with Section 853.5) of Title 3 of Part 2 of the Penal Code for violations of state or local animal control laws. Those employees shall not be authorized to take any person into custody even though the person to whom the notice is delivered does not give his or her written promise to appear in court. The authority of these employees is to be limited to the jurisdiction of the local agency authorizing the employees.

Education Code

Education Code § 35181.

The governing board of each school district may convene hearings, make findings, and adopt and issue policy statements setting forth the responsibilities of the pupils of that school district regarding academic performance, attendance, in-school behavior, and any other aspects of school life which the school district governing board may deem relevant to this task.

Education Code § 35183.

(a) The Legislature finds and declares each of the following:

(1) The children of this state have the right to an effective public school education. Both students and staff of the primary, elementary, junior and senior high school campuses have the constitutional right to be safe and secure in their persons at school. However, children in many of our public schools are forced to focus on the threat of violence and the messages of violence contained in many aspects of our society, particularly reflected in gang regalia that disrupts the learning environment.

(2) "Gang-related apparel" is hazardous to the health and safety of the school environment.

(3) Instructing teachers and administrators on the subtleties of identifying constantly changing gang regalia and gang affiliation takes an increasing amount of time away from educating our children.

(4) Weapons, including firearms and knives, have become common place upon even our elementary school campuses. Students often conceal weapons by wearing clothing, such as jumpsuits and overcoats, and by carrying large bags.

(5) The adoption of a schoolwide uniform policy is a reasonable way to provide some protection for students. A required uniform may protect students from being associated with any particular gang. Moreover, by requiring schoolwide uniforms teachers and administrators may not need to occupy as much of their time learning the subtleties of gang regalia.

(6) To control the environment in public schools to facilitate and maintain an effective learning environment and to keep the focus of the classroom on learning and not personal safety, schools need the authorization to implement uniform clothing requirements for our public school children.

(7) Many educators believe that school dress significantly influences pupil behavior. This influence is evident on school dressup days and color days. Schools that have adopted school uniforms experience a "coming together feeling," greater school pride, and better behavior in and out of the classroom.

(b) The governing board of any school district may adopt or rescind a reasonable dress code policy that requires pupils to wear a schoolwide uniform or prohibits pupils from wearing "gang-related apparel" if the governing board of the school district approves a plan that may be initiated by an individual school's principal, staff, and parents and determines that the policy is necessary for the health and safety of the school environment. Individual schools may include the reasonable dress code policy as part of its school safety plan, pursuant to Section 32281.

(c) Adoption and enforcement of a reasonable dress code policy pursuant to subdivision (b) is not a violation of Section 48950. For purposes of this section, Section 48950 shall apply to elementary, high school, and unified school districts. If a schoolwide uniform is required, the specific uniform selected shall be determined by the principal, staff, and parents of the individual school.

(d) A dress code policy that requires pupils to wear a schoolwide uniform shall not be implemented with less than six months' notice to parents and the availability of resources to assist economically disadvantaged pupils.

(e) The governing board shall provide a method whereby parents may choose not to have their children comply with an adopted school uniform policy.

(f) If a governing board chooses to adopt a policy pursuant to this section, the policy shall include a provision that no pupil shall be penalized academically or otherwise discriminated against nor denied attendance to school if the pupil's parents chose not to have the pupil comply with the school uniform policy. The governing board shall continue to have responsibility for the appropriate education of those pupils.

(g) A policy adopted pursuant to this section shall not preclude pupils that participate in a nationally recognized youth organization from wearing organization uniforms on days that the organization has a scheduled meeting.

Education Code § 38000.

(a) The governing board of any school district may establish a security department under the supervision of a chief of security or a police department under the supervision of a chief of police, as designated by, and under the direction of, the superintendent of the school district. In accordance with Chapter 5 (commencing with Section 45100) of Part 25, the governing board may employ personnel to ensure the safety of school district personnel and pupils and the security of the real and personal property of the school district. In addition, a school district may assign a school police reserve officer who is deputized pursuant to Section 35021.5 to a schoolsite to supplement the duties of school police personnel pursuant to this section. It is the intention of the Legislature in enacting this section that a school district police or security department is supplementary to city and county law enforcement agencies and is not vested with general police powers.

(b) The governing board of a school district that establishes a security department or a police department shall set minimum qualifications of employment for the chief of security or chief of police, respectively, including, but not limited to, prior employment as a peace officer or completion of any peace officer training course approved by the Commission on Peace Officer Standards and Training. A chief of security or chief of police shall comply with the prior employment or training requirement set forth in this subdivision as of January 1, 1993, or a date one year subsequent to the initial employment of the chief of security or chief of police by the school district, whichever occurs later. This subdivision shall not be construed to require the employment by a school district of any additional personnel.

Education Code § 38001.

Persons employed and compensated as members of a police department of a school district, when appointed and duly sworn, are peace officers, for the purposes of carrying out their duties of employment pursuant to Section 830.32 of the Penal Code.

Education Code § 38001.5.

(a) It is the intent of the Legislature to ensure the safety of pupils, staff, and the public on or near California's public schools, by providing school security officers with training that will enable them to deal with the increasingly diverse and dangerous situations they encounter.

(b) After July 1, 2000, every school security officer employed by a school district who works more than 20 hours a week as a school security officer shall complete a course of training developed no later than July 1, 1999, by the Bureau of Security and Investigative Services of the Department of Consumer Affairs in consultation with the Commission on Peace Officer Standards and Training pursuant to Section 7583.31 of the Business and Professions Code. If any school security officer subject to the requirements of this subdivision is required to carry a firearm while performing his or her duties, that school security officer shall additionally satisfy the training requirements of Section 832 of the Penal Code.

(c) For purposes of this chapter, "school security officer" means any person primarily employed or assigned pursuant to subdivision (b) to provide security services as a watchperson, security guard, or patrolperson on or about premises owned or operated by a school district to protect persons or property or to prevent the theft or unlawful taking of district property of any kind or to report any unlawful activity to the district and local law enforcement agencies.

(d) No school security officer shall be employed or shall continue to be employed by the district after July 1, 2000, until both of the following conditions have been met:

(1)(A) The applicant or employee has submitted to the district two copies of his or her fingerprints on forms or electronically, as prescribed by the Department of Justice. The district shall submit the fingerprints to the Department of Justice, which shall submit one copy of the fingerprints to the United States Federal Bureau of Investigation.

(B) An applicant or contracted employee who holds a permanent registration with the Bureau of Security and Investigative Services of the Department of Consumer Affairs as a security guard need only submit one copy of his or her fingerprints, which copy shall be submitted to the United States Federal Bureau of Investigation.

(C) An applicant or contracted employee who is registered by the Bureau of Security and Investigative Services of the Department of Consumer Affairs, and who holds a firearms qualification card as specified in Section 7583.22 of the Business and Professions Code, is exempt from the requirements of this subdivision.

(2) The applicant or employee has been determined not to be a person prohibited from employment by a school district pursuant to Sections 44237 and 45122.1, or by the Department of Justice from possessing a firearm if the applicant is required to carry a firearm. The Department of Justice may participate in the National Instant Criminal Background Check System (NICS) in lieu of submitting fingerprints to the United States Federal Bureau of Investigation in order to meet the requirements of this subdivision relating to firearms.

(e) Every school security officer employed by a school district prior to July 1, 2000, who works more than 20 hours a week as a school security officer shall meet the requirements of subdivision (b) by July 1, 2002, unless he or she has completed an equivalent course of instruction pursuant to Section 832.2 of the Penal Code.

Education Code § 39672.

Every school peace officer first employed by a K-12 public school district before July 1, 1999, shall, in order to retain his or her employment, fulfill both of the following conditions:

(a) The employee shall submit to the district one copy of his or her fingerprints on forms prescribed by the Department of Justice. The Department of Justice shall forward this copy to the United States Federal Bureau of Investigation.

(b) The employee shall be determined to be a person who is not prohibited from employment by a school district pursuant to Sections 44237 and 45122.1, and, if the employee is required to carry a firearm, shall be determined by the Department of Justice to be a person who is not prohibited from possessing a firearm. The Department of Justice may participate in the National Instant Criminal Background Check System (NICS) in lieu of submitting fingerprints to the United States Federal Bureau of Investigation in order to meet the requirements of this section relating to firearms.

Education Code § 44276.1.

(a) The Legislature finds and declares all of the following:

(1) The educational mission of schools may be thwarted when school campuses are not safe, secure, and peaceful.

(2) Effective school management can improve school safety and decrease violence and criminal behavior.

(3) In many school districts and neighborhoods, violence and criminal behavior are increasingly frequent.

(4) Teachers and other educators who are well prepared in principles of school safety may be able to mitigate, to some degree, the detrimental behavior of pupils and others on school campuses.

(b) Therefore, it is the intent of the Legislature that a comprehensive school safety plan be established pursuant to Section 35294.1 in order to achieve safe, secure, and peaceful school campuses. It is the further intent of the Legislature that the Commission on Teacher Credentialing adopt standards that address the principles of school safety in the preparation of future classroom teachers, school administrators, school counselors, and other pupil personnel service providers as a condition for licensing these prospective practitioners.

(c) Standards adopted by the commission pursuant to paragraph (3) of subdivision (b) of Section 44259, and pursuant to Sections 44266, 44270, 44277, and 44372, shall include the effective preparation of prospective classroom teachers, school administrators, school counselors, and other pupil personnel service providers in principles of school safety. In developing these standards, the commission shall consider, but is not limited to considering, the following principles of school safety:

(1) School management skills that emphasize crisis intervention and conflict resolution.

(2) Developing and maintaining a positive and safe school climate, including methods to prevent the possession of weapons on school campuses.

(3) Developing school safety plans.

(4) Developing ways to identify and defuse situations that may lead to conflict or violence.

(d) In developing standards relating to school safety, the commission shall consider the findings and recommendations of an advisory panel of experts on school violence.

(e) The commission shall allow an institution of postsecondary education to meet the standards developed by the commission relating to school safety by incorporating the principles of school safety in the program required by paragraph (3) of subdivision (b) of Section 44259.

(f) Implementation of subdivision (b) of this section as it applies to paragraph (3) of subdivision (b) of Section 44259 shall occur in conjunction with the review of requirements for earning and renewing multiple and single subject teaching credentials, as required by Section 44259.3.

(g) Instruction in principles of school safety shall be required of all candidates for credentials specified in Sections 44259, 44266, and 44270.

(h) A credential that was issued prior to January 1, 1994, shall remain in force as long as it is valid under the laws and regulations that were in effect on the date it was issued. The commission may not, by regulation, invalidate an otherwise valid credential, unless it issues to the holder of the credential, in substitution, a new credential authorized by another provision in this chapter that is no less restrictive than the credential for which it was substituted with respect to the kind of service authorized and the grades, classes, or types of schools in which it authorizes service.

(i) Notwithstanding this section, persons who were performing teaching, administrative, counseling, or other pupil personnel services as of January 1, 1994, pursuant to the language of this chapter that was in effect prior to that date, may continue to perform those services without complying with any requirements added by the amendments adding this section.

(j) The commission shall grant credentials based on the requirements for those credentials as of December 31, 1993, to candidates who, prior to the effective date of the commission's adoption of standards pursuant to this section, were in the process of meeting those credential requirements.

Education Code § 44276.6.

It is the intent of the Legislature that the Commission on Teacher Credentialing not duplicate the efforts of the State Department of Education, Office of Criminal Justice Planning, Department of the Youth Authority, and the School/Law Enforcement Partnership in undertaking leadership activities directed toward establishing appropriate standards of preparation for teachers and other certificated personnel concerning violent behavior by pupils. The commission shall consult with these agencies and consider policies, programs, guidelines, other resource and training materials, and experts, which these agencies have identified, funded, or developed to reduce violent behavior by pupils.

Education Code § 48900.

A pupil shall not be suspended from school or recommended for expulsion, unless the superintendent or the principal of the school in which the pupil is enrolled determines that the pupil has committed an act as defined pursuant to any of subdivisions (a) to (r), inclusive:

(a)(1) Caused, attempted to cause, or threatened to cause physical injury to another person.

(2) Willfully used force or violence upon the person of another, except in self-defense.

(b) Possessed, sold, or otherwise furnished a firearm, knife, explosive, or other dangerous object, unless, in the case of possession of an object of this type, the pupil had obtained written permission to possess the item from a certificated school employee, which is concurred in by the principal or the designee of the principal.

(c) Unlawfully possessed, used, sold, or otherwise furnished, or been under the influence of, a controlled substance listed in Chapter 2 (commencing with Section 11053) of Division 10 of the Health and Safety Code, an alcoholic beverage, or an intoxicant of any kind.

(d) Unlawfully offered, arranged, or negotiated to sell a controlled substance listed in Chapter 2 (commencing with Section 11053) of Division 10 of the Health and Safety Code, an alcoholic beverage, or an intoxicant of any kind, and either sold, delivered, or otherwise furnished to a person another liquid, substance, or material and represented the liquid, substance, or material as a controlled substance, alcoholic beverage, or intoxicant.

(e) Committed or attempted to commit robbery or extortion.

(f) Caused or attempted to cause damage to school property or private property.

(g) Stolen or attempted to steal school property or private property.

(h) Possessed or used tobacco, or products containing tobacco or nicotine products, including, but not limited to, cigarettes, cigars, miniature cigars, clove cigarettes, smokeless tobacco, snuff, chew packets, and betel. However, this section does not prohibit use or possession by a pupil of his or her own prescription products.

(i) Committed an obscene act or engaged in habitual profanity or vulgarity.

(j) Unlawfully possessed or unlawfully offered, arranged, or negotiated to sell drug paraphernalia, as defined in Section 11014.5 of the Health and Safety Code.

(k) Disrupted school activities or otherwise willfully defied the valid authority of supervisors, teachers, administrators, school officials, or other school personnel engaged in the performance of their duties.

(l) Knowingly received stolen school property or private property.

(m) Possessed an imitation firearm. As used in this section, "imitation firearm" means a replica of a firearm that is so substantially similar in physical properties to an existing firearm as to lead a reasonable person to conclude that the replica is a firearm.

(n) Committed or attempted to commit a sexual assault as defined in Section 261, 266c, 286, 288, 288a, or 289 of the Penal Code or committed a sexual battery as defined in Section 243.4 of the Penal Code.

(o) Harassed, threatened, or intimidated a pupil who is a complaining witness or a witness in a school disciplinary proceeding for the purpose of either preventing that pupil from being a witness or retaliating against that pupil for being a witness, or both.

(p) Unlawfully offered, arranged to sell, negotiated to sell, or sold the prescription drug Soma.

(q) Engaged in, or attempted to engage in, hazing. For purposes of this subdivision, "hazing" means a method of initiation or preinitiation into a pupil organization or body, whether or not the organization or body is officially recognized by an educational institution, which is likely to cause serious bodily injury or personal degradation or disgrace resulting in physical or mental harm to a former, current, or prospective pupil. For purposes of this subdivision, "hazing" does not include athletic events or school-sanctioned events.

(r) Engaged in an act of bullying, including, but not limited to, bullying committed by means of an electronic act, as defined in subdivisions (f) and (g) of Section 32261, directed specifically toward a pupil or school personnel.

(s) A pupil shall not be suspended or expelled for any of the acts enumerated in this section, unless that act is related to school activity or school attendance occurring within a school under the jurisdiction of the superintendent of the school district or principal or occurring within any other school district. A pupil may be suspended or expelled for acts that are enumerated in this section and related to school activity or attendance that occur at any time, including, but not limited to, any of the following:

(1) While on school grounds.

(2) While going to or coming from school.

(3) During the lunch period whether on or off the campus.

(4) During, or while going to or coming from, a school sponsored activity.

(t) A pupil who aids or abets, as defined in Section 31 of the Penal Code, the infliction or attempted infliction of physical injury to another person may be subject to suspension, but not expulsion, pursuant to this section, except that a pupil who has been adjudged by a juvenile court to have committed, as an aider and abettor, a crime of physical violence in which the victim suffered great bodily injury or serious bodily injury shall be subject to discipline pursuant to subdivision (a).

(u) As used in this section, "school property" includes, but is not limited to, electronic files and databases.

(v) A superintendent of the school district or principal may use his or her discretion to provide alternatives to suspension or expulsion, including, but not limited to, counseling and an anger management program, for a pupil subject to discipline under this section.

(w) It is the intent of the Legislature that alternatives to suspension or expulsion be imposed against a pupil who is truant, tardy, or otherwise absent from school activities.

Education Code § 48900.5.

Suspension shall be imposed only when other means of correction fail to bring about proper conduct. However, a pupil, including an individual with exceptional needs, as defined in Section 56026, may be suspended for any of the reasons enumerated in Section 48900 upon a first offense, if the principal or superintendent of schools determines that the pupil violated subdivision (a), (b), (c), (d), or (e) of Section 48900 or that the pupil's presence causes a danger to persons or property or threatens to disrupt the instructional process.

Education Code § 48902.

(a) The principal of a school or the principal's designee shall, prior to the suspension or expulsion of any pupil, notify the appropriate law enforcement authorities of the county or city in which the school is situated, of any acts of the pupil that may violate Section 245 of the Penal Code.

(b) The principal of a school or the principal's designee shall, within one schoolday after suspension or expulsion of any pupil, notify, by telephone or any other appropriate method chosen by the school, the appropriate law enforcement authority of the county or the school district in which the school is situated of any acts of the pupils that may violate subdivision (c) or (d) of Section 48900.

Education Code § 48915.

(a) Except as provided in subdivisions (c) and (e), the principal or the superintendent of schools shall recommend the expulsion of a pupil for any of the following acts committed at school or at a school activity off school grounds, unless the principal or superintendent finds that expulsion is inappropriate, due to the particular circumstance:

(1) Causing serious physical injury to another person, except in self-defense.

(2) Possession of any knife or other dangerous object of no reasonable use to the pupil.

(3) Unlawful possession of any controlled substance listed in Chapter 2 (commencing with Section 11053) of Division 10 of the Health and Safety Code, except for the first offense for the possession of not more than one avoirdupois ounce of marijuana, other than concentrated cannabis.

(4) Robbery or extortion.

(5) Assault or battery, as defined in Sections 240 and 242 of the Penal Code, upon any school employee.

(b) Upon recommendation by the principal, superintendent of schools, or by a hearing officer or administrative panel appointed pursuant to subdivision (d) of Section 48918, the governing board may order a pupil expelled upon finding that the pupil committed an act listed in subdivision (a) or in subdivision (a), (b), (c), (d), or (e) of Section 48900. A decision to expel shall be based on a finding of one or both of the following:

(1) Other means of correction are not feasible or have repeatedly failed to bring about proper conduct.

(2) Due to the nature of the act, the presence of the pupil causes a continuing danger to the physical safety of the pupil or others.

(c) The principal or superintendent of schools shall immediately suspend, pursuant to Section 48911, and shall recommend expulsion of a pupil that he or she determines has committed any of the following acts at school or at a school activity off school grounds:

(1) Possessing, selling, or otherwise furnishing a firearm. This subdivision does not apply to an act of possessing a firearm if the pupil had obtained prior written permission to possess the firearm from a certificated school employee, which is concurred in by the principal or the designee of the principal. This subdivision applies to an act of possessing a firearm only if the possession is verified by an employee of a school district.

(2) Brandishing a knife at another person.

(3) Unlawfully selling a controlled substance listed in Chapter 2 (commencing with Section 11053) of Division 10 of the Health and Safety Code.

(4) Committing or attempting to commit a sexual assault as defined in subdivision (n) of Section 48900 or committing a sexual battery as defined in subdivision (n) of Section 48900.

(5) Possession of an explosive.

(d) The governing board shall order a pupil expelled upon finding that the pupil committed an act listed in subdivision (c), and shall refer that pupil to a program of study that meets all of the following conditions:

(1) Is appropriately prepared to accommodate pupils who exhibit discipline problems.

(2) Is not provided at a comprehensive middle, junior, or senior high school, or at any elementary school.

(3) Is not housed at the schoolsite attended by the pupil at the time of suspension.

(e) Upon recommendation by the principal, superintendent of schools, or by a hearing officer or administrative panel appointed pursuant to subdivision (d) of Section 48918, the governing board may order a pupil expelled upon finding that the pupil, at school or at a school activity off of school grounds violated subdivision (f), (g), (h), (i), (j), (k), (l), or (m) of Section 48900, or Section 48900.2, 48900.3, or 48900.4, and either of the following:

(1) That other means of correction are not feasible or have repeatedly failed to bring about proper conduct.

(2) That due to the nature of the violation, the presence of the pupil causes a continuing danger to the physical safety of the pupil or others.

(f) The governing board shall refer a pupil who has been expelled pursuant to subdivision (b) or (e) to a program of study which meets all of the conditions specified in subdivision (d). Notwithstanding this subdivision, with respect to a pupil expelled pursuant to subdivision (e), if the county superintendent of schools certifies that an alternative program of study is not available at a site away from a comprehensive middle, junior, or senior high school, or an elementary school, and that the only option for placement is at another comprehensive middle, junior, or senior high school, or another elementary school, the pupil may be referred to a program of study that is provided at a comprehensive middle, junior, or senior high school, or at an elementary school.

(g) As used in this section, "knife" means any dirk, dagger, or other weapon with a fixed, sharpened blade fitted primarily for stabbing, a weapon with a blade fitted primarily for stabbing, a weapon with a blade longer than 31/2 inches, a folding knife with a blade that locks into place, or a razor with an unguarded blade.

(h) As used in this section, the term "explosive" means "destructive device" as described in Section 921 of Title 18 of the United States Code.

Education Code § 48915.5.

(a) An individual with exceptional needs, as defined in Section 56026, may be suspended or expelled from school in accordance with Section 1415(k) of Title 20 of the United States Code, the discipline provisions contained in Sections 300.530 to 300.537, inclusive, of Title 34 of the Code of Federal Regulations, and other provisions of this part that do not conflict with federal law and regulations.

(b) A free appropriate public education for individuals with exceptional needs suspended or expelled from school shall be in accordance with Section 1412(a)(1) of Title 20 of the United States Code and Section 300.530(d) of Title 34 of the Code of Federal Regulations.

(c) If an individual with exceptional needs is excluded from schoolbus transportation, the pupil is entitled to be provided with an alternative form of transportation at no cost to the pupil or parent or guardian provided that transportation is specified in the pupil's individualized education program.

Education Code § 48915.7.

It is the intent of the Legislature that where community school opportunities exist, the principal shall recommend for expulsion, and the governing board shall expel, any pupil who is found to be in possession of a firearm at school or at a school activity off school grounds and that the governing board shall request the county board of education to enroll the pupil in a community school.

Education Code § 48925.

As used in this article:

(a) "Day" means a calendar day unless otherwise specifically provided.

(b) "Expulsion" means removal of a pupil from

(1) the immediate supervision and control, or

(2) the general supervision, of school personnel, as those terms are used in Section 46300.

(c) "Schoolday" means a day upon which the schools of the district are in session or weekdays during the summer recess.

(d) "Suspension" means removal of a pupil from ongoing instruction for adjustment purposes. However, "suspension" does not mean any of the following:

(1) Reassignment to another education program or class at the same school where the pupil will receive continuing instruction for the length of day prescribed by the governing board for pupils of the same grade level.

(2) Referral to a certificated employee designated by the principal to advise pupils.

(3) Removal from the class, but without reassignment to another class or program, for the remainder of the class period without sending the pupil to the principal or the principal's designee as provided in Section 48910. Removal from a particular class shall not occur more than once every five schooldays.

(e) "Pupil" includes a pupil's parent or guardian or legal counsel.

Education Code § 49000.

The Legislature finds and declares that the protection against corporal punishment, which extends to other citizens in other walks of life, should include children while they are under the control of the public schools. Children of school age are at the most vulnerable and impressionable period of their lives and it is wholly reasonable that the safeguards to the integrity and sanctity of their bodies should be, at this tender age, at least equal to that afforded to other citizens.

Education Code § 49001.

(a) For the purposes of this section "corporal punishment" means the willful infliction of, or willfully causing the infliction of, physical pain on a pupil. An amount of force that is reasonable and necessary for a person employed by or engaged in a public school to quell a disturbance threatening physical injury to persons or damage to property, for purposes of self-defense, or to obtain possession of weapons or other dangerous objects within the control of the pupil, is not and shall not be construed to be corporal punishment within the meaning and intent of this section. Physical pain or discomfort caused by athletic competition or other such recreational activity, voluntarily engaged in by the pupil, is not and shall not be construed to be corporal punishment within the meaning and intent of this section.

(b) No person employed by or engaged in a public school shall inflict, or cause to be inflicted corporal punishment upon a pupil. Every resolution, bylaw, rule, ordinance, or other act or authority permitting or authorizing the infliction of corporal punishment upon a pupil attending a public school is void and unenforceable.

Education Code § 49330.

As used in this article "injurious object" shall mean those objects specified in Sections 653k, 12001, 12020, 12220, 12401, and 12402 of the Penal Code, and objects capable of inflicting substantial bodily damage, not necessary for the academic purpose of the pupil. As used in this section, "academic purpose" means any school sponsored activity or class of instruction scheduled during the schoolday. "Injurious object" does not include any personal possessions or items of apparel which a schoolage child reasonably may be expected either to have in his or her possession or to wear.

Education Code § 49331.

Any certificated employee of any school district and any classified employee of a school district who is designated by the governing board for such purposes may take from the personal possession of any pupil upon school premises or while under the authority of school personnel any injurious object in the possession of the pupil.

Education Code § 49332.

The parent or guardian of a pupil from whom an injurious object has been taken pursuant to this section may be notified by school personnel of the taking. School personnel may retain protective possession of any injurious object taken pursuant to this section until the risk of its use as a weapon has dissipated, unless prior to dissipation of the risk, the parent or guardian requests that the school personnel retain the object, in which case, the school personnel shall retain the object until the parent or guardian or another adult with the written consent of the parent or guardian appears personally to take possession of the injurious object from the school personnel.

Education Code § 49333.

Notwithstanding Section 49332, a pupil who brings an injurious object to school, and who presents the object to a certificated or classified employee, may have the object returned to him or her at the conclusion of the school day, provided such injurious object may be lawfully possessed off school grounds.

Education Code § 49334.

If a school employee initially notifies a law enforcement agency regarding a student or adult who possesses an injurious object while upon school premises or while under the authority of school personnel, the employee may not be subject to any civil or administrative proceeding, including any disciplinary action, for violation of any local policy or procedure relating to the notification of a law enforcement agency. The employee shall conform to locally adopted procedures after exercising his or her personal option to notify a law enforcement agency.

Education Code § 49335.

On or before April 1, 2001, the Superintendent of Public Instruction shall adopt a system that will shield the identity and provide protection to pupils who report the presence of injurious objects on school campuses that offer instruction in kindergarten and any of grades 1 to 12, inclusive.

Education Code § 49350.

(a) The Legislature finds and declares all of the following:

(1) Studies have shown that indicators of risk for violence are associated with a child's experiences at school. Antisocial behavior or aggressiveness, which is sometimes combined with isolation, withdrawal, hyperactivity, or attention deficit disorder, places children at increased risk of violence.

(2) These children are at risk of persistent antisocial behavior, such as skipping school, getting into fights, and misbehaving in class. Young people of both genders who engage in these activities are at increased risk of experiencing drug abuse, juvenile delinquency, violence, dropping out of school, and teen pregnancy.

(3) It is well-known that some youth, even though exposed to multiple risk factors, do not succumb to violent, antisocial behavior. One of the defining factors for this outcome is bonding--positive relationships with family members, teachers, police officers, sheriffs' deputies, and other adults.

(4) The Community Policing and Mentoring for School Safety Pilot Program brings this successful law enforcement strategy to California' s schools. By providing funding assistance, strict participation guidelines and assessments, the Community Policing and Mentoring for School Safety Pilot Program will bring highly trained law enforcement officers onto school campuses to work with students during and after school. Community policing in schools will provide the necessary opportunities for students' active involvement in positive activities, as well as trained personnel to teach them skills so that they may pursue later opportunities successfully. Community policing in schools provides a consistent system of recognition and reinforcement of positive behavior.

(5) Many school safety approaches, including metal detectors, drug-sniffing dogs, armed private security personnel, and similar security measures, are more one-dimensional in their approach to school safety. The Community Policing and Mentoring for School Safety Pilot Program takes a multidimensional approach by involving the community, schools, parents or guardians, and law enforcement personnel in the design of the program that will serve their schools. The relationships developed, as a result of this process and the programs

themselves, will be a strong preventative alternative to antisocial behavior in California's schools.

(b) As used in this article, "community policing" means an approach to crime prevention that is founded on developing positive relationships between law enforcement and the community. In community policing, law enforcement becomes an integral facet of the community because officers work directly with the community and develop positive relationships with members of the community. Community members become more involved in their community's activities because they know they have the personal support of law enforcement. Community policing identifies factors that put young people at risk for violence in order to reduce or eliminate these factors and strengthen protective factors such as positive relationships with adults.

Education Code § 49350.5.

(a) In order to ensure that students enrolled in the California public schools attend campuses that are safe, secure, orderly, and purposeful places in which students and staff are free to learn and teach without the threat of physical or psychological harm, it is the intent of the Legislature that two-year grants be provided to the ABC Unified School District and the Downey Unified School District to establish community policing school safety and mentoring programs.

(b) Grants under this article shall be awarded in order to develop and implement a plan that accomplishes both of the following:

(1) Provision for a continuum of responses to school safety needs by employees of school districts and local law enforcement agencies.

(2) Demonstration of a collaborative and integrated approach for implementing a system of providing safe and secure school environments between the school districts and local law enforcement agencies.

(c) Grant funds shall be expended as determined by the multiagency juvenile justice coordinating council, established pursuant to subdivision (b) of Section 49351.

(d) Grants under this article shall not be used to provide funding for school resource officers.

Education Code § 49351.

(a)(1) The Community Policing and Mentoring for School Safety Pilot Program is hereby established. The Community Policing and Mentoring for School Safety Pilot Program shall be administered by the State Department of Education for the purpose of reducing juvenile crime and delinquency. The Superintendent of Public Instruction shall award grants to the ABC Unified School District and the Downey Unified School District to accomplish the goals set forth in subdivision (b) of Section 49350.5.

(2) Programs funded pursuant to this article may include, but not necessarily be limited to, all of the following methods of community policing:

(A) Teaching conflict resolution classes.

(B) Teaching crime prevention classes.

(C) Operating afterschool programs.

(D) Provide mentoring.

(E) Patrolling the community that encompasses the school district participating in the Community Policing and Mentoring for School Safety Pilot Program.

(b) Each school district that receives a grant under this article shall be required to establish a multiagency juvenile justice coordinating council that shall develop and implement a continuum of community-based responses to juvenile crime in the school setting.

(c) The coordinating councils established pursuant to subdivision (b) shall, at a minimum, include the school district, law enforcement agency, a volunteer police representative, parents, and at least two community organizations. The coordinating councils shall develop a comprehensive, multiagency plan that identifies resources and strategies for providing an effective targeted community policing plan, for activities relating to prevention, intervention, supervision, and treatment of at-risk youths in school settings.

Education Code § 49352.

The coordinating council established pursuant to subdivision (b) of Section 49351 shall accomplish all of the following:

(a) Complete an identification and prioritization of the schools, and other areas in the community, that face a significant public safety risk from juvenile crime, such as gang activity, daylight burglary, late-night robbery, vandalism, truancy, controlled substance sales, firearm-related violence, and juvenile alcohol use within the council's jurisdiction.

(b) Develop information and intelligence sharing systems to ensure that school districts actions are fully coordinated with local law enforcement agencies, and to provide data for measuring the success of the grantee in achieving its goals. The plan shall develop goals related to the outcome measures that shall be used to determine the effectiveness of the program, at participating pilot sites.

(c) Identify outcome measures which shall include, but not necessarily be limited to, each of the following:

(1) The rate of drug- and alcohol-related offenses.

(2) The rate of crimes against persons.

(3) The rate of crimes against property.

(4) Incidence of students in possession of firearms or other weapons.

Education Code § 72330.

(a) The governing board of a community college district may establish a community college police department under the supervision of a community college chief of police and, in accordance with Chapter 4 (commencing with Section 88000) of Part 51, may employ personnel as necessary to enforce the law on or near the campus of the community college and on or near other grounds or properties owned, operated, controlled, or administered by the community college or by the state acting on behalf of the community college. Each campus of a multicampus community college district may designate a chief of police.

(b) The governing board of a community college district that establishes a community college police department under subdivision (a) may also establish a police reserve officer program to supplement that police department.

(c) Persons employed and compensated as members of a community college police department, when so appointed and duly sworn, are peace officers as defined in Chapter 4.5 (commencing with Section 830) of Title 3 of Part 2 of the Penal Code.

(d) The governing board of a community college district that establishes a community college police department shall set minimum qualifications of employment for the community college chief of police, including, but not limited to, prior employment as a peace officer or completion of any peace officer training course approved by the Commission on Peace Officer Standards and Training. A chief of security or chief of police shall be required to comply with the prior employment or training requirement set forth in this subdivision as of January 1, 1993, or a date one year subsequent to the initial employment of the chief of security or chief of police by the community college district, whichever occurs later. This subdivision may not be construed to require the employment by a community college district of any additional personnel.

Education Code § 72330.2.

Every member of a California Community College police department first employed by a California Community College district before July 1, 1999, shall, in order to retain his or her employment, fulfill both of the following conditions:

(a) The employee shall submit to the district one copy of his or her fingerprints on forms prescribed by the Department of Justice. The Department of Justice shall forward this copy to the United States Federal Bureau of Investigation.

(b) The employee shall be determined to be a person who is not prohibited from employment by the California Community College district, and, if the employee is required to carry a firearm, shall be determined by the Department of Justice to be a person who is not prohibited from possessing a firearm. The Department of Justice may participate in the National Instant Criminal Background Check System (NICS) in lieu of submitting fingerprints to the United States Federal Bureau of Investigation in order to meet the requirements of this section relating to firearms.

Education Code § 72330.5.

(a) It is the intent of the Legislature to ensure the safety of pupils, staff, and the public on or near California's community colleges, by providing community college security officers with training that will enable them to deal with the increasingly diverse and dangerous situations they encounter.

(b) After July 1, 2000, every school security officer employed by a community college district who works more than 20 hours a week as a school security officer shall complete a course of training developed no later than July 1, 1999, by the Bureau of Security and Investigative Services of the Department of Consumer Affairs in consultation with the Commission on Peace Officer Standards and Training pursuant to Section 7583.31 of the Business and Professions Code. If any community college security officer subject to the requirements of this subdivision is required to carry a firearm while employed, that security officer shall additionally satisfy the training requirements of Section 832 of the Penal Code.

(c) For purposes of this chapter, "security officer" means any person primarily employed or assigned pursuant to subdivision (b) to provide security services as a watchperson, security guard, or patrolperson on or about premises owned or operated by the community college district to protect persons or property or to prevent the theft or unlawful taking of district property of any kind or to report any unlawful activity to the district and local law enforcement.

(d) No security officer shall be employed or shall continue to be employed by the district after July 1, 2000, until both of the following conditions have been met:

(1)(A) The applicant or employee has submitted to the district two copies of his or her fingerprints on forms or electronically, as prescribed by the Department of Justice. The district shall submit the fingerprints to the Department of Justice, which shall submit one copy of the fingerprints to the United States Federal Bureau of Investigation.

(B) An applicant or employee who holds a permanent registration with the Bureau of Security and Investigative Services of the Department of Consumer Affairs as a security guard need only submit one copy of his or her fingerprints, which copy shall be submitted to the United States Federal Bureau of Investigation.

(C) An applicant or employee who is registered by the Bureau of Security and Investigative Services of the Department of Consumer Affairs, and who holds a firearms qualification card as specified in Section 7583.22 of the Business and Professions Code, is exempt from the requirements of this subdivision.

(2) The applicant or employee has been determined not to be a person legally prohibited from employment by the community college and has been determined by the Department of Justice not to be a person prohibited from possessing a firearm if the applicant is required to carry a firearm. The Department of Justice may participate in the National Instant Criminal Background Check System (NICS) in lieu of submitting fingerprints to the United States Federal Bureau of Investigation in order to meet the requirements of this subdivision relating to firearms.

(e) Every security officer employed by a community college district prior to July 1, 2000, who works more than 20 hours a week as a school security officer shall meet the requirements of subdivision (b) by July 1, 2002, unless he or she has completed an equivalent course of instruction pursuant to Section 832.2 of the Penal Code.

Elections Code

Elections Code § 18540.

(a) Every person who makes use of or threatens to make use of any force, violence, or tactic of coercion or intimidation, to induce or compel any other person to vote or refrain from voting at any election or to vote or refrain from voting for any particular person or measure at any election, or because any person voted or refrained from voting at any election or voted or refrained from voting for any particular person or measure at any election is guilty of a felony punishable by imprisonment in the state prison for 16 months or two or three years.

(b) Every person who hires or arranges for any other person to make use of or threaten to make use of any force, violence, or tactic of coercion or intimidation, to induce or compel any other person to vote or refrain from voting at any election or to vote or refrain from voting for any particular person or measure at any election, or because any person voted or refrained from voting at any election or voted or refrained from voting for any particular person or measure at any election is guilty of a felony punishable by imprisonment in the state prison for 16 months or two or three years.

Elections Code § 18544.

(a) Any person in possession of a firearm or any uniformed peace officer, private guard, or security personnel or any person who is wearing a uniform of a peace officer, guard, or security personnel, who is stationed in the immediate vicinity of, or posted at, a polling place without written authorization of the appropriate city or county elections official is punishable by a fine not exceeding ten thousand dollars ($10,000), by imprisonment in the state prison for 16 months or two or three years or in a county jail not exceeding one year, or by both the fine and imprisonment.

(b) This section shall not apply to any of the following:

(1) An unarmed uniformed guard or security personnel who is at the polling place to cast his or her vote.

(2) A peace officer who is conducting official business in the course of his or her public employment or who is at the polling place to cast his or her vote.

(3) A private guard or security personnel hired or arranged for by a city or county elections official.

(4) A private guard or security personnel hired or arranged for by the owner or manager of the facility or property in which the polling place is located if the guard or security personnel is not hired or arranged solely for the day on which an election is held.

Elections Code § 18545.

Any person who hires or arranges for any other person in possession of a firearm or any uniformed peace officer, private guard, or security personnel or any person who is wearing a uniform of a peace officer, guard, or security personnel, to be stationed in the immediate vicinity of, or posted at, a polling place without written authorization of the appropriate elections official is punishable by a fine not exceeding ten thousand dollars ($10,000), by imprisonment in the state prison for 16 months or two or three years or in a county jail not exceeding one year, or by both the fine and imprisonment. This section shall not apply to the owner or manager of the facility or property in which the polling place is located if the private guard or security personnel is not hired or arranged solely for the day on which the election is held.

Elections Code § 18546.

As used in this article:

(a) "Elections official" means the county elections official, registrar of voters, or city clerk.

(b) "Immediate vicinity" means the area within a distance of 100 feet from the room or rooms in which the voters are signing the roster and casting ballots.

Family Code

Family Code § 6218.

"Protective order" means an order that includes any of the following restraining orders, whether issued ex parte, after notice and hearing, or in a judgment:

(a) An order described in Section 6320 enjoining specific acts of abuse.

(b) An order described in Section 6321 excluding a person from a dwelling.

(c) An order described in Section 6322 enjoining other specified behavior.

Family Code § 6300.

An order may be issued under this part, with or without notice, to restrain any person for the purpose of preventing a recurrence of domestic violence and ensuring a period of separation of the persons involved, if an affidavit or, if necessary, an affidavit and any additional information provided to the court pursuant to Section 6306, shows, to the satisfaction of the court, reasonable proof of a past act or acts of abuse.

Family Code § 6304.

When making a protective order, as defined in Section 6218, where both parties are present in court, the court shall inform both the petitioner and the respondent of the terms of the order, including notice that the respondent is prohibited from owning, possessing, purchasing or receiving or attempting to own, possess, purchase or receive a firearm, and including notice of the penalty for violation.

Family Code § 6306.

(a) Prior to a hearing on the issuance or denial of an order under this part, the court shall ensure that a search is or has been conducted to determine if the subject of the proposed order has any prior criminal conviction for a violent felony specified in Section 667.5 of the Penal Code or a serious felony specified in Section 1192.7 of the Penal Code; has any misdemeanor conviction involving domestic violence, weapons, or other violence; has any outstanding warrant; is currently on parole or probation; or has any prior restraining order or any violation of a prior restraining order. The search shall be conducted of all records and data bases readily available and reasonably accessible to the court, including, but not limited to, the following:

(1) The Violent Crime Information Network (VCIN).

(2) The Supervised Release File.

(3) State summary criminal history information maintained by the Department of Justice pursuant to Section 11105 of the Penal Code.

(4) The Federal Bureau of Investigation's nationwide data base.

(5) Locally maintained criminal history records or data bases. However, a record or data base need not be searched if the information available in that record or data base can be obtained as a result of a search conducted in another record or data base.

(b)(1) Prior to deciding whether to issue an order under this part or when determining appropriate temporary custody and visitation orders, the court shall consider the following information obtained pursuant to a search conducted under subdivision (a): any conviction for a violent felony specified in Section 667.5 of the Penal Code or a serious felony specified in Section 1192.7 of the Penal Code; any misdemeanor conviction involving domestic violence, weapons, or other violence; any outstanding warrant; parole or probation status; any prior restraining order; and any violation of a prior restraining order.

(2) Information obtained as a result of the search that does not involve a conviction described in this subdivision shall not be considered by the court in making a determination regarding the issuance of an order pursuant to this part. That information shall be destroyed and shall not become part of the public file in this or any other civil proceeding.

(c)(1) After issuing its ruling, the court shall advise the parties that they may request the information described in subdivision (b) upon which the court relied. The court shall admonish the party seeking the proposed order that it is unlawful, pursuant to Sections 11142 and 13303 of the Penal Code, to willfully release the information, except as authorized by law.

(2) Upon the request of either party to obtain the information described in subdivision (b) upon which the court relied, the court shall release the information to the parties or, upon either party's request, to his or her attorney in that proceeding.

(3) The party seeking the proposed order may release the information to his or her counsel, court personnel, and court-appointed mediators for the purpose of seeking judicial review of the court's order or for purposes of court proceedings under Section 213.5 of the Welfare and Institutions Code.

(d) Any information obtained as a result of the search conducted pursuant to subdivision (a) and relied upon by the court shall be maintained in a confidential case file and shall not become part of the public file in the proceeding or any other civil proceeding. However, the contents of the confidential case file shall be disclosed to the court-appointed mediator assigned to the case or to a child custody evaluator appointed by the court pursuant to Section 3111 of the Family Code or Section 730 of the Evidence Code. All court-appointed mediators and child custody evaluators appointed or contracted by the court pursuant to Section 3111 of the Family Code or Section 730 of the Evidence Code who may receive information from the search conducted pursuant to subdivision (a) shall be subject to, and shall comply with, the California Law Enforcement Telecommunications System policies, practices, and procedures adopted pursuant to Section 15160 of the Government Code.

(e) If the results of the search conducted pursuant to subdivision (a) indicate that an outstanding warrant exists against the subject of the order, the court shall order the clerk of the court to immediately notify, by the most effective means available, appropriate law enforcement officials of the issuance and contents of any protective order and of any other information obtained through the search that the court determines is appropriate. The law enforcement officials so notified shall take all actions necessary to execute any outstanding warrants or any other actions, with respect to the restrained person, as appropriate and as soon as practicable.

(f) If the results of the search conducted pursuant to subdivision (a) indicate that the subject of the order is currently on parole or probation, the court shall order the clerk of the court to immediately notify, by the most effective means available, the appropriate parole or probation officer of the issuance and contents of any protective order issued by the court and of any other information obtained through the search that the court determines is appropriate. That officer shall take all actions necessary to revoke any parole or probation, or any other actions, with respect to the restrained person, as appropriate and as soon as practicable.

(g) Nothing in this section shall delay the granting of an application for an order that may otherwise be granted without the information resulting from the data base search. If the court finds that a protective order under this part should be granted on the basis of the affidavit presented with the petition, the court shall issue the protective order and shall then ensure that a search is conducted pursuant to subdivision (a) prior to the hearing.

Family Code § 6500.

A minor is an individual who is under 18 years of age. The period of minority is calculated from the first minute of the day on which the individual is born to the same minute of the corresponding day completing the period of minority.

Family Code § 6501.

An adult is an individual who is 18 years of age or older.

Family Code § 6502.

(a) The use of or reference to the words "age of majority," "age of minority," "adult," "minor," or words of similar intent in any instrument, order, transfer, or governmental communication made in this state:

(1) Before March 4, 1972, makes reference to individuals 21 years of age and older, or younger than 21 years of age.

(2) On or after March 4, 1972, makes reference to individuals 18 years of age and older, or younger than 18 years of age.

(b) Nothing in subdivision (a) or in Chapter 1748 of the Statutes of 1971 prevents amendment of any court order, will, trust, contract, transfer, or instrument to refer to the 18-year-old age of majority if the court order, will, trust, contract, transfer, or instrument satisfies all of the following conditions:

(1) It was in existence on March 4, 1972.

(2) It is subject to amendment by law, and amendment is allowable or not prohibited by its terms.

(3) It is otherwise subject to the laws of this state.

Financial Code

Financial Code § 21200.

(a) Except as otherwise provided in this chapter, no pawnbroker shall charge or receive compensation at a rate exceeding the sum of the following:

(1) Two and one-half percent per month on that portion of the unpaid principal balance of any loan up to, including, but not in excess of two hundred twenty-five dollars ($225).

(2) Two percent per month on that portion of the unpaid principal balance of the loan in excess of two hundred twenty-five dollars ($225) up to, including, but not exceeding nine hundred dollars ($900).

(3) One and one-half percent per month on that part of the unpaid principal balance in excess of nine hundred dollars ($900) up to and including, but not in excess of, one thousand six hundred fifty dollars ($1,650).

(4) One percent per month on any remainder of the unpaid principal balance in excess of one thousand six hundred fifty dollars ($1,650).

(5) A charge not exceeding three dollars ($3) a month on any loan when the monthly charge permitted by this section would otherwise be less than that minimum charge.

(b) One month's interest may be charged for any part of the month in which pawned property is redeemed.

Financial Code § 21200.1.

A loan setup fee not to exceed five dollars ($5) or 2 percent, whichever is greater, may be charged for each loan. However, the maximum loan setup fee shall not exceed ten dollars ($10). Loan setup fees are in addition to any other allowed charges.

Financial Code § 21200.5.

A pawnbroker may charge as prescribed in the following schedule: Schedule of Charges

(a) A charge not exceeding one dollar ($1) may be made on any loan for not more than 30 days which does not exceed fourteen dollars and ninety-nine cents ($14. 99).

(b) A charge not exceeding three dollars ($3) may be made on any loan for not more than 90 days of fifteen dollars ($15) or more, but not exceeding nineteen dollars and ninety-nine cents ($19.99).

(c) A charge not exceeding four dollars ($4) may be made on any loan for not more than 90 days of twenty dollars ($20) or more, but not exceeding twenty-four dollars and ninety-nine cents ($24.99).

(d) A charge not exceeding five dollars ($5) may be made on any loan for not more than 90 days of twenty-five dollars ($25) or more, but not exceeding thirty-nine dollars and ninety-nine cents ($39.99).

(e) A charge not exceeding six dollars ($6) may be made on any loan for not more than 90 days of forty dollars ($40) or more, but not exceeding forty-nine dollars and ninety-nine cents ($49.99).

(f) A charge not exceeding seven dollars and fifty cents ($7.50) may be made on any loan for not more than 90 days on any loan of fifty dollars ($50) or more, but not exceeding sixty-four dollars and ninety-nine cents ($64.99).

(g) A charge not exceeding eight dollars and fifty cents ($8.50) may be made on any loan for not more than 90 days of sixty-five dollars ($65) or more, but not exceeding seventy-four dollars and ninety-nine cents ($74.99).

(h) A charge not exceeding ten dollars ($10) may be made on any loan for not more than 90 days of seventy-five dollars ($75) or more, but not exceeding ninety-nine dollars and ninety-nine cents ($99.99).

(i) A charge not exceeding twelve dollars and fifty cents ($12.50) may be made on any loan for not more than 90 days of one hundred dollars ($100) or more, but not exceeding one hundred twenty-four dollars and ninety-nine cents ($124.99).

(j) A charge not exceeding thirteen dollars and fifty cents ($13.50) may be made on any loan for not more than 90 days of one hundred twenty-five dollars ($125) or more, but not exceeding one hundred forty-nine dollars and ninety-nine cents ($149.99).

(k) A charge not exceeding fifteen dollars ($15) may be made on any loan for not more than 90 days of one hundred fifty dollars ($150) or more, but not exceeding two hundred twenty-four dollars and ninety-nine cents ($224.99).

(l) A charge not exceeding twenty dollars ($20) may be made on any loan for not more than 90 days of two hundred twenty-five dollars ($225) or more, but not exceeding three hundred twenty-four dollars and ninety-nine cents ($324.99).

(m) A charge not exceeding twenty-five dollars ($25) may be made on any loan for not more than 90 days of three hundred twenty-five dollars ($325) or more, but not exceeding four hundred forty-nine dollars and ninety-nine cents ($449.99).

(n) A charge not exceeding thirty-five dollars ($35) may be made on any loan for not more than 90 days of four hundred fifty dollars ($450) or more, but not exceeding five hundred ninety-nine dollars and ninety-nine cents ($599.99).

(o) A charge not exceeding forty-five dollars ($45) may be made on any loan for not more than 90 days of six hundred dollars ($600) or more, but not exceeding seven hundred ninety-nine dollars and ninety-nine cents ($799.99).

(p) A charge not exceeding fifty-five dollars ($55) may be made on any loan for not more than 90 days of eight hundred dollars ($800) or more, but not exceeding nine hundred ninety-nine dollars and ninety-nine cents ($999.99).

(q) A charge not exceeding seventy dollars ($70) may be made in any loan for not more than 90 days of one thousand dollars ($1,000) or more, but not exceeding eleven hundred ninety-nine dollars and ninety-nine cents ($1,199.99).

(r) A charge not exceeding eighty-five dollars ($85) may be made on any loan for not more than 90 days of twelve hundred dollars ($1,200) or more, but not exceeding fourteen hundred ninety-nine dollars and ninety-nine cents ($1,499.99).

(s) A charge not exceeding one hundred dollars ($100) may be made on any loan for not more than 90 days of fifteen hundred dollars ($1,500) or more, but not exceeding seventeen hundred ninety-nine dollars and ninety-nine cents ($1,799.99).

(t) A charge not exceeding one hundred twenty dollars ($120) may be made on any loan for not more than 90 days of eighteen hundred dollars ($1,800) or more, but not exceeding two thousand ninety-nine dollars and ninety-nine cents ($2,099.99).

(u) A charge not exceeding one hundred forty dollars ($140) may be made on any loan for not more than 90 days of twenty-one hundred dollars ($2,100) or more, but not exceeding twenty-four hundred ninety-nine dollars and ninety-nine cents ($2,499.99).

(v) The charge for any extension or renewal of a loan covered by this section shall be computed in accordance with the provisions of Section 21200. The schedule of charges prescribed by this section shall be posted in a place clearly visible to the general public.

Financial Code § 21200.6.

(a) In addition to other allowed charges, at the time property is redeemed a pawnbroker may collect a handling and storage charge for certain pawned articles. Irrespective of the duration of the loan, the maximum amount that may be charged pursuant to this section is in accordance with the following schedule:

(1) Five dollars ($5) for any article that cannot be contained within one cubic foot.

(2) Ten dollars ($10) for any article that cannot be contained within three cubic feet.

(3) Twenty dollars ($20) for any article that cannot be contained within six cubic feet and one dollar ($1) for each additional cubic foot in excess of six cubic feet.

(b) No storage charge is allowed for any article that can be contained within one cubic foot.

(c) For purposes of this section, cubic feet shall be determined by multiplying the width of an article, at its greatest width, by the depth of an article, at its greatest depth, by the height of an article, at its greatest height.

Financial Code § 21200.7.

The maximum charge of compensation charged by a pawnbroker pursuant to the authority of Section 21200 shall be posted in a place clearly visible to the general public.

Financial Code § 21200.8.

In addition to other allowed charges, a pawnbroker may collect a processing charge of four dollars ($4) for each firearm pawned.

Fish and Game Code

Fish and Game Code § 1.

This code shall be known as the Fish and Game Code.

Fish and Game Code § 86.

"Take" means hunt, pursue, catch, capture, or kill, or attempt to hunt, pursue, catch, capture, or kill.

Fish and Game Code § 210.

(a) The commission shall provide copies of the regulations added, amended, or repealed pursuant to subdivision (e) of Section 206, subdivision (e) of Section 207, and subdivision (d) of Section 208 to each county clerk, each district attorney, and each judge of the superior court in the state.

(b) The commission and the department may do anything that is deemed necessary and proper to publicize and distribute regulations so that persons likely to be affected will be informed of them. The failure of the commission to provide any notice of its regulations, other than by filing them in accordance with Section 215, shall not impair the validity of the regulations.

(c) The department or the license agent may give a copy of the current applicable published regulations to each person issued a license at the time the license is issued.

(d) Notwithstanding any other provision of law, the commission and the department may contract with private entities to print regulations and other regulatory and public information. Printing contracts authorized by this subdivision and for which no state funds are expended are not subject to Chapter 2 (commencing with Section 10290) of Part 2 of Division 2 of the Public Contract Code, except for Article 2 (commencing with Section 10295) of Chapter 2.

Fish and Game Code § 211.

(a) Material printed pursuant to subdivision (d) of Section 210 that contains advertisements shall meet all specifications prescribed by the department. The printed material shall not contain advertisements for tobacco products, alcohol, firearms and devices prohibited pursuant to Sections 12020, 12220, and 12280 of the Penal Code, or firearms not authorized by the commission as a legal method of sport-hunting, political statements, solicitations for membership in organizations, or any other statement, solicitation, or product advertisement that is in conflict with the purposes for which the material is produced, as determined by the commission. The printing contract shall include criteria to ensure that the public information provided in the publication is easy to reference, read, and understand.

(b) Neither the department nor the commission shall contract with private entities to print the materials described in subdivision (d) of Section 210 if the letting of those contracts will result in the elimination of civil service positions.

Fish and Game Code § 312.

The commission may issue a permit authorizing any member of the armed forces of the United States or any student or faculty member of an elementary or secondary school in the public school system actually assigned to, and participating in, an organized survival training course to take fish, amphibia, birds, or mammals, except rare or endangered species, notwithstanding any other law or regulation, pursuant to the terms and conditions of such permit. A permit involving training by the armed forces of the United States shall be issued to the commanding officer of the unit having jurisdiction over the conduct of the survival training course. A permit involving training by an elementary or secondary school in the public school system shall be issued to the governing board or superintendent of the district having jurisdiction over such school and the conduct of the survival training course. A permit shall be applicable only to the area established for such survival training as designated by the commission in the permit and for the species and numbers designated in the permit.

The commission may revise any conditions of a permit if it finds such revision is necessary to properly protect the fish, amphibia, birds, or mammals in the area.

The term of such a permit shall be for not more than a calendar year.

A report shall be submitted on the expiration of the permit period, or as otherwise required by the commission, of all fish, amphibia, birds, or mammals taken during the period covered by the report in each permit area. No new permit may be issued until such report has been submitted and any existing permit may be canceled if such a report is not submitted when required by the commission.

No person engaged in such survival training taking fish, amphibia, birds, or mammals pursuant to such a permit may use any firearm, bow and arrow, steel trap, explosive, chemical, poison, drug, net or fish tackle except hooks or handlines or improvised poles and lines for the taking of fish.

Fish and Game Code § 2005.

(a) Except as otherwise authorized by this section, it is unlawful to use an artificial light to assist in the taking of game birds, game mammals, or game fish, except that this section shall not apply to sport fishing in ocean waters or other waters where night fishing is permitted if the lights are not used on or as part of the fishing tackle, commercial fishing, nor to the taking of mammals, the taking of which is governed by Article 2 (commencing with Section 4180) of Chapter 3 of Part 3 of Division 4.

(b) It is unlawful for any person, or one or more persons, to throw or cast the rays of any spotlight, headlight, or other artificial light on any highway or in any field, woodland, or forest where game mammals, fur-bearing mammals, or nongame mammals are commonly found, or upon any game mammal, fur-bearing mammal, or nongame mammal, while having in his or her possession or under his or her control any firearm or weapon with which that mammal could be killed, even though the mammal is not killed, injured, shot at, or otherwise pursued.

(c) It is unlawful to use or possess at any time any infrared or similar light used in connection with an electronic viewing device or any night vision equipment, optical devices, including, but not limited to, binoculars or scopes, that use light-amplifying circuits that are electrical or battery powered, to assist in the taking of birds, mammals, amphibians, or fish.

(d) The provisions of this section do not apply to any of the following:

(1) The use of a hand-held flashlight no larger, nor emitting more light, than a two-cell, three-volt flashlight, provided that light is not affixed in any way to a weapon, or to the use of a lamp or lantern that does not cast a directional beam of light.

(2) Headlights of a motor vehicle operated in a usual manner where there is no attempt or intent to locate a game mammal, fur-bearing mammal, or nongame mammal.

(3) To the owner, or his or her employee, of land devoted to the agricultural industry while on that land, or land controlled by such an owner and in connection with the agricultural industry.

(4) To those other uses as the commission may authorize by regulation.

(e) A person shall not be arrested for violation of this section except by a peace officer.

Fish and Game Code § 2006.

It is unlawful to possess a loaded rifle or shotgun in any vehicle or conveyance or its attachments which is standing on or along or is being driven on or along any public highway or other way open to the public. A rifle or shotgun shall be deemed to be loaded for the purposes of this section when there is an unexpended cartridge or shell in the firing chamber but not when the only cartridges or shells are in the magazine. The provisions of this section shall not apply to peace officers or members of the armed forces of this State or the United States, while on duty or going to or returning from duty.

Fish and Game Code § 2007.

It is unlawful to set, cause to be set, or placed any trap gun. A "trap gun" is a firearm loaded with other than blank cartridges and connected with a string or other contrivance contact with which will cause the firearm to be discharged.

Fish and Game Code § 2009.

(a) A person shall not willfully interfere with the participation of any individual in the lawful activity of shooting, hunting, fishing, falconry, or trapping at the location where that activity is taking place.

(b) A violation of this section is an infraction punishable by a fine of not less than one hundred dollars ($100) nor more than five hundred dollars ($500).

(c) If any person is convicted of a violation of this section and the offense occurred within two years of another separate violation of this section which resulted in a conviction, the violation is a misdemeanor punishable by a fine of not less than one hundred dollars ($100) nor more than one thousand dollars ($1,000), by imprisonment in the county jail for not more than one year, or by both that fine and imprisonment.

(d) This section does not apply to the actions of any peace officer or personnel of the department in the performance of their official duties. This section does not obstruct the rights and normal activities of landowners or tenants, including, but not limited to, farming, ranching, and limiting unlawful trespass.

(e) In order to be liable for a violation of this section, the person is required to have had the specific intent to interfere with the participation of an individual who was engaged in shooting, hunting, fishing, falconry, or trapping.

(f) For purposes of this section, "interfere with" means any action which physically impedes, hinders, or obstructs the lawful pursuit of any of the above-mentioned activities, including, but not limited to, actions taken for the purpose of frightening away animals from the location where the lawful activity is taking place.

Fish and Game Code § 2010.

It is unlawful to use or possess a shotgun larger than 10-gauge, or to use or possess a shotgun capable of holding more than six cartridges at one time to take any mammal or bird. However, the commission may, after public hearing, adopt regulations relative to the ammunition capacity of shotguns for taking mammals or birds that are further restrictive or that it determines may be needed to conform to federal law. Shotguns that have been modified with the insertion of a plug are deemed, for the purpose of this section, to have a cartridge capacity equal to the number of cartridges that can be loaded into the weapon as modified.

Fish and Game Code § 3001.

It is unlawful to take birds or mammals with firearms, BB devices as defined in subdivision (g) of Section 12001 of the Penal Code, crossbows, or with bow and arrow when intoxicated.

Fish and Game Code § 3002.

It is unlawful to shoot at any game bird or mammal, including a marine mammal as defined in Section 4500, from a powerboat, sailboat, motor vehicle, or airplane.

Fish and Game Code § 3003.

(a) It is unlawful for any person to shoot, shoot at, or kill any bird or mammal with any gun or other device accessed via an Internet connection in this state.

(b) It is further unlawful for any person, firm, corporation, partnership, limited liability company, association, or other business entity to do either of the following:

(1) Own or operate a shooting range, site, or gallery located in the state for purposes of the online shooting or spearing of any bird or mammal.

(2) Create, maintain, or utilize an Internet Web site, or a service or business via any other means, from any location within the state for purposes of the online shooting or spearing of any bird or mammal for the purposes of this section.

(c) It is unlawful to possess or confine any bird or mammal in furtherance of an activity prohibited by this section.

(d) It is unlawful for any person in this state to import into, or export from, this state any bird or mammal, or any part thereof, that is killed by any device accessed via an Internet connection.

(e) Any bird or mammal, or any part thereof, that is possessed in violation of this section shall be subject to seizure by the department.

(f) For the purposes of this section, "online shooting or spearing" means the use of a computer or any other device, equipment, software, or technology, to remotely control the aiming and discharge of any weapon, including, but not limited to, any firearm, bow and arrow, spear, slingshot, harpoon, or any other projectile device.

Fish and Game Code § 3004.

(a) It is unlawful for any person, other than the owner, person in possession of the premises, or a person having the express permission of the owner or person in possession of the premises, to hunt or to discharge while hunting, any firearm or other deadly weapon within 150 yards of any occupied dwelling house, residence, or other building or any barn or other outbuilding used in connection therewith. The 150-yard area is a "safety zone."

(b) It is unlawful for any person to intentionally discharge any firearm or release any arrow or crossbow bolt over or across any public road or way open to the public, in an unsafe manner.

Fish and Game Code § 3004.5.

(a) Nonlead centerfire rifle and pistol ammunition, as determined by the commission, shall be required when taking big game with rifle or pistol, as defined by Section 350 of the department's mammal hunting regulations, and when taking coyote, within the department's deer hunting zone A South, but excluding Santa Cruz, Alameda, Contra Costa, San Mateo, and San Joaquin Counties, areas west of Highway 101 within Santa Clara County, and areas between Highway 5 and Highway 99 within Stanislaus, Merced, Madera, Fresno, Kings, Tulare, and Kern Counties, and within deer hunting zones D7, D8, D9, D10, D11, and D13.

(b) By July 1, 2008, the commission shall establish, by regulation, a public process to certify centerfire rifle and pistol ammunition as nonlead ammunition, and shall define, by regulation, nonlead ammunition as including only centerfire rifle and pistol ammunition in which there is no lead content. The commission shall establish and annually update a list of certified centerfire rifle and pistol ammunition.

(c)(1) To the extent that funding is available, the commission shall establish a process that will provide hunters within the department's deer hunting zone A South, but excluding Santa Cruz, Alameda, Contra Costa, San Mateo, and San Joaquin Counties, areas west of Highway 101 within Santa Clara County, and areas between Highway 5 and Highway 99 within Stanislaus, Merced, Madera, Fresno, Kings, Tulare, and Kern Counties, and within deer hunting zones D7, D8, D9, D10, D11, and D13 with nonlead ammunition at no or reduced charge. The process shall provide that the offer for nonlead ammunition at no or reduced charge may be redeemed through a coupon sent to a permit holder with the appropriate permit tag. If available funding is not sufficient to provide nonlead ammunition at no charge, the commission shall set the value of the reduced charge coupon at the maximum value possible through available funding, up to the average cost within this state for nonlead ammunition, as determined by the commission.

(2) The nonlead ammunition coupon program described in paragraph (1) shall be implemented only to the extent that sufficient funding, as determined by the Department of Finance, is obtained from local, federal, public, or other nonstate sources in order to implement the program.

(3) If the nonlead ammunition coupon program is implemented, the commission shall issue a report on the usage and redemption rates of ammunition coupons. The report shall cover calendar years 2008, 2009, and 2012. Each report shall be issued by June of the following year.

(d) The commission shall issue a report on the levels of lead found in California condors. This report shall cover calendar years 2008, 2009, and 2012. Each report shall be issued by June of the following year.

(e) The department shall notify those hunters who may be affected by this section.

(f) A person who violates any provision of this section is guilty of an infraction punishable by a fine of five hundred dollars ($500). A second or subsequent offense shall be punishable by a fine of not less than one thousand dollars ($1,000) or more than five thousand dollars ($5,000).

Fish and Game Code § 3009.

Every person who while taking any bird or mammal kills or injures another person by the use of any firearm, bow and arrow, spear, slingshot, or other weapon or device used in such taking and who knowingly either abandons such person or fails to render to such injured person all necessary aid possible under the circumstances is guilty of a felony.

Fish and Game Code § 3660.

It is unlawful for any person to have in his possession the carcass, in such condition that the sex or species cannot be easily determined, of any pheasant while in the field or forest or while upon any highway, train, car, boat, or other conveyance when returning from any hunting trip with gun or other hunting equipment.

Fish and Game Code § 3801.6.

(a) Except as otherwise provided in this code or regulations made pursuant thereto, it is unlawful to possess the carcass, skin, or parts of any nongame bird. The feathers, carcass, skin, or parts of any nongame bird possessed by any person in violation of any of the provisions of this code shall be seized by the department and delivered to a California Native American tribal government or a scientific or educational institution, used by the department, or destroyed.

(b)(1) It shall be an affirmative defense to a violation of this section if the possessor of feathers, carcass, skin, or parts of a nongame bird legally acquired the feathers, carcass, skin, or parts, possesses them for tribal, cultural, or spiritual purposes, and satisfies either of the following criteria:

(A) The possessor is an enrolled member of a federally recognized Native American tribe or nonfederally recognized California Native American tribe listed on the California Tribal Consultation List maintained by the Native American Heritage Commission who has, in his or her immediate possession, valid tribal identification or other irrefutable proof of current enrollment.

(B) The possessor has a certificate of degree of Indian blood issued by the United States Bureau of Indian Affairs in his or her immediate possession.

(2) Nothing in this section allows any person to sell nongame bird feathers, carcasses, skins, or parts. Native Americans meeting the affirmative defense requirements may salvage dead nongame birds so long as the person salvaging these birds does not possess, nor is in the company of any person who possesses, a firearm, BB device as defined in subdivision (g) of Section 12001 of the Penal Code, trap, snare, net archery equipment, device capable of discharging a projectile, or any apparatus designed to take birds. Salvaging shall not take place by any person involved in the take of the nongame bird to be salvaged, any person present at the time of the take, or by any person who received related information originating from any person present at the time of the take of the nongame bird. Salvaging pursuant to this subdivision shall not take place if a bird has been struck with any thrown or discharged projectile, trapped, netted, caught, or snared.

(c) Notwithstanding subdivisions (a) and (b), any officer deputized pursuant to this code may interrupt any ongoing salvaging of dead nongame carcasses, feathers, skins, or parts if, in the officer's judgment, the activity causes a public disruption, safety hazard, or is detrimental to the ability of the department to prevent a possible violation of this section. The officer may seize any of the salvaged feathers, carcasses, skins, or parts and has the option of returning them to the general location from where they were salvaged.

Fish and Game Code § 4000.

The following are fur-bearing mammals: pine marten, fisher, mink, river otter, gray fox, red fox, kit fox, raccoon, beaver, badger, and muskrat.

Fish and Game Code § 4002.

Fur-bearing mammals may be taken only with a trap, a firearm, bow and arrow, poison under a proper permit, or with the use of dogs.

Fish and Game Code § 4003.

It is unlawful to use poison to take fur-bearing mammals without a permit from the department. The department may issue such a permit upon a written application indicating the kind of poison desired to be used and the time and place of use.

Fish and Game Code § 4181.5.

(a) Any owner or tenant of land or property that is being damaged or destroyed or is in immediate danger of being damaged or destroyed by deer may apply to the department for a permit to kill those deer. The department, upon satisfactory evidence of that damage or destruction, actual or immediately threatened, shall issue a revocable permit for the taking and disposition of those deer for a designated period not to exceed 60 days under regulations promulgated by the commission.

(b) The regulations of the commission shall include provisions concerning the type of weapons to be used to kill the deer. The weapons shall be those as will ensure humane killing, but the regulations of the commission shall provide for the use of a sufficient variety of weapons to permit the designation of particular types to be used in any particular locality commensurate with the need to protect persons and property. Firearms using .22-caliber rimfire cartridges may be used only when authorized by the director or his designee. No pistols shall be used. The caliber and type of weapon to be used by each permittee shall be specified in each permit by the issuing officer who shall take into consideration the location of the area, the necessity for clean kills, the safety factor, local firearms ordinances, and other factors that apply. Rifle ammunition used shall have expanding bullets; shotgun ammunition shall have only single slugs, or, if authorized by the department, 0 or 00 buckshot.

(c) The department shall issue tags similar to those provided for in Section 4331 at the same time the permit is issued. A permittee under this section shall carry the tags while hunting deer, and upon the killing of any deer, shall immediately fill out both parts of the tag and punch out clearly the date of the kill. One part of the tag shall be immediately attached to the antlers of antlered deer or to the ear of any other deer and kept attached until 10 days after the permit has expired. The other part of the tag shall be immediately sent to the department after it has been countersigned by any person authorized by Section 4341.

(d) A permit issued pursuant to this section may be renewed only after a finding by the department that further damage has occurred or will occur unless that permit is renewed. A person seeking renewal of the permit shall account for all prior tags issued at the time he or she received any prior permits, and if any tags are unused, he or she shall show either that any deer killed could not reasonably be tagged or why the killing was not accomplished within the allotted time and why that killing would be accomplished under a new time period.

Fish and Game Code § 4370.

In every area in which deer may lawfully be taken during the general open season there is an archery season for the taking of deer with bow and arrow. The season for each area shall be as the commission may prescribe, with a minimum interposing interval of three days immediately preceding the regular open season on deer in that area. No person taking or attempting to take deer during such archery season shall carry, or have under his immediate control, any firearm of any kind.

Fish and Game Code § 4750.

It is unlawful to take any bear with firearm, trap, or bow and arrow without first procuring a tag authorizing the taking of that bear in accordance with this chapter, but no iron or steel-jawed or any type of metal-jawed trap shall be used to take any bear.

Fish and Game Code § 6850.

As used in this article, "frog" means all species of frog.

Fish and Game Code § 6854.

It is unlawful to take frogs by the use of firearms of any caliber or type.

Fish and Game Code § 8664.2.

(a) Notwithstanding Sections 8693 and 8724, gill nets and trammel nets shall not be used offshore of San Nicolas Island in Ventura County in waters 20 fathoms or less in depth at mean lower low water.

(b) No person, except state, local, or federal employees in the performance of their official duties, shall discharge any firearm within the sea otter translocation zone surrounding San Nicolas Island.

(c) For purposes of this section, "sea otter translocation zone" includes San Nicolas Island, the nearby islet of Begg Rock, and surrounding waters within the following coordinates:
(North Latitude / West Longitude)

o	,	o	,	o	,	o	,
33	27.8	119	34.3	33	20.5	119	15.5
o	,	o	,	o	,	o	,
33	13.5	119	11.8	33	06.5	119	15.3
o	,	o	,	o	,	o	,
33	02.8	119	26.8	33	08.8	119	46.3
o	,	o	,	o	,	o	,
33	17.2	119	56.9	33	30.9	119	54.2

(d) The taking of a sea otter that is incidental to, and not for the purpose of, the carrying out of an otherwise lawful activity within the sea otter management zone described in subdivision

(e), is not a violation of the California Endangered Species Act, Chapter 1.5 (commencing with Section 2050) of Division 3, or Section 4700. (e) For purposes of this section, "sea otter management zone" includes all waters, islands, islets, and land areas seaward of mean high tide subject to the jurisdiction of the United States, including state tidelands, located south of Point Conception (34*26.9' N. Latitude), excepting therefrom any area within the sea otter translocation zone described in subdivision (c).

(f) This section shall become operative only upon the relocation and release of sea otters to San Nicolas Island. This section shall become inoperative if the sea otter translocation experiment is declared a failure pursuant to the provisions of Public Law 99-625.

Fish and Game Code § 9051.

(a) Spears, harpoons, and bows and arrows may be used for taking all varieties of skates, rays, and sharks, except soupfin sharks.

(b) This section shall become operative January 1, 1999.

Fish and Game Code § 10500.

Except under a permit or specific authorization, it is unlawful to do any of the following:

(a) To take or possess any bird or mammal, or part thereof, in any game refuge.

(b) To use or have in possession in a game refuge, any firearm, BB device as defined in subdivision (g) of Section 12001 of the Penal Code, crossbow, bow and arrow, or any trap or other contrivance designed to be, or capable of being, used to take birds or mammals, or to discharge any firearm or BB device or to release any arrow or crossbow bolt into any game refuge.

(c) To take or possess any species of fish or amphibian, or part thereof, in any fish refuge, or to use or have in possession in that refuge any contrivance designed to be used for catching fish.

(d) To take or possess any bird in, or to discharge any firearm or BB device, or to release any arrow or crossbow bolt within or into, any waterfowl refuge.

(e) To take or possess any quail in a quail refuge.

(f) To take or possess any invertebrate or specimen of marine plant life in a marine life refuge.

(g) To take or possess any clam in a clam refuge or to possess in such a refuge any instrument or apparatus capable of being used to dig clams.

Fish and Game Code § 10506.

Nothing in this code prohibits the possession of firearms, BB devices as defined in subdivision (g) of Section 12001 of the Penal Code, crossbows and bolts, or bows and arrows by persons when traveling through any game refuges when the firearms are taken apart or encased and unloaded and the bows are unstrung or stored separately from any arrow or bolt. When the traveling is done on a route other than a public highway or other public thoroughfare or right of way, notice shall be given to the department at least 24 hours before that traveling. The notice shall give the name and address of the person intending to travel through the refuge, the name of the refuge, the approximate route, and the approximate time when that person intends to travel through the refuge.

Fish and Game Code § 10651.

In the Mt. Tamalpais Game Refuge firearms may be possessed and used by members of any high school militia while on the grounds of the high school at which time they may be enrolled.

Fish and Game Code § 10659.

In the California Sea Otter Game Refuge, the lawful occupant of privately owned land, or the employees of such occupant, may possess firearms and traps and may take on such lands any nonprotected bird or mammal, and no permit is required for such taking.

Fish and Game Code § 10662.

Notwithstanding any other provision in this code, it shall be unlawful for any person to fire a firearm, but it shall not be unlawful to possess a firearm in the following areas: All of T. 5 S., R. 5 E., except Sections 1, 2, 11, 12, and 13, of Fish and Game District 4D.

Fish and Game Code § 10663.

In Fish and Game Refuge 4-D the lawful occupant of privately owned lands or the employees of such occupants may possess firearms without a permit.

Fish and Game Code § 10665.

Notwithstanding any provision of law to the contrary, in the Johnsville Game Refuge it shall be unlawful for any person to discharge a firearm or other device capable of killing or injuring any animal. However, it shall not be unlawful for the lawful occupants of privately owned lands or the employees of such occupants to possess firearms or other devices capable of killing or injuring an animal without a permit. Birds and animals lawfully taken and possessed outside of the boundaries of the Johnsville Game Refuge may be possessed within the refuge.

Food and Agricultural Code

Food and Agricultural Code § 5341.

To prevent the introduction into, or the spread within this state, of pests, the director shall maintain at such places within this state as he deems necessary plant quarantine inspection stations for the purpose of inspecting all conveyances which might carry plants or other things which are, or are liable to be, infested or infected with any pest.

Food and Agricultural Code § 5343.5.

At any inspection station maintained at or near the California border by the director pursuant to Section 5341, the following sign shall be conspicuously posted in block letters not less than four inches in height: "NOTICE: IF YOU ARE A CALIFORNIA RESIDENT, THE FEDERAL GUN CONTROL ACT MAY PROHIBIT YOU FROM BRINGING WITH YOU INTO THIS STATE FIREARMS THAT YOU ACQUIRED OUTSIDE OF THIS STATE. IN ADDITION, IF YOU ARE A NEW CALIFORNIA RESIDENT, STATE LAW REGULATES YOUR BRINGING INTO CALIFORNIA HANDGUNS AND OTHER DESIGNATED FIREARMS AND MANDATES THAT SPECIFIC PROCEDURES BE FOLLOWED. IF YOU HAVE ANY QUESTIONS ABOUT THE PROCEDURES TO BE FOLLOWED IN BRINGING FIREARMS INTO CALIFORNIA OR TRANSFERRING FIREARMS WITHIN CALIFORNIA, YOU SHOULD CONTACT THE CALIFORNIA DEPARTMENT OF JUSTICE OR A LOCAL CALIFORNIA LAW ENFORCEMENT AGENCY."

Food and Agricultural Code § 15201.

The Legislature hereby finds and declares that it is the joint responsibility of the Department of Food and Agriculture, the commissioner of each county under the direction and supervision of the director, and the Structural Pest Control Board to regulate the activities of structural pest control licensees. The Structural Pest Control Board has responsibility for licensing persons and companies engaged in structural pest control work. The department has primary responsibility for enforcing pesticide laws and regulations.

Food and Agricultural Code § 15205.

(a) Each registered structural pest control company shall make all existing records pertaining to pesticide and device use available to the director, the Structural Pest Control Board, or commissioner upon demand at the headquarters of the business during normal business hours. A registered structural pest control company or licensee may not prohibit onsite inspection for compliance with the Business and Professions Code and this division regarding pesticides and structural pest control devices and regulations adopted pursuant thereto. Except as provided in Section 8505.5 of the Business and Professions Code, nothing in this section shall be construed as requiring a registered structural pest control company or licensee to provide advance notice of the date, time, location of the application, type of device or pesticide application, or any other related information unless the information is contained in existing records available to the registered company or licensee, in which case the director, the Structural Pest Control Board, or commissioner may require that this information be produced at the company's place of business.

(b) Information and documents gathered by the director, the Structural Pest Control Board, or the commissioner pursuant to this section that are protected from disclosure under the California Public Records Act (Chapter 3.5 (commencing with Section 6250) of Division 7 of Title 1 of the Government Code) shall remain confidential while in the director's, the board's, or the commissioner's possession.

(c)(1) "Device," for purposes of this section, means any method, instrument, or contrivance intended to be used to prevent, eliminate, destroy, repel, attract, or mitigate any wood destroying pest, but does not include firearms, pesticides as defined in Section 12753, or equipment used for the application of pesticides when sold separately from a pesticide.

(2) "Wood destroying pest," for purposes of this section, includes, but is not limited to, insects such as wood borers and termites. "Wood destroying pest" does not include wood-decaying fungi, general household pests such as cockroaches, or vertebrate pests such as rats and mice.

Food and Agricultural Code § 15300.

For the purposes of this chapter, the following definitions apply:

(a) "Structural pest control device" or "device" means any method, instrument, or contrivance intended to be used to prevent, eliminate, destroy, repel, attract, or mitigate any wood destroying pest, but does not include firearms, pesticides as defined in Section 12753, or equipment used for the application of pesticides when sold separately from a pesticide.

(b) "Wood destroying pest" includes, but is not limited to, insects such as wood borers and termites. "Wood destroying pest" does not include wood-decaying fungi, general household pests such as cockroaches, or vertebrate pests such as rats and mice.

Government Code

Government Code § 830.

As used in this chapter:

(a) "Dangerous condition" means a condition of property that creates a substantial (as distinguished from a minor, trivial or insignificant) risk of injury when such property or adjacent property is used with due care in a manner in which it is reasonably foreseeable that it will be used.

(b) "Protect against" includes repairing, remedying or correcting a dangerous condition, providing safeguards against a dangerous condition, or warning of a dangerous condition.

(c) "Property of a public entity" and "public property" mean real or personal property owned or controlled by the public entity, but do not include easements, encroachments and other property that are located on the property of the public entity but are not owned or controlled by the public entity.

Government Code § 831.7.

(a) Neither a public entity nor a public employee is liable to any person who participates in a hazardous recreational activity, including any person who assists the participant, or to any spectator who knew or reasonably should have known that the hazardous recreational activity created a substantial risk of injury to himself or herself and was voluntarily in the place of risk, or having the ability to do so failed to leave, for any damage or injury to property or persons arising out of that hazardous recreational activity.

(b) As used in this section, "hazardous recreational activity" means a recreational activity conducted on property of a public entity which creates a substantial (as distinguished from a minor, trivial, or insignificant) risk of injury to a participant or a spectator. "Hazardous recreational activity" also means:

(1) Water contact activities, except diving, in places where or at a time when lifeguards are not provided and reasonable warning thereof has been given or the injured party should reasonably have known that there was no lifeguard provided at the time.

(2) Any form of diving into water from other than a diving board or diving platform, or at any place or from any structure where diving is prohibited and reasonable warning thereof has been given.

(3) Animal riding, including equestrian competition, archery, bicycle racing or jumping, mountain bicycling, boating, cross-country and downhill skiing, hang gliding, kayaking, motorized vehicle racing, off-road motorcycling or four-wheel driving of any kind, orienteering, pistol and rifle shooting, rock climbing, rocketeering, rodeo, spelunking, sky diving, sport parachuting, paragliding, body contact sports (i.e., sports in which it is reasonably foreseeable that there will be rough bodily contact with one or more participants), surfing, trampolining, tree climbing, tree rope swinging, waterskiing, white water rafting, and windsurfing. For the purposes of this subdivision, "mountain bicycling" does not include riding a bicycle on paved pathways, roadways, or sidewalks.

(c) Notwithstanding the provisions of subdivision (a), this section does not limit liability which would otherwise exist for any of the following:

(1) Failure of the public entity or employee to guard or warn of a known dangerous condition or of another hazardous recreational activity known to the public entity or employee that is not reasonably assumed by the participant as inherently a part of the hazardous recreational activity out of which the damage or injury arose.

(2) Damage or injury suffered in any case where permission to participate in the hazardous recreational activity was granted for a specific fee. For the purpose of this paragraph, a "specific fee" does not include a fee or consideration charged for a general purpose such as a general park admission charge, a vehicle entry or parking fee, or an administrative or group use application or permit fee, as distinguished from a specific fee charged for participation in the specific hazardous recreational activity out of which the damage or injury arose.

(3) Injury suffered to the extent proximately caused by the negligent failure of the public entity or public employee to properly construct or maintain in good repair any structure, recreational equipment or machinery, or substantial work of improvement utilized in the hazardous recreational activity out of which the damage or injury arose.

(4) Damage or injury suffered in any case where the public entity or employee recklessly or with gross negligence promoted the participation in or observance of a hazardous recreational activity. For purposes of this paragraph, promotional literature or a public announcement or advertisement which merely describes the available facilities and services on the property does not in itself constitute a reckless or grossly negligent promotion.

(5) An act of gross negligence by a public entity or a public employee which is the proximate cause of the injury. Nothing in this subdivision creates a duty of care or basis of liability for personal injury or for damage to personal property.

(d) Nothing in this section shall limit the liability of an independent concessionaire, or any person or organization other than the public entity, whether or not the person or organization has a contractual relationship with the public entity to use the public property, for injuries or damages suffered in any case as a result of the operation of a hazardous recreational activity on public property by the concessionaire, person, or organization.

Government Code § 6250.

In enacting this chapter, the Legislature, mindful of the right of individuals to privacy, finds and declares that access to information concerning the conduct of the people's business is a fundamental and necessary right of every person in this state.

Government Code § 6251.

This chapter shall be known and may be cited as the California Public Records Act.

Government Code § 6252.

As used in this chapter:

(a) "Local agency" includes a county; city, whether general law or chartered; city and county; school district; municipal corporation; district; political subdivision; or any board, commission or agency thereof; other local public agency; or entities that are legislative bodies of a local agency pursuant to subdivisions (c) and (d) of Section 54952.

(b) "Member of the public" means any person, except a member, agent, officer, or employee of a federal, state, or local agency acting within the scope of his or her membership, agency, office, or employment.

(c) "Person" includes any natural person, corporation, partnership, limited liability company, firm, or association.

(d) "Public agency" means any state or local agency.

(e) "Public records" includes any writing containing information relating to the conduct of the public's business prepared, owned, used, or retained by any state or local agency regardless of physical form or characteristics. "Public records" in the custody of, or maintained by, the Governor's office means any writing prepared on or after January 6, 1975.

(f) "State agency" means every state office, officer, department, division, bureau, board, and commission or other state body or agency, except those agencies provided for in Article IV (except Section 20 thereof) or Article VI of the California Constitution.

(g) "Writing" means any handwriting, typewriting, printing, photostating, photographing, photocopying, transmitting by electronic mail or facsimile, and every other means of recording upon any tangible thing any form of communication or representation, including letters, words, pictures, sounds, or symbols, or combinations thereof, and any record thereby created, regardless of the manner in which the record has been stored.

Government Code § 6252.5.

Notwithstanding the definition of "member of the public" in Section 6252, an elected member or officer of any state or local agency is entitled to access to public records of that agency on the same basis as any other person. Nothing in this section shall limit the ability of elected members or officers to access public records permitted by law in the administration of their duties. This section does not constitute a change in, but is declaratory of, existing law.

Government Code § 6252.6.

Notwithstanding paragraph (2) of subdivision (a) of Section 827 of the Welfare and Institutions Code, after the death of a foster child who is a minor, the name, date of birth, and date of death of the child shall be subject to disclosure by the county child welfare agency pursuant to this chapter.

Government Code § 6252.7.

Notwithstanding Section 6252.5 or any other provision of law, when the members of a legislative body of a local agency are authorized to access a writing of the body or of the agency as permitted by law in the administration of their duties, the local agency, as defined in Section 54951, shall not discriminate between or among any of those members as to which writing or portion thereof is made available or when it is made available.

Government Code § 6253.

(a) Public records are open to inspection at all times during the office hours of the state or local agency and every person has a right to inspect any public record, except as hereafter provided. Any reasonably segregable portion of a record shall be available for inspection by any person requesting the record after deletion of the portions that are exempted by law.

(b) Except with respect to public records exempt from disclosure by express provisions of law, each state or local agency, upon a request for a copy of records that reasonably describes an identifiable record or records, shall make the records promptly available to any person upon payment of fees covering direct costs of duplication, or a statutory fee if applicable. Upon request, an exact copy shall be provided unless impracticable to do so.

(c) Each agency, upon a request for a copy of records, shall, within 10 days from receipt of the request, determine whether the request, in whole or in part, seeks copies of disclosable public records in the possession of the agency and shall promptly notify the person making the request of the determination and the reasons therefor. In unusual circumstances, the time limit prescribed in this section may be extended by written notice by the head of the agency or his or her designee to the person making the request, setting forth the reasons for the extension and the date on which a determination is expected to be dispatched. No notice shall specify a date that would result in an extension for more than 14 days. When the agency dispatches the determination, and if the agency determines that the request seeks disclosable public records, the agency shall state the estimated date and time when the records will be made available. As used in this section, "unusual circumstances" means the following, but only to the extent reasonably necessary to the proper processing of the particular request:

(1) The need to search for and collect the requested records from field facilities or other establishments that are separate from the office processing the request.

(2) The need to search for, collect, and appropriately examine a voluminous amount of separate and distinct records that are demanded in a single request.

(3) The need for consultation, which shall be conducted with all practicable speed, with another agency having substantial interest in the determination of the request or among two or more components of the agency having substantial subject matter interest therein.

(4) The need to compile data, to write programming language or a computer program, or to construct a computer report to extract data.

(d) Nothing in this chapter shall be construed to permit an agency to delay or obstruct the inspection or copying of public records. The notification of denial of any request for records required by Section 6255 shall set forth the names and titles or positions of each person responsible for the denial.

(e) Except as otherwise prohibited by law, a state or local agency may adopt requirements for itself that allow for faster, more efficient, or greater access to records than prescribed by the minimum standards set forth in this chapter.

Government Code § 6253.1.

(a) When a member of the public requests to inspect a public record or obtain a copy of a public record, the public agency, in order to assist the member of the public make a focused and effective request that reasonably describes an identifiable record or records, shall do all of the following, to the extent reasonable under the circumstances:

(1) Assist the member of the public to identify records and information that are responsive to the request or to the purpose of the request, if stated.

(2) Describe the information technology and physical location in which the records exist.

(3) Provide suggestions for overcoming any practical basis for denying access to the records or information sought.

(b) The requirements of paragraph (1) of subdivision (a) shall be deemed to have been satisfied if the public agency is unable to identify the requested information after making a reasonable effort to elicit additional clarifying information from the requester that will help identify the record or records.

(c) The requirements of subdivision (a) are in addition to any action required of a public agency by Section 6253.

(d) This section shall not apply to a request for public records if any of the following applies:

(1) The public agency makes available the requested records pursuant to Section 6253.

(2) The public agency determines that the request should be denied and bases that determination solely on an exemption listed in Section 6254.

(3) The public agency makes available an index of its records.

Government Code § 6253.3.

A state or local agency may not allow another party to control the disclosure of information that is otherwise subject to disclosure pursuant to this chapter.

Government Code § 6254.

Except as provided in Sections 6254.7 and 6254.13, nothing in this chapter shall be construed to require disclosure of records that are any of the following:

(a) Preliminary drafts, notes, or interagency or intra-agency memoranda that are not retained by the public agency in the ordinary course of business, if the public interest in withholding those records clearly outweighs the public interest in disclosure.

(b) Records pertaining to pending litigation to which the public agency is a party, or to claims made pursuant to Division 3.6 (commencing with Section 810), until the pending litigation or claim has been finally adjudicated or otherwise settled.

(c) Personnel, medical, or similar files, the disclosure of which would constitute an unwarranted invasion of personal privacy.

(d) Contained in or related to any of the following:

(1) Applications filed with any state agency responsible for the regulation or supervision of the issuance of securities or of financial institutions, including, but not limited to, banks, savings and loan associations, industrial loan companies, credit unions, and insurance companies.

(2) Examination, operating, or condition reports prepared by, on behalf of, or for the use of, any state agency referred to in paragraph (1).

(3) Preliminary drafts, notes, or interagency or intra-agency communications prepared by, on behalf of, or for the use of, any state agency referred to in paragraph (1).

(4) Information received in confidence by any state agency referred to in paragraph (1).

(e) Geological and geophysical data, plant production data, and similar information relating to utility systems development, or market or crop reports, that are obtained in confidence from any person.

(f) Records of complaints to, or investigations conducted by, or records of intelligence information or security procedures of, the office of the Attorney General and the Department of Justice, the California Emergency Management Agency, and any state or local police agency, or any investigatory or security files compiled by any other state or local police agency, or any investigatory or security files compiled by any other state or local agency for correctional, law enforcement, or licensing purposes. However, state and local law enforcement agencies shall disclose the names and addresses of persons involved in, or witnesses other than confidential informants to, the incident, the description of any property involved, the date, time, and location of the incident, all diagrams, statements of the parties involved in the incident, the statements of all witnesses, other than confidential informants, to the victims of an incident, or an authorized representative thereof, an insurance carrier against which a claim has been or might be made, and any person suffering bodily injury or property damage or loss, as the result of the incident caused by arson, burglary, fire, explosion, larceny, robbery, carjacking, vandalism, vehicle theft, or a crime as defined by subdivision (b) of Section 13951, unless the disclosure would endanger the safety of a witness or other person involved in the investigation, or unless disclosure would endanger the successful completion of the investigation or a related investigation. However, nothing in this division shall require the disclosure of that portion of those investigative files that reflects the analysis or conclusions of the investigating officer. Customer lists provided to a state or local police agency by an alarm or security company at the request of the agency shall be construed to be records subject to this subdivision. Notwithstanding any other provision of this subdivision, state and local law enforcement agencies shall make public the following information, except to the extent that disclosure of a particular item of information would endanger the safety of a person involved in an investigation or would endanger the successful completion of the investigation or a related investigation:

(1) The full name and occupation of every individual arrested by the agency, the individual's physical description including date of birth, color of eyes and hair, sex, height and weight, the time and date of arrest, the time and date of booking, the location of the arrest, the factual circumstances surrounding the arrest, the amount of bail set, the time and manner of release or the location where the individual is currently being held, and all charges the individual is being held upon, including any outstanding warrants from other jurisdictions and parole or probation holds.

(2) Subject to the restrictions imposed by Section 841.5 of the Penal Code, the time, substance, and location of all complaints or requests for assistance received by the agency and the time and nature of the response thereto, including, to the extent the information regarding crimes alleged or committed or any other incident investigated is recorded, the time, date, and location of occurrence, the time and date of the report, the name and age of the victim, the factual circumstances surrounding the crime or incident, and a general description of any injuries, property, or weapons involved. The name of a victim of any crime defined by Section 220, 236.1, 261, 261.5,

262, 264, 264.1, 265, 266, 266a, 266b, 266c, 266e, 266f, 266j, 267, 269, 273a, 273d, 273.5, 285, 286, 288, 288a, 288.2, 288.3 (as added by Chapter 337 of the Statutes of 2006), 288.3 (as added by Section 6 of Proposition 83 of the November 7, 2006, statewide general election), 288.5, 288.7, 289, 422.6, 422.7, 422.75, 646.9, or 647.6 of the Penal Code may be withheld at the victim's request, or at the request of the victim's parent or guardian if the victim is a minor. When a person is the victim of more than one crime, information disclosing that the person is a victim of a crime defined in any of the sections of the Penal Code set forth in this subdivision may be deleted at the request of the victim, or the victim's parent or guardian if the victim is a minor, in making the report of the crime, or of any crime or incident accompanying the crime, available to the public in compliance with the requirements of this paragraph.

(3) Subject to the restrictions of Section 841.5 of the Penal Code and this subdivision, the current address of every individual arrested by the agency and the current address of the victim of a crime, where the requester declares under penalty of perjury that the request is made for a scholarly, journalistic, political, or governmental purpose, or that the request is made for investigation purposes by a licensed private investigator as described in Chapter 11.3 (commencing with Section 7512) of Division 3 of the Business and Professions Code. However, the address of the victim of any crime defined by Section 220, 236.1, 261, 261.5, 262, 264, 264.1, 265, 266, 266a, 266b, 266c, 266e, 266f, 266j, 267, 269, 273a, 273d, 273.5, 285, 286, 288, 288a, 288.2, 288.3 (as added by Chapter 337 of the Statutes of 2006), 288.3 (as added by Section 6 of Proposition 83 of the November 7, 2006, statewide general election), 288.5, 288.7, 289, 422.6, 422.7, 422.75, 646.9, or 647.6 of the Penal Code shall remain confidential. Address information obtained pursuant to this paragraph may not be used directly or indirectly, or furnished to another, to sell a product or service to any individual or group of individuals, and the requester shall execute a declaration to that effect under penalty of perjury. Nothing in this paragraph shall be construed to prohibit or limit a scholarly, journalistic, political, or government use of address information obtained pursuant to this paragraph.

(g) Test questions, scoring keys, and other examination data used to administer a licensing examination, examination for employment, or academic examination, except as provided for in Chapter 3 (commencing with Section 99150) of Part 65 of Division 14 of Title 3 of the Education Code.

(h) The contents of real estate appraisals or engineering or feasibility estimates and evaluations made for or by the state or local agency relative to the acquisition of property, or to prospective public supply and construction contracts, until all of the property has been acquired or all of the contract agreement obtained. However, the law of eminent domain shall not be affected by this provision.

(i) Information required from any taxpayer in connection with the collection of local taxes that is received in confidence and the disclosure of the information to other persons would result in unfair competitive disadvantage to the person supplying the information.

(j) Library circulation records kept for the purpose of identifying the borrower of items available in libraries, and library and museum materials made or acquired and presented solely for reference or exhibition purposes. The exemption in this subdivision shall not apply to records of fines imposed on the borrowers.

(k) Records, the disclosure of which is exempted or prohibited pursuant to federal or state law, including, but not limited to, provisions of the Evidence Code relating to privilege.

(l) Correspondence of and to the Governor or employees of the Governor's office or in the custody of or maintained by the Governor' s Legal Affairs Secretary. However, public records shall not be transferred to the custody of the Governor's Legal Affairs Secretary to evade the disclosure provisions of this chapter.

(m) In the custody of or maintained by the Legislative Counsel, except those records in the public database maintained by the Legislative Counsel that are described in Section 10248.

(n) Statements of personal worth or personal financial data required by a licensing agency and filed by an applicant with the licensing agency to establish his or her personal qualification for the license, certificate, or permit applied for.

(o) Financial data contained in applications for financing under Division 27 (commencing with Section 44500) of the Health and Safety Code, where an authorized officer of the California Pollution Control Financing Authority determines that disclosure of the financial data would be competitively injurious to the applicant and the data is required in order to obtain guarantees from the United States Small Business Administration. The California Pollution Control Financing Authority shall adopt rules for review of individual requests for confidentiality under this section and for making available to the public those portions of an application that are subject to disclosure under this chapter.

(p) Records of state agencies related to activities governed by Chapter 10.3 (commencing with Section 3512), Chapter 10.5 (commencing with Section 3525), and Chapter 12 (commencing with Section 3560) of Division 4, that reveal a state agency's deliberative processes, impressions, evaluations, opinions, recommendations, meeting minutes, research, work products, theories, or strategy, or that provide instruction, advice, or training to employees who do not have full collective bargaining and representation rights under these chapters. Nothing in this subdivision shall be construed to limit the disclosure duties of a state agency with respect to any other records relating to the activities governed by the employee relations acts referred to in this subdivision.

(q) Records of state agencies related to activities governed by Article 2.6 (commencing with Section 14081), Article 2.8 (commencing with Section 14087.5), and Article 2.91 (commencing with Section 14089) of Chapter 7 of Part 3 of Division 9 of the Welfare and Institutions Code, that reveal the special negotiator's deliberative processes, discussions, communications, or any other portion of the negotiations with providers of health care services, impressions, opinions, recommendations, meeting minutes, research, work product, theories, or strategy, or that provide instruction, advice, or training to employees. Except for the portion of a contract containing the rates of payment, contracts for inpatient services entered into pursuant to these articles, on or after April 1, 1984, shall be open to inspection one year after they are fully executed. If a contract for inpatient services that is entered into prior to April 1, 1984, is amended on or after April 1, 1984, the amendment, except for any portion containing the rates of payment, shall be open to inspection one year after it is fully executed. If the California Medical Assistance Commission enters into contracts with health care providers for other than inpatient hospital services, those contracts shall be open to inspection one year after they are fully executed. Three years after a contract or amendment is open to inspection under this subdivision, the portion of the contract or amendment containing the rates of payment shall be open to inspection. Notwithstanding any other provision of law, the entire contract or amendment shall be open to inspection by the Joint Legislative Audit Committee and the Legislative Analyst's Office. The committee and that office shall maintain the confidentiality of the contracts and amendments until the time a contract or amendment is fully open to inspection by the public.

(r) Records of Native American graves, cemeteries, and sacred places and records of Native American places, features, and objects described in Sections 5097.9 and 5097.993 of the Public Resources Code maintained by, or in the possession of, the Native

American Heritage Commission, another state agency, or a local agency.

(s) A final accreditation report of the Joint Commission on Accreditation of Hospitals that has been transmitted to the State Department of Health Care Services pursuant to subdivision (b) of Section 1282 of the Health and Safety Code.

(t) Records of a local hospital district, formed pursuant to Division 23 (commencing with Section 32000) of the Health and Safety Code, or the records of a municipal hospital, formed pursuant to Article 7 (commencing with Section 37600) or Article 8 (commencing with Section 37650) of Chapter 5 of Part 2 of Division 3 of Title 4 of this code, that relate to any contract with an insurer or nonprofit hospital service plan for inpatient or outpatient services for alternative rates pursuant to Section 10133 of the Insurance Code. However, the record shall be open to inspection within one year after the contract is fully executed.

(u)(1) Information contained in applications for licenses to carry firearms issued pursuant to Section 12050 of the Penal Code by the sheriff of a county or the chief or other head of a municipal police department that indicates when or where the applicant is vulnerable to attack or that concerns the applicant's medical or psychological history or that of members of his or her family.

(2) The home address and telephone number of peace officers, judges, court commissioners, and magistrates that are set forth in applications for licenses to carry firearms issued pursuant to Section 12050 of the Penal Code by the sheriff of a county or the chief or other head of a municipal police department.

(3) The home address and telephone number of peace officers, judges, court commissioners, and magistrates that are set forth in licenses to carry firearms issued pursuant to Section 12050 of the Penal Code by the sheriff of a county or the chief or other head of a municipal police department.

(v)(1) Records of the Managed Risk Medical Insurance Board related to activities governed by Part 6.3 (commencing with Section 12695) and Part 6.5 (commencing with Section 12700) of Division 2 of the Insurance Code, and that reveal the deliberative processes, discussions, communications, or any other portion of the negotiations with entities contracting or seeking to contract with the board, or the impressions, opinions, recommendations, meeting minutes, research, work product, theories, or strategy of the board or its staff, or records that provide instructions, advice, or training to employees.

(2)(A) Except for the portion of a contract that contains the rates of payment, contracts for health coverage entered into pursuant to Part 6.3 (commencing with Section 12695) or Part 6.5 (commencing with Section 12700) of Division 2 of the Insurance Code, on or after July 1, 1991, shall be open to inspection one year after their effective dates.

(B) If a contract that is entered into prior to July 1, 1991, is amended on or after July 1, 1991, the amendment, except for any portion containing the rates of payment, shall be open to inspection one year after the amendment has been fully executed.

(3) Three years after a contract or amendment is open to inspection pursuant to this subdivision, the portion of the contract or amendment containing the rates of payment shall be open to inspection.

(4) Notwithstanding any other provision of law, the entire contract or amendments to a contract shall be open to inspection by the Joint Legislative Audit Committee. The committee shall maintain the confidentiality of the contracts and amendments thereto, until the contracts or amendments to the contracts are open to inspection pursuant to paragraph (3).

(w)(1) Records of the Managed Risk Medical Insurance Board related to activities governed by Chapter 8 (commencing with Section 10700) of Part 2 of Division 2 of the Insurance Code, and that reveal the deliberative processes, discussions, communications, or any other portion of the negotiations with health plans, or the impressions, opinions, recommendations, meeting minutes, research, work product, theories, or strategy of the board or its staff, or records that provide instructions, advice, or training to employees.

(2) Except for the portion of a contract that contains the rates of payment, contracts for health coverage entered into pursuant to Chapter 8 (commencing with Section 10700) of Part 2 of Division 2 of the Insurance Code, on or after January 1, 1993, shall be open to inspection one year after they have been fully executed.

(3) Notwithstanding any other provision of law, the entire contract or amendments to a contract shall be open to inspection by the Joint Legislative Audit Committee. The committee shall maintain the confidentiality of the contracts and amendments thereto, until the contracts or amendments to the contracts are open to inspection pursuant to paragraph (2).

(x) Financial data contained in applications for registration, or registration renewal, as a service contractor filed with the Director of Consumer Affairs pursuant to Chapter 20 (commencing with Section 9800) of Division 3 of the Business and Professions Code, for the purpose of establishing the service contractor's net worth, or financial data regarding the funded accounts held in escrow for service contracts held in force in this state by a service contractor.

(y)(1) Records of the Managed Risk Medical Insurance Board related to activities governed by Part 6.2 (commencing with Section 12693) or Part 6.4 (commencing with Section 12699.50) of Division 2 of the Insurance Code, and that reveal the deliberative processes, discussions, communications, or any other portion of the negotiations with entities contracting or seeking to contract with the board, or the impressions, opinions, recommendations, meeting minutes, research, work product, theories, or strategy of the board or its staff, or records that provide instructions, advice, or training to employees.

(2)(A) Except for the portion of a contract that contains the rates of payment, contracts entered into pursuant to Part 6.2 (commencing with Section 12693) or Part 6.4 (commencing with Section 12699.50) of Division 2 of the Insurance Code, on or after January 1, 1998, shall be open to inspection one year after their effective dates.

(B) If a contract entered into pursuant to Part 6.2 (commencing with Section 12693) or Part 6.4 (commencing with Section 12699.50) of Division 2 of the Insurance Code is amended, the amendment shall be open to inspection one year after the amendment has been fully executed.

(3) Three years after a contract or amendment is open to inspection pursuant to this subdivision, the portion of the contract or amendment containing the rates of payment shall be open to inspection.

(4) Notwithstanding any other provision of law, the entire contract or amendments to a contract shall be open to inspection by the Joint Legislative Audit Committee. The committee shall maintain the confidentiality of the contracts and amendments thereto until the contract or amendments to a contract are open to inspection pursuant to paragraph (2) or (3).

(5) The exemption from disclosure provided pursuant to this subdivision for the contracts, deliberative processes, discussions, communications, negotiations, impressions, opinions, recommendations, meeting minutes, research, work product, theories, or strategy of the board or its staff shall also apply to the contracts, deliberative processes, discussions, communications, negotiations, impressions, opinions, recommendations, meeting minutes, research, work product, theories, or strategy of applicants pursuant to Part

6.4 (commencing with Section 12699.50) of Division 2 of the Insurance Code.

(z) Records obtained pursuant to paragraph (2) of subdivision (c) of Section 2891.1 of the Public Utilities Code.

(aa) A document prepared by or for a state or local agency that assesses its vulnerability to terrorist attack or other criminal acts intended to disrupt the public agency's operations and that is for distribution or consideration in a closed session.

(ab) Critical infrastructure information, as defined in Section 131(3) of Title 6 of the United States Code, that is voluntarily submitted to the California Emergency Management Agency for use by that office, including the identity of the person who or entity that voluntarily submitted the information. As used in this subdivision, "voluntarily submitted" means submitted in the absence of the office exercising any legal authority to compel access to or submission of critical infrastructure information. This subdivision shall not affect the status of information in the possession of any other state or local governmental agency.

(ac) All information provided to the Secretary of State by a person for the purpose of registration in the Advance Health Care Directive Registry, except that those records shall be released at the request of a health care provider, a public guardian, or the registrant's legal representative. (ad) The following records of the State Compensation Insurance Fund:

(1) Records related to claims pursuant to Chapter 1 (commencing with Section 3200) of Division 4 of the Labor Code, to the extent that confidential medical information or other individually identifiable information would be disclosed.

(2) Records related to the discussions, communications, or any other portion of the negotiations with entities contracting or seeking to contract with the fund, and any related deliberations.

(3) Records related to the impressions, opinions, recommendations, meeting minutes of meetings or sessions that are lawfully closed to the public, research, work product, theories, or strategy of the fund or its staff, on the development of rates, contracting strategy, underwriting, or competitive strategy pursuant to the powers granted to the fund in Chapter 4 (commencing with Section 11770) of Part 3 of Division 2 of the Insurance Code.

(4) Records obtained to provide workers' compensation insurance under Chapter 4 (commencing with Section 11770) of Part 3 of Division 2 of the Insurance Code, including, but not limited to, any medical claims information, policyholder information provided that nothing in this paragraph shall be interpreted to prevent an insurance agent or broker from obtaining proprietary information or other information authorized by law to be obtained by the agent or broker, and information on rates, pricing, and claims handling received from brokers.

(5)(A) Records that are trade secrets pursuant to Section 6276.44, or Article 11 (commencing with Section 1060) of Chapter 4 of Division 8 of the Evidence Code, including without limitation, instructions, advice, or training provided by the State Compensation Insurance Fund to its board members, officers, and employees regarding the fund's special investigation unit, internal audit unit, and informational security, marketing, rating, pricing, underwriting, claims handling, audits, and collections.

(B) Notwithstanding subparagraph (A), the portions of records containing trade secrets shall be available for review by the Joint Legislative Audit Committee, the Bureau of State Audits, Division of Workers' Compensation, and the Department of Insurance to ensure compliance with applicable law.

(6)(A) Internal audits containing proprietary information and the following records that are related to an internal audit:

(i) Personal papers and correspondence of any person providing assistance to the fund when that person has requested in writing that his or her papers and correspondence be kept private and confidential. Those papers and correspondence shall become public records if the written request is withdrawn, or upon order of the fund.

(ii) Papers, correspondence, memoranda, or any substantive information pertaining to any audit not completed or an internal audit that contains proprietary information.

(B) Notwithstanding subparagraph (A), the portions of records containing proprietary information, or any information specified in subparagraph (A) shall be available for review by the Joint Legislative Audit Committee, the Bureau of State Audits, Division of Workers' Compensation, and the Department of Insurance to ensure compliance with applicable law.

(7)(A) Except as provided in subparagraph (C), contracts entered into pursuant to Chapter 4 (commencing with Section 11770) of Part 3 of Division 2 of the Insurance Code shall be open to inspection one year after the contract has been fully executed.

(B) If a contract entered into pursuant to Chapter 4 (commencing with Section 11770) of Part 3 of Division 2 of the Insurance Code is amended, the amendment shall be open to inspection one year after the amendment has been fully executed.

(C) Three years after a contract or amendment is open to inspection pursuant to this subdivision, the portion of the contract or amendment containing the rates of payment shall be open to inspection.

(D) Notwithstanding any other provision of law, the entire contract or amendments to a contract shall be open to inspection by the Joint Legislative Audit Committee. The committee shall maintain the confidentiality of the contracts and amendments thereto until the contract or amendments to a contract are open to inspection pursuant to this paragraph.

(E) Nothing in this paragraph is intended to apply to documents related to contracts with public entities that are not otherwise expressly confidential as to that public entity.

(F) For purposes of this paragraph, "fully executed" means the point in time when all of the necessary parties to the contract have signed the contract. Nothing in this section prevents any agency from opening its records concerning the administration of the agency to public inspection, unless disclosure is otherwise prohibited by law. Nothing in this section prevents any health facility from disclosing to a certified bargaining agent relevant financing information pursuant to Section 8 of the National Labor Relations Act (29 U.S.C. Sec. 158).

Government Code § 6276.18.

Family counselor and client, confidential information, Section 4982, Business and Professions Code. Family Court, records, Section 1818, Family Law Code. Farm product processor license, confidentiality of financial statements, Section 55523.6, Food and Agricultural Code. Farm product processor licensee, confidentiality of grape purchases, Section 55601.5, Food and Agricultural Code. Fee payer information, prohibition against disclosure by Board of Equalization and others, Section 55381, Revenue and Taxation Code. Financial institutions, issuance of securities, reports and records of state agencies, subdivision (d), Section 6254, Government Code. Financial records, confidentiality of, Sections 7470, 7471, and 7473, Government Code. Financial statements of insurers, confidentiality of information received, Section 925.3, Insurance Code. Financial statements and questionnaires, of prospective bidders for the state, confidentiality of, Section 10165, Public Contract Code. Financial statements and questionnaires, of prospective bidders for California State University contracts, confidentiality of, Section 10763, Public Contract Code. Firearm license applications, subdivision (u), Section 6254, Government Code. Firearm sale or transfer, confidentiality of records, Section 12082, Penal Code. Firefighters Service Award, confidentiality of data filed with the Board of Administration of the Public Employees' Retirement System, Section 50955, Government Code. Fish and wildlife law enforcement agreements with other states, confidentiality of information, Section 391, Fish and Game Code. Fish and wildlife taken illegally, public record status of records of case, Section 2584, Fish and Game Code. Food stamps, disclosure of information, Section 18909, Welfare and Institutions Code. Foreign marketing of agricultural products, confidentiality of financial information, Section 58577, Food and Agricultural Code. Forest fires, anonymity of informants, Section 4417, Public Resources Code. Foster homes, identifying information, Section 1536, Health and Safety Code. Franchise Tax Board, access to Franchise Tax Board information by the State Department of Social Services, Section 11025, Welfare and Institutions Code. Franchise Tax Board, auditing, confidentiality of, Section 90005, Government Code. Franchises, applications, and reports filed with Commissioner of Corporations, disclosure and withholding from public inspection, Section 31504, Corporations Code. Fur dealer licensee, confidentiality of records, Section 4041, Fish and Game Code.

Government Code § 8550.

The state has long recognized its responsibility to mitigate the effects of natural, manmade, or war-caused emergencies which result in conditions of disaster or in extreme peril to life, property, and the resources of the state, and generally to protect the health and safety and preserve the lives and property of the people of the state. To ensure that preparations within the state will be adequate to deal with such emergencies, it is hereby found and declared to be necessary:

(a) To confer upon the Governor and upon the chief executives and governing bodies of political subdivisions of this state the emergency powers provided herein; and to provide for state assistance in the organization and maintenance of the emergency programs of such political subdivisions.

(b) To provide for a state agency to be known and referred to as the California Emergency Management Agency (Cal EMA), within the office of the Governor, and to prescribe the powers and duties of the secretary of that agency.

(c) To provide for the assignment of functions to state agencies to be performed during an emergency and for the coordination and direction of the emergency actions of such agencies.

(d) To provide for the rendering of mutual aid by the state government and all its departments and agencies and by the political subdivisions of this state in carrying out the purposes of this chapter.

(e) To authorize the establishment of such organizations and the taking of such actions as are necessary and proper to carry out the provisions of this chapter. It is further declared to be the purpose of this chapter and the policy of this state that all emergency services functions of this state be coordinated as far as possible with the comparable functions of its political subdivisions, of the federal government including its various departments and agencies, of other states, and of private agencies of every type, to the end that the most effective use may be made of all manpower, resources, and facilities for dealing with any emergency that may occur.

Government Code § 8551.

This chapter may be cited as the "California Emergency Services Act."

Government Code § 8556.

"Governor" means the Governor or the person upon whom the powers and duties of the office of Governor have devolved pursuant to Section 10 of Article V of the California Constitution.

Government Code § 8557.

(a) "Emergency Council" means the California Emergency Council.

(b) "State agency" means any department, division, independent establishment, or agency of the executive branch of the state government.

(c) "Political subdivision" includes any city, city and county, county, district, or other local governmental agency or public agency authorized by law.

(d) "Governing body" means the legislative body, trustees, or directors of a political subdivision.

(e) "Chief executive" means that individual authorized by law to act for the governing body of a political subdivision.

(f) "Disaster council" and "disaster service worker" have the meaning prescribed in Chapter 1 (commencing with Section 3201) of Part 1 of Division 4 of the Labor Code.

(g) "Public facility" means any facility of the state or a political subdivision, which facility is owned, operated, or maintained, or any combination thereof, through moneys derived by taxation or assessment.

(h) "Sudden and severe energy shortage" means a rapid, unforeseen shortage of energy, resulting from, but not limited to, events such as an embargo, sabotage, or natural disasters, and which has statewide, regional, or local impact.

Government Code § 8558.

Three conditions or degrees of emergency are established by this chapter:

(a) "State of war emergency" means the condition which exists immediately, with or without a proclamation thereof by the Governor, whenever this state or nation is attacked by an enemy of the United States, or upon receipt by the state of a warning from the federal government indicating that such an enemy attack is probable or imminent.

(b) "State of emergency" means the duly proclaimed existence of conditions of disaster or of extreme peril to the safety of persons and property within the state caused by such conditions as air pollution, fire, flood, storm, epidemic, riot, drought, sudden and severe energy shortage, plant or animal infestation or disease, the Governor's warning of an earthquake or volcanic prediction, or an earthquake, or other conditions, other than conditions resulting from a labor controversy or conditions causing a "state of war emergency," which, by reason of their magnitude, are or are likely to be beyond the control of the services, personnel, equipment, and facilities of any single county, city and county, or city and require the combined forces of a mutual aid region or regions to combat, or with respect to regulated energy utilities, a sudden and severe energy shortage requires extraordinary measures beyond the authority vested in the

California Public Utilities Commission.

(c) "Local emergency" means the duly proclaimed existence of conditions of disaster or of extreme peril to the safety of persons and property within the territorial limits of a county, city and county, or city, caused by such conditions as air pollution, fire, flood, storm, epidemic, riot, drought, sudden and severe energy shortage, plant or animal infestation or disease, the Governor's warning of an earthquake or volcanic prediction, or an earthquake, or other conditions, other than conditions resulting from a labor controversy, which are or are likely to be beyond the control of the services, personnel, equipment, and facilities of that political subdivision and require the combined forces of other political subdivisions to combat, or with respect to regulated energy utilities, a sudden and severe energy shortage requires extraordinary measures beyond the authority vested in the California Public Utilities Commission.

Government Code § 8559.

(a) A "mutual aid region" is a subdivision of the state emergency services organization, established to facilitate the coordination of mutual aid and other emergency operations within an area of the state consisting of two or more county operational areas.

(b) An "operational area" is an intermediate level of the state emergency services organization, consisting of a county and all political subdivisions within the county area.

Government Code § 8560.

(a) "Emergency plans" means those official and approved documents which describe the principles and methods to be applied in carrying out emergency operations or rendering mutual aid during emergencies. These plans include such elements as continuity of government, the emergency services of governmental agencies, mobilization of resources, mutual aid, and public information.

(b) "State Emergency Plan" means the State of California Emergency Plan as approved by the Governor.

Government Code § 8561.

"Master Mutual Aid Agreement" means the California Disaster and Civil Defense Master Mutual Aid Agreement, made and entered into by and between the State of California, its various departments and agencies, and the various political subdivisions of the state, to facilitate implementation of the purposes of this chapter.

Government Code § 8565.

The Governor shall have the powers granted by this article, which powers shall be in addition to any other powers granted to him by this chapter.

Government Code § 8566.

The Governor is empowered to expend any appropriation for support of the California Emergency Services Act to carry out the provisions of this chapter.

Government Code § 8567.

(a) The Governor may make, amend, and rescind orders and regulations necessary to carry out the provisions of this chapter. The orders and regulations shall have the force and effect of law. Due consideration shall be given to the plans of the federal government in preparing the orders and regulations. The Governor shall cause widespread publicity and notice to be given to all such orders and regulations, or amendments or rescissions thereof.

(b) Orders and regulations, or amendments or rescissions thereof, issued during a state of war emergency or state of emergency shall be in writing and shall take effect immediately upon their issuance. Whenever the state of war emergency or state of emergency has been terminated, the orders and regulations shall be of no further force or effect.

(c) All orders and regulations relating to the use of funds pursuant to Article 16 (commencing with Section 8645) shall be prepared in advance of any commitment or expenditure of the funds. Other orders and regulations needed to carry out the provisions of this chapter shall, whenever practicable, be prepared in advance of a state of war emergency or state of emergency.

(d) All orders and regulations made in advance of a state of war emergency or state of emergency shall be in writing, shall be exempt from Chapter 3.5 (commencing with Section 11340) of Part 1 of Division 3 of Title 2, but shall be subject to the approval of the Emergency Council. As soon thereafter as possible they shall be filed in the office of the Secretary of State and with the county clerk of each county.

Government Code § 8568.

The State Emergency Plan shall be in effect in each political subdivision of the state, and the governing body of each political subdivision shall take such action as may be necessary to carry out the provisions thereof.

Government Code § 8569.

The Governor shall coordinate the State Emergency Plan and those programs necessary for the mitigation of the effects of an emergency in this state; and he shall coordinate the preparation of plans and programs for the mitigation of the effects of an emergency by the political subdivisions of this state, such plans and programs to be integrated into and coordinated with the State Emergency Plan and the plans and programs of the federal government and of other states to the fullest possible extent.

Government Code § 8570.

The Governor may, in accordance with the State Emergency Plan and programs for the mitigation of the effects of an emergency in this state:

(a) Ascertain the requirements of the state or its political subdivisions for food, clothing, and other necessities of life in the event of an emergency.

(b) Plan for, procure, and pre-position supplies, medicines, materials, and equipment.

(c) Use and employ any of the property, services, and resources of the state as necessary to carry out the purposes of this chapter.

(d) Provide for the approval of local emergency plans.

(e) Provide for mobile support units.

(f) Provide for use of public airports.

(g) Institute training programs and public information programs.

(h) Make surveys of the industries, resources, and facilities, both public and private, within the state, as are necessary to carry out the purposes of this chapter.

(i) Plan for the use of any private facilities, services, and property and, when necessary, and when in fact used, provide for payment for that use under the terms and conditions as may be agreed upon.

(j) Take all other preparatory steps, including the partial or full mobilization of emergency organizations in advance of an actual emergency; and order those test exercises needed to insure the furnishing of adequately trained and equipped personnel in time of need.

Government Code § 8570.5.

The California Emergency Management Agency shall develop a guidance document to the state emergency plan to specify the response of the state and its political subdivisions to agriculture-related disasters. This document shall be completed by January 2002, and updated by January 2009, and shall include, but not be limited to, all of the following:

(a) The roles and responsibilities of the county agricultural commissioners.

(b) The roles and responsibilities of the Department of Agriculture and other relevant state agencies that are involved in the response to agriculture-related disasters.

(c) Coordination of initial and ongoing crop damage assessments.

(d) Disaster assistance between the time of the request for a federal disaster declaration and issuance of a federal declaration.

(e) State assistance available if a requested federal declaration is not issued.

(f) State assistance under a United States Department of Agriculture designation rather than a federal declaration.

(g) State assistance for long-term unemployment in areas with high unemployment rates prior to an emergency.

(h) Provision for the removal and elimination of extraordinary numbers of dead livestock for purposes of protecting public health and safety.

(i) Strategies to assist in the development of an integrated and coordinated response by community-based organizations to the victims of agriculture-related disasters.

(j) Procedures for the decontamination of individuals who have been or may have been exposed to hazardous materials, which may vary depending on the hazards posed by a particular hazardous material. The report shall specify that individuals shall be assisted in a humanitarian manner.

(k) Integration of various local and state emergency response plans, including, but not limited to, plans that relate to hazardous materials, oil spills, public health emergencies, and general disasters.

Government Code § 8571.

During a state of war emergency or a state of emergency the Governor may suspend any regulatory statute, or statute prescribing the procedure for conduct of state business, or the orders, rules, or regulations of any state agency, including subdivision (d) of Section 1253 of the Unemployment Insurance Code, where the Governor determines and declares that strict compliance with any statute, order, rule, or regulation would in any way prevent, hinder, or delay the mitigation of the effects of the emergency.

Government Code § 8571.5.

Nothing in this article shall authorize the seizure or confiscation of any firearm or ammunition from any individual who is lawfully carrying or possessing the firearm or ammunition, or authorize any order to that effect, provided however, that a peace officer who is acting in his or her official capacity may disarm an individual if the officer reasonably believes it is immediately necessary for the protection of the officer or another individual. The officer shall return the firearm to the individual before discharging the individual, unless the officer arrests that individual or seizes the firearm as evidence pursuant to an investigation for the commission of a crime.

Government Code § 8572..

In the exercise of the emergency powers hereby vested in him during a state of war emergency or state of emergency, the Governor is authorized to commandeer or utilize any private property or personnel deemed by him necessary in carrying out the responsibilities hereby vested in him as Chief Executive of the state and the state shall pay the reasonable value thereof. Notwithstanding the provisions of this section, the Governor is not authorized to commandeer any newspaper, newspaper wire service, or radio or television station, but may, during a state of war emergency or state of emergency, and if no other means of communication are available, utilize any news wire services, and the state shall pay the reasonable value of such use. In so utilizing any such facilities, the Governor shall interfere as little as possible with their use for the transmission of news.

Government Code § 8573.

The Governor may cooperate with the President and the heads of the armed forces and other agencies of the United States, and with officers and agencies of other states, on matters pertaining to emergencies; and he may take any steps he deems necessary to put into effect any rules, regulations, or suggestions made by such persons or agencies.

Government Code § 8574.

None of the provisions of this chapter shall limit, modify, or abridge the powers vested in the Governor under the Constitution or statutes of the state by proclamation, to declare any county, city and county, or city, or any portion thereof to be in a state of insurrection or to proclaim the existence of martial law and to exercise all the powers vested in him thereunder independent of, or in conjunction with, any of the provisions of this chapter.

Government Code § 8588.3.

(a) The Legislature finds and declares that it is the responsibility of the State of California to protect and preserve the right of its citizens to a safe and peaceful existence. To accomplish this goal and to minimize the destructive impact of disasters and other massive emergencies, the actions of numerous public agencies must be coordinated to effectively manage all four phases of emergency activity: preparedness, mitigation, response, and recovery. In order to ensure that the state's response to disasters or massive emergencies is effective, specialized training is necessary.

(b) The California Specialized Training Institute of the office of the Adjutant General is hereby transferred to the California Emergency Management Agency. The institute shall assist the Governor in providing, pursuant to subdivision (f) of Section 8570, training to state agencies, cities, and counties in their planning and preparation for disasters.

(c) The Secretary of California Emergency Management may solicit, receive, and administer funds or property from federal, state, or other public agency sources for the support and operation of the institute.

(d) The Secretary of California Emergency Management may solicit and receive firearms, other weaponry, explosive materials, chemical agents, and other items confiscated by or otherwise in the possession of law enforcement officers as donations to the institute if he or she deems them to be appropriate for the institute's training purposes.

(e) Any moneys received by the Secretary of California Emergency Management from charges or fees imposed in connection with the operation of the institute shall be deposited in the General Fund.

Government Code § 12811.3.

(a) Notwithstanding any other provision of law and subject to the provisions of subdivision (i), any employee of a department, board, or commission under the jurisdiction of the Department of Corrections and Rehabilitation, who is designated as a peace officer described in Chapter 4.5 (commencing with Section 830) of Title 3 of Part 2 of the Penal Code, may transfer from his or her current position to another department, board, or commission under the jurisdiction of the Department of Corrections and Rehabilitation.

(b) Any peace officer who desires to transfer to another department, board, or commission pursuant to subdivision (a), and who is prohibited from carrying a firearm pursuant to state or federal law may not transfer to a department, board, or commission that requires the use of a firearm.

(c) Any peace officer who desires to transfer to another department, board, or commission pursuant to subdivision (a) to a position requiring the ability to carry a firearm, as determined by the department, board, or commission, and who has not completed the required training pursuant to Section 832 of the Penal Code, shall successfully complete the required training before appointment to his or her new peace officer position.

(d)(1) Any peace officer who desires to transfer shall not be required to undergo a psychological screening pursuant to subdivision (f) of Section 1031 or subdivision (a) of Section 13601 of the Penal Code, unless the Secretary of the Department of Corrections and Rehabilitation, or his or her designee, makes a determination that a peace officer is required to undergo all or a portion of a psychological screening as described in subdivision (f) of Section 1031 of this code or subdivision (a) of Section 13601 of the Penal Code.

(2) The Secretary of the Department of Corrections and Rehabilitation shall promulgate emergency regulations in order to implement paragraph (1). Notwithstanding subdivision (b) of Section 11346.1, no showing of an emergency shall be necessary in order to adopt, amend, or repeal the emergency regulations required by this paragraph.

(e) Any peace officer who has successfully completed a course of training pursuant to Section 13602 of the Penal Code and who transfers to another department, board, or commission pursuant to subdivision (a) shall not be required to complete a new course of training pursuant to Section 13602 of the Penal Code. However, each department, board, or commission may prescribe additional training to be provided to an employee who transfers pursuant to subdivision (a) and shall provide that training within the first six months of appointment to his or her new peace officer position.

(f) Any peace officer who desires to transfer to another department, board, or commission pursuant to subdivision (a) shall not be required to undergo a new background investigation pursuant to Section 1029.1.

(g) Nothing in this section shall affect an employee's seniority calculation as provided for under current law or any memorandum of understanding between the state and any applicable bargaining unit agreement in effect upon the effective date of this section.

(h) The provisions of the Unit 6 Memorandum of Understanding, which expires July 2, 2006, as modified by the ratified addendum dated June 30, 2004, relating to the release of copies of videotaped incidents, shall be subject to the California Public Records Act.

(i) This section shall become operative only when the Secretary of the Department of Corrections and Rehabilitation certifies in writing that it is necessary to prevent or minimize employment actions, including, but not limited to, layoffs, demotions, reductions in time base, or involuntary transfers of employees. In addition, the Secretary of the Department of Corrections and Rehabilitation shall have the sole authority to designate any or all departments, boards, or commissions eligible to have its peace officer employees transfer pursuant to subdivision (a) and any or all departments, boards, or commissions that shall accept peace officer employees under this section.

Government Code § 25840.

The board of supervisors may prohibit and prevent the unnecessary firing and discharge of firearms on or into the highways and other public places and may pass all necessary ordinances regulating or forbidding such acts.

Government Code § 26616.

Upon the application of a licensee under the Private Investigator and Adjuster Act (commencing with Section 7500 of the Business and Professions Code), the sheriff shall furnish such licensee with a report stating whether any employee, or proposed employee, of such licensee has ever been convicted of a crime involving moral turpitude or the illegal possession of a dangerous weapon or of a felony; provided, that the information contained in the sheriff's report to the applying licensee shall be only a statement of whether or not a conviction of such a crime has occurred. The sheriff may charge a fee sufficient to cover the costs of furnishing such report. The application shall include:

(a) The full name, residence address, telephone number, date and place of birth, and the social security number of the employee or proposed employee.

(b) Three recent photographs of the employee or proposed employee of a type prescribed by the sheriff, and three classifiable sets of his fingerprints.

(c) Such other information, evidence, statements, or documents as may be required by the sheriff.

(d) A signed statement by the employee or proposed employee consenting to the application for such information.

Government Code § 27490.

The coroner shall hold inquests pursuant to this article.

Government Code § 27491.3.

(a) In any death into which the coroner is to inquire, the coroner may take charge of any and all personal effects, valuables, and property of the deceased at the scene of death or related to the inquiry and hold or safeguard them until lawful disposition thereof can be made. The coroner may lock the premises and apply a seal to the door or doors prohibiting entrance to the premises, pending arrival of a legally authorized representative of the deceased. However, this shall not be done in such a manner as to interfere with the investigation being conducted by other law enforcement agencies. Any costs arising from the premises being locked or sealed while occupied by property of the deceased may be a proper and legal charge against the estate of the deceased. Unless expressly permitted by law, any person who enters any premises or tampers with or removes any lock or seal in violation of this section is guilty of a misdemeanor.

(b) Any property or evidence related to the investigation or prosecution of any known or suspected criminal death may, with knowledge of the coroner, be delivered to a law enforcement agency or district attorney, receipt for which shall be acknowledged.

(c) Except as otherwise provided in subdivision (d), any person who searches for or removes any papers, moneys, valuable property or weapons constituting the estate of the deceased from the person of the deceased or from the premises, prior to arrival of the coroner or without the permission of the coroner, is guilty of a misdemeanor. At the scene of any death, when it is immediately apparent or when it has not been previously recognized and the coroner's examination reveals that police investigation or criminal prosecution may ensue, the coroner shall not further disturb the body or any related evidence until the law enforcement agency has had reasonable opportunity to respond to the scene, if their purposes so require and they so request. Custody and control of the body shall remain with the coroner at all times. Reasonable time at the scene shall be allowed by the coroner for criminal investigation by other law enforcement agencies, with the time and location of removal of the remains to a convenient place to be determined at the discretion of the coroner.

(d) A peace officer may search the person or property on or about the person of the deceased, whose death is due to a traffic accident, for a driver's license or identification card to determine if an anatomical donor card is attached. If a peace officer locates such an anatomical donor card which indicates that the deceased is an anatomical donor, the peace officer shall immediately furnish such information to the coroner having jurisdiction. "Peace officer," as used in this subdivision, means only those persons designated in Sections 830.1 and 830.2 of the Penal Code.

Government Code § 30061.

(a) There shall be established in each county treasury a Supplemental Law Enforcement Services Fund (SLESF), to receive all amounts allocated to a county for purposes of implementing this chapter.

(b) In any fiscal year for which a county receives moneys to be expended for the implementation of this chapter, the county auditor shall allocate the moneys in the county's SLESF, including any interest or other return earned on the investment of those moneys, within 30 days of the deposit of those moneys into the fund, and shall allocate those moneys in accordance with the requirements set forth in this subdivision. However, the auditor shall not transfer those moneys to a recipient agency until the Supplemental Law Enforcement Oversight Committee certifies receipt of an approved expenditure plan from the governing board of that agency. The moneys shall be allocated as follows:

(1) Five and fifteen-hundredths percent to the county sheriff for county jail construction and operation. In the case of Madera, Napa, and Santa Clara Counties, this allocation shall be made to the county director or chief of corrections.

(2) Five and fifteen-hundredths percent to the district attorney for criminal prosecution.

(3) Thirty-nine and seven-tenths percent to the county and the cities within the county, and, in the case of San Mateo, Kern, Siskiyou, and Contra Costa Counties, also to the Broadmoor Police Protection District, the Bear Valley Community Services District, the Stallion Springs Community Services District, the Lake Shastina Community Services District, and the Kensington Police Protection and Community Services District, in accordance with the relative population of the cities within the county and the unincorporated area of the county, and the Broadmoor Police Protection District in the County of San Mateo, the Bear Valley Community Services District and the Stallion Springs Community Services District in Kern County, the Lake Shastina Community Services District in Siskiyou County, and the Kensington Police Protection and Community Services District in Contra Costa County, as specified in the most recent January estimate by the population research unit of the Department of Finance, and as adjusted to provide a grant of at least one hundred thousand dollars ($100,000) to each law enforcement jurisdiction. For a newly incorporated city whose population estimate is not published by the Department of Finance, but that was incorporated prior to July 1 of the fiscal year in which an allocation from the SLESF is to be made, the city manager, or an appointee of the legislative body, if a city manager is not available, and the county administrative or executive officer shall prepare a joint notification to the Department of Finance and the county auditor with a population estimate reduction of the unincorporated area of the county equal to the population of the newly incorporated city by July 15, or within 15 days after the Budget Act is enacted, of the fiscal year in which an allocation from the SLESF is to be made. No person residing within the Broadmoor Police Protection District, the Bear Valley Community Services District, the Stallion Springs Community Services District, the Lake Shastina

Community Services District, or the Kensington Police Protection and Community Services District shall also be counted as residing within the unincorporated area of the County of San Mateo, Kern, Siskiyou, or Contra Costa, or within any city located within those counties. The county auditor shall allocate a grant of at least one hundred thousand dollars ($100,000) to each law enforcement jurisdiction. Moneys allocated to the county pursuant to this subdivision shall be retained in the county SLESF, and moneys allocated to a city pursuant to this subdivision shall be deposited in an SLESF established in the city treasury.

(4) Fifty percent to the county or city and county to implement a comprehensive multiagency juvenile justice plan as provided in this paragraph and to the Corrections Standards Authority for administrative purposes. Funding for the Corrections Standards Authority, as determined by the Department of Finance, shall not exceed two hundred seventy-five thousand dollars ($275,000). For the 2003-04 fiscal year, of the two hundred seventy-five thousand dollars ($275,000), up to one hundred seventy-six thousand dollars ($176,000) may be used for juvenile facility inspections. The juvenile justice plan shall be developed by the local juvenile justice coordinating council in each county and city and county with the membership described in Section 749.22 of the Welfare and Institutions Code. If a plan has been previously approved by the Corrections Standards Authority, the plan shall be reviewed and modified annually by the council. The plan or modified plan shall be approved by the county board of supervisors, and in the case of a city and county, the plan shall also be approved by the mayor. The plan or modified plan shall be submitted to the Corrections Standards Authority by May 1 of each year.

(A) Juvenile justice plans shall include, but not be limited to, all of the following components:

(i) An assessment of existing law enforcement, probation, education, mental health, health, social services, drug and alcohol, and youth services resources that specifically target at-risk juveniles, juvenile offenders, and their families.

(ii) An identification and prioritization of the neighborhoods, schools, and other areas in the community that face a significant public safety risk from juvenile crime, such as gang activity, daylight burglary, late-night robbery, vandalism, truancy, controlled substances sales, firearm-related violence, and juvenile substance abuse and alcohol use.

(iii) A local juvenile justice action strategy that provides for a continuum of responses to juvenile crime and delinquency and demonstrates a collaborative and integrated approach for implementing a system of swift, certain, and graduated responses for at-risk youth and juvenile offenders.

(iv) Programs identified in clause (iii) that are proposed to be funded pursuant to this subparagraph, including the projected amount of funding for each program.

(B) Programs proposed to be funded shall satisfy all of the following requirements:

(i) Be based on programs and approaches that have been demonstrated to be effective in reducing delinquency and addressing juvenile crime for any elements of response to juvenile crime and delinquency, including prevention, intervention, suppression, and incapacitation.

(ii) Collaborate and integrate services of all the resources set forth in clause (i) of subparagraph (A), to the extent appropriate.

(iii) Employ information sharing systems to ensure that county actions are fully coordinated, and designed to provide data for measuring the success of juvenile justice programs and strategies.

(iv) Adopt goals related to the outcome measures that shall be used to determine the effectiveness of the local juvenile justice action strategy.

(C) The plan shall also identify the specific objectives of the programs proposed for funding and specified outcome measures to determine the effectiveness of the programs and contain an accounting for all program participants, including those who do not complete the programs. Outcome measures of the programs proposed to be funded shall include, but not be limited to, all of the following:

(i) The rate of juvenile arrests per 100,000 population.

(ii) The rate of successful completion of probation.

(iii) The rate of successful completion of restitution and court-ordered community service responsibilities.

(iv) Arrest, incarceration, and probation violation rates of program participants.

(v) Quantification of the annual per capita costs of the program.

(D) The Corrections Standards Authority shall review plans or modified plans submitted pursuant to this paragraph within 30 days upon receipt of submitted or resubmitted plans or modified plans. The authority shall approve only those plans or modified plans that fulfill the requirements of this paragraph, and shall advise a submitting county or city and county immediately upon the approval of its plan or modified plan. The authority shall offer, and provide, if requested, technical assistance to any county or city and county that submits a plan or modified plan not in compliance with the requirements of this paragraph. The SLESF shall only allocate funding pursuant to this paragraph upon notification from the authority that a plan or modified plan has been approved.

(E) To assess the effectiveness of programs funded pursuant to this paragraph using the program outcome criteria specified in subparagraph (C), the following periodic reports shall be submitted:

(i) Each county or city and county shall report, beginning October 15, 2002, and annually each October 15 thereafter, to the county board of supervisors and the Corrections Standards Authority, in a format specified by the authority, on the programs funded pursuant to this chapter and program outcomes as specified in subparagraph (C).

(ii) The Corrections Standards Authority shall compile the local reports and, by March 15, 2003, and annually thereafter, make a report to the Governor and the Legislature on program expenditures within each county and city and county from the appropriation for the purposes of this paragraph, on the outcomes as specified in subparagraph (C) of the programs funded pursuant to this paragraph and the statewide effectiveness of the comprehensive multiagency juvenile justice plans.

(c) Subject to subdivision (d), for each fiscal year in which the county, each city, the Broadmoor Police Protection District, the Bear Valley Community Services District, the Stallion Springs Community Services District, the Lake Shastina Community Services District, and the Kensington Police Protection and Community Services District receive moneys pursuant to paragraph (3) of subdivision (b), the county, each city, and each district specified in this subdivision shall appropriate those moneys in accordance with the following procedures:

(1) In the case of the county, the county board of supervisors shall appropriate existing and anticipated moneys exclusively to provide frontline law enforcement services, other than those services specified in paragraphs (1) and (2) of subdivision (b), in the unincorporated areas of the county, in response to written requests submitted to the board by the county sheriff and the district attorney.

Any request submitted pursuant to this paragraph shall specify the frontline law enforcement needs of the requesting entity, and those personnel, equipment, and programs that are necessary to meet those needs. The board shall, at a public hearing held at a time determined by the board in each year that the Legislature appropriates funds for purposes of this chapter, or within 30 days after a request by a recipient agency for a hearing if the funds have been received by the county from the state prior to that request, consider and determine each submitted request within 60 days of receipt, pursuant to the decision of a majority of a quorum present. The board shall consider these written requests separate and apart from the process applicable to proposed allocations of the county general fund.

(2) In the case of a city, the city council shall appropriate existing and anticipated moneys exclusively to fund frontline municipal police services, in accordance with written requests submitted by the chief of police of that city or the chief administrator of the law enforcement agency that provides police services for that city. These written requests shall be acted upon by the city council in the same manner as specified in paragraph (1) for county appropriations.

(3) In the case of the Broadmoor Police Protection District within the County of San Mateo, the Bear Valley Community Services District or the Stallion Springs Community Services District within Kern County, the Lake Shastina Community Services District within Siskiyou County, or the Kensington Police Protection and Community Services District within Contra Costa County, the legislative body of that special district shall appropriate existing and anticipated moneys exclusively to fund frontline municipal police services, in accordance with written requests submitted by the chief administrator of the law enforcement agency that provides police services for that special district. These written requests shall be acted upon by the legislative body in the same manner specified in paragraph (1) for county appropriations.

(d) For each fiscal year in which the county, a city, or the Broadmoor Police Protection District within the County of San Mateo, the Bear Valley Community Services District or the Stallion Springs Community Services District within Kern County, the Lake Shastina Community Services District within Siskiyou County, or the Kensington Police Protection and Community Services District within Contra Costa County receives any moneys pursuant to this chapter, in no event shall the governing body of any of those recipient agencies subsequently alter any previous, valid appropriation by that body, for that same fiscal year, of moneys allocated to the county or city pursuant to paragraph (3) of subdivision (b).

(e) Effective April 1, 2009, the programs authorized by this chapter shall be funded from the Local Safety and Protection Account in the Transportation Fund authorized by Section 10752.2 of the Revenue and Taxation Code. Of the amount deposited in the Local Safety and Protection Account in the 2008-09 fiscal year, the Controller shall allocate 23.65 percent for purposes of paragraphs (1), (2), and (3) of subdivision (b), and shall allocate 23.65 percent for purposes of paragraph (4) of subdivision (b). These amounts shall be allocated in two installments, one on April 1, 2009 and one on July 1, 2009.

(f) In the 2009-10 fiscal year, and every fiscal year thereafter, the Controller shall allocate 21.30 percent of the amount deposited in the Local Safety and Protection Account for purposes of paragraphs (1), (2), and (3) of subdivision (b), and shall allocate 21.30 percent for purposes of paragraph (4) of subdivision (b).

(g) The Controller shall allocate funds to local jurisdictions for public safety in accordance with this section as annually calculated by the Director of Finance. The Controller shall allocate the amount appropriated for purposes of this chapter in the 2008 Budget Act in three installments, to be paid in September, December, and March. In the 2009 -10 fiscal year, and each fiscal year thereafter, the Controller shall allocate funds authorized for purposes of this chapter on a quarterly basis, beginning October 1.

(h) Funds received pursuant to subdivision (b) shall be expended or encumbered in accordance with this chapter no later than June 30 of the following fiscal year. A local agency that has not met this requirement shall remit unspent SLESF moneys received prior to April 1, 2009, to the Controller for deposit into the General Fund. A local agency that has not met the requirement of this subdivision shall remit unspent SLESF moneys received after April 1, 2009, to the Controller for deposit in the Local Safety and Protection Account.

(i) If a county, a city, a city and county, or a qualifying special district does not comply with the requirements of this chapter to receive an SLESF allocation, the Controller shall revert funds that were provided for the noncompliant entity prior to April 1, 2009, to the General Fund. Funds provided for the noncompliant entity after March 1, 2009, shall be reverted to the Local Safety and Protection Account.

Government Code § 50081.

(a) To the extent that funds have been made available to a local agency pursuant to Section 50082, the legislative body of a local agency shall furnish each newly hired police officer and deputy sheriff employed full time by the local agency with a service revolver or other suitable pistol, holster, belt and ammunition, a nightstick, handcuffs, raincoats, and rainboots.

(b) The following items are recommended to be provided by local agencies but are not reimbursable pursuant to Section 50082: (1) Offduty holster. (2) Whistle. (3) Flashlight, flashlight batteries, and flashlight bulb. (4) Chemical Mace and chemical Mace holder. (5) Utility jacket. (6) Protective vest.

(c) Issued equipment shall remain the property of the local agency and shall be returned upon request of the local agency. However, notwithstanding any other law, and as long as the item is not needed as evidence in a pending criminal or civil action or investigation, any local agency shall donate the personal effects, including pistols, revolvers, or other firearms capable of being concealed upon the person that have been rendered inoperable and shooting medals, of any police officer or deputy sheriff employed by the agency who is killed in the line of duty, to the family of the officer upon the request of the family. The officer's protective vest, ammunition, and chemical Mace shall not be made available to the family and shall remain the property of the local agency.

(d) Any requirement of a basic firearms safety certificate for persons who anticipate the transfer of a pistol, revolver, or other firearm capable of being concealed upon the person shall not apply to a person to whom an inoperable pistol, revolver, or other firearm capable of being concealed upon the person is donated pursuant to this section.

Government Code § 50911.

At the time of each annual tax levy, the legislative body shall direct the payment into the police relief and pension fund of the following amounts:

(a) Not less than 5 nor more than 10 percent of all money received from licenses for the keeping of places where spirituous, malt, or other intoxicating liquors are sold.

(b) One-half of all money received from taxes or dog licenses.

(c) All money received from fines paid by the members of the police force for violation of the regulations of the department.

(d) All proceeds of sales of unclaimed property.

(e) Not less than one-fourth nor more than one-half of all money received from licenses from pawnbrokers, billiardhall keepers, second-hand dealers, and junk stores.

(f) All money from fines for carrying concealed weapons.

(g) Twenty-five percent of fines paid for violation of the ordinances of the local agency.

(h) All rewards paid to members of the police force, other than those excepted by the chief of police.

Government Code § 53069.7.

A local agency, as defined in Section 54951, may offer and pay a reward, the amount thereof to be determined by the local agency, to any person who comes to the aid of any peace officer of the local agency or who furnishes information leading to the arrest and conviction of any person or persons killing or assaulting with a deadly weapon or inflicting serious bodily harm upon a peace officer of the local agency while such officer is acting in the line of duty.

Government Code § 53071.

It is the intention of the Legislature to occupy the whole field of regulation of the registration or licensing of commercially manufactured firearms as encompassed by the provisions of the Penal Code, and such provisions shall be exclusive of all local regulations, relating to registration or licensing of commercially manufactured firearms, by any political subdivision as defined in Section 1721 of the Labor Code.

Government Code § 53071.5.

By the enforcement of this section, the Legislature occupies the whole field of regulation of the manufacture, sale, or possession of imitation firearms, as defined in Section 12550 of the Penal Code, and that section shall preempt and be exclusive of all regulations relating to the manufacture, sale, or possession of imitation firearms, including regulations governing the manufacture, sale, or possession of BB devices and air rifles described in subdivision (g) of Section 12001 of the Penal Code.

Government Code § 54951.

As used in this chapter, "local agency" means a county, city, whether general law or chartered, city and county, town, school district, municipal corporation, district, political subdivision, or any board, commission or agency thereof, or other local public agency.

Government Code § 54957.8.

(a) For purposes of this section, "multijurisdictional law enforcement agency" means a joint powers entity formed pursuant to Article 1 (commencing with Section 6500) of Chapter 5 of Division 7 of Title 1 that provides law enforcement services for the parties to the joint powers agreement for the purpose of investigating criminal activity involving drugs; gangs; sex crimes; firearms trafficking or felony possession of a firearm; high technology, computer, or identity theft; human trafficking; or vehicle theft.

(b) Nothing contained in this chapter shall be construed to prevent the legislative body of a multijurisdictional law enforcement agency, or an advisory body of a multijurisdictional law enforcement agency, from holding closed sessions to discuss the case records of any ongoing criminal investigation of the multijurisdictional law enforcement agency or of any party to the joint powers agreement, to hear testimony from persons involved in the investigation, and to discuss courses of action in particular cases.

Health and Safety Code

Health and Safety Code § 11019.

"Narcotic drug" means any of the following, whether produced directly or indirectly by extraction from substances of vegetable origin, or independently by means of chemical synthesis, or by a combination of extraction and chemical synthesis: (a) Opium and opiate, and any salt, compound, derivative, or preparation of opium or opiate. (b) Any salt, compound, isomer, or derivative, whether natural or synthetic, of the substances referred to in subdivision (a), but not including the isoquinoline alkaloids of opium. (c) Opium poppy and poppy straw. (d) Coca leaves and any salt, compound, derivative, or preparation of coca leaves, but not including decocainized coca leaves or extractions of coca leaves which do not contain cocaine or ecgonine. (e) Cocaine, whether natural or synthetic, or any salt, isomer, derivative, or preparation thereof. (f) Ecgonine, whether natural or synthetic, or any salt, isomer, derivative, or preparation thereof. (g) Acetylfentanyl, the thiophene analog thereof, derivatives of either, and any salt, compound, isomer, or preparation of acetylfentanyl or the thiophene analog thereof.

Health and Safety Code § 11370.1.

(a) Notwithstanding Section 11350 or 11377 or any other provision of law, every person who unlawfully possesses any amount of a substance containing cocaine base, a substance containing cocaine, a substance containing heroin, a substance containing methamphetamine, a crystalline substance containing phencyclidine, a liquid substance containing phencyclidine, plant material containing phencyclidine, or a hand-rolled cigarette treated with phencyclidine while armed with a loaded, operable firearm is guilty of a felony punishable by imprisonment in the state prison for two, three, or four years. As used in this subdivision, "armed with" means having available for immediate offensive or defensive use.

(b) Any person who is convicted under this section shall be ineligible for diversion or deferred entry of judgment under Chapter 2.5 (commencing with Section 1000) of Title 6 of Part 2 of the Penal Code.

Health and Safety Code § 11550.

(a) No person shall use, or be under the influence of any controlled substance which is (1) specified in subdivision (b), (c), or (e), or paragraph (1) of subdivision (f) of Section 11054, specified in paragraph (14), (15), (21), (22), or (23) of subdivision (d) of Section 11054, specified in subdivision (b) or (c) of Section 11055, or specified in paragraph (1) or (2) of subdivision (d) or in paragraph (3) of subdivision (e) of Section 11055, or (2) a narcotic drug classified in Schedule III, IV, or V, except when administered by or under the direction of a person licensed by the state to dispense, prescribe, or administer controlled substances. It shall be the burden of the defense to show that it comes within the exception. Any person convicted of violating this subdivision is guilty of a misdemeanor and shall be sentenced to serve a term of not less than 90 days or more than one year in a county jail. The court may place a person convicted under this subdivision on probation for a period not to exceed five years and, except as provided in subdivision (c), shall in all cases in which probation is granted require, as a condition thereof, that the person be confined in a county jail for at least 90 days. Other than as provided by subdivision (c), in no event shall the court have the power to absolve a person who violates this subdivision from the obligation of spending at least 90 days in confinement in a county jail.

(b) Any person who (1) is convicted of violating subdivision (a) when the offense occurred within seven years of that person being convicted of two or more separate violations of that subdivision, and (2) refuses to complete a licensed drug rehabilitation program offered by the court pursuant to subdivision (c), shall be punished by imprisonment in a county jail for not less than 180 days nor more than one year. In no event does the court have the power to absolve a person convicted of a violation of subdivision (a) that is punishable under this subdivision from the obligation of spending at least 180 days in confinement in a county jail unless there are no licensed drug rehabilitation programs reasonably available. For the purpose of this section, a drug rehabilitation program shall not be considered reasonably available unless the person is required to pay no more than the court determines that he or she is reasonably able to pay, in order to participate in the program.

(c) The court may, when it would be in the interest of justice, permit any person convicted of a violation of subdivision (a) punishable under subdivision (a) or (b) to complete a licensed drug rehabilitation program in lieu of part or all of the imprisonment in the county jail. As a condition of sentencing, the court may require the offender to pay all or a portion of the drug rehabilitation program. In order to alleviate jail overcrowding and to provide recidivist offenders with a reasonable opportunity to seek rehabilitation pursuant to this subdivision, counties are encouraged to include provisions to augment licensed drug rehabilitation programs in their substance abuse proposals and applications submitted to the state for federal and state drug abuse funds.

(d) In addition to any fine assessed under this section, the judge may assess a fine not to exceed seventy dollars ($70) against any person who violates this section, with the proceeds of this fine to be used in accordance with Section 1463.23 of the Penal Code. The court shall, however, take into consideration the defendant's ability to pay, and no defendant shall be denied probation because of his or her inability to pay the fine permitted under this subdivision.

(e) Notwithstanding subdivisions (a) and (b) or any other provision of law, any person who is unlawfully under the influence of cocaine, cocaine base, heroin, methamphetamine, or phencyclidine while in the immediate personal possession of a loaded, operable firearm is guilty of a public offense punishable by imprisonment in a county jail for not exceeding one year or in state prison. As used in this subdivision "immediate personal possession" includes, but is not limited to, the interior passenger compartment of a motor vehicle.

(f) Every person who violates subdivision (e) is punishable upon the second and each subsequent conviction by imprisonment in the state prison for two, three, or four years.

(g) Nothing in this section prevents deferred entry of judgment or a defendant's participation in a preguilty plea drug court program under Chapter 2.5 (commencing with Section 1000) of Title 6 of Part 2 of the Penal Code unless the person is charged with violating subdivision (b) or (c) of Section 243 of the Penal Code. A person charged with violating this section by being under the influence of any controlled substance which is specified in paragraph (21), (22), or (23) of subdivision (d) of Section 11054 or in paragraph (3) of subdivision (e) of Section 11055 and with violating either subdivision (b) or (c) of Section 243 of the Penal Code or with a violation of subdivision (e) shall be ineligible for deferred entry of judgment or a preguilty plea drug court program.

Health and Safety Code § 11590.

(a) Except as provided in subdivisions (c) and (d), any person who is convicted in the State of California of any offense defined in Section 11350, 11351, 11351.5, 11352, 11353, 11353.5, 11353.7, 11354, 11355, 11357, 11358, 11359, 11360, 11361, 11363, 11366, 11366.5, 11366.6, 11368, 11378, 11378.5, 11379, 11379.5, 11379.6, 11380, 11380.5, 11383, or 11550, or subdivision (a) of Section 11377, or any person who is discharged or paroled from a penal institution where he or she was confined because of the commission of any such offense, or any person who is convicted in any other state of any offense which, if committed or attempted in this state, would have been punishable as one or more of the above-mentioned offenses, shall within 30 days of his or her coming into any county or city, or city and county in which he or she resides or is temporarily domiciled for that length of time, register with the chief of police of the city in which he or she resides or the sheriff of the county if he or she resides in an unincorporated area. For persons convicted of an offense defined in Section 11377, 11378, 11379, or 11380, this subdivision shall apply only to offenses involving controlled substances specified in paragraph (12) of subdivision (d) of Section 11054 and paragraph (2) of subdivision (d) of Section 11055, and to analogs of these substances, as defined in Section 11401. For persons convicted of an offense defined in Section 11379 or 11379.5, this subdivision shall not apply if the conviction was for transporting, offering to transport, or attempting to transport a controlled substance.

(b) Any person who is convicted in any federal court of any offense which, if committed or attempted in this state would have been punishable as one or more of the offenses enumerated in subdivision (a) shall within 30 days of his or her coming into any county or city, or city and county in which he or she resides or is temporarily domiciled for that length of time, register with the chief of police of the city in which he or she resides or the sheriff of the county if he or she resides in an unincorporated area.

(c) This section does not apply to a conviction of a misdemeanor under Section 11357, 11360, or 11377. (d) The registration requirements imposed by this section for the conviction of offenses defined in Section 11353.7, 11366.5, 11366.6, 11377, 11378, 11378.5, 11379, 11379.5, 11379.6, 11380, 11380.5, or 11383, shall apply to any person who commits any of those offenses on and after January 1, 1990.

Health and Safety Code § 12000.

For the purposes of this part, "explosives" means any substance, or combination of substances, the primary or common purpose of which is detonation or rapid combustion, and which is capable of a relatively instantaneous or rapid release of gas and heat, or any substance, the primary purpose of which, when combined with others, is to form a substance capable of a relatively instantaneous or rapid release of gas and heat. "Explosives" includes, but is not limited to, any explosives as defined in Section 841 of Title 18 of the United States Code and published pursuant to Section 555.23 of Title 27 of the Code of Federal Regulations, and any of the following:

(a) Dynamite, nitroglycerine, picric acid, lead azide, fulminate of mercury, black powder, smokeless powder, propellant explosives, detonating primers, blasting caps, or commercial boosters.

(b) Substances determined to be division 1.1, 1.2, 1.3, or 1.6 explosives as classified by the United States Department of Transportation.

(c) Nitro carbo nitrate substances (blasting agent) classified as division 1.5 explosives by the United States Department of Transportation.

(d) Any material designated as an explosive by the State Fire Marshal. The designation shall be made pursuant to the classification standards established by the United States Department of Transportation. The State Fire Marshal shall adopt regulations in accordance with the Government Code to establish procedures for the classification and designation of explosive materials or explosive devices that are not under the jurisdiction of the United States Department of Transportation pursuant to provisions of Section 841 of Title 18 of the United States Code and published pursuant to Section 555.23 of Title 27 of the Code of Federal Regulations that define explosives.

(e) Certain division 1.4 explosives as designated by the United States Department of Transportation when listed in regulations adopted by the State Fire Marshal.

(f) For the purposes of this part, "explosives" does not include any destructive device, as defined in Section 12301 of the Penal Code, nor does it include ammunition or small arms primers manufactured for use in shotguns, rifles, and pistols.

Health and Safety Code § 12001.

This part does not apply to any of the following:

(a) Any person engaged in the transportation of explosives regulated by, and when subject to, the provisions of Division 14 (commencing with Section 31600) of the Vehicle Code.

(b) Small arms ammunition of .75 caliber or less when designated as a division 1.4 explosive by the United States Department of Transportation.

(c) Fireworks regulated under Part 2 (commencing with Section 12500) of this division, including, but not limited to, special effects pyrotechnics regulated by the State Fire Marshal pursuant to Section 12555.

(d) Any explosives while in the course of transportation via railroad, aircraft, water, or highway when the explosives are in actual movement and under the jurisdiction of and in conformity with regulations adopted by the United States Department of Transportation, United States Coast Guard, or the Federal Aviation Agency. However, no explosives shall be sold, given away, or delivered except as provided in Section 12120.

(e) Special fireworks classified by the United States Department of Transportation as division 1.3 explosives when those special fireworks are regulated under Part 2 (commencing with Section 12500) of this division, when a permit has been issued pursuant to regulations of the State Fire Marshal.

(f)(1) Black powder in quantities of 25 pounds or less in the hands of a retailer having a permit issued under Article 2 (commencing with Section 6066) of Chapter 2 of Part 1 of Division 2 of the Revenue and Taxation Code and in quantities of five pounds or less in the hands of all others and smokeless powder in quantities of 20 pounds or less used, possessed, stored, sold, or transported that is exempted under, or authorized by, the Federal Organized Crime Control Act of 1970 (Public Law 91-452) and applicable federal regulations thereunder.

(2) All cities, counties, and special districts and county service areas providing fire protection shall require retailers in

possession of black powder to notify fire authorities.

Health and Safety Code § 12002.

Except when transporting explosives on highways and at safe stopping places established under the provisions of Division 14 (commencing with Section 31600) of the Vehicle Code, this part does not affect the operation of provisions of any city, county, or city and county ordinance respecting the delivery, storage, and handling of explosives which are at least as restrictive as the provisions of this part.

Health and Safety Code § 12003.

"Chief" means the Director of Forestry and Fire Protection and his or her authorized representatives, the chief of a fire department or fire protection agency maintained by a city, county, or city and county, or fire protection district and his or her authorized representatives, or the authorized representative of the United States Forest Service. In any area of the state in which there exists no organized fire protection agency responsible for the protection of the area, "chief," for the purpose of this part only, means the county sheriff and his or her authorized representatives. On any property that is owned by the state, the "chief," for the purpose of this part, shall be the official of the fire protection agency responsible for the suppression of fires in the area. On any state property where there is no fire protection agency responsible for the suppression of fires, the "chief," for the purpose of this part, shall be the State Fire Marshal. Upon request of the Director of Forestry and Fire Protection, the chief of a fire department or fire protection agency, or upon request of the county sheriff, the governing body of the area under the jurisdiction of the requesting chief or sheriff may designate any person as "chief" for the purposes of this part.

Health and Safety Code § 12004.

For the purposes of this part, the term "person" shall mean any person, organization, firm, corporation, association, city, county, city and county, and state, and shall include any of their employees and authorized representatives.

Health and Safety Code § 12005.

This part does not apply to the transportation and use of explosives by representatives of the California Highway Patrol, the State Bureau of Criminal Identification and Investigation, local police departments, sheriff's departments, and fire departments acting in their official capacity, nor shall this part apply to the transportation and use of explosives by any peace officer authorized to enforce the provisions of this part by Section 12020 when he is acting pursuant to such authority.

Health and Safety Code § 12005.5.

(a) This part shall not apply to the possession, handling, storage, transportation, or use of not more than 10 pounds of blasting agents (division 1.5 explosives), two pounds of division 1.1, 1.2, or 1.3 explosives, or 1,000 feet of detonating cord, or any combination thereof, by authorized employees of the Department of Transportation, acting within the scope of their employment, in the pursuit of seismic explorations.

(b) The Department of Transportation may not undertake that seismic exploration, unless the fire authority having jurisdiction in the area of the proposed seismic exploration has received a written notice from the department at least 48 hours prior to the commencement of the seismic exploration. The notice shall include the time and location of the proposed seismic exploration. In addition, the employee supervising the proposed seismic exploration, or his or her designated representative, shall consult with the fire authority to determine if the proposed handling, storage, transportation, or use of explosives would constitute an unreasonable hazard to life or property. If the fire authority determines that such a hazard would arise, the department shall not engage in that handling, storage, transportation, or use of explosives.

(c) The state shall be strictly liable for any injury to any person or property proximately caused by the handling, storage, transportation, or use of explosives by the Department of Transportation for the purpose of conducting seismic exploration. All claims for damages against the state arising under this section are governed by the procedures set forth in Part 3 (commencing with Section 900) and Part 4 (commencing with Section 940) of Division 3.6 of Title 1 of the Government Code.

Health and Safety Code § 12006.

The provisions of this part and the regulations adopted by the State Fire Marshal pursuant to this part do not apply when the use, handling, possession, storage and transportation is subject to the requirements of the Division of Occupational Safety and Health, Department of Industrial Relations, except as the provisions of this part and the regulations adopted by the State Fire Marshal may extend beyond the scope or authority of the Division of Occupational Safety and Health, Department of Industrial Relations.

Health and Safety Code § 12007.

(a) For the purposes of this part, the term "issuing authority" shall mean either the sheriff of a county, or the chief or other head of a municipal police department of any city or city and county, or the chief of a fire department or fire protection agency, and their authorized representatives, provided that, in the event the designated issuing authority is the chief of a fire department or fire protection agency, such fire department or fire protection agency is organized with regularly paid full-time personnel. The governing body of any county, city, or city and county shall designate one of the above as the issuing authority within its jurisdiction and shall notify the State Fire Marshal of the person so designated.

(b) If the governing body of any county, city, or city and county does not designate an issuing authority pursuant to subdivision (a), the State Fire Marshal shall designate the sheriff of the county as the issuing authority.

Health and Safety Code § 12020.

The chief and the issuing authority, as defined in Sections 12003 and 12007, respectively, shall in their areas of jurisdiction enforce the provisions of this part and the regulations adopted by the State Fire Marshal pursuant to this part. Any peace officer, as defined in Sections 830.1, 830.2, and subdivisions (a), (e), (k), and (l) of Section 830.3 of the Penal Code, and those officers listed in Section 830.6 of the Penal Code while acting in the course and scope of their employment as peace officers may enforce the provisions of this part.

Health and Safety Code § 12080.

(a) No person shall sell, give away, or transport any explosive which has not been classified as provided in Section 12000.

(b) The State Fire Marshal, upon receiving an application from any interested party, with the concurrence of the chief in the area affected, and if he determines that such action may be taken without jeopardizing the public welfare and safety, may authorize the transportation of unclassified explosives provided all other provisions of this part are met.

Health and Safety Code § 12082.

No explosives shall be sold, furnished, or given away to any person under 21 years of age, whether such person is acting for himself or for another person, nor shall any such person be eligible to obtain any permit to receive explosives governed by the provisions of this part. The reference to "under 21 years of age" in this section is unaffected by Section 1 of Chapter 1748 of the Statutes of 1971 or any other provision of that chapter.

Health and Safety Code § 12084.

No person shall willfully discharge any firearm within 500 feet of any magazine or any explosive manufacturing plant.

Health and Safety Code § 12085.

No person shall make, possess, or transport any explosive in a manner prohibited by this part or prohibited by any ordinance of a city, county, or city and county, or prohibited by the laws or regulations governing a harbor in those areas where such ordinance, laws, or regulations apply.

Health and Safety Code § 12086.

Any theft or loss of explosives, whether from a storage magazine, a vehicle in which they are being transported, or from a site on which they are being used, or from any other location, shall immediately be reported by the person having control of such explosives to the local police or county sheriff. The local police or county sheriff shall immediately transmit a report of such theft or loss of explosives to the State Bureau of Criminal Identification and Investigation at Sacramento.

Health and Safety Code § 12087.

No person shall abandon or otherwise dispose of any explosives in any manner which might, as the result of such abandonment or disposal, create any danger or threat of danger to life or property. Any person in possession or control of explosives required in the performance of his duties shall, when the need for such explosives no longer exists, either return the explosives to the source from which the explosives were obtained, or to an appropriate issuing authority for disposal or shall destroy the explosives in a safe manner so as not to make them available to persons who might obtain them and use them in a manner prejudicial to the safety of life and property. Magazines or temporary magazines used for storage purposes in any area where blasting is required shall, when the need for such storage no longer exists and the explosives have been removed or disposed of as above required, be removed or demolished, or signs, indicating the presence of explosives in such magazines or on the premises on which such magazines are located, shall be removed or effectively obliterated, and the issuing authority who issued the storage permit shall be immediately notified of the action taken.

Health and Safety Code § 12088.

The contents of a package containing explosives shall be plainly marked on the outside of the package at the time the package is delivered for transportation. It is unlawful for any person to deliver, or cause to be delivered, to any carrier for transportation any explosive under any false or deceptive marking, description, invoice, shipping order, or other declaration.

Health and Safety Code § 12089.

Except when transporting explosives received under Section 12102 of this code, every motor vehicle used in the transportation of explosives and which is subject to this part, shall have displayed thereon, signs conforming to the regulations of the United States Department of Transportation.

Health and Safety Code § 12090.

There shall not be included in any cargo of explosives any flammable or combustible liquids, acids, or corrosive liquids, oxidizers, or combustible materials, other than the explosives themselves, which may have such characteristics. Blasting caps or detonators shall not be transported upon the same vehicle with other explosives. The foregoing provisions of this section shall be subject to such exceptions as are permitted by the regulations of the United States.

Health and Safety Code § 12091.

Blasting caps or similar primary explosive initiation devices shall not be transported upon any vehicle equipped with a radio transmitter or other device which may cause detonation of such primary initiators unless such blasting caps or similar primary explosive initiation devices have been tested and proved safe for transportation by laboratory approved by the State Fire Marshal and there is affixed to the shipping container of such devices a label which states all of the following: (a) The type of primary explosive initiation devices in the container. (b) That such devices have been tested and proved safe for transportation upon any vehicle equipped with a radio transmitter or other device which may cause detonation of such primary initiators by a laboratory approved by the State Fire Marshal.

Health and Safety Code § 12092.

Any person who violates any of the requirements prescribed by regulation adopted pursuant to Section 12081 or 12151 shall be assessed a civil penalty of up to one thousand dollars ($1,000) for each violation.

Health and Safety Code § 12101.

(a) No person shall do any one of the following without first having made application for and received a permit in accordance with this section:

(1) Manufacture explosives.

(2) Sell, furnish, or give away explosives.

(3) Receive, store, or possess explosives.

(4) Transport explosives.

(5) Use explosives.

(6) Operate a terminal for handling explosives.

(7) Park or leave standing any vehicle carrying explosives, except when parked or left standing in or at a safe stopping place designated as such by the Department of the California Highway Patrol under Division 14 (commencing with Section 31600) of the Vehicle Code.

(b) Application for a permit shall be made to the appropriate issuing authority.

(c)(1) A permit shall be obtained from the issuing authority having the responsibility in the area where the activity, as specified in subdivision (a), is to be conducted.

(2) If the person holding a valid permit for the use or storage of explosives desires to purchase or receive explosives in a jurisdiction other than that of intended use or storage, the person shall first present the permit to the issuing authority in the jurisdiction of purchase or receipt for endorsement. The issuing authority may include any reasonable restrictions or conditions which the authority finds necessary for the prevention of fire and explosion, the preservation of life, safety, or the control and security of explosives within the authority's jurisdiction. If, for any reason, the issuing authority refuses to endorse the permit previously issued in the area of intended use or storage, the authority shall immediately notify both the issuing authority who issued the permit and the Department of Justice of the fact of the refusal and the reasons for the refusal.

(3) Every person who sells, gives away, delivers, or otherwise disposes of explosives to another person shall first be satisfied that the person receiving the explosives has a permit valid for that purpose. When the permit to receive explosives indicates that the intended storage or use of the explosives is other than in that area in which the permittee receives the explosives, the person who sells, gives away, delivers, or otherwise disposes of the explosives shall insure that the permit has been properly endorsed by a local issuing authority and, further, shall immediately send a copy of the record of sale to the issuing authority who originally issued the permit in the area of intended storage or use. The issuing authority in the area in which the explosives are received or sold shall not issue a permit for the possession, use, or storage of explosives in an area not within the authority's jurisdiction.

(d) In the event any person desires to receive explosives for use in an area outside of this state, a permit to receive the explosives shall be obtained from the State Fire Marshal.

(e) A permit may include any restrictions or conditions which the issuing authority finds necessary for the prevention of fire and explosion, the preservation of life, safety, or the control and security of explosives.

(f) A permit shall remain valid only until the time when the act or acts authorized by the permit are performed, but in no event shall the permit remain valid for a period longer than one year from the date of issuance of the permit.

(g) Any valid permit which authorizes the performance of any act shall not constitute authorization for the performance of any act not stipulated in the permit.

(h) An issuing authority shall not issue a permit authorizing the transportation of explosives pursuant to this section if the display of placards for that transportation is required by Section 27903 of the Vehicle Code, unless the driver possesses a license for the transportation of hazardous materials issued pursuant to Division 14.1 (commencing with Section 32000) of the Vehicle Code, or the explosives are a hazardous waste or extremely hazardous waste, as defined in Sections 25117 and 25115 of the Health and Safety Code, and the transporter is currently registered as a hazardous waste hauler pursuant to Section 25163 of the Health and Safety Code.

(i) An issuing authority shall not issue a permit pursuant to this section authorizing the handling or storage of division 1.1, 1.2, or 1.3 explosives in a building, unless the building has caution placards which meet the standards established pursuant to subdivision (g) of Section 12081.

(j)(1) A permit shall not be issued to a person who meets any of the following criteria:

(A) He or she has been convicted of a felony.

(B) He or she is addicted to a narcotic drug.

(C) He or she is in a class prohibited by state or federal law from possessing, receiving, owning, or purchasing a firearm.

(2) For purposes of determining whether a person meets any of the criteria set forth in this subdivision, the issuing authority shall obtain two sets of fingerprints on prescribed cards from all persons applying for a permit under this section and shall submit these cards to the Department of Justice. The Department of Justice shall utilize the fingerprint cards to make inquiries both within this state and to the Federal Bureau of Investigation regarding the criminal history of the applicant identified on the fingerprint card. This paragraph does not apply to any person possessing a current certificate of eligibility issued pursuant to paragraph (4) of subdivision (a) of Section 12071 or to any holder of a dangerous weapons permit or license issued pursuant to Section 12095, 12230, 12250, 12286, or 12305 of the Penal Code.

(k) An issuing authority shall inquire with the Department of Justice for the purposes of determining whether a person who is applying for a permit meets any of the criteria specified in subdivision (j). The Department of Justice shall determine whether a person who is applying for a permit meets any of the criteria specified in subdivision (j) and shall either grant or deny clearance for a permit to be issued pursuant to the determination. The Department of Justice shall not disclose the contents of a person's records to any person who is not authorized to receive the information in order to ensure confidentiality.

Health and Safety Code § 12101.5.

This chapter does not apply to any possession or use by a person licensed as a pyrotechnic operator--special effects first class of 20 pounds or less of smokeless powder, or five pounds or less of black sporting powder, if all of the following requirements are satisfied:

(a) All such powder is for use in the pursuit of the lawful business of such licensee and not for resale, and, in the case of black sporting powder, there shall be no gift, delivery or other disposition to another person who is not licensed as a pyrotechnic operator--special effects first class. Any such licensee may sell, give, deliver, or otherwise dispose of any smokeless or black sporting powder to another such licensee.

(b) The storage, use and handling of such smokeless and black powder conforms to rules, regulations, or ordinances of authorities having jurisdiction for fire prevention and suppression in the area of such storage, use, and handling of such explosives.

Health and Safety Code § 12102.

This chapter does not apply to any possession or use of 20 pounds or less of smokeless powder, or one pound or less of black sporting powder, provided that:

(a) Smokeless powder is intended only for hand loading of small arms ammunition of .75 caliber or less.

(b) Black sporting powder is intended for loading of small arms or small arms ammunition of .75 caliber or less.

(c) All such powder is for private use and not for resale, and, in the case of black sporting powder, there shall be no gift, delivery, or other disposition to another person.

(d) The storage, use and handling of such smokeless and black powder conforms to rules, regulations, or ordinances of authorities having jurisdiction for fire prevention and suppression in the area of such storage, use, and handling of such explosives.

Health and Safety Code § 12102.1.

Any person who sells, gives, delivers or otherwise disposes of 20 pounds or less of smokeless powder, or one pound or less of black sporting powder, shall first obtain a statement from the person who purchases or otherwise receives such powder, which statement shall include:

(a) The name, address and birth date of the person purchasing or receiving the powder.

(b) The purpose for which the powder is intended to be used, handled, stored, or possessed.

(c) The type and amount of the powder.

(d) The signature of the person purchasing or receiving the powder.

(e) The driver's license number, selective service card number, or other identifying information concerning the person purchasing or receiving the powder. Any person furnishing a fictitious name or address or knowingly furnishing an incorrect birth date and any person violating any of the provisions of this section is guilty of a misdemeanor.

Health and Safety Code § 12103.

Application for a permit, as required under Section 12101, shall be made by filing a statement on forms prescribed by the State Fire Marshal. Such statement shall contain, but shall not necessarily be limited to, the following:

(a) The name and address of the applicant.

(b) The name and address of the employee or authorized representatives designated by the applicant as being responsible for the use, handling, storage, possession, or transportation of explosives for the applicant and whether the employee or authorized representative has been issued a blaster's license by the Division of Industrial Safety to use or handle explosives.

(c) The place where, and the purpose for which, the explosives are intended to be used, handled, stored, or possessed. (d) The type and amount of explosives for which application is made.

(e) The signature of the applicant.

(f) The number of times purchases may be made and the frequency of such purchases.

(g) The routes, highways, and stopping places intended to be utilized in transporting the explosives.

Health and Safety Code § 12105.

If the issuing authority finds, after reviewing the application for a permit, that the applicant possesses sufficient and adequate facilities to conduct the acts specified in the application, and that the issuance of such permit would not appear to be contrary to the public welfare and safety, he shall issue a permit authorizing the applicant to engage in such specific acts. Before issuing a permit for the storage of explosives, the issuing authority shall first inspect and approve the storage facility. No application for such a permit shall be approved by the issuing authority unless the storage facility is in strict compliance with the regulations adopted by the State Fire Marshal pursuant to Section 12081. In addition, the issuing authority may, at his discretion, require the submission of any personal information relevant to the acts for which application is made. A permit shall not be issued until after the payment of a fee of ten dollars ($10), unless the quantity of explosives is 100 pounds or less, in which case the fee shall be two dollars ($2). The permit fee shall be equally divided and deposited into the treasury of the city, county, or city and county having jurisdiction over the issuing authority and into the State Treasury.

Health and Safety Code § 12105.1.

Except in a case in which the issuing authority determines that the explosives are necessary because of an emergency involving a danger to persons or property, no permit shall normally be issued until one week has elapsed after application is made. If the applicant gives evidence that he has previously been issued an explosives permit pursuant to this part and if the legitimacy of the purpose for which the current application is made is clearly apparent to the issuing authority, the issuing authority may in his discretion issue a permit before one week has elapsed. If no affirmative action is taken on the application within 14 days after the application is made, the issuing authority shall explain the cause for such delay to the applicant.

Health and Safety Code § 12105.2.

A copy of each permit issued shall be forwarded to the State Bureau of Criminal Identification and Investigation in Sacramento.

Health and Safety Code § 12106.

When required by and in amounts set forth in local ordinance, the applicant for a permit for explosives shall submit evidence that the applicant has a minimum and specified amount of funds available for the purpose of the payment of all damages to persons or property which arise from, or are caused by, the conduct of any act authorized by the permit and from which any legal judgment results. Such evidence, when required, shall be a bond issued by an authorized surety company or a public liability insurance policy or cash or other evidence of financial security acceptable to the State Fire Marshal. The minimum amount of any such bond or insurance policy shall be determined by the appropriate issuing authority. The provisions of this section do not apply to any public entity, as defined in Section 811.2 of the Government Code.

Health and Safety Code § 12107.

The issuing authority shall, in the exercise of reasonable discretion, deny a permit to any person if it is his opinion that the handling or use of explosives by such person would be hazardous to property or dangerous to any person. 12108. The form of the permits shall be prescribed by the State Fire Marshal. Permits shall be numbered by the local agency issuing the permit. The permit shall include on its face the date of expiration of the permit. It shall also include a statement to the effect that any unused portion of explosives authorized by the permit shall either be returned to the source from which the explosives were obtained, destroyed, or returned to an appropriate issuing authority in accordance with Section 12087 or, in lieu thereof, application for a new permit shall be made.

Health and Safety Code § 12109.

Except as provided in Section 12111, permits shall be valid for the period of time specified thereon.

Health and Safety Code § 12110.

No permit issued under the provisions of this chapter shall be transferable.

Health and Safety Code § 12111.

A permit may be suspended or revoked, after reasonable notice and hearing, by any chief or issuing authority in the area in which explosives are sold, used, stored, handled, or possessed, if the person to whom the permit was issued sells, uses, stores, or handles the explosives in a manner which is unlawful or which creates an unreasonable hazard to life and property. The chief or issuing authority taking action to suspend or revoke a permit shall immediately notify the agency who issued the permit of the action taken and shall also immediately notify the State Bureau of Criminal Identification and Investigation in Sacramento.

Health and Safety Code § 12112.

Any decision or action by any chief or issuing authority made pursuant to this part may be appealed to the governing body of the area in which such decision or action is made.

Health and Safety Code § 12120.

No person shall knowingly sell, give away, deliver, or otherwise dispose of any explosive to any person who does not possess a valid permit as required pursuant to Section 12101. The provisions of this section and subdivisions (e) and (f) of Section 12122 do not apply to transactions by the Department of Defense or to the transactions of an agency or organization acting pursuant to contract with the Department of Defense.

Health and Safety Code § 12121.

Every person who possesses, stores, uses, sells, gives away, delivers, or otherwise disposes of explosives shall keep an accurate journal, record book, or a record of sale in which he shall note each possession, storage, use, sale, delivery, gift, or other disposition of an explosive and the time when such disposition is made whether in the course of business or otherwise. Such journal, record book, or the record of sale shall be kept on file for a period of not less than three years. Field records required to be kept pursuant to Section 12123 need be kept in the appropriate county only for the period of the possession, storage, use, sale, gift, delivery, or other disposition of explosives within that county, after which time the field records may be destroyed.

Health and Safety Code § 12122.

Each notation in the journal, record book, or each record of sale, as required by Section 12121, shall legibly show:

(a) The date of each purchase or receipt, storage, use, sale, delivery, gift, or other disposition of explosives.

(b) The name and quantity of the explosives possessed, stored, used, sold, delivered, given away, or otherwise disposed of.

(c) The name, address, and business of the purchaser or transferee, where applicable.

(d) When the explosives are to be transported under Division 14 (commencing with Section 31600) of the Vehicle Code, the permit number issued by the California Highway Patrol; or when transported other than under Division 14 (commencing with Section 31600) of the Vehicle Code, the vehicle operator's license number or other comparable identification, the motor vehicle license number of the vehicle used, and the name and address of the individual to whom the explosives are to be delivered.

(e) The number of the permit to receive explosives.

(f) The name of the public agency which issued the permit and the name of the officer issuing such permit.

Health and Safety Code § 12123.

The journal, record book or record of sale shall be kept by the person required to keep it in his principal office or place of business. It shall be at all times, on proper demand, subject to the inspection and examination of any chief or other duly authorized law enforcement official. In addition, if the principal office or place of business is located in a place other than the county within which the explosives are possessed, stored, used, sold, given away, delivered, or otherwise disposed of, field records shall be kept in that county during the period of such possession, storage, use, sale, gift, delivery or other disposition.

Health and Safety Code § 12124.

The keeping of a journal, record book, or record of sale required by Sections 12121, 12122, and 12123 does not apply to those persons who are rendering a delivery service under a permit issued by the California Highway Patrol pursuant to Division 14 (commencing with Section 31600) of the Vehicle Code, nor does it apply to any possessor or user of explosives not required to have a permit under Section 12102. A journal, record book, or record of sale need not be kept by anyone who is in lawful possession of an explosive and who receives and detonates all such explosives within a 24-hour period.

Health and Safety Code § 12150.

Except for explosives kept only at an explosive manufacturing plant, no person shall possess, keep, or store any explosive which is not completely encased in a tight metal, wooden, or fiber container, or a container approved by the Interstate Commerce Commission. No person having any explosives in his possession or control shall under any circumstances permit or allow any grains or particles of such explosives to be or remain on the outside of, or about, the containers in which such explosives are kept.

Health and Safety Code § 12150.5.

Every person having any blasting caps (electric or nonelectric) in his possession or control shall keep the same securely deposited in a locked approved magazine, except when taken therefrom for actual use, transportation, or sale.

Health and Safety Code § 12151.

Except while in the custody of a common carrier or in course of transportation pending delivery to a consignee, all explosives shall be kept or stored as specified in the rules or regulations adopted by the State Fire Marshal pursuant to this part.

Health and Safety Code § 12303.

"Lawful possession of an explosive," as used in this chapter, means possessing explosives in accordance with the stated purpose and conditions of a valid permit obtained pursuant to the provisions of this part, unless such person is specifically excepted from the permit requirements by the provisions of this part.

Health and Safety Code § 12305.

Every person not in the lawful possession of an explosive who knowingly has any explosive in his possession is guilty of a felony.

Health and Safety Code § 12540.

The provisions of this part shall not apply to any of the following:

(a) Explosives regulated under Part 1 (commencing with Section 12000) of Division 11.

(b) Arms and handguns defined as firearms by the Federal Gun Control Act of 1968, as well as such devices and weapons classified under Section 12020 or 12301 of the Penal Code, including blank cartridge pistols of the type used at sporting events or theatrical productions.

(c) Research or experiments with rockets or missiles or the production or transportation of rockets or missiles by the Department of Defense of the United States, or by any agency or organization acting pursuant to a contract with the Department of Defense for the development and production of rockets or missiles.

(d) Paper caps which contain less than 0.25 grain of pyrotechnic composition per unit load.

Health and Safety Code § 12350.

Except as provided in subdivision (b) of Section 12080, any unclassified explosives which are sold, given away, or transported shall be subject to immediate seizure by any chief or police official.

Health and Safety Code § 12351.

Any explosives which are illegally manufactured, sold, given away, delivered, stored, used, possessed, or transported shall be subject to immediate seizure by any chief, issuing authority, or peace officer authorized to act under Section 12020. When a permit issued pursuant to this part has expired and is not immediately renewed, any explosives in the possession of the permittee shall be subject to immediate seizure by any chief, issuing authority, or peace officer authorized to act under Section 12020, unless first destroyed by the permittee in accordance with Section 12087.

Health and Safety Code § 12352.

When a permit issued pursuant to this part has been suspended or revoked any explosives in the possession of such permittee shall be subject to immediate seizure by the chief causing such suspension or revocation.

Health and Safety Code § 12353.

Any explosive seized under this chapter shall be stored in an approved manner and in accordance with regulations adopted by the State Fire Marshal. The person from whom such explosives have been seized may within 10 days after such seizure petition the governing body of the area in which such seizure was made to return the explosives upon the ground that such explosives were illegally or erroneously seized. Any such petition so filed shall be considered by the governing body within 15 days after filing and an oral hearing shall be granted the petitioner if requested. Notice of the decision of the governing body shall be served upon the petitioner.

Health and Safety Code § 12354.

If the governing body finds that the explosives were illegally or erroneously seized, the explosives shall be returned to the petitioner. The determination of the governing body is final unless within 60 days of the notice served pursuant to this chapter, an action is commenced in a court of competent jurisdiction in the State of California for the recovery of the explosives seized by the chief.

Health and Safety Code § 12355.

If no petition is received by the governing body within 10 days of seizure of any explosive, or if no action is commenced in a court of competent jurisdiction in the State of California within 60 days of the notice served pursuant to this chapter, the chief may dispose of the seized explosives in any manner which will not jeopardize public welfare and safety. When any explosive is disposed of pursuant to this section, the person from whom such disposed of explosives were seized shall not have any legal redress against the chief who caused the disposal of the explosives.

Health and Safety Code § 12400.

Except as provided in Chapter 7 (commencing with Section 12302), Part 1, Division 11 of the Health and Safety Code, every person who violates any provision of this part, or violates any regulation adopted by the State Fire Marshal pursuant to this part, is guilty of a misdemeanor, punishable by a fine of not more than one thousand dollars ($1,000), or by imprisonment for not more than six months, or by both such fine and imprisonment.

Health and Safety Code § 12401.

Every person who is found guilty of a felony as specified in this part is punishable by imprisonment in the state prison, or in a county jail not exceeding one year, or by fine not exceeding ten thousand dollars ($10,000), or by both such fine and imprisonment.

Insurance Code

Insurance Code § 14060.

Except as otherwise required to comply with the provisions of Article 6 (commencing with Section 14070), the proceedings under this article shall be conducted in accordance with Chapter 5 (commencing with Section 11500) of Part 1 of Division 3 of Title 2 of the Government Code and the commissioner shall have all the powers granted therein.

Insurance Code § 14061.

The commissioner may suspend or revoke a license issued under this chapter or may issue a restricted license in accordance with Section 14026.5 if he or she determines that the licensee, or his or her manager, if an individual, or if the licensee is a person other than an individual, that any of its officers, directors, partners, or its manager, has:

(a) Made any false statement or given any false information in connection with an application for a license or a renewal or reinstatement of a license.

(b) Violated any provisions of this chapter.

(c) Violated any rule of the commissioner adopted pursuant to the authority contained in this chapter.

(d) Been convicted of any crime substantially related to the qualifications, functions and duties of the holder of the registration or license in question.

(e) Impersonated, or permitted or aided and abetted an employee to impersonate a law enforcement officer or employee of the United States of America, or of any state or political subdivision thereof.

(f) Committed or permitted any employee to commit any act, while the license was expired which would be cause for the suspension or revocation of a license, or grounds for the denial of an application for a license.

(g) Willfully failed or refused to render to a client services or a report as agreed between the parties and for which compensation has been paid or tendered in accordance with the agreement of the parties.

(h) Committed assault, battery, or kidnapping, or used force or violence on any person, without proper justification.

(i) Knowingly violated, or advised, encouraged, or assisted the violation of any court order or injunction in the course of business as a licensee.

(j) Acted as a runner or capper for any attorney.

(k) Committed any act which is a ground for denial of an application for license under this chapter.

(l) Purchased, possessed, or transported any tear gas weapon except as authorized by law. A violation of this subdivision may be punished by the suspension of a license for a period to be determined by the commissioner.

Military and Veterans Code

Military and Veterans Code § 179.

(a) The Adjutant General shall establish a California State Military Museum and Resource Center as a repository for military artifacts, memorabilia, equipment, documents, and other items relating to the history of the California National Guard, in accordance with applicable regulations of the United States Army governing Army museum activities. The museum shall consist of the facility described in the Proclamation of the Governor dated May 11, 1994, and any branches as may currently exist or may from time to time be created throughout the state. Each facility shall be deemed to be an armory within the meaning of Section 430.

(b) The Adjutant General shall enter into an operating agreement with the California Military Museum Foundation, formerly known as the California National Guard Historical Society, an existing California nonprofit public benefit corporation that is tax exempt under Section 501(c)(3) of the Internal Revenue Code. Under the operating agreement with the Adjutant General, the foundation shall operate the California State Military Museum and Resource Center in coordination with the California State Military Reserve's California Center for Military History. The foundation shall develop, administer, interpret, and manage museum historical programs and related public services, and acquire and manage funding for museum programs and services.

(c) Volunteers, docents, members of the California State Military Reserve, or others working with or for the California Military Museum Foundation for purposes consistent with the mission of the organization, shall be considered volunteers under Sections 3118 and 3119 of the Government Code and Section 3363.5 of the Labor Code.

(d) The Board of Trustees of the California Military Museum Foundation shall include the Adjutant General, or the Assistant Adjutant General, or any Deputy Adjutant General designated by the Adjutant General, as an ex officio voting member of the board. The board of trustees of the foundation shall be the governing authority for operations funded through moneys received by the foundation. The board of trustees of the foundation shall submit an audit report annually to the Adjutant General. The board of trustees of the foundation shall submit copies of annual audit reports to the Director of Finance, the Chair of the Joint Legislative Audit Committee, and the Chair of the Joint Legislative Budget Committee. No funds raised or assets acquired by the foundation shall be used for purposes inconsistent with support of the museum.

(e) The Board of Trustees of the California Military Museum Foundation shall, no later than January 10 of each year, submit a business plan for the following fiscal year to the Adjutant General, the Director of Finance, and the Chair of the Joint Legislative Budget Committee for review and comment. The board of trustees shall also submit, not less than 30 days prior to adoption, any proposed formal amendments to the business plan to the Adjutant General, the Director of Finance, and the Chair of the Joint Legislative Budget Committee for review and comment.

(f)(1) The Adjutant General or the California State Military Museum Foundation may solicit, receive, and administer donations of funds or property for the support and improvement of the museum. Any grants or donations received may be expended or used for museum purposes.

(2) Property of historical military significance, not including real property, that is owned by the state and is determined by the Adjutant General to be in excess of the needs of the Military Department, shall be transferred to the museum.

(3) Property determined by the California State Military Museum Foundation to be in excess of the needs of the museum may be sold, donated, exchanged, or otherwise disposed of, at its discretion, in a manner appropriate to the historical and intrinsic value of the property, and the benefits from the disposition shall inure to the museum. This paragraph does not apply to property held in trust for the Controller pursuant to Section 1563 of the Code of Civil Procedure.

(g) The Adjutant General or the California State Military Museum Foundation may solicit and receive firearms and other weaponry confiscated by or otherwise in the possession of law enforcement officers as donations to the museum if he or she deems them to be of historical or military interest.

(h) The Adjutant General shall, in cooperation with the California State Military Museum Foundation, conduct a study of the future needs of the National Guard to preserve, display, and interpret artifacts, documents, photographs, films, literature, and other items relating to the history of the military in California.

(i)(1) The California State Military Museum Foundation may enter into agreements with other military museums in California, including, but not limited to, the Legion of Valor Museum, to loan property that is not real property and that is under the direct control of the foundation.

(2) The California State Military Museum may enter into agreements with other military museums in California to loan property held in trust for the Controller pursuant to Section 1563 of the Code of Civil Procedure.

Military and Veterans Code § 500.

The students of any college, community college or high school in this state, having 100 or more such students, 14 years of age or over, may be organized into a cadet company or companies under such rules and regulations as the governing body of the schools or colleges and the Adjutant General of the State of California may prescribe. Said company or companies shall be of such strength as may be prescribed by the Adjutant General.

Military and Veterans Code § 511.

A sufficient number of rifles suitable for drill purposes may be purchased by the board of high school trustees, board of education, board of directors or trustees of a college or community college, county superintendent of schools, the State Superintendent of Public Instruction, or the Adjutant General out of any funds available and not otherwise appropriated.

Penal Code

Penal Code § 15.

A crime or public offense is an act committed or omitted in violation of a law forbidding or commanding it, and to which is annexed, upon conviction, either of the following punishments:

1. Death;
2. Imprisonment;
3. Fine;
4. Removal from office; or,
5. Disqualification to hold and enjoy any office of honor, trust, or profit in this State.

Penal Code § 16.

Crimes and public offenses include:

1. Felonies;
2. Misdemeanors; and
3. Infractions.

Penal Code § 17.

(a) A felony is a crime which is punishable with death or by imprisonment in the state prison. Every other crime or public offense is a misdemeanor except those offenses that are classified as infractions.

(b) When a crime is punishable, in the discretion of the court, by imprisonment in the state prison or by fine or imprisonment in the county jail, it is a misdemeanor for all purposes under the following circumstances:

(1) After a judgment imposing a punishment other than imprisonment in the state prison.

(2) When the court, upon committing the defendant to the Youth Authority, designates the offense to be a misdemeanor.

(3) When the court grants probation to a defendant without imposition of sentence and at the time of granting probation, or on application of the defendant or probation officer thereafter, the court declares the offense to be a misdemeanor.

(4) When the prosecuting attorney files in a court having jurisdiction over misdemeanor offenses a complaint specifying that the offense is a misdemeanor, unless the defendant at the time of his or her arraignment or plea objects to the offense being made a misdemeanor, in which event the complaint shall be amended to charge the felony and the case shall proceed on the felony complaint.

(5) When, at or before the preliminary examination or prior to filing an order pursuant to Section 872, the magistrate determines that the offense is a misdemeanor, in which event the case shall proceed as if the defendant had been arraigned on a misdemeanor complaint.

(c) When a defendant is committed to the Youth Authority for a crime punishable, in the discretion of the court, by imprisonment in the state prison or by fine or imprisonment in the county jail, the offense shall, upon the discharge of the defendant from the Youth Authority, thereafter be deemed a misdemeanor for all purposes.

(d) A violation of any code section listed in Section 19.8 is an infraction subject to the procedures described in Sections 19.6 and 19.7 when:

(1) The prosecutor files a complaint charging the offense as an infraction unless the defendant, at the time he or she is arraigned, after being informed of his or her rights, elects to have the case proceed as a misdemeanor, or;

(2) The court, with the consent of the defendant, determines that the offense is an infraction in which event the case shall proceed as if the defendant had been arraigned on an infraction complaint.

(e) Nothing in this section authorizes a judge to relieve a defendant of the duty to register as a sex offender pursuant to Section 290 if the defendant is charged with an offense for which registration as a sex offender is required pursuant to Section 290, and for which the trier of fact has found the defendant guilty.

Penal Code § 18.

Except in cases where a different punishment is prescribed by any law of this state, every offense declared to be a felony, or to be punishable by imprisonment in a state prison, is punishable by imprisonment in any of the state prisons for 16 months, or two or three years; provided, however, every offense which is prescribed by any law of the state to be a felony punishable by imprisonment in any of the state prisons or by a fine, but without an alternate sentence to the county jail, may be punishable by imprisonment in the county jail not exceeding one year or by a fine, or by both.

Penal Code § 19.

Except in cases where a different punishment is prescribed by any law of this state, every offense declared to be a misdemeanor is punishable by imprisonment in the county jail not exceeding six months, or by fine not exceeding one thousand dollars ($1,000), or by both.

Penal Code § 19.2.

In no case shall any person sentenced to confinement in a county or city jail, or in a county or joint county penal farm, road camp, work camp, or other county adult detention facility, or committed to the sheriff for placement in any county adult detention facility, on conviction of a misdemeanor, or as a condition of probation upon conviction of either a felony or a misdemeanor, or upon commitment for civil contempt, or upon default in the payment of a fine upon conviction of either a felony or a misdemeanor, or for any reason except upon conviction of more than one offense when consecutive sentences have been imposed, be committed for a period in excess of one year; provided, however, that the time allowed on parole shall not be considered as a part of the period of confinement.

Penal Code § 19.4.

When an act or omission is declared by a statute to be a public offense and no penalty for the offense is prescribed in any statute, the act or omission is punishable as a misdemeanor.

Penal Code § 19.6.

An infraction is not punishable by imprisonment. A person charged with an infraction shall not be entitled to a trial by jury. A person charged with an infraction shall not be entitled to have the public defender or other counsel appointed at public expense to represent him or her unless he or she is arrested and not released on his or her written promise to appear, his or her own recognizance, or a deposit of bail.

Penal Code § 19.7.

Except as otherwise provided by law, all provisions of law relating to misdemeanors shall apply to infractions including, but not limited to, powers of peace officers, jurisdiction of courts, periods for commencing action and for bringing a case to trial and burden of proof.

Penal Code § 19.8.

The following offenses are subject to subdivision (d) of Section 17: Sections 193.8, 330, 415, 485, 490.7, 555, 652, and 853.7 of this code; subdivision (n) of Section 602 of this code; subdivision (b) of Section 25658 and Sections 21672, 25658.5, 25661, and 25662 of the Business and Professions Code; Section 27204 of the Government Code; subdivision (c) of Section 23109 and Sections 12500, 14601.1, 27150.1, 40508, and 42005 of the Vehicle Code, and any other offense which the Legislature makes subject to subdivision (d) of Section 17. Except where a lesser maximum fine is expressly provided for a violation of any of those sections, any violation which is an infraction is punishable by a fine not exceeding two hundred fifty dollars ($250).

Except for the violations enumerated in subdivision (d) of Section 13202.5 of the Vehicle Code, and Section 14601.1 of the Vehicle Code based upon failure to appear, a conviction for any offense made an infraction under subdivision (d) of Section 17 is not grounds for the suspension, revocation, or denial of any license, or for the revocation of probation or parole of the person convicted.

Penal Code § 136.

As used in this chapter:

(1) "Malice" means an intent to vex, annoy, harm, or injure in any way another person, or to thwart or interfere in any manner with the orderly administration of justice.

(2) "Witness" means any natural person,

(i) having knowledge of the existence or nonexistence of facts relating to any crime, or

(ii) whose declaration under oath is received or has been received as evidence for any purpose, or

(iii) who has reported any crime to any peace officer, prosecutor, probation or parole officer, correctional officer or judicial officer, or

(iv) who has been served with a subpoena issued under the authority of any court in the state, or of any other state or of the United States, or

(v) who would be believed by any reasonable person to be an individual described in subparagraphs (i) to (iv), inclusive.

(3) "Victim" means any natural person with respect to whom there is reason to believe that any crime as defined under the laws of this state or any other state or of the United States is being or has been perpetrated or attempted to be perpetrated.

Penal Code § 136.1.

(a) Except as provided in subdivision (c), any person who does any of the following is guilty of a public offense and shall be punished by imprisonment in a county jail for not more than one year or in the state prison:

(1) Knowingly and maliciously prevents or dissuades any witness or victim from attending or giving testimony at any trial, proceeding, or inquiry authorized by law.

(2) Knowingly and maliciously attempts to prevent or dissuade any witness or victim from attending or giving testimony at any trial, proceeding, or inquiry authorized by law.

(3) For purposes of this section, evidence that the defendant was a family member who interceded in an effort to protect the witness or victim shall create a presumption that the act was without malice.

(b) Except as provided in subdivision (c), every person who attempts to prevent or dissuade another person who has been the victim of a crime or who is witness to a crime from doing any of the following is guilty of a public offense and shall be punished by imprisonment in a county jail for not more than one year or in the state prison:

(1) Making any report of that victimization to any peace officer or state or local law enforcement officer or probation or parole or correctional officer or prosecuting agency or to any judge.

(2) Causing a complaint, indictment, information, probation or parole violation to be sought and prosecuted, and assisting in the prosecution thereof.

(3) Arresting or causing or seeking the arrest of any person in connection with that victimization.

(c) Every person doing any of the acts described in subdivision (a) or (b) knowingly and maliciously under any one or more of the following circumstances, is guilty of a felony punishable by imprisonment in the state prison for two, three, or four years under any of the following circumstances:

(1) Where the act is accompanied by force or by an express or implied threat of force or violence, upon a witness or victim or any third person or the property of any victim, witness, or any third person.

(2) Where the act is in furtherance of a conspiracy.

(3) Where the act is committed by any person who has been convicted of any violation of this section, any predecessor law hereto or any federal statute or statute of any other state which, if the act prosecuted was committed in this state, would be a violation

of this section.

(4) Where the act is committed by any person for pecuniary gain or for any other consideration acting upon the request of any other person. All parties to such a transaction are guilty of a felony.

(d) Every person attempting the commission of any act described in subdivisions (a), (b), and (c) is guilty of the offense attempted without regard to success or failure of the attempt. The fact that no person was injured physically, or in fact intimidated, shall be no defense against any prosecution under this section.

(e) Nothing in this section precludes the imposition of an enhancement for great bodily injury where the injury inflicted is significant or substantial.

(f) The use of force during the commission of any offense described in subdivision (c) shall be considered a circumstance in aggravation of the crime in imposing a term of imprisonment under subdivision (b) of Section 1170.

Penal Code § 136.2.

(a) Except as provided in subdivision (c), upon a good cause belief that harm to, or intimidation or dissuasion of, a victim or witness has occurred or is reasonably likely to occur, any court with jurisdiction over a criminal matter may issue orders including, but not limited to, the following:

(1) Any order issued pursuant to Section 6320 of the Family Code.

(2) An order that a defendant shall not violate any provision of Section 136.1.

(3) An order that a person before the court other than a defendant, including, but not limited to, a subpoenaed witness or other person entering the courtroom of the court, shall not violate any provisions of Section 136.1.

(4) An order that any person described in this section shall have no communication whatsoever with any specified witness or any victim, except through an attorney under any reasonable restrictions that the court may impose.

(5) An order calling for a hearing to determine if an order as described in paragraphs (1) to (4), inclusive, should be issued.

(6) An order that a particular law enforcement agency within the jurisdiction of the court provide protection for a victim or a witness, or both, or for immediate family members of a victim or a witness who reside in the same household as the victim or witness or within reasonable proximity of the victim's or witness' household, as determined by the court. The order shall not be made without the consent of the law enforcement agency except for limited and specified periods of time and upon an express finding by the court of a clear and present danger of harm to the victim or witness or immediate family members of the victim or witness. For purposes of this paragraph, "immediate family members" include the spouse, children, or parents of the victim or witness.

(7)(A) Any order protecting victims of violent crime from all contact by the defendant, or contact, with the intent to annoy, harass, threaten, or commit acts of violence, by the defendant. The court or its designee shall transmit orders made under this paragraph to law enforcement personnel within one business day of the issuance, modification, extension, or termination of the order, pursuant to subdivision (a) of Section 6380 of the Family Code. It is the responsibility of the court to transmit the modification, extension, or termination orders made under this paragraph to the same agency that entered the original protective order into the Domestic Violence Restraining Order System.

(B)(i) If a court does not issue an order pursuant to subparagraph (A) in a case in which the defendant is charged with a crime of domestic violence as defined in Section 13700, the court on its own motion shall consider issuing a protective order upon a good cause belief that harm to, or intimidation or dissuasion of, a victim or witness has occurred or is reasonably likely to occur, that provides as follows:

(I) The defendant shall not own, possess, purchase, receive, or attempt to purchase or receive, a firearm while the protective order is in effect.

(II) The defendant shall relinquish any firearms that he or she owns or possesses pursuant to Section 527.9 of the Code of Civil Procedure.

(ii) Every person who owns, possesses, purchases, or receives, or attempts to purchase or receive, a firearm while this protective order is in effect is punishable pursuant to subdivision (g) of Section 12021.

(C) Any order issued, modified, extended, or terminated by a court pursuant to this paragraph shall be issued on forms adopted by the Judicial Council of California and that have been approved by the Department of Justice pursuant to subdivision (i) of Section 6380 of the Family Code. However, the fact that an order issued by a court pursuant to this section was not issued on forms adopted by the Judicial Council and approved by the Department of Justice shall not, in and of itself, make the order unenforceable.

(b) Any person violating any order made pursuant to paragraphs (1) to (7), inclusive, of subdivision (a) may be punished for any substantive offense described in Section 136.1, or for a contempt of the court making the order. A finding of contempt shall not be a bar to prosecution for a violation of Section 136.1. However, any person so held in contempt shall be entitled to credit for any punishment imposed therein against any sentence imposed upon conviction of an offense described in Section 136.1. Any conviction or acquittal for any substantive offense under Section 136.1 shall be a bar to a subsequent punishment for contempt arising out of the same act.

(c)(1) Notwithstanding subdivisions (a) and (e), an emergency protective order issued pursuant to Chapter 2 (commencing with Section 6250) of Part 3 of Division 10 of the Family Code or Section 646.91 of the Penal Code shall have precedence in enforcement over any other restraining or protective order, provided the emergency protective order meets all of the following requirements:

(A) The emergency protective order is issued to protect one or more individuals who are already protected persons under another restraining or protective order.

(B) The emergency protective order restrains the individual who is the restrained person in the other restraining or protective order specified in subparagraph (A).

(C) The provisions of the emergency protective order are more restrictive in relation to the restrained person than are the provisions of the other restraining or protective order specified in subparagraph (A).

(2) An emergency protective order that meets the requirements of paragraph (1) shall have precedence in enforcement over the provisions of any other restraining or protective order only with respect to those provisions of the emergency protective order that are more restrictive in relation to the restrained person.

(d)(1) A person subject to a protective order issued under this section shall not own, possess, purchase, receive, or attempt to purchase or receive a firearm while the protective order is in effect.

(2) The court shall order a person subject to a protective order issued under this section to relinquish any firearms he or she owns or possesses pursuant to Section 527.9 of the Code of Civil Procedure.

(3) Every person who owns, possesses, purchases or receives, or attempts to purchase or receive a firearm while the protective order is in effect is punishable pursuant to subdivision (g) of Section 12021 of the Penal Code.

(e)(1) In all cases where the defendant is charged with a crime of domestic violence, as defined in Section 13700, the court shall consider issuing the above-described orders on its own motion. All interested parties shall receive a copy of those orders. In order to facilitate this, the court's records of all criminal cases involving domestic violence shall be marked to clearly alert the court to this issue.

(2) In those cases in which a complaint, information, or indictment charging a crime of domestic violence, as defined in Section 13700, has been issued, a restraining order or protective order against the defendant issued by the criminal court in that case has precedence in enforcement over any civil court order against the defendant, unless a court issues an emergency protective order pursuant to Chapter 2 (commencing with Section 6250) of Part 3 of Division 10 of the Family Code or Section 646.91 of the Penal Code, in which case the emergency protective order shall have precedence in enforcement over any other restraining or protective order, provided the emergency protective order meets the following requirements:

(A) The emergency protective order is issued to protect one or more individuals who are already protected persons under another restraining or protective order.

(B) The emergency protective order restrains the individual who is the restrained person in the other restraining or protective order specified in subparagraph (A).

(C) The provisions of the emergency protective order are more restrictive in relation to the restrained person than are the provisions of the other restraining or protective order specified in subparagraph (A).

(3) Custody and visitation with respect to the defendant and his or her minor children may be ordered by a family or juvenile court consistent with the protocol established pursuant to subdivision (f), but if ordered after a criminal protective order has been issued pursuant to this section, the custody and visitation order shall make reference to, and acknowledge the precedence of enforcement of, any appropriate criminal protective order. On or before July 1, 2006, the Judicial Council shall modify the criminal and civil court forms consistent with this subdivision.

(f) On or before January 1, 2003, the Judicial Council shall promulgate a protocol, for adoption by each local court in substantially similar terms, to provide for the timely coordination of all orders against the same defendant and in favor of the same named victim or victims. The protocol shall include, but shall not be limited to, mechanisms for assuring appropriate communication and information sharing between criminal, family, and juvenile courts concerning orders and cases that involve the same parties, and shall permit a family or juvenile court order to coexist with a criminal court protective order subject to the following conditions:

(1) Any order that permits contact between the restrained person and his or her children shall provide for the safe exchange of the children and shall not contain language either printed or handwritten that violates a "no contact order" issued by a criminal court.

(2) Safety of all parties shall be the courts' paramount concern. The family or juvenile court shall specify the time, day, place, and manner of transfer of the child, as provided in Section 3100 of the Family Code.

(g) On or before January 1, 2003, the Judicial Council shall modify the criminal and civil court protective order forms consistent with this section.

(h) In any case in which a complaint, information, or indictment charging a crime of domestic violence, as defined in Section 13700, has been filed, the court may consider, in determining whether good cause exists to issue an order under paragraph (1) of subdivision (a), the underlying nature of the offense charged, and the information provided to the court pursuant to Section 273.75.

Penal Code § 136.5.

Any person who has upon his person a deadly weapon with the intent to use such weapon to commit a violation of Section 136.1 is guilty of an offense punishable by imprisonment in the county jail for not more than one year, or in the state prison.

Penal Code § 139.

(a) Except as provided in Sections 71 and 136.1, any person who has been convicted of any felony offense specified in Section 12021.1 who willfully and maliciously communicates to a witness to, or a victim of, the crime for which the person was convicted, a credible threat to use force or violence upon that person or that person's immediate family, shall be punished by imprisonment in the county jail not exceeding one year or by imprisonment in the state prison for two, three, or four years.

(b) Any person who is convicted of violating subdivision (a) who subsequently is convicted of making a credible threat, as defined in subdivision (c), which constitutes a threat against the life of, or a threat to cause great bodily injury to, a person described in subdivision (a), shall be sentenced to consecutive terms of imprisonment as prescribed in Section 1170.13.

(c) As used in this section, "a credible threat" is a threat made with the intent and the apparent ability to carry out the threat so as to cause the target of the threat to reasonably fear for his or her safety or the safety of his or her immediate family.

(d) The present incarceration of the person making the threat shall not be a bar to prosecution under this section. (e) As used in this section, "malice," "witness," and "victim" have the meanings given in Section 136.

Penal Code § 148.

(a)(1) Every person who willfully resists, delays, or obstructs any public officer, peace officer, or an emergency medical technician, as defined in Division 2.5 (commencing with Section 1797) of the Health and Safety Code, in the discharge or attempt to discharge any duty of his or her office or employment, when no other punishment is prescribed, shall be punished by a fine not exceeding one thousand dollars ($1,000), or by imprisonment in a county jail not to exceed one year, or by both that fine and imprisonment.

(2) Except as provided by subdivision (d) of Section 653t, every person who knowingly and maliciously interrupts, disrupts, impedes, or otherwise interferes with the transmission of a communication over a public safety radio frequency shall be punished by a fine not exceeding one thousand dollars ($1,000), imprisonment in a county jail not exceeding one year, or by both that fine and imprisonment.

(b) Every person who, during the commission of any offense described in subdivision (a), removes or takes any weapon, other than a firearm, from the person of, or immediate presence of, a public officer or peace officer shall be punished by imprisonment in a county jail not to exceed one year or in the state prison.

(c) Every person who, during the commission of any offense described in subdivision (a), removes or takes a firearm from the person of, or immediate presence of, a public officer or peace officer shall be punished by imprisonment in the state prison.

(d) Except as provided in subdivision (c) and notwithstanding subdivision (a) of Section 489, every person who removes or takes without intent to permanently deprive, or who attempts to remove or take a firearm from the person of, or immediate presence of, a public officer or peace officer, while the officer is engaged in the performance of his or her lawful duties, shall be punished by imprisonment in a county jail not to exceed one year or in the state prison. In order to prove a violation of this subdivision, the prosecution shall establish that the defendant had the specific intent to remove or take the firearm by demonstrating that any of the following direct, but ineffectual, acts occurred:

(1) The officer's holster strap was unfastened by the defendant.

(2) The firearm was partially removed from the officer's holster by the defendant.

(3) The firearm safety was released by the defendant.

(4) An independent witness corroborates that the defendant stated that he or she intended to remove the firearm and the defendant actually touched the firearm.

(5) An independent witness corroborates that the defendant actually had his or her hand on the firearm and tried to take the firearm away from the officer who was holding it.

(6) The defendant's fingerprint was found on the firearm or holster.

(7) Physical evidence authenticated by a scientifically verifiable procedure established that the defendant touched the firearm.

(8) In the course of any struggle, the officer's firearm fell and the defendant attempted to pick it up.

(e) A person shall not be convicted of a violation of subdivision (a) in addition to a conviction of a violation of subdivision (b), (c), or (d) when the resistance, delay, or obstruction, and the removal or taking of the weapon or firearm or attempt thereof, was committed against the same public officer, peace officer, or emergency medical technician. A person may be convicted of multiple violations of this section if more than one public officer, peace officer, or emergency medical technician are victims.

(f) This section shall not apply if the public officer, peace officer, or emergency medical technician is disarmed while engaged in a criminal act.

Penal Code § 148.10.

(a) Every person who willfully resists a peace officer in the discharge or attempt to discharge any duty of his or her office or employment and whose willful resistance proximately causes death or serious bodily injury to a peace officer shall be punished by imprisonment in the state prison for two, three, or four years, or by a fine of not less than one thousand dollars ($1,000) or more than ten thousand dollars ($10,000), or by both that fine and imprisonment, or by imprisonment in a county jail for not more than one year, or by a fine of not more than one thousand dollars ($1,000), or by both that fine and imprisonment.

(b) For purposes of subdivision (a), the following facts shall be found by the trier of fact:

(1) That the peace officer's action was reasonable based on the facts or circumstances confronting the officer at the time.

(2) That the detention and arrest was lawful and there existed probable cause or reasonable cause to detain.

(3) That the person who willfully resisted any peace officer knew or reasonably should have known that the other person was a peace officer engaged in the performance of his or her duties.

(c) This section does not apply to conduct that occurs during labor picketing, demonstrations, or disturbing the peace.

(d) For purposes of this section, "serious bodily injury" is defined in paragraph (4) of subdivision (f) of Section 243.

Penal Code § 166.

(a) Except as provided in subdivisions (b), (c), and (d), every person guilty of any contempt of court, of any of the following kinds, is guilty of a misdemeanor:

(1) Disorderly, contemptuous, or insolent behavior committed during the sitting of any court of justice, in the immediate view and presence of the court, and directly tending to interrupt its proceedings or to impair the respect due to its authority.

(2) Behavior as specified in paragraph (1) committed in the presence of any referee, while actually engaged in any trial or hearing, pursuant to the order of any court, or in the presence of any jury while actually sitting for the trial of a cause, or upon any inquest or other proceedings authorized by law.

(3) Any breach of the peace, noise, or other disturbance directly tending to interrupt the proceedings of any court.

(4) Willful disobedience of the terms as written of any process or court order or out-of-state court order, lawfully issued by any court, including orders pending trial.

(5) Resistance willfully offered by any person to the lawful order or process of any court.

(6) The contumacious and unlawful refusal of any person to be sworn as a witness; or, when so sworn, the like refusal to answer any material question.

(7) The publication of a false or grossly inaccurate report of the proceedings of any court.

(8) Presenting to any court having power to pass sentence upon any prisoner under conviction, or to any member of the court, any affidavit or testimony or representation of any kind, verbal or written, in aggravation or mitigation of the punishment to be imposed upon the prisoner, except as provided in this code.

(b)(1) Any person who is guilty of contempt of court under paragraph (4) of subdivision (a) by willfully contacting a victim by telephone or mail, or directly, and who has been previously convicted of a violation of Section 646.9 shall be punished by imprisonment in a county jail for not more than one year, by a fine of five thousand dollars ($5,000), or by both that fine and imprisonment.

(2) For the purposes of sentencing under this subdivision, each contact shall constitute a separate violation of this subdivision.

(3) The present incarceration of a person who makes contact with a victim in violation of paragraph (1) is not a defense to a violation of this subdivision.

(c)(1) Notwithstanding paragraph (4) of subdivision (a), any willful and knowing violation of any protective order or stay-away court order issued pursuant to Section 136.2, in a pending criminal proceeding involving domestic violence, as defined in Section 13700, or issued as a condition of probation after a conviction in a criminal proceeding involving domestic violence, as defined in Section 13700, or elder or dependent adult abuse, as defined in Section 368, or that is an order described in paragraph (3), shall constitute contempt of court, a misdemeanor, punishable by imprisonment in a county jail for not more than one year, by a fine of not more than one thousand dollars ($1,000), or by both that imprisonment and fine.

(2) If a violation of paragraph (1) results in a physical injury, the person shall be imprisoned in a county jail for at least 48 hours, whether a fine or imprisonment is imposed, or the sentence is suspended.

(3) Paragraphs (1) and (2) apply to the following court orders:

(A) Any order issued pursuant to Section 6320 or 6389 of the Family Code.

(B) An order excluding one party from the family dwelling or from the dwelling of the other.

(C) An order enjoining a party from specified behavior that the court determined was necessary to effectuate the orders described in paragraph (1).

(4) A second or subsequent conviction for a violation of any order described in paragraph (1) occurring within seven years of a prior conviction for a violation of any of those orders and involving an act of violence or "a credible threat" of violence, as provided in subdivisions (c) and (d) of Section 139, is punishable by imprisonment in a county jail not to exceed one year, or in the state prison for 16 months or two or three years.

(5) The prosecuting agency of each county shall have the primary responsibility for the enforcement of the orders described in paragraph (1).

(d)(1) A person who owns, possesses, purchases, or receives a firearm knowing he or she is prohibited from doing so by the provisions of a protective order as defined in Section 136.2 of this code, Section 6218 of the Family Code, or Sections 527.6 or 527.8 of the Code of Civil Procedure, shall be punished under the provisions of subdivision (g) of Section 12021.

(2) A person subject to a protective order described in paragraph (1) shall not be prosecuted under this section for owning, possessing, purchasing, or receiving a firearm to the extent that firearm is granted an exemption pursuant to subdivision (h) of Section 6389 of the Family Code.

(e)(1) If probation is granted upon conviction of a violation of subdivision (c), the court shall impose probation consistent with the provisions of Section 1203.097 of the Penal Code.

(2) If probation is granted upon conviction of a violation of subdivision (c), the conditions of probation may include, in lieu of a fine, one or both of the following requirements:

(A) That the defendant make payments to a battered women's shelter, up to a maximum of one thousand dollars ($1,000).

(B) That the defendant provide restitution to reimburse the victim for reasonable costs of counseling and other reasonable expenses that the court finds are the direct result of the defendant's offense.

(3) For any order to pay a fine, make payments to a battered women' s shelter, or pay restitution as a condition of probation under this subdivision or subdivision (c), the court shall make a determination of the defendant's ability to pay. In no event shall any order to make payments to a battered women's shelter be made if it would impair the ability of the defendant to pay direct restitution to the victim or court-ordered child support.

(4) If the injury to a married person is caused in whole or in part by the criminal acts of his or her spouse in violation of subdivision (c), the community property may not be used to discharge the liability of the offending spouse for restitution to the injured spouse required by Section 1203.04, as operative on or before August 2, 1995, or Section 1202.4, or to a shelter for costs with regard to the injured spouse and dependents required by this subdivision, until all separate property of the offending spouse is exhausted.

(5) Any person violating any order described in subdivision (c) may be punished for any substantive offenses described under Section 136.1 or 646.9. No finding of contempt shall be a bar to prosecution for a violation of Section 136.1 or 646.9. However, any person held in contempt for a violation of subdivision (c) shall be entitled to credit for any punishment imposed as a result of that violation against any sentence imposed upon conviction of an offense described in Section 136.1 or 646.9. Any conviction or acquittal for any substantive offense under Section 136.1 or 646.9 shall be a bar to a subsequent punishment for contempt arising out of the same act.

Penal Code §171b.

(a) Any person who brings or possesses within any state or local public building or at any meeting required to be open to the public pursuant to Chapter 9 (commencing with Section 54950) of Part 1 of Division 2 of Title 5 of, or Article 9 (commencing with Section 11120) of Chapter 1 of Part 1 of Division 3 of Title 2 of, the Government Code, any of the following is guilty of a public offense punishable by imprisonment in a county jail for not more than one year, or in the state prison:

(1) Any firearm.

(2) Any deadly weapon described in Section 653k or 12020.

(3) Any knife with a blade length in excess of four inches, the blade of which is fixed or is capable of being fixed in an unguarded position by the use of one or two hands.

(4) Any unauthorized tear gas weapon.

(5) Any taser or stun gun, as defined in Section 244.5.

(6) Any instrument that expels a metallic projectile, such as a BB or pellet, through the force of air pressure, CO2 pressure, or spring action, or any spot marker gun or paint gun.

(b) Subdivision (a) shall not apply to, or affect, any of the following:

(1) A person who possesses weapons in, or transports weapons into, a court of law to be used as evidence.

(2)(A) A duly appointed peace officer as defined in Chapter 4.5 (commencing with Section 830) of Title 3 of Part 2, a retired peace officer with authorization to carry concealed weapons as described in subdivision (a) of Section 12027, a full-time paid peace officer of another state or the federal government who is carrying out official duties while in California, or any person summoned by any of these officers to assist in making arrests or preserving the peace while he or she is actually engaged in assisting the officer.

(B) Notwithstanding subparagraph (A), subdivision (a) shall apply to any person who brings or possesses any weapon specified therein within any courtroom if he or she is a party to an action pending before the court.

(3) A person holding a valid license to carry the firearm pursuant to Article 3 (commencing with Section 12050) of Chapter 1 of Title 2 of Part 4.

(4) A person who has permission to possess that weapon granted in writing by a duly authorized official who is in charge of the security of the state or local government building.

(5) A person who lawfully resides in, lawfully owns, or is in lawful possession of, that building with respect to those portions of the building that are not owned or leased by the state or local government.

(6) A person licensed or registered in accordance with, and acting within the course and scope of, Chapter 11.5 (commencing with Section 7512) or Chapter 11.6 (commencing with Section 7590) of Division 3 of the Business and Professions Code who has been hired by the owner or manager of the building if the person has permission pursuant to paragraph (5).

(7)(A) A person who, for the purpose of sale or trade, brings any weapon that may otherwise be lawfully transferred, into a gun show conducted pursuant to Sections 12071.1 and 12071.4.

(B) A person who, for purposes of an authorized public exhibition, brings any weapon that may otherwise be lawfully possessed, into a gun show conducted pursuant to Sections 12071.1 and 12071.4.

(c) As used in this section, "state or local public building" means a building that meets all of the following criteria:

(1) It is a building or part of a building owned or leased by the state or local government, if state or local public employees are regularly present for the purposes of performing their official duties. A state or local public building includes, but is not limited to, a building that contains a courtroom.

(2) It is not a building or facility, or a part thereof, that is referred to in Section 171c, 171d, 626.9, 626.95, or 626.10 of this code, or in Section 18544 of the Elections Code.

(3) It is a building not regularly used, and not intended to be used, by state or local employees as a place of residence.

Penal Code § 171c.

Any person, except a duly appointed peace officer as defined in Chapter 4.5 (commencing with Section 830) of Title 3 of Part 2, a full-time paid peace officer of another state or the federal government who is carrying out official duties while in California, any person summoned by any such officer to assist in making arrests or preserving the peace while he is actually engaged in assisting such officer, a member of the military forces of this state or the United States engaged in the performance of his duties, or a person holding a valid license to carry the firearm pursuant to Article 3 (commencing with Section 12050) of Chapter 1 of Title 2 of Part 4, who brings a loaded firearm into, or possesses a loaded firearm within, the State Capitol, any legislative office, any office of the Governor or other constitutional officer, or any hearing room in which any committee of the Senate or Assembly is conducting a hearing, or upon the grounds of the State Capitol, which is bounded by 10th, L, 15th, and N Streets in the City of Sacramento, shall be punished by imprisonment in the county jail for a period of not more than one year, a fine of not more than one thousand dollars ($1,000), or both such imprisonment and fine, or by imprisonment in the state prison.

Penal Code § 171d.

Any person, except a duly appointed peace officer as defined in Chapter 4.5 (commencing with Section 830) of Title 3 of Part 2, a full-time paid peace officer of another state or the federal government who is carrying out official duties while in California, any person summoned by that officer to assist in making arrests or preserving the peace while he or she is actually engaged in assisting the officer, a member of the military forces of this state or of the United States engaged in the performance of his or her duties, a person holding a valid license to carry the firearm pursuant to Article 3 (commencing with Section 12050) of Chapter 1 of Title 2 of Part 4, the Governor or a member of his or her immediate family or a person acting with his or her permission with respect to the Governor' s Mansion or any other residence of the Governor, any other constitutional officer or a member of his or her immediate family or a person acting with his or her permission with respect to the officer's residence, or a Member of the Legislature or a member of his or her immediate family or a person acting with his or her permission with respect to the Member's residence, shall be punished by imprisonment in a county jail for not more than one year, by fine of not more than one thousand dollars ($1,000), or by both the fine and imprisonment, or by imprisonment in the state prison, if he or she does any of the following:

(a) Brings a loaded firearm into, or possesses a loaded firearm within, the Governor's Mansion, or any other residence of the Governor, the residence of any other constitutional officer, or the residence of any Member of the Legislature.

(b) Brings a loaded firearm upon, or possesses a loaded firearm upon, the grounds of the Governor's Mansion or any other residence of the Governor, the residence of any other constitutional officer, or the residence of any Member of the Legislature.

Penal Code § 171e.

A firearm shall be deemed loaded for the purposes of Sections 171c and 171d whenever both the firearm and unexpended ammunition capable of being discharged from such firearm are in the immediate possession of the same person. In order to determine whether or not a firearm is loaded for the purpose of enforcing Section 171c or 171d, peace officers are authorized to examine any firearm carried by anyone on his person or in a vehicle while in any place or on the grounds of any place in or on which the possession of a loaded firearm is prohibited by Section 171c or 171d. Refusal to allow a peace officer to inspect a firearm pursuant to the provisions of this section constitutes probable cause for arrest for violation of Section 171c or 171d.

Penal Code § 171f.

No person or group of persons shall willfully and knowingly:

1. Enter or remain within or upon any part of the chamber of either house of the Legislature unless authorized, pursuant to rules adopted or permission granted by either such house, to enter or remain within or upon a part of the chamber of either such house;

2. Engage in any conduct within the State Capitol which disrupts the orderly conduct of official business. A violation of this section is a misdemeanor. As used in this section, "State Capitol" means the building which is intended primarily for use of the legislative department and situated in the area bounded by 10th, L, 15th, and N Streets in the City of Sacramento. Nothing in this section shall forbid

any act of any Member of the Legislature, or any employee of a Member of the Legislature, any officer or employee of the Legislature or any committee or subcommittee thereof, or any officer or employee of either house of the Legislature or any committee or subcommittee thereof, which is performed in the lawful discharge of his official duties.

Penal Code § 171.5.

(a) For purposes of this section:

(1) "Airport" means an airport, with a secured area, that regularly serves an air carrier holding a certificate issued by the United States Secretary of Transportation.

(2) "Passenger vessel terminal" means only that portion of a harbor or port facility, as described in Section 105.105(a)(2) of Title 33 of the Code of Federal Regulations, with a secured area that regularly serves scheduled commuter or passenger operations.

(3) "Sterile area" means a portion of an airport defined in the airport security program to which access generally is controlled through the screening of persons and property, as specified in Section 1540.5 of Title 49 of the Code of Federal Regulations, or a portion of any passenger vessel terminal to which, pursuant to the requirements set forth in Sections 105.255(a)(1), 105.255(c)(1), and 105.260(a) of Title 33 of the Code of Federal Regulations, access is generally controlled in a manner consistent with the passenger vessel terminal's security plan and the MARSEC level in effect at the time.

(b) It is unlawful for any person to knowingly possess, within any sterile area of an airport or a passenger vessel terminal, any of the items listed in subdivision (c).

(c) The following items are unlawful to possess as provided in subdivision (b):

(1) Any firearm.

(2) Any knife with a blade length in excess of four inches, the blade of which is fixed, or is capable of being fixed, in an unguarded position by the use of one or two hands.

(3) Any box cutter or straight razor.

(4) Any metal military practice hand grenade.

(5) Any metal replica hand grenade.

(6) Any plastic replica hand grenade.

(7) Any imitation firearm as defined in Section 417.4.

(8) Any frame, receiver, barrel, or magazine of a firearm.

(9) Any unauthorized tear gas weapon.

(10) Any taser or stun gun, as defined in Section 244.5.

(11) Any instrument that expels a metallic projectile, such as a BB or pellet, through the force of air pressure, CO2 pressure, or spring action, or any spot marker gun or paint gun.

(12) Any ammunition as defined in Section 12316.

(d) Subdivision (b) shall not apply to, or affect, any of the following:

(1) A duly appointed peace officer, as defined in Chapter 4.5 (commencing with Section 830) of Title 3 of Part 2, a retired peace officer with authorization to carry concealed weapons as described in subdivision (a) of Section 12027, a full-time paid peace officer of another state or the federal government who is carrying out official duties while in California, or any person summoned by any of these officers to assist in making arrests or preserving the peace while he or she is actually engaged in assisting the officer.

(2) A person who has authorization to possess a weapon specified in subdivision (c), granted in writing by an airport security coordinator who is designated as specified in Section 1542.3 of Title 49 of the Code of Federal Regulations, and who is responsible for the security of the airport.

(3) A person, including an employee of a licensed contract guard service, who has authorization to possess a weapon specified in subdivision (c) granted in writing by a person discharging the duties of Facility Security Officer or Company Security Officer pursuant to an approved United States Coast Guard facility security plan, and who is responsible for the security of the passenger vessel terminal.

(e) A violation of this section is punishable by imprisonment in a county jail for a period not exceeding six months, or by a fine not exceeding one thousand dollars ($1,000), or by both that fine and imprisonment.

(f) The provisions of this section are cumulative, and shall not be construed as restricting the application of any other law. However, an act or omission that is punishable in different ways by this and any other provision of law shall not be punished under more than one provision.

(g) Nothing in this section is intended to affect existing state or federal law regarding the transportation of firearms on airplanes in checked luggage, or the possession of the items listed in subdivision (c) in areas that are not "sterile areas."

Penal Code § 186.20.

This chapter shall be known and may be cited as the "California Street Terrorism Enforcement and Prevention Act."

Penal Code § 186.21.

The Legislature hereby finds and declares that it is the right of every person, regardless of race, color, creed, religion, national origin, gender, age, sexual orientation, or handicap, to be secure and protected from fear, intimidation, and physical harm caused by the activities of violent groups and individuals. It is not the intent of this chapter to interfere with the exercise of the constitutionally protected rights of freedom of expression and association. The Legislature hereby recognizes the constitutional right of every citizen to harbor and express beliefs on any lawful subject whatsoever, to lawfully associate with others who share similar beliefs, to petition lawfully constituted authority for a redress of perceived grievances, and to participate in the electoral process.

The Legislature, however, further finds that the State of California is in a state of crisis which has been caused by violent street gangs whose members threaten, terrorize, and commit a multitude of crimes against the peaceful citizens of their neighborhoods. These activities, both individually and collectively, present a clear and present danger to public order and safety and are not constitutionally protected. The Legislature finds that there are nearly 600 criminal street gangs operating in California, and that the number of gang-related murders is increasing. The Legislature also finds that in Los Angeles County alone there were 328 gang-related murders in 1986, and that gang homicides in 1987 have increased 80 percent over 1986. It is the intent of the Legislature in enacting this chapter to seek the eradication of criminal activity by street gangs by focusing upon patterns of criminal gang activity and upon the organized nature of street gangs, which together, are the chief source of terror created by street gangs. The Legislature further finds that an effective means of punishing and deterring the criminal activities of street gangs is through forfeiture of the profits, proceeds, and instrumentalities acquired, accumulated, or used by street gangs.

Penal Code § 186.22.

(a) Any person who actively participates in any criminal street gang with knowledge that its members engage in or have engaged in a pattern of criminal gang activity, and who willfully promotes, furthers, or assists in any felonious criminal conduct by members of that gang, shall be punished by imprisonment in a county jail for a period not to exceed one year, or by imprisonment in the state prison for 16 months, or two or three years.

(b)(1) Except as provided in paragraphs (4) and (5), any person who is convicted of a felony committed for the benefit of, at the direction of, or in association with any criminal street gang, with the specific intent to promote, further, or assist in any criminal conduct by gang members, shall, upon conviction of that felony, in addition and consecutive to the punishment prescribed for the felony or attempted felony of which he or she has been convicted, be punished as follows:

(A) Except as provided in subparagraphs (B) and (C), the person shall be punished by an additional term of two, three, or four years at the court's discretion.

(B) If the felony is a serious felony, as defined in subdivision (c) of Section 1192.7, the person shall be punished by an additional term of five years.

(C) If the felony is a violent felony, as defined in subdivision (c) of Section 667.5, the person shall be punished by an additional term of 10 years.

(2) If the underlying felony described in paragraph (1) is committed on the grounds of, or within 1,000 feet of, a public or private elementary, vocational, junior high, or high school, during hours in which the facility is open for classes or school-related programs or when minors are using the facility, that fact shall be a circumstance in aggravation of the crime in imposing a term under paragraph (1).

(3) The court shall order the imposition of the middle term of the sentence enhancement, unless there are circumstances in aggravation or mitigation. The court shall state the reasons for its choice of sentencing enhancements on the record at the time of the sentencing.

(4) Any person who is convicted of a felony enumerated in this paragraph committed for the benefit of, at the direction of, or in association with any criminal street gang, with the specific intent to promote, further, or assist in any criminal conduct by gang members, shall, upon conviction of that felony, be sentenced to an indeterminate term of life imprisonment with a minimum term of the indeterminate sentence calculated as the greater of:

(A) The term determined by the court pursuant to Section 1170 for the underlying conviction, including any enhancement applicable under Chapter 4.5 (commencing with Section 1170) of Title 7 of Part 2, or any period prescribed by Section 3046, if the felony is any of the offenses enumerated in subparagraph (B) or (C) of this paragraph.

(B) Imprisonment in the state prison for 15 years, if the felony is a home invasion robbery, in violation of subparagraph (A) of paragraph (1) of subdivision (a) of Section 213; carjacking, as defined in Section 215; a felony violation of Section 246; or a violation of Section 12022.55.

(C) Imprisonment in the state prison for seven years, if the felony is extortion, as defined in Section 519; or threats to victims and witnesses, as defined in Section 136.1.

(5) Except as provided in paragraph (4), any person who violates this subdivision in the commission of a felony punishable by imprisonment in the state prison for life shall not be paroled until a minimum of 15 calendar years have been served.

(c) If the court grants probation or suspends the execution of sentence imposed upon the defendant for a violation of subdivision (a), or in cases involving a true finding of the enhancement enumerated in subdivision (b), the court shall require that the defendant serve a minimum of 180 days in a county jail as a condition thereof.

(d) Any person who is convicted of a public offense punishable as a felony or a misdemeanor, which is committed for the benefit of, at the direction of or in association with, any criminal street gang with the specific intent to promote, further, or assist in any criminal conduct by gang members, shall be punished by imprisonment in the county jail not to exceed one year, or by imprisonment in the state prison for one, two, or three years, provided that any person sentenced to imprisonment in the county jail shall be imprisoned for a period not to exceed one year, but not less than 180 days, and shall not be eligible for release upon completion of sentence, parole, or any other basis, until he or she has served 180 days. If the court grants probation or suspends the execution of sentence imposed upon the defendant, it shall require as a condition thereof that the defendant serve 180 days in a county jail.

(e) As used in this chapter, "pattern of criminal gang activity" means the commission of, attempted commission of, conspiracy to commit, or solicitation of, sustained juvenile petition for, or conviction of two or more of the following offenses, provided at least one of these offenses occurred after the effective date of this chapter and the last of those offenses occurred within three years after a prior offense, and the offenses were committed on separate occasions, or by two or more persons:

(1) Assault with a deadly weapon or by means of force likely to produce great bodily injury, as defined in Section 245.

(2) Robbery, as defined in Chapter 4 (commencing with Section 211) of Title 8 of Part 1.

(3) Unlawful homicide or manslaughter, as defined in Chapter 1 commencing with Section 187) of Title 8 of Part 1.

(4) The sale, possession for sale, transportation, manufacture, offer for sale, or offer to manufacture controlled substances as defined in Sections 11054, 11055, 11056, 11057, and 11058 of the Health and Safety Code.

(5) Shooting at an inhabited dwelling or occupied motor vehicle, as defined in Section 246.

(6) Discharging or permitting the discharge of a firearm from a motor vehicle, as defined in subdivisions (a) and (b) of Section 12034.

(7) Arson, as defined in Chapter 1 (commencing with Section 450) of Title 13.

(8) The intimidation of witnesses and victims, as defined in Section 136.1.

(9) Grand theft, as defined in subdivision (a) or (c) of Section 487.

(10) Grand theft of any firearm, vehicle, trailer, or vessel.

(11) Burglary, as defined in Section 459.

(12) Rape, as defined in Section 261.

(13) Looting, as defined in Section 463.

(14) Money laundering, as defined in Section 186.10.

(15) Kidnapping, as defined in Section 207.

(16) Mayhem, as defined in Section 203.

(17) Aggravated mayhem, as defined in Section 205.

(18) Torture, as defined in Section 206.

(19) Felony extortion, as defined in Sections 518 and 520.

(20) Felony vandalism, as defined in paragraph (1) of subdivision (b) of Section 594.

(21) Carjacking, as defined in Section 215.

(22) The sale, delivery, or transfer of a firearm, as defined in Section 12072.

(23) Possession of a pistol, revolver, or other firearm capable of being concealed upon the person in violation of paragraph (1) of subdivision (a) of Section 12101.

(24) Threats to commit crimes resulting in death or great bodily injury, as defined in Section 422.

(25) Theft and unlawful taking or driving of a vehicle, as defined in Section 10851 of the Vehicle Code.

(26) Felony theft of an access card or account information, as defined in Section 484e.

(27) Counterfeiting, designing, using, attempting to use an access card, as defined in Section 484f.

(28) Felony fraudulent use of an access card or account information, as defined in Section 484g.

(29) Unlawful use of personal identifying information to obtain credit, goods, services, or medical information, as defined in Section 530.5.

(30) Wrongfully obtaining Department of Motor Vehicles documentation, as defined in Section 529.7.

(31) Prohibited possession of a firearm in violation of Section 12021.

(32) Carrying a concealed firearm in violation of Section 12025.

(33) Carrying a loaded firearm in violation of Section 12031.

(f) As used in this chapter, "criminal street gang" means any ongoing organization, association, or group of three or more persons, whether formal or informal, having as one of its primary activities the commission of one or more of the criminal acts enumerated in paragraphs (1) to (25), inclusive, or (31) to (33), inclusive, of subdivision (e), having a common name or common identifying sign or symbol, and whose members individually or collectively engage in or have engaged in a pattern of criminal gang activity.

(g) Notwithstanding any other law, the court may strike the additional punishment for the enhancements provided in this section or refuse to impose the minimum jail sentence for misdemeanors in an unusual case where the interests of justice would best be served, if the court specifies on the record and enters into the minutes the circumstances indicating that the interests of justice would best be served by that disposition.

(h) Notwithstanding any other provision of law, for each person committed to the Division of Juvenile Facilities for a conviction pursuant to subdivision (a) or (b) of this section, the offense shall be deemed one for which the state shall pay the rate of 100 percent of the per capita institutional cost of the Division of Juvenile Facilities, pursuant to Section 912.5 of the Welfare and Institutions Code.

(i) In order to secure a conviction or sustain a juvenile petition, pursuant to subdivision (a) it is not necessary for the prosecution to prove that the person devotes all, or a substantial part, of his or her time or efforts to the criminal street gang, nor is it necessary to prove that the person is a member of the criminal street gang. Active participation in the criminal street gang is all that is required.

(j) A pattern of gang activity may be shown by the commission of one or more of the offenses enumerated in paragraphs (26) to (30), inclusive, of subdivision (e), and the commission of one or more of the offenses enumerated in paragraphs (1) to (25), inclusive, or (31) to (33), inclusive of subdivision (e). A pattern of gang activity cannot be established solely by proof of commission of offenses enumerated in paragraphs (26) to (30), inclusive, of subdivision (e), alone.

Penal Code § 186.22a.

(a) Every building or place used by members of a criminal street gang for the purpose of the commission of the offenses listed in subdivision (e) of Section 186.22 or any offense involving dangerous or deadly weapons, burglary, or rape, and every building or place wherein or upon which that criminal conduct by gang members takes place, is a nuisance which shall be enjoined, abated, and prevented, and for which damages may be recovered, whether it is a public or private nuisance.

(b) Any action for injunction or abatement filed pursuant to subdivision (a), including an action filed by the Attorney General, shall proceed according to the provisions of Article 3 (commencing with Section 11570) of Chapter 10 of Division 10 of the Health and Safety Code, except that all of the following shall apply:

(1) The court shall not assess a civil penalty against any person unless that person knew or should have known of the unlawful acts.

(2) No order of eviction or closure may be entered.

(3) All injunctions issued shall be limited to those necessary to protect the health and safety of the residents or the public or those necessary to prevent further criminal activity.

(4) Suit may not be filed until 30-day notice of the unlawful use or criminal conduct has been provided to the owner by mail, return receipt requested, postage prepaid, to the last known address.

(c) Whenever an injunction is issued pursuant to subdivision (a), or Section 3479 of the Civil Code, to abate gang activity constituting a nuisance, the Attorney General or any district attorney or any prosecuting city attorney may maintain an action for money damages on behalf of the community or neighborhood injured by that nuisance. Any money damages awarded shall be paid by or collected from assets of the criminal street gang or its members. Only members of the criminal street gang who created, maintained, or contributed to the creation or maintenance of the nuisance shall be personally liable for the payment of the damages awarded. In a civil action for damages brought pursuant to this subdivision, the Attorney General, district attorney, or city attorney may use, but is not limited to the use of, the testimony of experts to establish damages suffered by the community or neighborhood injured by the nuisance. The damages recovered pursuant to this subdivision shall be deposited into a separate segregated fund for payment to the governing body of the city or county in whose political subdivision the community or neighborhood is located, and that governing body shall use those assets solely for the benefit of the community or neighborhood that has been injured by the nuisance.

(d) No nonprofit or charitable organization which is conducting its affairs with ordinary care or skill, and no governmental entity, shall be abated pursuant to subdivisions (a) and (b).

(e) Nothing in this chapter shall preclude any aggrieved person from seeking any other remedy provided by law.

(f)(1) Any firearm, ammunition which may be used with the firearm, or any deadly or dangerous weapon which is owned or possessed by a member of a criminal street gang for the purpose of the commission of any of the offenses listed in subdivision (e) of Section 186.22, or the commission of any burglary or rape, may be confiscated by any law enforcement agency or peace officer.

(2) In those cases where a law enforcement agency believes that the return of the firearm, ammunition, or deadly weapon confiscated pursuant to this subdivision, is or will be used in criminal street gang activity or that the return of the item would be likely to result in endangering the safety of others, the law enforcement agency shall initiate a petition in the superior court to determine if the item confiscated should be returned or declared a nuisance.

(3) No firearm, ammunition, or deadly weapon shall be sold or destroyed unless reasonable notice is given to its lawful owner if his or her identity and address can be reasonably ascertained. The law enforcement agency shall inform the lawful owner, at that person' s last known address by registered mail, that he or she has 30 days from the date of receipt of the notice to respond to the court clerk to confirm his or her desire for a hearing and that the failure to respond shall result in a default order forfeiting the confiscated firearm, ammunition, or deadly weapon as a nuisance.

(4) If the person requests a hearing, the court clerk shall set a hearing no later than 30 days from receipt of that request. The court clerk shall notify the person, the law enforcement agency involved, and the district attorney of the date, time, and place of the hearing.

(5) At the hearing, the burden of proof is upon the law enforcement agency or peace officer to show by a preponderance of the evidence that the seized item is or will be used in criminal street gang activity or that return of the item would be likely to result in endangering the safety of others. All returns of firearms shall be subject to Section 12021.3.

(6) If the person does not request a hearing within 30 days of the notice or the lawful owner cannot be ascertained, the law enforcement agency may file a petition that the confiscated firearm, ammunition, or deadly weapon be declared a nuisance. If the items are declared to be a nuisance, the law enforcement agency shall dispose of the items as provided in Section 12028.

Penal Code § 186.23.

This chapter does not apply to employees engaged in concerted activities for their mutual aid and protection, or the activities of labor organizations or their members or agents.

Penal Code § 186.24.

If any part or provision of this chapter, or the application thereof to any person or circumstance, is held invalid, the remainder of the chapter, including the application of that part or provision to other persons or circumstances, shall not be affected thereby and shall continue in full force and effect. To this end, the provisions of this chapter are severable.

Penal Code § 186.25.

Nothing in this chapter shall prevent a local governing body from adopting and enforcing laws consistent with this chapter relating to gangs and gang violence. Where local laws duplicate or supplement this chapter, this chapter shall be construed as providing alternative remedies and not as preempting the field.

Penal Code § 186.26.

(a) Any person who solicits or recruits another to actively participate in a criminal street gang, as defined in subdivision (f) of Section 186.22, with the intent that the person solicited or recruited participate in a pattern of criminal street gang activity, as defined in subdivision (e) of Section 186.22, or with the intent that the person solicited or recruited promote, further, or assist in any felonious conduct by members of the criminal street gang, shall be punished by imprisonment in the state prison for 16 months, or two or three years.

(b) Any person who threatens another person with physical violence on two or more separate occasions within any 30-day period with the intent to coerce, induce, or solicit any person to actively participate in a criminal street gang, as defined in subdivision (f) of Section 186.22, shall be punished by imprisonment in the state prison for two, three, or four years.

(c) Any person who uses physical violence to coerce, induce, or solicit another person to actively participate in any criminal street gang, as defined in subdivision (f) of Section 186.22, or to prevent the person from leaving a criminal street gang, shall be punished by imprisonment in the state prison for three, four, or five years.

(d) If the person solicited, recruited, coerced, or threatened pursuant to subdivision (a), (b), or (c) is a minor, an additional term of three years shall be imposed in addition and consecutive to the penalty prescribed for a violation of any of these subdivisions.

(e) Nothing in this section shall be construed to limit prosecution under any other provision of law.

Penal Code § 186.28.

(a) Any person, corporation, or firm who shall knowingly supply, sell, or give possession or control of any firearm to another shall be punished by imprisonment in the state prison, or in a county jail for a term not exceeding one year, or by a fine not exceeding one thousand dollars ($1,000), or by both that fine and imprisonment if all of the following apply:

(1) The person, corporation, or firm has actual knowledge that the person will use the firearm to commit a felony described

in subdivision (e) of Section 186.22, while actively participating in any criminal street gang, as defined in subdivision (f) of Section 186.22, the members of which engage in a pattern of criminal activity, as defined in subdivision (e) of Section 186.22.

(2) The firearm is used to commit the felony.

(3) A conviction for the felony violation under subdivision (e) of Section 186.22 has first been obtained of the person to whom the firearm was supplied, sold, or given possession or control pursuant to this section.

(b) This section shall only be applicable where the person is not convicted as a principal to the felony offense committed by the person to whom the firearm was supplied, sold, or given possession or control pursuant to this section.

Penal Code § 186.30.

(a) Any person described in subdivision (b) shall register with the chief of police of the city in which he or she resides, or the sheriff of the county if he or she resides in an unincorporated area, within 10 days of release from custody or within 10 days of his or her arrival in any city, county, or city and county to reside there, whichever occurs first.

(b) Subdivision (a) shall apply to any person convicted in a criminal court or who has had a petition sustained in a juvenile court in this state for any of the following offenses:

(1) Subdivision (a) of Section 186.22.

(2) Any crime where the enhancement specified in subdivision (b) of Section 186.22 is found to be true.

(3) Any crime that the court finds is gang related at the time of sentencing or disposition.

Penal Code § 186.31.

At the time of sentencing in adult court, or at the time of the dispositional hearing in the juvenile court, the court shall inform any person subject to Section 186.30 of his or her duty to register pursuant to that section. This advisement shall be noted in the court minute order. The court clerk shall send a copy of the minute order to the law enforcement agency with jurisdiction for the last known address of the person subject to registration under Section 186.30. The parole officer or the probation officer assigned to that person shall verify that he or she has complied with the registration requirements of Section 186.30.

Penal Code § 186.32.

(a) The registration required by Section 186.30 shall consist of the following:

(1) Juvenile registration shall include the following:

(A) The juvenile shall appear at the law enforcement agency with a parent or guardian.

(B) The law enforcement agency shall serve the juvenile and the parent with a California Street Terrorism Enforcement and Prevention Act notification which shall include, where applicable, that the juvenile belongs to a gang whose members engage in or have engaged in a pattern of criminal gang activity as described in subdivision (e) of Section 186.22.

(C) A written statement signed by the juvenile, giving any information that may be required by the law enforcement agency, shall be submitted to the law enforcement agency.

(D) The fingerprints and current photograph of the juvenile shall be submitted to the law enforcement agency.

(2) Adult registration shall include the following:

(A) The adult shall appear at the law enforcement agency. (B) The law enforcement agency shall serve the adult with a California Street Terrorism Enforcement and Prevention Act notification which shall include, where applicable, that the adult belongs to a gang whose members engage in or have engaged in a pattern of criminal gang activity as described in subdivision (e) of Section 186.22.

(C) A written statement, signed by the adult, giving any information that may be required by the law enforcement agency, shall be submitted to the law enforcement agency.

(D) The fingerprints and current photograph of the adult shall be submitted to the law enforcement agency.

(b) Within 10 days of changing his or her residence address, any person subject to Section 186.30 shall inform, in writing, the law enforcement agency with whom he or she last registered of his or her new address. If his or her new residence address is located within the jurisdiction of a law enforcement agency other than the agency where he or she last registered, he or she shall register with the new law enforcement agency, in writing, within 10 days of the change of residence.

(c) All registration requirements set forth in this article shall terminate five years after the last imposition of a registration requirement pursuant to Section 186.30.

(d) The statements, photographs and fingerprints required under this section shall not be open to inspection by any person other than a regularly employed peace or other law enforcement officer.

(e) Nothing in this section or Section 186.30 or 186.31 shall preclude a court in its discretion from imposing the registration requirements as set forth in those sections in a gang-related crime.

Penal Code § 186.33.

(a) Any person required to register pursuant to Section 186.30 who knowingly violates any of its provisions is guilty of a misdemeanor.

(b)(1) Any person who knowingly fails to register pursuant to Section 186.30 and is subsequently convicted of, or any person for whom a petition is subsequently sustained for a violation of, any of the offenses specified in Section 186.30, shall be punished by an additional term of imprisonment in the state prison for 16 months, or 2, or 3 years. The court shall order imposition of the middle term unless there are circumstances in aggravation or mitigation. The court shall state its reasons for the enhancement choice on the record at the time of sentencing.

(2) The existence of any fact bringing a person under this subdivision shall be alleged in the information, indictment, or petition, and be either admitted by the defendant or minor in open court, or found to be true or not true by the trier of fact.

Penal Code § 187.

(a) Murder is the unlawful killing of a human being, or a fetus, with malice aforethought.

(b) This section shall not apply to any person who commits an act that results in the death of a fetus if any of the following apply:

(1) The act complied with the Therapeutic Abortion Act, Article 2 (commencing with Section 123400) of Chapter 2 of Part 2 of Division 106 of the Health and Safety Code.

(2) The act was committed by a holder of a physician's and surgeon' s certificate, as defined in the Business and Professions Code, in a case where, to a medical certainty, the result of childbirth would be death of the mother of the fetus or where her death from childbirth, although not medically certain, would be substantially certain or more likely than not.

(3) The act was solicited, aided, abetted, or consented to by the mother of the fetus. (c) Subdivision (b) shall not be construed to prohibit the prosecution of any person under any other provision of law.

Penal Code § 189.

All murder which is perpetrated by means of a destructive device or explosive, a weapon of mass destruction, knowing use of ammunition designed primarily to penetrate metal or armor, poison, lying in wait, torture, or by any other kind of willful, deliberate, and premeditated killing, or which is committed in the perpetration of, or attempt to perpetrate, arson, rape, carjacking, robbery, burglary, mayhem, kidnapping, train wrecking, or any act punishable under Section 206, 286, 288, 288a, or 289, or any murder which is perpetrated by means of discharging a firearm from a motor vehicle, intentionally at another person outside of the vehicle with the intent to inflict death, is murder of the first degree. All other kinds of murders are of the second degree.

As used in this section, "destructive device" means any destructive device as defined in Section 12301, and "explosive" means any explosive as defined in Section 12000 of the Health and Safety Code.

As used in this section, "weapon of mass destruction" means any item defined in Section 11417. To prove the killing was "deliberate and premeditated," it shall not be necessary to prove the defendant maturely and meaningfully reflected upon the gravity of his or her act.

Penal Code § 190.

(a) Every person guilty of murder in the first degree shall be punished by death, imprisonment in the state prison for life without the possibility of parole, or imprisonment in the state prison for a term of 25 years to life. The penalty to be applied shall be determined as provided in Sections 190.1, 190.2, 190.3, 190.4, and 190.5. Except as provided in subdivision (b), (c), or (d), every person guilty of murder in the second degree shall be punished by imprisonment in the state prison for a term of 15 years to life.

(b) Except as provided in subdivision (c), every person guilty of murder in the second degree shall be punished by imprisonment in the state prison for a term of 25 years to life if the victim was a peace officer, as defined in subdivision (a) of Section 830.1, subdivision (a), (b), or (c) of Section 830.2, subdivision (a) of Section 830.33, or Section 830.5, who was killed while engaged in the performance of his or her duties, and the defendant knew, or reasonably should have known, that the victim was a peace officer engaged in the performance of his or her duties.

(c) Every person guilty of murder in the second degree shall be punished by imprisonment in the state prison for a term of life without the possibility of parole if the victim was a peace officer, as defined in subdivision (a) of Section 830.1, subdivision (a), (b), or (c) of Section 830.2, subdivision (a) of Section 830.33, or Section 830.5, who was killed while engaged in the performance of his or her duties, and the defendant knew, or reasonably should have known, that the victim was a peace officer engaged in the performance of his or her duties, and any of the following facts has been charged and found true:

(1) The defendant specifically intended to kill the peace officer.

(2) The defendant specifically intended to inflict great bodily injury, as defined in Section 12022.7, on a peace officer.

(3) The defendant personally used a dangerous or deadly weapon in the commission of the offense, in violation of subdivision (b) of Section 12022.

(4) The defendant personally used a firearm in the commission of the offense, in violation of Section 12022.5.

(d) Every person guilty of murder in the second degree shall be punished by imprisonment in the state prison for a term of 20 years to life if the killing was perpetrated by means of shooting a firearm from a motor vehicle, intentionally at another person outside of the vehicle with the intent to inflict great bodily injury.

(e) Article 2.5 (commencing with Section 2930) of Chapter 7 of Title 1 of Part 3 shall not apply to reduce any minimum term of a sentence imposed pursuant to this section. A person sentenced pursuant to this section shall not be released on parole prior to serving the minimum term of confinement prescribed by this section.

Penal Code § 190.2.

(a) The penalty for a defendant who is found guilty of murder in the first degree is death or imprisonment in the state prison for life without the possibility of parole if one or more of the following special circumstances has been found under Section 190.4 to be true:

(1) The murder was intentional and carried out for financial gain.

(2) The defendant was convicted previously of murder in the first or second degree. For the purpose of this paragraph, an offense committed in another jurisdiction, which if committed in California would be punishable as first or second degree murder, shall be deemed murder in the first or second degree.

(3) The defendant, in this proceeding, has been convicted of more than one offense of murder in the first or second degree.

(4) The murder was committed by means of a destructive device, bomb, or explosive planted, hidden, or concealed in any place, area, dwelling, building, or structure, and the defendant knew, or reasonably should have known, that his or her act or acts would create a great risk of death to one or more human beings.

(5) The murder was committed for the purpose of avoiding or preventing a lawful arrest, or perfecting or attempting to perfect, an escape from lawful custody.

(6) The murder was committed by means of a destructive device, bomb, or explosive that the defendant mailed or delivered, attempted to mail or deliver, or caused to be mailed or delivered, and the defendant knew, or reasonably should have known, that his or

her act or acts would create a great risk of death to one or more human beings.

(7) The victim was a peace officer, as defined in Section 830.1, 830.2, 830.3, 830.31, 830.32, 830.33, 830.34, 830.35, 830.36, 830.37, 830.4, 830.5, 830.6, 830.10, 830.11, or 830.12, who, while engaged in the course of the performance of his or her duties, was intentionally killed, and the defendant knew, or reasonably should have known, that the victim was a peace officer engaged in the performance of his or her duties; or the victim was a peace officer, as defined in the above-enumerated sections, or a former peace officer under any of those sections, and was intentionally killed in retaliation for the performance of his or her official duties.

(8) The victim was a federal law enforcement officer or agent who, while engaged in the course of the performance of his or her duties, was intentionally killed, and the defendant knew, or reasonably should have known, that the victim was a federal law enforcement officer or agent engaged in the performance of his or her duties; or the victim was a federal law enforcement officer or agent, and was intentionally killed in retaliation for the performance of his or her official duties.

(9) The victim was a firefighter, as defined in Section 245.1, who, while engaged in the course of the performance of his or her duties, was intentionally killed, and the defendant knew, or reasonably should have known, that the victim was a firefighter engaged in the performance of his or her duties.

(10) The victim was a witness to a crime who was intentionally killed for the purpose of preventing his or her testimony in any criminal or juvenile proceeding, and the killing was not committed during the commission or attempted commission, of the crime to which he or she was a witness; or the victim was a witness to a crime and was intentionally killed in retaliation for his or her testimony in any criminal or juvenile proceeding. As used in this paragraph, "juvenile proceeding" means a proceeding brought pursuant to Section 602 or 707 of the Welfare and Institutions Code.

(11) The victim was a prosecutor or assistant prosecutor or a former prosecutor or assistant prosecutor of any local or state prosecutor's office in this or any other state, or of a federal prosecutor's office, and the murder was intentionally carried out in retaliation for, or to prevent the performance of, the victim's official duties.

(12) The victim was a judge or former judge of any court of record in the local, state, or federal system in this or any other state, and the murder was intentionally carried out in retaliation for, or to prevent the performance of, the victim's official duties.

(13) The victim was an elected or appointed official or former official of the federal government, or of any local or state government of this or any other state, and the killing was intentionally carried out in retaliation for, or to prevent the performance of, the victim's official duties.

(14) The murder was especially heinous, atrocious, or cruel, manifesting exceptional depravity. As used in this section, the phrase "especially heinous, atrocious, or cruel, manifesting exceptional depravity" means a conscienceless or pitiless crime that is unnecessarily torturous to the victim.

(15) The defendant intentionally killed the victim by means of lying in wait.

(16) The victim was intentionally killed because of his or her race, color, religion, nationality, or country of origin.

(17) The murder was committed while the defendant was engaged in, or was an accomplice in, the commission of, attempted commission of, or the immediate flight after committing, or attempting to commit, the following felonies:

(A) Robbery in violation of Section 211 or 212.5.

(B) Kidnapping in violation of Section 207, 209, or 209.5.

(C) Rape in violation of Section 261.

(D) Sodomy in violation of Section 286.

(E) The performance of a lewd or lascivious act upon the person of a child under the age of 14 years in violation of Section 288.

(F) Oral copulation in violation of Section 288a.

(G) Burglary in the first or second degree in violation of Section 460.

(H) Arson in violation of subdivision (b) of Section 451.

(I) Train wrecking in violation of Section 219.

(J) Mayhem in violation of Section 203.

(K) Rape by instrument in violation of Section 289.

(L) Carjacking, as defined in Section 215.

(M) To prove the special circumstances of kidnapping in subparagraph (B), or arson in subparagraph (H), if there is specific intent to kill, it is only required that there be proof of the elements of those felonies. If so established, those two special circumstances are proven even if the felony of kidnapping or arson is committed primarily or solely for the purpose of facilitating the murder.

(18) The murder was intentional and involved the infliction of torture.

(19) The defendant intentionally killed the victim by the administration of poison.

(20) The victim was a juror in any court of record in the local, state, or federal system in this or any other state, and the murder was intentionally carried out in retaliation for, or to prevent the performance of, the victim's official duties.

(21) The murder was intentional and perpetrated by means of discharging a firearm from a motor vehicle, intentionally at another person or persons outside the vehicle with the intent to inflict death. For purposes of this paragraph, "motor vehicle" means any vehicle as defined in Section 415 of the Vehicle Code.

(22) The defendant intentionally killed the victim while the defendant was an active participant in a criminal street gang, as defined in subdivision (f) of Section 186.22, and the murder was carried out to further the activities of the criminal street gang.

(b) Unless an intent to kill is specifically required under subdivision (a) for a special circumstance enumerated therein, an actual killer, as to whom the special circumstance has been found to be true under Section 190.4, need not have had any intent to kill at the time of the commission of the offense which is the basis of the special circumstance in order to suffer death or confinement in the state prison for life without the possibility of parole.

(c) Every person, not the actual killer, who, with the intent to kill, aids, abets, counsels, commands, induces, solicits, requests, or assists any actor in the commission of murder in the first degree shall be punished by death or imprisonment in the state prison for life without the possibility of parole if one or more of the special circumstances enumerated in subdivision (a) has been found to be true under Section 190.4.

(d) Notwithstanding subdivision (c), every person, not the actual killer, who, with reckless indifference to human life and as a major participant, aids, abets, counsels, commands, induces, solicits, requests, or assists in the commission of a felony enumerated in paragraph (17) of subdivision (a) which results in the death of some person or persons, and who is found guilty of murder in the first degree therefor, shall be punished by death or imprisonment in the state prison for life without the possibility of parole if a special circumstance enumerated in paragraph (17) of subdivision (a) has been found to be true under Section 190.4. The penalty shall be determined as provided in this section and Sections 190.1, 190.3, 190.4, and 190.5.

Penal Code § 195.

Homicide is excusable in the following cases:

1. When committed by accident and misfortune, or in doing any other lawful act by lawful means, with usual and ordinary caution, and without any unlawful intent.

2. When committed by accident and misfortune, in the heat of passion, upon any sudden and sufficient provocation, or upon a sudden combat, when no undue advantage is taken, nor any dangerous weapon used, and when the killing is not done in a cruel or unusual manner.

Penal Code § 196.

Homicide is justifiable when committed by public officers and those acting by their command in their aid and assistance, either--

1. In obedience to any judgment of a competent Court; or,

2. When necessarily committed in overcoming actual resistance to the execution of some legal process, or in the discharge of any other legal duty; or,

3. When necessarily committed in retaking felons who have been rescued or have escaped, or when necessarily committed in arresting persons charged with felony, and who are fleeing from justice or resisting such arrest.

Penal Code § 197.

Homicide is also justifiable when committed by any person in any of the following cases:

1. When resisting any attempt to murder any person, or to commit a felony, or to do some great bodily injury upon any person; or,

2. When committed in defense of habitation, property, or person, against one who manifestly intends or endeavors, by violence or surprise, to commit a felony, or against one who manifestly intends and endeavors, in a violent, riotous or tumultuous manner, to enter the habitation of another for the purpose of offering violence to any person therein; or,

3. When committed in the lawful defense of such person, or of a wife or husband, parent, child, master, mistress, or servant of such person, when there is reasonable ground to apprehend a design to commit a felony or to do some great bodily injury, and imminent danger of such design being accomplished; but such person, or the person in whose behalf the defense was made, if he was the assailant or engaged in mutual combat, must really and in good faith have endeavored to decline any further struggle before the homicide was committed; or,

4. When necessarily committed in attempting, by lawful ways and means, to apprehend any person for any felony committed, or in lawfully suppressing any riot, or in lawfully keeping and preserving the peace.

Penal Code § 198.

A bare fear of the commission of any of the offenses mentioned in subdivisions 2 and 3 of Section 197, to prevent which homicide may be lawfully committed, is not sufficient to justify it. But the circumstances must be sufficient to excite the fears of a reasonable person, and the party killing must have acted under the influence of such fears alone.

Penal Code § 198.5.

Any person using force intended or likely to cause death or great bodily injury within his or her residence shall be presumed to have held a reasonable fear of imminent peril of death or great bodily injury to self, family, or a member of the household when that force is used against another person, not a member of the family or household, who unlawfully and forcibly enters or has unlawfully and forcibly entered the residence and the person using the force knew or had reason to believe that an unlawful and forcible entry occurred.

As used in this section, great bodily injury means a significant or substantial physical injury.

Penal Code § 199.

The homicide appearing to be justifiable or excusable, the person indicted must, upon his trial, be fully acquitted and discharged.

Penal Code § 219.

Every person who unlawfully throws out a switch, removes a rail, or places any obstruction on any railroad with the intention of derailing any passenger, freight or other train, car or engine and thus derails the same, or who unlawfully places any dynamite or other explosive material or any other obstruction upon or near the track of any railroad with the intention of blowing up or derailing any such train, car or engine and thus blows up or derails the same, or who unlawfully sets fire to any railroad bridge or trestle over which any such train, car or engine must pass with the intention of wrecking such train, car or engine, and thus wrecks the same, is guilty of a felony and punishable with death or imprisonment in the state prison for life without possibility of parole in cases where any person suffers death as a proximate result thereof, or imprisonment in the state prison for life with the possibility of parole, in cases where no person suffers death as a proximate result thereof. The penalty shall be determined pursuant to Sections 190.3 and 190.4.

Penal Code § 219.1

Every person who unlawfully throws, hurls or projects at a vehicle operated by a common carrier, while such vehicle is either in motion or stationary, any rock, stone, brick, bottle, piece of wood or metal or any other missile of any kind or character, or does any unlawful act, with the intention of wrecking such vehicle and doing bodily harm, and thus wrecks the same and causes bodily harm, is guilty of a felony and punishable by imprisonment in the state prison for two, four, or six years.

Penal Code § 240.

An assault is an unlawful attempt, coupled with a present ability, to commit a violent injury on the person of another.

Penal Code § 241.

(a) An assault is punishable by a fine not exceeding one thousand dollars ($1,000), or by imprisonment in the county jail not exceeding six months, or by both the fine and imprisonment.

(b) When an assault is committed against the person of a parking control officer engaged in the performance of his or her duties, and the person committing the offense knows or reasonably should know that the victim is a parking control officer, the assault is punishable by a fine not exceeding two thousand dollars ($2,000), or by imprisonment in the county jail not exceeding six months, or by both the fine and imprisonment.

(c) When an assault is committed against the person of a peace officer, firefighter, emergency medical technician, mobile intensive care paramedic, lifeguard, process server, traffic officer, code enforcement officer, or animal control officer engaged in the performance of his or her duties, or a physician or nurse engaged in rendering emergency medical care outside a hospital, clinic, or other health care facility, and the person committing the offense knows or reasonably should know that the victim is a peace officer, firefighter, emergency medical technician, mobile intensive care paramedic, lifeguard, process server, traffic officer, code enforcement officer, or animal control officer engaged in the performance of his or her duties, or a physician or nurse engaged in rendering emergency medical care, the assault is punishable by a fine not exceeding two thousand dollars ($2,000), or by imprisonment in the county jail not exceeding one year, or by both the fine and imprisonment. (d) As used in this section, the following definitions apply:

(1) Peace officer means any person defined in Chapter 4.5 (commencing with Section 830) of Title 3 of Part 2.

(2) "Emergency medical technician" means a person possessing a valid course completion certificate from a program approved by the State Department of Health Services for the medical training and education of ambulance personnel, and who meets the standards of Division 2.5 (commencing with Section 1797) of the Health and Safety Code.

(3) "Mobile intensive care paramedic" refers to those persons who meet the standards set forth in Division 2.5 (commencing with Section 1797) of the Health and Safety Code.

(4) "Nurse" means a person who meets the standards of Division 2.5 (commencing with Section 1797) of the Health and Safety Code.

(5) "Lifeguard" means a person who is:

(A) Employed as a lifeguard by the state, a county, or a city, and is designated by local ordinance as a public officer who has a duty and responsibility to enforce local ordinances and misdemeanors through the issuance of citations.

(B) Wearing distinctive clothing which includes written identification of the person's status as a lifeguard and which clearly identifies the employing organization.

(6) "Process server" means any person who meets the standards or is expressly exempt from the standards set forth in Section 22350 of the Business and Professions Code.

(7) "Traffic officer" means any person employed by a county or city to monitor and enforce state laws and local ordinances relating to parking and the operation of vehicles.

(8) "Animal control officer" means any person employed by a county or city for purposes of enforcing animal control laws or regulations.

(9)(A) "Code enforcement officer" means any person who is not described in Chapter 4.5 (commencing with Section 830) of Title 3 of Part 2 and who is employed by any governmental subdivision, public or quasi-public corporation, public agency, public service corporation, any town, city, county, or municipal corporation, whether incorporated or chartered, that has enforcement authority for health, safety, and welfare requirements, and whose duties include enforcement of any statute, rules, regulations, or standards, and who is authorized to issue citations, or file formal complaints.

(B) "Code enforcement officer" also includes any person who is employed by the Department of Housing and Community Development who has enforcement authority for health, safety, and welfare requirements pursuant to the Employee Housing Act (Part 1 (commencing with Section 17000) of Division 13 of the Health and Safety Code); the State Housing Law (Part 1.5 (commencing with Section 17910) of Division 13 of the Health and Safety Code); the Mobilehomes-Manufactured Housing Act (Part 2 (commencing with Section 18000) of Division 13 of the Health and Safety Code); the Mobilehome Parks Act (Part 2.1 (commencing with Section 18200) of Division 13 of the Health and Safety Code); and the Special Occupancy Parks Act (Part 2.3 (commencing with Section 18860) of Division 13 of the Health and Safety Code).

(10) "Parking control officer" means any person employed by a city, county, or city and county, to monitor and enforce state laws and local ordinances relating to parking.

Penal Code § 241.1.

When an assault is committed against the person of a custodial officer as defined in Section 831 or 831.5, and the person committing the offense knows or reasonably should know that such victim is such a custodial officer engaged in the performance of his duties, the offense shall be punished by imprisonment in the county jail not exceeding one year or by imprisonment in the state prison.

Penal Code § 241.2.

(a)(1) When an assault is committed on school or park property against any person, the assault is punishable by a fine not exceeding two thousand dollars ($2,000), or by imprisonment in the county jail not exceeding one year, or by both that fine and imprisonment.

(2) When a violation of this section is committed by a minor on school property, the court may, in addition to any other fine, sentence, or as a condition of probation, order the minor to attend counseling as deemed appropriate by the court at the expense of the minor's parents. The court shall take into consideration the ability of the minor's parents to pay, however, no minor shall be relieved of attending counseling because of the minor's parents' inability to pay for the counseling imposed by this section.

(b) "School," as used in this section, means any elementary school, junior high school, four-year high school, senior high school, adult school or any branch thereof, opportunity school, continuation high school, regional occupational center, evening high school, technical school, or community college.

(c) "Park," as used in this section, means any publicly maintained or operated park. It does not include any facility when used for professional sports or commercial events.

Penal Code § 241.3.

(a) When an assault is committed against any person on the property of, or on a motor vehicle of, a public transportation provider, the offense shall be punished by a fine not to exceed two thousand dollars ($2,000), or by imprisonment in a county jail not to exceed one year, or by both the fine and imprisonment.

(b) As used in this section, "public transportation provider" means a publicly or privately owned entity that operates, for the transportation of persons for hire, a bus, taxicab, streetcar, cable car, trackless trolley, or other motor vehicle, including a vehicle operated on stationary rails or on a track or rail suspended in air, or that operates a schoolbus.

(c) As used in this section, "on the property of" means the entire station where public transportation is available, including the parking lot reserved for the public who utilize the transportation system.

Penal Code § 241.4.

An assault is punishable by fine not exceeding one thousand dollars ($1,000), or by imprisonment in the county jail not exceeding six months, or by both. When the assault is committed against the person of a peace officer engaged in the performance of his or her duties as a member of a police department of a school district pursuant to Section 38000 of the Education Code, and the person committing the offense knows or reasonably should know that the victim is a peace officer engaged in the performance of his or her duties, the offense shall be punished by imprisonment in the county jail not exceeding one year or by imprisonment in the state prison.

Penal Code §241.5.

(a) When an assault is committed against a highway worker engaged in the performance of his or her duties and the person committing the offense knows or reasonably should know that the victim is a highway worker engaged in the performance of his or her duties, the offense shall be punishable by a fine not to exceed two thousand dollars ($2,000) or by imprisonment in a county jail up to one year or by both that fine and imprisonment.

(b) As used in this section, "highway worker" means an employee or contractor of the Department of Transportation who does one or more of the following:

(1) Performs maintenance, repair, or construction of state highway infrastructures and associated rights-of-way in highway work zones.

(2) Operates equipment on state highway infrastructures and associated rights-of-way in highway work zones.

(3) Performs any related maintenance work, as required, on state highway infrastructures in highway work zones.

Penal Code § 241.6.

When an assault is committed against a school employee engaged in the performance of his or her duties, or in retaliation for an act performed in the course of his or her duties, whether on or off campus, during the schoolday or at any other time, and the person committing the offense knows or reasonably should know the victim is a school employee, the assault is punishable by imprisonment in a county jail not exceeding one year, or by a fine not exceeding two thousand dollars ($2,000), or by both the fine and imprisonment. For purposes of this section, "school employee" has the same meaning as defined in subdivision (d) of Section 245.5. This section shall not apply to conduct arising during the course of an otherwise lawful labor dispute.

Penal Code § 241.7.

Any person who is a party to a civil or criminal action in which a jury has been selected to try the case and who, while the legal action is pending or after the conclusion of the trial, commits an assault against any juror or alternate juror who was selected and sworn in that legal action, shall be punished by a fine not to exceed two thousand dollars ($2,000), or by imprisonment in the county jail not exceeding one year, or by both such fine and imprisonment, or by imprisonment in the state prison.

Penal Code § 241.8.

(a) Any person who commits an assault against a member of the United States Armed Forces because of the victim's service in the United States Armed Forces shall be punished by a fine not exceeding two thousand dollars ($2,000), by imprisonment in a county jail for a period not exceeding one year, or by both that fine and imprisonment.

(b) "Because of" means that the bias motivation must be a cause in fact of the assault, whether or not other causes exist. When multiple concurrent motives exist, the prohibited bias must be a substantial factor in bringing about the assault.

Penal Code § 242.

A battery is any willful and unlawful use of force or violence upon the person of another.

Penal Code § 243.

(a) A battery is punishable by a fine not exceeding two thousand dollars ($2,000), or by imprisonment in a county jail not exceeding six months, or by both that fine and imprisonment.

(b) When a battery is committed against the person of a peace officer, custodial officer, firefighter, emergency medical technician, lifeguard, process server, traffic officer, code enforcement officer, or animal control officer engaged in the performance of his or her duties, whether on or off duty, including when the peace officer is in a police uniform and is concurrently performing the duties required of him or her as a peace officer while also employed in a private capacity as a part-time or casual private security guard or patrolman, or a nonsworn employee of a probation department engaged in the performance of his or her duties, whether on or off duty, or a physician or nurse engaged in rendering emergency medical care outside a hospital, clinic, or other health care facility, and the person committing the offense knows or reasonably should know that the victim is a peace officer, custodial officer, firefighter, emergency medical technician, lifeguard, process server, traffic officer, code enforcement officer, or animal control officer engaged in the performance of his or her duties, nonsworn employee of a probation department, or a physician or nurse engaged in rendering emergency medical care, the battery is punishable by a fine not exceeding two thousand dollars ($2,000), or by imprisonment in a county jail not exceeding one year, or by both that fine and imprisonment.

(c)(1) When a battery is committed against a custodial officer, firefighter, emergency medical technician, lifeguard, process server, traffic officer, or animal control officer engaged in the performance of his or her duties, whether on or off duty, or a nonsworn employee of a probation department engaged in the performance of his or her duties, whether on or off duty, or a physician or nurse engaged in rendering emergency medical care outside a hospital, clinic, or other health care facility, and the person committing the offense knows or reasonably should know that the victim is a nonsworn employee of a probation department, custodial officer, firefighter, emergency medical technician, lifeguard, process server, traffic officer, or animal control officer engaged in the performance of his or her duties, or a physician or nurse engaged in rendering emergency medical care, and an injury is inflicted on that victim, the battery is punishable by a fine of not more than two thousand dollars ($2,000), by imprisonment in a county jail not exceeding one year, or by both that fine and imprisonment, or by imprisonment in the state prison for 16 months, or two or three years.

(2) When the battery specified in paragraph (1) is committed against a peace officer engaged in the performance of his or her duties, whether on or off duty, including when the peace officer is in a police uniform and is concurrently performing the duties required of him or her as a peace officer while also employed in a private capacity as a part-time or casual private security guard or patrolman and the person committing the offense knows or reasonably should know that the victim is a peace officer engaged in the performance of his or her duties, the battery is punishable by a fine of not more than ten thousand dollars ($10,000), or by imprisonment in a county jail not exceeding one year or in the state prison for 16 months, or two or three years, or by both that fine and imprisonment.

(d) When a battery is committed against any person and serious bodily injury is inflicted on the person, the battery is punishable by imprisonment in a county jail not exceeding one year or imprisonment in the state prison for two, three, or four years.

(e)(1) When a battery is committed against a spouse, a person with whom the defendant is cohabiting, a person who is the parent of the defendant's child, former spouse, fiancé, or fiancee, or a person with whom the defendant currently has, or has previously had, a dating or engagement relationship, the battery is punishable by a fine not exceeding two thousand dollars ($2,000), or by imprisonment in a county jail for a period of not more than one year, or by both that fine and imprisonment. If probation is granted, or the execution or imposition of the sentence is suspended, it shall be a condition thereof that the defendant participate in, for no less than one year, and successfully complete, a batterer's treatment program, as defined in Section 1203.097, or if none is available, another appropriate counseling program designated by the court. However, this provision shall not be construed as requiring a city, a county, or a city and county to provide a new program or higher level of service as contemplated by Section 6 of Article XIIIB of the California Constitution.

(2) Upon conviction of a violation of this subdivision, if probation is granted, the conditions of probation may include, in lieu of a fine, one or both of the following requirements:

(A) That the defendant make payments to a battered women's shelter, up to a maximum of five thousand dollars ($5,000).

(B) That the defendant reimburse the victim for reasonable costs of counseling and other reasonable expenses that the court finds are the direct result of the defendant's offense. For any order to pay a fine, make payments to a battered women's shelter, or pay restitution as a condition of probation under this subdivision, the court shall make a determination of the defendant's ability to pay. In no event shall any order to make payments to a battered women's shelter be made if it would impair the ability of the defendant to pay direct restitution to the victim or court-ordered child support. Where the injury to a married person is caused in whole or in part by the criminal acts of his or her spouse in violation of this section, the community property may not be used to discharge the liability of the offending spouse for restitution to the injured spouse, required by Section 1203.04, as operative on or before August 2, 1995, or Section 1202.4, or to a shelter for costs with regard to the injured spouse and dependents, required by this section, until all separate property of the offending spouse is exhausted.

(3) Upon conviction of a violation of this subdivision, if probation is granted or the execution or imposition of the sentence is suspended and the person has been previously convicted of a violation of this subdivision and sentenced under paragraph (1), the person shall be imprisoned for not less than 48 hours in addition to the conditions in paragraph (1). However, the court, upon a showing of good cause, may elect not to impose the mandatory minimum imprisonment as required by this subdivision and may, under these circumstances, grant probation or order the suspension of the execution or imposition of the sentence.

(4) The Legislature finds and declares that these specified crimes merit special consideration when imposing a sentence so as to display society's condemnation for these crimes of violence upon victims with whom a close relationship has been formed.

(f) As used in this section:

(1) "Peace officer" means any person defined in Chapter 4.5 (commencing with Section 830) of Title 3 of Part 2.

(2) "Emergency medical technician" means a person who is either an EMT-I, EMT-II, or EMT-P (paramedic), and possesses a valid certificate or license in accordance with the standards of Division 2.5 (commencing with Section 1797) of the Health and Safety Code.

(3) "Nurse" means a person who meets the standards of Division 2.5 (commencing with Section 1797) of the Health and Safety Code.

(4) "Serious bodily injury" means a serious impairment of physical condition, including, but not limited to, the following: loss of consciousness; concussion; bone fracture; protracted loss or impairment of function of any bodily member or organ; a wound requiring extensive suturing; and serious disfigurement.

(5) "Injury" means any physical injury which requires professional medical treatment.

(6) "Custodial officer" means any person who has the responsibilities and duties described in Section 831 and who is employed by a law enforcement agency of any city or county or who performs those duties as a volunteer.

(7) "Lifeguard" means a person defined in paragraph (5) of subdivision (c) of Section 241.

(8) "Traffic officer" means any person employed by a city, county, or city and county to monitor and enforce state laws and local ordinances relating to parking and the operation of vehicles.

(9) "Animal control officer" means any person employed by a city, county, or city and county for purposes of enforcing animal control laws or regulations.

(10) "Dating relationship" means frequent, intimate associations primarily characterized by the expectation of affectional or sexual involvement independent of financial considerations.

(11)(A) "Code enforcement officer" means any person who is not described in Chapter 4.5 (commencing with Section 830) of Title 3 of Part 2 and who is employed by any governmental subdivision, public or quasi-public corporation, public agency, public service corporation, any town, city, county, or municipal corporation, whether incorporated or chartered, who has enforcement authority for health, safety, and welfare requirements, and whose duties include enforcement of any statute, rules, regulations, or standards, and who is authorized to issue citations, or file formal complaints.

(B) "Code enforcement officer" also includes any person who is employed by the Department of Housing and Community Development who has enforcement authority for health, safety, and welfare requirements pursuant to the Employee Housing Act (Part 1 (commencing with Section 17000) of Division 13 of the Health and Safety Code); the State Housing Law (Part 1.5 (commencing with Section 17910) of Division 13 of the Health and Safety Code); the Mobilehomes-Manufactured Housing Act (Part 2 (commencing with Section 18000) of Division 13 of the Health and Safety Code); the Mobilehome Parks Act (Part 2.1 (commencing with Section 18200) of Division 13 of the Health and Safety Code); and the Special Occupancy Parks Act (Part 2.3 (commencing with Section 18860) of Division 13 of the Health and Safety Code).

(g) It is the intent of the Legislature by amendments to this section at the 1981-82 and 1983-84 Regular Sessions to abrogate the holdings in cases such as People v. Corey, 21 Cal. 3d 738, and Cervantez v. J.C. Penney Co., 24 Cal. 3d 579, and to reinstate prior judicial interpretations of this section as they relate to criminal sanctions for battery on peace officers who are employed, on a part-time or casual basis, while wearing a police uniform as private security guards or patrolmen and to allow the exercise of peace officer powers concurrently with that employment.

Penal Code § 243.1.

When a battery is committed against the person of a custodial officer as defined in Section 831 of the Penal Code, and the person committing the offense knows or reasonably should know that the victim is a custodial officer engaged in the performance of his or her duties, and the custodial officer is engaged in the performance of his or her duties, the offense shall be punished by imprisonment in the state prison.

Penal Code § 243.2.

(a)(1) Except as otherwise provided in Section 243.6, when a battery is committed on school property, park property, or the grounds of a public or private hospital, against any person, the battery is punishable by a fine not exceeding two thousand dollars ($2,000), or by imprisonment in the county jail not exceeding one year, or by both the fine and imprisonment.

(2) When a violation of this section is committed by a minor on school property, the court may, in addition to any other fine, sentence, or as a condition of probation, order the minor to attend counseling as deemed appropriate by the court at the expense of the minor's parents. The court shall take into consideration the ability of the minor's parents to pay, however, no minor shall be relieved of attending counseling because of the minor's parents' inability to pay for the counseling imposed by this section.

(b) For the purposes of this section, the following terms have the following meanings:

(1) "Hospital" means a facility for the diagnosis, care, and treatment of human illness that is subject to, or specifically exempted from, the licensure requirements of Chapter 2 (commencing with Section 1250) of Division 2 of the Health and Safety Code.

(2) "Park" means any publicly maintained or operated park. It does not include any facility when used for professional sports or commercial events.

(3) "School" means any elementary school, junior high school, four-year high school, senior high school, adult school or any branch thereof, opportunity school, continuation high school, regional occupational center, evening high school, technical school, or community college.

(c) This section shall not apply to conduct arising during the course of an otherwise lawful labor dispute.

Penal Code § 243.25.

When a battery is committed against the person of an elder or a dependent adult as defined in Section 368, with knowledge that he or she is an elder or a dependent adult, the offense shall be punishable by a fine not to exceed two thousand dollars ($2,000), or by imprisonment in a county jail not to exceed one year, or by both that fine and imprisonment.

Penal Code § 243.3.

When a battery is committed against the person of an operator, driver, or passenger on a bus, taxicab, streetcar, cable car, trackless trolley, or other motor vehicle, including a vehicle operated on stationary rails or on a track or rail suspended in the air, used for the transportation of persons for hire, or against a schoolbus driver, or against the person of a station agent or ticket agent for the entity providing the transportation, and the person who commits the offense knows or reasonably should know that the victim, in the case of an operator, driver, or agent, is engaged in the performance of his or her duties, or is a passenger the offense shall be punished by a fine not exceeding ten thousand dollars ($10,000), or by imprisonment in a county jail not exceeding one year, or by both that fine and imprisonment. If an injury is inflicted on that victim, the offense shall be punished by a fine not exceeding ten thousand dollars ($10,000), or by imprisonment in a county jail not exceeding one year or in the state prison for 16 months, or two or three years, or by both that fine and imprisonment.

Penal Code § 243.35.

(a) Except as provided in Section 243.3, when a battery is committed against any person on the property of, or in a motor vehicle of, a public transportation provider, the offense shall be punished by a fine not to exceed two thousand dollars ($2,000), or by imprisonment in a county jail not to exceed one year, or by both the fine and imprisonment.

(b) As used in this section, "public transportation provider" means a publicly or privately owned entity that operates, for the transportation of persons for hire, a bus, taxicab, streetcar, cable car, trackless trolley, or other motor vehicle, including a vehicle operated on stationary rails or on a track or rail suspended in air, or that operates a schoolbus.

(c) As used in this section, "on the property of" means the entire station where public transportation is available, including the parking lot reserved for the public who utilize the transportation system.

Penal Code § 243.4

(a) Any person who touches an intimate part of another person while that person is unlawfully restrained by the accused or an accomplice, and if the touching is against the will of the person touched and is for the purpose of sexual arousal, sexual gratification, or sexual abuse, is guilty of sexual battery. A violation of this subdivision is punishable by imprisonment in a county jail for not more than one year, and by a fine not exceeding two thousand dollars ($2,000); or by imprisonment in the state prison for two, three, or four years, and by a fine not exceeding ten thousand dollars ($10,000).

(b) Any person who touches an intimate part of another person who is institutionalized for medical treatment and who is seriously disabled or medically incapacitated, if the touching is against the will of the person touched, and if the touching is for the purpose of sexual arousal, sexual gratification, or sexual abuse, is guilty of sexual battery. A violation of this subdivision is punishable by imprisonment in a county jail for not more than one year, and by a fine not exceeding two thousand dollars ($2,000); or by imprisonment in the state prison for two, three, or four years, and by a fine not exceeding ten thousand dollars ($10,000).

(c) Any person who touches an intimate part of another person for the purpose of sexual arousal, sexual gratification, or sexual abuse, and the victim is at the time unconscious of the nature of the act because the perpetrator fraudulently represented that the touching served a professional purpose, is guilty of sexual battery. A violation of this subdivision is punishable by imprisonment in a county jail for not more than one year, and by a fine not exceeding two thousand dollars ($2,000); or by imprisonment in the state prison for two, three, or four years, and by a fine not exceeding ten thousand dollars ($10,000).

(d) Any person who, for the purpose of sexual arousal, sexual gratification, or sexual abuse, causes another, against that person's will while that person is unlawfully restrained either by the accused or an accomplice, or is institutionalized for medical treatment and is seriously disabled or medically incapacitated, to masturbate or touch an intimate part of either of those persons or a third person, is guilty of sexual battery. A violation of this subdivision is punishable by imprisonment in a county jail for not more than one year, and by a fine not exceeding two thousand dollars ($2,000); or by imprisonment in the state prison for two, three, or four years, and by a fine not exceeding ten thousand dollars ($10,000).

(e)(1) Any person who touches an intimate part of another person, if the touching is against the will of the person touched, and is for the specific purpose of sexual arousal, sexual gratification, or sexual abuse, is guilty of misdemeanor sexual battery, punishable by a fine not exceeding two thousand dollars ($2,000), or by imprisonment in a county jail not exceeding six months, or by both that fine and imprisonment. However, if the defendant was an employer and the victim was an employee of the defendant, the misdemeanor sexual battery shall be punishable by a fine not exceeding three thousand dollars ($3,000), by imprisonment in a county jail not exceeding six months, or by both that fine and imprisonment. Notwithstanding any other provision of law, any amount of a fine above two thousand dollars ($2,000) which is collected from a defendant for a violation of this subdivision shall be transmitted to the State Treasury and, upon appropriation by the Legislature, distributed to the Department of Fair Employment and Housing for the purpose of enforcement of the California Fair Employment and Housing Act (Part 2.8 (commencing with Section 12900) of Division 3 of Title 2 of the Government Code), including, but not limited to, laws that proscribe sexual harassment in places of employment. However, in no event shall an amount over two thousand dollars ($2,000) be transmitted to the State Treasury until all fines, including any restitution fines that may have been imposed upon the defendant, have been paid in full.

(2) As used in this subdivision, "touches" means physical contact with another person, whether accomplished directly, through the clothing of the person committing the offense, or through the clothing of the victim.

(f) As used in subdivisions (a), (b), (c), and (d), "touches" means physical contact with the skin of another person whether accomplished directly or through the clothing of the person committing the offense.

(g) As used in this section, the following terms have the following meanings:

(1) "Intimate part" means the sexual organ, anus, groin, or buttocks of any person, and the breast of a female.

(2) "Sexual battery" does not include the crimes defined in Section 261 or 289.

(3) "Seriously disabled" means a person with severe physical or sensory disabilities.

(4) "Medically incapacitated" means a person who is incapacitated as a result of prescribed sedatives, anesthesia, or other medication.

(5) "Institutionalized" means a person who is located voluntarily or involuntarily in a hospital, medical treatment facility, nursing home, acute care facility, or mental hospital.

(6) "Minor" means a person under 18 years of age.

(h) This section shall not be construed to limit or prevent prosecution under any other law which also proscribes a course of conduct that also is proscribed by this section.

(i) In the case of a felony conviction for a violation of this section, the fact that the defendant was an employer and the victim was an employee of the defendant shall be a factor in aggravation in sentencing.

(j) A person who commits a violation of subdivision (a), (b), (c), or (d) against a minor when the person has a prior felony conviction for a violation of this section shall be guilty of a felony, punishable by imprisonment in the state prison for two, three, or four years and a fine not exceeding ten thousand dollars ($10,000).

Penal Code § 243.5.

(a) When a person commits an assault or battery on school property during hours when school activities are being conducted, a peace officer may, without a warrant, notwithstanding paragraph (2) or (3) of subdivision (a) of Section 836, arrest the person who commits the assault or battery:

(1) Whenever the person has committed the assault or battery, although not in the peace officer's presence.

(2) Whenever the peace officer has reasonable cause to believe that the person to be arrested has committed the assault or battery, whether or not it has in fact been committed.

(b) "School," as used in this section, means any elementary school, junior high school, four-year high school, senior high school, adult school or any branch thereof, opportunity school, continuation high school, regional occupational center, evening high school, technical school, or community college.

Penal Code § 243.6.

When a battery is committed against a school employee engaged in the performance of his or her duties, or in retaliation for an act performed in the course of his or her duties, whether on or off campus, during the schoolday or at any other time, and the person committing the offense knows or reasonably should know that the victim is a school employee, the battery is punishable by imprisonment in a county jail not exceeding one year, or by a fine not exceeding two thousand dollars ($2,000), or by both the fine and imprisonment. However, if an injury is inflicted on the victim, the battery shall be punishable by imprisonment in a county jail for not more than one year, or by a fine of not more than two thousand dollars ($2,000), or by imprisonment in the state prison for 16 months, or two or three years.

For purposes of this section, "school employee" has the same meaning as defined in subdivision (d) of Section 245.5. This section shall not apply to conduct arising during the course of an otherwise lawful labor dispute.

Penal Code § 243.65.

(a) When a battery is committed against the person of a highway worker engaged in the performance of his or her duties and the person committing the offense knows or reasonably should know that the victim is a highway worker engaged in the performance of his or her duties, the offense shall be punished by a fine not exceeding two thousand dollars ($2,000), or by imprisonment in a county jail not exceeding one year, or by both that fine and imprisonment.

(b) As used in this section, "highway worker" means an employee or contractor of the Department of Transportation who does one or more of the following:

(1) Performs maintenance, repair, or construction of state highway infrastructures and associated rights-of-way in highway work zones.

(2) Operates equipment on state highway infrastructures and associated rights-of-way in highway work zones.

(3) Performs any related maintenance work, as required, on state highway infrastructures in highway work zones.

Penal Code § 243.7.

Any person who is a party to a civil or criminal action in which a jury has been selected to try the case and who, while the legal action is pending or after the conclusion of the trial commits a battery against any juror or alternate juror who was selected and sworn in that legal action shall be punished by a fine not to exceed five thousand dollars ($5,000), or by imprisonment in the county jail not exceeding one year, or by both such fine and imprisonment, or by the imprisonment in the state prison for 16 months, or for two or three years.

Penal Code § 243.8.

(a) When a battery is committed against a sports official immediately prior to, during, or immediately following an interscholastic, intercollegiate, or any other organized amateur or professional athletic contest in which the sports official is participating, and the person who commits the offense knows or reasonably should know that the victim is engaged in the performance of his or her duties, the offense shall be punishable by a fine not exceeding two thousand dollars ($2,000), or by imprisonment in the county jail not exceeding one year, or by both that fine and imprisonment.

(b) For purposes of this section, "sports official" means any individual who serves as a referee, umpire, linesman, or who serves in a similar capacity but may be known by a different title or name and is duly registered by, or a member of, a local, state, regional, or national organization engaged in part in providing education and training to sports officials.

Penal Code § 243.83.

(a) It is unlawful for any person attending a professional sporting event to do any of the following:

(1) Throw any object on or across the court or field of play with the intent to interfere with play or distract a player.

(2) Enter upon the court or field of play without permission from an authorized person any time after the authorized participants of play have entered the court or field to begin the sporting event and until the participants of play have completed the playing time of the sporting event.

(b)(1) The owner of the facility in which a professional sporting event is to be held shall provide a notice specifying the unlawful activity prohibited by this section and the punishment for engaging in that prohibited activity.

(2) The notice shall be prominently displayed throughout the facility or may be provided by some other manner, such as on a big screen or by a general public announcement. In addition, notice shall be posted at all controlled entry areas of the sporting facility.

(3) Failure to provide the notice shall not be a defense to a violation of this section.

(c) For the purposes of this section, the following terms have the following meanings:

(1) "Player" includes any authorized participant of play, including, but not limited to, team members, referees however designated, and support staff, whether or not any of those persons receive compensation.

(2) "Professional sporting event" means a scheduled sporting event involving a professional sports team or organization or

a professional athlete for which an admission fee is charged to the public.

(d) A violation of subdivision (a) is an infraction punishable by a fine not exceeding two hundred fifty dollars ($250). The fine shall not be subject to penalty assessments as provided in Section 1464 or 1465.7 of this code or Section 76000 of the Government Code.

(e) This section shall apply to attendees at professional sporting events; this section shall not apply to players or to sports officials, as defined in Section 243.8.

(f) Nothing in this section shall be construed to limit or prevent prosecution under any applicable provision of law.

Penal Code § 244.

Any person who willfully and maliciously places or throws, or causes to be placed or thrown, upon the person of another, any vitriol, corrosive acid, flammable substance, or caustic chemical of any nature, with the intent to injure the flesh or disfigure the body of that person, is punishable by imprisonment in the state prison for two, three or four years. As used in this section, "flammable substance" means gasoline, petroleum products, or flammable liquids with a flashpoint of 150 degrees Fahrenheit or less.

Penal Code § 244.5.

(a) As used in this section, "stun gun" means any item, except a less lethal weapon, as defined in Section 12601, used or intended to be used as either an offensive or defensive weapon that is capable of temporarily immobilizing a person by the infliction of an electrical charge.

(b) Every person who commits an assault upon the person of another with a stun gun or less lethal weapon, as defined in Section 12601, shall be punished by imprisonment in a county jail for a term not exceeding one year, or by imprisonment in the state prison for 16 months, two, or three years.

(c) Every person who commits an assault upon the person of a peace officer or firefighter with a stun gun or less lethal weapon, as defined in Section 12601, who knows or reasonably should know that the person is a peace officer or firefighter engaged in the performance of his or her duties, when the peace officer or firefighter is engaged in the performance of his or her duties, shall be punished by imprisonment in the county jail for a term not exceeding one year, or by imprisonment in the state prison for two, three, or four years.

(d) This section shall not be construed to preclude or in any way limit the applicability of Section 245 in any criminal prosecution.

Penal Code § 245.

(a)(1) Any person who commits an assault upon the person of another with a deadly weapon or instrument other than a firearm or by any means of force likely to produce great bodily injury shall be punished by imprisonment in the state prison for two, three, or four years, or in a county jail for not exceeding one year, or by a fine not exceeding ten thousand dollars ($10,000), or by both the fine and imprisonment.

(2) Any person who commits an assault upon the person of another with a firearm shall be punished by imprisonment in the state prison for two, three, or four years, or in a county jail for not less than six months and not exceeding one year, or by both a fine not exceeding ten thousand dollars ($10,000) and imprisonment.

(3) Any person who commits an assault upon the person of another with a machinegun, as defined in Section 12200, or an assault weapon, as defined in Section 12276 or 12276.1, or a .50 BMG rifle, as defined in Section 12278, shall be punished by imprisonment in the state prison for 4, 8, or 12 years.

(b) Any person who commits an assault upon the person of another with a semiautomatic firearm shall be punished by imprisonment in the state prison for three, six, or nine years.

(c) Any person who commits an assault with a deadly weapon or instrument, other than a firearm, or by any means likely to produce great bodily injury upon the person of a peace officer or firefighter, and who knows or reasonably should know that the victim is a peace officer or firefighter engaged in the performance of his or her duties, when the peace officer or firefighter is engaged in the performance of his or her duties, shall be punished by imprisonment in the state prison for three, four, or five years.

(d)(1) Any person who commits an assault with a firearm upon the person of a peace officer or firefighter, and who knows or reasonably should know that the victim is a peace officer or firefighter engaged in the performance of his or her duties, when the peace officer or firefighter is engaged in the performance of his or her duties, shall be punished by imprisonment in the state prison for four, six, or eight years.

(2) Any person who commits an assault upon the person of a peace officer or firefighter with a semiautomatic firearm and who knows or reasonably should know that the victim is a peace officer or firefighter engaged in the performance of his or her duties, when the peace officer or firefighter is engaged in the performance of his or her duties, shall be punished by imprisonment in the state prison for five, seven, or nine years.

(3) Any person who commits an assault with a machinegun, as defined in Section 12200, or an assault weapon, as defined in Section 12276 or 12276.1, or a .50 BMG rifle, as defined in Section 12278, upon the person of a peace officer or firefighter, and who knows or reasonably should know that the victim is a peace officer or firefighter engaged in the performance of his or her duties, shall be punished by imprisonment in the state prison for 6, 9, or 12 years.

(e) When a person is convicted of a violation of this section in a case involving use of a deadly weapon or instrument or firearm, and the weapon or instrument or firearm is owned by that person, the court shall order that the weapon or instrument or firearm be deemed a nuisance, and it shall be confiscated and disposed of in the manner provided by Section 12028.

(f) As used in this section, "peace officer" refers to any person designated as a peace officer in Chapter 4.5 (commencing with Section 830) of Title 3 of Part 2. 245.1. As used in Sections 148.2, 241, 243, 244.5, and 245, "fireman" or "firefighter" includes any person who is an officer, employee or member of a fire department or fire protection or firefighting agency of the federal government, the State of California, a city, county, city and county, district, or other public or municipal corporation or political subdivision of this state, whether this person is a volunteer or partly paid or fully paid. As used in Section 148.2, "emergency rescue personnel" means any person who is an officer, employee or member of a fire department or fire protection or firefighting agency of the federal government, the State of California, a city, county, city and county, district, or other public or municipal corporation or political subdivision of this state, whether this person is a volunteer or partly paid or fully paid, while he or she is actually engaged in the on-the-site rescue of persons or property during an emergency as defined by subdivision (c) of Section 148.3.

Penal Code § 245.2.

Every person who commits an assault with a deadly weapon or instrument or by any means of force likely to produce great bodily injury upon the person of an operator, driver, or passenger on a bus, taxicab, streetcar, cable car, trackless trolley, or other motor vehicle, including a vehicle operated on stationary rails or on a track or rail suspended in the air, used for the transportation of persons for hire, or upon the person of a station agent or ticket agent for the entity providing such transportation, when the driver, operator, or agent is engaged in the performance of his or her duties, and where the person who commits the assault knows or reasonably should know that the victim is engaged in the performance of his or her duties, or is a passenger, shall be punished by imprisonment in the state prison for three, four, or five years.

Penal Code § 245.3.

Every person who commits an assault with a deadly weapon or instrument or by any means likely to produce great bodily injury upon the person of a custodial officer as defined in Section 831 or 831.5, and who knows or reasonably should know that such victim is such a custodial officer engaged in the performance of his duties, shall be punished by imprisonment in the state prison for three, four, or five years. When a person is convicted of a violation of this section in a case involving use of a deadly weapon or instrument, and such weapon or instrument is owned by such person, the court may, in its discretion, order that the weapon or instrument be deemed a nuisance and shall be confiscated and destroyed in the manner provided by Section 12028.

Penal Code § 245.5.

(a) Every person who commits an assault with a deadly weapon or instrument, other than a firearm, or by any means likely to produce great bodily injury upon the person of a school employee, and who knows or reasonably should know that the victim is a school employee engaged in the performance of his or her duties, when that school employee is engaged in the performance of his or her duties, shall be punished by imprisonment in the state prison for three, four, or five years, or in a county jail not exceeding one year.

(b) Every person who commits an assault with a firearm upon the person of a school employee, and who knows or reasonably should know that the victim is a school employee engaged in the performance of his or her duties, when the school employee is engaged in the performance of his or her duties, shall be punished by imprisonment in the state prison for four, six, or eight years, or in a county jail for not less than six months and not exceeding one year.

(c) Every person who commits an assault upon the person of a school employee with a stun gun or taser, and who knows or reasonably should know that the person is a school employee engaged in the performance of his or her duties, when the school employee is engaged in the performance of his or her duties, shall be punished by imprisonment in a county jail for a term not exceeding one year or by imprisonment in the state prison for two, three, or four years. This subdivision shall not be construed to preclude or in any way limit the applicability of Section 245 in any criminal prosecution.

(d) As used in the section, "school employee" means any person employed as a permanent or probationary certificated or classified employee of a school district on a part-time or full-time basis, including a substitute teacher. "School employee," as used in this section, also includes a student teacher, or a school board member. "School," as used in this section, has the same meaning as that term is defined in Section 626.

Penal Code § 246.

Any person who shall maliciously and willfully discharge a firearm at an inhabited dwelling house, occupied building, occupied motor vehicle, occupied aircraft, inhabited housecar, as defined in Section 362 of the Vehicle Code, or inhabited camper, as defined in Section 243 of the Vehicle Code, is guilty of a felony, and upon conviction shall be punished by imprisonment in the state prison for three, five, or seven years, or by imprisonment in the county jail for a term of not less than six months and not exceeding one year. As used in this section, "inhabited" means currently being used for dwelling purposes, whether occupied or not.

Penal Code § 246.1.

(a) Except as provided in subdivision (f), upon the conviction of any person found guilty of murder in the first or second degree, manslaughter, attempted murder, assault with a deadly weapon, the unlawful discharge or brandishing of a firearm from or at an occupied vehicle where the victim was killed, attacked, or assaulted from or in a motor vehicle by the use of a firearm on a public street or highway, or the unlawful possession of a firearm by a member of a criminal street gang, as defined in subdivision (f) of Section 186.22, while present in a vehicle the court shall order a vehicle used in the commission of that offense sold. Any vehicle ordered to be sold pursuant to this subdivision shall be surrendered to the sheriff of the county or the chief of police of the city in which the violation occurred. The officer to whom the vehicle is surrendered shall promptly ascertain from the Department of Motor Vehicles the names and addresses of all legal and registered owners of the vehicle and within five days of receiving that information, shall send by certified mail a notice to all legal and registered owners of the vehicle other than the defendant, at the addresses obtained from the department, informing them that the vehicle has been declared a nuisance and will be sold or otherwise disposed of pursuant to this section, and of the approximate date and location of the sale or other disposition. The notice shall also inform any legal owner of its right to conduct the sale pursuant to subdivision (b).

(b) Any legal owner which in the regular course of its business conducts sales of repossessed or surrendered motor vehicles may take possession and conduct the sale of the vehicle if it notifies the officer to whom the vehicle is surrendered of its intent to conduct the sale within 15 days of the mailing of the notice pursuant to subdivision (a). Sale of the vehicle pursuant to this subdivision may be conducted at the time, in the manner, and on the notice usually given by the legal owner for the sale of repossessed or surrendered vehicles. The proceeds of any sale conducted by the legal owner shall be disposed of as provided in subdivision (d).

(c) If the legal owner does not notify the officer to whom the vehicle is surrendered of its intent to conduct the sale as provided in subdivision (b), the officer shall offer the vehicle for sale at public auction within 60 days of receiving the vehicle. At least 10 days but not more than 20 days prior to the sale, not counting the day of sale, the officer shall give notice of the sale by advertising once in a newspaper of general circulation published in the city or county, as the case may be, in which the vehicle is located, which notice shall contain a description of the make, year, model, identification number, and license number of the vehicle, and the date, time, and location of the sale. For motorcycles, the engine number shall also be included. If there is no newspaper of general circulation published in the county, notice shall be given by posting a notice of sale containing the information required by this subdivision in three of the most public places in the city or county in which the vehicle is located and at the place where the vehicle is to be sold for 10 consecutive days prior to and including the day of the sale. (d) The proceeds of a sale conducted pursuant to this section shall be disposed of in the following priority:

(1) To satisfy the costs of the sale, including costs incurred with respect to the taking and keeping of the vehicle pending sale.

(2) To the legal owner in an amount to satisfy the indebtedness owed to the legal owner remaining as of the date of sale, including accrued interest or finance charges and delinquency charges.

(3) To the holder of any subordinate lien or encumbrance on the vehicle to satisfy any indebtedness so secured if written notification of demand is received before distribution of the proceeds is completed. The holder of a subordinate lien or encumbrance, if requested, shall reasonably furnish reasonable proof of its interest, and unless it does so on request is not entitled to distribution pursuant to this paragraph.

(4) To any other person who can establish an interest in the vehicle, including a community property interest, to the extent of his or her provable interest.

(5) The balance, if any, to the city or county in which the violation occurred, to be deposited in a special account in its general fund to be used exclusively to pay the costs or a part of the costs of providing services or education to prevent juvenile violence. The person conducting the sale shall disburse the proceeds of the sale as provided in this subdivision, and provide a written accounting regarding the disposition to all persons entitled to or claiming a share of the proceeds, within 15 days after the sale is conducted.

(e) If the vehicle to be sold under this section is not of the type that can readily be sold to the public generally, the vehicle shall be destroyed or donated to an eleemosynary institution.

(f) No vehicle may be sold pursuant to this section in either of the following circumstances:

(1) The vehicle is stolen, unless the identity of the legal and registered owners of the vehicle cannot be reasonably ascertained.

(2) The vehicle is owned by another, or there is a community property interest in the vehicle owned by a person other than the defendant and the vehicle is the only vehicle available to the defendant's immediate family which may be operated on the highway with a class 3 or class 4 driver's license.

(g) A vehicle is used in the commission of a violation of the offenses enumerated in subdivision (a) if a firearm is discharged either from the vehicle at another person or by an occupant of a vehicle other than the vehicle in which the victim is an occupant.

Penal Code § 246.3.

(a) Except as otherwise authorized by law, any person who willfully discharges a firearm in a grossly negligent manner which could result in injury or death to a person is guilty of a public offense and shall be punished by imprisonment in a county jail not exceeding one year, or by imprisonment in the state prison.

(b) Except as otherwise authorized by law, any person who willfully discharges a BB device in a grossly negligent manner which could result in injury or death to a person is guilty of a public offense and shall be punished by imprisonment in a county jail not exceeding one year.

(c) As used in this section, "BB device" means any instrument that expels a projectile, such as a BB or a pellet, through the force of air pressure, gas pressure, or spring action.

Penal Code § 247.

(a) Any person who willfully and maliciously discharges a firearm at an unoccupied aircraft is guilty of a felony.

(b) Any person who discharges a firearm at an unoccupied motor vehicle or an uninhabited building or dwelling house is guilty of a public offense punishable by imprisonment in the county jail for not more than one year or in the state prison. This subdivision does not apply to shooting at an abandoned vehicle, unoccupied vehicle, uninhabited building, or dwelling house with the permission of the owner. As used in this section and Section 246 "aircraft" means any contrivance intended for and capable of transporting persons through the airspace.

Penal Code § 247.5.

Any person who willfully and maliciously discharges a laser at an aircraft, whether in motion or in flight, while occupied, is guilty of a violation of this section, which shall be punishable as either a misdemeanor by imprisonment in the county jail for not more than one year or by a fine of one thousand dollars ($1,000), or a felony by imprisonment in the state prison for 16 months, two years, or three years, or by a fine of two thousand dollars ($2,000). This section does not apply to the conduct of laser development activity by or on behalf of the United States Armed Forces. As used in this section, "aircraft" means any contrivance intended for and capable of transporting persons through the airspace. As used in this section, "laser" means a device that utilizes the natural oscillations of atoms or molecules between energy levels for generating coherent electromagnetic radiation in the ultraviolet, visible, or infrared region of the spectrum, and when discharged exceeds one milliwatt continuous wave.

Penal Code § 248.

Any person who, with the intent to interfere with the operation of an aircraft, willfully shines a light or other bright device, of an intensity capable of impairing the operation of an aircraft, at an aircraft, shall be punished by a fine not exceeding one thousand dollars ($1,000), or by imprisonment in a county jail not exceeding one year, or by both that fine and imprisonment.

Penal Code § 273ab.

Any person who, having the care or custody of a child who is under eight years of age, assaults the child by means of force that to a reasonable person would be likely to produce great bodily injury, resulting in the child's death, shall be punished by imprisonment in the state prison for 25 years to life. Nothing in this section shall be construed as affecting the applicability of subdivision (a) of Section 187 or Section 189.

Penal Code § 273.5.

(a) Any person who willfully inflicts upon a person who is his or her spouse, former spouse, cohabitant, former cohabitant, or the mother or father of his or her child, corporal injury resulting in a traumatic condition, is guilty of a felony, and upon conviction thereof shall be punished by imprisonment in the state prison for two, three, or four years, or in a county jail for not more than one year, or by a fine of up to six thousand dollars ($6,000) or by both that fine and imprisonment.

(b) Holding oneself out to be the husband or wife of the person with whom one is cohabiting is not necessary to constitute cohabitation as the term is used in this section.

(c) As used in this section, "traumatic condition" means a condition of the body, such as a wound or external or internal injury, whether of a minor or serious nature, caused by a physical force.

(d) For the purpose of this section, a person shall be considered the father or mother of another person's child if the alleged male parent is presumed the natural father under Sections 7611 and 7612 of the Family Code.

(e) (1) Any person convicted of violating this section for acts occurring within seven years of a previous conviction under subdivision (a), or subdivision (d) of Section 243, or Section 243.4, 244, 244.5, or 245, shall be punished by imprisonment in a county jail for not more than one year, or by imprisonment in the state prison for two, four, or five years, or by both imprisonment and a fine of up to ten thousand dollars ($10,000).

(2) Any person convicted of a violation of this section for acts occurring within seven years of a previous conviction under subdivision (e) of Section 243 shall be punished by imprisonment in the state prison for two, three, or four years, or in a county jail for not more than one year, or by a fine of up to ten thousand dollars ($10,000), or by both that imprisonment and fine.

(f) If probation is granted to any person convicted under subdivision (a), the court shall impose probation consistent with the provisions of Section 1203.097.

(g) If probation is granted, or the execution or imposition of a sentence is suspended, for any defendant convicted under subdivision (a) who has been convicted of any prior offense specified in subdivision (e), the court shall impose one of the following conditions of probation:

(1) If the defendant has suffered one prior conviction within the previous seven years for a violation of any offense specified in subdivision (e), it shall be a condition thereof, in addition to the provisions contained in Section 1203.097, that he or she be imprisoned in a county jail for not less than 15 days.

(2) If the defendant has suffered two or more prior convictions within the previous seven years for a violation of any offense specified in subdivision (e), it shall be a condition of probation, in addition to the provisions contained in Section 1203.097, that he or she be imprisoned in a county jail for not less than 60 days.

(3) The court, upon a showing of good cause, may find that the mandatory imprisonment required by this subdivision shall not be imposed and shall state on the record its reasons for finding good cause.

(h) If probation is granted upon conviction of a violation of subdivision (a), the conditions of probation may include, consistent with the terms of probation imposed pursuant to Section 1203.097, in lieu of a fine, one or both of the following requirements:

(1) That the defendant make payments to a battered women's shelter, up to a maximum of five thousand dollars ($5,000), pursuant to Section 1203.097.

(2) That the defendant reimburse the victim for reasonable costs of counseling and other reasonable expenses that the court finds are the direct result of the defendant's offense. For any order to pay a fine, make payments to a battered women's shelter, or pay restitution as a condition of probation under this subdivision, the court shall make a determination of the defendant's ability to pay. In no event shall any order to make payments to a battered women's shelter be made if it would impair the ability of the defendant to pay direct restitution to the victim or court-ordered child support. Where the injury to a married person is caused in whole or in part by the criminal acts of his or her spouse in violation of this section, the community property may not be used to discharge the liability of the offending spouse for restitution to the injured spouse, required by Section 1203.04, as operative on or before August 2, 1995, or Section 1202.4, or to a shelter for costs with regard to the injured spouse and dependents, required by this section, until all separate property of the offending spouse is exhausted.

(i) Upon conviction under subdivision (a), the sentencing court shall also consider issuing an order restraining the defendant from any contact with the victim, which may be valid for up to 10 years, as determined by the court. It is the intent of the Legislature that the length of any restraining order be based upon the seriousness of the facts before the court, the probability of future violations, and the safety of the victim and his or her immediate family. This protective order may be issued by the court whether the defendant is sentenced to state prison, county jail, or if imposition of sentence is suspended and the defendant is placed on probation.

Penal Code § 273.6.

(a) Any intentional and knowing violation of a protective order, as defined in Section 6218 of the Family Code, or of an order issued pursuant to Section 527.6 or 527.8 of the Code of Civil Procedure, or Section 15657.03 of the Welfare and Institutions Code, is a misdemeanor punishable by a fine of not more than one thousand dollars ($1,000), or by imprisonment in a county jail for not more than one year, or by both that fine and imprisonment.

(b) In the event of a violation of subdivision (a) which results in physical injury, the person shall be punished by a fine of not more than two thousand dollars ($2,000), or by imprisonment in a county jail for not less than 30 days nor more than one year, or by both that fine and imprisonment. However, if the person is imprisoned in a county jail for at least 48 hours, the court may, in the interest of justice and for reasons stated on the record, reduce or eliminate the 30-day minimum imprisonment required by this subdivision. In determining whether to reduce or eliminate the minimum imprisonment pursuant to this subdivision, the court shall consider the seriousness of the facts before the court, whether there are additional allegations of a violation of the order during the pendency of the case before the court, the probability of future violations, the safety of the victim, and whether the defendant has successfully completed or is making progress with counseling.

(c) Subdivisions (a) and (b) shall apply to the following court orders:

(1) Any order issued pursuant to Section 6320 or 6389 of the Family Code.

(2) An order excluding one party from the family dwelling or from the dwelling of the other.

(3) An order enjoining a party from specified behavior which the court determined was necessary to effectuate the order described in subdivision (a).

(4) Any order issued by another state that is recognized under Part 5 (commencing with Section 6400) of Division 10 of the Family Code.

(d) A subsequent conviction for a violation of an order described in subdivision (a), occurring within seven years of a prior conviction for a violation of an order described in subdivision (a) and involving an act of violence or "a credible threat" of violence, as defined in subdivision (c) of Section 139, is punishable by imprisonment in a county jail not to exceed one year, or in the state prison.

(e) In the event of a subsequent conviction for a violation of an order described in subdivision (a) for an act occurring within one year of a prior conviction for a violation of an order described in subdivision (a) that results in physical injury to a victim, the person shall be punished by a fine of not more than two thousand dollars ($2,000), or by imprisonment in a county jail for not less than six months nor more than one year, by both that fine and imprisonment, or by imprisonment in the state prison. However, if the person is imprisoned in a county jail for at least 30 days, the court may, in the interest of justice and for reasons stated in the record, reduce or eliminate the six-month minimum imprisonment required by this subdivision. In determining whether to reduce or eliminate the minimum imprisonment pursuant to this subdivision, the court shall consider the seriousness of the facts before the court, whether there are additional allegations of a violation of the order during the pendency of the case before the court, the probability of future violations, the safety of the victim, and whether the defendant has successfully completed or is making progress with counseling.

(f) The prosecuting agency of each county shall have the primary responsibility for the enforcement of orders described in subdivisions (a), (b), (d), and (e).

(g)(1) Every person who owns, possesses, purchases, or receives a firearm knowing he or she is prohibited from doing so by the provisions of a protective order as defined in Section 136.2 of this code, Section 6218 of the Family Code, or Section 527.6 or 527.8 of the Code of Civil Procedure, or Section 15657.03 of the Welfare and Institutions Code, shall be punished under the provisions of subdivision (g) of Section 12021.

(2) Every person subject to a protective order described in paragraph (1) shall not be prosecuted under this section for owning, possessing, purchasing, or receiving a firearm to the extent that firearm is granted an exemption pursuant to subdivision (f) of Section 527.9 of the Code of Civil Procedure, or subdivision (h) of Section 6389 of the Family Code.

(h) If probation is granted upon conviction of a violation of subdivision (a), (b), (c), (d), or (e), the court shall impose probation consistent with the provisions of Section 1203.097, and the conditions of probation may include, in lieu of a fine, one or both of the following requirements:

(1) That the defendant make payments to a battered women's shelter or to a shelter for abused elder persons or dependent adults, up to a maximum of five thousand dollars ($5,000), pursuant to Section 1203.097.

(2) That the defendant reimburse the victim for reasonable costs of counseling and other reasonable expenses that the court finds are the direct result of the defendant's offense.

(i) For any order to pay a fine, make payments to a battered women' s shelter, or pay restitution as a condition of probation under subdivision (e), the court shall make a determination of the defendant's ability to pay. In no event shall any order to make payments to a battered women's shelter be made if it would impair the ability of the defendant to pay direct restitution to the victim or court-ordered child support.

Penal Code § 273.75.

(a) On any charge involving acts of domestic violence as defined in subdivisions (a) and (b) of Section 13700 of the Penal Code or Sections 6203 and 6211 of the Family Code, the district attorney or prosecuting city attorney shall perform or cause to be performed, by accessing the electronic databases enumerated in subdivision (b), a thorough investigation of the defendant's history, including, but not limited to, prior convictions for domestic violence, other forms of violence or weapons offenses and any current protective or restraining order issued by any civil or criminal court. This information shall be presented for consideration by the court

(1) when setting bond or when releasing a defendant on his or her own recognizance at the arraignment, if the defendant is in custody,

(2) upon consideration of any plea agreement, and

(3) when issuing a protective order pursuant to Section 136.2 of the Penal Code, in accordance with subdivision (h) of that section. In determining bail or release upon a plea agreement, the court shall consider the safety of the victim, the victim's children, and any other person who may be in danger if the defendant is released.

(b) For purposes of this section, the district attorney or prosecuting city attorney shall search or cause to be searched the following databases, when readily available and reasonably accessible:

(1) The Violent Crime Information Network (VCIN).

(2) The Supervised Release File.

(3) State summary criminal history information maintained by the Department of Justice pursuant to Section 11105 of the Penal Code.

(4) The Federal Bureau of Investigation's nationwide database.

(5) Locally maintained criminal history records or databases. However, a record or database need not be searched if the information available in that record or database can be obtained as a result of a search conducted in another record or database.

(c) If the investigation required by this section reveals a current civil protective or restraining order or a protective or restraining order issued by another criminal court and involving the same or related parties, and if a protective or restraining order is issued in the current criminal proceeding, the district attorney or prosecuting city attorney shall send relevant information regarding the contents of the order issued in the current criminal proceeding, and any information regarding a conviction of the defendant, to the other court immediately after the order has been issued. When requested, the information described in this subdivision may be sent to the appropriate family, juvenile, or civil court. When requested, and upon a showing of a compelling need, the information described in this section may be sent to a court in another state.

Penal Code § 374.

(a) Littering means the willful or negligent throwing, dropping, placing, depositing, or sweeping, or causing any such acts, of any waste matter on land or water in other than appropriate storage containers or areas designated for such purposes.

(b) Waste matter means discarded, used, or leftover substance including, but not limited to, a lighted or nonlighted cigarette, cigar, match, or any flaming or glowing material, or any garbage, trash, refuse, paper, container, packaging or construction material, carcass of a dead animal, any nauseous or offensive matter of any kind, or any object likely to injure any person or create a traffic hazard.

Penal Code § 374a.

A person giving information leading to the arrest and conviction of a person for a violation of Section 374c, 374.2, 374.3, 374.4, or 374.7 is entitled to a reward for providing the information. The amount of the reward for each arrest and conviction shall be 50 percent of the fine levied against and collected from the person who violated Section 374c, 374.2, 374.3, 374.4, or 374.7 and shall be paid by the court. If the reward is payable to two or more persons, it shall be divided equally. The amount of collected fine to be paid under this section shall be paid prior to any distribution of the fine that may be prescribed by any other section, including Section 1463.9, with respect to the same fine.

Penal Code § 374c.

Every person who shoots any firearm from or upon a public road or highway is guilty of a misdemeanor.

Penal Code § 375.

(a) It shall be unlawful to throw, drop, pour, deposit, release, discharge or expose, or to attempt to throw, drop, pour, deposit, release, discharge or expose in, upon or about any theater, restaurant, place of business, place of amusement or any place of public assemblage, any liquid, gaseous or solid substance or matter of any kind which is injurious to person or property, or is nauseous, sickening, irritating or offensive to any of the senses.

(b) It shall be unlawful to manufacture or prepare, or to possess any liquid, gaseous, or solid substance or matter of any kind which is injurious to person or property, or is nauseous, sickening, irritating or offensive, to any of the senses with intent to throw, drop, pour, deposit, release, discharge or expose the same in, upon or about any theater, restaurant, place of business, place of amusement, or any other place of public assemblage.

(c) Any person violating any of the provisions hereof shall be punished by imprisonment in the county jail for not less than three months and not more than one year, or by a fine of not less than five hundred dollars ($500) and not more than two thousand dollars ($2,000), or by both such fine and imprisonment.

(d) Any person who, in violating any of the provisions of subdivision (a), willfully employs or uses any liquid, gaseous or solid substance which may produce serious illness or permanent injury through being vaporized or otherwise dispersed in the air or who, in violating any of the provisions of subdivision (a), willfully employs or uses any tear gas, mustard gas or any of the combinations or compounds thereof, or willfully employs or uses acid or explosives, shall be guilty of a felony and shall be punished by imprisonment in the state prison.

Penal Code § 384h.

Every person who willfully or negligently, while hunting upon the inclosed lands of another, kills, maims, or wounds an animal, the property of another, is guilty of a misdemeanor.

Penal Code § 417.

(a)(1) Every person who, except in self-defense, in the presence of any other person, draws or exhibits any deadly weapon whatsoever, other than a firearm, in a rude, angry, or threatening manner, or who in any manner, unlawfully uses a deadly weapon other than a firearm in any fight or quarrel is guilty of a misdemeanor, punishable by imprisonment in a county jail for not less than 30 days.

(2) Every person who, except in self-defense, in the presence of any other person, draws or exhibits any firearm, whether loaded or unloaded, in a rude, angry, or threatening manner, or who in any manner, unlawfully uses a firearm in any fight or quarrel is punishable as follows:

(A) If the violation occurs in a public place and the firearm is a pistol, revolver, or other firearm capable of being concealed upon the person, by imprisonment in a county jail for not less than three months and not more than one year, by a fine not to exceed one thousand dollars ($1,000), or by both that fine and imprisonment.

(B) In all cases other than that set forth in subparagraph (A), a misdemeanor, punishable by imprisonment in a county jail for not less than three months.

(b) Every person who, except in self-defense, in the presence of any other person, draws or exhibits any loaded firearm in a rude, angry, or threatening manner, or who, in any manner, unlawfully uses any loaded firearm in any fight or quarrel upon the grounds of any day care center, as defined in Section 1596.76 of the Health and Safety Code, or any facility where programs, including day care programs or recreational programs, are being conducted for persons under 18 years of age, including programs conducted by a nonprofit organization, during the hours in which the center or facility is open for use, shall be punished by imprisonment in the state prison for 16 months, or two or three years, or by imprisonment in a county jail for not less than three months, nor more than one year.

(c) Every person who, in the immediate presence of a peace officer, draws or exhibits any firearm, whether loaded or unloaded, in a rude, angry, or threatening manner, and who knows, or reasonably should know, by the officer's uniformed appearance or other action of identification by the officer, that he or she is a peace officer engaged in the performance of his or her duties, and that peace officer is engaged in the performance of his or her duties, shall be punished by imprisonment in a county jail for not less than nine months and not to exceed one year, or in the state prison.

(d) Except where a different penalty applies, every person who violates this section when the other person is in the process of cleaning up graffiti or vandalism is guilty of a misdemeanor, punishable by imprisonment in a county jail for not less than three months nor more than one year.

(e) As used in this section, "peace officer" means any person designated as a peace officer pursuant to Chapter 4.5 (commencing with Section 830) of Title 3 of Part 2.

(f) As used in this section, "public place" means any of the following:

(1) A public place in an incorporated city.

(2) A public street in an incorporated city.

(3) A public street in an unincorporated area.

Penal Code § 417.25.

(a) Every person who, except in self-defense, aims or points a laser scope, as defined in subdivision (b), or a laser pointer, as defined in subdivision (c), at another person in a threatening manner with the specific intent to cause a reasonable person fear of bodily harm is guilty of a misdemeanor, punishable by imprisonment in a county jail for up to 30 days. For purposes of this section, the laser scope need not be attached to a firearm.

(b) As used in this section, "laser scope" means a portable battery-powered device capable of being attached to a firearm and capable of projecting a laser light on objects at a distance.

(c) As used in this section, "laser pointer" means any hand held laser beam device or demonstration laser product that emits a single point of light amplified by the stimulated emission of radiation that is visible to the human eye.

Penal Code § 417.26.

(a) Any person who aims or points a laser scope as defined in subdivision (b) of Section 417.25, or a laser pointer, as defined in subdivision (c) of that section, at a peace officer with the specific intent to cause the officer apprehension or fear of bodily harm and who knows or reasonably should know that the person at whom he or she is aiming or pointing is a peace officer, is guilty of a misdemeanor punishable by imprisonment in a county jail for a term not exceeding six months.

(b) Any person who commits a second or subsequent violation of subdivision (a) shall be punished by imprisonment in a county jail for not more than one year.

Penal Code § 417.27.

(a) No person, corporation, firm, or business entity of any kind shall knowingly sell a laser pointer to a person 17 years of age or younger, unless he or she is accompanied and supervised by a parent, legal guardian, or any other adult 18 years of age or older.

(b) No student shall possess a laser pointer on any elementary or secondary school premises unless possession of a laser pointer on the elementary or secondary school premises is for a valid instructional or other school-related purpose, including employment.

(c) No person shall direct the beam from a laser pointer directly or indirectly into the eye or eyes of another person or into a moving vehicle with the intent to harass or annoy the other person or the occupants of the moving vehicle.

(d) No person shall direct the beam from a laser pointer directly or indirectly into the eye or eyes of a guide dog, signal dog, service dog, or dog being used by a peace officer with the intent to harass or annoy the animal.

(e) A violation of subdivision (a), (b), (c), or (d) shall be an infraction that is punished by either a fine of fifty dollars ($50) or four hours of community service, and a second or subsequent violation of any of these subdivisions shall be an infraction that is punished by either a fine of one hundred dollars ($100) or eight hours of community service.

(f) As used in this section, "laser pointer" has the same meaning as set forth in subdivision (c) of Section 417.25.

(g) As used in this section, "guide dog," "signal dog," and "service dog," respectively, have the same meaning as set forth in subdivisions (d), (e), and (f) of Section 365.5.

Penal Code § 417.3.

Every person who, except in self-defense, in the presence of any other person who is an occupant of a motor vehicle proceeding on a public street or highway, draws or exhibits any firearm, whether loaded or unloaded, in a threatening manner against another person in such a way as to cause a reasonable person apprehension or fear of bodily harm is guilty of a felony punishable by imprisonment in the state prison for 16 months or two or three years or by imprisonment for 16 months or two or three years and a three thousand dollar ($3,000) fine. Nothing in this section shall preclude or prohibit prosecution under any other statute.

Penal Code § 417.4.

Every person who, except in self-defense, draws or exhibits an imitation firearm, as defined in Section 12550, in a threatening manner against another in such a way as to cause a reasonable person apprehension or fear of bodily harm is guilty of a misdemeanor punishable by imprisonment in a county jail for a term of not less than 30 days.

Penal Code § 417.6.

(a) If, in the commission of a violation of Section 417 or 417.8, serious bodily injury is intentionally inflicted by the person drawing or exhibiting the firearm or deadly weapon, the offense shall be punished by imprisonment in the county jail not exceeding one year or by imprisonment in the state prison.

(b) As used in this section, "serious bodily injury" means a serious impairment of physical condition, including, but not limited to, the following: loss of consciousness; concussion; bone fracture; protracted loss or impairment of function of any bodily member or organ; a wound requiring extensive suturing; and serious disfigurement.

(c) When a person is convicted of a violation of Section 417 or 417.8 and the deadly weapon or firearm used by the person is owned by that person, the court shall order that the weapon or firearm be deemed a nuisance and disposed of in the manner provided by Section 12028.

Penal Code § 417.8.

Every person who draws or exhibits any firearm, whether loaded or unloaded, or other deadly weapon, with the intent to resist or prevent the arrest or detention of himself or another by a peace officer shall be imprisoned in the state prison for two, three, or four years.

Penal Code §422.

Any person who willfully threatens to commit a crime which will result in death or great bodily injury to another person, with the specific intent that the statement, made verbally, in writing, or by means of an electronic communication device, is to be taken as a threat, even if there is no intent of actually carrying it out, which, on its face and under the circumstances in which it is made, is so unequivocal, unconditional, immediate, and specific as to convey to the person threatened, a gravity of purpose and an immediate prospect of execution of the threat, and thereby causes that person reasonably to be in sustained fear for his or her own safety or for his or her immediate family's safety, shall be punished by imprisonment in the county jail not to exceed one year, or by imprisonment in the state prison. For the purposes of this section, "immediate family" means any spouse, whether by marriage or not, parent, child, any person related by consanguinity or affinity within the second degree, or any other person who regularly resides in the household, or who, within the prior six months, regularly resided in the household. "Electronic communication device" includes, but is not limited to, telephones, cellular telephones, computers, video recorders, fax machines, or pagers. "Electronic communication" has the same meaning as the term defined in Subsection 12 of Section 2510 of Title 18 of the United States Code.

Penal Code § 422.75.

(a) Except in the case of a person punished under Section 422.7, a person who commits a felony that is a hate crime or attempts to commit a felony that is a hate crime, shall receive an additional term of one, two, or three years in the state prison, at the court's discretion.

(b) Except in the case of a person punished under Section 422.7 or subdivision (a) of this section, any person who commits a felony that is a hate crime, or attempts to commit a felony that is a hate crime, and who voluntarily acted in concert with another person, either personally or by aiding and abetting another person, shall receive an additional two, three, or four years in the state prison, at the court's discretion.

(c) For the purpose of imposing an additional term under subdivision (a) or (b), it shall be a factor in aggravation that the defendant personally used a firearm in the commission of the offense. Nothing in this subdivision shall preclude a court from also imposing a sentence enhancement pursuant to Section 12022.5, 12022.53, or 12022.55, or any other law.

(d) A person who is punished pursuant to this section also shall receive an additional term of one year in the state prison for each prior felony conviction on charges brought and tried separately in which it was found by the trier of fact or admitted by the defendant that the crime was a hate crime. This additional term shall only apply where a sentence enhancement is not imposed pursuant to Section 667 or 667.5.

(e) Any additional term authorized by this section shall not be imposed unless the allegation is charged in the accusatory pleading and admitted by the defendant or found to be true by the trier of fact.

(f) Any additional term imposed pursuant to this section shall be in addition to any other punishment provided by law.

(g) Notwithstanding any other provision of law, the court may strike any additional term imposed by this section if the court determines that there are mitigating circumstances and states on the record the reasons for striking the additional punishment.

Penal Code § 422.76.

Except where the court imposes additional punishment under Section 422.75 or in a case in which the person has been convicted of an offense subject to Section 1170.8, the fact that a person committed a felony or attempted to commit a felony that is a hate crime shall be considered a circumstance in aggravation of the crime in imposing a term under subdivision (b) of Section 1170.

Penal Code § 463.

(a) Every person who violates Section 459, punishable as a second-degree burglary pursuant to subdivision 2 of Section 461, during and within an affected county in a "state of emergency" or a "local emergency" resulting from an earthquake, fire, flood, riot, or other natural or manmade disaster shall be guilty of the crime of looting, punishable by imprisonment in a county jail for one year or in the state prison. Any person convicted under this subdivision who is eligible for probation and who is granted probation shall, as a condition thereof, be confined in a county jail for at least 180 days, except that the court may, in the case where the interest of justice would best be served, reduce or eliminate that mandatory jail sentence, if the court specifies on the record and enters into the minutes the circumstances indicating that the interest of justice would best be served by that disposition. In addition to whatever custody is ordered, the court, in its discretion, may require any person granted probation following conviction under this subdivision to serve up to 240 hours of community service in any program deemed appropriate by the court, including any program created to rebuild the community. For purposes of this section, the fact that the structure entered has been damaged by the earthquake, fire, flood, or other natural or manmade disaster shall not, in and of itself, preclude conviction.

(b) Every person who commits the crime of grand theft, as defined in Section 487, except grand theft of a firearm, during and within an affected county in a "state of emergency" or a "local emergency" resulting from an earthquake, fire, flood, riot, or other natural or unnatural disaster shall be guilty of the crime of looting, punishable by imprisonment in a county jail for one year or in the state prison. Every person who commits the crime of grand theft of a firearm, as defined in Section 487, during and within an affected county in a "state of emergency" or a "local emergency" resulting from an earthquake, fire, flood, riot, or other natural or unnatural disaster shall be guilty of the crime of looting, punishable by imprisonment in the state prison, as set forth in subdivision (a) of Section 489. Any person convicted under this subdivision who is eligible for probation and who is granted probation shall, as a condition thereof, be confined in a county jail for at least 180 days, except that the court may, in the case where the interest of justice would best be served, reduce or eliminate that mandatory jail sentence, if the court specifies on the record and enters into the minutes the circumstances indicating that the interest of justice would best be served by that disposition. In addition to whatever custody is ordered, the court, in its discretion, may require any person granted probation following conviction under this subdivision to serve up to 160 hours of community service in any program deemed appropriate by the court, including any program created to rebuild the community.

(c) Every person who commits the crime of petty theft, as defined in Section 488, during and within an affected county in a "state of emergency" or a "local emergency" resulting from an earthquake, fire, flood, riot, or other natural or manmade disaster shall be guilty of a misdemeanor, punishable by imprisonment in a county jail for six months. Any person convicted under this subdivision who is eligible for probation and who is granted probation shall, as a condition thereof, be confined in a county jail for at least 90 days, except that the court may, in the case where the interest of justice would best be served, reduce or eliminate that mandatory minimum jail sentence, if the court specifies on the record and enters into the minutes the circumstances indicating that the interest of justice would best be served by that disposition. In addition to whatever custody is ordered, the court, in its discretion, may require any person granted probation following conviction under this subdivision to serve up to 80 hours of community service in any program deemed appropriate by the court, including any program created to rebuild the community.

(d)(1) For purposes of this section, "state of emergency" means conditions which, by reason of their magnitude, are, or are likely to be, beyond the control of the services, personnel, equipment, and facilities of any single county, city and county, or city and require the combined forces of a mutual aid region or regions to combat.

(2) For purposes of this section, "local emergency" means conditions which, by reason of their magnitude, are, or are likely to be, beyond the control of the services, personnel, equipment, and facilities of any single county, city and county, or city and require the combined forces of a mutual aid region or regions to combat.

(3) For purposes of this section, a "state of emergency" shall exist from the time of the proclamation of the condition of the emergency until terminated pursuant to Section 8629 of the Government Code. For purposes of this section only, a "local emergency" shall exist from the time of the proclamation of the condition of the emergency by the local governing body until terminated pursuant to Section 8630 of the Government Code.

(4) Consensual entry into a commercial structure with the intent to commit a violation of Section 470, 476, 476a, 484f, or 484g of the Penal Code, shall not be charged as a violation under this section.

Penal Code § 464.

Any person who, with intent to commit crime, enters, either by day or by night, any building, whether inhabited or not, and opens or attempts to open any vault, safe, or other secure place by use of acetylene torch or electric arc, burning bar, thermal lance, oxygen lance, or any other similar device capable of burning through steel, concrete, or any other solid substance, or by use of nitroglycerine, dynamite, gunpowder, or any other explosive, is guilty of a felony and, upon conviction, shall be punished by imprisonment in the state prison for a term of three, five, or seven years.

Penal Code § 468.

Any person who knowingly buys, sells, receives, disposes of, conceals, or has in his possession a sniperscope shall be guilty of a misdemeanor, punishable by a fine not to exceed one thousand dollars ($1,000) or by imprisonment in the county jail for not more than one year, or by both such fine and imprisonment. As used in this section, sniperscope means any attachment, device or similar contrivance designed for or adaptable to use on a firearm which, through the use of a projected infrared light source and electronic telescope, enables the operator thereof to visually determine and locate the presence of objects during the nighttime. This section shall not prohibit the authorized use or possession of such sniperscope by a member of the armed forces of the United States or by police officers, peace officers, or law enforcement officers authorized by the properly constituted authorities for the enforcement of law or ordinances; nor shall this section prohibit the use or possession of such sniperscope when used solely for scientific research or educational purposes.

Penal Code § 484.1.

(a) Any person who knowingly gives false information or provides false verification as to the person's true identity or as to the person's ownership interest in property or the person's authority to sell property in order to receive money or other valuable consideration from a pawnbroker or secondhand dealer and who receives money or other valuable consideration from the pawnbroker or secondhand dealer is guilty of theft.

(b) Upon conviction of the offense described in subdivision (a), the court may require, in addition to any sentence or fine imposed, that the defendant make restitution to the pawnbroker or secondhand dealer in an amount not exceeding the actual losses sustained pursuant to the provisions of subdivision (c) of Section 13967 of the Government Code, as operative on or before September 28, 1994, if the defendant is denied probation, or Section 1203.04, as operative on or before August 2, 1995, if the defendant is granted probation or Section 1202.4.

(c) Upon the setting of a court hearing date for sentencing of any person convicted under this section, the probation officer, if one is assigned, shall notify the pawnbroker or secondhand dealer or coin dealer of the time and place of the hearing.

Penal Code § 485.

One who finds lost property under circumstances which give him knowledge of or means of inquiry as to the true owner, and who appropriates such property to his own use, or to the use of another person not entitled thereto, without first making reasonable and just efforts to find the owner and to restore the property to him, is guilty of theft.

Penal Code § 486.

Theft is divided into two degrees, the first of which is termed grand theft; the second, petty theft.

Penal Code § 487.

Grand theft is theft committed in any of the following cases:

(a) When the money, labor, or real or personal property taken is of a value exceeding four hundred dollars ($400), except as provided in subdivision (b).

(b) Notwithstanding subdivision (a), grand theft is committed in any of the following cases:

(1)(A) When domestic fowls, avocados, olives, citrus or deciduous fruits, other fruits, vegetables, nuts, artichokes, or other farm crops are taken of a value exceeding one hundred dollars ($100).

(B) For the purposes of establishing that the value of avocados or citrus fruit under this paragraph exceeds one hundred dollars ($100), that value may be shown by the presentation of credible evidence which establishes that on the day of the theft avocados or citrus fruit of the same variety and weight exceeded one hundred dollars ($100) in wholesale value.

(2) When fish, shellfish, mollusks, crustaceans, kelp, algae, or other aquacultural products are taken from a commercial or research operation which is producing that product, of a value exceeding one hundred dollars ($100).

(3) Where the money, labor, or real or personal property is taken by a servant, agent, or employee from his or her principal or employer and aggregates four hundred dollars ($400) or more in any 12 consecutive month period.

(c) When the property is taken from the person of another.

(d) When the property taken is any of the following:

(1) An automobile, horse, mare, gelding, any bovine animal, any caprine animal, mule, jack, jenny, sheep, lamb, hog, sow, boar, gilt, barrow, or pig.

(2) A firearm.

(e) This section shall become operative on January 1, 1997.

Penal Code § 489.

Grand theft is punishable as follows:

(a) When the grand theft involves the theft of a firearm, by imprisonment in the state prison for 16 months, 2, or 3 years.

(b) In all other cases, by imprisonment in a county jail not exceeding one year or in the state prison.

Penal Code § 600.

(a) Any person who willfully and maliciously and with no legal justification strikes, beats, kicks, cuts, stabs, shoots with a firearm, administers any poison or other harmful or stupefying substance to, or throws, hurls, or projects at, or places any rock, object, or other substance which is used in such a manner as to be capable of producing injury and likely to produce injury, on or in the path of, any horse being used by, or any dog under the supervision of, any peace officer in the discharge or attempted discharge of his or her duties, is guilty of a public offense. If the injury inflicted is a serious injury, as defined in subdivision (c), the person shall be punished by imprisonment in the state prison for 16 months, two or three years, or in a county jail for not exceeding one year, or by a fine not exceeding two thousand dollars ($2,000), or by both a fine and imprisonment. If the injury inflicted is not a serious injury, the person shall be punished by imprisonment in the county jail for not exceeding one year, or by a fine not exceeding one thousand dollars ($1,000), or by both a fine and imprisonment.

(b) Any person who willfully and maliciously and with no legal justification interferes with or obstructs any horse or dog being used by any peace officer in the discharge or attempted discharge of his or her duties by frightening, teasing, agitating, harassing, or hindering the horse or dog shall be punished by imprisonment in a county jail for not exceeding one year, or by a fine not exceeding one thousand dollars ($1,000), or by both a fine and imprisonment.

(c) Any person who, in violation of this section, and with intent to inflict such injury or death, personally causes the death, destruction, or serious physical injury including bone fracture, loss or impairment of function of any bodily member, wounds requiring extensive suturing, or serious crippling, of any horse or dog, shall, upon conviction of a felony under this section, in addition and consecutive to the punishment prescribed for the felony, be punished by an additional term of imprisonment in the state prison for one year.

(d) Any person who, in violation of this section, and with the intent to inflict such injury, personally causes great bodily injury, as defined in Section 12022.7, to any person not an accomplice, shall, upon conviction of a felony under this section, in addition and consecutive to the punishment prescribed for the felony, be punished by an additional term of imprisonment in the state prison for two years unless the conduct described in this subdivision is an element of any other offense of which the person is convicted or receives an enhancement under Section 12022.7.

(e) In any case in which a defendant is convicted of a violation of this section, the defendant shall be ordered to make restitution to the agency owning the animal and employing the peace officer for any veterinary bills, replacement costs of the animal if it is disabled or killed, and the salary of the peace officer for the period of time his or her services are lost to the agency.

Penal Code § 602.

Except as provided in paragraph (2) of subdivision (v), subdivision (x), and Section 602.8, every person who willfully commits a trespass by any of the following acts is guilty of a misdemeanor:

(a) Cutting down, destroying, or injuring any kind of wood or timber standing or growing upon the lands of another.

(b) Carrying away any kind of wood or timber lying on those lands.

(c) Maliciously injuring or severing from the freehold of another anything attached to it, or its produce.

(d) Digging, taking, or carrying away from any lot situated within the limits of any incorporated city, without the license of the owner or legal occupant, any earth, soil, or stone.

(e) Digging, taking, or carrying away from land in any city or town laid down on the map or plan of the city, or otherwise recognized or established as a street, alley, avenue, or park, without the license of the proper authorities, any earth, soil, or stone.

(f) Maliciously tearing down, damaging, mutilating, or destroying any sign, signboard, or notice placed upon, or affixed to, any property belonging to the state, or to any city, county, city and county, town or village, or upon any property of any person, by the state or by an automobile association, which sign, signboard or notice is intended to indicate or designate a road, or a highway, or is intended to direct travelers from one point to another, or relates to fires, fire control, or any other matter involving the protection of the property, or putting up, affixing, fastening, printing, or painting upon any property belonging to the state, or to any city, county, town, or village, or dedicated to the public, or upon any property of any person, without license from the owner, any notice, advertisement, or designation of, or any name for any commodity, whether for sale or otherwise, or any picture, sign, or device intended to call attention to it.

(g) Entering upon any lands owned by any other person whereon oysters or other shellfish are planted or growing; or injuring, gathering, or carrying away any oysters or other shellfish planted, growing, or on any of those lands, whether covered by water or not, without the license of the owner or legal occupant; or damaging, destroying, or removing, or causing to be removed, damaged, or destroyed, any stakes, marks, fences, or signs intended to designate the boundaries and limits of any of those lands.

(h)(1) Entering upon lands or buildings owned by any other person without the license of the owner or legal occupant, where signs forbidding trespass are displayed, and whereon cattle, goats, pigs, sheep, fowl, or any other animal is being raised, bred, fed, or held for the purpose of food for human consumption; or injuring, gathering, or carrying away any animal being housed on any of those lands, without the license of the owner or legal occupant; or damaging, destroying, or removing, or causing to be removed, damaged, or destroyed, any stakes, marks, fences, or signs intended to designate the boundaries and limits of any of those lands.

(2) In order for there to be a violation of this subdivision, the trespass signs under paragraph

(1) must be displayed at intervals not less than three per mile along all exterior boundaries and at all roads and trails entering the land.

(3) This subdivision shall not be construed to preclude prosecution or punishment under any other provision of law, including, but not limited to, grand theft or any provision that provides for a greater penalty or longer term of imprisonment.

(i) Willfully opening, tearing down, or otherwise destroying any fence on the enclosed land of another, or opening any gate, bar, or fence of another and willfully leaving it open without the written permission of the owner, or maliciously tearing down, mutilating, or destroying any sign, signboard, or other notice forbidding shooting on private property.

(j) Building fires upon any lands owned by another where signs forbidding trespass are displayed at intervals not greater than one mile along the exterior boundaries and at all roads and trails entering the lands, without first having obtained written permission from the owner of the lands or the owner's agent, or the person in lawful possession.

(k) Entering any lands, whether unenclosed or enclosed by fence, for the purpose of injuring any property or property rights or with the intention of interfering with, obstructing, or injuring any lawful business or occupation carried on by the owner of the land, the owner's agent or by the person in lawful possession.

(l) Entering any lands under cultivation or enclosed by fence, belonging to, or occupied by, another, or entering upon uncultivated or unenclosed lands where signs forbidding trespass are displayed at intervals not less than three to the mile along all exterior boundaries and at all roads and trails entering the lands without the written permission of the owner of the land, the owner's agent or of the person in lawful possession, and

(1) Refusing or failing to leave the lands immediately upon being requested by the owner of the land, the owner's agent or by the person in lawful possession to leave the lands, or

(2) Tearing down, mutilating, or destroying any sign, signboard, or notice forbidding trespass or hunting on the lands, or

(3) Removing, injuring, unlocking, or tampering with any lock on any gate on or leading into the lands, or

(4) Discharging any firearm.

(m) Entering and occupying real property or structures of any kind without the consent of the owner, the owner's agent, or the person in lawful possession.

(n) Driving any vehicle, as defined in Section 670 of the Vehicle Code, upon real property belonging to, or lawfully occupied by, another and known not to be open to the general public, without the consent of the owner, the owner's agent, or the person in lawful possession. This subdivision shall not apply to any person described in Section 22350 of the Business and Professions Code who is making a lawful service of process, provided that upon exiting the vehicle, the person proceeds immediately to attempt the service of process, and leaves immediately upon completing the service of process or upon the request of the owner, the owner's agent, or the person in lawful possession.

(o) Refusing or failing to leave land, real property, or structures belonging to or lawfully occupied by another and not open to the general public, upon being requested to leave by

(1) a peace officer at the request of the owner, the owner's agent, or the person in lawful possession, and upon being informed by the peace officer that he or she is acting at the request of the owner, the owner's agent, or the person in lawful possession, or

(2) the owner, the owner's agent, or the person in lawful possession. The owner, the owner's agent, or the person in lawful possession shall make a separate request to the peace officer on each occasion when the peace officer's assistance in dealing with a trespass is requested. However, a single request for a peace officer's assistance may be made to cover a limited period of time not to exceed 30 days and identified by specific dates, during which there is a fire hazard or the owner, owner's agent or person in lawful possession is absent from the premises or property. In addition, a single request for a peace officer's assistance may be made for a period not to exceed six months when the premises or property is closed to the public and posted as being closed. However, this subdivision shall not be applicable to persons engaged in lawful labor union activities which are permitted to be carried out on the property by the California Agricultural Labor Relations Act, Part 3.5 (commencing with Section 1140) of Division 2 of the Labor Code, or by the National Labor Relations Act. For purposes of this section, land, real property, or structures owned or operated by any housing authority for tenants as defined under Section 34213.5 of the Health and Safety Code constitutes property not open to the general public; however, this subdivision shall not apply to persons on the premises who are engaging in activities protected by the California or United States Constitution, or to persons who are on the premises at the request of a resident or management and who are not loitering or otherwise suspected of violating or actually violating any law or ordinance.

(p) Entering upon any lands declared closed to entry as provided in Section 4256 of the Public Resources Code, if the closed areas shall have been posted with notices declaring the closure, at intervals not greater than one mile along the exterior boundaries or along roads and trails passing through the lands.

(q) Refusing or failing to leave a public building of a public agency during those hours of the day or night when the building is regularly closed to the public upon being requested to do so by a regularly employed guard, watchman, or custodian of the public agency owning or maintaining the building or property, if the surrounding circumstances would indicate to a reasonable person that the person has no apparent lawful business to pursue.

(r) Knowingly skiing in an area or on a ski trail which is closed to the public and which has signs posted indicating the closure.

(s) Refusing or failing to leave a hotel or motel, where he or she has obtained accommodations and has refused to pay for those accommodations, upon request of the proprietor or manager, and the occupancy is exempt, pursuant to subdivision (b) of Section 1940 of the Civil Code, from Chapter 2 (commencing with Section 1940) of Title 5 of Part 4 of Division 3 of the Civil Code. For purposes of this subdivision, occupancy at a hotel or motel for a continuous period of 30 days or less shall, in the absence of a written agreement to the contrary, or other written evidence of a periodic tenancy of indefinite duration, be exempt from Chapter 2 (commencing with Section 1940) of Title 5 of Part 4 of Division 3 of the Civil Code.

(t) Entering upon private property, including contiguous land, real property, or structures thereon belonging to the same owner, whether or not generally open to the public, after having been informed by a peace officer at the request of the owner, the owner's agent, or the person in lawful possession, and upon being informed by the peace officer that he or she is acting at the request of the owner, the owner's agent, or the person in lawful possession, that the property is not open to the particular person; or refusing or failing to leave the property upon being asked to leave the property in the manner provided in this subdivision. This subdivision shall apply only to a person who has been convicted of a violent felony, as specified in subdivision (c) of Section 667.5, committed upon the particular private property. A single notification or request to the person as set forth above shall be valid and enforceable under this subdivision unless and until rescinded by the owner, the owner's agent, or the person in lawful possession of the property.

(u)(1) Knowingly entering, by an unauthorized person, upon any airport or passenger vessel terminal operations area if the area has been posted with notices restricting access to authorized personnel only and the postings occur not greater than every 150 feet along the exterior boundary, to the extent, in the case of a passenger vessel terminal, as defined in subparagraph (B) of paragraph (3), that the exterior boundary extends shoreside. To the extent that the exterior boundary of a passenger vessel terminal operations area extends waterside, this prohibition shall apply if notices have been posted in a manner consistent with the requirements for the shoreside exterior boundary, or in any other manner approved by the captain of the port.

(2) Any person convicted of a violation of paragraph (1) shall be punished as follows:

(A) By a fine not exceeding one hundred dollars ($100).

(B) By imprisonment in the county jail not exceeding six months, or by a fine not exceeding one thousand dollars ($1,000), or both, if the person refuses to leave the airport or passenger vessel terminal after being requested to leave by a peace officer or authorized personnel.

(C) By imprisonment in the county jail not exceeding six months, or by a fine not exceeding one thousand dollars ($1,000), or both, for a second or subsequent offense.

(3) As used in this subdivision the following definitions shall control:

(A) "Airport operations area" means that part of the airport used by aircraft for landing, taking off, surface maneuvering, loading and unloading, refueling, parking, or maintenance, where aircraft support vehicles and facilities exist, and which is not for public use or public vehicular traffic.

(B) "Passenger vessel terminal" means only that portion of a harbor or port facility, as described in Section 105.105(a)(2) of Title 33 of the Code of Federal Regulations, with a secured area that regularly serves scheduled commuter or passenger operations. For the purposes of this section, "passenger vessel terminal" does not include any area designated a public access area pursuant to Section 105.106 of Title 33 of the Code of Federal Regulations.

(C) "Authorized personnel" means any person who has a valid airport identification card issued by the airport operator or has a valid airline identification card recognized by the airport operator, or any person not in possession of an airport or airline identification card who is being escorted for legitimate purposes by a person with an airport or airline identification card. "Authorized personnel" also means any person who has a valid port identification card issued by the harbor operator, or who has a valid company identification card issued by a commercial maritime enterprise recognized by the harbor operator, or any other person who is being escorted for legitimate purposes by a person with a valid port or qualifying company identification card.

(D) "Airport" means any facility whose function is to support commercial aviation.

(v)(1) Except as permitted by federal law, intentionally avoiding submission to the screening and inspection of one's person and accessible property in accordance with the procedures being applied to control access when entering or reentering a sterile area of an airport or passenger vessel terminal, as defined in Section 171.5.

(2) A violation of this subdivision that is responsible for the evacuation of an airport terminal or passenger vessel terminal and is responsible in any part for delays or cancellations of scheduled flights or departures is punishable by imprisonment of not more than one year in a county jail if the sterile area is posted with a statement providing reasonable notice that prosecution may result from a trespass described in this subdivision.

(w) Refusing or failing to leave a battered women's shelter at any time after being requested to leave by a managing authority of the shelter.

(1) A person who is convicted of violating this subdivision shall be punished by imprisonment in a county jail for not more than one year.

(2) The court may order a defendant who is convicted of violating this subdivision to make restitution to a battered woman in an amount equal to the relocation expenses of the battered woman and her children if those expenses are incurred as a result of trespass by the defendant at a battered women's shelter.

(x)(1) Knowingly entering or remaining in a neonatal unit, maternity ward, or birthing center located in a hospital or clinic without lawful business to pursue therein, if the area has been posted so as to give reasonable notice restricting access to those with lawful business to pursue therein and the surrounding circumstances would indicate to a reasonable person that he or she has no lawful business to pursue therein. Reasonable notice is that which would give actual notice to a reasonable person, and is posted, at a minimum, at each entrance into the area.

(2) Any person convicted of a violation of paragraph (1) shall be punished as follows:

(A) As an infraction, by a fine not exceeding one hundred dollars ($100).

(B) By imprisonment in a county jail not exceeding one year, or by a fine not exceeding one thousand dollars ($1,000), or both, if the person refuses to leave the posted area after being requested to leave by a peace officer or other authorized person.

(C) By imprisonment in a county jail not exceeding one year, or by a fine not exceeding two thousand dollars ($2,000), or both, for a second or subsequent offense.

(D) If probation is granted or the execution or imposition of sentencing is suspended for any person convicted under this subdivision, it shall be a condition of probation that the person participate in counseling, as designated by the court, unless the court finds good cause not to impose this requirement. The court shall require the person to pay for this counseling, if ordered, unless good cause not to pay is shown.

(y) Except as permitted by federal law, intentionally avoiding submission to the screening and inspection of one's person and accessible property in accordance with the procedures being applied to control access when entering or reentering a courthouse or a city, county, city and county, or state building if entrances to the courthouse or the city, county, city and county, or state building have been posted with a statement providing reasonable notice that prosecution may result from a trespass described in this subdivision.

Penal Code § 626.

(a) As used in this chapter, the following definitions apply:

(1) "University" means the University of California, and includes any affiliated institution thereof and any campus or facility owned, operated, or controlled by the Regents of the University of California.

(2) "State university" means any California state university, and includes any campus or facility owned, operated, or controlled by the Trustees of the California State University.

(3) "Community college" means any public community college established pursuant to the Education Code.

(4) "School" means any public or private elementary school, junior high school, four-year high school, senior high school, adult school or any branch thereof, opportunity school, continuation high school, regional occupational center, evening high school, or technical school or any public right-of-way situated immediately adjacent to school property or any other place if a teacher and one or more pupils are required to be at that place in connection with assigned school activities.

(5) "Chief administrative officer" means either of the following:

(A) The president of the university or a state university, the Chancellor of the California State University, or the officer designated by the Regents of the University of California or pursuant to authority granted by the Regents of the University of California to administer and be the officer in charge of a campus or other facility owned, operated, or controlled by the Regents of the University of California, or the superintendent of a community college district.

(B) For a school, the principal of the school, a person who possesses a standard supervision credential or a standard administrative credential and who is designated by the principal, or a person who carries out the same functions as a person who possesses a credential and who is designated by the principal.

(b) For the purpose of determining the penalty to be imposed pursuant to this chapter, the court may consider a written report from the Department of Justice containing information from its records showing prior convictions; and that communication is prima facie evidence of the convictions, if the defendant admits them, regardless of whether or not the complaint commencing the proceedings has alleged prior convictions.

(c) As used in this code, the following definitions apply:

(1) "Pupil currently attending school" means a pupil enrolled in a public or private school who has been in attendance or has had an excused absence, for purposes of attendance accounting, for a majority of the days for which the pupil has been enrolled in that school during the school year.

(2) "Safe school zone" means an area that encompasses any of the following places during regular school hours or within 60 minutes before or after the schoolday or 60 minutes before or after a school-sponsored activity at the schoolsite:

(A) Within 100 feet of a bus stop, whether or not a public transit bus stop, that has been publicly designated by the school district as a schoolbus stop. This definition applies only if the school district has chosen to mark the bus stop as a schoolbus stop.

(B) Within 1,500 feet of a school, as designated by the school district.

Penal Code § 626.9.

(a) This section shall be known, and may be cited, as the Gun-Free School Zone Act of 1995.

(b) Any person who possesses a firearm in a place that the person knows, or reasonably should know, is a school zone, as defined in paragraph (1) of subdivision (e), unless it is with the written permission of the school district superintendent, his or her designee, or equivalent school authority, shall be punished as specified in subdivision (f).

(c) Subdivision (b) does not apply to the possession of a firearm under any of the following circumstances:

(1) Within a place of residence or place of business or on private property, if the place of residence, place of business, or private property is not part of the school grounds and the possession of the firearm is otherwise lawful.

(2) When the firearm is an unloaded pistol, revolver, or other firearm capable of being concealed on the person and is in a locked container or within the locked trunk of a motor vehicle. This section does not prohibit or limit the otherwise lawful transportation of any other firearm, other than a pistol, revolver, or other firearm capable of being concealed on the person, in accordance with state law.

(3) When the person possessing the firearm reasonably believes that he or she is in grave danger because of circumstances forming the basis of a current restraining order issued by a court against another person or persons who has or have been found to pose a threat to his or her life or safety. This subdivision may not apply when the circumstances involve a mutual restraining order issued pursuant to Division 10 (commencing with Section 6200) of the Family Code absent a factual finding of a specific threat to the person's life or safety. Upon a trial for violating subdivision (b), the trier of a fact shall determine whether the defendant was acting out of a reasonable belief that he or she was in grave danger.

(4) When the person is exempt from the prohibition against carrying a concealed firearm pursuant to subdivision (b), (d),

(e), or (h) of Section 12027.

(d) Except as provided in subdivision (b), it shall be unlawful for any person, with reckless disregard for the safety of another, to discharge, or attempt to discharge, a firearm in a school zone, as defined in paragraph (1) of subdivision (e). The prohibition contained in this subdivision does not apply to the discharge of a firearm to the extent that the conditions of paragraph (1) of subdivision (c) are satisfied.

(e) As used in this section, the following definitions shall apply:

(1) "School zone" means an area in, or on the grounds of, a public or private school providing instruction in kindergarten or grades 1 to 12, inclusive, or within a distance of 1,000 feet from the grounds of the public or private school.

(2) "Firearm" has the same meaning as that term is given in Section 12001.

(3) "Locked container" has the same meaning as that term is given in subdivision (c) of Section 12026.1.

(4) "Concealed firearm" has the same meaning as that term is given in Sections 12025 and 12026.1.

(f)(1) Any person who violates subdivision (b) by possessing a firearm in, or on the grounds of, a public or private school providing instruction in kindergarten or grades 1 to 12, inclusive, shall be punished by imprisonment in the state prison for two, three, or five years.

(2) Any person who violates subdivision (b) by possessing a firearm within a distance of 1,000 feet from the grounds of a public or private school providing instruction in kindergarten or grades 1 to 12, inclusive, shall be punished as follows:

(A) By imprisonment in the state prison for two, three, or five years, if any of the following circumstances apply:

(i) If the person previously has been convicted of any felony, or of any crime made punishable by Chapter 1 (commencing with Section 12000) of Title 2 of Part 4.

(ii) If the person is within a class of persons prohibited from possessing or acquiring a firearm pursuant to Section 12021 or 12021.1 of this code or Section 8100 or 8103 of the Welfare and Institutions Code.

(iii) If the firearm is any pistol, revolver, or other firearm capable of being concealed upon the person and the offense is punished as a felony pursuant to Section 12025.

(B) By imprisonment in a county jail for not more than one year or by imprisonment in the state prison for two, three, or five years, in all cases other than those specified in subparagraph (A).

(3) Any person who violates subdivision (d) shall be punished by imprisonment in the state prison for three, five, or seven years.

(g)(1) Every person convicted under this section for a misdemeanor violation of subdivision (b) who has been convicted previously of a misdemeanor offense enumerated in Section 12001.6 shall be punished by imprisonment in a county jail for not less than three months, or if probation is granted or if the execution or imposition of sentence is suspended, it shall be a condition thereof that he or she be imprisoned in a county jail for not less than three months.

(2) Every person convicted under this section of a felony violation of subdivision (b) or (d) who has been convicted previously of a misdemeanor offense enumerated in Section 12001.6, if probation is granted or if the execution of sentence is suspended, it shall be a condition thereof that he or she be imprisoned in a county jail for not less than three months.

(3) Every person convicted under this section for a felony violation of subdivision (b) or (d) who has been convicted previously of any felony, or of any crime made punishable by Chapter 1 (commencing with Section 12000) of Title 2 of Part 4, if probation is granted or if the execution or imposition of sentence is suspended, it shall be a condition thereof that he or she be imprisoned in a county jail for not less than three months.

(4) The court shall apply the three-month minimum sentence specified in this subdivision, except in unusual cases where the interests of justice would best be served by granting probation or suspending the execution or imposition of sentence without the minimum imprisonment required in this subdivision or by granting probation or suspending the execution or imposition of sentence with conditions other than those set forth in this subdivision, in which case the court shall specify on the record and shall enter on the minutes the circumstances indicating that the interests of justice would best be served by this disposition.

(h) Notwithstanding Section 12026, any person who brings or possesses a loaded firearm upon the grounds of a campus of, or buildings owned or operated for student housing, teaching, research, or administration by, a public or private university or college, that are contiguous or are clearly marked university property, unless it is with the written permission of the university or college president, his or her designee, or equivalent university or college authority, shall be punished by imprisonment in the state prison for two, three, or four years. Notwithstanding subdivision (k), a university or college shall post a prominent notice at primary entrances on noncontiguous property stating that firearms are prohibited on that property pursuant to this subdivision.

(i) Notwithstanding Section 12026, any person who brings or possesses a firearm upon the grounds of a campus of, or buildings owned or operated for student housing, teaching, research, or administration by, a public or private university or college, that are contiguous or are clearly marked university property, unless it is with the written permission of the university or college president, his or her designee, or equivalent university or college authority, shall be punished by imprisonment in the state prison for one, two, or three years. Notwithstanding subdivision (k), a university or college shall post a prominent notice at primary entrances on noncontiguous property stating that firearms are prohibited on that property pursuant to this subdivision.

(j) For purposes of this section, a firearm shall be deemed to be loaded when there is an unexpended cartridge or shell, consisting of a case that holds a charge of powder and a bullet or shot, in, or attached in any manner to, the firearm, including, but not limited to, in the firing chamber, magazine, or clip thereof attached to the firearm. A muzzle-loader firearm shall be deemed to be loaded when it is capped or primed and has a powder charge and ball or shot in the barrel or cylinder.

(k) This section does not require that notice be posted regarding the proscribed conduct.

(l) This section does not apply to a duly appointed peace officer as defined in Chapter 4.5 (commencing with Section 830) of Title 3 of Part 2, a full-time paid peace officer of another state or the federal government who is carrying out official duties while in California, any person summoned by any of these officers to assist in making arrests or preserving the peace while he or she is actually engaged in assisting the officer, a member of the military forces of this state or of the United States who is engaged in the performance of his or her duties, a person holding a valid license to carry the firearm pursuant to Article 3 (commencing with Section 12050) of Chapter 1 of Title 2 of Part 4, or an armored vehicle guard, engaged in the performance of his or her duties, as defined in subdivision (e) of Section

7521 of the Business and Professions Code.

(m) This section does not apply to a security guard authorized to carry a loaded firearm pursuant to Section 12031.

(n) This section does not apply to an existing shooting range at a public or private school or university or college campus.

(o) This section does not apply to an honorably retired peace officer authorized to carry a concealed or loaded firearm pursuant to subdivision (a) or (i) of Section 12027 or paragraph (1) or (8) of subdivision (b) of Section 12031.

Penal Code § 626.95.

(a) Any person who is in violation of paragraph (2) of subdivision (a), or subdivision (b), of Section 417 , or Section 12025 or 12031, upon the grounds of or within a playground, or a public or private youth center during hours in which the facility is open for business, classes, or school-related programs, or at any time when minors are using the facility, knowing that he or she is on or within those grounds, shall be punished by imprisonment in the state prison for one, two, or three years, or in a county jail not exceeding one year.

(b) State and local authorities are encouraged to cause signs to be posted around playgrounds and youth centers giving warning of prohibition of the possession of firearms upon the grounds of or within playgrounds or youth centers.

(c) For purposes of this section, the following definitions shall apply:

(1) "Playground" means any park or recreational area specifically designed to be used by children that has play equipment installed, including public grounds designed for athletic activities such as baseball, football, soccer, or basketball, or any similar facility located on public or private school grounds, or on city or county parks.

(2) "Youth center" means any public or private facility that is used to host recreational or social activities for minors while minors are present.

(d) It is the Legislature's intent that only an actual conviction of a felony of one of the offenses specified in this section would subject the person to firearms disabilities under the federal Gun Control Act of 1968 (P.L. 90-618; 18 U.S.C. Sec. 921).

Penal Code § 626.10.

(a) Any person, except a duly appointed peace officer as defined in Chapter 4.5 (commencing with Section 830) of Title 3 of Part 2, a full-time paid peace officer of another state or the federal government who is carrying out official duties while in this state, a person summoned by any officer to assist in making arrests or preserving the peace while the person is actually engaged in assisting any officer, or a member of the military forces of this state or the United States who is engaged in the performance of his or her duties, who brings or possesses any dirk, dagger, ice pick, knife having a blade longer than 2 ½ inches, folding knife with a blade that locks into place, a razor with an unguarded blade, a taser, or a stun gun, as defined in subdivision (a) of Section 244.5, any instrument that expels a metallic projectile such as a BB or a pellet, through the force of air pressure, CO 2 pressure, or spring action, or any spot marker gun, upon the grounds of, or within, any public or private school providing instruction in kindergarten or any of grades 1 to 12, inclusive, is guilty of a public offense, punishable by imprisonment in a county jail not exceeding one year, or by imprisonment in the state prison.

(b) Any person, except a duly appointed peace officer as defined in Chapter 4.5 (commencing with Section 830) of Title 3 of Part 2, a full-time paid peace officer of another state or the federal government who is carrying out official duties while in this state, a person summoned by any officer to assist in making arrests or preserving the peace while the person is actually engaged in assisting any officer, or a member of the military forces of this state or the United States who is engaged in the performance of his or her duties, who brings or possesses any dirk, dagger, ice pick, or knife having a fixed blade longer than 21/2 inches upon the grounds of, or within, any private university, the University of California, the California State University, or the California Community Colleges is guilty of a public offense, punishable by imprisonment in a county jail not exceeding one year, or by imprisonment in the state prison.

(c) Subdivisions (a) and (b) do not apply to any person who brings or possesses a knife having a blade longer than 21/2 inches or a razor with an unguarded blade upon the grounds of, or within, a public or private school providing instruction in kindergarten or any of grades 1 to 12, inclusive, or any private university, state university, or community college at the direction of a faculty member of the private university, state university, or community college, or a certificated or classified employee of the school for use in a private university, state university, community college, or school-sponsored activity or class.

(d) Subdivisions (a) and (b) do not apply to any person who brings or possesses an ice pick, a knife having a blade longer than 21/2 inches, or a razor with an unguarded blade upon the grounds of, or within, a public or private school providing instruction in kindergarten or any of grades 1 to 12, inclusive, or any private university, state university, or community college for a lawful purpose within the scope of the person's employment.

(e) Subdivision (b) does not apply to any person who brings or possesses an ice pick or a knife having a fixed blade longer than 21/2 inches upon the grounds of, or within, any private university, state university, or community college for lawful use in or around a residence or residential facility located upon those grounds or for lawful use in food preparation or consumption.

(f) Subdivision (a) does not apply to any person who brings an instrument that expels a metallic projectile such as a BB or a pellet, through the force of air pressure, CO2 pressure, or spring action, or any spot marker gun upon the grounds of, or within, a public or private school providing instruction in kindergarten or any of grades 1 to 12, inclusive, if the person has the written permission of the school principal or his or her designee.

(g) Any certificated or classified employee or school peace officer of a public or private school providing instruction in kindergarten or any of grades 1 to 12, inclusive, may seize any of the weapons described in subdivision (a), and any certificated or classified employee or school peace officer of any private university, state university, or community college may seize any of the weapons described in subdivision (b), from the possession of any person upon the grounds of, or within, the school if he or she knows, or has reasonable cause to know, the person is prohibited from bringing or possessing the weapon upon the grounds of, or within, the school.

(h) As used in this section, "dirk" or "dagger" means a knife or other instrument with or without a handguard that is capable of ready use as a stabbing weapon that may inflict great bodily injury or death.

(i) Any person who, without the written permission of the college or university president or chancellor or his or her designee, brings or possesses a less lethal weapon, as defined in Section 12601, or a stun gun, as defined in Section 12650, upon the grounds of or within, a public or private college or university campus is guilty of a misdemeanor.

Penal Code § 646.9.

(a) Any person who willfully, maliciously, and repeatedly follows or willfully and maliciously harasses another person and who makes a credible threat with the intent to place that person in reasonable fear for his or her safety, or the safety of his or her immediate family is guilty of the crime of stalking, punishable by imprisonment in a county jail for not more than one year, or by a fine of not more than one thousand dollars ($1,000), or by both that fine and imprisonment, or by imprisonment in the state prison.

(b) Any person who violates subdivision (a) when there is a temporary restraining order, injunction, or any other court order in effect prohibiting the behavior described in subdivision (a) against the same party, shall be punished by imprisonment in the state prison for two, three, or four years.

(c) (1) Every person who, after having been convicted of a felony under Section 273.5, 273.6, or 422, commits a violation of subdivision (a) shall be punished by imprisonment in a county jail for not more than one year, or by a fine of not more than one thousand dollars ($1,000), or by both that fine and imprisonment, or by imprisonment in the state prison for two, three, or five years.

(2) Every person who, after having been convicted of a felony under subdivision (a), commits a violation of this section shall be punished by imprisonment in the state prison for two, three, or five years.

(d) In addition to the penalties provided in this section, the sentencing court may order a person convicted of a felony under this section to register as a sex offender pursuant to Section 290.006.

(e) For the purposes of this section, "harasses" means engages in a knowing and willful course of conduct directed at a specific person that seriously alarms, annoys, torments, or terrorizes the person, and that serves no legitimate purpose.

(f) For the purposes of this section, "course of conduct" means two or more acts occurring over a period of time, however short, evidencing a continuity of purpose. Constitutionally protected activity is not included within the meaning of "course of conduct."

(g) For the purposes of this section, "credible threat" means a verbal or written threat, including that performed through the use of an electronic communication device, or a threat implied by a pattern of conduct or a combination of verbal, written, or electronically communicated statements and conduct, made with the intent to place the person that is the target of the threat in reasonable fear for his or her safety or the safety of his or her family, and made with the apparent ability to carry out the threat so as to cause the person who is the target of the threat to reasonably fear for his or her safety or the safety of his or her family. It is not necessary to prove that the defendant had the intent to actually carry out the threat. The present incarceration of a person making the threat shall not be a bar to prosecution under this section. Constitutionally protected activity is not included within the meaning of "credible threat."

(h) For purposes of this section, the term "electronic communication device" includes, but is not limited to, telephones, cellular phones, computers, video recorders, fax machines, or pagers. "Electronic communication" has the same meaning as the term defined in Subsection 12 of Section 2510 of Title 18 of the United States Code.

(i) This section shall not apply to conduct that occurs during labor picketing.

(j) If probation is granted, or the execution or imposition of a sentence is suspended, for any person convicted under this section, it shall be a condition of probation that the person participate in counseling, as designated by the court. However, the court, upon a showing of good cause, may find that the counseling requirement shall not be imposed.

(k) (1) The sentencing court also shall consider issuing an order restraining the defendant from any contact with the victim, that may be valid for up to 10 years, as determined by the court. It is the intent of the Legislature that the length of any restraining order be based upon the seriousness of the facts before the court, the probability of future violations, and the safety of the victim and his or her immediate family.

(2) This protective order may be issued by the court whether the defendant is sentenced to state prison, county jail, or if imposition of sentence is suspended and the defendant is placed on probation.

(l) For purposes of this section, "immediate family" means any spouse, parent, child, any person related by consanguinity or affinity within the second degree, or any other person who regularly resides in the household, or who, within the prior six months, regularly resided in the household.

(m) The court shall consider whether the defendant would benefit from treatment pursuant to Section 2684. If it is determined to be appropriate, the court shall recommend that the Department of Corrections and Rehabilitation make a certification as provided in Section 2684. Upon the certification, the defendant shall be evaluated and transferred to the appropriate hospital for treatment pursuant to Section 2684.

Penal Code § 653f.

(a) Every person who, with the intent that the crime be committed, solicits another to offer, accept, or join in the offer or acceptance of a bribe, or to commit or join in the commission of carjacking, robbery, burglary, grand theft, receiving stolen property, extortion, perjury, subornation of perjury, forgery, kidnapping, arson or assault with a deadly weapon or instrument or by means of force likely to produce great bodily injury, or, by the use of force or a threat of force, to prevent or dissuade any person who is or may become a witness from attending upon, or testifying at, any trial, proceeding, or inquiry authorized by law, shall be punished by imprisonment in a county jail for not more than one year or in the state prison, or by a fine of not more than ten thousand dollars ($10,000), or the amount which could have been assessed for commission of the offense itself, whichever is greater, or by both the fine and imprisonment.

(b) Every person who, with the intent that the crime be committed, solicits another to commit or join in the commission of murder shall be punished by imprisonment in the state prison for three, six, or nine years.

(c) Every person who, with the intent that the crime be committed, solicits another to commit rape by force or violence, sodomy by force or violence, oral copulation by force or violence, or any violation of Section 264.1, 288, or 289, shall be punished by imprisonment in the state prison for two, three, or four years.

(d) Every person who, with the intent that the crime be committed, solicits another to commit an offense specified in Section 11352, 11379, 11379.5, 11379.6, or 11391 of the Health and Safety Code shall be punished by imprisonment in a county jail not exceeding six months. Every person, who, having been convicted of soliciting another to commit an offense specified in this subdivision, is subsequently convicted of the proscribed solicitation, shall be punished by imprisonment in a county jail not exceeding one year, or in the state prison. This subdivision does not apply where the term of imprisonment imposed under other provisions of law would result in a longer term of imprisonment.

(e) Every person who, with the intent that the crime be committed, solicits another to commit an offense specified in Section 14014 of the Welfare and Institutions Code shall be punished by imprisonment in a county jail for not exceeding six months. Every person who, having been convicted of soliciting another to commit an offense specified in this subdivision, is subsequently convicted of the proscribed solicitation, shall be punished by imprisonment in a county jail not exceeding one year, or in the state prison.

(f) An offense charged in violation of subdivision (a), (b), or (c) shall be proven by the testimony of two witnesses, or of one witness and corroborating circumstances. An offense charged in violation of subdivision (d) or (e) shall be proven by the testimony of one witness and corroborating circumstances.

Penal Code § 653j.

(a) Every person 18 years of age or older who, in any voluntary manner, solicits, induces, encourages, or intimidates any minor with the intent that the minor shall commit a felony in violation of paragraph (1) of subdivision (c) of Section 136.1 or Section 187, 211, 215, 245, 246, 451, 459, or 520 of the Penal Code, or Section 10851 of the Vehicle Code, shall be punished by imprisonment in the state prison for a period of three, five, or seven years. If the minor is 16 years of age or older at the time of the offense, this section shall only apply when the adult is at least five years older than the minor at the time the offense is committed.

(b) In no case shall the court impose a sentence pursuant to subdivision (a) which exceeds the maximum penalty prescribed for the felony offense for which the minor was solicited, induced, encouraged, or intimidated to commit.

(c) Whenever a sentence is imposed under subdivision (a), the court shall consider the severity of the underlying crime as one of the circumstances in aggravation.

Penal Code § 653k.

Every person who possesses in the passenger's or driver's area of any motor vehicle in any public place or place open to the public, carries upon his or her person, and every person who sells, offers for sale, exposes for sale, loans, transfers, or gives to any other person a switchblade knife having a blade two or more inches in length is guilty of a misdemeanor.

For the purposes of this section, "switchblade knife" means a knife having the appearance of a pocketknife and includes a spring-blade knife, snap-blade knife, gravity knife or any other similar type knife, the blade or blades of which are two or more inches in length and which can be released automatically by a flick of a button, pressure on the handle, flip of the wrist or other mechanical device, or is released by the weight of the blade or by any type of mechanism whatsoever. "Switchblade knife" does not include a knife that opens with one hand utilizing thumb pressure applied solely to the blade of the knife or a thumb stud attached to the blade, provided that the knife has a detent or other mechanism that provides resistance that must be overcome in opening the blade, or that biases the blade back toward its closed position.

For purposes of this section, "passenger's or driver's area" means that part of a motor vehicle which is designed to carry the driver and passengers, including any interior compartment or space therein.

Penal Code § 667.

(a)(1) In compliance with subdivision (b) of Section 1385, any person convicted of a serious felony who previously has been convicted of a serious felony in this state or of any offense committed in another jurisdiction which includes all of the elements of any serious felony, shall receive, in addition to the sentence imposed by the court for the present offense, a five-year enhancement for each such prior conviction on charges brought and tried separately. The terms of the present offense and each enhancement shall run consecutively.

(2) This subdivision shall not be applied when the punishment imposed under other provisions of law would result in a longer term of imprisonment. There is no requirement of prior incarceration or commitment for this subdivision to apply.

(3) The Legislature may increase the length of the enhancement of sentence provided in this subdivision by a statute passed by majority vote of each house thereof.

(4) As used in this subdivision, "serious felony" means a serious felony listed in subdivision (c) of Section 1192.7.

(5) This subdivision shall not apply to a person convicted of selling, furnishing, administering, or giving, or offering to sell, furnish, administer, or give to a minor any methamphetamine-related drug or any precursors of methamphetamine unless the prior conviction was for a serious felony described in subparagraph (24) of subdivision (c) of Section 1192.7.

(b) It is the intent of the Legislature in enacting subdivisions (b) to (I), inclusive, to ensure longer prison sentences and greater punishment for those who commit a felony and have been previously convicted of serious and/or violent felony offenses.

(c) Notwithstanding any other law, if a defendant has been convicted of a felony and it has been pled and proved that the defendant has one or more prior felony convictions as defined in subdivision (d), the court shall adhere to each of the following:

(1) There shall not be an aggregate term limitation for purposes of consecutive sentencing for any subsequent felony conviction.

(2) Probation for the current offense shall not be granted, nor shall execution or imposition of the sentence be suspended for any prior offense.

(3) The length of time between the prior felony conviction and the current felony conviction shall not affect the imposition of sentence.

(4) There shall not be a commitment to any other facility other than the state prison. Diversion shall not be granted nor shall the defendant be eligible for commitment to the California Rehabilitation Center as provided in Article 2 (commencing with Section 3050) of Chapter 1 of Division 3 of the Welfare and Institutions Code.

(5) The total amount of credits awarded pursuant to Article 2.5 (commencing with Section 2930) of Chapter 7 of Title 1 of Part 3 shall not exceed one-fifth of the total term of imprisonment imposed and shall not accrue until the defendant is physically placed in the state prison.

(6) If there is a current conviction for more than one felony count not committed on the same occasion, and not arising from the same set of operative facts, the court shall sentence the defendant consecutively on each count pursuant to subdivision (e).

(7) If there is a current conviction for more than one serious or violent felony as described in paragraph (6), the court shall

impose the sentence for each conviction consecutive to the sentence for any other conviction for which the defendant may be consecutively sentenced in the manner prescribed by law.

(8) Any sentence imposed pursuant to subdivision (e) will be imposed consecutive to any other sentence which the defendant is already serving, unless otherwise provided by law.

(d) Notwithstanding any other law and for the purposes of subdivisions (b) to (i), inclusive, a prior conviction of a felony shall be defined as:

(1) Any offense defined in subdivision (c) of Section 667.5 as a violent felony or any offense defined in subdivision (c) of Section 1192.7 as a serious felony in this state. The determination of whether a prior conviction is a prior felony conviction for purposes of subdivisions (b) to (i), inclusive, shall be made upon the date of that prior conviction and is not affected by the sentence imposed unless the sentence automatically, upon the initial sentencing, converts the felony to a misdemeanor. None of the following dispositions shall affect the determination that a prior conviction is a prior felony for purposes of subdivisions (b) to (i), inclusive:

(A) The suspension of imposition of judgment or sentence.

(B) The stay of execution of sentence.

(C) The commitment to the State Department of Health Services as a mentally disordered sex offender following a conviction of a felony.

(D) The commitment to the California Rehabilitation Center or any other facility whose function is rehabilitative diversion from the state prison.

(2) A conviction in another jurisdiction for an offense that, if committed in California, is punishable by imprisonment in the state prison. A prior conviction of a particular felony shall include a conviction in another jurisdiction for an offense that includes all of the elements of the particular felony as defined in subdivision (c) of Section 667.5 or subdivision (c) of Section 1192.7.

(3) A prior juvenile adjudication shall constitute a prior felony conviction for purposes of sentence enhancement if:

(A) The juvenile was 16 years of age or older at the time he or she committed the prior offense.

(B) The prior offense is listed in subdivision (b) of Section 707 of the Welfare and Institutions Code or described in paragraph (1) or (2) as a felony.

(C) The juvenile was found to be a fit and proper subject to be dealt with under the juvenile court law.

(D) The juvenile was adjudged a ward of the juvenile court within the meaning of Section 602 of the Welfare and Institutions Code because the person committed an offense listed in subdivision (b) of Section 707 of the Welfare and Institutions Code.

(e) For purposes of subdivisions (b) to (i), inclusive, and in addition to any other enhancement or punishment provisions which may apply, the following shall apply where a defendant has a prior felony conviction:

(1) If a defendant has one prior felony conviction that has been pled and proved, the determinate term or minimum term for an indeterminate term shall be twice the term otherwise provided as punishment for the current felony conviction.

(2)(A) If a defendant has two or more prior felony convictions as defined in subdivision (d) that have been pled and proved, the term for the current felony conviction shall be an indeterminate term of life imprisonment with a minimum term of the indeterminate sentence calculated as the greater of:

(i) Three times the term otherwise provided as punishment for each current felony conviction subsequent to the two or more prior felony convictions.

(ii) Imprisonment in the state prison for 25 years.

(iii) The term determined by the court pursuant to Section 1170 for the underlying conviction, including any enhancement applicable under Chapter 4.5 (commencing with Section 1170) of Title 7 of Part 2, or any period prescribed by Section 190 or 3046.

(B) The indeterminate term described in subparagraph (A) shall be served consecutive to any other term of imprisonment for which a consecutive term may be imposed by law. Any other term imposed subsequent to any indeterminate term described in subparagraph (A) shall not be merged therein but shall commence at the time the person would otherwise have been released from prison.

(f)(1) Notwithstanding any other law, subdivisions (b) to (i), inclusive, shall be applied in every case in which a defendant has a prior felony conviction as defined in subdivision (d). The prosecuting attorney shall plead and prove each prior felony conviction except as provided in paragraph (2).

(2) The prosecuting attorney may move to dismiss or strike a prior felony conviction allegation in the furtherance of justice pursuant to Section 1385, or if there is insufficient evidence to prove the prior conviction. If upon the satisfaction of the court that there is insufficient evidence to prove the prior felony conviction, the court may dismiss or strike the allegation.

(g) Prior felony convictions shall not be used in plea bargaining as defined in subdivision (b) of Section 1192.7. The prosecution shall plead and prove all known prior felony convictions and shall not enter into any agreement to strike or seek the dismissal of any prior felony conviction allegation except as provided in paragraph (2) of subdivision (f).

(h) All references to existing statutes in subdivisions (c) to (g), inclusive, are to statutes as they existed on June 30, 1993.

(i) If any provision of subdivisions (b) to (h), inclusive, or the application thereof to any person or circumstance is held invalid, that invalidity shall not affect other provisions or applications of those subdivisions which can be given effect without the invalid provision or application, and to this end the provisions of those subdivisions are severable.

(j) The provisions of this section shall not be amended by the Legislature except by statute passed in each house by rollcall vote entered in the journal, two-thirds of the membership concurring, or by a statute that becomes effective only when approved by the electors.

Penal Code § 667.1.

Notwithstanding subdivision (h) of Section 667, for all offenses committed on or after the effective date of this act, all references to existing statutes in subdivisions (c) to (g), inclusive, of Section 667, are to those statutes as they existed on the effective date of this act, including amendments made to those statutes by the act enacted during the 2005-06 Regular Session that amended this section.

Penal Code § 667.5.

Enhancement of prison terms for new offenses because of prior prison terms shall be imposed as follows:

(a) Where one of the new offenses is one of the violent felonies specified in subdivision (c), in addition to and consecutive to any other prison terms therefor, the court shall impose a three-year term for each prior separate prison term served by the defendant where the prior offense was one of the violent felonies specified in subdivision (c). However, no additional term shall be imposed under this subdivision for any prison term served prior to a period of 10 years in which the defendant remained free of both prison custody and the commission of an offense which results in a felony conviction.

(b) Except where subdivision (a) applies, where the new offense is any felony for which a prison sentence is imposed, in addition and consecutive to any other prison terms therefor, the court shall impose a one-year term for each prior separate prison term served for any felony; provided that no additional term shall be imposed under this subdivision for any prison term served prior to a period of five years in which the defendant remained free of both prison custody and the commission of an offense which results in a felony conviction.

(c) For the purpose of this section, "violent felony" shall mean any of the following:

(1) Murder or voluntary manslaughter.

(2) Mayhem.

(3) Rape as defined in paragraph (2) or (6) of subdivision (a) of Section 261 or paragraph (1) or (4) of subdivision (a) of Section 262.

(4) Sodomy as defined in subdivision (c) or (d) of Section 286.

(5) Oral copulation as defined in subdivision (c) or (d) of Section 288a.

(6) Lewd or lascivious act as defined in subdivision (a) or (b) of Section 288.

(7) Any felony punishable by death or imprisonment in the state prison for life.

(8) Any felony in which the defendant inflicts great bodily injury on any person other than an accomplice which has been charged and proved as provided for in Section 12022.7, 12022.8, or 12022.9 on or after July 1, 1977, or as specified prior to July 1, 1977, in Sections 213, 264, and 461, or any felony in which the defendant uses a firearm which use has been charged and proved as provided in subdivision (a) of Section 12022.3, or Section 12022.5 or 12022.55.

(9) Any robbery.

(10) Arson, in violation of subdivision (a) or (b) of Section 451.

(11) Sexual penetration as defined in subdivision (a) or (j) of Section 289.

(12) Attempted murder.

(13) A violation of Section 12308, 12309, or 12310.

(14) Kidnapping.

(15) Assault with the intent to commit a specified felony, in violation of Section 220.

(16) Continuous sexual abuse of a child, in violation of Section 288.5.

(17) Carjacking, as defined in subdivision (a) of Section 215.

(18) Rape, spousal rape, or sexual penetration, in concert, in violation of Section 264.1.

(19) Extortion, as defined in Section 518, which would constitute a felony violation of Section 186.22 of the Penal Code

(20) Threats to victims or witnesses, as defined in Section 136.1, which would constitute a felony violation of Section 186.22 of the Penal Code.

(21) Any burglary of the first degree, as defined in subdivision (a) of Section 460, wherein it is charged and proved that another person, other than an accomplice, was present in the residence during the commission of the burglary.

(22) Any violation of Section 12022.53.

(23) A violation of subdivision (b) or (c) of Section 11418. The Legislature finds and declares that these specified crimes merit special consideration when imposing a sentence to display society's condemnation for these extraordinary crimes of violence against the person.

(d) For the purposes of this section, the defendant shall be deemed to remain in prison custody for an offense until the official discharge from custody or until release on parole, whichever first occurs, including any time during which the defendant remains subject to reimprisonment for escape from custody or is reimprisoned on revocation of parole. The additional penalties provided for prior prison terms shall not be imposed unless they are charged and admitted or found true in the action for the new offense.

(e) The additional penalties provided for prior prison terms shall not be imposed for any felony for which the defendant did not serve a prior separate term in state prison.

(f) A prior conviction of a felony shall include a conviction in another jurisdiction for an offense which, if committed in California, is punishable by imprisonment in the state prison if the defendant served one year or more in prison for the offense in the other jurisdiction. A prior conviction of a particular felony shall include a conviction in another jurisdiction for an offense which includes all of the elements of the particular felony as defined under California law if the defendant served one year or more in prison for the offense in the other jurisdiction.

(g) A prior separate prison term for the purposes of this section shall mean a continuous completed period of prison incarceration imposed for the particular offense alone or in combination with concurrent or consecutive sentences for other crimes, including any reimprisonment on revocation of parole which is not accompanied by a new commitment to prison, and including any reimprisonment after an escape from incarceration.

(h) Serving a prison term includes any confinement time in any state prison or federal penal institution as punishment for commission of an offense, including confinement in a hospital or other institution or facility credited as service of prison time in the jurisdiction of the confinement.

(i) For the purposes of this section, a commitment to the State Department of Mental Health as a mentally disordered sex offender following a conviction of a felony, which commitment exceeds one year in duration, shall be deemed a prior prison term.

(j) For the purposes of this section, when a person subject to the custody, control, and discipline of the Director of Corrections is incarcerated at a facility operated by the Department of the Youth Authority, that incarceration shall be deemed to be a term served in state prison.

(k) Notwithstanding subdivisions (d) and (g) or any other provision of law, where one of the new offenses is committed while the defendant is temporarily removed from prison pursuant to Section 2690 or while the defendant is transferred to a community facility pursuant to Section 3416, 6253, or 6263, or while the defendant is on furlough pursuant to Section 6254, the defendant shall be subject to the full enhancements provided for in this section. This subdivision shall not apply when a full, separate, and consecutive term is imposed pursuant to any other provision of law.

Penal Code § 667.61.

(a) Any person who is convicted of an offense specified in subdivision (c) under one or more of the circumstances specified in subdivision (d) or under two or more of the circumstances specified in subdivision (e) shall be punished by imprisonment in the state prison for 25 years to life.

(b) Except as provided in subdivision (a), any person who is convicted of an offense specified in subdivision (c) under one of the circumstances specified in subdivision (e) shall be punished by imprisonment in the state prison for 15 years to life. (c) This section shall apply to any of the following offenses:

(1) Rape, in violation of paragraph (2) or (6) of subdivision (a) of Section 261.

(2) Spousal rape, in violation of paragraph (1) or (4) of subdivision (a) of Section 262.

(3) Rape, spousal rape, or sexual penetration, in concert, in violation of Section 264.1.

(4) Lewd or lascivious act, in violation of subdivision (b) of Section 288.

(5) Sexual penetration, in violation of subdivision (a) of Section 289.

(6) Sodomy, in violation of paragraph (2) or (3) of subdivision (c), or subdivision (d), of Section 286.

(7) Oral copulation, in violation of paragraph (2) or (3) of subdivision (c), or subdivision (d), of Section 288a.

(8) Lewd or lascivious act, in violation of subdivision (a) of Section 288.

(9) Continuous sexual abuse of a child, in violation of Section 288.5.

(d) The following circumstances shall apply to the offenses specified in subdivision (c):

(1) The defendant has been previously convicted of an offense specified in subdivision (c), including an offense committed in another jurisdiction that includes all of the elements of an offense specified in subdivision (c).

(2) The defendant kidnapped the victim of the present offense and the movement of the victim substantially increased the risk of harm to the victim over and above that level of risk necessarily inherent in the underlying offense in subdivision (c).

(3) The defendant inflicted aggravated mayhem or torture on the victim or another person in the commission of the present offense in violation of Section 205 or 206.

(4) The defendant committed the present offense during the commission of a burglary of the first degree, as defined in subdivision (a) of Section 460, with intent to commit an offense specified in subdivision (c).

(5) The defendant committed the present offense in violation of Section 264.1, subdivision (d) of Section 286, or subdivision (d) of Section 288a, and, in the commission of that offense, any person committed any act described in paragraph (2), (3), or (4) of this subdivision.

(e) The following circumstances shall apply to the offenses specified in subdivision (c):

(1) Except as provided in paragraph (2) of subdivision (d), the defendant kidnapped the victim of the present offense in violation of Section 207, 209, or 209.5.

(2) Except as provided in paragraph (4) of subdivision (d), the defendant committed the present offense during the commission of a burglary in violation of Section 459.

(3) The defendant personally inflicted great bodily injury on the victim or another person in the commission of the present offense in violation of Section 12022.53, 12022.7, or 12022.8.

(4) The defendant personally used a dangerous or deadly weapon or a firearm in the commission of the present offense in violation of Section 12022, 12022.3, 12022.5, or 12022.53.

(5) The defendant has been convicted in the present case or cases of committing an offense specified in subdivision (c) against more than one victim.

(6) The defendant engaged in the tying or binding of the victim or another person in the commission of the present offense.

(7) The defendant administered a controlled substance to the victim in the commission of the present offense in violation of Section 12022.75.

(8) The defendant committed the present offense in violation of Section 264.1, subdivision (d) of Section 286, or subdivision (d) of Section 288a, and, in the commission of that offense, any person committed any act described in paragraph (1), (2), (3), (4), (6), or (7) of this subdivision.

(f) If only the minimum number of circumstances specified in subdivision (d) or (e) that are required for the punishment provided in subdivision (a) or (b) to apply have been pled and proved, that circumstance or those circumstances shall be used as the basis for imposing the term provided in subdivision (a) or (b), whichever is greater, rather than being used to impose the punishment authorized under any other provision of law, unless another provision of law provides for a greater penalty or the punishment under another provision of law can be imposed in addition to the punishment provided by this section. However, if any additional circumstance or circumstances specified in subdivision (d) or (e) have been pled and proved, the minimum number of circumstances shall be used as the basis for imposing the term provided in subdivision (a), and any other additional circumstance or circumstances shall be used to impose any punishment or enhancement authorized under any other provision of law.

(g) Notwithstanding Section 1385 or any other provision of law, the court shall not strike any allegation, admission, or finding of any of the circumstances specified in subdivision (d) or (e) for any person who is subject to punishment under this section.

(h) Notwithstanding any other provision of law, probation shall not be granted to, nor shall the execution or imposition of sentence be suspended for, any person who is subject to punishment under this section.

(i) For any offense specified in paragraphs (1) to (7), inclusive, of subdivision (c), the court shall impose a consecutive sentence for each offense that results in a conviction under this section if the crimes involve separate victims or involve the same victim on separate occasions as defined in subdivision (d) of Section 667.6.

(j) The penalties provided in this section shall apply only if the existence of any circumstance specified in subdivision (d) or

(e) is alleged in the accusatory pleading pursuant to this section, and is either admitted by the defendant in open court or found to be true by the trier of fact.

Penal Code § 667.7.

(a) Any person convicted of a felony in which the person inflicted great bodily injury as provided in Section 12022.53 or 12022.7, or personally used force which was likely to produce great bodily injury, who has served two or more prior separate prison terms as defined in Section 667.5 for the crime of murder; attempted murder; voluntary manslaughter; mayhem; rape by force, violence, or fear of immediate and unlawful bodily injury on the victim or another person; oral copulation by force, violence, duress, menace, or fear of immediate and unlawful bodily injury on the victim or another person; sodomy by force, violence, duress, menace, or fear of immediate and unlawful bodily injury on the victim or another person; lewd acts on a child under the age of 14 years by use of force, violence, duress, menace, or fear of immediate and unlawful bodily injury on the victim or another person; a violation of subdivision (a) of Section 289 where the act is accomplished against the victim's will by means of force, violence, duress, menace, or fear of immediate and unlawful bodily injury on the victim or another person; kidnapping as punished in former subdivision (d) of Section 208, or for ransom, extortion, or robbery; robbery involving the use of force or a deadly weapon; carjacking involving the use of a deadly weapon; assault with intent to commit murder; assault with a deadly weapon; assault with a force likely to produce great bodily injury; assault with intent to commit rape, sodomy, oral copulation, sexual penetration in violation of Section 289, or lewd and lascivious acts on a child; arson of a structure; escape or attempted escape by an inmate with force or violence in violation of subdivision (a) of Section 4530, or of Section 4532; exploding a destructive device with intent to murder in violation of Section 12308; exploding a destructive device which causes bodily injury in violation of Section 12309, or mayhem or great bodily injury in violation of Section 12310; exploding a destructive device with intent to injure, intimidate, or terrify, in violation of Section 12303.3; any felony in which the person inflicted great bodily injury as provided in Section 12022.53 or 12022.7; or any felony punishable by death or life imprisonment with or without the possibility of parole is a habitual offender and shall be punished as follows:

(1) A person who served two prior separate prison terms shall be punished by imprisonment in the state prison for life and shall not be eligible for release on parole for 20 years, or the term determined by the court pursuant to Section 1170 for the underlying conviction, including any enhancement applicable under Chapter 4.5 (commencing with Section 1170) of Title 7 of Part 2, or any period prescribed by Section 190 or 3046, whichever is greatest. Article 2.5 (commencing with Section 2930) of Chapter 7 of Title 1 of Part 3 shall apply to reduce any minimum term in a state prison imposed pursuant to this section, but the person shall not otherwise be released on parole prior to that time.

(2) Any person convicted of a felony specified in this subdivision who has served three or more prior separate prison terms, as defined in Section 667.5, for the crimes specified in subdivision (a) of this section shall be punished by imprisonment in the state prison for life without the possibility of parole.

(b) This section shall not prevent the imposition of the punishment of death or imprisonment for life without the possibility of parole. No prior prison term shall be used for this determination which was served prior to a period of 10 years in which the person remained free of both prison custody and the commission of an offense which results in a felony conviction. As used in this section, a commitment to the Department of the Youth Authority after conviction for a felony shall constitute a prior prison term. The term imposed under this section shall be imposed only if the prior prison terms are alleged under this section in the accusatory pleading, and either admitted by the defendant in open court, or found to be true by the jury trying the issue of guilt or by the court where guilt is established by a plea of guilty or nolo contendere or by a trial by the court sitting without a jury.

Penal Code § 692.

Lawful resistance to the commission of a public offense may be made:

1. By the party about to be injured;
2. By other parties.

Penal Code § 693.

Resistance sufficient to prevent the offense may be made by the party about to be injured:

1. To prevent an offense against his person, or his family, or some member thereof.
2. To prevent an illegal attempt by force to take or injure property in his lawful possession.

Penal Code § 694.

Any other person, in aid or defense of the person about to be injured, may make resistance sufficient to prevent the offense.

Penal Code § 813.

(a) When a complaint is filed with a magistrate charging a felony originally triable in the superior court of the county in which he or she sits, if, and only if, the magistrate is satisfied from the complaint that the offense complained of has been committed and that there is reasonable ground to believe that the defendant has committed it, the magistrate shall issue a warrant for the arrest of the defendant, except that, upon the request of the prosecutor, a summons instead of an arrest warrant shall be issued.

(b) A summons issued pursuant to this section shall be in substantially the same form as an arrest warrant and shall contain all of the following:

(1) The name of the defendant.

(2) The date and time the summons was issued.

(3) The city or county where the summons was issued.

(4) The signature of the magistrate, judge, justice, or other issuing authority who is issuing the summons with the title of his or her office and the name of the court or other issuing agency.

(5) The offense or offenses with which the defendant is charged.

(6) The time and place at which the defendant is to appear.

(7) Notification that the defendant is to complete the booking process on or before his or her first court appearance, as well as instructions for the defendant on completing the booking process.

(8) A provision for certification by the booking agency that the defendant has completed the booking process which shall be presented to the court by the defendant as proof of booking.

(c) If a defendant has been properly served with a summons and thereafter fails to appear at the designated time and place, a bench warrant for arrest shall issue. In the absence of proof of actual receipt of the summons by the defendant, a failure to appear shall not be used in any future proceeding.

(d) A defendant who responds to a summons issued pursuant to this section and who has not been booked as provided in subdivision (b) shall be ordered by the court to complete the booking process.

(e) The prosecutor shall not request the issuance of a summons in lieu of an arrest warrant as provided in this section under any of the following circumstances:

(1) The offense charged involves violence.

(2) The offense charged involves a firearm.

(3) The offense charged involves resisting arrest.

(4) There are one or more outstanding arrest warrants for the person.

(5) The prosecution of the offense or offenses with which the person is charged, or the prosecution of any other offense or offenses would be jeopardized.

(6) There is a reasonable likelihood that the offense or offenses would continue or resume, or that the safety of persons or property would be imminently endangered.

(7) There is reason to believe that the person would not appear at the time and place specified in the summons.

Penal Code § 827.

When a complaint is filed with a magistrate of the commission of a felony originally triable in the superior court of another county of the state than that in which the magistrate sits, but showing that the defendant is in the county where the complaint is filed, the same proceedings must be had as prescribed in this chapter, except that the warrant must require the defendant to be taken before the nearest or most accessible magistrate of the county in which the offense is triable, and the complaint must be delivered by the magistrate to the officer to whom the warrant is delivered.

Penal Code § 827.1.

A person who is specified or designated in a warrant of arrest for a misdemeanor offense may be released upon the issuance of a citation, in lieu of physical arrest, unless one of the following conditions exists:

(a) The misdemeanor cited in the warrant involves violence.

(b) The misdemeanor cited in the warrant involves a firearm.

(c) The misdemeanor cited in the warrant involves resisting arrest.

(d) The misdemeanor cited in the warrant involves giving false information to a peace officer.

(e) The person arrested is a danger to himself or herself or others due to intoxication or being under the influence of drugs or narcotics.

(f) The person requires medical examination or medical care or was otherwise unable to care for his or her own safety.

(g) The person has other ineligible charges pending against him or her.

(h) There is reasonable likelihood that the offense or offenses would continue or resume, or that the safety of persons or property would be immediately endangered by the release of the person.

(i) The person refuses to sign the notice to appear.

(j) The person cannot provide satisfactory evidence of personal identification.

(k) The warrant of arrest indicates that the person is not eligible to be released on a citation. The issuance of a citation under this section shall be undertaken in the manner set forth in Sections 853.6 to 853.8, inclusive.

Penal Code § 830.

Any person who comes within the provisions of this chapter and who otherwise meets all standards imposed by law on a peace officer is a peace officer, and notwithstanding any other provision of law, no person other than those designated in this chapter is a peace officer. The restriction of peace officer functions of any public officer or employee shall not affect his or her status for purposes of retirement.

Penal Code § 830.1.

(a) Any sheriff, undersheriff, or deputy sheriff, employed in that capacity, of a county, any chief of police of a city or chief, director, or chief executive officer of a consolidated municipal public safety agency that performs police functions, any police officer, employed in that capacity and appointed by the chief of police or chief, director, or chief executive of a public safety agency, of a city, any chief of police, or police officer of a district, including police officers of the San Diego Unified Port District Harbor Police, authorized by statute to maintain a police department, any marshal or deputy marshal of a superior court or county, any port warden or port police officer of the Harbor Department of the City of Los Angeles, or any inspector or investigator employed in that capacity in the office of a district attorney, is a peace officer. The authority of these peace officers extends to any place in the state, as follows:

(1) As to any public offense committed or which there is probable cause to believe has been committed within the political subdivision that employs the peace officer or in which the peace officer serves.

(2) Where the peace officer has the prior consent of the chief of police or chief, director, or chief executive officer of a consolidated municipal public safety agency, or person authorized by him or her to give consent, if the place is within a city, or of the sheriff, or person authorized by him or her to give consent, if the place is within a county.

(3) As to any public offense committed or which there is probable cause to believe has been committed in the peace officer's

presence, and with respect to which there is immediate danger to person or property, or of the escape of the perpetrator of the offense.

(b) The Attorney General and special agents and investigators of the Department of Justice are peace officers, and those assistant chiefs, deputy chiefs, chiefs, deputy directors, and division directors designated as peace officers by the Attorney General are peace officers. The authority of these peace officers extends to any place in the state where a public offense has been committed or where there is probable cause to believe one has been committed.

(c) Any deputy sheriff of the County of Los Angeles, and any deputy sheriff of the Counties of Butte, Calaveras, Glenn, Humboldt, Imperial, Inyo, Kern, Kings, Lake, Lassen, Mariposa, Mendocino, Plumas, Riverside, San Benito, San Diego, Santa Barbara, Shasta, Siskiyou, Solano, Sonoma, Stanislaus, Sutter, Tehama, Tulare, and Tuolumne who is employed to perform duties exclusively or initially relating to custodial assignments with responsibilities for maintaining the operations of county custodial facilities, including the custody, care, supervision, security, movement, and transportation of inmates, is a peace officer whose authority extends to any place in the state only while engaged in the performance of the duties of his or her respective employment and for the purpose of carrying out the primary function of employment relating to his or her custodial assignments, or when performing other law enforcement duties directed by his or her employing agency during a local state of emergency.

Penal Code § 830.2.

The following persons are peace officers whose authority extends to any place in the state:

(a) Any member of the Department of the California Highway Patrol including those members designated under subdivision (a) of Section 2250.1 of the Vehicle Code, provided that the primary duty of the peace officer is the enforcement of any law relating to the use or operation of vehicles upon the highways, or laws pertaining to the provision of police services for the protection of state officers, state properties, and the occupants of state properties, or both, as set forth in the Vehicle Code and Government Code.

(b) A member of the University of California Police Department appointed pursuant to Section 92600 of the Education Code, provided that the primary duty of the peace officer shall be the enforcement of the law within the area specified in Section 92600 of the Education Code.

(c) A member of the California State University Police departments appointed pursuant to Section 89560 of the Education Code, provided that the primary duty of the peace officer shall be the enforcement of the law within the area specified in Section 89560 of the Education Code.

(d)(1) Any member of the Office of Correctional Safety of the Department of Corrections and Rehabilitation, provided that the primary duties of the peace officer shall be the investigation or apprehension of inmates, wards, parolees, parole violators, or escapees from state institutions, the transportation of those persons, the investigation of any violation of criminal law discovered while performing the usual and authorized duties of employment, and the coordination of those activities with other criminal justice agencies.

(2) Any member of the Office of Internal Affairs of the Department of Corrections and Rehabilitation, provided that the primary duties shall be criminal investigations of Department of Corrections and Rehabilitation personnel and the coordination of those activities with other criminal justice agencies. For purposes of this subdivision, the member of the Office of Internal Affairs shall possess certification from the Commission on Peace Officer Standards and Training for investigators, or have completed training pursuant to Section 6126.1 of the Penal Code.

(e) Employees of the Department of Fish and Game designated by the director, provided that the primary duty of those peace officers shall be the enforcement of the law as set forth in Section 856 of the Fish and Game Code.

(f) Employees of the Department of Parks and Recreation designated by the director pursuant to Section 5008 of the Public Resources Code, provided that the primary duty of the peace officer shall be the enforcement of the law as set forth in Section 5008 of the Public Resources Code.

(g) The Director of Forestry and Fire Protection and employees or classes of employees of the Department of Forestry and Fire Protection designated by the director pursuant to Section 4156 of the Public Resources Code, provided that the primary duty of the peace officer shall be the enforcement of the law as that duty is set forth in Section 4156 of the Public Resources Code.

(h) Persons employed by the Department of Alcoholic Beverage Control for the enforcement of Division 9 (commencing with Section 23000) of the Business and Professions Code and designated by the Director of Alcoholic Beverage Control, provided that the primary duty of any of these peace officers shall be the enforcement of the laws relating to alcoholic beverages, as that duty is set forth in Section 25755 of the Business and Professions Code.

(i) Marshals and police appointed by the Board of Directors of the California Exposition and State Fair pursuant to Section 3332 of the Food and Agricultural Code, provided that the primary duty of the peace officers shall be the enforcement of the law as prescribed in that section.

(j) The Inspector General, pursuant to Section 6125, and the Chief Deputy Inspector General In Charge, the Senior Deputy Inspector General, the Deputy Inspector General, and those employees of the Inspector General as designated by the Inspector General, are peace officers, provided that the primary duty of these peace officers shall be conducting audits of investigatory practices and other audits, as well as conducting investigations, of the Department of Corrections and Rehabilitation, Division of Juvenile Justice and the Board of Parole Hearings.

Penal Code § 830.3.

The following persons are peace officers whose authority extends to any place in the state for the purpose of performing their primary duty or when making an arrest pursuant to Section 836 of the Penal Code as to any public offense with respect to which there is immediate danger to person or property, or of the escape of the perpetrator of that offense, or pursuant to Section 8597 or 8598 of the Government Code. These peace officers may carry firearms only if authorized and under those terms and conditions as specified by their employing agencies:

(a) Persons employed by the Division of Investigation of the Department of Consumer Affairs and investigators of the Medical Board of California and the Board of Dental Examiners, who are designated by the Director of Consumer Affairs, provided that the primary duty of these peace officers shall be the enforcement of the law as that duty is set forth in Section 160 of the Business and Professions Code.

(b) Voluntary fire wardens designated by the Director of Forestry and Fire Protection pursuant to Section 4156 of the Public Resources Code, provided that the primary duty of these peace officers shall be the enforcement of the law as that duty is set forth in Section 4156 of that code.

(c) Employees of the Department of Motor Vehicles designated in Section 1655 of the Vehicle Code, provided that the primary duty of these peace officers shall be the enforcement of the law as that duty is set forth in Section 1655 of that code.

(d) Investigators of the California Horse Racing Board designated by the board, provided that the primary duty of these peace officers shall be the enforcement of Chapter 4 (commencing with Section 19400) of Division 8 of the Business and Professions Code and Chapter 10 (commencing with Section 330) of Title 9 of Part 1 of this code.

(e) The State Fire Marshal and assistant or deputy state fire marshals appointed pursuant to Section 13103 of the Health and Safety Code, provided that the primary duty of these peace officers shall be the enforcement of the law as that duty is set forth in Section 13104 of that code.

(f) Inspectors of the food and drug section designated by the chief pursuant to subdivision (a) of Section 106500 of the Health and Safety Code, provided that the primary duty of these peace officers shall be the enforcement of the law as that duty is set forth in Section 106500 of that code.

(g) All investigators of the Division of Labor Standards Enforcement designated by the Labor Commissioner, provided that the primary duty of these peace officers shall be the enforcement of the law as prescribed in Section 95 of the Labor Code.

(h) All investigators of the State Departments of Health Care Services, Public Health, Social Services, Mental Health, and Alcohol and Drug Programs, the Department of Toxic Substances Control, the Office of Statewide Health Planning and Development, and the Public Employees' Retirement System, provided that the primary duty of these peace officers shall be the enforcement of the law relating to the duties of his or her department or office. Notwithstanding any other provision of law, investigators of the Public Employees' Retirement System shall not carry firearms.

(i) The Chief of the Bureau of Fraudulent Claims of the Department of Insurance and those investigators designated by the chief, provided that the primary duty of those investigators shall be the enforcement of Section 550.

(j) Employees of the Department of Housing and Community Development designated under Section 18023 of the Health and Safety Code, provided that the primary duty of these peace officers shall be the enforcement of the law as that duty is set forth in Section 18023 of that code.

(k) Investigators of the office of the Controller, provided that the primary duty of these investigators shall be the enforcement of the law relating to the duties of that office. Notwithstanding any other law, except as authorized by the Controller, the peace officers designated pursuant to this subdivision shall not carry firearms.

(l) Investigators of the Department of Corporations designated by the Commissioner of Corporations, provided that the primary duty of these investigators shall be the enforcement of the provisions of law administered by the Department of Corporations. Notwithstanding any other provision of law, the peace officers designated pursuant to this subdivision shall not carry firearms.

(m) Persons employed by the Contractors' State License Board designated by the Director of Consumer Affairs pursuant to Section 7011.5 of the Business and Professions Code, provided that the primary duty of these persons shall be the enforcement of the law as that duty is set forth in Section 7011.5, and in Chapter 9 (commencing with Section 7000) of Division 3, of that code. The Director of Consumer Affairs may designate as peace officers not more than three persons who shall at the time of their designation be assigned to the special investigations unit of the board. Notwithstanding any other provision of law, the persons designated pursuant to this subdivision shall not carry firearms.

(n) The Chief and coordinators of the Law Enforcement Division of the Office of Emergency Services.

(o) Investigators of the office of the Secretary of State designated by the Secretary of State, provided that the primary duty of these peace officers shall be the enforcement of the law as prescribed in Chapter 3 (commencing with Section 8200) of Division 1 of Title 2 of, and Section 12172.5 of, the Government Code. Notwithstanding any other provision of law, the peace officers designated pursuant to this subdivision shall not carry firearms.

(p) The Deputy Director for Security designated by Section 8880.38 of the Government Code, and all lottery security personnel assigned to the California State Lottery and designated by the director, provided that the primary duty of any of those peace officers shall be the enforcement of the laws related to assuring the integrity, honesty, and fairness of the operation and administration of the California State Lottery.

(q) Investigators employed by the Investigation Division of the Employment Development Department designated by the director of the department, provided that the primary duty of those peace officers shall be the enforcement of the law as that duty is set forth in Section 317 of the Unemployment Insurance Code. Notwithstanding any other provision of law, the peace officers designated pursuant to this subdivision shall not carry firearms.

(r) The chief and assistant chief of museum security and safety of the California Science Center, as designated by the executive director pursuant to Section 4108 of the Food and Agricultural Code, provided that the primary duty of those peace officers shall be the enforcement of the law as that duty is set forth in Section 4108 of the Food and Agricultural Code.

(s) Employees of the Franchise Tax Board designated by the board, provided that the primary duty of these peace officers shall be the enforcement of the law as set forth in Chapter 9 (commencing with Section 19701) of Part 10.2 of Division 2 of the Revenue and Taxation Code.

(t) Notwithstanding any other provision of this section, a peace officer authorized by this section shall not be authorized to carry firearms by his or her employing agency until that agency has adopted a policy on the use of deadly force by those peace officers, and until those peace officers have been instructed in the employing agency's policy on the use of deadly force. Every peace officer authorized pursuant to this section to carry firearms by his or her employing agency shall qualify in the use of the firearms at least every six months.

(u) Investigators of the Department of Managed Health Care designated by the Director of the Department of Managed Health Care, provided that the primary duty of these investigators shall be the enforcement of the provisions of laws administered by the Director of the Department of Managed Health Care. Notwithstanding any other provision of law, the peace officers designated pursuant to this subdivision shall not carry firearms.

(v) The Chief, Deputy Chief, supervising investigators, and investigators of the Office of Protective Services of the State Department of Developmental Services, provided that the primary duty of each of those persons shall be the enforcement of the law relating to the duties of his or her department or office.

Penal Code § 830.31.

The following persons are peace officers whose authority extends to any place in the state for the purpose of performing their primary duty or when making an arrest pursuant to Section 836 as to any public offense with respect to which there is immediate danger to person or property, or of the escape of the perpetrator of that offense, or pursuant to Section 8597 or 8598 of the Government Code. These peace officers may carry firearms only if authorized, and under the terms and conditions specified, by their employing agency.

(a) A police officer of the County of Los Angeles, if the primary duty of the officer is the enforcement of the law in or about properties owned, operated, or administered by his or her employing agency or when performing necessary duties with respect to patrons, employees, and properties of his or her employing agency.

(b) A person designated by a local agency as a park ranger and regularly employed and paid in that capacity, if the primary duty of the officer is the protection of park and other property of the agency and the preservation of the peace therein.

(c)(1) A peace officer of the Department of General Services of the City of Los Angeles designated by the general manager of the department, if the primary duty of the officer is the enforcement of the law in or about properties owned, operated, or administered by his or her employing agency or when performing necessary duties with respect to patrons, employees, and properties of his or her employing agency.

(2) A peace officer designated pursuant to this subdivision, and authorized to carry firearms by his or her employing agency, shall satisfactorily complete the introductory course of firearm training required by Section 832 and shall requalify in the use of firearms every six months.

(3) Notwithstanding any other provision of law, a peace officer designated pursuant to this subdivision who is authorized to carry a firearm by his or her employing agency while on duty shall not be authorized to carry a firearm when he or she is not on duty.

(d) A housing authority patrol officer employed by the housing authority of a city, district, county, or city and county or employed by the police department of a city and county, if the primary duty of the officer is the enforcement of the law in or about properties owned, operated, or administered by his or her employing agency or when performing necessary duties with respect to patrons, employees, and properties of his or her employing agency.

Penal Code § 830.32.

The following persons are peace officers whose authority extends to any place in the state for the purpose of performing their primary duty or when making an arrest pursuant to Section 836 as to any public offense with respect to which there is immediate danger to person or property, or of the escape of the perpetrator of that offense, or pursuant to Section 8597 or 8598 of the Government Code. Those peace officers may carry firearms only if authorized and under terms and conditions specified by their employing agency.

(a) Members of a California Community College police department appointed pursuant to Section 72330 of the Education Code, if the primary duty of the police officer is the enforcement of the law as prescribed in Section 72330 of the Education Code.

(b) Persons employed as members of a police department of a school district pursuant to Section 38000 of the Education Code, if the primary duty of the police officer is the enforcement of the law as prescribed in Section 38000 of the Education Code.

(c) Any peace officer employed by a K-12 public school district or California Community College district who has completed training as prescribed by subdivision (f) of Section 832.3 shall be designated a school police officer.

Penal Code § 830.33.

The following persons are peace officers whose authority extends to any place in the state for the purpose of performing their primary duty or when making an arrest pursuant to Section 836 as to any public offense with respect to which there is immediate danger to person or property, or of the escape of the perpetrator of that offense, or pursuant to Section 8597 or 8598 of the Government Code. Those peace officers may carry firearms only if authorized and under terms and conditions specified by their employing agency.

(a) A member of the San Francisco Bay Area Rapid Transit District Police Department appointed pursuant to Section 28767.5 of the Public Utilities Code, if the primary duty of the peace officer is the enforcement of the law in or about properties owned, operated, or administered by the district or when performing necessary duties with respect to patrons, employees, and properties of the district.

(b) Harbor or port police regularly employed and paid in that capacity by a county, city, or district other than peace officers authorized under Section 830.1, if the primary duty of the peace officer is the enforcement of the law in or about the properties owned, operated, or administered by the harbor or port or when performing necessary duties with respect to patrons, employees, and properties of the harbor or port.

(c) Transit police officers or peace officers of a county, city, transit development board, or district, if the primary duty of the peace officer is the enforcement of the law in or about properties owned, operated, or administered by the employing agency or when performing necessary duties with respect to patrons, employees, and properties of the employing agency.

(d) Any person regularly employed as an airport law enforcement officer by a city, county, or district operating the airport or by a joint powers agency, created pursuant to Article 1 (commencing with Section 6500) of Chapter 5 of Division 7 of Title 1 of the Government Code, operating the airport, if the primary duty of the peace officer is the enforcement of the law in or about properties owned, operated, and administered by the employing agency or when performing necessary duties with respect to patrons, employees, and properties of the employing agency.

(e)(1) Any railroad police officer commissioned by the Governor pursuant to Section 8226 of the Public Utilities Code, if the primary duty of the peace officer is the enforcement of the law in or about properties owned, operated, or administered by the employing agency or when performing necessary duties with respect to patrons, employees, and properties of the employing agency.

(2) Notwithstanding any other provision of law, a railroad police officer who has met the current requirements of the Commission on Peace Officer Standards and Training necessary for exercising the powers of a peace officer, and who has been commissioned by the Governor as described herein, and the officer's employing agency, may apply for access to information from the

California Law Enforcement Telecommunications System (CLETS) through a local law enforcement agency that has been granted direct access to CLETS, provided that, in addition to other review standards and conditions of eligibility applied by the Department of Justice, the CLETS Advisory Committee and the Attorney General, before access is granted the following are satisfied:

(A) The employing agency shall enter into a Release of CLETS Information agreement as provided for in the CLETS policies, practices, and procedures, and the required background check on the peace officer and other pertinent personnel has been completed, together with all required training.

(B) The Release of CLETS Information agreement shall be in substantially the same form as prescribed by the CLETS policies, practices, and procedures for public agencies of law enforcement who subscribe to CLETS services, and shall be subject to the provisions of Chapter 2.5 (commencing with Section 15150) of Title 2 of Division 3 of the Government Code and the CLETS policies, practices, and procedures.

(C)(i) The employing agency shall expressly waive any objections to jurisdiction in the courts of the State of California for any liability arising from use, abuse, or misuse of CLETS access or services or the information derived therefrom, or with respect to any legal actions to enforce provisions of California law relating to CLETS access, services, or information under this subdivision, and provided that this liability shall be in addition to that imposed by Public Utilities Code Section 8226.

(ii) The employing agency shall further agree to utilize CLETS access, services, or information only for law enforcement activities by peace officers who have met the current requirements of the Commission on Peace Officer Standards and Training necessary for exercising the powers of a peace officer, and who have been commissioned as described herein who are operating within the State of California, where the activities are directly related to investigations or arrests arising from conduct occurring within the State of California.

(iii) The employing agency shall further agree to pay to the Department of Justice and the providing local law enforcement agency all costs related to the provision of access or services, including, but not limited to, any and all hardware, interface modules, and costs for telephonic communications, as well as administrative costs.

Penal Code § 830.34.

The following persons are peace officers whose authority extends to any place in the state for the purpose of performing their primary duty or when making an arrest pursuant to Section 836 as to any public offense with respect to which there is immediate danger to person or property, or of the escape of the perpetrator of that offense, or pursuant to Section 8597 or 8598 of the Government Code. Those peace officers may carry firearms only if authorized and under terms and conditions specified by their employing agency.

(a) Persons designated as a security officer by a municipal utility district pursuant to Section 12820 of the Public Utilities Code, if the primary duty of the officer is the protection of the properties of the utility district and the protection of the persons thereon.

(b) Persons designated as a security officer by a county water district pursuant to Section 30547 of the Water Code, if the primary duty of the officer is the protection of the properties of the county water district and the protection of the persons thereon.

(c) The security director of the public utilities commission of a city and county, if the primary duty of the security director is the protection of the properties of the commission and the protection of the persons thereon. (d) Persons employed as a park ranger by a municipal water district pursuant to Section 71341.5 of the Water Code, if the primary duty of the park ranger is the protection of the properties of the municipal water district and the protection of the persons thereon.

Penal Code § 830.35.

The following persons are peace officers whose authority extends to any place in the state for the purpose of performing their primary duty or when making an arrest pursuant to Section 836 as to any public offense with respect to which there is immediate danger to person or property, or of the escape of the perpetrator of that offense, or pursuant to Section 8597 or 8598 of the Government Code. Those peace officers may carry firearms only if authorized and under terms and conditions specified by their employing agency.

(a) A welfare fraud investigator or inspector, regularly employed and paid in that capacity by a county, if the primary duty of the peace officer is the enforcement of the provisions of the Welfare and Institutions Code.

(b) A child support investigator or inspector, regularly employed and paid in that capacity by a district attorney's office, if the primary duty of the peace officer is the enforcement of the provisions of the Family Code and Section 270.

(c) The coroner and deputy coroners, regularly employed and paid in that capacity, of a county, if the primary duty of the peace officer are those duties set forth in Sections 27469 and 27491 to 27491.4, inclusive, of the Government Code.

Penal Code § 830.36.

The following persons are peace officers whose authority extends to any place in the state for the purpose of performing their primary duty or when making an arrest pursuant to Section 836 as to any public offense with respect to which there is immediate danger to person or property, or of the escape of the perpetrator of that offense, or pursuant to Section 8597 or 8598 of the Government Code. Those peace officers may carry firearms only if authorized and under terms and conditions specified by their employing agency.

(a) The Sergeant-at-Arms of each house of the Legislature, if the primary duty of the peace officer is the enforcement of the law in or about properties owned, operated, or administered by the employing agency or when performing necessary duties with respect to patrons, employees, and properties of the employing agency.

(b) Marshals of the Supreme Court and bailiffs of the courts of appeal, and coordinators of security for the judicial branch, if the primary duty of the peace officer is the enforcement of the law in or about properties owned, operated, or administered by the employing agency or when performing necessary duties with respect to patrons, employees, and properties of the employing agency.

(c) Court service officer in a county of the second class and third class, if the primary duty of the peace officer is the enforcement of the law in or about properties owned, operated, or administered by the employing agency or when performing necessary duties with respect to patrons, employees, and properties of the employing agency.

Penal Code § 830.37.

The following persons are peace officers whose authority extends to any place in the state for the purpose of performing their primary duty or when making an arrest pursuant to Section 836 as to any public offense with respect to which there is immediate danger to person or property, or of the escape of the perpetrator of that offense, or pursuant to Section 8597 or 8598 of the Government Code. These peace officers may carry firearms only if authorized and under terms and conditions specified by their employing agency:

(a) Members of an arson-investigating unit, regularly paid and employed in that capacity, of a fire department or fire protection agency of a county, city, city and county, district, or the state, if the primary duty of these peace officers is the detection and apprehension of persons who have violated any fire law or committed insurance fraud.

(b) Members other than members of an arson-investigating unit, regularly paid and employed in that capacity, of a fire department or fire protection agency of a county, city, city and county, district, or the state, if the primary duty of these peace officers, when acting in that capacity, is the enforcement of laws relating to fire prevention or fire suppression.

(c) Voluntary fire wardens as are designated by the Director of Forestry and Fire Protection pursuant to Section 4156 of the Public Resources Code, provided that the primary duty of these peace officers shall be the enforcement of the law as that duty is set forth in Section 4156 of the Public Resources Code.

(d) Firefighter/security guards by the Military Department, if the primary duty of the peace officer is the enforcement of the law in or about properties owned, operated, or administered by the employing agency or when performing necessary duties with respect to patrons, employees, and properties of the employing agency.

Penal Code § 830.38.

The officers of a state hospital under the jurisdiction of the State Department of Mental Health or the State Department of Developmental Services appointed pursuant to Section 4313 or 4493 of the Welfare and Institutions Code, are peace officers whose authority extends to any place in the state for the purpose of performing their primary duty or when making an arrest pursuant to Section 836 as to any public offense with respect to which there is immediate danger to person or property, or of the escape of the perpetrator of that offense, or pursuant to Section 8597 or 8598 of the Government Code provided that the primary duty of the peace officers shall be the enforcement of the law as set forth in Sections 4311, 4313, 4491, and 4493 of the Welfare and Institutions Code. Those peace officers may carry firearms only if authorized and under terms and conditions specified by their employing agency.

Penal Code § 830.39.

(a) Any regularly employed law enforcement officer of the Oregon State Police, the Nevada Department of Motor Vehicles and Public Safety, or the Arizona Department of Public Safety is a peace officer in this state if all of the following conditions are met:

(1) The officer is providing, or attempting to provide, law enforcement services within this state on the state or county highways and areas immediately adjacent thereto, within a distance of up to 50 statute miles of the contiguous border of this state and the state employing the officer.

(2) The officer is providing, or attempting to provide, law enforcement services pursuant to either of the following:

(A) In response to a request for services initiated by a member of the California Highway Patrol.

(B) In response to a reasonable belief that emergency law enforcement services are necessary for the preservation of life, and a request for services by a member of the Department of the California Highway Patrol is impractical to obtain under the circumstances. In those situations, the officer shall obtain authorization as soon as practical.

(3) The officer is providing, or attempting to provide, law enforcement services for the purpose of assisting a member of the California Highway Patrol to provide emergency service in response to misdemeanor or felony criminal activity, pursuant to the authority of a peace officer as provided in subdivision (a) of Section 830.2, or, in the event of highway-related traffic accidents, emergency incidents or other similar public safety problems, whether or not a member of the California Highway Patrol is present at the scene of the event. Nothing in this section shall be construed to confer upon the officer the authority to enforce traffic or motor vehicle infractions.

(4) An agreement pursuant to Section 2403.5 of the Vehicle Code is in effect between the Department of the California Highway Patrol and the agency of the adjoining state employing the officer, the officer acts in accordance with that agreement, and the agreement specifies that the officer and employing agency of the adjoining state shall be subject to the same civil immunities and liabilities as a peace officer and his or her employing agency in this state.

(5) The officer receives no separate compensation from this state for providing law enforcement services within this state.

(6) The adjoining state employing the officer confers similar rights and authority upon a member of the California Highway Patrol who renders assistance within that state.

(b) Whenever, pursuant to Nevada law, a Nevada correctional officer is working or supervising Nevada inmates who are performing conservation-related projects or fire suppression duties within California, the correctional officer may maintain custody of the inmates in California, and retake any inmate who should escape in California, to the same extent as if the correctional officer were a peace officer in this state and the inmate had been committed to his or her custody in proceedings under California law.

(c) Notwithstanding any other provision of law, any person who is acting as a peace officer in this state in the manner described in this section shall be deemed to have met the requirements of Section 1031 of the Government Code and the selection and training standards of the Commission on Peace Officer Standards and Training if the officer has completed the basic training required for peace officers in his or her state.

(d) In no case shall a peace officer of an adjoining state be authorized to provide services within a California jurisdiction during any period in which the regular law enforcement agency of the jurisdiction is involved in a labor dispute.

Penal Code § 830.4.

The following persons are peace officers whose authority extends to any place in the state for the purpose of performing their duties under the conditions as specified by statute. Those peace officers may carry firearms only if authorized and under terms and conditions specified by their employing agency.

(a) Members of the California National Guard have the powers of peace officers when they are involved in any or all of the following:

(1) Called or ordered into active state service by the Governor pursuant to the provisions of Section 143 or 146 of the Military and Veterans Code.

(2) Serving within the area wherein military assistance is required.

(3) Directly assisting civil authorities in any of the situations specified in Section 143 or 146. The authority of the peace officer under this subdivision extends to the area wherein military assistance is required as to a public offense committed or which there is reasonable cause to believe has been committed within that area. The requirements of Section 1031 of the Government Code are not applicable under those circumstances.

(b) Guards and messengers of the Treasurer's office when performing assigned duties as a guard or messenger.

(c) Security officers of the Department of Justice when performing assigned duties as security officers.

(d) Security officers of Hastings College of the Law. These officers shall have authority of peace officers only within the City and County of San Francisco. Notwithstanding any other provisions of law, the peace officers designated by this subdivision shall not be authorized by this subdivision to carry firearms either on or off duty. Notwithstanding any other provision of law, the act which designated the persons described in this subdivision as peace officers shall serve only to define those persons as peace officers, the extent of their jurisdiction, and the nature and scope of their authority, powers, and duties, and there shall be no change in the status of those persons for purposes of retirement, workers' compensation or similar injury or death benefits, or other employee benefits.

Penal Code § 830.5.

The following persons are peace officers whose authority extends to any place in the state while engaged in the performance of the duties of their respective employment and for the purpose of carrying out the primary function of their employment or as required under Sections 8597, 8598, and 8617 of the Government Code. Except as specified in this section, these peace officers may carry firearms only if authorized and under those terms and conditions specified by their employing agency:

(a) A parole officer of the Department of Corrections or the Department of the Youth Authority, probation officer, deputy probation officer, or a board coordinating parole agent employed by the Youthful Offender Parole Board. Except as otherwise provided in this subdivision, the authority of these parole or probation officers shall extend only as follows:

(1) To conditions of parole or of probation by any person in this state on parole or probation.

(2) To the escape of any inmate or ward from a state or local institution.

(3) To the transportation of persons on parole or probation.

(4) To violations of any penal provisions of law which are discovered while performing the usual or authorized duties of his or her employment.

(5) To the rendering of mutual aid to any other law enforcement agency. For the purposes of this subdivision, "parole agent" shall have the same meaning as parole officer of the Department of Corrections or of the Department of the Youth Authority. Any parole officer of the Department of Corrections, the Department of the Youth Authority, or the Youthful Offender Parole Board is authorized to carry firearms, but only as determined by the director on a case-by-case or unit-by-unit basis and only under those terms and conditions specified by the director or chairperson. The Department of the Youth Authority shall develop a policy for arming peace officers of the Department of the Youth Authority who comprise "high-risk transportation details" or "high-risk escape details" no later than June 30, 1995. This policy shall be implemented no later than December 31, 1995. The Department of the Youth Authority shall train and arm those peace officers who comprise tactical teams at each facility for use during "high-risk escape details."

(b) A correctional officer employed by the Department of Corrections or any employee of the Department of the Youth Authority having custody of wards or the Inspector General of the Youth and Adult Correctional Agency or any internal affairs investigator under the authority of the Inspector General or any employee of the Department of Corrections designated by the Director of Corrections or any correctional counselor series employee of the Department of Corrections or any medical technical assistant series employee designated by the Director of Corrections or designated by the Director of Corrections and employed by the State Department of Mental Health or employee of the Board of Prison Terms designated by the Secretary of the Youth and Adult Correctional Agency or employee of the Department of the Youth Authority designated by the Director of the Youth Authority or any superintendent, supervisor, or employee having custodial responsibilities in an institution operated by a probation department, or any transportation officer of a probation department.

(c) The following persons may carry a firearm while not on duty: a parole officer of the Department of Corrections or the Department of the Youth Authority, a correctional officer or correctional counselor employed by the Department of Corrections or any employee of the Department of the Youth Authority having custody of wards or any employee of the Department of Corrections designated by the Director of Corrections. A parole officer of the Youthful Offender Parole Board may carry a firearm while not on duty only when so authorized by the chairperson of the board and only under the terms and conditions specified by the chairperson. Nothing in this section shall be interpreted to require licensure pursuant to Section 12025. The director or chairperson may deny, suspend, or revoke for good cause a person's right to carry a firearm under this subdivision. That person shall, upon request, receive a hearing, as provided for in the negotiated grievance procedure between the exclusive employee representative and the Department of Corrections, the Department of the Youth Authority, or the Youthful Offender Parole Board, to review the director's or the chairperson's decision.

(d) Persons permitted to carry firearms pursuant to this section, either on or off duty, shall meet the training requirements of Section 832 and shall qualify with the firearm at least quarterly. It is the responsibility of the individual officer or designee to maintain his or her eligibility to carry concealable firearms off duty. Failure to maintain quarterly qualifications by an officer or designee with any concealable firearms carried off duty shall constitute good cause to suspend or revoke that person's right to carry firearms off duty.

(e) The Department of Corrections shall allow reasonable access to its ranges for officers and designees of either department to qualify to carry concealable firearms off duty. The time spent on the range for purposes of meeting the qualification requirements shall be the person's own time during the person's off-duty hours.

(f) The Director of Corrections shall promulgate regulations consistent with this section.

(g) "High-risk transportation details" and "high-risk escape details" as used in this section shall be determined by the Director of the Youth Authority, or his or her designee. The director, or his or her designee, shall consider at least the following in determining "high-risk transportation details" and "high-risk escape details": protection of the public, protection of officers, flight risk, and violence potential of the wards.

(h) "Transportation detail" as used in this section shall include transportation of wards outside the facility, including, but not limited to, court appearances, medical trips, and interfacility transfers.

Penal Code § 830.55.

(a) As used in this section, a correctional officer is a peace officer, employed by a city, county, or city and county which operates a facility described in Section 2910.5 of this code or Section 1753.3 of the Welfare and Institutions Code or facilities operated by counties pursuant to Section 6241 or 6242 of this code under contract with the Department of Corrections or the Department of the Youth Authority, who has the authority and responsibility for maintaining custody of specified state prison inmates or wards, and who performs tasks related to the operation of a detention facility used for the detention of persons who have violated parole or are awaiting parole back into the community or, upon court order, either for their own safekeeping or for the specific purpose of serving a sentence therein.

(b) A correctional officer shall have no right to carry or possess firearms in the performance of his or her prescribed duties, except, under the direction of the superintendent of the facility, while engaged in transporting prisoners, guarding hospitalized prisoners, or suppressing riots, lynchings, escapes, or rescues in or about a detention facility established pursuant to Section 2910.5 of this code or Section 1753.3 of the Welfare and Institutions Code.

(c) Each person described in this section as a correctional officer, within 90 days following the date of the initial assignment to that position, shall satisfactorily complete the training course specified in Section 832. In addition, each person designated as a correctional officer, within one year following the date of the initial assignment as an officer, shall have satisfactorily met the minimum selection and training standards prescribed by the Board of Corrections pursuant to Section 6035. Persons designated as correctional officers, before the expiration of the 90-day and one-year periods described in this subdivision, who have not yet completed the required training, may perform the duties of a correctional officer only while under the direct supervision of a correctional officer who has completed the training required in this section, and shall not carry or possess firearms in the performance of their prescribed duties.

(d) This section shall not be construed to confer any authority upon a correctional officer except while on duty. (e) A correctional officer may use reasonable force in establishing and maintaining custody of persons delivered to him or her by a law enforcement officer, may make arrests for misdemeanors and felonies within the local detention facility pursuant to a duly issued warrant, and may make warrantless arrests pursuant to Section 836.5 only during the duration of his or her job.

Penal Code § 830.6.

(a)(1) Whenever any qualified person is deputized or appointed by the proper authority as a reserve or auxiliary sheriff or city police officer, a reserve deputy sheriff, a reserve deputy marshal, a reserve police officer of a regional park district or of a transit district, a reserve park ranger, a reserve harbor or port police officer of a county, city, or district as specified in Section 663.5 of the Harbors and Navigation Code, a reserve deputy of the Department of Fish and Game, a reserve special agent of the Department of Justice, a reserve officer of a community service district which is authorized under subdivision (h) of Section 61600 of the Government Code to maintain a police department or other police protection, a reserve officer of a school district police department under Section 35021.5 of the Education Code, a reserve officer of a community college police department under Section 72330, a reserve officer of a police protection district formed under Part 1 (commencing with Section 20000) of Division 14 of the Health and Safety Code, or a reserve housing authority patrol officer employed by a housing authority defined in subdivision (d) of Section 830.31, and is assigned specific police functions by that authority, the person is a peace officer, if the person qualifies as set forth in Section 832.6. The authority of a person designated as a peace officer pursuant to this paragraph extends only for the duration of the person's specific assignment. A reserve park ranger or a transit, harbor, or port district reserve officer may carry firearms only if authorized by, and under those terms and conditions as are specified by, his or her employing agency.

(2) Whenever any qualified person is deputized or appointed by the proper authority as a reserve or auxiliary sheriff or city police officer, a reserve deputy sheriff, a reserve deputy marshal, a reserve park ranger, a reserve police officer of a regional park district, transit district, community college district, or school district, a reserve harbor or port police officer of a county, city, or district as specified in Section 663.5 of the Harbors and Navigation Code, a reserve officer of a community service district that is authorized under subdivision (h) of Section 61600 of the Government Code to maintain a police department or other police protection, or a reserve officer of a police protection district formed under Part 1 (commencing with Section 20000) of Division 14 of the Health and Safety Code, and is so designated by local ordinance or, if the local agency is not authorized to act by ordinance, by resolution, either individually or by class, and is assigned to the prevention and detection of crime and the general enforcement of the laws of this state by that authority, the person is a peace officer, if the person qualifies as set forth in paragraph (1) of subdivision (a) of Section 832.6. The authority of a person designated as a peace officer pursuant to this paragraph includes the full powers and duties of a peace officer as provided by Section 830.1. A transit, harbor, or port district reserve police officer, or a city or county reserve peace officer who is not provided with the powers and duties authorized by Section 830.1, has the powers and duties authorized in Section 830.33, or in the case of a reserve park ranger, the powers and duties that are authorized in Section 830.31, or in the case of a reserve housing authority patrol officer, the powers and duties that are authorized in subdivision (d) of Section 830.31, and a school district reserve police officer or a community college district reserve police officer has the powers and duties authorized in Section 830.32.

(b) Whenever any person designated by a Native American tribe recognized by the United States Secretary of the Interior is deputized or appointed by the county sheriff as a reserve or auxiliary sheriff or a reserve deputy sheriff, and is assigned to the prevention and detection of crime and the general enforcement of the laws of this state by the county sheriff, the person is a peace officer, if the person qualifies as set forth in paragraph (1) of subdivision (a) of Section 832.6. The authority of a peace officer pursuant to this subdivision includes the full powers and duties of a peace officer as provided by Section 830.1.

(c) Whenever any person is summoned to the aid of any uniformed peace officer, the summoned person is vested with the powers of a peace officer that are expressly delegated to him or her by the summoning officer or that are otherwise reasonably necessary to properly assist the officer.

Penal Code § 830.65.

(a) Any person who is a regularly employed police officer of a city or a regularly employed deputy sheriff of a county, or a reserve peace officer of a city or county and is appointed in the manner described in paragraph (1) or (2) of subdivision (a) of Section 832.6, may be appointed as a Campaign Against Marijuana Planting emergency appointee by the Attorney General pursuant to Section 5 of Chapter 1563 of the Statutes of 1985 to assist with a specific investigation, tactical operation, or search and rescue operation. When so appointed, the person shall be a peace officer of the Department of Justice, provided that the person's authority shall extend only for the duration of the specific assignment.

(b) Notwithstanding any other provision of law, any person who is appointed as a peace officer in the manner described in this section shall be deemed to have met the requirements of Section 1031 of the Government Code and the selection and training standards of the Commission on Peace Officer Standards and Training.

Penal Code § 830.7.

The following persons are not peace officers but may exercise the powers of arrest of a peace officer as specified in Section 836 during the course and within the scope of their employment, if they successfully complete a course in the exercise of those powers pursuant to Section 832:

(a) Persons designated by a cemetery authority pursuant to Section 8325 of the Health and Safety Code.

(b) Persons regularly employed as security officers for independent institutions of higher education, recognized under subdivision (b) of Section 66010 of the Education Code, if the institution has concluded a memorandum of understanding, permitting the exercise of that authority, with the sheriff or the chief of police within whose jurisdiction the institution lies.

(c) Persons regularly employed as security officers for health facilities, as defined in Section 1250 of the Health and Safety Code, that are owned and operated by cities, counties, and cities and counties, if the facility has concluded a memorandum of understanding, permitting the exercise of that authority, with the sheriff or the chief of police within whose jurisdiction the facility lies.

(d) Employees or classes of employees of the California Department of Forestry and Fire Protection designated by the Director of Forestry and Fire Protection, provided that the primary duty of the employee shall be the enforcement of the law as that duty is set forth in Section 4156 of the Public Resources Code.

(e) Persons regularly employed as inspectors, supervisors, or security officers for transit districts, as defined in Section 99213 of the Public Utilities Code, if the district has concluded a memorandum of understanding permitting the exercise of that authority, with, as applicable, the sheriff, the chief of police, or the Department of the California Highway Patrol within whose jurisdiction the district lies. For the purposes of this subdivision, the exercise of peace officer authority may include the authority to remove a vehicle from a railroad right-of-way as set forth in Section 22656 of the Vehicle Code.

(f) Nonpeace officers regularly employed as county parole officers pursuant to Section 3089.

(g) Persons appointed by the Executive Director of the California Science Center pursuant to Section 4108 of the Food and Agricultural Code.

(h) Persons regularly employed as investigators by the Department of Transportation for the City of Los Angeles and designated by local ordinance as public officers, to the extent necessary to enforce laws related to public transportation, and authorized by a memorandum of understanding with the chief of police, permitting the exercise of that authority. For the purposes of this subdivision, "investigator" means an employee defined in Section 53075.61 of the Government Code authorized by local ordinance to enforce laws related to public transportation. Transportation investigators authorized by this section shall not be deemed "peace officers" for purposes of Sections 241 and 243.

(i) Persons regularly employed by any department of the City of Los Angeles who are designated as security officers and authorized by local ordinance to enforce laws related to the preservation of peace in or about the properties owned, controlled, operated, or administered by any department of the City of Los Angeles and authorized by a memorandum of understanding with the Chief of Police of the City of Los Angeles permitting the exercise of that authority. Security officers authorized pursuant to this subdivision shall not be deemed peace officers for purposes of Sections 241 and 243.

(j) Illegal dumping enforcement officers, to the extent necessary to enforce laws related to illegal waste dumping, or littering, and authorized by a memorandum of understanding with, as applicable, the sheriff or chief of police within whose jurisdiction the person is employed, permitting the exercise of that authority. An "illegal dumping enforcement officer" is defined, for purposes of this section, as a person employed full-time, part-time, or as a volunteer after completing training prescribed by law, by a city, county, or city and county, whose duties include illegal dumping enforcement and is designated by local ordinance as a public officer. An illegal dumping control officer may also be a person who is not regularly employed by a city, county, or city and county, but who has met all training requirements and is directly supervised by a regularly employed dumping control officer. This person shall not have the power of arrest or access to summary criminal history information. No person may be appointed as an illegal dumping enforcement officer if that person is disqualified pursuant to the criteria set forth in Section 1029 of the Government Code. Persons regularly employed by a city, county, or city and county designated pursuant to this subdivision may be furnished state summary criminal history information upon a showing of compelling need pursuant to subdivision (c) of Section 11105.

Penal Code § 830.8.

(a) Federal criminal investigators and law enforcement officers are not California peace officers, but may exercise the powers of arrest of a peace officer in any of the following circumstances:

(1) Any circumstances specified in Section 836 or Section 5150 of the Welfare and Institutions Code for violations of state or local laws.

(2) When these investigators and law enforcement officers are engaged in the enforcement of federal criminal laws and exercise the arrest powers only incidental to the performance of these duties.

(3) When requested by a California law enforcement agency to be involved in a joint task force or criminal investigation.

(4) When probable cause exists to believe that a public offense that involves immediate danger to persons or property has just occurred or is being committed. In all of these instances, the provisions of Section 847 shall apply. These investigators and law enforcement officers, prior to the exercise of these arrest powers, shall have been certified by their agency heads as having satisfied the training requirements of Section 832, or the equivalent thereof. This subdivision does not apply to federal officers of the Bureau of Land

Management or the Forest Service of the Department of Agriculture. These officers have no authority to enforce California statutes without the written consent of the sheriff or the chief of police in whose jurisdiction they are assigned.

(b) Duly authorized federal employees who comply with the training requirements set forth in Section 832 are peace officers when they are engaged in enforcing applicable state or local laws on property owned or possessed by the United States government, or on any street, sidewalk, or property adjacent thereto, and with the written consent of the sheriff or the chief of police, respectively, in whose jurisdiction the property is situated.

(c) National park rangers are not California peace officers but may exercise the powers of arrest of a peace officer as specified in Section 836 and the powers of a peace officer specified in Section 5150 of the Welfare and Institutions Code for violations of state or local laws provided these rangers are exercising the arrest powers incidental to the performance of their federal duties or providing or attempting to provide law enforcement services in response to a request initiated by California state park rangers to assist in preserving the peace and protecting state parks and other property for which California state park rangers are responsible. National park rangers, prior to the exercise of these arrest powers, shall have been certified by their agency heads as having satisfactorily completed the training requirements of Section 832.3, or the equivalent thereof.

(d) Notwithstanding any other provision of law, during a state of war emergency or a state of emergency, as defined in Section 8558 of the Government Code, federal criminal investigators and law enforcement officers who are assisting California law enforcement officers in carrying out emergency operations are not deemed California peace officers, but may exercise the powers of arrest of a peace officer as specified in Section 836 and the powers of a peace officer specified in Section 5150 of the Welfare and Institutions Code for violations of state or local laws. In these instances, the provisions of Section 847 and of Section 8655 of the Government Code shall apply.

(e)(1) Any qualified person who is appointed as a Washoe tribal law enforcement officer is not a California peace officer, but may exercise the powers of a Washoe tribal peace officer when engaged in the enforcement of Washoe tribal criminal laws against any person who is an Indian, as defined in subsection (a) of Section 450b of Title 25 of the United States Code, on Washoe tribal land. The respective prosecuting authorities, in consultation with law enforcement agencies, may agree on who shall have initial responsibility for prosecution of specified infractions. This subdivision is not meant to confer cross-deputized status as California peace officers, nor to confer California peace officer status upon Washoe tribal law enforcement officers when enforcing state or local laws in the State of California. Nothing in this section shall be construed to impose liability upon or to require indemnification by the County of Alpine or the State of California for any act performed by an officer of the Washoe Tribe. Washoe tribal law enforcement officers shall have the right to travel to and from Washoe tribal lands within California in order to carry out tribal duties.

(2) Washoe tribal law enforcement officers are exempted from the provisions of subdivision (a) of Section 12025 and subdivision (a) of Section 12031 while performing their official duties on their tribal lands or while proceeding by a direct route to or from the tribal lands. Tribal law enforcement vehicles are deemed to be emergency vehicles within the meaning of Section 30 of the Vehicle Code while performing official police services.

(3) As used in this subdivision, the term "Washoe tribal lands" includes the following:

(A) All lands located in the County of Alpine within the limits of the reservation created for the Washoe Tribe of Nevada and California, notwithstanding the issuance of any patent and including rights-of-way running through the reservation and all tribal trust lands.

(B) All Indian allotments, the Indian titles to which have not been extinguished, including rights-of-way running through the same.

(4) As used in this subdivision, the term "Washoe tribal law" refers to the laws codified in the Law and Order Code of the Washoe Tribe of Nevada and California, as adopted by the Tribal Council of the Washoe Tribe of Nevada and California.

Penal Code § 830.9.

Animal control officers are not peace officers but may exercise the powers of arrest of a peace officer as specified in Section 836 and the power to serve warrants as specified in Sections 1523 and 1530 during the course and within the scope of their employment, if those officers successfully complete a course in the exercise of those powers pursuant to Section 832. That part of the training course specified in Section 832 pertaining to the carrying and use of firearms shall not be required for any animal control officer whose employing agency prohibits the use of firearms. For the purposes of this section, "firearms" includes capture guns, blowguns, carbon dioxide operated rifles and pistols, air guns, handguns, rifles, and shotguns.

Penal Code § 830.10.

Any uniformed peace officer shall wear a badge, nameplate, or other device which bears clearly on its face the identification number or name of the officer.

Penal Code § 830.11.

(a) The following persons are not peace officers but may exercise the powers of arrest of a peace officer as specified in Section 836 and the power to serve warrants as specified in Sections 1523 and 1530 during the course and within the scope of their employment, if they receive a course in the exercise of those powers pursuant to Section 832. The authority and powers of the persons designated under this section shall extend to any place in the state:

(1) Persons employed by the Department of Financial Institutions designated by the Commissioner of Financial Institutions, provided that the primary duty of these persons shall be the enforcement of, and investigations relating to, the provisions of law administered by the Commissioner of Financial Institutions.

(2) Persons employed by the Department of Real Estate designated by the Real Estate Commissioner, provided that the primary duty of these persons shall be the enforcement of the laws set forth in Part 1 (commencing with Section 10000) and Part 2 (commencing with Section 11000) of Division 4 of the Business and Professions Code. The Real Estate Commissioner may designate persons under this section, who at the time of their designation, are assigned to the Special Investigations Unit, internally known as the Crisis Response Team.

(3) Persons employed by the State Lands Commission designated by the executive officer, provided that the primary duty of these persons shall be the enforcement of the law relating to the duties of the State Lands Commission.

(4) Persons employed as investigators of the Investigations Bureau of the Department of Insurance, who are designated by the Chief of the Investigations Bureau, provided that the primary duty of these persons shall be the enforcement of the Insurance Code and other laws relating to persons and businesses, licensed and unlicensed by the Department of Insurance, who are engaged in the business of insurance.

(5) Persons employed as investigators and investigator supervisors of the Consumer Services Division or the Rail Safety and Carrier Division of the Public Utilities Commission who are designated by the commission's executive director and approved by the commission, provided that the primary duty of these persons shall be the enforcement of the law as that duty is set forth in Section 308.5 of the Public Utilities Code.

(6)(A) Persons employed by the State Board of Equalization, Investigations Division, who are designated by the board's executive director, provided that the primary duty of these persons shall be the enforcement of laws administered by the State Board of Equalization.

(B) Persons designated pursuant to this paragraph are not entitled to peace officer retirement benefits.

(7) Persons employed by the Department of Food and Agriculture and designated by the Secretary of Food and Agriculture as investigators, investigator supervisors, and investigator managers, provided that the primary duty of these persons shall be enforcement of, and investigations relating to, the Food and Agricultural Code or Division 5 (commencing with Section 12001) of the Business and Professions Code.

(b) Notwithstanding any other provision of law, persons designated pursuant to this section may not carry firearms.

(c) Persons designated pursuant to this section shall be included as "peace officers of the state" under paragraph (2) of subdivision (c) of Section 11105 for the purpose of receiving state summary criminal history information and shall be furnished that information on the same basis as peace officers of the state designated in paragraph (2) of subdivision (c) of Section 11105.

Penal Code § 830.12.

Notwithstanding any other provision of law, persons designated by a local agency as litter control officers, vehicle abatement officers, registered sanitarians, and solid waste specialists, are not peace officers, may not exercise the powers of arrest of a peace officer, as specified in Section 836, and shall not be authorized to carry or use firearms within the scope and course of their employment. These persons may, however, be authorized by the governing board of the particular local agency to issue citations involving violations of laws relating to abandoned vehicles and littering.

Penal Code § 830.13.

(a) The following persons are not peace officers but may exercise the power to serve warrants as specified in Sections 1523 and 1530 during the course and within the scope of their employment, if they receive a course in the exercise of that power pursuant to Section 832. The authority and power of the persons designated under this section shall extend to any place in the state:

(1) Persons employed as investigators of an auditor-controller or director of finance of any county or persons employed by a city and county who conduct investigations under the supervision of the controller of the city and county, who are regularly employed and paid in that capacity, provided that the primary duty of these persons shall be to engage in investigations related to the theft of funds or the misappropriation of funds or resources, or investigations related to the duties of the auditor-controller or finance director as set forth in Chapter 3.5 (commencing with Section 26880), Chapter 4 (commencing with Section 26900), Chapter 4.5 (commencing with Section 26970), and Chapter 4.6 (commencing with Section 26980) of Part 3 of Division 2 of Title 3 of the Government Code.

(2) Persons employed by the Department of Justice as investigative auditors, provided that the primary duty of these persons shall be to investigate financial crimes. Investigative auditors shall only serve warrants for the production of documentary evidence held by financial institutions, Internet service providers, telecommunications companies, and third parties who are not reasonably suspected of engaging or having engaged in criminal activity related to the documentary evidence for which the warrant is requested.

(b) Notwithstanding any other provision of law, persons designated pursuant to this section shall not carry firearms.

(c) Persons designated pursuant to this section shall be included as "peace officers of the state" under paragraph (2) of subdivision (c) of Section 11105 for the purpose of receiving state summary criminal history information and shall be furnished that information on the same basis as peace officers of the state designated in paragraph (2) of subdivision (c) of Section 11105.

(d) Unless otherwise specifically provided, this section confers to persons designated in this section the same authority and power to serve warrants as conferred by Section 830.11.

Penal Code § 830.14.

(a) A local or regional transit agency or a joint powers agency operating rail service identified in an implementation program adopted pursuant to Article 10 (commencing with Section 130450) of Chapter 4 of Division 12 of the Public Utilities Code may authorize by contract designated persons as conductors performing fare inspection duties who are employed by a railroad corporation that operates public rail commuter transit services for that agency to act as its agent in the enforcement of subdivisions (a) and (b) of Section 640 relating to the operation of the rail service if they complete the training requirement specified in this section.

(b) The governing board of the Altamont Commuter Express Authority, a joint powers agency duly formed pursuant to Article 1 (commencing with Section 6500) of Chapter 5 of Division 7 of Title 1 of the Government Code, by and between the Alameda Congestion Management Agency, the Santa Clara County Transit District, and the San Joaquin Regional Rail Commission, may contract with designated persons to act as its agents in the enforcement of subdivisions (a) and (b) of Section 640 relating to the operation of a public transportation system if these persons complete the training requirement specified in this section.

(c) The governing board of the Peninsula Corridor Joint Powers Board, a joint powers agency duly formed pursuant to Article 1 (commencing with Section 6500) of Chapter 5 of Division 7 of Title 1 of the Government Code, by and between the San Mateo County Transit District, the Santa Clara County Transit District, and the City and County of San Francisco, may appoint designated persons to act as its agents in the enforcement of subdivisions (a) and (b) of Section 640 relating to the operation of a public transportation system if these persons complete the training requirement specified in this section.

(d) The governing board of Foothill Transit, a joint powers agency duly formed pursuant to Article 1 (commencing with Section 6500) of Chapter 5 of Division 7 of Title 1 of the Government Code, by and between the Cities of Arcadia, Azusa, Baldwin Park, Bradbury, Claremont, Covina, Diamond Bar, Duarte, El Monte, Glendora, Industry, Irwindale, La Habra Heights, La Puente, La Verne, Monrovia, Pomona, San Dimas, South El Monte, Temple City, Walnut, West Covina, and the County of Los Angeles, may resolve to contract with designated persons to act as its agents in the enforcement of subdivisions (a) and (b) of Section 640 relating to the operation of a public transportation system if these persons complete the training requirement specified in this section.

(e) Persons authorized pursuant to this section to enforce subdivisions (a) and (b) of Section 640 shall complete a specialized fare compliance course which shall be provided by the authorizing agency. This training course shall include, but not be limited to, the following topics:

(1) An overview of barrier-free fare inspection concepts.

(2) The scope and limitations of inspector authority.

(3) Familiarization with the elements of the infractions enumerated in subdivisions (a) and (b) of Section 640.

(4) Techniques for conducting fare checks, including inspection procedures, demeanor, and contacting violators.

(5) Citation issuance and court appearances.

(6) Fare media recognition.

(7) Handling argumentative violators and diffusing conflict.

(8) The mechanics of law enforcement support and interacting with law enforcement for effective incident resolution.

(f) Persons described in this section are public officers, not peace officers, have no authority to carry firearms or any other weapon while performing the duties authorized in this section, and may not exercise the powers of arrest of a peace officer while performing the duties authorized in this section. These persons may be authorized by the agencies specified in this section to issue citations involving infractions relating to the operation of the rail service specified in this section.

(g) Nothing in this section shall affect the retirement or disability benefits provided to employees described in this section or be in violation of any collective bargaining agreement between a labor organization and a railroad corporation.

(h) Notwithstanding any other provision of this section, the primary responsibility of a conductor of a commuter passenger train shall be functions related to safe train operation.

Penal Code § 831.

(a) A custodial officer is a public officer, not a peace officer, employed by a law enforcement agency of a city or county who has the authority and responsibility for maintaining custody of prisoners and performs tasks related to the operation of a local detention facility used for the detention of persons usually pending arraignment or upon court order either for their own safekeeping or for the specific purpose of serving a sentence therein.

(b) A custodial officer shall have no right to carry or possess firearms in the performance of his or her prescribed duties.

(c) Each person described in this section as a custodial officer shall, within 90 days following the date of the initial assignment to the position, satisfactorily complete the training course specified in Section 832. In addition, each person designated as a custodial officer shall, within one year following the date of the initial assignment as a custodial officer, have satisfactorily met the minimum selection and training standards prescribed by the Board of Corrections pursuant to Section 6035. Persons designated as custodial officers, before the expiration of the 90-day and one-year periods described in this subdivision, who have not yet completed the required training, may perform the duties of a custodial officer only while under the direct supervision of a peace officer as described in Section 830.1, who has completed the training prescribed by the Commission on Peace Officer Standards and Training, or a custodial officer who has completed the training required in this section.

(d) At any time 20 or more custodial officers are on duty, there shall be at least one peace officer, as described in Section 830.1, on duty at the same time to supervise the performance of the custodial officers.

(e) This section shall not be construed to confer any authority upon any custodial officer except while on duty.

(f) A custodial officer may use reasonable force in establishing and maintaining custody of persons delivered to him or her by a law enforcement officer; may make arrests for misdemeanors and felonies within the local detention facility pursuant to a duly issued warrant; may release without further criminal process persons arrested for intoxication; and may release misdemeanants on citation to appear in lieu of or after booking.

Penal Code § 831.4.

(a) A sheriff's or police security officer is a public officer, employed by the sheriff of a county or police chief of a city, whose primary duty is the security of locations or facilities as directed by the sheriff or police chief. The duties of a sheriff' s or police security officer shall be limited to the physical security and protection of properties owned, operated, controlled, or administered by the county or city, or any municipality or special district contracting for police services from the county or city pursuant to Section 54981 of the Government Code, or necessary duties with respect to the patrons, employees, and properties of the employing county, city, or contracting entities.

(b) A sheriff's or police security officer is not a peace officer nor a public safety officer as defined in Section 3301 of the Government Code. A sheriff's or police security officer may carry or possess a firearm, baton, and other safety equipment and weapons authorized by the sheriff or police chief while performing the duties authorized in this section, and under the terms and conditions specified by the sheriff or police chief. These persons may not exercise the powers of arrest of a peace officer, but may issue citations for infractions if authorized by the sheriff or police chief.

(c) Each sheriff's or police security officer shall satisfactorily complete a course of training as specified in Section 832 prior to being assigned to perform his or her duties. Nothing in this subdivision shall preclude the sheriff or police chief from requiring additional training requirements.

(d) Notwithstanding any other law, nothing in this section shall be construed to confer any authority upon any sheriff's or police security officer except while on duty, or confer any additional retirement benefits to persons employed within this classification.

Penal Code § 831.5.

(a) As used in this section, a custodial officer is a public officer, not a peace officer, employed by a law enforcement agency of San Diego County, Fresno County, Kern County, Stanislaus County, Riverside County, Santa Clara County, or a county having a population of 425,000 or less who has the authority and responsibility for maintaining custody of prisoners and performs tasks related to the operation of a local detention facility used for the detention of persons usually pending arraignment or upon court order either for their own safekeeping or for the specific purpose of serving a sentence therein. Custodial officers of a county shall be employees of, and under the authority of, the sheriff, except in counties in which the sheriff, as of July 1, 1993, is not in charge of and the sole and exclusive authority to keep the county jail and the prisoners in it. A custodial officer includes a person designated as a correctional officer, jailer, or other similar title. The duties of a custodial officer may include the serving of warrants, court orders, writs, and subpoenas in the detention facility or under circumstances arising directly out of maintaining custody of prisoners and related tasks.

(b) A custodial officer has no right to carry or possess firearms in the performance of his or her prescribed duties, except, under the direction of the sheriff or chief of police, while engaged in transporting prisoners; guarding hospitalized prisoners; or suppressing jail riots, lynchings, escapes, or rescues in or about a detention facility falling under the care and custody of the sheriff or chief of police.

(c) Each person described in this section as a custodial officer shall, within 90 days following the date of the initial assignment to that position, satisfactorily complete the training course specified in Section 832. In addition, each person designated as a custodial officer shall, within one year following the date of the initial assignment as a custodial officer, have satisfactorily met the minimum selection and training standards prescribed by the Board of Corrections pursuant to Section 6035. Persons designated as custodial officers, before the expiration of the 90-day and one-year periods described in this subdivision, who have not yet completed the required training, shall not carry or possess firearms in the performance of their prescribed duties, but may perform the duties of a custodial officer only while under the direct supervision of a peace officer, as described in Section 830.1, who has completed the training prescribed by the Commission on Peace Officer Standards and Training, or a custodial officer who has completed the training required in this section.

(d) At any time 20 or more custodial officers are on duty, there shall be at least one peace officer, as described in Section 830.1, on duty at the same time to supervise the performance of the custodial officers.

(e) This section shall not be construed to confer any authority upon any custodial officer except while on duty.

(f) A custodial officer may use reasonable force in establishing and maintaining custody of persons delivered to him or her by a law enforcement officer; may make arrests for misdemeanors and felonies within the local detention facility pursuant to a duly issued warrant; may make warrantless arrests pursuant to Section 836.5 only during the duration of his or her job; may release without further criminal process persons arrested for intoxication; and may release misdemeanants on citation to appear in lieu of or after booking.

(g) Custodial officers employed by the Santa Clara County Department of Corrections are authorized to perform the following additional duties in the facility:

(1) Arrest a person without a warrant whenever the custodial officer has reasonable cause to believe that the person to be arrested has committed a misdemeanor or felony in the presence of the officer that is a violation of a statute or ordinance that the officer has the duty to enforce.

(2) Search property, cells, prisoners or visitors.

(3) Conduct strip or body cavity searches of prisoners pursuant to Section 4030.

(4) Conduct searches and seizures pursuant to a duly issued warrant.

(5) Segregate prisoners.

(6) Classify prisoners for the purpose of housing or participation in supervised activities. These duties may be performed at the Santa Clara Valley Medical Center as needed and only as they directly relate to guarding inpatient, in-custody inmates. This subdivision shall not be construed to authorize the performance of any law enforcement activity involving any person other than the inmate or his or her visitors.

(h) Nothing in this section shall authorize a custodial officer to carry or possess a firearm when the officer is not on duty.

(i) It is the intent of the Legislature that this section, as it relates to Santa Clara County, enumerate specific duties of custodial officers (known as "correctional officers" in Santa Clara County) and to clarify the relationships of the correctional officers and deputy sheriffs in Santa Clara County. These duties are the same duties of the custodial officers prior to the date of enactment of Senate Bill 1019 of the 1999-2000 Regular Session of the Legislature pursuant to local rules and judicial decisions. It is further the intent of the Legislature that all issues regarding compensation for custodial officers remain subject to the collective bargaining process between the County of Santa Clara and the authorized bargaining representative for the custodial officers. However, nothing in this section shall be construed to assert that the duties of custodial officers are equivalent to the duties of deputy sheriffs nor to affect the ability of the county to negotiate pay that reflects the different duties of custodial officers and deputy sheriffs.

(j) This section shall become operative on January 1, 2003. This act is an urgency statute necessary for the immediate preservation of the public peace, health, or safety within the meaning of Article IV of the Constitution and shall go into immediate effect. The facts constituting the necessity are: In order to finally, fully, and expeditiously implement the voters' wishes in creating the county department of corrections, giving it explicit direction to operate the county jails for all sentenced and unsentenced prisoners under authority of the county board of supervisors, it is necessary that this act take effect immediately.

Penal Code § 831.6.

(a) A transportation officer is a public officer, not a peace officer, appointed on a contract basis by a peace officer to transport a prisoner or prisoners.

(b) A transportation officer shall have the authority of a public officer, and shall have the right to carry or possess firearms, only while engaged in the transportation of a prisoner or prisoners for the duration of the contract.

(c) Each person described in this section as a transportation officer shall, prior to the transportation of any prisoner, have satisfactorily completed the training course specified in Section 832.

(d) A transportation officer may use reasonable force in establishing and maintaining custody of persons delivered to him or her by a peace officer.

Penal Code § 831.7.

(a) As used in this section, a custody assistant is a person who is a full-time employee, not a peace officer, employed by the county sheriff's department who assists peace officer personnel in maintaining order and security in a custody detention, court detention, or station jail facility of the sheriff's department. A custody assistant is responsible for maintaining custody of prisoners and performs tasks related to the operation of a local detention facility used for the detention of persons usually pending arraignment or upon court order either for their own safekeeping or for the specific purpose of serving a sentence therein. Custody assistants of the sheriff's department shall be employees of, and under the authority of, the sheriff.

(b) A custody assistant has no right to carry or possess firearms in the performance of his or her prescribed duties.

(c) Each person described in this section as a custody assistant shall satisfactorily complete a training course specified by the sheriff's department. In addition, each person designated as a custody assistant shall satisfactorily meet the minimum selection and training standards prescribed by the Department of Corrections and Rehabilitation pursuant to Section 6035.

(d) A custody assistant may use reasonable force in establishing and maintaining custody of persons housed at a local detention facility, court detention facility, or station jail facility.

(e) Custody assistants employed by the county sheriff's department are authorized to perform the following additional duties in a custody facility, court detention facility, or station jail facility:

(1) Assist in supervising the conduct of inmates in sleeping quarters, during meals and bathing, at recreation, and on work assignments.

(2) Assist in overseeing the work of, and instructing, a group of inmates assigned to various operational, maintenance, or other rehabilitative activities.

(3) Assist in the operation of main or dormitory control booths.

(4) Assist in processing inmates for court appearances.

(5) Control, or assist in the monitoring and control of, access to attorney rooms and visiting areas.

(6) Fingerprint, photograph, or operate livescan machines with respect to inmates, or assist in the fingerprinting or photographing of inmates.

(7) Obtain criminal history information relating to an inmate including any warrant or other hold, and update classification or housing information relating to an inmate, as necessary.

(8) Interview inmates and review records related to the classification process to determine the appropriate security level for an inmate or the eligibility of an inmate for transfer to another facility.

(9) Ensure compliance of a custody facility, court detention facility, or station jail facility with the provisions of Title 15 of the California Code of Regulations, or with any other applicable legislative or judicial mandate.

(10) Assist in receiving and processing inmates in a sheriff's station, court detention area, or type I jail facility.

(11) Secure inmates and their personal property and moneys as necessary in compliance with the rules and regulations of the sheriff' s department.

(12) Order, inspect, or serve meals to inmates.

(13) Maintain sanitary conditions within a custody facility, court detention facility, or station jail facility.

(14) Respond to public inquiries regarding any inmate.

(f) Notwithstanding any other law, nothing in this section shall be construed to confer any authority upon a custody assistant except while on duty, or to grant any additional retirement benefits to persons employed within this classification.

(g) This section shall apply only in a county of the first class, as established by Sections 28020 and 28022 of the Government Code, but shall not be operative in a county until adopted by resolution of the board of supervisors.

Penal Code § 832.

(a) Every person described in this chapter as a peace officer shall satisfactorily complete an introductory course of training prescribed by the Commission on Peace Officer Standards and Training. On or after July 1, 1989, satisfactory completion of the course shall be demonstrated by passage of an appropriate examination developed or approved by the commission. Training in the carrying and use of firearms shall not be required of any peace officer whose employing agency prohibits the use of firearms.

(b)(1) Every peace officer described in this chapter, prior to the exercise of the powers of a peace officer, shall have satisfactorily completed the course of training described in subdivision (a).

(2) Every peace officer described in Section 13510 or in subdivision (a) of Section 830.2 may satisfactorily complete the training required by this section as part of the training prescribed pursuant to Section 13510.

(c) Persons described in this chapter as peace officers who have not satisfactorily completed the course described in subdivision (a), as specified in subdivision (b), shall not have the powers of a peace officer until they satisfactorily complete the course.

(d) Any peace officer who, on March 4, 1972, possesses or is qualified to possess the basic certificate as awarded by the Commission on Peace Officer Standards and Training shall be exempted from this section.

(e)(1) Any person completing the training described in subdivision (a) who does not become employed as a peace officer within three years from the date of passing the examination described in subdivision (a), or who has a three-year or longer break in service as a peace officer, shall pass the examination described in subdivision (a) prior to the exercise of the powers of a peace officer, except for any person described in paragraph (2).

(2) The requirement in paragraph (1) does not apply to any person who meets any of the following requirements:

(A) Is returning to a management position that is at the second level of supervision or higher.

(B) Has successfully requalified for a basic course through the Commission on Peace Officer Standards and Training.

(C) Has maintained proficiency through teaching the course described in subdivision (a).

(D) During the break in California service, was continuously employed as a peace officer in another state or at the federal level.

(E) Has previously met the requirements of subdivision (a), has been appointed as a peace officer under subdivision (c) of Section 830.1, and has been continuously employed as a custodial officer as defined in Section 831 or 831.5 by the agency making the peace officer appointment since completing the training prescribed in subdivision (a).

(f) The commission may charge appropriate fees for the examination required by subdivision (e), not to exceed actual costs.

(g) Notwithstanding any other provision of law, the commission may charge appropriate fees for the examination required by subdivision (a) to each applicant who is not sponsored by a local or other law enforcement agency, or is not a peace officer employed by, or under consideration for employment by, a state or local agency, department, or district, or is not a custodial officer as defined in Sections 831 and 831.5. The fees shall not exceed actual costs.

Penal Code § 832.05.

(a) Each state or local department or agency that employs peace officers shall utilize a person meeting the requirements set forth in subdivision (f) of Section 1031 of the Government Code, applicable to emotional and mental examinations, for any emotional and mental evaluation done in the course of the department or agency' s screening of peace officer recruits or the evaluation of peace officers to determine their fitness for duty.

(b) This section shall become operative on January 1, 2005. 832.1. Any airport security officer, airport policeman, or airport special officer, regularly employed and paid by a city, county, city and county, or district who is a peace officer shall have completed a course of training relative to airport security approved by the Commission on Peace Officers Standards and Training. Any such airport officer so employed on the effective date of this section shall have completed the course of instruction required by this section by September 1, 1973. Any airport officer so employed after such effective date shall have completed the course of instruction within 90 days after such employment. Any officer who has not satisfactorily completed such course within such prescribed time shall not continue to have the powers of a peace officer until they have satisfactorily completed such course.

Penal Code § 832.2.

Every school police reserve officer, as described in Section 38000 of the Education Code, shall complete a course of training approved by the Commission on Peace Officer Standards and Training relating directly to the role of school police reserve officers. The school police reserve officer training course shall address guidelines and procedures for reporting offenses to other law enforcement agencies that deal with violence on campus and other school related matters, as determined by the Commission on Peace Officer Standards and Training.

Penal Code § 832.25.

(a) Notwithstanding any other provision of law, all welfare fraud investigators or inspectors who are appointed as peace officers pursuant to subdivision (a) of Section 830.35 on or after January 1, 2001, shall attend and complete a specialized investigators basic course approved by the Commission on Peace Officer Standards and Training within one year of being hired as a welfare investigator or inspector. Any welfare fraud investigator or inspector appointed prior to January 1, 2001, shall not be required to attend and complete the training required by this section, provided that he or she has been continuously employed in that capacity prior to January 1, 2001, by the county that made the appointment.

(b) Any investigator or inspector who possesses a valid basic peace officer certificate as awarded by the Commission on Peace Officer Standards and Training or who has successfully completed the regular basic course certified by the Commission on Peace Officer Standards and Training basic course within three years prior to appointment shall be exempt from the training requirements of subdivision (a).

Penal Code § 832.3.

(a) Except as provided in subdivision (e), any sheriff, undersheriff, or deputy sheriff of a county, any police officer of a city, and any police officer of a district authorized by statute to maintain a police department, who is first employed after January 1, 1975, shall successfully complete a course of training prescribed by the Commission on Peace Officer Standards and Training before exercising the powers of a peace officer, except while participating as a trainee in a supervised field training program approved by the Commission on Peace Officer Standards and Training. Each police chief, or any other person in charge of a local law enforcement agency, appointed on or after January 1, 1999, as a condition of continued employment, shall complete the course of training pursuant to this subdivision within two years of appointment. The training course for a sheriff, an undersheriff, and a deputy sheriff of a county, and a police chief and a police officer of a city or any other local law enforcement agency, shall be the same.

(b) For the purpose of ensuring competent peace officers and standardizing the training required in subdivision (a), the commission shall develop a testing program, including standardized tests that enable (1) comparisons between presenters of the training and (2) assessments of trainee achievement. The trainees' test scores shall be used only for the purposes enumerated in this subdivision and those research purposes as shall be approved in advance by the commission. The commission shall take all steps necessary to maintain the confidentiality of the test scores, test items, scoring keys, and other examination data used in the testing program required by this subdivision. The commission shall determine the minimum passing score for each test and the conditions for retesting students who fail. Passing these tests shall be required for successful completion of the training required in subdivision (a). Presenters approved by the commission to provide the training required in subdivision (a) shall administer the standardized tests or, at the commission's option, shall facilitate the commission's administration of the standardized tests to all trainees.

(c) Notwithstanding subdivision (c) of Section 84500 of the Education Code and any regulations adopted pursuant thereto, community colleges may give preference in enrollment to employed law enforcement trainees who shall complete training as prescribed by this section. At least 15 percent of each presentation shall consist of nonlaw enforcement trainees if they are available. Preference should only be given when the trainee could not complete the course within the time required by statute, and only when no other training program is reasonably available. Average daily attendance for these courses shall be reported for state aid.

(d) Prior to July 1, 1987, the commission shall make a report to the Legislature on academy proficiency testing scores. This report shall include an evaluation of the correlation between academy proficiency test scores and performance as a peace officer.

(e)(1) Any deputy sheriff described in subdivision (c) of Section 830.1 shall be exempt from the training requirements specified in subdivisions (a) and (b) as long as his or her assignments remain custodial related.

(2) Deputy sheriffs described in subdivision (c) of Section 830.1 shall complete the training for peace officers pursuant to subdivision (a) of Section 832, and within 120 days after the date of employment, shall complete the training required by the Board of Corrections for custodial personnel pursuant to Section 6035, and the training required for custodial personnel of local detention facilities pursuant to Division 1 (commencing with Section 100) of Title 15 of the California Code of Regulations.

(3) Deputy sheriffs described in subdivision (c) of Section 830.1 shall complete the course of training pursuant to subdivision (a) prior to being reassigned from custodial assignments to duties with responsibility for the prevention and detection of crime and the general enforcement of the criminal laws of this state.

(f) Any school police officer first employed by a K-12 public school district or California Community College district after July 1, 1999, shall successfully complete a basic course of training as prescribed by subdivision (a) before exercising the powers of a peace officer. A school police officer shall not be subject to this subdivision while participating as a trainee in a supervised field training program approved by the Commission on Peace Officer Standards and Training.

(g) The commission shall prepare a specialized course of instruction for the training of school peace officers, as defined in Section 830.32, to meet the unique safety needs of a school environment. This course is intended to supplement any other training requirements.

(h) Any school peace officer first employed by a K-12 public school district or California Community College district before July 1, 1999, shall successfully complete the specialized course of training prescribed in subdivision (g) no later than July 1, 2002. Any school police officer first employed by a K-12 public school district or California Community College district after July 1, 1999, shall successfully complete the specialized course of training prescribed in subdivision (g) within two years of the date of first employment.

Penal Code § 832.4.

(a) Any undersheriff or deputy sheriff of a county, any police officer of a city, and any police officer of a district authorized by statute to maintain a police department, who is first employed after January 1, 1974, and is responsible for the prevention and detection of crime and the general enforcement of the criminal laws of this state, shall obtain the basic certificate issued by the Commission on Peace Officer Standards and Training within 18 months of his or her employment in order to continue to exercise the powers of a peace officer after the expiration of the 18-month period.

(b) Every peace officer listed in subdivision (a) of Section 830.1, except a sheriff, or elected marshal, or a deputy sheriff described in subdivision (c) of Section 830.1, who is employed after January 1, 1988, shall obtain the basic certificate issued by the Commission on Peace Officer Standards and Training upon completion of probation, but in no case later than 24 months after his or her employment, in order to continue to exercise the powers of a peace officer after the expiration of the 24-month period. Deputy sheriffs described in subdivision (c) of Section 830.1 shall obtain the basic certificate issued by the Commission on Peace Officer Standards and Training within 24 months after being reassigned from custodial duties to general law enforcement duties. In those cases where the probationary period established by the employing agency is 24 months, the peace officers described in this subdivision may continue to exercise the powers of a peace officer for an additional three-month period to allow for the processing of the certification application.

(c) Each police chief, or any other person in charge of a local law enforcement agency, appointed on or after January 1, 1999, as a condition of continued employment, shall obtain the basic certificate issued by the Commission on Peace Officer Standards and Training within two years of appointment.

Penal Code § 832.5.

(a)(1) Each department or agency in this state that employs peace officers shall establish a procedure to investigate complaints by members of the public against the personnel of these departments or agencies, and shall make a written description of the procedure available to the public.

(2) Each department or agency that employs custodial officers, as defined in Section 831.5, may establish a procedure to investigate complaints by members of the public against those custodial officers employed by these departments or agencies, provided however, that any procedure so established shall comply with the provisions of this section and with the provisions of Section 832.7.

(b) Complaints and any reports or findings relating to these complaints shall be retained for a period of at least five years. All complaints retained pursuant to this subdivision may be maintained either in the peace or custodial officer's general personnel file or in a separate file designated by the department or agency as provided by department or agency policy, in accordance with all applicable requirements of law. However, prior to any official determination regarding promotion, transfer, or disciplinary action by an officer's employing department or agency, the complaints described by subdivision (c) shall be removed from the officer's general personnel file and placed in separate file designated by the department or agency, in accordance with all applicable requirements of law.

(c) Complaints by members of the public that are determined by the peace or custodial officer's employing agency to be frivolous, as defined in Section 128.5 of the Code of Civil Procedure, or unfounded or exonerated, or any portion of a complaint that is determined to be frivolous, unfounded, or exonerated, shall not be maintained in that officer's general personnel file. However, these complaints shall be retained in other, separate files that shall be deemed personnel records for purposes of the California Public Records Act (Chapter 3.5 (commencing with Section 6250) of Division 7 of Title 1 of the Government Code) and Section 1043 of the Evidence Code.

(1) Management of the peace or custodial officer's employing agency shall have access to the files described in this subdivision.

(2) Management of the peace or custodial officer's employing agency shall not use the complaints contained in these separate files for punitive or promotional purposes except as permitted by subdivision (f) of Section 3304 of the Government Code.

(3) Management of the peace or custodial officer's employing agency may identify any officer who is subject to the complaints maintained in these files which require counseling or additional training. However, if a complaint is removed from the officer's personnel file, any reference in the personnel file to the complaint or to a separate file shall be deleted.

(d) As used in this section, the following definitions apply:

(1) "General personnel file" means the file maintained by the agency containing the primary records specific to each peace or custodial officer's employment, including evaluations, assignments, status changes, and imposed discipline.

(2) "Unfounded" means that the investigation clearly established that the allegation is not true.

(3) "Exonerated" means that the investigation clearly established that the actions of the peace or custodial officer that formed the basis for the complaint are not violations of law or department policy.

Penal Code § 832.6.

(a) Every person deputized or appointed, as described in subdivision (a) of Section 830.6, shall have the powers of a peace officer only when the person is any of the following:

(1) A level I reserve officer deputized or appointed pursuant to paragraph (1) or (2) of subdivision (a) or subdivision (b) of Section 830.6 and assigned to the prevention and detection of crime and the general enforcement of the laws of this state, whether or not working alone, and the person has completed the basic training course for deputy sheriffs and police officers prescribed by the Commission on Peace Officer Standards and Training. For level I reserve officers appointed prior to January 1, 1997, the basic training requirement shall be the course that was prescribed at the time of their appointment. Reserve officers appointed pursuant to this paragraph shall satisfy the continuing professional training requirement prescribed by the commission.

(2) A level II reserve officer assigned to the prevention and detection of crime and the general enforcement of the laws of this state while under the immediate supervision of a peace officer who has completed the basic training course for deputy sheriffs and police officers prescribed by the Commission on Peace Officer Standards and Training, and the level II reserve officer has completed the course required by Section 832 and any other training prescribed by the commission. Level II reserve officers appointed pursuant to this paragraph may be assigned, without immediate supervision, to those limited duties that are authorized for level III reserve officers pursuant to paragraph (3). Reserve officers appointed pursuant to this paragraph shall satisfy the continuing professional training requirement prescribed by the commission.

(3) Level III reserve officers may be deployed and are authorized only to carry out limited support duties not requiring general law enforcement powers in their routine performance. Those limited duties shall include traffic control, security at parades and sporting events, report taking, evidence transportation, parking enforcement, and other duties that are not likely to result in physical arrests. Level III reserve officers while assigned these duties shall be supervised in the accessible vicinity by a level I reserve officer or a full-time, regular peace officer employed by a law enforcement agency authorized to have reserve officers. Level III reserve officers may transport prisoners without immediate supervision. Those persons shall have completed the training required under Section 832 and any other training prescribed by the commission for those persons.

(4) A person assigned to the prevention and detection of a particular crime or crimes or to the detection or apprehension of a particular individual or individuals while working under the supervision of a California peace officer in a county adjacent to the state border who possesses a basic certificate issued by the Commission on Peace Officer Standards and Training, and the person is a law enforcement officer who is regularly employed by a local or state law enforcement agency in an adjoining state and has completed the basic training required for peace officers in his or her state.

(5) For purposes of this section, a reserve officer who has previously satisfied the training requirements pursuant to this section, and has served as a level I or II reserve officer within the three-year period prior to the date of a new appointment shall be deemed to remain qualified as to the Commission on Peace Officer Standards and Training requirements if that reserve officer accepts a new appointment at the same or lower level with another law enforcement agency. If the reserve officer has more than a three-year break in service, he or she shall satisfy current training requirements. This training shall fully satisfy any other training requirements required by law, including those specified in Section 832. In no case shall a peace officer of an adjoining state provide services within a California jurisdiction during any period in which the regular law enforcement agency of the jurisdiction is involved in a labor dispute.

(b) Notwithstanding subdivision (a), a person who is issued a level I reserve officer certificate before January 1, 1981, shall have the full powers and duties of a peace officer as provided by Section 830.1 if so designated by local ordinance or, if the local agency is not authorized to act by ordinance, by resolution, either individually or by class, if the appointing authority determines the person is qualified to perform general law enforcement duties by reason of the person's training and experience. Persons who were qualified to be issued the level I reserve officer certificate before January 1, 1981, and who state in writing under penalty of perjury that they applied for but were not issued the certificate before January 1, 1981, may be issued the certificate before July 1, 1984. For purposes of this section, certificates so issued shall be deemed to have the full force and effect of any level I reserve officer certificate issued prior to January 1, 1981.

(c) In carrying out this section, the commission:

(1) May use proficiency testing to satisfy reserve training standards.

(2) Shall provide for convenient training to remote areas in the state.

(3) Shall establish a professional certificate for reserve officers as defined in paragraph (1) of subdivision (a) and may establish a professional certificate for reserve officers as defined in paragraphs (2) and (3) of subdivision (a).

(4) Shall facilitate the voluntary transition of reserve officers to regular officers with no unnecessary redundancy between the training required for level I and level II reserve officers.

(d) In carrying out paragraphs (1) and (3) of subdivision (c), the commission may establish and levy appropriate fees, provided the fees do not exceed the cost for administering the respective services. These fees shall be deposited in the Peace Officers' Training Fund established by Section 13520.

(e) The commission shall include an amount in its annual budget request to carry out this section.

Penal Code § 832.7.

(a) Peace officer or custodial officer personnel records and records maintained by any state or local agency pursuant to Section 832.5, or information obtained from these records, are confidential and shall not be disclosed in any criminal or civil proceeding except by discovery pursuant to Sections 1043 and 1046 of the Evidence Code. This section shall not apply to investigations or proceedings concerning the conduct of peace officers or custodial officers, or an agency or department that employs those officers, conducted by a grand jury, a district attorney's office, or the Attorney General's office.

(b) Notwithstanding subdivision (a), a department or agency shall release to the complaining party a copy of his or her own statements at the time the complaint is filed.

(c) Notwithstanding subdivision (a), a department or agency that employs peace or custodial officers may disseminate data regarding the number, type, or disposition of complaints (sustained, not sustained, exonerated, or unfounded) made against its officers if that information is in a form which does not identify the individuals involved.

(d) Notwithstanding subdivision (a), a department or agency that employs peace or custodial officers may release factual information concerning a disciplinary investigation if the officer who is the subject of the disciplinary investigation, or the officer's agent or representative, publicly makes a statement he or she knows to be false concerning the investigation or the imposition of disciplinary action. Information may not be disclosed by the peace or custodial officer's employer unless the false statement was published by an established medium of communication, such as television, radio, or a newspaper. Disclosure of factual information by the employing agency pursuant to this subdivision is limited to facts contained in the officer's personnel file concerning the disciplinary investigation or imposition of disciplinary action that specifically refute the false statements made public by the peace or custodial officer or his or her agent or representative.

(e)(1) The department or agency shall provide written notification to the complaining party of the disposition of the complaint within 30 days of the disposition.

(2) The notification described in this subdivision shall not be conclusive or binding or admissible as evidence in any separate or subsequent action or proceeding brought before an arbitrator, court, or judge of this state or the United States.

(f) Nothing in this section shall affect the discovery or disclosure of information contained in a peace or custodial officer's personnel file pursuant to Section 1043 of the Evidence Code.

Penal Code § 832.8.

As used in Section 832.7, "personnel records" means any file maintained under that individual's name by his or her employing agency and containing records relating to any of the following:

(a) Personal data, including marital status, family members, educational and employment history, home addresses, or similar information.

(b) Medical history.

(c) Election of employee benefits.

(d) Employee advancement, appraisal, or discipline.

(e) Complaints, or investigations of complaints, concerning an event or transaction in which he or she participated, or which he or she perceived, and pertaining to the manner in which he or she performed his or her duties.

(f) Any other information the disclosure of which would constitute an unwarranted invasion of personal privacy.

Penal Code § 832.9.

(a) A governmental entity employing a peace officer, as defined in Section 830, judge, court commissioner, or an attorney employed by the Department of Justice, the State Public Defender, or a county office of a district attorney or public defender shall reimburse the moving and relocation expenses of those employees, or any member of his or her immediate family residing with the officer in the same household or on the same property when it is necessary to move because the officer has received a credible threat that a life threatening action may be taken against the officer, judge, court commissioner, or an attorney employed by the Department of Justice, the State Public Defender, or a county office of the district attorney or public defender or his or her immediate family as a result of his or her employment.

(b) The person relocated shall receive actual and necessary moving and relocation expenses incurred both before and after the change of residence, including reimbursement for the costs of moving household effects either by a commercial household goods carrier or by the employee.

(1) Actual and necessary moving costs shall be those costs that are set forth in the Department of Personnel Administration rules governing promotional relocations while in the state service. The department shall not be required to administer this section.

(2) The public entity shall not be liable for any loss in value to a residence or for the decrease in value due to a forced sale.

(3) Except as provided in subdivision (c), peace officers, judges, court commissioners, and attorneys employed by the Department of Justice, the State Public Defender, or a county office of a district attorney or public defender shall receive approval of the appointing authority prior to incurring any cost covered by this section.

(4) Peace officers, judges, court commissioners, and attorneys employed by the Department of Justice, the State Public Defender, or a county office of a district attorney or public defender shall not be considered to be on duty while moving unless approved by the appointing authority.

(5) For a relocation to be covered by this section, the appointing authority shall be notified as soon as a credible threat has been received.

(6) Temporary relocation housing shall not exceed 60 days.

(7) The public entity ceases to be liable for relocation costs after 120 days of the original notification of a viable threat if the peace officer, judge, court commissioner, or attorney employed by the Department of Justice, the State Public Defender, or a county office of a district attorney or public defender has failed to relocate.

(c)(1) For purposes of the right to reimbursement of moving and relocation expenses pursuant to this section, judges shall be deemed to be employees of the State of California and a court commissioner is an employee of the court by which he or she is employed.

(2) For purposes of paragraph (3) of subdivision (b), a court commissioner shall receive approval by the presiding judge of the superior court in the county in which he or she is located.

(3) For purposes of paragraph (3) of subdivision (b), judges, including justices of the Supreme Court and the Courts of Appeal, shall receive approval from the Chief Justice, or his or her designee.

(d) As used in this section, "credible threat" means a verbal or written statement or a threat implied by a pattern of conduct or a combination of verbal or written statements and conduct made with the intent and the apparent ability to carry out the threat so as to cause the person who is the target of the threat to reasonably fear for his or her safety or the safety of his or her immediate family.

(e) As used in this section, "immediate family" means the spouse, parents, siblings, and children residing with the peace officer, judge, court commissioner, or attorney employed by the Department of Justice, the State Public Defender, or a county office of a district attorney or public defender.

Penal Code § 832.15.

(a) On and after October 1, 1993, the Department of Justice shall notify a state or local agency as to whether an individual applying for a position as a peace officer, as defined by this chapter, a custodial officer authorized by the employing agency to carry a firearm pursuant to Section 831.5, or a transportation officer pursuant to Section 831.6 authorized by the employing agency to carry a firearm, is prohibited from possessing, receiving, owning, or purchasing a firearm pursuant to state or federal law. If the prohibition is temporary, the notice shall indicate the date that the prohibition expires. However, the notice shall not provide any other information with respect to the basis for the prohibition.

(b) Before providing the information specified in subdivision (a), the applicant shall provide the Department of Justice with fingerprints and other identifying information deemed necessary by the department.

(c) The Department of Justice may charge the applicant a fee sufficient to reimburse its costs for furnishing the information specified in subdivision (a).

(d) The notice required by this section shall not apply to persons receiving treatment under subdivision (a) of Section 8100 of the Welfare and Institutions Code.

Penal Code § 832.16.

(a) On and after October 1, 1993, the Department of Justice shall notify a state or local agency employing a peace officer, as defined by this chapter, who is authorized by the employing agency to carry a firearm, as to whether a peace officer is prohibited from possessing, receiving, owning, or purchasing a firearm pursuant to state or federal law. If the prohibition is temporary, the notice shall indicate the date that the prohibition expires. However, the notice shall not provide any other information with respect to the basis for the prohibition.

(b) Before providing the information specified in subdivision (a), the agency employing the peace officer shall provide the Department of Justice with the officer's fingerprints and other identifying information deemed necessary by the department.

(c) The information specified in this section shall only be provided by the Department of Justice subject to the availability of funding.

(d) The notice required by this section shall not apply to persons receiving treatment under subdivision (a) of Section 8100 of the Welfare and Institutions Code.

Penal Code § 832.17.

(a) Upon request by a state or local agency, the Department of Justice shall notify the state or local agency as to whether an individual employed as a custodial or transportation officer and authorized by the employing agency to carry a firearm, is prohibited or subsequently becomes prohibited from possessing, receiving, owning, or purchasing a firearm pursuant to state or federal law. If the prohibition is temporary, the notice shall indicate the date on which the prohibition expires. However, the notice shall not provide any other information with respect to the basis for the prohibition.

(b) Before the department provides the information specified in subdivision (a), the officer shall provide the department with his or her fingerprints and other identifying information deemed necessary by the department.

(c) The department may charge the officer a fee sufficient to reimburse its costs for furnishing the information specified in subdivision (a). A local law enforcement agency may pay this fee for the officer.

(d) The notice required by this section shall not apply to persons receiving treatment under subdivision (a) of Section 8100 of the Welfare and Institutions Code.

Penal Code § 833.

A peace officer may search for dangerous weapons any person whom he has legal cause to arrest, whenever he has reasonable cause to believe that the person possesses a dangerous weapon. If the officer finds a dangerous weapon, he may take and keep it until the completion of the questioning, when he shall either return it or arrest the person. The arrest may be for the illegal possession of the weapon.

Penal Code § 833.5.

(a) In addition to any other detention permitted by law, if a peace officer has reasonable cause to believe that a person has a firearm or other deadly weapon with him or her in violation of any provision of law relating to firearms or deadly weapons the peace officer may detain that person to determine whether a crime relating to firearms or deadly weapons has been committed. For purposes of this section "reasonable cause to detain" requires that the circumstances known or apparent to the officer must include specific and articulable facts causing him or her to suspect that some offense relating to firearms or deadly weapons has taken place or is occurring or is about to occur and that the person he or she intends to detain is involved in that offense. The circumstances must be such as would cause any reasonable peace officer in like position, drawing when appropriate on his or her training and experience, to suspect the same offense and the same involvement by the person in question.

(b) Incident to any detention permitted pursuant to subdivision (a), a peace officer may conduct a limited search of the person for firearms or weapons if the peace officer reasonably concludes that the person detained may be armed and presently dangerous to the peace officer or others. Any firearm or weapon seized pursuant to a valid detention or search pursuant to this section shall be admissible in evidence in any proceeding for any purpose permitted by law.

(c) This section shall not be construed to otherwise limit the authority of a peace officer to detain any person or to make an arrest based on reasonable cause.

(d) This section shall not be construed to permit a peace officer to conduct a detention or search of any person at the person's residence or place of business absent a search warrant or other reasonable cause to detain or search.

(e) If a firearm or weapon is seized pursuant to this section and the person from whom it was seized owned the firearm or weapon and is convicted of a violation of any offense relating to the possession of such firearm or weapon, the court shall order the firearm or weapon to be deemed a nuisance and disposed of in the manner provided by Section 12028.

Penal Code § 834.

An arrest is taking a person into custody, in a case and in the manner authorized by law. An arrest may be made by a peace officer or by a private person.

Penal Code § 834a.

If a person has knowledge, or by the exercise of reasonable care, should have knowledge, that he is being arrested by a peace officer, it is the duty of such person to refrain from using force or any weapon to resist such arrest.

Penal Code § 835.

An arrest is made by an actual restraint of the person, or by submission to the custody of an officer. The person arrested may be subjected to such restraint as is reasonable for his arrest and detention.

Penal Code § 835a.

Any peace officer who has reasonable cause to believe that the person to be arrested has committed a public offense may use reasonable force to effect the arrest, to prevent escape or to overcome resistance. A peace officer who makes or attempts to make an arrest need not retreat or desist from his efforts by reason of the resistance or threatened resistance of the person being arrested; nor shall such officer be deemed an aggressor or lose his right to self-defense by the use of reasonable force to effect the arrest or to prevent escape or to overcome resistance.

Penal Code § 836.

(a) A peace officer may arrest a person in obedience to a warrant, or, pursuant to the authority granted to him or her by Chapter 4.5 (commencing with Section 830) of Title 3 of Part 2, without a warrant, may arrest a person whenever any of the following circumstances occur:

(1) The officer has probable cause to believe that the person to be arrested has committed a public offense in the officer's presence.

(2) The person arrested has committed a felony, although not in the officer's presence.

(3) The officer has probable cause to believe that the person to be arrested has committed a felony, whether or not a felony, in fact, has been committed.

(b) Any time a peace officer is called out on a domestic violence call, it shall be mandatory that the officer make a good faith effort to inform the victim of his or her right to make a citizen's arrest. This information shall include advising the victim how to safely execute the arrest.

(c)(1) When a peace officer is responding to a call alleging a violation of a domestic violence protective or restraining order issued under Section 527.6 of the Code of Civil Procedure, the Family Code, Section 136.2, 646.91, or paragraph (2) of subdivision (a) of Section 1203.097 of this code, Section 213.5 or 15657.03 of the Welfare and Institutions Code, or of a domestic violence protective or restraining order issued by the court of another state, tribe, or territory and the peace officer has probable cause to believe that the person against whom the order is issued has notice of the order and has committed an act in violation of the order, the officer shall, consistent with subdivision (b) of Section 13701, make a lawful arrest of the person without a warrant and take that person into custody whether or not the violation occurred in the presence of the arresting officer. The officer shall, as soon as possible after the arrest, confirm with the appropriate authorities or the Domestic Violence Protection Order Registry maintained pursuant to Section 6380 of the Family Code that a true copy of the protective order has been registered, unless the victim provides the officer with a copy of the protective order.

(2) The person against whom a protective order has been issued shall be deemed to have notice of the order if the victim presents to the officer proof of service of the order, the officer confirms with the appropriate authorities that a true copy of the proof of service is on file, or the person against whom the protective order was issued was present at the protective order hearing or was informed by a peace officer of the contents of the protective order.

(3) In situations where mutual protective orders have been issued under Division 10 (commencing with Section 6200) of the Family Code, liability for arrest under this subdivision applies only to those persons who are reasonably believed to have been the primary aggressor. In those situations, prior to making an arrest under this subdivision, the peace officer shall make reasonable efforts to identify, and may arrest, the primary aggressor involved in the incident. The primary aggressor is the person determined to be the most significant, rather than the first, aggressor. In identifying the primary aggressor, an officer shall consider

(A) the intent of the law to protect victims of domestic violence from continuing abuse,

(B) the threats creating fear of physical injury,

(C) the history of domestic violence between the persons involved, and

(D) whether either person involved acted in self-defense.

(d) Notwithstanding paragraph (1) of subdivision (a), if a suspect commits an assault or battery upon a current or former spouse, fiancé, fiancee, a current or former cohabitant as defined in Section 6209 of the Family Code, a person with whom the suspect currently is having or has previously had an engagement or dating relationship, as defined in paragraph (10) of subdivision (f) of Section 243, a person with whom the suspect has parented a child, or is presumed to have parented a child pursuant to the Uniform Parentage Act (Part 3 (commencing with Section 7600) of Division 12 of the Family Code), a child of the suspect, a child whose parentage by the suspect is the subject of an action under the Uniform Parentage Act, a child of a person in one of the above categories, any other person related to the suspect by consanguinity or affinity within the second degree, or any person who is 65 years of age or older and who is related to the suspect by blood or legal guardianship, a peace officer may arrest the suspect without a warrant where both of the following circumstances apply:

(1) The peace officer has probable cause to believe that the person to be arrested has committed the assault or battery, whether or not it has in fact been committed.

(2) The peace officer makes the arrest as soon as probable cause arises to believe that the person to be arrested has committed the assault or battery, whether or not it has in fact been committed.

(e) In addition to the authority to make an arrest without a warrant pursuant to paragraphs (1) and (3) of subdivision (a), a peace officer may, without a warrant, arrest a person for a violation of Section 12025 when all of the following apply:

(1) The officer has reasonable cause to believe that the person to be arrested has committed the violation of Section 12025.

(2) The violation of Section 12025 occurred within an airport, as defined in Section 21013 of the Public Utilities Code, in an area to which access is controlled by the inspection of persons and property.

(3) The peace officer makes the arrest as soon as reasonable cause arises to believe that the person to be arrested has committed the violation of Section 12025.

Penal Code § 836.1.

When a person commits an assault or battery against the person of a firefighter, emergency medical technician, or mobile intensive care paramedic while that person is on duty engaged in the performance of his or her duties in violation of subdivision (b) of Section 241 or subdivision (b) of Section 243, a peace officer may, without a warrant, arrest the person who commits the assault or battery:

(a) Whenever the peace officer has reasonable cause to believe that the person to be arrested has committed the assault or battery, although the assault or battery was not committed in the peace officer's presence.

(b) Whenever the peace officer has reasonable cause to believe that the person to be arrested has committed the assault or battery, whether or not the assault or battery has in fact been committed.

Penal Code § 836.3.

A peace officer may make an arrest in obedience to a warrant delivered to him, or may, without a warrant, arrest a person who, while charged with or convicted of a misdemeanor, has escaped from any county or city jail, prison, industrial farm or industrial road camp or from the custody of the officer or person in charge of him while engaged on any county road or other county work or going to or returning from such county road or other county work or from the custody of any officer or person in whose lawful custody he is when such escape is not by force or violence.

Penal Code § 836.5.

(a) A public officer or employee, when authorized by ordinance, may arrest a person without a warrant whenever the officer or employee has reasonable cause to believe that the person to be arrested has committed a misdemeanor in the presence of the officer or employee that is a violation of a statute or ordinance that the officer or employee has the duty to enforce.

(b) There shall be no civil liability on the part of, and no cause of action shall arise against, any public officer or employee acting pursuant to subdivision (a) and within the scope of his or her authority for false arrest or false imprisonment arising out of any arrest that is lawful or that the public officer or employee, at the time of the arrest, had reasonable cause to believe was lawful. No officer or employee shall be deemed an aggressor or lose his or her right to self-defense by the use of reasonable force to effect the arrest, prevent escape, or overcome resistance.

(c) In any case in which a person is arrested pursuant to subdivision (a) and the person arrested does not demand to be taken before a magistrate, the public officer or employee making the arrest shall prepare a written notice to appear and release the person on his or her promise to appear, as prescribed by Chapter 5C (commencing with Section 853.5). The provisions of that chapter shall thereafter apply with reference to any proceeding based upon the issuance of a written notice to appear pursuant to this authority.

(d) The governing body of a local agency, by ordinance, may authorize its officers and employees who have the duty to enforce a statute or ordinance to arrest persons for violations of the statute or ordinance as provided in subdivision (a).

(e) For purposes of this section, "ordinance" includes an order, rule, or regulation of any air pollution control district.

(f) For purposes of this section, a "public officer or employee" includes an officer or employee of a nonprofit transit corporation wholly owned by a local agency and formed to carry out the purposes of the local agency.

Penal Code § 836.6.

(a) It is unlawful for any person who is remanded by a magistrate or judge of any court in this state to the custody of a sheriff, marshal, or other police agency, to thereafter escape or attempt to escape from that custody.

(b) It is unlawful for any person who has been lawfully arrested by any peace officer and who knows, or by the exercise of reasonable care should have known, that he or she has been so arrested, to thereafter escape or attempt to escape from that peace officer.

(c) Any person who violates subdivision (a) or (b) is guilty of a misdemeanor, punishable by imprisonment in a county jail not to exceed one year. However, if the escape or attempted escape is by force or violence, and the person proximately causes a peace officer serious bodily injury, the person shall be punished by imprisonment in the state prison for two, three, or four years, or by imprisonment in a county jail not to exceed one year.

Penal Code § 837.

A private person may arrest another:

1. For a public offense committed or attempted in his presence.

2. When the person arrested has committed a felony, although not in his presence.

3. When a felony has been in fact committed, and he has reasonable cause for believing the person arrested to have committed it.

Penal Code § 838.

A magistrate may orally order a peace officer or private person to arrest any one committing or attempting to commit a public offense in the presence of such magistrate. 839. Any person making an arrest may orally summon as many persons as he deems necessary to aid him therein.

Penal Code § 840.

An arrest for the commission of a felony may be made on any day and at any time of the day or night. An arrest for the commission of a misdemeanor or an infraction cannot be made between the hours of 10 o'clock p.m. of any day and 6 o'clock a.m. of the succeeding day, unless:

(1) The arrest is made without a warrant pursuant to Section 836 or 837. (2) The arrest is made in a public place.

(3) The arrest is made when the person is in custody pursuant to another lawful arrest.

(4) The arrest is made pursuant to a warrant which, for good cause shown, directs that it may be served at any time of the day or night.

Penal Code § 841.

The person making the arrest must inform the person to be arrested of the intention to arrest him, of the cause of the arrest, and the authority to make it, except when the person making the arrest has reasonable cause to believe that the person to be arrested is actually engaged in the commission of or an attempt to commit an offense, or the person to be arrested is pursued immediately after its commission, or after an escape. The person making the arrest must, on request of the person he is arresting, inform the latter of the offense for which he is being arrested.

Penal Code § 841.5.

(a) Except as otherwise required by Chapter 10 (commencing with Section 1054) of Title 7, or by the United States Constitution or the California Constitution, no law enforcement officer or employee of a law enforcement agency shall disclose to any arrested person, or to any person who may be a defendant in a criminal action, the address or telephone number of any person who is a victim or witness in the alleged offense.

(b) Nothing in this section shall impair or interfere with the right of a defendant to obtain information necessary for the preparation of his or her defense through the discovery process.

(c) Nothing in this section shall impair or interfere with the right of an attorney to obtain the address or telephone number of any person who is a victim of, or a witness to, an alleged offense where a client of that attorney has been arrested for, or may be a defendant in, a criminal action related to the alleged offense.

(d) Nothing in this section shall preclude a law enforcement agency from releasing the entire contents of an accident report as required by Section 20012 of the Vehicle Code.

Penal Code § 842.

An arrest by a peace officer acting under a warrant is lawful even though the officer does not have the warrant in his possession at the time of the arrest, but if the person arrested so requests it, the warrant shall be shown to him as soon as practicable.

Penal Code § 843.

When the arrest is being made by an officer under the authority of a warrant, after information of the intention to make the arrest, if the person to be arrested either flees or forcibly resists, the officer may use all necessary means to effect the arrest.

Penal Code § 844.

To make an arrest, a private person, if the offense is a felony, and in all cases a peace officer, may break open the door or window of the house in which the person to be arrested is, or in which they have reasonable grounds for believing the person to be, after having demanded admittance and explained the purpose for which admittance is desired.

Penal Code § 845.

Any person who has lawfully entered a house for the purpose of making an arrest, may break open the door or window thereof if detained therein, when necessary for the purpose of liberating himself, and an officer may do the same, when necessary for the purpose of liberating a person who, acting in his aid, lawfully entered for the purpose of making an arrest, and is detained therein.

Penal Code § 846.

Any person making an arrest may take from the person arrested all offensive weapons which he may have about his person, and must deliver them to the magistrate before whom he is taken.

Penal Code § 847.

(a) A private person who has arrested another for the commission of a public offense must, without unnecessary delay, take the person arrested before a magistrate, or deliver him or her to a peace officer.

(b) There shall be no civil liability on the part of, and no cause of action shall arise against, any peace officer or federal criminal investigator or law enforcement officer described in subdivision (a) or (d) of Section 830.8, acting within the scope of his or her authority, for false arrest or false imprisonment arising out of any arrest under any of the following circumstances:

(1) The arrest was lawful, or the peace officer, at the time of the arrest, had reasonable cause to believe the arrest was lawful.

(2) The arrest was made pursuant to a charge made, upon reasonable cause, of the commission of a felony by the person to be arrested.

(3) The arrest was made pursuant to the requirements of Section 142, 837, 838, or 839.

Penal Code § 853.5.

(a) Except as otherwise provided by law, in any case in which a person is arrested for an offense declared to be an infraction, the person may be released according to the procedures set forth by this chapter for the release of persons arrested for an offense declared to be a misdemeanor. In all cases, except as specified in Sections 40302, 40303, 40305, and 40305.5 of the Vehicle Code, in which a person is arrested for an infraction, a peace officer shall only require the arrestee to present his or her driver' s license or other satisfactory evidence of his or her identity for examination and to sign a written promise to appear contained in a notice to appear. If the arrestee does not have a driver's license or other satisfactory evidence of identity in his or her possession, the officer may require the arrestee to place a right thumbprint, or a left thumbprint or fingerprint if the person has a missing or disfigured right thumb, on the notice to appear. Except for law enforcement purposes relating to the identity of the arrestee, no person or entity may sell, give away, allow the distribution of, include in a database, or create a database with, this print. Only if the arrestee refuses to sign a written promise, has no satisfactory identification, or refuses to provide a thumbprint or fingerprint may the arrestee be taken into custody.

(b) A person contesting a charge by claiming under penalty of perjury not to be the person issued the notice to appear may choose to submit a right thumbprint, or a left thumbprint if the person has a missing or disfigured right thumb, to the issuing court through his or her local law enforcement agency for comparison with the one placed on the notice to appear. A local law enforcement agency providing this service may charge the requester no more than the actual costs. The issuing court may refer the thumbprint submitted and the notice to appear to the prosecuting attorney for comparison of the thumbprints. When there is no thumbprint or fingerprint on the notice to appear, or when the comparison of thumbprints is inconclusive, the court shall refer the notice to appear or copy thereof back to the issuing agency for further investigation, unless the court finds that referral is not in the interest of justice.

(c) Upon initiation of the investigation or comparison process by referral of the court, the court shall continue the case and the speedy trial period shall be tolled for 45 days.

(d) Upon receipt of the issuing agency's or prosecuting attorney's response, the court may make a finding of factual innocence pursuant to Section 530.6 if the court determines that there is insufficient evidence that the person cited is the person charged and shall immediately notify the Department of Motor Vehicles of its determination. If the Department of Motor Vehicles determines the citation or citations in question formed the basis of a suspension or revocation of the person's driving privilege, the department shall immediately set aside the action.

(e) If the prosecuting attorney or issuing agency fails to respond to a court referral within 45 days, the court shall make a finding of factual innocence pursuant to Section 530.6, unless the court finds that a finding of factual innocence is not in the interest of justice.

Penal Code § 853.6.

(a) In any case in which a person is arrested for an offense declared to be a misdemeanor, including a violation of any city or county ordinance, and does not demand to be taken before a magistrate, that person shall, instead of being taken before a magistrate, be released according to the procedures set forth by this chapter. If the person is released, the officer or his or her superior shall prepare in duplicate a written notice to appear in court, containing the name and address of the person, the offense charged, and the time when, and place where, the person shall appear in court. If, pursuant to subdivision (i), the person is not released prior to being booked and the officer in charge of the booking or his or her superior determines that the person should be released, the officer or his or her superior shall prepare a written notice to appear in a court. In any case in which a person is arrested for a misdemeanor violation of a protective court order involving domestic violence, as defined in subdivision (b) of Section 13700, or arrested pursuant to a policy, as described in Section 13701, the person shall be taken before a magistrate instead of being released according to the procedures set forth in this chapter, unless the arresting officer determines that there is not a reasonable likelihood that the offense will continue or resume or that the safety of persons or property would be imminently endangered by release of the person arrested. Prior to adopting these provisions, each city, county, or city and county shall develop a protocol to assist officers to determine when arrest and release is appropriate, rather than taking the arrested person before a magistrate. The county shall establish a committee to develop the protocol, consisting of, at a minimum, the police chief or county sheriff within the jurisdiction, the district attorney, county counsel, city attorney, representatives from domestic violence shelters, domestic violence councils, and other relevant community agencies. Nothing in this subdivision shall be construed to affect a defendant's ability to be released on bail or on his or her own recognizance.

(b) Unless waived by the person, the time specified in the notice to appear shall be at least 10 days after arrest if the duplicate notice is to be filed by the officer with the magistrate.

(c) The place specified in the notice shall be the court of the magistrate before whom the person would be taken if the requirement of taking an arrested person before a magistrate were complied with, or shall be an officer authorized by that court to receive a deposit of bail.

(d) The officer shall deliver one copy of the notice to appear to the arrested person, and the arrested person, in order to secure release, shall give his or her written promise to appear in court as specified in the notice by signing the duplicate notice which shall be retained by the officer, and the officer may require the arrested person, if he or she has no satisfactory identification, to place a right thumbprint, or a left thumbprint or fingerprint if the person has a missing or disfigured right thumb, on the notice to appear. Except for law enforcement purposes relating to the identity of the arrestee, no person or entity may sell, give away, allow the distribution of, include in a database, or create a database with, this print. Upon the signing of the duplicate notice, the arresting officer shall immediately release the person arrested from custody.

(e) The officer shall, as soon as practicable, file the duplicate notice, as follows:

(1) It shall be filed with the magistrate if the offense charged is an infraction.

(2) It shall be filed with the magistrate if the prosecuting attorney has previously directed the officer to do so.

(3) The duplicate notice and underlying police reports in support of the charge or charges shall be filed with the prosecuting attorney in cases other than those specified in paragraphs (1) and (2). If the duplicate notice is filed with the prosecuting attorney, he or she, within his or her discretion, may initiate prosecution by filing the notice or a formal complaint with the magistrate specified in the duplicate notice within 25 days from the time of arrest. If the prosecution is not to be initiated, the prosecutor shall send notice to the person arrested at the address on the notice to appear. The failure by the prosecutor to file the notice or formal complaint within 25 days

of the time of the arrest shall not bar further prosecution of the misdemeanor charged in the notice to appear. However, any further prosecution shall be preceded by a new and separate citation or an arrest warrant. Upon the filing of the notice with the magistrate by the officer, or the filing of the notice or formal complaint by the prosecutor, the magistrate may fix the amount of bail that in his or her judgment, in accordance with Section 1275, is reasonable and sufficient for the appearance of the defendant and shall endorse upon the notice a statement signed by him or her in the form set forth in Section 815a. The defendant may, prior to the date upon which he or she promised to appear in court, deposit with the magistrate the amount of bail set by the magistrate. At the time the case is called for arraignment before the magistrate, if the defendant does not appear, either in person or by counsel, the magistrate may declare the bail forfeited, and may, in his or her discretion, order that no further proceedings shall be had in the case, unless the defendant has been charged with a violation of Section 374.3 or 374.7 of this code or of Section 11357, 11360, or 13002 of the Health and Safety Code, or a violation punishable under Section 5008.7 of the Public Resources Code, and he or she has previously been convicted of a violation of that section or a violation that is punishable under that section, except in cases where the magistrate finds that undue hardship will be imposed upon the defendant by requiring him or her to appear, the magistrate may declare the bail forfeited and order that no further proceedings be had in the case. Upon the making of the order that no further proceedings be had, all sums deposited as bail shall immediately be paid into the county treasury for distribution pursuant to Section 1463.

(f) No warrant shall be issued for the arrest of a person who has given a written promise to appear in court, unless and until he or she has violated that promise or has failed to deposit bail, to appear for arraignment, trial, or judgment or to comply with the terms and provisions of the judgment, as required by law.

(g) The officer may book the arrested person prior to release or indicate on the citation that the arrested person shall appear at the arresting agency to be booked or indicate on the citation that the arrested person shall appear at the arresting agency to be fingerprinted prior to the date the arrested person appears in court. If it is indicated on the citation that the arrested person shall be booked or fingerprinted prior to the date of the person's court appearance, the arresting agency at the time of booking or fingerprinting shall provide the arrested person with verification of the booking or fingerprinting by making an entry on the citation. If it is indicated on the citation that the arrested person is to be booked or fingerprinted, the magistrate, judge, or court shall, before the proceedings begin, order the defendant to provide verification that he or she was booked or fingerprinted by the arresting agency. If the defendant cannot produce the verification, the magistrate, judge, or court shall require that the defendant be booked or fingerprinted by the arresting agency before the next court appearance, and that the defendant provide the verification at the next court appearance unless both parties stipulate that booking or fingerprinting is not necessary.

(h) A peace officer shall use the written notice to appear procedure set forth in this section for any misdemeanor offense in which the officer has arrested a person without a warrant pursuant to Section 836 or in which he or she has taken custody of a person pursuant to Section 847.

(i) Whenever any person is arrested by a peace officer for a misdemeanor, that person shall be released according to the procedures set forth by this chapter unless one of the following is a reason for nonrelease, in which case the arresting officer may release the person, or the arresting officer shall indicate, on a form to be established by his or her employing law enforcement agency, which of the following was a reason for the nonrelease:

(1) The person arrested was so intoxicated that he or she could have been a danger to himself or herself or to others.

(2) The person arrested required medical examination or medical care or was otherwise unable to care for his or her own safety.

(3) The person was arrested under one or more of the circumstances listed in Sections 40302 and 40303 of the Vehicle Code.

(4) There were one or more outstanding arrest warrants for the person.

(5) The person could not provide satisfactory evidence of personal identification.

(6) The prosecution of the offense or offenses for which the person was arrested, or the prosecution of any other offense or offenses, would be jeopardized by immediate release of the person arrested.

(7) There was a reasonable likelihood that the offense or offenses would continue or resume, or that the safety of persons or property would be imminently endangered by release of the person arrested.

(8) The person arrested demanded to be taken before a magistrate or refused to sign the notice to appear.

(9) There is reason to believe that the person would not appear at the time and place specified in the notice. The basis for this determination shall be specifically stated. The form shall be filed with the arresting agency as soon as practicable and shall be made available to any party having custody of the arrested person, subsequent to the arresting officer, and to any person authorized by law to release him or her from custody before trial.

(j) Once the arresting officer has prepared the written notice to appear and has delivered a copy to the person arrested, the officer shall deliver the remaining original and all copies as provided by subdivision (e). Any person, including the arresting officer and any member of the officer's department or agency, or any peace officer, who alters, conceals, modifies, nullifies, or destroys, or causes to be altered, concealed, modified, nullified, or destroyed, the face side of the remaining original or any copy of a citation that was retained by the officer, for any reason, before it is filed with the magistrate or with a person authorized by the magistrate to receive deposit of bail, is guilty of a misdemeanor. If, after an arrested person has signed and received a copy of a notice to appear, the arresting officer determines that, in the interest of justice, the citation or notice should be dismissed, the arresting agency may recommend, in writing, to the magistrate that the charges be dismissed. The recommendation shall cite the reasons for the recommendation and shall be filed with the court. If the magistrate makes a finding that there are grounds for dismissal, the finding shall be entered in the record and the charges dismissed. Under no circumstances shall a personal relationship with any officer, public official, or law enforcement agency be grounds for dismissal.

(k)(1) A person contesting a charge by claiming under penalty of perjury not to be the person issued the notice to appear may choose to submit a right thumbprint, or a left thumbprint if the person has a missing or disfigured right thumb, to the issuing court through his or her local law enforcement agency for comparison with the one placed on the notice to appear. A local law enforcement agency providing this service may charge the requester no more than the actual costs. The issuing court may refer the thumbprint submitted and the notice to appear to the prosecuting attorney for comparison of the thumbprints. When there is no thumbprint or fingerprint on the notice to appear, or when the comparison of thumbprints is inconclusive, the court shall refer the notice to appear or copy thereof back to the issuing agency for further investigation, unless the court finds that referral is not in the interest of justice.

(2) Upon initiation of the investigation or comparison process by referral of the court, the court shall continue the case and the speedy trial period shall be tolled for 45 days.

(3) Upon receipt of the issuing agency's or prosecuting attorney's response, the court may make a finding of factual innocence pursuant to Section 530.6 if the court determines that there is insufficient evidence that the person cited is the person charged and shall immediately notify the Department of Motor Vehicles of its determination. If the Department of Motor Vehicles determines the citation or citations in question formed the basis of a suspension or revocation of the person's driving privilege, the department shall immediately set aside the action.

(4) If the prosecuting attorney or issuing agency fails to respond to a court referral within 45 days, the court shall make a finding of factual innocence pursuant to Section 530.6, unless the court finds that a finding of factual innocence is not in the interest of justice.

(5) The citation or notice to appear may be held by the prosecuting attorney or issuing agency for future adjudication should the arrestee who received the citation or notice to appear be found.

(l) For purposes of this section, the term "arresting agency" includes any other agency designated by the arresting agency to provide booking or fingerprinting services.

Penal Code § 853.6a.

(a) Except as provided in subdivision (b), if the person arrested appears to be under the age of 18 years, and the arrest is for a violation listed in Section 256 of the Welfare and Institutions Code, other than an offense involving a firearm, the notice under Section 853.6 shall instead provide that the person shall appear before the juvenile court, a juvenile court referee, or a juvenile hearing officer within the county in which the offense charged is alleged to have been committed, and the officer shall instead, as soon as practicable, file the duplicate notice with the prosecuting attorney unless the prosecuting attorney directs the officer to file the duplicate notice with the clerk of the juvenile court, the juvenile court referee, or the juvenile hearing officer. If the notice is filed with the prosecuting attorney, within 48 hours before the date specified on the notice to appear, the prosecutor, within his or her discretion, may initiate proceedings by filing the notice or a formal petition with the clerk of the juvenile court, or the juvenile court referee or juvenile hearing officer, before whom the person is required to appear by the notice.

(b) A juvenile court may exercise the option of not requiring a mandatory appearance of the juvenile before the court for infractions contained in the Vehicle Code, except those related to drivers' licenses as specified in Division 6 (commencing with Section 12500), those related to financial responsibility as specified in Division 7 (commencing with Section 16000), those related to speeding violations as specified in Division 11 (commencing with Section 21000) in which the speed limit was violated by 15 or more miles per hour, and those involving the use or possession of alcoholic beverages as specified in Division 11.5 (commencing with Section 23500).

(c) In counties where an Expedited Youth Accountability Program is operative, as established under Section 660.5 of the Welfare and Institutions Code, a peace officer may issue a citation and written promise to appear in juvenile court or record the minor's refusal to sign the promise to appear and serve notice to appear in juvenile court, according to the requirements and procedures provided in that section.

(d) This section may not be construed to limit the discretion of a peace officer or other person with the authority to enforce laws pertaining to juveniles to take the minor into custody pursuant to Article 15 (commencing with Section 625) of the Welfare and Institutions Code.

Penal Code § 853.7.

Any person who willfully violates his or her written promise to appear or a lawfully granted continuance of his or her promise to appear in court is guilty of a misdemeanor, regardless of the disposition of the charge upon which he or she was originally arrested.

Penal Code § 853.7a.

(a) In addition to the fees authorized or required by any other provision of law, a county may, by resolution of the board of supervisors, require the courts of that county to impose an assessment of fifteen dollars ($15) upon every person who violates his or her written promise to appear or a lawfully granted continuance of his or her promise to appear in court or before a person authorized to receive a deposit of bail, or who otherwise fails to comply with any valid court order for a violation of any provision of this code or local ordinance adopted pursuant to this code. This assessment shall apply whether or not a violation of Section 853.7 is concurrently charged or a warrant of arrest is issued pursuant to Section 853.8.

(b) The clerk of the court shall deposit the amounts collected under this section in the county treasury. All money so deposited shall be used first for the development and operation of an automated county warrant system. If sufficient funds are available after appropriate expenditures to develop, modernize, and maintain the automated warrant system, a county may use the balance to fund a warrant service task force for the purpose of serving all bench warrants within the county.

Penal Code § 853.8.

When a person signs a written promise to appear at the time and place specified in the written promise to appear and has not posted bail as provided in Section 853.6, the magistrate shall issue and have delivered for execution a warrant for his or her arrest within 20 days after his or her failure to appear as promised or within 20 days after his or her failure to appear after a lawfully granted continuance of his or her promise to appear.

Penal Code § 853.85.

This chapter shall not apply in any case where a person is arrested for an offense declared to be a felony.

Penal Code § 969.

In charging the fact of a previous conviction of felony, or of an attempt to commit an offense which, if perpetrated, would have been a felony, or of theft, it is sufficient to state, "That the defendant, before the commission of the offense charged herein, was in (giving the title of the court in which the conviction was had) convicted of a felony (or attempt, etc., or of theft)." If more than one previous conviction is charged, the date of the judgment upon each conviction may be stated, and all known previous convictions, whether in this State or elsewhere, must be charged.

Penal Code § 969a.

Whenever it shall be discovered that a pending indictment or information does not charge all prior felonies of which the defendant has been convicted either in this State or elsewhere, said indictment or information may be forthwith amended to charge such prior conviction or convictions, and if such amendment is made it shall be made upon order of the court, and no action of the grand jury (in the case of an indictment) shall be necessary. Defendant shall promptly be rearraigned on such information or indictment as amended and be required to plead thereto.

Penal Code § 969b.

For the purpose of establishing prima facie evidence of the fact that a person being tried for a crime or public offense under the laws of this State has been convicted of an act punishable by imprisonment in a state prison, county jail or city jail of this State, and has served a term therefor in any penal institution, or has been convicted of an act in any other state, which would be punishable as a crime in this State, and has served a term therefor in any state penitentiary, reformatory, county jail or city jail, or has been convicted of an act declared to be a crime by any act or law of the United States, and has served a term therefor in any penal institution, the records or copies of records of any state penitentiary, reformatory, county jail, city jail, or federal penitentiary in which such person has been imprisoned, when such records or copies thereof have been certified by the official custodian of such records, may be introduced as such evidence.

Penal Code § 969e.

In charging the fact of a previous conviction for a violation of Section 5652 of the Fish and Game Code, or of Section 13001 or 13002 of the Health and Safety Code or of Section 374b or 374d of the Penal Code or of Section 23111, 23112, or 23113 of the Vehicle Code, it is sufficient to state, "That the defendant, before the commission of the offense charged herein, was in (giving the title of the court in which the conviction was had) convicted of a violation of (specifying the section violated)."

Penal Code § 969f.

(a) Whenever a defendant has committed a serious felony as defined in subdivision (c) of Section 1192.7, the facts that make the crime constitute a serious felony may be charged in the accusatory pleading. However, the crime shall not be referred to as a serious felony nor shall the jury be informed that the crime is defined as a serious felony. This charge, if made, shall be added to and be a part of the count or each of the counts of the accusatory pleading which charged the offense. If the defendant pleads not guilty to the offense charged in any count which alleges that the defendant committed a serious felony, the question whether or not the defendant committed a serious felony as alleged shall be tried by the court or jury which tries the issue upon the plea of not guilty. If the defendant pleads guilty of the offense charged, the question whether or not the defendant committed a serious felony as alleged shall be separately admitted or denied by the defendant.

(b) In charging an act or acts that bring the defendant within the operation of paragraph (8) or (23) of subdivision (c) of Section 1192.7, it is sufficient for purposes of subdivision (a) if the pleading states the following: "It is further alleged that in the commission and attempted commission of the foregoing offense, the defendant ____, personally (inflicted great bodily injury on another person, other than an accomplice) (used a firearm, to wit: ____,) (used a dangerous and deadly weapon, to wit: ____,) within the meaning of Sections 667 and 1192.7 of the Penal Code."

Penal Code § 969.5.

(a) Whenever it shall be discovered that a pending complaint to which a plea of guilty has been made under Section 859a does not charge all prior felonies of which the defendant has been convicted either in this state or elsewhere, the complaint may be forthwith amended to charge the prior conviction or convictions and the amendments may and shall be made upon order of the court. The defendant shall thereupon be arraigned before the court to which the complaint has been certified and shall be asked whether he or she has suffered the prior conviction. If the defendant enters a denial, his or her answer shall be entered in the minutes of the court. The refusal of the defendant to answer is equivalent to a denial that he or she has suffered the prior conviction.

(b) Except as provided in subdivision (c), the question of whether or not the defendant has suffered the prior conviction shall be tried by a jury impaneled for that purpose unless a jury is waived, in which case it may be tried by the court.

(c) Notwithstanding the provisions of subdivision (b), the question of whether the defendant is the person who has suffered the prior conviction shall be tried by the court without a jury.

Penal Code § 1158.

Whenever the fact of a previous conviction of another offense is charged in an accusatory pleading, and the defendant is found guilty of the offense with which he is charged, the jury, or the judge if a jury trial is waived, must unless the answer of the defendant admits such previous conviction, find whether or not he has suffered such previous conviction. The verdict or finding upon the charge of previous conviction may be: "We (or I) find the charge of previous conviction true" or "We (or I) find the charge of previous conviction not true," according as the jury or the judge find that the defendant has or has not suffered such conviction. If more than one previous conviction is charged a separate finding must be made as to each.

Penal Code § 1158a.

(a) Whenever the fact that a defendant was armed with a weapon either at the time of his commission of the offense or at the time of his arrest, or both, is charged in accordance with section 969c of this code, in any count of the indictment or information to which the defendant has entered a plea of not guilty, the jury, if they find a verdict of guilty of the offense with which the defendant is charged, or of any offense included therein, must also find whether or not the defendant was armed as charged in the count to which the plea of not guilty was entered. The verdict of the jury upon a charge of being armed may be: "We find the charge of being armed contained in the _____ count true," or "We find the charge of being armed contained in the _____ count not true," as they find that the defendant was or was not armed as charged in any particular count of the indictment or information. A separate verdict upon the charge of being armed must be returned for each count which alleges that the defendant was armed.

(b) Whenever the fact that a defendant used a firearm is charged in accordance with Section 969d in any count of the indictment or information to which the defendant has entered a plea of not guilty, the jury if they find a verdict of guilty of the offense with which the defendant is charged must also find whether or not the defendant used a firearm as charged in the count to which the plea of not guilty was entered. A verdict of the jury upon a charge of using a firearm may be: "We find the charge of using a firearm contained in the _____ count true," or "We find the charge of using a firearm contained in the _____ count not true," as they find that the defendant used or did not use a firearm as charged in any particular count of the indictment or information. A separate verdict upon the charge of using a firearm shall be returned for each count which alleges that defendant used a firearm.

Penal Code § 1170.8.

(a) The fact that a robbery or an assault with a deadly weapon or instrument or by means of any force likely to produce great bodily injury was committed against a person while that person was in a church, synagogue, or building owned and occupied by a religious educational institution, or any other place primarily used as a place of worship where religious services are regularly conducted, shall be considered a circumstance in aggravation of the crime in imposing a term under subdivision (b) of Section 1170.

(b) Upon conviction of any person for a violation of Section 451 or 453, the fact that the person intentionally burned, or intended to burn, a church, synagogue, or building owned and occupied by a religious educational institution, or any other place primarily used as a place of worship where religious services are regularly conducted, shall be considered a circumstance in aggravation of the crime in imposing a term under subdivision (b) of Section 1170.

Penal Code § 1170.81.

The fact that the intended victim of an attempted life term crime was a peace officer, as described in subdivisions (a) and (b) of Section 830.1, or Section 830.2, 830.5 or 830.6, while the peace officer was engaged in the performance of his or her duties, and the defendant knew or reasonably should have known that the victim was a peace officer engaged in the performance of his or her duties, shall be considered a circumstance in aggravation of the crime in imposing a term under subdivision (b) of Section 1170.

Penal Code § 1170.82.

Upon a conviction of a violation of Section 11352, 11360, 11379, or 11379.5 of the Health and Safety Code, the fact that the person who committed the offense knew, or reasonably should have known, that any of the following circumstances existed with regard to the person to whom he or she unlawfully sold, furnished, administered, or gave away a controlled substance, shall be a circumstance in aggravation of the crime in imposing a term pursuant to subdivision (b) of Section 1170:

(a) The person was pregnant at the time of the selling, furnishing, administering, or giving away of the controlled substance.

(b) The person had been previously convicted of a violent felony, as defined in subdivision (c) of Section 667.5.

(c) The person was in psychological treatment for a mental disorder or for substance abuse at the time of the selling, furnishing, administering, or giving away of the controlled substance.

Penal Code § 1170.84.

Upon conviction of any serious felony, listed in subdivision (c) of Section 1192.7, it shall be considered a circumstance in aggravation of the crime in imposing a term under subdivision (b) of Section 1170 if, during the course of the serious felony, the person engaged in the tying, binding, or confining of any victim.

Penal Code § 1170.85.

(a) Upon conviction of any felony assault or battery offense, it shall be considered a circumstance in aggravation of the crime in imposing a term under subdivision (b) of Section 1170 if the offense was committed to prevent or dissuade a person who is or may become a witness from attending upon or testifying at any trial, proceeding, or inquiry authorized by law, or if the offense was committed because the person provided assistance or information to a law enforcement officer, or to a public prosecutor in a criminal or juvenile court proceeding.

(b) Upon conviction of any felony it shall be considered a circumstance in aggravation in imposing a term under subdivision (b) of Section 1170 if the victim of an offense is particularly vulnerable, or unable to defend himself or herself, due to age or significant disability.

Penal Code § 1170.86.

Upon conviction of a felony violation of Section 220, 261, 261.5, 264.1, or 266j the fact that the felony was committed within a safe school zone, as defined in subdivision (c) of Section 626, against a victim who was a pupil currently attending school, shall be considered a circumstance in aggravation in imposing a term under subdivision (b) of Section 1170.

Penal Code § 1170.89.

Where there is an applicable triad for an enhancement related to the possession of, being armed with, use of, or furnishing or supplying a firearm, set forth in Section 12021.5, 12022, 12022.2, 12022.3, 12022.4, 12022.5, or 12022.55 the fact that a person knew or had reason to believe that a firearm was stolen shall constitute a circumstance in aggravation of the enhancement justifying imposition of the upper term on that enhancement.

Penal Code § 1192.

Upon a plea of guilty, or upon conviction by the court without a jury, of a crime or attempted crime distinguished or divided into degrees, the court must, before passing sentence, determine the degree. Upon the failure of the court to so determine, the degree of the crime or attempted crime of which the defendant is guilty, shall be deemed to be of the lesser degree.

Penal Code § 1192.1.

Upon a plea of guilty to an information or indictment accusing the defendant of a crime or attempted crime divided into degrees when consented to by the prosecuting attorney in open court and approved by the court, such plea may specify the degree thereof and in such event the defendant cannot be punished for a higher degree of the crime or attempted crime than the degree specified.

Penal Code § 1192.2.

Upon a plea of guilty before a committing magistrate as provided in Section 859a, to a crime or attempted crime divided into degrees, when consented to by the prosecuting attorney in open court and approved by such magistrate, such plea may specify the degree thereof and in such event, the defendant cannot be punished for a higher degree of the crime or attempted crime than the degree specified.

Penal Code § 1192.3.

(a) A plea of guilty or nolo contendere to an accusatory pleading charging a public offense, other than a felony specified in Section 1192.5 or 1192.7, which public offense did not result in damage for which restitution may be ordered, made on the condition that charges be dismissed for one or more public offenses arising from the same or related course of conduct by the defendant which did result in damage for which restitution may be ordered, may specify the payment of restitution by the defendant as a condition of the plea or any probation granted pursuant thereto, so long as the plea is freely and voluntarily made, there is factual basis for the plea, and the plea and all conditions are approved by the court.

(b) If restitution is imposed which is attributable to a count dismissed pursuant to a plea bargain, as described in this section, the court shall obtain a waiver pursuant to People v. Harvey (1979) 25 Cal. 3d 754 from the defendant as to the dismissed count.

Penal Code § 1192.4.

If the defendant's plea of guilty pursuant to Section 1192.1 or 1192.2 is not accepted by the prosecuting attorney and approved by the court, the plea shall be deemed withdrawn and the defendant may then enter such plea or pleas as would otherwise have been available. The plea so withdrawn may not be received in evidence in any criminal, civil, or special action or proceeding of any nature, including proceedings before agencies, commissions, boards, and tribunals.

Penal Code § 1192.5.

Upon a plea of guilty or nolo contendere to an accusatory pleading charging a felony, other than a violation of paragraph (2), (3), or (6) of subdivision (a) of Section 261, paragraph (1) or (4) of subdivision (a) of Section 262, Section 264.1, Section 286 by force, violence, duress, menace or threat of great bodily harm, subdivision (b) of Section 288, Section 288a by force, violence, duress, menace or threat of great bodily harm, or subdivision (a) of Section 289, the plea may specify the punishment to the same extent as it may be specified by the jury on a plea of not guilty or fixed by the court on a plea of guilty, nolo contendere, or not guilty, and may specify the exercise by the court thereafter of other powers legally available to it. Where the plea is accepted by the prosecuting attorney in open court and is approved by the court, the defendant, except as otherwise provided in this section, cannot be sentenced on the plea to a punishment more severe than that specified in the plea and the court may not proceed as to the plea other than as specified in the plea. If the court approves of the plea, it shall inform the defendant prior to the making of the plea that (1) its approval is not binding, (2) it may, at the time set for the hearing on the application for probation or pronouncement of judgment, withdraw its approval in the light of further consideration of the matter, and (3) in that case, the defendant shall be permitted to withdraw his or her plea if he or she desires to do so. The court shall also cause an inquiry to be made of the defendant to satisfy itself that the plea is freely and voluntarily made, and that there is a factual basis for the plea. If the plea is not accepted by the prosecuting attorney and approved by the court, the plea shall be deemed withdrawn and the defendant may then enter the plea or pleas as would otherwise have been available. If the plea is withdrawn or deemed withdrawn, it may not be received in evidence in any criminal, civil, or special action or proceeding of any nature, including proceedings before agencies, commissions, boards, and tribunals.

Penal Code § 1192.6.

(a) In each felony case in which the charges contained in the original accusatory pleading are amended or dismissed, the record shall contain a statement explaining the reason for the amendment or dismissal.

(b) In each felony case in which the prosecuting attorney seeks a dismissal of a charge in the complaint, indictment, or information, he or she shall state the specific reasons for the dismissal in open court, on the record.

(c) When, upon a plea of guilty or nolo contendere to an accusatory pleading charging a felony, whether or not that plea is entered pursuant to Section 1192.5, the prosecuting attorney recommends what punishment the court should impose or how it should exercise any of the powers legally available to it, the prosecuting attorney shall state the specific reasons for the recommendation in open court, on the record. The reasons for the recommendation shall be transcribed and made part of the court file.

Penal Code § 1192.7.

(a)(1) It is the intent of the Legislature that district attorneys prosecute violent sex crimes under statutes that provide sentencing under a "one strike," "three strikes" or habitual sex offender statute instead of engaging in plea bargaining over those offenses.

(2) Plea bargaining in any case in which the indictment or information charges any serious felony, any felony in which it is alleged that a firearm was personally used by the defendant, or any offense of driving while under the influence of alcohol, drugs, narcotics, or any other intoxicating substance, or any combination thereof, is prohibited, unless there is insufficient evidence to prove the people's case, or testimony of a material witness cannot be obtained, or a reduction or dismissal would not result in a substantial change in sentence.

(3) If the indictment or information charges the defendant with a violent sex crime, as listed in subdivision (c) of Section 667.61, that could be prosecuted under Sections 269, 288.7, subdivisions (b) through (i) of Section 667, Section 667.61, or 667.71, plea bargaining is prohibited unless there is insufficient evidence to prove the people's case, or testimony of a material witness cannot be obtained, or a reduction or dismissal would not result in a substantial change in sentence. At the time of presenting the agreement to the court, the district attorney shall state on the record why a sentence under one of those sections was not sought.

(b) As used in this section "plea bargaining" means any bargaining, negotiation, or discussion between a criminal defendant, or his or her counsel, and a prosecuting attorney or judge, whereby the defendant agrees to plead guilty or nolo contendere, in exchange for any promises, commitments, concessions, assurances, or consideration by the prosecuting attorney or judge relating to any charge against the defendant or to the sentencing of the defendant.

(c) As used in this section, "serious felony" means any of the following:

(1) Murder or voluntary manslaughter;

(2) mayhem;

(3) rape;

(4) sodomy by force, violence, duress, menace, threat of great bodily injury, or fear of immediate and unlawful bodily injury on the victim or another person;

(5) oral copulation by force, violence, duress, menace, threat of great bodily injury, or fear of immediate and unlawful bodily injury on the victim or another person;

(6) lewd or lascivious act on a child under 14 years of age;

(7) any felony punishable by death or imprisonment in the state prison for life;

(8) any felony in which the defendant personally inflicts great bodily injury on any person, other than an accomplice, or any felony in which the defendant personally uses a firearm;

(9) attempted murder;

(10) assault with intent to commit rape or robbery;

(11) assault with a deadly weapon or instrument on a peace officer;

(12) assault by a life prisoner on a noninmate;

(13) assault with a deadly weapon by an inmate;

(14) arson;

(15) exploding a destructive device or any explosive with intent to injure;

(16) exploding a destructive device or any explosive causing bodily injury, great bodily injury, or mayhem;

(17) exploding a destructive device or any explosive with intent to murder;

(18) any burglary of the first degree;

(19) robbery or bank robbery;

(20) kidnapping;

(21) holding of a hostage by a person confined in a state prison;

(22) attempt to commit a felony punishable by death or imprisonment in the state prison for life;

(23) any felony in which the defendant personally used a dangerous or deadly weapon;

(24) selling, furnishing, administering, giving, or offering to sell, furnish, administer, or give to a minor any heroin, cocaine, phencyclidine (PCP), or any methamphetamine-related drug, as described in paragraph (2) of subdivision (d) of Section 11055 of the Health and Safety Code, or any of the precursors of methamphetamines, as described in subparagraph (A) of paragraph (1) of subdivision (f) of Section 11055 or subdivision (a) of Section 11100 of the Health and Safety Code;

(25) any violation of subdivision (a) of Section 289 where the act is accomplished against the victim's will by force, violence, duress, menace, or fear of immediate and unlawful bodily injury on the victim or another person;

(26) grand theft involving a firearm;

(27) carjacking;

(28) any felony offense, which would also constitute a felony violation of Section 186.22;

(29) assault with the intent to commit mayhem, rape, sodomy, or oral copulation, in violation of Section 220;

(30) throwing acid or flammable substances, in violation of Section 244;

(31) assault with a deadly weapon, firearm, machinegun, assault weapon, or semiautomatic firearm or assault on a peace officer or firefighter, in violation of Section 245;

(32) assault with a deadly weapon against a public transit employee, custodial officer, or school employee, in violation of Sections 245.2, 245.3, or 245.5;

(33) discharge of a firearm at an inhabited dwelling, vehicle, or aircraft, in violation of Section 246;

(34) commission of rape or sexual penetration in concert with another person, in violation of Section 264.1;

(35) continuous sexual abuse of a child, in violation of Section 288.5;

(36) shooting from a vehicle, in violation of subdivision (c) or (d) of Section 12034;

(37) intimidation of victims or witnesses, in violation of Section 136.1;

(38) criminal threats, in violation of Section 422;

(39) any attempt to commit a crime listed in this subdivision other than an assault;

(40) any violation of Section 12022.53;

(41) a violation of subdivision (b) or (c) of Section 11418; and

(42) any conspiracy to commit an offense described in this subdivision.

(d) As used in this section, "bank robbery" means to take or attempt to take, by force or violence, or by intimidation from the person or presence of another any property or money or any other thing of value belonging to, or in the care, custody, control, management, or possession of, any bank, credit union, or any savings and loan association. As used in this subdivision, the following terms have the following meanings:

(1) "Bank" means any member of the Federal Reserve System, and any bank, banking association, trust company, savings bank, or other banking institution organized or operating under the laws of the United States, and any bank the deposits of which are insured by the Federal Deposit Insurance Corporation.

(2) "Savings and loan association" means any federal savings and loan association and any "insured institution" as defined in Section 401 of the National Housing Act, as amended, and any federal credit union as defined in Section 2 of the Federal Credit Union Act. (3) "Credit union" means any federal credit union and any state-chartered credit union the accounts of which are insured by the Administrator of the National Credit Union administration.

(e) The provisions of this section shall not be amended by the Legislature except by statute passed in each house by rollcall vote entered in the journal, two-thirds of the membership concurring, or by a statute that becomes effective only when approved by the electors.

Penal Code § 1192.8.

(a) For purposes of subdivision (c) of Section 1192.7, "serious felony" also means any violation of Section 191.5, paragraph (1) of subdivision (c) of Section 192, subdivision (a), (b), or (c) of Section 192.5 of this code, or Section 2800.3, subdivision (b) of Section 23104, or Section 23153 of the Vehicle Code, when any of these offenses involve the personal infliction of great bodily injury on any person other than an accomplice, or the personal use of a dangerous or deadly weapon, within the meaning of paragraph (8) or (23) of subdivision (c) of Section 1192.7.

(b) It is the intent of the Legislature, in enacting subdivision (a), to codify the court decisions of People v. Gonzales, 29 Cal. App. 4th 1684, and People v. Bow, 13 Cal. App. 4th 1551, and to clarify that the crimes specified in subdivision (a) have always been, and continue to be, serious felonies within the meaning of subdivision (c) of Section 1192.7.

Penal Code § 1203.

(a) As used in this code, "probation" means the suspension of the imposition or execution of a sentence and the order of conditional and revocable release in the community under the supervision of a probation officer. As used in this code, "conditional sentence" means the suspension of the imposition or execution of a sentence and the order of revocable release in the community subject to conditions established by the court without the supervision of a probation officer. It is the intent of the Legislature that both conditional sentence and probation are authorized whenever probation is authorized in any code as a sentencing option for infractions or misdemeanors.

(b)(1) Except as provided in subdivision (j), if a person is convicted of a felony and is eligible for probation, before judgment is pronounced, the court shall immediately refer the matter to a probation officer to investigate and report to the court, at a specified time, upon the circumstances surrounding the crime and the prior history and record of the person, which may be considered either in aggravation or mitigation of the punishment.

(2)(A) The probation officer shall immediately investigate and make a written report to the court of his or her findings and recommendations, including his or her recommendations as to the granting or denying of probation and the conditions of probation, if granted.

(B) Pursuant to Section 828 of the Welfare and Institutions Code, the probation officer shall include in his or her report any information gathered by a law enforcement agency relating to the taking of the defendant into custody as a minor, which shall be considered for purposes of determining whether adjudications of commissions of crimes as a juvenile warrant a finding that there are circumstances in aggravation pursuant to Section 1170 or to deny probation.

(C) If the person was convicted of an offense that requires him or her to register as a sex offender pursuant to Section 290, the probation officer's report shall include the results of the State-Authorized Risk Assessment Tool for Sex Offenders (SARATSO) administered pursuant to Sections 290.04 to 290.06, inclusive, if applicable.

(D) The probation officer shall also include in the report his or her recommendation of both of the following:

(i) The amount the defendant should be required to pay as a restitution fine pursuant to subdivision (b) of Section 1202.4.

(ii) Whether the court shall require, as a condition of probation, restitution to the victim or to the Restitution Fund and the amount thereof.

(E) The report shall be made available to the court and the prosecuting and defense attorneys at least five days, or upon request of the defendant or prosecuting attorney nine days, prior to the time fixed by the court for the hearing and determination of the report, and shall be filed with the clerk of the court as a record in the case at the time of the hearing. The time within which the report shall be made available and filed may be waived by written stipulation of the prosecuting and defense attorneys that is filed with the court or an oral stipulation in open court that is made and entered upon the minutes of the court.

(3) At a time fixed by the court, the court shall hear and determine the application, if one has been made, or, in any case, the suitability of probation in the particular case. At the hearing, the court shall consider any report of the probation officer, including the results of the SARATSO, if applicable, and shall make a statement that it has considered the report, which shall be filed with the clerk of the court as a record in the case. If the court determines that there are circumstances in mitigation of the punishment prescribed by law or that the ends of justice would be served by granting probation to the person, it may place the person on probation. If probation is denied, the clerk of the court shall immediately send a copy of the report to the Department of Corrections and Rehabilitation at the prison or other institution to which the person is delivered.

(4) The preparation of the report or the consideration of the report by the court may be waived only by a written stipulation of the prosecuting and defense attorneys that is filed with the court or an oral stipulation in open court that is made and entered upon the minutes of the court, except that there shall be no waiver unless the court consents thereto. However, if the defendant is ultimately sentenced and committed to the state prison, a probation report shall be completed pursuant to Section 1203c.

(c) If a defendant is not represented by an attorney, the court shall order the probation officer who makes the probation report to discuss its contents with the defendant.

(d) If a person is convicted of a misdemeanor, the court may either refer the matter to the probation officer for an investigation and a report or summarily pronounce a conditional sentence. If the person was convicted of an offense that requires him or her to register as a sex offender pursuant to Section 290, the court shall refer the matter to the probation officer for the purpose of obtaining a report on the results of the State-Authorized Risk Assessment Tool for Sex Offenders administered pursuant to Sections 290.04 to 290.06, inclusive, if applicable, which the court shall consider. If the case is not referred to the probation officer, in sentencing the person, the court may consider any information concerning the person that could have been included in a probation report. The court shall inform the person of the information to be considered and permit him or her to answer or controvert the information. For this purpose, upon the request of the person, the court shall grant a continuance before the judgment is pronounced.

(e) Except in unusual cases where the interests of justice would best be served if the person is granted probation, probation shall not be granted to any of the following persons:

(1) Unless the person had a lawful right to carry a deadly weapon, other than a firearm, at the time of the perpetration of the crime or his or her arrest, any person who has been convicted of arson, robbery, carjacking, burglary, burglary with explosives, rape with force or violence, torture, aggravated mayhem, murder, attempt to commit murder, trainwrecking, kidnapping, escape from the state prison, or a conspiracy to commit one or more of those crimes and who was armed with the weapon at either of those times.

(2) Any person who used, or attempted to use, a deadly weapon upon a human being in connection with the perpetration of the crime of which he or she has been convicted.

(3) Any person who willfully inflicted great bodily injury or torture in the perpetration of the crime of which he or she has been convicted.

(4) Any person who has been previously convicted twice in this state of a felony or in any other place of a public offense which, if committed in this state, would have been punishable as a felony.

(5) Unless the person has never been previously convicted once in this state of a felony or in any other place of a public offense which, if committed in this state, would have been punishable as a felony, any person who has been convicted of burglary with explosives, rape with force or violence, torture, aggravated mayhem, murder, attempt to commit murder, trainwrecking, extortion, kidnapping, escape from the state prison, a violation of Section 286, 288, 288a, or 288.5, or a conspiracy to commit one or more of those crimes.

(6) Any person who has been previously convicted once in this state of a felony or in any other place of a public offense which, if committed in this state, would have been punishable as a felony, if he or she committed any of the following acts:

(A) Unless the person had a lawful right to carry a deadly weapon at the time of the perpetration of the previous crime or his or her arrest for the previous crime, he or she was armed with a weapon at either of those times.

(B) The person used, or attempted to use, a deadly weapon upon a human being in connection with the perpetration of the previous crime.

(C) The person willfully inflicted great bodily injury or torture in the perpetration of the previous crime.

(7) Any public official or peace officer of this state or any city, county, or other political subdivision who, in the discharge of the duties of his or her public office or employment, accepted or gave or offered to accept or give any bribe, embezzled public money, or was guilty of extortion.

(8) Any person who knowingly furnishes or gives away phencyclidine.

(9) Any person who intentionally inflicted great bodily injury in the commission of arson under subdivision (a) of Section 451 or who intentionally set fire to, burned, or caused the burning of, an inhabited structure or inhabited property in violation of subdivision (b) of Section 451.

(10) Any person who, in the commission of a felony, inflicts great bodily injury or causes the death of a human being by the discharge of a firearm from or at an occupied motor vehicle proceeding on a public street or highway.

(11) Any person who possesses a short-barreled rifle or a short-barreled shotgun under Section 12020, a machinegun under Section 12220, or a silencer under Section 12520.

(12) Any person who is convicted of violating Section 8101 of the Welfare and Institutions Code.

(13) Any person who is described in paragraph (2) or (3) of subdivision (g) of Section 12072.

(f) When probation is granted in a case which comes within subdivision (e), the court shall specify on the record and shall enter on the minutes the circumstances indicating that the interests of justice would best be served by that disposition.

(g) If a person is not eligible for probation, the judge shall refer the matter to the probation officer for an investigation of the facts relevant to determination of the amount of a restitution fine pursuant to subdivision (b) of Section 1202.4 in all cases where the determination is applicable. The judge, in his or her discretion, may direct the probation officer to investigate all facts relevant to the sentencing of the person. Upon that referral, the probation officer shall immediately investigate the circumstances surrounding the crime and the prior record and history of the person and make a written report to the court of his or her findings. The findings shall include a recommendation of the amount of the restitution fine as provided in subdivision (b) of Section 1202.4.

(h) If a defendant is convicted of a felony and a probation report is prepared pursuant to subdivision (b) or (g), the probation officer may obtain and include in the report a statement of the comments of the victim concerning the offense. The court may direct the probation officer not to obtain a statement if the victim has in fact testified at any of the court proceedings concerning the offense.

(i) No probationer shall be released to enter another state unless his or her case has been referred to the Administrator of the Interstate Probation and Parole Compacts, pursuant to the Uniform Act for Out-of-State Probationer or Parolee Supervision (Article 3 (commencing with Section 11175) of Chapter 2 of Title 1 of Part 4) and the probationer has reimbursed the county that has jurisdiction over his or her probation case the reasonable costs of processing his or her request for interstate compact supervision. The amount and method of reimbursement shall be in accordance with Section 1203.1b.

(j) In any court where a county financial evaluation officer is available, in addition to referring the matter to the probation officer, the court may order the defendant to appear before the county financial evaluation officer for a financial evaluation of the defendant's ability to pay restitution, in which case the county financial evaluation officer shall report his or her findings regarding restitution and other court-related costs to the probation officer on the question of the defendant's ability to pay those costs. Any order made pursuant to this subdivision may be enforced as a violation of the terms and conditions of probation upon willful failure to pay and at the discretion of the court, may be enforced in the same manner as a judgment in a civil action, if any balance remains unpaid at the end of the defendant's probationary period.

(k) Probation shall not be granted to, nor shall the execution of, or imposition of sentence be suspended for, any person who is convicted of a violent felony, as defined in subdivision (c) of Section 667.5, or a serious felony, as defined in subdivision (c) of Section 1192.7, and who was on probation for a felony offense at the time of the commission of the new felony offense.

Penal Code § 1203.055.

(a) Notwithstanding any other law, in sentencing a person convicted of committing or of attempting to commit one or more of the offenses listed in subdivision (b) against a person who is a passenger, operator, driver, or other occupant of any public transit vehicle whether the offense or attempt is committed within the vehicle or directed at the vehicle, the court shall require that the person serve some period of confinement. If probation is granted, it shall be a condition of probation that the person shall be confined in the county jail for some period of time. If the time spent in jail prior to arraignment is less than 24 hours, it shall not be considered to satisfy the requirement that some period of confinement be imposed. As used in this subdivision, "public transit vehicle" means any motor vehicle, streetcar, trackless trolley, bus, shuttle, light rail system, rapid transit system, subway, train, taxi cab, or jitney, which transports members of the public for hire.

(b) Subdivision (a) applies to the following crimes:

(1) Murder.

(2) A violation of Section 241, 241.3, 241.4, 244, 245, 245.2, or 246.

(3) Robbery, in violation of Section 211.

(4) Kidnapping, in violation of Section 207.

(5) Kidnapping, in violation of Section 209.

(6) Battery, in violation of Section 243, 243.1, or 243.3.

(7) Rape, in violation of Section 261, 262, 264, or 264.1. (8) Assault with intent to commit rape or sodomy, in violation of Section 220.

(9) Any other offense in which the defendant inflicts great bodily injury on any person other than an accomplice. As used in this paragraph, "great bodily injury" means "great bodily injury" as defined in Section 12022.7.

(10) Grand theft, in violation of subdivision (1) of Section 487.

(11) Throwing of a hard substance or shooting a missile at a transit vehicle, in violation of Section 219.2.

(12) Unlawfully causing a fire, in violation of Section 452. (13) Drawing, exhibiting, or using a firearm or deadly weapon, in violation of Section 417.

(14) A violation of Section 214.

(15) A violation of Section 215.

(16) Kidnapping, in violation of Section 209.5.

(c) Probation shall not be granted to, nor shall the execution or imposition of sentence be suspended for, any person convicted of a felony offense falling within this section if the person has been previously convicted and sentenced pursuant to this section.

(d)(1) The existence of any fact which would make a person ineligible for probation under subdivisions (a) and (c) shall be alleged in the accusatory pleading, and either admitted by the defendant in open court, or found to be true by the jury trying the issue of guilt or by the court where guilt is established by a plea of guilty or nolo contendere or by a trial by the court sitting without a jury. A finding bringing the defendant within this section shall not be stricken pursuant to Section 1385 or any provision of law.

(2) This subdivision does not prohibit the adjournment of criminal proceedings pursuant to Division 3 (commencing with Section 3000) or Division 6 (commencing with Section 6000) of the Welfare and Institutions Code.

(e) The court shall require, as a condition of probation for any person convicted of committing a crime which took place on a public transit vehicle, except in any case in which the court makes a finding and states on the record clear and compelling reasons why the condition would be inappropriate, that the person make restitution to the victim. If restitution is found to be inappropriate, the court shall require as a condition of probation, except in any case in which the court makes a finding and states on the record its reasons that the condition would be inappropriate, that the defendant perform specified community service. Nothing in this subdivision shall be construed to limit the authority of a court to provide additional conditions of probation.

(f) In any case in which a person is convicted of committing a crime which took place on a public transit vehicle, the probation officer shall immediately investigate and report to the court at a specified time whether, as a result of the crime, property damage or loss or personal injury was caused by the defendant, the amount of the damage, loss, or injury, and the feasibility of requiring restitution to be made by the defendant. When a probation report is required pursuant to Section 1203 the information required by this subdivision shall be added to that probation report.

Penal Code § 1203.06.

(a) Notwithstanding any other provision of law, probation shall not be granted to, nor shall the execution or imposition of sentence be suspended for, nor shall a finding bringing the defendant within this section be stricken pursuant to Section 1385 for, any of the following persons:

(1) Any person who personally used a firearm during the commission or attempted commission of any of the following crimes:

(A) Murder.

(B) Robbery, in violation of Section 211.

(C) Kidnapping, in violation of Section 207, 209, or 209.5.

(D) Lewd or lascivious act, in violation of Section 288.

(E) Burglary of the first degree, as defined in Section 460.

(F) Rape, in violation of Section 261, 262, or 264.1. (G) Assault with intent to commit a specified sexual offense, in violation of Section 220.

(H) Escape, in violation of Section 4530 or 4532.

(I) Carjacking, in violation of Section 215.

(J) Aggravated mayhem, in violation of Section 205.

(K) Torture, in violation of Section 206.

(L) Continuous sexual abuse of a child, in violation of Section 288.5.

(M) A felony violation of Section 136.1 or 137.

(N) Sodomy, in violation of Section 286.

(O) Oral copulation, in violation of Section 288a. (P) Sexual penetration, in violation of Section 289 or 264.1.

(Q) Aggravated sexual assault of a child, in violation of Section 269.

(2) Any person previously convicted of a felony specified in paragraph (1), or assault with intent to commit murder under former Section 217, who is convicted of a subsequent felony and who was personally armed with a firearm at any time during its commission or attempted commission or was unlawfully armed with a firearm at the time of his or her arrest for the subsequent felony.

(3) Aggravated arson, in violation of Section 451.5.

(b)(1) The existence of any fact that would make a person ineligible for probation under subdivision (a) shall be alleged in the accusatory pleading, and either admitted by the defendant in open court, or found to be true by the trier of fact.

(2) As used in subdivision (a), "used a firearm" means to display a firearm in a menacing manner, to intentionally fire it, to intentionally strike or hit a human being with it, or to use it in any manner that qualifies under Section 12022.5.

(3) As used in subdivision (a), "armed with a firearm" means to knowingly carry or have available for use a firearm as a means of offense or defense.

Penal Code § 1203.066.

(a) Notwithstanding Section 1203 or any other law, probation shall not be granted to, nor shall the execution or imposition of sentence be suspended for, nor shall a finding bringing the defendant within the provisions of this section be stricken pursuant to Section 1385 for, any of the following persons:

(1) A person who is convicted of violating Section 288 or 288.5 when the act is committed by the use of force, violence, duress, menace, or fear of immediate and unlawful bodily injury on the victim or another person.

(2) A person who caused bodily injury on the child victim in committing a violation of Section 288 or 288.5.

(3) A person who is convicted of a violation of Section 288 or 288.5 and who was a stranger to the child victim or befriended the child victim for the purpose of committing an act in violation of Section 288 or 288.5, unless the defendant honestly and reasonably believed the victim was 14 years of age or older.

(4) A person who used a weapon during the commission of a violation of Section 288 or 288.5.

(5) A person who is convicted of committing a violation of Section 288 or 288.5 and who has been previously convicted of a violation of Section 261, 262, 264.1, 266, 266c, 267, 285, 286, 288, 288.5, 288a, or 289, or of assaulting another person with intent to commit a crime specified in this paragraph in violation of Section 220, or who has been previously convicted in another state of an offense which, if committed or attempted in this state, would constitute an offense enumerated in this paragraph.

(6) A person who violated Section 288 or 288.5 while kidnapping the child victim in violation of Section 207, 209, or 209.5.

(7) A person who is convicted of committing a violation of Section 288 or 288.5 against more than one victim.

(8) A person who, in violating Section 288 or 288.5, has substantial sexual conduct with a victim who is under 14 years of age.

(9) A person who, in violating Section 288 or 288.5, used obscene matter, as defined in Section 311, or matter, as defined in Section 311, depicting sexual conduct, as defined in Section 311.3.

(b) "Substantial sexual conduct" means penetration of the vagina or rectum of either the victim or the offender by the penis of the other or by any foreign object, oral copulation, or masturbation of either the victim or the offender.

(c)(1) Except for a violation of subdivision (b) of Section 288, this section shall only apply if the existence of any fact required in subdivision (a) is alleged in the accusatory pleading and is either admitted by the defendant in open court, or found to be true by the trier of fact.

(2) For the existence of any fact under paragraph (7) of subdivision (a), the allegation must be made pursuant to this section.

(d)(1) If a person is convicted of a violation of Section 288 or 288.5, and the factors listed in subdivision (a) are not pled or proven, probation may be granted only if the following terms and conditions are met:

(A) If the defendant is a member of the victim's household, the court finds that probation is in the best interest of the child victim.

(B) The court finds that rehabilitation of the defendant is feasible and that the defendant is amenable to undergoing treatment, and the defendant is placed in a recognized treatment program designed to deal with child molestation immediately after the grant of probation or the suspension of execution or imposition of sentence.

(C) If the defendant is a member of the victim's household, probation shall not be granted unless the defendant is removed from the household of the victim until the court determines that the best interests of the victim would be served by his or her return. While removed from the household, the court shall prohibit contact by the defendant with the victim, with the exception that the court may permit supervised contact, upon the request of the director of the court-ordered supervised treatment program, and with the agreement of the victim and the victim's parent or legal guardian, other than the defendant.

(D) The court finds that there is no threat of physical harm to the victim if probation is granted.

(2) The court shall state its reasons on the record for whatever sentence it imposes on the defendant.

(3) The court shall order the psychiatrist or psychologist who is appointed pursuant to Section 288.1 to include a consideration of the factors specified in subparagraphs (A), (B), and (C) of paragraph (1) in making his or her report to the court.

(4) The court shall order the defendant to comply with all probation requirements, including the requirements to attend counseling, keep all program appointments, and pay program fees based upon ability to pay.

(5) No victim shall be compelled to participate in a program or counseling, and no program may condition a defendant's enrollment on participation by the victim.

(e) As used in subdivision (d), the following definitions apply:

(1) "Contact with the victim" includes all physical contact, being in the presence of the victim, communicating by any means, including by a third party acting on behalf of the defendant, or sending any gifts.

(2) "Recognized treatment program" means a program that consists of the following components:

(A) Substantial expertise in the treatment of child sexual abuse.

(B) A treatment regimen designed to specifically address the offense.

(C) The ability to serve indigent clients.

(D) Adequate reporting requirements to ensure that all persons who, after being ordered to attend and complete a program, may be identified for either failure to enroll in, or failure to successfully complete, the program, or for the successful completion of the program as ordered. The program shall notify the court and the probation department, in writing, within the period of time and in the manner specified by the court of any person who fails to complete the program. Notification shall be given if the program determines that the defendant is performing unsatisfactorily or if the defendant is not benefiting from the education, treatment, or counseling.

Penal Code § 1203.09.

(a) Notwithstanding any other law, probation shall not be granted to, nor shall the execution or imposition of sentence be suspended for, any person who commits or attempts to commit one or more of the crimes listed in subdivision (b) against a person who is 60 years of age or older; or against a person who is blind, a paraplegic, a quadriplegic, or a person confined to a wheelchair and that disability is known or reasonably should be known to the person committing the crime; and who during the course of the offense inflicts great bodily injury upon the person.

(b) Subdivision (a) applies to the following crimes:

(1) Murder.

(2) Robbery, in violation of Section 211.

(3) Kidnapping, in violation of Section 207.

(4) Kidnapping, in violation of Section 209.

(5) Burglary of the first degree, as defined in Section 460.

(6) Rape by force or violence, in violation of paragraph (2) or (6) of subdivision (a) of Section 261 or paragraph (1) or (4) of subdivision (a) of Section 262.

(7) Assault with intent to commit rape or sodomy, in violation of Section 220.

(8) Carjacking, in violation of Section 215.

(9) Kidnapping, in violation of Section 209.5.

(c) The existence of any fact which would make a person ineligible for probation under either subdivision (a) or (f) shall be alleged in the information or indictment, and either admitted by the defendant in open court, or found to be true by the jury trying the issue of guilt or by the court where guilt is established by plea of guilty or nolo contendere or by trial by the court sitting without a jury.

(d) As used in this section "great bodily injury" means "great bodily injury" as defined in Section 12022.7.

(e) This section shall apply in all cases, including those cases where the infliction of great bodily injury is an element of the offense.

(f) Except in unusual cases where the interests of justice would best be served if the person is granted probation, probation shall not be granted to, nor shall the execution or imposition of sentence be suspended for, any person convicted of having committed one or more of the following crimes against a person who is 60 years of age or older: assault with a deadly weapon or instrument, battery which results in physical injury which requires professional medical treatment, carjacking, robbery, or mayhem.

Penal Code § 1203.095.

(a) Except as provided in subdivision (b), but notwithstanding any other provision of law, if any person convicted of a violation of paragraph (2) of subdivision (a) of Section 245, of a violation of paragraph (1) of subdivision (d) of Section 245, of a violation of Section 246, or a violation of subdivision (c) of Section 417, is granted probation or the execution or imposition of sentence is suspended, it shall be a condition thereof that he or she be imprisoned for at least six months, and if any person convicted of a violation of paragraph (2) of subdivision (a) of Section 417 is granted probation or the execution or imposition of sentence is suspended, it shall be a condition thereof that he or she be imprisoned for at least three months.

(b) The provisions of subdivision (a) shall apply except in unusual cases where the interests of justice would best be served by granting probation or suspending the imposition or execution of sentence without the imprisonment required by subdivision (a), or by granting probation or suspending the imposition or execution of sentence with conditions other than those set forth in subdivision (a), in which case the court shall specify on the record and shall enter on the minutes the circumstances indicating that the interests of justice would best be served by such a disposition.

(c) This section does not prohibit the adjournment of criminal proceedings pursuant to Division 3 (commencing with Section 3000) or Division 6 (commencing with Section 6000) of the Welfare and Institutions Code.

Penal Code § 1203.1j.

In any case in which the defendant is convicted of assault, battery, or assault with a deadly weapon on a victim 65 years of age or older, and the defendant knew or reasonably should have known the elderly status of the victim, the court, as a condition of probation, shall order the defendant to make restitution for the costs of medical or psychological treatment incurred by the victim as a result of the crime, and that the defendant seek and maintain legitimate employment and apply that portion of his or her earnings specified by the court toward those costs.

The defendant shall be entitled to a hearing, concerning any modification of the amount of restitution, based on the costs of medical and psychological treatment incurred by the victim subsequent to the issuance of the order of probation.

Penal Code § 1203.1k.

For any order of restitution made under Section 1203.1, the court may order the specific amount of restitution and the manner in which restitution shall be made to a victim or the Restitution Fund, to the extent that the victim has received payment from the Victims of Crime Program, based on the probation officer's report or it may, with the consent of the defendant, order the probation officer to set the amount of restitution and the manner in which restitution shall be made to a victim or the Restitution Fund, to the extent that the victim has received payment from the Victims of Crime Program. The defendant shall have the right to a hearing before the judge to dispute the determinations made by the probation officer in regard to the amount or manner in which restitution is to be made to the victim or the Restitution Fund, to the extent that the victim has received payment from the Victims of Crime Program. If the court orders restitution to be made to the Restitution Fund, the court, and not the probation officer, shall determine the amount and the manner in which restitution is to be made to the Restitution Fund.

Penal Code § 1203.4.

(a) In any case in which a defendant has fulfilled the conditions of probation for the entire period of probation, or has been discharged prior to the termination of the period of probation, or in any other case in which a court, in its discretion and the interests of justice, determines that a defendant should be granted the relief available under this section, the defendant shall, at any time after the termination of the period of probation, if he or she is not then serving a sentence for any offense, on probation for any offense, or charged with the commission of any offense, be permitted by the court to withdraw his or her plea of guilty or plea of nolo contendere and enter a plea of not guilty; or, if he or she has been convicted after a plea of not guilty, the court shall set aside the verdict of guilty; and, in either case, the court shall thereupon dismiss the accusations or information against the defendant and except as noted below, he or she shall thereafter be released from all penalties and disabilities resulting from the offense of which he or she has been convicted, except as provided in Section 13555 of the Vehicle Code. The probationer shall be informed, in his or her probation papers, of this right and privilege and his or her right, if any, to petition for a certificate of rehabilitation and pardon. The probationer may make the application and change of plea in person or by attorney, or by the probation officer authorized in writing. However, in any subsequent prosecution of the defendant for any other offense, the prior conviction may be pleaded and proved and shall have the same effect as if probation had not been granted or the accusation or information dismissed. The order shall state, and the probationer shall be informed, that the order does not relieve him or her of the obligation to disclose the conviction in response to any direct question contained in any questionnaire or application for public office, for licensure by any state or local agency, or for contracting with the California State Lottery. Dismissal of an accusation or information pursuant to this section does not permit a person to own, possess, or have in his or her custody or control any firearm or prevent his or her conviction under Section 12021. Dismissal of an accusation or information underlying a conviction pursuant to this section does not permit a person prohibited from holding public office as a result of that conviction to hold public office. This subdivision shall apply to all applications for relief under this section which are filed on or after November 23, 1970.

(b) Subdivision (a) of this section does not apply to any misdemeanor that is within the provisions of subdivision (b) of Section 42001 of the Vehicle Code, to any violation of subdivision (c) of Section 286, Section 288, subdivision (c) of Section 288a, Section 288.5, or subdivision (j) of Section 289, any felony conviction pursuant to subdivision (d) of Section 261.5, or to any infraction.

(c)(1) Except as provided in paragraph (2), subdivision (a) does not apply to a person who receives a notice to appear or is otherwise charged with a violation of an offense described in subdivisions (a) to (e), inclusive, of Section 12810 of the Vehicle Code.

(2) If a defendant who was convicted of a violation listed in paragraph (1) petitions the court, the court in its discretion and in the interests of justice, may order the relief provided pursuant to subdivision (a) to that defendant.

(d) A person who petitions for a change of plea or setting aside of a verdict under this section may be required to reimburse the court for the actual costs of services rendered, whether or not the petition is granted and the records are sealed or expunged, at a rate to be determined by the court not to exceed one hundred twenty dollars ($120), and to reimburse the county for the actual costs of services rendered, whether or not the petition is granted and the records are sealed or expunged, at a rate to be determined by the county board of supervisors not to exceed one hundred twenty dollars ($120), and to reimburse any city for the actual costs of services rendered, whether or not the petition is granted and the records are sealed or expunged, at a rate to be determined by the city council not to exceed one hundred twenty dollars ($120). Ability to make this reimbursement shall be determined by the court using the standards set forth in paragraph (2) of subdivision (g) of Section 987.8 and shall not be a prerequisite to a person's eligibility under this section. The court may order reimbursement in any case in which the petitioner appears to have the ability to pay, without undue hardship, all or any portion of the costs for services established pursuant to this subdivision.

(e) Relief shall not be granted under this section unless the prosecuting attorney has been given 15 days' notice of the petition for relief. The probation officer shall notify the prosecuting attorney when a petition is filed, pursuant to this section. It shall be presumed that the prosecuting attorney has received notice if proof of service is filed with the court.

(f) If, after receiving notice pursuant to subdivision (e), the prosecuting attorney fails to appear and object to a petition for dismissal, the prosecuting attorney may not move to set aside or otherwise appeal the grant of that petition.

(g) Notwithstanding the above provisions or any other provision of law, the Governor shall have the right to pardon a person convicted of a violation of subdivision (c) of Section 286, Section 288, subdivision (c) of Section 288a, Section 288.5, or subdivision (j) of Section 289, if there are extraordinary circumstances.

Penal Code § 1270.1.

(a) Before any person who is arrested for any of the following crimes may be released on bail in an amount that is either more or less than the amount contained in the schedule of bail for the offense, or may be released on his or her own recognizance, a hearing shall be held in open court before the magistrate or judge:

(1) A serious felony, as defined in subdivision (c) of Section 1192.7, or a violent felony, as defined in subdivision (c) of Section 667.5, but not including a violation of subdivision (a) of Section 460 (residential burglary).

(2) A violation of Section 136.1 where punishment is imposed pursuant to subdivision (c) of Section 136.1, 262, 273.5, 422 where the offense is punished as a felony, or 646.9.

(3) A violation of paragraph (1) of subdivision (e) of Section 243.

(4) A violation of Section 273.6 if the detained person made threats to kill or harm, has engaged in violence against, or has gone to the residence or workplace of, the protected party.

(b) The prosecuting attorney and defense attorney shall be given a two court-day written notice and an opportunity to be heard on the matter. If the detained person does not have counsel, the court shall appoint counsel for purposes of this section only. The hearing required by this section shall be held within the time period prescribed in Section 825.

(c) At the hearing, the court shall consider evidence of past court appearances of the detained person, the maximum potential sentence that could be imposed, and the danger that may be posed to other persons if the detained person is released. In making the determination whether to release the detained person on his or her own recognizance, the court shall consider the potential danger to other persons, including threats that have been made by the detained person and any past acts of violence. The court shall also consider any evidence offered by the detained person regarding his or her ties to the community and his or her ability to post bond.

(d) If the judge or magistrate sets the bail in an amount that is either more or less than the amount contained in the schedule of bail for the offense, the judge or magistrate shall state the reasons for that decision and shall address the issue of threats made against the victim or witness, if they were made, in the record. This statement shall be included in the record.

Penal Code § 1274.

When the admission to bail is a matter of discretion, the Court or officer to whom the application is made must require reasonable notice thereof to be given to the District Attorney of the county.

Penal Code § 1275.

(a) In setting, reducing, or denying bail, the judge or magistrate shall take into consideration the protection of the public, the seriousness of the offense charged, the previous criminal record of the defendant, and the probability of his or her appearing at trial or hearing of the case. The public safety shall be the primary consideration. In considering the seriousness of the offense charged, the judge or magistrate shall include consideration of the alleged injury to the victim, and alleged threats to the victim or a witness to the crime charged, the alleged use of a firearm or other deadly weapon in the commission of the crime charged, and the alleged use or possession of controlled substances by the defendant.

(b) In considering offenses wherein a violation of Chapter 6 (commencing with Section 11350) of Division 10 of the Health and Safety Code is alleged, the judge or magistrate shall consider the following:

(1) the alleged amounts of controlled substances involved in the commission of the offense, and

(2) whether the defendant is currently released on bail for an alleged violation of Chapter 6 (commencing with Section 11350) of Division 10 of the Health and Safety Code.

(c) Before a court reduces bail below the amount established by the bail schedule approved for the county, in accordance with subdivisions (b) and (c) of Section 1269b, for a person charged with a serious felony, as defined in subdivision (c) of Section 1192.7, or a violent felony, as defined in subdivision (c) of Section 667.5, the court shall make a finding of unusual circumstances and shall set forth those facts on the record. For purposes of this subdivision, "unusual circumstances" does not include the fact that the defendant has made all prior court appearances or has not committed any new offenses.

Penal Code § 1299.02.

(a) No person, other than a certified law enforcement officer, shall be authorized to apprehend, detain, or arrest a bail fugitive unless that person meets one of the following conditions:

(1) Is a bail as defined in subdivision (b) of Section 1299.01 or a depositor of bail as defined in subdivision (c) of Section 1299.01. (2) Is a bail fugitive recovery person as defined in subdivision (d) of Section 1299.01.

(3) Holds a bail license issued by a state other than California or is authorized by another state to transact and post bail and is in compliance with the provisions of Section 847.5 with respect to the arrest of a bail fugitive.

(4) Is licensed as a private investigator as provided in Chapter 11.3 (commencing with Section 7512) of Division 3 of the Business and Professions Code.

(5) Holds a private investigator license issued by another state, is authorized by the bail or depositor of bail to apprehend a bail fugitive, and is in compliance with the provisions of Section 847.5 with respect to the arrest of a bail fugitive.

(b) This article shall not prohibit an arrest pursuant to Sections 837, 838, and 839.

Penal Code § 1299.10.

An individual authorized by Section 1299.02 to apprehend a bail fugitive shall not carry a firearm or other weapon unless in compliance with the laws of the state.

Penal Code § 1299.11. Penalties for violation of act

Any person who violates this act, or who conspires with another person to violate this act, or who hires an individual to apprehend a bail fugitive, knowing that the individual is not authorized by Section 1299.02 to apprehend a bail fugitive, is guilty of a misdemeanor punishable by a fine of five thousand dollars ($5,000) or by imprisonment in the county jail not to exceed one year, or by both that imprisonment and fine.

Penal Code § 1299.12.

This article shall remain in effect only until January 1, 2010, and as of that date is repealed, unless a later enacted statute, that is enacted before January 1, 2010, deletes or extends that date.

Penal Code § 1319.

(a) No person arrested for a violent felony, as described in subdivision (c) of Section 667.5, may be released on his or her own recognizance until a hearing is held in open court before the magistrate or judge, and until the prosecuting attorney is given notice and a reasonable opportunity to be heard on the matter. In all cases, these provisions shall be implemented in a manner consistent with the defendant's right to be taken before a magistrate or judge without unreasonable delay pursuant to Section 825.

(b) A defendant charged with a violent felony, as described in subdivision (c) of Section 667.5, shall not be released on his or her own recognizance where it appears, by clear and convincing evidence, that he or she previously has been charged with a felony offense and has willfully and without excuse from the court failed to appear in court as required while that charge was pending. In all other cases, in making the determination as to whether or not to grant release under this section, the court shall consider all of the following:

(1) The existence of any outstanding felony warrants on the defendant.

(2) Any other information presented in the report prepared pursuant to Section 1318.1. The fact that the court has not received the report required by Section 1318.1, at the time of the hearing to decide whether to release the defendant on his or her own recognizance, shall not preclude that release.

(3) Any other information presented by the prosecuting attorney.

(c) The judge or magistrate who, pursuant to this section, grants or denies release on a person's own recognizance, within the time period prescribed in Section 825, shall state the reasons for that decision in the record. This statement shall be included in the court's minutes. The report prepared by the investigative staff pursuant to subdivision (b) of Section 1318.1 shall be placed in the court file for that particular matter.

Penal Code § 1319.5.

(a) No person described in subdivision (b) who is arrested for a new offense may be released on his or her own recognizance until a hearing is held in open court before the magistrate or judge.

(b) Subdivision (a) shall apply to the following:

(1) Any person who is currently on felony probation or felony parole.

(2) Any person who has failed to appear in court as ordered, resulting in a warrant being issued, three or more times over the three years preceding the current arrest, except for infractions arising from violations of the Vehicle Code, and who is arrested for any of the following offenses:

(A) Any felony offense.

(B) Any violation of the California Street Terrorism Enforcement and Prevention Act (Chapter 11 (commencing with Section 186.20) of Title 7 of Part 1).

(C) Any violation of Chapter 9 (commencing with Section 240) of Title 8 of Part 1 (assault and battery).

(D) A violation of Section 484 (theft).

(E) A violation of Section 459 (burglary).

(F) Any offense in which the defendant is alleged to have been armed with or to have personally used a firearm.

Penal Code § 1542.

When a person charged with a felony is supposed by the magistrate before whom he is brought to have on his person a dangerous weapon, or anything which may be used as evidence of the commission of the offense, the magistrate may direct him to be searched in his presence, and the weapon or other thing to be retained, subject to his order, or to the order of the Court in which the defendant may be tried.

Penal Code § 2760.

The Department of Transportation of the State of California may employ or cause to be employed, prisoners confined in the state prisons in the improvement and maintenance of any state highway.

Penal Code § 2772.

Any person who, without authority, interferes with or in any way interrupts the work of any prisoners employed pursuant to this article, and any person not authorized by law, who gives or attempts to give to any prisoner so employed any controlled substances or any intoxicating liquors of any kind whatever, or firearms, weapons or explosives of any kind, is guilty of a felony and upon conviction thereof shall be punished by imprisonment in the state prison and shall be disqualified from holding any state office or position in the employ of this state. Any person who interferes with the discipline or good conduct of any prisoner employed pursuant to this article, while such prisoner is in the confines or limits of the state prison road camp is guilty of a misdemeanor and upon conviction thereof shall be punished by imprisonment in the county jail for a term not more than six months, or by a fine of not more than two hundred dollars ($200), or by both such fine and imprisonment. Any peace officer or any officer or guard of any state prison or any superintendent of such road work, having in charge the prisoners employed upon such highways or state roads, may arrest without a warrant any person violating any provisions of this article.

Penal Code § 3089.

(a) A county parole officer who is not a peace officer, as defined in Chapter 4.5 (commencing with Section 830) of Title 3 of Part 2, is a public officer who works at the direction of the County Board of Parole Commissioners, as provided for in Section 3075, and is responsible for supervising prisoners released on parole by the board.

(b) A county parole officer who is a public officer, as defined in subdivision (a), shall have no right to carry or possess firearms in the performance of his or her prescribed duties.

(c) A county parole officer, as defined in subdivision (a), shall comply with the standards for selection and training established by the Board of Corrections pursuant to Section 6035.

Penal Code § 4030.

(a) The Legislature finds and declares that law enforcement policies and practices for conducting strip or body cavity searches of detained persons vary widely throughout California. Consequently, some people have been arbitrarily subjected to unnecessary strip and body cavity searches after arrests for minor misdemeanor and infraction offenses. Some present search practices violate state and federal constitutional rights to privacy and freedom from unreasonable searches and seizures. It is the intent of the Legislature in enacting this section to protect the state and federal constitutional rights of the people of California by establishing a statewide policy strictly limiting strip and body cavity searches.

(b) The provisions of this section shall apply only to prearraignment detainees arrested for infraction or misdemeanor offenses and to any minor detained prior to a detention hearing on the grounds that he or she is a person described in Section 300, 601, or 602 of the Welfare and Institutions Code alleged to have committed a misdemeanor or infraction offense. The provisions of this section shall not apply to any person in the custody of the Director of the Department of Corrections or the Director of the Youth Authority.

(c) As used in this section, "strip search" means a search which requires a person to remove or arrange some or all of his or her clothing so as to permit a visual inspection of the underclothing, breasts, buttocks, or genitalia of such person.

(d) As used in this section:

(1) "Body cavity" only means the stomach or rectal cavity of a person, and vagina of a female person.

(2) "Visual body cavity search" means visual inspection of a body cavity.

(3) "Physical body cavity search" means physical intrusion into a body cavity for the purpose of discovering any object concealed in the body cavity.

(e) Notwithstanding any other provision of law, including Section 40304.5 of the Vehicle Code, when a person is arrested and taken into custody, that person may be subjected to patdown searches, metal detector searches, and thorough clothing searches in order to discover and retrieve concealed weapons and contraband substances prior to being placed in a booking cell.

(f) No person arrested and held in custody on a misdemeanor or infraction offense, except those involving weapons, controlled substances or violence nor any minor detained prior to a detention hearing on the grounds that he or she is a person described in Section 300, 601 or 602 of the Welfare and Institutions Code, except for those minors alleged to have committed felonies or offenses involving weapons, controlled substances or violence, shall be subjected to a strip search or visual body cavity search prior to placement in the general jail population, unless a peace officer has determined there is reasonable suspicion based on specific and articulable facts to believe such person is concealing a weapon or contraband, and a strip search will result in the discovery of the weapon or contraband. No strip search or visual body cavity search or both may be conducted without the prior written authorization of the supervising officer on duty. The authorization shall include the specific and articulable facts and circumstances upon which the reasonable suspicion determination was made by the supervisor.

(g)(1) Except pursuant to the provisions of paragraph (2), no person arrested and held in custody on a misdemeanor or infraction offense not involving weapons, controlled substances or violence, shall be confined in the general jail population unless all of the following are true:

(i) The person is not cited and released.

(ii) The person is not released on his or her own recognizance pursuant to Article 9 (commencing with Section 1318) of Chapter 1 of Title 10 of Part 2.

(iii) The person is not able to post bail within a reasonable time not less than three hours.

(2) No person may be housed in the general jail population prior to release pursuant to the provisions of paragraph (1) unless a documented emergency exists and there is no reasonable alternative to such placement. Such person shall be placed in the general population only upon prior written authorization documenting the specific facts and circumstances of the emergency. The written authorization shall be signed by the uniformed supervisor of the facility or by a uniformed watch commander. Any person confined in the general jail population pursuant to paragraph (1) shall retain all rights to release on citation, his or her own recognizance, or bail which were preempted as a consequence of the emergency.

(h) No person arrested on a misdemeanor or infraction offense, nor any minor described in subdivision (b), shall be subjected to a physical body cavity search except under the authority of a search warrant issued by a magistrate specifically authorizing the physical body cavity search.

(i) A copy of the prior written authorization required by subdivisions (f) and (g) and the search warrant required by subdivision (h) shall be placed in the agency's records and made available, on request, to the person searched or his or her authorized representative. With regard to any strip, visual or body search, the time, date and place of the search, the name and sex of the person conducting the search and a statement of the results of the search, including a list of any items removed from the person searched, shall be recorded in the agency's records and made available, upon request, to the person searched or his or her authorized representative.

(j) Persons conducting a strip search or a visual body cavity search shall not touch the breasts, buttocks, or genitalia of the person being searched.

(k) A physical body cavity search shall be conducted under sanitary conditions, and only by a physician, nurse practitioner, registered nurse, licensed vocational nurse or emergency medical technician Level II licensed to practice in this state. Any physician engaged in providing health care to detainees and inmates of the facility may conduct physical body cavity searches.

(l) All persons conducting or otherwise present during a strip search or visual or physical body cavity search shall be of the same sex as the person being searched, except for physicians or licensed medical personnel.

(m) All strip, visual and physical body cavity searches shall be conducted in an area of privacy so that the search cannot be observed by persons not participating in the search. Persons are considered to be participating in the search if their official duties relative to search procedure require them to be present at the time the search is conducted.

(n) A person who knowingly and willfully authorizes or conducts a strip, visual or physical body cavity search in violation of this section is guilty of a misdemeanor.

(o) Nothing in this section shall be construed as limiting any common law or statutory rights of any person regarding any action for damages or injunctive relief, or as precluding the prosecution under another provision of law of any peace officer or other person who has violated this section.

(p) Any person who suffers damage or harm as a result of a violation of this section may bring a civil action to recover actual damages, or one thousand dollars ($1,000), whichever is greater. In addition, the court may, in its discretion, award punitive damages, equitable relief as it deems necessary and proper, and costs, including reasonable attorney's fees.

Penal Code § 4500.

Every person while undergoing a life sentence, who is sentenced to state prison within this state, and who, with malice aforethought, commits an assault upon the person of another with a deadly weapon or instrument, or by any means of force likely to produce great bodily injury is punishable with death or life imprisonment without possibility of parole. The penalty shall be determined pursuant to the provisions of Sections 190.3 and 190.4; however, in cases in which the person subjected to such assault does not die within a year and a day after such assault as a proximate result thereof, the punishment shall be imprisonment in the state prison for life without the possibility of parole for nine years. For the purpose of computing the days elapsed between the commission of the assault and the death of the person assaulted, the whole of the day on which the assault was committed shall be counted as the first day. Nothing in this section shall be construed to prohibit the application of this section when the assault was committed outside the walls of any prison if the person committing the assault was undergoing a life sentence and was serving a sentence to a state prison at the time of the commission of the assault and was not on parole, on probation, or released on bail pending an appeal.

Penal Code § 4501.

Except as provided in Section 4500, every person confined in a state prison of this state who commits an assault upon the person of another with a deadly weapon or instrument, or by any means of force likely to produce great bodily injury, shall be guilty of a felony and shall be imprisoned in the state prison for two, four, or six years to be served consecutively.

Penal Code § 4502.

(a) Every person who, while at or confined in any penal institution, while being conveyed to or from any penal institution, or while under the custody of officials, officers, or employees of any penal institution, possesses or carries upon his or her person or has under his or her custody or control any instrument or weapon of the kind commonly known as a blackjack, slungshot, billy, sandclub, sandbag, or metal knuckles, any explosive substance, or fixed ammunition, any dirk or dagger or sharp instrument, any pistol, revolver, or other firearm, or any tear gas or tear gas weapon, is guilty of a felony and shall be punished by imprisonment in the state prison for two, three, or four years, to be served consecutively.

(b) Every person who, while at or confined in any penal institution, while being conveyed to or from any penal institution, or while under the custody of officials, officers, or employees of any penal institution, manufactures or attempts to manufacture any instrument or weapon of the kind commonly known as a blackjack, slungshot, billy, sandclub, sandbag, or metal knuckles, any explosive substance, or fixed ammunition, any dirk or dagger or sharp instrument, any pistol, revolver, or other firearm, or any tear gas or tear gas weapon, is guilty of a felony and shall be punished by imprisonment in the state prison for 16 months, or two or three years, to be served consecutively.

(c) For purposes of this section, "penal institution" means the state prison, a prison road camp, prison forestry camp, or other prison camp or farm, or a county jail or county road camp.

Penal Code § 4504.

For purposes of this chapter:

(a) A person is deemed confined in a "state prison" if he is confined in any of the prisons and institutions specified in Section 5003 by order made pursuant to law, including, but not limited to, commitments to the Department of Corrections or the Department of the Youth Authority, regardless of the purpose of such confinement and regardless of the validity of the order directing such confinement, until a judgment of a competent court setting aside such order becomes final.

(b) A person is deemed "confined in" a prison although, at the time of the offense, he is temporarily outside its walls or bounds for the purpose of serving on a work detail or for the purpose of confinement in a local correctional institution pending trial or for any other purpose for which a prisoner may be allowed temporarily outside the walls or bounds of the prison, but a prisoner who has been released on parole is not deemed "confined in" a prison for purposes of this chapter.

Penal Code § 4574.

(a) Except when otherwise authorized by law, or when authorized by the person in charge of the prison or other institution referred to in this section or by an officer of the institution empowered by the person in charge of the institution to give such authorization, any person, who knowingly brings or sends into, or knowingly assists in bringing into, or sending into, any state prison or prison road camp or prison forestry camp, or other prison camp or prison farm or any other place where prisoners of the state prison are located under the custody of prison officials, officers or employees, or any jail or any county road camp in this state, or within the grounds belonging or adjacent to any such institution, any firearms, deadly weapons, or explosives, and any person who, while lawfully confined in a jail or county road camp possesses therein any firearm, deadly weapon, explosive, tear gas or tear gas weapon, is guilty of a felony and punishable by imprisonment in the state prison for two, three, or four years.

(b) Except as provided in subdivision (a), any person who knowingly brings or sends into such places any tear gas or tear gas weapons which results in the release of such tear gas or use of such weapon is guilty of a felony and punishable by imprisonment in the state prison for two, three, or four years.

(c) Except as provided in subdivision (a), any person who knowingly brings or sends into such places any tear gas or tear gas weapons is guilty of a misdemeanor and punishable by imprisonment in the county jail not exceeding six months, or by fine not exceeding one thousand dollars ($1,000), or by both such fine and imprisonment.

Penal Code § 4852.01.

(a) Any person convicted of a felony who has been released from a state prison or other state penal institution or agency in California, whether discharged on completion of the term for which he or she was sentenced or released on parole prior to May 13, 1943, who has not been incarcerated in a state prison or other state penal institution or agency since his or her release and who presents satisfactory evidence of a three-year residence in this state immediately prior to the filing of the petition for a certificate of rehabilitation and pardon provided for by this chapter, may file the petition pursuant to the provisions of this chapter.

(b) Any person convicted of a felony who, on May 13, 1943, was confined in a state prison or other institution or agency to which he or she was committed and any person convicted of a felony after that date who is committed to a state prison or other institution or agency may file a petition for a certificate of rehabilitation and pardon pursuant to the provisions of this chapter.

(c) Any person convicted of a felony or any person who is convicted of a misdemeanor violation of any sex offense specified in Section 290, the accusatory pleading of which has been dismissed pursuant to Section 1203.4, may file a petition for certificate of rehabilitation and pardon pursuant to the provisions of this chapter if the petitioner has not been incarcerated in any prison, jail, detention facility, or other penal institution or agency since the dismissal of the accusatory pleading and is not on probation for the commission of any other felony, and the petitioner presents satisfactory evidence of five years residence in this state prior to the filing of the petition.

(d) This chapter shall not apply to persons serving a mandatory life parole, persons committed under death sentences, persons convicted of a violation of subdivision (c) of Section 286, Section 288, subdivision (c) of Section 288a, Section 288.5, or subdivision (j) of Section 289, or persons in the military service.

(e) Notwithstanding the above provisions or any other provision of law, the Governor shall have the right to pardon a person convicted of a violation of subdivision (c) of Section 286, Section 288, subdivision (c) of Section 288a, Section 288.5, or subdivision (j) of Section 289, if there are extraordinary circumstances.

Penal Code § 4852.16.

The certified copy of a certificate of rehabilitation transmitted to the Governor shall constitute an application for a full pardon upon receipt of which the Governor may, without any further investigation, issue a pardon to the person named therein, except that, pursuant to Section 8 of Article V of the Constitution, the Governor shall not grant a pardon to any person twice convicted of felony, except upon the written recommendation of a majority of the judges of the Supreme Court.

Penal Code § 4852.17.

Whenever a person is issued a certificate of rehabilitation or granted a pardon from the Governor under this chapter, the fact shall be immediately reported to the Department of Justice by the court, Governor, officer, or governmental agency by whose official action the certificate is issued or the pardon granted. The Department of Justice shall immediately record the facts so reported on the former criminal record of the person, and transmit those facts to the Federal Bureau of Investigation at Washington, D.C. When the criminal record is thereafter reported by the department, it shall also report the fact that the person has received a certificate of rehabilitation, or pardon, or both.

Whenever a person is granted a full and unconditional pardon by the Governor, based upon a certificate of rehabilitation, the pardon shall entitle the person to exercise thereafter all civil and political rights of citizenship, including but not limited to:

(1) the right to vote;

(2) the right to own, possess, and keep any type of firearm that may lawfully be owned and possessed by other citizens; except that this right shall not be restored, and Sections 12001 and 12021 shall apply, if the person was ever convicted of a felony involving the use of a dangerous weapon.

Penal Code § 4853.

In all cases in which a full pardon has been granted by the Governor of this state or will hereafter be granted by the Governor to a person convicted of an offense to which the pardon applies, it shall operate to restore to the convicted person, all the rights, privileges, and franchises of which he or she has been deprived in consequence of that conviction or by reason of any matter involved therein; provided, that nothing herein contained shall abridge or impair the power or authority conferred by law on any board or tribunal to revoke or suspend any right, privilege or franchise for any act or omission not involved in the conviction; provided further, that nothing in this article shall affect any of the provisions of the Medical Practice Act (Chapter 5 (commencing with Section 2000) of Division 2 of the Business and Professions Code) or the power or authority conferred by law on the Board of Medical Examiners therein, or the power or authority conferred by law upon any board that issues a certificate which permits any person or persons to apply his or her or their art or profession on the person of another.

Penal Code § 4854.

In the granting of a pardon to a person, the Governor may provide that the person is entitled to exercise the right to own, possess and keep any type of firearm that may lawfully be owned and possessed by other citizens; except that this right shall not be restored, and Sections 12001 and 12021 shall apply, if the person was ever convicted of a felony involving the use of a dangerous weapon.

Penal Code § 11105.

(a) (1) The Department of Justice shall maintain state summary criminal history information.

(2) As used in this section:

(A) "State summary criminal history information" means the master record of information compiled by the Attorney General pertaining to the identification and criminal history of any person, such as name, date of birth, physical description, fingerprints, photographs, date of arrests, arresting agencies and booking numbers, charges, dispositions, and similar data about the person.

(B) "State summary criminal history information" does not refer to records and data compiled by criminal justice agencies other than the Attorney General, nor does it refer to records of complaints to or investigations conducted by, or records of intelligence information or security procedures of, the office of the Attorney General and the Department of Justice.

(b) The Attorney General shall furnish state summary criminal history information to any of the following, if needed in the course of their duties, provided that when information is furnished to assist an agency, officer, or official of state or local government, a public utility, or any other entity, in fulfilling employment, certification, or licensing duties, Chapter 1321 of the Statutes of 1974 and Section 432.7 of the Labor Code shall apply:

(1) The courts of the state.

(2) Peace officers of the state, as defined in Section 830.1, subdivisions (a) and (e) of Section 830.2, subdivision (a) of Section

830.3, subdivisions (a) and (b) of Section 830.5, and subdivision (a) of Section 830.31.

(3) District attorneys of the state.

(4) Prosecuting city attorneys of any city within the state.

(5) City attorneys pursuing civil gang injunctions pursuant to Section 186.22a, or drug abatement actions pursuant to Section 3479 or 3480 of the Civil Code, or Section 11571 of the Health and Safety Code.

(6) Probation officers of the state.

(7) Parole officers of the state.

(8) A public defender or attorney of record when representing a person in proceedings upon a petition for a certificate of rehabilitation and pardon pursuant to Section 4852.08.

(9) A public defender or attorney of record when representing a person in a criminal case, or parole revocation or revocation extension proceeding, and if authorized access by statutory or decisional law.

(10) Any agency, officer, or official of the state if the criminal history information is required to implement a statute or regulation that expressly refers to specific criminal conduct applicable to the subject person of the state summary criminal history information, and contains requirements or exclusions, or both, expressly based upon that specified criminal conduct. The agency, officer, or official of the state authorized by this paragraph to receive state summary criminal history information may also transmit fingerprint images and related information to the Department of Justice to be transmitted to the Federal Bureau of Investigation.

(11) Any city or county, city and county, district, or any officer or official thereof if access is needed in order to assist that agency, officer, or official in fulfilling employment, certification, or licensing duties, and if the access is specifically authorized by the city council, board of supervisors, or governing board of the city, county, or district if the criminal history information is required to implement a statute, ordinance, or regulation that expressly refers to specific criminal conduct applicable to the subject person of the state summary criminal history information, and contains requirements or exclusions, or both, expressly based upon that specified criminal conduct. The city or county, city and county, district, or the officer or official thereof authorized by this paragraph may also transmit fingerprint images and related information to the Department of Justice to be transmitted to the Federal Bureau of Investigation.

(12) The subject of the state summary criminal history information under procedures established under Article 5 (commencing with Section 11120).

(13) Any person or entity when access is expressly authorized by statute if the criminal history information is required to implement a statute or regulation that expressly refers to specific criminal conduct applicable to the subject person of the state summary criminal history information, and contains requirements or exclusions, or both, expressly based upon that specified criminal conduct.

(14) Health officers of a city, county, city and county, or district when in the performance of their official duties enforcing Section 120175 of the Health and Safety Code.

(15) Any managing or supervising correctional officer of a county jail or other county correctional facility.

(16) Any humane society, or society for the prevention of cruelty to animals, for the specific purpose of complying with Section 14502 of the Corporations Code for the appointment of level I humane officers.

(17) Local child support agencies established by Section 17304 of the Family Code. When a local child support agency closes a support enforcement case containing summary criminal history information, the agency shall delete or purge from the file and destroy any documents or information concerning or arising from offenses for or of which the parent has been arrested, charged, or convicted, other than for offenses related to the parent's having failed to provide support for minor children, consistent with the requirements of Section 17531 of the Family Code.

(18) County child welfare agency personnel who have been delegated the authority of county probation officers to access state summary criminal history information pursuant to Section 272 of the Welfare and Institutions Code for the purposes specified in Section 16504.5 of the Welfare and Institutions Code. Information from criminal history records provided pursuant to this subdivision shall not be used for any purposes other than those specified in this section and Section 16504.5 of the Welfare and Institutions Code. When an agency obtains records obtained both on the basis of name checks and fingerprint checks, final placement decisions shall be based only on the records obtained pursuant to the fingerprint check.

(19) The court of a tribe, or court of a consortium of tribes, that has entered into an agreement with the state pursuant to Section 10553.1 of the Welfare and Institutions Code. This information may be used only for the purposes specified in Section 16504.5 of the Welfare and Institutions Code and for tribal approval or tribal licensing of foster care or adoptive homes. Article 6 (commencing with Section 11140) shall apply to officers, members, and employees of a tribal court receiving criminal record offender information pursuant to this section.

(20) Child welfare agency personnel of a tribe or consortium of tribes that has entered into an agreement with the state pursuant to Section 10553.1 of the Welfare and Institutions Code and to whom the state has delegated duties under paragraph (2) of subdivision (a) of Section 272 of the Welfare and Institutions Code. The purposes for use of the information shall be for the purposes specified in Section 16504.5 of the Welfare and Institutions Code and for tribal approval or tribal licensing of foster care or adoptive homes. When an agency obtains records on the basis of name checks and fingerprint checks, final placement decisions shall be based only on the records obtained pursuant to the fingerprint check. Article 6 (commencing with Section 11140) shall apply to child welfare agency personnel receiving criminal record offender information pursuant to this section.

(21) An officer providing conservatorship investigations pursuant to Sections 5351, 5354, and 5356 of the Welfare and Institutions Code.

(22) A court investigator providing investigations or reviews in conservatorships pursuant to Section 1826, 1850, 1851, or 2250.6 of the Probate Code.

(23) A person authorized to conduct a guardianship investigation pursuant to Section 1513 of the Probate Code.

(c) The Attorney General may furnish state summary criminal history information and, when specifically authorized by this subdivision, federal level criminal history information upon a showing of a compelling need to any of the following, provided that when information is furnished to assist an agency, officer, or official of state or local government, a public utility, or any other entity in fulfilling employment, certification, or licensing duties, Chapter 1321 of the Statutes of 1974 and Section 432.7 of the Labor Code shall apply:

(1) Any public utility, as defined in Section 216 of the Public Utilities Code, that operates a nuclear energy facility when access

is needed in order to assist in employing persons to work at the facility, provided that, if the Attorney General supplies the data, he or she shall furnish a copy of the data to the person to whom the data relates.

(2) To a peace officer of the state other than those included in subdivision (b).

(3) To an illegal dumping enforcement officer as defined in subdivision (j) of Section 830.7.

(4) To a peace officer of another country.

(5) To public officers, other than peace officers, of the United States, other states, or possessions or territories of the United States, provided that access to records similar to state summary criminal history information is expressly authorized by a statute of the United States, other states, or possessions or territories of the United States if the information is needed for the performance of their official duties.

(6) To any person when disclosure is requested by a probation, parole, or peace officer with the consent of the subject of the state summary criminal history information and for purposes of furthering the rehabilitation of the subject.

(7) The courts of the United States, other states, or territories or possessions of the United States.

(8) Peace officers of the United States, other states, or territories or possessions of the United States.

(9) To any individual who is the subject of the record requested if needed in conjunction with an application to enter the United States or any foreign nation.

(10) (A) Any public utility, as defined in Section 216 of the Public Utilities Code, or any cable corporation as defined in subparagraph (B), if receipt of criminal history information is needed in order to assist in employing current or prospective employees, contract employees, or subcontract employees who, in the course of their employment may be seeking entrance to private residences or adjacent grounds. The information provided shall be limited to the record of convictions and any arrest for which the person is released on bail or on his or her own recognizance pending trial. If the Attorney General supplies the data pursuant to this paragraph, the Attorney General shall furnish a copy of the data to the current or prospective employee to whom the data relates. Any information obtained from the state summary criminal history is confidential and the receiving public utility or cable corporation shall not disclose its contents, other than for the purpose for which it was acquired. The state summary criminal history information in the possession of the public utility or cable corporation and all copies made from it shall be destroyed not more than 30 days after employment or promotion or transfer is denied or granted, except for those cases where a current or prospective employee is out on bail or on his or her own recognizance pending trial, in which case the state summary criminal history information and all copies shall be destroyed not more than 30 days after the case is resolved. A violation of this paragraph is a misdemeanor, and shall give the current or prospective employee who is injured by the violation a cause of action against the public utility or cable corporation to recover damages proximately caused by the violations. Any public utility's or cable corporation's request for state summary criminal history information for purposes of employing current or prospective employees who may be seeking entrance to private residences or adjacent grounds in the course of their employment shall be deemed a "compelling need" as required to be shown in this subdivision. Nothing in this section shall be construed as imposing any duty upon public utilities or cable corporations to request state summary criminal history information on any current or prospective employees.

(B) For purposes of this paragraph, "cable corporation" means any corporation or firm that transmits or provides television, computer, or telephone services by cable, digital, fiber optic, satellite, or comparable technology to subscribers for a fee.

(C) Requests for federal-level criminal history information received by the Department of Justice from entities authorized pursuant to subparagraph (A) shall be forwarded to the Federal Bureau of Investigation by the Department of Justice. Federal-level criminal history information received or compiled by the Department of Justice may then be disseminated to the entities referenced in subparagraph (A), as authorized by law.

(D) (i) Authority for a cable corporation to request state or federal-level criminal history information under this paragraph shall commence July 1, 2005.

(ii) Authority for a public utility to request federal-level criminal history information under this paragraph shall commence July 1, 2005.

(11) To any campus of the California State University or the University of California, or any four-year college or university accredited by a regional accreditation organization approved by the United States Department of Education, if needed in conjunction with an application for admission by a convicted felon to any special education program for convicted felons, including, but not limited to, university alternatives and halfway houses. Only conviction information shall be furnished. The college or university may require the convicted felon to be fingerprinted, and any inquiry to the department under this section shall include the convicted felon's fingerprints and any other information specified by the department.

(d) Whenever an authorized request for state summary criminal history information pertains to a person whose fingerprints are on file with the Department of Justice and the department has no criminal history of that person, and the information is to be used for employment, licensing, or certification purposes, the fingerprint card accompanying the request for information, if any, may be stamped "no criminal record" and returned to the person or entity making the request.

(e) Whenever state summary criminal history information is furnished as the result of an application and is to be used for employment, licensing, or certification purposes, the Department of Justice may charge the person or entity making the request a fee that it determines to be sufficient to reimburse the department for the cost of furnishing the information. In addition, the Department of Justice may add a surcharge to the fee to fund maintenance and improvements to the systems from which the information is obtained. Notwithstanding any other law, any person or entity required to pay a fee to the department for information received under this section may charge the applicant a fee sufficient to reimburse the person or entity for this expense. All moneys received by the department pursuant to this section, Sections 11105.3 and 12054 of the Penal Code, and Section 13588 of the Education Code shall be deposited in a special account in the General Fund to be available for expenditure by the department to offset costs incurred pursuant to those sections and for maintenance and improvements to the systems from which the information is obtained upon appropriation by the Legislature.

(f) Whenever there is a conflict, the processing of criminal fingerprints and fingerprints of applicants for security guard or alarm agent registrations or firearms qualification permits submitted pursuant to Section 7583.9, 7583.23, 7596.3, or 7598.4 of the Business and Professions Code shall take priority over the processing of other applicant fingerprints.

(g) It is not a violation of this section to disseminate statistical or research information obtained from a record, provided that the identity of the subject of the record is not disclosed.

(h) It is not a violation of this section to include information obtained from a record in (1) a transcript or record of a judicial or administrative proceeding or (2) any other public record if the inclusion of the information in the public record is authorized by a court, statute, or decisional law.

(i) Notwithstanding any other law, the Department of Justice or any state or local law enforcement agency may require the submission of fingerprints for the purpose of conducting summary criminal history information checks that are authorized by law.

(j) The state summary criminal history information shall include any finding of mental incompetence pursuant to Chapter 6 (commencing with Section 1367) of Title 10 of Part 2 arising out of a complaint charging a felony offense specified in Section 290.

(k) (1) This subdivision shall apply whenever state or federal summary criminal history information is furnished by the Department of Justice as the result of an application by an authorized agency or organization and the information is to be used for peace officer employment or certification purposes. As used in this subdivision, a peace officer is defined in Chapter 4.5 (commencing with Section 830) of Title 3 of Part 2.

(2) Notwithstanding any other provision of law, whenever state summary criminal history information is furnished pursuant to paragraph (1), the Department of Justice shall disseminate the following information:

(A) Every conviction rendered against the applicant.

(B) Every arrest for an offense for which the applicant is presently awaiting trial, whether the applicant is incarcerated or has been released on bail or on his or her own recognizance pending trial.

(C) Every arrest or detention, except for an arrest or detention resulting in an exoneration, provided however that where the records of the Department of Justice do not contain a disposition for the arrest, the Department of Justice first makes a genuine effort to determine the disposition of the arrest.

(D) Every successful diversion.

(l) (1) This subdivision shall apply whenever state or federal summary criminal history information is furnished by the Department of Justice as the result of an application by a criminal justice agency or organization as defined in Section 13101 of the Penal Code, and the information is to be used for criminal justice employment, licensing, or certification purposes.

(2) Notwithstanding any other provision of law, whenever state summary criminal history information is furnished pursuant to paragraph (1), the Department of Justice shall disseminate the following information:

(A) Every conviction rendered against the applicant.

(B) Every arrest for an offense for which the applicant is presently awaiting trial, whether the applicant is incarcerated or has been released on bail or on his or her own recognizance pending trial.

(C) Every arrest for an offense for which the records of the Department of Justice do not contain a disposition or did not result in a conviction, provided that the Department of Justice first makes a genuine effort to determine the disposition of the arrest. However, information concerning an arrest shall not be disclosed if the records of the Department of Justice indicate or if the genuine effort reveals that the subject was exonerated, successfully completed a diversion or deferred entry of judgment program, or the arrest was deemed a detention.

(m) (1) This subdivision shall apply whenever state or federal summary criminal history information is furnished by the Department of Justice as the result of an application by an authorized agency or organization pursuant to Section 1522, 1568.09, 1569.17, or 1596.871 of the Health and Safety Code, or any statute that incorporates the criteria of any of those sections or this subdivision by reference, and the information is to be used for employment, licensing, or certification purposes.

(2) Notwithstanding any other provision of law, whenever state summary criminal history information is furnished pursuant to paragraph (1), the Department of Justice shall disseminate the following information:

(A) Every conviction of an offense rendered against the applicant.

(B) Every arrest for an offense for which the applicant is presently awaiting trial, whether the applicant is incarcerated or has been released on bail or on his or her own recognizance pending trial.

(C) Every arrest for an offense for which the Department of Social Services is required by paragraph (1) of subdivision (a) of Section 1522 of the Health and Safety Code to determine if an applicant has been arrested. However, if the records of the Department of Justice do not contain a disposition for an arrest, the Department of Justice shall first make a genuine effort to determine the disposition of the arrest.

(3) Notwithstanding the requirements of the sections referenced in paragraph (1) of this subdivision, the Department of Justice shall not disseminate information about an arrest subsequently deemed a detention or an arrest that resulted in either the successful completion of a diversion program or exoneration.

(n) (1) This subdivision shall apply whenever state or federal summary criminal history information, to be used for employment, licensing, or certification purposes, is furnished by the Department of Justice as the result of an application by an authorized agency, organization, or individual pursuant to any of the following:

(A) Paragraph (9) of subdivision (c), when the information is to be used by a cable corporation.

(B) Section 11105.3 or 11105.4.

(C) Section 15660 of the Welfare and Institutions Code.

(D) Any statute that incorporates the criteria of any of the statutory provisions listed in subparagraph (A), (B), or (C), or of this subdivision, by reference.

(2) With the exception of applications submitted by transportation companies authorized pursuant to Section 11105.3, and notwithstanding any other provision of law, whenever state summary criminal history information is furnished pursuant to paragraph (1), the Department of Justice shall disseminate the following information:

(A) Every conviction rendered against the applicant for a violation or attempted violation of any offense specified in subdivision (a) of Section 15660 of the Welfare and Institutions Code. However, with the exception of those offenses for which registration is required pursuant to Section 290, the Department of Justice shall not disseminate information pursuant to this subdivision unless the conviction occurred within 10 years of the date of the agency's request for information or the conviction is over 10 years old but the subject of the request was incarcerated within 10 years of the agency's request for information.

(B) Every arrest for a violation or attempted violation of an offense specified in subdivision (a) of Section 15660 of the

Welfare and Institutions Code for which the applicant is presently awaiting trial, whether the applicant is incarcerated or has been released on bail or on his or her own recognizance pending trial.

(o) (1) This subdivision shall apply whenever state or federal summary criminal history information is furnished by the Department of Justice as the result of an application by an authorized agency or organization pursuant to Section 261 or 550 of the Financial Code, or any statute that incorporates the criteria of either of those sections or this subdivision by reference, and the information is to be used for employment, licensing, or certification purposes.

(2) Notwithstanding any other provision of law, whenever state summary criminal history information is furnished pursuant to paragraph (1), the Department of Justice shall disseminate the following information:

(A) Every conviction rendered against the applicant for a violation or attempted violation of any offense specified in Section 550 of the Financial Code.

(B) Every arrest for a violation or attempted violation of an offense specified in Section 550 of the Financial Code for which the applicant is presently awaiting trial, whether the applicant is incarcerated or has been released on bail or on his or her own recognizance pending trial.

(p) (1) This subdivision shall apply whenever state or federal criminal history information is furnished by the Department of Justice as the result of an application by an agency, organization, or individual not defined in subdivision (k), (l), (m), (n), or (o), or by a transportation company authorized pursuant to Section 11105.3, or any statute that incorporates the criteria of that section or this subdivision by reference, and the information is to be used for employment, licensing, or certification purposes.

(2) Notwithstanding any other provisions of law, whenever state summary criminal history information is furnished pursuant to paragraph (1), the Department of Justice shall disseminate the following information:

(A) Every conviction rendered against the applicant.

(B) Every arrest for an offense for which the applicant is presently awaiting trial, whether the applicant is incarcerated or has been released on bail or on his or her own recognizance pending trial.

(q) All agencies, organizations, or individuals defined in subdivisions (k), (l), (m), (n), (o), and (p) may contract with the Department of Justice for subsequent arrest notification pursuant to Section 11105.2. This subdivision shall not supersede sections that mandate an agency, organization, or individual to contract with the Department of Justice for subsequent arrest notification pursuant to Section 11105.2.

(r) Nothing in this section shall be construed to mean that the Department of Justice shall cease compliance with any other statutory notification requirements.

(s) The provisions of Section 50.12 of Title 28 of the Code of Federal Regulations are to be followed in processing federal criminal history information.

Penal Code § 11106.

(a) In order to assist in the investigation of crime, the prosecution of civil actions by city attorneys pursuant to paragraph (3) of subdivision (c), the arrest and prosecution of criminals, and the recovery of lost, stolen, or found property, the Attorney General shall keep and properly file a complete record of all copies of fingerprints, copies of licenses to carry firearms issued pursuant to Section 12050, information reported to the Department of Justice pursuant to Section 12053, dealers' records of sales of firearms, reports provided pursuant to Section 12072 or 12078, forms provided pursuant to Section 12084, as that section read prior to being repealed by the act that amended this section, reports provided pursuant to Section 12071 that are not dealers' records of sales of firearms, and reports of stolen, lost, found, pledged, or pawned property in any city or county of this state, and shall, upon proper application therefor, furnish this information to the officers referred to in Section 11105.

(b)(1) Except as provided in subdivision (d), the Attorney General shall not retain or compile any information from reports filed pursuant to subdivision (a) of Section 12078 for firearms that are not handguns, from forms submitted pursuant to Section 12084, as that section read prior to being repealed by the act that amended this section, for firearms that are not handguns, or from dealers' records of sales for firearms that are not handguns. All copies of the forms submitted, or any information received in electronic form, pursuant to Section 12084, as that section read prior to being repealed by the act that amended this section, for firearms that are not handguns, or of the dealers' records of sales for firearms that are not handguns shall be destroyed within five days of the clearance by the Attorney General, unless the purchaser or transferor is ineligible to take possession of the firearm. All copies of the reports filed, or any information received in electronic form, pursuant to subdivision (a) of Section 12078 for firearms that are not handguns shall be destroyed within five days of the receipt by the Attorney General, unless retention is necessary for use in a criminal prosecution.

(2) A peace officer, the Attorney General, a Department of Justice employee designated by the Attorney General, or any authorized local law enforcement employee shall not retain or compile any information from a firearms transaction record, as defined in paragraph (5) of subdivision (c) of Section 12071, for firearms that are not handguns unless retention or compilation is necessary for use in a criminal prosecution or in a proceeding to revoke a license issued pursuant to Section 12071.

(3) A violation of this subdivision is a misdemeanor.

(c)(1) The Attorney General shall permanently keep and properly file and maintain all information reported to the Department of Justice pursuant to Sections 12071, 12072, 12078, 12082, and former Section 12084 or any other law, as to handguns and maintain a registry thereof.

(2) The registry shall consist of all of the following:

(A) The name, address, identification of, place of birth (state or country), complete telephone number, occupation, sex, description, and all legal names and aliases ever used by the owner or person being loaned the particular handgun as listed on the information provided to the department on the Dealers' Record of Sale, the Law Enforcement Firearms Transfer (LEFT), as defined in former Section 12084, or reports made to the department pursuant to Section 12078 or any other law.

(B) The name and address of, and other information about, any person (whether a dealer or a private party) from whom the owner acquired or the person being loaned the particular handgun and when the firearm was acquired or loaned as listed on the information provided to the department on the Dealers' Record of Sale, the LEFT, or reports made to the department pursuant to Section 12078 or any other law.

(C) Any waiting period exemption applicable to the transaction which resulted in the owner of or the person being loaned the particular handgun acquiring or being loaned that firearm.

(D) The manufacturer's name if stamped on the firearm, model name or number if stamped on the firearm, and, if applicable, the serial number, other number (if more than one serial number is stamped on the firearm), caliber, type of firearm, if the firearm is new or used, barrel length, and color of the firearm.

(3) Information in the registry referred to in this subdivision shall, upon proper application therefor, be furnished to the officers referred to in Section 11105, to a city attorney prosecuting a civil action, solely for use in prosecuting that civil action and not for any other purpose, or to the person listed in the registry as the owner or person who is listed as being loaned the particular handgun.

(4) If any person is listed in the registry as the owner of a firearm through a Dealers' Record of Sale prior to 1979, and the person listed in the registry requests by letter that the Attorney General store and keep the record electronically, as well as in the record's existing photographic, photostatic, or nonerasable optically stored form, the Attorney General shall do so within three working days of receipt of the request. The Attorney General shall, in writing, and as soon as practicable, notify the person requesting electronic storage of the record that the request has been honored as required by this paragraph.

(d)(1) Any officer referred to in paragraphs (1) to (6), inclusive, of subdivision (b) of Section 11105 may disseminate the name of the subject of the record, the number of the firearms listed in the record, and the description of any firearm, including the make, model, and caliber, from the record relating to any firearm's sale, transfer, registration, or license record, or any information reported to the Department of Justice pursuant to Section 12021.3, 12053, 12071, 12072, 12077, 12078, 12082, or 12285, if the following conditions are met:

(A) The subject of the record has been arraigned for a crime in which the victim is a person described in subdivisions (a) to (f), inclusive, of Section 6211 of the Family Code and is being prosecuted or is serving a sentence for the crime, or the subject of the record is the subject of an emergency protective order, a temporary restraining order, or an order after hearing, which is in effect and has been issued by a family court under the Domestic Violence Protection Act set forth in Division 10 (commencing with Section 6200) of the Family Code.

(B) The information is disseminated only to the victim of the crime or to the person who has obtained the emergency protective order, the temporary restraining order, or the order after hearing issued by the family court.

(C) Whenever a law enforcement officer disseminates the information authorized by this subdivision, that officer or another officer assigned to the case shall immediately provide the victim of the crime with a "Victims of Domestic Violence" card, as specified in subparagraph (H) of paragraph (9) of subdivision (c) of Section 13701.

(2) The victim or person to whom information is disseminated pursuant to this subdivision may disclose it as he or she deems necessary to protect himself or herself or another person from bodily harm by the person who is the subject of the record.

Penal Code § 11108.

(a) Each sheriff or police chief executive shall submit descriptions of serialized property, or nonserialized property that has been uniquely inscribed, which has been reported stolen, lost, found, recovered, held for safekeeping, or under observation, directly into the appropriate Department of Justice automated property system for firearms, stolen bicycles, stolen vehicles, or other property, as the case may be.

(b) Information about a firearm entered into the automated system for firearms shall remain in the system until the reported firearm has been found, recovered, is no longer under observation, or the record is determined to have been entered in error.

(c) Any costs incurred by the Department of Justice to implement subdivision (b) shall be reimbursed from funds other than fees charged and collected pursuant to subdivisions (e) and (f) of Section 12076.

Penal Code § 11108.3.

(a) In addition to the requirements of Section 11108 that apply to a local law enforcement agency's duty to report to the Department of Justice the recovery of a firearm, a police or sheriff' s department shall, and any other law enforcement agency or agent may, report to the department in a manner determined by the Attorney General in consultation with the Bureau of Alcohol, Tobacco, Firearms and Explosives all available information necessary to identify and trace the history of all recovered firearms that are illegally possessed, have been used in a crime, or are suspected of having been used in a crime.

(b) When the department receives information from a local law enforcement agency pursuant to subdivision (a), it shall promptly forward this information to the National Tracing Center of the federal Bureau of Alcohol, Tobacco, Firearms and Explosives to the extent practicable.

(c) The Department of Justice shall implement an electronic system by January 1, 2002, to receive comprehensive tracing information from each local law enforcement agency, and to forward this information to the National Tracing Center.

(d) In implementing this section, the Attorney General shall ensure to the maximum extent practical that both of the following apply:

(1) The information he or she provides to the federal Bureau of Alcohol, Tobacco, Firearms and Explosives enables that agency to trace the ownership of the firearm described in subdivision (a).

(2) Local law enforcement agencies can report all relevant information without being unduly burdened by this reporting function.

(e) Information collected pursuant to this section shall be maintained by the department for a period of not less than 10 years, and shall be available, under guidelines set forth by the Attorney General, for academic and policy research purposes.

(f) The Attorney General shall have the authority to issue regulations to further the purposes of this section.

Penal Code § 11108.5.

(a) If a law enforcement agency identifies serialized property that has been reported lost or stolen by the owner or a person entitled to possession of the property and the property has been entered into the appropriate Department of Justice automated property system pursuant to Section 11108, the agency shall notify the owner or person entitled to possession of the property of the location of the property within 15 days of making the identification. If the location of the property was reported by a licensed pawnbroker or secondhand dealer pursuant to Section 21630 of the Business and Professions Code, notice shall be given to the party who reported the property lost or stolen pursuant to Section 21647 of the Business and Professions Code.

(b) If the property is in the custody of the law enforcement agency and it is determined that the property is no longer required for use as evidence in a criminal case, the property shall be made available to the person entitled to possession pursuant to Section 1417.5.

(c) Subdivision (a) shall not apply to the return to an owner of a lost or stolen vehicle, as defined in Section 670 of the Vehicle Code.

Penal Code § 11108.9.

Each local law enforcement agency shall develop, in conjunction with and subject to the approval of the Department of Justice, a succinct Serial Number Restoration Plan setting forth the goals for reduction in the number of recovered firearms that cannot be traced due to obliterated serial numbers, and the methods that the local agency will follow in order to achieve these goals, including, but not limited to, establishing local programs for restoring serial numbers and accessing resources of the Department of Justice or the Bureau of Alcohol, Tobacco, and Firearms for restoring serial numbers. These plans shall be submitted to the Department of Justice by January 1, 2000.

Penal Code § 11108.10.

(a) In addition to the requirements of Sections 11108 and 11108.3, commencing January 1, 2009, every local law enforcement agency may cause to be entered into the United States Department of Justice, National Integrated Ballistic Information Network (NIBIN) information to ensure that representative samples of fired bullets and cartridge cases collected at crime scenes, from test-fires of firearms recovered at crime scenes, and other firearm information needed to investigate crimes, are recorded into the NIBIN in accordance with the protocol set forth in subdivision (b).

(b) The Attorney General, in cooperation with those law enforcement agencies that choose to do so, shall develop a protocol for the implementation of this section. The protocol shall be completed on or before July 1, 2008.

(c) The Attorney General shall have the authority to issue guidelines to further the purposes of this section.

Penal Code § 11160.

(a) Any health practitioner employed in a health facility, clinic, physician's office, local or state public health department, or a clinic or other type of facility operated by a local or state public health department who, in his or her professional capacity or within the scope of his or her employment, provides medical services for a physical condition to a patient whom he or she knows or reasonably suspects is a person described as follows, shall immediately make a report in accordance with subdivision (b):

(1) Any person suffering from any wound or other physical injury inflicted by his or her own act or inflicted by another where the injury is by means of a firearm.

(2) Any person suffering from any wound or other physical injury inflicted upon the person where the injury is the result of assaultive or abusive conduct.

(b) Any health practitioner employed in a health facility, clinic, physician's office, local or state public health department, or a clinic or other type of facility operated by a local or state public health department shall make a report regarding persons described in subdivision (a) to a local law enforcement agency as follows:

(1) A report by telephone shall be made immediately or as soon as practically possible.

(2) A written report shall be prepared on the standard form developed in compliance with paragraph (4) of this subdivision, and Section 11160.2, and adopted by the agency or agencies designated by the Director of Finance pursuant to Section 13820, or on a form developed and adopted by another state agency that otherwise fulfills the requirements of the standard form. The completed form shall be sent to a local law enforcement agency within two working days of receiving the information regarding the person.

(3) A local law enforcement agency shall be notified and a written report shall be prepared and sent pursuant to paragraphs (1) and (2) even if the person who suffered the wound, other injury, or assaultive or abusive conduct has expired, regardless of whether or not the wound, other injury, or assaultive or abusive conduct was a factor contributing to the death, and even if the evidence of the conduct of the perpetrator of the wound, other injury, or assaultive or abusive conduct was discovered during an autopsy.

(4) The report shall include, but shall not be limited to, the following:

(A) The name of the injured person, if known.

(B) The injured person's whereabouts.

(C) The character and extent of the person's injuries.

(D) The identity of any person the injured person alleges inflicted the wound, other injury, or assaultive or abusive conduct upon the injured person.

(c) For the purposes of this section, "injury" shall not include any psychological or physical condition brought about solely through the voluntary administration of a narcotic or restricted dangerous drug.

(d) For the purposes of this section, "assaultive or abusive conduct" shall include any of the following offenses:

(1) Murder, in violation of Section 187.

(2) Manslaughter, in violation of Section 192 or 192.5.

(3) Mayhem, in violation of Section 203.

(4) Aggravated mayhem, in violation of Section 205.

(5) Torture, in violation of Section 206.

(6) Assault with intent to commit mayhem, rape, sodomy, or oral copulation, in violation of Section 220.

(7) Administering controlled substances or anesthetic to aid in commission of a felony, in violation of Section 222.

(8) Battery, in violation of Section 242.

(9) Sexual battery, in violation of Section 243.4.

(10) Incest, in violation of Section 285.

(11) Throwing any vitriol, corrosive acid, or caustic chemical with intent to injure or disfigure, in violation of Section 244.

(12) Assault with a stun gun or taser, in violation of Section 244.5.

(13) Assault with a deadly weapon, firearm, assault weapon, or machinegun, or by means likely to produce great bodily injury, in violation of Section 245.

(14) Rape, in violation of Section 261.

(15) Spousal rape, in violation of Section 262.

(16) Procuring any female to have sex with another man, in violation of Section 266, 266a, 266b, or 266c.

(17) Child abuse or endangerment, in violation of Section 273a or 273d.

(18) Abuse of spouse or cohabitant, in violation of Section 273.5.

(19) Sodomy, in violation of Section 286.

(20) Lewd and lascivious acts with a child, in violation of Section 288.

(21) Oral copulation, in violation of Section 288a.

(22) Sexual penetration, in violation of Section 289.

(23) Elder abuse, in violation of Section 368.

(24) An attempt to commit any crime specified in paragraphs (1) to (23), inclusive.

(e) When two or more persons who are required to report are present and jointly have knowledge of a known or suspected instance of violence that is required to be reported pursuant to this section, and when there is an agreement among these persons to report as a team, the team may select by mutual agreement a member of the team to make a report by telephone and a single written report, as required by subdivision (b). The written report shall be signed by the selected member of the reporting team. Any member who has knowledge that the member designated to report has failed to do so shall thereafter make the report.

(f) The reporting duties under this section are individual, except as provided in subdivision (e).

(g) No supervisor or administrator shall impede or inhibit the reporting duties required under this section and no person making a report pursuant to this section shall be subject to any sanction for making the report. However, internal procedures to facilitate reporting and apprise supervisors and administrators of reports may be established, except that these procedures shall not be inconsistent with this article. The internal procedures shall not require any employee required to make a report under this article to disclose his or her identity to the employer.

(h) For the purposes of this section, it is the Legislature's intent to avoid duplication of information.

Penal Code § 11161.

Notwithstanding Section 11160, the following shall apply to every physician or surgeon who has under his or her charge or care any person described in subdivision (a) of Section 11160:

(a) The physician or surgeon shall make a report in accordance with subdivision (b) of Section 11160 to a local law enforcement agency.

(b) It is recommended that any medical records of a person about whom the physician or surgeon is required to report pursuant to subdivision (a) include the following:

(1) Any comments by the injured person regarding past domestic violence, as defined in Section 13700, or regarding the name of any person suspected of inflicting the wound, other physical injury, or assaultive or abusive conduct upon the person.

(2) A map of the injured person's body showing and identifying injuries and bruises at the time of the health care.

(3) A copy of the law enforcement reporting form.

(c) It is recommended that the physician or surgeon refer the person to local domestic violence services if the person is suffering or suspected of suffering from domestic violence, as defined in Section 13700.

Penal Code § 11161.9.

(a) A health practitioner who makes a report in accordance with this article shall not incur civil or criminal liability as a result of any report required or authorized by this article.

(b)(1) No person required or authorized to report pursuant to this article, or designated by a person required or authorized to report pursuant to this article, who takes photographs of a person suspected of being a person described in this article about whom a report is required or authorized shall incur any civil or criminal liability for taking the photographs, causing the photographs to be taken, or disseminating the photographs to local law enforcement with the reports required by this article in accordance with this article. However, this subdivision shall not be deemed to grant immunity from civil or criminal liability with respect to any other use of the photographs.

(2) A court may award attorney's fees to a commercial film and photographic print processor when a suit is brought against the processor because of a disclosure mandated by this article and the court finds that the suit is frivolous.

(c) A health practitioner who, pursuant to a request from an adult protective services agency or a local law enforcement agency, provides the requesting agency with access to the victim of a known or suspected instance of abuse shall not incur civil or criminal liability as a result of providing that access.

(d) No employee shall be discharged, suspended, disciplined, or harassed for making a report pursuant to this section.

(e) This section does not apply to mandated reporting of child abuse, as provided for in Article 2.5 (commencing with Section 11164).

Penal Code § 11162.

A violation of this article is a misdemeanor, punishable by imprisonment in a county jail not exceeding six months, or by a fine not exceeding one thousand dollars ($1,000), or by both that fine and imprisonment.

Penal Code § 11460.

(a) Any two or more persons who assemble as a paramilitary organization for the purpose of practicing with weapons shall be punished by imprisonment in a county jail for not more than one year or by a fine of not more than one thousand dollars ($1,000), or by both that fine and imprisonment. As used in this subdivision, "paramilitary organization" means an organization which is not an agency of the United States government or of the State of California, or which is not a private school meeting the requirements set forth in Section 48222 of the Education Code, but which engages in instruction or training in guerrilla warfare or sabotage, or which, as an organization, engages in rioting or the violent disruption of, or the violent interference with, school activities.

(b)(1) Any person who teaches or demonstrates to any other person the use, application, or making of any firearm, explosive, or destructive device, or technique capable of causing injury or death to persons, knowing or having reason to know or intending that these objects or techniques will be unlawfully employed for use in, or in the furtherance of a civil disorder, or any person who assembles with one or more other persons for the purpose of training with, practicing with, or being instructed in the use of any firearm, explosive, or destructive device, or technique capable of causing injury or death to persons, with the intent to cause or further a civil disorder, shall be punished by imprisonment in the county jail for not more than one year or by a fine of not more than one thousand dollars ($1,000), or by both that fine and imprisonment. Nothing in this subdivision shall make unlawful any act of any peace officer or a member of the military forces of this state or of the United States, performed in the lawful course of his or her official duties.

(2) As used in this section:

(A) "Civil disorder" means any disturbance involving acts of violence which cause an immediate danger of or results in damage or injury to the property or person of any other individual.

(B) "Destructive device" has the same meaning as in Section 12301.

(C) "Explosive" has the same meaning as in Section 12000 of the Health and Safety Code.

(D) "Firearm" means any device designed to be used as a weapon, or which may readily be converted to a weapon, from which is expelled a projectile by the force of any explosion or other form of combustion, or the frame or receiver of this weapon.

(E) "Peace officer" means any peace officer or other officer having the powers of arrest of a peace officer, specified in Chapter 4.5 (commencing with Section 830) of Title 3 of Part 2.

Penal Code § 12000.

This chapter shall be known and may be cited as "The Dangerous Weapons Control Law."

Penal Code § 12001.

(a)(1) As used in this title, the terms "pistol," "revolver," and "firearm capable of being concealed upon the person" shall apply to and include any device designed to be used as a weapon, from which is expelled a projectile by the force of any explosion, or other form of combustion, and that has a barrel less than 16 inches in length. These terms also include any device that has a barrel 16 inches or more in length which is designed to be interchanged with a barrel less than 16 inches in length.

(2) As used in this title, the term "handgun" means any "pistol," "revolver," or "firearm capable of being concealed upon the person."

(b) As used in this title, "firearm" means any device, designed to be used as a weapon, from which is expelled through a barrel, a projectile by the force of any explosion or other form of combustion.

(c) As used in Sections 12021, 12021.1, 12070, 12071, 12072, 12073, 12078, 12101, and 12801 of this code, and Sections 8100, 8101, and 8103 of the Welfare and Institutions Code, the term "firearm" includes the frame or receiver of the weapon.

(d) For the purposes of Sections 12025 and 12031, the term "firearm" also shall include any rocket, rocket propelled projectile launcher, or similar device containing any explosive or incendiary material whether or not the device is designed for emergency or distress signaling purposes.

(e) For purposes of Sections 12070, 12071, and paragraph (8) of subdivision (a), and subdivisions (b), (c), (d), and (f) of Section 12072, the term "firearm" does not include an unloaded firearm that is defined as an "antique firearm" in Section 921(a)(16) of Title 18 of the United States Code.

(f) Nothing shall prevent a device defined as a "handgun," "pistol," "revolver," or "firearm capable of being concealed upon the person" from also being found to be a short-barreled shotgun or a short-barreled rifle, as defined in Section 12020.

(g) For purposes of Sections 12551 and 12552, the term "BB device" means any instrument that expels a projectile, such as a BB or a pellet, not exceeding 6mm caliber, through the force of air pressure, gas pressure, or spring action, or any spot marker gun.

(h) As used in this title, "wholesaler" means any person who is licensed as a dealer pursuant to Chapter 44 (commencing with Section 921) of Title 18 of the United States Code and the regulations issued pursuant thereto who sells, transfers, or assigns firearms, or parts of firearms, to persons who are licensed as manufacturers, importers, or gunsmiths pursuant to Chapter 44 (commencing with Section 921) of Title 18 of the United States Code, or persons licensed pursuant to Section 12071, and includes persons who receive finished parts of firearms and assemble them into completed or partially completed firearms in furtherance of that purpose. "Wholesaler" shall not include a manufacturer, importer, or gunsmith who is licensed to engage in those activities pursuant to Chapter 44 (commencing with Section 921) of Title 18 of the United States Code or a person licensed pursuant to Section 12071 and the regulations issued pursuant thereto. A wholesaler also does not include those persons dealing exclusively in grips, stocks, and other parts of firearms that are not frames or receivers thereof.

(i) As used in Section 12071 or 12072, "application to purchase" means any of the following:

(1) The initial completion of the register by the purchaser, transferee, or person being loaned the firearm as required by subdivision (b) of Section 12076.

(2) The initial completion and transmission to the department of the record of electronic or telephonic transfer by the dealer on the purchaser, transferee, or person being loaned the firearm as required by subdivision (c) of Section 12076.

(j) For purposes of Section 12023, a firearm shall be deemed to be "loaded" whenever both the firearm and the unexpended ammunition capable of being discharged from the firearm are in the immediate possession of the same person.

(k) For purposes of Sections 12021, 12021.1, 12025, 12070, 12072, 12073, 12078, 12101, and 12801 of this code, and

Sections 8100, 8101, and 8103 of the Welfare and Institutions Code, notwithstanding the fact that the term "any firearm" may be used in those sections, each firearm or the frame or receiver of the same shall constitute a distinct and separate offense under those sections.

(l) For purposes of Section 12020, a violation of that section as to each firearm, weapon, or device enumerated therein shall constitute a distinct and separate offense.

(m) Each application that requires any firearms eligibility determination involving the issuance of any license, permit, or certificate pursuant to this title shall include two copies of the applicant's fingerprints on forms prescribed by the Department of Justice. One copy of the fingerprints may be submitted to the United States Federal Bureau of Investigation.

(n) As used in this chapter, a "personal handgun importer" means an individual who meets all of the following criteria:

(1) He or she is not a person licensed pursuant to Section 12071.

(2) He or she is not a licensed manufacturer of firearms pursuant to Chapter 44 (commencing with Section 921) of Title 18 of the United States Code.

(3) He or she is not a licensed importer of firearms pursuant to Chapter 44 (commencing with Section 921) of Title 18 of the United States Code and the regulations issued pursuant thereto.

(4) He or she is the owner of a handgun.

(5) He or she acquired that handgun outside of California.

(6) He or she moves into this state on or after January 1, 1998, as a resident of this state.

(7) He or she intends to possess that handgun within this state on or after January 1, 1998.

(8) The handgun was not delivered to him or her by a person licensed pursuant to Section 12071 who delivered that firearm following the procedures set forth in Section 12071 and subdivision (c) of Section 12072.

(9) He or she, while a resident of this state, had not previously reported his or her ownership of that handgun to the Department of Justice in a manner prescribed by the department that included information concerning him or her and a description of the firearm.

(10) The handgun is not a firearm that is prohibited by subdivision (a) of Section 12020.

(11) The handgun is not an assault weapon, as defined in Section 12276 or 12276.1.

(12) The handgun is not a machinegun, as defined in Section 12200.

(13) The person is 18 years of age or older.

(o) For purposes of paragraph (6) of subdivision (n):

(1) Except as provided in paragraph (2), residency shall be determined in the same manner as is the case for establishing residency pursuant to Section 12505 of the Vehicle Code.

(2) In the case of members of the Armed Forces of the United States, residency shall be deemed to be established when he or she was discharged from active service in this state.

(p) As used in this code, "basic firearms safety certificate" means a certificate issued by the Department of Justice pursuant to Article 8 (commencing with Section 12800) of Chapter 6 of Title 2 of Part 4, prior to January 1, 2003.

(q) As used in this code, "handgun safety certificate" means a certificate issued by the Department of Justice pursuant to Article 8 (commencing with Section 12800) of Chapter 6 of Title 2 of Part 4, as that article is operative on or after January 1, 2003.

(r) As used in this title, "gunsmith" means any person who is licensed as a dealer pursuant to Chapter 44 (commencing with Section 921) of Title 18 of the United States Code and the regulations issued pursuant thereto, who is engaged primarily in the business of repairing firearms, or making or fitting special barrels, stocks, or trigger mechanisms to firearms, or the agent or employee of that person.

(s) As used in this title, "consultant-evaluator" means a consultant or evaluator who, in the course of his or her profession is loaned firearms from a person licensed pursuant to Chapter 44 (commencing with Section 921) of Title 18 of the United States Code and the regulations issued pursuant thereto, for his or her research or evaluation, and has a current certificate of eligibility issued to him or her pursuant to Section 12071.

Penal Code § 12001.1.

(a) Any person in this state who commercially manufactures or causes to be commercially manufactured, or who knowingly imports into the state for commercial sale, or who knowingly exports out of this state for commercial, dealer, wholesaler, or distributor sale, or who keeps for commercial sale, or offers or exposes for commercial, dealer, wholesaler, or distributor sale, any undetectable knife is guilty of a misdemeanor. As used in this section, an "undetectable knife" means any knife or other instrument with or without a handguard that is capable of ready use as a stabbing weapon that may inflict great bodily injury or death that is commercially manufactured to be used as a weapon and is not detectable by a metal detector or magnetometer, either handheld or otherwise, that is set at standard calibration.

(b) Notwithstanding any other provision of law, commencing January 1, 2000, all knives or other instrument with or without a handguard that is capable of ready use as a stabbing weapon that may inflict great bodily injury or death that are commercially manufactured in this state that utilize materials that are not detectable by a metal detector or magnetometer, shall be manufactured to include materials that will ensure they are detectable by a metal detector or magnetometer, either handheld or otherwise, that is set at standard calibration.

(c) This section shall not apply to the manufacture or importation of undetectable knives for sale to a law enforcement or military entity with a valid agency, department, or unit purchase order, nor shall this section apply to the subsequent sale of these knives to a law enforcement or military entity.

(d) This section shall not apply to the manufacture or importation of undetectable knives for sale to federal, state, and local historical societies, museums, and institutional collections which are open to the public, provided that the undetectable knives are properly housed and secured from unauthorized handling, nor shall this section apply to the subsequent sale of the knives to these societies, museums, and collections.

Penal Code § 12001.5.

Except as expressly provided in Section 12020, and solely in accordance with Section 12020, no person may manufacture, import into this state, keep for sale, offer for sale, give, lend, or possess any short-barreled shotgun or short-barreled rifle, as defined in Section 12020, and nothing else in this chapter shall be construed as authorizing the manufacture, importation into the state, keeping for sale, offering for sale, or giving, lending, or possession of any short-barreled shotgun or short-barreled rifle, as defined in Section 12020.

Penal Code § 12001.6.

As used in this chapter, an offense which involves the violent use of a firearm includes any of the following:

(a) A violation of paragraph (2) or (3) of subdivision (a) of Section 245 or a violation of subdivision (d) of Section 245.

(b) A violation of Section 246.

(c) A violation of paragraph (2) of subdivision (a) of Section 417.

(d) A violation of subdivision (c) of Section 417.

Penal Code § 12002.

(a) Nothing in this chapter prohibits police officers, special police officers, peace officers, or law enforcement officers from carrying any wooden club, baton, or any equipment authorized for the enforcement of law or ordinance in any city or county.

(b) Nothing in this chapter prohibits a uniformed security guard, regularly employed and compensated by a person engaged in any lawful business, while actually employed and engaged in protecting and preserving property or life within the scope of his or her employment, from carrying any wooden club or baton if the uniformed security guard has satisfactorily completed a course of instruction certified by the Department of Consumer Affairs in the carrying and use of the club or baton. The training institution certified by the Department of Consumer Affairs to present this course, whether public or private, is authorized to charge a fee covering the cost of the training.

(c) The Department of Consumer Affairs, in cooperation with the Commission on Peace Officer Standards and Training, shall develop standards for a course in the carrying and use of the club or baton.

(d) Any uniformed security guard who successfully completes a course of instruction under this section is entitled to receive a permit to carry and use a club or baton within the scope of his or her employment, issued by the Department of Consumer Affairs. The department may authorize certified training institutions to issue permits to carry and use a club or baton. A fee in the amount provided by law shall be charged by the Department of Consumer Affairs to offset the costs incurred by the department in course certification, quality control activities associated with the course, and issuance of the permit.

(e) Any person who has received a permit or certificate which indicates satisfactory completion of a club or baton training course approved by the Commission on Peace Officer Standards and Training prior to January 1, 1983, shall not be required to obtain a baton or club permit or complete a course certified by the Department of Consumer Affairs.

(f) Any person employed as a county sheriff's or police security officer, as defined in Section 831.4, shall not be required to obtain a club or baton permit or to complete a course certified by the Department of Consumer Affairs in the carrying and use of a club or baton, provided that the person completes a course approved by the Commission on Peace Officer Standards and Training in the carrying and use of the club or baton, within 90 days of employment.

(g) Nothing in this chapter prohibits an animal control officer, as described in Section 830.9, or an illegal dumping enforcement officer, as described in Section 830.7, from carrying any wooden club or baton if the animal control officer or illegal dumping enforcement officer has satisfactorily completed a course of instruction certified by the Department of Consumer Affairs in the carrying and use of the club or baton. The training institution certified by the Department of Consumer Affairs to present this course, whether public or private, is authorized to charge a fee covering the cost of the training.

Penal Code § 12003.

If any section, subsection, sentence, clause or phrase of this chapter is for any reason held to be unconstitutional such decision shall not affect the validity of the remaining portions of this chapter. The Legislature hereby declares that it would have passed this act and each section, subsection, sentence, clause and phrase thereof, irrespective of the fact that any one or more other sections, subsections, sentences, clauses or phrases be declared unconstitutional.

Penal Code § 12010.

(a) The Attorney General shall establish and maintain an online database to be known as the Prohibited Armed Persons File. The purpose of the file is to cross-reference persons who have ownership or possession of a firearm on or after January 1, 1991, as indicated by a record in the Consolidated Firearms Information System, and who, subsequent to the date of that ownership or possession of a firearm, fall within a class of persons who are prohibited from owning or possessing a firearm.

(b) The information contained in the Prohibited Armed Persons File shall only be available to those entities specified in, and pursuant to, subdivision (b) or (c) of Section 11105, through the California Law Enforcement Telecommunications System, for the purpose of determining if persons are armed and prohibited from possessing firearms.

Penal Code § 12011.

The Prohibited Armed Persons File database shall function as follows:

(a) Upon entry into the Automated Criminal History System of a disposition for a conviction of any felony, a conviction for any firearms-prohibiting charge specified in Section 12021, a conviction for an offense described in Section 12021.1, a firearms prohibition pursuant to Section 8100 or 8103 of the Welfare and Institutions Code, or any firearms possession prohibition identified by the federal National Instant Criminal Background Check System, the Department of Justice shall determine if the subject has an entry in the Consolidated Firearms Information System indicating possession or ownership of a firearm on or after January 1, 1991, or an assault weapon registration, or a .50 BMG rifle registration.

(b) Upon an entry into any department automated information system that is used for the identification of persons who are prohibited by state or federal law from acquiring, owning, or possessing firearms, the department shall determine if the subject has an entry in the Consolidated Firearms Information System indicating ownership or possession of a firearm on or after January 1, 1991, or an assault weapon registration, or a .50 BMG rifle registration.

(c) If the department determines that, pursuant to subdivision (a) or (b), the subject has an entry in the Consolidated Firearms Information System indicating possession or ownership of a firearm on or after January 1, 1991, or an assault weapon registration, or a .50 BMG rifle registration, the following information shall be entered into the Prohibited Armed Persons File:

(1) The subject's name.

(2) The subject's date of birth.

(3) The subject's physical description.

(4) Any other identifying information regarding the subject that is deemed necessary by the Attorney General.

(5) The basis of the firearms possession prohibition.

(6) A description of all firearms owned or possessed by the subject, as reflected by the Consolidated Firearms Information System.

Penal Code § 12012.

The Attorney General shall provide investigative assistance to local law enforcement agencies to better ensure the investigation of individuals who are armed and prohibited from possessing a firearm.

Penal Code § 12020.

(a) Any person in this state who does any of the following is punishable by imprisonment in a county jail not exceeding one year or in the state prison:

(1) Manufactures or causes to be manufactured, imports into the state, keeps for sale, or offers or exposes for sale, or who gives, lends, or possesses any cane gun or wallet gun, any undetectable firearm, any firearm which is not immediately recognizable as a firearm, any camouflaging firearm container, any ammunition which contains or consists of any flechette dart, any bullet containing or carrying an explosive agent, any ballistic knife, any multiburst trigger activator, any nunchaku, any short-barreled shotgun, any short-barreled rifle, any metal knuckles, any belt buckle knife, any leaded cane, any zip gun, any shuriken, any unconventional pistol, any lipstick case knife, any cane sword, any shobi-zue, any air gauge knife, any writing pen knife, any metal military practice handgrenade or metal replica handgrenade, or any instrument or weapon of the kind commonly known as a blackjack, slungshot, billy, sandclub, sap, or sandbag.

(2) Commencing January 1, 2000, manufactures or causes to be manufactured, imports into the state, keeps for sale, or offers or exposes for sale, or who gives, or lends, any large-capacity magazine.

(3) Carries concealed upon his or her person any explosive substance, other than fixed ammunition.

(4) Carries concealed upon his or her person any dirk or dagger. However, a first offense involving any metal military practice handgrenade or metal replica handgrenade shall be punishable only as an infraction unless the offender is an active participant in a criminal street gang as defined in the Street Terrorism and Enforcement and Prevention Act (Chapter 11 (commencing with Section 186.20) of Title 7 of Part 1). A bullet containing or carrying an explosive agent is not a destructive device as that term is used in Section 12301.

(b) Subdivision (a) does not apply to any of the following:

(1) The sale to, purchase by, or possession of short-barreled shotguns or short-barreled rifles by police departments, sheriffs' offices, marshals' offices, the California Highway Patrol, the Department of Justice, the Department of Corrections and Rehabilitation, or the military or naval forces of this state or of the United States for use in the discharge of their official duties or the possession of short-barreled shotguns and short-barreled rifles by peace officer members of a police department, sheriff's office, marshal's office, the California Highway Patrol, the Department of Justice, or the Department of Corrections and Rehabilitation, when on duty and the use is authorized by the agency and is within the course and scope of their duties and the peace officer has completed a training course in the use of these weapons certified by the Commission on Peace Officer Standards and Training.

(2) The manufacture, possession, transportation or sale of short-barreled shotguns or short-barreled rifles when authorized by the Department of Justice pursuant to Article 6 (commencing with Section 12095) and not in violation of federal law.

(3) The possession of a nunchaku on the premises of a school which holds a regulatory or business license and teaches the arts of self-defense.

(4) The manufacture of a nunchaku for sale to, or the sale of a nunchaku to, a school which holds a regulatory or business license and teaches the arts of self-defense.

(5) Any antique firearm. For purposes of this section, "antique firearm" means any firearm not designed or redesigned for using rimfire or conventional center fire ignition with fixed ammunition and manufactured in or before 1898 (including any matchlock, flintlock, percussion cap, or similar type of ignition system or replica thereof, whether actually manufactured before or after the year 1898) and also any firearm using fixed ammunition manufactured in or before 1898, for which ammunition is no longer manufactured in the United States and is not readily available in the ordinary channels of commercial trade.

(6) Tracer ammunition manufactured for use in shotguns.

(7) Any firearm or ammunition that is a curio or relic as defined in Section 478.11 of Title 27 of the Code of Federal Regulations and which is in the possession of a person permitted to possess the items pursuant to Chapter 44 (commencing with Section 921) of Title 18 of the United States Code and the regulations issued pursuant thereto. Any person prohibited by Section 12021, 12021.1, or 12101 of this code or Section 8100 or 8103 of the Welfare and Institutions Code from possessing firearms or ammunition who obtains title to these items by bequest or intestate succession may retain title for not more than one year, but actual possession of these items at any time is punishable pursuant to Section 12021, 12021.1, or 12101 of this code or Section 8100 or 8103 of the Welfare and Institutions Code. Within the year, the person shall transfer title to the firearms or ammunition by sale, gift, or other disposition. Any person who violates this paragraph is in violation of subdivision (a).

(8) Any other weapon as defined in subsection (e) of Section 5845 of Title 26 of the United States Code and which is in the possession of a person permitted to possess the weapons pursuant to the federal Gun Control Act of 1968 (Public Law 90-618), as amended, and the regulations issued pursuant thereto. Any person prohibited by Section 12021, 12021.1, or 12101 of this code or Section 8100 or 8103 of the Welfare and Institutions Code from possessing these weapons who obtains title to these weapons by bequest or intestate succession may retain title for not more than one year, but actual possession of these weapons at any time is punishable pursuant

to Section 12021, 12021.1, or 12101 of this code or Section 8100 or 8103 of the Welfare and Institutions Code. Within the year, the person shall transfer title to the weapons by sale, gift, or other disposition. Any person who violates this paragraph is in violation of subdivision (a). The exemption provided in this subdivision does not apply to pen guns.

(9) Instruments or devices that are possessed by federal, state, and local historical societies, museums, and institutional collections which are open to the public, provided that these instruments or devices are properly housed, secured from unauthorized handling, and, if the instrument or device is a firearm, unloaded.

(10) Instruments or devices, other than short-barreled shotguns or short-barreled rifles, that are possessed or utilized during the course of a motion picture, television, or video production or entertainment event by an authorized participant therein in the course of making that production or event or by an authorized employee or agent of the entity producing that production or event.

(11) Instruments or devices, other than short-barreled shotguns or short-barreled rifles, that are sold by, manufactured by, exposed or kept for sale by, possessed by, imported by, or lent by persons who are in the business of selling instruments or devices listed in subdivision (a) solely to the entities referred to in paragraphs (9) and (10) when engaging in transactions with those entities.

(12) The sale to, possession of, or purchase of any weapon, device, or ammunition, other than a short-barreled rifle or short-barreled shotgun, by any federal, state, county, city and county, or city agency that is charged with the enforcement of any law for use in the discharge of their official duties, or the possession of any weapon, device, or ammunition, other than a short-barreled rifle or short-barreled shotgun, by peace officers thereof when on duty and the use is authorized by the agency and is within the course and scope of their duties.

(13) Weapons, devices, and ammunition, other than a short-barreled rifle or short-barreled shotgun, that are sold by, manufactured by, exposed or kept for sale by, possessed by, imported by, or lent by, persons who are in the business of selling weapons, devices, and ammunition listed in subdivision (a) solely to the entities referred to in paragraph (12) when engaging in transactions with those entities.

(14) The manufacture for, sale to, exposing or keeping for sale to, importation of, or lending of wooden clubs or batons to special police officers or uniformed security guards authorized to carry any wooden club or baton pursuant to Section 12002 by entities that are in the business of selling wooden batons or clubs to special police officers and uniformed security guards when engaging in transactions with those persons.

(15) Any plastic toy handgrenade, or any metal military practice handgrenade or metal replica handgrenade that is a relic, curio, memorabilia, or display item, that is filled with a permanent inert substance or that is otherwise permanently altered in a manner that prevents ready modification for use as a grenade.

(16) Any instrument, ammunition, weapon, or device listed in subdivision (a) that is not a firearm that is found and possessed by a person who meets all of the following:

(A) The person is not prohibited from possessing firearms or ammunition pursuant to Section 12021 or 12021.1 or paragraph (1) of subdivision (b) of Section 12316 of this code or Section 8100 or 8103 of the Welfare and Institutions Code.

(B) The person possessed the instrument, ammunition, weapon, or device no longer than was necessary to deliver or transport the same to a law enforcement agency for that agency's disposition according to law.

(C) If the person is transporting the listed item, he or she is transporting the listed item to a law enforcement agency for disposition according to law.

(17) Any firearm, other than a short-barreled rifle or short-barreled shotgun, that is found and possessed by a person who meets all of the following:

(A) The person is not prohibited from possessing firearms or ammunition pursuant to Section 12021 or 12021.1 or paragraph (1) of subdivision (b) of Section 12316 of this code or Section 8100 or 8103 of the Welfare and Institutions Code.

(B) The person possessed the firearm no longer than was necessary to deliver or transport the same to a law enforcement agency for that agency's disposition according to law.

(C) If the person is transporting the firearm, he or she is transporting the firearm to a law enforcement agency for disposition according to law.

(D) Prior to transporting the firearm to a law enforcement agency, he or she has given prior notice to that law enforcement agency that he or she is transporting the firearm to that law enforcement agency for disposition according to law.

(E) The firearm is transported in a locked container as defined in subdivision (d) of Section 12026.2.

(18) The possession of any weapon, device, or ammunition, by a forensic laboratory or any authorized agent or employee thereof in the course and scope of his or her authorized activities.

(19) The sale of, giving of, lending of, importation into this state of, or purchase of, any large-capacity magazine to or by any federal, state, county, city and county, or city agency that is charged with the enforcement of any law, for use by agency employees in the discharge of their official duties whether on or off duty, and where the use is authorized by the agency and is within the course and scope of their duties.

(20) The sale to, lending to, transfer to, purchase by, receipt of, or importation into this state of, a large-capacity magazine by a sworn peace officer as defined in Chapter 4.5 (commencing with Section 830) of Title 3 of Part 2 who is authorized to carry a firearm in the course and scope of his or her duties.

(21) The sale or purchase of any large-capacity magazine to or by a person licensed pursuant to Section 12071.

(22) The loan of a lawfully possessed large-capacity magazine between two individuals if all of the following conditions are met:

(A) The person being loaned the large-capacity magazine is not prohibited by Section 12021, 12021.1, or 12101 of this code or Section 8100 or 8103 of the Welfare and Institutions Code from possessing firearms or ammunition.

(B) The loan of the large-capacity magazine occurs at a place or location where the possession of the large-capacity magazine is not otherwise prohibited and the person who lends the large-capacity magazine remains in the accessible vicinity of the person to whom the large-capacity magazine is loaned.

(23) The importation of a large-capacity magazine by a person who lawfully possessed the large-capacity magazine in the state prior to January 1, 2000, lawfully took it out of the state, and is returning to the state with the large-capacity magazine previously lawfully

possessed in the state.

(24) The lending or giving of any large-capacity magazine to a person licensed pursuant to Section 12071, or to a gunsmith, for the purposes of maintenance, repair, or modification of that large-capacity magazine.

(25) The return to its owner of any large-capacity magazine by a person specified in paragraph (24).

(26) The importation into this state of, or sale of, any large-capacity magazine by a person who has been issued a permit to engage in those activities pursuant to Section 12079, when those activities are in accordance with the terms and conditions of that permit.

(27) The sale of, giving of, lending of, importation into this state of, or purchase of, any large-capacity magazine, to or by entities that operate armored vehicle businesses pursuant to the laws of this state.

(28) The lending of large-capacity magazines by the entities specified in paragraph (27) to their authorized employees, while in the course and scope of their employment for purposes that pertain to the entity's armored vehicle business.

(29) The return of those large-capacity magazines to those entities specified in paragraph (27) by those employees specified in paragraph (28).

(30)(A) The manufacture of a large-capacity magazine for any federal, state, county, city and county, or city agency that is charged with the enforcement of any law, for use by agency employees in the discharge of their official duties whether on or off duty, and where the use is authorized by the agency and is within the course and scope of their duties.

(B) The manufacture of a large-capacity magazine for use by a sworn peace officer as defined in Chapter 4.5 (commencing with Section 830) of Title 3 of Part 2 who is authorized to carry a firearm in the course and scope of his or her duties.

(C) The manufacture of a large-capacity magazine for export or for sale to government agencies or the military pursuant to applicable federal regulations.

(31) The loan of a large-capacity magazine for use solely as a prop for a motion picture, television, or video production.

(32) The purchase of a large-capacity magazine by the holder of a special weapons permit issued pursuant to Section 12095, 12230, 12250, 12286, or 12305, for any of the following purposes:

(A) For use solely as a prop for a motion picture, television, or video production.

(B) For export pursuant to federal regulations.

(C) For resale to law enforcement agencies, government agencies, or the military, pursuant to applicable federal regulations.

(c)(1) As used in this section, a "short-barreled shotgun" means any of the following:

(A) A firearm which is designed or redesigned to fire a fixed shotgun shell and having a barrel or barrels of less than 18 inches in length.

(B) A firearm which has an overall length of less than 26 inches and which is designed or redesigned to fire a fixed shotgun shell.

(C) Any weapon made from a shotgun (whether by alteration, modification, or otherwise) if that weapon, as modified, has an overall length of less than 26 inches or a barrel or barrels of less than 18 inches in length.

(D) Any device which may be readily restored to fire a fixed shotgun shell which, when so restored, is a device defined in subparagraphs (A) to (C), inclusive.

(E) Any part, or combination of parts, designed and intended to convert a device into a device defined in subparagraphs (A) to (C), inclusive, or any combination of parts from which a device defined in subparagraphs (A) to (C), inclusive, can be readily assembled if those parts are in the possession or under the control of the same person.

(2) As used in this section, a "short-barreled rifle" means any of the following:

(A) A rifle having a barrel or barrels of less than 16 inches in length.

(B) A rifle with an overall length of less than 26 inches.

(C) Any weapon made from a rifle (whether by alteration, modification, or otherwise) if that weapon, as modified, has an overall length of less than 26 inches or a barrel or barrels of less than 16 inches in length.

(D) Any device which may be readily restored to fire a fixed cartridge which, when so restored, is a device defined in subparagraphs (A) to (C), inclusive.

(E) Any part, or combination of parts, designed and intended to convert a device into a device defined in subparagraphs (A) to (C), inclusive, or any combination of parts from which a device defined in subparagraphs (A) to (C), inclusive, may be readily assembled if those parts are in the possession or under the control of the same person.

(3) As used in this section, a "nunchaku" means an instrument consisting of two or more sticks, clubs, bars or rods to be used as handles, connected by a rope, cord, wire, or chain, in the design of a weapon used in connection with the practice of a system of self-defense such as karate.

(4) As used in this section, a "wallet gun" means any firearm mounted or enclosed in a case, resembling a wallet, designed to be or capable of being carried in a pocket or purse, if the firearm may be fired while mounted or enclosed in the case.

(5) As used in this section, a "cane gun" means any firearm mounted or enclosed in a stick, staff, rod, crutch, or similar device, designed to be, or capable of being used as, an aid in walking, if the firearm may be fired while mounted or enclosed therein.

(6) As used in this section, a "flechette dart" means a dart, capable of being fired from a firearm, that measures approximately one inch in length, with tail fins that take up approximately five-sixteenths of an inch of the body.

(7) As used in this section, "metal knuckles" means any device or instrument made wholly or partially of metal which is worn for purposes of offense or defense in or on the hand and which either protects the wearer's hand while striking a blow or increases the force of impact from the blow or injury to the individual receiving the blow. The metal contained in the device may help support the hand or fist, provide a shield to protect it, or consist of projections or studs which would contact the individual receiving a blow.

(8) As used in this section, a "ballistic knife" means a device that propels a knifelike blade as a projectile by means of a coil spring, elastic material, or compressed gas. Ballistic knife does not include any device which propels an arrow or a bolt by means of any common bow, compound bow, crossbow, or underwater speargun.

(9) As used in this section, a "camouflaging firearm container" means a container which meets all of the following criteria:

(A) It is designed and intended to enclose a firearm.

(B) It is designed and intended to allow the firing of the enclosed firearm by external controls while the firearm is in the container.

(C) It is not readily recognizable as containing a firearm. "Camouflaging firearm container" does not include any camouflaging covering used while engaged in lawful hunting or while going to or returning from a lawful hunting expedition.

(10) As used in this section, a "zip gun" means any weapon or device which meets all of the following criteria:

(A) It was not imported as a firearm by an importer licensed pursuant to Chapter 44 (commencing with Section 921) of Title 18 of the United States Code and the regulations issued pursuant thereto.

(B) It was not originally designed to be a firearm by a manufacturer licensed pursuant to Chapter 44 (commencing with Section 921) of Title 18 of the United States Code and the regulations issued pursuant thereto.

(C) No tax was paid on the weapon or device nor was an exemption from paying tax on that weapon or device granted under Section 4181 and Subchapters F (commencing with Section 4216) and G (commencing with Section 4221) of Chapter 32 of Title 26 of the United States Code, as amended, and the regulations issued pursuant thereto.

(D) It is made or altered to expel a projectile by the force of an explosion or other form of combustion.

(11) As used in this section, a "shuriken" means any instrument, without handles, consisting of a metal plate having three or more radiating points with one or more sharp edges and designed in the shape of a polygon, trefoil, cross, star, diamond, or other geometric shape for use as a weapon for throwing.

(12) As used in this section, an "unconventional pistol" means a firearm that does not have a rifled bore and has a barrel or barrels of less than 18 inches in length or has an overall length of less than 26 inches.

(13) As used in this section, a "belt buckle knife" is a knife which is made an integral part of a belt buckle and consists of a blade with a length of at least 21/2 inches.

(14) As used in this section, a "lipstick case knife" means a knife enclosed within and made an integral part of a lipstick case.

(15) As used in this section, a "cane sword" means a cane, swagger stick, stick, staff, rod, pole, umbrella, or similar device, having concealed within it a blade that may be used as a sword or stiletto.

(16) As used in this section, a "shobi-zue" means a staff, crutch, stick, rod, or pole concealing a knife or blade within it which may be exposed by a flip of the wrist or by a mechanical action.

(17) As used in this section, a "leaded cane" means a staff, crutch, stick, rod, pole, or similar device, unnaturally weighted with lead.

(18) As used in this section, an "air gauge knife" means a device that appears to be an air gauge but has concealed within it a pointed, metallic shaft that is designed to be a stabbing instrument which is exposed by mechanical action or gravity which locks into place when extended.

(19) As used in this section, a "writing pen knife" means a device that appears to be a writing pen but has concealed within it a pointed, metallic shaft that is designed to be a stabbing instrument which is exposed by mechanical action or gravity which locks into place when extended or the pointed, metallic shaft is exposed by the removal of the cap or cover on the device.

(20) As used in this section, a "rifle" means a weapon designed or redesigned, made or remade, and intended to be fired from the shoulder and designed or redesigned and made or remade to use the energy of the explosive in a fixed cartridge to fire only a single projectile through a rifled bore for each single pull of the trigger.

(21) As used in this section, a "shotgun" means a weapon designed or redesigned, made or remade, and intended to be fired from the shoulder and designed or redesigned and made or remade to use the energy of the explosive in a fixed shotgun shell to fire through a smooth bore either a number of projectiles (ball shot) or a single projectile for each pull of the trigger.

(22) As used in this section, an "undetectable firearm" means any weapon which meets one of the following requirements:

(A) When, after removal of grips, stocks, and magazines, it is not as detectable as the Security Exemplar, by walk-through metal detectors calibrated and operated to detect the Security Exemplar.

(B) When any major component of which, when subjected to inspection by the types of X-ray machines commonly used at airports, does not generate an image that accurately depicts the shape of the component. Barium sulfate or other compounds may be used in the fabrication of the component.

(C) For purposes of this paragraph, the terms "firearm," "major component," and "Security Exemplar" have the same meanings as those terms are defined in Section 922 of Title 18 of the United States Code. All firearm detection equipment newly installed in nonfederal public buildings in this state shall be of a type identified by either the United States Attorney General, the Secretary of Transportation, or the Secretary of the Treasury, as appropriate, as available state-of-the-art equipment capable of detecting an undetectable firearm, as defined, while distinguishing innocuous metal objects likely to be carried on one's person sufficient for reasonable passage of the public.

(23) As used in this section, a "multiburst trigger activator" means one of the following devices:

(A) A device designed or redesigned to be attached to a semiautomatic firearm which allows the firearm to discharge two or more shots in a burst by activating the device.

(B) A manual or power-driven trigger activating device constructed and designed so that when attached to a semiautomatic firearm it increases the rate of fire of that firearm.

(24) As used in this section, a "dirk" or "dagger" means a knife or other instrument with or without a handguard that is capable of ready use as a stabbing weapon that may inflict great bodily injury or death. A nonlocking folding knife, a folding knife that is not prohibited by Section 653k, or a pocketknife is capable of ready use as a stabbing weapon that may inflict great bodily injury or death only if the blade of the knife is exposed and locked into position.

(25) As used in this section, "large-capacity magazine" means any ammunition feeding device with the capacity to accept more than 10 rounds, but shall not be construed to include any of the following:

(A) A feeding device that has been permanently altered so that it cannot accommodate more than 10 rounds.

(B) A .22 caliber tube ammunition feeding device.

(C) A tubular magazine that is contained in a lever-action firearm.

(d) Knives carried in sheaths which are worn openly suspended from the waist of the wearer are not concealed within the meaning of this section.

Penal Code § 12020.1.

Any person in this state who possesses, commercially manufactures or causes to be commercially manufactured, or who knowingly imports into the state for commercial sale, keeps for commercial sale, or offers or exposes for commercial sale, any composite knuckles or hard wooden knuckles is guilty of a misdemeanor. As used in this section, "composite knuckles" means any device or instrument made wholly or partially of composite materials, other than a medically prescribed prosthetic, that is not a metal knuckle as defined in paragraph (7) of subdivision (c) of Section 12020, that is worn for purposes of offense or defense in or on the hand, and that either protects the wearer's hand while striking a blow or increases the force of impact from the blow or injury to the individual receiving the blow. As used in this section, "hard wooden knuckles" means any device or instrument made wholly or partially of wood or paper products that is not a metal knuckle as defined in paragraph (7) of subdivision (c) of Section 12020, that is worn for purposes of offense or defense in or on the hand, and that either protects the wearer's hand while striking a blow, or increases the force of impact from the blow or injury to the individual receiving the blow. The composite materials, wood, or paper products contained in the device may help support the hand or fist, provide a shield to protect it, or consist of projections or studs that would contact the individual receiving a blow.

Penal Code § 12020.3.

Any person who, for commercial purposes, purchases, sells, manufacturers, ships, transports, distributes, or receives a firearm, where the coloration of the entire exterior surface of the firearm is bright orange or bright green, either singly, in combination, or as the predominant color in combination with other colors in any pattern, is liable for a civil fine in an action brought by the city attorney of the city or the district attorney for the county of not more than ten thousand dollars ($10,000).

Penal Code § 12020.5.

It shall be unlawful for any person, as defined in Section 12277, to advertise the sale of any weapon or device whose possession is prohibited by Section 12020, 12220, 12280, 12303, 12320, 12321, 12355, or 12520 in any newspaper, magazine, circular, form letter, or open publication that is published, distributed, or circulated in this state, or on any billboard, card, label, or other advertising medium, or by means of any other advertising device.

Penal Code § 12021.

(a)(1) Any person who has been convicted of a felony under the laws of the United States, the State of California, or any other state, government, or country or of an offense enumerated in subdivision (a), (b), or (d) of Section 12001.6, or who is addicted to the use of any narcotic drug, and who owns, purchases, receives, or has in his or her possession or under his or her custody or control any firearm is guilty of a felony.

(2) Any person who has two or more convictions for violating paragraph (2) of subdivision (a) of Section 417 and who owns, purchases, receives, or has in his or her possession or under his or her custody or control any firearm is guilty of a felony.

(b) Notwithstanding subdivision (a), any person who has been convicted of a felony or of an offense enumerated in Section 12001.6, when that conviction results from certification by the juvenile court for prosecution as an adult in an adult court under Section 707 of the Welfare and Institutions Code, and who owns or has in his or her possession or under his or her custody or control any firearm is guilty of a felony.

(c)(1) Except as provided in subdivision (a) or paragraph (2) of this subdivision, any person who has been convicted of a misdemeanor violation of Section 71, 76, 136.1, 136.5, or 140, subdivision (d) of Section 148, Section 171b, 171c, 171d, 186.28, 240, 241, 242, 243, 243.4, 244.5, 245, 245.5, 246.3, 247, 273.5, 273.6, 417, 417.6, 422, 626.9, 646.9, 12023, or 12024, subdivision (b) or (d) of Section 12034, Section 12040, subdivision (b) of Section 12072, subdivision (a) of former Section 12100, Section 12220, 12320, or 12590, or Section 8100, 8101, or 8103 of the Welfare and Institutions Code, any firearm-related offense pursuant to Sections 871.5 and 1001.5 of the Welfare and Institutions Code, or of the conduct punished in paragraph (3) of subdivision (g) of Section 12072, and who, within 10 years of the conviction, owns, purchases, receives, or has in his or her possession or under his or her custody or control, any firearm is guilty of a public offense, which shall be punishable by imprisonment in a county jail not exceeding one year or in the state prison, by a fine not exceeding one thousand dollars ($1,000), or by both that imprisonment and fine. The court, on forms prescribed by the Department of Justice, shall notify the department of persons subject to this subdivision. However, the prohibition in this paragraph may be reduced, eliminated, or conditioned as provided in paragraph (2) or (3).

(2) Any person employed as a peace officer described in Section 830.1, 830.2, 830.31, 830.32, 830.33, or 830.5 whose employment or livelihood is dependent on the ability to legally possess a firearm, who is subject to the prohibition imposed by this subdivision because of a conviction under Section 273.5, 273.6, or 646.9, may petition the court only once for relief from this prohibition. The petition shall be filed with the court in which the petitioner was sentenced. If possible, the matter shall be heard before the same judge who sentenced the petitioner. Upon filing the petition, the clerk of the court shall set the hearing date and shall notify the petitioner and the prosecuting attorney of the date of the hearing. Upon making each of the following findings, the court may reduce or eliminate the prohibition, impose conditions on reduction or elimination of the prohibition, or otherwise grant relief from the prohibition as the court deems appropriate:

(A) Finds by a preponderance of the evidence that the petitioner is likely to use a firearm in a safe and lawful manner.

(B) Finds that the petitioner is not within a prohibited class as specified in subdivision (a), (b), (d), (e), or (g) or Section 12021.1, and the court is not presented with any credible evidence that the petitioner is a person described in Section 8100 or 8103 of the Welfare and Institutions Code.

(C)(i) Finds that the petitioner does not have a previous conviction under this subdivision no matter when the prior conviction occurred.

(ii) In making its decision, the court shall consider the petitioner's continued employment, the interest of justice, any relevant evidence, and the totality of the circumstances. The court shall require, as a condition of granting relief from the prohibition under this section, that the petitioner agree to participate in counseling as deemed appropriate by the court. Relief from the prohibition shall not relieve any other person or entity from any liability that might otherwise be imposed. It is the intent of the Legislature that courts exercise broad discretion in fashioning appropriate relief under this paragraph in cases in which relief is warranted. However, nothing in this paragraph shall be construed to require courts to grant relief to any particular petitioner. It is the intent of the Legislature to permit persons who were convicted of an offense specified in Section 273.5, 273.6, or 646.9 to seek relief from the prohibition imposed by this subdivision.

(3) Any person who is subject to the prohibition imposed by this subdivision because of a conviction of an offense prior to that offense being added to paragraph (1) may petition the court only once for relief from this prohibition. The petition shall be filed with the court in which the petitioner was sentenced. If possible, the matter shall be heard before the same judge that sentenced the petitioner. Upon filing the petition, the clerk of the court shall set the hearing date and notify the petitioner and the prosecuting attorney of the date of the hearing. Upon making each of the following findings, the court may reduce or eliminate the prohibition, impose conditions on reduction or elimination of the prohibition, or otherwise grant relief from the prohibition as the court deems appropriate:

(A) Finds by a preponderance of the evidence that the petitioner is likely to use a firearm in a safe and lawful manner.

(B) Finds that the petitioner is not within a prohibited class as specified in subdivision (a), (b), (d), (e), or (g) or Section 12021.1, and the court is not presented with any credible evidence that the petitioner is a person described in Section 8100 or 8103 of the Welfare and Institutions Code.

(C)(i) Finds that the petitioner does not have a previous conviction under this subdivision, no matter when the prior conviction occurred.

(ii) In making its decision, the court may consider the interest of justice, any relevant evidence, and the totality of the circumstances. It is the intent of the Legislature that courts exercise broad discretion in fashioning appropriate relief under this paragraph in cases in which relief is warranted. However, nothing in this paragraph shall be construed to require courts to grant relief to any particular petitioner.

(4) Law enforcement officials who enforce the prohibition specified in this subdivision against a person who has been granted relief pursuant to paragraph (2) or (3) shall be immune from any liability for false arrest arising from the enforcement of this subdivision unless the person has in his or her possession a certified copy of the court order that granted the person relief from the prohibition. This immunity from liability shall not relieve any person or entity from any other liability that might otherwise be imposed.

(d)(1) Any person who, as an express condition of probation, is prohibited or restricted from owning, possessing, controlling, receiving, or purchasing a firearm and who owns, purchases, receives, or has in his or her possession or under his or her custody or control, any firearm but who is not subject to subdivision (a) or (c) is guilty of a public offense, which shall be punishable by imprisonment in a county jail not exceeding one year or in the state prison, by a fine not exceeding one thousand dollars ($1,000), or by both that imprisonment and fine. The court, on forms provided by the Department of Justice, shall notify the department of persons subject to this subdivision. The notice shall include a copy of the order of probation and a copy of any minute order or abstract reflecting the order and conditions of probation.

(2) For any person who is subject to subdivision (a), (b), or (c), the court shall, at the time judgment is imposed, provide on a form supplied by the Department of Justice, a notice to the defendant prohibited by this section from owning, purchasing, receiving, possessing or having under his or her custody or control, any firearm. The notice shall inform the defendant of the prohibition regarding firearms and include a form to facilitate the transfer of firearms. Failure to provide the notice shall not be a defense to a violation of this section.

(e) Any person who (1) is alleged to have committed an offense listed in subdivision (b) of Section 707 of the Welfare and Institutions Code, an offense described in subdivision (b) of Section 1203.073, any offense enumerated in paragraph (1) of subdivision (c), or any offense described in subdivision (a) of Section 12025, subdivision (a) of Section 12031, or subdivision (a) of Section 12034, and (2) is subsequently adjudged a ward of the juvenile court within the meaning of Section 602 of the Welfare and Institutions Code because the person committed an offense listed in subdivision (b) of Section 707 of the Welfare and Institutions Code, an offense described in subdivision (b) of Section 1203.073, any offense enumerated in paragraph (1) of subdivision (c), or any offense described in subdivision (a) of Section 12025, subdivision (a) of Section 12031, or subdivision (a) of Section 12034, shall not own, or have in his or her possession or under his or her custody or control, any firearm until the age of 30 years. A violation of this subdivision shall be punishable by imprisonment in a county jail not exceeding one year or in the state prison, by a fine not exceeding one thousand dollars ($1,000), or by both that imprisonment and fine. The juvenile court, on forms prescribed by the Department of Justice, shall notify the department of persons subject to this subdivision. Notwithstanding any other law, the forms required to be submitted to the department pursuant to this subdivision may be used to determine eligibility to acquire a firearm.

(f) Subdivision (a) shall not apply to a person who has been convicted of a felony under the laws of the United States unless either of the following criteria is satisfied:

(1) Conviction of a like offense under California law can only result in imposition of felony punishment.

(2) The defendant was sentenced to a federal correctional facility for more than 30 days, or received a fine of more than one thousand dollars ($1,000), or received both punishments.

(g)(1) Every person who purchases or receives, or attempts to purchase or receive, a firearm knowing that he or she is prohibited from doing so by a temporary restraining order or injunction issued pursuant to Section 527.6 or 527.8 of the Code of Civil Procedure, a protective order as defined in Section 6218 of the Family Code, a protective order issued pursuant to Section 136.2 or 646.91 of this code, or a protective order issued pursuant to Section 15657.03 of the Welfare and Institutions Code, is guilty of a public offense, which shall be punishable by imprisonment in a county jail not exceeding one year or in the state prison, by a fine not exceeding one thousand dollars ($1,000), or by both that imprisonment and fine.

(2) Every person who owns or possesses a firearm knowing that he or she is prohibited from doing so by a temporary restraining order or injunction issued pursuant to Section 527.6 or 527.8 of the Code of Civil Procedure, a protective order as defined in Section 6218 of the Family Code, a protective order issued pursuant to Section 136.2 or 646.91 of this code, or a protective order issued pursuant to Section 15657.03 of the Welfare and Institutions Code, is guilty of a public offense, which shall be punishable by imprisonment in a county jail not exceeding one year, by a fine not exceeding one thousand dollars ($1,000), or by both that imprisonment and fine.

(3) The Judicial Council shall provide notice on all protective orders that the respondent is prohibited from owning, possessing, purchasing, receiving, or attempting to purchase or receive a firearm while the protective order is in effect. The order shall also state that the firearm shall be relinquished to the local law enforcement agency for that jurisdiction or sold to a licensed gun dealer, and

that proof of surrender or sale shall be filed within a specified time of receipt of the order. The order shall state the penalties for a violation of the prohibition. The order shall also state on its face the expiration date for relinquishment.

(4) If probation is granted upon conviction of a violation of this subdivision, the court shall impose probation consistent with Section 1203.097.

(h)(1) A violation of subdivision (a), (b), (c), (d), or (e) is justifiable where all of the following conditions are met:

(A) The person found the firearm or took the firearm from a person who was committing a crime against him or her.

(B) The person possessed the firearm no longer than was necessary to deliver or transport the firearm to a law enforcement agency for that agency's disposition according to law.

(C) If the firearm was transported to a law enforcement agency, it was transported in accordance with paragraph (18) of subdivision (a) of Section 12026.2. (D) If the firearm is being transported to a law enforcement agency, the person transporting the firearm has given prior notice to the law enforcement agency that he or she is transporting the firearm to the law enforcement agency for disposition according to law.

(2) Upon the trial for violating subdivision (a), (b), (c), (d), or (e), the trier of fact shall determine whether the defendant was acting within the provisions of the exemption created by this subdivision.

(3) The defendant has the burden of proving by a preponderance of the evidence that he or she comes within the provisions of the exemption created by this subdivision.

(i) Subject to available funding, the Attorney General, working with the Judicial Council, the California Alliance Against Domestic Violence, prosecutors, and law enforcement, probation, and parole officers, shall develop a protocol for the implementation of the provisions of this section. The protocol shall be designed to facilitate the enforcement of restrictions on firearm ownership, including provisions for giving notice to defendants who are restricted, provisions for informing those defendants of the procedures by which defendants shall dispose of firearms when required to do so, provisions explaining how defendants shall provide proof of the lawful disposition of firearms, and provisions explaining how defendants may obtain possession of seized firearms when legally permitted to do so pursuant to this section or any other provision of law. The protocol shall be completed on or before January 1, 2005.

Penal Code § 12021.1.

(a) Notwithstanding subdivision (a) of Section 12021, any person who has been previously convicted of any of the offenses listed in subdivision (b) and who owns or has in his or her possession or under his or her custody or control any firearm is guilty of a felony. A dismissal of an accusatory pleading pursuant to Section 1203.4a involving an offense set forth in subdivision (b) does not affect the finding of a previous conviction. If probation is granted, or if the imposition or execution of sentence is suspended, it shall be a condition of the probation or suspension that the defendant serve at least six months in a county jail.

(b) As used in this section, a violent offense includes any of the following:

(1) Murder or voluntary manslaughter.

(2) Mayhem.

(3) Rape.

(4) Sodomy by force, violence, duress, menace, or threat of great bodily harm.

(5) Oral copulation by force, violence, duress, menace, or threat of great bodily harm.

(6) Lewd acts on a child under the age of 14 years.

(7) Any felony punishable by death or imprisonment in the state prison for life.

(8) Any other felony in which the defendant inflicts great bodily injury on any person, other than an accomplice, that has been charged and proven, or any felony in which the defendant uses a firearm which use has been charged and proven.

(9) Attempted murder.

(10) Assault with intent to commit rape or robbery.

(11) Assault with a deadly weapon or instrument on a peace officer.

(12) Assault by a life prisoner on a noninmate.

(13) Assault with a deadly weapon by an inmate.

(14) Arson.

(15) Exploding a destructive device or any explosive with intent to injure.

(16) Exploding a destructive device or any explosive causing great bodily injury.

(17) Exploding a destructive device or any explosive with intent to murder.

(18) Robbery.

(19) Kidnapping.

(20) Taking of a hostage by an inmate of a state prison.

(21) Attempt to commit a felony punishable by death or imprisonment in the state prison for life.

(22) Any felony in which the defendant personally used a dangerous or deadly weapon.

(23) Escape from a state prison by use of force or violence.

(24) Assault with a deadly weapon or force likely to produce great bodily injury.

(25) Any felony violation of Section 186.22.

(26) Any attempt to commit a crime listed in this subdivision other than an assault.

(27) Any offense enumerated in subdivision (a), (b), or (d) of Section 12001.6.

(28) Carjacking.

(29) Any offense enumerated in subdivision (c) of Section 12001.6 if the person has two or more convictions for violating paragraph (2) of subdivision (a) of Section 417.

(c) Any person previously convicted of any of the offenses listed in subdivision (b) which conviction results from certification by the juvenile court for prosecution as an adult in adult court under the provisions of Section 707 of the Welfare and Institutions Code, who owns or has in his or her possession or under his or her custody or control any firearm is guilty of a felony. If probation is granted, or if the imposition or execution of sentence is suspended, it shall be a condition of the probation or suspension that the defendant serve at least six months in a county jail.

(d) The court shall apply the minimum sentence as specified in subdivisions (a) and (c) except in unusual cases where the interests of justice would best be served by granting probation or suspending the imposition or execution of sentence without the imprisonment required by subdivisions (a) and (c), or by granting probation or suspending the imposition or execution of sentence with conditions other than those set forth in subdivisions (a) and (c), in which case the court shall specify on the record and shall enter on the minutes the circumstances indicating that the interests of justice would best be served by the disposition.

Penal Code § 12021.3.

(a)(1) Any person who claims title to any firearm that is in the custody or control of a court or law enforcement agency and who wishes to have the firearm returned to him or her shall make application for a determination by the Department of Justice as to whether he or she is eligible to possess a firearm. The application shall include the following:

(A) The applicant's name, date and place of birth, gender, telephone number, and complete address.

(B) Whether the applicant is a United States citizen. If the applicant is not a United States citizen, he or she shall also provide his or her country of citizenship and his or her alien registration or I-94 number.

(C) If the firearm is a handgun, the firearm's make, model, caliber, barrel length, handgun type, country of origin, and serial number.

(D) For residents of California, the applicant's valid California driver's license number or valid California identification card number issued by the Department of Motor Vehicles. For nonresidents of California, a copy of the applicant's military identification with orders indicating that the individual is stationed in California, or a copy of the applicant's valid driver's license from the state of residence, or a copy of the applicant's state identification card from the state of residence. Copies of the documents provided by non-California residents shall be notarized.

(E) The name of the court or law enforcement agency holding the firearm.

(F) The signature of the applicant and the date of signature.

(G) Any person furnishing a fictitious name or address or knowingly furnishing any incorrect information or knowingly omitting any information required to be provided for the application, including any notarized information pursuant to subparagraph (D) of paragraph (1) of subdivision (a) shall be guilty of a misdemeanor.

(2) A person who owns a firearm that is in the custody of a court or law enforcement agency and who does not wish to obtain possession of the firearm, and the firearm is an otherwise legal firearm, and the person otherwise has right to title of the firearm, shall be entitled to sell or transfer title of the firearm to a licensed dealer as defined in Section 12071.

(3) Any person furnishing a fictitious name or address, or knowingly furnishing any incorrect information or knowingly omitting any information required to be provided for the application, including any notarized information pursuant to subparagraph (D) of paragraph (1) of subdivision (a) is punishable as a misdemeanor.

(b) No law enforcement agency or court that has taken custody of any firearm may return the firearm to any individual unless the following requirements are satisfied:

(1) That individual presents to the agency or court notification of a determination by the department pursuant to subdivision (e) that the person is eligible to possess firearms.

(2) If the agency or court has direct access to the Automated Firearms System, the agency or court has verified that the firearm is not listed as stolen pursuant to Section 11108, and that the firearm has been recorded in the Automated Firearms System in the name of the individual who seeks its return.

(3) If the firearm has been reported lost or stolen pursuant to Section 11108, a law enforcement agency shall notify the owner or person entitled to possession pursuant to Section 11108.5. However, that person shall provide proof of eligibility to possess a firearm pursuant to subdivision (e). Nothing in this subdivision shall prevent the local law enforcement agency from charging the rightful owner or person entitled to possession of the firearm the fees described in subdivision (j). However, individuals who are applying for a background check to retrieve a firearm that comes into the custody or control of the court or law enforcement agency pursuant to subdivision (a) shall be exempt from the fees in subdivision (c) provided that the court or agency determines the firearm was reported stolen to a law enforcement agency prior to the date the firearm came into custody or control of the court or law enforcement agency or within five business days of the firearm being stolen from its owner. The court or agency shall notify the Department of Justice of this fee exemption in a manner prescribed by the department.

(c) The Department of Justice shall establish a fee of twenty dollars ($20) per request for return of a firearm, plus a three-dollar ($3) charge for each additional handgun being processed as part of the request to return a firearm, to cover its costs for processing firearm clearance determinations submitted pursuant to this section. The fees shall be deposited into the Dealers' Record of Sale Special Account. The department may increase the fee by using the California Consumer Price Index as compiled and reported by the California Department of Industrial Relations to determine an annual rate of increase. Any fee increase shall be rounded to the nearest dollar.

(d) When the Department of Justice receives a completed application pursuant to subdivision (a) accompanied with the fee required pursuant to subdivision (c), it shall conduct an eligibility check of the applicant to determine whether the applicant is eligible to possess firearms.

(e)(1) If the department determines that the applicant is eligible to possess the firearm, the department shall provide the applicant with written notification that includes the following:

(A) The identity of the applicant.

(B) A statement that the applicant is eligible to possess a firearm.

(C) If the firearm is a handgun, a description of the handgun by make, model, and serial number.

(2) If the firearm is a handgun, the department shall enter a record of the handgun into the Automated Firearms System.

(3) The department shall have 30 days from the date of receipt to complete the background check unless delayed by circumstances beyond the control of the department. The applicant may contact the department to inquire about the reason for the delay.

(f) If the department denies the application, and the firearm is an otherwise legal firearm, the department shall notify the applicant of the denial and provide a form for the applicant to use to sell or transfer the firearm to a licensed dealer as defined in Section

12071. The applicant may contact the department to inquire about the reason for the denial.

(g) Notwithstanding any other provision of law, no law enforcement agency or court shall be required to retain a firearm for more than 180 days after the owner of the firearm has been notified by the court or law enforcement agency that the firearm has been made available for return. An unclaimed firearm may be disposed of after the 180-day period has expired.

(h) Notwithstanding Section 11106, the department may retain personal information about an applicant in connection with a claim for a firearm that is not a handgun to allow for law enforcement confirmation of compliance with this section. The information retained may include personal identifying information regarding the individual applying for the clearance, but may not include information that identifies any particular firearm that is not a handgun.

(i)(1) If a law enforcement agency determines that the applicant is the legal owner of any firearm deposited with the law enforcement agency and is prohibited from possessing any firearm and the firearm is an otherwise legal firearm, the applicant shall be entitled to sell or transfer the firearm to a licensed dealer as defined in Section 12071.

(2) If the firearm has been lost or stolen, the firearm shall be restored to the lawful owner pursuant to Section 11108.5 upon his or her identification of the firearm and proof of ownership, and proof of eligibility to possess a firearm pursuant to subdivision (e). Nothing in this subdivision shall prevent the local law enforcement agency from charging the rightful owner of the firearm the fees described in subdivision (j).

(3) Subdivision (a) of Section 12070 shall not apply to deliveries, transfers, or returns of firearms made by a court or a law enforcement agency pursuant to this section.

(4) Subdivision (d) of Section 12072 shall not apply to deliveries, transfers, or returns of firearms made pursuant to this section.

(j)(1) A city, county, or city and county, or a state agency may adopt a regulation, ordinance, or resolution imposing a charge equal to its administrative costs relating to the seizure, impounding, storage, or release of firearms. The fees shall not exceed the actual costs incurred for the expenses directly related to taking possession of a firearm, storing the firearm, and surrendering possession of the firearm to a licensed firearms dealer or to the owner. Those administrative costs may be waived by the local or state agency upon verifiable proof that the firearm was reported stolen at the time the firearm came into the custody or control of the law enforcement agency.

(2) The following apply to any charges imposed for administrative costs pursuant to this subdivision:

(A) The charges shall only be imposed on the person claiming title to the firearms.

(B) Any charges shall be collected by the local or state authority only from the person claiming title to the firearm.

(C) The charges shall be in addition to any other charges authorized or imposed pursuant to this code.

(D) No charge may be imposed for any hearing or appeal relating to the removal, impound, storage, or release of a firearm unless that hearing or appeal was requested in writing by the legal owner of the firearm. In addition, the charge may be imposed only upon the person requesting that hearing or appeal.

(3) No costs for any hearing or appeal related to the release of a firearm shall be charged to the legal owner who redeems the firearm unless the legal owner voluntarily requests the post storage hearing or appeal. No city, county, city and county, or state agency shall require a legal owner to request a poststorage hearing as a requirement for release of the firearm to the legal owner.

(k) In a proceeding for the return of a firearm seized and not returned pursuant to this section, where the defendant or cross-defendant is a law enforcement agency, the court shall award reasonable attorney's fees to the prevailing party.

Penal Code § 12021.5.

(a) Every person who carries a loaded or unloaded firearm on his or her person, or in a vehicle, during the commission or attempted commission of any street gang crimes described in subdivision (a) or (b) of Section 186.22, shall, upon conviction of the felony or attempted felony, be punished by an additional term of imprisonment in the state prison for one, two, or three years. The court shall select the sentence enhancement which, in the court's discretion, best serves the interests of justice and shall state the reasons for its choice on the record at the time of sentence, in accordance with the provisions of subdivision (d) of Section 1170.1.

(b) Every person who carries a loaded or unloaded firearm together with a detachable shotgun magazine, a detachable pistol magazine, a detachable magazine, or a belt-feeding device on his or her person, or in a vehicle, during the commission or attempted commission of any street gang crimes described in subdivision (a) or (b) of Section 186.22, shall, upon conviction of the felony or attempted felony, be punished by an additional term of imprisonment in the state prison for two, three, or four years. The court shall select the sentence enhancement which, in the court's discretion, best serves the interests of justice and shall state the reasons for its choice on the record at the time of sentence, in accordance with the provisions of subdivision (d) of Section 1170.1.

(c) As used in this section, the following definitions shall apply:

(1) "Detachable magazine" means a device that is designed or redesigned to do all of the following:

(A) To be attached to a rifle that is designed or redesigned to fire ammunition.

(B) To be attached to, and detached from, a rifle that is designed or redesigned to fire ammunition.

(C) To feed ammunition continuously and directly into the loading mechanism of a rifle that is designed or redesigned to fire ammunition.

(2) "Detachable pistol magazine" means a device that is designed or redesigned to do all of the following:

(A) To be attached to a semiautomatic firearm that is not a rifle or shotgun that is designed or redesigned to fire ammunition.

(B) To be attached to, and detached from, a firearm that is not a rifle or shotgun that is designed or redesigned to fire ammunition.

(C) To feed ammunition continuously and directly into the loading mechanism of a firearm that is not a rifle or a shotgun that is designed or redesigned to fire ammunition.

(3) "Detachable shotgun magazine" means a device that is designed or redesigned to do all of the following:

(A) To be attached to a firearm that is designed or redesigned to fire a fixed shotgun shell through a smooth or rifled bore.

(B) To be attached to, and detached from, a firearm that is designed or redesigned to fire a fixed shotgun shell through a smooth bore.

(C) To feed fixed shotgun shells continuously and directly into the loading mechanism of a firearm that is designed or redesigned to fire a fixed shotgun shell.

(4) "Belt-feeding device" means a device that is designed or redesigned to continuously feed ammunition into the loading mechanism of a machinegun or a semiautomatic firearm.

(5) "Rifle" shall have the same meaning as specified in paragraph (20) of subdivision (c) of Section 12020.

(6) "Shotgun" shall have the same meaning as specified in paragraph (21) of subdivision (c) of Section 12020.

(d) This section shall remain in effect only until January 1, 2011, and as of that date is repealed, unless a later enacted statute, that is enacted before January 1, 2011, deletes or extends that date.

Penal Code § 12022.

(a)(1) Except as provided in subdivisions (c) and (d), any person who is armed with a firearm in the commission of a felony or attempted felony shall be punished by an additional and consecutive term of imprisonment in the state prison for one year, unless the arming is an element of that offense. This additional term shall apply to any person who is a principal in the commission of a felony or attempted felony if one or more of the principals is armed with a firearm, whether or not the person is personally armed with a firearm.

(2) Except as provided in subdivision (c), and notwithstanding subdivision (d), if the firearm is an assault weapon, as defined in Section 12276 or Section 12276.1, or a machinegun, as defined in Section 12200, or a .50 BMG rifle, as defined in Section 12278, the additional and consecutive term described in this subdivision shall be three years whether or not the arming is an element of the offense of which the person was convicted. The additional term provided in this paragraph shall apply to any person who is a principal in the commission of a felony or attempted felony if one or more of the principals is armed with an assault weapon or machinegun, or a .50 BMG rifle, whether or not the person is personally armed with an assault weapon or machinegun, or a .50 BMG rifle.

(b)(1) Any person who personally uses a deadly or dangerous weapon in the commission of a felony or attempted felony shall be punished by an additional and consecutive term of imprisonment in the state prison for one year, unless use of a deadly or dangerous weapon is an element of that offense.

(2) If the person described in paragraph (1) has been convicted of carjacking or attempted carjacking, the additional term shall be one, two, or three years.

(3) When a person is found to have personally used a deadly or dangerous weapon in the commission of a felony or attempted felony as provided in this subdivision and the weapon is owned by that person, the court shall order that the weapon be deemed a nuisance and disposed of in the manner provided in Section 12028.

(c) Notwithstanding the enhancement set forth in subdivision (a), any person who is personally armed with a firearm in the commission of a violation or attempted violation of Section 11351, 11351.5, 11352, 11366.5, 11366.6, 11378, 11378.5, 11379, 11379.5, or 11379.6 of the Health and Safety Code, shall be punished by an additional and consecutive term of imprisonment in the state prison for three, four, or five years.

(d) Notwithstanding the enhancement set forth in subdivision (a), any person who is not personally armed with a firearm who, knowing that another principal is personally armed with a firearm, is a principal in the commission of an offense or attempted offense specified in subdivision (c), shall be punished by an additional and consecutive term of imprisonment in the state prison for one, two, or three years.

(e) For purposes of imposing an enhancement under Section 1170.1, the enhancements under this section shall count as one, single enhancement.

(f) Notwithstanding any other provision of law, the court may strike the additional punishment for the enhancements provided in subdivision (c) or (d) in an unusual case where the interests of justice would best be served, if the court specifies on the record and enters into the minutes the circumstances indicating that the interests of justice would best be served by that disposition.

Penal Code § 12022.1.

(a) For the purposes of this section only:

(1) "Primary offense" means a felony offense for which a person has been released from custody on bail or on his or her own recognizance prior to the judgment becoming final, including the disposition of any appeal, or for which release on bail or his or her own recognizance has been revoked. In cases where the court has granted a stay of execution of a county jail commitment or state prison commitment, "primary offense" also means a felony offense for which a person is out of custody during the period of time between the pronouncement of judgment and the time the person actually surrenders into custody or is otherwise returned to custody.

(2) "Secondary offense" means a felony offense alleged to have been committed while the person is released from custody for a primary offense.

(b) Any person arrested for a secondary offense which was alleged to have been committed while that person was released from custody on a primary offense shall be subject to a penalty enhancement of an additional two years in state prison which shall be served consecutive to any other term imposed by the court.

(c) The enhancement allegation provided in subdivision (b) shall be pleaded in the information or indictment which alleges the secondary offense, or in the information or indictment of the primary offense if a conviction has already occurred in the secondary offense, and shall be proved as provided by law. The enhancement allegation may be pleaded in a complaint but need not be proved at the preliminary hearing or grand jury hearing.

(d) Whenever there is a conviction for the secondary offense and the enhancement is proved, and the person is sentenced on the secondary offense prior to the conviction of the primary offense, the imposition of the enhancement shall be stayed pending imposition of the sentence for the primary offense. The stay shall be lifted by the court hearing the primary offense at the time of sentencing for that offense and shall be recorded in the abstract of judgment. If the person is acquitted of the primary offense the stay shall be permanent.

(e) If the person is convicted of a felony for the primary offense, is sentenced to state prison for the primary offense, and is convicted of a felony for the secondary offense, any state prison sentence for the secondary offense shall be consecutive to the primary sentence.

(f) If the person is convicted of a felony for the primary offense, is granted probation for the primary offense, and is convicted of a felony for the secondary offense, any state prison sentence for the secondary offense shall be enhanced as provided in subdivision (b).

(g) If the primary offense conviction is reversed on appeal, the enhancement shall be suspended pending retrial of that felony. Upon retrial and reconviction, the enhancement shall be reimposed. If the person is no longer in custody for the secondary offense upon reconviction of the primary offense, the court may, at its discretion, reimpose the enhancement and order him or her recommitted to custody.

Penal Code § 12022.2.

(a) Any person who, while armed with a firearm in the commission or attempted commission of any felony, has in his or her immediate possession ammunition for the firearm designed primarily to penetrate metal or armor, shall upon conviction of that felony or attempted felony, in addition and consecutive to the punishment prescribed for the felony or attempted felony, be punished by an additional term of 3, 4, or 10 years. The court shall select the sentence enhancement which, in the court's discretion, best serves the interests of justice and shall state the reasons for its choice on the record at the time of the sentence in accordance with the provisions of subdivision (d) of Section 1170.1.

(b) Any person who wears a body vest in the commission or attempted commission of a violent offense, as defined in subdivision (b) of Section 12021.1, shall, upon conviction of that felony or attempted felony, in addition and consecutive to the punishment prescribed for the felony or attempted felony of which he or she has been convicted, be punished by an additional term of one, two, or five years. The court shall select the sentence enhancement which, in the court's discretion, best serves the interests of justice and shall state the reasons for its choice on the record at the time of the sentence in accordance with the provisions of subdivision (d) of Section 1170.1.

(c) As used in this section, "body vest" means any bullet-resistant material intended to provide ballistic and trauma protection for the wearer.

(d) This section shall remain in effect only until January 1, 2011, and as of that date is repealed, unless a later enacted statute, that is enacted before January 1, 2011, deletes or extends that date.

Penal Code § 12022.3.

For each violation of Section 220 involving a specified sexual offense, or for each violation or attempted violation of Section 261, 262, 264.1, 286, 288, 288a, or 289, and in addition to the sentence provided, any person shall receive the following:

(a) A 3-, 4-, or 10-year enhancement if the person uses a firearm or a deadly weapon in the commission of the violation.

(b) A one-, two-, or five-year enhancement if the person is armed with a firearm or a deadly weapon.

Penal Code § 12022.4.

(a) Any person who, during the commission or attempted commission of a felony, furnishes or offers to furnish a firearm to another for the purpose of aiding, abetting, or enabling that person or any other person to commit a felony shall, in addition and consecutive to the punishment prescribed by the felony or attempted felony of which the person has been convicted, be punished by an additional term of one, two, or three years in the state prison. The court shall select the sentence enhancement which, in the court's discretion, best serves the interests of justice and shall state the reasons for its choice on the record at the time of the sentence, in accordance with the provisions of subdivision (d) of Section 1170.1. The additional term provided in this section shall not be imposed unless the fact of the furnishing is charged in the accusatory pleading and admitted or found to be true by the trier of fact.

(b) This section shall remain in effect only until January 1, 2011, and as of that date is repealed, unless a later enacted statute, that is enacted before January 1, 2011, deletes or extends that date.

Penal Code § 12022.5.

(a) Except as provided in subdivision (b), any person who personally uses a firearm in the commission of a felony or attempted felony shall be punished by an additional and consecutive term of imprisonment in the state prison for 3, 4, or 10 years, unless use of a firearm is an element of that offense.

(b) Notwithstanding subdivision (a), any person who personally uses an assault weapon, as specified in Section 12276 or Section 12276.1, or a machinegun, as defined in Section 12200, in the commission of a felony or attempted felony, shall be punished by an additional and consecutive term of imprisonment in the state prison for 5, 6, or 10 years.

(c) Notwithstanding Section 1385 or any other provisions of law, the court shall not strike an allegation under this section or a finding bringing a person within the provisions of this section.

(d) Notwithstanding the limitation in subdivision (a) relating to being an element of the offense, the additional term provided by this section shall be imposed for any violation of Section 245 if a firearm is used, or for murder if the killing is perpetrated by means of shooting a firearm from a motor vehicle, intentionally at another person outside of the vehicle with the intent to inflict great bodily injury or death.

(e) When a person is found to have personally used a firearm, an assault weapon, a machinegun, or a .50 BMG rifle, in the commission of a felony or attempted felony as provided in this section and the firearm, assault weapon, machinegun, or a .50 BMG rifle, is owned by that person, the court shall order that the firearm be deemed a nuisance and disposed of in the manner provided in Section 12028.

(f) For purposes of imposing an enhancement under Section 1170.1, the enhancements under this section shall count as one, single enhancement.

Penal Code § 12022.53.

(a) This section applies to the following felonies:

(1) Section 187 (murder).

(2) Section 203 or 205 (mayhem).

(3) Section 207, 209, or 209.5 (kidnapping).

(4) Section 211 (robbery).

(5) Section 215 (carjacking).
(6) Section 220 (assault with intent to commit a specified felony).
(7) Subdivision (d) of Section 245 (assault with a firearm on a peace officer or firefighter).
(8) Section 261 or 262 (rape).
(9) Section 264.1 (rape or sexual penetration in concert).
(10) Section 286 (sodomy).
(11) Section 288 or 288.5 (lewd act on a child).
(12) Section 288a (oral copulation).
(13) Section 289 (sexual penetration).
(14) Section 4500 (assault by a life prisoner).
(15) Section 4501 (assault by a prisoner).
(16) Section 4503 (holding a hostage by a prisoner).
(17) Any felony punishable by death or imprisonment in the state prison for life.
(18) Any attempt to commit a crime listed in this subdivision other than an assault.

(b) Notwithstanding any other provision of law, any person who, in the commission of a felony specified in subdivision (a), personally uses a firearm, shall be punished by an additional and consecutive term of imprisonment in the state prison for 10 years. The firearm need not be operable or loaded for this enhancement to apply.

(c) Notwithstanding any other provision of law, any person who, in the commission of a felony specified in subdivision (a), personally and intentionally discharges a firearm, shall be punished by an additional and consecutive term of imprisonment in the state prison for 20 years.

(d) Notwithstanding any other provision of law, any person who, in the commission of a felony specified in subdivision (a), Section 246, or subdivision (c) or (d) of Section 12034, personally and intentionally discharges a firearm and proximately causes great bodily injury, as defined in Section 12022.7, or death, to any person other than an accomplice, shall be punished by an additional and consecutive term of imprisonment in the state prison for 25 years to life.

(e)(1) The enhancements provided in this section shall apply to any person who is a principal in the commission of an offense if both of the following are pled and proved:

(A) The person violated subdivision (b) of Section 186.22.

(B) Any principal in the offense committed any act specified in subdivision (b), (c), or (d).

(2) An enhancement for participation in a criminal street gang pursuant to Chapter 11 (commencing with Section 186.20) of Title 7 of Part 1 shall not be imposed on a person in addition to an enhancement imposed pursuant to this subdivision, unless the person personally used or personally discharged a firearm in the commission of the offense.

(f) Only one additional term of imprisonment under this section shall be imposed per person for each crime. If more than one enhancement per person is found true under this section, the court shall impose upon that person the enhancement that provides the longest term of imprisonment. An enhancement involving a firearm specified in Section 12021.5, 12022, 12022.3, 12022.4, 12022.5, or 12022.55 shall not be imposed on a person in addition to an enhancement imposed pursuant to this section. An enhancement for great bodily injury as defined in Section 12022.7, 12022.8, or 12022.9 shall not be imposed on a person in addition to an enhancement imposed pursuant to subdivision (d).

(g) Notwithstanding any other provision of law, probation shall not be granted to, nor shall the execution or imposition of sentence be suspended for, any person found to come within the provisions of this section.

(h) Notwithstanding Section 1385 or any other provision of law, the court shall not strike an allegation under this section or a finding bringing a person within the provisions of this section.

(i) The total amount of credits awarded pursuant to Article 2.5 (commencing with Section 2930) of Chapter 7 of Title 1 of Part 3 or pursuant to Section 4019 or any other provision of law shall not exceed 15 percent of the total term of imprisonment imposed on a defendant upon whom a sentence is imposed pursuant to this section.

(j) For the penalties in this section to apply, the existence of any fact required under subdivision (b), (c), or (d) shall be alleged in the accusatory pleading and either admitted by the defendant in open court or found to be true by the trier of fact. When an enhancement specified in this section has been admitted or found to be true, the court shall impose punishment for that enhancement pursuant to this section rather than imposing punishment authorized under any other provision of law, unless another enhancement provides for a greater penalty or a longer term of imprisonment.

(k) When a person is found to have used or discharged a firearm in the commission of an offense that includes an allegation pursuant to this section and the firearm is owned by that person, a coparticipant, or a coconspirator, the court shall order that the firearm be deemed a nuisance and disposed of in the manner provided in Section 12028.

(l) The enhancements specified in this section shall not apply to the lawful use or discharge of a firearm by a public officer, as provided in Section 196, or by any person in lawful self-defense, lawful defense of another, or lawful defense of property, as provided in Sections 197, 198, and 198.5.

Penal Code § 12022.55.

Notwithstanding Section 12022.5, any person who, with the intent to inflict great bodily injury or death, inflicts great bodily injury, as defined in Section 12022.7, or causes the death of a person, other than an occupant of a motor vehicle, as a result of discharging a firearm from a motor vehicle in the commission of a felony or attempted felony, shall be punished by an additional and consecutive term of imprisonment in the state prison for 5, 6, or 10 years.

Penal Code § 12022.6.

(a) When any person takes, damages, or destroys any property in the commission or attempted commission of a felony, with the intent to cause that taking, damage, or destruction, the court shall impose an additional term as follows:

(1) If the loss exceeds sixty-five thousand dollars ($65,000), the court, in addition and consecutive to the punishment

prescribed for the felony or attempted felony of which the defendant has been convicted, shall impose an additional term of one year.

(2) If the loss exceeds two hundred thousand dollars ($200,000), the court, in addition and consecutive to the punishment prescribed for the felony or attempted felony of which the defendant has been convicted, shall impose an additional term of two years.

(3) If the loss exceeds one million three hundred thousand dollars ($1,300,000), the court, in addition and consecutive to the punishment prescribed for the felony or attempted felony of which the defendant has been convicted, shall impose an additional term of three years.

(4) If the loss exceeds three million two hundred thousand dollars ($3,200,000), the court, in addition and consecutive to the punishment prescribed for the felony or attempted felony of which the defendant has been convicted, shall impose an additional term of four years.

(b) In any accusatory pleading involving multiple charges of taking, damage, or destruction, the additional terms provided in this section may be imposed if the aggregate losses to the victims from all felonies exceed the amounts specified in this section and arise from a common scheme or plan. All pleadings under this section shall remain subject to the rules of joinder and severance stated in Section 954.

(c) The additional terms provided in this section shall not be imposed unless the facts of the taking, damage, or destruction in excess of the amounts provided in this section are charged in the accusatory pleading and admitted or found to be true by the trier of fact.

(d) This section applies to, but is not limited to, property taken, damaged, or destroyed in violation of Section 502 or subdivision (b) of Section 502.7. This section shall also apply to applicable prosecutions for a violation of Section 350, 653h, 653s, or 653w.

(e) For the purposes of this section, the term "loss" has the following meanings:

(1) When counterfeit items of computer software are manufactured or possessed for sale, the "loss" from the counterfeiting of those items shall be equivalent to the retail price or fair market value of the true items that are counterfeited.

(2) When counterfeited but unassembled components of computer software packages are recovered, including, but not limited to, counterfeited computer diskettes, instruction manuals, or licensing envelopes, the "loss" from the counterfeiting of those components of computer software packages shall be equivalent to the retail price or fair market value of the number of completed computer software packages that could have been made from those components.

(f) It is the intent of the Legislature that the provisions of this section be reviewed within 10 years to consider the effects of inflation on the additional terms imposed. For that reason this section shall remain in effect only until January 1, 2018, and as of that date is repealed unless a later enacted statute, which is enacted before January 1, 2018, deletes or extends that date.

Penal Code § 12022.7.

(a) Any person who personally inflicts great bodily injury on any person other than an accomplice in the commission of a felony or attempted felony shall be punished by an additional and consecutive term of imprisonment in the state prison for three years.

(b) Any person who personally inflicts great bodily injury on any person other than an accomplice in the commission of a felony or attempted felony which causes the victim to become comatose due to brain injury or to suffer paralysis of a permanent nature, shall be punished by an additional and consecutive term of imprisonment in the state prison for five years. As used in this subdivision, "paralysis" means a major or complete loss of motor function resulting from injury to the nervous system or to a muscular mechanism.

(c) Any person who personally inflicts great bodily injury on a person who is 70 years of age or older, other than an accomplice, in the commission of a felony or attempted felony shall be punished by an additional and consecutive term of imprisonment in the state prison for five years.

(d) Any person who personally inflicts great bodily injury on a child under the age of five years in the commission of a felony or attempted felony shall be punished by an additional and consecutive term of imprisonment in the state prison for four, five, or six years.

(e) Any person who personally inflicts great bodily injury under circumstances involving domestic violence in the commission of a felony or attempted felony shall be punished by an additional and consecutive term of imprisonment in the state prison for three, four, or five years. As used in this subdivision, "domestic violence" has the meaning provided in subdivision (b) of Section 13700.

(f) As used in this section, "great bodily injury" means a significant or substantial physical injury.

(g) This section shall not apply to murder or manslaughter or a violation of Section 451 or 452. Subdivisions (a), (b), (c), and (d) shall not apply if infliction of great bodily injury is an element of the offense.

(h) The court shall impose the additional terms of imprisonment under either subdivision (a), (b), (c), or (d), but may not impose more than one of those terms for the same offense.

Penal Code § 12022.75.

(a) Except as provided in subdivision (b), any person who, for the purpose of committing a felony, administers by injection, inhalation, ingestion, or any other means, any controlled substance listed in Section 11054, 11055, 11056, 11057, or 11058 of the Health and Safety Code, against the victim's will by means of force, violence, or fear of immediate and unlawful bodily injury to the victim or another person, shall, in addition and consecutive to the penalty provided for the felony or attempted felony of which he or she has been convicted, be punished by an additional term of three years.

(b)(1) Any person who, in the commission or attempted commission of any offense specified in paragraph (2), administers any controlled substance listed in Section 11054, 11055, 11056, 11057, or 11058 of the Health and Safety Code to the victim shall be punished by an additional and consecutive term of imprisonment in the state prison for five years.

(2) This subdivision shall apply to the following offenses:

(A) Rape, in violation of paragraph (3) or (4) of subdivision (a) of Section 261.

(B) Sodomy, in violation of subdivision (f) or (i) of Section 286.

(C) Oral copulation, in violation of subdivision (f) or (i) of Section 288a.

(D) Sexual penetration, in violation of subdivision (d) or (e) of Section 289.

(E) Any offense specified in subdivision © of Section 667.61.

Penal Code § 12022.8.

Any person who inflicts great bodily injury, as defined in Section 12022.7, on any victim in a violation of Section 220 involving a specified sexual offense, or a violation or attempted violation of paragraph (2), (3), or (6) of subdivision (a) of Section 261, paragraph (1) or (4) of subdivision (a) of Section 262, Section 264.1, subdivision (b) of Section 288, subdivision (a) of Section 289, or sodomy or oral copulation by force, violence, duress, menace, or fear of immediate and unlawful bodily injury on the victim or another person as provided in Section 286 or 288a shall receive a five-year enhancement for each violation in addition to the sentence provided for the felony conviction.

Penal Code § 12022.85.

(a) Any person who violates one or more of the offenses listed in subdivision (b) with knowledge that he or she has acquired immune deficiency syndrome (AIDS) or with the knowledge that he or she carries antibodies of the human immunodeficiency virus at the time of the commission of those offenses, shall receive a three-year enhancement for each violation in addition to the sentence provided under those sections. (b) Subdivision (a) applies to the following crimes:

(1) Rape in violation of Section 261.

(2) Unlawful intercourse with a person under 18 years of age in violation of Section 261.5.

(3) Rape of a spouse in violation of Section 262.

(4) Sodomy in violation of Section 286.

(5) Oral copulation in violation of Section 288a.

(c) For purposes of proving the knowledge requirement of this section, the prosecuting attorney may use test results received under subdivision (c) of Section 1202.1 or subdivision (g) of Section 1202.6.

Penal Code § 12022.9.

Any person who, during the commission of a felony or attempted felony, knows or reasonably should know that the victim is pregnant, and who, with intent to inflict injury, and without the consent of the woman, personally inflicts injury upon a pregnant woman that results in the termination of the pregnancy shall be punished by an additional and consecutive term of imprisonment in the state prison for five years. The additional term provided in this subdivision shall not be imposed unless the fact of that injury is charged in the accusatory pleading and admitted or found to be true by the trier of fact. Nothing in this section shall be construed as affecting the applicability of subdivision (a) of Section 187.

Penal Code § 12022.95.

Any person convicted of a violation of Section 273a, who under circumstances or conditions likely to produce great bodily harm or death, willfully causes or permits any child to suffer, or inflicts thereon unjustifiable physical pain or injury that results in death, or having the care or custody of any child, under circumstances likely to produce great bodily harm or death, willfully causes or permits that child to be injured or harmed, and that injury or harm results in death, shall receive a four-year enhancement for each violation, in addition to the sentence provided for that conviction. Nothing in this paragraph shall be construed as affecting the applicability of subdivision (a) of Section 187 or Section 192. This section shall not apply unless the allegation is included within an accusatory pleading and admitted by the defendant or found to be true by the trier of fact.

Penal Code § 12023.

(a) Every person who carries a loaded firearm with the intent to commit a felony is guilty of armed criminal action.

(b) Armed criminal action is punishable by imprisonment in a county jail not exceeding one year, or in the state prison.

Penal Code § 12024.

Every person having upon him or her any deadly weapon, with intent to assault another, is guilty of a misdemeanor.

Penal Code § 12025.

(a) A person is guilty of carrying a concealed firearm when he or she does any of the following:

(1) Carries concealed within any vehicle which is under his or her control or direction any pistol, revolver, or other firearm capable of being concealed upon the person.

(2) Carries concealed upon his or her person any pistol, revolver, or other firearm capable of being concealed upon the person.

(3) Causes to be carried concealed within any vehicle in which he or she is an occupant any pistol, revolver, or other firearm capable of being concealed upon the person.

(b) Carrying a concealed firearm in violation of this section is punishable, as follows:

(1) Where the person previously has been convicted of any felony, or of any crime made punishable by this chapter, as a felony.

(2) Where the firearm is stolen and the person knew or had reasonable cause to believe that it was stolen, as a felony.

(3) Where the person is an active participant in a criminal street gang, as defined in subdivision (a) of Section 186.22, under the Street Terrorism Enforcement and Prevention Act (Chapter 11 (commencing with Section 186.20) of Title 7 of Part 1), as a felony.

(4) Where the person is not in lawful possession of the firearm, as defined in this section, or the person is within a class of persons prohibited from possessing or acquiring a firearm pursuant to Section 12021 or 12021.1 of this code or Section 8100 or 8103 of the Welfare and Institutions Code, as a felony.

(5) Where the person has been convicted of a crime against a person or property, or of a narcotics or dangerous drug violation, by imprisonment in the state prison, or by imprisonment in a county jail not to exceed one year, by a fine not to exceed one thousand dollars ($1,000), or by both that imprisonment and fine.

(6) By imprisonment in the state prison, or by imprisonment in a county jail not to exceed one year, by a fine not to exceed

one thousand dollars ($1,000), or by both that fine and imprisonment if both of the following conditions are met:

(A) Both the pistol, revolver, or other firearm capable of being concealed upon the person and the unexpended ammunition capable of being discharged from that firearm are either in the immediate possession of the person or readily accessible to that person, or the pistol, revolver, or other firearm capable of being concealed upon the person is loaded as defined in subdivision (g) of Section 12031.

(B) The person is not listed with the Department of Justice pursuant to paragraph (1) of subdivision (c) of Section 11106, as the registered owner of that pistol, revolver, or other firearm capable of being concealed upon the person.

(7) In all cases other than those specified in paragraphs (1) to (6), inclusive, by imprisonment in a county jail not to exceed one year, by a fine not to exceed one thousand dollars ($1,000), or by both that imprisonment and fine.

(c) A peace officer may arrest a person for a violation of paragraph (6) of subdivision (b) if the peace officer has probable cause to believe that the person is not listed with the Department of Justice pursuant to paragraph (1) of subdivision (c) of Section 11106 as the registered owner of the pistol, revolver, or other firearm capable of being concealed upon the person, and one or more of the conditions in subparagraph (A) of paragraph (6) of subdivision (b) is met.

(d)(1) Every person convicted under this section who previously has been convicted of a misdemeanor offense enumerated in Section 12001.6 shall be punished by imprisonment in a county jail for at least three months and not exceeding six months, or, if granted probation, or if the execution or imposition of sentence is suspended, it shall be a condition thereof that he or she be imprisoned in a county jail for at least three months.

(2) Every person convicted under this section who has previously been convicted of any felony, or of any crime made punishable by this chapter, if probation is granted, or if the execution or imposition of sentence is suspended, it shall be a condition thereof that he or she be imprisoned in a county jail for not less than three months.

(e) The court shall apply the three-month minimum sentence as specified in subdivision (d), except in unusual cases where the interests of justice would best be served by granting probation or suspending the imposition or execution of sentence without the minimum imprisonment required in subdivision (d) or by granting probation or suspending the imposition or execution of sentence with conditions other than those set forth in subdivision (d), in which case, the court shall specify on the record and shall enter on the minutes the circumstances indicating that the interests of justice would best be served by that disposition.

(f) Firearms carried openly in belt holsters are not concealed within the meaning of this section.

(g) For purposes of this section, "lawful possession of the firearm" means that the person who has possession or custody of the firearm either lawfully owns the firearm or has the permission of the lawful owner or a person who otherwise has apparent authority to possess or have custody of the firearm. A person who takes a firearm without the permission of the lawful owner or without the permission of a person who has lawful custody of the firearm does not have lawful possession of the firearm.

(h)(1) The district attorney of each county shall submit annually a report on or before June 30, to the Attorney General consisting of profiles by race, age, gender, and ethnicity of any person charged with a felony or a misdemeanor under this section and any other offense charged in the same complaint, indictment, or information.

(2) The Attorney General shall submit annually, a report on or before December 31, to the Legislature compiling all of the reports submitted pursuant to paragraph (1).

(3) This subdivision shall remain operative until January 1, 2005, and as of that date shall be repealed.

Penal Code § 12025.5.

(a) A violation of Section 12025 is justifiable when a person who possesses a firearm reasonably believes that he or she is in grave danger because of circumstances forming the basis of a current restraining order issued by a court against another person or persons who has or have been found to pose a threat to his or her life or safety. This section may not apply when the circumstances involve a mutual restraining order issued pursuant to Division 10 (commencing with Section 6200) of the Family Code absent a factual finding of a specific threat to the person's life or safety. It is not the intent of the Legislature to limit, restrict, or narrow the application of current statutory or judicial authority to apply this or other justifications to defendants charged with violating Section 12025 or of committing other similar offenses.

(b) Upon trial for violating Section 12025, the trier of fact shall determine whether the defendant was acting out of a reasonable belief that he or she was in grave danger.

Penal Code § 12026.

(a) Section 12025 shall not apply to or affect any citizen of the United States or legal resident over the age of 18 years who resides or is temporarily within this state, and who is not within the excepted classes prescribed by Section 12021 or 12021.1 of this code or Section 8100 or 8103 of the Welfare and Institutions Code, who carries, either openly or concealed, anywhere within the citizen' s or legal resident's place of residence, place of business, or on private property owned or lawfully possessed by the citizen or legal resident any pistol, revolver, or other firearm capable of being concealed upon the person.

(b) No permit or license to purchase, own, possess, keep, or carry, either openly or concealed, shall be required of any citizen of the United States or legal resident over the age of 18 years who resides or is temporarily within this state, and who is not within the excepted classes prescribed by Section 12021 or 12021.1 of this code or Section 8100 or 8103 of the Welfare and Institutions Code, to purchase, own, possess, keep, or carry, either openly or concealed, a pistol, revolver, or other firearm capable of being concealed upon the person within the citizen's or legal resident's place of residence, place of business, or on private property owned or lawfully possessed by the citizen or legal resident.

(c) Nothing in this section shall be construed as affecting the application of Section 12031.

Penal Code § 12026.1.

(a) Section 12025 shall not be construed to prohibit any citizen of the United States over the age of 18 years who resides or is temporarily within this state, and who is not prohibited by state or federal law from possessing, receiving, owning, or purchasing a firearm, from transporting or carrying any pistol, revolver, or other firearm capable of being concealed upon the person, provided that the following applies to the firearm:

(1) The firearm is within a motor vehicle and it is locked in the vehicle's trunk or in a locked container in the vehicle other than the utility or glove compartment.

(2) The firearm is carried by the person directly to or from any motor vehicle for any lawful purpose and, while carrying the firearm, the firearm is contained within a locked container.

(b) The provisions of this section do not prohibit or limit the otherwise lawful carrying or transportation of any pistol, revolver, or other firearm capable of being concealed upon the person in accordance with this chapter.

(c) As used in this section, "locked container" means a secure container which is fully enclosed and locked by a padlock, key lock, combination lock, or similar locking device.

Penal Code § 12026.2.

(a) Section 12025 does not apply to, or affect, any of the following:

(1) The possession of a firearm by an authorized participant in a motion picture, television, or video production or entertainment event when the participant lawfully uses the firearm as part of that production or event or while going directly to, or coming directly from, that production or event.

(2) The possession of a firearm in a locked container by a member of any club or organization, organized for the purpose of lawfully collecting and lawfully displaying pistols, revolvers, or other firearms, while the member is at meetings of the clubs or organizations or while going directly to, and coming directly from, those meetings.

(3) The transportation of a firearm by a participant when going directly to, or coming directly from, a recognized safety or hunter safety class, or a recognized sporting event involving that firearm.

(4) The transportation of a firearm by a person listed in Section 12026 directly between any of the places mentioned in Section 12026.

(5) The transportation of a firearm by a person when going directly to, or coming directly from, a fixed place of business or private residential property for the purpose of the lawful repair or the lawful transfer, sale, or loan of that firearm.

(6) The transportation of a firearm by a person listed in Section 12026 when going directly from the place where that person lawfully received that firearm to that person's place of residence or place of business or to private property owned or lawfully possessed by that person.

(7) The transportation of a firearm by a person when going directly to, or coming directly from, a gun show, swap meet, or similar event to which the public is invited, for the purpose of displaying that firearm in a lawful manner.

(8) The transportation of a firearm by an authorized employee or agent of a supplier of firearms when going directly to, or coming directly from, a motion picture, television, or video production or entertainment event for the purpose of providing that firearm to an authorized participant to lawfully use as a part of that production or event.

(9) The transportation of a firearm by a person when going directly to, or coming directly from, a target range, which holds a regulatory or business license, for the purposes of practicing shooting at targets with that firearm at that target range.

(10) The transportation of a firearm by a person when going directly to, or coming directly from, a place designated by a person authorized to issue licenses pursuant to Section 12050 when done at the request of the issuing agency so that the issuing agency can determine whether or not a license should be issued to that person to carry that firearm.

(11) The transportation of a firearm by a person when going directly to, or coming directly from, a lawful camping activity for the purpose of having that firearm available for lawful personal protection while at the lawful campsite. This paragraph shall not be construed to override the statutory authority granted to the Department of Parks and Recreation or any other state or local governmental agencies to promulgate rules and regulations governing the administration of parks and campgrounds.

(12) The transportation of a firearm by a person in order to comply with subdivision (c) or (i) of Section 12078 as it pertains to that firearm.

(13) The transportation of a firearm by a person in order to utilize subdivision (l) of Section 12078 as it pertains to that firearm.

(14) The transportation of a firearm by a person when going directly to, or coming directly from, a gun show or event, as defined in Section 478.100 of Title 27 of the Code of Federal Regulations, for the purpose of lawfully transferring, selling, or loaning that firearm in accordance with subdivision (d) of Section 12072.

(15) The transportation of a firearm by a person in order to utilize paragraph (6) of subdivision (a) of Section 12078 as it pertains to that firearm.

(16) The transportation of a firearm by a person who finds the firearm in order to comply with Article 1 (commencing with Section 2080) of Chapter 4 of Division 3 of the Civil Code as it pertains to that firearm and if that firearm is being transported to a law enforcement agency, the person gives prior notice to the law enforcement agency that he or she is transporting the firearm to the law enforcement agency.

(17) The transportation of a firearm by a person in order to comply with paragraph (2) of subdivision (f) of Section 12072 as it pertains to that firearm.

(18) The transportation of a firearm by a person who finds the firearm and is transporting it to a law enforcement agency for disposition according to law, if he or she gives prior notice to the law enforcement agency that he or she is transporting the firearm to the law enforcement agency for disposition according to law.

(19) The transportation of a firearm by a person in order to comply with paragraph (3) of subdivision (f) of Section 12072 as it pertains to that firearm.

(20) The transportation of a firearm by a person for the purpose of obtaining an identification number or mark assigned for that firearm from the Department of Justice pursuant to Section 12092.

(b) In order for a firearm to be exempted under subdivision (a), while being transported to or from a place, the firearm shall be unloaded, kept in a locked container, as defined in subdivision (d), and the course of travel shall include only those deviations between authorized locations as are reasonably necessary under the circumstances.

(c) This section does not prohibit or limit the otherwise lawful carrying or transportation of any pistol, revolver, or other firearm capable of being concealed upon the person in accordance with this chapter.

(d) As used in this section, "locked container" means a secure container which is fully enclosed and locked by a padlock, keylock, combination lock, or similar locking device. The term "locked container" does not include the utility or glove compartment of a motor vehicle.

Penal Code § 12027.

Section 12025 does not apply to, or affect, any of the following:

(a)(1)(A) Any peace officer, listed in Section 830.1 or 830.2, or subdivision (a) of Section 830.33, whether active or honorably retired, other duly appointed peace officers, honorably retired peace officers listed in subdivision (c) of Section 830.5, other honorably retired peace officers who during the course and scope of their employment as peace officers were authorized to, and did, carry firearms, full-time paid peace officers of other states and the federal government who are carrying out official duties while in California, or any person summoned by any of these officers to assist in making arrests or preserving the peace while he or she is actually engaged in assisting that officer. Any peace officer described in this paragraph who has been honorably retired shall be issued an identification certificate by the law enforcement agency from which the officer has retired. The issuing agency may charge a fee necessary to cover any reasonable expenses incurred by the agency in issuing certificates pursuant to this subdivision. As used in this section and Section 12031, the term "honorably retired" includes all peace officers who have qualified for, and have accepted, a service or disability retirement. For purposes of this section and Section 12031, the term "honorably retired" does not include an officer who has agreed to a service retirement in lieu of termination.

(B) Any officer, except an officer listed in Section 830.1 or 830.2, subdivision (a) of Section 830.33, or subdivision (c) of Section 830.5 who retired prior to January 1, 1981, shall have an endorsement on the identification certificate stating that the issuing agency approves the officer's carrying of a concealed firearm.

(C) No endorsement or renewal endorsement issued pursuant to paragraph (2) shall be effective unless it is in the format set forth in subparagraph (D), except that any peace officer listed in subdivision (f) of Section 830.2 or in subdivision (c) of Section 830.5, who is retired between January 2, 1981, and on or before December 31, 1988, and who is authorized to carry a concealed firearm pursuant to this section, shall not be required to have an endorsement in the format set forth in subparagraph (D) until the time of the issuance, on or after January 1, 1989, of a renewal endorsement pursuant to paragraph (2).

(D) A certificate issued pursuant to this paragraph for persons who are not listed in Section 830.1 or 830.2, subdivision (a) of Section 830.33, or subdivision (c) of Section 830.5 or for persons retiring after January 1, 1981, shall be in the following format: it shall be on a 2 X3 inch card, bear the photograph of the retiree, the retiree's name, date of birth, the date that the retiree retired, name and address of the agency from which the retiree retired, have stamped on it the endorsement "CCW Approved" and the date the endorsement is to be renewed. A certificate issued pursuant to this paragraph shall not be valid as identification for the sale, purchase, or transfer of a firearm.

(E) For purposes of this section and Section 12031, "CCW" means "carry concealed weapons."

(2) A retired peace officer, except an officer listed in Section 830.1 or 830.2, subdivision (a) of Section 830.33, or subdivision (c) of Section 830.5 who retired prior to January 1, 1981, shall petition the issuing agency for the renewal of his or her privilege to carry a concealed firearm every five years. An honorably retired peace officer listed in Section 830.1 or 830.2, subdivision (a) of Section 830.33, or subdivision (c) of Section 830.5 who retired prior to January 1, 1981, shall not be required to obtain an endorsement from the issuing agency to carry a concealed firearm. The agency from which a peace officer is honorably retired may, upon initial retirement of that peace officer, or at any time subsequent thereto, deny or revoke for good cause the retired officer's privilege to carry a concealed firearm. A peace officer who is listed in Section 830.1 or 830.2, subdivision (a) of Section 830.33, or subdivision (c) of Section 830.5 who retired prior to January 1, 1981, shall have his or her privilege to carry a concealed firearm denied or revoked by having the agency from which the officer retired stamp on the officer's identification certificate "No CCW privilege."

(3) An honorably retired peace officer who is listed in subdivision (c) of Section 830.5 and authorized to carry concealed firearms by this subdivision shall meet the training requirements of Section 832 and shall qualify with the firearm at least annually. The individual retired peace officer shall be responsible for maintaining his or her eligibility to carry a concealed firearm. The Department of Justice shall provide subsequent arrest notification pursuant to Section 11105.2 regarding honorably retired peace officers listed in subdivision (c) of Section 830.5 to the agency from which the officer has retired.

(b) The possession or transportation of unloaded pistols, revolvers, or other firearms capable of being concealed upon the person as merchandise by a person who is engaged in the business of manufacturing, importing, wholesaling, repairing, or dealing in firearms and who is licensed to engage in that business or the authorized representative or authorized agent of that person while engaged in the lawful course of the business.

(c) Members of the Army, Navy, Air Force, Coast Guard, or Marine Corps of the United States, or the National Guard, when on duty, or organizations which are by law authorized to purchase or receive those weapons from the United States or this state.

(d) The carrying of unloaded pistols, revolvers, or other firearms capable of being concealed upon the person by duly authorized military or civil organizations while parading, or the members thereof when going to and from the places of meeting of their respective organizations.

(e) Guards or messengers of common carriers, banks, and other financial institutions while actually employed in and about the shipment, transportation, or delivery of any money, treasure, bullion, bonds, or other thing of value within this state.

(f) Members of any club or organization organized for the purpose of practicing shooting at targets upon established target ranges, whether public or private, while the members are using pistols, revolvers, or other firearms capable of being concealed upon the person upon the target ranges, or transporting these firearms unloaded when going to and from the ranges.

(g) Licensed hunters or fishermen carrying pistols, revolvers, or other firearms capable of being concealed upon the person while engaged in hunting or fishing, or transporting those firearms unloaded when going to or returning from the hunting or fishing expedition.

(h) Transportation of unloaded firearms by a person operating a licensed common carrier or an authorized agent or employee thereof when transported in conformance with applicable federal law.

(i) Upon approval of the sheriff of the county in which they reside, honorably retired federal officers or agents of federal law enforcement agencies, including, but not limited to, the Federal Bureau of Investigation, the Secret Service, the United States Customs Service, the Federal Bureau of Alcohol, Tobacco, and Firearms, the Federal Bureau of Narcotics, the Drug Enforcement Administration, the United States Border Patrol, and officers or agents of the Internal Revenue Service who were authorized to carry weapons while on duty, who were assigned to duty within the state for a period of not less than one year, or who retired from active service in the state. Retired federal officers or agents shall provide the sheriff with certification from the agency from which they retired certifying their service in the state, the nature of their retirement, and indicating the agency's concurrence that the retired federal officer or agent should be accorded the privilege of carrying a concealed firearm. Upon that approval, the sheriff shall issue a permit to the retired federal officer or agent indicating that he or she may carry a concealed firearm in accordance with this subdivision. The permit shall be valid for a period not exceeding five years, shall be carried by the retiree while carrying a concealed firearm, and may be revoked for good cause. The sheriff of the county in which the retired federal officer or agent resides may require recertification prior to a permit renewal, and may suspend the privilege for cause. The sheriff may charge a fee necessary to cover any reasonable expenses incurred by the county.

(j) The carrying of a pistol, revolver, or other firearm capable of being concealed upon the person by a person who is authorized to carry that weapon in a concealed manner pursuant to Article 3 (commencing with Section 12050).

Penal Code § 12027.1.

(a)(1)(A)(i) Any peace officer employed by an agency and listed in Section 830.1 or 830.2 or subdivision (c) of Section 830.5 who retired after January 1, 1981, shall have an endorsement on the identification certificate stating that the issuing agency approves the officer's carrying of a concealed and loaded firearm.

(ii) Any peace officer listed in Section 830.1 or 830.2 or subdivision (c) of Section 830.5 who retired prior to January 1, 1981, is authorized to carry a concealed and loaded firearm if the agency issued the officer an identification certificate and the certificate has not been stamped as specified in paragraph (2) of subdivision (a) of Section 12027.

(iii) Peace officers not listed in clause (i) or (ii) who were authorized to, and did, carry firearms during the course and scope of their employment as peace officers, shall have an endorsement on the identification certificate stating that the issuing agency approves the officer's carrying of a concealed and loaded firearm.

(B) An identification certificate authorizing the officer to carry a concealed and loaded firearm or an endorsement on the certificate may be permanently revoked or denied by the issuing agency only upon a showing of good cause. Good cause shall be determined at a hearing, as specified in subdivision (d).

(C) An identification certificate authorizing the officer to carry a concealed and loaded firearm or an endorsement on the certificate may be immediately and temporarily revoked by the issuing agency when the conduct of a retired peace officer compromises public safety. Notice of this temporary revocation shall be effective upon personal service or upon receipt of the notice that was sent by first-class mail, postage prepaid, return receipt requested, to the retiree's last known place of residence. The retiree shall have 15 days to respond to the notification and request a hearing to determine if the temporary revocation should become permanent. A retired peace officer who fails to respond to the notice of hearing within the 15-day period shall forfeit his or her right to a hearing and the authority of the officer to carry a firearm shall be permanently revoked. The retired officer shall immediately return the identification certificate to the issuing agency. If a hearing is requested, good cause for permanent revocation shall be determined at the hearing, as specified in subdivision (d). The hearing shall be held no later than 120 days after the request by the retired officer for a hearing is received. The retiree may waive his or her right to a hearing and immediately return the identification to the issuing agency.

(2) A retired peace officer may have his or her privilege to carry a concealed and loaded firearm revoked or denied by violating any departmental rule, or state or federal law that, if violated by an officer on active duty, would result in that officer's arrest, suspension, or removal from the agency.

(b)(1) An identification certificate authorizing the officer to carry a concealed and loaded firearm or an endorsement may be permanently revoked or denied by the issuing agency only upon a showing of good cause. Good cause shall be determined at a hearing, as specified in subdivision (d).

(2) An identification certificate authorizing the officer to carry a concealed and loaded firearm or an endorsement may be permanently revoked only after a hearing, as specified in subdivision (d). Any retired peace officer whose identification certificate authorizing the officer to carry a concealed and loaded firearm or an endorsement is to be revoked shall have 15 days to respond to the notice of the hearing. Notice of the hearing shall be served either personally on the retiree or sent by first-class mail, postage prepaid, return receipt requested to the retiree's last known place of residence. From the date the retiree signs for the notice or upon the date the notice is served personally on the retiree, the retiree shall have 15 days to respond to the notification. A retired peace officer who fails to respond to the notice of the hearing shall forfeit his or her right to a hearing and the authority of the officer to carry a firearm shall be permanently revoked. The retired officer shall immediately return the identification certificate to the issuing agency. If a hearing is requested, good cause for permanent revocation shall be determined at the hearing, as specified in subdivision (d). The hearing shall be held no later than 120 days after the request by the retired officer for a hearing is received. The retiree may waive his or her right to a hearing and immediately return the identification certificate to the issuing agency.

(3) Issuance of an identification certificate authorizing the officer to carry a concealed and loaded firearm or an endorsement may be denied prior to a hearing. If a hearing is not conducted prior to the denial of an endorsement, a retired peace officer, within 15 days of the denial, shall have the right to request a hearing. A retired peace officer who fails to request a hearing pursuant to this paragraph shall forfeit his or her right to the hearing.

(c) A retired peace officer, when notified of the revocation of his or her privilege to carry a concealed and loaded firearm, after the hearing, or upon forfeiting his or her right to a hearing, shall immediately surrender to the issuing agency his or her identification certificate. The issuing agency shall reissue a new identification certificate without an endorsement. However, if the peace officer retired prior to January 1, 1981, and was at the time of his or her retirement a peace officer listed in Section 830.1 or 830.2 or subdivision (c) of Section 830.5, the issuing agency shall stamp on the identification certificate "No CCW privilege."

(d) Any hearing conducted under this section shall be held before a three-member hearing board. One member of the board shall be selected by the agency and one member shall be selected by the retired peace officer or his or her employee organization. The third member shall be selected jointly by the agency and the retired peace officer or his or her employee organization.

Any decision by the board shall be binding on the agency and the retired peace officer.

(e) No peace officer who is retired after January 1, 1989, because of a psychological disability shall be issued an endorsement to carry a concealed and loaded firearm pursuant to this section.

Penal Code § 12028.

(a) The unlawful concealed carrying upon the person of any explosive substance, other than fixed ammunition, dirk, or dagger, as provided in Section 12020, the unlawful carrying of any handguns in violation of Section 12025, and the unlawful possession or carrying of any item in violation of Section 653k is a nuisance.

(b)(1) Except as provided in paragraph (2), a firearm of any nature owned or possessed in violation of Section 12021, 12021.1, or 12101 of this code, or Chapter 3 (commencing with Section 8100) of Division 5 of the Welfare and Institutions Code, or used in the commission of any misdemeanor as provided in this code, any felony, or an attempt to commit any misdemeanor as provided in this code or any felony, is, upon a conviction of the defendant or upon a juvenile court finding that an offense which would be a misdemeanor or felony if committed by an adult was committed or attempted by the juvenile with the use of a firearm, a nuisance. A finding that the defendant was guilty of the offense but was insane at the time the offense was committed is a conviction for the purposes of this section.

(2) A firearm is not a nuisance pursuant to this subdivision if the firearm owner disposes of his or her firearm pursuant to paragraph (2) of subdivision (d) of Section 12021.

(c) Any weapon described in subdivision (a), or, upon conviction of the defendant or upon a juvenile court finding that an offense which would be a misdemeanor or felony if committed by an adult was committed or attempted by the juvenile with the use of a firearm, any weapon described in subdivision (b) shall be surrendered to the sheriff of a county or the chief of police or other head of a municipal police department of any city or city and county or the chief of police of any campus of the University of California or the California State University or the Commissioner of the California Highway Patrol. For purposes of this subdivision, the Commissioner of the California Highway Patrol shall receive only weapons that were confiscated by a member of the California Highway Patrol. The officers to whom the weapons are surrendered, except upon the certificate of a judge of a court of record, or of the district attorney of the county, that the retention thereof is necessary or proper to the ends of justice, may annually, between the 1st and 10th days of July, in each year, offer the weapons, which the officers in charge of them consider to have value with respect to sporting, recreational, or collection purposes, for sale at public auction to persons licensed pursuant to Section 12071 to engage in businesses involving any weapon purchased. If any weapon has been stolen and is thereafter recovered from the thief or his or her transferee, or is used in a manner as to constitute a nuisance pursuant to subdivision (a) or (b) without the prior knowledge of its lawful owner that it would be so used, it shall not be so offered for sale but shall be restored to the lawful owner, as soon as its use as evidence has been served, upon his or her identification of the weapon and proof of ownership, and after the law enforcement agency has complied with Section 12021.3.

(d) If, under this section, a weapon is not of the type that can be sold to the public, generally, or is not sold pursuant to subdivision (c), the weapon, in the month of July, next succeeding, or sooner, if necessary to conserve local resources including space and utilization of personnel who maintain files and security of those weapons, shall be destroyed so that it can no longer be used as such a weapon except upon the certificate of a judge of a court of record, or of the district attorney of the county, that the retention of it is necessary or proper to the ends of justice.

(e) This section does not apply to any firearm in the possession of the Department of Fish and Game or which was used in the violation of any provision of the Fish and Game Code or any regulation adopted pursuant thereto, or which is forfeited pursuant to Section 5008.6 of the Public Resources Code.

(f) No stolen weapon shall be sold or destroyed pursuant to subdivision (c) or (d) unless reasonable notice is given to its lawful owner, if his or her identity and address can be reasonably ascertained.

Penal Code § 12028.5.

(a) As used in this section, the following definitions shall apply:

(1) "Abuse" means any of the following:

(A) Intentionally or recklessly to cause or attempt to cause bodily injury.

(B) Sexual assault.

(C) To place a person in reasonable apprehension of imminent serious bodily injury to that person or to another.

(D) To molest, attack, strike, stalk, destroy personal property, or violate the terms of a domestic violence protective order issued pursuant to Part 4 (commencing with Section 6300) of Division 10 of the Family Code.

(2) "Domestic violence" means abuse perpetrated against any of the following persons:

(A) A spouse or former spouse.

(B) A cohabitant or former cohabitant, as defined in Section 6209 of the Family Code.

(C) A person with whom the respondent is having or has had a dating or engagement relationship.

(D) A person with whom the respondent has had a child, where the presumption applies that the male parent is the father of the child of the female parent under the Uniform Parentage Act (Part 3 (commencing with Section 7600) of Division 12 of the Family Code).

(E) A child of a party or a child who is the subject of an action under the Uniform Parentage Act, where the presumption applies that the male parent is the father of the child to be protected.

(F) Any other person related by consanguinity or affinity within the second degree.

(3) "Deadly weapon" means any weapon, the possession or concealed carrying of which is prohibited by Section 12020.

(b) A sheriff, undersheriff, deputy sheriff, marshal, deputy marshal, or police officer of a city, as defined in subdivision (a) of Section 830.1, a peace officer of the Department of the California Highway Patrol, as defined in subdivision (a) of Section 830.2, a member of the University of California Police Department, as defined in subdivision (b) of Section 830.2, an officer listed in Section 830.6 while acting in the course and scope of his or her employment as a peace officer, a member of a California State University Police Department, as defined in subdivision (c) of Section 830.2, a peace officer of the Department of Parks and Recreation, as defined in subdivision (f) of Section 830.2, a peace officer, as defined in subdivision (d) of Section 830.31, a peace officer, as defined in subdivisions (a) and (b) of Section 830.32, and a peace officer, as defined in Section 830.5, who is at the scene of a domestic violence incident involving a threat to human life or a physical assault, shall take temporary custody of any firearm or other deadly weapon in plain sight or discovered pursuant to a consensual or other lawful search as necessary for the protection of the peace officer or other persons present. Upon taking custody of a firearm or other deadly weapon, the officer shall give the owner or person who possessed the firearm a receipt. The receipt shall describe the firearm or other deadly weapon and list any identification or serial number on the firearm. The receipt shall indicate where the firearm or other deadly weapon can be recovered, the time limit for recovery as required by this section, and the date after which the owner or possessor can recover the firearm or other deadly weapon. No firearm or other deadly weapon shall be held less than 48 hours. Except as provided in subdivision (f), if a firearm or other deadly weapon is not retained for use as evidence related to criminal charges brought as a result of the domestic violence incident or is not retained because it was illegally possessed, the firearm or other deadly weapon shall be made available to the owner or person who was in lawful possession 48 hours after the seizure or as soon thereafter as possible, but no later than five business days after the owner or person who was in lawful possession demonstrates compliance with Section 12021.3. In any civil action or proceeding for the return of firearms or ammunition or other deadly weapon seized by any state or local law enforcement agency and not returned within five business days following the initial seizure, except as provided in subdivision (d), the court shall allow reasonable attorney's fees to the prevailing party.

(c) Any peace officer, as defined in subdivisions (a) and (b) of Section 830.32, who takes custody of a firearm or deadly weapon pursuant to this section shall deliver the firearm within 24 hours to the city police department or county sheriff's office in the jurisdiction where the college or school is located.

(d) Any firearm or other deadly weapon that has been taken into custody that has been stolen shall be restored to the lawful owner, as soon as its use for evidence has been served, upon his or her identification of the firearm or other deadly weapon and proof of ownership, and after the law enforcement agency has complied with Section 12021.3.

(e) Any firearm or other deadly weapon taken into custody and held by a police, university police, or sheriff's department or by a marshal's office, by a peace officer of the Department of the California Highway Patrol, as defined in subdivision (a) of Section 830.2, by a peace officer of the Department of Parks and Recreation, as defined in subdivision (f) of Section 830.2, by a peace officer, as defined in subdivision (d) of Section 830.31, or by a peace officer, as defined in Section 830.5, for longer than 12 months and not recovered by the owner or person who has lawful possession at the time it was taken into custody, shall be considered a nuisance and sold or destroyed as provided in subdivision (c) of Section 12028. Firearms or other deadly weapons not recovered within 12 months due to an extended hearing process as provided in subdivision (j), are not subject to destruction until the court issues a decision, and then only if the court does not order the return of the firearm or other deadly weapon to the owner.

(f) In those cases in which a law enforcement agency has reasonable cause to believe that the return of a firearm or other deadly weapon would be likely to result in endangering the victim or the person reporting the assault or threat, the agency shall advise the owner of the firearm or other deadly weapon, and within 60 days of the date of seizure, initiate a petition in superior court to determine if the firearm or other deadly weapon should be returned. The law enforcement agency may make an ex parte application stating good cause for an order extending the time to file a petition. Including any extension of time granted in response to an ex parte request, a petition must be filed within 90 days of the date of seizure of the firearm or other deadly weapon.

(g) The law enforcement agency shall inform the owner or person who had lawful possession of the firearm or other deadly weapon, at that person's last known address by registered mail, return receipt requested, that he or she has 30 days from the date of receipt of the notice to respond to the court clerk to confirm his or her desire for a hearing, and that the failure to respond shall result in a default order forfeiting the confiscated firearm or other deadly weapon. For the purposes of this subdivision, the person's last known address shall be presumed to be the address provided to the law enforcement officer by that person at the time of the family violence incident. In the event the person whose firearm or other deadly weapon was seized does not reside at the last address provided to the agency, the agency shall make a diligent, good faith effort to learn the whereabouts of the person and to comply with these notification requirements.

(h) If the person requests a hearing, the court clerk shall set a hearing no later than 30 days from receipt of that request. The court clerk shall notify the person, the law enforcement agency involved, and the district attorney of the date, time, and place of the hearing. Unless it is shown by a preponderance of the evidence that the return of the firearm or other deadly weapon would result in endangering the victim or the person reporting the assault or threat, the court shall order the return of the firearm or other deadly weapon and shall award reasonable attorney's fees to the prevailing party.

(i) If the person does not request a hearing or does not otherwise respond within 30 days of the receipt of the notice, the law enforcement agency may file a petition for an order of default and may dispose of the firearm or other deadly weapon as provided in Section 12028.

(j) If, at the hearing, the court does not order the return of the firearm or other deadly weapon to the owner or person who had lawful possession, that person may petition the court for a second hearing within 12 months from the date of the initial hearing. If there is a petition for a second hearing, unless it is shown by clear and convincing evidence that the return of the firearm or other deadly weapon would result in endangering the victim or the person reporting the assault or threat, the court shall order the return of the firearm or other deadly weapon and shall award reasonable attorney's fees to the prevailing party. If the owner or person who had lawful possession does not petition the court within this 12-month period for a second hearing or is unsuccessful at the second hearing in gaining return of the firearm or other deadly weapon, the firearm or other deadly weapon may be disposed of as provided in Section 12028.

(k) The law enforcement agency, or the individual law enforcement officer, shall not be liable for any act in the good faith exercise of this section.

Penal Code § 12028.7.

(a) When a firearm is taken into custody by a law enforcement officer, the officer shall issue the person who possessed the firearm a receipt describing the firearm, and listing any serial number or other identification on the firearm.

(b) The receipt shall indicate where the firearm may be recovered, any applicable time limit for recovery, and the date after which the owner or possessor may recover the firearm pursuant to Section 12021.3.

(c) Nothing in this section is intended to displace any existing law regarding the seizure or return of firearms.

Penal Code § 12029.

Except as provided in Section 12020, blackjacks, slungshots, billies, nunchakus, sandclubs, sandbags, shurikens, metal knuckles, short-barreled shotguns or short-barreled rifles as defined in Section 12020, and any other item which is listed in subdivision (a) of Section 12020 and is not listed in subdivision (a) of Section 12028 are nuisances, and the Attorney General, district attorney, or city attorney may bring an action to enjoin the manufacture of, importation of, keeping for sale of, offering or exposing for sale, giving, lending, or possession of, any of the foregoing items. These weapons shall be subject to confiscation and summary destruction whenever found within the state. These weapons shall be destroyed in the same manner as other weapons described in Section 12028, except that upon the certification of a judge or of the district attorney that the ends of justice will be subserved thereby, the weapon shall be preserved until the necessity for its use ceases.

Penal Code § 12030.

(a) The officer having custody of any firearms which may be useful to the California National Guard, the Coast Guard Auxiliary, or to any military or naval agency of the federal or state government, including, but not limited to, the California National Guard military museum and resource center, may, upon the authority of the legislative body of the city, city and county, or county by which he or she is employed and the approval of the Adjutant General, deliver the firearms to the commanding officer of a unit of the California National Guard, the Coast Guard Auxiliary, or any other military agency of the state or federal government in lieu of destruction as required by this chapter. The officer delivering the firearms shall take a receipt for them containing a complete description thereof and shall keep the receipt on file in his or her office as a public record.

(b) Any law enforcement agency which has custody of any firearms, or any parts of any firearms, which are subject to destruction as required by this chapter may, in lieu of destroying the weapons, retain and use any of them as may be useful in carrying out the official duties of the agency, or upon approval of a court, may release them to any other law enforcement agency for use in carrying out the official duties of that agency, or may turn over to the criminalistics laboratory of the Department of Justice or the criminalistics laboratory of a police department, sheriff's office, or district attorney's office any weapons which may be useful in carrying out the official duties of their respective agencies.

(c) Any firearm, or part of any firearm, which, rather than being destroyed, is used for official purposes pursuant to this section shall be destroyed by the agency using the weapon when it is no longer needed by the agency for use in carrying out its official duties. In the case of firearms or weaponry donated to the California National Guard military museum and resource center, they may be disposed of pursuant to Section 179 of the Military and Veterans Code.

(d) Any law enforcement agency which has custody of any firearms, or any parts of any firearms, which are subject to destruction as required by this chapter may, in lieu of destroying the firearms, obtain an order from the superior court directing the release of the firearms to the sheriff. The sheriff shall enter those weapons into the Automated Firearms System (AFS), via the California Law Enforcement Telecommunications System, with a complete description of each weapon, including the make, type, category, caliber, and serial number of the firearms, and the name of the academy receiving the weapon entered into the AFS miscellaneous field. The sheriff shall then release the firearms to the basic training academy certified by the Commission on Peace Officer Standards and Training, so that the firearms may be used for instructional purposes in the certified courses. As used in this section, the term "firearms" shall not include destructive devices, as defined in Section 12301. All firearms released to an academy shall be under the care, custody, and control of the particular academy. Any firearm, or part of any firearm, which is not destroyed, and is used for the purposes authorized by this section, shall be returned to the law enforcement agency which had original custody of the firearm when it is no longer needed by the basic training academy, or when the basic training academy is no longer certified by the commission. When those firearms are returned, the law enforcement agency to whom the firearms are returned, shall on the date of the return, enter into the Automated Firearms System (AFS), via the California Law Enforcement Telecommunications System, a complete description of each weapon, including the make, type, category, caliber, and serial number of the firearms, and the name of the entity returning the firearm.

(e) Any law enforcement agency that retains custody of any firearm pursuant to this section or that destroys a firearm pursuant to Section 12028 shall notify the Department of Justice of the retention or destruction. This notification shall consist of a complete description of each firearm, including the name of the manufacturer or brand name, model, caliber, and serial number.

Penal Code § 12031.

(a)(1) A person is guilty of carrying a loaded firearm when he or she carries a loaded firearm on his or her person or in a vehicle while in any public place or on any public street in an incorporated city or in any public place or on any public street in a prohibited area of unincorporated territory.

(2) Carrying a loaded firearm in violation of this section is punishable, as follows:

(A) Where the person previously has been convicted of any felony, or of any crime made punishable by this chapter, as a felony.

(B) Where the firearm is stolen and the person knew or had reasonable cause to believe that it was stolen, as a felony.

(C) Where the person is an active participant in a criminal street gang, as defined in subdivision (a) of Section 186.22, under the Street Terrorism Enforcement and Prevention Act (Chapter 11 (commencing with Section 186.20) of Title 7 of Part 1), as a felony.

(D) Where the person is not in lawful possession of the firearm, as defined in this section, or is within a class of persons prohibited from possessing or acquiring a firearm pursuant to Section 12021 or 12021.1 of this code or Section 8100 or 8103 of the Welfare and Institutions Code, as a felony.

(E) Where the person has been convicted of a crime against a person or property, or of a narcotics or dangerous drug violation, by imprisonment in the state prison, or by imprisonment in a county jail not to exceed one year, by a fine not to exceed one thousand dollars ($1,000), or by both that imprisonment and fine.

(F) Where the person is not listed with the Department of Justice pursuant to Section 11106, as the registered owner of the handgun, by imprisonment in the state prison, or by imprisonment in a county jail not to exceed one year, or by a fine not to exceed one thousand dollars ($1,000), or both that fine and imprisonment.

(G) In all cases other than those specified in subparagraphs (A) to (F), inclusive, as a misdemeanor, punishable by imprisonment in a county jail not to exceed one year, by a fine not to exceed one thousand dollars ($1,000), or by both that imprisonment and fine.

(3) For purposes of this section, "lawful possession of the firearm" means that the person who has possession or custody of the firearm either lawfully acquired and lawfully owns the firearm or has the permission of the lawful owner or person who otherwise has apparent authority to possess or have custody of the firearm. A person who takes a firearm without the permission of the lawful owner or without the permission of a person who has lawful custody of the firearm does not have lawful possession of the firearm.

(4) Nothing in this section shall preclude prosecution under Sections 12021 and 12021.1 of this code, Section 8100 or 8103 of the Welfare and Institutions Code, or any other law with a greater penalty than this section.

(5)(A) Notwithstanding paragraphs (2) and (3) of subdivision (a) of Section 836, a peace officer may make an arrest without a warrant:

(i) When the person arrested has violated this section, although not in the officer's presence.

(ii) Whenever the officer has reasonable cause to believe that the person to be arrested has violated this section, whether or not this section has, in fact, been violated.

(B) A peace officer may arrest a person for a violation of subparagraph (F) of paragraph (2), if the peace officer has probable cause to believe that the person is carrying a loaded handgun in violation of this section and that person is not listed with the Department of Justice pursuant to paragraph (1) of subdivision (c) of Section 11106 as the registered owner of that handgun.

(6)(A) Every person convicted under this section who has previously been convicted of an offense enumerated in Section 12001.6, or of any crime made punishable under this chapter, shall serve a term of at least three months in a county jail, or, if granted probation or if the execution or imposition of sentence is suspended, it shall be a condition thereof that he or she be imprisoned for a period of at least three months.

(B) The court shall apply the three-month minimum sentence except in unusual cases where the interests of justice would best be served by granting probation or suspending the imposition or execution of sentence without the minimum imprisonment required in this subdivision or by granting probation or suspending the imposition or execution of sentence with conditions other than those set forth in this subdivision, in which case, the court shall specify on the record and shall enter on the minutes the circumstances indicating that the interests of justice would best be served by that disposition.

(7) A violation of this section which is punished by imprisonment in a county jail not exceeding one year shall not constitute a conviction of a crime punishable by imprisonment for a term exceeding one year for the purposes of determining federal firearms eligibility under Section 922(g)(1) of Title 18 of the United States Code.

(b) Subdivision (a) shall not apply to any of the following:

(1) Peace officers listed in Section 830.1 or 830.2, or subdivision (a) of Section 830.33, whether active or honorably retired, other duly appointed peace officers, honorably retired peace officers listed in subdivision (c) of Section 830.5, other honorably retired peace officers who during the course and scope of their employment as peace officers were authorized to, and did, carry firearms, full-time paid peace officers of other states and the federal government who are carrying out official duties while in California, or any person summoned by any of those officers to assist in making arrests or preserving the peace while the person is actually engaged in assisting that officer. Any peace officer described in this paragraph who has been honorably retired shall be issued an identification certificate by the law enforcement agency from which the officer has retired. The issuing agency may charge a fee necessary to cover any reasonable expenses incurred by the agency in issuing certificates pursuant to this paragraph and paragraph (3).

Any officer, except an officer listed in Section 830.1 or 830.2, subdivision (a) of Section 830.33, or subdivision (c) of Section 830.5 who retired prior to January 1, 1981, shall have an endorsement on the identification certificate stating that the issuing agency approves the officer's carrying of a loaded firearm.

No endorsement or renewal endorsement issued pursuant to paragraph (2) shall be effective unless it is in the format set forth in subparagraph (D) of paragraph (1) of subdivision (a) of Section 12027, except that any peace officer listed in subdivision (f) of Section 830.2 or in subdivision (c) of Section 830.5, who is retired between January 2, 1981, and on or before December 31, 1988, and who is authorized to carry a loaded firearm pursuant to this section, shall not be required to have an endorsement in the format set forth in subparagraph (D) of paragraph (1) of subdivision (a) of Section 12027 until the time of the issuance, on or after January 1, 1989, of a renewal endorsement pursuant to paragraph (2).

(2) A retired peace officer, except an officer listed in Section 830.1 or 830.2, subdivision (a) of Section 830.33, or subdivision (c) of Section 830.5 who retired prior to January 1, 1981, shall petition the issuing agency for renewal of his or her privilege to carry a loaded firearm every five years. An honorably retired peace officer listed in Section 830.1 or 830.2, subdivision (a) of Section 830.33, or subdivision (c) of Section 830.5 who retired prior to January 1, 1981, shall not be required to obtain an endorsement from the issuing agency to carry a loaded firearm. The agency from which a peace officer is honorably retired may, upon initial retirement of the peace officer, or at any time subsequent thereto, deny or revoke for good cause the retired officer's privilege to carry a loaded firearm. A peace officer who is listed in Section 830.1 or 830.2, subdivision (a) of Section 830.33, or subdivision (c) of Section 830.5 who is retired prior to January 1, 1981, shall have his or her privilege to carry a loaded firearm denied or revoked by having the agency from which the officer retired stamp on the officer's identification certificate "No CCW privilege."

(3) An honorably retired peace officer who is listed in subdivision (c) of Section 830.5 and authorized to carry loaded firearms by this subdivision shall meet the training requirements of Section 832 and shall qualify with the firearm at least annually. The individual retired peace officer shall be responsible for maintaining his or her eligibility to carry a loaded firearm. The Department of Justice shall provide subsequent arrest notification pursuant to Section 11105.2 regarding honorably retired peace officers listed in subdivision (c) of Section 830.5 to the agency from which the officer has retired.

(4) Members of the military forces of this state or of the United States engaged in the performance of their duties.

(5) Persons who are using target ranges for the purpose of practice shooting with a firearm or who are members of shooting clubs while hunting on the premises of those clubs.

(6) The carrying of handguns by persons as authorized pursuant to Article 3 (commencing with Section 12050) of Chapter 1 of Title 2 of Part 4.

(7) Armored vehicle guards, as defined in Section 7521 of the Business and Professions Code,

(A) if hired prior to January 1, 1977, or (B) if hired on or after that date, if they have received a firearms qualification card from the Department of Consumer Affairs, in each case while acting within the course and scope of their employment.

(8) Upon approval of the sheriff of the county in which they reside, honorably retired federal officers or agents of federal law enforcement agencies, including, but not limited to, the Federal Bureau of Investigation, the Secret Service, the United States Customs Service, the Federal Bureau of Alcohol, Tobacco, and Firearms, the Federal Bureau of Narcotics, the Drug Enforcement Administration, the United States Border Patrol, and officers or agents of the Internal Revenue Service who were authorized to carry weapons while on duty, who were assigned to duty within the state for a period of not less than one year, or who retired from active service in the state.

Retired federal officers or agents shall provide the sheriff with certification from the agency from which they retired certifying their service in the state, the nature of their retirement, and indicating the agency's concurrence that the retired federal officer or agent should be accorded the privilege of carrying a loaded firearm.

Upon approval, the sheriff shall issue a permit to the retired federal officer or agent indicating that he or she may carry a loaded firearm in accordance with this paragraph. The permit shall be valid for a period not exceeding five years, shall be carried by the retiree while carrying a loaded firearm, and may be revoked for good cause.

The sheriff of the county in which the retired federal officer or agent resides may require recertification prior to a permit renewal, and may suspend the privilege for cause. The sheriff may charge a fee necessary to cover any reasonable expenses incurred by the county.

(c) Subdivision (a) shall not apply to any of the following who have completed a regular course in firearms training approved by the Commission on Peace Officer Standards and Training:

(1) Patrol special police officers appointed by the police commission of any city, county, or city and county under the express terms of its charter who also, under the express terms of the charter, (A) are subject to suspension or dismissal after a hearing on charges duly filed with the commission after a fair and impartial trial, (B) are not less than 18 years of age or more than 40 years of age, (C) possess physical qualifications prescribed by the commission, and (D) are designated by the police commission as the owners of a certain beat or territory as may be fixed from time to time by the police commission.

(2) The carrying of weapons by animal control officers or zookeepers, regularly compensated as such by a governmental agency when acting in the course and scope of their employment and when designated by a local ordinance or, if the governmental agency is not authorized to act by ordinance, by a resolution, either individually or by class, to carry the weapons, or by persons who are authorized to carry the weapons pursuant to Section 14502 of the Corporations Code, while actually engaged in the performance of their duties pursuant to that section.

(3) Harbor police officers designated pursuant to Section 663.5 of the Harbors and Navigation Code.

(d) Subdivision (a) shall not apply to any of the following who have been issued a certificate pursuant to Section 12033. The certificate shall not be required of any person who is a peace officer, who has completed all training required by law for the exercise of his or her power as a peace officer, and who is employed while not on duty as a peace officer.

(1) Guards or messengers of common carriers, banks, and other financial institutions while actually employed in and about the shipment, transportation, or delivery of any money, treasure, bullion, bonds, or other thing of value within this state.

(2) Guards of contract carriers operating armored vehicles pursuant to California Highway Patrol and Public Utilities Commission authority (A) if hired prior to January 1, 1977, or (B) if hired on or after January 1, 1977, if they have completed a course in the carrying and use of firearms which meets the standards prescribed by the Department of Consumer Affairs.

(3) Private investigators and private patrol operators who are licensed pursuant to Chapter 11.5 (commencing with Section 7512) of, and alarm company operators who are licensed pursuant to Chapter 11.6 (commencing with Section 7590) of, Division 3 of the Business and Professions Code, while acting within the course and scope of their employment.

(4) Uniformed security guards or night watch persons employed by any public agency, while acting within the scope and course of their employment.

(5) Uniformed security guards, regularly employed and compensated in that capacity by persons engaged in any lawful business, and uniformed alarm agents employed by an alarm company operator, while actually engaged in protecting and preserving the property of their employers or on duty or en route to or from their residences or their places of employment, and security guards and alarm agents en route to or from their residences or employer-required range training. Nothing in this paragraph shall be construed to prohibit cities and counties from enacting ordinances requiring alarm agents to register their names.

(6) Uniformed employees of private patrol operators and private investigators licensed pursuant to Chapter 11.5 (commencing with Section 7512) of Division 3 of the Business and Professions Code, while acting within the course and scope of their employment.

(e) In order to determine whether or not a firearm is loaded for the purpose of enforcing this section, peace officers are authorized to examine any firearm carried by anyone on his or her person or in a vehicle while in any public place or on any public street in an incorporated city or prohibited area of an unincorporated territory. Refusal to allow a peace officer to inspect a firearm pursuant to this section constitutes probable cause for arrest for violation of this section.

(f) As used in this section, "prohibited area" means any place where it is unlawful to discharge a weapon.

(g) A firearm shall be deemed to be loaded for the purposes of this section when there is an unexpended cartridge or shell, consisting of a case that holds a charge of powder and a bullet or shot, in, or attached in any manner to, the firearm, including, but not limited to, in the firing chamber, magazine, or clip thereof attached to the firearm; except that a muzzle-loader firearm shall be deemed to be loaded when it is capped or primed and has a powder charge and ball or shot in the barrel or cylinder.

(h) Nothing in this section shall prevent any person engaged in any lawful business, including a nonprofit organization, or any officer, employee, or agent authorized by that person for lawful purposes connected with that business, from having a loaded firearm within the person's place of business, or any person in lawful possession of private property from having a loaded firearm on that property.

(i) Nothing in this section shall prevent any person from carrying a loaded firearm in an area within an incorporated city while engaged in hunting, provided that the hunting at that place and time is not prohibited by the city council.

(j)(1) Nothing in this section is intended to preclude the carrying of any loaded firearm, under circumstances where it would otherwise be lawful, by a person who reasonably believes that the person or property of himself or herself or of another is in immediate, grave danger and that the carrying of the weapon is necessary for the preservation of that person or property. As used in this subdivision, "immediate" means the brief interval before and after the local law enforcement agency, when reasonably possible, has been notified of the danger and before the arrival of its assistance.

(2) A violation of this section is justifiable when a person who possesses a firearm reasonably believes that he or she is in grave danger because of circumstances forming the basis of a current restraining order issued by a court against another person or persons who has or have been found to pose a threat to his or her life or safety. This paragraph may not apply when the circumstances involve a mutual restraining order issued pursuant to Division 10 (commencing with Section 6200) of the Family Code absent a factual finding of a specific threat to the person's life or safety. It is not the intent of the Legislature to limit, restrict, or narrow the application of current statutory or judicial authority to apply this or other justifications to defendants charged with violating Section 12025 or of committing other similar offenses.

Upon trial for violating this section, the trier of fact shall determine whether the defendant was acting out of a reasonable belief that he or she was in grave danger.

(k) Nothing in this section is intended to preclude the carrying of a loaded firearm by any person while engaged in the act of making or attempting to make a lawful arrest.

(l) Nothing in this section shall prevent any person from having a loaded weapon, if it is otherwise lawful, at his or her place of residence, including any temporary residence or campsite.

Penal Code § 12031.1.

Nothing in Section 12031 shall prevent any person from storing aboard any vessel or aircraft any loaded or unloaded rocket, rocket propelled projectile launcher, or similar device designed primarily for emergency or distress signaling purposes, or from possessing such a device while in a permitted hunting area or traveling to or from such area and carrying a valid California permit or license to hunt.

Penal Code § 12032.

Notwithstanding any provision of law or of any local ordinance to the contrary, when any firearm is in the possession of any officer of the state, or of a county, city and county or city, or of any campus of the University of California or the California State University, and the firearm is an exhibit filed in any criminal action or proceeding which is no longer needed or is unclaimed or abandoned property, which has been in the possession of the officer for at least 180 days, the firearm shall be sold, or destroyed, as provided for in Section 12028. This section shall not apply to any firearm in the possession of the Department of Fish and Game or which was used in the violation of any provision of law, or regulation thereunder, in the Fish and Game Code.

Penal Code § 12033.

The Department of Consumer Affairs may issue a certificate to any person referred to in subdivision (d) of Section 12031, upon notification by the school where the course was completed, that the person has successfully completed a course in the carrying and use of firearms and a course of training in the exercise of the powers of arrest which meet the standards prescribed by the department pursuant to Section 7583.5 of the Business and Professions Code.

Penal Code § 12034.

(a) It is a misdemeanor for a driver of any motor vehicle or the owner of any motor vehicle, whether or not the owner of the vehicle is occupying the vehicle, knowingly to permit any other person to carry into or bring into the vehicle a firearm in violation of Section 12031 of this code or Section 2006 of the Fish and Game Code.

(b) Any driver or owner of any vehicle, whether or not the owner of the vehicle is occupying the vehicle, who knowingly permits any other person to discharge any firearm from the vehicle is punishable by imprisonment in the county jail for not more than one year or in state prison for 16 months or two or three years.

(c) Any person who willfully and maliciously discharges a firearm from a motor vehicle at another person other than an occupant of a motor vehicle is guilty of a felony punishable by imprisonment in state prison for three, five, or seven years.

(d) Except as provided in Section 3002 of the Fish and Game Code, any person who willfully and maliciously discharges a firearm from a motor vehicle is guilty of a public offense punishable by imprisonment in the county jail for not more than one year or in the state prison.

Penal Code § 12035.

(a) As used in this section, the following definitions apply:

(1) "Locking device" means a device that is designed to prevent the firearm from functioning and when applied to the firearm, renders the firearm inoperable.

(2) "Loaded firearm" has the same meaning as set forth in subdivision (g) of Section 12031.

(3) "Child" means a person under 18 years of age.

(4) "Great bodily injury" has the same meaning as set forth in Section 12022.7.

(5) "Locked container" has the same meaning as set forth in subdivision (d) of Section 12026.2.

(b)(1) Except as provided in subdivision (c), a person commits the crime of "criminal storage of a firearm of the first degree" if he or she keeps any loaded firearm within any premises that are under his or her custody or control and he or she knows or reasonably should know that a child is likely to gain access to the firearm without the permission of the child's parent or legal guardian and the child obtains access to the firearm and thereby causes death or great bodily injury to himself, herself, or any other person.

(2) Except as provided in subdivision (c), a person commits the crime of "criminal storage of a firearm of the second degree" if he or she keeps any loaded firearm within any premises that are under his or her custody or control and he or she knows or reasonably should know that a child is likely to gain access to the firearm without the permission of the child's parent or legal guardian and the child obtains access to the firearm and thereby causes injury, other than great bodily injury, to himself, herself, or any other person, or carries the firearm either to a public place or in violation of Section 417.

(c) Subdivision (b) shall not apply whenever any of the following occurs:

(1) The child obtains the firearm as a result of an illegal entry to any premises by any person.

(2) The firearm is kept in a locked container or in a location that a reasonable person would believe to be secure.

(3) The firearm is carried on the person or within such a close proximity thereto that the individual can readily retrieve and use the firearm as if carried on the person.

(4) The firearm is locked with a locking device that has rendered the firearm inoperable.

(5) The person is a peace officer or a member of the armed forces or National Guard and the child obtains the firearm during, or incidental to, the performance of the person's duties.

(6) The child obtains, or obtains and discharges, the firearm in a lawful act of self-defense or defense of another person, or persons.

(7) The person who keeps a loaded firearm on any premise that is under his or her custody or control has no reasonable expectation, based on objective facts and circumstances, that a child is likely to be present on the premises.

(d) Criminal storage of a firearm is punishable as follows:

(1) Criminal storage of a firearm in the first degree, by imprisonment in the state prison for 16 months, or two or three years, by a fine not exceeding ten thousand dollars ($10,000), or by both that imprisonment and fine; or by imprisonment in a county jail not exceeding one year, by a fine not exceeding one thousand dollars ($1,000), or by both that fine and imprisonment.

(2) Criminal storage of a firearm in the second degree, by imprisonment in a county jail not exceeding one year, by a fine not exceeding one thousand dollars ($1,000), or by both that imprisonment and fine.

(e) If the person who allegedly violated this section is the parent or guardian of a child who is injured or who dies as the result of an accidental shooting, the district attorney shall consider, among other factors, the impact of the injury or death on the person alleged to have violated this section when deciding whether to prosecute an alleged violation. It is the Legislature's intent that a parent or guardian of a child who is injured or who dies as the result of an accidental shooting shall be prosecuted only in those instances in which the parent or guardian behaved in a grossly negligent manner or where similarly egregious circumstances exist. This subdivision shall not otherwise restrict, in any manner, the factors that a district attorney may consider when deciding whether to prosecute alleged violations of this section.

(f) If the person who allegedly violated this section is the parent or guardian of a child who is injured or who dies as the result of an accidental shooting, no arrest of the person for the alleged violation of this section shall occur until at least seven days after the date upon which the accidental shooting occurred. In addition to the limitation contained in this subdivision, a law enforcement officer shall consider the health status of a child who suffers great bodily injury as the result of an accidental shooting prior to arresting a person for a violation of this section, if the person to be arrested is the parent or guardian of the injured child. The intent of this subdivision is to encourage law enforcement officials to delay the arrest of a parent or guardian of a seriously injured child while the child remains on life-support equipment or is in a similarly critical medical condition.

(g)(1) The fact that the person who allegedly violated this section attended a firearm safety training course prior to the purchase of the firearm that is obtained by a child in violation of this section shall be considered a mitigating factor by a district attorney when he or she is deciding whether to prosecute the alleged violation.

(2) In any action or trial commenced under this section, the fact that the person who allegedly violated this section attended a firearm safety training course prior to the purchase of the firearm that is obtained by a child in violation of this section, shall be admissible.

(h) Every person licensed under Section 12071 shall post within the licensed premises the notice required by paragraph (7) of subdivision (b) of that section, disclosing the duty imposed by this section upon any person who keeps a loaded firearm.

Penal Code § 12036.

(a) As used in this section, the following definitions shall apply:

(1) "Locking device" means a device that is designed to prevent the firearm from functioning and when applied to the firearm, renders the firearm inoperable.

(2) "Child" means a person under the age of 18 years.

(3) "Off-premises" means premises other than the premises where the firearm was stored.

(4) "Locked container" has the same meaning as set forth in subdivision (d) of Section 12026.2.

(b) A person who keeps a pistol, revolver, or other firearm capable of being concealed upon the person, loaded or unloaded, within any premises that are under his or her custody or control and he or she knows or reasonably should know that a child is likely to gain access to that firearm without the permission of the child's parent or legal guardian and the child obtains access to that firearm and thereafter carries that firearm off-premises, shall be punished by imprisonment in a county jail not exceeding one year, by a fine not exceeding one thousand dollars ($1,000), or by both that imprisonment and fine.

(c) A person who keeps any firearm within any premises that is under his or her custody or control and he or she knows or reasonably should know that a child is likely to gain access to the firearm without the permission of the child's parent or legal guardian and the child obtains access to the firearm and thereafter carries that firearm off-premises to any public or private preschool, elementary school, middle school, high school, or to any school-sponsored event, activity, or performance whether occurring on school grounds or elsewhere, shall be punished by imprisonment in a county jail not exceeding one year, by a fine not exceeding five thousand dollars ($5,000), or by both that imprisonment and fine.

(d) A pistol, revolver, or other firearm capable of being concealed upon the person that a child gains access to and carries off-premises in violation of this section shall be deemed "used in the commission of any misdemeanor as provided in this code or any felony" for the purpose of subdivision (b) of Section 12028 regarding the authority to confiscate firearms and other deadly weapons as a nuisance.

(e) This section shall not apply if any one of the following circumstances exists:

(1) The child obtains the firearm as a result of an illegal entry into any premises by any person.

(2) The firearm is kept in a locked container or in a location that a reasonable person would believe to be secure.

(3) The firearm is locked with a locking device that has rendered the firearm inoperable.

(4) The firearm is carried on the person within such a close range that the individual can readily retrieve and use the firearm as if carried on the person.

(5) The person is a peace officer or a member of the Armed Forces or National Guard and the child obtains the firearm during, or incidental to, the performance of the person's duties.

(6) The child obtains, or obtains and discharges, the firearm in a lawful act of self-defense or defense of another person or persons.

(7) The person who keeps a firearm has no reasonable expectation, based on objective facts and circumstances, that a child is likely to be present on the premises.

(f) If the person who allegedly violated this section is the parent or guardian of a child who is injured or who dies as the result of an accidental shooting, the district attorney shall consider, among other factors, the impact of the injury or death on the person alleged to have violated this section when deciding whether to prosecute the alleged violation. It is the Legislature's intent that a parent or guardian of a child who is injured or who dies as the result of an accidental shooting shall be prosecuted only in those instances in which the parent or guardian behaved in a grossly negligent manner or where similarly egregious circumstances exist. This subdivision shall not otherwise restrict, in any manner, the factors that a district attorney may consider when deciding whether to prosecute alleged violations of this section.

(g) If the person who allegedly violated this section is the parent or guardian of a child who is injured or who dies as the result of an accidental shooting, no arrest of the person for the alleged violation of this section shall occur until at least seven days after the date upon which the accidental shooting occurred. In addition to the limitation contained in this subdivision, a law enforcement officer shall consider the health status of a child who suffers great bodily injury as the result of an accidental shooting prior to arresting a person for a violation of this section, if the person to be arrested is the parent or guardian of the injured child. The intent of this subdivision is to encourage law enforcement officials to delay the arrest of a parent or guardian of a seriously injured child while the child remains on life-support equipment or is in a similarly critical medical condition.

(h)(1) The fact that the person who allegedly violated this section attended a firearm safety training course prior to the purchase of the firearm that is obtained by a child in violation of this section shall be considered a mitigating factor by a district attorney when he or she is deciding whether to prosecute the alleged violation.

(2) In any action or trial commenced under this section, the fact that the person who allegedly violated this section attended a firearm safety training course prior to the purchase of the firearm that is obtained by a child in violation of this section, shall be admissible.

(i) Every person licensed under Section 12071 shall post within the licensed premises the notice required by paragraph (7) of subdivision (b) of that section, disclosing the duty imposed by this section upon any person who keeps any firearm.

Penal Code § 12039.

The Attorney General shall provide the Legislature on or before April 15 of each year, commencing in 1998, a written report on the specific types of firearms used in the commission of crimes based upon information obtained from state and local crime laboratories. The report shall include all of the following information regarding crimes in which firearms were used:

(a) A description of the relative occurrence of firearms most frequently used in the commission of violent crimes, distinguishing whether the firearms used were handguns, rifles, shotguns, assault weapons, or other related types of weapons.

(b) A description of specific types of firearms that are used in homicides or street gang and drug trafficking crimes.

(c) The frequency with which stolen firearms were used in the commission of the crimes.

(d) The frequency with which fully automatic firearms were used in the commission of the crimes.

(e) Any trends of importance such as those involving specialized ammunition or firearms modifications, such as conversion to a fully automatic weapon, removal of serial number, shortening of barrel, or use of a suppressor.

Penal Code § 12040.

(a) A person commits criminal possession of a firearm when he or she carries a firearm in a public place or on any public street while masked so as to hide his or her identity.

(b) Criminal possession of a firearm is punishable by imprisonment in the state prison or by imprisonment in a county jail not to exceed one year.

(c) Subdivision (a) shall not apply to the following:

(1) A peace officer who is in the performance of his or her duties.

(2) Full-time paid peace officers of other states and the federal government who are carrying out official duties while in this state.

(3) Any person summoned by any of the officers enumerated in paragraph (1) or (2) to assist in making arrests or preserving the peace while he or she is actually engaged in assisting that officer.

(4) The possession of an unloaded firearm or a firearm loaded with blank ammunition by an authorized participant in, or while rehearsing for, a motion picture, television, video production, entertainment event, entertainment activity, or lawfully organized and conducted activity when the participant lawfully uses the firearm as part of that production, event, or activity.

(5) The possession of a firearm by a licensed hunter while actually engaged in lawful hunting, or while going directly to or returning directly from the hunting expedition.

Penal Code § 12050.

(a)(1)(A) The sheriff of a county, upon proof that the person applying is of good moral character, that good cause exists for the issuance, and that the person applying satisfies any one of the conditions specified in subparagraph (D) and has completed a course of training as described in subparagraph (E), may issue to that person a license to carry a pistol, revolver, or other firearm capable of being concealed upon the person in either one of the following formats:

(i) A license to carry concealed a pistol, revolver, or other firearm capable of being concealed upon the person.

(ii) Where the population of the county is less than 200,000 persons according to the most recent federal decennial census, a license to carry loaded and exposed in only that county a pistol, revolver, or other firearm capable of being concealed upon the person.

(B) The chief or other head of a municipal police department of any city or city and county, upon proof that the person applying is of good moral character, that good cause exists for the issuance, and that the person applying is a resident of that city and has completed a course of training as described in subparagraph (E), may issue to that person a license to carry a pistol, revolver, or other firearm capable of being concealed upon the person in either one of the following formats:

(i) A license to carry concealed a pistol, revolver, or other firearm capable of being concealed upon the person.

(ii) Where the population of the county in which the city is located is less than 200,000 persons according to the most recent federal decennial census, a license to carry loaded and exposed in only that county a pistol, revolver, or other firearm capable of being concealed upon the person.

(C) The sheriff of a county or the chief or other head of a municipal police department of any city or city and county, upon proof that the person applying is of good moral character, that good cause exists for the issuance, and that the person applying is a person who has been deputized or appointed as a peace officer pursuant to subdivision (a) or (b) of Section 830.6 by that sheriff or that chief of police or other head of a municipal police department, may issue to that person a license to carry concealed a pistol, revolver, or other firearm capable of being concealed upon the person. Direct or indirect fees for the issuance of a license pursuant to this subparagraph may be waived. The fact that an applicant for a license to carry a pistol, revolver, or other firearm capable of being concealed upon the person has been deputized or appointed as a peace officer pursuant to subdivision (a) or (b) of Section 830.6 shall be considered only for the purpose of issuing a license pursuant to this subparagraph, and shall not be considered for the purpose of issuing a license pursuant to subparagraph (A) or (B).

(D) For the purpose of subparagraph (A), the applicant shall satisfy any one of the following:

(i) Is a resident of the county or a city within the county.

(ii) Spends a substantial period of time in the applicant's principal place of employment or business in the county or a city within the county.

(E)(i) For new license applicants, the course of training may be any course acceptable to the licensing authority, shall not exceed 16 hours, and shall include instruction on at least firearm safety and the law regarding the permissible use of a firearm. Notwithstanding this clause, the licensing authority may require a community college course certified by the Commission on Peace Officer Standards and Training, up to a maximum of 24 hours, but only if required uniformly of all license applicants without exception.

(ii) For license renewal applicants, the course of training may be any course acceptable to the licensing authority, shall be no less than four hours, and shall include instruction on at least firearm safety and the law regarding the permissible use of a firearm. No course of training shall be required for any person certified by the licensing authority as a trainer for purposes of this subparagraph, in order for that person to renew a license issued pursuant to this section.

(2)(A)(i) Except as otherwise provided in clause (ii), subparagraphs (C) and (D) of this paragraph, and subparagraph (B) of paragraph (4) of subdivision (f), a license issued pursuant to subparagraph (A) or (B) of paragraph (1) is valid for any period of time not to exceed two years from the date of the license.

(ii) If the licensee's place of employment or business was the basis for issuance of the license pursuant to subparagraph (A) of paragraph (1), the license is valid for any period of time not to exceed 90 days from the date of the license. The license shall be valid only in the county in which the license was originally issued. The licensee shall give a copy of this license to the licensing authority of the city, county, or city and county in which he or she resides. The licensing authority that originally issued the license shall inform the licensee verbally and in writing in at least 16-point type of this obligation to give a copy of the license to the licensing authority of the city, county, or city and county of residence. Any application to renew or extend the validity of, or reissue, the license may be granted only upon the concurrence of the licensing authority that originally issued the license and the licensing authority of the city, county, or city and county in which the licensee resides.

(B) A license issued pursuant to subparagraph (C) of paragraph (1) to a peace officer appointed pursuant to Section 830.6 is valid for any period of time not to exceed four years from the date of the license, except that the license shall be invalid upon the conclusion of the person's appointment pursuant to Section 830.6 if the four-year period has not otherwise expired or any other condition imposed pursuant to this section does not limit the validity of the license to a shorter time period.

(C) A license issued pursuant to subparagraph (A) or (B) of paragraph (1) is valid for any period of time not to exceed three years from the date of the license if the license is issued to any of the following individuals:

(i) A judge of a California court of record.

(ii) A full-time court commissioner of a California court of record.

(iii) A judge of a federal court.

(iv) A magistrate of a federal court.

(D) A license issued pursuant to subparagraph (A) or (B) of paragraph (1) is valid for any period of time not to exceed four years from the date of the license if the license is issued to a custodial officer who is an employee of the sheriff as provided in Section 831.5, except that the license shall be invalid upon the conclusion of the person's employment pursuant to Section 831.5 if the four-year period has not otherwise expired or any other condition imposed pursuant to this section does not limit the validity of the license to a shorter time period.

(3) For purposes of this subdivision, a city or county may be considered an applicant's "principal place of employment or business" only if the applicant is physically present in the jurisdiction during a substantial part of his or her working hours for purposes of that employment or business.

(b) A license may include any reasonable restrictions or conditions which the issuing authority deems warranted, including restrictions as to the time, place, manner, and circumstances under which the person may carry a pistol, revolver, or other firearm capable of being concealed upon the person.

(c) Any restrictions imposed pursuant to subdivision (b) shall be indicated on any license issued.

(d) A license shall not be issued if the Department of Justice determines that the person is prohibited by state or federal law from possessing, receiving, owning, or purchasing a firearm.

(e)(1) The license shall be revoked by the local licensing authority if at any time either the local licensing authority is notified by the Department of Justice that a licensee is prohibited by state or federal law from owning or purchasing firearms, or the local licensing authority determines that the person is prohibited by state or federal law from possessing, receiving, owning, or purchasing a firearm.

(2) If at any time the Department of Justice determines that a licensee is prohibited by state or federal law from possessing, receiving, owning, or purchasing a firearm, the department shall immediately notify the local licensing authority of the determination.

(3) If the local licensing authority revokes the license, the Department of Justice shall be notified of the revocation pursuant to Section 12053. The licensee shall also be immediately notified of the revocation in writing.

(f)(1) A person issued a license pursuant to this section may apply to the licensing authority for an amendment to the license to do one or more of the following:

(A) Add or delete authority to carry a particular pistol, revolver, or other firearm capable of being concealed upon the person.

(B) Authorize the licensee to carry concealed a pistol, revolver, or other firearm capable of being concealed upon the person.

(C) If the population of the county is less than 200,000 persons according to the most recent federal decennial census, authorize the licensee to carry loaded and exposed in only that county a pistol, revolver, or other firearm capable of being concealed upon the person.

(D) Change any restrictions or conditions on the license, including restrictions as to the time, place, manner, and circumstances under which the person may carry a pistol, revolver, or other firearm capable of being concealed upon the person.

(2) When the licensee changes his or her address, the license shall be amended to reflect the new address and a new license shall be issued pursuant to paragraph (3).

(3) If the licensing authority amends the license, a new license shall be issued to the licensee reflecting the amendments.

(4)(A) The licensee shall notify the licensing authority in writing within 10 days of any change in the licensee's place of residence.

(B) If the license is one to carry concealed a pistol, revolver, or other firearm capable of being concealed upon the person, then it may not be revoked solely because the licensee changes his or her place of residence to another county if the licensee has not breached any conditions or restrictions set forth in the license and has not become prohibited by state or federal law from possessing, receiving, owning, or purchasing a firearm. However, any license issued pursuant to subparagraph (A) or (B) of paragraph (1) of subdivision (a) shall expire 90 days after the licensee moves from the county of issuance if the licensee's place of residence was the basis for issuance of the license.

(C) If the license is one to carry loaded and exposed a pistol, revolver, or other firearm capable of being concealed upon the person, the license shall be revoked immediately if the licensee changes his or her place of residence to another county.

(5) An amendment to the license does not extend the original expiration date of the license and the license shall be subject to renewal at the same time as if the license had not been amended.

(6) An application to amend a license does not constitute an application for renewal of the license.

(g) Nothing in this article shall preclude the chief or other head of a municipal police department of any city from entering an agreement with the sheriff of the county in which the city is located for the sheriff to process all applications for licenses, renewals of licenses, and amendments to licenses, pursuant to this article.

Penal Code § 12050.2.

Within three months of the effective date of the act adding this section, each licensing authority shall publish and make available a written policy summarizing the provisions of subparagraphs (A) and (B) of paragraph (1) of subdivision (a) of Section 12050.

Penal Code § 12051.

(a)(1) The standard application form for licenses described in paragraph (3) shall require information from the applicant including, but not limited to, the name, occupation, residence and business address of the applicant, his or her age, height, weight, color of eyes and hair, and reason for desiring a license to carry the weapon. Applications for licenses shall be filed in writing, and signed by the applicant. Any license issued upon the application shall set forth the licensee's name, occupation, residence and business address, his or her age, height, weight, color of eyes and hair, the reason for desiring a license to carry the weapon, and shall, in addition, contain a description of the weapon or weapons authorized to be carried, giving the name of the manufacturer, the serial number, and the caliber. The license issued to the licensee may be laminated.

(2) Applications for amendments to licenses shall be filed in writing and signed by the applicant, and shall state what type of amendment is sought pursuant to subdivision (f) of Section 12050 and the reason for desiring the amendment.

(3)(A) Applications for amendments to licenses, applications for licenses, amendments to licenses, and licenses shall be uniform throughout the state, upon forms to be prescribed by the Attorney General. The Attorney General shall convene a committee composed of one representative of the California State Sheriffs' Association, one representative of the California Police Chiefs' Association, and one representative of the Department of Justice to review, and as deemed appropriate, revise the standard application form for licenses. The committee shall meet for this purpose if two of the committee's members deem that necessary. The application shall include a section summarizing the statutory provisions of state law that result in the automatic denial of a license.

(B) The forms shall contain a provision whereby the applicant attests to the truth of statements contained in the application.

(C) An applicant shall not be required to complete any additional application or form for a license, or to provide any information other than that necessary to complete the standard application form described in subparagraph (A), except to clarify or interpret information provided by the applicant on the standard application form.

(D) The standard application form described in subparagraph (A) is deemed to be a local form expressly exempt from the requirements of the Administrative Procedures Act, Chapter 3.5 (commencing with Section 11340) of Part 1 of Division 3 of Title 2 of the Government Code.

(b) Any person who files an application required by subdivision (a) knowing that statements contained therein are false is guilty of a misdemeanor.

(c) Any person who knowingly makes a false statement on the application regarding any of the following shall be guilty of a felony:

(1) The denial or revocation of a license, or the denial of an amendment to a license, issued pursuant to Section 12050.

(2) A criminal conviction.

(3) A finding of not guilty by reason of insanity.

(4) The use of a controlled substance.
(5) A dishonorable discharge from military service.
(6) A commitment to a mental institution.
(7) A renunciation of United States citizenship.

Penal Code § 12052.

(a) The fingerprints of each applicant shall be taken and two copies on forms prescribed by the Department of Justice shall be forwarded to the department. Upon receipt of the fingerprints and the fee as prescribed in Section 12054, the department shall promptly furnish the forwarding licensing authority a report of all data and information pertaining to any applicant of which there is a record in its office, including information as to whether the person is prohibited by state or federal law from possessing, receiving, owning, or purchasing a firearm. No license shall be issued by any licensing authority until after receipt of the report from the department.

(b) However, if the license applicant has previously applied to the same licensing authority for a license to carry firearms pursuant to Section 12050 and the applicant's fingerprints and fee have been previously forwarded to the Department of Justice, as provided by this section, the licensing authority shall note the previous identification numbers and other data that would provide positive identification in the files of the Department of Justice on the copy of any subsequent license submitted to the department in conformance with Section 12053 and no additional application form or fingerprints shall be required.

(c) If the license applicant has a license issued pursuant to Section 12050 and the applicant's fingerprints have been previously forwarded to the Department of Justice, as provided in this section, the licensing authority shall note the previous identification numbers and other data that would provide positive identification in the files of the Department of Justice on the copy of any subsequent license submitted to the department in conformance with Section 12053 and no additional fingerprints shall be required.

Penal Code § 12052.5.

The licensing authority shall give written notice to the applicant indicating if the license is approved or denied within 90 days of the initial application for a new license or a license renewal or 30 days after receipt of the applicant's criminal background check from the Department of Justice, whichever is later.

Penal Code § 12053.

(a) A record of the following shall be maintained in the office of the licensing authority:
(1) The denial of a license.
(2) The denial of an amendment to a license.
(3) The issuance of a license.
(4) The amendment of a license.
(5) The revocation of a license.

(b) Copies of each of the following shall be filed immediately by the issuing officer or authority with the Department of Justice:
(1) The denial of a license.
(2) The denial of an amendment to a license.
(3) The issuance of a license.
(4) The amendment of a license.
(5) The revocation of a license.

(c) Commencing on or before January 1, 2000, and annually thereafter, each licensing authority shall submit to the Attorney General the total number of licenses issued to peace officers, pursuant to subparagraph (C) of paragraph (1) of subdivision (a) of Section 12050, and to judges, pursuant to subparagraph (A) or (B) of paragraph (1) of subdivision (a) of Section 12050. The Attorney General shall collect and record the information submitted pursuant to this subdivision by county and licensing authority.

Penal Code § 12054.

(a) Each applicant for a new license or for the renewal of a license shall pay at the time of filing his or her application a fee determined by the Department of Justice not to exceed the application processing costs of the Department of Justice for the direct costs of furnishing the report required by Section 12052. After the department establishes fees sufficient to reimburse the department for processing costs, fees charged shall increase at a rate not to exceed the legislatively approved annual cost-of-living adjustments for the department's budget. The officer receiving the application and the fee shall transmit the fee, with the fingerprints if required, to the Department of Justice. The licensing authority of any city, city and county, or county may charge an additional fee in an amount equal to the actual costs for processing the application for a new license, excluding fingerprint and training costs, but in no case to exceed one hundred dollars ($100), and shall transmit the additional fee, if any, to the city, city and county, or county treasury. The first 20 percent of this additional local fee may be collected upon filing of the initial application. The balance of the fee shall be collected only upon issuance of the license. The licensing authority may charge an additional fee, not to exceed twenty-five dollars ($25), for processing the application for a license renewal, and shall transmit an additional fee, if any, to the city, city and county, or county treasury. These local fees may be increased at a rate not to exceed any increase in the California Consumer Price Index as compiled and reported by the California Department of Industrial Relations.

(b) In the case of an amended license pursuant to subdivision (f) of Section 12050, the licensing authority of any city, city and county, or county may charge a fee, not to exceed ten dollars ($10), except that the fee may be increased at a rate not to exceed any increase in the California Consumer Price Index as compiled and reported by the California Department of Industrial Relations, for processing the amended license and shall transmit the fee to the city, city and county, or county treasury.

(c) If psychological testing on the initial application is required by the licensing authority, the license applicant shall be referred to a licensed psychologist used by the licensing authority for the psychological testing of its own employees. The applicant may be charged for the actual cost of the testing in an amount not to exceed one hundred fifty dollars ($150). Additional psychological testing of an applicant seeking license renewal shall be required only if there is compelling evidence to indicate that a test is necessary. The cost to the applicant for this additional testing shall not exceed one hundred fifty dollars ($150).

(d) Except as authorized pursuant to subdivisions (a), (b), and (c), no requirement, charge, assessment, fee, or condition that requires the payment of any additional funds by the applicant may be imposed by any licensing authority as a condition of the application for a license.

Penal Code § 12060

As used in this article, the following terms apply:

(a) "Department" means the Department of Justice.

(b) "Handgun ammunition" means handgun ammunition as defined in subdivision (a) of Section 12323, but excluding ammunition designed and intended to be used in an "antique firearm" as defined in Section 921(a)(16) of Title 18 of the United States Code. Handgun ammunition does not include blanks.

(c) "Handgun ammunition vendor" or "vendor" means any person, firm, corporation, dealer, or any other business enterprise that is engaged in the retail sale of any handgun ammunition, or that holds itself out as engaged in the business of selling any handgun ammunition.

Penal Code § 12061

(a) A vendor shall comply with all of the following conditions, requirements and prohibitions:

(1) A vendor shall not permit any employee who the vendor knows or reasonably should know is a person described in Section 12021 or 12021.1 of this code or Section 8100 or 8103 of the Welfare and Institutions Code to handle, sell, or deliver handgun ammunition in the course and scope of his or her employment.

(2) A vendor shall not sell or otherwise transfer ownership of, offer for sale or otherwise offer to transfer ownership of, or display for sale or display for transfer of ownership of any handgun ammunition in a manner that allows that ammunition to be accessible to a purchaser or transferee without the assistance of the vendor or employee thereof.

(3) Commencing February 1, 2011, a vendor shall not sell or otherwise transfer ownership of any handgun ammunition without, at the time of delivery, legibly recording the following information:

(A) The date of the sale or other transaction.

(B) The purchaser's or transferee's driver's license or other identification number and the state in which it was issued.

(C) The brand, type, and amount of ammunition sold or otherwise transferred.

(D) The purchaser's or transferee's signature.

(E) The name of the salesperson who processed the sale or other transaction.

(F) The right thumbprint of the purchaser or transferee on the above form.

(G) The purchaser's or transferee's full residential address and telephone number.

(H) The purchaser's or transferee's date of birth.

(4) Commencing February 1, 2011, the records required by this section shall be maintained on the premises of the vendor for a period of not less than five years from the date of the recorded transfer.

(5) Commencing February 1, 2011, the records referred to in paragraph (3) shall be subject to inspection at any time during normal business hours by any peace officer employed by a sheriff, city police department, or district attorney as provided in subdivision (a) of Section 830.1, or employed by the department as provided in subdivision (b) of Section 830.1, provided the officer is conducting an investigation where access to those records is or may be relevant to that investigation, is seeking information about persons prohibited from owning a firearm or ammunition, or is engaged in ensuring compliance with the Dangerous Weapons Control Law (Chapter 1 (commencing with Section 12000) of Title 2 of Part 4), or any other laws pertaining to firearms or ammunition. The records shall also be subject to inspection at any time during normal business hours by any other employee of the department, provided that employee is conducting an investigation where access to those records is or may be relevant to that investigation, is seeking information about persons prohibited from owning a firearm or ammunition, or is engaged in ensuring compliance with the Dangerous Weapons Control Law (Chapter 1 (commencing with Section 12000) of Title 2 of Part 4), or any other laws pertaining to firearms or ammunition.

(6) Commencing February 1, 2011, the vendor shall not knowingly make a false entry in, fail to make a required entry in, fail to obtain the required thumbprint, or otherwise fail to maintain in the required manner records prepared in accordance with paragraph (2). If the right thumbprint is not available, then the vendor shall have the purchaser or transferee use his or her left thumb, or any available finger, and shall so indicate on the form. If the purchaser or transferee is physically unable to provide a thumbprint or fingerprint, the vendor shall so indicate on the form.

(7) Commencing February 1, 2011, no vendor shall refuse to permit a person authorized under paragraph (5) to examine any record prepared in accordance with this section during any inspection conducted pursuant to this section, or refuse to permit the use of any record or information by those persons.

(b) Paragraph (3) of subdivision (a) shall not apply to or affect sales or other transfers of ownership of handgun ammunition by handgun ammunition vendors to any of the following, if properly identified:

(1) A person licensed pursuant to Section 12071.

(2) A handgun ammunition vendor.

(3) A person who is on the centralized list maintained by the department pursuant to Section 12083.

(4) A target facility which holds a business or regulatory license.

(5) Gunsmiths.

(6) Wholesalers.

(7) Manufacturers or importers of firearms licensed pursuant to Chapter 44 (commencing with Section 921) of Title 18 of the United States Code, and the regulations issued pursuant thereto.

(8) Sales or other transfers of ownership made to authorized law enforcement representatives of cities, counties, cities and counties, or state or federal governments for exclusive use by those government agencies if, prior to the delivery, transfer, or sale of

handgun ammunition, written authorization from the head of the agency authorizing the transaction is presented to the person from whom the purchase, delivery, or transfer is being made. Proper written authorization is defined as verifiable written certification from the head of the agency by which the purchaser, transferee, or person otherwise acquiring ownership is employed, identifying the employee as an individual authorized to conduct the transaction, and authorizing the transaction for the exclusive use of the agency by which he or she is employed.

(c)(1) A violation of paragraph (3), (4), (6), or (7) of subdivision (a) is a misdemeanor.

(2) The provisions of this subdivision are cumulative, and shall not be construed as restricting the application of any other law. However, an act or omission punishable in different ways by different provisions of law shall not be punished under more than one provision.

Penal Code § 12070.

(a) No person shall sell, lease, or transfer firearms unless he or she has been issued a license pursuant to Section 12071. Any person violating this section is guilty of a misdemeanor.

(b) Subdivision (a) does not apply to any of the following:

(1) The sale, lease, or transfer of any firearm by a person acting pursuant to operation of law, a court order, or pursuant to the Enforcement of Judgments Law (Title 9 (commencing with Section 680.010) of Part 2 of the Code of Civil Procedure), or by a person who liquidates a personal firearm collection to satisfy a court judgment.

(2) A person acting pursuant to subdivision (e) of Section 186.22a or subdivision (c) of Section 12028.

(3) The sale, lease, or transfer of a firearm by a person who obtains title to the firearm by intestate succession or by bequest or as a surviving spouse pursuant to Chapter 1 (commencing with Section 13500) of Part 2 of Division 8 of the Probate Code, provided the person disposes of the firearm within 60 days of receipt of the firearm.

(4) The infrequent sale, lease, or transfer of firearms.

(5) The sale, lease, or transfer of used firearms other than handguns, at gun shows or events, as specified in Section 12071, by a person other than a licensee or dealer, provided the person has a valid federal firearms license and a current certificate of eligibility issued by the Department of Justice, as specified in Section 12071, and provided all the sales, leases, or transfers fully comply with subdivision (d) of Section 12072. However, the person shall not engage in the sale, lease, or transfer of used firearms other than handguns at more than 12 gun shows or events in any calendar year and shall not sell, lease, or transfer more than 15 used firearms other than handguns at any single gun show or event. In no event shall the person sell more than 75 used firearms other than handguns in any calendar year.

A person described in this paragraph shall be known as a "Gun Show Trader."

The Department of Justice shall adopt regulations to administer this program and shall recover the full costs of administration from fees assessed applicants.

As used in this paragraph, the term "used firearm" means a firearm that has been sold previously at retail and is more than three years old.

(6) Deliveries, sales, or transfers of firearms between or to importers and manufacturers of firearms licensed to engage in business pursuant to Chapter 44 (commencing with Section 921) of Title 18 of the United States Code and the regulations issued pursuant thereto.

(7) The sale, delivery, or transfer of firearms by manufacturers or importers licensed pursuant to Chapter 44 (commencing with Section 921) of Title 18 of the United States Code and the regulations issued pursuant thereto to dealers or wholesalers.

(8) Deliveries and transfers of firearms made pursuant to Section 12028, 12028.5, or 12030.

(9) The loan of a firearm for the purposes of shooting at targets, if the loan occurs on the premises of a target facility which holds a business or regulatory license or on the premises of any club or organization organized for the purposes of practicing shooting at targets upon established ranges, whether public or private, if the firearm is at all times kept within the premises of the target range or on the premises of the club or organization.

(10) Sales, deliveries, or transfers of firearms by manufacturers, importers, or wholesalers licensed pursuant to Chapter 44 (commencing with Section 921) of Title 18 of the United States Code and the regulations issued pursuant thereto to persons who reside outside this state who are licensed pursuant to Chapter 44 (commencing with Section 921) of Title 18 of the United States Code and the regulations issued pursuant thereto, if the sale, delivery, or transfer is in accordance with Chapter 44 (commencing with Section 921) of Title 18 of the United States Code and the regulations issued pursuant thereto.

(11) Sales, deliveries, or transfers of firearms by persons who reside outside this state and are licensed outside this state pursuant to Chapter 44 (commencing with Section 921) of Title 18 of the United States Code and the regulations issued pursuant thereto to wholesalers, manufacturers, or importers, if the sale, delivery, or transfer is in accordance with Chapter 44 (commencing with Section 921) of Title 18 of the United States Code and the regulations issued pursuant thereto.

(12) Sales, deliveries, or transfers of firearms by wholesalers to dealers.

(13) Sales, deliveries, or transfers of firearms by persons who reside outside this state to persons licensed pursuant to Section 12071, if the sale, delivery, or transfer is in accordance with Chapter 44 (commencing with Section 921) of Title 18 of the United States Code, and the regulations issued pursuant thereto.

(14) Sales, deliveries, or transfers of firearms by persons who reside outside this state and are licensed pursuant to Chapter 44 (commencing with Section 921) of Title 18 of the United States Code and the regulations issued pursuant thereto to dealers, if the sale, delivery, or transfer is in accordance with Chapter 44 (commencing with Section 921) of Title 18 of the United States Code and the regulations issued pursuant thereto.

(15) The delivery, sale, or transfer of an unloaded firearm by one wholesaler to another wholesaler if that firearm is intended as merchandise in the receiving wholesaler's business.

(16) The loan of an unloaded firearm or the loan of a firearm loaded with blank cartridges for use solely as a prop for a motion picture, television, or video production or entertainment or theatrical event.

(17) The delivery of an unloaded firearm that is a curio or relic, as defined in Section 478.11 of Title 27 of the Code of Federal Regulations, by a person licensed as a collector pursuant to Chapter 44 (commencing with Section 921) of Title 18 of the United

States Code and the regulations issued pursuant thereto with a current certificate of eligibility issued pursuant to Section 12071 to a dealer.

(18) Loans or returns of firearms to or from a gunsmith for service or repair.

(19) The delivery, sale, return, or transfer of a firearm regulated pursuant to Article 6 (commencing with Section 12095) of Chapter 1, Chapter 2 (commencing with Section 12200), Chapter 2.3 (commencing with Section 12275), or Chapter 2.5 (commencing with Section 12301) by a person who holds a permit issued pursuant to Section 12095, 12230, 12287, or 12305, if the delivery, sale, return, or transfer is conducted in accordance with the terms and conditions of the permit.

(c)(1) As used in this section, "infrequent" means:

(A) For handguns, less than six transactions per calendar year.

For this purpose, "transaction" means a single sale, lease, or transfer of any number of handguns.

(B) For firearms other than handguns, occasional and without regularity.

(2) As used in this section, "operation of law" includes, but is not limited to, any of the following:

(A) The executor or administrator of an estate, if the estate includes firearms.

(B) A secured creditor or an agent or employee thereof when the firearms are possessed as collateral for, or as a result of, a default under a security agreement under the Commercial Code.

(C) A levying officer, as defined in Section 481.140, 511.060, or 680.260 of the Code of Civil Procedure.

(D) A receiver performing his or her functions as a receiver, if the receivership estate includes firearms.

(E) A trustee in bankruptcy performing his or her duties, if the bankruptcy estate includes firearms.

(F) An assignee for the benefit of creditors performing his or her functions as an assignee, if the assignment includes firearms.

(G) A transmutation of property between spouses pursuant to Section 850 of the Family Code.

(H) Firearms received by the family of a police officer or deputy sheriff from a local agency pursuant to Section 50081 of the Government Code.

(I) The transfer of a firearm by a law enforcement agency to the person who found the firearm where the delivery is to the person as the finder of the firearm pursuant to Article 1 (commencing with Section 2080) of Chapter 4 of Division 3 of the Civil Code.

Penal Code § 12071.

(a)(1) As used in this chapter, the term "licensee," "person licensed pursuant to Section 12071," or "dealer" means a person who has all of the following:

(A) A valid federal firearms license.

(B) Any regulatory or business license, or licenses, required by local government.

(C) A valid seller's permit issued by the State Board of Equalization.

(D) A certificate of eligibility issued by the Department of Justice pursuant to paragraph (4).

(E) A license issued in the format prescribed by paragraph (6).

(F) Is among those recorded in the centralized list specified in subdivision (e).

(2) The duly constituted licensing authority of a city, county, or a city and county shall accept applications for, and may grant licenses permitting, licensees to sell firearms at retail within the city, county, or city and county. The duly constituted licensing authority shall inform applicants who are denied licenses of the reasons for the denial in writing.

(3) No license shall be granted to any applicant who fails to provide a copy of his or her valid federal firearms license, valid seller's permit issued by the State Board of Equalization, and the certificate of eligibility described in paragraph (4).

(4) A person may request a certificate of eligibility from the Department of Justice. The Department of Justice shall examine its records and records available to the department in the National Instant Criminal Background Check System in order to determine if the applicant is prohibited by state or federal law from possessing, receiving, owning, or purchasing a firearm and issue a certificate to an applicant if the department's records indicate that the applicant is not a person who is prohibited by state or federal law from possessing firearms.

(5) The department shall adopt regulations to administer the certificate of eligibility program and shall recover the full costs of administering the program by imposing fees assessed to applicants who apply for those certificates.

(6) A license granted by the duly constituted licensing authority of any city, county, or city and county, shall be valid for not more than one year from the date of issuance and shall be in one of the following forms:

(A) In the form prescribed by the Attorney General.

(B) A regulatory or business license that states on its face "Valid for Retail Sales of Firearms" and is endorsed by the signature of the issuing authority.

(C) A letter from the duly constituted licensing authority having primary jurisdiction for the applicant's intended business location stating that the jurisdiction does not require any form of regulatory or business license or does not otherwise restrict or regulate the sale of firearms.

(7) Local licensing authorities may assess fees to recover their full costs of processing applications for licenses.

(b) A license is subject to forfeiture for a breach of any of the following prohibitions and requirements:

(1)(A) Except as provided in subparagraphs (B) and (C), the business shall be conducted only in the buildings designated in the license.

(B) A person licensed pursuant to subdivision (a) may take possession of firearms and commence preparation of registers for the sale, delivery, or transfer of firearms at gun shows or events, as defined in Section 478.100 of Title 27 of the Code of Federal Regulations, or its successor, if the gun show or event is not conducted from any motorized or towed vehicle. A person conducting business pursuant to this subparagraph shall be entitled to conduct business as authorized herein at any gun show or event in the state without regard to the jurisdiction within this state that issued the license pursuant to subdivision (a), provided the person complies with (i) all applicable laws, including, but not limited to, the waiting period specified in subparagraph (A) of paragraph (3), and (ii) all applicable local laws, regulations, and fees, if any.

A person conducting business pursuant to this subparagraph shall publicly display his or her license issued pursuant to subdivision (a), or a facsimile thereof, at any gun show or event, as specified in this subparagraph.

(C) A person licensed pursuant to subdivision (a) may engage in the sale and transfer of firearms other than pistols, revolvers, or other firearms capable of being concealed upon the person, at events specified in subdivision (g) of Section 12078, subject to the prohibitions and restrictions contained in that subdivision.

A person licensed pursuant to subdivision (a) also may accept delivery of firearms other than pistols, revolvers, or other firearms capable of being concealed upon the person, outside the building designated in the license, provided the firearm is being donated for the purpose of sale or transfer at an auction or similar event specified in subdivision (g) of Section 12078.

(D) The firearm may be delivered to the purchaser, transferee, or person being loaned the firearm at one of the following places:

(i) The building designated in the license.

(ii) The places specified in subparagraph (B) or (C).

(iii) The place of residence of, the fixed place of business of, or on private property owned or lawfully possessed by, the purchaser, transferee, or person being loaned the firearm.

(2) The license or a copy thereof, certified by the issuing authority, shall be displayed on the premises where it can easily be seen.

(3) No firearm shall be delivered:

(A) Within 10 days of the application to purchase, or, after notice by the department pursuant to subdivision (d) of Section 12076, within 10 days of the submission to the department of any correction to the application, or within 10 days of the submission to the department of any fee required pursuant to subdivision (e) of Section 12076, whichever is later.

(B) Unless unloaded and securely wrapped or unloaded and in a locked container.

(C) Unless the purchaser, transferee, or person being loaned the firearm presents clear evidence of his or her identity and age to the dealer.

(D) Whenever the dealer is notified by the Department of Justice that the person is prohibited by state or federal law from processing, owning, purchasing, or receiving a firearm. The dealer shall make available to the person in the prohibited class a prohibited notice and transfer form, provided by the department, stating that the person is prohibited from owning or possessing a firearm, and that the person may obtain from the department the reason for the prohibition.

(4) No pistol, revolver, or other firearm or imitation thereof capable of being concealed upon the person, or placard advertising the sale or other transfer thereof, shall be displayed in any part of the premises where it can readily be seen from the outside.

(5) The licensee shall agree to and shall act properly and promptly in processing firearms transactions pursuant to Section 12082.

(6) The licensee shall comply with Sections 12073, 12076, and 12077, subdivisions (a) and (b) and paragraph (1) of subdivision (f) of Section 12072, and subdivision (a) of Section 12316.

(7) The licensee shall post conspicuously within the licensed premises the following warnings in block letters not less than one inch in height:

(A) "IF YOU KEEP A LOADED FIREARM WITHIN ANY PREMISES UNDER YOUR CUSTODY OR CONTROL, AND A PERSON UNDER 18 YEARS OF AGE OBTAINS IT AND USES IT, RESULTING IN INJURY OR DEATH, OR CARRIES IT TO A PUBLIC PLACE, YOU MAY BE GUILTY OF A MISDEMEANOR OR A FELONY UNLESS YOU STORED THE FIREARM IN A LOCKED CONTAINER OR LOCKED THE FIREARM WITH A LOCKING DEVICE, TO KEEP IT FROM TEMPORARILY FUNCTIONING."

(B) "IF YOU KEEP A PISTOL, REVOLVER, OR OTHER FIREARM CAPABLE OF BEING CONCEALED UPON THE PERSON, WITHIN ANY PREMISES UNDER YOUR CUSTODY OR CONTROL, AND A PERSON UNDER 18 YEARS OF AGE GAINS ACCESS TO THE FIREARM, AND CARRIES IT OFF-PREMISES, YOU MAY BE GUILTY OF A MISDEMEANOR, UNLESS YOU STORED THE FIREARM IN A LOCKED CONTAINER, OR LOCKED THE FIREARM WITH A LOCKING DEVICE, TO KEEP IT FROM TEMPORARILY FUNCTIONING."

(C) "IF YOU KEEP ANY FIREARM WITHIN ANY PREMISES UNDER YOUR CUSTODY OR CONTROL, AND A PERSON UNDER 18 YEARS OF AGE GAINS ACCESS TO THE FIREARM, AND CARRIES IT OFF-PREMISES TO A SCHOOL OR SCHOOL-SPONSORED EVENT, YOU MAY BE GUILTY OF A MISDEMEANOR, INCLUDING A FINE OF UP TO FIVE THOUSAND DOLLARS ($5,000), UNLESS YOU STORED THE FIREARM IN A LOCKED CONTAINER, OR LOCKED THE FIREARM WITH A LOCKING DEVICE."

(D) "DISCHARGING FIREARMS IN POORLY VENTILATED AREAS, CLEANING FIREARMS, OR HANDLING AMMUNITION MAY RESULT IN EXPOSURE TO LEAD, A SUBSTANCE KNOWN TO CAUSE BIRTH DEFECTS, REPRODUCTIVE HARM, AND OTHER SERIOUS PHYSICAL INJURY. HAVE ADEQUATE VENTILATION AT ALL TIMES. WASH HANDS THOROUGHLY AFTER EXPOSURE."

(E) "FEDERAL REGULATIONS PROVIDE THAT IF YOU DO NOT TAKE PHYSICAL POSSESSION OF THE FIREARM THAT YOU ARE ACQUIRING OWNERSHIP OF WITHIN 30 DAYS AFTER YOU COMPLETE THE INITIAL BACKGROUND CHECK PAPERWORK, THEN YOU HAVE TO GO THROUGH THE BACKGROUND CHECK PROCESS A SECOND TIME IN ORDER TO TAKE PHYSICAL POSSESSION OF THAT FIREARM."

(F) "NO PERSON SHALL MAKE AN APPLICATION TO PURCHASE MORE THAN ONE PISTOL, REVOLVER, OR OTHER FIREARM CAPABLE OF BEING CONCEALED UPON THE PERSON WITHIN ANY 30-DAY PERIOD AND NO DELIVERY SHALL BE MADE TO ANY PERSON WHO HAS MADE AN APPLICATION TO PURCHASE MORE THAN ONE PISTOL, REVOLVER, OR OTHER FIREARM CAPABLE OF BEING CONCEALED UPON THE PERSON WITHIN ANY 30-DAY PERIOD.

(8)(A) Commencing April 1, 1994, and until January 1, 2003, no pistol, revolver, or other firearm capable of being concealed upon the person shall be delivered unless the purchaser, transferee, or person being loaned the firearm presents to the dealer a basic firearms safety certificate.

(B) Commencing January 1, 2003, no dealer may deliver a handgun unless the person receiving the handgun presents to the dealer a valid handgun safety certificate. The firearms dealer shall retain a photocopy of the handgun safety certificate as proof of compliance with this requirement.

(C) Commencing January 1, 2003, no handgun may be delivered unless the purchaser, transferee, or person being loaned the firearm presents documentation indicating that he or she is a California resident. Satisfactory documentation shall include a utility bill from within the last three months, a residential lease, a property deed, or military permanent duty station orders indicating assignment within this state, or other evidence of residency as permitted by the Department of Justice. The firearms dealer shall retain a photocopy of the documentation as proof of compliance with this requirement.

(D) Commencing January 1, 2003, except as authorized by the department, no firearms dealer may deliver a handgun unless the recipient performs a safe handling demonstration with that handgun. The demonstration shall commence with the handgun unloaded and locked with the firearm safety device with which it is required to be delivered, if applicable. While maintaining muzzle awareness, that is, the firearm is pointed in a safe direction, preferably down at the ground, and trigger discipline, that is, the trigger finger is outside of the trigger guard and along side of the handgun frame, at all times, the handgun recipient shall correctly and safely perform the following:

(i) If the handgun is a semiautomatic pistol:

(I) Remove the magazine.

(II) Lock the slide back. If the model of firearm does not allow the slide to be locked back, pull the slide back, visually and physically check the chamber to ensure that it is clear.

(III) Visually and physically inspect the chamber, to ensure that the handgun is unloaded.

(IV) Remove the firearm safety device, if applicable. If the firearm safety device prevents any of the previous steps, remove the firearm safety device during the appropriate step.

(V) Load one bright orange, red, or other readily identifiable dummy round into the magazine. If no readily identifiable dummy round is available, an empty cartridge casing with an empty primer pocket may be used.

(VI) Insert the magazine into the magazine well of the firearm.

(VII) Manipulate the slide release or pull back and release the slide.

(VIII) Remove the magazine.

(IX) Visually inspect the chamber to reveal that a round can be chambered with the magazine removed.

(X) Lock the slide back to eject the bright orange, red, or other readily identifiable dummy round. If the handgun is of a model that does not allow the slide to be locked back, pull the slide back and physically check the chamber to ensure that the chamber is clear. If no readily identifiable dummy round is available, an empty cartridge casing with an empty primer pocket may be used.

(XI) Apply the safety, if applicable.

(XII) Apply the firearm safety device, if applicable. This requirement shall not apply to an Olympic competition pistol if no firearms safety device, other than a cable lock that the department has determined would damage the barrel of the pistol, has been approved for the pistol, and the pistol is either listed in paragraph (2) of subdivision (h) of Section 12132 or is subject to paragraph (3) of subdivision (h) of Section 12132.

(ii) If the handgun is a double-action revolver.

(I) Open the cylinder.

(II) Visually and physically inspect each chamber, to ensure that the revolver is unloaded.

(III) Remove the firearm safety device. If the firearm safety device prevents any of the previous steps, remove the firearm safety device during the appropriate step.

(IV) While maintaining muzzle awareness and trigger discipline, load one bright orange, red, or other readily identifiable dummy round into a chamber of the cylinder and rotate the cylinder so that the round is in the next-to-fire position. If no readily identifiable dummy round is available, an empty cartridge casing with an empty primer pocket may be used.

(V) Close the cylinder.

(VI) Open the cylinder and eject the round.

(VII) Visually and physically inspect each chamber to ensure that the revolver is unloaded.

(VIII) Apply the firearm safety device, if applicable. This requirement shall not apply to an Olympic competition pistol if no firearms safety device, other than a cable lock that the department has determined would damage the barrel of the pistol, has been approved for the pistol, and the pistol is either listed in paragraph (2) of subdivision (h) of Section 12132 or is subject to paragraph (3) of subdivision (h) of Section 12132.

(iii) If the handgun is a single-action revolver:

(I) Open the loading gate.

(II) Visually and physically inspect each chamber, to ensure that the revolver is unloaded.

(III) Remove the firearm safety device required to be sold with the handgun. If the firearm safety device prevents any of the previous steps, remove the firearm safety device during the appropriate step.

(IV) Load one bright orange, red, or other readily identifiable dummy round into a chamber of the cylinder, close the loading gate and rotate the cylinder so that the round is in the next-to-fire position. If no readily identifiable dummy round is available, an empty cartridge casing with an empty primer pocket may be used.

(V) Open the loading gate and unload the revolver.

(VI) Visually and physically inspect each chamber to ensure that the revolver is unloaded.

(VII) Apply the firearm safety device, if applicable. This requirement shall not apply to an Olympic competition pistol if no firearms safety device, other than a cable lock that the department has determined would damage the barrel of the pistol, has been approved for the pistol, and the pistol is either listed in paragraph (2) of subdivision (h) of Section 12132 or is subject to paragraph (3) of subdivision (h) of Section 12132.

(E) The recipient shall receive instruction regarding how to render that handgun safe in the event of a jam.

(F) The firearms dealer shall sign and date an affidavit stating that the requirements of subparagraph (D) have been met. The firearms dealer shall additionally obtain the signature of the handgun purchaser on the same affidavit. The firearms dealer shall retain the original affidavit as proof of compliance with this requirement.

(G) The recipient shall perform the safe handling demonstration for a department-certified instructor.

(H) No demonstration shall be required if the dealer is returning the handgun to the owner of the handgun.

(I) Department-certified instructors who may administer the safe handling demonstration shall meet the requirements set forth in subdivision (j) of Section 12804.

(J) The persons who are exempt from the requirements of subdivision (b) of Section 12801, pursuant to Section 12807, are also exempt from performing the safe handling demonstration.

(9) Commencing July 1, 1992, the licensee shall offer to provide the purchaser or transferee of a firearm, or person being loaned a firearm, with a copy of the pamphlet described in Section 12080 and may add the cost of the pamphlet, if any, to the sales price of the firearm.

(10) The licensee shall not commit an act of collusion as defined in Section 12072.

(11) The licensee shall post conspicuously within the licensed premises a detailed list of each of the following:

(A) All charges required by governmental agencies for processing firearm transfers required by Sections 12076, 12082, and 12806.

(B) All fees that the licensee charges pursuant to Sections 12082 and 12806.

(12) The licensee shall not misstate the amount of fees charged by a governmental agency pursuant to Sections 12076, 12082, and 12806.

(13) Except as provided in subparagraphs (B) and (C) of paragraph (1) of subdivision (b), all firearms that are in the inventory of the licensee shall be kept within the licensed location. The licensee shall report the loss or theft of any firearm that is merchandise of the licensee, any firearm that the licensee takes possession of pursuant to Section 12082, or any firearm kept at the licensee's place of business within 48 hours of discovery to the appropriate law enforcement agency in the city, county, or city and county where the licensee's business premises are located.

(14) Except as provided in subparagraphs (B) and (C) of paragraph (1) of subdivision (b), any time when the licensee is not open for business, all inventory firearms shall be stored in the licensed location. All firearms shall be secured using one of the following methods as to each particular firearm:

(A) Store the firearm in a secure facility that is a part of, or that constitutes, the licensee's business premises.

(B) Secure the firearm with a hardened steel rod or cable of at least one-eighth inch in diameter through the trigger guard of the firearm. The steel rod or cable shall be secured with a hardened steel lock that has a shackle. The lock and shackle shall be protected or shielded from the use of a boltcutter and the rod or cable shall be anchored in a manner that prevents the removal of the firearm from the premises.

(C) Store the firearm in a locked fireproof safe or vault in the licensee's business premises.

(15) The licensing authority in an unincorporated area of a county or within a city may impose security requirements that are more strict or are at a higher standard than those specified in paragraph (14).

(16) Commencing January 1, 1994, the licensee shall, upon the issuance or renewal of a license, submit a copy of the same to the Department of Justice.

(17) The licensee shall maintain and make available for inspection during business hours to any peace officer, authorized local law enforcement employee, or Department of Justice employee designated by the Attorney General, upon the presentation of proper identification, a firearms transaction record.

(18)(A) On the date of receipt, the licensee shall report to the Department of Justice in a format prescribed by the department the acquisition by the licensee of the ownership of a pistol, revolver, or other firearm capable of being concealed upon the person.

(B) The provisions of this paragraph shall not apply to any of the following transactions:

(i) A transaction subject to the provisions of subdivision (n) of Section 12078.

(ii) The dealer acquired the firearm from a wholesaler.

(iii) The dealer acquired the firearm from a person who is licensed as a manufacturer or importer to engage in those activities pursuant to Chapter 44 (commencing with Section 921) of Title 18 of the United States Code and any regulations issued pursuant thereto.

(iv) The dealer acquired the firearm from a person who resides outside this state who is licensed pursuant to Chapter 44 (commencing with Section 921) of Title 18 of the United States Code and any regulations issued pursuant thereto.

(v) Until July 1, 2010, the dealer is also licensed as a secondhand dealer pursuant to Article 4 (commencing with Section 21625) of Chapter 9 of Division 8 of the Business and Professions Code, acquires a handgun, and reports its acquisition pursuant to Section 21628 of the Business and Professions Code.

(vi) Commencing July 1, 2010, the dealer is also licensed as a secondhand dealer pursuant to Article 4 (commencing with Section 21625) of Chapter 9 of Division 8 of the Business and Professions Code, acquires a handgun, and reports its acquisition pursuant to Section 21628.2 of the Business and Professions Code.

(19) The licensee shall forward in a format prescribed by the Department of Justice, information as required by the department on any firearm that is not delivered within the time period set forth in Section 478.102 (c) of Title 27 of the Code of Federal Regulations.

(20)(A) Firearms dealers may require any agent who handles, sells, or delivers firearms to obtain and provide to the dealer a certificate of eligibility from the department pursuant to paragraph (4) of subdivision (a). The agent or employee shall provide on the application, the name and California firearms dealer number of the firearms dealer with whom he or she is employed.

(B) The department shall notify the firearms dealer in the event that the agent or employee who has a certificate of eligibility is or becomes prohibited from possessing firearms.

(C) If the local jurisdiction requires a background check of the agents or employees of the firearms dealer, the agent or employee shall obtain a certificate of eligibility pursuant to subparagraph (A).

(D) Nothing in this paragraph shall be construed to preclude a local jurisdiction from conducting an additional background check pursuant to Section 11105 or prohibiting employment based on criminal history that does not appear as part of obtaining a certificate of eligibility, provided however, that the local jurisdiction may not charge a fee for the additional criminal history check.

(E) The licensee shall prohibit any agent who the licensee knows or reasonably should know is within a class of persons prohibited from possessing firearms pursuant to Section 12021 or 12021.1 of this code, or Section 8100 or 8103 of the Welfare and Institutions Code, from coming into contact with any firearm that is not secured and from accessing any key, combination, code, or other means to open any of the locking devices described in clause (ii) of subparagraph (G) of this paragraph.

(F) Nothing in this paragraph shall be construed as preventing a local government from enacting an ordinance imposing additional conditions on licensees with regard to agents.

(G) For purposes of this section, the following definitions shall apply:

(i) An "agent" is an employee of the licensee.

(ii) "Secured" means a firearm that is made inoperable in one or more of the following ways:

(I) The firearm is inoperable because it is secured by a firearms safety device listed on the department's roster of approved firearms safety devices pursuant to subdivision (d) of Section 12088 of this chapter.

(II) The firearm is stored in a locked gun safe or long-gun safe which meets the standards for department-approved gun safes set forth in Section 12088.2.

(III) The firearm is stored in a distinct locked room or area in the building that is used to store firearms that can only be unlocked by a key, a combination, or similar means.

(IV) The firearm is secured with a hardened steel rod or cable that is at least one-eighth of an inch in diameter through the trigger guard of the firearm. The steel rod or cable shall be secured with a hardened steel lock that has a shackle. The lock and shackle shall be protected or shielded from the use of a boltcutter and the rod or cable shall be anchored in a manner that prevents the removal of the firearm from the premises.

(c)(1) As used in this article, "clear evidence of his or her identity and age" means either of the following:

(A) A valid California driver's license.

(B) A valid California identification card issued by the Department of Motor Vehicles.

(2) As used in this section, a "secure facility" means a building that meets all of the following specifications:

(A) All perimeter doorways shall meet one of the following:

(i) A windowless steel security door equipped with both a dead bolt and a doorknob lock.

(ii) A windowed metal door that is equipped with both a dead bolt and a doorknob lock. If the window has an opening of five inches or more measured in any direction, the window shall be covered with steel bars of at least ½ -inch diameter or metal grating of at least 9 gauge affixed to the exterior or interior of the door.

(iii) A metal grate that is padlocked and affixed to the licensee's premises independent of the door and doorframe.

(B) All windows are covered with steel bars.

(C) Heating, ventilating, air-conditioning, and service openings are secured with steel bars, metal grating, or an alarm system.

(D) Any metal grates have spaces no larger than six inches wide measured in any direction.

(E) Any metal screens have spaces no larger than three inches wide measured in any direction.

(F) All steel bars shall be no further than six inches apart.

(3) As used in this section, "licensed premises," "licensed place of business," "licensee's place of business," or "licensee's business premises" means the building designated in the license.

(4) For purposes of paragraph (17) of subdivision (b):

(A) A "firearms transaction record" is a record containing the same information referred to in subdivision (a) of Section 478.124, Section 478.124a, and subdivision (e) of Section 478.125 of Title 27 of the Code of Federal Regulations.

(B) A licensee shall be in compliance with the provisions of paragraph (17) of subdivision (b) if he or she maintains and makes available for inspection during business hours to any peace officer, authorized local law enforcement employee, or Department of Justice employee designated by the Attorney General, upon the presentation of proper identification, the bound book containing the same information referred to in Section 478.124a and subdivision (e) of Section 478.125 of Title 27 of the Code of Federal Regulations and the records referred to in subdivision (a) of Section 478.124 of Title 27 of the Code of Federal Regulations.

(d) Upon written request from a licensee, the licensing authority may grant an exemption from compliance with the requirements of paragraph (14) of subdivision (b) if the licensee is unable to comply with those requirements because of local ordinances, covenants, lease conditions, or similar circumstances not under the control of the licensee.

(e)(1) Except as otherwise provided in this paragraph, the Department of Justice shall keep a centralized list of all persons licensed pursuant to subparagraphs (A) to (E), inclusive, of paragraph (1) of subdivision (a). The department may remove from this list any person who knowingly or with gross negligence violates this article. Upon removal of a dealer from this list, notification shall be provided to local law enforcement and licensing authorities in the jurisdiction where the dealer's business is located.

(2) The department shall remove from the centralized list any person whose federal firearms license has expired or has been revoked.

(3) Information compiled from the list shall be made available, upon request, for the following purposes only:

(A) For law enforcement purposes.

(B) When the information is requested by a person licensed pursuant to Chapter 44 (commencing with Section 921) of Title 18 of the United States Code for determining the validity of the license for firearm shipments.

(C) When information is requested by a person promoting, sponsoring, operating, or otherwise organizing a show or event as defined in Section 478.100 of Title 27 of the Code of Federal Regulations, or its successor, who possesses a valid certificate of eligibility issued pursuant to Section 12071.1, if that information is requested by the person to determine the eligibility of a prospective participant in a gun show or event to conduct transactions as a firearms dealer pursuant to subparagraph (B) of paragraph (1) of subdivision (b).

(4) Information provided pursuant to paragraph (3) shall be limited to information necessary to corroborate an individual's current license status as being one of the following:

(A) A person licensed pursuant to subparagraphs (A) to (E), inclusive, of paragraph (1) of subdivision (a).

(B) A person licensed pursuant to Chapter 44 (commencing with Section 921) of Title 18 of the United States Code and who is not subject to the requirement that he or she be licensed pursuant to subparagraphs (A) to (E), inclusive, of paragraph (1) of subdivision (a).

(f) The Department of Justice may inspect dealers to ensure compliance with this article. The department may assess an annual fee, not to exceed one hundred fifteen dollars ($115), to cover the reasonable cost of maintaining the list described in subdivision (e), including the cost of inspections. Dealers whose place of business is in a jurisdiction that has adopted an inspection program to ensure compliance with firearms law shall be exempt from that portion of the department's fee that relates to the cost of inspections. The applicant is responsible for providing evidence to the department that the jurisdiction in which the business is located has the inspection program.

(g) The Department of Justice shall maintain and make available upon request information concerning the number of inspections conducted and the amount of fees collected pursuant to subdivision (f), a listing of exempted jurisdictions, as defined in subdivision (f), the number of dealers removed from the centralized list defined in subdivision (e), and the number of dealers found to have violated this article with knowledge or gross negligence.

(h) Paragraph (14) or (15) of subdivision (b) shall not apply to a licensee organized as a nonprofit public benefit or mutual benefit corporation organized pursuant to Part 2 (commencing with Section 5110) or Part 3 (commencing with Section 7110) of Division 2 of the Corporations Code, if both of the following conditions are satisfied:

(1) The nonprofit public benefit or mutual benefit corporation obtained the dealer's license solely and exclusively to assist that corporation or local chapters of that corporation in conducting auctions or similar events at which firearms are auctioned off to fund the activities of that corporation or the local chapters of the corporation.

(2) The firearms are not pistols, revolvers, or other firearms capable of being concealed upon the person.

Penal Code § 12071.1.

(a) No person shall produce, promote, sponsor, operate, or otherwise organize a gun show or event, as specified in subparagraph (B) of paragraph (1) of subdivision (b) of Section 12071, unless that person possesses a valid certificate of eligibility from the Department of Justice. Unless the department's records indicate that the applicant is a person prohibited from possessing firearms, a certificate of eligibility shall be issued by the Department of Justice to an applicant provided the applicant does all of the following:

(1) Certifies that he or she is familiar with the provisions of this section and Section 12071.4.

(2) Ensures that liability insurance is in effect for the duration of an event or show in an amount of not less than one million dollars ($1,000,000).

(3) Provides an annual list of the gun shows or events that the applicant plans to promote, produce, sponsor, operate, or otherwise organize during the year for which the certificate of eligibility is issued, including the date, time, and location of the gun shows or events.

(b) If during that year the information required by paragraph (3) of subdivision (a) changes, or additional gun shows or events will be promoted, produced, sponsored, operated, or otherwise organized by the applicant, the producer shall notify the Department of Justice no later than 30 days prior to the gun show or event.

(c) As used in this section, a "licensed gun show producer" means a person who has been issued a certificate of eligibility by the Department of Justice pursuant to subdivision (a). No regulations shall be required to implement this subdivision.

(d) The Department of Justice shall adopt regulations to administer the certificate of eligibility program under this section and shall recover the full costs of administering the program by fees assessed applicants who apply for certificates. A licensed gun show producer shall be assessed an annual fee of eighty-five dollars ($85) by the department.

(e)(1) A willful failure by a gun show producer to comply with any of the requirements of this section, except for the posting of required signs, shall be a misdemeanor punishable by a fine not to exceed two thousand dollars ($2,000), and shall render the producer ineligible for a gun show producer license for one year from the date of the conviction.

(2) The willful failure of a gun show producer to post signs as required by this section shall be a misdemeanor punishable by a fine not to exceed one thousand dollars ($1,000) for the first offense and not to exceed two thousand dollars ($2,000) for the second or subsequent offense, and with respect to the second or subsequent offense, shall render the producer ineligible for a gun show producer license for one year from the date of the conviction.

(3) Multiple violations charged pursuant to paragraph (1) arising from more than one gun show or event shall be grounds for suspension of a producer's certificate of eligibility pending adjudication of the violations.

(f) Prior to the commencement of a gun show or event, the producer thereof shall, upon written request, within 48 hours, or a later time specified by the requesting law enforcement agency, make available to the requesting law enforcement agency with jurisdiction over the facility, a complete and accurate list of all persons, entities, and organizations that have leased or rented, or are known to the producer to intend to lease or rent, any table, display space, or area at the gun show or event for the purpose of selling, leasing, or transferring firearms. The producer shall thereafter, upon written request, for every day the gun show or event operates, within 24 hours, or a later time specified by the requesting law enforcement agency, make available to the requesting law enforcement agency with jurisdiction over the facility, an accurate, complete, and current list of the persons, entities, and organizations that have leased or rented, or are known to the producer to intend to lease or rent, any table, display space, or area at the gun show or event for the purpose of selling, leasing, or transferring firearms. This subdivision applies to persons, entities, and organizations whether or not they participate in the entire gun show or event, or only a portion thereof.

(g) The information that may be requested by the law enforcement agency with jurisdiction over the facility, and that shall be provided by the producer upon request, may include, but is not limited to, the following information relative to a vendor who offers for sale firearms manufactured after December 31, 1898: his or her complete name, and a driver's license or identification card number.

(h) The producer and facility manager shall prepare an annual event and security plan and schedule that shall include, at a minimum, the following:

(1) The type of shows or events including, but not limited to, antique or general firearms.

(2) The estimated number of vendors offering firearms for sale or display.

(3) The estimated number of attendees.

(4) The number of entrances and exits at the gun show or event site.

(5) The location, dates, and times of the shows or events.

(6) The contact person and telephone number for both the producer and the facility.

(7) The number of sworn peace officers employed by the producer or the facilities manager who will be present at the show or event.

(8) The number of nonsworn security personnel employed by the producer or the facility's manager who will be present at the show or event.

(i) The annual event and security plan shall be submitted by either the producer or the facility's manager to the Department of Justice and the law enforcement agency with jurisdiction over the facility. Not later than 15 days prior to the commencement of the gun show or event, the producer shall submit to the department, the law enforcement agency with jurisdiction over the facility site, and the facility's manager a revised event and security plan if significant changes have been made since the annual plan was submitted, including a revised list of vendors that the producer knows, or reasonably should know, will be renting tables, space, or otherwise participating in the gun show or event. The event and security plan shall be approved by the facility's manager prior to the event or show after consultation with the law enforcement agency with jurisdiction over the facility. No gun show or event shall commence unless the requirements of this subdivision are met.

(j) The producer shall be responsible for informing prospective gun show vendors of the requirements of this section and of Section 12071.4 that apply to vendors.

(k) The producer shall, within seven calendar days of the commencement of the show or event, but not later than noon on Friday for a show or event held on a weekend, submit a list of all prospective vendors and designated firearms transfer agents who are licensed firearms dealers to the Department of Justice for the purpose of determining whether these prospective vendors and designated firearms transfer agents possess valid licenses and are thus eligible to participate as licensed dealers at the show or event. The department shall examine its records and if it determines that a dealer's license is not valid, it shall notify the show or event producer of that fact prior to the commencement of the show or event.

(l) If a licensed firearms dealer fails to cooperate with a producer or fails to comply with the applicable requirements of this section or Section 12071.4, that person shall not be allowed to participate in that show or event.

(m) If a producer fails to comply with subdivision (j) or (k), the gun show or event shall not commence until those requirements are met.

(n) All producers shall have written contracts with all gun show vendors selling firearms at the show or event.

(o) The producer shall require that signs be posted in a readily visible location at each public entrance to the show containing, but not limited to, the following notices:

(1) This gun show follows all federal, state, and local firearms and weapons laws without exception.

(2) All firearms carried onto the premises by members of the public will be checked, cleared of any ammunition, secured in a manner that prevents them from being operated, and an identification tag or sticker will be attached to the firearm prior to the person being allowed admittance to the show.

(3) No member of the public under the age of 18 years shall be admitted to the show unless accompanied by a parent, grandparent, or legal guardian.

(4) All firearms transfers between private parties at the show shall be conducted through a licensed dealer in accordance with applicable state and federal laws.

(5) Persons possessing firearms on this facility must have in their immediate possession government-issued photo identification, and display it upon request to any security officer or any peace officer, as defined in Section 830.

(p) The show producer shall post, in a readily visible location at each entrance to the parking lot at the show, signage that states: "The transfer of firearms on the parking lot of this facility is a crime."

(q) It is the intent of the Legislature that the certificate of eligibility program established pursuant to this section be incorporated into the certificate of eligibility program established pursuant to Section 12071 to the maximum extent practicable.

Penal Code § 12071.4.

(a) This section shall be known, and may be cited as, the Gun Show Enforcement and Security Act of 2000.

(b) All gun show or event vendors shall certify in writing to the producer that they:

(1) Will not display, possess, or offer for sale any firearms, knives, or weapons for which possession or sale is prohibited.

(2) Acknowledge that they are responsible for knowing and complying with all applicable federal, state, and local laws dealing with the possession and transfer of firearms.

(3) Will not engage in activities that incite or encourage hate crimes.

(4) Will process all transfers of firearms through licensed firearms dealers as required by state law.

(5) Will verify that all firearms in their possession at the show or event will be unloaded, and that the firearms will be secured in a manner that prevents them from being operated except for brief periods when the mechanical condition of a firearm is being demonstrated to a prospective buyer.

(6) Have complied with the requirements of subdivision (e).

(7) Will not display or possess black powder, or offer it for sale.

(c) All firearms transfers at the gun show or event shall be in accordance with applicable state and federal laws.

(d) Except for purposes of showing ammunition to a prospective buyer, ammunition at a gun show or event may be displayed only in closed original factory boxes or other closed containers.

(e) Prior to the commencement of a gun show or event, each vendor shall provide to the producer all of the following information relative to the vendor, the vendor's employees, and other persons, compensated or not, who will be working or otherwise providing services to the public at the vendor's display space if firearms manufactured after December 31, 1898, will be offered for sale:

(1) His or her complete name.

(2) His or her driver's license or state-issued identification card number.

(3) His or her date of birth. The producer shall keep the information at the show's or event's onsite headquarters for the duration of the show or event, and at the producer's regular place of business for two weeks after the conclusion of the show or event, and shall make the information available upon request to any sworn peace officer for purposes of the officer's official law enforcement duties.

(f) Vendors and employees of vendors shall wear name tags indicating first and last name.

(g) No person at a gun show or event, other than security personnel or sworn peace officers, shall possess at the same time both a firearm and ammunition that is designed to be fired in the firearm. Vendors having those items at the show for sale or exhibition are exempt from this prohibition.

(h) No member of the public who is under the age of 18 years shall be admitted to, or be permitted to remain at, a gun show or event unless accompanied by a parent or legal guardian. Any member of the public who is under the age of 18 shall be accompanied by his or her parent, grandparent, or legal guardian while at the show or event.

(i) Persons other than show or event security personnel, sworn peace officers, or vendors, who bring firearms onto the gun show or event premises shall sign in ink the tag or sticker that is attached to the firearm prior to being allowed admittance to the show or event, as provided for in subdivision (j).

(j) All firearms carried onto the premises of a gun show or event by members of the public shall be checked, cleared of any ammunition, secured in a manner that prevents them from being operated, and an identification tag or sticker shall be attached to the firearm, prior to the person being allowed admittance to the show. The identification tag or sticker shall state that all firearms transfers between private parties at the show or event shall be conducted through a licensed dealer in accordance with applicable state and federal laws. The person possessing the firearm shall complete the following information on the tag before it is attached to the firearm:

(1) The gun owner's signature.

(2) The gun owner's printed name.

(3) The identification number from the gun owner's government-issued photo identification.

(k) All persons possessing firearms at the gun show or event shall have in his or her immediate possession, government-issued photo identification, and display it upon request, to any security officer, or any peace officer.

(l) Unless otherwise specified, a first violation of this section is an infraction. Any second or subsequent violation is a misdemeanor. Any person who commits an act which he or she knows to be a violation of this section is guilty of a misdemeanor for a first offense.

Penal Code § 12072.

(a)(1) No person, corporation, or firm shall knowingly supply, deliver, sell, or give possession or control of a firearm to any person within any of the classes prohibited by Section 12021 or 12021.1.

(2) No person, corporation, or dealer shall sell, supply, deliver, or give possession or control of a firearm to any person whom he or she has cause to believe to be within any of the classes prohibited by Section 12021 or 12021.1 of this code or Section 8100 or 8103 of the Welfare and Institutions Code.

(3)(A) No person, corporation, or firm shall sell, loan, or transfer a firearm to a minor, nor sell a handgun to an individual under 21 years of age.

(B) Subparagraph (A) shall not apply to or affect those circumstances set forth in subdivision (p) of Section 12078.

(4) No person, corporation, or dealer shall sell, loan, or transfer a firearm to any person whom he or she knows or has cause to believe is not the actual purchaser or transferee of the firearm, or to any person who is not the person actually being loaned the firearm, if the person, corporation, or dealer has either of the following:

(A) Knowledge that the firearm is to be subsequently loaned, sold, or transferred to avoid the provisions of subdivision (c) or (d).

(B) Knowledge that the firearm is to be subsequently loaned, sold, or transferred to avoid the requirements of any exemption to the provisions of subdivision (c) or (d).

(5) No person, corporation, or dealer shall acquire a firearm for the purpose of selling, transferring, or loaning the firearm, if the person, corporation, or dealer has either of the following:

(A) In the case of a dealer, intent to violate subdivision (b) or (c).

(B) In any other case, intent to avoid either of the following:

(i) The provisions of subdivision (d).

(ii) The requirements of any exemption to the provisions of subdivision (d).

(6) The dealer shall comply with the provisions of paragraph (18) of subdivision (b) of Section 12071.

(7) The dealer shall comply with the provisions of paragraph (19) of subdivision (b) of Section 12071.

(8) No person shall sell or otherwise transfer his or her ownership in a handgun unless the firearm bears either:

(A) The name of the manufacturer, the manufacturer's make or model, and a manufacturer's serial number assigned to that firearm.

(B) The identification number or mark assigned to the firearm by the Department of Justice pursuant to Section 12092.

(9)(A) No person shall make an application to purchase more than one handgun within any 30-day period.

(B) Subparagraph (A) shall not apply to any of the following:

(i) Any law enforcement agency.

(ii) Any agency duly authorized to perform law enforcement duties.

(iii) Any state or local correctional facility.

(iv) Any private security company licensed to do business in California.

(v) Any person who is properly identified as a full-time paid peace officer, as defined in Chapter 4.5 (commencing with Section 830) of Title 3 of Part 2, and who is authorized to, and does carry a firearm during the course and scope of his or her employment as a peace officer.

(vi) Any motion picture, television, or video production company or entertainment or theatrical company whose production by its nature involves the use of a firearm.

(vii) Any person who may, pursuant to Section 12078, claim an exemption from the waiting period set forth in subdivision (c) of this section.

(viii) Any transaction conducted through a licensed firearms dealer pursuant to Section 12082.

(ix) Any person who is licensed as a collector pursuant to Chapter 44 (commencing with Section 921) of Title 18 of the

United States Code and the regulations issued pursuant thereto and who has a current certificate of eligibility issued to him or her by the Department of Justice pursuant to Section 12071.

(x) The exchange of a handgun where the dealer purchased that firearm from the person seeking the exchange within the 30-day period immediately preceding the date of exchange or replacement.

(xi) The replacement of a handgun when the person's handgun was lost or stolen, and the person reported that firearm lost or stolen prior to the completion of the application to purchase to any local law enforcement agency of the city, county, or city and county in which he or she resides.

(xii) The return of any handgun to its owner.

(xiii) Community colleges that are certified by the Commission on Peace Officer Standards and Training to present the law enforcement academy basic course or other commission-certified law enforcement training.

(b) No person licensed under Section 12071 shall supply, sell, deliver, or give possession or control of a handgun to any person under the age of 21 years or any other firearm to a person under the age of 18 years.

(c) No dealer, whether or not acting pursuant to Section 12082, shall deliver a firearm to a person, as follows:

(1) Within 10 days of the application to purchase, or, after notice by the department pursuant to subdivision (d) of Section 12076, within 10 days of the submission to the department of any correction to the application, or within 10 days of the submission to the department of any fee required pursuant to subdivision (e) of Section 12076, whichever is later.

(2) Unless unloaded and securely wrapped or unloaded and in a locked container.

(3) Unless the purchaser, transferee, or person being loaned the firearm presents clear evidence of his or her identity and age, as defined in Section 12071, to the dealer.

(4) Whenever the dealer is notified by the Department of Justice that the person is prohibited by state or federal law from possessing, receiving, owning, or purchasing a firearm.

(5)(A) Commencing April 1, 1994, and until January 1, 2003, no handgun shall be delivered unless the purchaser, transferee, or person being loaned the firearm presents to the dealer a basic firearms safety certificate.

(B) Commencing January 1, 2003, no handgun shall be delivered unless the purchaser, transferee, or person being loaned the handgun presents a handgun safety certificate to the dealer.

(6) No handgun shall be delivered whenever the dealer is notified by the Department of Justice that within the preceding 30-day period the purchaser has made another application to purchase a handgun and that the previous application to purchase involved none of the entities specified in subparagraph (B) of paragraph (9) of subdivision (a).

(d) Where neither party to the transaction holds a dealer's license issued pursuant to Section 12071, the parties to the transaction shall complete the sale, loan, or transfer of that firearm through a licensed firearms dealer pursuant to Section 12082.

(e) No person may commit an act of collusion relating to Article 8 (commencing with Section 12800) of Chapter 6. For purposes of this section and Section 12071, collusion may be proven by any one of the following factors:

(1) Answering a test applicant's questions during an objective test relating to firearms safety.

(2) Knowingly grading the examination falsely.

(3) Providing an advance copy of the test to an applicant.

(4) Taking or allowing another person to take the basic firearms safety course for one who is the applicant for a basic firearms safety certificate or a handgun safety certificate.

(5) Allowing another to take the objective test for the applicant, purchaser, or transferee.

(6) Using or allowing another to use one's identification, proof of residency, or thumbprint.

(7) Allowing others to give unauthorized assistance during the examination.

(8) Reference to unauthorized materials during the examination and cheating by the applicant.

(9) Providing originals or photocopies of the objective test, or any version thereof, to any person other than as authorized by the department.

(f)(1)(A) Commencing July 1, 2008, a person who is licensed pursuant to Chapter 44 (commencing with Section 921) of Title 18 of the United States Code may not deliver, sell, or transfer a firearm to a person in California who is licensed pursuant to Chapter 44 (commencing with Section 921) of Title 18 of the United States Code unless, prior to delivery, the person intending to deliver, sell, or transfer the firearm obtains a verification number via the Internet for the intended delivery, sale, or transfer, from the department. If Internet service is unavailable to either the department or the licensee due to a technical or other malfunction, or a federal firearms licensee who is located outside of California does not possess a computer or have Internet access, alternate means of communication, including facsimile or telephone, shall be made available for a licensee to obtain a verification number in order to comply with this section.

(B) For every verification number request received pursuant to this section, the department shall determine whether the intended recipient is on the centralized list of firearms dealers pursuant to this section, or the centralized list of exempted federal firearms licensees pursuant to subdivision (a) of Section 12083, or the centralized list of firearms manufacturers pursuant to subdivision (f) of Section 12086.

(C) If the department finds after the reviews specified in subparagraph (B) that the intended recipient is authorized to receive the firearm shipment, the department shall issue to the inquiring party a unique verification number for the intended delivery, sale, or transfer. One verification number shall be issued for each delivery, sale, or transfer, which may involve multiple firearms. In addition to the unique verification number, the department may provide to the inquiring party information necessary for determining the eligibility of the intended recipient to receive the firearm. The person intending to deliver, sell, or transfer the firearm shall provide the unique verification number to the recipient along with the firearm upon delivery, in a manner to be determined by the department.

(D) If the department finds after the reviews specified in subparagraph (B) that the intended recipient is not authorized to receive the firearm shipment, the department shall notify the inquiring party that the intended recipient is ineligible to receive the shipment.

(E) The department shall prescribe the manner in which the verification numbers may be requested via the Internet, or by alternate means of communication, such as by facsimile or telephone, including all required enrollment information and procedures.

(2)(A) On or after January 1, 1998, within 60 days of bringing a handgun into this state, a personal handgun importer shall do one of the following:

(i) Forward by prepaid mail or deliver in person to the Department of Justice, a report prescribed by the department including information concerning that individual and a description of the firearm in question.

(ii) Sell or transfer the firearm in accordance with the provisions of subdivision (d) or in accordance with the provisions of an exemption from subdivision (d).

(iii) Sell or transfer the firearm to a dealer licensed pursuant to Section 12071.

(iv) Sell or transfer the firearm to a sheriff or police department.

(B) If the personal handgun importer sells or transfers the handgun pursuant to subdivision (d) of Section 12072 and the sale or transfer cannot be completed by the dealer to the purchaser or transferee, and the firearm can be returned to the personal handgun importer, the personal handgun importer shall have complied with the provisions of this paragraph.

(C) The provisions of this paragraph are cumulative and shall not be construed as restricting the application of any other law. However, an act or omission punishable in different ways by this section and different provisions of the Penal Code shall not be punished under more than one provision.

(D)(i) On and after January 1, 1998, the department shall conduct a public education and notification program regarding this paragraph to ensure a high degree of publicity of the provisions of this paragraph.

(ii) As part of the public education and notification program described in this subparagraph, the department shall do all of the following:

(I) Work in conjunction with the Department of Motor Vehicles to ensure that any person who is subject to this paragraph is advised of the provisions of this paragraph, and provided with blank copies of the report described in clause (i) of subparagraph (A) at the time that person applies for a California driver's license or registers his or her motor vehicle in accordance with the Vehicle Code.

(II) Make the reports referred to in clause (i) of subparagraph (A) available to dealers licensed pursuant to Section 12071.

(III) Make the reports referred to in clause (i) of subparagraph (A) available to law enforcement agencies.

(IV) Make persons subject to the provisions of this paragraph aware of the fact that reports referred to in clause (i) of subparagraph (A) may be completed at either the licensed premises of dealers licensed pursuant to Section 12071 or at law enforcement agencies, that it is advisable to do so for the sake of accuracy and completeness of the reports, that prior to transporting a handgun to a law enforcement agency in order to comply with subparagraph (A), the person should give prior notice to the law enforcement agency that he or she is doing so, and that in any event, the handgun should be transported unloaded and in a locked container.

(iii) Any costs incurred by the department to implement this paragraph shall be absorbed by the department within its existing budget and the fees in the Dealers' Record of Sale Special Account allocated for implementation of this subparagraph pursuant to Section 12076.

(3) Where a person who is licensed as a collector pursuant to Chapter 44 (commencing with Section 921) of Title 18 of the United States Code and the regulations issued pursuant thereto, whose licensed premises are within this state, acquires a handgun that is a curio or relic, as defined in Section 478.11 of Title 27 of the Code of Federal Regulations, outside of this state, takes actual possession of that firearm outside of this state pursuant to the provisions of subsection (j) of Section 923 of Title 18 of the United States Code, as amended by Public Law 104-208, and transports that firearm into this state, within five days of that licensed collector transporting that firearm into this state, he or she shall report to the department in a format prescribed by the department his or her acquisition of that firearm.

(4)(A) It is the intent of the Legislature that a violation of paragraph (2) or (3) shall not constitute a "continuing offense" and the statute of limitations for commencing a prosecution for a violation of paragraph (2) or (3) commences on the date that the applicable grace period specified in paragraph (2) or (3) expires.

(B) Paragraphs (2) and (3) shall not apply to a person who reports his or her ownership of a handgun after the applicable grace period specified in paragraph (2) or (3) expires if evidence of that violation arises only as the result of the person submitting the report described in paragraph (2) or (3).

(g)(1) Except as provided in paragraph (2), (3), or (5), a violation of this section is a misdemeanor.

(2) If any of the following circumstances apply, a violation of this section is punishable by imprisonment in the state prison for two, three, or four years.

(A) If the violation is of paragraph (1) of subdivision (a).

(B) If the defendant has a prior conviction of violating the provisions, other than paragraph (9) of subdivision (a), of this section or former Section 12100 of this code or Section 8101 of the Welfare and Institutions Code.

(C) If the defendant has a prior conviction of violating any offense specified in subdivision (b) of Section 12021.1 or of a violation of Section 12020, 12220, or 12520, or of former Section 12560.

(D) If the defendant is in a prohibited class described in Section 12021 or 12021.1 of this code or Section 8100 or 8103 of the Welfare and Institutions Code.

(E) A violation of this section by a person who actively participates in a "criminal street gang" as defined in Section 186.22.

(F) A violation of subdivision (b) involving the delivery of any firearm to a person who the dealer knows, or should know, is a minor.

(3) If any of the following circumstances apply, a violation of this section shall be punished by imprisonment in a county jail not exceeding one year or in the state prison, or by a fine not to exceed one thousand dollars ($1,000), or by both that fine and imprisonment.

(A) A violation of paragraph (2), (4), or (5) of subdivision (a).

(B) A violation of paragraph (3) of subdivision (a) involving the sale, loan, or transfer of a handgun to a minor.

(C) A violation of subdivision (b) involving the delivery of a handgun.

(D) A violation of paragraph (1), (3), (4), (5), or (6) of subdivision (c) involving a pistol, revolver, or other firearm capable of being concealed upon the person.

(E) A violation of subdivision (d) involving a handgun.

(F) A violation of subdivision (e).

(4) If both of the following circumstances apply, an additional term of imprisonment in the state prison for one, two, or three years shall be imposed in addition and consecutive to the sentence prescribed.

(A) A violation of paragraph (2) of subdivision (a) or subdivision (b).

(B) The firearm transferred in violation of paragraph (2) of subdivision (a) or subdivision (b) is used in the subsequent commission of a felony for which a conviction is obtained and the prescribed sentence is imposed.

(5)(A) A first violation of paragraph (9) of subdivision (a) is an infraction punishable by a fine of fifty dollars ($50).

(B) A second violation of paragraph (9) of subdivision (a) is an infraction punishable by a fine of one hundred dollars ($100).

(C) A third or subsequent violation of paragraph (9) of subdivision (a) is a misdemeanor.(D) For purposes of this paragraph each application to purchase a handgun in violation of paragraph (9) of subdivision (a) shall be deemed a separate offense.

Penal Code § 12072.5.

(a) For purposes of this section, "ballistics identification systems" includes, but is not limited to, any automated image analysis system that is capable of storing firearm ballistic markings and tracing those markings to the firearm that produced them.

(b) The Attorney General shall conduct a study to evaluate ballistics identification systems to determine the feasibility and potential benefits to law enforcement of utilizing a statewide ballistics identification system capable of maintaining a data base of ballistic images and information from test fired and sold firearms. The study shall include an evaluation of ballistics identification systems currently used by state and federal law enforcement agencies and the firearms industry. The Attorney General shall consult with law enforcement agencies, firearms industry representatives, private technology providers, and other appropriate parties in conducting the study.

(c) In evaluating ballistics identification systems to determine the feasibility of utilizing a statewide system as required pursuant to subdivision (b), the Attorney General shall consider, at a minimum, the following:

(1) The development of methods by which firearm manufacturers, importers, and dealers may potentially capture ballistic images from firearms prior to sale in California and forward that information to the Attorney General.

(2) The development of methods by which the Attorney General will receive, store, and make available to law enforcement ballistic images submitted by firearm manufacturers, importers, and dealers prior to sale in California.

(3) The potential financial costs to the Attorney General of implementing and operating a statewide ballistics identification system, including the process for receipt of information from firearm manufacturers, importers, and dealers.

(4) The capability of a ballistics identification system maintaining a data base of ballistic images and information from test fired firearms for all firearms sold in California.

(5) The compatibility of a ballistics identification system with ballistics identification systems that are currently used by law enforcement agencies in California.

(6) A method to ensure that state and local law enforcement agencies can forward ballistic identification information to the Attorney General for inclusion in a statewide ballistics identification system.

(7) The feasibility and potential benefits to law enforcement of requiring firearm manufacturers, importers, and dealers to provide the Attorney General with ballistic images from any, or a selected number of, test fired firearms prior to the sale of those firearms in California.

(d) The Attorney General shall submit a report to the Legislature with the results of the study not later than June 1, 2001. In the event the report includes a determination that a ballistics identification system and data base is feasible and would benefit law enforcement, the report shall also recommend a strategy for implementation.

Penal Code § 12073.

(a) As required by the Department of Justice, every dealer shall keep a register or record of electronic or telephonic transfer in which shall be entered the information prescribed in Section 12077.

(b) This section shall not apply to any of the following transactions:

(1) The delivery, sale, or transfer of an unloaded firearm that is not a handgun by a dealer to another dealer upon proof of compliance with the requirements of paragraph (1) of subdivision (f) of Section 12072.

(2) The delivery, sale, or transfer of an unloaded firearm by a dealer to another dealer if that firearm is intended as merchandise in the receiving dealer's business upon proof of compliance with the requirements of paragraph (1) of subdivision (f) of Section 12072.

(3) The delivery, sale, or transfer of an unloaded firearm by a dealer to a person licensed as an importer or manufacturer pursuant to Chapter 44 (commencing with Section 921) of Title 18 of the United States Code and any regulations issued pursuant thereto.

(4) The delivery, sale, or transfer of an unloaded firearm by a dealer who sells, transfers, or delivers the firearm to a person who resides outside this state who is licensed pursuant to Chapter 44 (commencing with Section 921) of Title 18 of the United States Code and any regulations issued pursuant thereto.

(5) The delivery, sale, or transfer of an unloaded firearm by a dealer to a wholesaler if that firearm is being returned to the wholesaler and is intended as merchandise in the wholesaler's business.

(6) The delivery, sale, or transfer of an unloaded firearm that is not a handgun by a dealer to himself or herself.

(7) The loan of an unloaded firearm by a dealer who also operates a target facility which holds a business or regulatory license on the premises of the building designated in the license or whose building designated in the license is on the premises of any club or organization organized for the purpose of practicing shooting at targets upon established ranges, whether public or private, to a person at that target facility or club or organization, if the firearm is kept at all times within the premises of the target range or on the premises of the club or organization.

(8) The delivery of an unloaded firearm by a dealer to a gunsmith for service or repair.

(9) The return of an unloaded firearm to the owner of that firearm by a dealer, if the owner initially delivered the firearm to the dealer for service or repair.

(10) The loan of an unloaded firearm by a dealer to a person who possesses a valid entertainment firearms permit issued pursuant to Section 12081, for use solely as a prop in a motion picture, television, video, theatrical, or other entertainment production or event.

(11) The loan of an unloaded firearm by a dealer to a consultant-evaluator, if the loan does not exceed 45 days from the date

of delivery of the firearm by the dealer to the consultant-evaluator.

(c) A violation of this section is a misdemeanor.

Penal Code § 12074.

(a) The register shall be prepared by and obtained from the State Printer and shall be furnished by the State Printer only to dealers on application at a cost to be determined by the Department of General Services for each 100 leaves in quadruplicate, one original and three duplicates for the making of carbon copies. The original and duplicate copies shall differ in color, and shall be in the form provided by this article.

(b) Where the electronic transfer of applicant information is used, the Department of Justice shall develop the standards for all appropriate electronic equipment and telephone numbers to effect the transfer of information to the department.

Penal Code § 12075.

The State Printer upon issuing a register shall forward to the Department of Justice the name and business address of the dealer together with the series and sheet numbers of the register. The register shall not be transferable. If the dealer moves his business to a different location he shall notify the department of such fact in writing within 48 hours.

Penal Code § 12076.

(a)(1) Before January 1, 1998, the Department of Justice shall determine the method by which a dealer shall submit firearm purchaser information to the department and the information shall be in one of the following formats:

(A) Submission of the register described in Section 12077.

(B) Electronic or telephonic transfer of the information contained in the register described in Section 12077.

(2) On or after January 1, 1998, electronic or telephonic transfer, including voice or facsimile transmission, shall be the exclusive means by which purchaser information is transmitted to the department.

(3) On or after January 1, 2003, except as permitted by the department, electronic transfer shall be the exclusive means by which information is transmitted to the department. Telephonic transfer shall not be permitted for information regarding sales of any firearms.

(b)(1) Where the register is used, the purchaser of any firearm shall be required to present clear evidence of his or her identity and age, as defined in Section 12071, to the dealer, and the dealer shall require him or her to sign his or her current legal name and affix his or her residence address and date of birth to the register in quadruplicate. The salesperson shall affix his or her signature to the register in quadruplicate as a witness to the signature and identification of the purchaser. Any person furnishing a fictitious name or address or knowingly furnishing any incorrect information or knowingly omitting any information required to be provided for the register and any person violating any provision of this section is guilty of a misdemeanor, provided however, that any person who is prohibited from obtaining a firearm pursuant to Section 12021 or 12021.1 of this code, or Section 8100 or 8103 of the Welfare and Institutions Code who knowingly furnishes a fictitious name or address or knowingly furnishes any incorrect information or knowingly omits any information required to be provided for the register shall be punished by imprisonment in a county jail not exceeding one year or imprisonment in the state prison for a term of 8, 12, or 18 months.

(2) The original of the register shall be retained by the dealer in consecutive order. Each book of 50 originals shall become the permanent register of transactions that shall be retained for not less than three years from the date of the last transaction and shall be available for the inspection of any peace officer, Department of Justice employee designated by the Attorney General, or agent of the federal Bureau of Alcohol, Tobacco, Firearms, and Explosives upon the presentation of proper identification, but no information shall be compiled therefrom regarding the purchasers or other transferees of firearms that are not pistols, revolvers, or other firearms capable of being concealed upon the person.

(3) Two copies of the original sheet of the register, on the date of the application to purchase, shall be placed in the mail, postage prepaid, and properly addressed to the Department of Justice in Sacramento.

(4) If requested, a photocopy of the original shall be provided to the purchaser by the dealer.

(5) If the transaction is a private party transfer conducted pursuant to Section 12082, a photocopy of the original shall be provided to the seller or purchaser by the dealer, upon request. The dealer shall redact all of the purchaser's personal information, as required pursuant to paragraph (1) of subdivision (b) and paragraph (1) of subdivision (c) of Section 12077, from the seller's copy, and the seller's personal information from the purchaser's copy.

(c)(1) Where the electronic or telephonic transfer of applicant information is used, the purchaser shall be required to present clear evidence of his or her identity and age, as defined in Section 12071, to the dealer, and the dealer shall require him or her to sign his or her current legal name to the record of electronic or telephonic transfer. The salesperson shall affix his or her signature to the record of electronic or telephonic transfer as a witness to the signature and identification of the purchaser. Any person furnishing a fictitious name or address or knowingly furnishing any incorrect information or knowingly omitting any information required to be provided for the electronic or telephonic transfer and any person violating any provision of this section is guilty of a misdemeanor, provided however, that any person who is prohibited from obtaining a firearm pursuant to Section 12021 or 12021.1 of this code, or Section 8100 or 8103 of the Welfare and Institutions Code who knowingly furnishes a fictitious name or address or knowingly furnishes any incorrect information or knowingly omits any information required to be provided for the register shall be punished by imprisonment in a county jail not exceeding one year or imprisonment in the state prison for a term of 8, 12, or 18 months.

(2) The record of applicant information shall be transmitted to the Department of Justice in Sacramento by electronic or telephonic transfer on the date of the application to purchase.

(3) The original of each record of electronic or telephonic transfer shall be retained by the dealer in consecutive order. Each original shall become the permanent record of the transaction that shall be retained for not less than three years from the date of the last transaction and shall be provided for the inspection of any peace officer, Department of Justice employee designated by the Attorney General, or agent of the federal Bureau of Alcohol, Tobacco, Firearms, and Explosives upon the presentation of proper identification, but no information shall be compiled therefrom regarding the purchasers or other transferees of firearms that are not pistols, revolvers, or

other firearms capable of being concealed upon the person.

(4) If requested, a copy of the record of electronic or telephonic transfer shall be provided to the purchaser by the dealer.

(5) If the transaction is a private party transfer conducted pursuant to Section 12082, a copy shall be provided to the seller or purchaser by the dealer, upon request. The dealer shall redact all of the purchaser's personal information, as required pursuant to paragraph (1) of subdivision (b) and paragraph (1) of subdivision (c) of Section 12077, from the seller's copy, and the seller's personal information from the purchaser's copy.

(d)(1) The department shall examine its records, as well as those records that it is authorized to request from the State Department of Mental Health pursuant to Section 8104 of the Welfare and Institutions Code, in order to determine if the purchaser is a person described in subparagraph (A) of paragraph (9) of subdivision (a) of Section 12072, or is prohibited by state or federal law from possessing, receiving, owning, or purchasing a firearm.

(2) To the extent that funding is available, the Department of Justice may participate in the National Instant Criminal Background Check System (NICS), as described in subsection (t) of Section 922 of Title 18 of the United States Code, and, if that participation is implemented, shall notify the dealer and the chief of the police department of the city or city and county in which the sale was made, or if the sale was made in a district in which there is no municipal police department, the sheriff of the county in which the sale was made, that the purchaser is a person prohibited from acquiring a firearm under federal law.

(3) If the department determines that the purchaser is prohibited by state or federal law from possessing, receiving, owning, or purchasing a firearm or is a person described in subparagraph (A) of paragraph (9) of subdivision (a) of Section 12072, it shall immediately notify the dealer and the chief of the police department of the city or city and county in which the sale was made, or if the sale was made in a district in which there is no municipal police department, the sheriff of the county in which the sale was made, of that fact.

(4) If the department determines that the copies of the register submitted to it pursuant to paragraph (3) of subdivision (b) contain any blank spaces or inaccurate, illegible, or incomplete information, preventing identification of the purchaser or the pistol, revolver, or other firearm to be purchased, or if any fee required pursuant to subdivision (e) is not submitted by the dealer in conjunction with submission of copies of the register, the department may notify the dealer of that fact. Upon notification by the department, the dealer shall submit corrected copies of the register to the department, or shall submit any fee required pursuant to subdivision (e), or both, as appropriate and, if notification by the department is received by the dealer at any time prior to delivery of the firearm to be purchased, the dealer shall withhold delivery until the conclusion of the waiting period described in Sections 12071 and 12072.

(5) If the department determines that the information transmitted to it pursuant to subdivision (c) contains inaccurate or incomplete information preventing identification of the purchaser or the pistol, revolver, or other firearm capable of being concealed upon the person to be purchased, or if the fee required pursuant to subdivision (e) is not transmitted by the dealer in conjunction with transmission of the electronic or telephonic record, the department may notify the dealer of that fact. Upon notification by the department, the dealer shall transmit corrections to the record of electronic or telephonic transfer to the department, or shall transmit any fee required pursuant to subdivision (e), or both, as appropriate, and if notification by the department is received by the dealer at any time prior to delivery of the firearm to be purchased, the dealer shall withhold delivery until the conclusion of the waiting period described in Sections 12071 and 12072.

(e) The Department of Justice may require the dealer to charge each firearm purchaser a fee not to exceed fourteen dollars ($14), except that the fee may be increased at a rate not to exceed any increase in the California Consumer Price Index as compiled and reported by the California Department of Industrial Relations. The fee shall be no more than is necessary to fund the following:

(1)(A) The department for the cost of furnishing this information.

(B) The department for the cost of meeting its obligations under paragraph (2) of subdivision (b) of Section 8100 of the Welfare and Institutions Code.

(2) Local mental health facilities for state-mandated local costs resulting from the reporting requirements imposed by Section 8103 of the Welfare and Institutions Code.

(3) The State Department of Mental Health for the costs resulting from the requirements imposed by Section 8104 of the Welfare and Institutions Code.

(4) Local mental hospitals, sanitariums, and institutions for state-mandated local costs resulting from the reporting requirements imposed by Section 8105 of the Welfare and Institutions Code.

(5) Local law enforcement agencies for state-mandated local costs resulting from the notification requirements set forth in subdivision (a) of Section 6385 of the Family Code.

(6) Local law enforcement agencies for state-mandated local costs resulting from the notification requirements set forth in subdivision (c) of Section 8105 of the Welfare and Institutions Code.

(7) For the actual costs associated with the electronic or telephonic transfer of information pursuant to subdivision (c).

(8) The Department of Food and Agriculture for the costs resulting from the notification provisions set forth in Section 5343.5 of the Food and Agricultural Code.

(9) The department for the costs associated with subparagraph (D) of paragraph (2) of subdivision (f) of Section 12072.

(10) The department for the costs associated with funding Department of Justice firearms-related regulatory and enforcement activities related to the sale, purchase, loan, or transfer of firearms pursuant to this chapter. The fee established pursuant to this subdivision shall not exceed the sum of the actual processing costs of the department, the estimated reasonable costs of the local mental health facilities for complying with the reporting requirements imposed by paragraph (2) of this subdivision, the costs of the State Department of Mental Health for complying with the requirements imposed by paragraph (3) of this subdivision, the estimated reasonable costs of local mental hospitals, sanitariums, and institutions for complying with the reporting requirements imposed by paragraph (4) of this subdivision, the estimated reasonable costs of local law enforcement agencies for complying with the notification requirements set forth in subdivision (a) of Section 6385 of the Family Code, the estimated reasonable costs of local law enforcement agencies for complying with the notification requirements set forth in subdivision (c) of Section 8105 of the Welfare and Institutions Code imposed by paragraph (6) of this subdivision, the estimated reasonable costs of the Department of Food and Agriculture for the costs resulting from the notification provisions set forth in Section 5343.5 of the Food and Agricultural Code, the estimated reasonable costs of the department for the costs

associated with subparagraph (D) of paragraph (2) of subdivision (f) of Section 12072, and the estimated reasonable costs of department firearms-related regulatory and enforcement activities related to the sale, purchase, loan, or transfer of firearms pursuant to this chapter.

(f)(1) The Department of Justice may charge a fee sufficient to reimburse it for each of the following but not to exceed fourteen dollars ($14), except that the fee may be increased at a rate not to exceed any increase in the California Consumer Price Index as compiled and reported by the California Department of Industrial Relations:

(A) For the actual costs associated with the preparation, sale, processing, and filing of forms or reports required or utilized pursuant to Section 12078.

(B) For the actual processing costs associated with the submission of a Dealers' Record of Sale to the department.

(C) For the actual costs associated with the preparation, sale, processing, and filing of reports utilized pursuant to subdivision (l) of Section 12078 or paragraph (18) of subdivision (b) of Section 12071, or clause (i) of subparagraph (A) of paragraph (2) of subdivision (f) of Section 12072, or paragraph (3) of subdivision (f) of Section 12072.

(D) For the actual costs associated with the electronic or telephonic transfer of information pursuant to subdivision (c).

(2) If the department charges a fee pursuant to subparagraph (B) of paragraph (1) of this subdivision, it shall be charged in the same amount to all categories of transaction that are within that subparagraph.

(3) Any costs incurred by the Department of Justice to implement this subdivision shall be reimbursed from fees collected and charged pursuant to this subdivision. No fees shall be charged to the dealer pursuant to subdivision (e) for implementing this subdivision.

(g) All money received by the department pursuant to this section shall be deposited in the Dealers' Record of Sale Special Account of the General Fund, which is hereby created, to be available, upon appropriation by the Legislature, for expenditure by the department to offset the costs incurred pursuant to this section, paragraph (1) and subparagraph (D) of paragraph (2) of subdivision (f) of Section 12072, Sections 12083 and 12099, subdivision (c) of Section 12131, Sections 12234, 12289, and 12289.5, and subdivisions (f) and (g) of Section 12305.

(h) Where the electronic or telephonic transfer of applicant information is used, the department shall establish a system to be used for the submission of the fees described in subdivision (e) to the department.

(i)(1) Only one fee shall be charged pursuant to this section for a single transaction on the same date for the sale of any number of firearms that are not pistols, revolvers, or other firearms capable of being concealed upon the person or for the taking of possession of those firearms.

(2) In a single transaction on the same date for the delivery of any number of firearms that are pistols, revolvers, or other firearms capable of being concealed upon the person, the department shall charge a reduced fee pursuant to this section for the second and subsequent firearms that are part of that transaction.

(j) Only one fee shall be charged pursuant to this section for a single transaction on the same date for taking title or possession of any number of firearms pursuant to paragraph (18) of subdivision (b) of Section 12071 or subdivision (c) or (i) of Section 12078.

(k) Whenever the Department of Justice acts pursuant to this section as it pertains to firearms other than pistols, revolvers, or other firearms capable of being concealed upon the person, the department's acts or omissions shall be deemed to be discretionary within the meaning of the California Tort Claims Act pursuant to Division 3.6 (commencing with Section 810) of Title 1 of the Government Code.

(l) As used in this section, the following definitions apply:

(1) "Purchaser" means the purchaser or transferee of a firearm or a person being loaned a firearm.

(2) "Purchase" means the purchase, loan, or transfer of a firearm.

(3) "Sale" means the sale, loan, or transfer of a firearm.

(4) "Seller" means, if the transaction is being conducted pursuant to Section 12082, the person selling, loaning, or transferring the firearm.

Penal Code § 12076.5.

(a) The Firearms Safety and Enforcement Special Fund is hereby established in the State Treasury and shall be administered by the Department of Justice. Notwithstanding Section 13340 of the Government Code, all moneys in the fund are continuously appropriated to the Department of Justice without regard to fiscal years for the purpose of implementing and enforcing the provisions of Article 8 (commencing with Section 12800), as added by the Statutes of 2001, enforcing the provisions of this title, and for the establishment, maintenance and upgrading of equipment and services necessary for firearms dealers to comply with Section 12077.

(b) The Department of Justice may require firearms dealers to charge each person who obtains a firearm a fee not to exceed five dollars ($5) for each transaction. Revenues from this fee shall be deposited in the Firearms Safety and Enforcement Special Fund.

Penal Code § 12077.

(a) The Department of Justice shall prescribe the form of the register and the record of electronic transfer pursuant to Section 12074.

(b)(1) For handguns, information contained in the register or record of electronic transfer shall be the date and time of sale, make of firearm, peace officer exemption status pursuant to subdivision (a) of Section 12078 and the agency name, dealer waiting period exemption pursuant to subdivision (n) of Section 12078, dangerous weapons permit holder waiting period exemption pursuant to subdivision (r) of Section 12078, curio and relic waiting period exemption pursuant to subdivision (t) of Section 12078, California Firearms Dealer number issued pursuant to Section 12071, for transactions occurring prior to January 1, 2003, the purchaser's basic firearms safety certificate number issued pursuant to Sections 12805 and 12809, for transactions occurring on or after January 1, 2003, the purchaser's handgun safety certificate number issued pursuant to Article 8 (commencing with Section 12800), manufacturer's name if stamped on the firearm, model name or number, if stamped on the firearm, if applicable, serial number, other number (if more than one serial number is stamped on the firearm), any identification number or mark assigned to the firearm pursuant to Section 12092, caliber, type of firearm, if the firearm is new or used, barrel length, color of the firearm, full name of purchaser, purchaser's complete date of birth, purchaser's local address, if current address is temporary, complete permanent address of purchaser, identification of purchaser, purchaser's place of birth (state or country), purchaser's complete telephone number, purchaser's occupation, purchaser's sex, purchaser's physical description, all legal names and aliases ever used by the purchaser, yes or no answer to questions that prohibit purchase including, but not limited to, conviction of a felony as described in Section 12021 or an offense described in Section 12021.1, the purchaser's status as a person described in Section 8100 of the Welfare and Institutions Code, whether the purchaser is a person who has been adjudicated by a court to be a danger to others or found not guilty by reason of insanity, whether the purchaser is a person who has been found incompetent to stand trial or placed under conservatorship by a court pursuant to Section 8103 of the Welfare and Institutions Code, signature of purchaser, signature of salesperson (as a witness to the purchaser's signature), salesperson's certificate of eligibility number if he or she has obtained a certificate of eligibility, name and complete address of the dealer or firm selling the firearm as shown on the dealer's license, the establishment number, if assigned, the dealer's complete business telephone number, any information required by Section 12082, any information required to determine whether or not paragraph (6) of subdivision (c) of Section 12072 applies, and a statement of the penalties for any person signing a fictitious name or address or for knowingly furnishing any incorrect information or for knowingly omitting any information required to be provided for the register.

(2) Effective January 1, 2003, the purchaser shall provide his or her right thumbprint on the register in a manner prescribed by the department. No exception to this requirement shall be permitted except by regulations adopted by the department.

(3) The firearms dealer shall record on the register or record of electronic transfer the date that the handgun is delivered.

(c)(1) For firearms other than handguns, information contained in the register or record of electronic transfer shall be the date and time of sale, peace officer exemption status pursuant to subdivision (a) of Section 12078 and the agency name, auction or event waiting period exemption pursuant to subdivision (g) of Section 12078, California Firearms Dealer number issued pursuant to Section 12071, dangerous weapons permit holder waiting period exemption pursuant to subdivision (r) of Section 12078, curio and relic waiting period exemption pursuant to paragraph (1) of subdivision (t) of Section 12078, full name of purchaser, purchaser's complete date of birth, purchaser's local address, if current address is temporary, complete permanent address of purchaser, identification of purchaser, purchaser's place of birth (state or country), purchaser's complete telephone number, purchaser's occupation, purchaser's sex, purchaser' s physical description, all legal names and aliases ever used by the purchaser, yes or no answer to questions that prohibit purchase, including, but not limited to, conviction of a felony as described in Section 12021 or an offense described in Section 12021.1, the purchaser's status as a person described in Section 8100 of the Welfare and Institutions Code, whether the purchaser is a person who has been adjudicated by a court to be a danger to others or found not guilty by reason of insanity, whether the purchaser is a person who has been found incompetent to stand trial or placed under conservatorship by a court pursuant to Section 8103 of the Welfare and Institutions Code, signature of purchaser, signature of salesperson (as a witness to the purchaser's signature), salesperson' s certificate of eligibility number if he or she has obtained a certificate of eligibility, name and complete address of the dealer or firm selling the firearm as shown on the dealer's license, the establishment number, if assigned, the dealer's complete business telephone number, any information required by Section 12082, and a statement of the penalties for any person signing a fictitious name or address or for knowingly furnishing any incorrect information or for knowingly omitting any information required to be provided for the register.

(2) Effective January 1, 2003, the purchaser shall provide his or her right thumbprint on the register in a manner prescribed by the department. No exception to this requirement shall be permitted except by regulations adopted by the department.

(3) The firearms dealer shall record on the register or record of electronic transfer the date that the firearm is delivered.

(d) Where the register is used, the following shall apply:

(1) Dealers shall use ink to complete each document.

(2) The dealer or salesperson making a sale shall ensure that all information is provided legibly. The dealer and salespersons shall be informed that incomplete or illegible information will delay sales.

(3) Each dealer shall be provided instructions regarding the procedure for completion of the form and routing of the form. Dealers shall comply with these instructions which shall include the information set forth in this subdivision.

(4) One firearm transaction shall be reported on each record of sale document. For purposes of this subdivision, a "transaction" means a single sale, loan, or transfer of any number of firearms that are not handguns.

(e) The dealer or salesperson making a sale shall ensure that all required information has been obtained from the purchaser. The dealer and all salespersons shall be informed that incomplete information will delay sales.

(f) Effective January 1, 2003, the purchaser's name, date of birth, and driver's license or identification number shall be obtained electronically from the magnetic strip on the purchaser's driver's license or identification and shall not be supplied by any other means except as authorized by the department. This requirement shall not apply in either of the following cases:

(1) The purchaser's identification consists of a military identification card.

(2) Due to technical limitations, the magnetic stripe reader is unable to obtain the required information from the purchaser's identification. In those circumstances, the firearms dealer shall obtain a photocopy of the identification as proof of compliance.

(3) In the event that the dealer has reported to the department that the dealer's equipment has failed, information pursuant to this subdivision shall be obtained by an alternative method to be determined by the department.

(g) As used in this section, the following definitions shall control:

(1) "Purchaser" means the purchaser or transferee of a firearm or the person being loaned a firearm.

(2) "Purchase" means the purchase, loan, or transfer of a firearm.

(3) "Sale" means the sale, loan, or transfer of a firearm.

Penal Code § 12077.5.

(a) An individual may request that the Department of Justice perform a firearms eligibility check for that individual. The applicant requesting the eligibility check shall provide the information required by subdivision (c) of Section 12077 to the department, in an application specified by the department.

(b) The department shall charge a fee of twenty dollars ($20) for performing the eligibility check authorized by this section, but not to exceed the actual processing costs of the department. After the department establishes fees sufficient to reimburse the department for processing costs, fees charged may increase at a rate not to exceed the legislatively approved cost-of-living adjustment for the department's budget or as otherwise increased through the Budget Act.

(c) An applicant for the eligibility check pursuant to subdivision (a) shall complete the application, have it notarized by any licensed California Notary Public, and submit it by mail to the department. Upon receipt of a notarized application and fee, the department shall do all of the following:

(1) Examine its records, and the records it is authorized to request from the State Department of Mental Health pursuant to Section 8104 of the Welfare and Institutions Code, to determine if the purchaser is prohibited by state or federal law from possessing, receiving, owning, or purchasing a firearm.

(2) Notify the applicant by mail of its determination of whether the applicant is prohibited by state or federal law from possessing, receiving, owning, or purchasing a firearm. The department's notification shall state either "eligible to possess firearms as of the date the check was completed" or "ineligible to possess firearms as of the date the check was completed."

(d) If the department determines that the information submitted to it in the application contains any blank spaces, or inaccurate, illegible, or incomplete information, preventing identification of the applicant, or if the required fee is not submitted, the department shall not be required to perform the firearms eligibility check.

(e) The department shall make applications to conduct a firearms eligibility check as described in this section available to licensed firearms dealers and on the department's Web site.

(f) The department shall be immune from any liability arising out of the performance of the firearms eligibility check, or any reliance upon the firearms eligibility check.

(g) No person or agency may require or request another person to obtain a firearms eligibility check or notification of a firearms eligibility check pursuant to this section. A violation of this subdivision is a misdemeanor.

(h) The department shall include on the application specified in subdivision (a) and the notification of eligibility specified in subdivision (c) the following statements: "No person or agency may require or request another person to obtain a firearms eligibility check or notification of firearms eligibility check pursuant to Section 12077.5 of the Penal Code. A violation of these provisions is a misdemeanor." "If the applicant for a firearms eligibility check purchases, transfers, or receives a firearm through a licensed dealer as required by law, a waiting period and background check are both required."

Penal Code § 12078.

(a)(1) The waiting periods described in Sections 12071 and 12072 shall not apply to the deliveries, transfers, or sales of firearms made to persons properly identified as full-time paid peace officers as defined in Chapter 4.5 (commencing with Section 830) of Title 3 of Part 2, provided that the peace officers are authorized by their employer to carry firearms while in the performance of their duties. Proper identification is defined as verifiable written certification from the head of the agency by which the purchaser or transferee is employed, identifying the purchaser or transferee as a peace officer who is authorized to carry firearms while in the performance of his or her duties, and authorizing the purchase or transfer. The certification shall be delivered to the dealer at the time of purchase or transfer and the purchaser or transferee shall identify himself or herself as the person authorized in the certification. The dealer shall keep the certification with the record of sale. On the date that the delivery, sale, or transfer is made, the dealer delivering the firearm shall transmit to the Department of Justice an electronic or telephonic report of the transaction as is indicated in subdivision (b) or (c) of Section 12077.

(2) Subdivision (b) of Section 12801 and the preceding provisions of this article do not apply to deliveries, transfers, or sales of firearms made to authorized law enforcement representatives of cities, counties, cities and counties, or state or federal governments for exclusive use by those governmental agencies if, prior to the delivery, transfer, or sale of these firearms, written authorization from the head of the agency authorizing the transaction is presented to the person from whom the purchase, delivery, or transfer is being made. Proper written authorization is defined as verifiable written certification from the head of the agency by which the purchaser or transferee is employed, identifying the employee as an individual authorized to conduct the transaction, and authorizing the transaction for the exclusive use of the agency by which he or she is employed. Within 10 days of the date a handgun is acquired by the agency, a record of the same shall be entered as an institutional weapon into the Automated Firearms System (AFS) via the California Law Enforcement Telecommunications System (CLETS) by the law enforcement or state agency. Those agencies without access to AFS shall arrange with the sheriff of the county in which the agency is located to input this information via this system.

(3) Subdivision (b) of Section 12801 and the preceding provisions of this article do not apply to the loan of a firearm made by an authorized law enforcement representative of a city, county, or city and county, or the state or federal government to a peace officer employed by that agency and authorized to carry a firearm for the carrying and use of that firearm by that peace officer in the course and scope of his or her duties.

(4) Subdivision (b) of Section 12801 and the preceding provisions of this article do not apply to the delivery, sale, or transfer of a firearm by a law enforcement agency to a peace officer pursuant to Section 10334 of the Public Contract Code. Within 10 days of the date that a handgun is sold, delivered, or transferred pursuant to Section 10334 of the Public Contract Code to that peace officer, the name of the officer and the make, model, serial number, and other identifying characteristics of the firearm being sold, transferred, or delivered shall be entered into the Automated Firearms System (AFS) via the California Law Enforcement Telecommunications System (CLETS) by the law enforcement or state agency that sold, transferred, or delivered the firearm. Those agencies without access to AFS shall arrange with the sheriff of the county in which the agency is located to input this information via this system.

(5) Subdivision (b) of Section 12801 and the preceding provisions of this article do not apply to the delivery, sale, or transfer of a firearm by a law enforcement agency to a retiring peace officer who is authorized to carry a firearm pursuant to Section 12027.1. Within 10 days of the date that a handgun is sold, delivered, or transferred to that retiring peace officer, the name of the officer and the make, model, serial number, and other identifying characteristics of the firearm being sold, transferred, or delivered shall be entered into the Automated Firearms System (AFS) via the California Law Enforcement Telecommunications System (CLETS) by the law enforcement or state agency that sold, transferred, or delivered the firearm. Those agencies without access to AFS shall arrange with the sheriff of the county in which the agency is located to input this information via this system.

(6) Subdivision (d) of Section 12072 and subdivision (b) of Section 12801 do not apply to sales, deliveries, or transfers of firearms to authorized representatives of cities, cities and counties, counties, or state or federal governments for those governmental agencies where the entity is acquiring the weapon as part of an authorized, voluntary program where the entity is buying or receiving weapons from private individuals. Any weapons acquired pursuant to this paragraph shall be disposed of pursuant to the applicable

provisions of Section 12028 or 12032.

(7) Subdivision (d) of Section 12072 and subdivision (b) of Section 12801 shall not apply to the sale, loan, delivery, or transfer of a firearm made by an authorized law enforcement representative of a city, county, city and county, state, or the federal government to any public or private nonprofit historical society, museum, or institutional collection or the purchase or receipt of that firearm by that public or private nonprofit historical society, museum, or institutional collection if all of the following conditions are met:

(A) The entity receiving the firearm is open to the public.

(B) The firearm prior to delivery is deactivated or rendered inoperable.

(C) The firearm is not subject to Section 12028, 12028.5, 12030, or 12032.

(D) The firearm is not prohibited by other provisions of law from being sold, delivered, or transferred to the public at large.

(E) Prior to delivery, the entity receiving the firearm submits a written statement to the law enforcement representative stating that the firearm will not be restored to operating condition, and will either remain with that entity, or if subsequently disposed of, will be transferred in accordance with the applicable provisions of this article and, if applicable, Section 12801.

(F) Within 10 days of the date that the firearm is sold, loaned, delivered, or transferred to that entity, the name of the government entity delivering the firearm, and the make, model, serial number, and other identifying characteristics of the firearm and the name of the person authorized by the entity to take possession of the firearm shall be reported to the department in a manner prescribed by the department.

(G) In the event of a change in the status of the designated representative, the entity shall notify the department of a new representative within 30 days.

(8) Subdivision (d) of Section 12072 and subdivision (b) of Section 12801 shall not apply to the sale, loan, delivery, or transfer of a firearm made by any person other than a representative of an authorized law enforcement agency to any public or private nonprofit historical society, museum, or institutional collection if all of the following conditions are met:

(A) The entity receiving the firearm is open to the public.

(B) The firearm is deactivated or rendered inoperable prior to delivery.

(C) The firearm is not of a type prohibited from being sold, delivered, or transferred to the public.

(D) Prior to delivery, the entity receiving the firearm submits a written statement to the person selling, loaning, or transferring the firearm stating that the firearm will not be restored to operating condition, and will either remain with that entity, or if subsequently disposed of, will be transferred in accordance with the applicable provisions of this article and, if applicable, Section 12801.

(E) If title to a handgun is being transferred to the public or private nonprofit historical society, museum, or institutional collection, then the designated representative of that public or private historical society, museum, or institutional collection, within 30 days of taking possession of that handgun, shall forward by prepaid mail or deliver in person to the Department of Justice, a single report signed by both parties to the transaction, that includes information identifying the person representing that public or private historical society, museum, or institutional collection, how title was obtained and from whom, and a description of the firearm in question, along with a copy of the written statement referred to in subparagraph (D). The report forms that are to be completed pursuant to this paragraph shall be provided by the Department of Justice.

(F) In the event of a change in the status of the designated representative, the entity shall notify the department of a new representative within 30 days.

(b)(1) Section 12071, subdivisions (c) and (d) of Section 12072, and subdivision (b) of Section 12801 shall not apply to deliveries, sales, or transfers of firearms between or to importers and manufacturers of firearms licensed to engage in that business pursuant to Chapter 44 (commencing with Section 921) of Title 18 of the United States Code and the regulations issued pursuant thereto.

(2) Subdivision (b) of Section 12801 shall not apply to the delivery, sale, or transfer of a handgun to a person licensed pursuant to Section 12071, where the licensee is receiving the handgun in the course and scope of his or her activities as a person licensed pursuant to Section 12071.

(c)(1) Subdivision (d) of Section 12072 shall not apply to the infrequent transfer of a firearm that is not a handgun by gift, bequest, intestate succession, or other means by one individual to another if both individuals are members of the same immediate family.

(2) Subdivision (d) of Section 12072 shall not apply to the infrequent transfer of a handgun by gift, bequest, intestate succession, or other means by one individual to another if both individuals are members of the same immediate family and all of the following conditions are met:

(A) The person to whom the firearm is transferred shall, within 30 days of taking possession of the firearm, forward by prepaid mail or deliver in person to the Department of Justice, a report that includes information concerning the individual taking possession of the firearm, how title was obtained and from whom, and a description of the firearm in question. The report forms that individuals complete pursuant to this paragraph shall be provided to them by the Department of Justice.

(B) The person taking title to the firearm shall first obtain a handgun safety certificate.

(C) The person receiving the firearm is 18 years of age or older.

(3) As used in this subdivision, "immediate family member" means any one of the following relationships:

(A) Parent and child.

(B) Grandparent and grandchild.

(d)(1) Subdivision (d) of Section 12072 shall not apply to the infrequent loan of firearms between persons who are personally known to each other for any lawful purpose, if the loan does not exceed 30 days in duration and, when the firearm is a handgun, commencing January 1, 2003, the individual being loaned the handgun has a valid handgun safety certificate.

(2) Subdivision (d) of Section 12072, and subdivision (b) of Section 12801 shall not apply to the loan of a firearm where all of the following conditions exist:

(A) The person loaning the firearm is at all times within the presence of the person being loaned the firearm.

(B) The loan is for a lawful purpose.

(C) The loan does not exceed three days in duration.

(D) The individual receiving the firearm is not prohibited by state or federal law from possessing, receiving, owning, or purchasing a firearm.

(E) The person loaning the firearm is 18 years of age or older.

(F) The person being loaned the firearm is 18 years of age or older.

(e)(1) Section 12071, subdivisions (c) and (d) and paragraph (1) of subdivision (f) of Section 12072, and subdivision (b) of Section 12801 shall not apply to the delivery of a firearm to a gunsmith for service or repair, or to the return of the firearm to its owner by the gunsmith, or to the delivery of a firearm by a gunsmith to a person licensed pursuant to Chapter 44 (commencing with Section 921) of Title 18 of the United States Code for service or repair and the return of the firearm to the gunsmith.

(2) Paragraph (1) of subdivision (f) of Section 12072 shall not apply to the delivery, sale, or transfer of any firearm in any of the following circumstances:

(A) Where the transferor and the transferee are the same person or corporation.

(B) Where the transfer is to or from a person who has a valid entertainment firearms permit under Section 12081 and the transfer involves the loan or return of firearms used solely as props in television, film, or theatrical productions.

(f) Subdivision (d) of Section 12072 and subdivision (b) of Section 12801 shall not apply to the sale, delivery, or transfer of firearms by persons who reside in this state to persons who reside outside this state who are licensed pursuant to Chapter 44 (commencing with Section 921) of Title 18 of the United States Code and the regulations issued pursuant thereto, if the sale, delivery, or transfer is in accordance with Chapter 44 (commencing with Section 921) of Title 18 of the United States Code and the regulations issued pursuant thereto.

(g)(1) Subdivision (d) of Section 12072 shall not apply to the infrequent sale or transfer of a firearm, other than a handgun, at auctions or similar events conducted by nonprofit mutual or public benefit corporations organized pursuant to the Corporations Code.

As used in this paragraph, the term "infrequent" shall not be construed to prohibit different local chapters of the same nonprofit corporation from conducting auctions or similar events, provided the individual local chapter conducts the auctions or similar events infrequently. It is the intent of the Legislature that different local chapters, representing different localities, be entitled to invoke the exemption created by this paragraph, notwithstanding the frequency with which other chapters of the same nonprofit corporation may conduct auctions or similar events.

(2) Subdivision (d) of Section 12072 shall not apply to the transfer of a firearm other than a handgun, if the firearm is donated for an auction or similar event described in paragraph (1) and the firearm is delivered to the nonprofit corporation immediately preceding, or contemporaneous with, the auction or similar event.

(3) The waiting period described in Sections 12071 and 12072 shall not apply to a dealer who delivers a firearm other than a handgun at an auction or similar event described in paragraph (1), as authorized by subparagraph (C) of paragraph (1) of subdivision (b) of Section 12071. Within two business days of completion of the application to purchase, the dealer shall forward by prepaid mail to the Department of Justice a report of the same as is indicated in subdivision (c) of Section 12077. If the electronic or telephonic transfer of applicant information is used, within two business days of completion of the application to purchase, the dealer delivering the firearm shall transmit to the Department of Justice an electronic or telephonic report of the same as is indicated in subdivision (c) of Section 12077.

(h) Subdivision (d) of Section 12072 and subdivision (b) of Section 12801 shall not apply to the loan of a firearm to a person 18 years of age or older for the purposes of shooting at targets if the loan occurs on the premises of a target facility that holds a business or regulatory license or on the premises of any club or organization organized for the purposes of practicing shooting at targets upon established ranges, whether public or private, if the firearm is at all times kept within the premises of the target range or on the premises of the club or organization.

(i)(1) Subdivision (d) of Section 12072 shall not apply to a person who takes title or possession of a firearm that is not a handgun by operation of law if the person is not prohibited by state or federal law from possessing, receiving, owning, or purchasing a firearm.

(2) Subdivision (d) of Section 12072 shall not apply to a person who takes title or possession of a handgun by operation of law if the person is not prohibited by state or federal law from possessing, receiving, owning, or purchasing a firearm and all of the following conditions are met:

(A) If the person taking title or possession is neither a levying officer as defined in Section 481.140, 511.060, or 680.210 of the Code of Civil Procedure, nor a person who is receiving that firearm pursuant to subparagraph (G), (I), or (J) of paragraph (2) of subdivision (u), the person shall, within 30 days of taking possession, forward by prepaid mail or deliver in person to the Department of Justice, a report of information concerning the individual taking possession of the firearm, how title or possession was obtained and from whom, and a description of the firearm in question. The reports that individuals complete pursuant to this paragraph shall be provided to them by the department.

(B) If the person taking title or possession is receiving the firearm pursuant to subparagraph (G) of paragraph (2) of subdivision (u), the person shall do both of the following:

(i) Within 30 days of taking possession, forward by prepaid mail or deliver in person to the department, a report of information concerning the individual taking possession of the firearm, how title or possession was obtained and from whom, and a description of the firearm in question. The reports that individuals complete pursuant to this paragraph shall be provided to them by the department.

(ii) Prior to taking title or possession of the firearm, the person shall obtain a handgun safety certificate.

(C) Where the person receiving title or possession of the handgun is a person described in subparagraph (I) of paragraph (2) of subdivision (u), on the date that the person is delivered the firearm, the name and other information concerning the person taking possession of the firearm, how title or possession of the firearm was obtained and from whom, and a description of the firearm by make, model, serial number, and other identifying characteristics shall be entered into the Automated Firearms System (AFS) via the California Law Enforcement Telecommunications System (CLETS) by the law enforcement or state agency that transferred or delivered the firearm. Those agencies without access to AFS shall arrange with the sheriff of the county in which the agency is located to input this information via this system.

(D) Where the person receiving title or possession of the handgun is a person described in subparagraph (J) of paragraph (2) of subdivision (u), on the date that the person is delivered the firearm, the name and other information concerning the person taking possession of the firearm, how title or possession of the firearm was obtained and from whom, and a description of the firearm by make, model, serial number, and other identifying characteristics shall be entered into the AFS via the CLETS by the law enforcement or state agency that transferred or delivered the firearm. Those agencies without access to AFS shall arrange with the sheriff of the county in which the agency is located to input this information via this system. In addition, that law enforcement agency shall not deliver that handgun to the person referred to in this subparagraph unless, prior to the delivery of the same, the person presents proof to the agency that he or she is the holder of a handgun safety certificate.

(3) Subdivision (d) of Section 12072 shall not apply to a person who takes possession of a firearm by operation of law in a representative capacity who subsequently transfers ownership of the firearm to himself or herself in his or her individual capacity. In the case of a handgun, the individual shall obtain a handgun safety certificate prior to transferring ownership to himself or herself, or taking possession of a handgun in an individual capacity.

(j) Subdivision (d) of Section 12072 and subdivision (b) of Section 12801 shall not apply to deliveries, transfers, or returns of firearms made pursuant to Section 12021.3, 12028, 12028.5, or 12030.

(k) Section 12071, subdivision (c) of Section 12072, and subdivision (b) of Section 12801 shall not apply to any of the following:

(1) The delivery, sale, or transfer of unloaded firearms that are not handguns by a dealer to another dealer upon proof of compliance with the requirements of paragraph (1) of subdivision (f) of Section 12072.

(2) The delivery, sale, or transfer of unloaded firearms by dealers to persons who reside outside this state who are licensed pursuant to Chapter 44 (commencing with Section 921) of Title 18 of the United States Code and the regulations issued pursuant thereto.

(3) The delivery, sale, or transfer of unloaded firearms to a wholesaler if the firearms are being returned to the wholesaler and are intended as merchandise in the wholesaler's business.

(4) The delivery, sale, or transfer of unloaded firearms by one dealer to another dealer if the firearms are intended as merchandise in the receiving dealer's business upon proof of compliance with the requirements of paragraph (1) of subdivision (f) of Section 12072.

(5) The delivery, sale, or transfer of an unloaded firearm that is not a handgun by a dealer to himself or herself.

(6) The loan of an unloaded firearm by a dealer who also operates a target facility that holds a business or regulatory license on the premises of the building designated in the license or whose building designated in the license is on the premises of any club or organization organized for the purposes of practicing shooting at targets upon established ranges, whether public or private, to a person at that target facility or that club or organization, if the firearm is at all times kept within the premises of the target range or on the premises of the club or organization.

(l) A person who is exempt from subdivision (d) of Section 12072 or is otherwise not required by law to report his or her acquisition, ownership, or disposal of a handgun or who moves out of this state with his or her handgun may submit a report of the same to the Department of Justice in a format prescribed by the department.

(m) Subdivision (d) of Section 12072 and subdivision (b) of Section 12801 shall not apply to the delivery, sale, or transfer of unloaded firearms to a wholesaler as merchandise in the wholesaler's business by manufacturers or importers licensed to engage in that business pursuant to Chapter 44 (commencing with Section 921) of Title 18 of the United States Code and the regulations issued pursuant thereto, or by another wholesaler, if the delivery, sale, or transfer is made in accordance with Chapter 44 (commencing with Section 921) of Title 18 of the United States Code.

(n)(1) The waiting period described in Section 12071 or 12072 shall not apply to the delivery, sale, or transfer of a handgun by a dealer in either of the following situations:

(A) The dealer is delivering the firearm to another dealer and it is not intended as merchandise in the receiving dealer's business.

(B) The dealer is delivering the firearm to himself or herself and it is not intended as merchandise in his or her business.

(2) In order for this subdivision to apply, both of the following shall occur:

(A) If the dealer is receiving the firearm from another dealer, the dealer receiving the firearm shall present proof to the dealer delivering the firearm that he or she is licensed pursuant to Section 12071 by complying with paragraph (1) of subdivision (f) of Section 12072.

(B) Whether the dealer is delivering, selling, or transferring the firearm to himself or herself or to another dealer, on the date that the application to purchase is completed, the dealer delivering the firearm shall forward by prepaid mail to the Department of Justice a report of the same and the type of information concerning the purchaser or transferee as is indicated in subdivision (b) of Section 12077. Where the electronic or telephonic transfer of applicant information is used, on the date that the application to purchase is completed, the dealer delivering the firearm shall transmit an electronic or telephonic report of the same and the type of information concerning the purchaser or transferee as is indicated in subdivision (b) of Section 12077.

(o) Section 12071 and subdivisions (c) and (d) of Section 12072 shall not apply to the delivery, sale, or transfer of a firearm regulated pursuant to Section 12020, Chapter 2 (commencing with Section 12200), Chapter 2.3 (commencing with Section 12275), or Chapter 2.5 (commencing with Section 12301), if the delivery, sale, or transfer of that firearm is conducted in accordance with the applicable provisions of Section 12020, Chapter 2 (commencing with Section 12200), Chapter 2.3 (commencing with Section 12275), or Chapter 2.5 (commencing with Section 12301).

(p)(1) Paragraph (3) of subdivision (a) and subdivision (d) of Section 12072 shall not apply to the loan of a firearm that is not a handgun to a minor, with the express permission of the parent or legal guardian of the minor, if the loan does not exceed 30 days in duration and is for a lawful purpose.

(2) Paragraph (3) of subdivision (a) of Section 12072, subdivision (d) of Section 12072, and subdivision (b) of Section 12801 shall not apply to the loan of a handgun to a minor by a person who is not the parent or legal guardian of the minor if all of the following circumstances exist:

(A) The minor has the written consent of his or her parent or legal guardian that is presented at the time of, or prior to the time of, the loan, or is accompanied by his or her parent or legal guardian at the time the loan is made.

(B) The minor is being loaned the firearm for the purpose of engaging in a lawful, recreational sport, including, but not limited to, competitive shooting, or agricultural, ranching, or hunting activity, or a motion picture, television, or video production, or entertainment or theatrical event, the nature of which involves the use of a firearm.

(C) The duration of the loan does not exceed the amount of time that is reasonably necessary to engage in the lawful, recreational sport, including, but not limited to, competitive shooting, or agricultural, ranching, or hunting activity, or a motion picture, television, or video production, or entertainment or theatrical event, the nature of which involves the use of a firearm.

(D) The duration of the loan does not, in any event, exceed 10 days.

(3) Paragraph (3) of subdivision (a), and subdivision (d), of Section 12072, and subdivision (b) of Section 12801 shall not apply to the loan of a handgun to a minor by his or her parent or legal guardian if both of the following circumstances exist:

(A) The minor is being loaned the firearm for the purposes of engaging in a lawful, recreational sport, including, but not limited to, competitive shooting, or agricultural, ranching, or hunting activity, or a motion picture, television, or video production, or entertainment or theatrical event, the nature of which involves the use of a firearm.

(B) The duration of the loan does not exceed the amount of time that is reasonably necessary to engage in the lawful, recreational sport, including, but not limited to, competitive shooting, or agricultural, ranching, or hunting activity, or a motion picture, television, or video production, or entertainment or theatrical event, the nature of which involves the use of a firearm.

(4) Paragraph (3) of subdivision (a), and subdivision (d), of Section 12072 shall not apply to the transfer or loan of a firearm that is not a handgun to a minor by his or her parent or legal guardian.

(5) Paragraph (3) of subdivision (a), and subdivision (d), of Section 12072 shall not apply to the transfer or loan of a firearm that is not a handgun to a minor by his or her grandparent who is not the legal guardian of the minor if the transfer is done with the express permission of the parent or legal guardian of the minor.

(6) Subparagraph (A) of paragraph (3) of subdivision (a) of Section 12072 shall not apply to the sale of a handgun if both of the following requirements are satisfied:

(A) The sale is to a person who is at least 18 years of age.

(B) The firearm is an antique firearm as defined in paragraph (16) of subsection (a) of Section 921 of Title 18 of the United States Code.

(q) Subdivision (d) of Section 12072 shall not apply to the loan of a firearm that is not a handgun to a licensed hunter for use by that licensed hunter for a period of time not to exceed the duration of the hunting season for which that firearm is to be used.

(r) The waiting period described in Section 12071 or 12072 shall not apply to the delivery, sale, or transfer of a firearm to the holder of a special weapons permit issued by the Department of Justice issued pursuant to Section 12095, 12230, 12250, or 12305. On the date that the application to purchase is completed, the dealer delivering the firearm shall transmit to the Department of Justice an electronic or telephonic report of the same as is indicated in subdivision (b) or (c) of Section 12077.

(s)(1) Subdivision (d) of Section 12072 and subdivision (b) of Section 12801 shall not apply to the infrequent loan of an unloaded firearm by a person who is neither a dealer as defined in Section 12071 nor a federal firearms licensee pursuant to Chapter 44 (commencing with Section 921) of Title 18 of the United States Code, to a person 18 years of age or older for use solely as a prop in a motion picture, television, video, theatrical, or other entertainment production or event.

(2) Subdivision (d), and paragraph (1) of subdivision (f), of Section 12072, and subdivision (b) of Section 12801 shall not apply to the loan of an unloaded firearm by a person who is not a dealer as defined in Section 12071 but who is a federal firearms licensee pursuant to Chapter 44 (commencing with Section 921) of Title 18 of the United States Code, to a person who possesses a valid entertainment firearms permit issued pursuant to Section 12081, for use solely as a prop in a motion picture, television, video, theatrical, or other entertainment production or event. The person loaning the firearm pursuant to this paragraph shall retain a photocopy of the entertainment firearms permit as proof of compliance with this requirement.

(3) Subdivision (b) of Section 12071, subdivision (c) of, and paragraph (1) of subdivision (f) of, Section 12072, and subdivision (b) of Section 12801 shall not apply to the loan of an unloaded firearm by a dealer as defined in Section 12071, to a person who possesses a valid entertainment firearms permit issued pursuant to Section 12081, for use solely as a prop in a motion picture, television, video, theatrical, or other entertainment production or event. The dealer shall retain a photocopy of the entertainment firearms permit as proof of compliance with this requirement.

(4) Subdivision (b) of Section 12071, subdivision (c) and paragraph (1) of subdivision (f) of Section 12072, and subdivision (b) of Section 12801 shall not apply to the loan of an unloaded firearm to a consultant-evaluator by a person licensed pursuant to Section 12071 if the loan does not exceed 45 days from the date of delivery. At the time of the loan, the consultant-evaluator shall provide the following information, which the dealer shall retain for two years:

(A) A photocopy of a valid, current, government-issued identification to determine the consultant-evaluator's identity, including, but not limited to, a California driver's license, identification card, or passport.

(B) A photocopy of the consultant-evaluator's valid, current certificate of eligibility.

(C) A letter from the person licensed as an importer, manufacturer, or dealer pursuant to Chapter 44 (commencing with Section 921) of Title 18 of the United States Code, with whom the consultant-evaluator has a bona fide business relationship. The letter shall detail the bona fide business purposes for which the firearm is being loaned and confirm that the consultant-evaluator is being loaned the firearm as part of a bona fide business relationship.

(D) The signature of the consultant-evaluator on a form indicating the date the firearm is loaned and the last day the firearm may be returned.

(t)(1) The waiting periods described in Sections 12071 and 12072 shall not apply to the sale, delivery, loan, or transfer of a firearm that is a curio or relic, as defined in Section 478.11 of Title 27 of the Code of Federal Regulations, or its successor, by a dealer to a person who is licensed as a collector pursuant to Chapter 44 (commencing with Section 921) of Title 18 of the United States Code and the regulations issued pursuant thereto who has a current certificate of eligibility issued to him or her by the Department of Justice pursuant to Section 12071. On the date that the delivery, sale, or transfer is made, the dealer delivering the firearm shall transmit to the Department of Justice an electronic or telephonic report of the transaction as is indicated in subdivision (b) or (c) of Section 12077.

(2) Subdivision (d) and paragraph (1) of subdivision (f) of Section 12072 shall not apply to the infrequent sale, loan, or transfer of a firearm that is not a handgun, which is a curio or relic manufactured at least 50 years prior to the current date, but not including replicas thereof, as defined in Section 478.11 of Title 27 of the Code of Federal Regulations, or its successor.

(u) As used in this section:

(1) "Infrequent" has the same meaning as in paragraph (1) of subdivision (c) of Section 12070.

(2) "A person taking title or possession of firearms by operation of law" includes, but is not limited to, any of the following instances wherein an individual receives title to, or possession of, firearms:

(A) The executor or administrator of an estate if the estate includes firearms.

(B) A secured creditor or an agent or employee thereof when the firearms are possessed as collateral for, or as a result of, a default under a security agreement under the Commercial Code.

(C) A levying officer, as defined in Section 481.140, 511.060, or 680.260 of the Code of Civil Procedure.

(D) A receiver performing his or her functions as a receiver if the receivership estate includes firearms.

(E) A trustee in bankruptcy performing his or her duties if the bankruptcy estate includes firearms.

(F) An assignee for the benefit of creditors performing his or her functions as an assignee, if the assignment includes firearms.

(G) A transmutation of property consisting of firearms pursuant to Section 850 of the Family Code.

(H) Firearms passing to a surviving spouse pursuant to Chapter 1 (commencing with Section 13500) of Part 2 of Division 8 of the Probate Code.

(I) Firearms received by the family of a police officer or deputy sheriff from a local agency pursuant to Section 50081 of the Government Code.

(J) The transfer of a firearm by a law enforcement agency to the person who found the firearm where the delivery is to the person as the finder of the firearm pursuant to Article 1 (commencing with Section 2080) of Chapter 4 of Division 3 of the Civil Code.

Penal Code § 12079.

(a) Upon a showing that good cause exists, the Department of Justice may issue permits for the possession, transportation, or sale between a person licensed pursuant to Section 12071 and an out-of-state client, of large capacity magazines.

(b) For purposes of this section, "large capacity magazine" shall have the same meaning as that set forth in paragraph (25) of subdivision (c) of Section 12020.

Penal Code § 12080.

(a) The Department of Justice shall prepare a pamphlet which summarizes California firearms laws as they pertain to persons other than law enforcement officers or members of the armed services.

(b) The pamphlet shall include the following matters:

(1) Lawful possession.

(2) Licensing procedures.

(3) Transportation and use of firearms.

(4) Acquisition of hunting licenses.

(5) The safe handling and use of firearms.

(6) Various methods of safe storage and child proofing of firearms.

(7) The availability of firearms safety programs and devices.

(8) The responsibilities of firearms ownership.

(9) The operation of various types of firearms.

(10) The lawful use of deadly force.

(c) The department shall offer copies of the pamphlet at actual cost to firearms dealers licensed pursuant to Section 12071 who shall have copies of the most current version available for sale to retail purchasers or transferees of firearms. The cost of the pamphlet, if any, may be added to the sale price of the firearm. Other interested parties may purchase copies directly from the Department of General Services. The pamphlet shall declare that it is merely intended to provide a general summary of laws applicable to firearms and is not designed to provide individual guidance for specific areas. Individuals having specific questions shall be directed to contact their local law enforcement agency or private counsel.

(d) The Department of Justice or any other public entity shall be immune from any liability arising from the drafting, publication, or dissemination of the pamphlet or any reliance upon it. All receipts from the sale of these pamphlets shall be deposited as reimbursements to the support appropriation for the Department of Justice.

Penal Code § 12081.

(a) Any person who is at least 21 years of age may apply for an entertainment firearms permit from the Department of Justice that authorizes the permit holder to possess firearms loaned to him or her for use solely as a prop in a motion picture, television, video, theatrical, or other entertainment production or event. Upon receipt of an initial or renewal application submitted as specified in subdivision (b), the department shall examine its records, records the department is authorized to request from the State Department of Mental Health pursuant to Section 8104 of the Welfare and Institutions Code, and records of the National Instant Criminal Background Check System as described in subsection (t) of Section 922 of Title 18 of the United States Code, in order to determine if the applicant is prohibited from possessing or receiving firearms. The department shall issue an entertainment firearms permit only if the records indicate that the applicant is not prohibited from possessing or receiving firearms pursuant to any federal, state, or local law.

(b)(1) Requests for entertainment firearms permits shall be made on application forms prescribed by the Department of Justice that require applicant information, including, but not limited to, the following:

(A) Complete name.

(B) Residential and mailing address.

(C) Telephone number.

(D) Date of birth.

(E) Place of birth.

(F) Country of citizenship and, if other than United States, alien number or admission number.

(G) Valid driver's license number or valid identification card number issued by the California Department of Motor Vehicles.

(H) Social security number.

(I) Signature.

(2) All applications must be submitted with the appropriate fee as specified in subdivision (c).

(3) An initial application for an entertainment firearms permit shall require the submission of fingerprint images and related information in a manner prescribed by the department, for the purpose of obtaining information as to the existence and nature of a record of state or federal level convictions and state or federal level arrests for which the department establishes that the individual was released on bail or on his or her own recognizance pending trial as needed to determine whether the applicant may be issued the permit. Requests for federal level criminal offender record information received by the Department of Justice pursuant to this section shall be forwarded by the department to the Federal Bureau of Investigation.

(4) The Department of Justice shall review the criminal offender record information specified in subdivision (l) of Section 11105 for entertainment firearms permit applicants.

(5) The Department of Justice shall review subsequent arrests, pursuant to Section 11105.2, to determine the continuing validity of the permit as specified in subdivision (d) for all entertainment firearms permit holders.

(6) Any person who furnishes a fictitious name or address or knowingly furnishes any incorrect information or knowingly omits any information required to be provided on this application is guilty of a misdemeanor.

(c) The Department of Justice shall recover the full costs of administering the program by assessing the following application fees:

(1) For the initial application: one hundred four dollars ($104). Of this sum, fifty-six dollars ($56) shall be deposited into the Fingerprint Fee Account, and forty-eight dollars ($48) shall be deposited into the Dealer Record of Sale Account.

(2) For each annual renewal application: twenty-nine dollars ($29), which shall be deposited into the Dealer Record of Sale Account.

(d) The implementation of subdivisions (a), (b), and (c) by the department is exempt from the Administrative Procedure Act (Chapter 3.5 (commencing with Section 11340) of Part 1 of Division 3 of Title 2 of the Government Code).

(e) The department shall annually review and shall adjust the fees specified in subdivision (c), if necessary, to fully fund, but not to exceed the actual costs of, the permit program provided for by this section, including enforcement of the program.

(f) An entertainment firearms permit issued by the Department of Justice shall be valid for one year from the date of issuance. If at any time during that year the permit holder becomes prohibited from possessing or receiving firearms pursuant to any federal, state, or local law, his or her entertainment firearms permit shall be no longer valid.

Penal Code § 12082.

(a) A person shall complete any sale, loan, or transfer of a firearm through a person licensed pursuant to Section 12071 in accordance with this section in order to comply with subdivision (d) of Section 12072. The seller or transferor or the person loaning the firearm shall deliver the firearm to the dealer who shall retain possession of that firearm. The dealer shall then deliver the firearm to the purchaser or transferee or the person being loaned the firearm, if it is not prohibited, in accordance with subdivision (c) of Section 12072. If the dealer cannot legally deliver the firearm to the purchaser or transferee or the person being loaned the firearm, the dealer shall forthwith, without waiting for the conclusion of the waiting period described in Sections 12071 and 12072, return the firearm to the transferor or seller or the person loaning the firearm. The dealer shall not return the firearm to the seller or transferor or the person loaning the firearm when to do so would constitute a violation of subdivision (a) of Section 12072. If the dealer cannot legally return the firearm to the transferor or seller or the person loaning the firearm, then the dealer shall forthwith deliver the firearm to the sheriff of the county or the chief of police or other head of a municipal police department of any city or city and county who shall then dispose of the firearm in the manner provided by Sections 12028 and 12032. The purchaser or transferee or person being loaned the firearm may be required by the dealer to pay a fee not to exceed ten dollars ($10) per firearm, and no other fee may be charged by the dealer for a sale, loan, or transfer of a firearm conducted pursuant to this section, except for the applicable fees that may be charged pursuant to Sections 12076, 12076.5, and 12088.9 and forwarded to the Department of Justice, and the fees set forth in Section 12805. Nothing in these provisions shall prevent a dealer from charging a smaller fee. The dealer may not charge any additional fees.

(b) The Attorney General shall adopt regulations under this section to do all of the following:

(1) Allow the seller or transferor or the person loaning the firearm, and the purchaser or transferee or the person being loaned the firearm, to complete a sale, loan, or transfer through a dealer, and to allow those persons and the dealer to comply with the requirements of this section and Sections 12071, 12072, 12076, and 12077 and to preserve the confidentiality of those records.

(2) Where a personal handgun importer is selling or transferring a pistol, revolver, or other firearm capable of being concealed upon the person to comply with clause (ii) of subparagraph (A) of paragraph (2) of subdivision (f) of Section 12072, to allow a personal handgun importer's ownership of the pistol, revolver, or other firearm capable of being concealed upon the person being sold or transferred to be recorded in a manner that if the firearm is returned to that personal handgun importer because the sale or transfer cannot be completed, the Department of Justice will have sufficient information about that personal handgun importer so that a record of his or her ownership can be maintained in the registry provided by subdivision (c) of Section 11106.

(3) Ensure that the register or record of electronic transfer shall state the name and address of the seller or transferor of the firearm or the person loaning the firearm and whether or not the person is a personal handgun importer in addition to any other information required by Section 12077.

(c) Notwithstanding any other provision of law, a dealer who does not sell, transfer, or keep an inventory of handguns is not required to process private party transfers of handguns.

(d) A violation of this section by a dealer is a misdemeanor.

Penal Code § 12083.

(a) Commencing January 1, 2008, the Department of Justice shall keep a centralized list of persons who identify themselves as being licensed pursuant to Chapter 44 (commencing with Section 921) of Title 18 of the United States Code as a dealer, importer, or manufacturer of firearms whose licensed premises are within this state and who declare to the department an exemption from the firearms dealer licensing requirements of Section 12070. The list shall be known as the centralized list of exempted federal firearms licensees. To qualify for placement on the centralized list, an applicant shall do all of the following:

(1) Possess a valid federal firearms license pursuant to Chapter 44 (commencing with Section 921) of Title 18 of the United States Code as a dealer, importer, or manufacturer of firearms.

(2) Possess a current, valid certificate of eligibility pursuant to Section 12071.

(3) Maintain with the department a signed declaration enumerating the applicant's statutory exemptions from licensing requirements of Section 12070. Any person furnishing a fictitious name, knowingly furnishing any incorrect information, or knowingly omitting any information for the declaration shall be guilty of a misdemeanor.

(b) Commencing January 1, 2008, the department shall assess an annual fee of one hundred fifteen dollars ($115) to cover its costs of maintaining the centralized list of exempted federal firearms licensees prescribed by subdivision (a), conducting inspections in accordance with this section, and for the cost of maintaining the firearm shipment verification number system described in subdivision (f) of Section 12072. A person who is not licensed pursuant to Section 12071, who has been issued a permit pursuant to Section 12095, 12287, 12230, or 12305, and who is placed on the centralized list of exempted federal firearms licensees shall not be charged the fee. The department may increase the fee at a rate not to exceed the increase in the California Consumer Price Index as compiled and reported by the Department of Industrial Relations. The fees collected shall be deposited in the Dealers' Record of Sale Special Account.

(c)(1) Any person licensed pursuant to Chapter 44 (commencing with Section 921) of Title 18 of the United States Code as a dealer, importer, or manufacturer of firearms whose licensed premises are within this state shall not import or receive firearms from any source unless listed on the centralized list of firearms dealers pursuant to Section 12071, or the centralized list of exempted federal firearms licensees pursuant to subdivision (a), or the centralized list of firearms manufacturers pursuant to subdivision (f) of Section 12086.

(2) A violation of this subdivision is a misdemeanor.

(d)(1) All persons on the centralized list of exempted federal firearms licensees prescribed by subdivision (a) shall record and keep on file for three years, the verification number that shall accompany firearms received from other federal firearms licensees pursuant to subdivision (f) of Section 12072.

(2) A violation of this subdivision is cause for immediate removal from the centralized list.

(e) Information compiled from the list described in subdivision (a) shall be made available for the following purposes:

(1) Requests from local, state, and federal law enforcement agencies and the duly constituted city, county, and city and county licensing authorities.

(2) When the information is requested by a person licensed pursuant to Chapter 44 (commencing with Section 921) of Title 18 of the United States Code for determining the validity of the license for firearm shipments.

(f) The department may conduct onsite inspections at the business premises of a person on the centralized list described in subdivision (a) to determine compliance with firearms laws pursuant to Article 4 (commencing with Section 12070) of Chapter 1 of Title 2 of Part 4 of the Penal Code. The department shall work in consultation with the Bureau of Alcohol, Tobacco, Firearms, and Explosives to ensure that licensees are not subject to duplicative inspections. During the inspection the following firearm records shall be made available for review:

(1) Federal records referred to in subdivision (a) of Section 478.125 of Title 27 of the Code of Federal Regulations and the bound book containing the same information referred to in Section 478.124a and subdivision (e) of Section 478.125 of Title 27 of the Code of Federal Regulations.

(2) Verification numbers issued pursuant to subdivision (f) of Section 12072.

(3) Any other records requested by the department to determine compliance with this article.

(g) The department may remove from the centralized list described in subdivision (a), any person who violates this article.

(h) The department may adopt regulations as necessary to carry out the provisions of this section, subdivision (f) of Section 12072, and Section 12071. The department shall work in consultation with the Bureau of Alcohol, Tobacco, Firearms, and Explosives to ensure that state regulations are not duplicative of federal regulations.

Penal Code § 12085.

(a) Commencing July 1, 1999, no person, firm, or corporation licensed to manufacture firearms pursuant to Chapter 44 (commencing with Section 921) of Title 18 of the United States Code may manufacture firearms within this state unless licensed pursuant to Section 12086.

(b) Subdivision (a) does not apply to a person licensed to manufacture firearms pursuant to Chapter 44 (commencing with Section 921) of Title 18 of the United States Code who manufactures fewer than 100 firearms in a calendar year within this state.

(c) If a person, firm, or corporation required to be licensed pursuant to Section 12086 ceases operations, then the records required pursuant to paragraphs (6) and (10) of subdivision (c) of Section 12086 shall be forwarded to the federal Bureau of Alcohol, Tobacco, and Firearms within three days of the closure of business.

(d) A violation of this section is a misdemeanor.

(e)(1) As used in this section and Section 12086, the term "firearm" includes the frame or receiver of the weapon.

(2) As used in this section and Section 12086, the term "firearm" includes the unfinished frame or receiver of a weapon that can be readily converted to the functional condition of a finished frame or receiver.

(3) For purposes of this section and Section 12086, the term "firearm" does not include an unloaded firearm that is defined as an "antique firearm" in paragraph (16) of subsection (a) of Section 921 of Title 18 of the United States Code.

Penal Code § 12086.

(a)(1) As used in this section, "licensee" means a person, firm, or corporation that satisfies both of the following:

(A) Has a license issued pursuant to paragraph (2) of subdivision (b).

(B) Is among those recorded in the centralized list specified in subdivision (f).

(2) As used in this section, "department" means the Department of Justice.

(b)(1) The Department of Justice shall accept applications for, and shall grant licenses permitting, the manufacture of firearms within this state. The department shall inform applicants who are denied licenses of the reasons for the denial in writing.

(2) No license shall be granted by the department unless and until the applicant presents proof that he or she has all of the following:

(A) A valid license to manufacture firearms issued pursuant to Chapter 44 (commencing with Section 921) of Title 18 of the United States Code.

(B) Any regulatory or business license, or licenses, required by local government.

(C) A valid seller's permit or resale certificate issued by the State Board of Equalization, if applicable.

(D) A certificate of eligibility issued by the Department of justice pursuant to paragraph (4) of subdivision (a) of Section 12071.

(3) The department shall adopt regulations to administer this section and Section 12085 and shall recover the full costs of administering the program by collecting fees from license applicants. Recoverable costs shall include, but not be limited to, the costs of inspections and maintaining a centralized list of licensed firearm manufacturers. The fee for licensed manufacturers who produce fewer than 500 firearms in a calendar year within this state shall not exceed two hundred fifty dollars ($250) per year or the actual costs of inspections and maintaining a centralized list of firearm manufacturers and any other duties of the department required pursuant to this section and Section 12085, whichever is less. (4) A license granted by the department shall be valid for no more than one year from the date of issuance and shall be in the form prescribed by the Attorney General.

(c) A licensee shall comply with the following prohibitions and requirements:

(1) The business shall be conducted only in the buildings designated in the license.

(2) The license or a copy thereof, certified by the department, shall be displayed on the premises where it can easily be seen.

(3) Whenever a licensee discovers that a firearm has been stolen or is missing from the licensee's premises, the licensee shall report the loss or theft within 48 hours of the discovery to all of the following:

(A) The Department of Justice, in a manner prescribed by the department.

(B) The federal Bureau of Alcohol, Tobacco, and Firearms.

(C) The police department in the city or city and county where the building designated in the license is located.

(D) If there is no police department in the city or city and county where the building designated in the license is located, the sheriff of the county where the building designated in the license is located.

(4)(A) The licensee shall require that each employee obtain a certificate of eligibility pursuant to paragraph (4) of subdivision (a) of Section 12071, which shall be renewed annually, prior to being allowed to come into contact with any firearm.

(B) The licensee shall prohibit any employee who the licensee knows or reasonably should know is prohibited by state or federal law from possessing, receiving, owning, or purchasing a firearm from coming into contact with any firearm.

(5)(A) Each firearm the licensee manufactures in this state shall be identified with a unique serial number stamped onto the firearm utilizing the method of compression stamping.

(B) Licensed manufacturers who produce fewer than 500 firearms in a calendar year within this state may serialize long guns only by utilizing a method of compression stamping or by engraving the serial number onto the firearm.

(C) The licensee shall stamp the serial number onto the firearm within one business day of the time the receiver or frame is manufactured.

(D) The licensee shall not use the same serial number for more than one firearm.

(6)(A) The licensee shall record the type, model, caliber, or gauge, and serial number of each firearm manufactured or acquired, and the date of the manufacture or acquisition, within one business day of the manufacture or acquisition.

(B) The licensee shall maintain permanently within the building designated in the license the records required pursuant to subparagraph (A).

(C) Backup copies of the records described in subparagraph (A), whether electronic or hard copy, shall be made at least once a month. These backup records shall be maintained in a facility separate from the one in which the primary records are stored.

(7)(A) The licensee shall allow the department to inspect the building designated in the license to ensure compliance with the requirements of this section.

(B) The licensee shall allow any peace officer, authorized law enforcement employee, or Department of Justice employee designated by the Attorney General, upon the presentation of proper identification, to inspect facilities and records during business hours to ensure compliance with the requirements of this section.

(8) The licensee shall store in a secure facility all firearms manufactured and all barrels for firearms manufactured.

(9)(A) The licensee shall notify the chief of police or other head of the municipal police department in the city or city and county where the building designated in the license is located that the licensee is manufacturing firearms within that city or city and county and the location of the licensed premises.

(B) If there is no police department in the city or city and county where the building designated in the license is located, the licensee shall notify the sheriff of the county where the building designated in the license is located that the licensee is manufacturing firearms within that county and the location of the licensed premises.

(10) For at least 10 years, the licensee shall maintain records of all firearms that are lost or stolen, as prescribed by the department.

(d) Except as otherwise provided in subdivision (e), as used in this section, a "secure facility" means that the facility satisfies all of the following:

(1) The facility is equipped with a burglar alarm with central monitoring.

(2) All perimeter entries to areas in which firearms are stored other than doors, including windows and skylights, are secured with steel window guards or an audible, silent, or sonic alarm to detect entry.

(3) All perimeter doorways are designed in one of the following ways:

(A) A windowless steel security door equipped with both a deadbolt and a doorknob lock.

(B) A windowed metal door equipped with both a deadbolt and a doorknob lock. If the window has an opening of five inches or more measured in any direction, the window is covered with steel bars of at least one-half inch diameter or metal grating of at least nine gauge affixed to the exterior or interior of the door.

(C) A metal grate that is padlocked and affixed to the licensee's premises independent of the door and doorframe.

(D) Hinges and hasps attached to doors by welding, riveting, or bolting with nuts on the inside of the door.

(E) Hinges and hasps installed so that they cannot be removed when the doors are closed and locked.

(4) Heating, ventilating, air-conditioning, and service openings are secured with steel bars, metal grating, or an alarm system.

(5) No perimeter metal grates are capable of being entered by any person.

(6) Steel bars used to satisfy the requirements of this subdivision are not capable of being entered by any person.

(7) Perimeter walls of rooms in which firearms are stored are constructed of concrete or at least 10-gauge expanded steel wire mesh utilized along with typical wood frame and drywall construction. If firearms are not stored in a vault, the facility shall use an exterior security-type door along with a high security, single-key deadbolt, or other door that is more secure. All firearms shall be stored in a separate room away from any general living area or work area. Any door to the storage facility shall be locked while unattended.

(8) Perimeter doorways, including the loading dock area, are locked at all times when not attended by paid employees or contracted employees, including security guards.

(9) Except when a firearm is currently being tested, any ammunition on the premises is removed from all manufactured guns and stored in a separate and locked room, cabinet, or box away from the storage area for the firearms. Ammunition may be stored with a weapon only in a locked safe.

(e) For purposes of this section, any licensed manufacturer who produces fewer than 500 firearms in a calendar year within this state may maintain a "secure facility" by complying with all of the requirements described in subdivision (d), or may design a security plan that is approved by the Department of Justice or the federal Bureau of Alcohol, Tobacco, and Firearms.

(1) If a security plan is approved by the federal Bureau of Alcohol, Tobacco, and Firearms, the approved plan, along with proof of approval, shall be filed with the Department of Justice and the local police department. If there is no police department, the filing shall be with the county sheriff's office.

(2) If a security plan is approved by the Department of Justice, the approved plan, along with proof of approval, shall be filed with the local police department. If there is no police department, the filing shall be with the county sheriff's office.

(f)(1) Except as otherwise provided in this subdivision, the Department of Justice shall maintain a centralized list of all persons licensed pursuant to paragraph (2) of subdivision (b). The centralized list shall be provided annually to each police department and county sheriff within the state.

(2) Except as provided in paragraph (3), the license of any licensee who violates this section may be revoked.

(3) The license of any licensee who knowingly or with gross negligence violates this section or violates this section three times shall be revoked, and that person, firm, or corporation shall become permanently ineligible to obtain a license pursuant to this section.

(g)(1) Upon the revocation of the license, notification shall be provided to local law enforcement authorities in the jurisdiction where the licensee's business is located and to the federal Bureau of Alcohol, Tobacco, and Firearms.

(2) The department shall make information concerning the location and name of a licensee available, upon request, for the following purposes only:

(A) Law enforcement.

(B) When the information is requested by a person licensed pursuant to Chapter 44 (commencing with Section 921) of Title 18 of the United States Code for determining the validity of the license for firearm shipments.

(3) Notwithstanding paragraph (2), the department shall make the name and business address of a licensee available to any person upon written request.

(h) The Department of Justice shall maintain and make available upon request information concerning the number of inspections conducted and the amount of fees collected pursuant to paragraph (3) of subdivision (b), the number of licensees removed from the centralized list described in subdivision (f), and the number of licensees found to have violated this section.

Penal Code § 12087.

This article shall be known and may be cited as the "Aroner-Scott-Hayden Firearms Safety Act of 1999."

Penal Code § 12087.5.

The Legislature makes the following findings:

(a) In the years 1987 to 1996, nearly 2,200 children in the United States under the age of 15 years died in unintentional shootings. In 1996 alone, 138 children were shot and killed unintentionally. Thus, more than 11 children every month, or one child every three days, were shot or killed unintentionally in firearms-related incidents.

(b) The United States leads the industrialized world in the rates of children and youth lost to unintentional, firearms-related deaths. A 1997 study from the federal Centers for Disease Control and Prevention reveals that for unintentional firearm-related deaths for children under the age of 15, the rate in the United States was nine times higher than in 25 other industrialized countries combined.

(c) While the number of unintentional deaths from firearms is an unacceptable toll on America's children, nearly eight times that number are treated in U.S. hospital emergency rooms each year for nonfatal unintentional gunshot wounds.

(d) A study of unintentional firearm deaths among children in California found that unintentional gunshot wounds most often involve handguns.

(e) A study in the December 1995 issue of the Archives of Pediatric and Adolescent Medicine found that children as young as three years old are strong enough to fire most commercially available handguns. The study revealed that 25 percent of three to four year olds and 70 percent of five to six year olds had sufficient finger strength to fire 59 (92 percent) of the 64 commonly available handguns referenced in the study.

(f) The Government Accounting Office (GAO), in its March 1991 study, "Accidental Shootings: Many Deaths and Injuries Caused by Firearms Could be Prevented," estimates that 31 percent of accidental deaths caused by firearms might be prevented by the addition of two safety devices: a child-resistant safety device that automatically engages and a device that indicates whether the gun is loaded.

According to the study results, of the 107 unintentional firearms-related fatalities the GAO examined for the calendar years 1988 and 1989, 8 percent could have been prevented had the firearm been equipped with a child-resistant safety device. This 8 percent represents instances in which children under the age of six unintentionally shot and killed themselves or other persons.

(g) Currently, firearms are the only products manufactured in the United States that are not subject to minimum safety standards.

(h) A 1997 public opinion poll conducted by the National Opinion Research Center at the University of Chicago in conjunction with the Johns Hopkins Center for Gun Policy and Research found that 74 percent of Americans support safety regulation of the firearms industry.

(i) Some currently available trigger locks and other similar devices are inadequate to prevent the accidental discharge of the firearms to which they are attached, or to prevent children from gaining access to the firearm.

Penal Code § 12087.6.

As used in this article:

(a) "Firearms safety device" means a device other than a gun safe that locks and is designed to prevent children and unauthorized users from firing a firearm. The device may be installed on a firearm, be incorporated into the design of the firearm, or prevent access to the firearm.

(b) "Gun safe" means a locking container that fully contains and secures one or more firearms, and that meets the standards for gun safes adopted pursuant to Section 12088.2.

(c) "Long-gun safe" means a locking container designed to fully contain and secure a rifle as defined in paragraph (20) of subdivision (c) of Section 12020 or a shotgun as defined in paragraph (21) of subdivision (c) of Section 12020, that has a locking system consisting of either a mechanical combination lock or an electronic combination lock that has at least 1,000 possible unique combinations consisting of a minimum of three numbers, letters, or symbols per combination, and that is not listed on the roster maintained pursuant to subdivision (d) of Section 12088.

Penal Code § 12088.

(a) The Department of Justice shall certify laboratories to verify compliance with standards for firearms safety devices set forth in Section 12088.2.

(b) The Department of Justice may charge any laboratory that is seeking certification to test firearms safety devices a fee not exceeding the costs of certification, including costs associated with the development and approval of regulations and standards pursuant to Section 12088.2.

(c) The certified laboratory shall, at the manufacturer's or dealer's expense, test the firearms safety device and submit a copy of the final test report directly to the Department of Justice along with the firearms safety device. The department shall notify the manufacturer or dealer of its receipt of the final test report and the department's determination as to whether the firearms safety device tested may be sold in this state.

(d) On and after July 1, 2001, the Department of Justice shall compile, publish, and thereafter maintain a roster listing all of the firearms safety devices that have been tested by a certified testing laboratory, have been determined to meet the department's standards for firearms safety devices and may be sold in this state.

(e) The roster shall list, for each firearms safety device, the manufacturer, model number, and model name.

(f) The department may randomly retest samples obtained from sources other than directly from the manufacturer of the firearms safety device listed on the roster to ensure compliance with the requirements of this article.

(g) Firearms safety devices used for random sample testing and obtained from sources other than the manufacturer shall be in new, unused condition, and still in the manufacturer's original and unopened package.

Penal Code § 12088.1.

(a) All firearms sold or transferred in this state by a licensed firearms dealer, including private transfers through a dealer, and all firearms manufactured in this state, shall include or be accompanied by a firearms safety device that is listed on the Department of Justice's roster of approved firearms safety devices and that is identified as appropriate for that firearm by reference to either the manufacturer and model of the firearm, or to the physical characteristics of the firearm that match those listed on the roster for use with the device.

(b) All firearms sold or transferred in this state by a licensed firearms dealer, including private transfers through a dealer, and all firearms manufactured in this state shall be accompanied with warning language or labels as described in Section 12088.3.

(c)(1) All long-gun safes commercially sold or transferred in this state, or manufactured in this state for sale in this state, that do not meet the standards for gun safes adopted pursuant to Section 12088.2 shall be accompanied by the following warning: "WARNING: This gun safe does not meet the safety standards for gun safes specified in California Penal Code Section 12088.2. It does not satisfy the requirements of Penal Code Section 12088.1, which mandates that all firearms sold in California be accompanied by a firearms safety device or proof of ownership, as required by law, of a gun safe that meets the Section 12088.2 minimum safety standards developed by the California Attorney General."

(2) This warning shall be conspicuously displayed in its entirety on the principal display panel of the gun safe's package, on any descriptive materials that accompany the gun safe, and on a label affixed to the front of the gun safe.

(3) This warning shall be displayed in both English and Spanish in conspicuous and legible type in contrast by typography, layout, or color with other printed matter on the package or descriptive materials in a manner consistent with Part 1500.121 of Title 16 of the Code of Federal Regulations, or successor regulations thereto.

(d) The sale or transfer of a firearm shall be exempt from subdivision (a) if both of the following apply:

(1) The purchaser or transferee owns a gun safe that meets the standards set forth in Section 12088.2. Gun safes shall not be required to be tested, and therefore may meet the standards without appearing on the Department of Justice roster.

(2) The purchaser or transferee presents an original receipt for purchase of the gun safe, or other proof of purchase or

ownership of the gun safe as authorized by the Attorney General, to the firearms dealer. The dealer shall maintain a copy of this receipt or proof of purchase with the dealers' record of sales of firearms.

(e) The sale or transfer of a firearm shall be exempt from subdivision (a) if all of the following apply:

(1) The purchaser or transferee purchases an approved safety device no more than 30 days prior to the day the purchaser or transferee takes possession of the firearm.

(2) The purchaser or transferee presents the approved safety device to the firearms dealer when picking up the firearm.

(3) The purchaser or transferee presents an original receipt to the firearms dealer which shows the date of purchase, the name, and the model number of the safety device.

(4) The firearms dealer verifies that the requirements in (1) to (3), inclusive, have been satisfied.

(5) The firearms dealer maintains a copy of the receipt along with the dealers' record of sales of firearms.

Penal Code § 12088.15.

(a) No person shall keep for commercial sale, offer, or expose for commercial sale, or commercially sell any firearms safety device that is not listed on the roster maintained pursuant to subdivision (d) of Section 12088, or that does not comply with the standards for firearms safety devices adopted pursuant to Section 12088.2.

(b) No person may distribute as part of an organized firearm safety program, with or without consideration, any firearm safety device that is not listed on the roster maintained pursuant to subdivision (d) of Section 12088 or does not comply with the standards for firearms safety devices adopted pursuant to Section 12088.2.

(c) No long-gun safe may be manufactured in this state for sale in this state that does not comply with the standards for gun safes adopted pursuant to Section 12088.2, unless the long-gun safe is labeled by the manufacturer consistent with the requirements of Section 12088.1.

(d)(1) Any person who keeps for commercial sale, offers, or exposes for commercial sale, or who commercially sells a long-gun safe that does not comply with the standards for gun safes adopted pursuant to Section 12088.2, and who knows or has reason to know, that the long-gun safe in question does not meet the standards for gun safes adopted pursuant to Section 12088.2, is in violation of this section, and is punishable as provided in subdivision (e), unless the long-gun safe is labeled pursuant to Section 12088.1.

(2) Any person who keeps for commercial sale, offers, or exposes for commercial sale, or who commercially sells a long-gun safe that does not comply with the standards for gun safes adopted pursuant to Section 12088.2, and who removes or causes to be removed from the long-gun safe, the label required pursuant to Section 12088.1, is in violation of this section, and is punishable as provided in subdivision (e).

(e) A violation of this section is punishable by a civil fine of up to five hundred dollars ($500). A second violation of this section that occurs within five years of the date of a previous offense is punishable by a civil fine of up to one thousand dollars ($1,000) and, if the violation is committed by a licensed firearms dealer, the dealer shall be ineligible to sell firearms in this state for 30 days. A third or subsequent violation that occurs within five years of two or more previous offenses is punishable by a civil fine of up to five thousand dollars ($5,000) and, if the violation is committed by a licensed firearms dealer, the firearms dealer shall be permanently ineligible to sell firearms in this state.

(f) The Attorney General, a district attorney, or a city attorney may bring a civil action for a violation of the provisions of this section.

Penal Code § 12088.2.

(a) No later than January 1, 2000, the Attorney General shall commence development of regulations to implement a minimum safety standard for firearms safety devices and gun safes to significantly reduce the risk of firearms-related injuries to children 17 years of age and younger. The final standard shall do all of the following:

(1) Address the risk of injury from unintentional gunshot wounds.

(2) Address the risk of injury from self-inflicted gunshot wounds by unauthorized users.

(3) Include provisions to ensure that all firearms safety devices and gun safes are reusable and of adequate quality and construction to prevent children and unauthorized users from firing the firearm and to ensure that these devices cannot be readily removed from the firearm or that the firearm cannot be readily removed from the gun safe except by an authorized user utilizing the key, combination, or other method of access intended by the manufacturer of the device.

(4) Include additional provisions as appropriate.

(b) The Attorney General may consult, for the purposes of guidance in development of the standards, test protocols such as those described in Title 16 (commencing with Part 1700) of the Code of Federal Regulations, relating to poison prevention packaging standards. These protocols may be consulted to provide suggestions for potential methods to utilize in developing standards and shall serve as guidance only. The Attorney General shall also give appropriate consideration to the use of devices that are not detachable, but are permanently installed and incorporated into the design of a firearm. The Attorney General shall adopt and issue regulations implementing a final standard not later than January 1, 2001. The Attorney General shall report to the Legislature on these standards by January 1, 2001. The final standard shall be effective January 1, 2002.

Penal Code § 12088.3.

(a) The packaging of any firearm and any descriptive materials that accompany any firearm sold or transferred in this state, or delivered for sale in this state, by any licensed manufacturer, or licensed dealer, shall bear a label containing the following warning statement: WARNING Children are attracted to and can operate firearms that can cause severe injuries or death. Prevent child access by always keeping guns locked away and unloaded when not in use. If you keep a loaded firearm where a child obtains and improperly uses it, you may be fined or sent to prison. A yellow triangle containing an exclamation mark shall appear immediately before the word "Warning" on the label.

(b) If the firearm is sold or transferred without accompanying packaging, the warning label or notice shall be affixed to the firearm itself by a method to be prescribed by regulation of the Attorney General.

(c) The warning statement required under subdivisions (a) and (b) shall be:

(1) Displayed in its entirety on the principal display panel of the firearm's package, and on any descriptive materials that accompany the firearm.

(2) Displayed in both English and Spanish in conspicuous and legible type in contrast by typography, layout, or color with other printed matter on that package or descriptive materials in a manner consistent with Part 1500.121 of Title 16, of the Code of Federal Regulations, or successor regulations thereto.

Penal Code § 12088.4.

If at any time the Attorney General determines that a gun safe or firearms safety device subject to the provisions of this article and sold after January 1, 2002, does not conform with the standards required by subdivision (a) of Section 12088.1 or Section 12088.2, the Attorney General may order the recall and replacement of the gun safe or firearms safety device, or order that the gun safe or firearm safety device be brought into conformity with those requirements. If the firearms safety device cannot be separated from the firearm without damaging the firearm, the Attorney General may order the recall and replacement of the firearm. If the firearms safety device can be separated and reattached to the firearm without damaging the firearm, the licensed manufacturer or licensed firearms dealer shall immediately provide a conforming replacement as instructed by the Attorney General.

Penal Code § 12088.5.

Each lead law enforcement agency investigating an incident shall report to the State Department of Health Services any information obtained that reasonably supports the conclusion that:

(a) A child 18 years of age or younger suffered an unintentional or self-inflicted gunshot wound inflicted by a firearm that was sold or transferred in this state, or manufactured in this state.

(b) Whether as a result of that incident the child died, suffered serious injury, or was treated for an injury by a medical professional.

Penal Code § 12088.6.

Any violation of Section 12088.1 or Section 12088.3 is punishable by a fine of one thousand dollars ($1,000). On the second violation of any of those sections, the licensed firearm manufacturer shall be ineligible to manufacture, or the licensed firearm dealer shall be ineligible to sell, firearms in this state for 30 days, and shall be punished by a fine of one thousand dollars ($1,000). On the third violation of any of those sections, a firearm manufacturer shall be permanently ineligible to manufacture firearms in this state. On the third violation of any of those sections, a licensed firearm dealer shall be permanently ineligible to sell firearms in this state.

Penal Code § 12088.7.

Compliance with the requirements set forth in this article shall not relieve any person from liability to any other person as may be imposed pursuant to common law, statutory law, or local ordinance.

Penal Code § 12088.8.

(a) This article does not apply to the commerce of any firearm defined as an "antique firearm" in paragraph (16) of subsection (a) of Section 921 of Title 18 of the United States Code.

(b) This article shall not apply to the commerce of any firearm intended to be used by a salaried, full-time peace officer as defined in Chapter 4.5 (commencing with Section 830) of Title 3 of Part 2 for purposes of law enforcement. Nothing in this article shall preclude local governments, local agencies, or state law enforcement agencies from requiring their peace officers to store their firearms in gun safes or attach firearms safety devices to those firearms.

Penal Code § 12088.9.

(a) The Department of Justice may require each dealer to charge each firearm purchaser or transferee a fee not to exceed one dollar ($1) for each firearm transaction. The fee shall be for the purpose of supporting department program costs related to this act, including the establishment, maintenance, and upgrading of related data base systems and public rosters.

(b) There is hereby created within the General Fund the Firearm Safety Account. Revenue from the fee imposed by subdivision (a) shall be deposited into the Firearm Safety Account and shall be available for expenditure by the Department of Justice upon appropriation by the Legislature. Expenditures from the Firearm Safety Account shall be limited to program expenditures as defined by subdivision (a).

Penal Code § 12090.

Any person who changes, alters, removes or obliterates the name of the maker, model, manufacturer's number, or other mark of identification, including any distinguishing number or mark assigned by the Department of Justice on any pistol, revolver, or any other firearm, without first having secured written permission from the department to make such change, alteration or removal shall be punished by imprisonment in the state prison.

Penal Code § 12092.

The Department of Justice upon request may assign a distinguishing number or mark of identification to any firearm whenever it is without a manufacturer's number, or other mark of identification or whenever the manufacturer's number or other mark of identification or the distinguishing number or mark assigned by the department has been destroyed or obliterated.

Penal Code § 12093.

Any person may place or stamp on any pistol, revolver, or other firearm any number or identifying indicium, provided the number or identifying indicium does not change, alter, remove, or obliterate the manufacturer's name, number, model, or other mark of identification. This section does not prohibit restoration by the owner of the name of the maker, model, or of the original manufacturer's number or other mark of identification when such restoration is authorized by the department, nor prevent any manufacturer from placing in the ordinary course of business the name of the maker, model, manufacturer's number, or other mark of identification upon a new firearm.

Penal Code § 12094.

(a) Any person with knowledge of any change, alteration, removal, or obliteration described herein, who buys, receives, disposes of, sells, offers for sale, or has in his or her possession any pistol, revolver, or other firearm which has had the name of the maker, model, or the manufacturer's number or other mark of identification including any distinguishing number or mark assigned by the Department of Justice changed, altered, removed, or obliterated is guilty of a misdemeanor. (b) Subdivision (a) does not apply to any of the following:

(1) The acquisition or possession of a firearm described in subdivision (a) by any member of the military forces of this state or of the United States, while on duty and acting within the scope and course of his or her employment.

(2) The acquisition or possession of a firearm described in subdivision (a) by any peace officer described in Chapter 4.5 (commencing with Section 830) of Title 3 of Part 2, while on duty and acting within the scope and course of his or her employment.

(3) The acquisition or possession of a firearm described in subdivision (a) by any employee of a forensic laboratory, while on duty and acting within the scope and course of his or her employment.

(4) The possession and disposition of a firearm described in subdivision (a) by a person who meets all of the following:

(A) He or she is not prohibited by state or federal law from possessing, receiving, owning, or purchasing a firearm.

(B) The person possessed the firearm no longer than was necessary to deliver the same to a law enforcement agency for that agency's disposition according to law.

(C) If the person is transporting the firearm, he or she is transporting the firearm to a law enforcement agency in order to deliver the firearm to the law enforcement agency for the agency's disposition according to law.

(D) If the person is transporting the firearm to a law enforcement agency, he or she has given prior notice to the law enforcement agency that he or she is transporting the firearm to that law enforcement agency for that agency's disposition according to law.

(E) The firearm is transported in a locked container as defined in subdivision (d) of Section 12026.2.

Penal Code § 12095.

(a) If it finds that it does not endanger the public safety, the Department of Justice may issue permits initially valid for a period of one year, and renewable annually thereafter, for the manufacture, possession, transportation, or sale of short-barreled shotguns or short-barreled rifles upon a showing that good cause exists for the issuance thereof to the applicant for the permit. No permit shall be issued to a person who is under 18 years of age.

(b) Good cause, for the purposes of this section, shall be limited to only the following:

(1) The permit is sought for the manufacture, possession, or use with blank cartridges, of a short-barreled rifle or short-barreled shotgun, solely as props for a motion picture, television, or video production or entertainment event.

(2) The permit is sought for the manufacture of, exposing for sale, keeping for sale, sale of, importation or lending of short-barreled rifles or short-barreled shotguns to the entities listed in paragraph (1) of subdivision (b) of Section 12020 by persons who are licensed as dealers or manufacturers under the provisions of Chapter 53 (commencing with Section 5801) of Title 26 of the United States Code, as amended, and the regulations issued pursuant thereto.

Penal Code § 12096.

Applications for permits shall be filed in writing, signed by the applicant if an individual, or by a member or officer qualified to sign if the applicant is a firm or corporation, and shall state the name, business in which engaged, business address, and a full description of the use to which the short-barreled shotguns or short-barreled rifles are to be put. Applications and permits shall be uniform throughout the state on forms prescribed by the Department of Justice. Each applicant for a permit shall pay at the time of filing his or her application a fee determined by the Department of Justice not to exceed the application processing costs of the Department of Justice. A permit granted pursuant to this article may be renewed one year from the date of issuance, and annually thereafter, upon the filing of a renewal application and the payment of a permit renewal fee not to exceed the application processing costs of the Department of Justice. After the department establishes fees sufficient to reimburse the department for processing costs, fees charged shall increase at a rate not to exceed the legislatively approved annual cost-of-living adjustments for the department's budget.

Penal Code § 12097.

(a) Every person, firm, or corporation to whom a permit is issued shall keep it on his or her person or at the place where the short-barreled shotguns or short-barreled rifles are kept. The permit shall be open to inspection by any peace officer or any other person designated by the authority issuing the permit.

(b) Every short-barreled shotgun or short-barreled rifle possessed pursuant to the provisions of this article shall bear a unique identifying number. If a weapon does not bear a unique identifying number, the Department of Justice shall assign a number which shall be placed or stamped on that weapon.

Penal Code § 12098.

Permits issued in accordance with this article may be revoked by the issuing authority at any time when it appears that the need for the short-barreled shotguns or short-barreled rifles has ceased or that the holder of the permit has used the short-barreled shotguns or short-barreled rifles for purposes other than those allowed by the permit or that the holder of the permit has not exercised great care in retaining custody of any weapons possessed under the permit.

Penal Code § 12099.

(a) Except as provided in subdivision (b), the Department of Justice shall, for every person, firm, or corporation to whom a permit is issued pursuant to this article, annually conduct an inspection for security and safe storage purposes, and to reconcile the inventory of short-barreled shotguns and short-barreled rifles.

(b) A person, firm, or corporation with an inventory of fewer than five devices that require any Department of Justice permit shall be subject to an inspection for security and safe storage purposes, and to reconcile inventory, once every five years, or more frequently if determined by the department.

Penal Code § 12101.

(a)(1) A minor shall not possess a pistol, revolver, or other firearm capable of being concealed upon the person.

(2) Paragraph (1) shall not apply if one of the following circumstances exists:

(A) The minor is accompanied by his or her parent or legal guardian, and the minor is actively engaged in, or is in direct transit to or from, a lawful, recreational sport, including, but not limited to, competitive shooting, or agricultural, ranching, or hunting activity, or a motion picture, television, or video production, or entertainment or theatrical event, the nature of which involves this use of a firearm.

(B) The minor is accompanied by a responsible adult, the minor has the prior written consent of his or her parent or legal guardian, and the minor is actively engaged in, or is in direct transit to or from, a lawful, recreational sport, including, but not limited to, competitive shooting, or agricultural, ranching, or hunting activity, or a motion picture, television, or video production, or entertainment or theatrical event, the nature of which involves the use of a firearm.

(C) The minor is at least 16 years of age, the minor has the prior written consent of his or her parent or legal guardian and the minor is actively engaged in, or is in direct transit to or from, a lawful recreational sport, including, but not limited to, competitive shooting, or agricultural, ranching, or hunting activity, or a motion picture, television, or video production, or entertainment or theatrical event, the nature of which involves the use of a firearm.

(D) The minor has the prior written consent of his or her parent or legal guardian, the minor is on lands owned or lawfully possessed by his or her parent or legal guardian, and the minor is actively engaged in, or is in direct transit to or from, a lawful, recreational sport, including, but not limited to, competitive shooting, or agricultural, ranching, or hunting activity, or a motion picture, television, or video production, or entertainment or theatrical event, the nature of which involves the use of a firearm.

(b)(1) A minor shall not possess live ammunition. (2) Paragraph (1) shall not apply if one of the following circumstances exists:

(A) The minor has the written consent of his or her parent or legal guardian to possess live ammunition.

(B) The minor is accompanied by his or her parent or legal guardian.

(C) The minor is actively engaged in, or is going to or from, a lawful, recreational sport, including, but not limited to, competitive shooting, or agricultural, ranching, or hunting activity, the nature of which involves the use of a firearm.

(c) Every minor who violates this section shall be punished as follows:

(1) By imprisonment in the state prison or in a county jail if one of the following applies:

(A) The minor has been found guilty previously of violating this section.

(B) The minor has been found guilty previously of an offense specified in subdivision (b) of Section 12021.1 or in Section 12020, 12220, 12520, or 12560.

(C) The minor has been found guilty of a violation of paragraph (1) of subdivision (a).

(2) Violations of this section other than those violations specified in paragraph (1) shall be punishable as a misdemeanor.

(d) In a proceeding to enforce this section brought pursuant to Article 14 (commencing with Section 601) of Chapter 2 of Part 1 of the Welfare and Institutions Code, the court may require the custodial parent or legal guardian of a minor who violates this section to participate in classes on parenting education that meet the requirements established in Section 16507.7 of the Welfare and Institutions Code.

(e) As used in this section, "responsible adult" means a person at least 21 years of age who is not prohibited by state or federal law from possessing, receiving, owning, or purchasing a firearm.

(f) It is not the intent of the Legislature in enacting the amendments to this section or to Section 12078 to expand or narrow the application of current statutory or judicial authority as to the rights of minors to be loaned or to possess live ammunition or a firearm for the purpose of self-defense or the defense of others.

Penal Code § 12125.

(a) Commencing January 1, 2001, any person in this state who manufactures or causes to be manufactured, imports into the state for sale, keeps for sale, offers or exposes for sale, gives, or lends any unsafe handgun shall be punished by imprisonment in a county jail not exceeding one year.

(b) This section shall not apply to any of the following:

(1) The manufacture in this state, or importation into this state, of any prototype pistol, revolver, or other firearm capable of being concealed upon the person when the manufacture or importation is for the sole purpose of allowing an independent laboratory certified by the Department of Justice pursuant to Section 12130 to conduct an independent test to determine whether that pistol, revolver, or other firearm capable of being concealed upon the person is prohibited by this chapter, and, if not, allowing the department to add the firearm to the roster of pistols, revolvers, and other firearms capable of being concealed upon the person that may be sold in this state pursuant to Section 12131.

(2) The importation or lending of a pistol, revolver, or other firearm capable of being concealed upon the person by employees or authorized agents of entities determining whether the weapon is prohibited by this section.

(3) Firearms listed as curios or relics, as defined in Section 478.11 of Title 27 of the Code of Federal Regulations.

(4) The sale or purchase of any pistol, revolver or other firearm capable of being concealed upon the person, if the pistol, revolver, or other firearm is sold to, or purchased by, the Department of Justice, any police department, any sheriff's official, any marshal's office, the Youth and Adult Correctional Agency, the California Highway Patrol, any district attorney's office, or the military or naval forces

of this state or of the United States for use in the discharge of their official duties. Nor shall anything in this section prohibit the sale to, or purchase by, sworn members of these agencies of any pistol, revolver, or other firearm capable of being concealed upon the person.

(c) Violations of subdivision (a) are cumulative with respect to each handgun and shall not be construed as restricting the application of any other law. However, an act or omission punishable in different ways by this section and other provisions of law shall not be punished under more than one provision, but the penalty to be imposed shall be determined as set forth in Section 654.

Penal Code § 12126.

As used in this chapter, "unsafe handgun" means any pistol, revolver, or other firearm capable of being concealed upon the person, as defined in subdivision (a) of Section 12001, for which any of the following is true:

(a) For a revolver:

(1) It does not have a safety device that, either automatically in the case of a double-action firing mechanism, or by manual operation in the case of a single-action firing mechanism, causes the hammer to retract to a point where the firing pin does not rest upon the primer of the cartridge.

(2) It does not meet the firing requirement for handguns pursuant to Section 12127.

(3) It does not meet the drop safety requirement for handguns pursuant to Section 12128.

(b) For a pistol:

(1) It does not have a positive manually operated safety device, as determined by standards relating to imported guns promulgated by the federal Bureau of Alcohol, Tobacco, and Firearms.

(2) It does not meet the firing requirement for handguns pursuant to Section 12127.

(3) It does not meet the drop safety requirement for handguns pursuant to Section 12128.

(4) Commencing January 1, 2006, for a center fire semiautomatic pistol that is not already listed on the roster pursuant to Section 12131, it does not have either a chamber load indicator, or a magazine disconnect mechanism.

(5) Commencing January 1, 2007, for all center fire semiautomatic pistols that are not already listed on the roster pursuant to Section 12131, it does not have both a chamber load indicator and if it has a detachable magazine, a magazine disconnect mechanism.

(6) Commencing January 1, 2006, for all rimfire semiautomatic pistols that are not already listed on the roster pursuant to Section 12131, it does not have a magazine disconnect mechanism, if it has a detachable magazine.

(7) Commencing January 1, 2010, for all semiautomatic pistols that are not already listed on the roster pursuant to Section 12131, it is not designed and equipped with a microscopic array of characters that identify the make, model, and serial number of the pistol, etched or otherwise imprinted in two or more places on the interior surface or internal working parts of the pistol, and that are transferred by imprinting on each cartridge case when the firearm is fired, provided that the Department of Justice certifies that the technology used to create the imprint is available to more than one manufacturer unencumbered by any patent restrictions. The Attorney General may also approve a method of equal or greater reliability and effectiveness in identifying the specific serial number of a firearm from spent cartridge casings discharged by that firearm than that which is set forth in this paragraph, to be thereafter required as otherwise set forth by this paragraph where the Attorney General certifies that this new method is also unencumbered by any patent restrictions. Approval by the Attorney General shall include notice of that fact via regulations adopted by the Attorney General for purposes of implementing that method for purposes of this paragraph. The microscopic array of characters required by this section shall not be considered the name of the maker, model, manufacturer's number, or other mark of identification, including any distinguishing number or mark assigned by the Department of Justice, within the meaning of Sections 12090 and 12094.

(c) As used in this section, a "chamber load indicator" means a device that plainly indicates that a cartridge is in the firing chamber. A device satisfies this definition if it is readily visible, has incorporated or adjacent explanatory text or graphics, or both, and is designed and intended to indicate to a reasonably foreseeable adult user of the pistol, without requiring the user to refer to a user's manual or any other resource other than the pistol itself, whether a cartridge is in the firing chamber.

(d) As used in this section, a "magazine disconnect mechanism" means a mechanism that prevents a semiautomatic pistol that has a detachable magazine from operating to strike the primer of ammunition in the firing chamber when a detachable magazine is not inserted in the semiautomatic pistol.

(e) As used in this section, a "semiautomatic pistol" means a pistol, as defined in subdivision (a) of Section 12001, the operating mode of which uses the energy of the explosive in a fixed cartridge to extract a fired cartridge and chamber a fresh cartridge with each single pull of the trigger.

Penal Code § 12127.

(a) As used in this chapter, the "firing requirement for handguns" means a test in which the manufacturer provides three handguns of the make and model for which certification is sought to an independent testing laboratory certified by the Attorney General pursuant to Section 12130. These handguns may not be refined or modified in any way from those that would be made available for retail sale if certification is granted. The magazines of a tested pistol shall be identical to those that would be provided with the pistol to a retail customer. The laboratory shall fire 600 rounds from each gun, stopping after each series of 50 rounds has been fired for 5 to 10 minutes to allow the weapon to cool, stopping after each series of 100 rounds has been fired to tighten any loose screws and clean the gun in accordance with the manufacturer's instructions, and stopping as needed to refill the empty magazine or cylinder to capacity before continuing. The ammunition used shall be of the type recommended by the handgun manufacturer in the user manual, or if none is recommended, any standard ammunition of the correct caliber in new condition that is commercially available. A handgun shall pass this test if each of the three test guns meets both of the following:

(1) Fires the first 20 rounds without a malfunction that is not due to ammunition that fails to detonate.

(2) Fires the full 600 rounds with no more than six malfunctions that are not due to ammunition that fails to detonate and without any crack or breakage of an operating part of the handgun that increases the risk of injury to the user.

(b) If a pistol or revolver fails the requirements of either paragraph (1) or (2) of subdivision (a) due to ammunition that fails to detonate, the pistol or revolver shall be retested from the beginning of the "firing requirement for handguns" test. A new model of the pistol or revolver that failed due to ammunition that fails to detonate may be submitted for the test to replace the pistol or revolver that failed.

(c) As used in this section, "malfunction" means a failure to properly feed, fire, or eject a round, or failure of a pistol to accept or eject the magazine, or failure of a pistol's slide to remain open after the magazine has been expended.

Penal Code § 12128.

As used in this chapter, the "drop safety requirement for handguns" means that at the conclusion of the firing requirements for handguns described in Section 12127, the same certified independent testing laboratory shall subject the same three handguns of the make and model for which certification is sought, to the following test: A primed case (no powder or projectile) shall be inserted into the chamber. For pistols, the slide shall be released, allowing it to move forward under the impetus of the recoil spring, and an empty magazine shall be inserted. For both pistols and revolvers, the weapon shall be placed in a drop fixture capable of dropping the pistol from a drop height of 1m + 1cm (39.4 + 0.4 in.) onto the largest side of a slab of solid concrete having minimum dimensions of 7.5 X 15 X 15 cm (3 X 6 X 6 in.). The drop distance shall be measured from the lowermost portion of the weapon to the top surface of the slab. The weapon shall be dropped from a fixture and not from the hand. The weapon shall be dropped in the condition that it would be in if it were dropped from a hand (cocked with no manual safety applied). If the design of a pistol is such that upon leaving the hand a "safety" is automatically applied by the pistol, this feature shall not be defeated. An approved drop fixture is a short piece of string with the weapon attached at one end and the other end held in an air vise until the drop is initiated. The following six drops shall be performed:

(a) Normal firing position with barrel horizontal.

(b) Upside down with barrel horizontal.

(c) On grip with barrel vertical.

(d) On muzzle with barrel vertical.

(e) On either side with barrel horizontal.

(f) If there is an exposed hammer or striker, on the rearmost point of that device, otherwise on the rearmost point of the weapon. The primer shall be examined for indentations after each drop. If indentations are present, a fresh primed case shall be used for the next drop. The handgun shall pass this test if each of the three test guns does not fire the primer.

Penal Code § 12129.

Every person who is licensed as a manufacturer of firearms pursuant to Chapter 44 (commencing with Section 921) of Title 18 of the United States Code who manufactures firearms in this state, and every person who imports into the state for sale, keeps for sale, or offers or exposes for sale any firearm, shall certify under penalty of perjury and any other remedy provided by law that every model, kind, class, style, or type of pistol, revolver, or other firearm capable of being concealed upon the person that he or she manufactures or imports, keeps, or exposes for sale is not an unsafe handgun as prohibited by this chapter.

Penal Code § 12130.

(a) Any pistol, revolver, or other firearm capable of being concealed upon the person manufactured in this state, imported into the state for sale, kept for sale, or offered or exposed for sale, shall be tested within a reasonable period of time by an independent laboratory certified pursuant to subdivision (b) to determine whether that pistol, revolver, or other firearm capable of being concealed upon the person meets or exceeds the standards defined in Section 12126.

(b) On or before October 1, 2000, the Department of Justice shall certify laboratories to verify compliance with the standards defined in Section 12126. The department may charge any laboratory that is seeking certification to test any pistol, revolver, or other firearm capable of being concealed upon the person pursuant to this chapter a fee not exceeding the costs of certification.

(c) The certified testing laboratory shall, at the manufacturer's or importer's expense, test the firearm and submit a copy of the final test report directly to the Department of Justice along with a prototype of the weapon to be retained by the department. The department shall notify the manufacturer or importer of its receipt of the final test report and the department's determination as to whether the firearm tested may be sold in this state.

(d)(1) Commencing January 1, 2006, no center-fire semiautomatic pistol may be submitted for testing pursuant to this chapter if it does not have either a chamber load indicator as defined in subdivision (c) of Section 12126, or a magazine disconnect mechanism as defined in subdivision (d) of Section 12126 if it has a detachable magazine.

(2) Commencing January 1, 2007, no center-fire semiautomatic pistol may be submitted for testing pursuant to this chapter if it does not have both a chamber load indicator as defined in subdivision (c) of Section 12126 and a magazine disconnect mechanism as defined in subdivision (d) of Section 12126.

(3) Commencing January 1, 2006, no rimfire semiautomatic pistol may be submitted for testing pursuant to this chapter if it has a detachable magazine, and does not have a magazine disconnect mechanism as defined in subdivision (d) of Section 12126.

Penal Code § 12131.

(a) On and after January 1, 2001, the Department of Justice shall compile, publish, and thereafter maintain a roster listing all of the pistols, revolvers, and other firearms capable of being concealed upon the person that have been tested by a certified testing laboratory, have been determined not to be unsafe handguns, and may be sold in this state pursuant to this title. The roster shall list, for each firearm, the manufacturer, model number, and model name.

(b)(1) The department may charge every person in this state who is licensed as a manufacturer of firearms pursuant to Chapter 44 (commencing with Section 921) of Title 18 of the United States Code, and any person in this state who manufactures or causes to be manufactured, imports into the state for sale, keeps for sale, or offers or exposes for sale any pistol, revolver, or other firearm capable of being concealed upon the person in this state, an annual fee not exceeding the costs of preparing, publishing, and maintaining the roster pursuant to subdivision (a) and the costs of research and development, report analysis, firearms storage, and other program infrastructure costs necessary to implement this chapter.

(2) Any pistol, revolver, or other firearm capable of being concealed upon the person that is manufactured by a manufacturer who manufactures or causes to be manufactured, imports into the state for sale, keeps for sale, or offers or exposes for sale any pistol,

revolver, or other firearm capable of being concealed upon the person in this state, and who fails to pay any fee required pursuant to paragraph (1), may be excluded from the roster.

(3) If a purchaser has initiated a transfer of a handgun that is listed on the roster as not unsafe, and prior to the completion of the transfer, the handgun is removed from the roster of not unsafe handguns because of failure to pay the fee required to keep that handgun listed on the roster, the handgun shall be deliverable to the purchaser if the purchaser is not otherwise prohibited from purchasing or possessing the handgun. However, if a purchaser has initiated a transfer of a handgun that is listed on the roster as not unsafe, and prior to the completion of the transfer, the handgun is removed from the roster pursuant to subdivision (f), the handgun shall not be deliverable to the purchaser.

(c) The Attorney General may annually retest up to 5 percent of the handgun models that are listed on the roster described in subdivision (a).

(d) The retesting of a handgun model pursuant to subdivision (c) shall conform to the following:

(1) The Attorney General shall obtain from retail or wholesale sources, or both, three samples of the handgun model to be retested.

(2) The Attorney General shall select the certified laboratory to be used for the retesting.

(3) The ammunition used for the retesting shall be of a type recommended by the manufacturer in the user manual for the handgun. If the user manual for the handgun model makes no ammunition recommendation, the Attorney General shall select the ammunition to be used for the retesting. The ammunition shall be of the proper caliber for the handgun, commercially available, and in new condition.

(e) The retest shall be conducted in the same manner as the testing prescribed in Sections 12127 and 12128.

(f) If the handgun model fails retesting, the Attorney General shall remove the handgun model from the roster maintained pursuant to subdivision (a).

(g) A handgun model removed from the roster pursuant to subdivision (f) may be reinstated on the roster if all of the following are met:

(1) The manufacturer petitions the Attorney General for reinstatement of the handgun model.

(2) The manufacturer pays the Department of Justice for all of the costs related to the reinstatement testing of the handgun model, including the purchase price of the handguns, prior to reinstatement testing.

(3) The reinstatement testing of the handguns shall be in accordance with subdivisions (d) and (e).

(4) The three handgun samples shall be tested only once for reinstatement. If the sample fails it may not be retested.

(5) If the handgun model successfully passes testing for reinstatement, and if the manufacturer of the handgun is otherwise in compliance with this chapter, the Attorney General shall reinstate the handgun model on the roster maintained pursuant to subdivision (a).

(6) The manufacturer shall provide the Attorney General with the complete testing history for the handgun model.

(7) Notwithstanding subdivision (c), the Attorney General may, at any time, further retest any handgun model that has been reinstated to the roster.

Penal Code § 12131.5.

(a) A firearm shall be deemed to satisfy the requirements of subdivision (a) of Section 12131 if another firearm made by the same manufacturer is already listed and the unlisted firearm differs from the listed firearm only in one or more of the following features:

(1) Finish, including, but not limited to, bluing, chrome-plating, oiling, or engraving.

(2) The material from which the grips are made.

(3) The shape or texture of the grips, so long as the difference in grip shape or texture does not in any way alter the dimensions, material, linkage, or functioning of the magazine well, the barrel, the chamber, or any of the components of the firing mechanism of the firearm.

(4) Any other purely cosmetic feature that does not in any way alter the dimensions, material, linkage, or functioning of the magazine well, the barrel, the chamber, or any of the components of the firing mechanism of the firearm.

(b) Any manufacturer seeking to have a firearm listed under this section shall provide to the Department of Justice all of the following:

(1) The model designation of the listed firearm.

(2) The model designation of each firearm that the manufacturer seeks to have listed under this section.

(3) A statement, under oath, that each unlisted firearm for which listing is sought differs from the listed firearm only in one or more of the ways identified in subdivision (a) and is in all other respects identical to the listed firearm.

(c) The department may, in its discretion and at any time, require a manufacturer to provide to the department any model for which listing is sought under this section, to determine whether the model complies with the requirements of this section.

Penal Code § 12132.

This chapter shall not apply to any of the following:

(a) The sale, loan, or transfer of any firearm pursuant to Section 12082 in order to comply with subdivision (d) of Section 12072.

(b) The sale, loan, or transfer of any firearm that is exempt from the provisions of subdivision (d) of Section 12072 pursuant to any applicable exemption contained in Section 12078, if the sale, loan, or transfer complies with the requirements of that applicable exemption to subdivision (d) of Section 12072.

(c) The sale, loan, or transfer of any firearm as described in paragraph (3) of subdivision (b) of Section 12125.

(d) The delivery of a pistol, revolver, or other firearm capable of being concealed upon the person to a person licensed pursuant to Section 12071 for the purposes of the service or repair of that firearm.

(e) The return of a pistol, revolver, or other firearm capable of being concealed upon the person by a person licensed pursuant to Section 12071 to its owner where that firearm was initially delivered in the circumstances set forth in subdivisions (a), (d), (f) or (j).

(f) The delivery of a pistol, revolver, or other firearm capable of being concealed upon the person to a person licensed pursuant to Section 12071 for the purpose of a consignment sale or as collateral for a pawnbroker loan.

(g) The sale, loan, or transfer of any pistol, revolver, or other firearm capable of being concealed upon the person listed as a curio or relic, as defined in Section 178.11 of the Code of Federal Regulations.

(h)(1) The Legislature finds a significant public purpose in exempting pistols that are designed expressly for use in Olympic target shooting events. Therefore, those pistols that are sanctioned by the International Olympic Committee and by USA Shooting, the national governing body for international shooting competition in the United States, and that are used for Olympic target shooting purposes at the time that the act adding this subdivision is enacted, and that fall within the definition of "unsafe handgun" pursuant to paragraph (3) of subdivision (b) of Section 12126 shall be exempt, as provided in paragraphs (2) and (3).

(2) This chapter shall not apply to any of the following pistols, because they are consistent with the significant public purpose expressed in paragraph (1):

MANUFACTURER	MODEL	CALIBER
ANSCHUTZ	FP	.22LR
BENELLI	MP90	.22LR
BENELLI	MP90	.32 S&W LONG
BENELLI	MP95	.22LR
BENELLI	MP95	.32 S&W LONG
DRULOV	FP	.22LR
GREEN	ELECTROARM	.22LR
HAMMERLI	100	.22LR
HAMMERLI	101	.22LR
HAMMERLI	102	.22LR
HAMMERLI	162	.22LR
HAMMERLI	280	.22LR
HAMMERLI	280	.32 S&W LONG
HAMMERLI	FP10	.22LR
HAMMERLI	MP33	.22LR
HAMMERLI	SP20	.22LR
HAMMERLI	SP20	.32 S&W LONG
MORINI	CM102E	.22LR
MORINI	22M	.22LR
MORINI	32M	.22LR
MORINI	CM80	.22LR
PARDINI	GP	.22 SHORT
PARDINI	GPO	.22 SHORT
PARDINI	GP-SCHUMANN	.22 SHORT
PARDINI	HP	.32 S&W LONG

PARDINI	K22	.22LR
PARDINI	MP	.32 S&W LONG
PARDINI	PGP75	.22LR
PARDINI	SP	.22LR
PARDINI	SPE	.22LR
SAKO	FINMASTER	.22LR
STEYR	FP	.22LR
VOSTOK	IZH NO. 1	.22LR
VOSTOK	MU55	.22LR
VOSTOK	TOZ35	.22LR
WALTHER	FP	.22LR
WALTHER	GSP	.22LR
WALTHER	GSP	.32 S&W LONG
WALTHER	OSP	.22 SHORT
WALTHER	OSP-2000	.22 SHORT

(3) The department shall create a program that is consistent with the purpose stated in paragraph (1) to exempt new models of competitive firearms from this chapter. The exempt competitive firearms may be based on recommendations by USA Shooting consistent with the regulations contained in the USA Shooting Official Rules or may be based on the recommendation or rules of any other organization that the department deems relevant.

(i) The sale, loan, or transfer of any semiautomatic pistol that is to be used solely as a prop during the course of a motion picture, television, or video production by an authorized participant therein in the course of making that production or event or by an authorized employee or agent of the entity producing that production or event.

(j) The delivery of a pistol, revolver, or other firearm capable of being concealed upon the person to a person licensed pursuant to Section 12071 where the firearm is being loaned by the licensee to a consultant-evaluator.

(k) The delivery of a pistol, revolver, or other firearm capable of being concealed upon the person by a person licensed pursuant to Section 12071 where the firearm is being loaned by the licensee to a consultant-evaluator.

(l) The return of a pistol, revolver, or other firearm capable of being concealed upon the person to a person licensed pursuant to Section 12071 where it was initially delivered pursuant to subdivision (k).

Penal Code § 12133.

(a) The provisions of this chapter shall not apply to a single-action revolver that has at least a 5-cartridge capacity with a barrel length of not less than three inches, and meets any of the following specifications:

(1) Was originally manufactured prior to 1900 and is a curio or relic, as defined in Section 478.11 of Title 27 of the Code of Federal Regulations.

(2) Has an overall length measured parallel to the barrel of at least 7 1/2 inches when the handle, frame or receiver, and barrel are assembled.

(3) Has an overall length measured parallel to the barrel of at least 7 1/2 inches when the handle, frame or receiver, and barrel are assembled and that is currently approved for importation into the United States pursuant to the provisions of paragraph (3) of subsection (d) of Section 925 of Title 18 of the United States Code.

(b) The provisions of this chapter shall not apply to a single-shot pistol with a barrel length of not less than six inches and that has an overall length of at least 10 1/2 inches when the handle, frame or receiver, and barrel are assembled.

Penal Code § 12200.

The term "machinegun" as used in this chapter means any weapon which shoots, is designed to shoot, or can readily be restored to shoot, automatically more than one shot, without manual reloading, by a single function of the trigger. The term shall also include the frame or receiver of any such weapon, any part designed and intended solely and exclusively, or combination of parts designed and intended, for use in converting a weapon into a machinegun, and any combination of parts from which a machinegun can be assembled if such parts are in the possession or under the control of a person. The term also includes any weapon deemed by the federal Bureau of Alcohol, Tobacco, and Firearms as readily convertible to a machinegun under Chapter 53 (commencing with Section 5801) of Title 26 of the United States Code.

Penal Code § 12201.

Nothing in this chapter shall affect or apply to any of the following:

(a) The sale to, purchase by, or possession of machineguns by police departments, sheriffs' offices, marshals' offices, district attorneys' offices, the California Highway Patrol, the Department of Justice, the Department of Corrections for use by the department's Special Emergency Response Teams and Law Enforcement Liaison/Investigations Unit, or the military or naval forces of this state or of the United States for use in the discharge of their official duties, provided, however, that any sale to these entities be transacted by a person who is permitted pursuant to Section 12230 and licensed pursuant to Section 12250.

(b) The possession of machineguns by regular, salaried, full-time peace officer members of a police department, sheriff's office, marshal's office, district attorney's office, the California Highway Patrol, the Department of Justice, or the Department of Corrections for use by the department's Special Emergency Response Teams and Law Enforcement Liaison/Investigations Unit when on duty and if the use is within the scope of their duties.

Penal Code § 12220.

(a) Any person, firm, or corporation, who within this state possesses or knowingly transports a machinegun, except as authorized by this chapter, is guilty of a public offense and upon conviction thereof shall be punished by imprisonment in the state prison, or by a fine not to exceed ten thousand dollars ($10,000), or by both such fine and imprisonment.

(b) Any person, firm, or corporation who within this state intentionally converts a firearm into a machinegun, or who sells, or offers for sale, or knowingly manufactures a machinegun, except as authorized by this chapter, is punishable by imprisonment in the state prison for four, six, or eight years.

Penal Code § 12230.

The Department of Justice may issue permits for the possession, manufacture, and transportation or possession, manufacture, or transportation of machineguns, upon a satisfactory showing that good cause exists for the issuance thereof to the applicant for the permit, but no permit shall be issued to a person who is under 18 years of age.

Penal Code § 12231.

Applications for permits shall be filed in writing, signed by the applicant if an individual, or by a member or officer qualified to sign if the applicant is a firm or corporation, and shall state the name, business in which engaged, business address and a full description of the use to which the firearms are to be put. Applications and permits shall be uniform throughout the state on forms prescribed by the Department of Justice. Each applicant for a permit shall pay at the time of filing his or her application a fee determined by the Department of Justice not to exceed the application processing costs of the Department of Justice. A permit granted pursuant to this article may be renewed one year from the date of issuance, and annually thereafter, upon the filing of a renewal application and the payment of a permit renewal fee not to exceed the application processing costs of the Department of Justice. After the department establishes fees sufficient to reimburse the department for processing costs, fees charged shall increase at a rate not to exceed the legislatively approved annual cost-of-living adjustments for the department's budget.

Penal Code § 12232.

Every person, firm or corporation to whom a permit is issued shall keep it on his person or at the place where the firearms are kept. The permit shall be open to inspection by any peace officer or any other person designated by the authority issuing the permit.

Penal Code § 12233.

Permits issued in accordance with this chapter may be revoked by the issuing authority at any time when it appears that the need for the firearms has ceased or that the holder of the permit has used the firearms for purposes other than those allowed by the permit or that the holder of the permit has not exercised great care in retaining custody of any weapons possessed under the permit.

Penal Code § 12234.

(a) Except as provided in subdivision (b), the Department of Justice shall, for every person, firm, or corporation to whom a permit is issued pursuant to this article, annually conduct an inspection for security and safe storage purposes, and to reconcile the inventory of machine guns.

(b) A person, firm, or corporation with an inventory of fewer than five devices that require any Department of Justice permit shall be subject to an inspection for security and safe storage purposes, and to reconcile inventory, once every five years, or more frequently if determined by the department.

Penal Code § 12250.

(a) The Department of Justice may grant licenses in a form to be prescribed by it effective for not more than one year from the date of issuance, to permit the sale at the place specified in the license of machineguns subject to all of the following conditions, upon breach of any of which the license shall be revoked:

1. The business shall be carried on only in the place designated in the license.

2. The license or a certified copy thereof must be displayed on the premises in a place where it may easily be read.

3. No machinegun shall be delivered to any person not authorized to receive the same under the provisions of this chapter.

4. A complete record must be kept of sales made under the authority of the license, showing the name and address of the purchaser, the descriptions and serial numbers of the weapons purchased, the number and date of issue of the purchaser's permit, if any, and the signature of the purchaser or purchasing agent. This record shall be open to the inspection of any peace officer or other person designated by the Attorney General.

(b) Applications for licenses shall be filed in writing, signed by the applicant if an individual or by a member or officer qualified to sign if the applicant is a firm or corporation, and shall state the name, business in which engaged, business address and a full description of the use to which the firearms are to be put. Applications and licenses shall be uniform throughout the state on forms prescribed by the Department of Justice. Each applicant for a license shall pay at the time of filing his or her application a fee determined by the Department of Justice not to exceed the application processing costs of the Department of Justice. A license granted pursuant to this article may be renewed one year from the date of issuance, and annually thereafter, upon the filing of a renewal application and the payment of a license renewal fee not to exceed the application processing costs of the Department of Justice. After the department establishes fees sufficient to reimburse the department for processing costs, fees charged shall increase at a rate not to exceed the legislatively approved annual cost-of-living adjustments for the department's budget.

Penal Code § 12251.

It shall be a public nuisance to possess any machinegun in violation of this chapter, and the Attorney General, any district attorney or any city attorney may bring an action before the superior court to enjoin the possession of any such machinegun. Any such machinegun found to be in violation of this chapter shall be surrendered to the Department of Justice, and the department shall destroy such machinegun so as to render it unusable and unrepairable as a machinegun, except upon the filing of a certificate with the department by a judge or district attorney stating that the preservation of such machinegun is necessary to serve the ends of justice.

Penal Code § 12275.

This chapter shall be known as the Roberti-Roos Assault Weapons Control Act of 1989 and the .50 Caliber BMG Regulation Act of 2004.

Penal Code § 12275.5.

(a) The Legislature hereby finds and declares that the proliferation and use of assault weapons poses a threat to the health, safety, and security of all citizens of this state. The Legislature has restricted the assault weapons specified in Section 12276 based upon finding that each firearm has such a high rate of fire and capacity for firepower that its function as a legitimate sports or recreational firearm is substantially outweighed by the danger that it can be used to kill and injure human beings. It is the intent of the Legislature in enacting this chapter to place restrictions on the use of assault weapons and to establish a registration and permit procedure for their lawful sale and possession. It is not, however, the intent of the Legislature by this chapter to place restrictions on the use of those weapons which are primarily designed and intended for hunting, target practice, or other legitimate sports or recreational activities.

(b) The Legislature hereby finds and declares that the proliferation and use of .50 BMG rifles, as defined in Section 12278, poses a clear and present terrorist threat to the health, safety, and security of all residents of, and visitors to, this state, based upon findings that those firearms have such a high capacity for long distance and highly destructive firepower that they pose an unacceptable risk to the death and serious injury of human beings, destruction or serious damage of vital public and private buildings, civilian, police and military vehicles, power generation and transmission facilities, petrochemical production and storage facilities, and transportation infrastructure. It is the intent of the Legislature in enacting this chapter to place restrictions on the use of these rifles and to establish a registration and permit procedure for their lawful sale and possession.

Penal Code § 12276.

As used in this chapter, "assault weapon" shall mean the following designated semiautomatic firearms:

(a) All of the following specified rifles:

(1) All AK series including, but not limited to, the models identified as follows:

(A) Made in China AK, AKM, AKS, AK47, AK47S, 56, 56S, 84S, and 86S.

(B) Norinco 56, 56S, 84S, and 86S.

(C) Poly Technologies AKS and AK47.

(D) MAADI AK47 and ARM.

(2) UZI and Galil.

(3) Beretta AR-70.

(4) CETME Sporter.

(5) Colt AR-15 series.

(6) Daewoo K-1, K-2, Max 1, Max 2, AR 100, and AR 110C.

(7) Fabrique Nationale FAL, LAR, FNC, 308 Match, and Sporter.

(8) MAS 223.

(9) HK-91, HK-93, HK-94, and HK-PSG-1.

(10) The following MAC types:

(A) RPB Industries Inc. sM10 and sM11.

(B) SWD Incorporated M11.

(11) SKS with detachable magazine.

(12) SIG AMT, PE-57, SG 550, and SG 551.

(13) Springfield Armory BM59 and SAR-48.

(14) Sterling MK-6.

(15) Steyer AUG.

(16) Valmet M62S, M71S, and M78S.

(17) Armalite AR-180.

(18) Bushmaster Assault Rifle.

(19) Calico M-900.

(20) J&R ENG M-68.

(21) Weaver Arms Nighthawk.

(b) All of the following specified pistols:

(1) UZI.

(2) Encom MP-9 and MP-45.

(3) The following MAC types:

(A) RPB Industries Inc. sM10 and sM11.

(B) SWD Incorporated M-11.

(C) Advance Armament Inc. M-11.

(D) Military Armament Corp. Ingram M-11.

(4) Intratec TEC-9.

(5) Sites Spectre.

(6) Sterling MK-7.

(7) Calico M-950.

(8) Bushmaster Pistol.

(c) All of the following specified shotguns:

(1) Franchi SPAS 12 and LAW 12.

(2) Striker 12.

(3) The Streetsweeper type S/S Inc. SS/12.

(d) Any firearm declared by the court pursuant to Section 12276.5 to be an assault weapon that is specified as an assault weapon in a list promulgated pursuant to Section 12276.5.

(e) The term "series" includes all other models that are only variations, with minor differences, of those models listed in subdivision (a), regardless of the manufacturer.

(f) This section is declaratory of existing law, as amended, and a clarification of the law and the Legislature's intent which bans the weapons enumerated in this section, the weapons included in the list promulgated by the Attorney General pursuant to Section 12276.5, and any other models which are only variations of those weapons with minor differences, regardless of the manufacturer. The Legislature has defined assault weapons as the types, series, and models listed in this section because it was the most effective way to identify and restrict a specific class of semiautomatic weapons.

Penal Code § 12276.1.

(a) Notwithstanding Section 12276, "assault weapon" shall also mean any of the following:

(1) A semiautomatic, centerfire rifle that has the capacity to accept a detachable magazine and any one of the following:

(A) A pistol grip that protrudes conspicuously beneath the action of the weapon.

(B) A thumbhole stock.

(C) A folding or telescoping stock.

(D) A grenade launcher or flare launcher.

(E) A flash suppressor.

(F) A forward pistol grip.

(2) A semiautomatic, centerfire rifle that has a fixed magazine with the capacity to accept more than 10 rounds.

(3) A semiautomatic, centerfire rifle that has an overall length of less than 30 inches.

(4) A semiautomatic pistol that has the capacity to accept a detachable magazine and any one of the following:

(A) A threaded barrel, capable of accepting a flash suppressor, forward handgrip, or silencer.

(B) A second handgrip.

(C) A shroud that is attached to, or partially or completely encircles, the barrel that allows the bearer to fire the weapon without burning his or her hand, except a slide that encloses the barrel.

(D) The capacity to accept a detachable magazine at some location outside of the pistol grip.

(5) A semiautomatic pistol with a fixed magazine that has the capacity to accept more than 10 rounds.

(6) A semiautomatic shotgun that has both of the following:

(A) A folding or telescoping stock.

(B) A pistol grip that protrudes conspicuously beneath the action of the weapon, thumbhole stock, or vertical handgrip.

(7) A semiautomatic shotgun that has the ability to accept a detachable magazine.

(8) Any shotgun with a revolving cylinder.

(b) The Legislature finds a significant public purpose in exempting pistols that are designed expressly for use in Olympic target shooting events. Therefore, those pistols that are sanctioned by the International Olympic Committee and by USA Shooting, the national governing body for international shooting competition in the United States, and that are used for Olympic target shooting purposes at the time the act adding this subdivision is enacted, and that would otherwise fall within the definition of "assault weapon" pursuant to this section are exempt, as provided in subdivision (c).

(c) "Assault weapon" does not include either of the following:

(1) Any antique firearm.

(2) Any of the following pistols, because they are consistent with the significant public purpose expressed in subdivision (b):

MANUFACTURER	MODEL	CALIBER
BENELLI	MP90	.22LR
BENELLI	MP90	.32 S&W LONG
BENELLI	MP95	.22LR

BENELLI	MP95	.32 S&W LONG
HAMMERLI	280	.22LR
HAMMERLI	280	.32 S&W LONG
HAMMERLI	SP20	.22LR
HAMMERLI	SP20	.32 S&W LONG
PARDINI	GPO	.22 SHORT
PARDINI	GP-SCHUMANN	.22 SHORT
PARDINI	HP	.32 S&W LONG
PARDINI	MP	.32 S&W LONG
PARDINI	SP	.22LR
PARDINI	SPE	.22LR
WALTHER	GSP	.22LR
WALTHER	GSP	.32 S&W LONG
WALTHER	OSP	.22 SHORT
WALTHER	OSP-2000	.22 SHORT

(3) The Department of Justice shall create a program that is consistent with the purposes stated in subdivision (b) to exempt new models of competitive pistols that would otherwise fall within the definition of "assault weapon" pursuant to this section from being classified as an assault weapon. The exempt competitive pistols may be based on recommendations by USA Shooting consistent with the regulations contained in the USA Shooting Official Rules or may be based on the recommendation or rules of any other organization that the department deems relevant.

(d) The following definitions shall apply under this section:

(1) "Magazine" shall mean any ammunition feeding device.

(2) "Capacity to accept more than 10 rounds" shall mean capable of accommodating more than 10 rounds, but shall not be construed to include a feeding device that has been permanently altered so that it cannot accommodate more than 10 rounds.

(3) "Antique firearm" means any firearm manufactured prior to January 1, 1899.

(e) This section shall become operative January 1, 2000.

Penal Code § 12276.5.

(a) The Attorney General shall prepare a description for identification purposes, including a picture or diagram, of each assault weapon listed in Section 12276, and any firearm declared to be an assault weapon pursuant to this section, and shall distribute the description to all law enforcement agencies responsible for enforcement of this chapter. Those law enforcement agencies shall make the description available to all agency personnel.

(b)(1) Until January 1, 2007, the Attorney General shall promulgate a list that specifies all firearms designated as assault weapons in Section 12276 or declared to be assault weapons pursuant to this section. The Attorney General shall file that list with the Secretary of State for publication in the California Code of Regulations. Any declaration that a specified firearm is an assault weapon shall be implemented by the Attorney General who, within 90 days, shall promulgate an amended list which shall include the specified firearm declared to be an assault weapon. The Attorney General shall file the amended list with the Secretary of State for publication in the California Code of Regulations. Any firearm declared to be an assault weapon prior to January 1, 2007, shall remain on the list filed with the Secretary of State.

(2) Chapter 3.5 (commencing with Section 11340) of Division 3 of Title 2 of the Government Code, pertaining to the adoption of rules and regulations, shall not apply to any list of assault weapons promulgated pursuant to this section.

(c) The Attorney General shall adopt those rules and regulations that may be necessary or proper to carry out the purposes and intent of this chapter.

Penal Code § 12277.

As used in this chapter, "person" means an individual, partnership, corporation, limited liability company, association, or any other group or entity, regardless of how it was created.

Penal Code § 12278.

(a) As used in this chapter, a ".50 BMG rifle" means a center fire rifle that can fire a .50 BMG cartridge and is not already an assault weapon pursuant to Section 12276, 12276.1, or 12276.5, or a machinegun, as defined in Section 12200.

(b) As used in this chapter, a ".50 BMG cartridge" means a cartridge that is designed and intended to be fired from a center fire rifle and that meets all of the following criteria:

(1) It has an overall length of 5.54 inches from the base to the tip of the bullet.

(2) The bullet diameter for the cartridge is from .510 to, and including, .511 inch.

(3) The case base diameter for the cartridge is from .800 inch to, and including, .804 inch.

(4) The cartridge case length is 3.91 inches.

(c) A ".50 BMG rifle" does not include any "antique firearm," nor any curio or relic as defined in Section 178.11 of Title 27 of the Code of Federal Regulations.

(d) As used in this section, "antique firearm" means any firearm manufactured prior to January 1, 1899.

Penal Code § 12280.

(a)(1) Any person who, within this state, manufactures or causes to be manufactured, distributes, transports, or imports into the state, keeps for sale, or offers or exposes for sale, or who gives or lends any assault weapon or any .50 BMG rifle, except as provided by this chapter, is guilty of a felony, and upon conviction shall be punished by imprisonment in the state prison for four, six, or eight years.

(2) In addition and consecutive to the punishment imposed under paragraph (1), any person who transfers, lends, sells, or gives any assault weapon or any .50 BMG rifle to a minor in violation of paragraph (1) shall receive an enhancement of one year.

(3) Except in the case of a first violation involving not more than two firearms as provided in subdivisions (b) and (c), for purposes of this section, if more than one assault weapon or .50 BMG rifle is involved in any violation of this section, there shall be a distinct and separate offense for each.

(b) Any person who, within this state, possesses any assault weapon, except as provided in this chapter, shall be punished by imprisonment in a county jail for a period not exceeding one year, or by imprisonment in the state prison. However, a first violation of these provisions is punishable by a fine not exceeding five hundred dollars ($500) if the person was found in possession of no more than two firearms in compliance with subdivision (c) of Section 12285 and the person meets all of the following conditions:

(1) The person proves that he or she lawfully possessed the assault weapon prior to the date it was defined as an assault weapon pursuant to Section 12276, 12276.1, or 12276.5.

(2) The person has not previously been convicted of a violation of this section.

(3) The person was found to be in possession of the assault weapon within one year following the end of the one-year registration period established pursuant to subdivision (a) of Section 12285.

(4) The person relinquished the firearm pursuant to Section 12288, in which case the assault weapon shall be destroyed pursuant to Section 12028.

(c) Any person who, within this state, possesses any .50 BMG rifle, except as provided in this chapter, shall be punished by a fine of one thousand dollars ($1,000), imprisonment in a county jail for a period not to exceed one year, or by both that fine and imprisonment. However, a first violation of these provisions is punishable by a fine not exceeding five hundred dollars ($500) if the person was found in possession of no more than two firearms in compliance with subdivision (a) of Section 12285 and the person meets the conditions set forth in paragraphs (1), (2), and (3):

(1) The person proves that he or she lawfully possessed the .50 BMG rifle prior to January 1, 2005.

(2) The person has not previously been convicted of a violation of this section.

(3) The person was found to be in possession of the .50 BMG rifle within one year following the end of the .50 BMG rifle registration period established pursuant to subdivision (a) of Section 12285.

(4) Firearms seized pursuant to this subdivision from persons who meet all of the conditions set forth in paragraphs (1), (2), and (3) shall be returned unless the court finds in the interest of public safety, after notice and hearing, that the .50 BMG rifle should be destroyed pursuant to Section 12028. Firearms seized from persons who do not meet the conditions set forth in paragraphs (1), (2), and (3) shall be destroyed pursuant to Section 12028.

(d) Notwithstanding Section 654 or any other provision of law, any person who commits another crime while violating this section may receive an additional, consecutive punishment of one year for violating this section in addition and consecutive to the punishment, including enhancements, which is prescribed for the other crime.

(e) Subdivisions (a), (b), and (c) shall not apply to the sale to, purchase by, importation of, or possession of assault weapons or a . 50 BMG rifle by the Department of Justice, police departments, sheriffs' offices, marshals' offices, the Department of Corrections and Rehabilitation, the Department of the California Highway Patrol, district attorneys' offices, Department of Fish and Game, Department of Parks and Recreation, or the military or naval forces of this state or of the United States, or any federal law enforcement agency for use in the discharge of their official duties.

(f)(1) Subdivisions (b) and (c) shall not prohibit the possession or use of assault weapons or a .50 BMG rifle by sworn peace officer members of those agencies specified in subdivision (e) for law enforcement purposes, whether on or off duty.

(2) Subdivisions (a), (b), and (c) shall not prohibit the delivery, transfer, or sale of an assault weapon or a .50 BMG rifle to, or the possession of an assault weapon or a .50 BMG rifle by, a sworn peace officer member of an agency specified in subdivision (e) if the peace officer is authorized by his or her employer to possess or receive the assault weapon or the .50 BMG rifle. Required authorization is defined as verifiable written certification from the head of the agency, identifying the recipient or possessor of the assault weapon as a peace officer and authorizing him or her to receive or possess the specific assault weapon. For this exemption to apply, in the case of a peace officer who possesses or receives the assault weapon prior to January 1, 2002, the officer shall register the assault weapon pursuant to Section 12285 on or before April 1, 2002, and in the case of a peace officer who possesses or receives the assault weapon on or after January 1, 2002, the officer shall register the assault weapon pursuant to Section 12285 not later than 90 days after possession or receipt. In the case of a peace officer who possesses or receives a .50 BMG rifle on or before January 1, 2005, the officer shall register the .50 BMG rifle on or before April 30, 2006. In the case of a peace officer who possesses or receives a .50 BMG rifle after January 1, 2005, the officer shall register the .50 BMG rifle not later than one year after possession or receipt. The peace officer must include with the registration, a copy of the authorization required pursuant to this paragraph.

(3) Nothing in this section shall be construed to limit or prohibit the delivery, transfer, or sale of an assault weapon or a .50 BMG rifle to, or the possession of an assault weapon or a .50 BMG rifle by, a member of a federal law enforcement agency provided that person is authorized by the employing agency to possess the assault weapon or .50 BMG rifle.

(g) Subdivision (b) shall not apply to the possession of an assault weapon during the 90-day period immediately after the date it was specified as an assault weapon pursuant to Section 12276.5, or during the one-year period after the date it was defined as an assault weapon pursuant to Section 12276.1, if all of the following are applicable:

(1) The person is eligible under this chapter to register the particular assault weapon.

(2) The person lawfully possessed the particular assault weapon prior to the date it was specified as an assault weapon pursuant to Section 12276.5, or prior to the date it was defined as an assault weapon pursuant to Section 12276.1.

(3) The person is otherwise in compliance with this chapter.

(h) Subdivisions (a), (b), and (c) shall not apply to the manufacture by persons who are issued permits pursuant to Section 12287 of assault weapons or .50 BMG rifles for sale to the following:

(1) Exempt entities listed in subdivision (e).

(2) Entities and persons who have been issued permits pursuant to Section 12286 or 12287.

(3) Entities outside the state who have, in effect, a federal firearms dealer's license solely for the purpose of distribution to an entity listed in paragraphs (4) to (6), inclusive.

(4) Federal military and law enforcement agencies.

(5) Law enforcement and military agencies of other states.

(6) Foreign governments and agencies approved by the United States State Department.

(i) Subdivision (a) shall not apply to a person who is the executor or administrator of an estate that includes an assault weapon or a .50 BMG rifle registered under Section 12285 or that was possessed pursuant to paragraph (1) of subdivision (f) that is disposed of as authorized by the probate court, if the disposition is otherwise permitted by this chapter.

(j) Subdivisions (b) and (c) shall not apply to a person who is the executor or administrator of an estate that includes an assault weapon or a .50 BMG rifle registered under Section 12285 or that was possessed pursuant to paragraph (1) of subdivision (f) if the assault weapon or .50 BMG rifle is possessed at a place set forth in paragraph (1) of subdivision (c) of Section 12285 or as authorized by the probate court.

(k) Subdivision (a) shall not apply to either of the following:

(1) A person who lawfully possesses and has registered an assault weapon or .50 BMG rifle pursuant to this chapter who lends that assault weapon or .50 BMG rifle to another if all the following apply:

(A) The person to whom the assault weapon or .50 BMG rifle is lent is 18 years of age or over and is not prohibited by state or federal law from possessing, receiving, owning, or purchasing a firearm.

(B) The person to whom the assault weapon or .50 BMG rifle is lent remains in the presence of the registered possessor of the assault weapon or .50 BMG rifle.

(C) The assault weapon or .50 BMG rifle is possessed at any of the following locations:

(i) While on a target range that holds a regulatory or business license for the purpose of practicing shooting at that target range.

(ii) While on the premises of a target range of a public or private club or organization organized for the purpose of practicing shooting at targets.

(iii) While attending any exhibition, display, or educational project that is about firearms and that is sponsored by, conducted under the auspices of, or approved by a law enforcement agency or a nationally or state recognized entity that fosters proficiency in, or promotes education about, firearms.

(2) The return of an assault weapon or .50 BMG rifle to the registered possessor, or the lawful possessor, which is lent by the same pursuant to paragraph (1).

(l) Subdivisions (b) and (c) shall not apply to the possession of an assault weapon or .50 BMG rifle by a person to whom an assault weapon or .50 BMG rifle is lent pursuant to subdivision (k).

(m) Subdivisions (a), (b), and (c) shall not apply to the possession and importation of an assault weapon or a .50 BMG rifle into this state by a nonresident if all of the following conditions are met:

(1) The person is attending or going directly to or coming directly from an organized competitive match or league competition that involves the use of an assault weapon or a .50 BMG rifle.

(2) The competition or match is conducted on the premises of one of the following:

(A) A target range that holds a regulatory or business license for the purpose of practicing shooting at that target range.

(B) A target range of a public or private club or organization that is organized for the purpose of practicing shooting at targets.

(3) The match or competition is sponsored by, conducted under the auspices of, or approved by, a law enforcement agency or a nationally or state recognized entity that fosters proficiency in, or promotes education about, firearms.

(4) The assault weapon or .50 BMG rifle is transported in accordance with Section 12026.1 or 12026.2.

(5) The person is 18 years of age or over and is not in a class of persons prohibited from possessing firearms by virtue of Section 12021 or 12021.1 of this code or Section 8100 or 8103 of the Welfare and Institutions Code.

(n) Subdivisions (b) and (c) shall not apply to any of the following persons:

(1) A person acting in accordance with Section 12286 or 12287.

(2) A person who has a permit to possess an assault weapon or a .50 BMG rifle issued pursuant to Section 12286 or 12287 when he or she is acting in accordance with Section 12285, 12286, or 12287.

(o) Subdivisions (a), (b), and (c) shall not apply to any of the following persons:

(1) A person acting in accordance with Section 12285.

(2) A person acting in accordance with Section 12286, 12287, or 12290.

(p) Subdivisions (b) and (c) shall not apply to the registered owner of an assault weapon or a .50 BMG rifle possessing that firearm in accordance with subdivision (c) of Section 12285.

(q) Subdivision (a) shall not apply to the importation into this state of an assault weapon or a .50 BMG rifle by the registered owner of that assault weapon or a .50 BMG rifle if it is in accordance with the provisions of subdivision (c) of Section 12285.

(r) Subdivision (a) shall not apply during the first 180 days of the 2005 calendar year to the importation into this state of a .50 BMG rifle by a person who lawfully possessed that .50 BMG rifle in this state prior to January 1, 2005.

(s) Subdivision (c) shall not apply to the possession of a .50 BMG rifle that is not defined or specified as an assault weapon pursuant to this chapter, by any person prior to May 1, 2006, if all of the following are applicable:

(1) The person is eligible under this chapter to register that .50 BMG rifle.

(2) The person lawfully possessed the .50 BMG rifle prior to January 1, 2005.

(3) The person is otherwise in compliance with this chapter.

(t) Subdivisions (a), (b), and (c) shall not apply to the sale of assault weapons or .50 BMG rifles by persons who are issued permits pursuant to Section 12287 to any of the following:

(1) Exempt entities listed in subdivision (e).

(2) Entities and persons who have been issued permits pursuant to Section 12286 or 12287.

(3) Federal military and law enforcement agencies.

(4) Law enforcement and military agencies of other states.

(5) Foreign governments and agencies approved by the United States State Department.

(6) Officers described in subdivision (f) who are authorized to possess assault weapons or .50 BMG rifles pursuant to subdivision (f).

(u) As used in this chapter, the date a firearm is an assault weapon is the earliest of the following:

(1) The effective date of an amendment to Section 12276 that adds the designation of the specified firearm.

(2) The effective date of the list promulgated pursuant to Section 12276.5 that adds or changes the designation of the specified firearm.

(3) The operative date of Section 12276.1, as specified in subdivision (d) of that section.

Penal Code § 12281.

(a) Any person who, or firm, company, or corporation that, operated a retail or other commercial firm, company, or corporation, and manufactured, distributed, transported, imported, possessed, possessed for sale, offered for sale, or transferred, for commercial purpose, an SKS rifle in California between January 1, 1992, and December 19, 1997, shall be immune from criminal prosecution under Section 12280. The immunity provided in this subdivision shall apply retroactively to any person who, or firm, company, or corporation that, is or was charged by complaint or indictment with a violation of Section 12280 for conduct related to an SKS rifle, whether or not the case of that person, firm, company, or corporation is final.

(b) Any person who possessed, gave, loaned, or transferred an SKS rifle in California between January 1, 1992, and December 19, 1997, shall be immune from criminal prosecution under Section 12280. The immunity provided in this subdivision shall apply retroactively to any person who was charged by complaint or indictment with a violation of Section 12280 for conduct related to an SKS rifle, whether or not the case of that person is final.

(c) Any SKS rifle in the possession of any person who, or firm, company, or corporation that, is described in subdivision (a) or (b), shall not be subject to seizure by law enforcement for violation of Section 12280 prior to January 1, 2000.

(d) Any person, firm, company, or corporation, convicted under Section 12280 for conduct relating to an SKS rifle, shall be permitted to withdraw his or her plea of guilty or nolo contendere, or to reopen his or her case and assert the immunities provided in this section, if the court determines that the allowance of the immunity is in the interests of justice. The court shall interpret this section liberally to the benefit of the defendant.

(e) The Department of Justice shall notify all district attorneys on or before January 31, 1999, of the provisions of this section. The department shall identify all criminal prosecutions in the state for conduct related to SKS rifles within 90 days of the effective date of this section. In all cases so identified by the Attorney General, the district attorneys shall inform defense counsel, or the defendant if the defendant is in propria persona, in writing, of the provisions of this section within 120 days of the effective date of this section.

(f)(1) Any person, firm, company, or corporation that is in possession of an SKS rifle shall do one of the following on or before January 1, 2000:

(A) Relinquish the SKS rifle to the Department of Justice pursuant to subdivision (h).

(B) Relinquish the SKS rifle to a law enforcement agency pursuant to Section 12288.

(C) Dispose of the SKS rifle as permitted by Section 12285.

(2) Any person who has obtained title to an SKS rifle by bequest or intestate succession shall be required to comply with subparagraph (A) or (B) of paragraph (1) of this subdivision unless he or she otherwise complies with paragraph (1) of subdivision (b) of Section 12285.

(3) Any SKS rifle relinquished to the department pursuant to this subdivision shall be in a manner prescribed by the department.

(4) The department shall conduct a public education and notification program as described in Section 12289, commencing no later than January 1, 1999.

(g) Any person who complies with subdivision (f) shall be exempt from the prohibitions set forth in subdivision (a) or (b) of Section 12280 for those acts by that person associated with complying with the requirements of subdivision (f).

(h)(1) The department shall purchase any SKS rifle relinquished pursuant to subdivision (f) from funds appropriated for this purpose by the act amending this section in the 1997-98 Regular Session of the Legislature or by subsequent budget acts or other legislation. The department shall adopt regulations for this purchase program that include, but are not limited to, the manner of delivery, the reimbursement to be paid, and the manner in which persons shall be informed of the state purchase program.

(2) Any person who relinquished possession of an SKS rifle to a law enforcement agency pursuant to Section 12288 prior to the effective date of the purchase program set forth in paragraph (1) shall be eligible to be reimbursed from the purchase program. The

procedures for reimbursement pursuant to this paragraph shall be part of the regulations adopted by the department pursuant to paragraph (1).

(i) Notwithstanding paragraph (11) of subdivision (a) of Section 12276, an "SKS rifle" under this section means all SKS rifles commonly referred to as "SKS Sporter" versions, manufactured to accept a detachable AK-47 magazine and imported into this state and sold by a licensed gun dealer, or otherwise lawfully possessed in this state by a resident of this state who is not a licensed gun dealer, between January 1, 1992, and December 19, 1997.

(j) Failure to comply with subdivision (f) is a public offense punishable by imprisonment in the state prison, or in a county jail, not exceeding one year.

(k) In addition to the regulations required pursuant to subdivision (h), emergency regulations for the purchase program described in subdivision (h) shall be adopted pursuant to Chapter 3.5 (commencing with Section 11340) of Part 1 of Division 3 of Title 2 of the Government Code.

Penal Code § 12282.

(a) Except as provided in Section 12280, possession of any assault weapon, as defined in Section 12276, 12276.1, or 12276.5, or of any .50 BMG rifle, as defined in Section 12278, in violation of this chapter is a public nuisance, solely for purposes of this section and subdivision (d) of Section 12028. The Attorney General, any district attorney, or any city attorney, may, in lieu of criminal prosecution, bring a civil action or reach a civil compromise in any superior court to enjoin the possession of the assault weapon or .50 BMG rifle that is a public nuisance.

(b) Upon motion of the Attorney General, district attorney, or city attorney, a superior court may impose a civil fine not to exceed three hundred dollars ($300) for the first assault weapon or .50 BMG rifle deemed a public nuisance pursuant to subdivision (a) and up to one hundred dollars ($100) for each additional assault weapon or .50 BMG rifle deemed a public nuisance pursuant to subdivision (a).

(c) Any assault weapon or .50 BMG rifle deemed a public nuisance under subdivision (a) shall be destroyed in a manner so that it may no longer be used, except upon a finding by a court, or a declaration from the Department of Justice, district attorney, or city attorney stating that the preservation of the assault weapon or .50 BMG rifle is in the interest of justice.

(d) Upon conviction of any misdemeanor or felony involving the illegal possession or use of an assault weapon, the assault weapon shall be deemed a public nuisance and disposed of pursuant to subdivision (d) of Section 12028.

Penal Code § 12285.

(a)(1) Any person who lawfully possesses an assault weapon, as defined in Section 12276, prior to June 1, 1989, shall register the firearm by January 1, 1991, and any person who lawfully possessed an assault weapon prior to the date it was specified as an assault weapon pursuant to Section 12276.5 shall register the firearm within 90 days with the Department of Justice pursuant to those procedures that the department may establish. Except as provided in subdivision (a) of Section 12280, any person who lawfully possessed an assault weapon prior to the date it was defined as an assault weapon pursuant to Section 12276.1, and which was not specified as an assault weapon under Section 12276 or 12276.5, shall register the firearm within one year of the effective date of Section 12276.1, with the department pursuant to those procedures that the department may establish. The registration shall contain a description of the firearm that identifies it uniquely, including all identification marks, the full name, address, date of birth, and thumbprint of the owner, and any other information that the department may deem appropriate. The department may charge a fee for registration of up to twenty dollars ($20) per person but not to exceed the actual processing costs of the department. After the department establishes fees sufficient to reimburse the department for processing costs, fees charged shall increase at a rate not to exceed the legislatively approved annual cost-of-living adjustment for the department's budget or as otherwise increased through the Budget Act. The fees shall be deposited into the Dealers' Record of Sale Special Account.

(2) Except as provided in subdivision (a) of Section 12280, any person who lawfully possesses any .50 BMG rifle prior to January 1, 2005, that is not specified as an assault weapon under Section 12276 or 12276.5 or defined as an assault weapon pursuant to Section 12276.1, shall register the .50 BMG rifle with the department no later than April 30, 2006, pursuant to those procedures that the department may establish. The registration shall contain a description of the firearm that identifies it uniquely, including all identification marks, the full name, address, date of birth, and thumbprint of the owner, and any other information that the department may deem appropriate. The department may charge a fee for registration of twenty-five dollars ($25) per person to cover the actual processing and public education campaign costs of the department. The fees shall be deposited into the Dealers' Record of Sale Special Account. Data-processing costs associated with modifying the department's data system to accommodate .50 caliber BMG rifles shall not be paid from the Dealers Record of Sale Special Account.

(b)(1) Except as provided in paragraph (2), no assault weapon possessed pursuant to this section may be sold or transferred on or after January 1, 1990, to anyone within this state other than to a licensed gun dealer, as defined in subdivision (c) of Section 12290, or as provided in Section 12288. Any person who (A) obtains title to an assault weapon registered under this section or that was possessed pursuant to paragraph (1) of subdivision (f) of Section 12280 by bequest or intestate succession, or (B) lawfully possessed a firearm subsequently declared to be an assault weapon pursuant to Section 12276.5, or subsequently defined as an assault weapon pursuant to Section 12276.1, shall, within 90 days, render the weapon permanently inoperable, sell the weapon to a licensed gun dealer, obtain a permit from the Department of Justice in the same manner as specified in Article 3 (commencing with Section 12230) of Chapter 2, or remove the weapon from this state. A person who lawfully possessed a firearm that was subsequently declared to be an assault weapon pursuant to Section 12276.5 may alternatively register the firearm within 90 days of the declaration issued pursuant to subdivision (f) of Section 12276.5.

(2) A person moving into this state, otherwise in lawful possession of an assault weapon, shall do one of the following:

(A) Prior to bringing the assault weapon into this state, that person shall first obtain a permit from the Department of Justice in the same manner as specified in Article 3 (commencing with Section 12230) of Chapter 2.

(B) The person shall cause the assault weapon to be delivered to a licensed gun dealer, as defined in subdivision (c) of Section

12290, in this state in accordance with Chapter 44 (commencing with Section 921) of Title 18 of the United States Code and the regulations issued pursuant thereto. If the person obtains a permit from the Department of Justice in the same manner as specified in Article 3 (commencing with Section 12230) of Chapter 2, the dealer shall redeliver that assault weapon to the person. If the licensed gun dealer, as defined in subdivision (c) of Section 12290, is prohibited from delivering the assault weapon to a person pursuant to this paragraph, the dealer shall possess or dispose of the assault weapon as allowed by this chapter.

(3) Except as provided in paragraph (4), no .50 BMG rifle possessed pursuant to this section may be sold or transferred on or after January 1, 2005, to anyone within this state other than to a licensed gun dealer, as defined in subdivision (c) of Section 12290, or as provided in Section 12288. Any person who obtains title to a . 50 BMG rifle registered under this section or that was possessed pursuant to paragraph (1) of subdivision (f) of Section 12280 by bequest or intestate succession shall, within 180 days of receipt, render the weapon permanently inoperable, sell the weapon to a licensed gun dealer, obtain a permit from the Department of Justice in the same manner as specified in Article 3 (commencing with Section 12230) of Chapter 2, or remove the weapon from this state.

(4) A person moving into this state, otherwise in lawful possession of a .50 BMG rifle, shall do one of the following:

(A) Prior to bringing the .50 BMG rifle into this state, that person shall first obtain a permit from the Department of Justice in the same manner as specified in Article 3 (commencing with Section 12230) of Chapter 2.

(B) The person shall cause the .50 BMG rifle to be delivered to a licensed gun dealer, as defined in subdivision (c) of Section 12290 in this state in accordance with Chapter 44 (commencing with Section 921) of Title 18 of the United States Code and the regulations issued pursuant thereto. If the person obtains a permit from the Department of Justice in the same manner as specified in Article 3 (commencing with Section 12230) of Chapter 2, the dealer shall redeliver that .50 BMG rifle to the person. If the licensed gun dealer, as defined in subdivision (c) of Section 12290 is prohibited from delivering the . 50 caliber BMG rifle to a person pursuant to this paragraph, the dealer shall dispose of the .50 BMG rifle as allowed by this chapter.

(c) A person who has registered an assault weapon or registered a .50 BMG rifle under this section may possess it only under any of the following conditions unless a permit allowing additional uses is first obtained under Section 12286:

(1) At that person's residence, place of business, or other property owned by that person, or on property owned by another with the owner's express permission.

(2) While on the premises of a target range of a public or private club or organization organized for the purpose of practicing shooting at targets.

(3) While on a target range that holds a regulatory or business license for the purpose of practicing shooting at that target range.

(4) While on the premises of a shooting club which is licensed pursuant to the Fish and Game Code.

(5) While attending any exhibition, display, or educational project which is about firearms and which is sponsored by, conducted under the auspices of, or approved by a law enforcement agency or a nationally or state recognized entity that fosters proficiency in, or promotes education about, firearms.

(6) While on publicly owned land if the possession and use of a firearm described in Section 12276, 12276.1, 12276.5, or 12278, is specifically permitted by the managing agency of the land.

(7) While transporting the assault weapon or .50 BMG rifle between any of the places mentioned in this subdivision, or to any licensed gun dealer, as defined in subdivision (c) of Section 12290, for servicing or repair pursuant to subdivision (b) of Section 12290, if the assault weapon is transported as required by Section 12026.1.

(d) No person who is under the age of 18 years, and no person who is prohibited by state or federal law from possessing, receiving, owning, or purchasing a firearm may register or possess an assault weapon or .50 BMG rifle.

(e) The department's registration procedures shall provide the option of joint registration for assault weapons or .50 BMG rifle owned by family members residing in the same household.

(f) For 90 days following January 1, 1992, a forgiveness period shall exist to allow persons specified in subdivision (b) of Section 12280 to register with the Department of Justice assault weapons that they lawfully possessed prior to June 1, 1989.

(g)(1) Any person who registered a firearm as an assault weapon pursuant to the provisions of law in effect prior to January 1, 2000, where the assault weapon is thereafter defined as an assault weapon pursuant to Section 12276.1, shall be deemed to have registered the weapon for purposes of this chapter and shall not be required to reregister the weapon pursuant to this section.

(2) Any person who legally registered a firearm as an assault weapon pursuant to the provisions of law in effect prior to January 1, 2005, where the assault weapon is thereafter defined as a .50 caliber BMG rifle pursuant to Section 12278, shall be deemed to have registered the weapon for purposes of this chapter and shall not be required to reregister the weapon pursuant to this section.

(h) Any person who registers his or her assault weapon during the 90-day forgiveness period described in subdivision (f), and any person whose registration form was received by the Department of Justice after January 1, 1991, and who was issued a temporary registration prior to the end of the forgiveness period, shall not be charged with a violation of subdivision (b) of Section 12280, if law enforcement becomes aware of that violation only as a result of the registration of the assault weapon. This subdivision shall have no effect upon persons charged with a violation of subdivision (b) of Section 12280 of the Penal Code prior to January 1, 1992, provided that law enforcement was aware of the violation before the weapon was registered.

Penal Code § 12286.

Any person who lawfully acquired an assault weapon before June 1, 1989, or a .50 BMG rifle before January 1, 2005, and wishes to use it in a manner different than specified in subdivision (c) of Section 12285, who lawfully acquired an assault weapon between June 1, 1989, and January 1, 1990, and wishes to keep it after January 1, 1990, or who wishes to acquire an assault weapon after January 1, 1990, or a .50 BMG rifle after January 1, 2005, shall first obtain a permit from the Department of Justice in the same manner as specified in Article 3 (commencing with Section 12230) of Chapter 2.

Penal Code § 12287.

(a) The Department of Justice may, upon a finding of good cause, issue permits for the manufacture or sale of assault weapons or .50 BMG rifles for the sale to, purchase by, or possession of assault weapons or .50 BMG rifles by, any of the following:

(1) The agencies listed in subdivision (e), and the officers described in subdivision (f) of Section 12280.

(2) Entities and persons who have been issued permits pursuant to this section or Section 12286.

(3) Entities outside the state who have, in effect, a federal firearms dealer's license solely for the purpose of distribution to an entity listed in paragraphs (4) to (6), inclusive.

(4) Federal law enforcement and military agencies.

(5) Law enforcement and military agencies of other states.

(6) Foreign governments and agencies approved by the United States State Department.

(b) Application for the permits, the keeping and inspection thereof, and the revocation of permits shall be undertaken in the same manner as specified in Article 3 (commencing with Section 12230) of Chapter 2.

Penal Code § 12288.

Any individual may arrange in advance to relinquish an assault weapon or a .50 BMG rifle to a police or sheriff's department. The assault weapon or .50 BMG rifle shall be transported in accordance with Section 12026.1.

Penal Code § 12288.5.

(a) No peace officer or dispatcher shall broadcast over a police radio that an individual has registered, or has obtained a permit to possess, an assault weapon or .50 BMG rifle pursuant to this chapter, unless there exists a reason to believe in good faith that one of the following conditions exist:

(1) The individual has engaged, or may be engaged, in criminal conduct.

(2) The police are responding to a call in which the person allegedly committing a criminal violation may gain access to the assault weapon or .50 BMG rifle.

(3) The victim, witness, or person who reported the alleged criminal violation may be using the assault weapon or .50 BMG rifle to hold the person allegedly committing the criminal violation or may be using the weapon in defense of himself, herself, or other persons.

(b) This section shall not prohibit a peace officer or dispatcher from broadcasting over a police radio that an individual has not registered, or has not obtained a permit to possess, an assault weapon or .50 BMG rifle pursuant to this chapter.

(c) This section does not limit the transmission of an assault weapon or a .50 BMG rifle ownership status via law enforcement computers or any other medium that is legally accessible only to peace officers or other authorized personnel.

Penal Code § 12289.

(a) The Department of Justice shall conduct a public education and notification program regarding the registration of assault weapons and the definition of the weapons set forth in Section 12276.1. The public education and notification program shall include outreach to local law enforcement agencies and utilization of public service announcements in a variety of media approaches, to ensure maximum publicity of the limited forgiveness period of the registration requirement specified in subdivision (f) of Section 12285 and the consequences of nonregistration. The department shall develop posters describing gunowners' responsibilities under this chapter which shall be posted in a conspicuous place in every licensed gun store in the state during the forgiveness period. For . 50 BMG rifles, the department's education campaign shall provide materials to dealers of .50 BMG rifles, and to recognized national associations that specialize in .50 BMG rifles.

(b) Any costs incurred by the Department of Justice to implement this section which cannot be absorbed by the department shall be funded from the Dealers' Record of Sale Special Account, as set forth in subdivision (d) of Section 12076, upon appropriation by the Legislature.

Penal Code § 12289.5.

(a) Except as provided in subdivision (b), the Department of Justice shall, for every person, firm, or corporation to whom a permit is issued pursuant to this article, annually conduct an inspection for security and safe storage purposes, and to reconcile the inventory of assault weapons.

(b) A person, firm, or corporation with an inventory of fewer than five devices that require any Department of Justice permit shall be subject to an inspection for security and safe storage purposes, and to reconcile inventory, once every five years, or more frequently if determined by the department.

Penal Code § 12290.

(a) Any licensed gun dealer, as defined in subdivision (c), who lawfully possesses an assault weapon or .50 BMG rifle pursuant to Section 12285, in addition to the uses allowed in Section 12285, may transport the firearm between dealers or out of the state if that person is permitted pursuant to the National Firearms Act, display it at any gun show licensed by a state or local governmental entity, sell it to a resident outside the state, or sell it to a person who has been issued a permit pursuant to Section 12286. Any transporting allowed by this section must be done as required by Section 12026.1.

(b)(1) Any licensed gun dealer, as defined in subdivision (c), may take possession of any assault weapon or .50 BMG rifle for the purposes of servicing or repair from any person to whom it is legally registered or who has been issued a permit to possess it pursuant to this chapter.

(2) Any licensed gun dealer, as defined in subdivision (c), may transfer possession of any assault weapon or .50 BMG rifle received pursuant to paragraph (1), to a gunsmith for purposes of accomplishing service or repair of the same. Transfers are permissible only to the following persons:

(A) A gunsmith who is in the dealer's employ.

(B) A gunsmith with whom the dealer has contracted for gunsmithing services. In order for this subparagraph to apply, the gunsmith receiving the assault weapon or .50 BMG rifle shall hold all of the following:

(i) A dealer's license issued pursuant to Chapter 44 (commencing with Section 921) of Title 18 of the United States Code and the regulations issued pursuant thereto.

(ii) Any business license required by a state or local governmental entity.

(c) The term "licensed gun dealer," as used in this article, means a person who is licensed pursuant to Section 12071 and who has a permit to sell assault weapons or .50 BMG rifles pursuant to Section 12287.

Penal Code § 12301.

(a) The term "destructive device," as used in this chapter, shall include any of the following weapons:

(1) Any projectile containing any explosive or incendiary material or any other chemical substance, including, but not limited to, that which is commonly known as tracer or incendiary ammunition, except tracer ammunition manufactured for use in shotguns.

(2) Any bomb, grenade, explosive missile, or similar device or any launching device therefor.

(3) Any weapon of a caliber greater than 0.60 caliber which fires fixed ammunition, or any ammunition therefor, other than a shotgun (smooth or rifled bore) conforming to the definition of a "destructive device" found in subsection (b) of Section 479.11 of Title 27 of the Code of Federal Regulations, shotgun ammunition (single projectile or shot), antique rifle, or an antique cannon. For purposes of this section, the term "antique cannon" means any cannon manufactured before January 1, 1899, which has been rendered incapable of firing or for which ammunition is no longer manufactured in the United States and is not readily available in the ordinary channels of commercial trade. The term "antique rifle" means a firearm conforming to the definition of an "antique firearm" in Section 479.11 of Title 27 of the Code of Federal Regulations.

(4) Any rocket, rocket-propelled projectile, or similar device of a diameter greater than 0.60 inch, or any launching device therefor, and any rocket, rocket-propelled projectile, or similar device containing any explosive or incendiary material or any other chemical substance, other than the propellant for that device, except those devices as are designed primarily for emergency or distress signaling purposes.

(5) Any breakable container which contains a flammable liquid with a flashpoint of 150 degrees Fahrenheit or less and has a wick or similar device capable of being ignited, other than a device which is commercially manufactured primarily for the purpose of illumination.

(6) Any sealed device containing dry ice ($CO2$) or other chemically reactive substances assembled for the purpose of causing an explosion by a chemical reaction.

(b) The term "explosive," as used in this chapter, shall mean any explosive defined in Section 12000 of the Health and Safety Code.

Penal Code § 12302.

Nothing in this chapter shall prohibit the sale to, purchase by, or possession, transportation, storage, or use of, destructive devices or explosives by:

(a) Any peace officer listed in Section 830.1 or 830.2, or any peace officer in the Department of Justice authorized by the Attorney General, while on duty and acting within the scope and course of his or her employment.

(b) Any member of the Army, Navy, Air Force, or Marine Corps of the United States, or the National Guard, while on duty and acting within the scope and course of his or her employment. Nothing in this chapter prohibits the sale to, or the purchase, possession, transportation, storage, or use by any person who is a regularly employed and paid officer, employee, or member of a fire department or fire protection or firefighting agency of the federal government, the State of California, a city, county, city and county, district, or other public or municipal corporation or political subdivision of this state, while on duty and acting within the scope and course of his or her employment, of any equipment used by that department or agency in the course of fire suppression.

Penal Code § 12303.

Any person, firm, or corporation who, within this state, possesses any destructive device, other than fixed ammunition of a caliber greater than .60 caliber, except as provided by this chapter, is guilty of a public offense and upon conviction thereof shall be punished by imprisonment in the county jail for a term not to exceed one year, or in state prison, or by a fine not to exceed ten thousand dollars ($10,000) or by both such fine and imprisonment.

Penal Code § 12303.1.

Every person who willfully does any of the following is guilty of a felony and is punishable by imprisonment in the state prison for two, four, or six years:

(a) Carries any explosive or destructive device on any vessel, aircraft, car, or other vehicle that transports passengers for hire.

(b) Places or carries any explosive or destructive device, while on board any such vessel, aircraft, car or other vehicle, in any hand baggage, roll, or other container.

(c) Places any explosive or destructive device in any baggage which is later checked with any common carrier.

Penal Code § 12303.2.

Every person who recklessly or maliciously has in his possession any destructive device or any explosive on a public street or highway, in or near any theater, hall, school, college, church, hotel, other public building, or private habitation, in, on, or near any aircraft, railway passenger train, car, cable road or cable car, vessel engaged in carrying passengers for hire, or other public place ordinarily passed by human beings is guilty of a felony, and shall be punishable by imprisonment in the state prison for a period of two, four, or six years.

Penal Code § 12303.3.

Every person who possesses, explodes, ignites, or attempts to explode or ignite any destructive device or any explosive with intent to injure, intimidate, or terrify any person, or with intent to wrongfully injure or destroy any property, is guilty of a felony, and shall be punished by imprisonment in the state prison for a period of three, five, or seven years.

Penal Code § 12303.6.

Any person, firm, or corporation who, within this state, sells, offers for sale, or knowingly transports any destructive device, other than fixed ammunition of a caliber greater than .60 caliber, except as provided by this chapter, is guilty of a felony and is punishable by imprisonment in the state prison for two, three or four years.

Penal Code § 12304.

Any person, firm or corporation who, within this state, sells, offers for sale, possesses or knowingly transports any fixed ammunition of a caliber greater than .60 caliber, except as provided in this chapter, is guilty of a public offense and upon conviction thereof shall be punished by imprisonment in the county jail for a term not to exceed six months or by a fine not to exceed one thousand dollars ($1,000), or by both such fine and imprisonment.

A second or subsequent conviction shall be punished by imprisonment in the county jail for a term not to exceed one year, or by imprisonment in the state prison, or by a fine not to exceed three thousand dollars ($3,000), or by both such fine and imprisonment.

Penal Code § 12305.

(a) Every dealer, manufacturer, importer, and exporter of any destructive device, or any motion picture or television studio using destructive devices in the conduct of its business, shall obtain a permit for the conduct of that business from the Department of Justice.

(b) Any person, firm, or corporation not mentioned in subdivision (a) shall obtain a permit from the Department of Justice in order to possess or transport any destructive device. No permit shall be issued to any person who meets any of the following criteria:

(1) Has been convicted of any felony.

(2) Is addicted to the use of any narcotic drug.

(3) Is prohibited by state or federal law from possessing, receiving, owning, or purchasing a firearm.

(c) Applications for permits shall be filed in writing, signed by the applicant if an individual, or by a member or officer qualified to sign if the applicant is a firm or corporation, and shall state the name, business in which engaged, business address and a full description of the use to which the destructive devices are to be put.

(d) Applications and permits shall be uniform throughout the state on forms prescribed by the Department of Justice.

(e) Each applicant for a permit shall pay at the time of filing his or her application a fee not to exceed the application processing costs of the Department of Justice. A permit granted pursuant to this article may be renewed one year from the date of issuance, and annually thereafter, upon the filing of a renewal application and the payment of a permit renewal fee not to exceed the application processing costs of the Department of Justice. After the department establishes fees sufficient in amount to cover processing costs, the amount of the fees shall only increase at a rate not to exceed the legislatively approved cost-of-living adjustment for the department.

(f) Except as provided in subdivision (g), the Department of Justice shall, for every person, firm, or corporation to whom a permit is issued pursuant to this article, annually conduct an inspection for security and safe storage purposes, and to reconcile the inventory of destructive devices.

(g) A person, firm, or corporation with an inventory of fewer than five devices that require any Department of Justice permit shall be subject to an inspection for security and safe storage purposes, and to reconcile inventory, once every five years, or more frequently if determined by the department.

Penal Code § 12307.

The possession of any destructive device in violation of this chapter shall be deemed to be a public nuisance and the Attorney General or district attorney of any city, county, or city and county may bring an action before the superior court to enjoin the possession of any destructive device. Any destructive device found to be in violation of this chapter shall be surrendered to the Department of Justice, or to the sheriff or chief of police, if the sheriff or chief of police has elected to perform the services required by this section. The department, sheriff, or chief of police shall destroy the destructive device so as to render it unusable and unrepairable as a destructive device, except upon the filing of a certificate with the department by a judge or district attorney stating that the preservation of the destructive device is necessary to serve the ends of justice.

Penal Code § 12308.

Every person who explodes, ignites, or attempts to explode or ignite any destructive device or any explosive with intent to commit murder is guilty of a felony, and shall be punished by imprisonment in the state prison for life with the possibility of parole.

Penal Code § 12309.

Every person who willfully and maliciously explodes or ignites any destructive device or any explosive which causes bodily injury to any person is guilty of a felony, and shall be punished by imprisonment in the state prison for a period of five, seven, or nine years.

Penal Code § 12310.

(a) Every person who willfully and maliciously explodes or ignites any destructive device or any explosive which causes the death of any person is guilty of a felony, and shall be punished by imprisonment in the state prison for life without the possibility of parole.

(b) Every person who willfully and maliciously explodes or ignites any destructive device or any explosive which causes mayhem or great bodily injury to any person is guilty of a felony, and shall be punished by imprisonment in the state prison for life.

Penal Code § 12311.

No person convicted of a violation of this chapter shall be granted probation, and the execution of the sentence imposed upon such person shall not be suspended by the court.

Penal Code § 12312.

Every person who possesses any substance, material, or any combination of substances or materials, with the intent to make any destructive device or any explosive without first obtaining a valid permit to make such destructive device or explosive, is guilty of a felony, and is punishable by imprisonment in the state prison for two, three, or four years.

Penal Code § 12316.

(a)(1) Any person, corporation, or dealer who does any of the following shall be punished by imprisonment in a county jail for a term not to exceed six months, or by a fine not to exceed one thousand dollars ($1,000), or by both the imprisonment and fine:

(A) Sells any ammunition or reloaded ammunition to a person under 18 years of age.

(B) Sells any ammunition or reloaded ammunition designed and intended for use in a handgun to a person under 21 years of age. As used in this subparagraph, "ammunition" means handgun ammunition as defined in subdivision (a) of Section 12323. Where ammunition or reloaded ammunition may be used in both a rifle and a handgun, it may be sold to a person who is at least 18 years of age, but less than 21 years of age, if the vendor reasonably believes that the ammunition is being acquired for use in a rifle and not a handgun.

(C) Supplies, delivers, or gives possession of any ammunition to any minor who he or she knows, or using reasonable care should know, is prohibited from possessing that ammunition at that time pursuant to Section 12101.

(2) Proof that a person, corporation, or dealer, or his or her agent or employee, demanded, was shown, and acted in reasonable reliance upon, bona fide evidence of majority and identity shall be a defense to any criminal prosecution under this subdivision. As used in this subdivision, "bona fide evidence of majority and identity" means a document issued by a federal, state, county, or municipal government, or subdivision or agency thereof, including, but not limited to, a motor vehicle operator's license, California state identification card, identification card issued to a member of the Armed Forces, or other form of identification that bears the name, date of birth, description, and picture of the person.

(b)(1) No person prohibited from owning or possessing a firearm under Section 12021 or 12021.1 of this code or Section 8100 or 8103 of the Welfare and Institutions Code shall own, possess, or have under his or her custody or control, any ammunition or reloaded ammunition.

(2) For purposes of this subdivision, "ammunition" shall include, but not be limited to, any bullet, cartridge, magazine, clip, speed loader, autoloader, or projectile capable of being fired from a firearm with a deadly consequence. "Ammunition" does not include blanks.

(3) A violation of paragraph (1) of this subdivision is punishable by imprisonment in a county jail not to exceed one year or in the state prison, by a fine not to exceed one thousand dollars ($1,000), or by both the fine and imprisonment.

(4) A person who is not prohibited by paragraph (1) from owning, possessing, or having under his or her custody or control, any ammunition or reloaded ammunition, but who is enjoined from engaging in activity pursuant to an injunction issued pursuant to Section 3479 of the Civil Code against that person as a member of a criminal street gang, as defined in Section 186.22, may not own, possess, or have under his or her custody or control, any ammunition or reloaded ammunition.

(5) A violation of paragraph (4) of this subdivision is a misdemeanor.

(c) Unless it is with the written permission of the school district superintendent, his or her designee, or equivalent school authority, no person shall carry ammunition or reloaded ammunition onto school grounds, except sworn law enforcement officers acting within the scope of their duties or persons exempted under subparagraph (A) of paragraph (1) of subdivision (a) of Section 12027. This subdivision shall not apply to a duly appointed peace officer as defined in Chapter 4.5 (commencing with Section 830) of Title 3 of Part 2, a full-time paid peace officer of another state or the federal government who is carrying out official duties while in California, any person summoned by any of these officers to assist in making an arrest or preserving the peace while he or she is actually engaged in assisting the officer, a member of the military forces of this state or of the United States who is engaged in the performance of his or her duties, a person holding a valid license to carry the firearm pursuant to Article 3 (commencing with Section 12050) of Chapter 1 of Title 2 of Part 4, or an armored vehicle guard, who is engaged in the performance of his or her duties, as defined in subdivision (e) of Section 7521 of the Business and Professions Code. A violation of this subdivision is punishable by imprisonment in a county jail for a term not to exceed six months, a fine not to exceed one thousand dollars ($1,000), or both the imprisonment and fine.

(d)(1) A violation of paragraph (1) or (4) of subdivision (b) is justifiable where all of the following conditions are met:

(A) The person found the ammunition or reloaded ammunition or took the ammunition or reloaded ammunition from a person who was committing a crime against him or her.

(B) The person possessed the ammunition or reloaded ammunition no longer than was necessary to deliver or transport the ammunition or reloaded ammunition to a law enforcement agency for that agency's disposition according to law.

(C) The person is prohibited from possessing any ammunition or reloaded ammunition solely because that person is prohibited from owning or possessing a firearm only by virtue of Section 12021 or ammunition or reloaded ammunition because of paragraph (4) of subdivision (b).

(2) Upon the trial for violating paragraph (1) or (4) of subdivision (b), the trier of fact shall determine whether the defendant is subject to the exemption created by this subdivision.

(3) The defendant has the burden of proving by a preponderance of the evidence that he or she is subject to the exemption provided by this subdivision.

Penal Code § 12317

(a) Any person, corporation, or firm who supplies, delivers, sells, or gives possession or control of, any ammunition to any person who he or she knows or using reasonable care should know is prohibited from owning, possessing, or having under his or her custody or control, any ammunition or reloaded ammunition pursuant to paragraph (1) or (4) of subdivision (b) of Section 12316, is guilty of a misdemeanor, punishable by imprisonment in a county jail not exceeding one year, or a fine not exceeding one thousand dollars ($1,000), or by both that fine and imprisonment.

(b) The provisions of this section are cumulative and shall not be construed as restricting the application of any other law. However, an act or omission punishable in different ways by this section and another provision of law shall not be punished under more than one provision.

(c) For purposes of this section, "ammunition" shall include, but not be limited to, any bullet, cartridge, magazine, clip, speed loader, autoloader, or projectile capable of being fired from a firearm with deadly consequence. "Ammunition" does not include blanks.

Penal Code § 12318

(a) Commencing February 1, 2011, the delivery or transfer of ownership of handgun ammunition may only occur in a face-to-face transaction with the deliverer or transferor being provided bona fide evidence of identity from the purchaser or other transferee. A violation of this section is a misdemeanor.

(b) For purposes of this section:

(1) "Bona fide evidence of identity" means a document issued by a federal, state, county, or municipal government, or subdivision or agency thereof, including, but not limited to, a motor vehicle operator's license, state identification card, identification card issued to a member of the Armed Forces, or other form of identification that bears the name, date of birth, description, and picture of the person.

(2) "Handgun ammunition" means handgun ammunition as defined in subdivision (a) of Section 12323, but excluding ammunition designed and intended to be used in an "antique firearm" as defined in Section 921(a)(16) of Title 18 of the United States Code. Handgun ammunition does not include blanks.

(3) "Handgun ammunition vendor" has the same meaning as set forth in Section 12060.

(c) Subdivision (a) shall not apply to or affect the deliveries, transfers, or sales of, handgun ammunition to any of the following:

(1) Authorized law enforcement representatives of cities, counties, cities and counties, or state and federal governments for exclusive use by those government agencies if, prior to the delivery, transfer, or sale of the handgun ammunition, written authorization from the head of the agency employing the purchaser or transferee, is obtained identifying the employee as an individual authorized to conduct the transaction, and authorizing the transaction for the exclusive use of the agency employing the individual.

(2) Sworn peace officers, as defined in Chapter 4.5 (commencing with Section 830) of Title 3 of Part 2 who are authorized to carry a firearm in the course and scope of their duties.

(3) Importers and manufacturers of handgun ammunition or firearms licensed to engage in business pursuant to Chapter 44 (commencing with Section 921) of Title 18 of the United States Code and the regulations issued pursuant thereto.

(4) Persons who are on the centralized list maintained by the Department of Justice pursuant to Section 12083.

(5) Persons whose licensed premises are outside this state who are licensed as dealers or collectors of firearms pursuant to Chapter 44 (commencing with Section 921) of Title 18 of the United States Code and the regulations issued pursuant thereto.

(6) Persons licensed as collectors of firearms pursuant to Chapter 44 (commencing with Section 921) of Title 18 of the United States Code and the regulations issued pursuant thereto whose licensed premises are within this state who has a current certificate of eligibility issued to him or her by the Department of Justice pursuant to Section 12071.

(7) A handgun ammunition vendor.

(8) A consultant-evaluator, as defined in subdivision (s) of Section 12001.

Penal Code § 12320.

Any person, firm, or corporation who, within this state knowingly possesses any handgun ammunition designed primarily to penetrate metal or armor is guilty of a public offense and upon conviction thereof shall be punished by imprisonment in the state prison, or in the county jail for a term not to exceed one year, or by a fine not to exceed five thousand dollars ($5,000), or by both such fine and imprisonment.

Penal Code § 12321.

Any person, firm, or corporation who, within this state, manufactures, imports, sells, offers to sell, or knowingly transports any handgun ammunition designed primarily to penetrate metal or armor is guilty of a felony and upon conviction thereof shall be punished by imprisonment in state prison, or by a fine not to exceed five thousand dollars ($5,000), or by both such fine and imprisonment.

Penal Code § 12322.

Nothing in this chapter shall apply to or affect either of the following:

(a) The sale to, purchase by, possession of, or use of any ammunition by any member of the Army, Navy, Air Force, or Marine Corps of the United States, or the National Guard, while on duty and acting within the scope and course of his or her employment, or any police agency or forensic laboratory or any person who is the holder of a valid permit issued pursuant to Section 12305.

(b) The possession of handgun ammunition designed primarily to penetrate metal or armor by a person who found the ammunition, if he or she is not prohibited from possessing firearms or ammunition pursuant to Section 12021, 12021.1, or paragraph (1) of subdivision (b) of Section 12316 of this code or Section 8100 or 8103 of the Welfare and Institutions Code and is transporting the ammunition to a law enforcement agency for disposition according to law.

Penal Code § 12323.

As used in this chapter, the following definitions shall apply:

(a) "Handgun ammunition" means ammunition principally for use in pistols, revolvers, and other firearms capable of being concealed upon the person, as defined in subdivision (a) of Section 12001, notwithstanding that the ammunition may also be used in some rifles.

(b) "Handgun ammunition designed primarily to penetrate metal or armor" means any ammunition, except a shotgun shell or ammunition primarily designed for use in rifles, that is designed primarily to penetrate a body vest or body shield, and has either of the following characteristics:

(1) Has projectile or projectile core constructed entirely, excluding the presence of traces of other substances, from one or a combination of tungsten alloys, steel, iron, brass, beryllium copper, or depleted uranium, or any equivalent material of similar density

or hardness.

(2) Is primarily manufactured or designed, by virtue of its shape, cross-sectional density, or any coating applied thereto, including, but not limited to, ammunition commonly known as "KTW ammunition," to breach or penetrate a body vest or body shield when fired from a pistol, revolver, or other firearm capable of being concealed upon the person.

(c) "Body vest or shield" means any bullet-resistant material intended to provide ballistic and trauma protection for the wearer or holder.

(d) "Rifle" shall have the same meaning as defined in paragraph (20) of subdivision (c) of Section 12020.

Penal Code § 12324.

Nothing in this chapter shall prohibit the possession, importation, sale, attempted sale, or transport of ammunition from which the propellant has been removed and the primer has been permanently deactivated.

Penal Code § 12325.

Nothing in this chapter shall prohibit the manufacture of ammunition under contracts approved by agencies of the state or federal government.

Penal Code § 12355.

(a) Except as provided in Chapter 2.5 (commencing with Section 12301), any person who assembles, maintains, places, or causes to be placed a boobytrap device as described in subdivision (c) is guilty of a felony punishable by imprisonment in the state prison for two, three, or five years.

b) Possession of any device with the intent to use the device as a boobytrap is punishable by imprisonment in state prison, or in a county jail not exceeding one year, or by a fine not exceeding five thousand dollars ($5,000), or by both that fine and imprisonment.

(c) For purposes of this section, "boobytrap" means any concealed or camouflaged device designed to cause great bodily injury when triggered by an action of any unsuspecting person coming across the device. Boobytraps may include, but are not limited to, guns, ammunition, or explosive devices attached to trip wires or other triggering mechanisms, sharpened stakes, and lines or wire with hooks attached.

Penal Code § 12360.

No body armor shall be acquired by the commissioner pursuant to Section 2259.5 of the Vehicle Code unless, pursuant to subdivision (a) of Section 12361, the Department of Justice has certified such body armor.

Penal Code § 12361.

(a) Before a body armor may be purchased for use by state peace officers the Department of Justice, after consultation with the Department of the California Highway Patrol, shall establish minimum ballistic performance standards, and shall determine that the armor satisfies those standards.

(b) Only body armor that meets state requirements under subdivision (a) for acquisition or purchase shall be eligible for testing for certification under the ballistic performance standards established by the Department of Justice; and only body armor that is certified as acceptable by the department shall be purchased for use by state peace officers.

Penal Code § 12362.

Any person engaged in the manufacture or sale of body armor may apply to the Department of Justice for certification that a particular type of body armor manufactured or sold by that person is acceptable. The applicant shall reimburse the state for any actual expenses incurred by the state in testing and certifying a particular type of body armor.

Penal Code § 12363.

Any application submitted pursuant to Section 12362 shall contain all of the following:

(a) Full written reports of any investigation conducted for the purpose of determining whether such body armor is acceptable.

(b) A full written statement of the design of such body armor.

(c) A full written statement of the methods used in, and the facilities and controls used for, the manufacture of such body armor.

(d) Such samples of body armor and its components as the department may require.

(e) Specimens of the instructions and advertisements used or proposed to be used for such body armor.

Penal Code § 12364.

The Department of Justice, in cooperation with the Office of Procurement of the Department of General Services, shall establish a schedule for ballistic testing for certification pursuant to subdivision (b) of Section 12361.

Penal Code § 12365.

The department shall issue an order refusing to certify a body armor as acceptable if, after due notice to the applicant, the department finds any of the following:

(a) That the body armor does not satisfy the ballistic performance standards established by the department pursuant to subdivision (b) of Section 12361.

(b) That the application contains any misrepresentation of a material fact.

(c) That the application is materially incomplete. (d) That the applicant has failed to reimburse the state as required by Section 12362.

Penal Code § 12366.

The department shall issue an order revoking certification if, after due notice to the applicant, the department finds any of the following:

(a) That the experience or additional testing show that the body armor does not comply with the department's ballistic performance standards.

(b) That the application contains any misrepresentation of a material fact.

(c) The body armor must be retested for certification under new department standards.

Penal Code § 12367.

The department shall adopt and promulgate regulations for the fair and efficient enforcement of this chapter.

Penal Code § 12368.

(a) All purchases of certified body armor under the provisions of this chapter shall be made by the Department of General Services on behalf of an authorized state agency or department. Purchases of body armor shall be based upon written requests submitted by an authorized state agency or department to the Department of General Services..

(b) The Department of General Services shall make certified body armor available to peace officers of the Department of Justice, as defined by Section 830.3 of the Penal Code, while engaged in law enforcement activities.

Penal Code § 12369.

The Department of General Services shall, pursuant to departmental regulation, after consultation with the Department of the California Highway Patrol, define the term "enforcement activities" for purposes of this chapter, and develop standards regarding what constitutes sufficient wear on body armor to necessitate replacement thereof.

Penal Code § 12370.

(a) Any person who has been convicted of a violent felony, as defined in subdivision (c) of Section 667.5, under the laws of the United States, the State of California, or any other state, government, or country, who purchases, owns, or possesses body armor, as defined by Section 942 of Title 11 of the California Code of Regulations, except as authorized under subdivision (b), is guilty of a felony, punishable by imprisonment in a state prison for 16 months, or two or three years.

(b) Any person whose employment, livelihood, or safety is dependent on the ability to legally possess and use body armor, who is subject to the prohibition imposed by subdivision (a) due to a prior violent felony conviction, may file a petition with the chief of police or county sheriff of the jurisdiction in which he or she seeks to possess and use the body armor for an exception to this prohibition. The chief of police or sheriff may reduce or eliminate the prohibition, impose conditions on reduction or elimination of the prohibition, or otherwise grant relief from the prohibition as he or she deems appropriate, based on the following:

(1) A finding that the petitioner is likely to use body armor in a safe and lawful manner.

(2) A finding that the petitioner has a reasonable need for this type of protection under the circumstances. In making its decision, the chief of police or sheriff shall consider the petitioner's continued employment, the interests of justice, any relevant evidence, and the totality of the circumstances. It is the intent of the Legislature that law enforcement officials exercise broad discretion in fashioning appropriate relief under this paragraph in cases in which relief is warranted. However, this paragraph may not be construed to require law enforcement officials to grant relief to any particular petitioner. Relief from this prohibition does not relieve any other person or entity from any liability that might otherwise be imposed.

(c) The chief of police or sheriff shall require, as a condition of granting an exception under subdivision (b), that the petitioner agree to maintain on his or her person a certified copy of the law enforcement official's permission to possess and use body armor, including any conditions or limitations.

(d) Law enforcement officials who enforce the prohibition specified in subdivision (a) against a person who has been granted relief pursuant to subdivision (b), shall be immune from any liability for false arrest arising from the enforcement of this subdivision unless the person has in his or her possession a certified copy of the permission granting the person relief from the prohibition, as required by subdivision (c). This immunity from liability does not relieve any person or entity from any other liability that might otherwise be imposed.

(e) For purposes of this section only, "violent felony" refers to the specific crimes listed in subdivision (c) of Section 667.5, and to crimes defined under the applicable laws of the United States or any other state, government, or country that are reasonably equivalent to the crimes listed in subdivision (c) of Section 667.5.

Penal Code § 12401.

"Tear gas" as used in this chapter shall apply to and include all liquid, gaseous or solid substances intended to produce temporary physical discomfort or permanent injury through being vaporized or otherwise dispersed in the air, but does not apply to, and shall not include, any substance registered as an economic poison as provided in Chapter 2 (commencing with Section 12751) of Division 7 of the Agricultural Code provided that such substance is not intended to be used to produce discomfort or injury to human beings.

Penal Code § 12402.

The term "tear gas weapon" as used in this chapter shall apply to and include:

(a) Any shell, cartridge, or bomb capable of being discharged or exploded, when the discharge or explosion will cause or permit the release or emission of tear gases.

(b) Any revolvers, pistols, fountain pen guns, billies, or other form of device, portable or fixed, intended for the projection or release of tear gas except those regularly manufactured and sold for use with firearm ammunition.

Penal Code § 12403.

Nothing in this chapter shall prohibit any person who is a peace officer, as defined in Chapter 4.5 (commencing with Section

830) of Title 3 of Part 2, from purchasing, possessing, transporting, or using any tear gas or tear gas weapon if the person has satisfactorily completed a course of instruction approved by the Commission on Peace Officer Standards and Training in the use of tear gas.

Penal Code § 12403.1.

Nothing in this chapter shall prohibit any member of the military and naval forces of this state or of the United States or any federal law enforcement officer from purchasing, possessing, or transporting any tear gas or tear gas weapon for official use in the discharge of his duties.

Penal Code § 12403.5.

Notwithstanding any other provision of law, a person holding a license as a private investigator or private patrol operator issued pursuant to Chapter 11 (commencing with Section 7500), Division 3 of the Business and Professions Code, or uniformed patrolmen employees of a private patrol operator, may purchase, possess, or transport any tear gas weapon, if it is used solely for defensive purposes in the course of the activity for which the license was issued and if the person has satisfactorily completed a course of instruction approved by the Department of Consumer Affairs in the use of tear gas.

Penal Code § 12403.7.

Notwithstanding any other law, any person may purchase, possess, or use tear gas and tear gas weapons for the projection or release of tear gas if the tear gas and tear gas weapons are used solely for self-defense purposes, subject to the following requirements:

(a) No person convicted of a felony or any crime involving an assault under the laws of the United States, the State of California, or any other state, government, or country or convicted of misuse of tear gas under subdivision (g) shall purchase, possess, or use tear gas or tear gas weapons.

(b) No person who is addicted to any narcotic drug shall purchase, possess, or use tear gas or tear gas weapons.

(c) No person shall sell or furnish any tear gas or tear gas weapon to a minor.

(d) No person who is a minor shall purchase, possess, or use tear gas or tear gas weapons.

(e)(1) No person shall purchase, possess, or use any tear gas weapon that expels a projectile, or that expels the tear gas by any method other than an aerosol spray, or that contains more than 2.5 ounces net weight of aerosol spray.

(2) Every tear gas container and tear gas weapon that may be lawfully purchased, possessed, and used pursuant to this section shall have a label that states: "WARNING: The use of this substance or device for any purpose other than self-defense is a crime under the law. The contents are dangerous--use with care."

(3) After January 1, 1984, every tear gas container and tear gas weapon that may be lawfully purchased, possessed, and used pursuant to this section shall have a label that discloses the date on which the useful life of the tear gas weapon expires.

(4) Every tear gas container and tear gas weapon that may be lawfully purchased pursuant to this section shall be accompanied at the time of purchase by printed instructions for use.

(f) Effective March 1, 1994, every tear gas container and tear gas weapon that may be lawfully purchased, possessed, and used pursuant to this section shall be accompanied by an insert including directions for use, first aid information, safety and storage information, and explanation of the legal ramifications of improper use of the tear gas container or tear gas product.

(g) Any person who uses tear gas or tear gas weapons except in self-defense is guilty of a public offense and is punishable by imprisonment in a state prison for 16 months, or two or three years or in a county jail not to exceed one year or by a fine not to exceed one thousand dollars ($1,000), or by both the fine and imprisonment, except that, if the use is against a peace officer, as defined in Chapter 4.5 (commencing with Section 830) of Title 3 of Part 2, engaged in the performance of his or her official duties and the person committing the offense knows or reasonably should know that the victim is a peace officer, the offense is punishable by imprisonment in a state prison for 16 months or two or three years or by a fine of one thousand dollars ($1,000), or by both the fine and imprisonment.

Penal Code § 12403.8.

(a) Notwithstanding paragraph (4) of subdivision (a) of Section 12403.7, a minor who has attained the age of 16 years may purchase and possess tear gas or tear gas weapons pursuant to this chapter if he or she is accompanied by a parent or guardian, or has the written consent of his or her parent or guardian.

(b) Notwithstanding paragraph (3) of subdivision (a) of Section 12403.7, a person may sell or furnish tear gas or a tear gas weapon to a minor who has attained the age of 16 years and who is accompanied by a parent or guardian, or who presents a statement of consent signed by the minor's parent or guardian.

(c) Any civil liability of a minor arising out of his or her use of tear gas or a tear gas weapon other than for self-defense is imposed upon the person, parent, or guardian who signed the statement of consent specified in subdivision (b) who shall be jointly and severally liable with the minor for any damages proximately resulting from the negligent or wrongful act or omission of the minor in the use of the tear gas or a tear gas weapon.

Penal Code § 12403.9.

Custodial officers of any county may carry tear gas weapons pursuant to Section 12403 only while on duty. These custodial officers may carry tear gas weapons while off duty only in accordance with all other laws.

Penal Code § 12404.

Nothing in this chapter authorizes the possession of tear gas or tear gas weapons in any institution described in Section 4574, or within the grounds belonging or adjacent to any such institution, except where authorized by the person in charge of such institution.

Penal Code § 12420.

Any person, firm, or corporation who within this state knowingly sells or offers for sale, possesses, or transports any tear gas or tear gas weapon, except as permitted under the provisions of this chapter, is guilty of a public offense and upon conviction thereof shall be punishable by imprisonment in the county jail for not exceeding one year or by a fine not to exceed two thousand dollars ($2,000), or by both.

Penal Code § 12421.

Each tear gas weapon sold, transported or possessed under the authority of this chapter shall bear the name of the manufacturer and a serial number applied by him.

Penal Code § 12422.

Any person who changes, alters, removes or obliterates the name of the manufacturer, the serial number or any other mark of identification on any tear gas weapon is guilty of a public offense and, upon conviction, shall be punished by imprisonment in the state prison or by a fine of not more than two thousand dollars ($2,000) or by both. Possession of any such weapon upon which the same shall have been changed, altered, removed, or obliterated, shall be presumptive evidence that such possessor has changed, altered, removed, or obliterated the same.

Penal Code § 12423.

The Department of Justice may issue a permit for the possession and transportation of tear gas or tear gas weapons that are not intended or certified for personal self-defense purposes, upon proof that good cause exists for the issuance thereof to the applicant for this permit. The permit may also allow the applicant to install, maintain, and operate a protective system involving the use of tear gas or tear gas weapons in any place which is accurately and completely described in the application for the permit.

Penal Code § 12424.

Applications for permits shall be filed in writing, signed by the applicant if an individual, or by a member or officer qualified to sign if the applicant is a firm or corporation, and shall state the name, business in which engaged, business address and a full description of the place or vehicle in which the tear gas or tear gas weapons are to be transported, kept, installed, or maintained. If the tear gas or tear gas weapons are to be used in connection with, or to constitute, a protective system, the application shall also contain the name of the person who is to install the protective system. Applications and permits shall be uniform throughout the state upon forms prescribed by the Department of Justice. Each applicant for a permit shall pay at the time of filing his or her application a fee determined by the Department of Justice not to exceed the application processing costs of the Department of Justice. A permit granted pursuant to this article may be renewed one year from the date of issuance, and annually thereafter, upon the filing of a renewal application and the payment of a permit renewal fee not to exceed the application processing costs of the Department of Justice. After the department establishes fees sufficient to reimburse the department for processing costs, fees charged shall increase at a rate not to exceed the legislatively approved annual cost-of-living adjustments for the department's budget.

Penal Code § 12424.5.

Notwithstanding Section 12423, a bank, a savings and loan association, a credit union, or an industrial loan company which maintains more than one office or branch may make a single annual application for a permit. In addition to the requirements set forth in this article, that application shall separately state the business address and a full description of each office or branch in which the tear gas or tear gas weapons are to be kept, installed, or maintained. Any location additions or deletions as to offices or branches shall be reported to the department within 60 days of the change. A single permit issued under this section shall allow for the possession, operation, and maintenance of tear gas at each office or branch named in the application, including location changes.

Penal Code § 12425.

Every person, firm or corporation to whom a permit is issued shall either carry the permit upon his person or keep it in the place described in the permit. The permit shall be open to inspection by any peace officer or other person designated by the authority issuing the permit.

Penal Code § 12426.

Permits issued in accordance with this article may be revoked or suspended by the issuing authority at any time when it appears that the need for the possession or transportation of the tear gas or tear gas weapons or protective system involving the use thereof, has ceased, or that the holder of the permit has engaged in an unlawful business or occupation or has wrongfully made use of the tear gas or tear gas weapons or the permit issued.

Penal Code § 12500.

The term "silencer" as used in this chapter means any device or attachment of any kind designed, used, or intended for use in silencing, diminishing, or muffling the report of a firearm. The term "silencer" also includes any combination of parts, designed or redesigned, and intended for use in assembling a silencer or fabricating a silencer and any part intended only for use in such assembly or fabrication.

Penal Code § 12501.

Section 12520 shall not apply to, or affect, any of the following:

(a) The sale to, purchase by, or possession of silencers by agencies listed in Section 830.1, or the military or naval forces of this state or of the United States for use in the discharge of their official duties.

(b) The possession of silencers by regular, salaried, full-time peace officers who are employed by an agency listed in Section 830.1, or by the military or naval forces of this state or of the United States when on duty and when the use of silencers is authorized by the agency and is within the course and scope of their duties.

(c) The manufacture, possession, transportation, or sale or other transfer of silencers to an entity described in subdivision

(a) by dealers or manufacturers registered under Chapter 53 (commencing with Section 5801) of Title 26 of the United States Code, and the regulations issued pursuant thereto.

Penal Code § 12520.

Any person, firm, or corporation who within this state possesses a silencer is guilty of a felony and upon conviction thereof shall be punished by imprisonment in the state prison or by a fine not to exceed ten thousand dollars ($10,000) or by both.

Penal Code § 12550.

As used in this article, the following definitions apply:

(a) "BB device" is defined in subdivision (g) of Section 12001.

(b) "Firearm" is defined in subdivision (b) of Section 12001.

(c) "Imitation firearm" means any BB device, toy gun, replica of a firearm, or other device that is so substantially similar in coloration and overall appearance to an existing firearm as to lead a reasonable person to perceive that the device is a firearm.

Penal Code § 12551.

Every person who sells to a minor any BB device is guilty of a misdemeanor.

Penal Code § 12552.

(a) Every person who furnishes any BB device to any minor, without the express or implied permission of the parent or legal guardian of the minor, is guilty of a misdemeanor.

(b) As used in this section, "furnishes" means any of the following:

(1) A loan.

(2) A transfer that does not involve a sale.

Penal Code § 12553.

(a)(1) Any person who changes, alters, removes, or obliterates any coloration or markings that are required by any applicable state or federal law or regulation, for any imitation firearm, or device described in subdivision (c) of Section 12555, in any way that makes the imitation firearm or device look more like a firearm is guilty of a misdemeanor.

(2) This subdivision shall not apply to a manufacturer, importer, or distributor of imitation firearms or to the lawful use in theatrical productions, including motion pictures, television, and stage productions.

(b) Any manufacturer, importer, or distributor of imitation firearms that fails to comply with any applicable federal law or regulation governing the marking of a toy, look-alike or imitation firearm as defined by federal law or regulation is guilty of a misdemeanor.

Penal Code § 12554.

(a) Any imitation firearm manufactured after July 1, 2005, shall, at the time of offer for sale in this state, be accompanied by a conspicuous advisory in writing as part of the packaging, but not necessarily affixed to the imitation firearm, to the effect that the product may be mistaken for a firearm by law enforcement officers or others, that altering the coloration or markings required by state or federal law or regulations so as to make the product look more like a firearm is dangerous, and may be a crime, and that brandishing or displaying the product in public may cause confusion and may be a crime.

(b) Any manufacturer, importer, or distributor that fails to comply with this advisory for any imitation firearm manufactured after July 1, 2005, shall be liable for a civil fine for each action brought by a city attorney or district attorney of not more than one thousand dollars ($1,000) for the first action, five thousand dollars ($5,000) for the second action, and ten thousand dollars ($10,000) for the third action and each subsequent action.

Penal Code § 12555.

(a) Any person who, for commercial purposes, purchases, sells, manufactures, ships, transports, distributes, or receives, by mail order or in any other manner, an imitation firearm except as authorized by this section shall be liable for a civil fine in an action brought by the city attorney or the district attorney of not more than ten thousand dollars ($10,000) for each violation.

(b) The manufacture, purchase, sale, shipping, transport, distribution, or receipt, by mail or in any other manner, of imitation firearms is authorized if the device is manufactured, purchased, sold, shipped, transported, distributed, or received for any of the following purposes:

(1) Solely for export in interstate or foreign commerce.

(2) Solely for lawful use in theatrical productions, including motion picture, television, and stage productions.

(3) For use in a certified or regulated sporting event or competition.

(4) For use in military or civil defense activities, or ceremonial activities.

(5) For public displays authorized by public or private schools.

(c) As used in this section, "imitation firearm" does not include any of the following:

(1) A nonfiring collector's replica that is historically significant, and is offered for sale in conjunction with a wall plaque or presentation case.

(2) A BB device, as defined in subdivision (g) of Section 12001.

(3) A device where the entire exterior surface of the device is white, bright red, bright orange, bright yellow, bright green, bright blue, bright pink, or bright purple, either singly or as the predominant color in combination with other colors in any pattern, as provided by federal regulations governing imitation firearms, or where the entire device is constructed of transparent or translucent materials which permits unmistakable observation of the device's complete contents, as provided by federal regulations governing imitation firearms.

Penal Code § 12556.

(a) No person may openly display or expose any imitation firearm, as defined in Section 12550, in a public place.

(b) Violation of this section, except as provided in subdivision (c), is an infraction punishable by a fine of one hundred dollars ($100) for the first offense, and three hundred dollars ($300) for a second offense.

(c) A third or subsequent violation of this section is punishable as a misdemeanor.

(d) Subdivision (a) shall not apply to the following, when the imitation firearm is:

(1) Packaged or concealed so that it is not subject to public viewing.

(2) Displayed or exposed in the course of commerce, including commercial film or video productions, or for service, repair, or restoration of the imitation firearm.

(3) Used in a theatrical production, a motion picture, video, television, or stage production.

(4) Used in conjunction with a certified or regulated sporting event or competition.

(5) Used in conjunction with lawful hunting, or lawful pest control activities.

(6) Used or possessed at certified or regulated public or private shooting ranges.

(7) Used at fairs, exhibitions, expositions, or other similar activities for which a permit has been obtained from a local or state government.

(8) Used in military, civil defense, or civic activities, including flag ceremonies, color guards, parades, award presentations, historical reenactments, and memorials.

(9) Used for public displays authorized by public or private schools or displays that are part of a museum collection.

(10) Used in parades, ceremonies, or other similar activities for which a permit has been obtained from a local or state government.

(11) Displayed on a wall plaque or in a presentation case.

(12) Used in areas where the discharge of a firearm is lawful.

(13) A device where the entire exterior surface of the device is white, bright red, bright orange, bright yellow, bright green, bright blue, bright pink, or bright purple, either singly or as the predominant color in combination with other colors in any pattern, or where the entire device is constructed of transparent or translucent materials which permits unmistakable observation of the device's complete contents. Merely having an orange tip as provided in federal law and regulations does not satisfy this requirement. The entire surface must be colored or transparent or translucent.

(e) For purposes of this section, the term "public place" means an area open to the public and includes streets, sidewalks, bridges, alleys, plazas, parks, driveways, front yards, parking lots, automobiles, whether moving or not, and buildings open to the general public, including those that serve food or drink, or provide entertainment, and the doorways and entrances to buildings or dwellings, and shall include public schools and a public or private college or university.

(f) Nothing in this section shall be construed to preclude prosecution for a violation of Section 171b, 171.5, or 626.10.

Penal Code § 12580.

"Blowgun," as used in this article, means a hollow tube designed and intended to be used as a tube through which a dart is propelled by the force of the breath of the user.

Penal Code § 12581.

"Blowgun ammunition," as used in this article, means a dart designed and intended for use in a blowgun.

Penal Code § 12582.

Any person who knowingly manufactures, sells, offers for sale, possesses, or uses a blowgun or blowgun ammunition in this state is guilty of a misdemeanor.

Penal Code § 12583.

Nothing in this article shall prohibit the sale to, purchase by, possession of, or use of blowguns or blowgun ammunition by zookeepers, animal control officers, Department of Fish and Game personnel, humane officers whose names are maintained in the county record of humane officers pursuant to Section 14502 of the Corporations Code, or veterinarians in the course and scope of their business in order to administer medicine to animals.

Penal Code § 12590.

(a) Any person who does any of the following acts while engaged in picketing, or other informational activities in a public place relating to a concerted refusal to work, is guilty of a misdemeanor:

(1) Carries concealed upon his person or within any vehicle which is under his or her control or direction any pistol, revolver, or other firearm capable of being concealed upon the person.

(2) Carries a loaded firearm upon his or her person or within any vehicle which is under his or her control or direction.

(3) Carries a deadly weapon.

(4) Wears the uniform of a peace officer, whether or not the person is a peace officer.

(b) This section shall not be construed to authorize or ratify any picketing or other informational activities not otherwise authorized by law.

(c) Section 12027 shall not be construed to authorize any conduct described in paragraph (1) of subdivision (a), nor shall subdivision (b) of Section 12031 be construed to authorize any conduct described in paragraph (2) of subdivision (a).

Penal Code § 12600.

A person who is a peace officer or a custodial officer as defined in Chapter 4.5 (commencing with Section 830) of Title 3 of Part 2 may if authorized by and under the terms and conditions as are specified by his or her employing agency purchase, possess, or transport any less lethal weapon or ammunition therefor, for official use in the discharge of his or her duties.

Penal Code § 12601.

(a) "Less lethal weapon" means any device that is designed to or that has been converted to expel or propel less lethal ammunition by any action, mechanism, or process for the purpose of incapacitating, immobilizing, or stunning a human being through the infliction of any less than lethal impairment of physical condition, function, or senses, including physical pain or discomfort. It is not necessary that a weapon leave any lasting or permanent incapacitation, discomfort, pain, or other injury or disability in order to qualify as a less lethal weapon.

(b) Less lethal weapon includes the frame or receiver of any weapon described in subdivision (a), but does not include any of the following unless the part or weapon has been converted as described in subdivision (a):

(1) Pistol, revolver, or firearm as defined in Section 12001.

(2) Machinegun as defined in Section 12200.

(3) Rifle or shotgun using fixed ammunition consisting of standard primer and powder and not capable of being concealed upon the person.

(4) Pistols, rifles, and shotguns that are firearms having a barrel less than 0.18 inches in diameter and that are designed to expel a projectile by any mechanical means or by compressed air or gas.

(5) When used as designed or intended by the manufacturer, any weapon commonly regarded as a toy gun, and that as such is incapable of inflicting any impairment of physical condition, function, or senses.

(6) A destructive device as defined in Section 12301.

(7) A tear gas weapon as defined in Section 12402.

(8) A bow or crossbow designed to shoot arrows.

(9) A device commonly known as a slingshot.

(10) A device designed for the firing of stud cartridges, explosive rivets, or similar industrial ammunition.

(11) A device designed for signaling, illumination, or safety.

(12) An assault weapon as defined in Section 12276 or 12276.1.

(c) "Less lethal ammunition" means any ammunition that (1) is designed to be used in any less lethal weapon or any other kind of weapon (including, but not limited to, firearms, pistols, revolvers, shotguns, rifles, and spring, compressed air, and compressed gas weapons) and (2) when used in the less lethal weapon or other weapon is designed to immobilize or incapacitate or stun a human being through the infliction of any less than lethal impairment of physical condition, function, or senses, including physical pain or discomfort.

Penal Code § 12650.

"Stun gun" as used in this chapter shall include any item, except a taser, used or intended to be used as either an offensive or defensive weapon capable of temporarily immobilizing a person by the infliction of an electrical charge.

Penal Code § 12651.

Notwithstanding any other provision of law, any person may purchase, possess, or use a stun gun, subject to the following requirements:

(a) No person convicted of a felony or any crime involving an assault under the laws of the United States, of the State of California, or any other state, government, or country or convicted of misuse of a stun gun under Section 244.5, shall purchase, possess, or use stun guns.

(b) No person who is addicted to any narcotic drug shall purchase, possess, or use a stun gun.

(c) No person shall sell or furnish any stun gun to a minor unless the minor is at least 16 years of age and has the written consent of his or her parent or legal guardian. Violation of this subdivision shall be a public offense punishable by a fifty dollar ($50) fine for the first offense. Any subsequent violation of this subdivision is a misdemeanor.

(d) No minor shall possess any stun gun unless the minor is at least 16 years of age and has the written consent of his or her parent or legal guardian.

Penal Code § 12652.

Each stun gun sold shall contain both of the following:

(a) The name of the manufacturer stamped on the stun gun.

(b) The serial number applied by the manufacturer.

Penal Code § 12653.

Unless otherwise specified, any violation of this article is a misdemeanor.

Penal Code § 12654.

Each stun gun sold in this state shall be accompanied by an instruction booklet. Violation of this section shall be a public offense punishable by a fifty dollar ($50) fine for each weapon sold without the booklet.

Penal Code § 12655.

Any person who sells a less lethal weapon, as defined in Section 12601, to a person under the age of 18 years is guilty of a misdemeanor, punishable by imprisonment in the county jail for up to six months or by a fine of not more than one thousand dollars ($1,000), or by both that imprisonment and fine.

Penal Code § 12800.

It is the intent of the Legislature in enacting this article to require that persons who obtain handguns have a basic familiarity with those firearms, including, but not limited to, the safe handling and storage of those firearms. It is not the intent of the Legislature to require a handgun safety certificate for the mere possession of a firearm.

Penal Code § 12801.

(a) As used in this article, the following definitions shall apply:

(1) "Department" means the Department of Justice.

(2) "DOJ Certified Instructor" or "certified instructor" means a person designated as a handgun safety instructor by the Department of Justice pursuant to subdivision (d) of Section 12804.

(b) No person shall do either of the following:

(1) Purchase or receive any handgun, except an antique firearm, as defined in paragraph (16) of subsection (a) of Section 921 of Title 18 of the United States Code, without a valid handgun safety certificate.

(2) Sell, deliver, loan, or transfer any handgun, except an antique firearm, as defined in paragraph (16) of subsection (a) of Section 921 of Title 18 of the United States Code, to any person who does not have a valid handgun safety certificate.

(c) Any person who violates subdivision (b) is guilty of a misdemeanor.

(d) The provisions of this section are cumulative, and shall not be construed as restricting the application of any other law. However, an act or omission punishable in different ways by different provisions of this code shall not be punished under more than one provision.

Penal Code § 12802.

(a) No person may commit an act of collusion as specified in Section 12072.

(b) Any person who alters, counterfeits, or falsifies a handgun safety certificate, or who uses or attempts to use any altered, counterfeited, or falsified handgun safety certificate to purchase a handgun is guilty of a misdemeanor.

(c) The provisions of this section are cumulative and shall not be construed as restricting the application of any other law. However, an act or omission punishable in different ways by this section and different provisions of this code shall not be punished under more than one provision.

Penal Code § 12803.

(a) No certified instructor may issue a handgun safety certificate to any person who has not complied with this article. Proof of compliance shall be forwarded to the department by certified instructors as frequently as the department may determine.

(b) No certified instructor may issue a handgun safety certificate to any person who is under 18 years of age.

(c) A violation of this section shall be grounds for the department to revoke the instructor's certification to issue handgun safety certificates.

Penal Code § 12804.

(a) The department shall develop an instruction manual in English and in Spanish by October 1, 2002. The department shall make the instructional manual available to firearms dealers licensed pursuant to Section 12071, who shall make it available to the general public. Essential portions of the manual may be included in the pamphlet described in Section 12080.

(b) The department shall develop audiovisual materials in English and in Spanish by March 1, 2003, to be issued to instructors certified by the department.

(c)(1) The department shall develop a written objective test, in English and in Spanish, and prescribe its content, form, and manner, to be administered by an instructor certified by the department. If the person taking the test is unable to read, the examination shall be administered orally. The test shall cover, but not be limited to, all of the following:

(A) The laws applicable to carrying and handling firearms, particularly handguns.

(B) The responsibilities of ownership of firearms, particularly handguns.

(C) Current law as it relates to the private sale and transfer of firearms.

(D) Current law as it relates to the permissible use of lethal force.

(E) What constitutes safe firearm storage.

(F) Issues associated with bringing a handgun into the home.

(G) Prevention strategies to address issues associated with bringing firearms into the home.

(2) If the person taking the test is unable to read English or Spanish, the test may be applied orally by a translator.

(d) The department shall prescribe a minimum level of skill, knowledge and competency to be required of all handgun safety certificate instructors.

(e) If a dealer licensed pursuant to Section 12071 or his or her employee, or where the managing officer or partner is certified as an instructor pursuant to this article, he or she shall also designate a separate room or partitioned area for a person to take the objective test, and maintain adequate supervision to assure that no acts of collusion occur while the objective test is being administered.

(f) The department shall solicit input from any reputable association or organization, including any law enforcement association that has as one of its objectives the promotion of firearms safety, in the development of the handgun safety certificate instructional materials.

(g) The department shall develop handgun safety certificates to be issued by instructors certified by the department, to those persons who have complied with this article.

(h) The department shall be immune from any liability arising from implementing this section.

(i) The department shall update test materials related to this article every five years.

(j) Department Certified Instructor applicants shall have a certification to provide training from one of the following organizations as specified, or any entity found by the department to give comparable instruction in firearms safety, or the applicant shall have similar or equivalent training to that provided by the following, as determined by the department:

(1) Department of Consumer Affairs, State of California-Firearm Training Instructor.

(2) Director of Civilian Marksmanship, Instructor or Rangemaster.

(3) Federal Government, Certified Rangemaster or Firearm Instructor.

(4) Federal Law Enforcement Training Center, Firearm Instructor Training Program or Rangemaster.

(5) United States Military, Military Occupational Specialty (MOS) as marksmanship or firearms instructor. Assignment as Range Officer or Safety Officer are not sufficient.

(6) National Rifle Association-Certified Instructor, Law Enforcement Instructor, Rangemaster, or Training Counselor.

(7) Commission on Peace Officer Standards and Training (POST), State of California-Firearm Instructor or Rangemaster.

(8) Authorization from a State of California accredited school to teach a firearm training course.

Penal Code § 12805.

(a) An applicant for a handgun safety certificate shall successfully pass the objective test referred to in paragraph (1) of subdivision (c) of Section 12804, with a passing grade of at least 75 percent. Any person receiving a passing grade on the objective test shall immediately be issued a handgun safety certificate by the instructor.

(b) An applicant who fails to pass the objective test upon the first attempt shall be offered additional instructional materials by the instructor such as a videotape or booklet. The person may not retake the objective test under any circumstances until 24 hours have elapsed after the failure to pass the objective test upon the first attempt. The person failing the test on the first attempt shall take another version of the test upon the second attempt. All tests shall be taken from the same instructor except upon permission by the department, which shall be granted only for good cause shown. The instructor shall make himself or herself available to the applicant during regular business hours in order to retake the test.

(c) The certified instructor may charge a fee of twenty-five dollars ($25), fifteen dollars ($15) of which is to be paid to the department pursuant to subdivision (e).

(d) An applicant to renew a handgun safety certificate shall be required to pass the objective test. The certified instructor may charge a fee of twenty-five dollars ($25), fifteen dollars ($15) of which is to be forwarded to the department pursuant to subdivision (e).

(e) The department may charge the certified instructor up to fifteen dollars ($15) for each handgun safety certificate issued by that instructor to cover the department's cost in carrying out and enforcing this article, and enforcing this title, as determined annually by the department.

(f) All money received by the department pursuant to this article shall be deposited into the Firearms Safety and Enforcement Special Fund created pursuant to Section 12076.5.

(g) The department shall conduct enforcement activities, including, but not limited to, law enforcement activities to ensure compliance with Title 2 (commencing with Section 12000) of Part 4.

Penal Code § 12806.

(a) A handgun safety certificate shall include, but not be limited to, the following information:

(1) A unique handgun safety certificate identification number.

(2) The holder's full name.

(3) The holder's date of birth.

(4) The holder's driver's license or identification number.

(5) The holder's signature.

(6) The signature of the issuing instructor.

(7) The date of issuance.

(b) The handgun safety certificate shall expire five years after the date that it was issued by the certified instructor.

Penal Code § 12807.

(a) The following persons, properly identified, are exempted from the handgun safety certificate requirement in subdivision (b) of Section 12801:

(1) Any active or honorably retired peace officer, as defined in Chapter 4.5 (commencing with Section 830) of Title 3 of Part 2.

(2) Any active or honorably retired federal officer or law enforcement agent.

(3) Any reserve peace officer, as defined in Section 832.6.

(4) Any person who has successfully completed the course of training specified in Section 832.

(5) A firearms dealer licensed pursuant to Section 12071, who is acting in the course and scope of his or her activities as a person licensed pursuant to Section 12071.

(6) A federally licensed collector who is acquiring or being loaned a handgun that is a curio or relic, as defined in Section 478.11 of Title 27 of the Code of Federal Regulations, who has a current certificate of eligibility issued to him or her by the department pursuant to Section 12071.

(7) A person to whom a handgun is being returned, where the person receiving the firearm is the owner of the firearm.

(8) A family member of a peace officer or deputy sheriff from a local agency who receives a firearm pursuant to Section 50081 of the Government Code.

(9) Any individual who has a valid concealed weapons permit issued pursuant to Section 12050.

(10) An active, or honorably retired member of the United States Armed Forces, the National Guard, the Air National Guard, the active reserve components of the United States, where individuals in those organizations are properly identified. For purposes of this section, proper identification includes the Armed Forces Identification Card, or other written documentation certifying that the individual is an active or honorably retired member.

(11) Any person who is authorized to carry loaded firearms pursuant to subdivision (c) or (d) of Section 12031.

(12) Persons who are the holders of a special weapons permit issued by the department pursuant to Section 12095, 12230,

12250, or 12305.

(b) The following persons who take title or possession of a handgun by operation of law in a representative capacity, until or unless they transfer title ownership of the handgun to themselves in a personal capacity, are exempted from the handgun safety certificate requirement in subdivision (b) of Section 12801:

(1) The executor or administrator of an estate.

(2) A secured creditor or an agent or employee thereof when the firearms are possessed as collateral for, or as a result of, or an agent or employee thereof when the firearms are possessed as collateral for, or as a result of, a default under a security agreement under the Commercial Code.

(3) A levying officer, as defined in Section 481.140, 511.060, or 680.260 of the Code of Civil Procedure.

(4) A receiver performing his or her functions as a receiver.

(5) A trustee in bankruptcy performing his or her duties.

(6) An assignee for the benefit of creditors performing his or her functions as an assignee.

Penal Code § 12808.

(a) In the case of loss or destruction of a handgun safety certificate, the issuing instructor shall issue a duplicate certificate upon request and proof of identification to the certificate holder.

(b) The department may authorize the issuing instructor to charge a fee not to exceed fifteen dollars ($15), for a duplicate certificate. Revenues from this fee shall be deposited in the Firearms Safety and Enforcement Special Fund, created pursuant to Section 12076.5.

Penal Code § 12809.

Except for the provisions of Section 12804, this article shall become operative on January 1, 2003.

Public Contracts Code

Public Contracts Code § 10334.

(a) No state employee shall acquire any goods from the state, unless the goods are offered to the general public in the regular course of the state's business on the same terms and conditions as those applicable to the employee. "State employee," as used in this section, means any employee of the state included within Section 82009 of the Government Code, and all officers and employees included within Section 4 of Article VII of the California Constitution, except those persons excluded from the definition of "designated employee" under the last paragraph of Section 82019 of the Government Code.

(b) Notwithstanding subdivision (a), any peace officer as defined in Chapter 4.5 (commencing with Section 830) of Title 3 of Part 2 of the Penal Code, employed by the State of California for a period of more than 120 months who has been duly retired through a service retirement or a peace officer retiring from a job-incurred disability not related to a mental or emotional disorder and who has been granted the legal right to carry a concealed firearm pursuant to subdivision (a) of Section 12027 of the Penal Code may be authorized by the person's department head to purchase his or her state-issued handgun. Disability retired peace officers need not meet the 120-month employment requirement. The cost of the handgun shall be the fair market value as listed in the annual Blue Book of Gun Values or replacement cost, whichever is less, of the handgun issued as determined by the appointing power, plus a charge for the cost of handling. The retiring officer shall request to purchase his or her handgun in writing to the department within 30 calendar days of his or her retirement date.

(c) Notwithstanding subdivision (a), any peace officer described in Chapter 4.5 (commencing with Section 830) of Title 3 of Part 2 of the Penal Code employed by the State of California who is authorized to carry firearms may purchase his or her state-issued service firearm if the person's department head directs the department to change its state-issued service weapon system. The cost of the service firearm shall be the fair market value as listed in the annual Blue Book of Gun Values or replacement cost, whichever is less, of the firearm issued as determined by the department head, plus a charge for the cost of handling. The requesting officer shall request to purchase his or her firearm in writing to the department within 10 calendar days of receiving the new state-issued weapon.

Public Resources Code

Public Resources Code § 4332.

Whenever it is necessary in the interests of public peace or safety, the director, with the consent of the Governor, may order closed to camping, hunting, trapping, or the use of firearms, any area in any state park or state forest. The director shall post and enforce such closure order in such area.

Public Resources Code § 4333.

Any order which is issued pursuant to Section 4332 shall be published twice in at least one newspaper of general circulation in any county that is affected by the order. The publication shall be separated by a period of not less than one week and not more than two weeks. The order shall also be posted in such public places in each county as the director may direct, and along roads and trails which pass through such areas declared to be closed to camping or entry.

Public Resources Code § 4445.

A person shall not fire or cause to be fired from any rifle or other device capable of discharging ammunition, any bullet, projectile, or other ammunition which contains the components of thermite, magnesium, or aluminum, or any other component capable of causing a fire and commonly known as tracer or incendiary ammunition within any forest-covered area, brush-covered area, grass-covered area or grain-covered area.

Public Resources Code § 5164.

(a)(1) A county or city or city and county or special district shall not hire a person for employment, or hire a volunteer to perform services, at a county or city or city and county or special district operated park, playground, recreational center, or beach used for recreational purposes, in a position having supervisory or disciplinary authority over any minor, if that person has been convicted of any offense specified in paragraph (2).

(2)(A) Violations or attempted violations of Section 220, 261.5, 262, 273a, 273d, or 273.5 of the Penal Code, or any sex offense listed in Section 290 of the Penal Code, except for the offense specified in subdivision (d) of Section 243.4 of the Penal Code.

(B) Any felony or misdemeanor conviction specified in subparagraph (C) within 10 years of the date of the employer's request.

(C) Any felony conviction that is over 10 years old, if the subject of the request was incarcerated within 10 years of the employer's request, for a violation or attempted violation of any of the offenses specified in Chapter 3 (commencing with Section 207) of Title 8 of Part 1 of the Penal Code, Section 211 or 215 of the Penal Code, wherein it is charged and proved that the defendant personally used a deadly or dangerous weapon, as provided in subdivision (b) of Section 12022 of the Penal Code, in the commission of that offense, Section 217.1 of the Penal Code, Section 236 of the Penal Code, any of the offenses specified in Chapter 9 (commencing with Section 240) of Title 8 of Part 1 of the Penal Code, or any of the offenses specified in subdivision (c) of Section 667.5 of the Penal Code, provided that no record of a misdemeanor conviction shall be transmitted to the requester unless the subject of the request has a total of three or more misdemeanor convictions, or a combined total of three or more misdemeanor and felony convictions, for violations listed in this section within the 10-year period immediately preceding the employer's request or has been incarcerated for any of those convictions within the preceding 10 years.

(b)(1) To give effect to this section, a county or city or city and county or special district shall require each such prospective employee or volunteer to complete an application that inquires as to whether or not that individual has been convicted of any offense specified in subdivision (a). The county or city or city and county or special district shall screen, pursuant to Section 11105.3 of the Penal Code, any such prospective employee or volunteer, having supervisory or disciplinary authority over any minor, for that person' s criminal background.

(2) Any local agency requests for Department of Justice records pursuant to this subdivision shall include the prospective employee's or volunteer's fingerprints, which may be taken by the local agency, and any other data specified by the Department of Justice. The request shall be made on a form approved by the Department of Justice. No fee shall be charged to the local agency for requesting the records of a prospective volunteer pursuant to this subdivision.

Public Resources Code § 33211.5.

(a) The following conditions of use apply to property owned or subject to the management of the conservancy:

(1) Opening and closing hours shall be posted on any property upon which public use is permitted.

(2) Property may be closed to public use only when fire, mudslide, landslide, or flood dangers pose a substantial risk of injury or loss of life, or when a federal, state, or local disaster or emergency declaration has been made by an authorized person or public agency, or where there is an emergency or potential emergency situation of a temporary nature that involves substantial risk or potential risk to life or property, and the temporary closure or restriction of access is necessary to protect the public health and safety. Any property closed shall be reopened as soon as the fire, mudslide, landslide, or flood dangers no longer pose a danger of injury or loss of life, or when a federal, state, or local disaster or emergency declaration is no longer in effect, or where there is no longer an emergency or potential emergency situation of a temporary nature that involves substantial risk or potential risk to life or property.

(3) Vehicles shall park only in designated areas and may not be operated off of roads or other areas designated for vehicle use. All vehicle use, including bicycles, shall conform to posted signs.

(b) Trails, campsites, and other public use areas on property owned or subject to the management of the conservancy shall be designated and posted with prohibited activities and use restrictions clearly indicated, including, but not limited to, the prohibition or restriction of smoking, fires, fireworks, animals, possession of dangerous weapons, or other activities that affect the safety of visitors, campers, trail users, or the natural or historic resources of the property.

(c) Determining and posting conditions of use pursuant to subdivisions (a) and (b) may not be considered the adoption of regulations within the meaning of the Administrative Procedure Act (Chapter 3.5 (commencing with Section 11340) of Part 1 of Division

3 of Title 2 of the Government Code).

(d)(1) The conditions of use and types of uses of property owned or subject to the management of the conservancy are considered to be of statewide significance. The types of uses and the management policies affecting those uses shall be consistent with the policies for permitted uses of lands within the state park system.

(2) Notwithstanding any other law, ordinance, rule, or regulation, the conservancy may exercise its discretion in determining whether to authorize any license, permit for special use, easement, project, activity, or other entitlement to be undertaken by the conservancy or its agents, for the use of conservancy owned or managed land. This subdivision shall not be construed to restrict the authority of the conservancy to lease lands consistent with the purposes of this division and the requirements of Section 33206.

Vehicle Code

Vehicle Code § 115.

An "armored car" is a vehicle that is equipped with materials on either the front, sides, or rear for the protection of persons therein from missiles discharged from firearms.

Vehicle Code § 10653.

Whenever any vehicle of a type subject to registration under this code which shows evidence of having been struck by a bullet is stored in a garage or repair shop, the keeper thereof shall within 24 hours after receiving the vehicle report such fact to the sheriff's office of the county or police department of the city wherein the garage or repair shop is located, giving the motor or other number of the vehicle, the license number if ascertainable, and the name and address of the person storing the same or the name and address of the owner shown by the registration card, if the same is attached to the vehicle in a clearly discernible place.

Vehicle Code § 13202.4.

(a)(1) For each conviction of a minor who commits a public offense involving a pistol, revolver, or other firearm capable of being concealed upon the person, the court may suspend the minor' s driving privilege for five years. If the minor convicted does not yet have the privilege to drive, the court may order the department to delay issuing the privilege to drive for five years subsequent to the time the person becomes legally eligible to drive. For each successive offense, the court may suspend the minor's driving privilege for those possessing a license or delay the eligibility for those not in possession of a license at the time of their conviction for one additional year.

(2)(A) Any minor whose driving privilege is suspended pursuant to this section may elect to reduce the period of suspension or delay imposed by the court by performing community service under the supervision of the probation department if both of the following conditions are met:

(i) At least 50 percent of the suspension or delay period has expired.

(ii) The person has not been the subject of any other criminal conviction during the suspension or delay period.

(B) If the conditions specified in subparagraph (A) are met, the period of suspension or delay ordered under paragraph (1) shall be reduced at the rate of one day for each hour of community service performed.

(3) As used in this section, the term "conviction" includes the findings in juvenile proceedings specified in Section 13105.

(b)(1) Whenever the court suspends driving privileges pursuant to subdivision (a), the court in which the conviction is had shall require all driver's licenses held by the person to be surrendered to the court. The court shall, within 10 days following the conviction, transmit a certified abstract of the conviction, together with any driver's licenses surrendered, to the department.

(2) Violations of restrictions imposed pursuant to this section are subject to Section 14603.

(c) When the court is considering suspending or delaying driving privileges pursuant to subdivision (a), the court shall consider if a personal or family hardship exists that requires the person to have a driver's license for his or her own, or a member of his or her family's, employment or medically related purposes.

(d) The suspension, restriction, or delay of driving privileges pursuant to this section shall be in addition to any penalty imposed upon conviction for the offense.

Vehicle Code § 13210.

In addition to the penalties set forth in subdivision (a) of Section 245 of the Penal Code, the court may order the suspension of the driving privilege of any operator of a motor vehicle who commits an assault as described in subdivision (a) of Section 245 of the Penal Code on an operator or passenger of another motor vehicle, an operator of a bicycle, or a pedestrian and the offense occurs on a highway. The suspension period authorized under this section for an assault commonly known as "road rage," shall be six months for a first offense and one year for a second or subsequent offense to commence, at the discretion of the court, either on the date of the person's conviction, or upon the person's release from confinement or imprisonment. The court may, in lieu of or in addition to the suspension of the driving privilege, order a person convicted under this section to complete a court-approved anger management or "road rage" course, subsequent to the date of the current violation.

Vehicle Code § 13351.5.

(a) Upon receipt of a duly certified abstract of the record of any court showing that a person has been convicted of a felony for a violation of Section 245 of the Penal Code and that a vehicle was found by the court to constitute the deadly weapon or instrument used to commit that offense, the department immediately shall revoke the privilege of that person to drive a motor vehicle.

(b) The department shall not reinstate a privilege revoked under subdivision (a) under any circumstances.

(c) Notwithstanding subdivision (b), the department shall terminate any revocation order issued under this section on or after January 1, 1995, for a misdemeanor conviction of violating Section 245 of the Penal Code.

Vehicle Code § 21464.

(a) A person, without lawful authority, may not deface, injure, attach any material or substance to, knock down, or remove, nor may a person shoot at, any official traffic control device, traffic guidepost, traffic signpost, motorist callbox, or historical marker placed or erected as authorized or required by law, nor may a person without lawful authority deface, injure, attach any material or substance to, or remove, nor may a person shoot at, any inscription, shield, or insignia on any device, guide, or marker.

(b) A person may not use, and a vehicle, other than an authorized emergency vehicle or a public transit passenger vehicle, may not be equipped with, any device, including, but not limited to, a mobile infrared transmitter, that is capable of sending a signal that interrupts or changes the sequence patterns of an official traffic control signal unless that device or use is authorized by the Department of Transportation pursuant to Section 21350 or by local authorities pursuant to Section 21351.

(c) A person may not buy, possess, manufacture, install, sell, offer for sale, or otherwise distribute a device described in subdivision (b), including, but not limited to, a mobile infrared transmitter (MIRT), unless the purchase, possession, manufacture, installation, sale, offer for sale, or distribution is for the use of the device by a peace officer or other person authorized to operate an authorized emergency vehicle or a public transit passenger vehicle, in the scope of his or her duties.

(d) Any willful violation of subdivision (a), (b), or (c) that results in injury to, or the death of, a person is punishable by imprisonment in the state prison, or by imprisonment in a county jail for a period of not more than six months, and by a fine of not less than five thousand dollars ($5,000) nor more than ten thousand dollars ($10,000).

(e) Any willful violation of subdivision (a), (b), or (c) that does not result in injury to, or the death of, a person is punishable by a fine of not more than five thousand dollars ($5,000).

(f) The court shall allow the offender to perform community service designated by the court in lieu of all or part of any fine imposed under this section.

Vehicle Code § 31600.

For the purposes of this division "explosive" or "explosives" means any substance, or combination of substances, the primary or common purpose of which is detonation or rapid combustion and which is capable of a relatively instantaneous or rapid release of gas and heat. "Explosive" or "explosives" includes, but is not necessarily limited to, explosives as defined in Section 12000 of the Health and Safety Code, and any of the following:

(a) Dynamite, nitroglycerine, picric acid, lead azide, fulminate of mercury, black powder, smokeless powder, propellant explosives, detonating primers, blasting caps, commercial boosters, ammonium nitrate-fuel oil mixture (blasting agent), or any explosives as defined in Section 841 of Title 18 of the United States Code and published pursuant to Section 555.23 of Title 27 of the Code of Federal Regulations, when transported in a combined load with any explosive, as defined in this section.

(b) Substances determined to be division 1.1, 1.2, 1.3, or 1.6 explosives as classified by the United States Department of Transportation.

(c) "Explosive" or "explosives" does not include small arms ammunition or any other division 1.4 explosive.

(d) This division shall not apply to special fireworks classified by the United States Department of Transportation as division 1.2 or 1.3 explosives when those special fireworks are regulated by and in conformance with Part 2 (commencing with Section 12500) of Division 11 of the Health and Safety Code.

(e) Nothing in this chapter supersedes any regulations for the transportation of hazardous materials as defined in Section 2402.7 or as regulated in Division 14.1 (commencing with Section 32000).

Vehicle Code § 31601.

(a) This division shall apply to the operation of any motor vehicle on any highway, and to the operation and parking of any vehicle on any property designated pursuant to this division as a safe stopping place for the purpose of transporting any explosive in any amount when the transportation is rendered as a delivery service or for hire, or in any other event for the purpose of transporting any explosive or a combined load of any explosive and ammonium nitrate-fuel oil mixture (blasting agent) in an amount in excess of 1,000 pounds. The transportation of quantities of explosives of 1,000 pounds or less, or other than on a public highway, is governed by Division 11 (commencing at Section 12000) of the Health and Safety Code. Notwithstanding other provisions of this section, a license required by Section 31602 may be used to transport quantities of less than 1,000 pounds of explosives if all other requirements of this division are met.

(b) It is the legislative intention in enacting this division and with particular reference to requiring licenses for transportation of explosives as set forth herein that such provisions shall apply uniformly throughout the State of California and that such license to be obtained from the Department of the California Highway Patrol, as provided in Chapter 2.5 (commencing with Section 2500) of Division 2, shall be in lieu of any requirement for any license to be obtained by any such owner from any local authority within the state.

Vehicle Code § 31602.

(a) It is a misdemeanor for any owner of a vehicle to drive or permit the driving of the vehicle on any public highway for the purpose of transporting any explosive as defined herein and within the scope of Section 31601 unless the owner then holds a valid license for the transportation of explosives as provided in this division, except such persons as are expressly exempted in this division.

(b) It is a misdemeanor for the owner, or authorized agent of the owner, of any vehicle transporting explosives to drive, or to permit the driving of the vehicle, or for the driver to drive such vehicle, upon any public highway, not designated in regulations adopted by the Department of the California Highway Patrol as a route for the transportation of explosives, unless the use of the highway is required to permit delivery of, or the loading of, explosives at a point not on a highway designated as a route for the transportation of explosives, or unless the use of the highway is required to permit the vehicle to proceed to, and return from, a point designated as an inspection stop pursuant to this division.

(c) It is a misdemeanor for the driver of any vehicle transporting explosives to stop at any place not designated as a safe stopping place unless the vehicle is disabled or except when necessary to avoid conflict with other traffic or to comply with the orders of a peace officer or an official traffic control device. A safe stopping place is any location designated by the Department of the California Highway Patrol where the driver may stop for food, fuel or other necessary reasons and any location designated by the Department of the California Highway Patrol as a safe parking place, a safe stopping place, or as an inspection stop for purposes of this division.

(d) In the event the owner of a vehicle leases the same to be used in the transportation of explosives for which a license is required, the lessee shall be deemed the owner for the purposes of this division.

Vehicle Code § 31607.

(a) Any person operating or permitting the operation of a vehicle or combination of vehicles used in the transportation of explosives and subject to this division shall make or cause to be made an inspection of every said vehicle or combination of vehicles as hereinafter set forth.

(b) Such inspection as called for in Section 31608 shall be made immediately preceding the actual transportation of explosives by the vehicle and whenever there is an interchange of any vehicle operating in combination with any other vehicle in the transportation of explosives.

(c) Inspection of tires and brakes shall also be made en route at suitable intervals, off the roadway, at inspection stops established by the Department of the California Highway Patrol, at regular stops, terminal points, or driver-change points.

Vehicle Code § 31608.

The inspection of a vehicle required under subdivision (b) of Section 31607 shall include inspection of the following:

(a) Brakes and the brake system.

(b) The ignition and lighting systems.

(c) All tires on the equipment.

(d) All supplemental equipment as required by Section 31610.

Vehicle Code § 31609.

Every person operating a vehicle or combination of vehicles in the transportation of explosives subject to this division shall complete a record of every inspection which is required under Sections 31607 and 31608 in such form as approved by the Department of the California Highway Patrol showing the time and place of every inspection. The person making the inspection shall certify the fact in the record. The forms may be based upon the type used by the United States Department of Transportation. The record of every inspection shall be made at the time such inspection is conducted. The driver of the vehicle shall display the record upon demand of any member of the California Highway Patrol or any police officer of a city who is on duty for the exclusive or main purpose of enforcing the provisions of this code.

Vehicle Code § 31610.

Every vehicle or combination of vehicles used in the transportation of explosives and subject to this division, in addition to any other equipment required by law, shall be equipped and maintained as required by this section.

(a) Brakes and the brake system shall be maintained in good and safe operating condition.

(b) The ignition and lighting systems shall be maintained in good operating condition.

(c) All tires shall be in good condition, properly matched and inflated. Except as may be necessary to cause immediate replacement, no vehicle shall be driven unless all tires in actual use on the vehicle are properly inflated.

(d) Fire extinguishers and other safety equipment prescribed by regulations adopted by the department pursuant to subdivision (f) of Section 34500 and Section 34501 shall be carried in each vehicle or combination of vehicles.

(e) No flare, fusee, oil lantern, or any signal device producing a flame shall be carried upon any vehicle or combination of vehicles.

Vehicle Code § 31611.

Every owner of a vehicle used in the transportation of explosives and subject to this division shall make available in each vehicle the latest map showing the routes which are to be used for the transportation of explosives which has been furnished for the vehicle by the Department of the California Highway Patrol and a list of the safe stopping places prescribed by the regulations of the Department of the California Highway Patrol for vehicles transporting explosives. The owner shall require that the driver be thoroughly familiar with the provisions of this division before operating any vehicle in the transportation of explosives.

Vehicle Code § 31612.

Persons operating vehicles, or combinations of vehicles, in the transportation of explosives and subject to this division, shall not accept any explosives for transportation unless the shipment is accompanied by a bill of lading or other shipping paper supplied by the shipper, showing the kind of explosives and bearing a statement that they have been packaged, labeled and marked in accordance with regulations of the United States Department of Transportation, and the bill of lading or other shipping paper shall be carried in the vehicle while en route and shall be displayed upon demand of any member of the California Highway Patrol or any police officer of a city who is on duty for the exclusive or main purpose of enforcing the provisions of this code.

Vehicle Code § 31613.

There shall not be included in any cargo of explosives any flammable liquids, acids, or corrosive liquids, oxidizers, or combustible materials, other than the explosives themselves, which may have such characteristics. Blasting caps or detonators shall not be transported upon the same vehicle with other explosives, nor shall electric blasting caps be transported upon any vehicle equipped with a radio transmitter. The foregoing provisions of this section shall be subject to such exceptions as are permitted by the United States Department of Transportation loading chart for cargoes of explosives.

Vehicle Code § 31614.

The following provisions shall apply to any vehicle transporting explosives subject to this division:

(a) When transporting explosives through or into a city or any other congested area for which a route has not been designated by the Department of the California Highway Patrol, drivers shall follow such routes as may be prescribed or established by local authorities.

(b) Where routes are not prescribed by local authority, every driver of a vehicle transporting explosives shall avoid, so far as practicable, and, where feasible, by prearrangement of routes, driving into or through congested thoroughfares, places where crowds are assembled, streetcar tracks, tunnels, viaducts, and dangerous crossings.

(c) No driver or other person in charge of any vehicle on any public or private property shall permit any explosive to be loaded into, or on, or to be unloaded from any motor vehicle with the engine running, and, whenever any loading operation is in progress, the parking brake on the motor vehicle shall be securely set and all reasonable precautions taken to prevent movement of the motor vehicle during loading or unloading.

(d) No driver or other person in charge of such vehicle shall operate or permit the operation of any vehicle transporting explosives unless all of that portion of the lading which consists of explosives is contained entirely within the body of the motor vehicle or within the horizontal outline thereof, without overhang or projection of any part of the load, and if such motor vehicle has a tailboard or tailgate it shall be closed and secured in place during such transportation.

(e) Every motor vehicle transporting explosives shall have either a closed body or have the explosive cargo covered with a fire- and water-resistant tarpaulin, and in either event, care shall be taken to protect the load from moisture and sparks. Subject to other exceptions as are permitted by the United States Department of Transportation regulations, explosives may be transported on flat-bed vehicles if the explosive portion of the load on each vehicle is packed in fire- and water-resistant containers or covered with a fire- and water-resistant tarpaulin.

(f) No person shall operate any vehicle transporting explosives past any fire of any kind burning on or near the highway until the driver ascertains that such passing can be made with safety.

(g) No motor vehicle transporting explosives shall be left unattended upon any street or highway except in extreme emergency. The vehicle shall be deemed attended whenever a driver or person in charge thereof is in or upon the vehicle or is in a position to observe the vehicle at all times. The driver or person in charge of a vehicle transporting explosives may, however, leave the vehicle unattended at any place designated as a safe parking place on the list of safe stopping places prepared by the Department of the California Highway Patrol unless conditions exist, which are known to the driver, which make it unreasonable to do so.

(h) No driver or other person shall smoke or light any match or otherwise have or produce any fire or flame while in, upon, or near any vehicle transporting explosives.

(i) No person shall transport any explosives in a passenger vehicle, or bus, which is subject to this division.

Vehicle Code § 31615.

Nothing contained in this division shall be deemed to exempt any vehicle transporting explosives and subject to this division, or the owner or any other person, from other provisions of this code, but all such other provisions relating to the driving and movement of vehicles, the size, weight, and equipment thereof, shall be deemed to apply as applicable to each and every vehicle engaged in transporting explosives subject to this division.

Vehicle Code § 31616.

The Department of the California Highway Patrol, after consultation with the officials having the responsibility for the prevention and suppression of fire in communities through which routes for the transporting of explosives pass, representatives of transportation companies concerned, explosives manufacturers, and the State Fire Marshal shall, by regulation, designate the routes in this state which are to be used for the transportation of explosives. The Department of the California Highway Patrol shall prepare for distribution to persons engaged in the transportation of explosives, maps which clearly indicate the routes, as established in regulations, which are to be used for the transportation of explosives. The Department of the California Highway Patrol shall prepare for distribution to persons engaged in the transportation of explosives a list of locations of required inspection stops, safe parking places, and safe stopping places and shall revise the list to keep it current. Notwithstanding any other provision of law, regulations adopted pursuant to this section shall be adopted in accordance with Chapter 3.5 (commencing with Section 11340) of Part 1 of Division 3 of Title 2 of the Government Code, except that, for the purposes of subdivision (a) of Section 11346.4 of the Government Code, the public comment period shall be 30 days, and the regulations shall become effective upon filing with the Secretary of State. 31616.5. Notwithstanding Section 11349.3 of the Government Code, the review by the Office of Administrative Law of regulations adopted pursuant to Section 31616 shall be completed within 15 days after the regulations have been submitted to the Office of Administrative Law for review.

Vehicle Code § 31617.

In the event of an emergency, the Department of the California Highway Patrol is authorized to suspend or change any designated route for the transportation of explosives or to temporarily designate new or additional routes for such transportation. The Department of the California Highway Patrol shall, unless the nature of the emergency makes it impracticable to do so, consult with local fire officials in the area or areas affected before making any such changes or new designations. If the changes or new designations are made before they can be discussed with those officials, the Department of the California Highway Patrol shall immediately notify the appropriate officials of his action. The change in or new designation of routes shall not be effective for more than 90 days from the date of such action, unless the Department of the California Highway Patrol determines that the change or new designation should become permanent, in which case the Department of the California Highway Patrol shall, within the 90-day period, initiate action to make the change or new designation permanent in accordance with the provisions of Section 31616 and in which case the emergency change or designation shall remain in effect until superseded by a regulation of the Department of the California Highway Patrol.

Vehicle Code § 31618.

Where not specifically provided otherwise, it is a misdemeanor for any person to violate any provision of this division. Every person convicted of a misdemeanor for a violation of any of the provisions of this division shall be punished as follows:

(a) For a first violation, by a fine of not less than one thousand dollars ($1,000), or by imprisonment for not more than six months, or by both fine and imprisonment.

(b) For a second or subsequent violation, by a fine of not less than two thousand dollars ($2,000) or by imprisonment for not more than six months, or by both fine and imprisonment.

Vehicle Code § 31619.

When not in conflict with any local ordinance pertaining to the transportation of explosives, it shall be lawful to transport smokeless powder in an amount not exceeding 100 pounds if packed in containers prescribed by the United States Department of Transportation upon a highway not designated by the Department of the California Highway Patrol as a route for the transportation of explosives.

Vehicle Code § 31620.

The Department of the California Highway Patrol, upon application of any interested party, with the concurrence of the fire chief or chiefs in the area or areas affected, and if he determines that such action may be taken without jeopardizing the public safety, may suspend, or waive compliance with, the whole or any part of the requirements of this division insofar as they apply to the delivery or transportation of explosives in sparsely populated, unincorporated areas or in any area where there may be practical difficulties or unnecessary or unreasonable hardship in carrying out the provisions of this division. No person shall be charged with any crime for any violation of the provisions of this division when such a suspension or waiver by the Department of the California Highway Patrol is in effect in the area in which the alleged violation occurs.

Vehicle Code § 38318.

(a) Any person who throws any substance at an off-highway motor vehicle or occupant thereof is guilty of a misdemeanor and shall be punished pursuant to Section 42002 by a fine of not more than one thousand dollars ($1,000) or by imprisonment in the county jail for not more than six months, or by both the fine and imprisonment.

(b) Any person who, with intent to do great bodily injury, maliciously and willfully throws or projects any rock, brick, bottle, metal, or other missile, projects any other substance capable of doing serious bodily harm, or discharges a firearm at an off-highway motor vehicle or occupant thereof is guilty of a felony.

Vehicle Code § 40000.19.

A violation of any of the following provisions is a misdemeanor, and not an infraction:

(a) Section 31303, relating to transportation of hazardous waste.

(b) Division 14 (commencing with Section 31600), relating to transportation of explosives.

(c) Division 14.1 (commencing with Section 32000), relating to the transportation of hazardous material.

(d) Division 14.3 (commencing with Section 32100), relating to transportation of inhalation hazards.

(e) Division 14.5 (commencing with Section 33000), relating to transportation of radioactive materials.

(f) Division 14.7 (commencing with Section 34001), relating to flammable liquids.

Water Code

Water Code § 71660.

A district may construct, maintain, improve, and operate public recreational facilities appurtenant to facilities operated or contracted to be operated by the district. It may by ordinance provide regulations binding upon all persons to govern the use of such facilities, including regulations imposing reasonable charges for the use thereof. Violation of district regulations relating to vehicle or boat speed limits, defacement of district property, the use, possession or discharge of firearms, weapons or fireworks, the creation of fire hazards, being under the influence of intoxicating beverages or dangerous drugs, or remaining on, or reentering district premises after an authorized district officer or employee has specifically withdrawn consent for a person to utilize district facilities, is a misdemeanor. Violation of any other regulation of the district adopted pursuant to this section is an infraction.

Welfare and Institutions Code

Welfare and Institutions Code § 602.

(a) Except as provided in subdivision (b), any person who is under the age of 18 years when he or she violates any law of this state or of the United States or any ordinance of any city or county of this state defining crime other than an ordinance establishing a curfew based solely on age, is within the jurisdiction of the juvenile court, which may adjudge such person to be a ward of the court.

(b) Any person who is alleged, when he or she was 14 years of age or older, to have committed one of the following offenses shall be prosecuted under the general law in a court of criminal jurisdiction:

(1) Murder, as described in Section 187 of the Penal Code, if one of the circumstances enumerated in subdivision (a) of Section 190.2 of the Penal Code is alleged by the prosecutor, and the prosecutor alleges that the minor personally killed the victim.

(2) The following sex offenses, if the prosecutor alleges that the minor personally committed the offense, and if the prosecutor alleges one of the circumstances enumerated in the One Strike law, subdivision (d) or (e) of Section 667.61 of the Penal Code, applies:

(A) Rape, as described in paragraph (2) of subdivision (a) of Section 261 of the Penal Code.

(B) Spousal rape, as described in paragraph (1) of subdivision (a) of Section 262 of the Penal Code.

(C) Forcible sex offenses in concert with another, as described in Section 264.1 of the Penal Code.

(D) Forcible lewd and lascivious acts on a child under the age of 14 years, as described in subdivision (b) of Section 288 of the Penal Code.

(E) Forcible sexual penetration, as described in subdivision (a) of Section 289 of the Penal Code.

(F) Sodomy or oral copulation in violation of Section 286 or 288a of the Penal Code, by force, violence, duress, menace, or fear of immediate and unlawful bodily injury on the victim or another person.

(G) Lewd and lascivious acts on a child under the age of 14 years, as defined in subdivision (a) of Section 288, unless the defendant qualifies for probation under subdivision (c) of Section 1203.066 of the Penal Code.

Welfare and Institutions Code § 602.3.

(a) Notwithstanding any other law and pursuant to the provisions of this section, the juvenile court shall commit any minor adjudicated to be a ward of the court for the personal use of a firearm in the commission of a violent felony, as defined in subdivision (c) of Section 667.5 of the Penal Code, to placement in a juvenile hall, ranch, camp, or with the Department of the Youth Authority.

(b) A court may impose a treatment-based alternative placement order on any minor subject to this section if the court finds the minor has a mental disorder requiring intensive treatment. Any alternative placement order under this subdivision shall be made on the record, in writing, and in accordance with Article 3 (commencing with Section 6550) of Chapter 2 of Part 2 of Division 6.

Welfare and Institutions Code § 625.

A peace officer may, without a warrant, take into temporary custody a minor:

(a) Who is under the age of 18 years when such officer has reasonable cause for believing that such minor is a person described in Section 601 or 602, or

(b) Who is a ward of the juvenile court or concerning whom an order has been made under Section 636 or 702, when such officer has reasonable cause for believing that person has violated an order of the juvenile court or has escaped from any commitment ordered by the juvenile court, or

(c) Who is under the age of 18 years and who is found in any street or public place suffering from any sickness or injury which requires care, medical treatment, hospitalization, or other remedial care. In any case where a minor is taken into temporary custody on the ground that there is reasonable cause for believing that such minor is a person described in Section 601 or 602, or that he has violated an order of the juvenile court or escaped from any commitment ordered by the juvenile court, the officer shall advise such minor that anything he says can be used against him and shall advise him of his constitutional rights, including his right to remain silent, his right to have counsel present during any interrogation, and his right to have counsel appointed if he is unable to afford counsel.

Welfare and Institutions Code § 625.3.

Notwithstanding Section 625, a minor who is 14 years of age or older and who is taken into custody by a peace officer for the personal use of a firearm in the commission or attempted commission of a felony or any offense listed in subdivision (b) of Section 707 shall not be released until that minor is brought before a judicial officer.

Welfare and Institutions Code § 660.5.

(a) This section shall be known as the Expedited Youth Accountability Program. It shall be operative in the superior court in Los Angeles County. It shall also be operative in any other county in which a committee consisting of the sheriff, the chief probation officer, the district attorney, the public defender, and the presiding judge of the superior court votes to participate in the program, upon approval by the board of supervisors.

(b) It is the intent of the Legislature to hold nondetained, delinquent youth accountable for their crimes in a swift and certain manner.

(c) Each county participating in the Expedited Youth Accountability Program shall establish agreed upon time deadlines for law enforcement, probation, district attorney, and court functions which shall assure that a case which is to proceed pursuant to this section shall be ready to be heard within 60 calendar days after the minor is cited to the court.

(d)(1) Notwithstanding Sections 658, 659, and 660, if a minor is not detained for any misdemeanor or felony offense and is not cited to Informal Juvenile and Traffic Court pursuant to paragraphs (1) to (15), inclusive, of Section 256 and Section 853.6a of the Penal Code, the peace officer or probation officer releasing the minor shall issue a citation and obtain a written promise to appear in juvenile court, or record the minor's refusal to sign the promise to appear and serve a notice to appear in juvenile court. The appearance shall not be set for more than 60 calendar days nor less than 10 calendar days from the issuance of the citation. If the 60th day falls on a court holiday, the appearance date shall be on the next date that the court is in session. The date set for the appearance of the minor shall allow for sufficient time for the probation department to evaluate eligible minors for informal handling under Section 654 or any other disposition provided by law. However, nothing in this section shall be construed to limit or conflict with Sections 653.1 and 653.5.

(2) Upon receipt of the citation and petition, but in no event less than 72 hours, excluding nonjudicial days and holidays prior to the hearing, the clerk of the juvenile court shall issue a copy of the citation and petition to the public defender or the minor's attorney of record. If a copy of the citation and petition is not provided at least 72 hours, excluding nonjudicial days and holidays prior to the hearing, it shall be grounds to request a continuance pursuant to Sections 682 and 700. At a hearing conducted under Section 700, the minor and minor's parent or guardian shall be furnished a copy of the petition and any other material required to be provided under Section 659.

(3) The original citation and promise or notice to appear shall be retained by the court if a petition is filed. In addition, there shall be three copies of the citation and promise or notice to appear, which shall be distributed as follows:

(A) One copy shall be provided to the person to whom the citation is issued.

(B) One copy shall be provided to the probation department.

(C) If a petition is requested, the second copy of the citation shall go to the district attorney along with the petition request, and the third copy shall be retained by the agency issuing the citation.

(4) The original citation shall include a copy of all police reports relating to the citation and a petition request. The citation shall contain the following information:

(A) Date, time, and location of the issuance of the citation.

(B) The name, address, telephone number if known, driver's license number, age, date of birth, sex, race, height, weight, hair color, and color of eyes of the person to whom the citation is issued.

(C) A list of the offenses and the location where the offense or offenses were committed.

(D) Date and time of the required court appearance.

(E) Address of the juvenile court where the person to whom the citation is issued is to appear.

(F) A preprinted promise to appear which is signed by the person to whom the citation is issued, or where the person refused to sign the written promise, the notice to appear.

(G) A preprinted declaration under penalty of perjury that the above information is true and correct, signed by the peace officer or probation officer issuing the citation.

(H) A statement that the failure to appear is punishable as a misdemeanor.

(e) The minor's parent or guardian shall be issued a citation in the same manner as described in subdivision (b).

(f) The willful failure to appear in court pursuant to a citation or notice issued as required pursuant to this section is a misdemeanor.

(g)(1) Notwithstanding Section 662, if a parent or guardian to whom a citation has been issued pursuant to this section fails to appear, a warrant of arrest may issue for that person. A warrant of arrest may also issue for a parent or guardian who is not personally served where efforts to effect personal service have been unsuccessful, upon an affidavit, under penalty of perjury, signed by a peace officer stating facts sufficient to establish that all reasonable efforts to locate the person have failed or that the person has willfully evaded service of process.

(2) Notwithstanding Section 663, if a minor to whom a citation has been issued pursuant to this section fails to appear, and the minor' s parent or guardian has either appeared or the prerequisite conditions for issuing a warrant against the minor's parent or guardian under paragraph (1) have been met, a warrant of arrest may issue for the minor.

(3) A warrant of arrest may also issue for a minor who is not personally served where each of the following occur:

(A) Efforts to effect personal service have been unsuccessful.

(B) An affidavit is submitted under penalty of perjury, signed by a peace officer, stating facts sufficient to establish that all reasonable efforts to locate the minor have failed or that minor has willfully evaded service of process.

(C) The minor's parent or guardian has either appeared or the prerequisite conditions for issuing a warrant against the minor's parent or guardian under paragraph (1) have been met.

(h)(1) Notwithstanding Section 654 or any other provision of law, a probation officer in a county in which this subdivision is applicable may, in lieu of filing a petition or proceeding under Section 654, issue a citation in the form described in subdivision (d) to the Informal Juvenile and Traffic Court pursuant to Section 256 for any misdemeanor except the following:

(A) Any crime involving a firearm.

(B) Any crime involving violence.

(C) Any crime involving a sex-related offense.

(D) Any minor who has previously been declared a ward of the court.

(E) Any minor who has previously been referred to juvenile traffic court pursuant to this section.

(2) This subdivision shall apply only if the case will be heard by a juvenile hearing officer who meets the minimum qualifications of a juvenile court referee and only in those counties in which a committee consisting of the sheriff, the chief probation officer, the district attorney, the public defender, and the presiding judge of the superior court vote for this subdivision to apply and then only upon approval of the board of supervisors. This approval shall be required in Los Angeles and all other counties participating in the program, and shall be in addition to that required by subdivision (a) for participation in the Expedited Youth Accountability Program.

(3) In counties in which this subdivision is applicable, the probation department shall conduct a risk and needs assessment for each minor eligible for citation to the Informal Juvenile and Traffic Court pursuant to paragraph (1). The risk and needs assessment shall consider the best interest of the minor and the protection of the community. It shall also include an assessment of whether the child has any significant problems in the home, school, or community, whether the matter appears to have arisen from a temporary problem within the family which has been or can be resolved, and whether any agency or other resource in the community is better suited to serve the needs of the child, the parent or guardian, or both.

(i) In the event that the probation officer places a minor on informal probation or cites the minor to Informal Juvenile and Traffic Court, or elects some other lawful disposition not requiring the hearing set forth in subdivision (b), the probation officer shall so inform the minor and his or her parent or guardian no later than 72 hours, excluding nonjudicial days and holidays, prior to the hearing, that a court appearance is not required.

(j) Except as modified by this section, the requirements of this chapter shall remain in full force and effect.

(k) This section shall be operative on January 1, 1998, and shall be implemented in all branches of the juvenile court in Los Angeles County on or before July 1, 1998.

(l) It is the intent of the Legislature that an interim hearing be conducted by appropriate policy committees in the Legislature prior to January 1, 2002, to examine the success of the program in expediting punishment for juvenile offenses, reducing delinquent behavior, and promoting greater accountability on the part of juvenile offenders.

Welfare and Institutions Code § 675.

(a) All cases under the provisions of this chapter shall be heard at a special or separate session of the court, and no other matter shall be heard at that session. Except as provided in subdivision (b), no person on trial, awaiting trial, or under accusation of crime, other than a parent, guardian, or relative of the minor, shall be permitted to be present at any such session, except as a witness.

(b) Hearings for two or more minors may be heard upon the same rules of joinder, consolidation, and severance as apply to trials in a court of criminal jurisdiction.

Welfare and Institutions Code § 676.

(a) Unless requested by the minor concerning whom the petition has been filed and any parent or guardian present, the public shall not be admitted to a juvenile court hearing. Nothing in this section shall preclude the attendance of up to two family members of a prosecuting witness for the support of that witness, as authorized by Section 868.5 of the Penal Code. The judge or referee may nevertheless admit those persons he or she deems to have a direct and legitimate interest in the particular case or the work of the court. However, except as provided in subdivision (b), members of the public shall be admitted, on the same basis as they may be admitted to trials in a court of criminal jurisdiction, to hearings concerning petitions filed pursuant to Section 602 alleging that a minor is a person described in Section 602 by reason of the violation of any one of the following offenses:

(1) Murder.

(2) Arson of an inhabited building.

(3) Robbery while armed with a dangerous or deadly weapon.

(4) Rape with force or violence or threat of great bodily harm.

(5) Sodomy by force, violence, duress, menace, or threat of great bodily harm.

(6) Oral copulation by force, violence, duress, menace, or threat of great bodily harm.

(7) Any offense specified in subdivision (a) of Section 289 of the Penal Code.

(8) Kidnapping for ransom.

(9) Kidnapping for purpose of robbery.

(10) Kidnapping with bodily harm.

(11) Assault with intent to murder or attempted murder.

(12) Assault with a firearm or destructive device.

(13) Assault by any means of force likely to produce great bodily injury.

(14) Discharge of a firearm into an inhabited dwelling or occupied building.

(15) Any offense described in Section 1203.09 of the Penal Code. (16) Any offense described in Section 12022.5 or 12022.53 of the Penal Code.

(17) Any felony offense in which a minor personally used a weapon listed in subdivision (a) of Section 12020 of the Penal Code.

(18) Burglary of an inhabited dwelling house or trailer coach, as defined in Section 635 of the Vehicle Code, or the inhabited portion of any other building, if the minor previously has been adjudged a ward of the court by reason of the commission of any offense listed in this section, including an offense listed in this paragraph.

(19) Any felony offense described in Section 136.1 or 137 of the Penal Code.

(20) Any offense as specified in Sections 11351, 11351.5, 11352, 11378, 11378.5, 11379, and 11379.5 of the Health and Safety Code.

(21) Criminal street gang activity which constitutes a felony pursuant to Section 186.22 of the Penal Code.

(22) Manslaughter as specified in Section 192 of the Penal Code. (23) Driveby shooting or discharge of a weapon from or at a motor vehicle as specified in Sections 246, 247, and 12034 of the Penal Code.

(24) Any crime committed with an assault weapon, as defined in Section 12276 of the Penal Code, including possession of an assault weapon as specified in subdivision (b) of Section 12280 of the Penal Code.

(25) Carjacking, while armed with a dangerous or deadly weapon.

(26) Kidnapping, in violation of Section 209.5 of the Penal Code.

(27) Torture, as described in Sections 206 and 206.1 of the Penal Code.

(28) Aggravated mayhem, in violation of Section 205 of the Penal Code.

(b) Where the petition filed alleges that the minor is a person described in Section 602 by reason of the commission of rape with force or violence or great bodily harm; sodomy by force, violence, duress, menace, or threat of great bodily harm; oral copulation by force, violence, duress, menace, or threat of great bodily harm; or any offense specified in Section 289 of the Penal Code, members of the public shall not be admitted to the hearing in either of the following instances:

(1) Upon a motion for a closed hearing by the district attorney, who shall make the motion if so requested by the victim.

(2) During the victim's testimony, if, at the time of the offense the victim was under 16 years of age.

(c) The name of a minor found to have committed one of the offenses listed in subdivision (a) shall not be confidential, unless the court, for good cause, so orders. As used in this subdivision, "good cause" shall be limited to protecting the personal safety of the minor, a victim, or a member of the public. The court shall make a written finding, on the record, explaining why good cause exists to make the name of the minor confidential.

(d) Notwithstanding Sections 827 and 828 and subject to subdivisions (e) and (f), when a petition is sustained for any offense listed in subdivision (a), the charging petition, the minutes of the proceeding, and the orders of adjudication and disposition of the court that are contained in the court file shall be available for public inspection. Nothing in this subdivision shall be construed to authorize public access to any other documents in the court file.

(e) The probation officer or any party may petition the juvenile court to prohibit disclosure to the public of any file or record. The juvenile court shall prohibit the disclosure if it appears that the harm to the minor, victims, witnesses, or public from the public disclosure outweighs the benefit of public knowledge. However, the court shall not prohibit disclosure for the benefit of the minor unless the court makes a written finding that the reason for the prohibition is to protect the safety of the minor.

(f) Nothing in this section shall be applied to limit the disclosure of information as otherwise provided for by law.

(g) The juvenile court shall for each day that the court is in session, post in a conspicuous place which is accessible to the general public, a written list of hearings that are open to the general public pursuant to this section, the location of those hearings, and the time when the hearings will be held.

Welfare and Institutions Code § 707.

(a)(1) In any case in which a minor is alleged to be a person described in subdivision (a) of Section 602 by reason of the violation, when he or she was 16 years of age or older, of any criminal statute or ordinance except those listed in subdivision (b), upon motion of the petitioner made prior to the attachment of jeopardy the court shall cause the probation officer to investigate and submit a report on the behavioral patterns and social history of the minor being considered for a determination of unfitness. Following submission and consideration of the report, and of any other relevant evidence that the petitioner or the minor may wish to submit, the juvenile court may find that the minor is not a fit and proper subject to be dealt with under the juvenile court law if it concludes that the minor would not be amenable to the care, treatment, and training program available through the facilities of the juvenile court, based upon an evaluation of the following criteria:

(A) The degree of criminal sophistication exhibited by the minor.

(B) Whether the minor can be rehabilitated prior to the expiration of the juvenile court's jurisdiction.

(C) The minor's previous delinquent history.

(D) Success of previous attempts by the juvenile court to rehabilitate the minor.

(E) The circumstances and gravity of the offense alleged in the petition to have been committed by the minor. A determination that the minor is not a fit and proper subject to be dealt with under the juvenile court law may be based on any one or a combination of the factors set forth above, which shall be recited in the order of unfitness. In any case in which a hearing has been noticed pursuant to this section, the court shall postpone the taking of a plea to the petition until the conclusion of the fitness hearing, and no plea that may have been entered already shall constitute evidence at the hearing.

(2)(A) This paragraph shall apply to a minor alleged to be a person described in Section 602 by reason of the violation, when he or she has attained 16 years of age, of any felony offense when the minor has been declared to be a ward of the court pursuant to Section 602 on one or more prior occasions if both of the following apply:

(i) The minor has previously been found to have committed two or more felony offenses.

(ii) The offenses upon which the prior petition or petitions were based were committed when the minor had attained 14 years of age.

(B) Upon motion of the petitioner made prior to the attachment of jeopardy the court shall cause the probation officer to investigate and submit a report on the behavioral patterns and social history of the minor being considered for a determination of unfitness. Following submission and consideration of the report, and of any other relevant evidence that the petitioner or the minor may wish to submit, the minor shall be presumed to be not a fit and proper subject to be dealt with under the juvenile court law unless the juvenile court concludes, based upon evidence, which evidence may be of extenuating or mitigating circumstances, that the minor would be amenable to the care, treatment, and training program available through the facilities of the juvenile court based upon an evaluation of the following criteria:

(i) The degree of criminal sophistication exhibited by the minor.

(ii) Whether the minor can be rehabilitated prior to the expiration of the juvenile court's jurisdiction.

(iii) The minor's previous delinquent history.

(iv) Success of previous attempts by the juvenile court to rehabilitate the minor.

(v) The circumstances and gravity of the offense alleged in the petition to have been committed by the minor. A determination that the minor is a fit and proper subject to be dealt with under the juvenile court law shall be based on a finding of amenability after consideration of the criteria set forth above, and findings therefore recited in the order as to each of the above criteria that the minor is fit and proper under each and every one of the above criteria. In making a finding of fitness, the court may consider extenuating and mitigating circumstances in evaluating each of the above criteria. In any case in which the hearing has been noticed pursuant to this section, the court shall postpone the taking of a plea to the petition until the conclusion of the fitness hearing and no plea which may have been entered already shall constitute evidence at the hearing. If the minor is found to be a fit and proper subject to be dealt with under the juvenile court law pursuant to this subdivision, the minor shall be committed to placement in a juvenile hall, ranch camp, forestry camp, boot camp, or secure juvenile home pursuant to Section 730, or in any institution operated by the Department of Corrections and Rehabilitation, Division of Juvenile Facilities.

(3) If, pursuant to this subdivision, the minor is found to be not a fit and proper subject for juvenile court treatment and is tried in a court of criminal jurisdiction and found guilty by the trier of fact, the judge may commit the minor to the Department of Corrections and Rehabilitation, Division of Juvenile Facilities, in lieu of sentencing the minor to the state prison, unless the limitations specified in Section 1732.6 apply.

(b) Subdivision (c) shall be applicable in any case in which a minor is alleged to be a person described in Section 602 by reason of the violation of one of the following offenses:

(1) Murder.

(2) Arson, as provided in subdivision (a) or (b) of Section 451 of the Penal Code.

(3) Robbery.

(4) Rape with force, violence, or threat of great bodily harm.

(5) Sodomy by force, violence, duress, menace, or threat of great bodily harm.

(6) A lewd or lascivious act as provided in subdivision (b) of Section 288 of the Penal Code.

(7) Oral copulation by force, violence, duress, menace, or threat of great bodily harm.

(8) An offense specified in subdivision (a) of Section 289 of the Penal Code.

(9) Kidnapping for ransom.

(10) Kidnapping for purposes of robbery.

(11) Kidnapping with bodily harm.

(12) Attempted murder.

(13) Assault with a firearm or destructive device.

(14) Assault by any means of force likely to produce great bodily injury.

(15) Discharge of a firearm into an inhabited or occupied building.

(16) An offense described in Section 1203.09 of the Penal Code.

(17) An offense described in Section 12022.5 or 12022.53 of the Penal Code.

(18) A felony offense in which the minor personally used a weapon listed in subdivision (a) of Section 12020 of the Penal Code.

(19) A felony offense described in Section 136.1 or 137 of the Penal Code.

(20) Manufacturing, compounding, or selling one-half ounce or more of a salt or solution of a controlled substance specified in subdivision (e) of Section 11055 of the Health and Safety Code.

(21) A violent felony, as defined in subdivision (c) of Section 667.5 of the Penal Code, which also would constitute a felony violation of subdivision (b) of Section 186.22 of the Penal Code.

(22) Escape, by the use of force or violence, from a county juvenile hall, home, ranch, camp, or forestry camp in violation of subdivision (b) of Section 871 if great bodily injury is intentionally inflicted upon an employee of the juvenile facility during the commission of the escape.

(23) Torture as described in Sections 206 and 206.1 of the Penal Code.

(24) Aggravated mayhem, as described in Section 205 of the Penal Code.

(25) Carjacking, as described in Section 215 of the Penal Code, while armed with a dangerous or deadly weapon.

(26) Kidnapping for purposes of sexual assault, as punishable in subdivision (b) of Section 209 of the Penal Code.

(27) Kidnapping as punishable in Section 209.5 of the Penal Code.

(28) The offense described in subdivision (c) of Section 12034 of the Penal Code.

(29) The offense described in Section 12308 of the Penal Code.

(30) Voluntary manslaughter, as described in subdivision (a) of Section 192 of the Penal Code.

(c) With regard to a minor alleged to be a person described in Section 602 by reason of the violation, when he or she was 14 years of age or older, of any of the offenses listed in subdivision (b), upon motion of the petitioner made prior to the attachment of jeopardy the court shall cause the probation officer to investigate and submit a report on the behavioral patterns and social history of the minor being considered for a determination of unfitness. Following submission and consideration of the report, and of any other relevant evidence that the petitioner or the minor may wish to submit, the minor shall be presumed to be not a fit and proper subject to be dealt with under the juvenile court law unless the juvenile court concludes, based upon evidence, which evidence may be of extenuating or mitigating circumstances, that the minor would be amenable to the care, treatment, and training program available through the facilities of the juvenile court based upon an evaluation of each of the following criteria:

(1) The degree of criminal sophistication exhibited by the minor.

(2) Whether the minor can be rehabilitated prior to the expiration of the juvenile court's jurisdiction.

(3) The minor's previous delinquent history.

(4) Success of previous attempts by the juvenile court to rehabilitate the minor.

(5) The circumstances and gravity of the offenses alleged in the petition to have been committed by the minor. A determination that the minor is a fit and proper subject to be dealt with under the juvenile court law shall be based on a finding of amenability after consideration of the criteria set forth above, and findings therefore recited in the order as to each of the above criteria that the minor is fit and proper under each and every one of the above criteria. In making a finding of fitness, the court may consider extenuating or mitigating circumstances in evaluating each of the above criteria. In any case in which a hearing has been noticed pursuant to this section, the court shall postpone the taking of a plea to the petition until the conclusion of the fitness hearing and no plea which may have been entered already shall constitute evidence at the hearing. If, pursuant to this subdivision, the minor is found to be not a fit and proper subject for juvenile court treatment and is tried in a court of criminal jurisdiction and found guilty by the trier of fact, the judge may commit the minor to the Department of Corrections and Rehabilitation, Division of Juvenile Facilities, in lieu of sentencing the minor to the state prison, unless the limitations specified in Section 1732.6 apply.

(d)(1) Except as provided in subdivision (b) of Section 602, the district attorney or other appropriate prosecuting officer may file an accusatory pleading in a court of criminal jurisdiction against any minor 16 years of age or older who is accused of committing an offense enumerated in subdivision (b).

(2) Except as provided in subdivision (b) of Section 602, the district attorney or other appropriate prosecuting officer may file an accusatory pleading against a minor 14 years of age or older in a court of criminal jurisdiction in any case in which any one or more of the following circumstances apply:

(A) The minor is alleged to have committed an offense that if committed by an adult would be punishable by death or imprisonment in the state prison for life.

(B) The minor is alleged to have personally used a firearm during the commission or attempted commission of a felony, as described in Section 12022.5 or 12022.53 of the Penal Code.

(C) The minor is alleged to have committed an offense listed in subdivision (b) in which any one or more of the following circumstances apply:

(i) The minor has previously been found to be a person described in Section 602 by reason of the commission of an offense listed in subdivision (b).

(ii) The offense was committed for the benefit of, at the direction of, or in association with any criminal street gang, as defined in subdivision (f) of Section 186.22 of the Penal Code, with the specific intent to promote, further, or assist in criminal conduct by gang members.

(iii) The offense was committed for the purpose of intimidating or interfering with any other person's free exercise or enjoyment of a right secured to him or her by the Constitution or laws of this state or by the Constitution or laws of the United States and because of the other person's race, color, religion, ancestry, national origin, disability, gender, or sexual orientation, or because the minor perceives that the other person has one or more of those characteristics, as described in Title 11.6 (commencing with Section 422.55) of Part 1 of the Penal Code.

(iv) The victim of the offense was 65 years of age or older, or blind, deaf, quadriplegic, paraplegic, developmentally disabled, or confined to a wheelchair, and that disability was known or reasonably should have been known to the minor at the time of the commission of the offense.

(3) Except as provided in subdivision (b) of Section 602, the district attorney or other appropriate prosecuting officer may file an accusatory pleading in a court of criminal jurisdiction against any minor 16 years of age or older who is accused of committing one or more of the following offenses, if the minor has previously been found to be a person described in Section 602 by reason of the violation of a felony offense, when he or she was 14 years of age or older:

(A) A felony offense in which it is alleged that the victim of the offense was 65 years of age or older, or blind, deaf, quadriplegic, paraplegic, developmentally disabled, or confined to a wheelchair, and that disability was known or reasonably should have been known to the minor at the time of the commission of the offense.

(B) A felony offense committed for the purposes of intimidating or interfering with any other person's free exercise or enjoyment of a right secured to him or her by the Constitution or laws of this state or by the Constitution or laws of the United States and because of the other person's race, color, religion, ancestry, national origin, disability, gender, or sexual orientation, or because the minor perceived that the other person had one or more of those characteristics, as described in Title 11.6 (commencing with Section 422.55) of Part 1 of the Penal Code.

(C) The offense was committed for the benefit of, at the direction of, or in association with any criminal street gang as prohibited by Section 186.22 of the Penal Code.

(4) In any case in which the district attorney or other appropriate prosecuting officer has filed an accusatory pleading against a minor in a court of criminal jurisdiction pursuant to this subdivision, the case shall then proceed according to the laws applicable to a criminal case. In conjunction with the preliminary hearing as provided in Section 738 of the Penal Code, the magistrate shall make a finding that reasonable cause exists to believe that the minor comes within this subdivision. If reasonable cause is not established, the criminal court shall transfer the case to the juvenile court having jurisdiction over the matter.

(5) For an offense for which the prosecutor may file the accusatory pleading in a court of criminal jurisdiction pursuant to this subdivision, but elects instead to file a petition in the juvenile court, if the minor is subsequently found to be a person described in subdivision (a) of Section 602, the minor shall be committed to placement in a juvenile hall, ranch camp, forestry camp, boot camp, or secure juvenile home pursuant to Section 730, or in any institution operated by the Department of Corrections and Rehabilitation, Division of Juvenile Facilities.

(6) If, pursuant to this subdivision, the minor is found to be not a fit and proper subject for juvenile court treatment and is tried in a court of criminal jurisdiction and found guilty by the trier of fact, the judge may commit the minor to the Department of Corrections and Rehabilitation, Division of Juvenile Facilities, in lieu of sentencing the minor to the state prison, unless the limitations specified in Section 1732.6 apply.

(e) A report submitted by a probation officer pursuant to this section regarding the behavioral patterns and social history of the minor being considered for a determination of unfitness shall include any written or oral statement offered by the victim, the victim's parent or guardian if the victim is a minor, or if the victim has died, the victim's next of kin, as authorized by subdivision (b) of Section 656.2. Victims' statements shall be considered by the court to the extent they are relevant to the court's determination of unfitness.

Welfare and Institutions Code § 871.5.

(a) Except as authorized by law, or when authorized by the person in charge of any county juvenile hall, ranch, camp, or forestry camp, or by an officer of any juvenile hall or camp empowered by the person in charge to give that authorization, any person who knowingly brings or sends into, or who knowingly assists in bringing into, or sending into, any county juvenile hall, ranch, camp, or forestry camp, or any person who while confined in any of those institutions possesses therein, any controlled substance, the possession of which is prohibited by Division 10 (commencing with Section 11000) of the Health and Safety Code, any firearm, weapon, or explosive of any kind, or any tear gas or tear gas weapon shall be punished by imprisonment in a county jail for not more than one year or by imprisonment in the state prison.

(b) Except as otherwise authorized in the manner provided in subdivision (a), any person who knowingly uses tear gas or uses a tear gas weapon in an institution or camp specified in subdivision (a) is guilty of a felony.

(c) A sign shall be posted at the entrance of each county juvenile hall, ranch, camp, or forestry camp specifying the conduct prohibited by this section and the penalties therefor.

(d) Except as otherwise authorized in the manner provided in subdivision (a), any person who knowingly brings or sends into, or who knowingly assists in bringing into, or sending into, any county juvenile hall, ranch, camp, or forestry camp, or any person who while confined in such an institution knowingly possesses therein, any alcoholic beverage shall be guilty of a misdemeanor.

(e) This section shall not be construed to preclude or in any way limit the applicability of any other law proscribing a course of conduct also proscribed by this section.

Welfare and Institutions Code § 1000.

Commencing July 1, 2005, any reference to the Department of the Youth Authority refers to the Department of Corrections and Rehabilitation, Division of Juvenile Facilities, which has jurisdiction over all educational training and treatment institutions now or hereafter established and maintained in the state as correctional schools for the reception of wards of the juvenile court and other persons committed to the department.

Welfare and Institutions Code § 1001.5.

(a) Except when authorized by law, or when authorized by the person in charge of an institution or camp administered by the Youth Authority, or by an officer of the institution or camp empowered by the person in charge of the institution or camp to give that authorization, any person who knowingly brings or sends into, or who knowingly assists in bringing into, or sending into, any institution or camp, or the grounds belonging to any institution or camp, administered by the Youth Authority, or any person who, while confined in the institution or camp knowingly possesses therein, any controlled substance, the possession of which is prohibited by Division 10 (commencing with Section 11000) of the Health and Safety Code; any alcoholic beverage; any firearm, weapon or explosive of any kind; or any tear gas or tear gas weapon shall be punished by imprisonment in a county jail for not more than one year or by imprisonment in the state prison.

(b) Except as otherwise authorized in the manner provided in subdivision (a), any person who knowingly uses tear gas or uses a tear gas weapon in any institution or camp specified in subdivision (a) is guilty of a felony.

(c) This section shall not be construed to preclude or in any way limit the applicability of any other law proscribing a course of conduct also proscribed by this section.

Welfare and Institutions Code § 1768.8.

(a) An assault or battery by any person confined in an institution under the jurisdiction of the Department of the Youth Authority upon the person of any individual who is not confined therein shall be punishable by a fine not exceeding two thousand dollars ($2,000), or by imprisonment in the county jail not exceeding one year, or by both a fine and imprisonment.

(b) An assault by any person confined in an institution under the jurisdiction of the Department of the Youth Authority upon the person of any individual who is not confined therein, with a deadly weapon or instrument, or by any means of force likely to produce great bodily injury, is a felony punishable by imprisonment in the state prison for two, four, or six years.

Welfare and Institutions Code § 5350.

A conservator of the person, of the estate, or of the person and the estate may be appointed for any person who is gravely disabled as a result of mental disorder or impairment by chronic alcoholism. The procedure for establishing, administering, and terminating a conservatorship under this chapter shall be the same as that provided in Division 4 (commencing with Section 1400) of the Probate Code, except as follows:

(a) A conservator may be appointed for a gravely disabled minor.

(b)(1) Appointment of a conservator under this part, including the appointment of a conservator for a person who is gravely disabled, as defined in subparagraph (A) of paragraph (1) of subdivision (h) of Section 5008, shall be subject to the list of priorities in Section 1812 of the Probate Code unless the officer providing conservatorship investigation recommends otherwise to the superior court.

(2) In appointing a conservator, as defined in subparagraph (B) of paragraph (1) of subdivision (h) of Section 5008, the court shall consider the purposes of protection of the public and the treatment of the conservatee. Notwithstanding any other provision of this section, the court shall not appoint the proposed conservator if the court determines that appointment of the proposed conservator will not result in adequate protection of the public.

(c) No conservatorship of the estate pursuant to this chapter shall be established if a conservatorship or guardianship of the estate exists under the Probate Code. When a gravely disabled person already has a guardian or conservator of the person appointed under the Probate Code, the proceedings under this chapter shall not terminate the prior proceedings but shall be concurrent with and superior thereto. The superior court may appoint the existing guardian or conservator of the person or another person as conservator of the person under this chapter.

(d) The person for whom conservatorship is sought shall have the right to demand a court or jury trial on the issue whether he or she is gravely disabled. Demand for court or jury trial shall be made within five days following the hearing on the conservatorship petition. If the proposed conservatee demands a court or jury trial before the date of the hearing as provided for in Section 5365, the demand shall constitute a waiver of the hearing. Court or jury trial shall commence within 10 days of the date of the demand, except that the court shall continue the trial date for a period not to exceed 15 days upon the request of counsel for the proposed conservatee. This right shall also apply in subsequent proceedings to reestablish conservatorship.

(e)(1) Notwithstanding subparagraph (A) of paragraph (1) of subdivision (h) of Section 5008, a person is not "gravely disabled" if that person can survive safely without involuntary detention with the help of responsible family, friends, or others who are both willing and able to help provide for the person's basic personal needs for food, clothing, or shelter.

(2) However, unless they specifically indicate in writing their willingness and ability to help, family, friends, or others shall not be considered willing or able to provide this help.

(3) The purpose of this subdivision is to avoid the necessity for, and the harmful effects of, requiring family, friends, and others to publicly state, and requiring the court to publicly find, that no one is willing or able to assist the mentally disordered person in providing for the person's basic needs for food, clothing, or shelter.

(4) This subdivision does not apply to a person who is gravely disabled, as defined in subparagraph (B) of paragraph (1) of subdivision (h) of Section 5008.

(f) Conservatorship investigation shall be conducted pursuant to this part and shall not be subject to Section 1826 or Chapter 2 (commencing with Section 1850) of Part 3 of Division 4 of the Probate Code.

(g) Notice of proceedings under this chapter shall be given to a guardian or conservator of the person or estate of the proposed conservatee appointed under the Probate Code.

(h) As otherwise provided in this chapter.

Welfare and Institutions Code § 5357.

All conservators of the estate shall have the general powers specified in Chapter 6 (commencing with Section 2400) of Part 4 of Division 4 of the Probate Code and shall have the additional powers specified in Article 11 (commencing with Section 2590) of Chapter 6 of Part 4 of Division 4 of the Probate Code as the court may designate. The report shall set forth which, if any, of the additional powers it recommends. The report shall also recommend for or against the imposition of each of the following disabilities on the proposed conservatee:

(a) The privilege of possessing a license to operate a motor vehicle. If the report recommends against this right and if the court follows the recommendation, the agency providing conservatorship investigation shall, upon the appointment of the conservator, so notify the Department of Motor Vehicles.

(b) The right to enter into contracts. The officer may recommend against the person having the right to enter specified types of transactions or transactions in excess of specified money amounts.

(c) The disqualification of the person from voting pursuant to Section 2208 of the Elections Code.

(d) The right to refuse or consent to treatment related specifically to the conservatee's being gravely disabled. The conservatee shall retain all rights specified in Section 5325.

(e) The right to refuse or consent to routine medical treatment unrelated to remedying or preventing the recurrence of the conservatee's being gravely disabled. The court shall make a specific determination regarding imposition of this disability.

(f) The disqualification of the person from possessing a firearm pursuant to subdivision (e) of Section 8103.

Welfare and Institutions Code § 6500.

On and after July 1, 1971, no mentally retarded person may be committed to the State Department of Developmental Services pursuant to this article, unless he or she is a danger to himself or herself, or others. For the purposes of this article, dangerousness to self or others shall be considered to include, but not be limited to, a finding of incompetence to stand trial pursuant to the provisions of Chapter 6 (commencing with Section 1367) of Title 10 of Part 2 of the Penal Code when the defendant has been charged with murder, mayhem, aggravated mayhem, a violation of Section 207, 209, or 209.5 of the Penal Code in which the victim suffers intentionally inflicted great bodily injury, robbery perpetrated by torture or by a person armed with a dangerous or deadly weapon or in which the victim suffers great bodily injury, carjacking perpetrated by torture or by a person armed with a dangerous or deadly weapon or in which the victim suffers great bodily injury, a violation of subdivision (b) of Section 451 of the Penal Code, a violation of paragraph (1) or (2) of subdivision (a) of Section 262 or paragraph (2) or (3) of subdivision (a) of Section 261 of the Penal Code, a violation of Section 288 of the Penal Code, any of the following acts when committed by force, violence, duress, menace, fear of immediate and unlawful bodily injury on the victim or another person: a violation of paragraph (1) or (2) of subdivision (a) of Section 262 of the Penal Code, a violation of Section 264.1, 286, or 288a of the Penal Code, or a violation of subdivision (a) of Section 289 of the Penal Code; a violation of Section 459 of the Penal Code in the first degree, assault with intent to commit murder, a violation of Section 220 of the Penal Code in which the victim suffers great bodily injury, a violation of Section 12303.1, 12303.3, 12308, 12309, or 12310 of the Penal Code, or if the defendant has been charged with a felony involving death, great bodily injury, or an act which poses a serious threat of bodily harm to another person. If the mentally retarded person is in the care or treatment of a state hospital, developmental center, or other facility at the time a petition for commitment is filed pursuant to this article, proof of a recent overt act while in the care and treatment of a state hospital, developmental center, or other facility is not required in order to find that the person is a danger to self or others. Any order of commitment made pursuant to this article shall expire automatically one year after the order of commitment is made. This section shall not be construed to prohibit any party enumerated in Section 6502 from filing subsequent petitions for additional periods of commitment. In the event subsequent petitions are filed, the procedures followed shall be the same as with an initial petition for commitment. In any proceedings conducted under the authority of this article, the alleged mentally retarded person shall be informed of his or her right to counsel by the court, and if the person does not have an attorney for the proceedings, the court shall immediately appoint the public defender or other attorney to represent him or her. The person shall pay the cost for the legal services if he or she is able to do so. At any judicial proceeding under the provisions of this article, allegations that a person is mentally retarded and a danger to himself or herself or to others shall be presented by the district attorney for the county unless the board of supervisors, by ordinance or resolution, delegates this authority to the county counsel.

Welfare and Institutions Code § 8100.

(a) A person shall not have in his or her possession or under his or her custody or control, or purchase or receive, or attempt to purchase or receive, any firearms whatsoever or any other deadly weapon, if on or after January 1, 1992, he or she has been admitted to a facility and is receiving inpatient treatment and, in the opinion of the attending health professional who is primarily responsible for the patient's treatment of a mental disorder, is a danger to self or others, as specified by Section 5150, 5250, or 5300, even though the patient has consented to that treatment. A person is not subject to this subdivision once he or she is discharged from the facility.

(b)(1) A person shall not have in his or her possession or under his or her custody or control, or purchase or receive, or attempt to purchase or receive, any firearms whatsoever or any other deadly weapon for a period of six months whenever, on or after January 1, 1992, he or she communicates to a licensed psychotherapist, as defined in subdivisions (a) to (e), inclusive, of Section 1010 of the Evidence Code, a serious threat of physical violence against a reasonably identifiable victim or victims. The six-month period shall commence from the date that the licensed psychotherapist reports to the local law enforcement agency the identity of the person making the communication. The prohibition provided for in this subdivision shall not apply unless the licensed psychotherapist notifies a local law enforcement agency of the threat by that person. The person, however, may own, possess, have custody or control over, or receive or purchase any firearm if a superior court, pursuant to paragraph (3) and upon petition of the person, has found, by a preponderance of the evidence, that the person is likely to use firearms or other deadly weapons in a safe and lawful manner.

(2) Upon receipt of the report from the local law enforcement agency pursuant to subdivision (c) of Section 8105, the Department of Justice shall notify by certified mail, return receipt requested, a person subject to this subdivision of the following:

(A) That he or she is prohibited from possessing, having custody or control over, receiving, or purchasing any firearm or other deadly weapon for a period of six months commencing from the date that the licensed psychotherapist reports to the local law enforcement agency the identity of the person making the communication. The notice shall state the date when the prohibition commences and ends.

(B) That he or she may petition a court, as provided in this subdivision, for an order permitting the person to own, possess, control, receive, or purchase a firearm.

(3) Any person who is subject to paragraph (1) may petition the superior court of his or her county of residence for an order that he or she may own, possess, have custody or control over, receive, or purchase firearms. At the time the petition is filed, the clerk of the court shall set a hearing date and notify the person, the Department of Justice, and the district attorney. The people of the State of California shall be the respondent in the proceeding and shall be represented by the district attorney. Upon motion of the district attorney, or upon its own motion, the superior court may transfer the petition to the county in which the person resided at the time of the statements, or the county in which the person made the statements. Within seven days after receiving notice of the petition, the Department of Justice shall file copies of the reports described in Section 8105 with the superior court. The reports shall be disclosed upon request to the person and to the district attorney. The district attorney shall be entitled to a continuance of the hearing to a date of not less than 14 days after the district attorney is notified of the hearing date by the clerk of the court. The court, upon motion of the petitioner establishing that confidential information is likely to be discussed during the hearing that would cause harm to the person, shall conduct the hearing in camera with only the relevant parties present, unless the court finds that the public interest would be better served by conducting the hearing in public. Notwithstanding any other provision of law, declarations, police reports, including criminal history information, and any other material and relevant evidence that is not excluded under Section 352 of the Evidence Code, shall be admissible at the hearing under this paragraph. If the court finds by a preponderance of the evidence that the person would be likely to use firearms in a safe and lawful manner, the court shall order that the person may have custody or control over, receive, possess, or purchase firearms. A copy of the order shall be submitted to the Department of Justice. Upon receipt of the order, the department shall delete any reference to the prohibition against firearms from the person's state summary criminal history information.

(c) "Discharge," for the purposes of this section, does not include a leave of absence from a facility.

(d) "Attending health care professional," as used in this section, means the licensed health care professional primarily responsible for the person's treatment who is qualified to make the decision that the person has a mental disorder and has probable cause to believe that the person is a danger to self or others.

(e) "Deadly weapon," as used in this section and in Sections 8101, 8102, and 8103, means any weapon, the possession or concealed carrying of which is prohibited by Section 12020 of the Penal Code.

(f) "Danger to self," as used in subdivision (a), means a voluntary person who has made a serious threat of, or attempted, suicide with the use of a firearm or other deadly weapon.

(g) A violation of subdivision (a) of, or paragraph (1) of subdivision (b) of, this section shall be a public offense, punishable by imprisonment in the state prison, or in a county jail for not more than one year, by a fine not exceeding one thousand dollars ($1,000), or by both that imprisonment and fine.

(h) The prohibitions set forth in this section shall be in addition to those set forth in Section 8103.

(i) Any person admitted and receiving treatment prior to January 1, 1992, shall be governed by this section, as amended by Chapter 1090 of the Statutes of 1990, until discharged from the facility.

Welfare and Institutions Code § 8101.

(a) Any person who shall knowingly supply, sell, give, or allow possession or control of a deadly weapon to any person described in Section 8100 or 8103 shall be punishable by imprisonment in the state prison, or in a county jail for a period of not exceeding one year, by a fine of not exceeding one thousand dollars ($1,000), or by both the fine and imprisonment.

(b) Any person who shall knowingly supply, sell, give, or allow possession or control of a firearm to any person described in Section 8100 or 8103 shall be punished by imprisonment in the state prison for two, three, or four years.

(c) "Deadly weapon," as used in this section has the meaning prescribed by Section 8100.

Welfare and Institutions Code § 8102.

(a) Whenever a person, who has been detained or apprehended for examination of his or her mental condition or who is a person described in Section 8100 or 8103, is found to own, have in his or her possession or under his or her control, any firearm whatsoever, or any other deadly weapon, the firearm or other deadly weapon shall be confiscated by any law enforcement agency or peace officer, who shall retain custody of the firearm or other deadly weapon. "Deadly weapon," as used in this section, has the meaning prescribed by Section 8100.

(b) Upon confiscation of any firearm or other deadly weapon from a person who has been detained or apprehended for examination of his or her mental condition, the peace officer or law enforcement agency shall notify the person of the procedure for the return of any firearm or other deadly weapon which has been confiscated. Where the person is released, the professional person in charge of the facility, or his or her designee, shall notify the person of the procedure for the return of any firearm or other deadly weapon which may have been confiscated. Health facility personnel shall notify the confiscating law enforcement agency upon release of the detained person, and shall make a notation to the effect that the facility provided the required notice to the person regarding the procedure to obtain return of any confiscated firearm.

(c) Upon the release of a person as described in subdivision (b), the confiscating law enforcement agency shall have 30 days to initiate a petition in the superior court for a hearing to determine whether the return of a firearm or other deadly weapon would be likely to result in endangering the person or others, and to send a notice advising the person of his or her right to a hearing on this issue. The law enforcement agency may make an ex parte application stating good cause for an order extending the time to file a petition. Including any extension of time granted in response to an ex parte request, a petition must be filed within 60 days of the release of the person from a health facility.

(d) If the law enforcement agency does not initiate proceedings within the 30-day period, or the period of time authorized by the court in an ex parte order issued pursuant to subdivision (c), it shall make the weapon available for return.

(e) The law enforcement agency shall inform the person that he or she has 30 days to respond to the court clerk to confirm his or her desire for a hearing, and that the failure to respond will result in a default order forfeiting the confiscated firearm or weapon. For the purpose of this subdivision, the person's last known address shall be the address provided to the law enforcement officer by the person at the time of the person's detention or apprehension.

(f) If the person responds and requests a hearing, the court clerk shall set a hearing, no later than 30 days from receipt of the request. The court clerk shall notify the person and the district attorney of the date, time, and place of the hearing.

(g) If the person does not respond within 30 days of the notice, the law enforcement agency may file a petition for order of default.

Welfare and Institutions Code § 8103.

(a)(1) No person who after October 1, 1955, has been adjudicated by a court of any state to be a danger to others as a result of a mental disorder or mental illness, or who has been adjudicated to be a mentally disordered sex offender, shall purchase or receive, or attempt to purchase or receive, or have in his or her possession, custody, or control any firearm or any other deadly weapon unless there has been issued to the person a certificate by the court of adjudication upon release from treatment or at a later date stating that the person may possess a firearm or any other deadly weapon without endangering others, and the person has not, subsequent to the issuance of the certificate, again been adjudicated by a court to be a danger to others as a result of a mental disorder or mental illness.

(2) The court shall immediately notify the Department of Justice of the court order finding the individual to be a person described in paragraph (1). The court shall also notify the Department of Justice of any certificate issued as described in paragraph (1).

(b)(1) No person who has been found, pursuant to Section 1026 of the Penal Code or the law of any other state or the United States, not guilty by reason of insanity of murder, mayhem, a violation of Section 207, 209, or 209.5 of the Penal Code in which the victim suffers intentionally inflicted great bodily injury, carjacking or robbery in which the victim suffers great bodily injury, a violation of Section 451 or 452 of the Penal Code involving a trailer coach, as defined in Section 635 of the Vehicle Code, or any dwelling house, a violation of paragraph (1) or (2) of subdivision (a) of Section 262 or paragraph (2) or (3) of subdivision (a) of Section 261 of the Penal Code, a violation of Section 459 of the Penal Code in the first degree, assault with intent to commit murder, a violation of Section 220 of the Penal Code in which the victim suffers great bodily injury, a violation of Section 12303.1, 12303.2, 12303.3, 12308, 12309, or 12310 of the Penal Code, or of a felony involving death, great bodily injury, or an act which poses a serious threat of bodily harm to another person, or a violation of the law of any other state or the United States that includes all the elements of any of the above felonies as defined under California law, shall purchase or receive, or attempt to purchase or receive, or have in his or her possession or under his or her custody or control any firearm or any other deadly weapon.

(2) The court shall immediately notify the Department of Justice of the court order finding the person to be a person described in paragraph (1).

(c)(1) No person who has been found, pursuant to Section 1026 of the Penal Code or the law of any other state or the United States, not guilty by reason of insanity of any crime other than those described in subdivision (b) shall purchase or receive, or attempt to purchase or receive, or shall have in his or her possession, custody, or control any firearm or any other deadly weapon unless the court of commitment has found the person to have recovered sanity, pursuant to Section 1026.2 of the Penal Code or the law of any other state or the United States.

(2) The court shall immediately notify the Department of Justice of the court order finding the person to be a person described in paragraph (1). The court shall also notify the Department of Justice when it finds that the person has recovered his or her sanity.

(d)(1) No person found by a court to be mentally incompetent to stand trial, pursuant to Section 1370 or 1370.1 of the Penal Code or the law of any other state or the United States, shall purchase or receive, or attempt to purchase or receive, or shall have in his or her possession, custody, or control any firearm or any other deadly weapon, unless there has been a finding with respect to the person of restoration to competence to stand trial by the committing court, pursuant to Section 1372 of the Penal Code or the law of any other state or the United States.

(2) The court shall immediately notify the Department of Justice of the court order finding the person to be mentally incompetent as described in paragraph (1). The court shall also notify the Department of Justice when it finds that the person has recovered his or her competence.

(e)(1) No person who has been placed under conservatorship by a court, pursuant to Section 5350 or the law of any other state or the United States, because the person is gravely disabled as a result of a mental disorder or impairment by chronic alcoholism shall purchase or receive, or attempt to purchase or receive, or shall have in his or her possession, custody, or control any firearm or any other deadly weapon while under the conservatorship if, at the time the conservatorship was ordered or thereafter, the court which imposed the conservatorship found that possession of a firearm or any other deadly weapon by the person would present a danger to the safety of the person or to others. Upon placing any person under conservatorship, and prohibiting firearm or any other deadly weapon possession by the person, the court shall notify the person of this prohibition.

(2) The court shall immediately notify the Department of Justice of the court order placing the person under conservatorship and prohibiting firearm or any other deadly weapon possession by the person as described in paragraph (1). The notice shall include the date the conservatorship was imposed and the date the conservatorship is to be terminated. If the conservatorship is subsequently terminated before the date listed in the notice to the Department of Justice or the court subsequently finds that possession of a firearm or any other deadly weapon by the person would no longer present a danger to the safety of the person or others, the court shall immediately notify the Department of Justice.

(3) All information provided to the Department of Justice pursuant to paragraph (2) shall be kept confidential, separate, and apart from all other records maintained by the Department of Justice, and shall be used only to determine eligibility to purchase or possess firearms or other deadly weapons. Any person who knowingly furnishes that information for any other purpose is guilty of a misdemeanor. All the information concerning any person shall be destroyed upon receipt by the Department of Justice of notice of the termination of conservatorship as to that person pursuant to paragraph (2).

(f)(1) No person who has been (A) taken into custody as provided in Section 5150 because that person is a danger to himself, herself, or to others, (B) assessed within the meaning of Section 5151, and (C) admitted to a designated facility within the meaning of Sections 5151 and 5152 because that person is a danger to himself, herself, or others, shall own, possess, control, receive, or purchase, or attempt to own, possess, control, receive, or purchase any firearm for a period of five years after the person is released from the facility. A person described in the preceding sentence, however, may own, possess, control, receive, or purchase, or attempt to own, possess, control, receive, or purchase any firearm if the superior court has, pursuant to paragraph (5), found that the People of the State of California have not met their burden pursuant to paragraph (6).

(2) For each person subject to this subdivision, the facility shall immediately, on the date of admission, submit a report to the Department of Justice, on a form prescribed by the Department of Justice, containing information that includes, but is not limited to, the identity of the person and the legal grounds upon which the person was admitted to the facility. Any report prescribed by this subdivision shall be confidential, except for purposes of the court proceedings described in this subdivision and for determining the eligibility of the person to own, possess, control, receive, or purchase a firearm.

(3) Prior to, or concurrent with, the discharge, the facility shall inform a person subject to this subdivision that he or she is prohibited from owning, possessing, controlling, receiving, or purchasing any firearm for a period of five years. Simultaneously, the facility shall inform the person that he or she may request a hearing from a court, as provided in this subdivision, for an order permitting the person to own, possess, control, receive, or purchase a firearm. The facility shall provide the person with a form for a request for a hearing. The Department of Justice shall prescribe the form. Where the person requests a hearing at the time of discharge, the facility shall forward the form to the superior court unless the person states that he or she will submit the form to the superior court.

(4) The Department of Justice shall provide the form upon request to any person described in paragraph (1). The Department of Justice shall also provide the form to the superior court in each county. A person described in paragraph (1) may make a single request for a hearing at any time during the five-year period. The request for hearing shall be made on the form prescribed by the department or in a document that includes equivalent language.

(5) Any person who is subject to paragraph (1) who has requested a hearing from the superior court of his or her county of residence for an order that he or she may own, possess, control, receive, or purchase firearms shall be given a hearing. The clerk of the court shall set a hearing date and notify the person, the Department of Justice, and the district attorney. The People of the State of California shall be the plaintiff in the proceeding and shall be represented by the district attorney. Upon motion of the district attorney, or on its own motion, the superior court may transfer the hearing to the county in which the person resided at the time of his or her detention, the county in which the person was detained, or the county in which the person was evaluated or treated. Within seven days after the request for a hearing, the Department of Justice shall file copies of the reports described in this section with the superior court. The reports shall be disclosed upon request to the person and to the district attorney. The court shall set the hearing within 30 days of receipt of the request for a hearing. Upon showing good cause, the district attorney shall be entitled to a continuance not to exceed 14 days after the district attorney was notified of the hearing date by the clerk of the court. If additional continuances are granted, the total length of time for continuances shall not exceed 60 days. The district attorney may notify the county mental health director of the hearing who shall provide information about the detention of the person that may be relevant to the court and shall file that information with the superior court. That information shall be disclosed to the person and to the district attorney. The court, upon motion of the person subject to paragraph (1) establishing that confidential information is likely to be discussed during the hearing that would cause harm to the person, shall conduct the hearing in camera with only the relevant parties present, unless the court finds that the public interest would be better served by conducting the hearing in public. Notwithstanding any other law, declarations, police reports, including criminal history information, and any other material and relevant evidence that is not excluded under Section 352 of the Evidence Code, shall be admissible at the hearing under this section.

(6) The people shall bear the burden of showing by a preponderance of the evidence that the person would not be likely to use firearms in a safe and lawful manner.

(7) If the court finds at the hearing set forth in paragraph (5) that the people have not met their burden as set forth in paragraph (6), the court shall order that the person shall not be subject to the five-year prohibition in this section on the ownership, control, receipt, possession or purchase of firearms. A copy of the order shall be submitted to the Department of Justice. Upon receipt of the order, the Department of Justice shall delete any reference to the prohibition against firearms from the person's state mental health firearms prohibition system information.

(8) Where the district attorney declines or fails to go forward in the hearing, the court shall order that the person shall not be subject to the five-year prohibition required by this subdivision on the ownership, control, receipt, possession, or purchase of firearms. A copy of the order shall be submitted to the Department of Justice. Upon receipt of the order, the Department of Justice shall, within 15 days, delete any reference to the prohibition against firearms from the person's state mental health firearms prohibition system information.

(9) Nothing in this subdivision shall prohibit the use of reports filed pursuant to this section to determine the eligibility of persons to own, possess, control, receive, or purchase a firearm if the person is the subject of a criminal investigation, a part of which involves the ownership, possession, control, receipt, or purchase of a firearm.

(g)(1) No person who has been certified for intensive treatment under Section 5250, 5260, or 5270.15 shall own, possess, control, receive, or purchase, or attempt to own, possess, control, receive, or purchase any firearm for a period of five years. Any person who meets the criteria contained in subdivision (e) or (f) who is released from intensive treatment shall nevertheless, if applicable, remain subject to the prohibition contained in subdivision (e) or (f).

(2) For each person certified for intensive treatment under paragraph (1), the facility shall immediately submit a report to the Department of Justice, on a form prescribed by the department, containing information regarding the person, including, but not limited to, the legal identity of the person and the legal grounds upon which the person was certified. Any report submitted pursuant to this paragraph shall only be used for the purposes specified in paragraph (2) of subdivision (f).

(3) Prior to, or concurrent with, the discharge of each person certified for intensive treatment under paragraph (1), the facility shall inform the person of that information specified in paragraph (3) of subdivision (f).

(4) Any person who is subject to paragraph (1) may petition the superior court of his or her county of residence for an order that he or she may own, possess, control, receive, or purchase firearms. At the time the petition is filed, the clerk of the court shall set

a hearing date and notify the person, the Department of Justice, and the district attorney. The People of the State of California shall be the respondent in the proceeding and shall be represented by the district attorney. Upon motion of the district attorney, or on its own motion, the superior court may transfer the petition to the county in which the person resided at the time of his or her detention, the county in which the person was detained, or the county in which the person was evaluated or treated. Within seven days after receiving notice of the petition, the Department of Justice shall file copies of the reports described in this section with the superior court. The reports shall be disclosed upon request to the person and to the district attorney. The district attorney shall be entitled to a continuance of the hearing to a date of not less than 14 days after the district attorney was notified of the hearing date by the clerk of the court. The district attorney may notify the county mental health director of the petition, and the county mental health director shall provide information about the detention of the person that may be relevant to the court and shall file that information with the superior court. That information shall be disclosed to the person and to the district attorney. The court, upon motion of the person subject to paragraph (1) establishing that confidential information is likely to be discussed during the hearing that would cause harm to the person, shall conduct the hearing in camera with only the relevant parties present, unless the court finds that the public interest would be better served by conducting the hearing in public. Notwithstanding any other provision of law, any declaration, police reports, including criminal history information, and any other material and relevant evidence that is not excluded under Section 352 of the Evidence Code, shall be admissible at the hearing under this section. If the court finds by a preponderance of the evidence that the person would be likely to use firearms in a safe and lawful manner, the court may order that the person may own, control, receive, possess, or purchase firearms. A copy of the order shall be submitted to the Department of Justice. Upon receipt of the order, the Department of Justice shall delete any reference to the prohibition against firearms from the person's state mental health firearms prohibition system information.

(h) For all persons identified in subdivisions (f) and (g), facilities shall report to the Department of Justice as specified in those subdivisions, except facilities shall not report persons under subdivision (g) if the same persons previously have been reported under subdivision (f). Additionally, all facilities shall report to the Department of Justice upon the discharge of persons from whom reports have been submitted pursuant to subdivision (f) or (g). However, a report shall not be filed for persons who are discharged within 31 days after the date of admission.

(i) Every person who owns or possesses or has under his or her custody or control, or purchases or receives, or attempts to purchase or receive, any firearm or any other deadly weapon in violation of this section shall be punished by imprisonment in the state prison or in a county jail for not more than one year.

(j) "Deadly weapon," as used in this section, has the meaning prescribed by Section 8100.

Welfare and Institutions Code § 8104.

The State Department of Mental Health shall maintain in a convenient central location and shall make available to the Department of Justice those records that the State Department of Mental Health has in its possession that are necessary to identify persons who come within Section 8100 or 8103. These records shall be made available to the Department of Justice upon request. The Department of Justice shall make these requests only with respect to its duties with regard to applications for permits for, or to carry, or the possession, purchase, or transfer of, explosives as defined in Section 12000 of the Health and Safety Code, devices defined in Section 12001 of the Penal Code, machineguns as defined in Section 12200 of the Penal Code, short-barreled shotguns or short-barreled rifles as defined in Section 12020 of the Penal Code, assault weapons as defined in Section 12276 of the Penal Code, and destructive devices as defined in Section 12301 of the Penal Code, or to determine the eligibility of a person to acquire, carry, or possess a firearm, explosive, or destructive device by a person who is subject to a criminal investigation, a part of which involves the acquisition, carrying, or possession of a firearm by that person. These records shall not be furnished or made available to any person unless the department determines that disclosure of any information in the records is necessary to carry out its duties with respect to applications for permits for, or to carry, or the possession, purchase, or transfer of, explosives, destructive devices, devices as defined in Section 12001 of the Penal Code, short-barreled shotguns, short-barreled rifles, assault weapons, and machineguns, or to determine the eligibility of a person to acquire, carry, or possess a firearm, explosive, or destructive device by a person who is subject to a criminal investigation, a part of which involves the acquisition, carrying, or possession of a firearm by that person.

Welfare and Institutions Code § 8105.

(a) The Department of Justice shall request each public and private mental hospital, sanitarium, and institution to submit to the department that information that the department deems necessary to identify those persons who are within subdivision (a) of Section 8100, in order to carry out its duties in relation to firearms, destructive devices, and explosives.

(b) Upon request of the Department of Justice pursuant to subdivision (a), each public and private mental hospital, sanitarium, and institution shall submit to the department that information which the department deems necessary to identify those persons who are within subdivision (a) of Section 8100, in order to carry out its duties in relation to firearms, destructive devices, and explosives.

(c) A licensed psychotherapist shall immediately report to a local law enforcement agency the identity of a person subject to subdivision (b) of Section 8100. Upon receipt of the report, the local law enforcement agency, on a form prescribed by the Department of Justice, shall immediately notify the department of the person who is subject to subdivision (b) of Section 8100.

(d) All information provided to the Department of Justice pursuant to this section shall be kept confidential, separate and apart from all other records maintained by the department. The information provided to the Department of Justice pursuant to this section shall be used only for any of the following purposes:

(1) By the department to determine eligibility of a person to acquire, carry, or possess firearms, destructive devices, or explosives.

(2) For the purposes of the court proceedings described in subdivision (b) of Section 8100 to determine the eligibility of the person who is bringing the petition pursuant to paragraph (3) of subdivision (b) of Section 8100.

(3) To determine the eligibility of a person to acquire, carry, or possess firearms, destructive devices, or explosives who is the subject of a criminal investigation, if a part of the criminal investigation involves the acquisition, carrying, or possession of firearms, explosives, or destructive devices by that person.

(e) Reports shall not be required or requested under this section where the same person has been previously reported pursuant to Section 8103 or 8104.

Welfare and Institutions Code § 8108.

Mental hospitals, health facilities, or other institutions, or treating health professionals or psychotherapists who provide reports subject to this chapter shall be civilly immune for making any report required or authorized by this chapter. This section is declaratory of existing law.

Welfare and Institutions Code § 15610.07.

"Abuse of an elder or a dependent adult" means either of the following:

(a) Physical abuse, neglect, financial abuse, abandonment, isolation, abduction, or other treatment with resulting physical harm or pain or mental suffering.

(b) The deprivation by a care custodian of goods or services that are necessary to avoid physical harm or mental suffering.

Welfare and Institutions Code § 15657.03.

(a) An elder or dependent adult who has suffered abuse as defined in Section 15610.07 may seek protective orders as provided in this section.

(b) For the purposes of this section, "protective order" means an order that includes any of the following restraining orders, whether issued ex parte, after notice and hearing, or in a judgment:

(1) An order enjoining a party from abusing, intimidating, molesting, attacking, striking, stalking, threatening, sexually assaulting, battering, harassing, telephoning, including, but not limited to, annoying telephone calls as described in Section 653m of the Penal Code, destroying personal property, contacting, either directly or indirectly, by mail or otherwise, or coming within a specified distance of, or disturbing the peace of the petitioner.

(2) An order excluding a party from the petitioner's residence or dwelling, except that this order shall not be issued if legal or equitable title to, or lease of, the residence or dwelling is in the sole name of the party to be excluded, or is in the name of the party to be excluded and any other party besides the petitioner.

(3) An order enjoining a party from specified behavior that the court determines is necessary to effectuate orders described in paragraph (1) or (2).

(c) An order may be issued under this section, with or without notice, to restrain any person for the purpose of preventing a recurrence of abuse, if an affidavit shows, to the satisfaction of the court, reasonable proof of a past act or acts of abuse of the petitioning elder or dependent adult.

(d)(1) Upon filing a petition for protective orders under this section, the petitioner may obtain a temporary restraining order in accordance with Section 527 of the Code of Civil Procedure, except to the extent this section provides a rule that is inconsistent. The temporary restraining order may include any of the protective orders described in subdivision (b). However, the court may issue an ex parte order excluding a party from the petitioner's residence or dwelling only on a showing of all of the following:

(A) Facts sufficient for the court to ascertain that the party who will stay in the dwelling has a right under color of law to possession of the premises.

(B) That the party to be excluded has assaulted or threatens to assault the petitioner.

(C) That physical or emotional harm would otherwise result to the petitioner.

(2) If a temporary restraining order is granted without notice, the matter shall be made returnable on an order requiring cause to be shown why a permanent order should not be granted, on the earliest day that the business of the court will permit, but not later than 20 days or, if good cause appears to the court, 25 days from the date the temporary restraining order is granted, unless the order is otherwise modified or terminated by the court.

(e) The court may issue, upon notice and a hearing, any of the orders set forth in subdivision (b). The court may issue, after notice and hearing, an order excluding a person from a residence or dwelling if the court finds that physical or emotional harm would otherwise result to the petitioner.

(f) In the discretion of the court, an order issued after notice and a hearing under this section may have a duration of not more than three years, subject to termination or modification by further order of the court either on written stipulation filed with the court or on the motion of a party. These orders may be renewed upon the request of a party, either for three years or permanently, without a showing of any further abuse since the issuance of the original order, subject to termination or modification by further order of the court either on written stipulation filed with the court or on the motion of a party. The failure to state the expiration date on the face of the form creates an order with a duration of three years from the date of issuance.

(g) Upon the filing of a petition for protective orders under this section, the respondent shall be personally served with a copy of the petition, notice of the hearing or order to show cause, temporary restraining order, if any, and any affidavits in support of the petition. Service shall be made at least five days before the hearing. The court may, on motion of the petitioner or on its own motion, shorten the time for service on the respondent.

(h) The court may, upon the filing of an affidavit by the applicant that the respondent could not be served within the time required by statute, reissue an order previously issued and dissolved by the court for failure to serve the respondent. The reissued order shall be made returnable on the earliest day that the business of the court will permit, but not later than 20 days or, if good cause appears to the court, 25 days from the date of reissuance. The reissued order shall state on its face the date of expiration of the order.

(i)(1) If the person named in a temporary restraining order is personally served with the order and notice of hearing with respect to a restraining order or protective order based thereon, but the person does not appear at the hearing, either personally or by counsel, and the terms and conditions of the restraining order or protective order are identical to the temporary restraining order, except for the duration of the order, then the restraining order or protective order may be served on the person by first-class mail sent to that person at the most current address for the person available to the court.

(2) The judicial form for orders issued pursuant to this subdivision shall contain a statement in substantially the following form: "NO ADDITIONAL PROOF OF SERVICE IS REQUIRED IF THE FACE OF THIS FORM INDICATES THAT BOTH PARTIES WERE

PERSONALLY PRESENT AT THE HEARING WHERE THE ORDER WAS ISSUED. IF YOU HAVE BEEN PERSONALLY SERVED WITH A TEMPORARY RESTRAINING ORDER OR EMERGENCY PROTECTIVE ORDER AND NOTICE OF HEARING, BUT YOU DO NOT APPEAR AT THE HEARING EITHER IN PERSON OR BY COUNSEL, AND A RESTRAINING ORDER OR PROTECTIVE ORDER IS ISSUED AT THE HEARING THAT DOES NOT DIFFER FROM THE PRIOR TEMPORARY RESTRAINING ORDER OR EMERGENCY PROTECTIVE ORDER, A COPY OF THE ORDER WILL BE SERVED UPON YOU BY MAIL AT THE FOLLOWING ADDRESS ____. IF THAT ADDRESS IS NOT CORRECT OR YOU WISH TO VERIFY THAT THE TEMPORARY OR EMERGENCY ORDER WAS MADE PERMANENT WITHOUT SUBSTANTIVE CHANGE, CALL THE CLERK OF THE COURT AT ____."

(j)(1) The court shall order the petitioner or the attorney for the petitioner to deliver, or the clerk of the court to mail, a copy of an order issued under this section, or a reissuance, extension, modification, or termination of the order, and any subsequent proof of service, by the close of the business day on which the order, reissuance, extension, modification, or termination was made, to each local law enforcement agency designated by the petitioner or the attorney for the petitioner having jurisdiction over the residence of the petitioner, and to any additional law enforcement agencies within the court's discretion as are requested by the petitioner. Each appropriate law enforcement agency shall make available information as to the existence and current status of these orders to law enforcement officers responding to the scene of reported abuse.

(2) An order issued under this section shall, on request of the petitioner, be served on the respondent, whether or not the respondent has been taken into custody, by any law enforcement officer who is present at the scene of reported abuse involving the parties to the proceeding. The petitioner shall provide the officer with an endorsed copy of the order and a proof of service, which the officer shall complete and send to the issuing court.

(3) Upon receiving information at the scene of an incident of abuse that a protective order has been issued under this section, or that a person who has been taken into custody is the respondent to that order, if the protected person cannot produce an endorsed copy of the order, a law enforcement officer shall immediately attempt to verify the existence of the order.

(4) If the law enforcement officer determines that a protective order has been issued, but not served, the officer shall immediately notify the respondent of the terms of the order and where a written copy of the order can be obtained, and the officer shall at that time also enforce the order. The law enforcement officer's verbal notice of the terms of the order shall constitute service of the order and is sufficient notice for the purposes of this section and for the purposes of Section 273.6 of the Penal Code.

(k) Nothing in this section shall preclude either party from representation by private counsel or from appearing on the party's own behalf.

(l) There is no filing fee for a petition, response, or paper seeking the reissuance, modification, or enforcement of a protective order filed in a proceeding brought pursuant to this section.

(m) Pursuant to paragraph (4) of subdivision (b) of Section 6103.2 of the Government Code, a petitioner shall not be required to pay a fee for law enforcement to serve an order issued under this chapter.

(n) The prevailing party in any action brought under this section may be awarded court costs and attorney's fees, if any.

(o)(1) An order issued pursuant to this section shall prohibit the person subject to it from owning, possessing, purchasing, receiving, or attempting to purchase or receive, a firearm.

(2) Paragraph (1) shall not apply to a case consisting solely of financial abuse unaccompanied by force, threat, harassment, intimidation, or any other form of abuse.

(3) The court shall order a person subject to a protective order issued under this section to relinquish any firearms he or she owns or possesses pursuant to Section 527.9 of the Code of Civil Procedure.

(4) Every person who owns, possesses, purchases, or receives, or attempts to purchase or receive a firearm while the protective order is in effect is punishable pursuant to subdivision (g) of Section 12021 of the Penal Code.

(p) Any willful disobedience of any temporary restraining order or restraining order after hearing granted under this section is punishable pursuant to Section 273.6 of the Penal Code.

(q) This section does not apply to any action or proceeding covered by Title 1.6C (commencing with Section 1788) of Part 4 of Division 3 of the Civil Code, by Chapter 3 (commencing with Section 525) of Title 7 of Part 2 of the Code of Civil Procedure, or by Division 10 (commencing with Section 6200) of the Family Code. Nothing in this section shall preclude a petitioner's right to use other existing civil remedies.

(r) The Judicial Council shall promulgate forms and instructions therefor, rules for service of process, scheduling of hearings, and any other matters required by this section. The petition and response forms shall be simple and concise.

(s) This section shall remain in effect only until January 1, 2010, and as of that date is repealed, unless a later enacted statute, that is enacted before January 1, 2010, deletes or extends that date.

Welfare and Institutions Code § 16507.7.

Each agency or entity, except for a community college, which offers a parenting course as part of a family maintenance or family reunification effort for a parent or parents of a child who has been adjudicated or is in the process of being adjudicated a dependent child of the court under Section 300, or whose family is participating in a voluntary family maintenance program, shall meet all of the requirements specified in this section. Effective July 1, 1992, organizations which receive state funding for the purpose of providing parenting courses shall meet those requirements as a condition of receiving state funding. The requirements are as follows:

(a) Each parenting course shall be no more than six months in duration, and shall meet for a specified number of hours determined by each program as sufficient for the program to meet all of the requirements listed in subdivision (b).

(b) The curriculum shall include all of the following components:

(1) Building self-esteem, including, but not limited to, parents' building a positive parental identity and building the self-esteem of their children.

(2) Handling stress and anger.

(3) The growth and development of children, including, but not limited to, safety, nutrition, and health.

(4) Developing and increasing communication skills in order that a parent may learn to listen to and speak with his or her child or children.

(5) Learning to use positive disciplinary mechanisms as alternatives to the physical punishment of a child, including, but not limited to, learning what constitutes abuse and neglect.

(6) Learning the boundaries of permissible sexual conduct by adults with regard to children.

(7) Respect for, and sensitivity to, cultural differences in child rearing practices in addressing all of the topics listed in paragraphs (1) to (6), inclusive.

(c) Each parenting course is encouraged to have a maximum parent to teacher ratio of 15 parents for each teacher.

(d) Each parenting course is encouraged to conduct an initial assessment and interview of each parent enrolled in the course.

(e) Each parenting course shall give a preliminary examination prior to the start of the parenting course and an examination at the conclusion of the parenting course to measure changes in parental attitudes.

(f) Each parenting course shall enter into a written agreement with each parent with respect to the responsibilities a parent must satisfy in order to pass the course.

(g) The staff of each parenting course shall have training in the following areas:

(1) The prevention of child abuse and neglect.

(2) Parenting techniques.

(h) Each parenting course shall provide all of the following information to the county welfare department of the county in which the course is taught, for clients referred through child welfare services programs:

(1) Level of participation by parents.

(2) Number of course hours completed.

(3) Topics covered during attendance in class by a parent and topics covered during a parent's absence from class.

(4) Assessment of a parent's gain in his or her knowledge about parenting as demonstrated by tests prior to and after the parenting course.

Appendix Three

Famous Gun Quotes

"A free people ought to be armed." - George Washington

"That rifle on the wall of the labourer's cottage or working class flat is the symbol of democracy. It is our job to see that it stays there." - George Orwell

"Our task of creating a Socialist America can only succeed when those who resist us are totally disarmed." - Sarah Brady

"Firearms are second only to the Constitution in importance; they are the peoples' liberty's teeth." - George Washington

"...the right to defend one's home and one's person when attacked has been guaranteed through the ages by common law." Martin Luther King

" A free people ought not only to be armed and disciplined, but they should have sufficient arms and ammunition to maintain a status of independence from any who might attempt to abuse them, which would include their own government." - George Washington

"If I could have banned them all - Mr. And Mrs. America turn in your guns - I would have!" - Diane Feinstein

"A woman who demands further gun control legislation is like a chicken who roots for Colonel Sanders." - Larry Elder

"Those who would give up essential liberty to purchase a little temporary safety, deserve neither liberty nor safety." - Benjamin Franklin

"But if someone has a gun and is trying to kill you...it would be reasonable to shoot back with your own gun." Dalai Lama

"The strongest reason for people to retain the right to keep and bear arms is, as a last resort, to protect themselves against tyranny in government." - Thomas Jefferson

"We would just go out and line up a bunch of cans and shoot with rifles, handguns, and at times, submachine guns...When I wa a kid it was a controlled atmosphere, we weren't shooting at humans...we were shooting at cans and bottles mostly. I will certainly take my kids out for target practice." - Johnny Depp

"My view of guns is simple. I hate guns and I cannot imagine why anyone would want to own one. If I had my way, guns for sport would be registered, and all other guns would be banned." - Deborah Prothrow-Stith, Dean of Harvard School of Public Health

"No free man shall ever be debarred the use of arms." - Thomas Jefferson

"The laws that forbid the carrying of arms are laws of such a nature. They disarm only those who are neither inclined nor determined to commit crimes.... Such laws make things worse for the assaulted and better for the assailants; they serve rather to encourage than to prevent homicides, for an unarmed man may be attacked with greater confidence than an armed man." - Thomas Jefferson quoting Cesare Beccaria

"Among other evils which being unarmed brings you, it causes you to be despised." - Charlton Heston

"A strong body makes the mind strong. As to the species of exercises, I advise the gun. While this gives moderate exercise to the body, it gives boldness, enterprise and independence to the mind. Games played with the ball, and others of that nature, are too violent for the body and stamp no character on the mind. Let your gun therefore be your constant companion of your walks." - Thomas Jefferson

"There are no dangerous weapons. There are only dangerous men." - Robert A. Heinlein

The Constitution of most of our states (and of the United States) assert that all power is inherent in the people; that they may exercise it by themselves; that it is their right and duty to be at all times armed." - Thomas Jefferson

"Arms in the hands of citizens may be used at individual discretion in private self defense." - John Adams

"An armed society is a polite society." - Robert A. Heinlein

"All political power comes from the barrel of a gun. The communist party must command all the guns, that way, no guns may ever be used to command the party." - Mao Tse Tung

"To disarm the people is the most effectual way to enslave them." - George Mason

"A fear of weapons is a sign of retarded sexual and emotional maturity." - Sigmund Freud

"I ask sir, what is the militia? It is the whole people except for a few politicians." - George Mason

To my mind it is wholly irresponsible to go into the world incapable of preventing violence, injury, crime, and death. How feeble is the mindset to accept defenselessness. How unnatural. How cheap. How cowardly. How pathetic." - Ted Nugent

"All we ask for is registration, just like we do for cars." - Charles Schumer

"Before a standing army can rule, the people must be disarmed, as they are in almost every country in Europe." - Noah Webster

"There are hundreds of millions of gun owners in this country, and not one of them will have an accident today. The only misuse of guns comes in environments where there are drugs, alcohol, bad parents, and undisciplined children. Period." - Ted Nugent

"Good intentions will always be pleaded for every assumption of authority....The Constitution was made to guard against the dangers of good intentions. There are men in all ages who mean to govern well, but they mean to govern. They promise to be good masters, but they mean to be masters." - Noah Webster

"I have a love interest in every one of my films - a gun." - Arnold Schwarzenegger

"When we got organized as a country, [and] wrote a fairly radical Constitution, with a radical Bill of Rights, giving radical amounts of freedom to Americans, it was assumed that Americans who had that freedom would use it responsibly....When personal freedom is being abused, you have to move to limit it." - Bill Clinton

"The supreme power in America cannot enforce unjust laws by the sword; because the whole body of the people are armed, and constitute a force superior to any band of regular troops." - Noah Webster

"The most foolish mistake we could possibly make would be to allow the subject races to possess arms. History shows that all conquerors who have allowed their subject races to carry arms have prepared their own downfall by so doing. Indeed, I would go so far as to say that the supply of arms to the underdogs is a sine qua non for the overthrow of any sovereignty." - Adolf Hitler

"I have a very strict gun control policy: if there's a gun around, I want to be in control of it." - Clint Eastwood

"A government resting on the minority is an aristocracy, not a Republic, and could not be safe with a numerical and physical force against it, without a standing army, an enslaved press and a disarmed populace." - James Madison

"Waiting periods are only a step. Registration is only a step. The prohibition of private firearms is the goal." - Attorney General Janet Reno

"The world is filled with violence. Because criminals carry guns, we decent law-abiding citizens should also have guns. Otherwise, they will win and the decent people will lose." - James Earl Jones

"Americans have the right and advantage of being armed, unlike the peoples of other countries, whose leaders are afraid to trust them with arms." - James Madison

"The right of the people to keep and bear arms shall not be infringed. A well regulated militia, composed of the body of the people, trained to arms, is the best and most natural defense of a free country." - James Madison

"The measures adopted to restore public order are: First of all, the elimination of the so-called subversive elements....They were elements of disorder and subversion. On the morrow of each conflict I gave the categorical order to confiscate the largest possible number of weapons of every sort and kind. This confiscation, which continues with the utmost energy, has given satisfactory results." - Benito Mussolini

"The ultimate authority resides in the people alone." - James Madison

"Necessity is the plea for every infringement of human freedom. It is the argument of tyrants; it is the creed of slaves." - William Pitt

"To preserve liberty, it is essential that the whole body of the people always possess arms, and be taught alike, especially when young, how to use them." - Richard Henry Lee

"I don't care about crime; I just want to get the guns." - Senator Howard Metzenbaum

"A militia, when properly formed, are in fact the people themselves....and include all men capable of bearing arms." - Richard Henry Lee

"Guard with jealous attention the public liberty. Suspect everyone who approaches that jewel. Unfortunately, nothing will preserve it but downright force, you are ruined....The great object is that every man be armed. Everyone who is able might have a gun." - Patrick Henry

"This may be considered as the true palladium of liberty....The right of self defense is the first law of nature: in most governments it has been the study of rulers to confine this right within the narrowest limits possible. Wherever standing armies are kept up, and the right of the people to keep and bear arms is, under any color or pretext whatsoever, prohibited, liberty, if not already annihilated, is on the brink of destruction." - St. George Tucker

"We are bending the law as far as we can to ban an entirely new class of guns." - Rahm Emmanuel

"The Constitution shall never be construed to prevent the people of the United States who are peaceable citizens from keeping their own arms." - Samuel Adams

"The right of the citizens to keep and bear arms has been justly considered, as the palladium of the liberties of the republic; since it offers a strong moral check against the usurpation and arbitrary power of rulers; and will generally, even if these are successful in the first instance, enable the people to resist and triumph over them." - Joseph Story

""What, Sir, is the use of a militia? It is to prevent the establishment of a standing army, the bane of liberty....Whenever Governments mean to invade the rights and liberties of the people, they always attempt to destroy the militia, in order to raise an army upon their ruins." - Elbridge Gerry

"...for it is a truth, which the experience of all ages has attested, that the people are commonly most in danger when the means of insuring their rights are in the possession of those of whom they entertain the least suspicion." - Alexander Hamilton

"You cannot invade the mainland United States. There would be a rifle behind each blade of grass." Admiral Isoroku Yamamoto

"We must get rid of all the guns." - Sarah Brady

"If the constitutional right to keep and bear arms is to mean anything, it must, as a general matter, permit a person to possess, carry and sometimes conceal arms to maintain the security of his private residence or privately operated business." David Prosser, Wisconsin Supreme Court Justice

"If the opposition disarms, well and good. If it refuses to disarm, we shall disarm it ourselves." - Joseph Stalin

"As a card-carrying member of the liberal media, producing this piece was an eye opening experience. I have to admit that I saw guns as inherently evil, violence begets violence, and so on. I have learned, however, that in trained hands, just the presence of a gun can be a real "man stopper." I am sorry that women have had to resort to this, but wishing it wasn't so won't make it any safer out there." - Jill Fieldstein, CBS Producer of Street Stories: Women and Guns

"Gun control? It's the best thing you can do for crooks and gangsters. I want you to have nothing. If I'm the bad guy, I'm always gonna have a gun. Safety locks? You can pull the trigger with the lock on, and I'll pull the trigger. We'll see who wins. - Sammy "The Bull" Gavano

If gun laws in fact worked, the sponsors of this type of legislation should have no difficulty drawing upon long lists of examples of crime rates reduced by such legislation. That they cannot do so after a century and a half of trying – that they must sweep under the rug the southern attempts at gun control of the 1870-1910 period, the northeastern attempts in the 1920-1939 period, the attempts at both Federal and State levels in 1965-1976 – establishes the repeated, complete, and inevitable failure of gun laws to control serious crime. - Senator Orrin Hatch

"Germans who wish to use firearms should join the SS or SA - ordinary citizens don't need guns, as their having guns doesn't serve the state." - Heinrich Himmler

Ordering Copies of This Book

If you wish to purchase additional copies of this book, you may order it over the internet with a credit card at:

www.cagunlaw.com

Substantial discounts may be had for dealers and instructors when ordering in quantities of fifteen books for more. Please use the "Contact Us" form at the website listed above to inquire.

Consider joining or donating to these fine organizations, all dedicated to protecting your rights under the Second Amendment:[2312]

Calguns Foundation
California Pistol and Rifle Association
Gun Owners of America
Gun Owners of California
Gun Owners of Nevada
Jews for the Preservation of Firearms Ownership
National Rifle Association
Second Amendment Foundation

My suggestion that you consider joining or donating to these organizations is not to be construed as an endorsement of this book by these organizations.

[2312]Mr. Bergin's recommended organizations are simply listed alphabetically, and not arranged in any certain order of importance or significance.